PAST AND PRESENT
VEGETATION OF THE ISLE OF SKYE
A PALAEOECOLOGICAL STUDY

PAST AND PRESENT VEGETATION OF THE ISLE OF SKYE

A PALAEOECOLOGICAL STUDY

H. J. B. BIRKS

Fellow of Sidney Sussex College and Assistant in Research, Botany School
University of Cambridge

CAMBRIDGE
AT THE UNIVERSITY PRESS
1973

Published by the Syndics of the Cambridge University Press
Bentley House, 200 Euston Road, London NW1 2DB
American Branch: 32 East 57th Street, New York, N.Y.10022

Library of Congress Catalogue Card Number: 76-189591

ISBN: 0 521 08533 0

Printed in Great Britain
at the University Printing House, Cambridge
(Brooke Crutchley, University Printer)

To Hilary

CONTENTS

PART III. THE PALAEOECOLOGICAL INVESTIGATIONS

CONTENTS

PART IV. THE LATE-DEVENSIAN FLORA AND VEGETATION OF THE ISLE OF SKYE

PART V. CONCLUSIONS

PREFACE

The study described in this book formed the basis of my Ph.D. dissertation submitted to the University of Cambridge in 1969. The laboratory work was carried out in the University Sub-Department of Quaternary Research, Botany School, Cambridge, between October 1966 and December 1969. During the first year I was supported by a Science Research Council Research Studentship and the Frank Smart Studentship, and from October 1967 to December 1969 by a Research Fellowship at Sidney Sussex College. The writing of this book was started while I was a visiting Research Fellow at the Limnological Research Center, Department of Geology, University of Minnesota from January 1970 to December 1970, where I was supported by a National Science Foundation research grant. The manuscript was completed during tenure of a University Assistantship in Quaternary Research in Cambridge and a Fellowship at Sidney Sussex College. The Royal Society and the Botany School (Brooks Fund) provided generous grants towards publication costs of this book.

The project was supervised by Dr R. G. West, F.R.S., and I wish to thank him most sincerely for his continual and friendly interest, encouragement, and support. I owe much to Dr E. J. Cushing, University of Minnesota, for many stimulating discussions about techniques and approaches, for his generous supply of ideas, and for his critical reading of parts of the manuscript. I am also indebted to Dr D. A. Ratcliffe, The Nature Conservancy, not only for encouraging my interests in the flora and vegetation of northern and western Britain, but for his valuable and continual advice and criticism.

My interests in Continental phytosociology developed largely from discussions in the field on Skye with Dr K. Rybniček, Czechoslovak Academy of Sciences, Brno. My interests in glacial geomorphology owe much to similar discussions with Mr F. M. Synge, Geological Survey of Ireland.

Other people to whom I am grateful for the discussion of ideas and concepts include Dr S. Th. Andersen, Dr B. E. Berglund, Dr J. Dransfield, Professor K. Faegri, Professor Sir Harry Godwin, F.R.S., the late Dr J. Iversen, Dr C. R. Janssen, Dr A. J. C. Malloch, Mrs Rona M. Pitman (née Peck), Dr B. Seddon, Dr D. W. Shimwell, Mrs W. Tutin, Professor W. A. Watts, and Professor H. E. Wright, Jr.

Financial support for the fieldwork was provided by the Sir Albert Howard Travel Exhibition (1966) and the Frank Smart Studentship (1967). I am grateful to Dr H. H. Birks, the late Mr I. S. C. Campbell, Dr J. Dransfield, Dr F. A. Hibbert, Mr J. Johansen, Dr K. Rybniček, and Dr R. G. West for their assistance in the field, frequently in inclement weather.

I am indebted to Miss R. Andrew of the Sub-Department in Cambridge, who maintains the most extensive pollen reference collection anywhere in Britain, for her advice on pollen identifications.

The radiocarbon dates were supplied by Dr V. R. Switsur of the Radiocarbon Dating Laboratory, University of Cambridge, and I am indebted to him and his staff for obtaining the dates from such difficult material.

Several taxonomic specialists have assisted in the identification of vascular plants, bryophytes, lichens, and fossil diatoms and hystrichosphaerids, particularly Mr A. C. Crundwell, Dr C. Downie, Dr J. Dransfield, Mrs J. W. Fitzgerald, Miss E. Y. Haworth, Mrs J. A. Paton, and Mr P. D. Sell.

I am grateful to Mr and Mrs R. Murray, Prabost, Isle of Skye for their friendliness and kind hospitality during my visits to the Island, and for many stimulating discussions about its geology and botany.

For help in the production of this book I am grateful to Mr R. Darling, University of Minnesota for his expert drafting of the pollen diagrams, to Mrs M. E. Pettit for assistance in data processing, and to Miss Ruth Braverman, Mrs Anne Robinson, and Mrs Vera Taylor for typing the manuscript. I am indebted to my father, Dr J. B. Birks, for his meticulous and critical reading of the manuscript.

I wish to express my appreciation to Professor Sir Harry Godwin, F.R.S. for encouraging my interests in palynology and in vegetational history over the last ten years.

My greatest debt is, however, to my wife, Dr H. H. Birks. All the fieldwork has been done with Hilary; she has assisted in the identification of many specimens; and she has patiently discussed and criticised the work, both vegetational and palynological. Besides undertaking her own extensive and demanding research programme in the Scottish Highlands, she has provided a home and an environment where ideas could both freely and comfortably develop.

Sidney Sussex College, Cambridge H.J.B.B.
November 1971

PART I

INTRODUCTION

1

THE NATURE OF THE INVESTIGATION

Ecology considers the relationships between living organisms and their present environment. Palaeoecology is concerned with the relationships between past organisms and the environment in which they lived. Ecology aims at the understanding of present ecosystems; palaeoecology aims at the reconstruction of past ecosystems. Although the two disciplines have related aims and invoke many of the same principles, they differ in several of their concepts and working methods. These differences arise because the past ecosystem cannot be observed directly; its components and characteristics must be inferred from observations of fossils and the sediments in which they are found.

The ecologist can select the particular organisms and environmental factors to be studied. The palaeoecologist is limited to the study of past organisms whose fossils are preserved, and he is usually not able to study directly the physical and chemical attributes of past ecosystems. The ecologist can establish and operate within defined boundaries of space and time, which serve to delimit the modern ecosystem under study. The palaeoecologist has much less control over the range in space and time represented by the sedimentary fossil evidence. He must accept his evidence where it can be found. Some uncertainty in the range of space and time represented by this evidence arises due to the processes of transportation, diagenesis, and redeposition. Due to transportation, the evidence may be found in regions outside the system of interest, and it may then be mixed with and indistinguishable from that from other systems. The organisms which are preserved as fragmentary fossils cannot necessarily be assumed to have lived in the system within which their fossils are found today. Due to diagenesis, evidence that originated in one region of space and time, but that is transported outside that region, may be modified by processes operating in other ecosystems within the same or subsequent time intervals. Due to redeposition, evidence that originated in one period of time may be deposited and preserved with that derived from a different period. Fortunately the limitations imposed on palaeoecology by the processes of transportation, diagenesis, and redeposition are not insuperable, since in many cases the processes can be identified and their effects evaluated and allowed for.

Despite these limitations, palaeoecology can provide reconstructions of past ecosystems which appear to be valid and useful. Although such reconstructions are inevitably rather gross and unsophisticated, they enable comparisons to be made with ecosystems from other periods of time, including the present, so that the causes and mechanisms of change within an ecosystem over time can be postulated. Because many biological processes that are important to an understanding of ecosystem structure and dynamics operate over long time intervals, modern ecology can benefit from the results of palaeoecology. The historical perspective of the development of modern ecosystems which is provided by palaeoecology provides a basis for the formulation of models in which predictions about the future effects of environmental changes can be made.

In attempting the reconstruction of past ecosystems, the palaeoecologist must face decisions about sampling which can generally be avoided by the ecologist. In addition to selecting where and how to sample, the palaeoecologist is also faced with the problems of deciding what the samples represent and where the fossils came from. These difficulties have inevitably resulted in simplifications, both in techniques and interpretation. The commonest approach is to compare observations of the fossils and their lithologies with modern situations. Although the environmental conditions of the past ecosystem are largely unknown – indeed, it is often the primary aim of a palaeoecological study to determine them – generalisations about processes within modern ecosystems may be extended backwards in time, provided the generalisations are sufficiently broad. The present is used to model the past, but the model is simplified, not because of a reduction in the number of environmental factors, but because of observational limitations. The use of quantitative models in palaeoecology shows considerable promise (for example;

Fox, 1968; Imbrie & Kipp, 1971), but often the models are inadequate to deal with all the complexities of past ecosystems.

Palaeoecology is practiced by scientists of varying disciplines, who tend to work either on a particular group of organisms or on a particular division of geological time. The bulk of the fossiliferous rocks of the Palaeozoic and Mesozoic eras are marine in their origin, and studies of the palaeoecology of this time are concerned with the marine environment and with organisms such as echinoderms, molluscs, and brachiopods that have readily preservable hard parts. Deposits of Quaternary age are largely continental in origin, and their palaeoecology has attracted considerable attention. The period of time represented by these deposits has probably been studied more intensively than any other time span of comparable magnitude.

Quaternary palaeoecology considers primarily those groups of organisms that appear as abundant fossils – molluscs, vertebrates, arthropods, algae, bryophytes, and vascular plants. Of the various types of organic remains preserved in Quaternary sediments, few are more abundant than the pollen grains and spores of vascular plants. Studies of Quaternary palaeoecology have been largely based, therefore, on the technique of stratigraphical pollen analysis, the results of which can provide a basis for the reconstruction of the past flora and vegetation. The historical development of Quaternary palaeoecology using pollen analysis closely parallels that of vegetational ecology. Qualitative studies of vegetation and of pollen floras in Quaternary sediments were made towards the end of the nineteenth century. Quantitative studies of vegetation began in the first two decades of this century, and in 1916 the potentialities of the quantitative analysis of pollen grains in Quaternary sediments was first realised by the Swedish geologist Lennart von Post. Analyses of the percentage frequencies of different pollen types from successive layers were represented diagrammatically, and von Post was able to demonstrate the similarities of the pollen sequences within a small region and the differences between those from widely spaced regions. Pollen analysis added new detail to the dimension of time in the study of vegetation, at a period when critical problems of the nature of vegetation, vegetational history, and climatic changes were arising.

The early success of pollen analysis as a method in Quaternary palaeoecology led to its adoption throughout Europe and North America, and subsequently in other parts of the world, and many thousands of pollen diagrams have now been produced. The methods of analysis and data interpretation have been greatly refined in the last twenty years or so, partly by improved microscopy and increased knowledge of pollen morphology, partly by an increased understanding of the relationships between vegetation and modern pollen rain, and partly by the introduction of radiocarbon dating. Attention has been increasingly focused on some of the basic assumptions and techniques of pollen analysis as a palaeoecological technique, particularly in the interpretation of palynological data in terms of past flora and vegetation.

As in other branches of palaeoecology, the interpretations of Quaternary pollen analytical data are derived mainly from the extension of present-day ecological observations backwards in time. Past ecosystems are reconstructed by analogy with the present floristic composition of vegetational types, and with the known ecological preferences of the taxa or vegetational types involved. This corresponds to the implicit assumption of the principle of methodological uniformitarianism (*sensu* Gould, 1965) by which natural laws, which are established by observing present situations, are extrapolated backwards in time. While this principle is probably acceptable for the relatively short time interval of the Quaternary, biological evolution and taxonomic differentiation are continuous and active processes (cf. G. H. Scott, 1963) so that the present may not necessarily always be the key to the past.

The reconstruction of a past ecosystem by pollen analysis involves obtaining answers to the following questions.

(i) What taxa were present? The answer can be only partial, since some taxa produce pollen that is either not preserved or that is not dispersed. The degree of information that is extracted depends on the quality and reliability of the pollen indentification and on the taxonomic level to which it is carried out.

(ii) What were the relative abundances of the taxa present? This involves an interpretation of the numerical data of the pollen spectra. The constant of proportionality (R) between pollen percentages and taxon frequencies, which is commonly assumed to exist, varies by many orders of magnitude between taxa – abundant species in the vegetation may produce little or no pollen, rare species may produce abundant pollen. Modern pollen spectra may be used to estimate R within a particular vegetational type, but unless similar communities can be identified within the fossil assemblage, it is unwise to assume a similar value of *R*, since the latter can be strongly influenced by changes in community structure and composition. Fossil pollen spectra will always tend to be dominated by taxa with high values of *R*.

(iii) What plant communities were present? This involves comparisons of the pollen spectra of modern associations with the fossil pollen spectra, and the identification of pollen of 'indicator species' within the pollen assemblage. Since the pollen spectra generally originate from several plant associations, the analysis involves a detailed knowledge of their ecology.

(iv) What space did the ecosystem occupy? This is critically dependent on the processes of pollen transport and dispersal and on the choice of site, which depends on a detailed study of the topography.

(v) What time did the ecosystem occur? Radiocarbon dating of the sediments can potentially give an exact answer to this question, but large errors can arise in the dating of lake sediments of low organic content. Comparison of the pollen and sediment stratigraphy of related sites can provide a supplementary means of correlation.

(vi) What was the environment of the ecosystem? A detailed study of the local topography may provide information on the geological and geomorphological history. Some information about the physical and chemical attributes of the environment may be obtained from the sediments. However, almost all the information about the environment is obtained indirectly from the present ecology of the taxa and/or communities that are found to have occurred in the past. Attention is often focused on the estimation of past climatic variables from palynological data. Besides requiring information about the distribution of the fossils in space and in time, the essential requisites are a thorough knowledge of the present ecological requirements of the taxa that the fossils represent. From such autecological information, the past occurrence of a particular taxon may indicate the possible range of environmental variables present at the time and place of sampling.

Besides the limitations imposed by the problems of pollen preservation and identification, the principal limitations of pollen analysis as a technique in palaeoecology is in the interpretation of the numerical data that result from a count of the pollen types present in a sample of sediment. The relationship between the pollen frequency and the number of individuals of the corresponding taxon in the vegetation surrounding the site of deposition is complex and it depends on a number of independent variables such as pollen production, plant abundance, wind velocity, and processes of dispersal, sedimentation, and preservation. The difficulties of inferring past vegetation from fossil pollen assemblages are being increasingly appreciated (Davis, 1963), and attempts at achieving a more factual and objective approach to the reconstruction of past vegetation have been made by investigating modern pollen rain in relation to present vegetation. A further limitation is that a pollen assemblage in a site of deposition is derived from an undefinable source area, so that pollen spectra do not yield any direct information about the composition or distribution of communities in space, except in the rare cases when the latter are homogeneous. Such information has therefore to be sought by inferential methods.

Many of the assumptions of the pollen analytical method have been recently subjected to adequate tests, and others are under study. Many refinements remain to be made, however, before all the criticisms levelled at pollen analysis can be satisfactorily refuted. The current sceptical mood that prevails in many quarters, although it has led to several new and important investigations, is not likely to result in a sound methodology so long as the scepticism is directed only at the approaches and conclusions of an earlier generation of pollen analysts. Unless the new approaches and conclusions are examined as thoroughly as the old ones, the result may merely be a change from one orthodoxy to another.

With this background of recent developments and problems in the use of pollen analysis in Quaternary palaeoecology, a project was designed to test the applicability of the technique to the reconstruction of the past landscape of an area, including the topography, soils, and climate, and the organisms that populated it, during the closing phases of the last glaciation. It was wished to demonstrate whether pollen analysis could be used to discriminate any differences in floral, vegetational, and ecological history between sites that could be attributed to differences in habitat conditions within a fairly small region. The Isle of Skye, with its varied geology and topography and its rich and diverse flora, is an ideal area for such an investigation. The choice of the Isle of Skye offered the additional advantages of studying the vegetational history in an area where no detailed work had been done, for at the time this project was initiated, no pollen diagrams had been published from the Hebrides. The only information then available about the vegetational history at the end of the last glaciation in Scotland north of the Great Glen was a single profile from Loch Droma in Ross and Cromarty (Kirk & Godwin, 1963). Since the beginning of the project two pollen diagrams from the Isle of Skye have been published by Vasari & Vasari (1968), and one from Ross and Cromarty by Pennington & Lishman (1971).

The study of the past and present vegetation of the Isle of Skye has involved several related stages. First, a survey was made of the present vegetation of the island and this is presented in Chapter 4. This survey was designed to provide a basis for considering the role of environmental factors such as climate, soils, and land use (Chapter 3) in influencing the composition and distribution of the present vegetation, and to form a background of the present ecological tolerances and requirements of the individual species and vegetational types within Skye today, against which the palaeoecological reconstructions could be made. The principal ecological factors influencing the floristic and vegetational differentiation within the island are considered in Chapter 5, and a phytogeographical analysis of the present vascular-plant flora is discussed in Chapter 6, as a basis for considering the geographical affinities of the past flora.

Five sites were selected for palaeoecological investigation after assessment of the present floristic, vegetational, and ecological variation within the island (Chapter 9), in order to compare the past and present patterns of flora and vegetation. The methods of sampling and analysis of the samples are described in Chapter 7, and the criteria for the determination of many of the pollen and spore types are presented in Chapter 8. Besides the pollen analytical studies, attention was also given to the sediment lithology of the profiles investigated, to obtain independent evidence of depositional environments, and to the macrofossil content of the sediments. These results are presented in Chapter 9. The pollen stratigraphical data obtained from the five sites investigated were classified into a series of pollen zones, and these biostratigraphic units are defined and described in Chapter 10. A study of the relationships between modern pollen rain and vegetational types in Scotland is discussed in Chapter 11, as a basis for the interpretation of fossil pollen assemblages in terms of modern vegetational analogues.

With this background of the present environment, flora, vegetation, and pollen rain of the Isle of Skye, Chapters 12, 13, and 14 are concerned with the reconstruction of the flora, vegetation, and landscape or palaeoecosystem of the island during the interval of time considered. These chapters attempt to interpret the data in terms of the floristic, vegetational, and ecological history of the island, and are of a more speculative nature. The past flora (Chapter 12), as reconstructed from pollen analytical and macrofossil data, is considered both as a single unit for an analysis of its phytogeographical affinities, and as smaller, regional units for consideration of floristic changes between areas on Skye. The vegetational history (Chapter 13) is reconstructed independently for each site, by means of comparisons between the modern and fossil pollen assemblages and from the fossil occurrence of pollen and spore types of taxa of narrow ecological amplitude today. The pollen assemblage zones are ordered stratigraphically within Skye, and correlated in time by radiocarbon dating. Comparisons and correlations with pollen stratigraphical sequences from other areas are also discussed in Chapter 13.

Attempts at the reconstruction of the landscape, including its topography and the organisms that populated it, are presented in Chapter 14. This reconstruction is only attempted after all the data on chronologically and stratigraphically related biota and lithologies have been assembled. The reconstruction of the palaeolandscape of Skye, including the spatial distribution of flora and vegetation within it, from the observable evidence of the sediments and their fossils, enables the nature and interaction of environmental forces within that landscape – the palaeoecosystem – to be inferred. Causes of change and of differentiation within the landscape are discussed, and tentative reconstructions of the past climate of Skye are proposed. Several problems in the reconstruction of the landscape remain unsolved, however, and these are discussed in Chapter 14.

This book attempts to describe the various stages involved in the reconstruction of the past flora, vegetation, and landscape of Skye. It emphasises and evaluates the shortcomings of the methods adopted and of the project as a whole when viewed as a study in palaeoecology. It is hoped, however, that it will lead to a greater appreciation of the interdependence of modern ecology and Quaternary palaeoecology, and that it will contribute to the redefinition of problems and approaches in further studies.

2

NOMENCLATURE AND TERMINOLOGY

The botanical nomenclature follows that of Clapham, Tutin & Warburg (1962) for vascular plants; Warburg (1963) for mosses; Paton (1965) for liverworts; and James (1965) for lichens. For taxa not considered by these authors, the relevant authorities are cited when the taxa are first mentioned in the text.

The spelling of place names follows that of the Ordnance Survey (Seventh Series, One Inch, 1:63360) maps.

The term 'Late-Devensian' is used in the sense proposed by Shotton & West (1969) to describe the youngest substage and subage of the Devensian Stage and Age, respectively. The Devensian Stage and Age of the British Quaternary succession encompass the deposits and the time interval, respectively, of the last glaciation in the British Isles. They are correlated with the Weichselian Stage and Age of North-West Europe. The term 'Devensian' is derived from Devenses, those living by the River Deva (Dee) in the English Midlands, the area of the principal stratigraphic localities of deposits of the last glaciation in the British Isles. The Late-Devensian Substage refers to deposits dating from '26000 radiocarbon years before present to the end of zone III' at the base of the Flandrian Stage (Shotton & West, 1969). The Late-Devensian Subage refers to the time interval during which Late-Devensian sediments were deposited. The term 'Late-Devensian', as used here, is a unit of the standard stratigraphical scale (*sensu* Geological Society of London, 1967; 1969), with upper and lower marker or boundary points defined at a specific type locality. It is preferred to the more widely used and rather ambiguous term 'late-glacial'.

The term 'late-glacial' has been used in several different ways by Quaternary stratigraphers to refer to various distinct stratigraphic units, including biostratigraphic units (for example pollen zones I, II, and III), lithostratigraphic units (for example Older Dryas, Allerød, and Younger Dryas Beds), geologic-time or chronomeric (*sensu* Geological Society of London, 1967; 1969) units (the 'Late-glacial Period'), and geologic-climatic units (Allerød interstade and post-Allerød climatic deterioration or stade). The term 'late-glacial' has also been used in a variety of geographical and ecological settings to refer to local events or episodes of landscape and/or vegetational development, such as the time between the first appearance of the land surface from beneath the wasting ice to the final disappearance of active ice from a particular area, to inferred climatic changes, and to specific glacial retreats and/or readvances. The use of the same term for the description and nomenclature of both stratigraphic units and episodes can lead to confusion, and as a result the term 'late-glacial' with its related terms 'post-glacial' and 'full-glacial' are considered to be too general for use in the precise subdivision and nomenclature of stratigraphic sequences, geologic time, or episodes in the earth's history.

The term 'Flandrian' is used to refer to the youngest stage and age of the British Quaternary succession (Suggate & West, 1967). It is generally equivalent in its meaning to the more widely used, but rather ambiguous, terms 'Post-glacial Period', 'Holocene Epoch', and 'Holocene Series'. The lower base or boundary point of the Flandrian Stage is defined in sediments 'at the beginning of the spread of thermophilous and deciduous trees following the climatic amelioration which caused the end of the Weichselian (i.e. Devensian) glaciation' (West, 1967, p. 5) and at 'the base of pollen zone IV (FI)' (Shotton & West, 1969). The upper boundary is not defined, as the stage encompasses sediments extending to the present day. The Flandrian Age refers to that interval of time during which Flandrian sediments were deposited. The name 'Flandrian' is used in accordance with the custom in North-West Europe of naming temperate, interglacial stages and ages after the marine transgression most characteristic of them (Suggate & West, 1967).

In discussing the pollen stratigraphical evidence, it is considered essential to keep the observed changes in pollen stratigraphy distinct from the inferred changes in climatic and glacial history until independent evidence is available to establish how they are related in space and time. The use of the traditional pollen zonational divisions of the Late-Devensian Substage (pollen zones I, II, and III) has been deliberately avoided in view of the different stratigraphical concepts (biostratigraphical, lithostratigraphical, geologic–climatic, time–stratigraphical, geochronological, morphostratigraphical) by which these divisions have been made by pollen analysts, glacial geologists, and Quaternary stratigraphers. To avoid such ambiguities, biostratigraphic units of the assemblage zone type (see Chapter 10 and Cushing, 1964*a*; 1967*a*) are defined on the basis of the observed pollen and spore content of the sediments examined. Pending the establishment of the temporal relationships of these biostratigraphic units, terms such as '*Lycopodium*–Cyperaceae' time are used informally to refer to the time interval during which the sediments containing a particular pollen assemblage zone were deposited at the site under discussion.

All radiocarbon dates quoted are calculated on a half-life of 5568 ± 30 radiocarbon years, as specified in the journal *Radiocarbon*, and they are given as radiocarbon years before present (B.P.) with the zero datum at the year 1950 A.D.

PART II

THE PRESENT FLORA AND VEGETATION OF THE ISLE OF SKYE

3

THE ENVIROMENTAL BACKGROUND

1. LOCATION

The Isle of Skye lies off the north-west coast of Scotland between latitudes 57° 03′ N and 57° 44′ N, and longitudes 6° 46′ W and 5° 38′ W. It is the largest island in the Inner Hebrides and it forms part of the political county of Inverness-shire. It is separated from the mainland of Scotland (Fig. 1) by the Sound of Sleat, Kyle Rhea, Loch Alsh, and the Inner Sound, and from the Outer Hebrides by the Minch and the Little Minch. The island is 48 miles (77 km) long from Rubha Hunish in the north to the Point of Sleat in the south, and 52 miles (84 km) wide from Oisgill Bay in the west to Kyle Rhea in the east. The coast is deeply indented so that no part of the island is more than 5 miles (8 km) from the sea. It has a total area of 670 square miles (1720 km²).

2. GEOLOGY AND TOPOGRAPHY

The geology of the Isle of Skye has been described in detail in the *Memoirs of the Geological Survey* (Anderson & Dunham, 1966; Clough & Harker, 1904; Harker, 1904; Peach *et al.* 1910) and in Richey (1961); therefore only a brief account is given here. The solid geology and the topography of the island are shown in a simplified form in Figs. 2 and 3 respectively. Skye is conveniently divided, topographically as well as geologically, into several regions.

(i) the Sleat Peninsula,
(ii) Suardal,
(iii) the Kyleakin region,
(iv) northern Skye,
(v) the Cuillin Hills, and
(vi) the Red Hills.

The boundaries of these regions are delimited in Chapter 5 (see p. 170 and Fig. 5).

The *Sleat Peninsula* consists exclusively of Palaeozoic rocks, and although there are no areas above 1000 feet (304 m), the topography is rugged, with steep, bare rock-outcrops, peat-filled hollows and small lochans, and several deeply-cut ravines with waterfalls. Lewisian gneiss occurs quite extensively in the eastern part of the Sleat Peninsula, and it is separated from Torridonian rocks to the west by the Moine Thrust Plane. The Lewisian rocks consist largely of hard foliated hornblende gneiss and granulite, with occasional outcrops of hornblende schist, often rich in chlorite and epidote; the Torridonian rocks are felspathic sandstones, shales, and grits. In the south and south-west region of the Sleat Peninsula there are outcrops of basic Moine phyllites and schistose grits. The structural relationships of these three series on Skye are complex due to overthrusting from the east along the Moine Thrust Plane.

Suardal. Cambrian, and possibly Early Ordovician, rocks outcrop locally in the Sleat near Ord and more extensively to the north of Loch Eishort and to the south-west of Broadford in Strath Suardal. The rocks at Ord have probably been moved from the east by overthrusting, and they were probably once largely covered by Torridonian rocks that were then also thrust forward along thrust-planes. The thrusts have been folded into anticlines, in the centres of which the Cambrian rocks are exposed. Cambrian Quartzites, Fucoid Beds, and Serpulite Grits are overlain by Durness limestones and dolomites, the probable age of which is Early Ordovician (Phemister, 1960). These limestone outcrops are important topographically in that they occur as low scarps and as fragmentary areas of limestone pavement with some karstic landforms such as clint and grike structures, especially on Ben Suardal and at Torrin. The limestones and dolomites of Ben Suardal are in part altered to marble by the Tertiary intrusions, and they have developed many metamorphic minerals, for example chondrodite, humite, fluoborite, datolite, harkerite, monticellite, and magnetite (Richey, 1961).

The Kyleakin region consists primarily of Torridonian sandstones, rising to form two peaks (Sgùrr na Coinnich and Beinn na Caillich) above 2000 feet (610 m). The topography is rather subdued with few extensive cliffs or rock outcrops, but there are many deep ravines with waterfalls, formed by streams

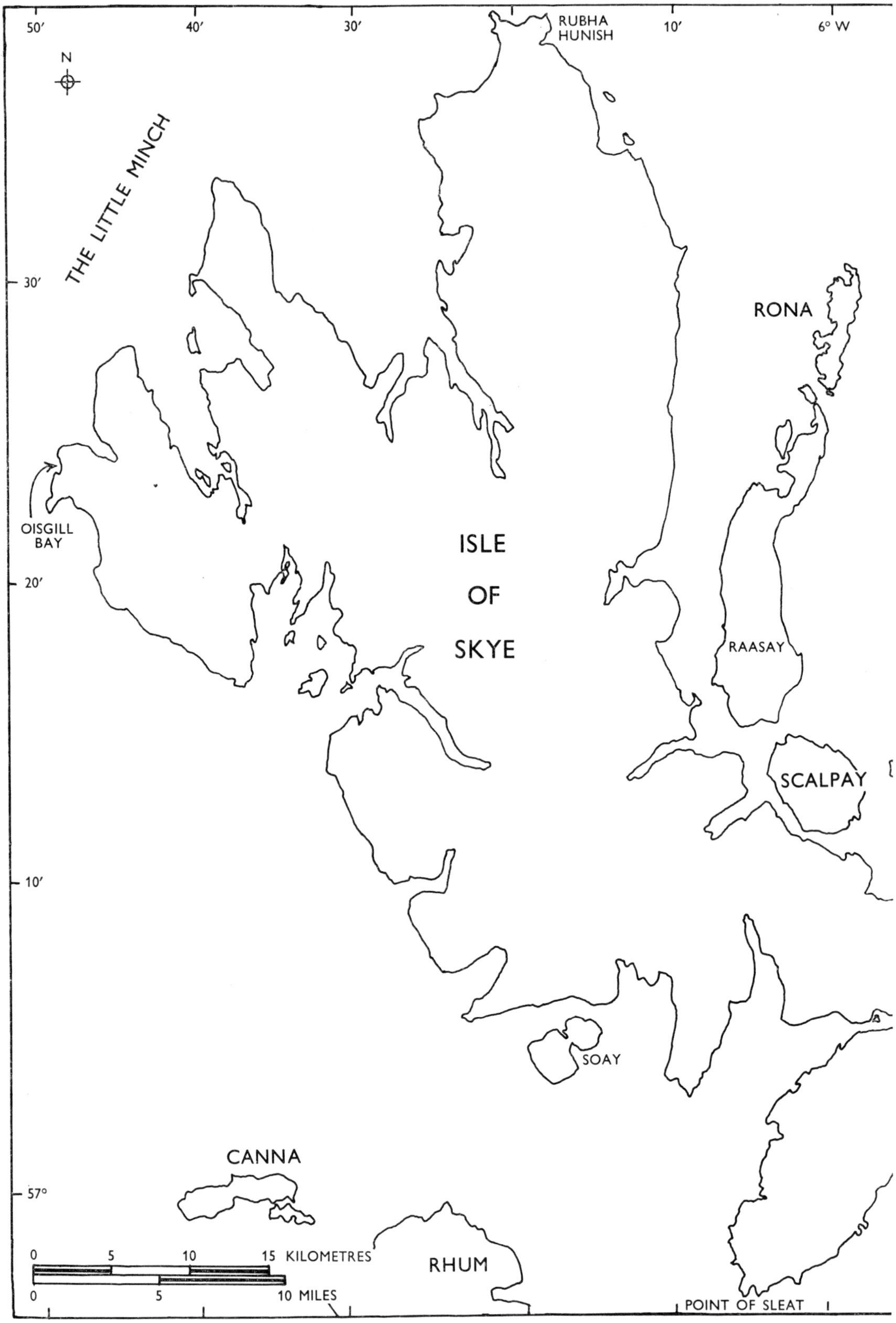

Figure 1. Map showing the location of the Isle of Skye in relation

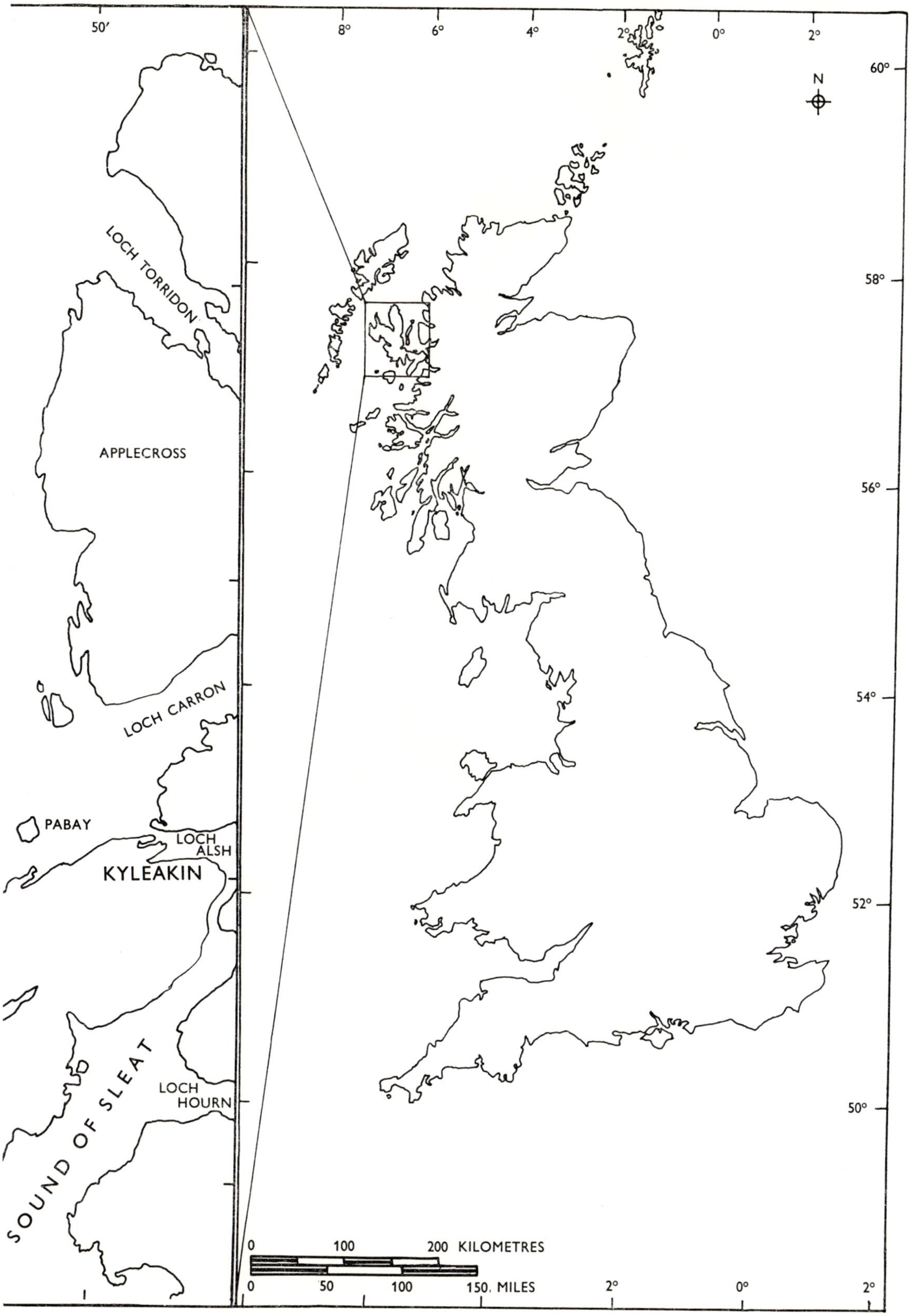

to the British Isles (right) and to the Scottish mainland (left).

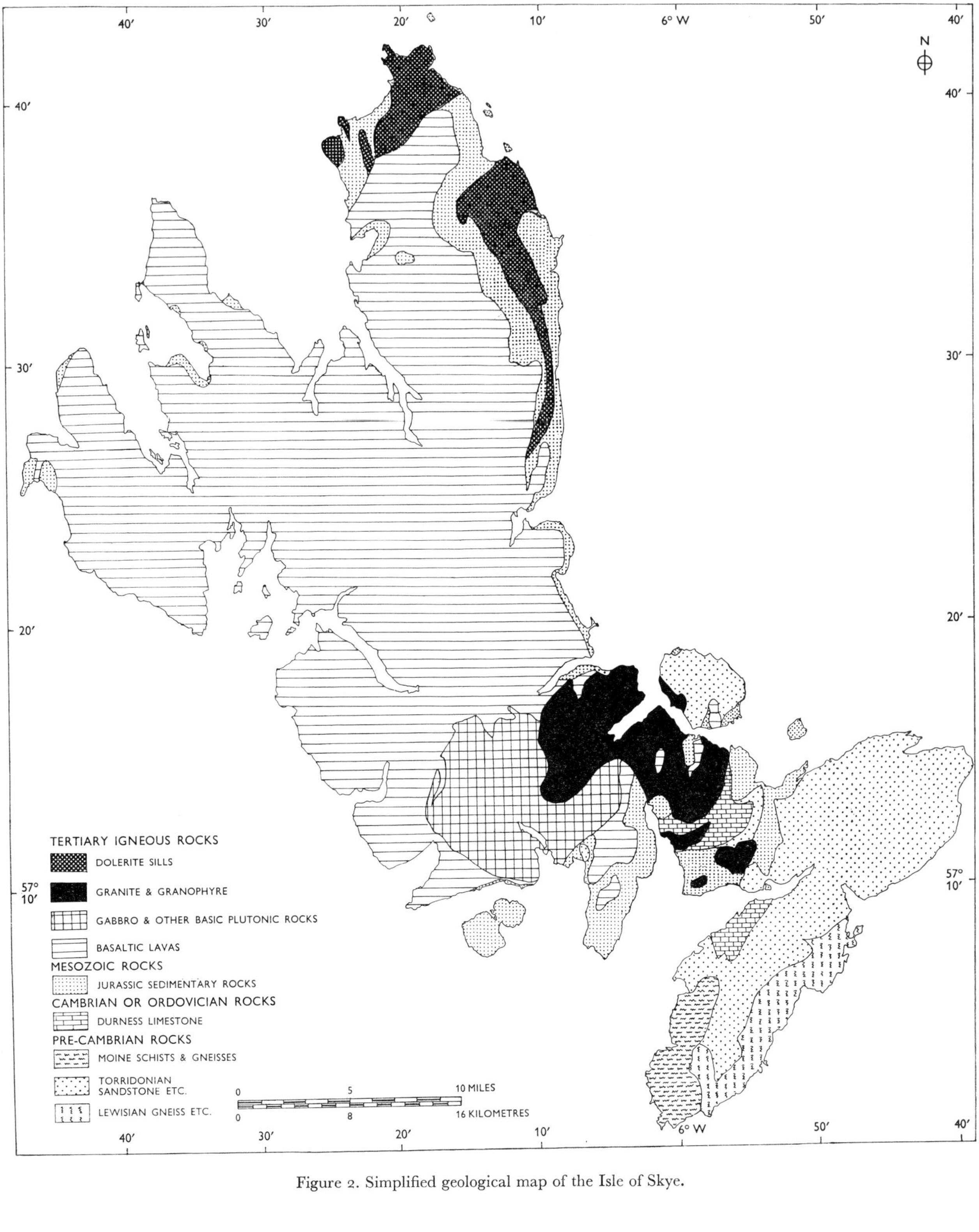

Figure 2. Simplified geological map of the Isle of Skye.

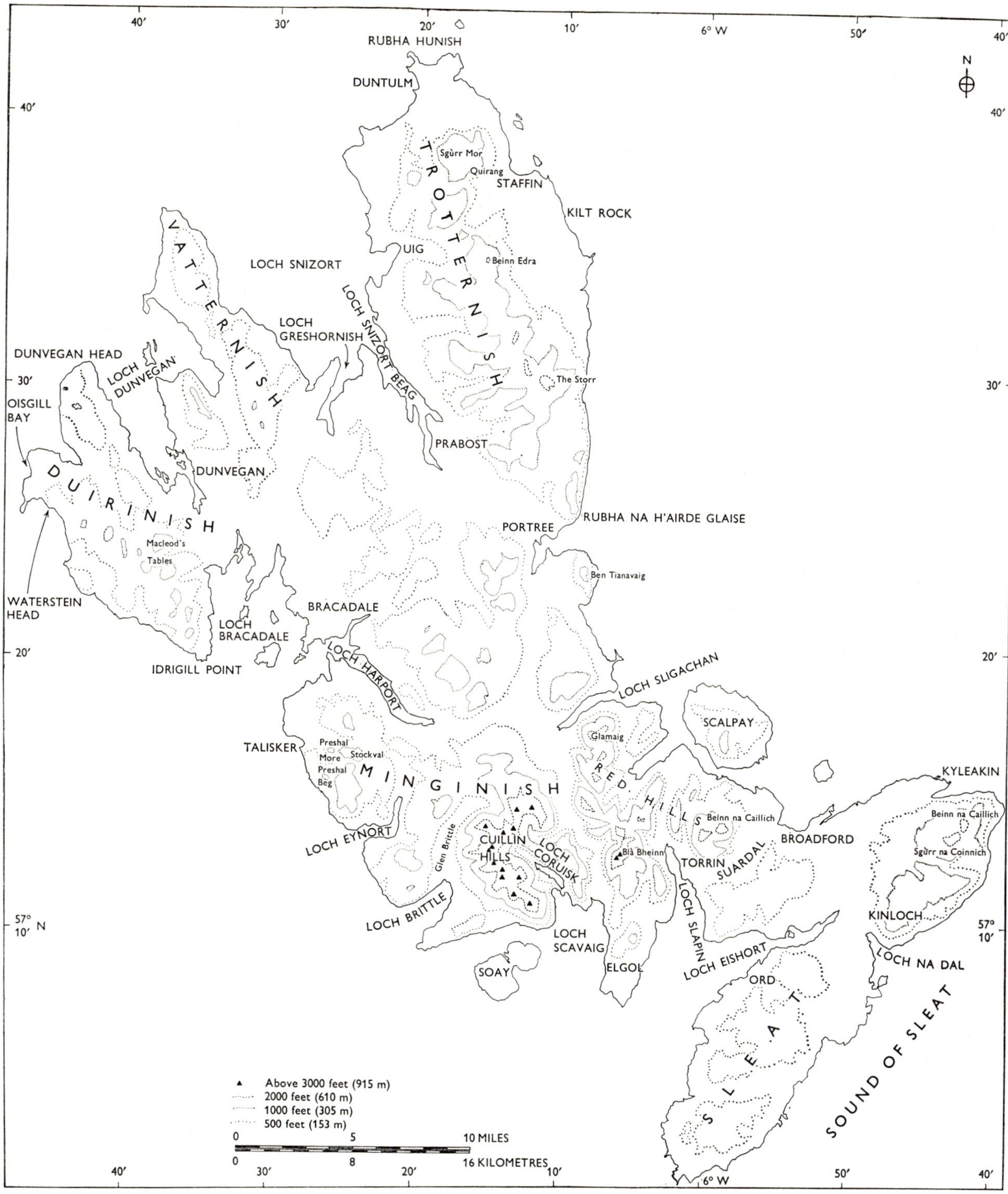

Figure 3. Topographical map of the Isle of Skye, with contours at 500 feet (153 m), 1000 feet (305 m), 2000 feet (610 m), and 3000 feet (915 m).

descending radially from the high ground, for example to the east of Kinloch and Loch na Dal.

Northern Skye consists largely of three peninsulas, Trotternish, Vatternish, and Duirinish. The central area around Portree is nowhere above 1000 feet (305 m) except for a small group of flat-topped hills to the south-west of Portree. The area has an extensive drift cover, with complex drainage systems and numerous small lochans and peat-filled hollows. The central area is separated from the Trotternish Peninsula to the north by a low-lying strath which runs north-westwards from Portree to Loch Snizort Beag. It is separated from the Vaternish and Duirinish Peninsulas by Loch Greshornish, the valleys of the Red Burn and Caroy River, and Loch Bracadale.

The Trotternish Peninsula consists of Jurassic rocks, outcropping primarily along the east coast, overlain by a considerable thickness of Tertiary volcanic rocks. Elsewhere the Jurassic rocks lie largely below sea-level, and are only sporadically exposed by minor folds, as in Loch Bay and in the extreme west near Oisgill Bay. The Mesozoic rocks are lithologically varied, with sandstones, shales, limestones, ironstones, lignites, and oil shales, representing a lower marine series (Lias and Inferior Oolite), followed by the Great Estuarine Series (estuarine deposits), after which marine conditions led to the deposition of the Oxford Clay, the Corallian, and the Kimmeridge Clay. After the close of the Jurassic these sediments were folded into a gentle syncline with a slight northerly pitch to its north-north-east axis. The syncline was later eroded apparently to base-level, for the overlying Tertiary lavas were seemingly extruded over a smooth peneplane.

Tertiary volcanic activity, beginning perhaps in the Eocene, was marked initially by a considerable thickness of water-deposited tuffs, and subsequently by extensive lava sheets, attaining thicknesses of up to 4000 feet (1220 m). The lavas occur as flows, usually about 50 feet (15 m) thick, consisting of hard olivine-basalt, commonly exhibiting columnar jointing and interspaced with softer amygdaloidal slag. The differential resistance of these layers to erosion produces the characteristic low, broad flat-topped hills and terraced slopes of much of northern Skye. Lapses in volcanic activity were sometimes long enough for local soil and vegetational development. Thin lateritic soil and plant beds are preserved in a few areas. The plant remains have not been examined in detail, but macrofossils of *Ginkgo*, *Cryptomeria*, *Sequoia*, and *Platanus* have been reported (Anderson & Dunham, 1966).

The topography of northern Skye is rugged, rocky, and often spectacular, although there are large areas of hummocky, peat-covered ground in the lowlands. The Trotternish Peninsula is traversed for most of its length by the impressive east-facing basalt escarpment rising to 2360 feet (723 m) at The Storr, and gradually descending to Meall nan Suireamach (1779 feet, 582 m) in the north. The escarpment is probably the most extensive inland cliff system in Britain, with several vertical buttresses over 500 feet (153 m) high. Along the scarp there are frequent screes and rocky gullies, and there are many extensive landslips caused by rotational slipping and slumping producing a mass of collapsed basalt columns, tumbled rocks, block litters, and detached pinnacles that extend for some considerable distance (up to 7000 feet, 2170 m at The Quirang) away from the cliffs (see Anderson & Dunham, 1966). In contrast the western slopes of the Trotternish ridge are gentler, they are extensively peat covered, and they largely follow the low westward dip of the lavas. In one place, Glen Uig, the River Conon has cut through the lavas to expose in an amphitheatre the underlying Jurassic sediments. The slopes are dissected by consequent streams rising in the high ground and flowing rather sinuously through open alluvial valleys into Loch Snizort. Springs and diffuse areas of surface-water seepage are numerous and occur at all levels in northern Skye.

The Vatternish and Duirinish Peninsulas have little ground over 1000 feet (310 m) and, as the base of the lavas occur at or below sea-level, landslips are only developed in one or two places, such as Score Horan, Waterstein Head, and Beinn Bhreac. The coastline is extremely precipitous with spectacular sea-cliffs descending vertically in places for nearly 1000 feet (310 m). Biod an Athair near Dunvegan Head rises almost vertically from the sea to 1025 feet (314 m), and Waterstein Head is a near-vertical face 967 feet (294 m) high. The coastal cliffs are cut by several deep ravines and waterfalls. The Macleod's Tables, consisting of Healaval Mhor (1538 feet, 470 m) and Healaval Beag (1601 feet, 490 m) are the highest points in north-west Skye, and they are characteristic flat-topped terraced, basalt hills.

The central area of Skye, comprising the *Cuillin Hills* (including Blà Bheinn), the *Red Hills*, and the *Elgol Peninsula*, is one of marked geological and topographical diversity. The Elgol Peninsula is a lowlying area consisting primarily of Jurassic limestones, shales, and sandstones with some overlying basalts and intruded dolerite sills. The Cuillin Hills contain the highest peak on Skye (Sgùrr Alasdair; 3309 feet, 1014 m) and twenty-two other peaks over 3000 feet (920 m). These hills and the nearby Blà Bheinn have a characteristic form with serrated peaks, narrow summit ridges, deeply cut corries often with high cliffs and small, moraine-bounded lochans, and extensive scree- and boulder-strewn slopes (see Haynes, 1968). They consist of basic and ultra-basic plutonic rocks, mainly hard gabbro rich in olivine and labradorite feldspar, that were intruded into the surrounding low-lying lavas. Other ultra-basic rocks in the Cuillins, for example on Sgùrr Dubh, include peridotite, dunite, picrite, and allivalite. It is this rapid variation in rock type that gives rise to the serrated outline of the Cuillins, as many of the gullies represent basic dykes which have been more easily eroded than the gabbro they traverse. At a later stage there were intrusions of granite and granophyre to the north and east of the Cuillins, forming the Red Hills. These are topographically more subdued than the Cuillin Hills, with gently contoured slopes, broad watersheds, and summit plateaux attaining 2537 feet (780 m) on Sgùrr Mhair and 2400 feet (740 m) on Beinn na Caillich, Broadford. In the Red Hills there are fewer corries and cliffs than in the Cuillins.

There are several examples in the Red Hills and the Cuillins of the intermingling of, and reaction between, acid and basic materials, one or both of which were in the liquid state. For example, on Marsco a hybrid rock termed marscoite was interpreted by Harker (1904) as an instance of the acidification of a basic magma by the inclusion of granitic material.

The last igneous phase was a complex series of minor intrusions forming radially-arranged composite horizontal sills and basic dyke swarms consisting of trachytes, mugearites, andesites, olivine–dolerites, and pitchstones. Several of these sills form impressive inland crags, such as Preshal More, Preshal Beg, and Stockval near Talisker. Rockfalls formed by debris from the scarp of columnar-jointed dolerite sills are rare on Skye, but two fine examples occur near Rubha Garbhaig, Staffin and Cnoc Roll, just south of Duntulm. Sills within the Jurassic sediments of northern Skye (not shown in detail on Fig. 2) have produced many spectacular cliff-forms, such as the Kilt Rock near Staffin, where columnar dolerite forms the upper half of a 170 foot (52 m) vertical sea-cliff. Rubha na h-Airde Glaise, near Portree, rises to 1286 feet (420 m) above sea-level as a step-like cliff of Jurassic rocks and included dolerite sills. At Rubha Hunish a near-vertical dolerite sill 380 feet (124 m) high forms the northernmost tip of the island. Along the east coast of the Trotternish Peninsula many of the streams follow rocky, turbulent courses along their entire length, but are often broken in places by sheer drops of great depth to the sea, as at Bearreraig River, River Lealt, and the Rigg Burn north of Portree.

In contrast, the coastline of southern Skye is less rugged, with large rather sheltered sea-lochs. The inland Loch Coruisk within the Cuillins occupies a steep sided rock-basin 125 feet (39 m) deep, which is cut 100 feet (30 m) below sea-level (see Harker, 1901). In several of the sea-lochs and around the low-lying coast, raised shoreline features are conspicuous, with level wave-cut rock platforms, beach gravels, and sea-caves (Donner, 1959; McCann, 1966).

3. CLIMATE

The Isle of Skye has a cool, oceanic climate, with a relatively small temperature range, a high and evenly distributed annual rainfall, strong winds, and high cloud cover. From its position on the western seaboard, Skye is one of the most oceanic regions in Britain with mountain peaks of 3000 feet (920 m) or more. Considering its high latitude (57°N), Skye possesses some anomalous climatic features. These stem from the warm North Atlantic ocean currents and the regional atmospheric circulation, which maintain a cool, but mild, maritime air stream over the island for much of the year. Climatic variations within the island are governed largely by topography. Meteorological data for Skye are available from two low-lying stations; Duntulm in northern Skye, and from Prabost in a rather dry coastal area of western Skye. Additional information for Staffin is given by Slesser (1970).

Average monthly values of daily mean temperature, daily maximum temperature, and daily minimum temperature for the period 1901–30 for lowland Skye (*Climatological Atlas*, 1952) are given in Table 3.1.

No temperature records are available for high levels in Skye comparable to those from Dun Fell (Manley, 1945) and Ben Nevis (Manley, 1952). Average monthly values of daily mean temperatures for the period 1901–30 have therefore been estimated for The Storr and Sgùrr Alasdair, the highest point on Skye, from the corresponding records at lowland

TABLE 3.1 *Average monthly values of temperature for lowland Skye* (°C)

	Jan.	Feb.	Mar.	Apr.	May	June	July	Aug.	Sept.	Oct.	Nov.	Dec.
Daily mean (1901–30)	4.2	4.7	5.3	6.9	9.5	11.7	13.6	13.6	11.7	9.2	5.8	5.3
Daily maximum (1901–30)	6.8	7.2	8.3	10.6	13.3	15.5	18.3	16.7	14.4	13.9	8.3	6.8
Daily minimum (1901–30)	2.2	2.2	2.2	3.3	5.5	8.3	10.6	10.0	7.7	5.5	3.9	2.2

TABLE 3.2 *Estimated average monthly values of daily mean temperature for The Storr and Sgùrr Alasdair* (°C)

Locality	Altitude (m)	Jan.	Feb.	Mar.	Apr.	May	June	July	Aug.	Sept.	Oct.	Nov.	Dec.
Broadford	0	4.2	4.7	5.3	6.9	9.5	11.7	13.6	13.6	11.7	9.2	5.8	5.3
The Storr	723	−0.7	−0.1	0.4	2.1	5.4	5.9	8.8	8.8	5.9	4.3	1.0	0.4
Sgùrr Alasdair	1014	−2.7	−2.1	−1.6	0.1	2.6	4.8	6.2	6.2	4.8	2.3	−1.0	−1.6

stations, assuming a lapse rate of 1 °F (0.56 °C) for every 270 feet (82 m) altitude (Manley, 1952). The values, which can only be considered as approximate, are listed in Table 3.2.

The daily mean temperatures calculated for each month at 1000 feet (305 m) in Snowdonia (Ratcliffe, 1959) are similar to those at sea-level on Skye, illustrating the important gradient of decreasing warmth from south to north in Britain (see Spence, 1960). The range of mean monthly temperatures is 16 °F (8.3 °C) on Skye, in contrast to 21 °F (11.7 °C) in the eastern Highlands. The growing season has been defined in various ways; as the length of time with temperatures above 42 °F (5.6 °C) (Manley, 1952); or in terms of accumulated temperatures above 42.8 °F (6 °C) (Gregory, 1954; Fairbairn, 1968). Low-lying ground on Skye experiences between 833 and 1111 day-degrees C, in contrast to the higher ground above 3000 feet (920 m) with less than 300 day-degrees C. The short growing season and the low temperatures during much of the winter on the higher summits cause soil instability and solifluction. Although variations in temperature are related mainly to altitude, aspect may also be important by affecting insolation, tending to reduce temperatures on shaded, steep north-west to north-east slopes, especially during the winter. Low ground on Skye is generally free from air-frosts from mid-April to late November.

Total annual average rainfall on Skye is between 65 and 80 inches (165–203 cm) in the lowlands, increasing with altitude to at least 90 inches (228 cm) on The Storr, whereas a limited area centred around the Cuillins probably receives at least 125 inches (318 cm) a year (*Annual Average Rainfall Map*, 1967). Broadford, in the lee of the Red Hills and the Cuillins, receives over 100 inches (254 cm) a year at sea level (Slesser, 1970). Rainfall does not show a simple relation to altitude for, although it tends to increase with height on any one slope, the zone of highest precipitation usually extends some distance to the leeward of the highest ground, thus affecting low ground as well. This may also be followed by a rain shadow. The rainfall along the coast is almost invariably less than it is a little distance inland, due mainly to disturbances of air flow resulting from changes in relief. Rainfall is distributed rather evenly throughout the year (see Table 3.3), and although prolonged and heavy rain may fall in any one month, there are few lengthy drought periods in the lowlands (except for remarkable summers, such as 1968). The winter months are the wettest, though July and August are highly placed in the order of monthly rainfall.

TABLE 3.3 *Average monthly rainfall (mm) at Portree (sea-level) for the period 1916–1950*
(*from* Annual Average Rainfall Map, 1967)

Jan.	Feb.	Mar.	Apr.	May	June	July	Aug.	Sept.	Oct.	Nov.	Dec.	Total for year (mm)
205	140	115	115	95	105	120	140	170	220	200	190	1815

Relative humidity is generally high (>75%) throughout the year. The average annual number of rain-days (a day with at least 0.01 inches (0.2 mm) rain) is about 250 (*Climatological Atlas*, 1952) and there are 200–220 wet-days (a day with at least 0.04 inches (1 mm) rain) throughout the island, increasing to 220+ in the uplands (Ratcliffe, 1968). The average annual potential water deficit (soil water deficit) is insignificant (<0.5 inches, 1.27 cm) throughout the island (Green, 1959; 1964), but this probably varies locally with topography, aspect and soil characteristics. For example, steep north- and east-facing slopes tend to be wetter in both atmosphere and soil, for the reduction of insolation reduces evaporation and transpiration rates. In contrast, on wind-exposed slopes and summit plateaux where the severe winds aid dessication and where there are no ground-water sources to replenish water losses, short term increases in potential water deficit may occur.

Cloud cover is correlated with rainfall, and the Cuillins and the Trotternish Peninsula experience a high cloud-cover, whereas the Red Hills and the Kyleakin Hills appear to experience a lower amount of cloud. Mist is frequent on ground above 1000 feet (305 m) at all times of the year. Besides maintaining a regionally high air humidity, prolonged low cloud reduces incident radiation and air temperature, thus potentially limiting plant growth.

There is a striking west–east gradient across Skye in the average daily duration of bright sunshine (*Climatological Atlas*, 1952) with the Duirinish, Glenbrittle, Elgol, and Sleat Peninsulas receiving a greater total sunshine than any other parts of the island. The importance of this in terms of plant growth is strikingly shown by the luxuriance of hedgebanks and crops in the Sleat Peninsula.

In contrast to its importance in the eastern Highlands, snow appears to have limited effects on the montane vegetation of Skye. The duration of snow-lie varies greatly from one winter to another. A little snow usually falls on the Cuillin summits before the end of October, and during the rest of the winter there are alternating and variable periods of snow-cover and thaw until the end of March. Snow-patches only persist very locally in high-lying sheltered depressions and shaded gullies with a northerly aspect until late July following winters when accumulation has been heavy, and after a cold spring with little warm, heavy rain. Such areas support a characteristic vegetation (see Chapter 4). The *Climatological Atlas* (1952) shows annual averages of 10–20 mornings with snow lying in the lowlands in the period 1912–38, increasing to 30 mornings in the Cuillins, and of 20–25 days with snow falling on low ground. These figures contrast with figures of over 100 mornings and 30–35 days, respectively, in the Cairngorms. Records of snow-cover at various altitudes in the Cuillins are given in the *Snow Survey of Great Britain* (1948–56). The mean annual number of days with snow lying at 3000 feet (920 m) is about 75 days, decreasing to 25 days at 1000 feet (305 m). This contrasts with 45–60 days in Snowdonia and over 140 days on Ben Nevis and the Cairngorms at 3000 feet (920 m), and with 215 days at 4000 feet (1220 m) on Ben Nevis. Manley (1952) has calculated that the present snow-line would be 5300 feet (1620 m) on Ben Nevis.

Prevailing wind directions are largely north-west to south, influenced by North Atlantic depressions, and the average wind-speed is about 6.7 $m\,s^{-1}$ at 33 feet (10 m) above ground level in open situations (*Climatological Atlas*, 1952). There are no measurements of wind speeds on high ground on Skye, but discounting shelter effects, wind-exposure increases with altitude, and it is extreme on the highest summits. Average wind-speeds on the Cuillins are probably between those on Ben Nevis (13.4 $m\,s^{-1}$) and Dun Fell (8.9 $m\,s^{-1}$) (figures from Manley, 1945; 1952). At sea-level Skye experiences gale-force winds (a wind greater than 16.4 $m\,s^{-1}$) on 20–30 days a year (*Climatological Atlas*, 1952), and although wind-exposure can vary locally with topography, there will be a greater frequency of gale-force winds at higher altitudes, perhaps between 150 and 200 days a year. This would be a rather lower frequency than the summit of Ben Nevis where over a period of 16 years, the average annual frequency of gale-force winds was 261 days.

4. LAND USE

The present population of the Isle of Skye is about 7400 people, 2500 of whom live in Portree or Broadford. The remainder are divided among about 180 townships that are mostly situated in fertile areas near the coast. At the beginning of the nineteenth century the population was at a maximum of 23074 people (Murray, 1966), mainly engaged in crofting, fishing, and kelp-burning. Between 1840 and 1880 sheep-farming was introduced, and there were many evictions of crofters. The dispossessed people mainly drifted southwards to the developing industrial areas or emigrated to America or Australia, although some accepted tiny holdings offered to them along the coast. Since the 1886–1911 Small Landholders (Scotland) Acts the land has been redistributed, and during the present century government grants for land improvement have become available, resulting in the reclamation, reseeding, and general improvement of over 250 hectares since 1956.

Crofted land is used for growing crops of potatoes and oats, or for hay for livestock. The only part of Skye that is climatically suitable for growing other crops is the Sleat, but the soils are rather poor for profitable yields. There are more fertile soils on the basalts in the northern part of the island, but the climate there is more severe.

Most of the island is managed as upland hill pasture, and it is grazed mainly by sheep. There are over 100 000 sheep on Skye, primarily Black-faced sheep, and about 11 000 cattle, mostly Highland breeds. The stocking rates of breeding sheep are rather low, with one sheep per 4 hectares or more over much of the island, increasing to one sheep per 2.2 hectares on the more fertile pastures in the Trotternish Peninsula (King & Nicholson, 1964). The grazing pressures are not uniformly distributed over the island, for quite apart from differences in management of different flocks, there is selective grazing both by wild and domestic animals of the more productive and fertile areas. Further differences arise from the fact that sheep tend to graze less on steep, rocky sites than on unbroken slopes, and that the higher summit areas are usually grazed during the summer only. Many of the more fertile grasslands on the basalt soils in Trotternish are badly overgrazed, both by sheep and by rabbits, resulting in the loss of vegetational cover, and consequent sheet and gully erosion and loss of soil on many of the steeper slopes (McVean & Lockie, 1969).

There is little game preservation on Skye, except for some stalking of red-deer (*Cervus elephus* L.) in the Cuillins and Red Hills, and some shooting of grouse (*Lagopus lagopus* L.) on some of the more remote moors. Although moor-burning is not greatly in evidence at present, there are indications that it has been widely practised in the past. There have been many attempts at drainage of wet ground in the lowlands, and locally a great amount of peat is still cut for fuel, especially near the coastal townships. Most areas of bog, both in the lowlands and the uplands, have been burnt and cut at some time, often resulting in peat erosion and bog degeneration.

Over 2000 hectares of lowland moorland and bog have been planted recently with introduced conifers by the Forestry Commission, and these activities are increasing. All the surviving areas of deciduous woodland appear to have been exploited to some degree for timber in the past.

Due to a rapidly increasing tourist trade, many of the roads on Skye have been improved and rebuilt, but despite the increased communications with the rest of Britain, there is likely to be little change in the land-use practices on Skye in the near future.

4

THE VEGETATION

1. INTRODUCTION

A survey of the present flora and vegetation of the Isle of Skye was undertaken to provide a modern ecological basis for the subsequent palaeoecological investigations. The survey was made in a period of fifteen weeks during the summers of 1966, 1967, 1968, and 1969 in association with the author's wife, Dr Hilary H. Birks. The aims of the survey were:

1. to characterise and to delimit, on floristic criteria, the principal vegetational types occurring on Skye today,
2. to describe the range of floristic variation between the vegetational types as an aid to the recognition of the main directions of variation in the floristic and sociological composition of the present vegetation,
3. to provide a basis on which to consider the role of environmental factors in influencing the spatial distribution and floristic composition of the present vegetation,
4. to permit floristic and vegetational comparisons to be made within Skye, with other areas of the British Isles, and elsewhere in Europe, and
5. to place the present floristic and vegetational patterns in a suitable ecological context that could be used in the interpretation of the palaeoecological data.

The theoretical and practical problems involved in the description of vegetation, and the organisation and delimitation of vegetational units have been extensively discussed by Dahl (1956), Greig-Smith (1964), Lambert & Dale (1964), and Poore (1955*a*, 1955*b*, 1956, 1962).

In any ecological study of vegetation the plant ecologist must adopt certain methods to describe and to simplify and organise the vegetational complex of an area, in an attempt to discover and to clarify the relationships between the vegetation and the environment. The approach adopted depends largely upon the purpose of the investigation and the nature of the problems involved, but it is also conditioned by the implicit views of the ecologist about the general nature of vegetation and its structural complexity (see Yarranton, 1967*a*). The aim of the present study has been to abstract meaningful entities from the complex of plant assemblages that comprise the present vegetational cover of the Isle of Skye, solely on floristic criteria. Such entities may then be related to the observable environmental factors. The approach was thus essentially floristic, although naturally the data were collected from as wide a range of habitats as possible.

In any vegetational study there is a potential conflict in approach between the recognition of discrete vegetational units on the one hand, and the continuous variation in vegetation and environment on the other (see Goodall, 1963; Greig-Smith, 1964; McIntosh, 1967). Goodall (1954) has emphasised the importance of treating variation in vegetation as a continuous variable, rather than imposing arbitrary classificatory divisions upon it. Goodall thus advocated the use of ordination methods rather than classification procedures in vegetational description. In ordination methods, stands of similar floristic composition and abundance are initially arranged together on a relatively small number of axes of variation within a multidimensional system ('vegetational space' *sensu* Goodall, 1963), the distances between stands being some property of their floristic similarity. Environmental factors and individual species distributions can then be plotted on the stand ordination, and correlations attempted between species occurrence and abundance and environmental factors. In classificatory approaches, a similar analytical procedure is followed. Floristically similar groups of stands are initially assembled together, in an attempt to simplify a large and complex mass of raw data, and the relationships of these groups to habitat factors can then be considered. Both ordination and classification are essentially 'structuring' techniques (Lambert & Dale, 1964), in that both approaches are aimed at seeking organisation and simplification of the original data. Classificatory methods are frequently criticised as being arbitrary in that the limits to the groupings are set by the investigator; but many ordination procedures are equally arbitrary in that the number of axes adopted is also determined by the investigator (Lambert & Dale, 1964).

The applications of objective ordination techniques to either primary surveys or intensive studies of European vegetation have, so far, largely resulted in ecological hypotheses and conclusions closely similar to those arrived at independently by classificatory methods (see Rogers, 1970; van Groenewoud, 1965). When applied to carefully selected problems of detailed distribution of species in relation to small and rather subtle environmental differences, ordination approaches may produce results commensurate with the work involved. Both classification and ordination are valuable tools in vegetational description, in that they can serve different needs and may thus be complementary to each other (Anderson, 1965; Gittins, 1965; Goodall, 1963, 1970). In attempting a reconnaissance vegetational survey of an area as large and as diverse as Skye, a semi-quantitative classificatory approach appeared to be the most appropriate.

The classification of plant communities is a matter of considerable controversy, which has been discussed by Whittaker (1962). Many of the differences between the British, Scandinavian, and Continental ecological aims and methods have been greatly exaggerated in the past, and as a result much common ground may have been ignored (Moore, 1962).

The descriptive phytosociological approach was chosen as the most suitable of the methods of vegetational classification for the present study. Descriptive phytosociology is one of the most established and widely accepted methods of primary vegetational survey in Europe, it is economical in time and effort, and it provides a means of comparison of vegetational units both within and outside the area of study. The alternative approach of association analysis and related numerical techniques is less concerned with the construction of an abstract vegetational classification that can be applied within and between areas than with the treatment of each investigated area as a separate entity in order to extract the maximum ecological information from it (Lambert & Dale, 1964). This results in a large number of individual studies that cannot readily be grouped into a single unified scheme.

Ivimey-Cook & Proctor (1966*a*) have applied association-analysis and the related 'nodal-analysis' to data obtained in a primary vegetational survey using descriptive phytosociological techniques. In general, the association-analysis confirmed the phytosociological classification, and it also proved a useful technique for the determination of constant, faithful, and differential species. Moore & O'Sullivan (1970) have compared the classification obtained in a vegetational survey of Irish grasslands using descriptive phytosociological techniques with those obtained by agglomerative analysis using two different coefficients of floristic similarity. The classifications obtained by the cluster analyses closely corresponded to the original phytosociological classification. Lambert & Dale (1964) have argued that the proper application of association analysis to primary vegetational survey involves abandonment of the phytosociological method of selective sampling of plots for description in the field, and its replacement by the sampling of the vegetation by a regular grid of plots. This latter approach is clearly only applicable if a relatively small area is studied, but for a primary survey of a large area, it raises two serious practical problems. It is extremely difficult to set out regularly, or indeed randomly, distributed plots accurately and objectively in an area as large and as topographically diverse as the Isle of Skye, and even if this were possible, vegetational types that occupy large areas of terrain would tend to be represented by a very large number of relevés, whereas more restricted or local types would be represented by a few relevés, or even none at all. A great deal of time and effort would have to be expended on repetitive sampling of common vegetation types if the less common types are to be sampled at all adequately (see Moore, Fitzsimmons, Lambe & White, 1970).

Moore *et al.* (1970) conducted a comparison of the relative efficiencies of association analysis, cluster analysis, ordination, and descriptive phytosociology when applied to the same vegetational data from three different areas. They concluded that descriptive phytosociology was the most efficient tool for primary vegetational survey, as it was most economical in terms of the time and effort involved in the sampling, recording, and processing of the data, and it yielded results at least as informative and as valuable in the subsequent generation of ecological hypotheses as anything obtainable from association analysis, ordination, or cluster analysis when considered separately. In view of the present consensus of opinion in favour of descriptive phytosociology being ideally suited for primary vegetational surveys and subsequent comparison with other areas, it was adopted for the present study. The value of descriptive phytosociology as a tool in vegetational description and in plant ecology as a whole, is perhaps most clearly demonstrated by the advanced and organised state of knowledge in those countries where such techniques have been applied widely, as opposed to those areas where a preoccupation with concepts and techniques has inhibited the extensive applications of any one method.

To summarise, the classificatory methods of descriptive phytosociology were considered the most appropriate for the present purposes because of the time and labour available, the limited state of knowledge of the flora and vegetation prior to the survey, and the comparatively large area to be surveyed. The Isle of Skye, with its varied geology and topography (see Chapter 3) and its rich and diverse flora (see Chapter 6), provided an ideal area for such a study.

The phytosociological classification presented here attempts to abstract meaningful and consistent entities from the complex of plant assemblages that comprise the present vegetation of the Isle of Skye. The value of such an approach is five-fold: it provides a description of the vegetation and a classification of the vegetational data; it allows comparisons to be made of the vegetational types within the area of study and with other areas; it establishes an initial but admittedly a rather general framework for considering the ecological and spatial relationships of the individual species and of the vegetational types; it reveals most readily and most efficiently the principal directions of variation within the vegetational and floristic complex; and it permits the generation of working hypotheses concerning the role of environmental factors in influencing the flora and vegetation in an area as large as Skye. The testing of such ecological hypotheses requires further and more detailed observations on specific problems.

2. FIELD AND LABORATORY METHODS

The field methods adopted were generally similar to those of Dahl (1956), McVean & Ratcliffe (1962), and Poore (1955*a*, 1955*b*). Areas of vegetation (*stands*) that appeared as uniform as possible were selected for description in the field. A uniform or homogeneous stand of vegetation is here defined as one that shows no obvious variation in the spatial distribution, physiognomy, or relative abundance of at least the major species present, and that shows little or no variation in ecological conditions within the stand, as far as these features can be determined by inspection.

A standard plot size of 4 square metres was normally used for description within a uniform stand, but in some cliff and boulder vegetation types, smaller plots were necessary, and in the woodland stands, larger plots of 16 square metres were generally selected. The sample size for each plot analysed is shown in the floristic tables. No attempt was made to assess a 'minimal area' statistically as this concept has been considered by Dahl (1956), Nordhagen (1927), and Poore (1955*a*), to be of less value in the field than ecological experience and general assessment of the 'scale' of the vegetation.

All the taxa occurring within the plots were recorded in the field, and those of doubtful identity were collected and subsequently determined in the laboratory. Certain identification problems were encountered. In some bryophyte genera, for example *Cephalozia*, *Lejeunea*, *Campylium*, *Thuidium*, and *Ulota*, several closely related species often occurred together and could not always be distinguished in the field. The identifications listed in the tables are considered reliable, but occasionally one species may have been overlooked in the presence of another. Although an attempt was made to identify all 'critical' taxa occurring within the stands, immature or non-flowing individuals of *Euphrasia*, *Hieracium*, and *Taraxacum* were frequently encountered, and these could only be referred to the aggregate taxon. In closely-grazed grasslands it was often difficult to estimate the relative proportions of *Festuca ovina* and *F. vivipara*, since the specific identifications depended on inflorescences, whereas the estimates of cover-abundance referred to vegetative growth. Much of the field work was done in late July and August, and hence vernal species, such as *Ranunculus ficaria*, though probably common, may not have been recorded. Subject to the above limitations, the plant lists are considered to be comprehensive and accurate.

The cover and abundance of all the taxa occurring within the plots were estimated visually on the 10-point Domin scale:

1. Cover less than 4%; very rare, one or a few individuals.
2. Cover less than 4%; scattered individuals.
3. Cover less than 4%; frequent individuals.
4. Cover 4–10%.
5. Cover 10–25%.
6. Cover 25–33%.
7. Cover 33–50%.
8. Cover 50–75%.
9. Cover 75–90%.
10. Cover 90–100%.

Cover is here defined as the estimate of the space covered by a vertical projection on the soil of all the living, above-ground parts of the plants. When more than one vegetational layer was present, each stratum was estimated separately. Total vegetational cover within the plot was also recorded. Species absent from the plot, but occurring in the stand immediately adjacent to the plot, were also recorded, and these are indicated by a + in the tables. For a few plots only a species list was made: species occurrence within a plot is indicated by a × in the tables. No 'index of sociability', such as Braun-Blanquet's scale (1951), was used, because of the potential ambiguities in such scales discussed by Poore (1955*a*).

The descriptive methods used proved to be practicable, despite the limited time available, the variable weather, and the general remoteness of much of the terrain on Skye. They are considered to represent a reasonable practical compromise between the more time-consuming statistical approaches and the rather scanty vegetational descriptions prevalent in much of the British ecological literature (Poore, 1962). As Poore (1962) has emphasised, no vegetational description can ever describe all the attributes of even the simplest community at one moment of time, no matter how exact is the method used. Criticisms have been frequently levelled at the use of subjective estimates of cover and abundance in the description of vegetation. Such criticisms are certainly valid if the conclusions that are drawn are themselves more detailed than the original observations. The purpose of the vegetational descriptions in this study was not only to give an accurate and reliable record of the actual vegetation analysed, but also to permit comparisons to be made between one description and another. Such comparisons were, however, usually concerned with differences in the presence or absence of species, and with significant and consistent differences in species abundance. With such aims the field methods were considered to be justified and to provide the most economical means of obtaining the required information. In primary surveys such as this, it was clearly advantageous to use standard and efficient field techniques in order to facilitate the subsequent task of comparing large numbers of field descriptions.

Each plot analysed was given a reference number in the field. Habitat features, such as aspect, slope, attitude, soil type, geology, and the relationships of the stands to nearby vegetation types, were also noted in the field. Aspect was measured with a compass, and expressed in degrees to the nearest cardinal point. Slope was either estimated by eye or measured with a hand level. When there was an imperceptible slope but a distinct direction of drainage, the latter was noted; for example 0° N refers to a drainage towards the north. Altitude was estimated from the Ordnance Survey maps.

Soil samples were collected of the top 5 cm of soil, or of the combined A horizons where the depth was less than 5 cm. The pH values of the soil samples were measured within 12 hours of collection, using a minimal addition of distilled water, a glass electrode, and a Pye portable pH meter. Samples of water from freshwater lochs, mires, and springs adjacent to the vegetational plots were collected in plastic bottles. These samples were filtered through No. 44 Whatman papers as soon as possible after collection, and their pH values were determined using a glass electrode. The water samples were stored at 5 °C until analysis, a drop of toluene being added to prevent microbial growth. The conductivity was measured with a Mullard conductivity bridge, the reading being corrected for water temperature and hydrogen ion conductivity and expressed as the corrected specific conductivity (K_{corr}) at 20 °C in reciprocal megohms (μmhos) (Sjörs, 1950*a*). Calcium and magnesium ion concentrations were determined with an Eel atomic absorption spectrophotometer. Sodium and potassium ion concentrations were determined with an Eel flame photometer. All ionic concentrations were expressed in milligrams/litre.

3. PHYTOSOCIOLOGICAL TERMINOLOGY AND CLASSIFICATION

A *stand* (or *Bestand*) of vegetation is here defined as an actual area of vegetation in the field from which a plot has been described. A *relevé* (or *Aufnahme*) is an annotated list of species and related site characteristics recorded in the description of a plot within a homogeneous stand of vegetation. A *community* is any aggregation of plants constituting a certain spatial whole. It is used here as an abstract unit of vegetation of any classificatory standing (association, facies, order, etc.) whose nature is not indicated. It is regarded as synonymous with Poore's (1955*a*) general term 'nodum'.

Although the vegetational relevés were collected from as wide a range of habitats as possible, the relevés have been grouped solely on the basis of floristic affinities, irrespective of habitat. In many cases there were such obvious similarities in the floristic composition of the species lists for different relevés that they could be grouped readily into vegetational units. In other cases, where such similarities were less clear cut and the relevés fell less readily into distinct groups, the lists were arranged by inspection, using a 'process of successive approximation' (Poore, 1956, 1962) in which floristic similarities between lists were compared and lists that upset the consistency of a group were rejected. Repeated sorting of the lists to find consistent species combinations resulted in the formation of vegetational units containing a number of relevés with a consistent combination of constant, faithful, differential, and, to some degree, dominant species not found as such in any other vegetational unit. A *constant species* is here defined as one that occurs in 81–100% (Constancy or Presence Class V; Braun-Blanquet, 1951) of the relevés within a vegetational type; a *dominant species* of a given layer is the one with the highest cover-abundance value in the relevés; a *faithful species* is one that shows a high degree of fidelity (exclusive, selective, preferential; see Braun-Blanquet, 1951; Poore, 1955*b*) towards a particular vegetational type; and a *differential species* is a non-faithful species which can be used to distinguish between two closely related groups of relevés. Relatively little use was made of the concept of fidelity in this work. The selection of a particular species as exclusive to a particular vegetational unit from inspection of the vegetational analyses was frequently invalidated by the field observation of its occurrence in fragmentary or mixed stands of other communities which had not been analysed.

As a test for floristic homogeneity or 'homotoneity' (Nordhagen, 1943) within a group of relevés, Raunkiaer's (1934) 'Law of Frequencies' provides a useful empirical tool which has a certain theoretical basis (Dahl, 1956; Dahl & Hadač, 1949; Goodall, 1970; cf. McIntosh, 1962). A group of at least five relevés is required for such a test, and if the group conforms to the homogeneity test it is termed an association. An *association* is here defined as a plant community containing certain specified plant taxa in which the number of taxa in Constancy Class V (constants *sensu stricto*) exceeds or is equal to the number of taxa in Constancy Class IV (61–80%), and which differs from other communities in its floristic composition, particularly in its constant, dominant, and faithful taxa. It is an abstraction, obtained by the comparison of a number of relevés made in selected stands in the field. It is defined solely by floristic composition, and *not* by habitat.

Within an association so defined there may be considerable floristic variation, and in some cases the associations were divided into *subassociations*. These contain the constant and faithful taxa of the given association, but differ from it in the occurrence of certain clearly definable differential taxa; these taxa are absent from the other subassociations of the given association, but they may occur in other vegetational types. When less than five relevés are available, or where the vegetational unit is rather heterogeneous, it is termed a *nodum*. The word is italicised when it is used to refer to a specific vegetational unit that does not merit the rank of association. If used otherwise, it refers to any abstract vegetational unit of unspecified rank (Poore, 1955*a*). When there is an obvious floristic discontinuity within an association, but one that is hardly significant to warrant the delimitation of further units, it is termed a *facies*.

The use of the constancy test for floristic homogeneity is only strictly valid when all the lists have been prepared from equal sized plots (Dahl, 1956). Although it was necessary to depart from a standard plot size in some cases, species occurring outside the plot (+) were recorded from the immediate surroundings only, thus reducing any discrepancies resulting from plots of unequal size. In cases where plots of unequal size were used and compared, there was no significant positive correlation between the number of species recorded and the size of plot used. It was concluded that the unequal sample size did not, in these instances at least, introduce any appreciable error into the comparisons (see Dahl, 1956). The analyses were therefore treated as comparable in spite of the unequal plot size.

As the work progressed it became increasingly apparent that much of the variation in the vegetation was virtually continuous, with rather gradual spatial changes between some vegetational types. Although fairly sharp discontinuities occurred locally between some vegetational types, it was often possible to find a series of intermediates to link related vegetational types on examination of a larger area. It was thus important to select a sufficient number of arbitrary vegetational 'reference points' to provide as adequate a representation as possible of the total range of variation in the present vegetation. The concept of vegetational 'reference points' in a field of more or less continuous variation has been expressed by Poore (1955*a*, 1962) in his term 'nodum', and by Goodall (1963) in his concept of 'clusters' within a multidimensional vegetational space. It is around such clusters that lines of arbitrary boundaries can be drawn to delimit vegetational units or 'reference points.' An important practical problem arises, however, in the spacing of such 'reference points' in the field – whether to take a large number close together, or a smaller number from a larger area that may overlap in composition. In practice the first alternative was adopted in species-rich and heterogeneous vegetation types, where spatial changes were frequently rapid, whereas the second alternative was followed in more homogeneous, floristically-poor vegetation where spatial changes are more gradual. The selection of 'reference points' is clearly rather subjective, but the present survey involved the recording of 550 relevés collected from all over the island. The relevés were subsequently grouped into 81 vegetational units, and these units are considered to provide an adequate representation of at least the major plant communities occurring on Skye today.

About two thirds of the vegetational units were classified as associations. In order to demonstrate the full range of the vegetational units on Skye, and to emphasise the connections between them, all the available floristic analyses were considered for potential groupings. This has involved a certain sacrifice of the homogeneity of the individual units, but it represents a reasonable compromise between a neat classification covering only a small proportion of the possible vegetational types, and a comprehensive, but undigested, mass of raw data. Following this procedure, only seven out of the total of 550 relevés remained unclassified.

The homogeneity of any vegetational unit depends, to some degree, on the initial choice of stands for analysis and on the choice of lists in the compilation of the floristic tables. It might be possible to promote more vegetational units to association status by more careful selection at both these stages. Although a high measure of homogeneity in a particular vegetational unit is desirable in that it simplifies attempts at characterising vegetation in terms of consistent features, it is unwise to force the units to conform to any prescribed standard of uniformity *per se*, since there are real as well as artificial variations in vegetational homogeneity, related to instability and spatial variations of habitat, to chance as it influences plant dispersal, and to forms of vegetative spread and morphological pattern. As the degree of selection has been kept within similar bounds throughout, the defined units are considered to represent a fair reflection of the natural range in the floristic composition of the present vegetation of Skye.

By applying numerical methods to measure the degree of similarity between floristic lists (see Češka, 1966; Dahl, 1956; Poore, 1955*c*), it should eventually be possible to provide numerical criteria for the delineation of vegetational units, thereby giving a more even spacing of 'reference points' or noda, and aiding in the objective definition of the limits of the units themselves (associations, subassociations, *noda*, etc.). Such an approach might, however, involve the rejection of many lists, with a corresponding loss of potentially useful information. The simpler methods adopted in this study, although more subjective, are considered adequate for the present purpose.

No attempt has been made to maintain the distinction proposed by Du Rietz (1930) between an association (a vegetational unit characterised mainly by faithful and differential species) and a sociation (a vegetational unit characterised mainly by dominance in the different layers). Both types of units are designed to serve the same function in vegetational classification, and it is difficult to decide *a priori* by which criteria vegetational units should be distinguished. In species-rich communities, faithful taxa may be useful in delimiting vegetational types; in species-poor communities dominant taxa may be important in vegetational characterisation. In several vegetational types it is often useful to employ several criteria for their characterisation (Dahl, 1956), and this has been the case in the present work.

The vegetational tables are arranged in a format similar to those of McVean & Ratcliffe (1962). The more typical Continental arrangement of vegetational tables has not been attempted, as little is known about species fidelity, both in associations and in higher vegetational units, in western Scotland. Associations, subassociations, and *noda* have been named according to their most prominent species or genera (dominants or constants); faithful species were not used for this purpose. Wherever the vegetational unit could be clearly identified with a previously named community that name was used, and the relevant authority given.

The *noda*, subassociations, and associations have been arranged for convenience into a hierarchy of higher units – alliances, orders, and classes. Some British ecologists have objected to this type of hierarchical arrangement and have indicated a preference for a multidimensional system of vegetation types or ecological gradients (Webb, 1954). In an area such as the Isle of Skye with a rich and diverse vegetation, a multidimensional classification of all the vegetation types does, however, raise serious practical problems of computation, presentation, and visualization (cf. Gams, 1941). In a descriptive account such as this, the communities can only be arranged in a linear sequence. This is readily done without destroying the essential form of a hierarchical or two-dimensional classification, but a multidimensional arrangement cannot be dealt with in this way. The nature and value of any classificatory scheme should be judged in relation to the purpose for which it is required (Gilmour & Walters, 1963), and, in the present work, a hierarchical system is considered to be the most convenient approach.

The arrangement and nomenclature of the classes, orders, and alliances follows, with some modifications, the schemes proposed by Lohmeyer *et al.* (1962), Oberdorfer (1957, 1970), Oberdorfer *et al.* (1967), and Westhoff & Den Held (1969). It was considered desirable to adopt an established and widely accepted mode of classification rather than to formulate a new and local system of higher units. The scheme of higher units introduced by the Continental phytosociologists is not commonly used or known in Britain. Although the higher units are nominally defined by concepts of fidelity, they were originally conceived in broader ecological and physiognomic terms and, in practice, they frequently correspond to contrasting habitat conditions (Braun-Blanquet, 1948–50; Dahl, 1956; Nordhagen, 1936; Oberdorfer, 1957; Westhoff & Den Held, 1969). Associations belonging to the same alliance are usually found either occupying broadly similar habitats, or occupying comparable ecological niches in different geographical regions. The classes are broadly arranged in an order of 'sociological progression', starting with the simplest and most poorly integrated types and culminating in the most complex and highly organised woodland communities. Thus, in general, seral stages are placed early in the arrangement, and climax vegetation types towards the end.

The complete analyses of floristic composition are presented in the floristic tables (Tables 4.1–4.15 and 4.17–4.56) and only the salient features of each vegetational type are discussed in this chapter. These include the range of floristic variation shown by each type and the criteria which distinguish them from other related types, the geographical extent on Skye, the habitat range of each type, and the spatial and ecological relationships to other vegetational types, and the relevant ecological features. Wherever possible the vegetational types are compared with similar communities occurring elsewhere in the British Isles. This comparison is based mainly on the author's field experience in south-west England, north Wales, Lakeland, the Pennines, Southern Uplands, Scottish Highlands, and western Ireland, but any relevant literature is also cited. A similar comparison of the Skye communities with those of Scandinavia and the rest of Europe is based largely on published material. The terminology of soil-types follows that of Fitzpatrick (1964).

In the floristic tables (Tables 4.1–4.56, which are grouped at end of Chapter 4) the reference number of each relevé is divided into an upper line giving the initial of the recorder's name and the year of the record, and a lower line giving the recorder's serial number for that year. Each plot is located by a full six-figure Ordnance Survey National Grid Reference, with eastings in the upper line, and northings in the lower line. All grid references on the Isle of Skye fall within the 100 km square 18 or NG. A separate list of localities is also given at the bottom of the tables. Altitude of the plot is expressed in feet without the metric equivalent, but the altitudinal range of each vegetational type is given in both feet and metres in the text. Aspect of the plot is given in degrees to the nearest cardinal point, and slope is expressed in degrees. For plots from aquatic habitats, the depth of water is given in centimetres. The figure for percentage total vegetational cover does not distinguish between plots with bare rock and those with unvegetated soil. This is considered in the text. The area of each plot sampled is given in square metres. A point (·) in the relevant column indicates that the particular feature was not determined or not determinable.

The species are arranged in alphabetical order within the following broad categories: trees, shrubs, and dwarf shrubs; pteridophytes; grasses; other monocotyledons; dicotyledon herbs; mosses; liverworts; lichens; algae. A few taxa are not considered within the group to which they belong in the strict sense, for example *Thymus drucei* is grouped as a herb rather than as a dwarf shrub. In the body of the tables, the figures represent combined cover-abundance values on the 10-point Domin scale, with the addition of + for taxa immediately within the stand but not in the sample plot itself, and × for taxa in the sample plot but whose cover-abundance values were not determined. Taxa that only occur once in a table are grouped together at the bottom. Where the cover and abundance of several taxa, for example *Festuca ovina* and *F. vivipara*, have been estimated together, the combined value is printed in italics, and repeated for each of the taxa concerned. The constancy of each taxon in all associations, and subassociations with 5 or more relevés is given in the column labelled C, with Constancy Class V representing presence in 81–100% of the plots, IV representing 61–80% presence, III representing 41–60% presence, II representing

21–40% presence, and I representing 0–20% presence. The mean Domin value for each taxon is given in the column labelled D. All association or *nodum* constants have been printed in bold type; the main differential and faithful species are mentioned in the text, and shown in the synthetic table (Table 4.57). The total number of species recorded in each plot, and in each nodum is given at the bottom. The mean number of species per plot within a vegetational unit is also given. In tables where relevés for two or more noda are presented, the total number of species in each nodum is shown.

Subspecies and varieties are generally not distinguished in the tables, but they are distinguished in the footnotes. Throughout the tables the following abbreviations have been used:

Asplenium adiantum-nigrum	=	*A. adiantum-nigrum* ssp. *adiantum-nigrum*
Viola riviniana	=	*V. riviniana* ssp. *riviniana*
Silene dioica	=	*S. dioica* ssp. *dioica*
Salix atrocinerea	=	*S. cinerea* ssp. *atrocinerea*
Armeria maritima	=	*A. maritima* ssp. *maritima*
Veronica serpyllifolia	=	*V. serpyllifolia* ssp. *serpyllifolia*
Tripleurospermum maritimum	=	*T. maritimum* ssp. *maritimum*
Trichophorum cespitosum	=	*T. cespitosum* ssp. *germanicum*

In several critical genera, for example *Hieracium*, *Taraxacum*, *Cochlearia*, and *Euphrasia*, the records are referred to the aggregate species, when immature or non-flowering individuals were encountered.

The occurrence of all the species in the principal vegetational types on Skye are tabulated in Table 4.57 on the basis of the five constancy or presence classes (Braun-Blanquet, 1951). Species that occur in only one community with a constancy of II or less are listed separately at the bottom of the table. Species with similar sociological amplitudes have been grouped together as far as possible, but in the case of species with a wide sociological amplitude, for example *Rumex acetosa*, the species are repeated in different parts of the table. The table serves to summarise the constant, differential, and faithful species of each vegetational type. There are, however, extremely few exclusive species of high constancy, suggesting that in the case of the present vegetation of Skye, a vegetational classification based on faithful species only would not be justified, or indeed possible. Although specific taxa can be selected from inspection of the tables as being exclusive to a particular vegetational type, this selection is frequently invalidated by further field observations (Poore, 1955*c*). However, all the species can be used as differential species between one community and another, and this procedure is invaluable in analysing the sociological characteristics and the possible ecological factors that differentiate one community from another. The floristic interrelations of the communities are, however, complex. The most striking feature of the table is the gradient running from the left-hand top to the right-hand base. Virtually none of the species are restricted to one community or even to groups of communities, and many species occur in a wide range of vegetational types. The communities that are floristically most distinctive are often the most specialised ones, for example lichen communities on boulders, montane spring communities, and salt-marsh vegetation. The overall impression from the table is that the vegetation is essentially a continuum in which the delimitation of units can only be rather arbitrary. As discussed by Poore (1955*c*) and McVean & Ratcliffe (1962), vegetational units delimited in a study such as this should be regarded as 'reference points' within a field of more or less continuous variation and not as discrete units that can be traced directly from one area to another.

4. CONSPECTUS OF THE PLANT COMMUNITIES

1. EPIPETRETEA LICHENOSA Massé 1964
   RHIZOCARPETALIA Massé 1964
   Parmelion saxatilis Massé 1964
   Hedwigia ciliata–Parmelia saxatilis Association

2. THLASPIETEA ROTUNDIFOLII Braun-Blanquet 1947
   ANDROSACETALIA ALPINAE Braun-Blanquet 1926
   Androsacion alpinae Braun-Blanquet 1926
   Scree Communities
   Koenigia islandica Scree Community
   River gravel Communities

3. ASPLENIETEA RUPESTRIS Braun-Blanquet 1934
   POTENTILLETALIA CAULESCENTIS Braun-Blanquet 1926
   Potentillion caulescentis Braun-Blanquet 1926
   Asplenium marinum–Grimmia maritima Association
   Asplenium trichomanes–Fissidens cristatus Association

4. CHENOPODIETEA (Braun-Blanquet 1951) Lohmeyer, J. Tüxen & R. Tüxen 1961
POLYGONO-CHENOPODIETALIA (R. Tüxen & Lohmeyer 1950) J. Tüxen 1961
Weed Communities

5. PLANTAGINETEA MAJORIS R. Tüxen & Preising 1950
PLANTAGINETALIA MAJORIS R. Tüxen (1947) 1950
Lolio–Plantaginion Sissingh 1969
Lolium perenne–Plantago major Association

6. ISOETO–NANOJUNCETEA Braun-Blanquet & R. Tüxen 1943
NANOCYPERETALIA Klika 1935
Nanocyperion flavescentis W. Koch 1926
Isolepis setacea–Blasia pusilla Communities

7. AMMOPHILETEA Braun-Blanquet & R. Tüxen 1943
ELYMO-AMMOPHILETALIA ARENARIAE Géhu & Géhu 1969
Agropyrion Boreoatlanticum Géhu & Géhu 1969
Fore-dune Communities
Ammophilion Borealis (R. Tüxen 1955) Géhu & Géhu 1969
Grey dune Turfs

8. ASTERETEA TRIPOLIUM Westhoff & Beeftink 1962
GLAUCETO-PUCCINELLIETALIA Beeftink & Westhoff 1962
Puccinellion maritimae (Christiansen 1927 *pro parte*) R. Tüxen 1937
Puccinellietum maritimae Association (Warming 1890) Christiansen 1927
Puccinellia maritima–Ascophyllum nodosum Subassociation
Puccinellia maritima–Festuca rubra Subassociation
Armerion maritimae Braun-Blanquet & De Leeuw 1936
Juncus gerardii–Carex extensa Association
Armeria maritima–Grimmia maritima Association

9. CAKILETEA MARITIMAE R. Tüxen & Preising 1950
CAKILETALIA MARITIMAE R. Tüxen & Preising in Oberdorfer 1949
Atriplicion littoralis (Nordhagen 1940) R. Tüxen 1950
Atriplex glabriuscula–Rumex crispus Association

10. LITTORELLETEA Braun-Blanquet & R. Tüxen 1943
LITTORELLETALIA W. Koch 1926
Littorellion uniflorae W. Koch 1926
Littorella uniflora–Lobelia dortmanna Association

11. POTAMETEA R. Tüxen & Preising 1942
MAGNOPOTAMETALIA Den Hartog & Segal 1964
Nymphaeion albae Oberdorfer 1957
Potamogeton natans–Nymphaea alba nodum
PARVOPOTAMETALIA Den Hartog & Segal 1964
Callitricho–Batrachion Den Hartog & Segal 1964
River Communities

12. PHRAGMITETEA R. Tüxen & Preising 1942
PHRAGMITETALIA EUROSIBIRICA (W. Koch 1926) R. Tüxen & Preising 1942
Phragmition communis W. Koch 1926
Brackish Water Communities
Schoenoplectus lacustris–Phragmites communis Association
Phragmites communis–Equisetum fluviatile Subassociation
Schoenoplectus lacustris–Equisetum fluviatile Subassociation
Magnocaricion elatae W. Koch 1926
Carex rostrata–Menyanthes trifoliata Association
Glycerio–Sparganion Braun-Blanquet & Sissingh 1942
Oenanthe crocata Communities

13. SCHEUCHZERIO–CARICETEA FUSCAE (Nordhagen 1936) R. Tüxen 1937
SCHEUCHZERIETALIA PALUSTRIS Nordhagen 1936
Rhynchosporion albae W. Koch 1926
Eriophorum angustifolium–Sphagnum cuspidatum Association
Caricion lasiocarpae Vanden Berghen 1949
Carex lasiocarpa–Menyanthes trifoliata Association
Carex rostrata–C. limosa nodum
CARICETALIA FUSCAE (W. Koch 1926) Nordhagen 1936
Caricion canescentis–fuscae (W. Koch 1926) Nordhagen 1936
Trichophorum cespitosum–Carex panicea Association
Molinia caerulea–Myrica gale Association
Sphagneto–Juncetum effusi Association McVean & Ratcliffe 1962
Carex–Sphagnum recurvum nodum

Sphagno–Tomenthypnion Dahl 1956
Carex rostrata–Aulacomnium palustre Association
TOFIELDIETALIA Preising in Oberdorfer 1949
Eriophorion latifoliae Braun-Blanquet & R. Tüxen 1943
Carex rostrata–Scorpidium scorpioides Association
Carex panicea–Campylium stellatum Association
Eriophorum latifolium–Carex hostiana Association
Schoenus nigricans Association
Carex–Saxifraga aizoides nodum

14. OXYCOCCO–SPHAGNETEA Braun-Blanquet & R. Tüxen 1943
ERICETALIA TETRALICIS Moore (1964) 1968
Ericion tetralicis Schwickerath 1933
Trichophoreto–Callunetum Association McVean & Ratcliffe 1962
Molinieto–Callunetum Association McVean & Ratcliffe 1962
SPHAGNETALIA MAGELLANICI Moore (1964) 1968
Erico–Sphagnion Moore (1964) 1968
Trichophoreto–Eriophoretum Association McVean & Ratcliffe 1962
Calluneto–Eriophoretum Association McVean & Ratcliffe 1962

15. MONTIO–CARDAMINETEA Braun-Blanquet & R. Tüxen 1943
MONTIO–CARDAMINETALIA Pawłowski 1928
Cardamino–Montion Braun-Blanquet 1925
Philonoto–Saxifragetum stellaris Association Nordhagen 1943
Koenigia islandica–Carex demissa nodum
Anthelia julacea banks
Cratoneurion commutati W. Koch 1928
Cratoneuron commutatum–Saxifraga aizoides nodum
Saxifragetum aizoidis Association McVean & Ratcliffe 1962

16. MOLINIO–ARRHENATHERETEA R. Tüxen 1937
MOLINIETALIA COERULEAE W. Koch 1926
Filipendulo–Petasition Braun-Blanquet 1947
Juncus acutiflorus–Filipendula ulmaria Association
ARRHENATHERETALIA Pawłowski 1928
Cynosurion cristati R. Tüxen 1947
Centaureo–Cynosuretum Association Braun-Blanquet & R. Tüxen 1952
Maritime grassland nodum

17. ELYNO–SESLERIETEA Braun-Blanquet 1948
ELYNO–DRYADETALIA Braun-Blanquet 1948
Kobresio–Dryadion Nordhagen (1936) 1943
Dryas octopetala–Carex flacca Association

18. CARICETEA CURVULAE Braun-Blanquet 1948
CARICETALIA CURVULAE Braun-Blanquet 1926
Arctostaphyleto–Cetrarion nivalis Dahl 1956
Cariceto–Rhacomitretum lanuginosi Association McVean & Ratcliffe 1962
Festuca ovina–Luzula spicata nodum
Rhacomitreto–Callunetum Association McVean & Ratcliffe 1962
Juniperus nana nodum
Rhacomitreto–Empetretum Association McVean & Ratcliffe 1962
Alchemilla alpina–Vaccinium myrtillus nodum

19. SALICETEA HERBACEAE Braun-Blanquet 1947
DESCHAMPSIETO–MYRTILLETALIA Dahl 1956
Nardeto–Caricion bigelowii (Nordhagen 1936) Dahl 1956
Nardus stricta–Vaccinium myrtillus Association

20. NARDO–CALLUNETEA Preising 1949
NARDETALIA (Oberdorfer 1949) Preising 1949
Nardo–Galion saxatilis Preising 1949
Agrosto–Festucetum (species-poor) Association McVean & Ratcliffe 1962
Alchemilleto–Agrosto–Festucetum Association McVean & Ratcliffe 1962
Agrosto–Festucetum (species-rich) Association McVean & Ratcliffe 1962
Dwarf herb nodum McVean & Ratcliffe 1962
Nardo–Juncetum squarrosi Association
CALLUNO–ULICETALIA (Quantin 1935) R. Tüxen 1937
Ericion cinereae Böcher 1943
Callunetum vulgaris Association McVean & Ratcliffe 1962
Calluna vulgaris–Sieglingia decumbens Association
Calluna vulgaris–Arctostaphylos uva-ursi nodum
Myrtillion boreale Böcher 1943
Vaccineto–Callunetum hepaticosum Association McVean & Ratcliffe 1962

21. BETULO–ADENOSTYLETEA Braun-Blanquet 1948
ADENOSTYLETALIA Braun-Blanquet 1931
Dryoptero–Calamagrostidion purpureae Nordhagen 1943
Luzula sylvatica–Vaccinium myrtillus Association

Mulgedion alpini Nordhagen 1943
Luzula sylvatica–Silene dioica Association
Betula pubescens–Cirsium heterophyllum Association
Sedum rosea–Alchemilla glabra Association

22. ALNETEA GLUTINOSAE Braun-Blanquet & R. Tüxen 1943
ALNETALIA GLUTINOSAE R. Tüxen 1937
Alnion glutinosae (Malcuit 1929) Meijer-Drees 1936
Alnus glutinosa Woods

23. QUERCETEA ROBORI–PETRAEAE Braun-Blanquet & R. Tüxen 1943
QUERCETALIA ROBORI–PETRAEAE R. Tüxen (1931) 1937
Quercion robori–petraeae (Malcuit 1929) Braun-Blanquet 1932
Betula pubescens–Vaccinium myrtillus Association
Corylus avellana–Oxalis acetosella Association
Oxalis acetosella–Rhytidiadelphus loreus Association
Hymenophyllum wilsonii–Isothecium myosuroides Association
Open Boulder Association

24. QUERCO–FAGETEA Braun-Blanquet & Vlieger 1937
FAGETALIA SYLVATICAE Pawłowski 1928
Fagion sylvaticae R. Tüxen & Diemont 1936
Fraxinus excelsior–Brachypodium sylvaticum Association

25. EPIPHYTIC COMMUNITIES
Epiphytes of Alnus glutinosa Woods
Epiphytes of Betula pubescens–Vaccinium myrtillus Association
Epiphytes of Corylus avellana–Oxalis acetosella Association
Decaying Log Communities

26. LIMESTONE PAVEMENT COMMUNITIES

5. THE PLANT COMMUNITIES

1. EPIPETRETEA LICHENOSA Massé 1964
Saxicolous lichen and bryophyte communities.

RHIZOCARPETALIA Massé 1964
Communities of dry acidic rocks.

Parmelion saxatilis Massé 1964
Hedwigia ciliata–Parmelia saxatilis Association

This is a distinctive but rather local association of large, dry, sun-exposed, south- to west-facing angular, detached blocks at moderate elevations (Table 4.1). It occurs most frequently on bare gabbro, peridotite, and basaltic rocks, and more rarely on granite. *Hedwigia ciliata*, *Hypnum cupressiforme*, *Rhacomitrium fasciculare*, *R. heterostichum*, *Lecidea cyathoides*, *Parmelia omphalodes*, and *P. saxatilis* are constants, and *Antitrichia curtipendula*, *Glyphomitrium daviesii*, *Grimmia ovalis*, *Hedwigia integrifolia*, *Ulota hutchinsiae*, *Frullania germana*, *Gymnomitrion crenulatum*, *Umbilicaria pustulata*, and *U. torrefacta* are notable components. The Mediterranean–Atlantic moss *Campylopus polytrichoides* has its northernmost known world localities on Skye, occurring in this community near sea-level with *Pterogonium gracile* and *Ptychomitrium polyphyllum*. With the gradual accumulation of humus, *Aira praecox*, *Agrostis tenuis*, *Rumex acetosella*, *Sedum anglicum*, and *Polytrichum piliferum* become more prominent in small depressions, crevices, and on gently sloping (5–25°) tops of boulders, often near the sea (cf. the *Aira praecox–Sedum anglicum* Association; Braun-Blanquet & Tüxen, 1952).

At higher altitudes (above about 1000 feet, 305 m) *Andreaea* spp. are prominent, forming a distinctive community on blocks and irrigated rock slabs. This community has not been examined. These and closely related communities occur on igneous rocks throughout much of northern and western Britain, for example on the Dartmoor granite (Yarranton, 1967*b*), and elsewhere in Europe (von Hübschmann, 1967).

2. THLASPIETEA ROTUNDIFOLII Braun-Blanquet 1947
Scree and gravel communities of the alpine and sub-alpine zones.

ANDROSACETALIA ALPINAE Braun-Blanquet 1926
Androsacion alpinae Braun-Blanquet 1926
Communities of non-calcareous montane screes and gravels.

Scree Communities

Extensive areas of exposed, angular rock debris cover much of the steeper slopes (30° or more) of the Cuillins and the Red Hills above 1500 feet (460 m). Most of the ground is unstable and is almost devoid of vegetation; the bare screes in the Red Hills probably result from soil erosion following repeated burning and intensive grazing (McVean & Lockie, 1969), whereas in the stone-shoots covering the steep backwalls of the Cuillin corries, constant addition of rock from above by frost shattering maintains the instability. In the few more stable areas, often with large angular blocks, such as in Coire Uaigneach on Blà Bheinn, and on the south slopes of Glamaig, some plant cover occurs, including *Cryptogramma crispa*, *Deschampsia flexuosa*, *Dryopteris abbreviata*, *Festuca ovina*, *Lycopodium selago*, *Ditrichum zonatum*, *Grimmia doniana*, *Rhacomitrium lanuginosum*, *Gymnomitrion concinnatum*, *G. obtusum*, *Marsupella adusta*, *M. stableri*, and *Stereocaulon* spp. Similar communities with *Cryptogramma crispa* occur widely in montane Britain (Leach, 1930; Tallis, 1958) but they tend to be rather local in the Scottish Highlands. In ungrazed, stablised areas on the larger screes *Luzula sylvatica–Vaccinium myrtillus* stands occasionally occur (Lists 4, 5; Table 4.45), that are rather similar in floristic composition to ungrazed vegetation of acidic cliffs.

Koenigia islandica Scree Community

The extensive fine-grained red-brown basalt screes above 1000 feet (305 m) on the steep slopes below the east-facing cliff escarpment of Trotternish are highly unstable and support a sparse but rather characteristic flora (Table 4.2). *Cardaminopsis petraea*, *Cherleria sedoides*, *Luzula spicata*, *Koenigia islandica*, *Oxyria digyna*, *Poa glauca*, and *Sagina subulata* are notable components of this community. Such areas probably result from both the inherent instability of the steep basalt slopes, and from the loss of vegetational cover by sheep and rabbit grazing with subsequent sheet and gully erosion (McVean & Lockie, 1969), as there are obvious floristic similarities between the open scree communities and the nearby closed Alchemilleto–Agrosto–Festucetum grasslands (Tables 4.40, 4.57). Related basaltic scree communities are described from south-west Iceland by Tüxen & Böttcher (1969).

River gravel Communities

Stabilised areas of river gravel are extremely rare on Skye. The delta of Abhainn an t-Sratha Mhòir, Loch Slapin, supports a rich and varied flora, listed below, which includes several montane taxa, presumably washed down from the nearby hills.

Reference Number: B67/144 Altitude: 20 feet Plot area: 16 square metres Grid Reference: 18/563227
Total plant cover: 30%

Aira praecox	+	*Linum catharticum*	3
Alchemilla alpina	6	*Lotus corniculatus*	4
Anthoxanthum odoratum	4	*Oxyria digyna*	3
Bellis perennis	3	*Plantago lanceolata*	3
Calluna vulgaris	1	*P. maritima*	1
Cardaminopsis petraea	3	*Polygala serpyllifolia*	1
Cerastium holosteoides	2	*Potentilla erecta*	2
Erica cinerea	1	*Prunella vulgaris*	3
Euphrasia nemorosa	3	*Ranunculus acris*	3
Festuca rubra	5	*Saxifraga aizoides*	4
F. vivipara	6	*S. oppositifolia*	4
Galium saxatile	3	*Silene acaulis*	5
Hieracium pilosella	1	*Teucrium scorodonia*	+
Hypericum pulchrum	2	*Thymus drucei*	4
Polytrichum piliferum	3	*R. fasciculare*	3
Rhacomitrium canescens	8	*R. lanuginosum*	2

A similar area of gravel occurs at the delta of the River Haultin, Loch Snizort Beag (18/417518) and supports, *i.a.*, *Anthyllis vulneraria* and *Cherleria sedoides*. Similar gravel communities occur locally throughout Scotland, particularly in the eastern Highlands, and floristically related stands also occur on recently colonised glacial outwash gravels in Norway (Faegri, 1933).

3. ASPLENIETEA RUPESTRIS Braun-Blanquet 1934

Open rock-crevice and wall communities, characterised largely in the British Isles and elsewhere in north-west Europe by small ferns.

POTENTILLETALIA CAULESCENTIS Braun-Blanquet 1926

Crevice communities of basic, calcareous rocks. Although *Potentilla caulescens* does not occur in north-west Europe, there are strong floristic relationships between central and north-west European communities, with *Asplenium ruta-muraria*, *A. trichomanes*, and *A. viride* as widespread faithful species (Braun-Blanquet, 1948–50; Oberdorfer, 1957). Oberdorfer *et al.* (1967) have suggested that Asplenietalia rutae-murariae is a more appropriate name for this order than Potentilletalia caulescentis.

Potentillion caulescentis Braun-Blanquet 1926

This is the principal alliance, occurring throughout most of Europe, and it has the basic characters of the order. Related alliances are largely characterised by local endemics (Braun-Blanquet, 1948; 1966–67; Tüxen & Oberdorfer, 1958).

Asplenium marinum–Grimmia maritima Association (Asplenietum marini Braun-Blanquet & R. Tüxen 1952 *pro parte.*)

This association (Table 4.3) occurs locally in sheltered rock-crevices near the sea and on rock-faces under overhangs of sea-cliffs. It appears to favour more sheltered sites than the related *Armeria maritima–Grimmia maritima* Association (Table 4.8) into which it frequently merges. *Asplenium marinum*, *Grimmia maritima*, and *Trichostomum brachydontium* are constants, and *Ligusticum scoticum* and *Sedum rosea* are rare but notable components. *Asplenium marinum* appears to favour mildly basic rocks, as does *Trichostomum brachydontium*, but they also occur more rarely on sandstones and limestones (Lists 2, 3; Table 4.3). The community is often subject to sea-spray, especially during storms. *Asplenium adiantum-nigrum* may also be present, or even dominate the community (Lists 7, 8; Table 4.3).

Related communities occur locally along the rocky coasts of western Britain (Braun-Blanquet & Tüxen, 1952; Ivimey-Cook & Proctor, 1966*b*; Malloch, 1971) and elsewhere in western Europe (Rodriguez, 1966). Such communities are probably sufficiently distinctive in their floristic composition to justify the creation of a new alliance, or even an order, for western Europe with *Asplenium adiantum-nigrum*, *A. marinum*, and *Phyllitis scolopendrium* as possible characteristic species (Nordhagen, 1936).

Asplenium trichomanes–Fissidens cristatus Association (Asplenio–Cystopteridetum Oberdorfer 1949 *pro parte*.)

This chasmophytic association (Table 4.4) occurs widely but locally on Skye in sheltered basic rock-crevices in walls of ravines (Lists 1–4, 9–12), on shaded inland cliff-faces (Lists 5, 6, 13, 14), or in grikes of limestone pavement (Lists 7, 8). It is naturally a rather heterogeneous group and, with more data, it is possible that several distinct noda could be usefully delimited. *Asplenium trichomanes*, *Festuca ovina*, and *Fissidens cristatus* are the only constants in the association.

Three floristic facies are distinguished, however, and these are correlated with either the solid geology or the altitude of the stand. Lists 1–4 are from mildly basic basalt ravines, with *Trichostomum crispulum*, *Lejeunea cavifolia*, and *Metzgeria furcata* as differential species for the basalt facies. Lists 5–12 are from a variety of low-lying limestones (Jurassic: Lists 5, 6, 11, 12; Durness: Lists 7–10), and they are distinguished by the occurrence of *Asplenium ruta-muraria*, *A. viride*, *Cystopteris fragilis*, *Phyllitis scolopendrium*, *Ctenidium molluscum*, *Neckera crispa*, *Tortella tortuosa*, *Gyalecta jenensis*, and *Solorina saccata*, along with several rather local bryophytes such as *Anomodon viticulosus*, *Cololejeunea calcarea*, *Eucladium verticillatum*, and *Metzgeria pubescens*. Many of these taxa are classed as 'exacting calcicoles' by McVean & Ratcliffe (1962) or 'calciphiles' by Ferreira (1963), and their rarity or even absence on much of the basic, but non-calcareous, basalts of Skye is very striking. A similar distributional pattern is shown on Skye by many of the montaine phanerogams (for example *Saxifraga aizoides*, *Dryas octopetala*) and this is discussed in Chapter 5.

The montane facies (Lists 13, 14) is characterised by *Polystichum lonchitis*, *Anoectangium aestivum*, *Isopterygium pulchellum*, *Orthothecium rufescens*, and *Pohlia cruda*, as well as several local montane phanerogams and bryophytes. The facies is extremely rare on Skye, and it is only known to occur above 1000 feet (305 m) on Jurassic limestone outcrops in Coire Uaigneach, Blà Bheinn, and above 1200 feet (360 m) on the calcareous basalt cliffs of Sgùrr Mor, The Storr, and the Quirang. Stands of this facies have many species in common with the Saxifragetum aizoidis (Tables 4.31, 4.57) into which the *Asplenium trichomanes–Fissidens cristatus* Association frequently merges.

Although some of the Skye populations of *Asplenium trichomanes* can be referred to either the diploid ssp. *bivalens* D. E. Meyer or the tetraploid ssp. *quadrivalens* D. E. Meyer on the basis of the length of rhizome scale and spore size, the majority of the plants examined (23 out of a total of 33) are morphologically intermediate, with spore sizes between 38 and 42 μm, and rhizome scales between 2.4 and 3.2 mm (Wood, 1969).

This association or related communities can be recognised on stone-walls and basic-rock outcrops throughout most of the British Isles. Communities on stone-walls differ from this association, however, in the frequent occurrence of *Cymbalaria muralis*, *Barbula convoluta*, *B. rigidula*, *B. vinealis*, *Bryum capillare*, *Eurhynchium murale*, and *Tortula muralis* (Tortulo–Cymbalarietalia; Segal, 1969). The limestone facies occurs widely on the Carboniferous limestones in western Ireland, often with *Ceterach officinarum* (Ivimey-Cook & Proctor, 1966*b*), and in the Pennines, whereas the montane facies is restricted to basic-rock outcrops at high altitudes in Snowdonia, Lakeland, and the Scottish Highlands, with isolated occurrences in north-western Ireland, the northern Pennines, and the Moffat Hills. *Woodsia alpina* is a notable but rare component of some of the Scottish and Welsh stands. The montane facies appears to correspond in part to the Norwegian Asplenion viridis subarcticum Alliance (Nordhagen, 1936), and in part to the subalpine Asplenio–Cystopteridetum Association (Oberdorfer, 1957).

4. CHENOPODIETEA (Braun-Blanquet 1951) Lohmeyer, J. Tüxen & R. Tüxen 1961.

Communities of weeds and ruderals on nutrient-rich soils.

POLYGONO–CHENOPODIETALIA (R. Tüxen & Lohmeyer 1950) J. Tüxen 1961

Weed Communities

Weed communities are not well represented on Skye, but occasional fragments occur around derelict crofts and in townships. The following two relevés are from old crofting sites.

	1	2
Reference number	B69 005	B69 017
Map Reference	643 242	386 636
Altitude (feet)	30	10
Cover (per cent)	100	50
Plot area (square metres)	4	4
Agropyron repens	2	3
Atriplex patula	.	3
Bromus mollis agg.	.	3
Capsella bursa-pastoris	3	6
Cerastium holosteoides	1	2
Galeopsis bifida	.	+
Galium aparine	3	3
Holcus lanatus	5	3
Lamium purpureum	.	3
Lolium perenne	3	2
Matricaria matricarioides	4	5
Plantago lanceolata	5	3
Poa annua	2	4
P. pratensis	4	3
Polygonum persicaria	3	4
Potentilla anserina	.	2
Ranunculus repens	3	1
Rumex obtusifolius	6	4
Senecio vulgaris	3	6
Sherardia arvensis	+	.
Sonchus asper	.	1
Spergula arvensis	.	4
Stellaria media	2	3
Trifolium repens	4	3
Urtica dioica	4	4
Veronica persica	2	.
Total number of species (26)	19	24

Localities: 1. Corry Lodge, 2. Uig.

Similar, rather heterogeneous assemblages of 'nitrophilous' tall biennial and perennial weeds and ruderals occur widely but locally elsewhere in western Scotland, and they are clearly related to the well characterised weed communities of central Europe (Oberdorfer, 1957; Oberdorfer *et al.*, 1967; Westhoff & Den Held, 1969).

5. PLANTAGINETEA MAJORIS R. Tüxen & Preising 1950

PLANTAGINETALIA MAJORIS R. Tüxen (1947) 1950

Lolio–Plantaginion Sissingh 1969

Anthropogenic communities of trampled habitats.

Lolium perenne–Plantago major Association Beger 1930

Thisassociation (Table 4.5) appears to occur, with little variation, in heavily trampled habitats throughout the lowlands of the British Isles (Braun-Blanquet & Tüxen, 1952; Ivimey-Cook & Proctor, 1966*b*) and throughout most of Europe outside the Mediterranean region (Géhu, 1961; Segal, 1969; Sissingh, 1969; Tüxen, 1950; Tüxen & Oberdorfer, 1958). It is a rather local community on Skye, occurring at low altitudes on roadside laybys, gravel paths, and farm tracks. *Lolium perenne*, *Bellis perennis*, and *Plantago major* are constants in this association. There are several species in this association that also occur in communities from pastures and hay-meadows (see Table 4.57), but this association is distinctive, both floristically and ecologically. It is the principal habitat on Skye and elsewhere in Britain for the introduced species *Juncus tenuis* (cf. the Juncetum tenuis Association; Westhoff & Den Held, 1969; and Plantagini–Juncetum macri Association; Oberdorfer, 1957) and *Matricaria matricarioides*, and for several ruderal bryophytes (for example *Bryum bicolor*, *Barbula* spp., and *Ceratodon purpureus*.)

6. ISOETO–NANOJUNCETEA Braun-Blanquet & R. Tüxen 1943

NANOCYPERETALIA Klika 1935

Nanocyperion flavescentis W. Koch 1926

Therophyte communities of temporarily open sites on periodically moist sandy, peaty, or muddy soils in northern and western Europe with, for example, *Juncus bufonius*, *Gnaphalium uliginosum*, *Montia fontana*, *Anagallis minima*, *Isolepis setacea*, and *Pohlia* spp.

Isolepis setacea–Blasia pusilla Communities

These fragmentary communities are rare on Skye, occurring on bare, moist sand or gravel in seasonally water-logged hollows by paths and in waste-ground at low altitudes. The best example seen occurs on the floor of a derelict quarry near Kyleakin, where the following relevé was made.

Reference Number: B68/367. Altitude: 75 feet. Grid Reference: 18/715255. Plot area: 4 square metres. Total plant cover 70%.

Agrostis stolonifera	4	*Isolepis setacea*	6
Anagallis minima	2	*Juncus articulatus*	6
Carex demissa	3	*J. bufonius*	4
Epilobium nerterioides	5	*Ranunculus flammula*	3
Gnaphalium uliginosum	+	*Sagina procumbens*	4

Acrocladium cuspidatum	4	*Drepanocladus aduncus*	5
Archidium alternifolium	2	*Ephemerum serratum* var. *serratum*	2
Bryum pallens	1	*Philonotis fontana*	1
Ceratodon purpureus	1	*Pohlia annotina*	3
Dicranella schreberana	2	*Rhytidiadelphus squarrosus*	1
Blasia pusilla	4	*Nardia scalaris*	3
Fossombronia incurva	2	*Riccardia incurvata*	2
F. wondraczekii	1	*Scapania irrigua*	3
Haplomitrium hookeri	1		

A related assemblage occurs around the sandy margins of shallow lochans, with, for example, *Callitriche hermaphroditica*, *Isolepis setacea*, *Montia fontana*, *Archidium alternifolium*, *Fossombronia foveolata*, *Haplomitrium hookeri*, *Riccardia incurvata*, and *Riccia sorocarpa*. These lowland habitats of *Haplomitrium hookeri* contrast with the recent discoveries of it growing above 2000 feet (610 m) in late snow-bed vegetation in the Scottish Highlands (Paton & Corley, 1969).

Related communities occur widely but locally in similar, lowland habitats in northern and western Britain (Braun-Blanquet & Tüxen, 1952) and elsewhere in Europe (Braun-Blanquet, 1948–50; Géhu, 1961; Oberdorfer, 1957; Tüxen, 1937; von Hübschmann, 1967; Westhoff & Den Held, 1969). The general assemblage, especially of bryophytes, is rather similar to that found in moist, coastal 'dune-slacks' (Birse, 1958).

7. AMMOPHILETEA Braun-Blanquet & R. Tüxen 1943

Communities of young and mobile maritime sand-dunes of the Atlantic and Mediterranean coasts of Europe.

ELYMO–AMMOPHILETALIA ARENARIAE Géhu & Géhu 1969

Communities of mobile maritime sand-dunes in northern Europe with *Ammophila arenaria*, *Agropyron unceiforme*, and *Elymus arenarius*.

Agropyrion Boreoatlanticum Géhu and Géhu 1969

Fore-dune communities

One of the few areas of coastal sand-dune on Skye is at the southern end of Glenbrittle. Fragmentary examples of an *Agropyron junceiforme* fore-dune community occur with *Carex arenaria*, *Honkenya peploides*, *Potentilla anserina*, and *Sonchus asper* (Table 4.6). Other species of note that occur in these fore-dune communities at Glenbrittle include *Cakile maritima* and *Polygonum raii*. *Elymus arenarius* and *Salsola kali* have their sole Skye stations in this community elsewhere on the island. Similar communities characterise fore-dunes in western and northern Britain (Gimingham, 1964*a*; Tansley, 1949). The exact phytosociological relationships of the Glenbrittle community are not known, for it has floristic affinities with the order Salsolo–Minuartion peploidis R. Tüxen 1950 in the class Cakiletea maritimae R. Tüxen & Preising 1950 (see p. 37), and with the Agropyrion boreoatlanticum Géhu & Géhu 1969 of the class Ammophiletea Braun-Blanquet & R. Tüxen 1943 in which it is classified here.

Ammophilion Borealis (R. Tüxen 1955) Géhu & Géhu 1969

Communities of stable maritime sand-dunes in northern Europe.

Grey dune Turfs

At Glenbrittle there is a narrow zone of stable grey-dune turf between the fore-dune communities and farmland. This zone supports a *Festuca rubra-Galium verum* turf (Table 4.6) with *Lotus corniculatus*, *Sedum acre*, *Thalictrum minus*, and *Tortula ruraliformis*. Identical communities are described from Canna in the Inner Hebrides by Asprey (1947), and they are clearly related to the species-rich 'machair' vegetation developed on blown shell-sands in the Outer Hebrides. The exact phytosociological relationships of this community remain to be determined.

8. ASTERETEA TRIPOLIUM Westhoff & Beeftink 1962

Halophytic communities of saltmarshes and sea-cliffs along the coasts of northern and western Europe.

GLAUCETO-PUCCINELLIETALIA Beeftink & Westhoff 1962

West European and Baltic halophyte communities. Much of the coastline of Skye is extremely precipitous, and the more exposed cliff-faces provide habitats for halophytic vegetation. In addition, limited areas of saltmarsh occur at the heads of many of the more sheltered sea-lochs.

Puccinellion maritimae (Christiansen 1927 *pro parte*) R. Tüxen 1937

Puccinellietum maritimae Association (Warming 1890) Christiansen 1927

This association (Table 4.7) comprises the vegetation of the lower parts of the saltmarshes from about mean high water to a few centimetres below mean spring high-water, and of very exposed sea-cliffs on Skye. *Armeria maritima*, *Glaux maritima*, *Plantago maritima*, and *Puccinellia maritima* are constants of the association. It varies little in floristic composition, though there may be a considerable range in the relative prominence of the different species. Essentially the same association occurs around the coasts of the British Isles (Braun-Blanquet & Tüxen, 1952; Ivimey-Cook & Proctor, 1966*b*; Tansley, 1949), although the lower saltmarshes of southern Britain are often more species-rich, including, for example, *Limonium* spp., *Halimione portulacoides*, and *Parapholis strigosa*, than in Scotland. Similar associations occur elsewhere in western Europe (Beeftink, 1965, 1968; Dahl & Hadač, 1941; Hocquette, Géhu & Fauquet, 1965; Skogen, 1965).

Two subassociations within this association have been delimited on Skye (Table 4.7).

Puccinellia-maritima–Ascophyllum nodosum Subassociation

This community occurs in the lowest parts of many of the salt-marshes on Skye and it consists of heavily sheep- and cattle-grazed turf dominated by *Puccinellia maritima* and the turf ecad *mackaii* of *Ascophyllum nodosum* (Gibb, 1957), and with a characteristic group of halophytes, including *Armeria maritima*, *Aster tripolium*, *Glaux maritima*, *Plantago maritima*, and *Spergularia media*. It is submerged by the tide for at least 8 hours a day. It is characterised floristically by the constancy of *Ascophyllum nodosum* and by the absence of species of the upper saltmarsh zones such as *Festuca rubra*, *Carex extensa*, and *Juncus gerardii* (see Table 4.57). The pioneer communities of *Salicornia* spp. that are common on the saltmarshes of southern Britain (Tansley, 1949) are virtually absent from Skye, perhaps as a result of the rather coarse, sandy texture of many of the Skye marshes.

Puccinellia maritima–Festuca rubra Subassociation.

The upper and rather drier parts of the *Puccinellia maritima* zone in the Skye saltmarshes are characterised by the consistent presence of *Festuca rubra* and the absence of *Ascophyllum nodosum*. *Catapodium marinum* has its sole Skye station in this habitat. A related, but more species-rich, assemblage occurs on rather shallow dry soils on very exposed cliff-faces, with *Plantago coronopus*, *P. lanceolata*, and *Trichostomum brachydontium* (Lists 11, 12; Table 4.7). These latter two relevés resemble the '*Plantago* swards' described from exposed sea-cliffs in western Ireland (Tansley, 1949), Sanday (Asprey, 1947), St Kilda (McVean, 1961*a*), and the Faeröes (Ostenfeld, 1908).

Armerion maritimae Braun-Blanquet & DeLeeuv 1936

Although *Armeria maritima* is constant within all the halophytic communities on Skye, this alliance is effectively distinguished from the Puccinellion maritimae Alliance by the absence of *Puccinellia maritima*. Armerion maritimae is a rather diverse alliance, but on the basis of the available data (Table 4.8) only two associations can be consistently recognised.

Juncus gerardii–Carex extensa Association

(Junco–Caricetum extensae Braun-Blanquet & De Leeuw 1936 *pro parte*.) (Scirpetum rufi (G. E. & G. Du Rietz 1925) Gillner 1960 *pro parte*.)

Within this association (Table 4.8) the stands analysed are from two distinct habitats:

(i) Lists 1–12 represent closed turf of the upper saltmarshes extending from mean spring high water into the storm zone. They are characterised by the constancy of *Armeria maritima*, *Festuca rubra*, *Glaux maritima*, *Plantago maritima*, and *Agrostis stolonifera*. *Carex extensa* and *C. scandinavica* are frequent and apparently exclusive to this association. The presence of *Leontodon autumnalis* and *Agrostis stolonifera* probably indicates less saline conditions than in the lower saltmarshes (Gillham, 1957). The occurrence of *Grimmia maritima* in closed saltmarsh turf contrasts with its typical open rupestral habitats in the *Asplenium marinum–Grimmia maritima* and *Armeria maritima–Grimmia maritima* Associations.

(ii) Lists 13–17 represent an open assemblage occurring on stony ground at the landward edge o saltmarshes or on wave-scoured rock platforms of low sea-cliffs. *Juncus gerardii* is prominent, with frequent *Blysmus rufus*, *Carex flacca*, *C. distans*, *C. extensa*, and *C. serotina*, and occasional *Eleocharis uniglumis*. The rare moss *Myurium hebridarum* is found occasionally on exposed or shaded coastal rocks in this habitat. *Spergularia marina* occurs rarely, with *Festuca rubra*, *Plantago coronopus*, *Sagina maritima*, and *S. nodosa* in open, eroded patches within this community in the upper saltmarsh zone (cf. the habitat of *Spergularia media* on Skye).

The association occurs widely around the British coasts, often with *Juncus maritimus*, and it tends to characterise the upper saltmarsh zones (Gimingham, 1964*a*; Ivimey-Cook & Proctor, 1966*b*; Tansley, 1949). In some localities in southern Britain there may be considerably more spatial overlap between the species of the *Juncus gerardii* and the *Puccinellia maritima* communities than is found on Skye. Related associations but generally lacking *Blysmus rufus* occur along the coasts of western Europe (Beeftink, 1965; Hocquette *et al.*, 1965; Rodriguez, 1966), and reach as far north as southern Scandinavia (Beeftink, 1965).

Armeria maritima–Grimmia maritima Association

This is an exclusively open maritime community (Table 4.8) that occurs on rather dry and shallow soil in rock crevices, on small ledges, and on steep rock-faces above the main *Xanthoria parietina* zone on sea-cliffs that are usually less exposed to sea-spray than those supporting *Puccinellia maritima–Festuca rubra* turfs. *Armeria maritima*, *Festuca rubra*, *Grimmia maritima*, and *Plantago maritima* are constant, whereas the annual *Cerastium atrovirens* and the lichens *Anaptychia fusca*, *Ramalina curnowii*, *R. siliquosa*, *Verrucaria maura*, and *Xanthoria parietina* are exclusive to this association. Other cryptogams of interest occurring in this community on Skye, but not recorded from the stands examined, include *Arthopyrenia halodytes* (often on barnacles), *Haematomma coccineum*, *Lecanora atra*, *Lichina pygmaea*, and *Ulota phyllantha* (also on trees, see p. 69). It is the main habitat on Skye for *Sedum anglicum* and *Ligusticum scoticum*, although the latter also occurs in the related *Asplenium marinum–Grimmia maritima* Association (Lists 1, 3; Table 4.3) and, more rarely, in shingle-beach vegetation (Lists 4, 5; Table 4.9). On more sheltered sites with deeper, moister soils, this association grades into ledge communities of 'tall herbs', including *Sedum rosea* (Table 446).

Several of the larger sea-cliffs on Skye support large populations of sea-birds. Several of the ledges below nesting sites support a diverse and lush vegetation including *Athyrium filix-femina*, *Cochlearia officinalis*, *Angelica sylvestris*, *Festuca rubra*, *Montia fontana*, *Poa annua*, *Silene dioica*, *Stellaria media*, and *Urtica dioica*. The lichen *Candelariella vitellina* is frequent on sea-cliffs below bird perches. These communities have not been examined in detail.

The association occurs widely on exposed sea-cliffs in western Europe, and it has been briefly described from Scotland by Asprey (1947) and Gimingham (1964*a*), from the Faeröes by Ostenfeld (1908), and from Norway by Nordhagen (1922), Skogen (1965), and Störmer (1938). Related, but more species-rich communities, with *Crithmum maritimum*, *Spergularia rupicola*, and *Inula crithmoides*, are described from south-west England by Malloch (1971) and from France by Géhu (1964*a*, 1964*b*).

The classification of this association within the alliance Armerion maritimae is rather questionable (Malloch, 1971), for although the association contains some of the characteristic species (*Armeria maritima*, *Festuca rubra*), it lacks other equally characteristic taxa such as *Glaux maritima* and *Juncus gerardii* (Beeftink, 1965, 1968). The association similarly lacks several of the characteristic Mediterranean–Atlantic taxa of the class Crithmo–Staticetea Braun-Blanquet 1947, such as *Spergularia rupicola* and *Crithmum maritimum*. The association is probably sufficiently distinctive in its floristic composition to justify the delimitation of a new alliance based on relevés from areas that are outside the range of the Ibero-Mediterranean species (cf. Malloch, 1971).

9. CAKILETEA MARITIMAE R. Tüxen & Preising 1950

Open nitrophilous weedy communities of sandy strandlines and shingle beaches.

CAKILETALIA MARITIMAE R. Tüxen & Preising in Oberdorfer 1949

The principal order for western and north European communities.

Atriplicion littoralis (Nordhagen 1940) R. Tüxen 1950

Communities of shingle beaches and strandlines of western Europe and the Baltic.

Atriplex glabriuscula–Rumex crispus Association

Along the shores of several of the more sheltered sea-lochs on Skye shingle beaches occur near the high-water mark. The shingle beaches generally consist of rounded pebbles (about 5–15 cm diameter), mixed with coarse sand, silt, and decaying sea-weed debris ('wrack'). They frequently support interesting 'nitrophilous' communities of therophytes. Although the floristic composition and structure of such communities vary with the substrate, stability, drainage, and age (Scott, 1963*a*), a fairly consistent association occurs on Skye (Table 4.9) with *Atriplex glabriuscula*, *Galium aparine*, *Rumex crispus* var. *triangulatus*, and *Stellaria media* as constant species. This habitat provides the main localities for *Carex otrubae*, *Lycopus europaeus*, and *Scutellaria galericulata* on Skye, in contrast to their typically inland, mire habitats in southern Britain. *Cakile maritima*, *Mertensia maritima*, and *Pottia heimii* have their sole Skye stations in this association. The occurrence of several so-called 'weed' species, such as *Agropyron repens*, *Polygonum persicaria*, *Plantago major*, *Sagina procumbens*, and *Stellaria media*, in an apparently non-anthropogenic community is of interest.

This association is found widely around the Scottish coasts (Gimingham, 1964*a*; Scott, 1963*b*), and related communities occur elsewhere in the British Isles (Braun-Blanquet & Tüxen, 1952; Ivimey-Cook & Proctor, 1966*b*), in Norway (Dahl & Hadač, 1941; Nordhagen, 1940), and in south-west Iceland (Hadač, 1970). The precise phytosociological relationships of the Skye association are not clear, however, for the association has some floristic affinities with the alliances Atriplicion littoralis (Nordhagen 1940) R. Tüxen 1950 and Salsolo–Minuartion peploidis R. Tüxen 1950 of the class Cakiletea maritimae, with the alliance Agropyro–Rumicion crispus Nordhagen 1940 of the class Plantaginetea majoris R. Tüxen & Preising 1950, and with the class Agropyretea pungentis Géhu & Géhu, 1969 (see Beeftink, 1965; Géhu & Géhu, 1969; Hadač, 1970; Nordhagen, 1940; Tüxen, 1950).

10. LITTORELLETEA Braun-Blanquet & R. Tüxen 1943

LITTORELLETALIA W. Koch 1926

Communities of margins of freshwater lakes and ponds, that are usually permanently submerged or exposed for a very short period in the summer, growing on sand, gravel, marl, or mud in clear water.

Littorellion uniflorae W. Koch 1926

This alliance comprises communities of silty or stony margins of clear, usually oligotrophic, lakes in northern and western Europe.

Littorella uniflora–Lobelia dortmanna Association (Isoeto–Lobelietum (W. Koch 1926) R. Tüxen 1937 *pro parte*.)

A distinctive and widespread association (Table 4.10) that occurs on intensively wave-eroded stony and sandy margins of freshwater locks in water between 15 and 30 cm depth (mean = 27 cm) on Skye. Although generally an oligotrophic community, it also occurs on calcareous silty marls at Loch Cill Chriosd (List 7), but there it lacks *Lobelia dortmanna* (cf. the *Littorella uniflora–Baldellia ranunculoides* Association of the Burren Lakes; Ivimey-Cook & Proctor, 1966*b*). Besides the association constants *Littorella uniflora* and *Lobelia dortmanna*, the community provides the main habitat on Skye for *Isoetes lacustris*, *Juncus bulbosus* forma *fluitans*, *Subularia aquatica*, and *Baldellia ranunculoides*. Primarily a lowland community, it ascends to 1700 feet (520 m) in some of the corrie lochans of the Cuillins.

This association occurs widely in Scotland (Spence, 1964), the Lake District, north Wales, and western Ireland (Braun-Blanquet & Tüxen, 1952). Related communities are noted in Scandinavia (Lohammar, 1965), the Faeröes (Ostenfeld, 1908), and in parts of western Europe (Tüxen, 1937; Vanden Berghen, 1968; Westhoff & Den Held, 1969).

11. POTAMETEA R. Tüxen & Preising 1942

Communities of rooted, floating, and submerged aquatics in fresh or slightly brackish waters.

MAGNOPOTAMETALIA Den Hartog & Segal 1964

Communities of large floating-leaved aquatics (nymphaeids *sensu* Den Hartog & Segal, 1964) in open water of depth 1 m or more.

Nymphaeion albae Oberdorfer 1957

Communities containing species of *Myriophyllum*, *Nymphaea*, *Potamogeton*, and *Sparganium* are locally frequent in shallow water (1 m or less) in some of the freshwater lochs in Skye. The available relevé data are rather limited and heterogeneous, and a more detailed study may reveal several distinct noda.

Potamogeton natans–Nymphaea alba nodum

Stands of floating-leaved aquatics (Table 4.11) are rather rare and local in small lochans or in the sheltered bays, generally on the southern or western shores, of the larger lowland lochs. The *nodum* often occurs as an indistinct zone outside the *Phragmites communis*, *Schoenoplectus lacustris* or, more rarely, *Carex rostrata* reedswamps, in water of depths between 52 and 90 cm (mean = 75 cm) on a variety of substrata. The floating aquatics often overlap with the reed-swamp plants. Typical spatial relationships of these communities are shown in Figs. 15 and 17. Floating-leaved species of *Potamogeton* occurring in this community on Skye include *P. alpinus*, *P. coloratus*, *P. gramineus*, and *P. natans*. Submerged-leaved species also occur in this community, including *P. lucens*, *P. perfoliatus*, *P. praelongus*, and *Myriophyllum alterniflorum*.

Similar communities are widespread in Britain (Ivimey-Cook & Proctor, 1966*b*; Spence, 1964; Tansley, 1949) and Europe (Oberdorfer, 1957; Oberdorfer *et al.*, 1967; Tüxen, 1937; Westhoff & Den Held, 1969).

PARVOPOTAMETALIA Den Hartog & Segal 1964

Communities of submerged aquatics in shallow (less than 1 m depth), fresh or slightly brackish water.

Callitricho–Batrachion Den Hartog & Segal 1964

Communities composed largely of species of batrachian *Ranunculus* and *Callitriche* occurring in ditches, rivers, shallow pools, etc.

River Communities

The majority of streams and rivers on Skye are steep, rocky and fast-flowing and although they often support a characteristic cryptogamic assemblage, with, for example, *Brachythecium plumosum*, *B. rivulare*, *Eurhynchium riparioides*, *Fontinalis squamosa*, *Rhacomi-*

trium aciculare, *Marsupella emarginata*, *Nardia compressa*, *Scapania undulata*, and *Ephebe lanata*, they have not been examined in detail (cf. Endocarpion Alliance; Braun-Blanquet, 1948–50).

In the slow-flowing stream between Loch Leathan and L. Fada a stand dominated by *Ranunculus trichophyllus* was examined.

Reference Number: B68/069. Altitude: 450 feet. Grid Reference: 18/495503. Plot area: 4 square metres. Total plant cover: 50%.

Callitriche stagnalis	4	*Potamogeton perfoliatus*	+
Glyceria fluitans	4	*Ranunculus flammula*	2
Myriophyllum alterniflorum	3	*R. trichophyllus*	8–9

This stand occurs in water of at least 100 cm depth, and, although batrachian *Ranunculus* communities occur widely in rivers and streams throughout Britain (Tansley, 1949), this is the only known station for the sub-genus (other than *R. hederaceus*) on Skye.

12. PHRAGMITETEA R. Tüxen & Preising 1942
PHRAGMITETALIA EUROSIBERICA (W. Koch 1926) R. Tüxen & Preising 1942
Reedswamp communities.

Phragmition communis W. Koch 1926

This alliance comprises tall reed-swamps of lakes, slow-flowing rivers, and estuaries. It is effectively defined by life-form, although there are some floristic connections between the rather diverse communities contained within the alliance.

Brackish Water Communities
(Scirpetum maritimi (W. Christiansen, 1934) R. Tüxen 1937 *pro parte.*)

Stands of *Scirpus maritimus* (Table 4.12) occur in ungrazed areas when freshwater streams enter the upper edges of either saltmarshes (Lists 1, 2) or shingle beaches (List 3), or as a marginal reedswamp around slightly brackish pools (Lists 4, 5). The stands are characterised by *Agrostis stolonifera*, *Eleocharis palustris*, and *Scirpus maritimus* as constants and by a mixture of halophytic species, for example *Juncus gerardii* and *Glaux maritima*, and inland mire plants, for example *Carex nigra* and *Potentilla palustris*. *Catabrosa aquatica* and *Samolus valerandi* have their few Skye stations in this community. *Hydrocotyle vulgaris* is commoner in this community than in any other on Skye, in contrast to its wide ecological amplitude elsewhere in Britain. In western Norway it also tends to be rather coastal in its habitat preferences (Faegri, 1960; Nordhagen, 1922).

Similar communities are frequent elsewhere in Britain (Tansley, 1949) and in Europe (Berglund, 1963; Braun-Blanquet, 1966–67; Dahl & Hadač, 1941; Rodriguez, 1966).

Schoenoplectus lacustris–Phragmites communis Association
(Scirpo–Phragmitetum W. Koch 1926 *pro parte.*)
(Scirpetum lacustris (Allorge 1922) Chouard 1924 *pro parte.*)

This is the characteristic tall-reedswamp association (Table 4.13) of deepish water in the lowland lochs on Skye, commonly occurring as a zone between the floating-leaved aquatic communities and the *Carex rostrata* marginal reedswamps (see Figs. 15, 17). It is characterised by the luxuriance of the dominant species. The association occurs widely in Britain (Ivimey-Cook & Proctor, 1966*b*; Spence, 1964; Tansley, 1949) and elsewhere in Europe (Géhu, 1961; Oberdorfer, 1957; Rodriguez, 1966; Tüxen, 1937; Westhoff & Den Held, 1969).

Two subassociations are distinguished on the basis of the dominant taxon, and they appear to differ in both their range of water depths and their substrate preferences. *Equisetum fluviatile* is the only constant in common in the two subassociations.

Phragmites communis–Equisetum fluviatile Subassociation

Stands of almost pure *Phragmites communis* occur in water depths between 23 and 52 cm (mean = 35 cm), on highly organic substrata. The stands in shallow water often contain floating-leaved aquatics (for example *Nymphaea alba*, *Potamogeton* spp.) and, like the *Potamogeton natans–Nymphaea alba nodum*, the *Phragmites* communities are restricted to small lochs or to the more sheltered areas of large lowland lochs. This community occurs widely but rather locally on Skye.

Schoenoplectus lacustris–Equisetum fluviatile Subassociation

Extensive stands of *Schoenoplectus lacustris* characteristically occur on silty substrata in rather more exposed areas, and in deeper water (42–90 cm; mean = 67 cm) than the related *Phragmites communis* community. In exposed sites the *Schoenoplectus lacustris* stands grade into *Littorella uniflora–Lobelia dortmanna* stands in shallower water, often with abundant *Eleocharis palustris*, whereas in more sheltered sites it grades into either Magnocaricion or *Phragmites communis* communities.

Magnocaricion elatae W. Koch 1926

Marginal reedswamp and riverside communities dominated by large sedges and marsh plants, generally developed in stagnant water. The alliance is divided into suballiances Caricion rostratae and Caricion gracilis by Balátová-Tuláčková (1963). Such a division is useful floristically and it appears to reflect differences in substrate and water depth (see Oberdorfer *et al.*, 1967).

Carex rostrata–Menyanthes trifoliata Association (Caricetum rostratae Rübel 1912 *pro parte.*)

This is the major reedswamp association (Table 4.14) of shallow, stagnant water (15–45 cm; mean = 32 cm) in the lowland lochs (generally below 1000 feet, 305 m) on Skye, and it is characterised by the constancy and dominance of *Carex rostrata* and the constancy of *Menyanthes trifoliata.* It differs floristically from the *Carex rostrata* dominated communities of the Scheuchzerio–Caricetea fuscae in the virtual absence of bryophytes (see Table 4.57). In shallower water this association merges into *Carex lasiocarpa–Menyanthes trifoliata*, *Carex rostrata–Aulacomnium palustre*, or, more rarely, *Carex rostrata–Scorpidium scorpioides* fens, and in deeper water it overlaps with *Schoenoplectus lacustris–Phragmites communis* or floating-leaved aquatic stands. Although it can occur on silty substrata of low organic content, it generally favours highly organic muds. It is the principal habitat for *Eriocaulon septangulare* on Skye (cf. the Irish associations Eriocauleto–Lobelietum; Braun-Blanquet & Tüxen, 1952; and Eriocauletum septangularis; Schoof-van Pelt & Westhoff, 1969 within the alliance Littorellion).

It is the typical marginal reedswamp association of shallow waters in northern Britain (Holdgate, 1955*a*; Spence, 1964), and related communities occur in Scandinavia (Mörnsjö, 1969; Nordhagen, 1927, 1943; Persson, 1961) and elsewhere in Europe (Balátová-Tuláčková, 1968; Oberdorfer, 1957; Tüxen, 1937). It clearly belongs to Balátová-Tuláčková's (1963) Caricion rostratae Suballiance.

Glycerio–Sparganion Braun-Blanquet & Sissingh 1942

'Reedswamp' communities of shallow, muddy margins of lakes, ponds, small streams and ditches, typically with *Glyceria* spp., *Veronica beccabunga*, *Rorippa nasturtium–aquaticum*, *Sparganium erectum*, *S. emersum*, etc. This alliance is not well represented on Skye.

Oenanthe crocata Communities

Table 4.15 presents two relevés from a small, slowly flowing eutrophic stream near sea-level at Camas Mor, Kilmuir. The stands examined are dominated by *Oenanthe crocata*, and they contain several introduced species, for example *Aegopodium podagraria*, *Astrantia major*, and *Mimulus guttatus. Chrysanthemum vulgare*, *Cicerbita macrophylla*, *Salix pentandra*, *S. viminalis*, and *S. aurita* × *S. vimianalis* occur nearby on the stream-bank.

Related assemblages occur rather locally elsewhere in western Britain (Braun-Blanquet & Tüxen, 1952), and in south-west Europe (Iglesias, 1968; Rodriguez, 1966).

13. SCHEUCHZERIO–CARICETEA FUSCAE (Nordhagen 1936) R. Tüxen 1937

Communities of bog-hollows and of fens.

There is considerable variation in the use of general descriptive terms in mire ecology, and it is felt necessary to define their use in this account. The term *mire* is used here as a habitat or geographical term to denote an area of ground where the water-table is permanently at or near the ground surface, where the vegetation (particularly the root system) is adapted to the water-logged substrata and the associated anaerobic conditions, and where organic materials (generally peat) may accumulate (Godwin, 1956). As used here the term mire is not a vegetational concept, but is a geographical term. The vegetation of a mire is often a mosaic of different vegetational types.

An *ombrotrophic* mire or peatland (generally termed a *bog* or moss) is an area of ground in which the permanently high water-table is maintained solely by atmospheric precipitation (ombrogenous) falling on the bog surface. As this is the major source of mineral ions, the bog water is generally very deficient in mineral salts (oligotrophic), causing a low cation saturation of the peat, a low pH value, and a general nutrient deficiency. It supports bog vegetation, which is generally rather poor in diversity of vascular plant species.

A *minerotrophic* mire (generally termed a *fen*) is an area of ground in which the permanently high water-table is maintained by both atmospheric precipitation and ground water (geogenous). The latter provides an additional supply of ions derived largely from percolation through mineral soils. The mire water is therefore richer in mineral nutrients (mesotrophic and eutrophic) and it has a higher pH value than in ombrotrophic mires. It supports fen vegetation, which is generally richer in species of vascular plants than is bog vegetation. In minerotrophic mires or fens, the high water-table can arise either by impeded drainage within closed basins, channels, or hollows (*topogenous*), or by water movement, either as surface run-off or as percolating ground-water from nearby slopes, springs, or rills (*soligenous*).

The distinction between these two principal types of mire habitat, namely bog and fen, is generally supported by floristic and vegetational characteristics (Sjörs, 1948; Du Rietz, 1949, 1954). The transition between bogs and fens corresponds, in hydrotopographical terms, to the *mineralbodenwassergrenze* of Thunmark (1940), and in floristic terms to the 'fen plant limit' of Sjörs (1948) and the *mineralbodenwasserzeigergrenze* of Du Rietz (1954). Fens can be sub-divided on habitat criteria into topogenous and soligenous fens, or on floristic criteria into poor-fens and rich-fens (Du Rietz, 1949, 1954), although, as emphasised by Sjörs (1950*a*), these two types frequently intergrade. The division between poor- and rich-fens usually reflects the varying base status of the fens (Sjörs, 1950*a*; Witting, 1947).

The definitions adopted above correspond to those in current Scandinavian ecological usage (Ingram, 1967; Sonesson, 1970). The alternative terminology proposed by McVean & Ratcliffe (1962) and Ratcliffe (1964) who retain the term 'bog' for an ombrotrophic mire, but who use the terms 'fen' and 'mire' in a more restricted sense to refer to topogenous and soligenous mires, respectively, is less useful in the present context and it has not been followed. As there are frequent floristic and environmental gradations from soligenous to topogenous mires, a classification based on floristics alone, rather than on habitat and hydrotopographical features, is considered desirable.

The concept of 'directions of variation' in mire vegetation (Tuomikoski, 1942) as discussed by Sjörs (1948, 1950*b*), is of considerable use in the classification and discussion of the mire types on Skye. Both the bog/poor-fen/rich-fen gradient, and the hummock/lawn/carpet/mud-bottom vegetational series appear to be relevant.

The classification adopted here attempts to incorporate both these directions of variation: the hummock and lawn communities of bogs are classed, along with the wet-heaths, in the class Oxycocco–Sphagnetea, whereas the communities of fens and of bog-hollows are grouped in the class Scheuchzerio–Caricetea fuscae. Floristic and vegetational distinctions made within this class appear to reflect variations in base status, hydrology, water-table, and altitude. The present scheme represents one of the various possible modes of classification of a multi-dimensional variation (see Du Rietz, 1949, 1954; Duvigneaud, 1949; Malmer, 1968; Nordhagen, 1936, 1943; Oberdorfer *et al.*, 1967; Sjörs, 1948; Westhoff & Den Held, 1969).

All pH and conductivity values and ion concentrations quoted for bog, fen, and spring communities on Skye were determined on water samples, unless otherwise stated (Table 4.16).

SCHEUCHZERIETALIA PALUSTRIS Nordhagen 1936

Communities of wet hollows, generally containing stagnant or slowly moving water, in bogs and fens with a permanently high water-table. The intricate mosaic of hummock and hollow complexes on bog surfaces can present problems of delimitation and vegetational classification. Duvigneaud (1949) has placed all mire communities into a series of orders within one large class (Sphagno–Caricetea fuscae), whereas Du Rietz (1949) has united hummock and hollow communities of bogs into regional alliances though recognising them as distinct associations. The more generally accepted scheme of Nordhagen (1936, 1943) and Vanden Berghen (1952) is followed here, although problems of delimitation can sometimes arise.

Rhynchosporion albae W. Koch 1926

Communities of bog-hollows and pools, and characterised by *Carex limosa*, *Rhynchospora alba*, *Scheuchzeria palustris*, *Sphagnum cuspidatum*, and *Cladopodiella fluitans*.

Eriophorum angustifolium–Sphagnum cuspidatum Association

(Cuspidato–Scheuchzerietum palustris (R. Tüxen 1937) Preising & R. Tüxen 1958 *pro parte.*)
(Caricetum limosae Braun-Blanquet 1921 *pro parte.*)

Within the wetter stands of Trichophoreto–Eriophoretum bog that have developed on level or gently sloping low-lying ground, a mosaic of hummocks and hollows commonly occurs, often with a complex system of pools. These surface patterns may occur as aligned features, the origin and development of which is a matter of much controversy (Boatman & Armstrong, 1968; Pearsall, 1956; Ratcliffe & Walker, 1958).

There are broadly two pool types on the patterned

bogs on Skye. There are deep, irregularly-shaped, steep-sided pools, often with eroded margins and a sparse vegetation, usually of scattered plants of *Menyanthes trifoliata*, *Sphagnum cuspidatum*, and *Utricularia* spp. and often with a rich algal flora of, for example, *Batrachospermum* spp., *Rhizoclonium* spp., and *Zygogonium ericetorum* (Dillw) Kütz. These areas represent 'mud-bottom' communities (Sjörs, 1948) on unconsolidated aquatic *Sphagnum* peat, but they have not been examined in detail.

Shallower pools have an almost continuous *Sphagnum cuspidatum* carpet, and often with abundant *Eriophorum angustifolium* (Table 4.17). *Rhynchospora alba* and *Sphagnum subsecundum* var. *auriculatum* are locally frequent in the shallowest hollows. *Rhynchospora alba* may be particularly abundant in a narrow vertical zone from about water level to the base of *Sphagnum* hummocks. *Carex limosa*, *Cladopodiella fluitans*, and *Sphagnum pulchrum* are notable components of some stands. The water of these pools is base deficient and acid (pH range 4.0–4.1; see Table 4.16). All intermediate stages can be recognised from these pool communities to hummock and lawn stands. The developmental sequence is complicated, however, by different trends, often involving erosion and degeneration (see Ratcliffe & Walker, 1958). The community is distinctive in its floristic composition, and differs from other bog communities on Skye in the constancy and abundance of *Sphagnum cuspidatum* and the absence of ericoid dwarf-shrubs (see Table 4.57). As the community is dependent on a high water-table in undrained peat areas, it is now extremely local on Skye.

Similar communities occur on patterned bogs in northern and western Scotland (Pearsall, 1956; Ratcliffe & Walker, 1958) and in Ireland (Morrison, 1959). They are widely recorded in Scandinavia (Malmer, 1962; Sjörs, 1948; Svensson, 1965) and elsewhere in Europe (Burrichter, 1969; Jahns, 1969; Rybniček, 1970; Stamer, 1967).

In Britain *Hammarbya paludosa* and *Rhynchospora fusca* are rare and local components of this association, and *Scheuchzeria palustris* has its sole known Scottish station in this community.

Caricion lasiocarpae Vanden Berghen 1949

Communities of fen-hollows. Characteristic species include *Carex lasiocarpa*, *C. diandra*, *C. chordorrhiza*, and *Eriophorum gracile*.

Carex lasiocarpa–Menyanthes trifoliata Association (Sphagno–Caricetum lasiocarpae (Gadeçeau 1909) Steffen 1931 *pro parte.*) (Caricetum lasiocarpae W. Koch 1926 *pro parte.*) (Scorpidio–Caricetum diandrae (W. Koch 1926) Westhoff 1969 *pro parte.*)

This association (Table 4.18) and the closely related *Carex rostrata–Carex limosa nodum* (Table 4.18) are the characteristic 'mud-bottom' communities in hollows within the lowland fens on Skye. *Carex lasiocarpa*, *C. limosa*, *C. nigra*, *C. rostrata*, *Equisetum fluviatile*, and *Menyanthes trifoliata* are association constants. The association differs from the Magnocaricion communities (Table 4.14) in the presence of well developed bryophyte carpets. *Carex diandra* and *C. lasiocarpa* are exclusive to the association on Skye, and it is the principal habitat for *Carex limosa*, *Sparganium minimum*, and *Acrocladium giganteum* on Skye. The substratum is always a highly organic black fen-peat or lake-mud of considerable depth (up to 8 m) with the water-level generally not more than 20 cm above ground-level. The stands examined range from rather base-poor floating peat-rafts (Lists 1, 2, 8; pH range 4.8–4.9; see Table 4.16) with *Sphagnum palustre* and *S. recurvum* (cf. Caricetum lasiocarpae Sphagnetosum; Vanden Berghen, 1952; Sphagno-Caricetum lasiocarpae; Westhoff & Den Held, 1969) to more basic stands (Lists 3–7; pH range 5.8–6.0) occurring within either *Carex rostrata–Aulacomnium palustre* intermediate-fens or *Carex rostrata–Scorpidium scorpioides* rich-fens, and with *Sphagnum subsecundum* var. *inundatum* and *Scorpidium scorpioides* (cf. Caricetum lasiocarpae Scorpidietosum; Vanden Berghen, 1952). With increasing water depth the association merges into Magnocaricion or, more rarely, Phragmition communities, with a marked decrease in species richness.

The association occurs locally throughout Britain (Holdgate, 1955*a*; Ivimey-Cook & Proctor, 1966*b*), occasionally with *Eriophorum gracile* in southern England and Ireland, whereas in Sutherland *Carex chordorrhiza* grows in its only known British locality in this community. Related communities occur widely in Scandinavia (Mörnsjö, 1969; Nordhagen, 1927, 1943; Sjörs, 1948) and elsewhere in Europe (Braun, 1968; Oberdorfer, 1957; Rybniçek, 1970; Segal, 1966; Vanden Berghen, 1952).

CARICETALIA FUSCAE (W. Koch 1926) Nordhagen 1936

Communities of poor- and intermediate-fens (acid to mildly basic), generally dominated by *Carex* spp. (for example *C. echinata* and *C. nigra*) or *Juncus effusus*, with a moss layer predominantly of *Polytrichum commune*, *Sphagnum palustre*, *S. recurvum*, *S. subsecundum* (mainly var. *inundatum*) and, more rarely, *S. girgensohnii* and *S. plumulosum*, and with associated herbs such as *Epilobium palustre*, *Ranunculus flammula*, and *Viola palustris*. Rich-fens are placed in the next order. This is generally a fairly satisfactory division, although as emphasised by Duvigneaud (1949) there is a continuous gradation from acid bog hollows to the most calcareous fens. If anything it appears to be more difficult to maintain such a division between the various orders and alliances in the British Isles than on the Continent, as there is often considerable overlap in the tolerance of species which are regarded as faithful to one order or alliance in central Europe.

Caricion canescentis–fuscae (W. Koch 1926) Nordhagen 1936

Communities of poor-fens (*sensu* Du Reitz, 1949, 1954) that are commonly developed in soligenous sites and fed by moving geogenous water, or in flushed ground around springs, rills, or streams.

Trichophorum cespitosum–Carex panicea Association (Trichophoreto–Eriophoretum caricetosum McVean & Ratcliffe 1962.) (Narthecio–Ericetum tetralicis Moore 1968 *pro parte.*)

This is a widespread but rather local association on Skye (Table 4.19), that is characteristic of 'water-tracks' (Ingram, 1967; Sjörs, 1948) or soligenous soaks (Malmer, 1962) within stands of Trichophoreto–Eriophoretum bog (Table 4.26). Stands are rarely extensive in area. The constants *Carex echinata*, *C. panicea*, *Erica tetralix*, *Molinia caerulea*, *Narthecium ossifragum*, and *Sphagnum palustre*, and the frequent occurrence of *Carex demissa*, *Eleocharis multicaulis*, *Equisetum palustre*, *Euphrasia scottica*, *Pinguicula vulgaris*, *Riccardia pinguis*, *Schoenus nigricans*, *Selaginella selaginoides*, *Sphagnum plumulosum*, and *Succisa pratensis* all indicate soligenous conditions, and they serve to distinguish this association floristically from the related Trichophoreto–Eriophoretum bog community (see Table 4.57). An extensive stand of a *Narthecium ossifragum* flush (List 8) appears to belong here.

The community occurs on fairly shallow, humified peats, overlying a gleyed mineral substratum, often in sloping areas (5° or less) up to 900 feet (275 m) altitude. The pH values range from 4.4 to 4.8 and the specific conductivity values range from 81 to 108 μmhos, and they are thus higher than in the related Trichophoreto–Eriophoretum bog communities (see Table 4.16). It frequently merges, often rather gradually, into Trichophoreto–Eriophoretum, Trichophoreto–Callunetum, or *Molinia caerulea–Myrica gale* Associations. *Campylopus atrovirens* var. *falcatus*, *C. setifolius*, and *C. shawii* occasionally occur in this community, especially in areas of shallow but wet peat and in seepage channels. The alga *Gleocapsa magna* is locally common in open areas, and *Acrocladium sarmentosum* occurs occasionally.

The association commonly occurs, with little floristic variation, in western Scotland (McVean & Ratcliffe, 1962) and western Ireland, and more locally in north Wales (Edgell, 1969) and Lakeland. Related communities are described from western Norway by Nordhagen (1922), and from elsewhere in western Europe by Braun-Blanquet (1948).

Molinia caerulea–Myrica gale Association (*Molinia–Myrica* nodum McVean & Ratcliffe 1962.)

This distinctive community (Table 4.20) is dominated by *Molinia caerulea* and *Myrica gale*, and it commonly occurs on periodically flooded ground by stream-sides and rills, generally within areas of bog (Lists 1–4, 6, 7) and, more rarely, on deep peat in seepage areas within valley-floors (List 5). It occurs widely but rather locally throughout Skye. The stands are rather poor floristically, as the dominants are frequently so luxuriant, especially when the dense, tussock habit of *Molinia caerulea* is developed. Jefferies (1915) attributed this growth habit to a continuous supply of well-aerated water, and Webster (1962) has demonstrated experimentally that in stagnant conditions the growth of *Molinia* tillers is considerably less than under conditions of moving water. This reduction in growth probably results from an oxygen deficiency and carbon dioxide and hydrogen sulphide accumulation around the roots, which tends to depress the plants' metabolic activities and ion uptake (Armstrong & Boatman, 1967; Sheikh, 1970).

Besides the two dominants, *Carex echinata*, *Pinguicula vulgaris*, *Potentilla erecta*, and *Sphagnum palustre* are also constant. *Carex panicea*, *Sphagnum plumulosum*, and *S. recurvum* are frequent, and they are indicative of soligenous conditions. Notable but rare components of this association include *Anagallis tenella*, *Drosera intermedia*, *Sphagnum contortum*, a lax form of *S. imbricatum*, and *S. strictum*. Several of the stands are poor in bryophytes, perhaps due to the accumulation of dense mats of dead leaves of *Molinia*.

The association occurs in sloping areas (8° or less) at low altitudes (100–500 feet, 31–152 m) on shallow (40–80 cm), highly humified, silty peats, frequently overlying alluvium, with pH values ranging between 5.2 and 5.9 and specific conductivities between 99 and 115 μmhos (Table 4.16). It commonly grades into Trichophoreto–Eriophoretum, Molinieto–Callunetum, or *Trichophorum cespitosum–Carex panicea* mires. The association is common in western Scotland (McVean & Ratcliffe, 1962; Ratcliffe & Walker, 1958) and western Ireland, and it occurs locally in north Wales and south-west Lakeland. Related associations are described from western Scandinavia by Böcher (1943) and Skogen (1965).

Sphagneto–Juncetum effusi Association McVean & Ratcliffe 1962
(Juncetum effusi Jonas 1935 *pro parte.*)

This is a distinctive, floristically consistent mire type on Skye (Table 4.21) with *Juncus effusus* as the physiognomic dominant, although *Carex echinata, Galium saxatile, Potentilla erecta, Polytrichum commune, Sphagnum palustre*, and *S. recurvum* are also constants. It is the main habitat for *Viola palustris* and *Sphagnum girgensohnii* on Skye. Many of the associated taxa, for example *Agrostis canina, Anthoxanthum odoratum, Festuca* spp., *Luzula campestris, Lophocolea bidentata*, and *Rhytidiadelphus squarrosus*, are characteristic of Agrosto–Festucetum grassland communities (see Table 4.57) within which this mire community commonly occurs, either in waterlogged hollows in level ground (Lists 4, 5) or along gently sloping (5° or less) stream-sides or rills (Lists 1, 2, 3) wherever drainage is impeded. The association is widespread, but never extensive, on Skye, and it favours shallow gleyed peaty silts (with abundant *Sphagnum* spp.) or gley podsols (with abundant *Polytrichum commune*) in sites with a fluctuating water-table. Standing water is generally rare. The pH range is from 4.5 to 4.7 and the specific conductivity range is from 122 to 150 μmhos (Table 4.16). The association occurs from near sea-level to 1000 feet (305 m) altitude.

The association occurs commonly with little floristic variation throughout Scotland (McVean & Ratcliffe, 1962), northern England (Eddy, Welch & Rawes, 1969), Wales (Ratcliffe, 1959), south-west England, and Ireland (Moore, 1960). A comparable Juncetum effusi Association is described from the Netherlands by Westhoff & Den Held (1969), and a related Violo–Juncetum effusi Association is described from Switzerland by Berset (1969). *Juncus effusus* is considered by Ratcliffe (1964) to be commonly associated with biotic disturbances, and the association may thus be largely anthropogenic. It is of interest that a related community occurs in central Europe (Hadač & Vaňa, 1967) except that *Juncus filiformis* is the physiognomic dominant, rather than *J. effusus*. In Britain *J. filiformis* is a rare, lake-margin plant, whose present distribution is largely centred on Lakeland.

Carex-Sphagnum recurvum nodum
(Sphagneto–Caricetum sub-alpinum McVean & Ratcliffe 1962.)

This *nodum* (Table 4.21) is closely related to the Sphagneto–Juncetum effusi Association, except that *Eriophorum angustifolium* is the physiognomic dominant, with abundant *Carex echinata*, and that *Juncus effusus* and many of the associated grassland species are absent. Of the *Sphagnum* species present, *S. palustre*, *S. recurvum*, and *S. subsecundum* (both var. *auriculatum* and var. *inundatum*) are the most frequent, and form a nearly continuous lawn. The pH and specific conductivity values are similar to those for the Sphagneto–Juncetum effusi (see Table 4.16) but the water-table is permanently high in this *nodum*. It occurs on shallow peat in waterlogged seepage channels amidst eroding Trichophoreto–Callunetum bog at moderate elevations. It can occur more rarely in waterlogged hollows within blanket bog, but only where there is some indication of water movement through the peat. In contrast to the Sphagneto–Juncetum effusi community, this *nodum* occurs on predominantly organic soils. The *nodum* is rather rare on Skye, but it occurs more widely elsewhere in Scotland (McVean & Ratcliffe, 1962), in northern England (Eddy *et al.*, 1969), Wales (Edgell, 1969), and Ireland, and it is the principal habitat for *Carex paupercula* in Britain.

Sphagno–Tomenthypnion Dahl 1956

Communities of intermediate-fens (*sensu* Sjörs, 1950*a*) that are characterised by a mixture of poor-fen species (for example *Carex echinata, C. nigra, Juncus effusus, Sphagnum recurvum*, and *S. palustre*) and rich-fen species (for example *Carex dioica, Juncus articulatus, Campylium stellatum, Sphagnum contortum, S. teres*, and *S. warnstorfianum* (see Table 4.57)).

Carex rostrata–Aulacomnium palustre Association
(*Carex rostrata–Sphagnum warnstorfianum nodum* McVean & Ratcliffe 1962 *pro parte.*)

This mire type (Table 4.22) occurs rather locally as a marginal reedswamp community on deep, highly organic fen-peat or lake-mud (up to 8 m depth) at the edge of several lowland lochs. Stands are rarely extensive on Skye. The water-table is generally slightly below ground-level and there appears to be little or no lateral water movement. It is dominated by *Carex rostrata* growing amidst an almost continuous bryophyte carpet that is composed primarily of *Sphagnum recurvum*, *S. teres*, *S. contortum*, *Acrocladium cuspidatum*, and *Aulacomnium palustre*. Other constants in the association include *Equisetum palustre*, *Carex echinata*, *C. nigra*, *Eriophorum angustifolium*, *Pedicularis palustris*, *Potentilla palustris*, and *Ranunculus flammula*.

The association has floristic affinities with communities of the orders Caricetalia fuscae, Tofieldietalia, and Molinietalia (see Table 4.57). It commonly merges into *Juncus acutiflorus–Filipendula ulmaria* (Molinietalia) meadows (Table 4.32) on shallower, drier, silty peats, and it has several species in common with these meadows, for example *Holcus lanatus*, *Caltha palustris*, *Filipendula ulmaria*, *Lychnis flos-cuculi*, and *Acrocladium cuspidatum* (see Table 4.57). It differs, however, in the dominance of sedges rather than rushes, and in the richer and more varied bryophyte flora. It is the principal habitat for *Myosotis scorpioides*, *Veronica scutellata*, *Acrocladium cordifolium*, *A. stramineum*, *Aulacomnium palustre*, *Dicranum bonjeani*, *Mnium pseudo-punctatum*, *M. seligeri*, *Sphagnum squarrosum*, *S. teres*, and *S. warnstorfianum* on Skye. In wetter sites it grades into stands of the Magnocaricion or into *Carex lasiocarpa* communities, with reduced floristic richness. The pH values are between 4.8 and 5.5, and the specific conductivity ranges from 110 to 137 μmhos (see Table 4.16).

This and related associations occur locally throughout northern Britain, but they have only rarely been described (Eddy *et al.*, 1969; McVean & Ratcliffe, 1962; Spence, 1964). It is the principal habitat for *Camptothecium nitens* in Britain. Comparable communities occur widely in Scandinavia (Dahl, 1956; Fransson, 1963; Mörnsjö, 1969; Nordhagen, 1943; Persson, 1961; Sonesson, 1970; Svensson, 1965) and elsewhere in Europe (Rybniček, 1970).

TOFIELDIETALIA Preising in Oberdorfer 1949

Communities of rich-fens (*sensu* Du Rietz, 1949; 1954).

Eriophorion latifoliae Braun-Blanquet & R. Tüxen 1943

Communities of lowland and sub-alpine calcareous rich-fens with, for example, *Carex hostiana*, *Eleocharis quinqueflora*, *Eriophorum latifolium*, *Schoenus nigricans*, *Campylium stellatum*, *Drepanocladus revolvens*, and *Scorpidium scorpioides*. As the rate of humus decomposition depends on the base status as well as the soil aeration, rich-fens tend to have less accumulation of organic soils than poor-fens or bogs. Where the water flow is strong, there is not only rapid humus decomposition, but mineral particles are transported as well, resulting in bare silty-muds, characteristic of open flush communities. The ground water in these communities is generally highly calcareous and with a high pH and specific conductivity (see Table 4.16).

Carex rostrata–Scorpidium scorpioides Association

(*Carex rostrata*–brown moss *nodum* McVean & Ratcliffe 1962.)

This association (Table 4.23) is rather local and diverse on Skye, with *Carex rostrata* as the physiognomic dominant within an almost continuous carpet of pleurocarpous 'brown mosses' such as *Campylium stellatum*, *Drepanocladus revolvens* var. *intermedius*, and *Scorpidium scorpioides*. *Carex nigra*, *C. panicea*, *Equisetum palustre*, *Eriophorum augustifolium*, and *Menyanthes trifoliata* are also constant. This association differs from the *Carex rostrata–Menyanthes trifoliata* Association (Magnocaricion) in its well-developed bryophyte carpet.

The association occurs in strongly soligenous channels within areas of blanket bog below 500 feet (152 m) altitude (Lists 1–3) in hollows and pools within lowland fens, or as marginal pioneer fen communities around lowland lochs (Lists 4–7). It favours wet highly organic fen-peats or lake-muds of depths up to 8 m, with the water-table permanently at or slightly above ground-level. In many instances there is little evidence for any water movement. The pH values are between 5.2 and 6.0 and the specific conductivity values range between 147 and 182 μmhos (Table 4.16). With increasing water-depth it merges into Magnocaricion or *Carex lasiocarpa* stands, and this community may often form a complex mosaic within the rather drier and less base-demanding *Carex rostrata–Aulacomnium palustre* intermediate-fens. *Carex serotina*, *Utricularia minor*, *U. intermedia*, *Acrocladium giganteum*, *Cinclidium stygium*, and *Sphagnum contortum* are notable but rather rare components of the association.

The association occurs locally in the Scottish Highlands (McVean & Ratcliffe, 1962) and in the Carboniferous limestone areas of northern England (Holdgate, 1955*a*). Comparable associations are described from Scandinavia (Dahl, 1956; Fransson, 1963; Nordhagen, 1943; Sjörs, 1948) and elsewhere in Europe (Braun, 1968; Rybniček, 1964, 1966, 1970).

Carex panicea–Campylium stellatum Association McVean & Ratcliffe 1962

This is a widespread but local association (Table 4.24) on Skye, occurring as a closely-grazed sedge-dominated sward, and containing a wide range of basiphilous herbs and mosses. *Carex panicea, Juncus articulatus, Pinguicula vulgaris, Potentilla erecta, Selaginella selaginoides, Breutelia chrysocoma,* and *Campylium stellatum* are constants. Associated sedges of high constancy or cover include *Carex demissa, C. echinata, C. nigra,* and *C. pulicaris,* and *Eleocharis quinqueflora* can be locally abundant. Additional species of interest in this association include *Euphrasia scottica, Pinguicula lusitanica, Thalictrum alpinum,* and *Drepanocladus revolvens* var. *intermedius.* The community commonly occurs as a narrow zone along small rills (Lists 1–4) or adjoining open calcareous flushes (Lists 5, 6) on slopes between 5 and 20°, and it ascends to 1100 feet (335 m). It favours very moist silty peats that are often highly organic and shallow (30 cm or less). The pH values are between 5.6 and 6.2 and the specific conductivity values range from 149 to 166 μmhos (Table 4.16). It frequently merges rather abruptly into basic grasslands on drier soils or into *Trichophorum cespitosum–Carex panicea* mires, often with abundant *Erica tetralix,* in less soligenous sites within areas of bog.

The association occurs widely but rather locally in Scotland (McVean & Ratcliffe, 1962; Poore, 1955*c*), the Southern Uplands, Lakeland, and on the Carboniferous limestones of northern England, and it appears to correspond in part to the wet, calcareous pastures of upper Teesdale that contain *Carex capillaris, Equisetum variegatum, Gentiana verna, Kobresia simpliciuscula,* and *Primula farinosa* (Pigott, 1956). A rather species-poor variant of this association occurs in north Wales (Edgell, 1969). Related communities occur in Scandinavia (Hallberg, 1971; Nordhagen, 1927, 1943; Persson, 1961; Svensson, 1965), but some of the Scandinavian stands differ in their great abundance of *Salix* spp. Comparable communities are described from central Europe (Braun, 1968; Rybníček, 1964, 1970), but they differ from the Scottish association in their great species richness.

Eriophorum latifolium–Carex hostiana Association (Cariceto–Saxifragetum aizoidis McVean & Ratcliffe 1962 *pro parte.*)

This is a floristically distinctive open flush association (Table 4.25) commonly occurring below calcareous springs (Cratoneurion commutati) where the rate of water flow is greatest. The vegetational cover is generally low (50–80%), but the association is floristically rich with 83 taxa recorded in eleven relevés, with a mean of 29 taxa per stand. *Carex demissa, C. panicea, Eleocharis quinqueflora, Eriophorum latifolium, Schoenus nigricans, Pinguicula vulgaris, Campylium stellatum,* and *Scorpidium scorpioides* are constants, and *Carex dioica, C. lepidocarpa, Drosera anglica, Euphrasia scottica, Pinguicula lusitanica, Utricularia minor, Cinclidium stygium, Sphagnum contortum, S. warnstorfianum,* and *Splachnum ampullaceum* are notable but rather rare components. It is the principal habitat for *Acrocladium trifarium* on Skye (cf. Proctor, 1959; Rybníček, 1966). The association favours sloping ground (3–10°) at altitudes up to 750 feet (225 m) on moist silt, sand, or gravel with a low humus content. The pH and specific conductivity values are high (6.4–7.2 and 196–417 μmhos, respectively; see Table 4.16). The surface is often littered with partially embedded stones, and it generally has a water-scoured appearance, although the open character may also result from grazing. There are indications in some stands that the open flushes are enlarging at the expense of the surrounding vegetation. At some sites on the slopes of the Cuillins, the community has developed on the mineral soil exposed by recent peat erosion and gullying. Extensive cattle and sheep trampling can result in the vegetational cover becoming discontinuous. The exposed peat or soil is then rapidly washed away by rain and by melting snow, and the underlying mineral substratum is thus exposed. The association is rather local in its distribution on Skye, being centred on the limestones of the Suardal area and the basic igneous rocks of northern Skye and the Cuillins.

List 11 is from a heavily cattle-grazed area by Loch Cill Chriosd, near Ben Suardal, and it consists of a mosaic of turf hummocks (up to 50 cm high) scattered within open, calcareous mud and gravel kept more or less permanently wet by a continual seepage of water from nearby springs. The hummocks support a diverse flora, including *Dactylorchis purpurella, Linum catharticum, Platanthera bifolia, Thalictrum alpinum, Barbula fallax, Philonotis calcarea, Leiocolea bantriensis, L. muelleri,* and *Scapania aspera,* whereas the hummock sides have *Orthothecium rufescens,* a species otherwise restricted to calcareous cliff-vegetation on Skye. The hummocks, which are most frequent just below the springs, consist of a thin cap of humus-rich silt overlying calcareous silts and gravels. The area lies within a cattle pasture, and it is likely that the hummocks represent residual pieces of the surrounding continuous turf, as the soil profiles are similar.

Although the springs slowly eat back into the marsh, the principal erosive agent appears to be cattle-trampling resulting in disruption of the turf. Subsequent washing away of the silty mud during wet periods results in the accumulation of coarse gravel and stones between the hummocks. That the marsh would be continuous turf in the absence of cattle is confirmed nearby, for where a fence crosses the area, there is an almost closed turf dominated by *Schoenus nigricans* (List 14: Table 4.25). This stand of hummocks closely resembles the 'turfy marshes' in upper Teesdale (Pigott, 1956), at Tarn Moor, Westmorland (Holdgate, 1955*b*), and at Great Close Mire, Yorkshire.

The stands of the association occur amidst a wide range of vegetation types, for example ombrotrophic bogs (Lists 1, 3, 5–10), grasslands (List 2), or marginal reedswamps (List 9). The flushes generally merge in less sloping areas into dense *Schoenus nigricans* stands, and may be bordered by a low sedge-sward of the *Carex panicea–Campylium stellatum* Association. There is often a very striking change in vegetation and soil type within a comparatively short distance, the junction frequently being marked by a fairly steep bank.

Similar flushes occur locally in calcareous areas of western Scotland (McVean & Ratcliffe, 1962), northern England (Pigott, 1956), and Scandinavia (Coombe & White, 1951). Related but rather more closed communities occur in lowland fens in southern England, Ireland, and elsewhere in Europe (Braun, 1968; Sjörs, 1948; Tüxen, 1937).

Schoenus nigricans Association

(Schoenetum nigricantis W. Koch 1926 *pro parte.*)

This mire type is dominated by dense tussocks of *Schoenus nigricans* (Table 4.25), and, although it has several constants in common with the previous association (*Carex panicea*, *Schoenus nigricans*, *Pinguicula vulgaris*, *Campylium stellatum*, *Scorpidium scorpioides*), it is floristically poorer with a mean of 18 taxa per stand. It differs from the *Eriophorum latifolium–Carex hostiana* Association, however, in the virtual absence of *Carex demissa*, *C. hostiana*, *Triglochin palustre*, and *Blindia acuta*, and in the greater abundance of *Sphagnum subsecundum* var. *inundatum*. The occurrence of *Rhynchospora alba* in this rich-fen association is of interest, in view of its frequent occurrence in bog communities on Skye, such as the *Eriophorum angustifolium–Sphagnum cuspidatum* and Trichophoreto–Eriophoretum Associations (cf. Rybniček, 1970). The *Schoenus* community commonly occurs associated with calcareous springs and *Eriophorum latifolium* gravel-flushes, but it appears to favour flat or gently sloping areas (2–5°) with generally lower rates of water-movement (Lists 12, 17, 18). It also occurs in soligenous seepage areas within *Carex rostrata–Scorpidium scorpioides* fens, receiving drainage-water either from limestones (Lists 13, 14) or ultra-basic rocks (List 16). It occurs up to 750 feet (225 m) altitude, and it favours calcareous peats or marls rather than silts and gravels. The pH and specific conductivity values are high (6.4–7.0 and 278–400 μmhos, respectively; see Table 4.16), and they are similar to those of the *Eriophorum latifolium* stands. Like the *E. latifolium* Association, it is rather local on Skye today, and it frequently merges into a wide range of vegetation types with improved drainage.

Similar associations occur locally in basic areas of western Scotland (McVean & Ratcliffe, 1962; Spence, 1970), northern England (often with *Primula farinosa*; Holdgate, 1955*b*), western Ireland (Ivimey-Cook & Proctor, 1966*b*), and southern England (with *Epipactis palustris*, *Liparis loeselii*, and, in East Anglia, *Leiocolea rutheana*). Related communities, often with *Schoenus ferrugineus*, are described from Scandinavia (Malmer, 1965; Skogen, 1965) and elsewhere in Europe (Allorge, 1921–22; Görs, 1964; Oberdorfer, 1957; Tüxen, 1937; Vanden Berghen, 1952).

Schoenus nigricans has a wide ecological amplitude in Britain (see Sparling, 1968); for example in western Ireland it occurs in both rich-fens and bogs* (see the *Pleurozia purpurea–Erica tetralix* Association; Braun-Blanquet & Tüxen, 1952). On Skye, and in Scotland generally, its occurrence in bogs invariably indicates some water-movement and soligenous influence, as judged by its associated species. On Skye it can also occur on intermittently flushed limestone or ultra-basic (gabbro or peridotite) cliffs, on rocks by the sea, and in brackish-water communities. It is possible that *Schoenus nigricans* has a preference for both saline and calcareous conditions, and it is probable that no one single environmental factor can be invoked to explain its autecology (cf. Aletsee, 1967; Boatman, 1961; Sparling, 1967; Tansley, 1949).

Carex–Saxifraga aizoides nodum

(Cariceto–Saxifragetum aizoidis McVean & Ratcliffe 1962 *pro parte.*)

The four available lists of this *nodum* (Table 4.25) differ from the closely related *Eriophorum latifolium–Carex hostiana* Association in the occurrence of the

* A similar habitat range occurs in *Cladium mariscus*, *Campylium stellatum*, and *Scorpidium scorpioides*.

montane taxa *Juncus biglumis*, *J. triglumis*, *Dryas octopetala*, *Saxifraga aizoides*, and *Thalictrum alpinum*, and the virtual absence of *Carex hostiana*, *Drosera anglica*, and *Eriophorum latifolium*. The *nodum* is thus regarded as a montane equivalent of the *Eriophorum latifolium–Carex hostiana* Association. It closely corresponds to the Cariceto–Saxifragetum aizoidis Association of the Scottish Highlands (McVean & Ratcliffe, 1962). It favours similar ecological situations to the *Eriophorum latifolium* stands, except that it occurs at higher altitudes. It is restricted on Skye to the Suardal region, northern Skye, and the Cuillins. The pH values are between 6.2 and 6.8, whereas the specific conductivity values are between 96 and 116 μmhos (see Table 4.16), and are thus considerably lower than in other communities in this order.

This *nodum* strictly belongs to the alpine alliance Caricion bicoloris-atrofuscae Nordhagen 1936. There are, however, such strong affinities on Skye with the lowland Eriophorion latifoliae Alliance (Schoenion ferruginei; Nordhagen, 1936) that such a division would result in an arbitrary separation between closely related noda.

This open community occurs locally in the Scottish Highlands, supporting such rarities as *Carex atrofusca*, *C. microglochin*, *C. saxatilis*, *Juncus castaneus*, and *Kobresia simpliciuscula*, along with taxa that are extremely rare or curiously absent from Skye, for example *Equisetum variegatum*, *Juncus alpinoarticulatus*, *Tofieldia pusilla*, *Amblyodon dealbatus*, *Catascopium nigritum*, and *Meesia uliginosa*. It occurs locally in Lakeland and upper Teesdale (with *Bartsia alpina*, *Kobresia simpliciuscula*, *Minuartia stricta*, and *Primula farinosa*; Pigott, 1956) and similar communities, but lacking *Saxifraga aizoides*, occur locally in north Wales and the Moffat Hills. Related communities occur widely in Scandinavia (Coombe & White, 1951; Nordhagen, 1927, 1943; Persson, 1961) and elsewhere in Europe (Braun-Blanquet, 1948–50; Oberdorfer, 1957).

14. OXYCOCCO-SPHAGNETEA Braun-Blanquet & R. Tüxen 1943

Communities of bog-hummocks and lawns, and of wet-heaths generally dominated by ericaceous dwarf-shrubs and *Sphagnum* spp. The phytosociological classification for the class Oxycocco–Sphagnetea proposed by Moore (1968) is adopted here (cf. Tüxen, 1969).

ERICETALIA TETRALICIS Moore (1964) 1968

Ericion tetralicis Schwickerath 1933

Communities of wet-heaths and bogs on shallow peat in western Europe.

Trichophoreto–Callunetum Association McVean & Ratcliffe 1962

(Trichophoretum germanici brittanicum Duvigneaud 1949 *pro parte*.)

This association (Table 4.26) is characterised by the co-dominance and constancy of *Trichophorum cespitosum* spp. *germanicum* and *Calluna vulgaris*. There are only two other constants, *Erica tetralix* and *Potentilla erecta*. The association is widespread and very extensive on Skye, occurring on moderate slopes (0–15°) that are generally too well-drained to support the wetter Trichophoreto–Eriophoretum or Calluneto–Eriophoretum bogs, and that are too moist to support Callunetum vulgaris or Agrosto–Festucetum stands. It occurs from sea level to 1600 feet (490 m) on well humified peats up to 2 m deep. It may occur on the thin layer of waterlogged peat left after peat-cutting. The pH values are between 3.8 and 4.2, and the specific conductivity values are low (24–29 μmhos; see Table 4.16). On ground above 1000 feet (305 m) this bog-type is frequently undergoing sheet erosion, and it occurs in a complex mosaic with *Carex–Sphagnum recurvum* stands in wetter areas. It is characterised from other bog communities on Skye by the absence of *Myrica gale*, *Polygala serpyllifolia*, and *Sphagnum palustre* (see Table 4.57).

Three facies are distinguished:

(i) *Sphagnum-rich* facies (Lists 1–6) with abundant *Sphagnum palustre*, *S. papillosum*, and *S. rubellum*. This is closely related to the Trichophoreto–Eriophoretum Association, but it lacks *Myrica gale*, *Pleurozia purpurea*, and *Sphagnum compactum*. It tends to occur at higher altitudes and often occupies small depressions, rather than slopes, in areas that are apparently unaffected by recent burning or drainage.

(ii) *Rhacomitrium-rich* facies (Lists 7–11) with large, conspicuous hummocks of *Rhacomitrium lanuginosum*, and a rather low *Sphagnum* cover. This and the succeeding facies appear to reflect drying of the bog surface resulting from a complex of factors, including repeated moor-burning, grazing, and subsequent gully and sheet erosion. Abundant hummocks of *Rhacomitrium lanuginosum* are characteristic of disturbed and rather dry bogs both in western Scotland (Ratcliffe, 1964) and in western Norway (Skogen, 1965).

(iii) *Lichen-rich* facies (Lists 12–14) with much bare peat, rich in crustose lichens (for example *Icmadophila ericetorum*) and small hepatics (for example *Lepidozia setacea*, *Lophozia incisa*, *L. ventricosa*, *Mylia anomala*, *Nowellia curvifolia*, and *Odontoschisma denudatum*), many of which also occur on decaying logs in

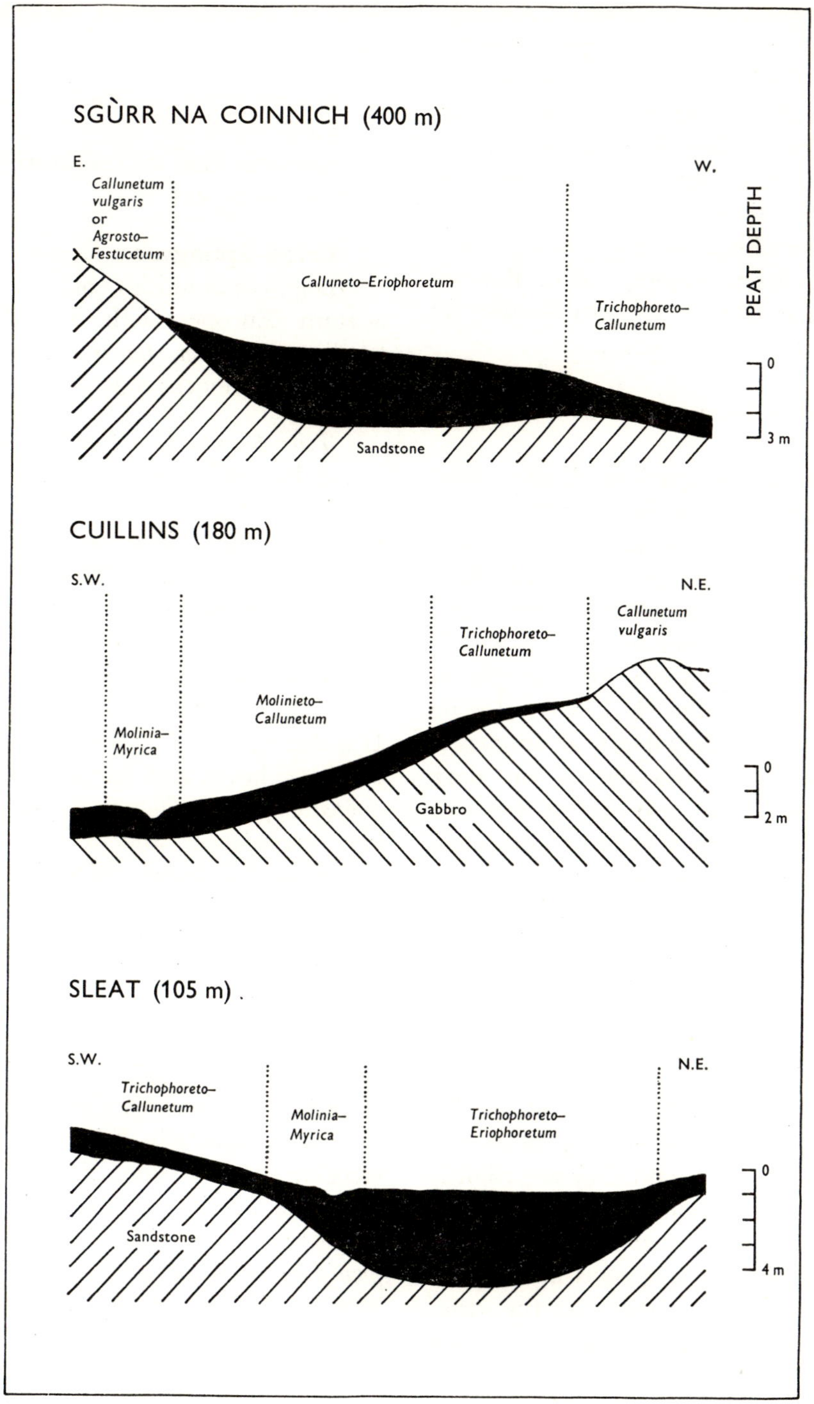

Figure 4. Relationships of bog communities to peat depth, slope, and altitude in the Kyleakin area, the Cuillins, and the Sleat Peninsula.

woods (see Table 4.54). Peaty banks are the main habitat for *Calypogeia neesiana* var. *neesiana*, *Cephalozia bicuspidata* var. *lammersiana*, and *C. leucantha* on Skye. The introduced moss *Campylopus introflexus* grows in this facies, with *Dicranella cerviculata*, *Funaria obtusa*, and *Polytrichum alpestre*, and also in recently abandoned peat cuttings. The ecological factors that differentiate this facies from the *Rhacomitrium* facies are not clear.

It is a diverse association, with floristic affinities with bog communities, with Agrosto–Festucetum grasslands, and with Callunetum vulgaris heaths (see Table 4.57) into which it frequently merges on better drained ground (see Fig. 4). This bog-type is the main habitat for *Campylopus brevipilus* and *C. schwarzii* on Skye, although they are absent or poorly represented in the lists. *Campylopus setifolius*, *C. shawii*, *Sphagnum molle*, and *S. strictum* occur occasionally, especially in moist areas of low *Sphagnum* cover.

The association occurs widely throughout Scotland (McVean & Ratcliffe, 1962), and in some western hill-districts of northern England (Eddy *et al.*, 1969), north Wales, and Ireland (Moore, 1960). Related communities are described from western Norway by Faegri (1960) and Nordhagen (1922).

Molinieto–Callunetum Association McVean & Ratcliffe 1962

This association (Table 4.27) is distinguished from other bog communities on Skye by the abundance and co-dominance of *Molinia caerulea* and *Calluna vulgaris*. Other association constants include *Erica tetralix*, *Narthecium ossifragum*, *Potentilla erecta*, and *Trichophorum cespitosum*. The community occurs widely on Skye, and it covers large areas, for example on the lower slopes of the Cuillins. It favours sloping ground (up to 15°) or valley-floors at moderate elevations (300–1500 feet, 180–460 m) on dark brown, highly humified, silty peat of 1 m depth or less. The habitat is not strictly that of an ombrotrophic bog, for it is clearly influenced by a moderate rate of water movement through the peat. Associated species such as *Carex dioica*, *C. echinata*, *C. panicea*, *Pinguicula lusitanica*, and *Schoenus nigricans* are all typical 'fen-plants'. It is the principal habitat for *Sphagnum strictum* on Skye, and *Campylopus atrovirens* var. *falcatus*, *C. setifolius*, *C. shawii*, and a lax-form of *Sphagnum imbricatum* occasionally occur. The pH and specific conductivity ranges are 4.5–4.8 and 35–42 μmhos, respectively, (see Table 4.16), and they are slightly higher than those of the previous association.

The association often grades into *Molinia caerulea–Myrica gale* mires where the soligenous influence is more marked, whereas its relation to the drier Trichophoreto–Callunetum bog clearly reflects slope and drainage differences (Fig. 4). When the ground-water becomes stagnant, as in hollows, it frequently merges into Trichophoreto–Eriophoretum bog. Almost pure stands of *Molinia caerulea* occur locally, perhaps resulting from the loss of *Calluna vulgaris* and other dwarf shrubs following repeated burning.

The association occurs widely in western Scotland (McVean & Ratcliffe, 1962), in parts of south-west Scotland, and in Ireland (Braun-Blanquet & Tüxen, 1952; Moore, 1960), and more locally in north Wales and northern England. Comparable associations are described from western Norway (Knaben, 1950).

SPHAGNETALIA MAGELLANICI Moore (1964) 1968

Communities of ombrotrophic *Sphagnum*-rich bogs on deep peat.

Erico–Sphagnion Moore (1964) 1968

Bog communities of the atlantic sector of western Europe, with an abundance of *Erica tetralix*. *Sphagnum fuscum* is absent or occurs as isolated hummocks only.

Trichophoreto–Eriophoretum Association McVean & Ratcliffe 1962

(Erico–Sphagnetum magellanici Moore 1968 *pro parte.*) (*Pleurozia purpurea–Erica tetralix* Association Braun-Blanquet & R. Tüxen 1952 *pro parte.*) (Trichophoro–Sphagnetum papillosi J. Tüxen 1969 *pro parte.*)

This is a characteristic western bog-type (Table 4.28), occurring widely but rather locally on Skye. It is distinguished by the presence of well-developed *Sphagnum* lawns and hummocks, mainly of *Sphagnum compactum*, *S. papillosum*, *S. rubellum*, *S. subsecundum* var. *auriculatum*, and *S. tenellum*, but also with occasional hummocks of *S. fuscum* and *S. imbricatum*, and scattered patches of *Campylopus atrovirens* (including *C. atrovirens* var. *falcatus*), *C. setifolius*, *C. shawii*, *Rhacomitrium lanuginosum*, *Pleurozia purpurea*, and *Cladonia uncialis*. There is a wide range of dwarf-shrubs and herbs, including *Calluna vulgaris*, *Erica tetralix*, *Myrica gale*, *Narthecium ossifragum*, and *Rhynchospora alba*. Association constants are *Calluna vulgaris*, *Erica tetralix*, *Eriophorum angustifolium*, *Molinia caerulea*, *Myrica gale*, *Narthecium ossifragum*, *Trichophorum cespitosum*, *Pleurozia purpurea*, *Sphagnum compactum*, *S. papillosum*, and *S. rubellum*. *Carex pauciflora*, *Drosera anglica*, *Pedicularis sylvatica* ssp. *hibernica* (Webb, 1956), *Sphagnum imbricatum*, and *Pleurozia purpurea* are strongly characteristic.

The association favours deep, humified peats (up to 4 m depth) on level or gently sloping ground (less than 5°; Fig. 4) at low altitudes (up to 600 feet, 360 m). The pH values range from 3.6 to 4.3 and the specific conductivity values are from 20 to 30 μmhos (see Table 4.16). Much of the low-lying peatlands on Skye would once have supported this community, but a long history of peat cutting for fuel by crofters has restricted its distribution, as have recent attempts at drainage for forestry plantations. The stands examined range from rather dry dwarf-shrub-dominated bog (Lists 6, 14) to wet *Sphagnum*-dominated lawns (Lists 4, 13), reflecting differences in water-table and bog morphology (Ratcliffe & Walker, 1958). Lists 8–11 are from hummock and lawn communities within areas of *Sphagnum*-dominated patterned bogs, with a mosaic structure of pools, lawns, and hummocks. The pool vegetation has been described separately on p. 41. Undisturbed hummocks of *Sphagnum fuscum* and *S. imbricatum* frequently support a characteristic hepatic flora including *Calypogeia sphagnicola*, *Cephalozia connivens*, *C. loitlesbergeri*, *C. macrostachya*, *C. media*, *Lepidozia setacea*, and *Mylia anomala*. There is often an abundance of *Mylia taylori* and *Odontoschisma sphagni* in these bogs, either creeping over *Sphagnum* or in dense pure patches especially in areas where the *Sphagnum* growth appears to be unhealthy. *Pleurozia purpurea* can be locally plentiful in these bogs.

The association occurs widely but rather locally in western and south-west Scotland (McVean & Ratcliffe, 1962; Pearsall, 1956; Ratcliffe & Walker, 1958), and very locally in south-west Lakeland, north Wales, and on Dartmoor. *Andromeda polifolia* and *Vaccinium oxycoccos* are absent from this association throughout its range. A similar association occurs widely in western Ireland (see Boatman, 1960; Braun-Blanquet & Tüxen, 1952), but the Irish stands often differ in their abundance of *Schoenus nigricans*, which appears as an ecological replacement of *Trichophorum cespitosum* or *Eriophorum vaginatum*. The British distribution of the association as a whole is markedly western, falling within the zone of 180+ 'wet-days' (map in Ratcliffe, 1968) or 240+ 'rain-days' a year.

Calluneto–Eriophoretum Association McVean & Ratcliffe 1962

(Vaccinio–Ericetum tetralicis Moore 1962 *pro parte.*)

This is a rare but distinctive bog association (Table 4.29) on Skye, differing from the Trichophoreto–Eriophoretum Association in its abundance and constancy of *Empetrum nigrum*, *Eriophorum vaginatum*, *Calluna vulgaris*, *Hylocomium splendens*, *Pleurozium schreberi*, and *Sphagnum capillaceum*, and by the absence of such plants as *Drosera anglica*, *Myrica gale*, and *Narthecium ossifragum* (see Table 4.57). Although *Sphagnum capillaceum* is constant and has a high cover in this association, bryophytes other than *Sphagnum* are frequent (for example *Hylocomium splendens*, *Hypnum cupressiforme* var. *ericetorum*, *Pleurozium schreberi*, and *Rhytidiadelphus loreus*). It occurs at moderate elevations (400–1250 feet, 122–382 m) in relatively undisturbed areas on flat or gently-sloping ground (5° or less), often forming plateau-bogs on relatively deep (2–3 m), humified peats with a slightly lower water-table than in the Trichophoreto–Eriophoretum bogs. Pools are generally rare. Plateau-bog is rather local on Skye, due to the rugged topography, but where high-level peat does occur, the vegetation is often dominated by *Juncus squarrosus* (see Lists 6–9, Table 3.41). These stands are probably derived by repeated burning and grazing of Calluneto–Eriophoretum bog (Ratcliffe, 1959; Welch, 1966). The community is subjected to sheep-grazing and periodic burning. In the early stages of recovery after burning, *Eriophorum vaginatum* becomes prominent at the expense of *Calluna*, but in the later stages *Calluna* may become dominant. The association generally grades into the Callunetum vulgaris Association on better drained sites (see Fig. 4), whereas on shallower peat it merges into Trichophoreto–Callunetum bog, often with abundant *Rhacomitrium lanuginosum*. The ecological differentiation between *Trichophorum cespitosum* and *Eriophorum vaginatum* in these bog communities is far from clear (Moore, 1960).

The association is a widespread upland bog-type in northern Britain, forming extensive areas of peatland in the eastern Highlands (McVean & Ratcliffe, 1962), often with *Rubus chamaemorus* and, more rarely, with *Arctous alpinus*, *Betula nana*, *Chamaepericlymenum suecicum*, and *Vaccinium microcarpon*. It corresponds to the less disturbed blanket-peats of the Pennines (Eddy *et al.*, 1969; Pearsall, 1941; Tansley, 1949), and it also occurs in upland areas of the eastern half of the Southern Uplands (Birse & Robertson, 1967), the Cheviots, Lakeland, north Wales (Edgell, 1969; Ratcliffe, 1959; Tallis, 1969), and central and eastern Ireland (Moore, 1960). The association has floristic affinities with both the western alliance Erico–Sphagnion and the more continental and boreal alliance Sphagnion fusci (Moore, 1968).

15. MONTIO–CARDAMINETEA Braun-Blanquet & R. Tüxen 1943

MONTIO–CARDAMINETALIA Pawłowski 1928

Communities of springs fed by water of more or less even temperature, commonly dominated by bryophytes.

Cardamino–Montion Braun-Blanquet 1925

Communities of springs fed by waters poor in calcium in western and montane areas of Europe.

Philonoto–Saxifragetum stellaris Association Nordhagen 1943
(Philonotido–Montietum Büker & R. Tüxen 1941 *pro parte.*)

This association (Table 4.30), dominated by *Philonotis fontana*, occurs widely but rather locally on Skye around spring-heads on flat or gently-sloping ground. It generally occurs above 1000 feet (305 m), although related stands do occur at lower levels (for example List 1), but they often lack many of the characteristic montane taxa (for example *Saxifraga stellaris*). The water-supply is rather base-poor (see Table 4.16) with a pH range of 5.0 to 6.2, although, judging by the rather considerable floristic variation between stands (cf. Lists 4 and 7), there is probably a greater range in water chemistry than the data suggest. Water temperatures can reach up to 10 °C (cf. Dahl, 1956). *Montia fontana* ssp. *fontana*, *Saxifraga stellaris*, *Stellaria alsine*, *Dicranella palustris*, and *Philonotis fontana* are constant, and *Caltha palustris* ssp. *minor*, *Epilobium alsinifolium*, *E. anagallidifolium*, *Poa subcaerulea* Sm., *Bryum weigelii*, *Oncophorus virens*, *Pohlia wahlenbergii* var. *glacialis*, *Scapania paludosa*, *S. uliginosa*, *Tritomaria polita*, and a dwarf form of *Geum rivale* are exclusive to the association. It is the principal Skye habitat for *Euphrasia frigida*, *Acrocladium sarmentosum*, *Drepanocladus exannulatus*, and *Solenostoma cordifolium*. Although there are some floristic affinities with the Caricetalia fuscae, this spring association is floristically and ecologically very distinct. Several species of the association may also be found by streams and rills, and in areas of slowly moving water. The springs emerge amidst a range of montane communities, and there is frequently an abrupt change from the wet moss-dominated springs to the drier surrounds. A shallow layer (10–15 cm) of silty peat is generally present, overlying water-saturated anaerobic blue-grey silts. The springs may, in some instances, be fed by snow meltwater for part of the year. The association occurs in all the hill regions on Skye.

Similar associations occur widely throughout the Scottish Highlands (McVean & Ratcliffe, 1962), Southern Uplands, northern Pennines (Eddy *et al.*, 1969), Lakeland, north Wales (Edgell, 1969), and Ireland, supporting such rarities as *Alopecurus alpinus*, *Cerastium cerastoides*, *Phleum alpinum*, *Saxifraga hirculus*, *Sedum villosum*, *Bryum schleicheri* var. *latifolium*, and *Splachnum vasculosum*. Related communities also occur in Scandinavia (Dahl, 1956; Fransson, 1963; Nordhagen, 1943; Persson, 1961), Greenland (Böcher, 1954), the Faeröes (Ostenfeld, 1908), Iceland (Hadač, 1971), and central Europe (Braun-Blanquet, 1948; 1948–50; Oberdorfer, 1957).

Koenigia islandica–Carex demissa nodum

This is a rare but distinctive vegetational type (Table 4.30) on Skye, being restricted to ground above 1700 feet (520 m) on the Trotternish basalt ridge. It is an open, strongly irrigated community, consisting of a bryophyte-dominated carpet (*Acrocladium sarmentosum*, *Blindia acuta*, *Scapania undulata*) with a sparse vascular cover that includes *Carex demissa*, *Deschampsia alpina*, *Juncus biglumis*, *J. bulbosus* s.s., *J. triglumis*, *Euphrasia frigida*, *Koenigia islandica*, *Sagina saginoides*, and *Saxifraga stellaris*. It commonly occurs in open stony or silty rills fed by Philonoto–Saxifragetum stellaris springs amidst *Rhacomitrium* heath or *Festuca ovina–Luzula spicata* erosion ground. The water chemistry (Table 4.16) is very similar to that of the Philonoto–Saxifragetum stellaris springs, with a pH range of 5.8 to 6.1, and a generally low base content. *Koenigia islandica* is found mainly in this habitat on Skye (Raven, 1952), although it may also be locally frequent in some of the basalt screes (Table 4.2) and, more rarely, in open 'fell-field' communities (List 16; Table 4.36).

Koenigia islandica is reported from a range of communities in Scandinavia, the Faeröes, Greenland, Iceland, and North America (Böcher, 1937, 1954; Dahl, 1963; Gjaerevoll, 1956; Hadač, 1971; Hansen, 1930; Nordhagen, 1943; Ostenfeld, 1908; Steindórsson, 1963). They are all open, periodically moist communities adjacent to pools or streams, or associated with snow-beds. Associations rather similar to the Skye communities occur in Scandinavia, for example the *Carex rufina–Koenigia–Acrocladium sarmentosum* Association described by Gjaerevoll (1956) and by Lid (1959), and also in Iceland (Hadač, 1971; Sörensen, 1942; Steindórsson, 1963).

The Skye stands have several species in common with the spring community Philonoto–Saxifragetum stellaris, and they are thus classified here in the alliance Cardamino–Montion. The stands do, however, have floristic affinities with the alliance Koenigio–Microjuncion described from Iceland by Sörensen (1942), with such species in common as *Koenigia islandica*, *Juncus triglumis*, *Deschampsia alpina*, and *Saxifraga stellaris*.

Anthelia julacea banks

This is a distinctive, but extremely rare, spring community (Table 4.30) on Skye, consisting of a firm, grey mat of *Anthelia julacea*, with scattered herbs growing within it, for example *Deschampsia cespitosa*, *Juncus bulbosus* s.s., and *Thalictrum alpinum*. The two stands known on Skye are both at high altitudes and they are influenced, for much of the year, by snow-meltwater. They appear to experience a slower rate of water-movement than the related Philonoto–Saxifragetum stellaris springs.

Anthelia banks occur locally in the Scottish Highlands (McVean & Ratcliffe, 1962), and they are rather similar to the *Anthelia*-dominated snow-bed flushes described in Scandinavia by Gjaerevoll (1956) and Nordhagen (1927).

Cratoneurion commutati W. Koch 1928
Communities of springs fed by calcareous waters.

Cratoneuron commutatum–Saxifraga aizoides nodum McVean & Ratcliffe 1962
(Cratoneureto–Saxifragetum aizoidis Nordhagen 1943 *pro parte.*) (Pinguiculo–Cratoneuretum Oberdorfer 1957 *pro parte.*)

This is a characteristic spring community (Table 4.31) dominated by *Cratoneuron commutatum* (including var. *falcatum*), and supporting a sparse but consistent assemblage of associates, that includes *Festuca rubra*, *Pinguicula vulgaris*, *Saxifraga aizoides*, *Drepanocladus revolvens*, *Gymnostomum aeruginosum*, *G. recurvirostrum*, and *Riccardia pinguis*. Species of interest occurring in these springs include *Crepis paludosa* and *Philonotis calcarea*. The association is always associated with limestone springs, and there is often incipient tufa-formation. A shallow layer (10 cm) of silty moss peat is generally present, overlying wet silts or tufa. The pH and the specific conductivity values are very high (6.8–7.4 and 208–500 μmhos, respectively), and the calcium and magnesium concentrations are both greater than 7.6 milligrams/litre (Table 4.16). The *nodum* is rare on Skye, being restricted to the Jurassic and Durness limestones, and only four relevés are available. It occurs at a range of altitudes (up to 1400 feet, 460 m) on Skye. The stands are rarely more than a few square metres in extent and they commonly drain into *Eriophorum latifolium–Carex hostiana* (lowland) or *Carex–Saxifraga aizoides* (upland) flushes, or into Saxifragetum aizoidis banks on irrigated calcareous cliff-faces. The nodum has floristic affinities with all these communities (see Table 4.57).

The association occurs locally in the calcareous areas of the Scottish Highlands (McVean & Ratcliffe, 1962), occasionally with *Cratoneuron decipiens*. Comparable communities occur in the Southern Uplands, northern England (Eddy *et al.*, 1969), and north Wales, but only in Lakeland and Teesdale do they contain *Saxifraga aizoides*. Similar communities occur in Scandinavia (Dahl, 1956; Nordhagen, 1943; Persson, 1961) and elsewhere in Europe (Braun, 1968; Braun-Blanquet, 1948, 1948–50; Oberdorfer, 1957).

Saxifragetum aizoidis Association McVean & Ratcliffe 1962

This is a characteristic, but very local, association on Skye (Table 4.31), occurring on continuously irrigated, steep (60–75°) calcareous cliff-faces, generally of north or east aspect above 1000 feet (305 m). Association constants are *Alchemilla glabra*, *Deschampsia cespitosa*, *Festuca rubra*, *Pinguicula vulgaris*, *Ranunculus acris*, *Saxifraga aizoides*, *S. oppositifolia*, *Selaginella selaginoides*, *Blindia acuta*, and *Orthothecium rufescens*. Notable species occurring in this association include *Alchemilla alpina*, *Asplenium viride*, *Carex lepidocarpa*, *Oxyria digyna*, *Polystichum lonchitis*, *Saussurea alpina*, *Sedum rosea*, *Silene acaulis*, *Thalictrum alpinum*, *Barbula ferruginascens*, *Cololejeunea calcarea*, *Pohlia cruda*, *Leiocolea bantriensis*, *L. muelleri*, *Solenostoma sphaerocarpoidea*, and *Tritomaria quinquedentata*. The association is clearly related to the *Cratoneuron commutatum* springs (see Table 4.57), but it also has floristic affinities with both the montane facies of the *Asplenium trichomanes–Fissidens cristatus* Association (Table 4.4), and the 'tall herb' communities. (Table 4.47). The association is floristically rich with 81 taxa recorded in seven relevés, and a mean of 30 taxa per relevé. Soils tend to be rather shallow (20 cm or less) wet silts with varying amount of stones and humus and high pH values (6.8–7.2).

The association occurs on metamorphosed Jurassic limestone cliffs in Coire Uaigneach, Blà Bheinn, and on calcareous basalts at Sgùrr Mor. It merges into *Asplenium trichomanes–Fissidens cristatus* stands in crevices, whereas the drier cliff-faces support open, heterogeneous assemblages ('inops' *sensu* Segal, 1969) that are often rich in rare montane species, for example *Draba incana*, *Dryas octopetala*, *Poa alpina*, *Saxifraga nivalis*, *Grimmia funalis*, and *G. torquata*. The description of such open and often fragmentary stands or 'inops' is difficult, and it has not been attempted. A general floristic account is given in Chapter 5. On irrigated ungrazed ledges nearby, communities of 'tall herbs' frequently occur, and on the grazed slopes below the cliffs, Agrosto–Festucetum (species-rich) grasslands are common.

The association occurs locally in the Scottish Highlands (McVean & Ratcliffe, 1962) and it supports such rarities as *Cystopteris montana* and *Hypnum bambergeri*. Fragmentary stands also occur rather rarely in Lakeland and in north-west Ireland. Comparable communities occur more widely in Scandinavia but generally not on such steep ground as in Scotland (Coombe & White, 1951; Gjaerevoll, 1956; Nordhagen, 1927).

16. MOLINIO-ARRHENATHERETEA R. Tüxen 1937

Communities of fresh or periodically wet hay-meadows and pastures.

MOLINIETALIA COERULEAE W. Koch 1926

Communities of natural or semi-natural wet or periodically damp meadows.

Filipendulo–Petasition Braun-Blanquet 1947

'Tall herb' communities of natural or semi-natural wet meadows.

Juncus acutiflorus–Filipendula ulmaria Association

(*Juncus acutiflorus–Senecio aquaticus* nodum Ivimey-Cook & Proctor 1966 *pro parte.*)

This is a characteristic, but rather variable, meadow association (Table 3.32) on Skye, centred on the lowland basalt areas of northern Skye, and it is generally dominated by *Juncus acutiflorus*. Other association constants include *Equisetum palustre*, *Filipendula ulmaria*, *Holcus lanatus*, *Lychnis flos-cuculi*, *Ranunculus repens*, *Acrocladium cuspidatum*, and *Rhytidiadelphus squarrosus*. There is a variety of 'tall herbs' including *Angelica sylvestris*, *Cirsium heterophyllum*, *C. palustre*, *Crepis paludosa*, *Filipendula ulmaria*, *Trollius europaeus*, and *Valeriana officinalis*. It is floristically rich with 107 taxa recorded in 10 relevés, with a mean of 34 taxa per relevé. Notable components include *Euphrasia brevipila*, *Galium boreale*, *Gymnadenia conopsea*, and *Lathyrus montanus*, whilst *Lythrum salicaria* and *Peucedanum ostruthium* have their sole Skye stations in this community. It is the principal habitat for *Achillea ptarmica*, *Equisetum sylvaticum*, *Hypericum tetrapterum*, *Lotus pedunculatus*, *Myosotis secunda*, *Parnassia palustris*, *Rumex longifolius*, *Senecio aquaticus*, *Climacium dendroides*, and *Trichocolea tomentella* on Skye.

The association occurs on moist, poorly-drained, silty peats, peaty-gleys, or fertile brown earths (pH range 5.6–6.2) along stream-banks that are liable to seasonable flooding (Lists 3, 4, 8–10), in waterlogged hollows within ungrazed meadows (Lists 5–7), or more rarely in fens (Lists 1, 2) where the stands are dominated by *Molinia caerulea*. These two stands represent floristically a transition type between *Carex rostrata–Aulacomnium palustre* intermediate-fens and *Juncus*-dominated meadows. Fragmentary stands also occur on roadside verges. Lists 9 and 10 show increased abundance of *Equisetum palustre*, with a corresponding decrease in the cover of *Juncus acutiflorus*, suggesting an ecological or life-form replacement. The meadows are not mown for hay or grazed by animals to any extent, and their fertility appears to be largely maintained by periodic irrigation and flushing rather than by fertilisation by man (cf. Sjörs, 1954). Where flushing is less active and where the soil is free-draining, leaching commences and a pronounced illuvial horizon is often present. *Juncus effusus* often predominates in these areas (cf. the Sphagneto–Juncetum effusi Association).

The association is clearly diverse in its floristic composition, and its classificatory position is debatable. The stands show floristic affinities with the annually mown hay-meadows and pastures of the Centaureo–Cynosuretum Association (for example *Cynosurus cristatus*, *Holcus lanatus*, *Ranunculus repens*, *Trifolium pratense*), with lowland poor- and intermediate-fens of the order Caricetalia fuscae, especially the *Carex rostrata–Aulacomnium palustre* Association (for example *Carex echinata*, *C. nigra*, *Filipendula ulmaria*, *Lychnis flos-cuculi*), and with Adenostyletalia communities (see Table 4.57). The *Juncus acutiflorus–Filipendula ulmaria* meadows frequently intergrade with the Centaureo–Cynosuretum on drier sites, and with *Carex rostrata–Aulacomnium palustre* fens on wetter peaty soils. Duvigneaud (1949) has proposed that the Filipendulo–Petasition Alliance, and the related Molinion and Calthion Alliances should be grouped, with Scheuchzerio–Caricetea fuscae into a single order Molinio–Caricetalia fuscae. The classification of the Skye communities follows the schemes generally adopted by central European workers (Balátová-Tuláčková, 1968; Meisel, 1969; Oberdorfer, 1957; Oberdorfer *et al.*, 1967; Tüxen, 1937, 1955, 1970; Tüxen & Preising, 1951; Westhoff & Den Held, 1969; Williams, 1968) although it is clear that the Skye stands trangress, to some degree, the limits of the alliances Molinion, Calthion, Juncion acutiflori, and Filipendulo–Petasition, as given by the above authors. A similar problem also occurs in Ireland (O'Sullivan, 1968*a*). Judging from the published relevés, *Juncus acutiflorus* appear to have a wider ecological range in western Britain than it does in central Europe.

Similar associations occur locally in western Scotland (for example in south Argyll) and western Ireland (Ivimey-Cook & Proctor, 1966*b*) and related associations, which lack many of the 'tall herbs', are described from Scotland and Wales by Birse & Robertson (1967), McVean & Ratcliffe (1962), and Ratcliffe (1959).

ARRHENATHERETALIA Pawłowski 1928

Anthropogenic herb, grassland, and allied communities on damp, fertile, but well-aerated and manured, basic to slightly acid soils.

Cynosurion cristati R. Tüxen 1937

Communities of lowland grazed pastures and related habitats.

Centaureo–Cynosuretum Association Braun-Blanquet & R. Tüxen 1952

This association (Table 4.33) is the characteristic lowland, enclosed hay-meadow community on Skye, occurring on well-drained sites within townships. It is largely dominated by grasses, especially *Anthoxanthum odoratum*, *Cynosurus cristatus*, *Festuca rubra*, *Holcus lanatus*, and *Poa pratensis*. There is a constant assemblage of common meadow and agricultural grassland species, including *Centaurea nigra*, *Plantago lanceolata*, *Ranunculus repens*, *Trifolium pratense*, and *T. repens*. Other constants of the association are *Chrysanthemum leucanthemum*, *Euphrasia brevipila*, *Rhinanthus minor* ssp. *stenophyllus*, and *Senecia jacobea*. It is the main habitat on Skye for *Platanthera chlorantha* and the introduced *Veronica filiformis*, and other species of interest occurring in this community include *Dactylorchis purpurella*, *Conopodium majus*, and *Gymnadenia conopsea*.

It is closely related to the *Juncus acutiflorus–Filipendula ulmaria* Association, but it differs in the virtual absence of rushes and of 'tall herbs', and in the low cover of bryophytes. The two associations frequently occur together, with the *Juncus acutiflorus* stands always favouring the wetter ungrazed situations that are not artificially manured. Transitional stands can often be found (for example List 10; Table 4.33) with *Filipendula ulmaria*, *Carex* spp., and *Lychnis flos-cuculi*. The Centaureo–Cynosuretum stands are generally restricted to well-drained sites, and the soils are commonly fertile brown earths, with good crumb structure and abundant earthworms (pH range 5.0–5.8). More rarely the soils may be more clayey, or even gleyed in areas of impeded drainage.

Unlike the *Juncus acutiflorus* meadows, the Centaureo–Cynosuretum hay-meadows are mown annually, usually in late June or early July, but the hay may not be removed until late September. The meadows are lightly grazed by sheep and cattle in the autumn and winter. The fertility is largely maintained by manuring, and some stands (for example Lists 1, 2) have been reseeded at some stage with grasses of higher agricultural yield, such as *Dactylis glomerata*, *Alopecurus pratensis*, *Lolium perenne*, *Phleum pratensis*, and *P. bertolonii*. In some meadows where fertilising activities are low and the sites are well drained, surface leaching commonly occurs, resulting in a reduction in hay yield. Species such as *Juncus effusus*, *Agrostis tenuis*, *Galium saxatile*, and *Potentilla erecta* become prominent (Lists 11, 12), and *Chrysanthemum segetum* is a characteristic but local species of these poorer meadows.

The association is very similar in floristic composition to meadow and pasture communities described from elsewhere in western Britain (Braun-Blanquet & Tüxen, 1952; Ivimey-Cook & Proctor, 1966*b*; O'Sullivan, 1968*b*).

Maritime grassland nodum

On the stable tops of many of the large basalt sea-cliffs of north Skye there is often a narrow zone of closed-grassland between the *Calluna vulgaris–Sieglingia decumbens* heath (Table 4.43) and the more open cliff vegetation (Table 4.8). At the unstable cliff-edge there are often open, fragmentary stands with, for example, *Alchemilla alpina*, *Armeria maritima*, *Antennaria dioica*, *Anthyllis vulneraria*, *Carex pulicaris*, *Draba incana*, *Plantago maritima*, *Rubus saxatilis*, *Saxifraga hypnoides*, *Silene acaulis*, and *S. maritima*, but these have not been analysed. These stands are rather similar to the vegetation on the upper ledges and cliff-faces of the larger basalt sea-cliffs (see Chapter 5), and contain several maritime species as well as species of lowland meadows (Table 4.57).

The grassland (Table 4.34) is dominated by *Agrostis stolonifera*, *Dactylis glomerata*, *Holcus lanatus*, and *Festuca rubra*. Other constants are *Plantago lanceolata* and *P. maritima*. Rarer components include *Anthyllis vulneraria*, *Euphrasia brevipila*, *Heracleum sphondylium*, *Plantago coronopus*, *Salix repens* ssp. *argentea*, *Sedum anglicum*, *Silene maritima*, and *Funaria attenuata*.

The grassland is lightly grazed by sheep, and it frequently merges into 'tall herb' communities on inaccessible cliff ledges. The soils are well-drained moderately deep (20 cm) brown earths (pH range of 5.2 to 6.1), often with some accumulation of litter, and they are clearly influenced by sea-spray. On Skye the *nodum* is found only on basaltic rocks. It is possible that several distinct noda could be usefully distinguished, but the Skye data are too limited.

Related maritime grasslands occur widely in western Britain (Gimingham, 1964*a*; Ivimey-Cook &

Proctor, 1966*b*; Malloch, 1971; McVean, 1961*a*; Tansley, 1949) and elsewhere in Europe (Géhu, 1964*a*).

17. ELYNO–SESLERIETEA Braun-Blanquet 1948

Chionophobous montane grass and dwarf-shrub heaths of calcareous soils.

ELYNO–DRYADETALIA Braun-Blanquet 1948

Kobresio–Dryadion Nordhagen (1936) 1943

Chionophobous montane grass and dwarf-shrub heaths on well-drained calcareous soils in Scotland and Scandinavia.

Dryas octopetala–Carex flacca Association

(*Dryas octopetala* noda McVean & Ratcliffe 1962 *pro parte.*) (Plantagino–Dryadetum Shimwell 1969 *pro parte.*)

This association (Table 4.35) is restricted on Skye to the Durness limestone of the Ben Suardal area between sea-level and 500 feet (152 m). It occurs as extensive areas on shallow, highly organic, black, well-drained rendzina soils developed over bare limestone (pH range 5.6–7.2), and it is characterised by the constancy and dominance of *Dryas octopetala.* It is heavily-grazed by sheep and, to some degree, by rabbits. *Carex flacca, Festuca vivipara, Hieracium pilosella, Thymus drucei, Ctenidium molluscum,* and *Tortella tortuosa* are also constant, and *Antennaria dioica, Rubus saxatilis, Thalictrum alpinum, Entodon concinnus,* and *Scapania aspera* are notable but rare components.

Four facies are distinguished:

(i) *Typicum* (Lists 1, 2) with dominant *Dryas octopetala* and several species of mesophilous grassland. The stands are rather poor floristically (mean number of species per relevé = 19). Soil pH values range from 6.2 to 6.7.

(ii) *Flushed* facies (Lists 3–5) with *Carex panicea, Pinguicula vulgaris, Saxifraga aizoides, Selaginella selaginoides,* and *Schoenus nigricans* occurring on shallow soils that are intermittently irrigated. The soil pH range is 6.8 to 7.2.

(iii) *Leached* facies (Lists 6–9), characterised by the consistent occurrence of *Calluna vulgaris* amidst the *Dryas* turf. *Erica cinerea* and *Vaccinium myrtillus* occur more rarely, with *Dicranum scoparium, Hylocomium splendens, Rhytidiadelphus loreus,* and *R. triquetrus.* This assemblage is considered to reflect surface leaching and soil acidification (cf. Grime, 1963). Soil pH values range from 5.6 to 6.4. This facies often merges into *Calluna vulgaris–Sieglingia decumbens* heath (Table 4.43) on deeper more acid soils, with the disappearance of many of the more demanding calcicoles (for example *Euphrasia confusa, Ctenidium molluscum, Tortella tortuosa*) and a progressive reduction in species richness. All intermediate stages can be found, but the mosaic structure of the community is probably maintained temporally and spatially by the fissure structure of the underlying limestone.

(iv) *Arctostaphylos* facies (Lists 10–12). *Arctostaphylos uva-ursi* may be the sole dominant (List 12). *Calluna vulgaris* is absent throughout. Otherwise these relevés differ little from those of the other facies. Similar mixed communities of *Arctostaphylos* and *Dryas* occur in west Sutherland, western Ireland (Ivimey-Cook & Proctor, 1966*b*), and Norway (Coombe & White, 1951; Nordhagen, 1936), and it seems reasonable to regard *Arctostaphylos uva-ursi* as a life-form replacement for *Dryas* in these stands.

Apart from *Dryas octopetala* heaths, *Arctostaphylos uva-ursi* occurs in a range of dwarf-shrub communities on Skye, for it is apparently indifferent to soil base-status, and it favours dry, sun-exposed rocky areas that have not been recently burnt (for example the Rhacomitreto–Callunetum Association, List 1; Table 4.36, and the *Calluna vulgaris–Sieglingia decumbens* Association, Lists 11–14; Table 4.43).

The *Dryas octopetala–Carex flacca* Association is the main habitat for *Dryas octopetala* on Skye, although small colonies also occur on a few dry limestone or calcareous basalt cliffs up to an altitude of 1500 feet (460 m). The association also occurs locally at low elevations on outcrops of Durness limestone and on calcareous blown shell-sands in north-west Sutherland (McVean & Ratcliffe, 1962; Shimwell, 1969), and on Triassic limestone on Rhum. There is also an inland occurrence on Dalradian limestone in Glencoe. A similar association occurs near sea-level on the Carboniferous limestones of the Burren in western Ireland, supporting the rarities *Euphrasia salisburgensis, Gentiana verna,* and *Helianthemum canum* (Ivimey-Cook & Proctor, 1966*b*). Although the Irish stands have several constants in common with the Skye association, they differ in the occurrence of *Asperula cynanchica, Carlina vulgaris, Koeleria cristata,* and *Spiranthes spiralis.* These species are generally associated with lowland or limestone grasslands of southern England (Shimwell, 1971), whilst the abundance of *Sesleria albicans* in the Burren suggests affinities with the limestone grasslands of northern England (cf. Seslerio–Caricetum pulicaris; Shimwell, 1969).

Related lowland *Dryas* communities, characterised by the occurrence of *Carex rupestris,* also occur on

Durness limestone outcrops in north-west Sutherland and in west Ross. A rare *Dryas octopetala–Salix reticulata* ledge-community (Salico–Dryadetum Association; Shimwell, 1969) occurs above 2000 feet (610 m) on calcareous schistose cliffs often of south or east aspect in the central Highlands, with an outlier in west Ross. This community supports such rarities as *Astragalus alpinus*, *Bartsia alpina*, *Carex atrata*, *C. rupestris*, *Minuartia rubella*, *Potentilla crantzii*, *Salix arbuscula*, *Veronica fruticans*, *Encalypta alpina*, and *Saelania glaucescens*. *Sesleria albicans* has some of its few Scottish stations in this habitat. *Dryas octopetala* grows in similar but less species-rich cliff-habitats in several of its southern British localities, for example in Lakeland, north Wales, and west Donegal (Birks, Birks & Ratcliffe, 1969*a*).

It is clear that the high altitude *Dryas octopetala* association in Scotland belongs to the montane alliance Kobresio–Dryadion (Nordhagen, 1936; 1955) but the classification of the lowland *Dryas* communities is more difficult. They cannot be classified satisfactorily in either the Elyno–Seslerietea or Festuco–Brometea, as defined elsewhere in Europe, and they clearly occupy an intermediate position. They appear to have more affinities with the former class (Shimwell, 1969) and they have thus been grouped in the Elyno–Seslerietea. Braun-Blanquet & Tüxen (1952) and Ivimey-Cook & Proctor (1966*b*) grouped the Irish associations into the alliance Mesobromion erecti of the class Festuco–Brometea Braun-Blanquet & R. Tüxen 1943, because of the presence of several species characteristic of lowland mesic limestone grasslands. The Scottish lowland *Dryas* heaths lack many of these Mesobromion species, however, and they have therefore been grouped with the high-level *Dryas* communities into the alliance Kobriesio–Dryadion (McVean & Ratcliffe, 1962; Shimwell, 1969), although there are some affinities with the limestone grasslands of northern England, which are referable to Oberdorfer's (1957) Seslerio–Mesobromion Suballiance (Shimwell, 1969). This suballiance appears to represent an altitudinal and latitudinal transition between the Festuco–Brometea and the Elyno–Seslerietea Classes.

18. CARICETEA CURVULAE Braun-Blanquet 1948

CARICETALIA CURVULAE Braun-Blanquet 1926

Arctostaphyleto–Cetrarion nivalis Dahl 1956

Chionophobous montane grass and dwarf-shrub heaths of poor soils. The classification proposed by Dahl (1956) is followed, where both grass and dwarf-shrub heaths are united into a single class, rather than the scheme of Nordhagen (1936) based primarily on physiognomy in which grass heaths are grouped into the Caricetalia curvulae, and dwarf-shrub heaths in the Rhodoretalia ferruginei.

Cariceto–Rhacomitretum lanuginosi Association McVean & Ratcliffe 1962

(Rhacomitreto–Caricetum bigelowii Dahl 1956 *pro parte*.)

This association (Table 4.36) forms the main summit-heath vegetation on Skye, occupying many acres of summit plateaux in northern Skye, the Red Hills, and the Kyleakin Hills. It occurs from 1500 to 2600 feet (460–800 m) and it favours wind-exposed level or gently sloping (3° or less) ground. It is dominated by *Rhacomitrium lanuginosum*, with *Alchemilla alpina*, *Carex bigelowii*, *Galium saxatile*, *Festuca vivipara*, *Vaccinium myrtillus*, and *Cladonia uncialis* as the other association constants. Notable components include *Gnaphalium supinum*, *Lycopodium alpinum*, *Plantago maritima*, *Salix herbacea*, *Polytrichum alpinum*, and *Cetraria islandica*. *Thamnolia vermicularis* has its sole Skye station in this community. A 'cushion-herb' facies (Lists 10–13) occurs on slightly steeper ground (5–8°), with *Armeria maritima*, *Cherleria sedoides*, *Polygonum viviparum*, *Silene acaulis*, *Thalictrum alpinum*, and *Aulacomnium turgidum*. The community is most extensively developed on the extensive summit plateau of the Trotternish basalt ridge.

The community is dominated by an almost continuous mat of *Rhacomitrium languinosum*, often as much as 5 cm thick, and with its shoots generally growing away from the direction of the prevailing wind. The associated species of vascular plants are scattered through this mat, for example the rhizomes of *Carex bigelowii* run in or just below the moss mat. This sedge rarely flowers in this habitat on Skye, and it is rather stunted in its growth compared with its performance in more sheltered cliff-localities. *Salix herbacea* is also dwarfed in this habitat, but it grows much larger on sheltered cliff-faces.

The soils are shallow rankers, incipient or well-developed podsols or, on the deeper basalt soils, virtually undifferentiated, with pH values between 3.8 and 4.8. There may be a humus layer up to 3 cm thick. The community is locally influenced by solifluction and wind-ablation. Solifluction earth-hummocks with a closed vegetation occur on level ground on the Storr, and terraces are frequent on steeper ground (5–18°). These slopes support a more open *Rhacomitrium* heath, with abundant *Gnaphalium supinum* and *Salix herbacea*, whereas open *Festuca ovina–Luzula spicata* 'fell-field' communities occur on the terrace flats. With increasing snow-lie and/or waterlogging, *Rhacomitrium* heath merges into *Nardus stricta–Vaccinium myrtillus* snow-beds (Table 4.39) or *Juncus squarrosus* bogs (Table 4.41), whilst in broken, rocky ground Rhacomitreto–Empetretum (Table 4.38) or even open scree communities occur. There is often an abrupt transition along an erosion edge, from the closed *Rhacomitrium* heath to open *Festuca ovina-Luzula spicata* 'fell-field' vegetation, and at lower altitudes the *Rhacomitrium* heath may merge into Rhacomitreto–Callunetum (Table 4.37) or *Juniperus communis* ssp. *nana* (Table 4.37) communities in slightly less exposed areas.

The association occurs widely, and often extensively, in the Scottish Highlands (McVean & Ratcliffe, 1962; Poore, 1955*c*), whereas the 'cushion-herb' facies, approaching the Polygoneto–Rhacomitretum lanuginosi Association in floristic composition, is characteristic of north-west Scotland. *Rhacomitrium* heath occurs more locally in summit areas in the Southern Uplands, Lakeland, northern Pennines, north Wales (Tallis, 1958), and Ireland. It also occurs in western Norway (Dahl, 1956), the Faeröes (Böcher, 1937; Ostenfeld, 1908), Iceland (Hansen, 1930; McVean, 1955), and Greenland (Trapnell, 1933).

Festuca ovina–Luzula spicata nodum
(*Juncus trifidus–Festuca ovina nodum* McVean & Ratcliffe 1962 *pro parte.*)

This *nodum* (Table 4.36) occurs on windswept ridges, solifluction terraces, cols, and exposed summits in many of the hill regions on Skye, but often as fragmentary, unanalysable stands (for example in the Cuillins.) The four relevés available are characterised by the constancy of *Festuca ovina*, *F. vivipara*, *Luzula spicata*, *Salix herbacea*, *Oligotrichum hercynicum*, and *Rhacomitrium lanuginosum*, and they occur on flat or gently sloping ground from 1500 to 3200 feet (460–980 m). The vegetational cover is very low (20–30%), and notable components include *Cerastium arcticum*, *Juncus trifidus*, *Koenigia islandica*, *Anthelia juratzkana*, and *Conostomum tetragonum*. *Gymnomitrion corallioides* has its two Skye stations in this community, in contrast to the commoner *G. concinnatum*, *G. crenulatum*, and *G. obtusum* which occur on rock-faces and detached blocks in screes and boulder-fields. *G. concinnatum* also occurs on rather dry basaltic lithosols on Skye (cf. Haapasaari, 1966).

The soils of this community are generally rather shallow and skeletal (20 cm or less in depth), and they are frequently truncated. The surface layers are often stony. They have a pH range of 4.0 to 4.5 and often have an ill-defined humus-rich crust. Solifluction phenomena are common, for example small terraces and up-ended rock-slabs ('gravestones'), but structured solifluction features such as small-scale sorted stone-polygons and sorted stone-stripes are less frequent. The stands frequently occur within *Rhacomitrium* heath, often with a sharp discontinuity between the two vegetational types suggesting that the open areas may, in some places at least, be derived from erosion of *Rhacomitrium* heath. The open character of the vegetation appears to be maintained largely by extreme wind-exposure, causing erosion and destruction of the vegetation cover, and re-exposure of the rock debris, although soil instability may also be important. In some areas there is evidence to suggest cyclical alternation between *Rhacomitrium* heath and the open erosion ground or rock debris, perhaps reflecting local variations in wind erosion. It is closely related in floristics to the Cariceto–Rhacomitretum lanuginosi Association (see Table 4.57).

The *nodum* is clearly related to the *Juncus trifidus–Festuca ovina nodum* described by McVean & Ratcliffe (1962). *Juncus trifidus* is rare in this community on Skye, however, being primarily a plant of acid rock-ledges growing amidst *Rhacomitrium* spp. and *Salix herbacea*. The community as a whole is confined in Britain to the north-west Highlands within a zone experiencing 25+ days a year with gale-force winds at sea-level (McVean & Ratcliffe, 1962). The Scottish *nodum* supports the rarities *Artemisia norvegica*, *Diapensia lapponica*, and *Luzula arcuata*.

Similar 'fell-field' (Warming, 1902) or *fjaeldmark* vegetation is described from Shetland and from the Isle of Rhum (with *Arenaria norvegica*, *Cardaminopsis petraea*, and, in the Shetland stands, *Cerastium nigrescens*) by Spence (1957, 1970), from the Faeröes (with *Ranunculus glacialis* L.) by Böcher (1937) and Ostenfeld (1908), from Norway by Nordhagen (1927) and Engelskjön (1970), from Greenland by Böcher (1954), and from Iceland by Hansen (1930).

Rhacomitreto–Callunetum Association McVean & Ratcliffe 1962

This association (Table 4.37) consists of a wind-clipped prostrate mat of *Calluna vulgaris*, with abundant *Rhacomitrium lanuginosum* and it occurs on level or gently sloping wind-exposed cols and lower summits between 500 and 2000 feet (152–610 m). It occurs widely but locally throughout Skye. *Calluna vulgaris, Festuca vivipara, Potentilla erecta, Rhacomitrium lanuginosum, Cladonia uncialis,* and *Sphaerophorus globosus* are constant, and notable components include *Antennaria dioica, Euphrasia micrantha, Leucorchis albida, Salix herbacea, Solidago virgaurea* (the so-called var. *cambrica*), and *Ochrolechia frigida. Arctostaphylos uva-ursi* occurs rarely (List 1). The soils are shallow rankers or incipient podsols (pH range 4.2–4.8) rich in raw humus, developed on bare rock. The community grades into Callunetum vulgaris (Table 4.42) or Trichophoreto–Callunetum bog on more sheltered ground, into *Nardus stricta–Vaccinium myrtillus* stands (Table 4.39) with increasing snow-lie or, at higher altitudes, into *Rhacomitrium* heath in more exposed sites. It has floristic affinities with all these communities (see Table 4.57).

The association occurs locally in north-west Scotland (McVean & Ratcliffe, 1962), often with *Arctous alpinus* and *Loiseleuria procumbens*. Related but more lichen-rich associations occur more widely in the Scottish Highlands (McVean & Ratcliffe, 1962) and in Scandinavia (Dahl, 1956; Nordhagen, 1927, 1943).

Juniperus nana nodum

(Juniperetum nanae McVean & Ratcliffe 1962.)

This *nodum* (Table 4.37) is rare on Skye and only four relevés are available. Besides the dominance of the prostrate *Juniperus communis* ssp. *nana*, the relevés are very similar, both floristically and ecologically, to the previous association, although the stands are all above 1700 feet (520 m). The soils are shallow rankers (pH range 4.0–4.5) of raw juniper-humus directly overlying bare rock. Prostrate *Juniperus communis* ssp. *nana* does, however, occur near sea-level, for example on ungrazed ledges of cliffs (Lists 1, 3; Table 4.46) or in ravines (Lists 13, 14; Table 4.43). The restriction of the community to high ground on Skye probably results from the greater occurrence in the lowlands of burning, to which dwarf juniper is particularly sensitive (McVean, 1961*b*). The stands are blown clear of snow in the winter, and in hollows and poorly drained situations, it is replaced by Callunetum vulgaris or Trichophoreto–Callunetum bog on shallow peat.

The *nodum* occurs locally in north-west Scotland (McVean & Ratcliffe, 1962), often with *Arctostaphylos uva-ursi*, and in western Ireland (White, 1968).

Rhacomitreto–Empetretum Association McVean & Ratcliffe 1962

This association (Table 4.38), which is characterised by the dominance of *Rhacomitrium lanuginosum* and *Empetrum hermaphroditum*, occurs on summit block-detritus, on steep but stable block screes, and on acidic cliff-ledges between 1400 and 2400 feet (425–710 m) in all the hill regions on Skye. *Carex bigelowii, Empetrum hermaphroditum, Festuca vivipara, Galium saxatile, Vaccinium myrtillus, Rhacomitrium lanuginosum, Diplophyllum albicans,* and *Cladonia uncialis* are constant, and *Alchemilla alpina, Armeria maritima, Lycopodium alpinum, Plantago maritima, Salix herbacea, Sedum rosea,* and *Silene acaulis* are notable components. On north- or east-facing shaded cliff-ledges the association often supports a wide variety of Atlantic bryophytes, such as *Dicranodontium uncinatum, Anastrepta orcadensis, Bazzania pearsonii, B. tricrenata, Mylia taylori, Mastigophora woodsii, Plagiochila carringtonii, P. spinulosa, Scapania gracilis, S. nimbosa,* and *S. ornithopodioides*, along with the filmy fern *Hymenophyllum wilsonii.* This cryptogamic assemblage only occurs in this association and in the Vaccineto–Callunetum hepaticosum Association (Table 4.44). The soils are shallow rankers, with damp raw humus (pH range 4.2 to 4.7) resting directly on angular rock debris or bedrock. It may merge rather sharply into *Rhacomitrium* heath or *Festuca ovina–Luzula spicata* 'fell-field' communities in summit localities, and it has strong floristic affinities with these communities (see Table 4.57).

The association occurs widely in the Scottish Highlands, but it is largely centred on the north-west Highlands (McVean & Ratcliffe, 1962). Related communities occur in the Faeröes as described by Böcher (1937).

Alchemilla alpina–Vaccinium myrtillus nodum

(Festuceto–Vaccinetum McVean & Ratcliffe 1962 *pro parte.*)

This *nodum* (Table 4.38) is characterised by an abundance of *Alchemilla alpina, Festuca ovina, Vaccinium myrtillus,* and *Rhacomitrium lanuginosum.* It differs from the previous association in the absence of *Empetrum hermaphroditum*, and of several of the other association constants (see Table 4.57). It occurs locally on Skye on acidic to mildly basic cliff-ledges or on steep slopes below cliffs between 800 and 2300 feet (245–705 m) in all the hill regions, and it favours north-west to north-east aspects. It frequently merges into Agrosto–Festucetum grasslands on grazed slopes below cliffs. Soils are generally rather shallow peaty podsols, with pH values between 4.0 and 4.8.

The status of this *nodum* is obscure. It has floristic similarities with the mixed *Vaccinium*-grass heaths of southern Scotland, northern England, and north Wales, which are considered to be biotically derived from sub-montane dwarf Callunetum (McVean & Ratcliffe, 1962). On the other hand it also has some floristic affinities with ungrazed acidic ledge communities, such as the *Luzula sylvatica–Vaccinium myrtillus* Association (Table 4.45). The Skye stands are rather similar to those of the Festuceto–Vaccinetum Association (rhacomitrosum–facies) of the north-west Scottish Highlands (McVean & Ratcliffe, 1962). Comparable communities are described from Norway (Nordhagen, 1927, 1943).

19. SALICETEA HERBACEAE Braun-Blanquet 1947
Chionophilous communities.

DESCHAMPSIETO–MYRTILLETALIA Dahl 1956
Chionophilous or seasonally wet montane communities of stable, acidic soils.

Nardeto–Caricion bigelowii (Nordhagen 1936) Dahl 1956
Oligotrophic seasonally wet communities with a snow-cover melting before the end of June ('snow-patch' *sensu* Molenaar, 1968). The effects of prolonged snow-lie on vegetation are complex (Braun-Blanquet, 1948; Dahl, 1956; McVean, 1958*a*; McVean & Ratcliffe, 1962). It is often difficult to separate the direct effects of frost-protection and of a reduced growing-season from the influence of irrigation and impeded drainage. This alliance comprises communities in which these effects are barely distinguishable (Dahl, 1956).

Snow-lie is not prolonged on Skye (see Chapter 3), and chionophilous vegetation is rare. All the stands examined are grouped into a single association.

Nardus stricta–Vaccinium myrtillus Association
This association (Table 4.39), which is characterised by the constancy and dominance of *Nardus stricta*, occurs on gently sloping ground (5–15°) between 1800 and 2900 feet (550–890 m) in all the hill regions of Skye. *Carex bigelowii, Galium saxatile, Lycopodium alpinum, L. selago, Nardus stricta, Potentilla erecta, Vaccinium myrtillus, Rhacomitrium lanuginosum, Rhytidiadelphus loreus, Cetraria islandica*, and *Cladonia uncialis* are association constants, and *Gnaphalium supinum, Polygonum viviparum*, and *Salix herbacea* are notable components. The association differs from the anthropogenic Nardo–Juncetum squarrosi Association (Table 4.41) in the occurrence of *Carex bigelowii* and *Cetraria islandica*, in the constancy of *Lycopodium alpinum*, and in the absence of *Juncus squarrosus* (see Table 4.57).

The stands are rarely extensive in area, and they occur in sheltered hollows within *Rhacomitrium* heath (Lists 7, 8), in the tops of north or east-facing gullies Lists 5, 6), or in the lee of exposed ridges (Lists 1–4, 9–11). Direct observations indicate that these areas generally support snow until early June at least. Soils are generally moist rather shallow podsols, often somewhat peaty, with a pH range of 4.2 to 4.6, resting directly on stony detritus and boulders. Lists 10 and 11 form a *Vaccinium*-rich facies with dominant *Vaccinium myrtillus* and a low *Nardus stricta* cover. These stands are rich in hepatics with *Anastrepta orcadensis, Barbilophozia barbata, Mylia taylori, Ptilidium ciliare*, and *Scapania gracilis*. The ecological distinction between *Nardus stricta* and *Vaccinium myrtillus* in chionophilous vegetation has been discussed by Dahl (1956), Gjaerevoll (1956), McVean & Ratcliffe (1962), and Nordhagen (1927, 1943). It is generally considered that *Nardus stricta* attains dominance when the growing-season is too short for *Vaccinium myrtillus* and/or where impeded drainage occurs. The *Vaccinium*-rich facies may reflect a better drained ground, being on Torridonian sandstone, rather than a difference in duration of snow-lie.

Similar mixed *Nardus stricta–Vaccinium myrtillus* communities occur widely in the Scottish Highlands, but they are rather western in distribution (McVean & Ratcliffe, 1962). The Scottish noda described by McVean & Ratcliffe are rather diverse, and the Skye stands are similar to their *Nardus stricta–Rhacomitrium lanuginosum* (Lists 1–8), Deschampsieto–Rhytidiadelphetum (List 9), and Vaccineto–Empetretum (Lists 10, 11) noda. The Skye data are, however, too limited to justify any such divisions. Similar communities occur locally in the Southern Uplands, Lakeland, and north Wales, but they usually merge imperceptibly into biotically derived *Vaccinium* heaths or *Nardus* grasslands, and in place are indistinguishable. Related associations are described from the low-alpine regions of Scandinavia, particularly in western districts (Gjaerevoll, 1956; Knaben, 1950; Nordhagen, 1927, 1943), and also from the Faeröes (Böcher, 1937).

20. NARDO–CALLUNETEA Preising 1949
Dwarf-shrub dry heaths and derived grassland communities of western and northern Europe.

NARDETALIA (Oberdorfer 1949) Preising 1949
Nardo–Galion saxatilis Preising 1949
Communities of anthropogenic heathy grasslands.

Agrosto–Festucetum (species-poor) Association McVean & Ratcliffe 1962

(Nardo–Caricetum binervis Braun-Blanquet & R. Tüxen 1952 *pro parte.*)

This is a widespread grassland community (Table 4.40) on Skye, occurring as extensive stands from near sea-level to 1750 feet (535 m), and it is characterised by the co-dominance and constancy of *Agrostis canina*, *A. tenuis*, *Anthoxanthum odoratum*, and *Festuca ovina* agg., with *Galium saxatile*, *Potentilla erecta*, and *Hylocomium splendens* as additional association constants. It is floristically poor with only 29 taxa recorded in 8 stands (mean = 20). It consists of a closely cropped grass-sward less than 10 cm high, often with numerous dwarf shoots of *Calluna vulgaris*. It favours well-drained slopes (5–12°) or alluvial-flats. On slopes of north or east aspect, the stands are often rich in hypnaceous mosses. The soils are rather dry, shallow podsols or skeletal brown-earths often developed on alluvium (pH range 4.4–5.1). The grasslands in these situations are often bordered by river gravel and shingle. With decreasing slope and/or increased water-logging, the association generally merges into Trichophoreto–Callunetum bog, whereas on steep rocky ground it may grade rather gradually into Callunetum vulgaris heath (Table 4.42).

The association is the principal sheep pasture of northern Britain, and it occurs widely in the Scottish Highlands (McVean & Ratcliffe, 1962), Southern Uplands (Birse & Robertson, 1967), northern England, north and central Wales (Edgell, 1969; Ratcliffe, 1959), and parts of Ireland (Braun-Blanquet & Tüxen, 1952). Although essentially the same as the Scottish association, the equivalent communities of the southern hills tend to be dominated by *Festuca ovina* rather than by *Agrostis* spp., probably resulting from the effects of a longer grazing history (Eddy *et al.*, 1969).

Alchemilleto–Agrosto–Festucetum Association McVean & Ratcliffe 1962

This distinctive grassland (Table 4.40) is centred on Skye on the steep well-drained slopes of the basalt areas in northern Skye. The association constants are *Agrostis tenuis*, *Alchemilla alpina*, *Festuca ovina*, *Oxalis acetosella*, *Rumex acetosa*, *Thymus drucei*, *Viola riviniana*, and *Hylocomium splendens*. It is floristically richer than the previous association with 87 taxa recorded in 6 stands (mean = 32.3) and is distinguished from it by the abundance of *Alchemilla* spp. Although *Alchemilla alpina* is generally dominant, *A. filicaulis*, *A. vestita*, *A. xanthochlora* and, more rarely, *A. wichurae* can occur in some abundance. *Ranunculus acris* and *Selaginella selaginoides* are of high constancy. On steep north- or east-facing slopes, the stands are often bryophyte-rich (for example Lists 12, 14) with *Anastrepta orcadensis*, *Barbilophozia lycopodioides*, *Bazzania tricrenata*, *Herberta straminea*, *Isothecium myosuroides* var. *brachythecioides*, *Scapania ornithopodioides*, and (not in the lists) *Lophozia obtusa* and *Mastigophora woodsii*. All the stands are heavily sheep- and rabbit-grazed, and they are closely cropped swards less than 10 cm high. The association occurs from 800 to 1800 feet (245–550 m) on slopes up to 30°, and it is clearly influenced in places by irrigation from the steep basalt cliffs above. The soils are rather shallow well-drained silty brown-earths with mull humus (pH range 5.2–5.4), developed on colluvium or fine scree. The grassland commonly merges into open basalt screes, formed largely as a result of over-grazing and loss of vegetational cover.

The association occurs widely but locally in the Scottish Highlands (McVean & Ratcliffe, 1962), and it is otherwise restricted in the British Isles to Lakeland. Related communities are described from the Faeröes by Böcher (1937) and Hansen (1967).

Agrosto-Festucetum (*species-rich*) Association McVean & Ratcliffe 1962

This grassland (Table 4.40) is restricted on Skye to the fertile soils developed on limestones and basalts. *Agrostis tenuis*, *Anthoxanthum odoratum*, *Carex pulicaris*, *Festuca ovina*, *Lotus corniculatus*, *Potentilla erecta*, *Prunella vulgaris*, *Thymus drucei*, *Viola riviniana*, *Ctenidium molluscum*, *Hylocomium splendens*, *Hypnum cupressiforme*, and *Pseudoscleropodium purum* are association constants. *Anthyllis vulneraria*, *Botrychium lunaria*, *Galium boreale*, *Polygonum viviparum*, *Saxifraga aizoides*, *Silene maritima*, *Antitrichia curtipendula*, and *Peltigera apthosa* are notable but rare components. *Carex caryophyllea* and *Ophioglossum vulgatum* have their sole Skye stations in this community. It is the principal habitat for *Coeloglossum viride*, *Helictotrichon pratense*, and *H. pubescens* on Skye. The stands are generally grass-dominated, but with a rich assemblage of basiphilous herbs. The stands are heavily sheep-grazed to a sward less than 10 cm high. Occasional dwarf 'tall herbs' occur, for example *Epilobium montanum* and *Filipendula ulmaria*. It is a floristically rich association with a mean of 35.8 taxa per relevé. The floristic distinctions between this association and the other Agrosto–Festucetum grasslands are shown in Tables 4.40 and 4.57. It rarely occurs as extensive stands, and it favours well-drained slopes (40° or less) up to 1300 feet (400 m). In many sites the grassland is enriched both by intermittent irrigation from basic rock outcrops nearby, and by downwash of mineral particles from unstable cliffs. The soils are well-drained, humus-rich brown-earths with a good crumb structure (pH range 5.0 to 6.4). The stands frequently merge into Alchemilleto–Agrosto–Festucetum grasslands in drier, less flushed sites, or into 'tall herb' stands in areas protected, to some degree, from grazing animals.

In comparable situations, but at higher altitudes, the closely related Dwarf herb *nodum* (Lists 21, 22; Table 4.40) occurs with *Cherleria sedoides*, *Sibbaldia procumbens*, and *Silene acaulis*. Other species of interest found in this community on Skye include *Sedum rosea* (a low-growing, dwarf form) and *Marsupella alpina*. Soils are very similar to those supporting Agrosto–Festucetum (species-rich) grassland, being flushed fertile brown-earths with some surface accumulation of mull-humus.

Both noda occur widely, but locally, in the Scottish Highlands (McVean & Ratcliffe, 1962; Poore, 1955*c*), the Dwarf herb *nodum* supporting such rarities as *Cerastium alpinum*, *Draba norvegica*, *Erigeron borealis*, *Gentiana nivalis*, *Minuartia rubella*, *Myosotis alpestris*, *Potentilla crantzii*, and *Veronica fruticans*. Species-rich Agrosto–Festucetum grasslands are found more widely in the Scottish Highlands (McVean & Ratcliffe, 1962; Spence, 1970). Comparable communities also occur on Carboniferous limestones in the northern Pennines, but they differ in the local abundance of *Minuartia verna* and *Sesleria albicans* (Eddy *et al.*, 1969), and in the occurrence in upper Teesdale of the rarities *Carex capillaris*, *C. ericetorum*, *Gentiana verna*, and *Myosotis alpestris* (Pigott, 1956). Related grasslands are found locally in Lakeland, and north Wales (Edgell, 1969; Ratcliffe, 1959), and they occur elsewhere in Europe (Nordhagen, 1943; Jurko, 1969, 1971) and in Iceland (Tüxen & Böttcher, 1969).

The classificatory position of the Agrosto–Festucetum grassland complex on Skye is debatable. The species-poor association is clearly related to the alliance Nardo–Galion saxatilis Preising 1949, having such character species as *Galium saxatile*, *Pedicularis sylvatica*, and *Polygala serpyllifolia* in common with the central European stands (Oberdorfer, 1957). The Alchemilleto and species-rich associations on Skye contain several species of high constancy (see Table 4.57) that are considered characteristic of the class Molinio–Arrhenatheretea R. Tüxen 1937 (*Festuca rubra*, *Holcus lanatus*, *Poa pratensis*, *Prunella vulgaris*, *Plantago lanceolata*, *Ranunculus acris*, *Rumex acetosa*, *Rhytidiadelphus squarrosus*), of the order Arrhenatheretalia Pawłowski 1928 (*Achillea millefolium*, *Bellis perennis*, *Lotus corniculatus*), and of the alliance Cynosurion cristati R. Tüxen 1947 (*Cynosurus cristatus*, *Trifolium repens*) in central Europe (Oberdorfer, 1957; Tüxen & Preising, 1951). Communities closely related to the species-rich association on Skye have been classified by Eddy *et al.* (1969) in the order Arrhenatheretalia on the basis of central European character species, whereas McVean & Ratcliffe (1962) comment that the Agrosto–Festucetum grasslands as a whole in Scotland are virtually unclassifiable since they are almost entirely anthropogenic. They suggest that these grasslands may be referable to the Nardeto–Agrostion tenuis Nordhagen 1943 within the Arrhenatheretalia. Similarly Jurko (1969, 1971) has classified mountain pasture communities in Czechoslovakia that are closely related to the species-rich association on Skye within the alliance Cynosurion of the order Arrhenatheretalia.

Despite the strong floristic affinities of the Agrosto–Festucetum (species-rich) Association, and, to a lesser degree, the Alchemilleto–Agrosto–Festucetum Association on Skye with the Arrhenatheretalia, as delimited in central Europe, the associations are so closely related, floristically and ecologically, to the species-poor association that separation of these associations into different phytosociological classes would result in an arbitrary separation between closely related communities. The systematic affinities of the widespread anthropogenic grasslands of northern and western Britain require further study and classification.

Nardo–Juncetum squarrosi Association

(Nardetum sub-alpinum McVean & Ratcliffe 1962 *pro parte.*) (Juncetum squarrosi McVean & Ratcliffe 1962 *pro parte.*) (Nardeto-Juncetum squarrosi Büker 1942 *pro parte.*) (Juncetum squarrosi Nordhagen 1922 *pro parte.*)

This association (Table 4.41) differs from the Agrosto–Festucetum Associations in its abundance of *Nardus stricta* and/or *Juncus squarrosus*. The association is rather rare and floristically variable on Skye, with the dominant taxon being *Nardus stricta* (Lists 1–3) or *Juncus squarrosus* (Lists 6–9), or both (Lists 4, 5). It is only known in northern Skye. *Galium saxatile* and *Potentilla erecta* are also constant. Only nine relevés are available and with more data it is possible that several distinct noda could be usefully delimited. It favours flat or gently sloping sites (10° or less) that are moister than those supporting Agrosto–Festucetum grasslands. Nardo–Juncetum squarrosi stands generally occur at moderate altitudes (1500–2100 feet, 460–645 m). Soils are generally podsols (pH range 4.3–5.1), often somewhat gleyed, but Lists 6–9, with dominant *Juncus squarrosus* and abundant *Sphagnum papillosum*, occur on wet peaty or gleyed podsols, or on shallow peats with a seasonally high water table. *Juncus squarrosus* becomes an important component of bog vegetation following burning, grazing, manuring, and erosion, and these stands may represent a biotic derivative of Trichophoreto–Callunetum or Calluneto–Eriophoretum bog (Ratcliffe, 1959; Welch, 1966). The association rarely occupies large areas of ground and it frequently occurs in a mosaic with other vegetation types. On drier ground it grades into Agrosto–Festucetum grasslands, on deep, wet peat into blanket-bog communities, and on wind-exposed sites into wind-blasted Rhacomitreto–Callunetum or Cariceto–Rhacomitretum lanuginosi heaths.

Similar associations occur widely, and often extensively, in Scotland (Birse & Robertson, 1967; McVean & Ratcliffe, 1962), northern England (Eddy *et al.*, 1969; Welch, 1967; Williams & Varley, 1967), north Wales (Edgell, 1969; Ratcliffe, 1959), and Ireland (Braun-Blanquet & Tüxen, 1952; Moore, 1960). Comparable associations also occur in western Norway (Nordhagen, 1922), the Faeröes (Hansen, 1967), and elsewhere in Europe (Duvigneaud, 1949; Jurko, 1971; Oberdorfer, 1957; Rodriguez, 1966; Tüxen, 1955), but they often differ from the British communities in having a greater frequency of dwarf-shrubs, perhaps reflecting differences in land-use and grazing pressures.

CALLUNO-ULICETALIA (Quantin 1935) R. Tüxen 1937

Atlantic and Sub-Atlantic dwarf-shrub heaths.

Ericion cinereae Böcher 1943

Atlantic 'Eu-Oceanic' dwarf-shrub heaths of well-drained soils.

Callunetum vulgaris Association McVean & Ratcliffe 1962

(Ericeto-Caricetum binervis Braun-Blanquet & R. Tüxen 1952 *pro parte.*)

This is a floristically poor and rather uniform association (Table 4.42) that is dominated by *Calluna vulgaris*. *Erica cinerea*, *Potentilla erecta*, *Hypnum cupressiforme* var. *ericetorum*, and *Pleurozium schreberi* are also constant, and *Agrostis tenuis* and *Carex binervis* are of high constancy. *Lycopodium clavatum* is selective for this association on Skye. Floristically, the association is distinguished from other dwarf-shrub heaths on Skye by the overwhelming dominance of *Calluna vulgaris*, the virtual absence of *Empetrum* spp. and *Vaccinium* spp., and the constancy and abundance of *Hypnum cupressiforme* var. *ericetorum* and *Pleurozium schreberi*, combined with low amounts of *Rhacomitrium lanuginosum* and *Sphagnum* spp. Callunetum vulgaris occurs from near sea-level to 1600 feet (490 m) on well-drained south- or west-facing ground of moderate slope. Soils are generally iron-humus podsols, with a pH range of 3.8 to 4.7, and often with a thick accumulation of raw-humus. More rarely, the soil may be a peaty podsol. There is some variation in floristic richness associated with different ages of the dominant *Calluna vulgaris* following burning. Recently burnt areas are rather open with much bare peat and soil, supporting many crustose lichens (List 8), whereas medium age (6–12 years) stands ('building phase' *sensu* Watt, 1947; Barclay-Estrup & Gimingham, 1969) are dense, with abundant *Erica cinerea* and a limited growth of grasses and herbs (Lists 4, 5). Stands of 12 or more years old are more open ('mature phase'), and they support many associated grasses, herbs, and bryophytes.

The association occurs widely throughout the island, but the stands are rarely extensive on Skye and they commonly merge into Agrosto–Festucetum grasslands on well drained-sites. In wetter areas Callunetum vulgaris grades into Trichophoreto–Callunetum or Molinieto–Callunetum bog.

The association occurs widely throughout Scotland (McVean & Ratcliffe, 1962; Spence, 1960). Related communities, but often with *Ulex gallii*, are locally frequent in western England, Wales (Edgell, 1969; Ratcliffe, 1959), Ireland (with *Daboecia cantabrica* in Mayo and Galway; Braun-Blanquet & Tüxen, 1952; Clark, 1968; Moore, 1960), south-west England (with *Agrostis setacea* and *Erica vagans*), and northern France (Lemée, 1937; Vanden Berghen, 1958). Communities similar to the Skye association are described from the Faeröes by Böcher (1940), and from western Norway by Böcher (1940) and Nordhagen (1922). The geographical relationships of this and the succeeding association to other *Calluna vulgaris*-dominated communities described from elsewhere in Europe are discussed by Böcher (1943) and Gimingham (1961, 1969) in terms of two axes – a

R. carringtonii,* *Sticta canariensis*,* and *S. dufourii*. Many of the liverworts occur mixed together on open rock habitats, though some also grow as epiphytes on larger bryophytes. *Metzgeria conjugata* and *M. hamata* commonly grow as wefts loosely attached to the rock surface, or amidst other more robust bryophytes on shaded ledges. *Bartramia hallerana*, *Dicranodontium uncinatum*, *Rhabdoweisia crenulata*, *R. denticulata*, *Trichostomum hibernicum*, *T. tenuirostre*, *T. tenuirostre* var. *holtii*, and *Plectocolea paroica* occur on small ledges with a thin soil covering, the last four taxa favouring ledges where water drips or spray falls at times. *Dryopteris aemula* is restricted to larger ledges with some accumulation of raw humus, and it is usually associated with *Blechnum spicant* and *Luzula sylvatica*. *Fissidens celticus** J. A. Paton is restricted on Skye to shady loamy and clayey banks by streams. On steep, dry rocks in less deeply shaded situations *Dicranum scottianum*, *Plagiochila punctata*, and *Lepidozia pinnata* are often prominent, and *Tetraphis browniana* generally occurs under small, shaded overhangs. The most striking feature of these ravines is the great luxuriance of bryophyte growth. This largely results from the profusion of robust and rather common species, including *Breutelia chrysocoma*, *Hookeria lucens*, *Hypnum cupressiforme*, *Isothecium myosuroides*, *Ptilium crista-castrensis*, *Rhytidiadelphus loreus*, *Sphagnum quinquefarium*, *Thuidium delicatulum*, *T. tamariscinum*, *Bazzania trilobata*, *B. tricrenata*, *Diplophyllum albicans*, *Frullania tamarisci*, *Herberta adunca*, *Plagiochila spinulosa*, *Saccogyna viticulosa*, *Scapania gracilis*, and the filmy fern *Hymenophyllum wilsonii*.

Periodically flooded blocks in the beds of the ravines provide habitats for *Grimmia hartmanii*, *Heterocladium heteropterum*, *Hygrohypnum eugyrium*, *Hyocomium flagellare*, and *Trichostomum tenuirostre*. Constantly wet, dripping rocks and shaded recesses support *Fissidens crassipes*, *F. curnowii*, *Jubula hutchinsiae*,* and *Riccardia sinuata*. Although wooded gorges are the richest localities for these plants, many of the Atlantic species also occur on shady rocks and caves near the sea, on treeless but shaded slopes, cliff-faces, and gullies generally of north to east aspect on a range of rock types up to 1500 feet (460 m), and in block litters, wherever there is a moist, shaded environment.

Similar assemblages occur locally in shaded ravines in western Scotland, Lakeland, north Wales, western Ireland, and, more sparingly, in south-west England. Notable species of these habitats not known on Skye include *Cyclodictyon laetevirens* (Jura),† *Daltonia splachnoides* (west Ross), *Fissidens polyphyllus* (south-west Norway), *Isothecium holtii* (western Norway), *Dumortiera hirsuta* (Jura), *Lejeunea diversiloba* (west Galway), *L. holtii* (west Galway), *Porella pinnata* (Lakeland), *Radula holtii* (west Mayo), *R. voluta* (Argyll), and *Trichomanes speciosum* (Argyll).

The classificatory position of the *Betula pubescens–Vaccinium myrtillus* woods on Skye is debatable. McVean & Ratcliffe (1962) assign floristically similar woods to the class Vaccinio–Piceetea. They do, however, comment that this and the next association transgress the limits of Vaccinio–Piceetea and show some of the characteristic species of the class Quercetea robori–petraeae. It is considered that both the birch and hazel woods on Skye represent a northern facies of the mixed deciduous woodlands that are more widespread in western Britain, as described by Braun-Blanquet & Tüxen (1952), Klötzli (1970), and Tittensor & Steele (1971), and elsewhere in western Europe (Allorge, 1921–2). It is perhaps significant that the understorey of the one known sessile oakwood on Skye (List 2; Table 4.49) is identical to that of the birchwoods. Tittensor & Steele (1971) suggest that the herb vegetation in comparable communities at Loch Lomond is not dependent upon the composition of the tree layer. It is suggestive that many of the birch and hazel woods of southern Skye are derived, climatically or serally, from oak rather than from coniferous woods, and they are thus most meaningfully grouped within the class Quercetea robori–petraeae. Similar birchwoods, with their associated micro-communities of boulders, epiphytes, and decaying logs occur in north-west Scotland. Within western Scotland, oak becomes increasingly prominent in areas such as Ardnamurchan, Argyll, and Knapdale (Tittensor & Steele, 1971), and in areas further south such as Lakeland, Wales, south-west England, and Ireland.

Corylus avellana–Oxalis acetosella Association

(*Betula*-herb *nodum* McVean & Ratcliffe 1962 *pro parte*.) (Blechno–Quercetum Klötzli 1970 *pro parte*.) (Dryopterido–Fraxinetum Klötzli 1970 *pro parte*.)

Hazel scrub (Table 4.49) occurs widely but locally on Skye in sheltered areas on basalt, limestone, gabbro, or sandstone. *Anthoxanthum odoratum*, *Corylus avellana*, *Deschampsia cespitosa*, *Galium saxatile*, *Oxalis acetosella*, *Primula vulgaris*, *Viola riviniana*, *Hylocomium brevirostre*, and *Thuidium tamariscinum* are constant, and *Carex pallescens*, *C. remota*, *Circaea*

* The species indicated occur in or near their northernmost world localities on Skye.

† The northernmost known world locality of each species is shown in parentheses.

west–east climatic gradient of oceanicity and a north–south gradient of temperature. Within this network the Skye associations fall in the Euoceanic series because of the high representation of Atlantic species. This interpretation of the floristic variation in western European heath communities appears to be more satisfactory in interpreting the range of British heath types than does the scheme proposed by Braun-Blanquet (1966–67). In Braun-Blanquet's scheme the dry heaths are split into northern and southern alliances solely (in Britain) on the presence of *Ulex minor* and *U. gallii* in the southern alliance (Erico–Ulicetalia) and their absence in the northern alliance (Erico–Genistetalia) (see also Harrison, 1970).

Calluna vulgaris–Sieglingia decumbens Association

This association (Table 4.43) is clearly related to the previous one, but it has a lower cover of dwarf-shrubs and is floristically richer with 94 taxa in 10 relevés (mean = 33.2; cf. 17.2 in Callunetum vulgaris–see Table 4.57). *Agrostis canina, Calluna vulgaris, Carex pulicaris, Erica cinerea, Festuca ovina, F. vivipara, Lotus corniculatus, Potentilla erecta, Sieglingia decumbens, Hylocomium splendens,* and *Pleurozium schreberi* are association constants. Notable components include *Antennaria dioica, Euphrasia micrantha, Galium boreale, G. verum, Gentianella campestris, Lathyrus montanus, Plantago maritima, Pyrola media, Rubus saxatilis, Salix repens* ssp. *argentea,* and *Silene acaulis.* It is the principal habitat for *Orobanche alba* and *Trifolium medium* on Skye. The association occurs at low altitudes on dry, well-drained south- or west-facing slopes, commonly near the sea, in northern Skye, the Sleat, and the Suardal areas. Soils are iron-humus podsols or brown earths (pH range 4.9–6.1) developed over basalt or limestone. It covers extensive areas on sea-cliff tops, and it is clearly influenced by sea-spray and extreme exposure, for the growth-habit of the *Calluna* bushes is a rather open, low, closely wind-pruned form often growing to leeward and dying away to the windward side. *Erica cinerea* also shows a prostrate, diffusely branching growth habit similar to that described by Grubb, Green & Merrifield (1969) from chalk-heath communities in southern England. It is possible that sea-spray may result in some nutrient enrichment of the soils. The stands frequently grade into maritime grasslands with increased exposure towards the edge of sea-cliffs or, more rarely, into *Dryas octopetala–Carex flacca* (leached-facies) heaths on Durness limestone. A feature of ecological interest is the intimate mixture of so-called calcifuge species with plants of a calcicole tendency, or at least, basiphile tendency growing closely together in this association. A similar situation is described from 'chalk heath' in southern England by Grubb *et al.* (1969), and from coastal heaths in south-west England by Malloch (1971).

Four related stands (Lists 11–14) are characterised by the occurrence of *Arctostaphylos uva-ursi,* with *Juniperus communis* ssp. *nana* and *Lonicera periclymenum,* forming a *Calluna vulgaris–Arctostaphylos uva-ursi nodum,* occurring in identical situations to the *Calluna vulgaris–Sieglingia decumbens* Association. It is the main habitat for *Carlina vulgaris* and (not in the table) *Vicia orobus* on Skye, whereas *Frullania fragilifolia* is a notable but rare component.

Comparable associations occur from Shetland (Spence, 1960) through western Scotland (Gimingham, 1964*b*; McVean & Ratcliffe, 1962; Spence, 1970) to south Wales and south-west England (Coombe & Frost, 1956; Malloch, 1971). The Skye noda have floristic affinities both with the herb-rich facies of McVean & Ratcliffe's (1962) Callunetum vulgaris Association, and with their rather eastern Arctostaphyleto–Callunetum Association. Related species-rich heath communities are described from the Faeröes by Böcher (1940) and Ostenfeld (1908), from western Norway by Böcher (1940), Faegri (1960), Gimingham (1961), and Skogen (1965), and from northern France by Vanden Berghen (1958).

Myrtillion boreale Böcher 1943

Northern Atlantic dwarf-shrub heaths rich in bryophytes, characterised by Northern and Atlantic species.

Vaccineto–Callunetum hepaticosum Association McVean & Ratcliffe 1962

Mixed *Vaccinium myrtillus–Calluna vulgaris* stands (Table 4.44) are rather rare on Skye. The association is restricted to steep (30–45°) boulder-strewn north- or north-east-facing slopes between sea-level and 1700 feet (520 m) in all the hill regions on Skye. The association constants are *Blechnum spicant, Calluna vulgaris, Hymenophyllum wilsonii, Potentilla erecta, Vaccinium myrtillus, Campylopus atrovirens, Hypnum cupressiforme, Rhacomitrium lanuginosum, Rhytidiadelphus loreus, Sphagnum capillaceum, Anastrepta orcadensis, Bazzania tricrenata, Diplophyllum albicans, Herberta adunca, Mylia taylori, Plagiochila spinulosa,* and *Scapania gracilis.* It is the principal habitat for *Listera cordata* on Skye, and *Campylopus setifolius, Dicranodontium uncinatum, Hylocomium umbratum, Myurium hebridarum, Ptilium crista-castrensis, Sphagnum quinquefarium, S. robustum, Frullania germana, Lepidozia trichoclados, Mastigophora woodsii,*

Pleurozia purpurea, *Saccogyna viticulosa*, and *Scapania ornithopodioides* are notable components. *Colura calyptrifolia*, *Harpalejeunea ovata*, and *Parmelia physodes* occasionally occur, growing on heather stems.

The association is extremely rare on Skye, presumably due to the destruction of the habitat by moor-burning and grazing (McVean & Ratcliffe, 1962; Ratcliffe, 1968). Small stands occur on protected ledges in low-lying ravines, often with well-developed mixed hepatic mats. Fragments persist at 1700 feet (520 m) in sheltered areas within the north-facing corries of Beinn na Caillich, Broadford (with the addition of *Bazzania pearsonii*, *Lepidozia pearsonii*, and *Plagiochila carringtonii*) suggesting that the association may once have been commoner on Skye in areas of suitable topography and climate. It frequently grades laterally into burnt Callunetum vulgaris heath or Trichophoreto–Callunetum bog on gentler slopes. Soils are shallow, well humified peats or raw humus (pH range 3.8–4.5) overlying coarse, angular block scree with occasional pockets of leached mineral soil between the peat and the stones. Although many of the Atlantic hepatics occur in other associations on Skye (for example in Rhacomitreto–Empetretum heaths and Alchemilleto–Agrosto–Festucetum grasslands), in no association do they attain such abundance and luxuriance as in this one. It is this abundance of bryophytes that is the main floristic character of the association (see Table 4.57). The luxuriance depends to some extent on the shelter provided by the dwarf-shrubs, but generally the bryophyte growth is finest in the openings between the shrubs and in caves and shaded recesses amidst the blocks.

This association occurs locally in the north-west Highlands (McVean & Ratcliffe, 1962) with the addition of *Scapania nimbosa*,* *Anastrophyllum donianum*, and *A. joergensenii* at higher altitudes, and in west Donegal, west Mayo, west Galway, and Kerry. *Adelanthus unciformis* is a notable, but rare, component of some of the Irish stands. The association is clearly dependent on a high regional humidity, and its distribution in the British Isles falls within the zone of 220+ 'wet-days' a year (see Fig. 4 in Ratcliffe, 1968), with the exception of the outlying Cairngorm stands, which are influenced by late snow-lie. Related communities, but lacking some of the large leafy hepatics, occur locally in south-west Scotland, Lakeland, north Wales, and south-west Norway (Lye, 1966).

The classification of this association within the Myrtillion Boreale Alliance is not entirely satisfactory, for although the Skye association has a large number of species in common with the alliance as defined by Böcher (1943), it also contains many distinctive Atlantic bryophytes of high constancy and fidelity. The association in western Britain is probably sufficiently distinctive in its floristic composition to justify the creation of a new alliance within the Calluno–Ulicetalia.

21. BETULO–ADENOSTYLETEA Braun-Blanquet 1948

ADENOSTYLETALIA Braun-Blanquet 1931

Communities of 'tall herbs' and broad-leaved grass, generally of the sub-alpine and low-alpine zones.

Dryoptero–Calamagrostidion purpureae Nordhagen 1943

Fern- and grass-dominated communities of damp, acid soils.

Luzula sylvatica–Vaccinium myrtillus Association

(*Vaccinium–Luzula* treeless facies McVean & Ratcliffe 1962.) (*Luzula silvatica Gesellschaft* Braun-Blanquet & Tüxen 1952.)

This is a characteristic, but rather diverse, association (Table 4.45) of ungrazed unburnt acidic-ledges occurring throughout Skye from near sea-level to 1700 feet (520 m). It is dominated by *Luzula sylvatica*, with abundant *Vaccinium myrtillus* and ferns. Association constants are *Blechnum spicant*, *Deschampsia flexuosa*, *Luzula sylvatica*, *Oxalis acetosella*, *Vaccinium myrtillus*, and *Thuidium tamariscinum*. It is the principal habitat for *Dryopteris aemula* on Skye, whereas *D. borreri*, *Hypericum androsaemum*, *Hymenophyllum wilsonii*, *Thelypteris dryopteris*, *T. phegopteris*, *Hylocomium umbratum*, *Lepidozia pearsonii*, *L. pinnata*, *Ptilium crista-castrensis*, and *Sphagnum quinquefarium* are further notable components. The association is differentiated floristically from other associations in the Adenostyletalia on Skye by the absence of many basiphilous 'tall herbs' such as *Angelica sylvestris*, *Trollius europaeus*, and *Valeriana officinalis*, and from the Vaccineto–Callunetum hepaticosum by the absence of many of the large leafy liverworts (see Table 4.57). Stands occur widely but locally on Skye, but they are rarely very extensive. They are restricted to areas protected, in some way, from grazing animals, for example on inaccessible ledges in wooded ravines (List 1), on ledges of inland cliffs (List 2), or within areas of block screes (Lists 3–5). They also occur on ungrazed tops of large detached blocks and on ungrazed islands in lochs, and related

* *Scapania nimbosa* occurs on Skye, but its one known station is on cliff-ledges supporting the Rhacomitreto–Empetretum Association.

communities occur on north-facing sheltered acid sea-cliffs. *Geocalyx graveolens* has its sole Skye station in this habitat, growing with *Cephalozia connivens* and *Harpanthus scutatus* (Birks, Birks & Ratcliffe, 1969*b*).

The association favours gently sloping ledges (3–40°) of north or east aspect, and it is floristically poor (mean of 30 taxa per relevé) compared with other associations of the class. Soils consists of deep (up to 50 cm), raw humus (pH range 3.8–4.3), resting directly on rock. It commonly merges into dwarf-shrub heath or grassland communities on grazed slopes nearby. List 1 has affinities with the *Betula pubescens–Vaccinium myrtillus* woodlands (Table 4.49), whereas List 5, with *Cryptogramma crispa*, *Dryopteris abbreviata*, and *Lycopodium selago*, is the nearest approach to the Cryptogrammeto–Athyrietum chionophilum Association (McVean & Ratcliffe, 1962; Nordhagen, 1943) on Skye.

Similar associations occur widely, but rather locally, in northern and western Britain (Braun-Blanquet & Tüxen, 1952; McVean & Ratcliffe, 1962; Spence, 1960; Tittensor & Steele, 1971), in western Norway ('Macroluzuletum' of Nordhagen, 1922), and in the Faeröes (Ostenfeld, 1908).

Mulgedion alpini Nordhagen 1943
'Tall herb' communities of damp, basic soils.

Luzula sylvatica–Silene dioica Association

This association (Table 4.46) occurs on inaccessible north-facing ledges of basalt sea-cliffs (Lists 1–6), or in basalt ravines near the sea (List 7) in northern Skye and the Cuillins. Association constants are *Angelica sylvestris*, *Calluna vulgaris*, *Festuca ovina*, *Luzula sylvatica*, *Rumex acetosa*, *Sedum rosea*, and *Silene dioica*. It is the main habitat for *Sorbus rupicola* and *Vicia sylvatica* on Skye, and other notable components include *Chamaenerion angustifolium*, *Cirsium heterophyllum*, *Crepis paludosa*, *Juniperus communis* ssp. *nana*, *Lathyrus montanus*, *Orchis mascula*, *Osmunda regalis*, *Populus tremula*, *Rubus saxatilis*, and *Trollius europaeus*. Related communities occur on moist Jurassic limestone sea-cliffs, with the addition of *Agrimonia eupatoria*, *Allium ursinum*, *Carex laevigata*, *C. sylvatica*, *Equisetum telmateia*, *Eupatorium cannabinum*, *Hypericum androsaemum*, *Oenanthe crocata*, *Phyllitis scolopendrium*, and *Torilis japonica*. These stands are rather fragmentary and have not been analysed.

Calluna vulgaris is often abundant, and although *Luzula sylvatica* is present it rarely attains the luxuriance of the previous association. The stands are floristically richer than the previous association, with a mean of 34 taxa per relevé. There is always a luxuriance of 'tall herbs', including *Epilobium montanum*, *Filipendula ulmaria*, *Geum rivale*, and *Valeriana officinalis*. *Sedum rosea* is often a conspicuous component. Some of the stands support some growth of trees and shrubs, such as *Juniperus communis* ssp. *nana*, *Lonicera periclymenum*, *Populus tremula*, *Salix aurita*, *Sorbus aucuparia*, and *S. rupicola*. Soils are fertile brown earths (pH range 5.3–6.5) that are frequently irrigated by drainage water from above. Where this enrichment is reduced, *Luzula sylvatica–Vaccinium myrtillus* communities occur, but on more exposed sites the association merges into open *Armeria maritima–Grimmia maritima* stands. On the accessible grazed cliff-tops and on slopes below, *Calluna vulgaris–Sieglingia decumbens* heaths or maritime grasslands are frequent.

Similar communities occur locally in comparable situations in north-west Scotland (for example at the Point of Stoer in Sutherland), on Canna (Asprey, 1947), and on Shetland and South Uist (Spence, 1960). Related assemblages occur on sea-cliffs in western Norway ('Rhodioletum roseae' of Nordhagen, 1922; Engelskjön, 1970; Skogen, 1965) and the Faeröes (Ostenfeld, 1908).

Betula pubescens–Cirsium heterophyllum Association

This association (Table 4.47) occurs at low altitudes in steep, rocky woodlands (Lists 1, 3, 5), or on large, stable damp inaccessible ledges in basic wooded ravines (Lists 2, 4, 6, 7) of a north or east aspect. Besides the trees *Betula pubescens* ssp. *odorata*, *Corylus avellana*, and *Sorbus aucuparia*, other association constants include *Cirsium heterophyllum*, *Deschampsia cespitosa*, *Filipendula ulmaria*, *Geum rivale*, *Primula vulgaris*, *Mnium undulatum*, and *Rhytidiadelphus triquetrus*. The stands are very rich floristically with 122 taxa recorded in 7 relevés (mean = 40.3). Notable components include *Crepis paludosa*, *Galium odoratum*, *Listera ovata*, *Polystichum aculeatum*, *Populus tremula*, *Ribes spicatum*, *Rubus saxatilis*, *Sanicula europaea*, *Trollius europaeus*, *Valeriana officinalis*, and *Hylocomium brevirostre*. *Melica nutans*, *Mercurialis perennis*, *Paris quadrifolia*, and *Prunus padus* have some of their few Skye stations in this association.

The association is floristically related to the *Juncus acutiflorus–Filipendula ulmaria* Association of ungrazed hay-meadows (Table 4.32), but the present association differs by the absence of, for example, *Equisetum palustre*, *Juncus* spp., and *Lychnis flos-cuculi*. It differs from the previous association in the virtual absence of *Calluna vulgaris*, *Sedum rosea*, and *Silene dioica*. It grades into *Corylus avellana–Oxalis acetosella* or *Betula pubescens–Vaccinium myrtillus* woodlands where there is no protection from grazing animals. Stands are generally not extensive, and they are restricted to basalt or limestone areas. Soils are fertile, well-aerated brown earths, often with abundant silt, and with a pH range of 6.2–6.9; in many instances they are irrigated by basic drainage-water from small springs. Fragmentary stands occur on small ledges in almost all the lowlying basic ravines on Skye, and in all cases they are restricted to areas inaccessible to grazing animals.

Related associations occur locally either in woodland or in derived hay-meadows throughout northern Britain at low altitudes. Comparable examples have been seen, for example, by Loch Tay, Perthshire, on Morrone near Braemar, at Blackhope, Moffat, in upper Teesdale (Bradshaw, 1962; Pigott, 1956), by the River Irthing, Cumberland, and in the Craven and Derbyshire Pennines. *Geranium sylvaticum* is frequently a conspicuous component of stands south of the Great Glen, and *Polemonium caeruleum* is a notable rarity of some Pennine stands. Other local species occurring in such communities include *Aquilegia vulgaris*, *Campanula latifolia*, *Crepis mollis*, *Myosotis sylvatica*, *Polygonatum verticillatum*, and *Stellaria nemorum*. Comparable communities are described from ungrazed wooded fragments on islands in Scottish lochs (Spence, 1960). The association is clearly similar to the communities of 'tall herb' birch woods of Scandinavia (Hämet-Ahti, 1963; Holmen, 1965; Nordhagen, 1927, 1943) and Greenland (Böcher, 1954).

Sedum rosea–Alchemilla glabra Association
(Tall herb *nodum* McVean & Ratcliffe 1962.)

This association (Table 4.47) occurs on north- or east-facing damp, stable basic ledges between 600 and 1600 feet (180–490 m) in northern Skye and the Cuillins. Trees are generally absent, and *Alchemilla glabra*, *Angelica sylvestris*, *Deschampsia cespitosa*, *Filipendula ulmaria*, *Geum rivale*, *Luzula sylvatica*, *Ranunculus acris*, *Rumex acetosa*, *Sedum rosea*, *Ctenidium molluscum*, and *Herberta straminea* are association constants. Notable components include *Asplenium viride*, *Cirsium heterophyllum*, *Cochlearia officinalis* ssp. *alpina*, *Draba incana*, *Galium boreale*, *Oxyria digyna*, *Poa glauca*, *Polystichum lonchitis*, *Rhinanthus borealis*, *Saxifraga aizoides*, *S. hypnoides*, *S. oppositifolia*, *Silene acaulis*, *Thalictrum alpinum*, *Trollius europaeus*, *Distichium capillaceum*, *Mastigophora woodsii*, *Metzgeria hamata*, *Orthothecium rufescens*, *Plagiobryum zierii*, *Trichostomum hibernicum*, and *Solorina saccata*. *Saussurea alpina*, *Herberta straminea*, and *Leptodontium recurvifolium* are virtually exclusive to the association, and *Salix myrsinites* has its sole Skye station in this community. *S. phylicifolia* has three known Skye localities, occurring either in this association or along streamsides at moderate elevations. The occurrence of *Chamaenerion angustifolium* in this and the related *Luzula sylvatica–Silene dioica* Association (Table 4.46) is of interest.

The association is very rich floristically with 156 taxa recorded in 7 relevés (mean = 49.8). The stands are rarely extensive and they are restricted to broad ledges on steep, precipitous basalt or limestone cliffs that are inaccessible to grazing animals. Soils are fresh, well-aerated brown earths, with much silt accummulation and a pH range of 5.5–6.7. They vary considerably in depth and moisture content. The stands are constantly irrigated by water draining from the cliffs above and enriched by downwash of mineral particles from unstable basic-rock outcrops. The association grades into Saxifragetum aizoidis banks on flushed, near-vertical, cliff-faces, or into the drier rather open and fragmentary cliff-face vegetation (p. 196), and on the grazed slopes below, Agrosto–Festucetum or Dwarf herb grasslands are frequent. On more acidic, less irrigated, ledges *Luzula sylvatica–Vaccinium myrtillus* stands may occur. The association has floristic affinities with all these communities (Table 4.57).

Similar associations occur widely but locally in the Scottish Highlands (Bradshaw, 1962; McVean & Ratcliffe, 1962) supporting such rarities as *Cicerbita alpina*, *Gnaphalium norvegicum*, *Salix arbuscula*, *S. lanata*, and *S. lapponum*, in the Moffat Hills, in Lakeland (with *Potentilla fruticosa*), and in north Wales (with *Mecanopsis cambrica*). The Scottish stands are clearly related to the sub-alpine birch and willow scrub and low-alpine 'tall herb' communities of Scandinavia (Dahl, 1956; Nordhagen, 1927, 1943; Rune, 1965), Greenland (Böcher, 1954), and Iceland (Steindórsson, 1945).

22. ALNETEA GLUTINOSAE Braun-Blanquet & R. Tüxen 1943

ALNETALIA GLUTINOSAE R. Tüxen 1937

Alnion glutinosae (Malcuit 1929) Meijer-Drees 1936

Communities of alder woods on damp soils.

Alnus glutinosa Woods

Occasional trees of *Alnus glutinosa* occur along lowland streams and, more rarely, in hazel and birch woods on Skye. Only one area of alder-dominated wood is known on the island (Table 4.48). The trees are up to 25 feet (8 m) high and they occur on a steep but water-logged north-facing slope below a spring line. *Deschampsia cespitosa* dominates the understorey, and in clearings *Dryopteris carthusiana*, *Filipendula ulmaria*, and *Iris pseudacorus* are abundant. *Carex remota* is frequent in very wet soaks with the wood. Pure alder woods are infrequent in Scotland, and the Skye example appears to fall within the community types 1*b* and 2*b* described by McVean & Ratcliffe (1962) in their Table B. Similar communities are described from southern Scotland (Birse & Robertson, 1967).

The trees support a distinctive epiphyte flora (Table 4.48) with an abundance of *Parmelia* spp. (cf. the alliance Parmelion saxatilis; Barkman, 1958). The microlichen *Stenocybe pullatula* occurs on the upper twigs of alders in this wood, and it appears to be exclusive to alder trees in Britain.

23. QUERCETEA ROBORI-PETRAEAE Braun-Blanquet & R. Tüxen 1943

QUERCETALIA ROBORI–PETRAEAE R. Tüxen (1931) 1937

Quercion robori–petraeae (Malcuit 1929) Braun-Blanquet 1932

West European deciduous woodlands and their semi-natural derivatives on acidic to mildly basic soils.

Betula pubescens–Vaccinium myrtillus Association

(Betuletum Oxaleto–Vaccinetum McVean & Ratcliffe 1962 *pro parte.*) (Blechno–Quercetum Braun-Blanquet & R. Tüxen 1952 *pro parte.*)

Woodlands are not common on Skye, occurring mainly in sheltered areas in the south and east of the island. This woodland association (Table 4.49) is characterised by the constants *Anthoxanthum odoratum*, *Betula pubescens* ssp. *odorata*, *Blechnum spicant*, *Calluna vulgaris*, *Deschampsia flexuosa*, *Galium saxatile*, *Oxalis acetosella*, *Potentilla erecta*, *Pteridium aquilinum*, *Sorbus aucuparia*, *Vaccinium myrtillus*, *Hylocomium splendens*, *Plagiothecium undulatum*, *Pleurozium schreberi*, *Polytrichum formosum*, *Rhytidiadelphus loreus*, *Scapania gracilis*, *Thuidium delicatulum*, and *T. tamariscinum*. *Dicranum majus*, *Sphagnum fimbriatum*, and *S. quinquefarium* are present with a constancy of class IV. Notable but rather rare components include *Carex sylvatica*, *Dryopteris aemula*, *Hymenophyllum wilsonii*, *Melampyrum pratense*, *Dicranodontium denudatum*, *Hylocomium umbratum*, and *Ptilium crista-castrensis*.

This association is distinguished floristically from the *Corylus avellana–Oxalis acetosella* Association by the prominence of *Calluna vulgaris*, *Deschampsia flexuosa*, *Vaccinium myrtillus*, and several bryophytes, and by the absence of *Deschampsia cespitosa* and several basiphilous herbs such as *Primula vulgaris* and *Filipendula ulmaria* in the *Betula pubescens–Vaccinium myrtillus* Association (see Table 4.57).

The woods favour north- or east-facing slopes (5–30°) at low altitudes (less than 800 feet, 245 m). *Betula pubescens* ssp. *odorata* is the dominant tree, and it generally has a low, rather gnarled habit attaining up to 30 feet (9 m) height. List 2 is from a *Quercus petraea*-dominated wood. *Sorbus aucuparia* is a constant, but rather rare, component of the tree layer, and *Ilex aquifolium*, *Lonicera periclymenum*, and *Salix* spp. are always rare. The forest floor is grass- or *Vaccinium myrtillus*-dominated, although the bryophyte luxuriance is the most striking feature of the woods. Soils range from humus-rich podsols to brown earths with a pH range of 3.7–4.9, developed over sandstone or granite. Soil cover is rarely continuous, for the floor is generally block-strewn. The boulders support a characteristic and often luxuriant bryophyte growth, the composition of which appears to depend on block size and shape. It contrast to the herb layer there appears to be little differentiation in these boulder communities within *Betula pubescens–Vaccinium myrtillus* and *Corylus avellana–Oxalis acetosella* woods, and accordingly lists from the two woodland types are grouped together. Three associations have been distinguished:

(i) *Oxalis acetosella–Rhytidiadelphus loreus* Association (Table 4.50) is characterised by an abundance of hypnaceous mosses, in particular *Hylocomium* spp., *Pleurozium schreberi*, *Rhytidiadelphus loreus*, and *Thuidium delicatulum*. Grasses and herbs are frequent with *Deschampsia flexuosa* and *Oxalis acetosella* as association constants. The association approaches in floristic composition the ground-communities of the woods already described, and they frequently merge in less rocky ground. The stands occur on flat or gently sloping (3–20°) tops of boulders, on which a thick (10–20 cm) humus mat mixed with mineral particles has accumulated.

(ii) *Hymenophyllum wilsonii–Isothecium myosuroides* Association. (Hymenophylletum Braun-Blanquet & R. Tüxen 1952 *pro parte.*) This association (Table 4.51) is characterised by an abundance of *Hymenophyllum wilsonii*, with *Isothecium myosuroides*, *Dicranum scoparium*, *Plagiochila spinulosa*, and *Scapania gracilis* as additional association constants. Herbs and grasses are virtually absent. The association occurs on steep (45–90°) sides of blocks, forming a dense but unstable humus mat. It is the principal habitat for

Adelanthus decipiens, *Dicranum scottianum*, and *Sphaerophorus melanocarpus* (cf. Lye, 1969) on Skye, and additional notable components include *Bazzania tricrenata*, *B. trilobata*, *Frullania germana*, *Lepidozia pinnata*, *Plagiochila punctata*, and several foliose lichens.

(iii) *Open boulder* Association (Table 4.52) is characterized by a sparse bryophyte cover (50–70%) growing on steeply inclined (60–80°) blocks that are intermittently irrigated by water. *Diplophyllum albicans*, *Heterocladium heteropterum*, *Hyocomium flagellare*, *Lejeunea patens*, *Rhacomitrium aquaticum*, and *Scapania gracilis* are constant, and *Grimmia hartmanii*, *Hypnum callichroum*, and *Trichostomum tenuirostre* are highly characteristic. *Campylostelium saxicola* and *Sematophyllum novae-caesareae* have their sole Skye stations in this community. *Harpanthus scutatus* and *Scapania umbrosa* are notable but rare components of this community.

All these boulder communities can generally be recognised in deciduous woodlands in western Ireland (Richards, 1938), Dartmoor, north Wales, Lakeland, western Scotland (McVean & Ratcliffe, 1962), and south-west Norway (Lye, 1966, 1969). There are, however, obvious floristic differences between the areas; for example, there is the greatest representation of Southern Atlantic species in the woods of south-west Ireland, including *Adelanthus decipiens*, *Hymenophyllum tunbridgense*, *Lejeunea flava*, and *Sematophyllum demissum*. Although *Adelanthus decipiens* and *Hymenophyllum tunbridgense* have their northernmost known world localities on Skye, the filmy-fern only grows there in sheltered crevices in wooded ravines, and it does not occur in boulder communities within woods. The three associations have been recognised as seral stages in a succession (Richards, 1938), perhaps best regarded as a potential series, for development can be arrested permanently at any stage by gravity (see Lye, 1967*a*), and on the steepest rocks a closed community never develops.

The birch trees support a sparse but characteristic epiphytic flora. General lists from the six woods examined are given in Table 4.53. At least two communities are represented in the lists. Twigs and smaller branches typically support *Ulota bruchii*, *U. crispa*, and *Frullania tamarisci*, with *Aphanolejeunea microscopica*, *Lejeunea ulicina*, *Ulota phyllantha*, and *Usnea rubiginea* (cf. associations of the alliance Ulotion crispae; Barkman, 1958). The trunks and tree bases invariably support *Dicranum scoparium*, *Hymenophyllum wilsonii*, *Hypnum cupressiforme*, *Isothecium myosuroides*, *Plagiochila punctata*, *P. spinulosa*, and *Scapania gracilis*. Notable components of the trunk and tree-base community include *Douinia ovata*, *Frullania germana*, *Mylia cuneifolia*, *Plagiochila tridenticulata*, *Lobaria laetevirens*, *Menegazzia terebrata*, *Mycoblastus sanguinarius*, *Pseudocyphellaria crocata*, *P. thouarsii*, *Sphaerophorus globosus*, *Sticta fuliginosa*, and *S. sylvatica*. This assemblage closely matches the Hymenophylleto–Isothecium myosuroidis community described by Barkman (1958). Similar communities occur frequently in birch and oak woods in western Scotland, south-west England, and western Ireland, and more rarely in Lakeland and north Wales (Martin, 1938; Proctor, 1962).

Moist decaying logs in the woods support an interesting and characteristic assemblage of bryophytes (Table 4.54), some of which also occur as epiphytes or ground-layer species. *Cephalozia catenulata*, *C. connivens*, *C. media*, *Lophocolea heterophylla*, *Lophozia incisa*, *L. ventricosa*, *Nowellia curvifolia*, *Riccardia latifrons*, *R. palmata*, *Scapania umbrosa*, *Tetraphis pellucida*, *Tritomaria exsecta*, and *T. exsectiformis* are characteristic of decaying logs, although several of them also occur on bare peat in bogs and heaths (see Table 4.26). It is interesting that, although there are many differences in the epiphyte floras on living birch and hazel trees (Table 4.53), no such differences are discernible on rotting, decorticated logs. Similar communities occur widely in western Britain and clearly belong to the alliances Blepharostomion (Barkman, 1958) or Nowellion curvifoliae (Philippi, 1965).

The richest localities for Atlantic bryophytes on Skye, as elsewhere, are low-lying damp wooded ravines, rocky gullies, and waterfalls where a high atmospheric humidity combined with a shaded, sheltered aspect provides a wide range of microhabitats. There are several such gorges on Skye, occurring within either *Betula pubescens–Vaccinium myrtillus* or *Corylus avellana–Oxalis acetosella* woods. Many of these gorges support an interesting and characteristic cryptogamic flora. The openness and heterogeneity of the habitats discourages attempts at their detailed description. Notable components of shaded, dry or slightly damp, acidic or mildly basic ravine walls on Skye include *Hymenophyllum tunbridgense*,* *Acrobolbus wilsonii*,* *Aphanolejeunea microscopica*, *Cephaloziella pearsonii*, *Colura calyptrifolia*, *Douinia ovata*, *Drepanolejeunea hamatifolia*, *Frullania fragilifolia*, *F. germana*, *F. microphylla*, *Harpalejeunea ovata*, *Lejeuena lamacerina* var. *lamacerina*, *L. lamacerina* var. *azorica*, *L. mandonii*,* *L. patens*, *Lophocolea fragrans*, *Plagiochila tridenticulata*, *Porella laevigata*, *Radula aquilegia*,

* The species indicated occur in or near their northernmost world localities on Skye.

intermedia, *Polystichum aculeatum*, *Prunus padus*, *Thelypteris phegopteris*, and *Hypnum callichroum* are notable components. The association is slightly richer floristically than the *Betula pubescens–Vaccinium myrtillus* Association with a mean of 40.1 taxa per relevé (cf. mean of 38.5 taxa in the *Betula pubescens–Vaccinium myrtillus* Association). *Corylus avellana* is generally the dominant canopy-forming tree growing to 10 m high, although mixed birch-hazel stands are quite common. *Sorbus aucuparia* and *Quercus petraea* are generally rather rare in these woods. The understorey is intensively grazed throughout the year and it is dominated by basiphilous herbs and grasses, but in many woods the floor is boulder-strewn. These support a luxuriant bryophyte growth, similar to that described above (Tables 4.50–4.52). List 14 (Table 4.49) is of the ground flora under a dense stand of *Pteridium aquilinum*, the dense shade of the bracken fronds acting as a canopy. The association is distinguished floristically from the previous woodland association by the virtual absence of *Vaccinium myrtillus*, *Deschampsia flexuosa*, and *Sphagnum* spp., and by the occurrence of, or increase in, *Deschampsia cespitosa*, *Circaea intermedia*, *Conopodium majus*, *Filipendula vulgaris*, *Lysimachia nemorum*, *Primula vulgaris*, *Ranunculus ficaria*, *Thelypteris phegopteris*, *Viola riviniana*, *Eurhynchium striatum*, *Hylocomium brevirostre*, and *Mnium undulatum*.

The association favours a north or east aspect on slopes of 5–35° at low altitudes (less than 500 feet, 152 m). Soils are commonly intermittently irrigated fertile brown earths with a pH range of 5.1–6.0 with fresh mull humus. It clearly favours richer sites than do *Betula pubescens–Vaccinium myrtillus* woods, for when the two woodland types occur together, as, for example, at Ord, the *Betula pubescens–Vaccinium myrtillus* stands are restricted to the poorer rocks (sandstones and quartzites), whereas the *Corylus avellana–Oxalis acetosella* woods only occur on either the Durness limestone or on flushed sandstone areas. A similar vegetational pattern can be seen in Coille Gaireallach near Ben Suardal (see p. 262).

Hazel trees support an interesting and characteristic epiphytic flora (Table 4.53). At least three communities are represented in the general lists. Twigs and upper branches support a sparse growth of *Ulota vittata*, *Frullania dilatata*, and *F. germana*, with *Dimerella lutea*, *Lejeunea ulicina*, *Leptogium burgessii*, *Normandina pulchella*, *Pannaria pezizoides*, *P. rubiginosa*, *Parmeliella corallinoides*, *P. plumbea*, *Pyrenula nitida*, *Ulota bruchii*, *U. crispa*, and *U. phyllantha* (cf. Uloteto–Frullanietum germanae; Barkman, 1958). The trunks are covered by a dense growth of *Hypnum cupressiforme*, *Isothecium myosuroides*, *Neckera complanata*, *Metzgeria furcata*, and *Radula complanata* (cf. Scoparieto–Hypnetum filiformis; Barkman, 1958). This is the principal habitat for the large foliose lichens on Skye (*Lobaria* spp., *Nephroma laevigatum*, *Pseudocyphellaria thouarsii*, *Sticta* spp.), although many of them also occur on blocks in woods or on shaded coastal rocks. Tree bases support *Eurhynchium striatum*, *Hylocomium breviorstre*, *Isothecium myurum*, and *Mnium hornum*, which belong essentially to the ground layer (cf. Eurhynchietum striati; Barkman, 1958). The same three or related communities can be recognised on hazel trees elsewhere in western Britain (for example Ivimey-Cook & Proctor, 1966*b*). They are floristically richer (mean of 29 taxa per list) than the equivalent epiphytic communities of birch trees (mean = 20) but the causes of this floristic difference are not clear. Factors such as the microtopography of the bark, the nutrient content of the bark, and local microclimate may all be important. The flora of decaying logs in these woods (Table 4.54) is very similar to that in birch woods, as discussed above.

This association represents a floristically intermediate-type between the birch and oakwoods on acidic soils, and the ashwoods on limestone soils (see Table 4.57). Woods with a similar herb-rich understorey, but with dominant oak, ash, and elm, and with hazel in the shrub layer occur widely in northern Britain on a range of basic soils (Birse & Robertson, 1967; Klötzli, 1970; Tansley, 1949; Tittensor & Steele, 1971). The Skye association has floristic affinities with both the Quercetea robori–petraeae and the Querco–Fagetea, but in view of its close affinities, both floristically and ecologically, with the previous association, the hazel woods are classified within the Quercetea robori–petraeae. The systematic position of all the woodland types in northern and western Britain requires further clarification.

Low-growing dense hazel shrub also occurs on Skye on steep, exposed and ungrazed slopes, for example on talus below sea-cliffs. Due to the low, wind-pruned gnarled growth of the bushes, and the steep, rocky slopes, the herb-rich understorey typical of more sheltered woods is almost eliminated. These areas have not been examined in detail.

24. QUERCO–FAGETEA Braun-Blanquet & Vlieger 1937

Central and west European deciduous woodlands and scrub on base-rich soils and their semi-natural derivatives.

FAGETALIA SYLVATICAE Pawłowski 1928
Deciduous woodlands on fresh, moderately damp soils.

Fagion sylvaticae R. Tüxen & Diemont 1936
Principally woodlands of light-demanding trees on calcareous, moist soils.

Fraxinus excelsior–Brachypodium sylvaticum Association
(Dryopterido–Fraxinetum Klötzli 1970 *pro parte.*)
(Hyperico–Fraxinetum Klötzli 1970 *pro parte.*)
(Corylo–Fraxinetum Braun-Blanquet & Tüxen 1952 *pro parte.*)

This is a rare but distinctive woodland type on Skye (Table 4.55), with the constants *Agrostis tenuis*, *Brachypodium sylvaticum*, *Corylus avellana*, *Filipendula ulmaria*, *Fraxinus excelsior*, *Oxalis acetosella*, *Primula vulgaris*, *Viola riviniana*, and *Thuidium tamariscinum*. *Corylus avellana* dominates the tree layer, forming a dense canopy up to 40 feet (12 m) high, and scattered *Betula pubescens*, *Fraxinus excelsior*, and *Ulmus glabra* form an open tree layer overtopping the hazel. *Brachypodium sylvaticum* dominates the floristically rich ground-layer (mean = 43 taxa per relevé). Notable components include *Allium ursinum*, *Carex sylvatica*, *Listera ovata*, *Prunus padus*, *Thelypteris phegopteris*, *Anomodon viticulosus*, *Marchesinia mackaii*, and *Metzgeria pubescens*, and it is the principal habitat for *Circaea lutetiana* and *Viburnum opulus* on Skye. The trees support a rather similar epiphytic flora to the *Corylus avellana–Oxalis acetosella* woods (Table 4.53), but the larger ash trees often support numerous foliose lichens, including *Collema furfuraceum*, *Nephroma parile*, *Parmelia caperata*, *P. crinita*, *P. borreri*, and *P. perlata*, and the bryophytes *Neckera pumila*, *Orthotrichum striatum*, and *Zygodon conoideus*.

The association is restricted to Durness limestone pavements (Lists 2–5) or to Jurassic limestone outcrops (List 1) on Skye, the pavement relevés being characterised by a greater abundance of calcicolous mosses, such as *Ctenidium molluscum*, *Hylocomium brevirostre*, and *Tortella tortuosa*. In these stands mosses frequently cover more of the ground than do herbs. The woodland stands are not extensive, frequently merging into *Corylus avellana–Oxalis acetosella* woods (Table 4.49) on sites away from limestone pavement, into 'tall herb' dominated vegetation (Table 4.46) in ungrazed, inaccessible areas, or into treeless limestone pavement (Table 4.56). It differs from the other woodlands on Skye in the abundance of *Brachypodium sylvaticum* in the field-layer. The association favours gently sloping, sheltered areas of north or north-west aspect at low altitudes (less than 300 feet, 91 m). Soils are organic rendzinas or deep brown earths (pH range 5.5–6.4) resting directly on bedrock.

Wooded limestone ravines support a characteristic and distinct flora of pteridophytes, bryophytes, and lichens. Sheltered rock crevices support stands of the limestone facies of the *Asplenium trichomanes–Fissidens cristatus* Association (Table 4.4), and on shaded ravine-walls and ledges *Calamogrostis epigejos*, *Melica nutans*, *Phyllitis scolopendrium*, *Polystichum aculeatum*, *Amblystegiella sprucei*, *Anomdon viticulosus*, *Barbula tophacea*, *Camptothecium lutescens*, *Eucladium verticillatum*, *Gymnostomum calcareum*, *Heterocladium heteropterum* var. *flaccidum*, *Neckera complanata*, *N. crispa*, *Orthothecium intricatum*, *Seligeria acutifolia* var. *longiseta*, *S. doniana*, *Cololejeunea calcarea*, *Leiocolea badensis*, *L. turbinata*, *Marchesinia mackaii*, *Metzgeria pubescens*, *Porella cordeana*, *Gyalecta jenensis*, and *Solorina saccata* are characteristic and notable components.

Comparable woods are very rare in Scotland. The finest example is Rassal wood in west Ross developed on Durness limestone pavement (McVean & Ratcliffe, 1962). Similar ashwoods are, however, widespread and characteristic of the Carboniferous limestones in western Ireland (Ivimey-Cook & Proctor, 1966*b*; Klötzli, 1970) and northern England (Klötzli, 1970; Pigott, 1969; Tansley, 1949), with such rarities as *Actaea spicata*, *Cardamine impatiens*, *Carex digitata*, *C. ornithopoda*, *Convallaria majalis*, *Cypripedium calceolus*, *Daphne mezereum*, *Epipactis atrorubens*, and *Polygonatum odoratum* occurring in some of the woods.

Although the ashwoods of northern and western Britain contain some of the characteristic species of the central European alliance Fagion sylvaticae (Oberdorfer, 1957), for example *Actaea spicata*, *Festuca altissima*, and *Plagiochila asplenioides*, the absence of *Fagus sylvatica* and of such characteristic species as *Cephalanthera damasonium*, *Dentaria bulbifera*, and *Phyteuma spicatum* suggests the establishment of a new alliance, the Fraxino–Brachypodion (Shimwell, personal communication), for British woods on calcareous soils beyond the northern and western limits of *Fagus sylvatica* and as a geographical vicariant of the alliance Fagion.

25. LIMESTONE PAVEMENT COMMUNITIES

There are several quite extensive areas of exposed Durness limestone pavement on Skye. The majority of this is bare treeless limestone supporting a diverse but rather fragmentary vegetation. Fissured limestone pavement is one of the most micro-topographically diverse habitats, with its complex of clints and grikes, resulting in marked micro-climatic gradients within very small areas (Dickinson, Pearson & Webb, 1964; Yarranton & Beasleigh, 1969).

General floristic lists for all the limestone pavements on Skye are presented in Table 4.56. These lists serve to demonstrate the considerable floristic diversity of this habitat. It is clear that species characteristic of several different vegetational types are well represented, for example the *Asplenium trichomanes–Fissidens cristatus* (Table 4.4), *Dryas octopetala–Carex flacca* (Table 4.35), Agrosto–Festucetum (species-rich) (Table 4.40), and *Fraxinus excelsior–Brachypodium sylvaticum* (Table 4.55) Associations. There is also present a small group of species that are virtually restricted on Skye to limestone pavements. This group includes *Epipactis helleborine*, *E. atrorubens*, *Paris quadrifolia*, and *Collema crispum*. There is also a group of species which, although not restricted to pavement habitats, is particularly prominent in that habitat. This group includes *Geranium robertianum*, *Rubus saxatilis*, *Teucrium scorodonia*, *Encalypta streptocarpa*, and *Orthotrichum anomalum*.

Such a species-rich mosaic of fragmentary stands of saxicolous, grassland, dwarf-shrub, and woodland communities is equally typical of the more extensive Carboniferous limestone pavements of western Ireland (Ivimey-Cook & Proctor, 1966*b*) and northern England. Notable plants of these pavement areas that are extremely rare or absent in Scotland include *Actaea spicata*, *Adiantum capillus-veneris*, *Carex ornithopoda*, *Ceterach officinarum*, *Dryopteris villarii*, and *Thelypteris robertiana*. The striking environmental and floristic diversity of limestone pavement has convincingly been demonstrated by statistical analysis (Yarranton & Beasleigh, 1968).

TABLE 4.1

Class	EPIPETRETEA LICHENOSA								
Order	RHIZOCARPETALIA								
Alliance	**Parmelion saxatilis**								
Association	*Hedwigia ciliata–Parmelia saxatilis*								
	1	2	3	4	5	6	7		
Reference Number	B68	B68	B68	B68	B67	B66	B68		
	155	156	157	190	88A	003	94A		
Map Reference	504	504	508	156	512	430	524		
	446	446	448	555	198	190	627		
Altitude (feet)	200	200	150	400	200	350	200		
Aspect (degrees)	180	135	135	270	270	180	270		
Slope (degrees)	10	40	15	10	10	15	10		
Cover (per cent)	85	90	80	90	90	80	75		
Plot area (square metres)	0.5	1	1	1	1	1	0.5	C	D
Festuca rubra	.	.	2	.	×	.	.	II	0.5
Sedum anglicum	.	.	.	3	×	×	×	III	0.8
Antitrichia curtipendula	.	.	3	.	.	×	.	II	0.8
Dicranum scoparium	.	.	2	3	×	×	.	III	1.3
Glyphomitrium daviesii	.	.	.	2	.	×	×	III	0.5
Grimmia trichophylla	2	.	1	.	×	×	.	III	0.8
Hedwigia ciliata	6	5	6	4	×	×	×	V	5.3
Hypnum cupressiforme	2	1	2	4	×	×	×	V	2.3
Isothecium myosuroides	.	3	.	4	.	×	×	III	1.8
Pterogonium gracile	3	.	.	.	×	.	.	II	0.8
Ptychomitrium polyphyllum	.	.	4	.	.	×	×	III	1.0
Rhacomitrium fasciculare	1	3	3	7	×	×	×	V	4.5
R. heterostichum	7	7	5	6	×	×	×	V	6.3
Ulota hutchinsiae	.	.	2	.	.	×	.	II	0.5
Frullania germana	.	.	.	3	.	×	×	III	0.8
F. tamarisci	.	.	3	.	.	×	×	III	0.8
Scapania gracilis	.	.	.	4	×	.	×	III	1.0
Cladonia subcervicornis	.	1	1	.	.	.	.	II	0.5
Lecanora dispersa	.	2	1	.	.	.	×	III	0.8
Lecidea cyathoides	6	4	5	5	×	×	×	V	5.0
Ochrolechia parella	5	4	.	3	.	.	.	III	4.0
O. tartarea	.	5	.	.	×	.	.	II	1.3
**Parmelia glabratula*	3	.	.	.	×	.	×	II	0.8
P. omphalodes	4	5	3	5	×	×	×	V	4.3
P. saxatilis	4	6	6	4	×	×	×	V	5.0
Total number of species (38)	11	14	18	16	18	20	16		

* var. *fuliginosa* in 1. Mean number of species per relevé = 16.

ADDITIONAL SPECIES IN LIST

2. *Rhacomitrium aciculare* 4, *Caloplaca ferruginea* 1.
3. *Ulota phyllantha* 2, *Xanthoria parietina* 1.
4. *Aira praecox* +, *Rhacomitrium lanuginosum* 4.
5. *Andreaea rothii* ×, *Hedwigia integrifolia* ×, *Umbilicaria torrefacta* ×.
6. *Grimmia ovalis* ×, *Rhacomitrium ellipticum* ×, *Gymnomitrion crenulatum* ×, *Umbilicaria pustulata* ×.

LOCALITIES

1, 2, 3. Rubha na h'Airde Glaise; 4. Dunvegan Head; 5. Camasunary; 6. An Sgùman; 7. Rubha nam Braithairean.

TABLE 4.2

Class	THLASPIETEA ROTUNDIFOLII
Order	ANDROSACETALIA ALPINAE
Alliance	**Androsacion alpinae**
	Koenigia islandica scree community

	1	2	3	4
Reference Number	B68	B67	B66	B67
	033	131	002	129
Map Reference	499	456	500	456
	540	618	540	613
Altitude (feet)	1600	1750	1600	1600
Aspect (degrees)	90	90	90	90
Slope (degrees)	45	60	35	20
Cover (per cent)	10	10	20	40
Plot area (square metres)	4	4	4	4
Agrostis canina	3	4	×	5
Festuca vivipara	5	6	×	5
Poa glauca	3	.	×	.
Carex demissa	.	.	.	3
Luzula spicata	.	3	.	1
Alchemilla alpina	6	4	×	3
Cardaminopsis petraea	3	2	×	5
Cerastium holosteoides	.	3	×	.
Cherleria sedoides	.	2	.	.
Galium saxatile	.	.	.	3
Koenigia islandica	7	5	×	4
Oxyria digyna	+	.	.	.
Sagina subulata	3	3	×	.
Saxifraga hypnoides	.	×	.	.
S. stellaris	.	.	.	2
Sibbaldia procumbens	.	.	.	5
Silene acaulis	.	2	.	2
Thymus drucei	4	1	×	5
Viola riviniana	3	.	.	.
Andreaea rothii	.	.	.	2
Oligotrichum hercynicum	3	3	×	2
Polytrichum urnigerum	.	2	.	.
Rhacomitrium canescens	3	.	×	.
R. ellipticum	.	.	.	1
R. lanuginosum	.	.	.	2
Nardia scalaris	+	.	×	.
Stereocaulon vesuvianum	.	.	.	1
Total number of species (27)	13	14	12	17

Mean number of species per relevé = 14.

LOCALITIES

1, 3. The Storr; 2. Beinn Edra; 4. Bealach Amadal.

TABLE 4.3

Class	ASPLENIETEA RUPESTRIS
Order	POTENTILLETALIA CAULESCENTIS
Alliance	**Potentillion caulescentis**
Association	*Asplenium marinum–Grimmia maritima*

	1	2	3	4	5	6	7	8		
Reference Number	B68	B68	B68	B68	B68	B68	B68	B68		
	147	158	211	288	325	004	200	202		
Map reference	141	504	583	558	508	410	222	323		
	477	444	189	157	186	762	613	385		
Altitude (feet)	100	50	25	10	30	50	5	20		
Aspect (degrees)	90	135	270	90	90	315	0	270		
Slope (degrees)	80	90	75	80	90	80	90	80		
Cover (per cent)	60	50	60	80	100	50	40	60		
Plot area (square metres)	1	0.5	2	4	1	1	0.5	2	C	D
Asplenium adiantum-nigrum	.	.	.	.	.	.	3	8	II	1.4
A. marinum	9	8	8	8	9	8	8	.	V	7.3
Festuca rubra	.	4	4	3	.	4	3	4	IV	2.8
Armeria maritima	3	.	5	.	4	.	4	4	IV	2.5
Ligusticum scoticum	2	.	2	.	.	.	.	.	II	0.5
Plantago maritima	.	.	.	.	1	2	5	3	III	1.4
Tripleurospermum maritimum	4	.	.	3	.	3	.	.	II	1.3
Grimmia maritima	2	3	.	3	4	3	3	4	V	2.8
***Trichostomum brachydontium**	3	2	3	4	3	2	.	3	V	2.5
Total number of species (20)	7	5	8	6	6	8	6	8		

* var. littorale in 5. Mean number of species per relevé = 6.7.

ADDITIONAL SPECIES IN LIST

1. *Conocephalum conicum* +.
2. *Asplenium ruta-muraria* 5.
3. *Agrostis stolonifera* 3, *Euphrasia officinalis* agg. 1, *Leontodon autumnalis* 2.
4. *Cochlearia officinalis* agg. 4.
5. *Bryum alpinum* 2.
6. *Sedum rosea* 1, *Ramalina siliquosa* 3.
8. *Polypodium vulgare*, 3, *Sedum anglicum* 4.

LOCALITIES

1. Waterstein Head; 2. Rubha na h'Airde Glaise; 3. Camas Malag; 4. Drinen; 5. Loch Scavaig; 6. Meall Tuath; 7. Ard Beag; 8. Ullinish Bay.

Notes to Table 4.4.

ADDITIONAL SPECIES IN LIST

2. *Hypericum pulchrum* 2, *Sagina procumbens* 1, *Amphidium mougeotii* 6, *Saccogyna viticulosa* 1.
3. *Hymenophyllum wilsonii* 3, *Plagiochila spinulosa* 1.
4. *Polypodium vulgare* 2, *Hypnum cupressiforme* 3, *Rhytidiadelphus triquetrus* 3, *Lobaria scrobiculata* 1, *Sticta fuliginosa* 1.
5. *Rhynchostegiella tenella* 4.
6. *Asplenium adiantum-nigrum* 5, *Bellis perennis* 3, *Prunella vulgaris* 2, *Anomodon viticulosus* 3, *Bryum capillare* 2, *Porella platyphylla* 1, *Protoblastenia rupestris* 3.
8. *Breutelia chrysocoma* 4, *Metzgeria pubescens* 1.
9. *Primula vulgaris* 1, *Collema* sp. 3.
11. *Crepis paludosa* 2, *Gymnostomum aeruginosum* 4, *Heterocladium heteropterum* 2, *Mnium punctatum* 1.
12. *Anemone nemorosa* 2, *Campylium protensum* 1, *Pohlia wahlenbergii* 1, *Leiocolea muelleri* 2.
13. *Ranunculus acris* 3, *Saxifraga oppositifolia* 3, *Ditrichum flexicaule* 3, *Tritomaria quinquedentata* 1.
14. *Barbula ferruginascens* 2, *Distichium capillaceum* 4, *Radula aquilegia* 1, *R. lindbergiana* 2, *Metzgeria hamata* 1.

LOCALITIES

1. Bay River; 2. Red Burn; 3, 4. Sumerdale River; 5, 6. Rubha na h'Airde Glaise; 7. Camas Malag; 8. Ben Suardal; 9. Coille Gaireallach; 10. Tokavaig; 11, 12. Allt na Dunaiche; 13, 14. Coire Uaigneach, Blá Bheinn.

TABLE 4.4

Class	ASPLENIETEA RUPESTRIS
Order	POTENTILLETALIA CAULESCENTIS
Alliance	**Potentillion caulescentis**
Association	*Asplenium trichomanes–Fissidens cristatus*

Facies	Basalt				Limestone								Montane			
	1	2	3	4	5	6	7	8	9	10	11	12	13	14		
Reference Number	B68	B68	B68	B68	B68	B68	B68	B68	B68	B68	B68	B68	B68	B68		
	152	191	207	208	159	154	217	304	257	301	231	230	236	238		
Map Reference	272	317	377	377	504	504	584	618	611	615	558	560	539	537		
	531	507	364	364	444	446	187	195	200	120	217	217	216	213		
Altitude (feet)	50	200	300	300	150	250	75	100	75	300	120	100	1500	1600		
Aspect (degrees)	90	45	45	90	180	90	270	315	90	0	0	0	315	315		
Slope (degrees)	90	75	80	90	80	90	80	75	80	90	90	90	80	75		
Cover (per cent)	100	80	80	100	50	50	100	100	100	100	100	100	100	100		
Plot area (square metres)	0.5	2	4	4	2	4	2	1	2	1	2	1	2	2	C	D
Asplenium ruta-muraria	.	.	.	.	7	5	4	5	7	3	.	.	.	.	III	2.2
A. trichomanes	8	7	8	8	6	6	7	7	5	7	7	7	3	6	V	6.6
A. viride	.	.	.	.	.	.	.	5	6	2	3	6	8	7	III	2.8
Cystopteris fragilis	.	.	.	.	.	.	.	3	+	4	5	+	4	3	III	1.5
Phyllitis scolopendrium	.	.	.	.	.	.	1	2	.	2	4	.	.	.	II	0.6
Polystichum aculeatum	.	3	.	1	.	.	3	.	1	.	1	.	.	.	II	0.6
P. lonchitis	.	.	.	.	.	.	.	.	.	.	.	.	3	4	I	0.5
Selaginella selaginoides	.	.	.	.	.	.	.	.	.	.	.	.	1	3	I	0.3
Arrhenatherum elatius	.	.	.	.	3	3	3	.	.	.	.	.	.	.	II	0.6
Festuca ovina	2	3	3	3	5	5	2	3	.	2	1	.	4	2	V	2.5
Allium ursinum	.	.	.	.	.	.	4	.	.	.	2	.	.	.	I	0.4
Carex pulicaris	2	.	.	.	.	.	2	.	.	.	.	.	.	.	I	0.1
Chrysosplenium oppositifolium	.	.	4	3	.	.	.	.	.	.	2	.	.	1	II	0.7
Geranium robertianum	.	.	.	4	2	3	4	3	.	3	.	.	.	.	III	1.4
Epilobium montanum	.	2	.	2	.	.	.	1	.	.	1	.	.	.	II	0.4
Fragaria vesca	.	3	.	4	.	.	.	.	.	.	.	.	.	.	I	0.5
Linum catharticum	.	.	.	.	.	3	2	+	.	.	.	.	.	.	II	0.4
Oxalis acetosella	2	2	4	3	.	.	.	1	.	.	2	.	.	2	III	1.1
Thymus drucei	1	.	.	.	.	1	3	3	.	.	.	.	.	.	II	0.6
Anoectangium aestivum	.	.	.	.	.	.	.	.	.	.	.	.	4	4	I	0.6
Camptothecium sericeum	1	.	.	.	.	5	1	.	.	.	.	.	.	.	II	0.5
Ctenidium molluscum	.	.	.	1	.	.	.	5	6	4	6	6	5	.	III	2.4
Eucladium verticillatum	.	.	.	.	2	.	.	.	.	.	2	.	.	.	I	0.3
Fissidens cristatus	4	2	3	3	2	3	4	4	4	5	4	4	3	3	V	3.4
Isopterygium pulchellum	.	.	.	.	.	.	.	.	.	.	.	.	2	2	I	0.3
Neckera complanata	.	.	.	.	.	2	.	.	.	.	.	4	.	.	I	0.4
N. crispa	.	.	.	.	.	.	4	3	.	.	.	.	.	.	I	0.5
Orthothecium rufescens	.	.	.	.	.	.	.	.	1	.	.	1	1	3	II	0.4
Pohlia cruda	.	.	.	.	.	.	.	.	.	.	.	.	2	3	I	0.4
Thamnium alopecurum	.	.	.	2	.	.	.	.	.	3	2	1	.	.	II	0.6
Tortella tortuosa	.	.	.	.	.	.	3	3	4	5	.	.	6	.	III	1.5
Trichostomum crispulum	6	3	3	3	.	.	.	.	3	4	.	3	.	.	III	1.8
Cololejeunea calcarea	.	.	.	.	.	.	.	.	.	1	2	.	.	.	I	0.2
Conocephalum conicum	.	.	3	3	.	.	.	.	.	3	3	4	.	.	II	1.1
Frullania tamarisci	3	.	.	.	.	.	.	.	.	.	.	.	1	.	I	0.3
Lejeunea cavifolia	3	1	5	3	.	.	.	.	.	.	.	.	.	1	II	1.0
Metzgeria furcata	.	2	6	4	.	.	.	.	.	.	3	.	.	.	II	1.0
Pellia endiviifolia	.	.	.	.	.	.	.	.	.	.	.	.	1	3	I	0.3
P. epiphylla	.	.	.	.	.	.	.	.	.	.	1	.	.	2	I	0.2
Plagiochila asplenioides	.	3	4	3	.	.	.	3	5	.	.	2	1	1	III	1.6
Preissia quadrata	3	.	.	.	.	.	.	.	1	.	.	.	3	3	II	0.7
Scapania aspera	.	.	.	.	.	.	.	3	1	.	.	.	1	.	II	0.4
Gyalecta jenensis	.	.	.	.	.	2	.	2	.	3	.	.	.	2	II	0.6
Solorina saccata	.	.	.	.	.	.	.	2	2	.	.	.	.	.	I	0.3
Total number of species (86)	11	15	12	21	8	18	15	21	16	15	22	15	22	24		

Mean number of species per relevé = 16.8.

For notes see facing page.

TABLE 4.5

Class	PLANTAGINETEA MAJORIS
Order	PLANTAGINETALIA MAJORIS
Alliance	**Lolio–Plantaginion**
Association	*Lolium perenne–Plantago major*

	1	2	3	4	5	6	7	8		
Reference number	B68 088	B68 206	B68 256	B68 287	B68 346	B68 358	B68 362	B68 052		
Map Reference	518 605	377 364	611 203	554 166	532 323	696 116	672 099	478 388		
Altitude (feet)	300	300	50	50	50	75	100	120		
Cover (per cent)	100	100	100	100	100	90	100	80		
Plot area (square metres)	4	4	4	4	4	4	4	4	C	D
Agrostis stolonifera	.	.	.	.	1	2	.	4	II	0.9
A. tenuis	2	5	.	.	.	.	.	.	II	0.9
Anthoxanthum odoratum	.	.	.	.	4	.	2	.	II	0.8
Cynosurus cristatus	5	4	4	3	.	.	.	2	IV	2.3
Festuca ovina	.	.	3	.	.	.	.	4	II	0.9
F. rubra	5	.	.	.	.	.	.	5	II	1.3
Holcus lanatus	2	5	.	.	.	.	.	4	II	1.4
Lolium perenne	5	5	5	6	5	6	6	5	V	5.4
Poa anua	.	2	4	.	2	3	.	7	IV	2.3
Carex ovalis	.	.	.	.	.	.	1	+	II	0.3
Juncus articulatus	2	.	.	.	.	.	2	.	II	0.5
Achillea millefolium	.	5	4	3	.	.	.	.	II	1.5
Bellis perennis	5	6	3	3	.	1	4	4	V	3.3
Cerastium holosteoides	2	1	.	.	1	.	.	3	III	0.9
Euphrasia brevipila	.	.	.	3	.	.	1	.	II	0.5
Plantago lanceolata	3	.	4	1	.	3	3	+	IV	1.9
P. major	6	5	8	8	6	7	8	6	V	6.8
Prunella vulgaris	3	2	.	.	.	.	3	3	III	1.4
Ranunculus repens	3	3	1	2	.	.	.	2	IV	1.4
Rumex acetosella	.	2	.	2	.	.	.	1	II	0.6
R. obtusifolius	.	.	.	.	3	2	.	.	II	0.6
Sagina procumbens	2	3	.	.	.	.	.	3	II	1.0
Taraxacum officinale agg.	1	.	2	.	1	.	3	.	III	0.9
Thymus drucei	.	.	2	.	.	.	.	2	II	0.5
Trifolium repens	.	4	.	2	6	4	3	4	IV	2.9
Acrocladium cuspidatum	1	.	.	.	.	.	.	1	II	0.3
Brachythecium rutabulum	.	.	.	.	2	.	1	3	II	0.8
Bryum bicolor	.	.	.	.	.	.	1	2	II	0.4
Ceratodon purpureus	.	.	.	.	1	1	3	3	III	1.0
Total number of species (49)	17	20	14	12	11	9	16	28		

Mean number of species per relevé = 15.9.

ADDITIONAL SPECIES IN LIST

1. *Alopecurus geniculatus* 3, *Plantago maritima* 1.
2. *Viola riviniana* 2, *Eurhynchium praelongum* 1, *Hylocomium splendens* 1, *Pseudoscleropodium purum* 1, *Polytrichum urnigerum* 1, *Rhytidiadelphus squarrosus* 2.
3. *Agropyron repens* 2, *Hieracium pilosella* 1, *Potentilla anserina* 1.
4. *Leontodon autumnalis* 1, *Polygonum aviculare* 2.
7. *Juncus tenuis* 2, *Archidium alternifolium* 3.
8. *Juncus bulbosus* 3, *Aira praecox* 2, *Veronica agrestis* 2, *Barbula unguiculata* 1, *Bryum capillare* 2, *B. pallens* +.

LOCALITIES

1. Lealt; 2. Loch Harport; 3. Broadford; 4. Drinen; 5. Sconser; 6. Camas Croise; 7. Teangue; 8. Varragill.

TABLE 4.6

Class			AMMOPHILETEA		
Order			ELYMO-AMMOPHILETALIA ARENARIAE		
Alliance			**Agropyrion boreoatlanticum**		
			Fore-dune communities		
	1	2		1	2
Reference Number	B68	B68			
	347	365			
Map Reference	412	412			
	205	205			
Cover (per cent)	90	80			
Plot area (square metres)	4	4			
Agropyron junceiforme	8	7	*Honkenya peploides*	5	4
Agrostis stolonifera	3	3	*Lotus corniculatus*	4	2
Ammophila arenaria	.	4	*Potentilla anserina*	5	4
Festuca rubra	4	5	*Rumex crispus*	+	.
Carex arenaria	6	5	*Sonchus asper*	3	3
Cirsium vulgare	2	+			

Alliance			**Ammophilion borealis**		
			Grey dune Turfs		
	3	4		3	4
Reference number	B68	B68			
	349	366			
Map Reference	412	412			
	222	220			
Cover (per cent)	60	80			
Plot area (square metres)	4	4			
Festuca rubra	7	8	*Sedum acre*	1	3
Achillea millefolium	5	3	*Senecio jacobea*	2	1
Centaurea nigra	3	3	*Thalictrum minus*	4	3
Galium verum	6	5	*Trifolium repens*	3	2
Heracleum sphondylium	+	.	*Bryum argenteum*	1	.
Leontodon autumnalis	2	.	*B. capillare*	1	3
Lotus corniculatus	4	5	*Tortula ruraliformis*	2	2
Plantago lanceolata	3	1			

LOCALITY: 1, 2, 3, 4, Glenbrittle.

TABLE 4.7

Class	ASTERETEA TRIPOLIUM															
Order	GLAUCETO–PUCCINELLIETALIA															
Alliance	**Puccinellion maritimae**															
Association	*Puccinellietum maritimae*															
Subassociation	*Puccinellia–Ascophyllum nodosum*								*Puccinellia–Festuca rubra*							
	1	2	3	4	5	6			7	8	9	10	11	12		
Reference Number	B68	B68	B68	B68	B68	B68			B68	B68	B68	B68	B68	B68		
	133	134	289	277	357	205			058	142	141	057	092	093		
Map reference	540	540	565	703	699	323			495	416	415	495	527	527		
	273	273	222	158	116	385			305	519	520	305	627	627		
Altitude (feet)	.	.	.	.	.	.			.	.	.	.	75	60		
Cover (per cent)	100	100	100	100	100	100			90	100	100	95	75	100		
Plot area (square metres)	4	4	4	4	4	4	C	D	4	4	4	4	4	4	C	D
Festuca rubra	.	.	.	.	.	.			3	6	5	5	4	5	V	4.6
Puccinellia maritima	8	8	8	7	6	8	V	7.5	6	8	7	5	9	7	V	7.0
Armeria maritima	5	4	5	8	3	7	V	5.3	8	5	4	3	5	3	V	4.7
Aster tripolium	.	.	.	.	2	7	II	1.5	.	.	.	.	.	.		
Euphrasia officinalis agg.	.	.	.	.	.	.			.	.	.	.	2	3	II	0.8
Glaux maritima	4	5	5	4	3	5	V	4.3	5	5	3	+	.	.	IV	2.3
Leontodon autumnalis	.	.	.	.	.	.			.	.	.	+	+	.	II	0.3
Plantago coronopus	.	.	.	.	.	.			.	.	.	.	4	4	II	1.3
P. lanceolata	.	.	.	.	.	.			.	.	.	.	2	4	II	1.0
P. maritima	6	6	5	5	7	3	V	5.3	4	5	4	9	6	4	V	5.3
Spergularia media	.	.	.	3	.	4	II	1.2	.	.	4	.	.	.	I	0.7
Trichostomum brachydontium	.	.	.	.	.	.			.	.	.	.	3	3	II	1.0
Ascophyllum nodosum	7	5	6	5	3	.	V	4.3	.	.	.	.	.	.		
Total number of species (20)	5	5	5	6	6	8			5	5	7	7	10	10		

Mean number of species per relevé = 5.8.
Total number of species in subassociation = 9.

Mean number of species per relevé = 7.3.
Total number of species in subassociation = 16.

ADDITIONAL SPECIES IN LIST

6. *Cochlearia officinalis* agg. 2, *Triglochin maritima* 3.
9. *Salicornia europaea* 2.
10. *Grimmia maritima* +.
11. *Daucus carota* 3.
12. *Senecio vulgaris* 2, *Campylium protensum* 1.

LOCALITIES

1, 2. Loch Ainort; 3. Loch Slapin; 4. Loch na Dal; 5. Camas Croise; 6. Ullinish; 7, 10. Loch Sligachan; 8, 9. Loch Eyre; 11, 12. Lealt.

TABLE 4.8

Class	ASTERETEA TRIPOLIUM																													
Order	GLAUCETO – PUCCINELLIETALIA																													
Alliance	**Armerion maritimae**																													
Association	*Juncus gerardii–Carex extensa*																			*Armeria maritima–Grimmia maritima*										
	1	2	3	4	5	6	7	8	9	10	11	12	13	14	15	16	17			18	19	20	21	22	23	24	25	26		
Reference Number	B68	B68	B68	B68	B68	B68	B68	B68	B68	B68	B68	B68	B68	B68	B68	B68	B68			B68	B68	B68	B68	B68	B68	B68	B68	B68		
Map Reference	129	119	131	127	132	278	290	135	143	177	178	355	116	117	126	130	144			094	148	175	145	176	199	203	204	212		
	597	305	597	596	540	703	565	485	416	273	273	698	308	308	596	597	416			527	154	297	131	297	222	323	323	583		
	269	437	269	268	273	158	222	418	519	433	433	116	427	427	268	269	519			627	507	420	475	420	613	385	385	189		
Altitude (feet)	.	.	.	.	.	.	.	.	.	.	.	.	.	.	.	.	.			20	25	30	250	25	10	25	20	30		
Cover (percent)	100	100	100	100	100	100	100	100	100	100	100	100	20	75	90	60	100			50	50	30	100	25	100	50	90	100		
Plot area (square metres)	4	4	4	4	4	4	4	4	4	4	4	4	4	4	4	4	4	C	D	1	2	4	4	4	4	2	4	4	C	D
Agrostis stolonifera	.	4	3	3	4	4	3	3	.	3	3	4	4	4	5	3	.	V	3.2	.	.	.	.	.	.	.	.	.	I	0.4
Festuca rubra	.	3	4	3	2	5	4	2	3	4	3	4	4	6	3	.	5	V	3.3	3	5	6	7	2	6	3	5	5	V	4.6
Blysmus rufus	.	.	2	.	.	.	.	2	4	2	.	4	.	.	.	5	6	III	1.5	.	.	.	.	.	.	.	.	.		
Carex extensa	.	1	3	3	4	.	.	.	3	2	.	3	.	.	3	.	3	III	1.6	.	.	.	.	.	.	.	.	.		
C. flacca	.	.	.	.	.	.	.	.	.	.	.	.	3	4	3	.	1	II	0.6	.	.	.	.	.	.	.	.	.		
C. scandinavica	.	.	2	.	.	.	3	.	2	2	.	.	.	.	.	.	.	II	0.5	.	.	.	.	.	.	.	.	.		
Juncus gerardii	5	9	3	4	6	5	5	7	7	3	8	7	8	9	8	8	6	V	6.3	.	.	.	.	.	.	.	.	.		
Triglochin maritima	.	.	.	.	.	.	.	1	2	3	3	3	.	2	.	4	+	III	1.1	.	.	.	.	.	.	.	.	.		
Armeria maritima	6	4	4	8	2	7	4	4	3	6	4	3	3	5	6	4	3	V	4.5	9	8	8	7	9	8	7	8	8	V	8.0
Aster tripolium	.	.	.	.	.	.	.	5	.	5	4	4	.	.	.	.	.	II	1.0	.	.	.	.	.	.	.	.	.		
Cochlearia officinalis agg.	.	.	.	.	.	.	.	+	.	.	.	1	.	1	.	.	.	I	0.2	5	.	.	.	1	.	.	.	1	II	0.8
Glaux maritima	5	3	3	.	3	3	4	5	4	4	3	4	.	5	4	4	4	V	3.4	.	.	.	.	.	.	.	.	.		
Leontodon autumnalis	.	.	.	.	1	2	3	+	.	.	.	.	.	.	.	.	3	II	0.6	.	.	.	4	.	.	.	.	4	II	0.9
Ligusticum scoticum	.	.	.	.	.	.	.	.	.	.	.	.	.	.	.	.	.			.	.	.	.	.	.	2	.	3	II	0.6
Plantago coronopus	.	.	.	3	3	3	1	.	.	.	.	.	.	.	.	.	.	II	0.6	.	.	.	3	.	1	.	.	.	II	0.4
P. maritima	8	7	8	3	7	7	6	6	4	7	3	5	4	3	4	3	4	V	5.2	3	5	5	3	3	2	5	6	5	V	4.1
Sagina maritima	.	.	.	5	3	.	.	.	.	.	.	.	+	.	.	.	.	I	0.5	.	+	.	.	1	.	2	.	3	III	0.8
Sedum anglicum	.	.	.	.	.	.	.	.	.	.	.	.	.	.	.	.	.			.	.	.	.	.	.	4	.	2	II	0.6
Spergularia media	.	.	.	.	.	.	.	.	.	.	1	2	.	.	.	.	.	I	0.2	.	.	.	.	.	.	.	.	.		
Thymus drucei	.	.	.	.	.	.	.	.	.	.	.	.	.	.	.	.	.			.	.	.	2	.	.	.	.	1	II	0.3
Amblystegium serpens	.	+	.	3	.	.	.	.	.	.	.	.	.	.	.	.	.	I	0.2	.	.	.	.	.	.	.	.	.		
Grimmia maritima	.	.	1	1	4	.	3	.	.	.	.	.	3	1	.	.	1	II	0.7	4	4	5	4	4	2	3	3	3	V	3.6
Trichostomum brachydontium	.	.	.	.	.	.	.	.	.	.	.	.	.	.	.	.	.			.	.	.	.	1	1	.	.	.	II	0.2
Anaptychia fusca	.	.	.	.	.	.	.	.	.	.	.	.	.	.	.	.	.			.	2	.	2	.	3	.	4	.	III	1.2
Ramalina siliquosa	.	.	.	.	.	.	.	.	.	.	.	.	.	.	.	.	.			.	4	.	.	3	.	.	5	4	III	1.8
Xanthoria parietina	.	.	.	.	.	.	.	.	.	.	.	.	+	.	.	.	.			.	3	2	.	.	.	.	4	.	II	1.0
Total number of species (43)	5	8	10	10	11	8	11	11	9	11	9	12	11	13	8	7	13			5	8	7	9	8	7	10	11	13		

Mean number of species per relevé = 9.8.
Total number of species in association = 28.

Mean number of species per relevé = 8.7.
Total number of species per association = 26.

ADDITIONAL SPECIES IN LIST

1. *Suaeda maritima* 3.
7. *Bryum* sp. 1.
13. *Puccinellia maritima* 1, *Frullania germana* 2.
14. *Carex distans* 2, *C. serotina* 2, *Eleocharis uniglumis* 2.
17. *Eriophorum angustifolium* 1, *Cratoneuron filicinum* +.
20. *Ochrolechia parella* 3, *Parmelia glabratula* 3.
21. *Cerastium atrovirens* 4.
24. *Lotus corniculatus*, 2, *Verrucaria maura* 2.
25. *Empetrum nigrum* 2, *Rumex crispus* 1, *Ramalina curnowii* 1.
26. *Camptothecium sericeum* 2, *Collema* sp. 1.

LOCALITIES

1, 3, 4, 15, 16. Caolas Scalpay; 2, 13, 14. Loch Caroy; 5. Loch Ainort; 6. Loch na Dal; 7. Loch Slapin; 8. Loch Portree; 9, 17. Loch Eyre; 10, 11. Roag; 12. Camas Croise; 18. Lealt; 19, Meanish; 20, 22. Loch Caroy (west side); 21. Neist; 23. Trumpan; 24, 25. Ullinish; 26. Camas Malag.

TABLE 4.9

Class	CAKILETEA MARITIMAE										
Order	CAKILETALIA MARITIMAE										
Alliance	**Atriplicion littoralis**										
Association	*Atriplex glabriuscula–Rumex crispus*										
	1	2	3	4	5	6	7	8	9		
Reference Number	B68 118	B68 153	B68 140	B68 198	B68 201	B68 038	B68 128	B68 036	B68 037		
Map Reference	305 437	260 566	415 520	222 612	323 385	376 663	596 268	375 661	376 663		
Altitude (feet)	20	20	15	10	25	25	5	10	25		
Cover (per cent)	50	70	50	100	100	80	40	60	75		
Plot area (square metres)	16	4	16	4	4	4	4	4	4	C	D
Equisetum arvense	.	1	.	.	.	3	.	.	+	II	0.6
Agrostis stolonifera	.	.	+	3	3	2	.	.	.	III	1.0
Agropyron repens	.	2	.	.	2	.	.	.	.	II	0.4
Festuca rubra	2	.	3	4	3	3	.	.	.	III	1.6
Holcus lanatus	.	3	.	.	1	.	.	.	.	II	0.4
Juncus bufonius	.	2	.	.	+	3	.	3	.	III	1.0
J. gerardii	.	.	.	.	.	.	.	3	3	II	0.7
Scirpus maritimus	.	.	.	.	.	.	.	7	6	II	1.4
Triglochin maritima	+	2	.	.	.	.	.	2	.	II	0.4
Armeria maritima	+	3	4	2	+	.	4	.	.	IV	1.7
Atriplex glabriuscula	8	7	6	6	6	6	7	4	3	V	5.9
Cochlearia officinalis agg.	.	.	2	.	.	.	1	.	.	II	0.3
Galium aparine	2	3	3	5	4	6	.	2	3	V	3.1
Glaux maritima	3	1	4	.	.	.	3	.	.	III	1.2
Leontodon autumnalis	.	.	.	.	2	1	.	.	.	II	0.3
Ligusticum scoticum	.	.	.	5	1	.	.	.	.	II	0.7
Lycopus europaeus	.	2	.	.	+	.	.	.	.	II	0.3
Plantago maritima	.	.	3	.	.	.	.	+	.	II	0.4
Polygonum persicaria	1	+	.	.	.	.	.	.	.	I	0.2
Rumex crispus* var. *triangulatus	4	5	5	7	6	3	3	3	3	V	4.3
Sonchus arvensis	.	5	.	.	.	.	.	.	+	II	0.7
Stellaria media	5	+	4	5	3	.	6	+	+	V	2.9
Tripleurospermum maritimum	3	3	3	1	8	.	.	.	+	IV	2.1
Total number of species (48)	11	18	12	13	19	13	9	15	13		

Mean number of species per relevé = 13.6.

ADDITIONAL SPECIES IN LIST

1. *Rumex acetosa* 1.
2. *Carex otrubae* 4, *Juncus articulatus* 2.
4. *Lolium perenne* 1, *Plantago coronopus* 1, *Silene maritima* 4.
5. *Galium verum* +, *Ranunculus acris* 1, *Sedum rosea* 1, *Senecio jacobea* 1.
6. *Agropyron junceiforme* 2, *Myosotis discolor* +, *Plantago major* 2, *Sagina procumbens* 3.
7. *Salicornia europaea* 2, *Spergularia media* 3, *Suaeda maritima* 6.
8. *Eleocharis palustris* +, *Amblystegium serpens* 1, *Grimmia maritima* +, *Pottia heimii* +, *Trichostomum brachydontium* 2.
9. *Achillea ptarmica* +, *Scutellaria galericulata* +.

LOCALITIES

1. Loch Caroy; 2. Waternish; 3. Loch Eyre; 4. Ard Beag; 5. Ullinish; 6, 8, 9. Totscore; 7. Caolas Scalpay.

TABLE 4.10

Class	LITTORELLETEA
Order	LITTORELLETALIA
Alliance	**Littorellion uniflorae**
Association	*Littorella uniflora–Lobelia dortmanna*

	1	2	3	4	5	6	7	8	9	10	11		
Reference Number	B68	B68	B68	B68	B68	B68	B68	B68	B68	B68	B68		
	354	025	044	175	225	327	253	07B	291	295	296		
Map Reference	590	472	502	222	679	683	606	416	676	656	657		
	106	306	652	412	205	203	203	182	105	113	110		
Altitude (feet)	250	300	250	800	150	200	50	275	200	350	350		
Cover (per cent)	50	20	40	50	50	50	50	50	100	100	100		
Plot area (square metres)	4	4	4	4	4	4	4	4	4	4	4		
Water depth (centimetres)	21	25	23	30	30	21	15	26	26	23	27	C	D
Equisetum fluviatile	.	.	+	.	5	.	.	.	+	.	.	II	0.6
Isoetes lacustris	.	3	.	.	.	.	.	.	.	5	.	I	0.7
Baldellia ranunculoides	.	.	.	.	.	4	5	2	.	.	.	II	1.0
Carex nigra	.	.	.	.	4	3	.	2	1	.	.	II	0.9
Eleocharis palustris	.	.	.	.	3	.	.	4	5	4	9	III	2.1
Eleogiton fluitans	.	.	.	.	.	.	.	3	5	3	.	II	1.0
Juncus articulatus	5	3	4	.	.	3	4	+	1	3	.	IV	2.3
J. bulbosus	1	.	.	4	6	4	3	.	3	5	3	IV	2.6
J. effusus	.	.	.	.	2	+	.	.	.	.	.	I	0.3
Littorella uniflora	9	5	9	5	.	.	8	5	7	7	3	V	5.3
Lobelia dortmanna	.	7	3	8	8	8	.	7	6	6	3	V	5.1
Myriophyllum alterniflorum	.	.	+	.	.	.	3	.	.	.	2	II	0.6
Ranunculus flammula	3	3	+	3	5	4	.	2	+	3	.	IV	2.3
Total number of species (18)	4	6	6	4	7	7	8	8	9	8	5		

Mean number of species per relevé = 6.6.

ADDITIONAL SPECIES IN LIST

2. *Eriocaulon septangulare* 4.
3. *Nitella* sp. +.
7. *Potamogeton coloratus* 1, *P. gramineus* 2, *P. natans* 3.

LOCALITIES

1. Loch Gauscavaig; 2. Loch nan Eilean; 3. Loch Mealt; 4. Ollisdal; 5. Lochain Dubha; 6. Loch Airigh na Saorach; 7. Loch Cill Chriosd; 8. Loch Coir' a' Ghobhainn; 9. Loch nan Dùbhrachan; 10, 11. Loch Meodal.

TABLE 4.11

Class	POTAMETEA							
Order	MAGNOPOTAMETALIA							
Alliance	**Nymphaeion albae**							
Nodum	*Potamogeton natans–Nymphaea alba*							
	1	2	3	4	5	6		
Reference Number	B68 292	B68 224	B68 023	B68 043	B68 067	B68 194		
Map Reference	676 106	679 205	472 306	502 652	494 487	233 605		
Altitude (feet)	200	150	300	250	450	200		
Cover (per cent)	100	90	75	50	50	90		
Plot area (square metres)	4	4	4	4	4	4		
Water depth (centimeters)	75	90	90	75	70	52	C	D
Equisetum fluviatile	3	3	3	3	.	.	IV	2.0
Eleogiton fluitans	5	.	.	.	5	.	II	1.7
Potamogeton natans	.	7	7	8	8	5	V	5.8
P. perfoliatus	.	.	.	3	2	7	III	2.0
Sparganium angustifolium	7	.	.	5	3	4	IV	3.2
Myriophyllum alterniflorum	3	.	.	+	4	5	IV	2.2
**Nymphaea alba*	6	8	6	.	3	.	IV	3.8
Chara spp.	.	.	2	.	.	3	II	0.8
Total number of species (13)	5	3	8	5	7	5		

* ssp. *occidentalis* in 2. Mean number of species per relevé = 5.5.

ADDITIONAL SPECIES IN LIST

3. *Carex rostrata* 4, *Juncus bulbosus* 3, *Sparganium minimum* +, *Menyanthes trifoliata* 4.
5. *Callitriche stagnalis* +.

LOCALITIES

1. Loch nan Dùbhrachan; 2. Lochain Dubha; 3. Loch nan Eilean; 4. Loch Mealt; 5. Loch Fada; 6. Cnoc a'Chatha.

TABLE 4.12

Class	PHRAGMITETEA
Order	PHRAGMITETALIA EUROSIBIRICA
Alliance	**Phragmition communis**
	Brackish water communities

	1	2	3	4	5		
Reference number	B68	B68	B68	B68	B68		
	149	136	356	351	352		
Map Reference	154	485	698	578	578		
	307	418	116	086	086		
Altitude (feet)	25	20	15	15	15		
Cover (per cent)	100	100	100	100	100		
Plot area (square metres)	4	4	4	4	4	C	D
Agrostis stolonifera	3	4	3	3	3	V	3.2
Phragmites communis	8	8	.	.	.	II	3.2
Carex nigra	2	.	.	5	3	III	1.4
Eleocharis palustris	3	3	1	5	2	V	2.8
Iris pseudacorus	.	.	1	2	.	II	0.6
Juncus articulatus	2	3	1	.	3	IV	1.8
J. bufonius	.	.	2	.	2	II	0.8
J. gerardii	4	4	2	.	3	IV	2.6
Scirpus maritimus	3	4	9	8	9	V	6.6
Triglochin maritima	3	2	2	3	.	IV	2.0
Caltha palustris	.	.	3	4	2	III	1.8
Cochlearia officinalis agg.	.	3	1	.	2	III	1.2
Galium palustre	.	.	1	2	1	III	0.8
Glaux maritima	5	3	3	2	.	IV	1.6
Hydrocotyle vulgaris	.	.	.	2	4	II	1.2
Plantago maritima	3	2	.	.	.	II	1.0
Potentilla anserina	.	.	4	.	2	II	1.2
Ranunculus flammula	.	.	3	3	3	III	1.8
Viola palustris	.	.	2	2	.	II	0.8
Drepanocladus aduncus	2	.	1	.	4	III	1.4
Total number of species (32)	13	11	20	12	19		

Mean number of species per relevé = 15.

ADDITIONAL SPECIES IN LIST

1. *Armeria maritima* 4, *Grimmia maritima* 2.
2. *Blysmus rufus* 3.
3. *Epilobium palustre* 2, *Rumex crispus* 2, *Sagina procumbens* 3, *Stellaria media* 4.
5. *Myosotis scorpioides* +, *Potentilla palustris* 3, *Acrocladium cuspidatum* 2, *Campylium stellatum* 1, *Riccardia pinguis* 1.

LOCALITIES

1. Meanish; 2. Loch Portree; 3. Camas Croise; 4, 5. Rubha Sloc an Eòrna, Tarskavaig.

TABLE 4.13

Class	PHRAGMITETEA
Order	PHRAGMITETALIA EUROSIBIRICA
Alliance	**Phragmition communis**
Association	*Schoenoplectus lacustris–Phragmites communis*

Subassociation	*Phragmites–Equisetum fluviatile*								*Schoenoplectus–Equisetum fluviatile*								
	1	2	3	4	5	6			7	8	9	10	11	12	13		
Reference number	B68	B68	B68	B68	B68	B68			B68	B68	B68	B68	B68	B68	B68		
	251	248	254	193	015	017			293	294	040	066	249	014	252		
Map reference	614	611	606	233	574	574			674	656	503	494	613	572	614		
	205	204	203	605	018	018			104	113	652	487	203	012	205		
Altitude (feet)	50	50	50	200	200	200			200	350	250	450	50	200	50		
Cover (per cent)	100	100	100	60	75	90			80	90	50	40	90	50	100		
Plot area (square metres)	4	4	4	4	4	4			4	4	4	4	4	4	4		
Water depth (centimetres)	52	36	30	45	26	23	C	D	90	60	60	65	60	42	90	C	D
Equisetum fluviatile	3	3	·	3	3	3	V	2.5	·	2	4	3	3	3	3	V	2.6
Phragmites communis	10	9	9	9	9	9	V	9.1	·	·	·	·	·	·	·		
Schoenoplectus lacustris	·	·	·	·	·	·			9	8	8	9	9	8	9	V	8.6
Carex rostrata	2	4	4	·	3	·	IV	2.2	·	3	4	3	3	3	·	IV	2.3
Eleocharis palustris	·	·	·	2	·	·	I	0.3	3	·	·	4	·	·	·	II	1.0
Juncus bulbosus	·	·	·	4	·	2	II	1.0	·	·	·	·	4	2	·	II	0.8
Potamogeton natans	·	·	·	3	3	·	III	1.0	·	3	3	·	2	·	4	III	1.7
P. polygonifolius	·	·	·	·	+	3	II	0.7	·	·	·	·	·	·	4	III	0.6
Menyanthes trifoliata	·	4	4	1	·	3	IV	2.0	·	·	3	·	4	3	·	III	1.4
**Nymphaea alba*	·	·	6	·	2	4	III	2.0	·	·	·	·	·	3	·	I	0.4
Potentilla palustris	·	·	·	·	+	3	II	0.7	·	·	·	·	·	3	·	I	0.4
Utricularia minor	·	·	2	·	·	·	I	0.5	·	·	·	·	·	1	·	I	0.1
Total number of species (28)	3	5	6	7	11	10			2	4	5	8	6	10	4		

Mean number of species per relevé = 7.
Total number of species in subassociation = 20.

Mean number of species per relevé = 5.6.
Total number of species in subassociation = 17.

* ssp. *occidentalis* in 5, 6, and 12.

ADDITIONAL SPECIES IN LIST

2. *Potamogeton coloratus* 1.
3. *Eriophorum angustifolium* 3.
4. *Chara* sp. 4.
5. *Juncus articulatus* 3, *Potamogeton gramineus* +, *Sparganium minimum* +.
6. *Carex panicea* 2, *Utricularia intermedia* 1, *Sphagnum subsecundum* var. *inundatum* 2.
10. *Glyceria fluitans* +, *Potamogeton perfoliatus* 3, *Sparganium angustifolium* +, *Myriophyllum alterniflorum* 2.
12. *Galium palustre* 2, *Ranunculus flammula* 2.
13. *Potamogeton lucens* 1.

LOCALITIES

1, 2, 3, 11, 13. Loch Cill Chriosd; 4. Cnoc a'Chatha; 5, 6, 12. Loch Aruisg; 7. Loch nan Dùbhrachan; 8. Loch Meodal, 9. Loch Mealt; 10. Loch Fada.

TABLE 4.14

Class	PHRAGMITETEA
Order	PHRAGMITETALIA EUROSIBIRICA
Alliance	**Magnocaricion elatae**
Association	*Carex rostrata–Menyanthes trifoliata*

	1	2	3	4	5	6	7	8		
Reference number	B68 041	B68 07A	B68 046	B68 020	B68 022	B68 068	B68 247	B68 018		
Map reference	503 652	416 182	502 652	472 304	272 306	494 487	611 204	656 113		
Altitude (feet)	250	275	250	300	300	450	50	350		
Cover (per cent)	70	60	60	60	70	80	100	75		
Plot area (square metres)	4	4	4	4	4	4	4	4		
Water depth (centimetres)	45	45	36	36	36	15	15	15	C	D
Equisetum fluviatile	3	3	4	.	.	4	3	5	IV	2.8
Carex nigra	.	.	1	3	5	.	.	3	III	1.5
C. rostrata	8	8	8	8	7	9	9	9	V	8.3
Eleocharis palustris	3	.	.	3	3	4	.	3	IV	2.0
Eriocaulon septangulare	.	.	.	5	2	.	.	.	II	0.9
Juncus articulatus	.	.	.	+	2	.	.	.	II	0.4
J. bulbosus	.	.	.	3	+	.	.	.	II	0.5
Potamogeton natans	3	.	.	.	4	.	.	.	II	0.9
P. polygonifolius	.	+	.	.	.	.	4	3	II	1.0
Schoenoplectus lacustris	2	.	3	.	.	.	.	3	II	1.0
Lobelia dortmanna	.	.	.	.	3	.	.	3	II	0.8
Menyanthes trifoliata	5	3	5	5	5	3	5	1	V	4.0
**Nymphaea alba*	.	3	.	2	3	.	.	.	II	1.0
Potentilla palustris	3	.	.	.	.	3	.	.	II	0.8
Ranunculus flammula	.	4	.	4	3	.	.	3	III	1.8
Total number of species (19)	7	6	6	11	11	5	5	9		

* ssp. *occidentalis* in 2. Mean number of species per relevé = 7.5.

ADDITIONAL SPECIES IN LIST

3. *Potamogeton perfoliatus* 2.
4. *Schoenus nigricans* +, *Scorpidium scorpioides* +.
7. *Phragmites communis* 4.

LOCALITIES

1, 3. Loch Mealt; 2. Loch Coir' a' Ghobhainn; 4, 5. Loch nan Eilean; 6. Loch Fada; 7. Loch Cill Chriosd; 8. Loch Meodal.

TABLE 4.15

Class	PHRAGMITETEA				
Order	PHRAGMITETALIA EUROSIBIRICA				
Alliance	**Glycerio–Sparganion**				
	Oenanthe crocata communities				
	1	2		1	2
Reference Number	B69 018	B69 019	Reference Number	B69 018	B69 019
Map Reference	373 707	373 707	Map Reference	373 707	373 707
Cover (per cent)	100	100	Cover (per cent)	100	100
Plot area (square metres)	4	4	Plot area (square metres)	4	4
Aegopodium podagraria	.	3	*Mentha aquatica*	1	3
Astrantia major	3	.	*Mimulus guttatus*	5	4
Berula erecta	3	3	*Myosotis scorpioides*	1	3
Caltha palustris	4	3	*Oenanthe crocata*	7	8
Cardamine pratensis	1	+	*Phalaris arundinacea*	6	4
Equisetum fluviatile	4	3	*Potentilla anserina*	1	1
Filipendula ulmaria	5	3	*Ranunculus repens*	.	2
Galium palustre	3	1	*Rorippa nasturtium–aquaticum*	3	4
Glyceria fluitans	4	3	*Rumex obtusifolius*	3	3
Hypericum tetrapterum	.	1	*Urtica dioica*	2	1
Iris pseudacorus	5	3	*Veronica beccabunga*	3	4
Lathyrus pratensis	+	.			

LOCALITY: Camas Mor, Kilmuir

TABLE 4.16

	pH	K_{corr} (μmhos)	Ca	Mg	Na	K	Relevé number	Locality
			(milligrams/litre)					
OXYCOCCO-SPHAGNETEA								
ERICETALIA TETRALICIS								
Ericion tetralicis								
Trichophoreto–Callunetum	4.0	26	0.4	0.7	4.6	1.2	67/079	Kirkibost
	4.0	25	0.1	0.5	1.4	1.8	.	Ben Suardal
	4.0	25	0.4	1.9	9.7	0.8	67/023	Blà Bheinn
	3.8	24	0.4	1.7	5.5	0.6	68/009	S. of Glenbrittle
	4.2	29	0.1	1.2	9.9	3.1	68/049	Biod Buidhe
Molinieto–Callunetum	4.8	35	0.3	1.0	2.3	1.3	68/008	Lochan Coir' a' Ghobhainn
	4.6	42	0.3	0.7	2.3	0.7	67/088	Sligachan
	4.5	38	0.2	0.9	2.3	1.4	67/080	Kirkibost
	4.8	40	0.3	0.7	2.1	1.2	67/027	Carbost
SPHAGNETALIA MAGELLANICI								
Erico–Sphagnion								
Trichophoreto–Eriophoretum	4.1	26	0.3	0.6	2.5	2.5	68/229	Loch Airigh na Saorach
	3.6	20	0.3	2.4	11.5	1.0	.	S. of Broadford
	4.3	30	0.4	0.6	3.2	1.1	67/005	Blà Bheinn
	4.0	25	0.4	1.6	6.7	1.1	67/140	Loch nan Eilean
Calluneto–Eriophoretum	3.8	47	0.6	1.9	9.2	4.7	69/111	Coire Mhic Eachainn
SCHEUCHZERIO-CARICETEA FUSCAE								
SCHEUCHZERIETALIA								
Rhynchosporion albae								
Eriophorum angustifolium–Sphagnum cuspidatum	4.1	33	0.6	0.9	6.4	1.7	68/228	Loch Airigh na Saorach
	4.0	53	0.4	1.1	10.6	0.8	68/56A	Loch Sligachan
	4.0	42	0.5	1.0	3.9	0.9	68/311A	Kyleakin
Caricion lasiocarpae								
Carex lasiocarpa–Menyanthes trifoliata	4.9	143	1.4	1.5	11.2	2.9	68/223	Lochain Dubha
	4.8	114	1.4	1.7	9.7	0.7	68/226	Lochain Dubha
	5.8	117	3.2	3.3	9.2	0.3	68/250	Loch Cill Chriosd
	6.0	152	1.2	3.1	9.2	1.0	68/010	Loch Meodal
	5.9	164	2.0	2.7	9.6	1.5	68/011	Loch Meodal
	6.8	128	1.6	3.2	5.9	1.0	68/064	Loch Fada

	pH	K_{corr} (μmhos)	Ca (milligrams/litre)	Mg	Na	K	Relevé number	Locality
CARICETALIA FUSCAE								
Caricion canescentis–fuscae								
Trichophorum cespitosum–Carex panicea	4.8	81	1.1	2.9	13.6	1.0	68/097	N. of Uig
	4.6	84	0.9	1.2	5.1	0.9	.	The Storr
	4.5	99	2.0	0.9	8.1	2.0	68/125	Carn Liath
	4.5	83	1.2	1.2	5.9	0.8	68/310	Sligachan
	4.4	108	0.6	1.2	6.5	1.5	.	Blà Bheinn
Molinia caerulea–Myrica gale	5.9	115	1.4	2.2	9.9	0.9	68/013	Aird of Sleat
	5.4	102	1.3	0.4	6.9	1.9	67/045	Coille Gaireallach
	5.2	99	1.2	1.7	7.6	0.6	67/009	Blà Bheinn
	5.2	104	1.4	0.6	3.7	1.4	67/008	Blà Bheinn
Sphagneto–Juncetum effusi	4.6	150	0.2	2.4	10.8	6.3	.	near Staffin
	4.7	122	0.3	1.6	9.6	6.3	68/027	The Storr
	4.5	143	0.3	0.9	4.1	5.7	.	The Storr
	4.6	136	0.2	1.4	6.2	6.3	.	The Storr
Carex–Sphagnum recurvum	4.4	103	0.4	1.7	10.8	2.8	68/050	Biod Bhuidhe
	4.5	100	0.6	1.7	9.2	1.8	68/051	Biod Bhuidhe
Sphagno–Tomenthypnion								
Carex rostrata–Aulacomnium palustre	4.8	118	2.5	1.9	9.6	2.5	67/091	Loch Meodal
	5.3	122	2.3	2.2	7.4	0.6	67/091	Loch Meodal
	5.1	137	2.4	2.4	5.8	0.5	68/062	Loch Fada
	4.8	110	2.2	2.2	2.8	1.7	67/136	Loch Mealt
	5.5	120	2.2	2.2	4.1	0.7	68/042	Loch Mealt
TOFIELDIETALIA								
Eriophorion latifoliae								
Carex rostrata–Scorpidium scorpioides	5.9	182	4.2	1.2	7.4	2.0	67/042	Loch Cill Chriosd
	5.4	164	3.2	1.8	10.3	1.9	68/019	Loch Meodal
	5.8	151	3.6	2.1	6.7	0.9	.	Loch nan Eilean
	5.2	184	4.0	1.5	6.2	0.6	68/053	Glen Varragill
	5.4	147	3.2	1.6	6.7	2.9	68/065	Loch Fada
	6.0	148	5.4	3.8	11.0	1.3	68/045	Loch Mealt
Carex panicea–Campylium stellatum	6.1	149	3.1	4.2	10.4	0.9	67/037	Preshal More
	6.2	165	3.6	1.2	8.7	1.3	67/076	Faoilean
	5.6	152	2.4	1.5	5.3	1.1	68/323	Kyleakin
	5.8	166	3.0	0.9	4.1	0.9	.	Blà Bheinn
	5.9	153	3.2	2.8	7.8	1.3	68/098	near Uig
	6.0	160	3.1	2.9	8.1	1.2	.	Ben Suardal
Eriophorum latifolium–Carex hostiana	6.8	358	8.6	8.3	9.9	1.1	67/011	Blà Bheinn
	6.7	211	7.0	4.6	11.9	2.0	68/349	Kyleakin
	6.8	333	11.4	2.4	11.0	2.0	67/044	Loch Cill Chriosd
	7.2	417	14.8	3.3	11.0	1.2	.	Loch Cill Chriosd
	6.4	358	7.8	5.6	22.1	1.9	68/012	Aird of Sleat
	6.8	196	8.2	3.4	10.2	3.9	68/024	Loch nan Eilean
Schoenus nigricans	6.4	310	12.2	2.9	11.0	1.4	67/043	Loch Cill Chriosd
	7.0	400	13.4	3.3	11.9	1.6	68/255	Loch Cill Chriosd
	6.8	278	10.6	2.8	12.2	1.2	67/043	Loch Cill Chriosd
	6.8	333	8.0	4.6	17.0	1.7	68/321	Kyleakin
	6.4	294	8.0	1.8	5.5	2.7	67/010	Blà Bheinn
Carex–Saxifraga aizoides	6.8	108	0.8	3.2	4.6	0.7	68/234	Blà Bheinn
	6.4	116	0.3	2.8	6.9	0.9	68/105	Sgùrr Mor
	6.2	96	0.4	1.9	4.1	0.7	68/107	Sgùrr Mor
MONTIO–CARDAMINETEA								
MONTIO–CARDAMINETALIA								
Cardamino–Montion								
Philonoto–Saxifragetum stellaris	5.8	97	1.0	1.2	5.5	1.1	67/021	Blà Bheinn
	5.0	93	0.2	1.2	9.6	0.8	68/106	Sgùrr Mor
	5.8	96	0.1	0.8	9.6	1.4	68/075	Sgùrr Mor
	5.8	97	0.1	0.8	5.1	1.0	.	The Storr
	6.2	80	0.1	1.0	4.6	0.6	.	Beinn Edra
	6.2	106	0.2	1.7	6.4	0.8	68/072	The Storr
Koenigia islandica–Carex demissa	5.8	97	0.1	0.6	4.1	0.8	68/076	The Storr
	6.1	95	0.1	0.5	5.3	0.8	68/034	The Storr
	6.0	96	0.2	0.9	3.7	0.4	.	The Storr
	6.0	96	0.1	0.7	4.6	0.5	.	The Storr
Cratoneurion commutati								
Cratoneuron commutatum–Saxifraga aizoides	6.8	208	8.2	8.3	7.6	0.5	68/232	Allt na Dunaich
	7.1	313	7.6	8.9	8.8	1.6	.	Blà Bheinn
	7.2	500	8.8	10.9	31.0	2.1	68/090	Lealt
	7.4	370	9.6	17.1	31.0	2.6	68/091	Lealt

TABLE 4.17

Class	SCHEUCHZERIO–CARICETEA FUSCAE						
Order	SCHEUCHZERIETALIA PALUSTRIS						
Alliance	**Rhynchosporion albae**						
Association	*Eriophorum angustifolium–Sphagnum cuspidatum*						
	1	2	3	4	5		
Reference Number	B68	B67	B68	B68	B66		
	228	085A	056A	311A	001		
Map Reference	676	516	488	748	423		
	203	193	302	258	212		
Altitude (feet)	200	150	25	100	600		
Cover (per cent)	100	100	100	100	100		
Plot area (square metres)	4	4	4	4	4	C	D
Carex limosa	5	.	.	.	×	II	1.3
Eleocharis multicaulis	3	2	.	.	.	II	1.3
Eriophorum angustifolium	6	6	7	7	×	V	6.5
Narthecium ossifragum	.	4	4	3	×	IV	3.8
Potamogeton polygonifolius	.	4	2	.	.	II	1.5
Rhynchospora alba	4	3	4	6	.	IV	4.3
Drosera anglica	3	3	3	1	×	V	2.5
D. rotundifolia	2	3	3	3	×	V	3.8
Menyanthes trifoliata	4	1	5	.	×	IV	2.5
Utricularia minor	4	.	2	.	.	II	1.5
Sphagnum cuspidatum	8	6	7	7	×	V	7.0
S. magellanicum	2	.	.	3	×	III	1.3
S. palustre	2	3	4	.	×	IV	2.3
S. plumulosum	.	2	.	.	×	II	0.5
S. pulchrum	5	2	.	.	.	II	1.8
**S. subsecundum*	2	6	4	.	×	IV	3.0
Gymnocolea inflata	.	1	2	.	.	II	0.8
Total number of species (21)	15	15	12	8	12		

Mean number of species per relevé = 12·4.

* var. *auriculatum* in 1, 2, 3 and 5.

ADDITIONAL SPECIES IN LIST

1. *Carex pauciflora* 2, *Juncus kochii* 1.
2. *Schoenus nigricans* 2.
4. *Cladopodiella fluitans* 1.

LOCALITIES

1. West of Loch Airigh na Saorach; 2. Camasunary; 3. Loch Sligachan; 4. Kyleakin; 5. Sgùrr Dearg.

TABLE 4.18

Class	SCHEUCHZERIO–CARICETEA FUSCAE										
Order	SCHEUCHZERIETALIA PALUSTRIS										
Alliance	**Caricion lasiocarpae**										
Association	*Carex lasiocarpa–Menyanthes trifoliata*								*Carex rostrata–Carex limosa nodum*		
	1	2	3	4	5	6			7	8	
Reference number	B68 226	B68 223	B68 010	B68 011	B68 016	B68 064			B68 250	B68 174	
Map Reference	678 206	679 205	656 113	656 113	574 018	494 487			612 203	220 412	
Altitude (feet)	150	150	350	350	200	450			50	800	
Cover (per cent)	80	100	75	90	75	100			100	100	
Plot area (square metres)	4	4	4	4	4	4	C	D	4	4	D
Equisetum fluviatile	3	5	2	4	.	3	V	2.8	3	3	3.0
Molinia caerulea	.	2	.	1	.	.	II	0.5	.	.	
Carex echinata	.	.	2	2	.	3	III	1.2	.	.	
C. lasiocarpa	9	8	8	8	8	3	V	7.3	.	.	
C. limosa	3	5	+	2	.	2	V	2.2	4	3	3.5
C. nigra	2	3	3	2	3	4	V	2.8	.	2	1.0
C. rostrata	.	2	3	5	5	8	V	3.8	8	9	8.5
Eriophorum angustifolium	.	1	.	2	.	.	II	0.5	.	5	2.5
Juncus articulatus	.	.	.	.	3	1	I	0.7	3	.	1.5
J. kochii	5	4	3	2	.	.	IV	2.3	4	2	3.0
Potamogeton polygonifolius	.	.	3	3	3	.	III	1.5	.	.	
Sparganium minimum	.	.	.	+	.	.	I	0.2	4	.	2.0
Triglochin palustre	.	.	.	.	3	.	I	0.5	+	.	0.5
Drosera rotundifolia	.	.	.	2	3	.	I	0.8	.	.	
Galium palustre	.	.	1	1	.	3	III	0.8	.	.	
Menyanthes trifoliata	5	2	5	3	4	4	V	3.8	4	5	4.5
Pedicularis palustris	.	.	1	2	.	.	II	0.5	.	.	
Potentilla palustris	.	.	3	1	.	4	III	1.3	1	.	0.5
Ranunculus flammula	.	.	3	2	2	.	III	1.2	+	1	1.0
Acrocladium giganteum	.	.	.	.	.	3	I	0.5	2	.	1.0
Drepanocladus fluitans	.	.	2	.	2	.	II	0.7	.	.	2.0
Scorpidium scorpioides	.	.	.	.	3	2	II	0.8	4	.	2.0
Sphagnum palustre	5	2	4	.	.	.	III	1.8	.	4	2.0
S. recurvum	3	3	4	.	.	.	III	1.7	.	6	3.0
**S. subsecundum*	.	4	3	4	2	.	IV	2.2	3	.	1.5
Total number of species (43)	12	12	19	21	12	15			15	13	

* var. *inundatum* in 2, 3, 4, and 7.

Mean number of species per relevé = 15.2.
Total number of species in association = 38.

Mean number of species per relevé = 14.
Total number of species in *nodum* = 20.

ADDITIONAL SPECIES IN LIST

1. *Eleocharis multicaulis* 3, *Eriocaulon septangulare* 1, *Utricularia minor* 2, *Sphagnum cuspidatum* 4.
3. *Agrostis stolonifera* +, *Carex dioica* 3.
4. *Potentilla erecta* 2, *Succisa pratensis* 2, *Viola palustris* 2.
6. *Carex curta* 3, *C. diandra* 4, *C. panicea* 2, *Mentha aquatica* 2.
7. *Utricularia vulgaris* agg. 3, *Drepanocladus revolvens* 1.
8. *Narthecium ossifragum* 3, *Polytrichum commune* 2, *Sphagnum squarrosum*, 3.

LOCALITIES

1, 2. Lochain Dubha; 3, 4. Loch Meodal; 5. Loch Aruisg; 6. Loch Fada; 7. Loch Cill Chriosd; 8. Ollisdal.

TABLE 4.19

Class	SCHEUCHZERIO–CARICETEA FUSCAE
Order	CARICETALIA FUSCAE
Alliance	**Caricion canescentis–fuscae**
Association	*Trichophorum cespitosum–Carex panicea*

	1	2	3	4	5	6	7	8		
Reference Number	B68 160	B68 112	B68 125	B68 209	B68 097	B67 032	B68 310	B67 053		
Map Reference	243 455	390 420	510 565	398 336	395 645	317 328	494 282	443 256		
Altitude (feet)	200	500	700	350	400	250	150	900		
Aspect (degrees)	90	135	90	.	180	90	270	315		
Slope (degrees)	3	5	5	o.N.	5	3	5	5		
Cover (per cent)	100	100	100	100	100	100	100	75		
Plot area (square metres)	4	4	4	4	4	4	4	4	C	D
Calluna vulgaris	5	3	.	2	4	.	3	.	IV	2.2
Erica tetralix	4	5	4	6	5	4	4	3	V	4.4
Myrica gale	5	.	5	4	.	.	6	.	III	2.5
Equisetum palustre	.	1	2	.	3	.	2	.	III	1.0
Selaginella selaginoides	2	2	.	2	+	.	.	.	III	0.9
Deschampsia flexuosa	.	.	2	.	.	1	.	.	II	0.4
Molinia caerulea	5	5	3	4	4	2	5	4	V	4.0
Carex demissa	.	2	2	.	.	3	.	.	II	0.9
C. echinata	4	5	5	5	5	2	5	3	V	4.3
C. nigra	3	.	.	+	4	.	.	.	II	1.0
C. panicea	.	1	2	4	4	2	4	2	V	2.4
C. pulicaris	2	.	3	.	3	.	.	.	II	1.0
C. rostrata	.	.	3	.	.	.	4	.	II	0.9
Eriophorum angustifolium	4	2	5	6	5	6	2	3	V	4.1
Juncus squarrosus	.	.	.	.	.	1	.	3	II	0.5
Narthecium ossifragum	.	4	3	4	3	3	3	8	V	3.5
Schoenus nigricans	.	.	3	.	.	.	6	.	II	1.3
Trichophorum cespitosum	7	7	7	7	8	8	7	5	V	7.0
Drosera rotundifolia	2	2	2	2	1	2	3	.	V	1.6
Euphrasia scottica	.	1	1	.	1	.	.	.	II	0.4
Pedicularis sylvatica	.	2	.	.	.	2	.	1	II	0.6
Pinguicula vulgaris	.	.	1	.	2	1	.	2	III	0.8
Polygala serpyllifolia	1	2	.	.	.	2	.	1	III	0.8
Potentilla erecta	2	1	2	1	2	2	1	.	V	1.4
Succisa pratensis	3	3	2	.	3	.	.	.	III	1.4
Breutelia chrysocoma	.	2	3	.	3	.	.	2	III	1.3
**Campylopus atrovirens*	.	.	.	1	4	3	.	4	III	1.5
C. setifolius	.	.	1	3	.	4	.	.	II	1.0
C. shawii	.	.	.	.	3	3	.	.	II	0.8
†*Hypnum cupressiforme*	3	.	.	1	.	.	.	.	II	0.5
Rhacomitrium lanuginosum	.	.	.	.	.	3	.	3	II	0.8
Sphagnum compactum	.	.	2	.	3	3	3	5	IV	2.0
S. palustre	3	4	3	4	3	3	+	.	V	2.6
S. plumulosum	3	4	.	.	3	3	2	+	IV	2.0
S. rubellum	4	2	.	1	.	2	.	.	III	1.1
‡*S. subsecundum*	.	3	.	5	5	.	4	2	IV	2.4
S. tenellum	.	.	1	.	.	2	.	.	II	0.4
Pleurozia purpurea	.	.	+	+	.	.	.	3	II	0.6
Riccardia pinguis	.	.	.	2	+	.	.	.	II	0.4
Total number of species (62)	24	25	27	21	28	27	21	19		

Mean number of species per relevé = 24.0.

* var. *falcatus* in 8. † var. *ericetorum* in 1 and 4. ‡ var. *auriculatum* in 8. var. *inundatum* in 2, 4, 5, and 7.

ADDITIONAL SPECIES IN LIST

1. *Vaccinium myrtillus* 1, *Eriophorum vaginatum* 3, *Aulacomnium palustre* 1, *Hylocomium splendens* 1, *Rhytidiadelphus loreus* 2, *Scapania irrigua* 1.
2. *Carex pauciflora* 4, *Sphagnum recurvum* 1, *Odontoschisma sphagni* 1.
3. *Carex hostiana* 3, *Eleocharis multicaulis* 3.
5. *Juncus kochii* 4, *Ranunculus flammula* 3, *Sphagnum strictum* +.
6. *Acrocladium cuspidatum* 1, *A. sarmentosum* +, *Dicranum scoparium* 1.
7. *Carex limosa* 3, *Juncus articulatus* 3, *Rhynchospora alba* 2, *Drosera anglica* 2.
8. *Marsupella emarginata* 3, *Scapania undulata* 2.

LOCALITIES

1. Osdale; 2. Beinn a'Mhadaidh; 3. Carn Liath; 4. Uchd Mòr; 5. N. of Uig; 6. Fiskavaig; 7. Sligachan; 8. Coire na Creiche.

TABLE 4.20

Class	SCHEUCHZERIO–CARICETEA FUSCAE
Order	CARICETALIA FUSCAE
Alliance	**Caricion canescentis–fuscae**
Association	*Molinia caerulea–Myrica gale*

	1	2	3	4	5	6	7		
Reference Number	B67 008	B67 009	B67 094	B68 013	B68 007	B67 038	B67 045		
Map Reference	556 216	596 216	657 113	572 007	416 182	707 158	610 203		
Altitude (feet)	350	350	400	300	275	100	150		
Aspect (degrees)	90	90	90	270	0	225	0		
Slope (degrees)	2	.	.	o.N.	2	5	8		
Cover (per cent)	100	100	100	100	100	100	100		
Plot area (square metres)	4	4	4	4	4	4	4	C	D
Calluna vulgaris	3	4	1	3	.	.	2	IV	1.9
Erica tetralix	.	.	2	3	1	4	2	IV	1.7
Myrica gale	7	6	7	8	6	7	7	V	6.9
Salix aurita	.	.	.	3	+	.	.	II	0.6
Blechnum spicant	2	.	.	.	.	.	2	II	0.6
Deschampsia flexuosa	.	.	.	2	.	2	2	III	0.9
Festuca vivipara	.	.	2	.	.	.	1	II	0.4
Molinia caerulea	8	7	7	7	7	8	7	V	7.3
Carex demissa	.	.	3	4	.	.	1	III	1.1
C. echinata	1	.	4	3	2	3	3	V	2.3
C. panicea	.	.	4	4	1	2	2	IV	1.9
C. pulicaris	2	.	2	.	3	2	.	III	1.3
C. rostrata	.	.	3	.	+	.	.	II	0.6
**Dactylorchis maculata*	.	.	+	1	+	1	1	IV	0.7
Eriophorum angustifolium	3	.	.	2	2	.	1	III	1.1
Juncus effusus	.	.	.	2	.	.	2	II	0.6
Narthecium ossifragum	.	.	3	3	3	2	2	IV	1.9
Drosera rotundifolia	.	1	.	3	1	1	.	III	0.9
Galium saxatile	2	.	.	1	.	.	.	II	0.4
Pinguicula vulgaris	1	2	3	1	+	1	1	V	1.4
Polygala serpyllifolia	2	2	1	.	.	1	1	IV	1.0
Potentilla erecta	4	3	3	2	2	1	2	V	2.4
Breutelia chrysocoma	.	.	.	.	1	.	3	II	0.6
Drepanocladus revolvens	.	.	.	1	1	.	.	II	0.3
Sphagnum capillaceum	.	.	3	2	.	.	.	II	0.7
S. compactum	3	1	.	.	.	.	.	II	0.6
S. palustre	3	2	3	6	1	5	3	V	3.3
S. plumulosum	2	.	2	4	3	.	.	III	1.6
S. recurvum	4	2	.	3	2	.	2	IV	1.9
S. rubellum	.	.	1	.	2	2	2	III	1.0
†*S. subsecundum*	.	.	.	.	+	3	.	II	0.6
Splachnum ampullaceum	.	.	+	.	.	.	2	II	0.4
Total number of species (55)	16	10	25	29	26	18	25		

Mean number of species per relevé = 21.3.

* ssp. *ericetorum* in 3, 4, 5, and 6. † var. *auriculatum* in 6. var. *inundatum* in 5 and 6.

ADDITIONAL SPECIES IN LIST

1. *Campylium stellatum* 1.
3. *Carex nigra* 2, *Potamogeton polygonifolius* +, *Pedicularis sylvatica* 1, *Aulacomnium palustre* 2.
4. *Carex dioica* 2, *Eleocharis palustris* 3, *Juncus kochii* 1, *Triglochin palustre* 1, *Anagallis tenella* 3, *Drosera intermedia* +, *Hypericum pulchrum* +, *Scorpidium scorpioides* 1.
5. *Schoenus nigricans* 3, *Cirsium palustre* +, *Pedicularis palustris* +, *Sphagnum contortum* 1, *S. imbricatum* +.
6. *Lycopodium selago* +, *Hypnum cupressiforme* var. *ericetorum* 1.
7. *Equisetum palustre* +, *Juncus squarrosus* +, *Rhacomitrium lanuginosum*, 2.

LOCALITIES

1, 2. Blà Bheinn; 3. near Loch Meodal; 4. Aird of Sleat; 5. Lochan Coir' a' Ghobhainn; 6. E. side of Loch na Dal; 7. Coille Gaireallach.

TABLE 4.21

Class	SCHEUCHZERIO–CARICETEA FUSCAE										
Order	CARICETALIA FUSCAE										
Alliance	**Caricion canescentis–fuscae**										
Association	*Sphagneto–Juncetum effusi*							*Carex–Sphagnum recurvum nodum*			
	1	2	3	4	5			6	7	8	
Reference number	B67 036	B68 027	B68 364	B67 086	B68 060			B68 050	B68 051	B68 071	
Map reference	335 300	502 523	514 545	513 190	493 310			438 678	438 678	496 535	
Altitude (feet)	650	500	650	30	50			950	950	1600	
Aspect (degrees)	0	90	90	.	.			0	.	.	
Slope (degrees)	5	5	5	.	.			5	.	.	
Cover (per cent)	100	100	100	100	100			100	100	100	
Plot area (square metres)	4	4	4	4	4	C	D	4	4	4	D
Erica tetralix	.	.	.	.	.			3	3	.	2.0
Agrostis canina	.	4	.	.	4	II	1.6	.	.	.	
Anthoxanthum odoratum	.	+	3	2	.	III	1.2	.	.	3	1.0
Deschampsia flexuosa	3	3	3	.	.	III	1.8	.	.	2	0.7
Festuca ovina	2	.	.	3	.	II	1.0	.	.	.	
F. vivipara	.	.	.	3	.	I	0.6	.	3	4	2.3
Molinia caerulea	.	.	2	.	.	I	0.4	2	.	3	1.7
Carex echinata	2	+	2	3	3	V	2.2	5	7	5	5.7
C. nigra	3	.	3	1	3	IV	2.0	3	3	3	3.0
C. panicea	.	.	.	3	.	I	0.6	2	.	3	1.7
Eriophorum angustifolium	2	.	.	2	.	II	0.8	8	6	8	7.3
Juncus effusus	8	8	8	7	9	V	8.0	.	.	.	
J. kochii	.	.	.	.	.			3	2	.	1.7
J. squarrosus	.	2	.	.	.	I	0.4	.	.	4	1.3
Luzula campestris	.	+	1	1	.	III	0.6	.	.	.	
Galium saxatile	3	4	2	5	4	V	3.6	.	.	.	
Pinguicula vulgaris	.	.	.	.	.			2	.	2	1.3
Polygala serpyllifolia	1	.	.	2	.	II	0.6	.	2	.	0.7
Potentilla erecta	2	3	3	4	3	V	3.0	.	4	.	1.3
Rumex acetosa	.	4	2	.	.	II	1.2	.	.	.	
Viola palustris	.	3	2	.	5	III	2.0	.	.	2	0.7
Hylocomium splendens	2	5	.	4	.	III	2.2	.	.	+	0.3
Polytrichum commune	3	3	5	5	4	V	4.0	.	3	.	1.0
Rhytidiadelphus squarrosus	.	3	1	3	3	IV	2.0	.	.	.	
Sphagnum girgensohnii	.	3	3	.	.	II	1.2	.	.	.	
S. palustre	6	4	3	4	3	V	4.0	5	6	3	4.7
S. plumulosum	.	.	.	.	.			2	4	.	2.0
S. recurvum	8	6	7	7	7	V	7.0	6	6	5	5.7
S. rubellum	1	.	.	2	.	II	0.6	.	.	.	
**S. subsecundum*	.	.	.	.	.			3	3	4	3.3
Thuidium tamariscinum	1	3	.	3	.	III	1.4	.	.	.	
Lophocolea bidentata	.	2	2	2	2	IV	1.6	.	.	.	
Pleurozia purpurea	.	.	.	.	.			2	.	+	1.0
Total number of species (58)	17	23	17	23	18			17	15	20	

Mean number of species per relevé = 19.6
Total number of species in association = 42.

Mean number of species per relevé = 17.3.
Total number of species in *nodum* = 32.

* var. *inundatum* in 6 and 7. var. *auriculatum* in 8.

ADDITIONAL SPECIES IN LIST

1. *Plagiothecium undulatum* 1, *Pleurozium schreberi* 1.
2. *Equisetum palustre* 4, *Cirsium palustre* 3, *Epilobium palustre* 2, *Pseudoscleropodium purum* +.
4. *Parnassia palustris* 3, *Succisa pratensis* 1, *Hypnum cupressiforme* 4.
5. *Carex ovalis* 3, *Cardamine pratensis* 4, *Stellaria alsine* 2, *Acrocladium cuspidatum* 4, *Eurhynchium praelongum* 1, *Peltigera canina* 1.
6. *Carex pauciflora* 3, *Narthecium ossifragum* 3, *Drosera rotundifolia* +, *Tetraplodon mnioides* +.
7. *Calluna vulgaris* 2, *Breutelia chrysocoma* 1.
8. *Selaginella selaginoides* +, *Nardus stricta* 3, *Carex demissa* 2, *Juncus articulatus* 3.

LOCALITIES

1. Preshal More; 2. The Storr; 3. Tottrome; 4. Camasunary; 5. Loch Sligachan; 6, 7. Biod Bhuidhe; 8. Bealach Beag.

TABLE 4.22

Class	SCHEUCHZERIO–CARICETEA FUSCAE
Order	CARICETALIA FUSCAE
Alliance	**Sphagno–Tomenthypnion**
Association	*Carex rostrata–Aulacomnium palustre*

	1	2	3	4	5		
Reference Number	B68	B68	B67	B68	B67		
	192	042	136	062	091		
Map Reference	233	502	502	493	656		
	604	652	652	486	113		
Altitude (feet)	200	250	250	450	350		
Cover (per cent)	100	100	100	100	100		
Plot area (square metres)	4	4	4	4	4	C	D
Myrica gale	.	2	.	.	3	II	1.0
Equisetum palustre	1	2	1	5	2	V	2.2
Agrostis canina	.	3	.	.	3	II	1.2
Holcus lanatus	+	.	3	4	.	III	1.6
Molinia caerulea	4	3	2	.	2	IV	2.2
Carex curta	.	+	2	2	.	III	1.0
C. dioica	.	.	1	+	.	II	0.4
C. echinata	3	2	2	4	4	V	3.0
C. nigra	5	3	3	5	4	V	4.0
C. rostrata	8	7	7	8	7	V	7.4
Eleocharis palustris	.	.	2	.	4	II	1.2
Eriophorum angustifolium	1	2	2	3	3	V	2.2
Juncus acutiflorus	1	.	3	2	.	III	1.2
J. articulatus	.	3	3	2	.	III	1.6
J. effusus	1	.	2	2	.	III	1.0
J. kochii	2	.	.	.	2	II	0.8
Luzula multiflora	.	.	1	3	.	II	0.8
Caltha palustris	.	4	6	3	.	III	2.6
Cardamine pratensis	2	1	2	.	.	III	1.0
Cirsium palustre	.	.	.	+	+	II	0.4
Epilobium palustre	3	2	.	1	.	III	1.2
Filipendula ulmaria	.	2	5	3	.	III	2.0
Galium palustre	.	3	5	2	+	IV	2.2
Lychnis flos-cuculi	3	+	1	2	.	IV	1.4
Mentha aquatica	.	3	3	2	.	III	1.6
Menyanthes trifoliata	4	3	.	4	2	IV	2.6
Myosotis scorpioides	+	1	+	2	.	IV	1.0
Pedicularis palustris	1	4	4	3	3	V	3.0
Potentilla palustris	5	7	6	5	3	V	5.2
Ranunculus flammula	2	2	4	3	2	V	2.6
Rhinanthus minor	.	+	.	2	.	II	0.6
Rumex acetosa	1	2	3	.	.	III	1.2
Succisa pratensis	.	+	1	.	3	III	1.0
Viola palustris	1	.	.	3	.	II	0.8
Acrocladium cuspidatum	4	4	3	3	3	V	3.4
Aulacomnium palustre	3	2	3	2	2	V	2.4
Bryum pseudotriquetrum	2	.	.	1	.	II	0.6
Mnium pseudopunctatum	+	3	.	2	.	III	1.2
M. seligeri	+	2	3	.	.	III	1.2
Rhytidiadelphus squarrosus	.	3	.	2	.	II	1.0
Sphagnum contortum	.	2	3	.	.	II	1.0
S. palustre	.	.	.	1	5	II	1.2
S. recurvum	2	3	2	4	6	V	3.4
S. squarrosum	.	1	.	2	1	III	0.8
**S. subsecundum*	.	+	.	3	.	II	0.8
S. teres	.	+	2	2	.	III	1.0
S. warnstorfianum	.	.	.	2	1	II	0.6
Splachnum ampullaceum	+	.	.	.	+	II	0.4
Chiloscyphus pallescens	.	1	1	+	.	III	0.6
Pellia neesiana	2	1	.	+	.	III	0.8
Total number of species (75)	35	41	38	44	27		

Mean number of species per relevé = 37.0.

* var. *inundatum* in 2 and 4.

ADDITIONAL SPECIES IN LIST

1. *Juncus squarrosus* 2, *Achillea ptarmica* 3, *Senecio aquaticus* 1, *Acrocladium giganteum* +, *Campylium stellatum* 3, *Drepanocladus revolvens* 2, *Sphagnum plumulosum* 1.
2. *Salix aurita* 2, *Iris pseudacorus* +, *Acrocladium cordifolium* 2, *Lophocolea cuspidata* 1.
3. *Deschampsia flexuosa* 2, *Triglochin palustre* 2, *Pinguicula vulgaris* +, *Dicranum bonjeani* 1, *Trichocolea tomentella* 1.
4. *Parnassia palustris* 3, *Potentilla erecta* 3, *Valeriana officinalis* 3, *Acrocladium stramineum* +, *Dicranella palustris* 1.
5. *Carex panicea* 4, *C. pulicaris* 2, *Drosera rotundifolia* 1, *Galium saxatile* 1.

LOCALITIES

1. Cnoc a' Chatha; 2, 3. Loch Mealt; 4. Loch Fada; 5. Loch Meodal.

TABLE 4.23

Class	SCHEUCHZERIO–CARICETEA FUSCAE								
Order	TOFIELDIETALIA								
Alliance	**Eriophorion latifoliae**								
Association	*Carex rostrata–Scorpidium scorpioides*								
	1	2	3	4	5	6	7		
Reference Number	B68	B68	B68	B68	B68	B68	B67		
	053	055	114	045	019	065	042		
Map Reference	468	467	385	502	656	494	605		
	342	334	414	652	113	487	203		
Altitude (feet)	300	350	500	250	350	450	50		
Aspect (degrees)	.	270	.	.	.	.	.		
Slope (degrees)	.	2	.	.	.	.	.		
Cover (per cent)	75	75	100	90	100	100	100		
Plot area (square metres)	4	4	4	4	4	4	4	C	D
Myrica gale	1	3	.	.	.	.	4	III	1.1
Equisetum palustre	3	3	.	4	1	2	1	V	2.0
Molinia caerulea	.	.	5	.	.	.	3	II	1.1
Carex demissa	.	4	3	.	.	.	.	II	1.0
C. dioica	4	.	4	3	.	.	1	III	1.7
C. echinata	.	2	2	.	.	+	3	III	1.1
C. hostiana	.	.	5	.	.	.	3	II	1.1
C. limosa	.	3	3	.	.	.	.	II	0.9
C. nigra	.	3	4	3	2	3	2	V	2.4
C. panicea	5	4	4	5	3	3	3	V	3.9
C. pulicaris	.	.	2	.	.	.	1	II	0.4
C. rostrata	7	7	6	6	8	9	7	V	7.1
C. serotina	.	.	.	4	.	3	.	II	1.0
Eleocharis quinqueflora	.	+	3	2	.	.	2	III	1.1
Eriophorum angustifolium	5	3	4	3	2	+	4	V	3.0
Juncus articulatus	.	.	1	4	.	.	.	II	0.7
J. kochii	.	.	2	.	2	.	.	II	0.6
Potamogeton polygonifolius	2	+	.	.	.	2	.	III	0.7
Triglochin palustre	.	.	2	.	.	+	.	II	0.4
Caltha palustris	.	.	.	.	+	.	1	II	0.3
Galium palustre	.	.	.	.	3	3	.	II	0.9
Mentha aquatica	.	.	.	2	.	+	.	II	0.4
Menyanthes trifoliata	.	4	3	7	5	2	3	V	3.4
Pedicularis palustris	.	.	1	4	+	+	.	III	1.0
Pinguicula vulgaris	3	.	2	.	.	.	.	II	0.7
Potentilla erecta	.	.	+	.	2	.	2	III	0.7
P. palustris	.	.	.	4	4	3	.	III	1.6
Ranunculus flammula	.	.	2	2	3	4	.	III	1.6
Succisa pratensis	.	.	2	.	.	.	2	II	0.6
Utricularia minor	2	+	.	.	3	.	.	III	0.9
Bryum pseudotriquetrum	.	.	.	1	.	+	.	II	0.3
Campylium stellatum	5	3	4	4	.	4	3	V	3.3
†***Drepanocladus revolvens***	3	4	4	3	2	.	+	V	2.4
Scorpidium scorpioides	6	4	3	3	3	3	4	V	3.7
Sphagnum contortum	.	4	.	3	.	.	4	III	1.6
S. palustre	.	5	.	.	.	.	2	II	1.0
S. plumulosum	3	.	2	.	.	.	2	III	1.0
S. recurvum	.	2	.	.	4	.	.	II	0.9
**S. subsecundum*	3	3	.	.	3	.	2	III	1.6
Total number of species (64)	16	22	29	24	20	19	32		

Mean number of species per relevé = 23.1.

* var. *inundatum* in 1, 2, 5, and 7.   † var. *intermedius* in 1, 2, 3, 4, 5, and 7

ADDITIONAL SPECIES IN LIST

1. *Narthecium ossifragum* 2, *Drosera rotundifolia* 3.
2. *Epilobium palustre* 2, *Viola palustris* 3.
3. *Selaginella selaginoides* 3, *Dactylorchis incarnata* 1, *Trichophorum cespitosum* 3, *Euphrasia scottica* +.
4. *Acrocladium giganteum* 1, *Cinclidium stygium* 5, *Mnium pseudopunctatum* 3, *Philonotis calcarea* +, *Sphagnum teres* 2.
5. *Cirsium palustre* 3, *Utricularia intermedia* +.
6. *Riccardia pinguis* +.
7. *Phragmites communis* +, *Dactylorchis purpurella* 1, *Eleocharis palustris* 2, *Platanthera bifolia* +, *Schoenus nigricans* 3, *Drosera anglica* 1, *Acrocladium cuspidatum* 2, *Breutelia chrysocoma* 3, *Splachnum ampullaceum* +.

LOCALITIES

1, 2. Glen Varragill; 3. Beinn a' Mhadaidh; 4. Loch Mealt; 5. Loch Meodal; 6. Loch Fada; 7. Loch Cill Chriosd.

TABLE 4.24

Class	SCHEUCHZERIO–CARICETEA FUSCAE							
Order	TOFIELDIETALIA							
Alliance	**Eriophorion latifoliae**							
Association	*Carex panicea–Campylium stellatum*							
	1	2	3	4	5	6		
Reference Number	B67 061	B67 037	B67 076	B67 115	B68 098	B68 323		
Map Reference	752 210	331 300	567 201	510 403	395 645	753 260		
Altitude (feet)	1100	600	100	600	400	200		
Aspect (degrees)	225	0	90	225	180	0		
Slope (degrees)	15	10	20	12	5	5		
Cover (per cent)	60	70	80	75	100	100		
Plot area (square metres)	4	4	4	4	4	4	C	D
Erica tetralix	2	.	.	2	1	3	IV	1.3
Equisetum palustre	.	2	.	.	5	.	II	1.2
Selaginella selaginoides	2	3	3	2	3	2	V	2.5
Anthoxanthum odoratum	1	4	.	.	.	.	II	0.8
Carex demissa	5	.	.	4	2	3	IV	2.3
C. dioica	.	.	.	2	.	4	II	1.0
C. echinata	.	3	4	2	4	5	IV	3.0
C. flacca	.	.	.	4	4	2	III	1.7
C. hostiana	.	.	.	.	4	3	II	1.2
C. nigra	2	3	2	.	.	.	III	1.2
C. panicea	6	6	6	7	7	6	V	6.3
C. pulicaris	2	.	.	4	3	.	III	1.5
Eleocharis palustris	1	3	.	.	.	.	II	0.7
E. quinqueflora	3	3	.	3	6	.	IV	2.5
Eriophorum angustifolium	3	2	2	.	4	.	IV	1.8
Juncus articulatus	2	3	.	3	3	3	V	2.3
J. kochii	1	.	.	1	4	.	III	1.0
J. squarrosus	1	1	2	.	3	.	IV	1.2
Narthecium ossifragum	2	.	.	.	.	2	II	0.7
Drosera rotundifolia	.	.	2	1	2	.	III	0.8
Euphrasia scottica	.	.	3	2	.	3	III	1.3
Pedicularis sylvatica	1	2	.	3	.	.	III	1.0
Pinguicula vulgaris	3	2	3	3	.	1	V	2.0
Potentilla erecta	3	1	2	.	3	2	V	1.8
Ranunculus acris	.	3	3	3	.	.	III	1.5
R. flammula	1	.	.	.	.	3	II	0.7
Taraxacum officinale agg.	1	2	.	.	.	.	II	0.5
Blindia acuta	1	1	.	2	.	.	III	0.7
Breutelia chrysocoma	3	1	3	2	3	.	V	2.0
Bryum pseudotriquetrum	1	2	.	.	.	.	II	0.5
Campylium stellatum	5	4	5	6	6	5	V	5.2
Ctenidium molluscum	2	.	.	2	.	5	III	1.5
**Drepanocladus revolvens*	4	1	2	.	5	.	IV	2.0
Mnium punctatum	1	2	.	.	.	.	II	0.5
Scorpidium scorpioides	4	.	3	4	.	.	III	1.8
Riccardia pinguis	.	.	1	.	2	.	II	0.5
Total number of species (62)	31	27	24	26	23	18		

Mean number of species per relevé = 24.8.

* var. *intermedius* in 1, 2, 3, and 5.

ADDITIONAL SPECIES IN LIST

1. *Calluna vulgaris* 1, *Thalictrum alpinum* 4, *Fissidens adianthoides* 2.
2. *Triglochin palustre* 1, *Caltha palustris* 3, *Pedicularis palustris* 2, *Acrocladium cuspidatum* 2, *Mnium seligeri* 2.
3. *Cynosurus cristatus* 1, *Parnassia palustris* 2, *Prunella vulgaris* 2, *Rhinanthus minor* 1, *Viola riviniana* 2, *Philonotis fontana* 1, *Sphagnum squarrosum* 1, *Thuidium tamariscinum* 3.
4. *Deschampsia cespitosa* 3, *Festuca rubra* 2, *Juncus effusus* +, *Polygala serpyllifolia* +, *Sphagnum palustre* 1.
5. *Potamogeton polygonifolius* 4, *Pinguicula lusitanica* 3, *Riccardia sinuata* 1.
6. *Molinia caerulea* 4, *Succisa pratensis* 2.

LOCALITIES

1. Sgùrr na Coinnich; 2. Preshal More; 3. Faoilean; 4. Ben Tianavaig; 5. near Uig; 6. Kyleakin.

TABLE 4.25

Class	SCHEUCHZERIO-CARICETEA FUSCAE																										
Order	TOFIELDIETALIA																										
Alliance	**Eriophorion latifoliae**																										
Association	*Eriophorum latifolium–Carex hostiana*													*Schoenus nigricans*									*Carex–Saxifraga aizoides nodum*				
	1	2	3	4	5	6	7	8	9	10	11			12	13	14	15	16	17	18			19	20	21	22	
Reference Number	B67	B67	B68	B68	B68	B68	B68	B68	B68	B68	B67			B67	B68	B67	B68	B67	B67	B68			B67	B68	B68	B68	
	011	113	012	024	322	349	350	359	124	123	044			010	255	043	021	083	039	321			075	234	105	107	
Map Reference	555	597	587	472	753	412	412	415	503	502	601			555	605	602	472	528	707	753			594	544	449	449	
	614	198	007	306	260	222	222	199	567	567	200			614	202	202	304	187	158	260			200	215	699	699	
Altitude (feet)	350	100	200	300	200	150	150	250	700	750	150			350	50	50	250	750	100	200			100	800	1550	1550	
Aspect (degrees)	45	0	135	180	0	270	270	270	90	45	0			90	.	.	.	270	270	0			0	135	90	90	
Slope (degrees)	5	10	10	5	5	3	3	10	5	5	.			5	.	.	.	5	2	5			5	5	5	5	
Cover (per cent)	50	50	100	60	50	60	75	85	100	100	70			100	100	80	100	100	100	100			40	60	40	60	
Plot area (square metres)	4	4	4	4	4	4	4	4	4	4	4	C	D	4	4	4	4	4	4	4	C	D	4	4	4	4	D
Calluna vulgaris	.	.	.	3	.	.	.	.	+	2	.	II	0.5	.	.	.	2	.	.	.	I	0.3	.	.	.	.	
Erica tetralix	2	.	2	3	.	1	2	1	3	1	.	IV	1.4	.	1	.	2	.	1	4	III	1.1	.	.	.	.	
Myrica gale	.	.	4	3	.	.	.	.	2	4	4	III	1.5	2	3	.	4	.	.	.	III	1.3	.	.	.	.	
Equisetum palustre	.	2	.	.	.	.	.	.	4	4	.	II	0.9	.	.	.	.	.	.	.			.	.	.	.	
Selaginella selaginoides	1	3	3	.	.	1	2	3	2	.	3	IV	1.6	2	4	1	2	3	2	.	V	2.0	2	3	.	3	2.0
Festuca ovina	.	2	.	.	4	3	3	.	.	.	2	III	1.3	.	.	.	.	.	.	.			3	.	3	.	1.5
F. rubra	.	.	.	.	.	.	.	.	.	.	.			.	.	.	.	.	.	.			.	.	4	3	1.8
F. vivipara	.	.	.	.	.	.	.	.	.	.	.			.	.	.	.	.	.	.			2	5	3	3	3.3
Molinia caerulea	.	.	3	2	.	2	.	.	.	3	4	III	1.3	.	3	.	3	.	2	2	III	1.4	.	4	.	.	1.0
Carex demissa	3	4	5	3	3	2	3	3	3	2	3	V	3.1	.	.	.	.	.	.	.			3	2	5	6	4.0
C. dioica	2	2	.	2	4	3	2	2	.	3	.	IV	1.8	.	.	.	2	.	2	.	II	0.6	.	1	3	.	1.0
C. echinata	2	.	4	2	.	.	.	.	.	4	2	III	1.3	4	2	.	4	2	1	.	IV	1.9	.	2	2	.	1.0
C. flacca	3	3	5	4	3	.	.	.	.	3	1	IV	2.0	.	.	.	.	1	.	.	I	0.1	5	3	4	5	4.3
C. hostiana	4	4	3	3	3	4	3	4	4	4	4	V	3.6	.	2	3	.	.	.	.	II	0.7	.	3	.	.	0.8
C. lepidocarpa	.	5	.	.	.	.	.	.	.	.	5	I	0.9	.	.	3	.	.	.	.	I	0.4	2	.	.	.	0.5
C. nigra	1	.	.	+	.	3	.	.	+	3	.	III	0.8	.	4	2	4	.	.	.	III	1.4	.	.	.	.	
C. panicea	5	3	4	4	2	3	3	4	3	4	4	V	3.5	4	3	3	4	4	4	3	V	3.6	3	3	4	4	3.5
C. pulicaris	.	3	.	3	.	3	.	.	.	2	2	III	1.2	.	1	.	.	.	.	.	I	0.1	2	4	3	.	2.3
C. rostrata	.	.	.	.	.	.	.	.	+	7	.	I	0.7	.	2	4	5	.	.	.	III	1.6	3	.	.	.	0.8
Eleocharis palustris	.	.	.	.	.	.	.	.	5	.	.	I	0.4	.	.	2	.	.	.	.	I	0.3	.	.	.	.	
E. quinqueflora	2	3	2	.	.	4	4	3	6	3	3	V	2.7	.	2	2	.	.	3	4	III	1.6	.	2	.	.	0.5
Eriophorum angustifolium	.	.	.	.	.	.	2	.	.	.	.	I	0.2	.	.	.	3	2	1	.	III	0.9	.	1	.	.	0.3
E. latifolium	7	8	6	7	8	6	6	8	7	7	6	V	6.9	3	2	+	.	.	.	.	II	0.9	.	.	.	.	
Juncus articulatus	.	.	5	3	4	4	3	1	.	.	.	III	1.8	.	.	.	.	.	.	.			2	4	.	.	1.5
J. kochii	1	.	2	4	.	.	.	3	.	4	.	III	1.3	.	.	.	3	.	.	.	I	0.4	.	.	.	.	
J. triglumis	.	.	.	.	.	.	.	.	.	.	.			.	.	.	.	.	.	.			.	.	4	4	2.0
Narthecium ossifragum	.	.	1	3	.	.	1	2	3	.	1	III	0.9	.	.	2	3	3	.	3	III	1.6	.	1	.	.	0.3
Potamogeton polygonifolius	3	.	3	.	.	.	1	.	4	2	2	III	1.4	3	.	2	.	.	2	.	III	1.0	.	.	.	.	
Rhynchospora alba	.	.	.	.	.	.	.	.	.	.	.			.	1	.	+	.	1	.	II	0.4	.	.	.	.	
Schoenus nigricans	4	5	6	6	5	5	6	6	6	5	5	V	5.4	8	8	9	9	8	8	9	V	8.4	4	5	.	.	2.3
Triglochin palustre	.	3	+	.	.	1	.	.	.	1	2	III	0.7	.	.	.	.	.	.	.			.	.	.	.	
Drosera anglica	.	.	.	.	3	3	3	4	.	.	4	III	1.5	2	4	2	4	.	3	4	V	2.7	.	1	.	.	0.3
D. rotundifolia	.	.	3	.	.	.	1	3	2	.	.	II	0.8	.	.	2	3	3	2	2	IV	1.7	.	.	.	.	
Euphrasia scottica	.	1	1	.	.	.	1	.	.	3	2	III	0.7	.	.	.	.	.	.	.			2	4	1	3	2.5
Hypericum pulchrum	.	.	1	.	.	.	.	.	.	.	1	I	0.2	.	.	.	.	.	.	.			1	.	.	.	0.3
Menyanthes trifoliata	.	.	.	.	.	.	.	.	5	+	1	I	0.6	.	4	3	.	.	.	.	II	1.0	.	.	.	.	
Pedicularis palustris	.	2	1	.	.	.	.	.	.	.	+	II	0.4	.	.	.	.	.	.	.			.	.	.	.	
Pinguicula lusitanica	.	.	3	.	3	.	.	.	4	.	.	II	0.9	.	.	.	.	.	.	1	I	0.1	.	.	.	.	
P. vulgaris	3	1	3	3	2	2	4	2	.	1	2	V	2.1	1	2	.	1	2	2	2	V	1.4	4	2	4	3	3.3
Plantago maritima	.	4	.	.	.	.	.	.	.	.	3	I	0.6	.	.	.	.	.	.	.			1	.	.	.	0.3

Potentilla erecta	.	.	.	.	.	.	.	I	.	2	.	I	0.3	.	.	.	.	I	.	.	I	0.1	.	.	.	.	
Ranunculus flammula	.	.	2	.	.	.	.	.	.	I	.	I	0.3	.	.	.	.	.	.	.			.	.	3	3	1.5
Saxifraga aizoides	.	.	.	.	.	.	.	.	.	.	.			.	.	.	.	.	.	.			5	8	7	7	6.8
Succisa pratensis	.	3	2	+	.	.	I	3	.	I	+	IV	1.1	.	I	.	.	.	.	I	II	0.1	.	.	.	.	
Thalictrum alpinum	.	.	.	.	.	.	.	.	.	.	2	I	0.2	.	.	.	.	.	.	.			2	.	2	3	1.8
Thymus drucei	.	.	.	.	.	.	.	.	.	.	.			.	.	.	.	.	.	.			3	I	.	.	1.0
Utricularia minor	+	.	+	.	.	.	+	.	.	.	.	II	0.3	.	3	.	2	.	.	I	III	0.9	.	.	.	.	
Acrocladium sarmentosum	.	.	.	.	.	2	.	.	+	.	.	I	0.3	.	.	.	.	.	.	.			.	.	.	.	
A. trifarium	3	.	.	3	.	.	.	.	.	.	.	I	0.5	.	.	.	.	.	.	.			.	.	.	.	
Blindia acuta	.	2	+	2	3	I	3	3	.	.	+	IV	1.5	.	.	.	.	I	.	.	I	0.1	3	3	6	6	4.5
Breutelia chrysocoma	.	.	.	.	.	.	2	2	I	.	.	II	0.5	.	.	.	I	.	.	.	I	0.1	.	.	.	.	
Bryum pseudotriquetrum	.	.	3	2	.	.	I	.	.	.	3	II	0.8	.	.	.	.	.	.	.			2	I	.	.	1.0
Campylium stellatum	3	3	4	4	4	4	4	4	4	5	4	V	3.9	4	3	4	3	4	3	5	V	3.7	4	3	5	4	4.0
Cinclidium stygium	.	2	.	.	.	.	.	.	.	.	4	I	0.5	.	.	.	.	.	.	.			.	.	.	.	
Cratoneuron commutatum	.	6	.	.	.	.	.	.	.	.	3	I	0.8	.	.	.	.	.	.	.			4	5	.	I	2.5
Ctenidium molluscum	.	.	2	.	.	.	.	3	.	I	3	II	0.8	.	.	.	.	.	.	.			3	.	.	2	1.3
**Drepanocladus revolvens*	.	2	4	.	.	3	.	+	3	4	4	III	1.9	.	.	2	2	.	.	.	II	0.6	4	3	4	I	3.0
Fissidens adianthoides	.	2	.	.	.	.	.	.	.	3	I	II	0.5	.	I	.	.	.	.	.	I	0.1	.	2	.	.	0.5
Scorpidium scorpioides	6	6	4	5	2	5	4	4	4	3	5	V	4.4	3	6	5	3	5	4	3	V	4.1	2	5	3	2	3.0
Sphagnum contortum	.	.	+	.	.	.	.	.	+	+	2	II	0.5	.	.	4	.	.	.	.	I	0.6	.	.	.	.	
S. plumulosum	.	.	.	.	.	.	.	+	+	.	.	I	0.2	.	.	.	.	.	.	.			.	.	.	.	
†**S. subsecundum**	3	.	.	2	.	.	.	I	5	I	.	III	1.1	2	4	5	3	2	I	.	V	2.4	.	.	.	.	
Splachnum ampullaceum	.	.	.	.	.	I	I	I	.	.	.	II	0.3	.	.	.	.	.	.	.			.	.	.	.	
Tortella tortuosa	.	.	.	.	.	.	.	I	.	.	I	I	0.2	.	.	.	.	.	.	.			.	.	.	.	
Pellia epiphylla	.	.	.	.	.	.	.	.	I	I	I	II	0.3	.	.	.	+	.	.	.	I	0.1	.	.	.	.	
Riccardia pinguis	.	.	I	I	.	I	.	2	.	.	.	III	0.5	.	.	.	.	.	.	.			I	I	2	2	1.5
Total number of species (98)	20	28	35	26	15	25	26	31	31	36	50			12	23	20	25	14	17	15			30	28	22	22	

Mean number of species per relevé = 29.4.
Total number of species in association = 83.

Mean number of species per relevé = 18.0
Total number of species in association = 41.

Mean number of species per relevé = 25.5.
Total number of species in nodum = 47.

* var. *intermedius* in 2, 3, 6, 8, 9, 10, 11, 14, 15, and 22. † var. *inundatum* in 4, 8, 9, 13, 14, and 15. var. *auriculatum* in 1, 12, 16, and 17.

ADDITIONAL SPECIES IN LIST

2. *Mnium undulatum* 2, *Chara* sp. 4.
3. *Prunella vulgaris* 1.
6. *Splachnum sphaericum* 1.
8. *Riccardia multifida* 1.
9. *Empetrum nigrum* +, *Carex limosa* 3, *Sphagnum palustre* 1.
10. *Carex curta*, *Sphagnum warnstorfianum* 1.
11. *Dactylorchis purpurella* 1, *Platanthera bifolia* 1, *Linum catharticum* +, *Acrocladium cuspidatum* 1, *Barbula fallax* +, *Cratoneuron filicinum* 1, *Mnium seligeri* +, *Orthothecium rufescens* 2, *Philonotis calcarea* 2, *Pseudoscleropodium purum* 1, *Leiocolea bantriensis* 2, *L. muelleri* 2, *Scapania aspera* 2.
13. *Phragmites communis* +.
19. *Dryas octopetala* 2, *Parnassia palustris* 1, *Gymnostomum recurvirostrum* 2.
21. *Juncus biglumis* +, *Lotus corniculatus* 3.
22. *Viola riviniana* 2, *Anthelia julacea* 2, *Riccardia sinuata* +.

LOCALITIES

1, 12, 20. Blà Bheinn; 2, 19. Ben Suardal; 3. Aird of Sleat; 4, 15. Loch an Eilean; 5, 18. Kyleakin; 6, 7. Glenbrittle; 8. Sgùrr Sgumain; 9, 10. Carn Liath; 11, 13, 14. Loch Cill Chriosd; 16. Slat Bheinn; 17. E. side, Loch na Dal; 21, 22. Sgùrr Mor.

TABLE 4.26

Class	OXYCOCCO-SPHAGNETEA															
Order	ERICETALIA TETRALICIS															
Alliance	**Ericion tetralicis**															
Association	*Trichophoreto–Callunetum*															
Facies	*Sphagnum–rich*						*Rhacomitrium–rich*					*Lichen–rich*				
	1	2	3	4	5	6	7	8	9	10	11	12	13	14		
Reference Number	B67	B67	B68	B68	B68	B68	B68	B67	B67	B68	B67	B68	B67	B67		
	079	112	087	180	333	029	009	023	111	049	122	332	095	060		
Map Reference	547	241	506	165	504	500	416	540	241	438	435	504	657	752		
	183	551	557	543	286	535	182	208	551	675	606	286	113	210		
Altitude (feet)	300	300	700	650	1300	1000	300	1400	300	950	1000	1200	400	1000		
Aspect (degrees)	225	315	45	45	0	90	90	135	315	.	0	0	270	225		
Slope (degrees)	5	5	4	5	5	2	8	10	5	E.	10	15	10	10		
Cover (per cent)	100	100	100	100	100	100	90	80	80	100	100	90	70	70		
Plot area (square metres)	4	4	4	4	4	4	4	4	4	4	4	4	4	4	C	D
Calluna vulgaris	6	5	7	4	7	5	5	5	7	6	7	7	6	5	V	5.9
Empetrum nigrum	.	.	.	3	2	2	.	.	2	.	3	.	.	1	III	0.9
Erica cinerea	.	.	.	.	.	.	4	.	2	2	.	4	2	.	II	1.0
E. tetralix	3	3	4	4	3	2	3	.	3	3	3	+	3	3	V	2.7
Vaccinium myrtillus	.	.	.	.	1	2	.	.	.	.	2	.	.	2	II	0.5
Lycopodium selago	.	.	.	.	.	.	.	.	.	1	1	.	.	.	I	0.1
Agrostis canina	.	.	.	.	.	.	1	.	.	.	.	1	.	.	I	0.1
Molinia caerulea	3	2	.	3	.	3	3	.	3	.	.	2	4	.	III	1.6
Nardus stricta	.	.	.	.	2	.	.	.	.	.	.	2	.	.	I	0.3
Carex binervis	.	.	.	.	.	.	.	.	4	.	.	1	+	.	II	0.4
C. echinata	1	.	.	.	1	.	.	.	1	.	.	.	.	.	II	0.2
C. nigra	.	2	.	.	.	1	.	.	1	.	.	.	.	.	II	0.3
C. panicea	.	.	.	.	.	.	2	.	2	.	.	.	.	+	II	0.4
C. rostrata	.	.	3	.	.	2	.	.	.	.	.	.	.	.	I	0.4
**Dactylorchis maculata*	.	+	.	.	.	.	+	.	.	.	.	.	.	.	I	0.1
Eriophorum angustifolium	3	3	3	4	3	3	.	.	2	4	2	+	.	3	IV	2.2
E. vaginatum	3	4	4	4	4	4	.	.	5	.	2	.	.	3	IV	2.4
Juncus squarrosus	3	2	.	.	4	2	4	5	3	+	1	.	2	2	IV	2.1
Narthecium ossifragum	1	.	3	1	.	+	3	.	.	3	2	.	.	2	III	1.1
Trichophorum cespitosum	8	6	7	7	7	7	7	8	8	8	6	8	8	7	V	7.3
Drosera rotundifolia	.	.	1	2	.	3	.	.	.	2	.	.	.	1	II	0.6
Pedicularis sylvatica	.	+	.	.	.	.	1	.	.	.	.	.	2	.	II	0.3
Pinguicula vulgaris	.	.	.	3	.	.	.	2	.	2	.	.	.	.	II	0.5
Polygala serpyllifolia	+	2	.	.	.	.	.	2	1	.	.	1	.	2	III	0.6
Potentilla erecta	3	4	3	3	3	4	3	3	3	3	3	3	3	2	V	3.1
Succisa pratensis	.	.	.	1	.	.	.	.	.	.	.	.	2	.	II	0.2
Breutelia chrysocoma	1	.	.	.	.	1	.	2	.	2	1	.	1	.	III	0.6
Campylopus atrovirens	1	.	3	.	.	.	1	4	.	.	1	2	.	.	III	0.9
‡*C. flexuosus*	2	.	+	.	.	.	1	.	.	1	.	3	1	.	III	0.9

C. setifolius	+	.	2	.	.	.	.	.	.	.	.	1	.	.	II	0.3
Dicranella heteromalla	.	.	.	.	.	.	.	.	.	.	.	2	.	1	I	0.2
Dicranum scoparium	3	.	.	+	.	.	.	1	.	.	.	.	1	.	II	0.4
†*Hypnum cupressiforme*	3	.	.	.	.	3	.	1	2	.	4	2	3	1	III	1.4
Pleurozium schreberi	2	.	.	+	2	.	.	3	.	2	+	.	.	.	III	0.8
Polytrichum commune	.	.	.	.	3	+	.	.	.	.	.	.	.	.	I	0.3
Rhacomitrium lanuginosum	1	3	3	.	.	.	4	5	5	7	7	2	3	3	IV	3.1
Rhytidiadelphus loreus	.	.	.	.	3	3	.	.	.	.	.	.	.	.	I	0.4
Sphagnum capillaceum	.	.	.	.	.	.	.	.	3	3	3	2	3	4	III	1.3
S. compactum	2	.	.	.	.	.	.	.	.	.	.	3	1	2	II	0.6
S. imbricatum	+	.	.	.	.	.	.	.	.	.	+	.	.	.	I	0.1
S. palustre	.	3	.	5	5	3	.	.	.	.	2	.	.	3	III	1.5
S. papillosum	.	1	4	4	.	.	.	3	.	.	.	.	1	.	II	0.9
S. plumulosum	.	.	1	.	.	.	.	.	.	.	2	.	.	.	I	0.2
S. rubellum	4	3	4	3	6	5	.	.	.	.	.	.	1	.	III	1.9
S. tenellum	.	.	3	1	.	.	.	.	.	4	.	.	2	1	II	0.8
Cephalozia bicuspidata	.	.	.	.	.	.	2	.	.	.	.	1	.	.	I	0.2
Diplophyllum albicans	.	.	.	.	1	.	.	.	.	1	.	2	1	.	II	0.4
Lepidozia setacea	.	.	.	.	.	.	.	.	.	.	.	3	.	1	I	0.3
Lophozia ventricosa	.	.	.	.	1	.	.	.	.	.	.	.	.	1	I	0.1
Mylia taylori	.	.	.	.	1	.	1	.	.	+	.	.	1	1	II	0.4
Odontoschisma sphagni	1	1	1	.	.	.	1	.	.	.	1	1	.	.	III	0.4
Pleurozia purpurea	.	.	2	.	.	.	.	.	.	2	2	+	.	1	II	0.6
Scapania gracilis	.	.	.	.	.	.	.	.	.	.	1	.	2	.	I	0.2
Cladonia arbuscula	.	.	.	.	.	.	.	.	.	4	3	.	3	.	II	0.7
C. coccifera	1	.	.	.	.	.	.	.	.	1	.	3	3	2	II	0.7
C. uncialis	1	1	.	.	.	.	.	.	.	3	3	.	3	3	III	1.0
Total number of species (80)	26	20	19	18	21	21	23	13	19	25	26	26	31	31		

Mean number of species per relevé = 22.8.

* ssp. *ericetorum* in 2 and 7. † var. *ericetorum* in 1, 6, 8, 9, 10, 11, 12, 13, and 14. ‡ var. *zonatus* in 3.

ADDITIONAL SPECIES IN LIST

1. *Nowellia curvifolia* +.
2. *Campylopus brevipilus* 2, *Splachnum sphaericum* +.
5. *Festuca vivipara* 2, *Luzula sylvatica* 2.
6. *Hylocomium splendens* 3.
7. *Carex binervis* 2, *Melampyrum pratense* +, *Campylopus shawii* 3, *Pohlia nutans* 2, *Sphagnum strictum* 2.
9. *Juncus effusus* 2.
10. *Vaccinium vitis–idaea* 2, *Deschampsia flexuosa* 3.
11. *Tetraplodon mnioides* 1.
12. *Cladonia pyxidata* 1.
13. *Blechnum spicant* 2, *Cladonia digitata* 1, *C. floerkiana* 1, *C. rangiformis* 1, *Icmadophila ericetorum* 2.
14. *Campylopus introflexus* +, *Lophozia incisa* +, *Mylia anomala* 1, *Odontoschisma denudatum* 1, *Cladonia impexa* 1.

LOCALITIES

1. Kirkibost; 2, 9. Lovaig Bay; 3. Carn Liath; 4. Dunvegan Head; 5, 12. Druim na Ruaige; 6. The Storr; 7. S. of Glenbrittle; 8. Blà Bheinn; 10. Biod Biudhe; 11. Coire Amadal; 13. near Loch Meodal; 14. Glen Arroch.

TABLE 4.27

Class	OXYCOCCO–SPHAGNETEA
Order	ERICETALIA TETRALICIS
Alliance	**Ericion tetralicis**
Association	*Molinieto–Callunetum*

	1	2	3	4	5	6	7	8	9		
Reference Number	B68 008	B68 326	B67 050	B67 052	B67 084	B67 088	B67 080	B67 027	B68 181		
Map Reference	416 182	492 195	437 257	441 256	516 193	512 199	542 185	370 305	165 543		
Altitude (feet)	300	150	400	650	300	200	250	500	650		
Aspect (degrees)	90	270	270	225	270	270	270	225	45		
Slope (degrees)	12	15	15	15	15	12	15	5	5		
Cover (per cent)	100	100	100	100	100	100	100	100	100		
Plot area (square metres)	4	4	4	4	4	4	4	4	4	C	D
Calluna vulgaris	5	5	5	5	6	6	5	8	7	V	5.8
Empetrum nigrum	.	.	.	.	.	.	.	2	3	II	0.6
Erica cinerea	2	.	.	1	.	2	.	.	.	II	0.6
E. tetralix	.	4	3	3	1	3	2	2	4	V	2.4
Myrica gale	.	3	.	2	.	.	.	.	.	II	0.6
Deschampsia flexuosa	.	.	.	.	1	.	3	.	.	II	0.4
Molinia caerulea	7	8	8	6	7	6	8	5	7	V	6.9
Carex echinata	2	2	.	.	.	.	2	.	.	II	0.7
**Dactylorchis maculata*	1	.	.	.	.	.	.	.	1	II	0.2
Eriophorum vaginatum	3	.	.	.	.	.	.	3	3	II	1.0
Juncus squarrosus	.	.	1	1	.	3	.	1	+	III	0.8
Narthecium ossifragum	3	3	2	3	2	3	3	.	3	V	2.4
Schoenus nigricans	.	1	.	.	.	1	.	.	.	II	0.2
Trichophorum cespitosum	3	2	3	2	2	3	3	1	.	V	2.1
Drosera rotundifolia	2	1	.	.	.	2	.	.	2	III	0.8
Pedicularis sylvatica	2	.	2	2	+	2	2	.	.	IV	1.2
Polygala serpyllifolia	.	.	1	2	.	2	.	2	.	III	0.8
Potentilla erecta	3	2	3	3	3	3	3	3	4	V	3.0
Succisa pratensis	.	2	.	.	.	.	.	.	+	II	0.3
Breutelia chrysocoma	.	1	.	.	.	.	+	1	.	II	0.3
†*Campylopus atrovirens*	.	4	2	.	1	3	1	.	.	III	1.2
Hylocomium splendens	.	.	.	.	.	.	.	4	3	II	0.8
‡*Hypnum cupressiforme*	.	.	.	.	.	.	.	2	1	II	0.3
Rhacomitrium lanuginosum	.	3	3	4	2	2	1	.	.	IV	1.7
Sphagnum capillaceum	4	.	.	.	.	.	4	5	2	III	1.7
S. compactum	.	3	3	.	1	1	.	.	.	III	0.9
S. imbricatum	.	.	+	.	.	+	.	.	.	II	0.2
S. palustre	.	.	.	.	.	.	2	3	1	II	0.7
S. papillosum	3	.	.	.	.	.	.	3	.	II	0.7
S. plumulosum	2	.	.	.	.	2	.	.	.	II	0.4
S. recurvum	.	.	.	.	.	.	2	3	.	II	0.6
S. strictum	.	2	.	.	2	+	.	.	3	III	0.9
S. tenellum	.	.	1	1	.	1	.	4	.	III	0.8
Pleurozia purpurea	.	3	2	2	3	2	1	.	1	IV	1.6
Cladonia arbuscula	.	3	.	.	.	1	.	2	.	II	0.7
C. impexa	.	.	.	1	2	.	1	.	.	II	0.4
C. uncialis	.	2	.	.	3	+	.	2	.	III	0.9
Total number of species (59)	18	20	17	15	16	26	18	24	21		

Mean number of species per relevé = 19.4.

* ssp. *ericetorum* in 1 and 9. † var. *falcatus* in 2 and 6. ‡ var. *ericetorum* in 8 and 9.

ADDITIONAL SPECIES IN LIST

1. *Carex dioica* 1, *C. panicea* 2, *Pinguicula lusitanica* +, *Leucobryum glaucum* 2.
2. *Splachnum sphaericum* 1.
3. *Lycopodium selago* 1, *Melampyrum pratense* 2.
5. *Campylopus flexuosus* 1.
6. *Pinguicula vulgaris* 1, *Campylopus setifolius* 1, *C. shawii* 1, *Sphagnum molle* +.
7. *Thuidium tamariscinum* +.
8. *Dicranum scoparium* 3, *Rhytidiadelphus loreus* 2, *Sphagnum cuspidatum* 2, *Mylia taylori* 2, *Odontoschisma sphagni* 1.
9. *Selaginella selaginoides* +, *Eriophorum angustifolium* 2, *Plagiothecium undulatum* 3, *Pleurozium schreberi* 2.

LOCALITIES

1. Lochan Coir' a' Ghobhainn; 2. Loch Coruisk; 3, 4. Coire na Creiche; 5. Camasunary; 6. Sligachan; 7. Kirkibost; 8. Carbost; 9. Dunvegan Head.

TABLE 4.28

Class	OXYCOCCO–SPHAGNETEA
Order	SPHAGNETALIA MAGELLANICI
Alliance	**Erico–Sphagnion**
Association	*Trichophoreto–Eriophoretum*

	1	2	3	4	5	6	7	8	9	10	11	12	12	14	15		
Reference Number	B67	B67	B67	B68	B68	B68	B67	B68	B68	B68	B68	B67	B67	B67	B67		
	090	093	140	113	210	207	048	056	229	309	311	085	005	006	051		
Map Reference	540	657	472	385	398	675	618	488	676	493	748	516	561	558	440		
	177	113	306	414	336	205	198	302	203	282	258	193	216	214	256		
Altitude (feet)	150	400	250	500	350	200	500	25	200	100	100	200	100	250	600		
Aspect (degrees)	.	.	0	.	.	.	30	.	.	.	.	.	45	90	45		
Slope (degrees)	.	.	2	.	.	.	2	.	.	.	.	.	3	3	5		
Cover (per cent)	100	100	100	100	100	100	100	100	100	100	100	100	100	100	100		
Plot area (square metres)	4	4	4	4	4	4	4	4	4	4	4	4	4	4	4	C	D
Calluna vulgaris	5	3	5	4	6	7	6	5	7	3	4	6	6	7	5	V	5.3
Erica tetralix	4	3	3	4	4	4	3	3	4	3	4	3	3	3	3	V	3.4
Myrica gale	4	5	6	2	5	5	3	4	.	5	2	3	5	5	4	V	4.2
Deschampsia flexuosa	.	.	.	3	.	.	.	.	.	.	.	.	1	3	.	I	0 5
Molinia caerulea	4	3	5	4	5	5	3	4	5	6	5	4	5	5	3	V	4.4
Carex echinata	2	2	3	.	.	.	.	3	.	.	1	1	1	.	1	III	0.9
C. limosa	.	.	+	2	.	.	.	.	.	2	.	.	.	.	.	I	0.3
C. pauciflora	2	2	3	3	.	.	.	.	.	1	.	.	.	.	.	II	0.7
Eriophorum angustifolium	5	5	3	6	5	4	3	6	3	4	5	4	3	2	3	V	4.1
E. vaginatum	3	2	.	3	4	3	2	+	2	2	3	.	.	.	2	IV	1.8
Juncus squarrosus	1	.	2	.	.	.	.	2	.	.	.	2	.	.	.	II	0.5
Schoenus nigricans	2	.	+	.	.	.	.	.	.	4	.	.	.	2	.	II	0.6
Narthecium ossifragum	3	2	3	2	2	+	1	4	2	3	3	2	3	3	1	V	2.3
Rhynchospora alba	.	+	.	1	.	2	.	2	4	3	.	+	.	.	.	III	0.9
Trichophorum cespitosum	4	3	4	5	5	3	4	3	6	5	7	6	4	3	4	V	4.4
Drosera anglica	2	2	2	3	2	1	.	3	3	2	1	2	.	.	1	IV	1.6
D. rotundifolia	1	2	.	3	3	3	2	3	3	2	3	2	2	1	+	V	2.1
Menyanthes trifoliata	.	.	+	.	.	.	.	+	.	2	.	.	.	.	.	I	0.3
Pedicularis sylvatica	.	.	2	+	.	.	1	.	.	1	.	.	.	1	.	II	0.4
Pinguicula vulgaris	.	.	.	1	.	.	2	.	.	1	.	.	2	+	.	II	0 5
Polygala serpyllifolia	1	2	.	.	.	+	1	1	.	.	.	.	2	3	2	III	0.9
Potentilla erecta	2	.	.	1	2	+	2	3	.	2	2	2	3	1	2	IV	1.5
Aulacomnium palustre	.	1	.	.	.	.	.	.	.	.	1	.	.	.	.	I	0.1
Breutelia chrysocoma	.	1	2	.	.	.	.	.	.	1	.	.	2	.	.	II	0.4
**Campylopus atrovirens*	.	.	1	2	1	2	2	.	3	.	.	3	2	.	.	IV	1.1
C. flexuosus	.	.	.	.	.	1	.	.	.	.	1	.	.	.	.	I	0.1
C. setifolius	.	.	.	.	.	.	.	.	.	1	.	2	1	.	.	I	0.3
C. shawii	.	.	.	.	.	.	3	2	.	2	.	3	.	.	.	II	0.7
†*Hypnum cupressiforme*	.	.	2	.	.	.	+	.	.	1	1	.	.	2	.	II	0.5
Leucobryum glaucum	.	.	.	.	.	.	1	.	2	.	.	.	.	.	+	II	0.3
Rhacomitrium lanuginosum	.	3	2	3	3	3	.	.	6	4	.	3	3	+	3	IV	2.3
Sphagnum compactum	.	2	2	3	3	4	2	1	.	2	1	2	4	2	1	V	1.9
S. cuspidatum	.	3	.	3	.	3	1	2	.	.	.	.	.	.	.	II	0.8
S. imbricatum	3	4	1	2	.	.	.	.	3	.	.	3	.	.	.	II	1.1
S. magellanicum	.	.	.	5	3	3	.	.	4	.	3	.	.	.	.	II	1.2
S. palustre	4	3	.	.	.	.	2	5	.	2	.	2	.	.	.	II	1.2
S. papillosum	3	.	5	4	4	3	3	3	3	3	3	3	3	2	3	V	3.0
S. plumulosum	.	.	.	2	.	3	.	.	.	3	.	.	.	.	.	I	0.5
S. rubellum	5	5	4	5	4	4	4	5	3	4	3	3	5	4	4	V	4.1
S. strictum	.	.	.	.	.	.	+	.	.	.	.	1	.	.	.	I	0.1
‡*S. subsecundum*	.	1	+	3	2	.	2	4	.	1	.	2	1	1	.	IV	1.2
S. tenellum	.	.	.	.	3	2	2	.	.	.	.	1	.	.	2	II	0.7
Cephalozia bicuspidata	.	.	.	.	.	1	.	.	.	.	+	.	.	.	.	I	0.1
Diplophyllum albicans	.	.	.	.	.	1	.	.	.	1	2	.	.	.	.	I	0.3
Gymnocolea inflata	.	1	.	.	.	1	1	1	.	.	.	.	.	.	.	II	0.3
Lepidozia setacea	.	.	.	.	.	.	.	.	1	1	1	.	.	.	.	I	0.2
Odontoschisma sphagni	.	.	.	1	.	2	1	.	1	1	1	.	.	.	.	II	0.5
Pleurozia purpurea	1	2	2	1	3	3	2	2	4	2	2	3	3	2	2	V	2.3
Riccardia latifrons	.	.	.	.	.	1	.	.	1	1	.	.	.	.	.	I	0 2
Cladonia arbuscula	.	1	1	1	.	1	3	.	.	.	.	.	.	.	+	II	0 5
C. uncialis	.	3	3	1	2	2	3	.	1	.	1	.	.	.	.	III	1.1
Total number of species (73)	22	28	28	32	21	31	33	26	29	37	26	26	22	21	21		

Mean number of species per relevé = 26.9.

* var. *falcatus* in 12. † var. *ericetorum* in 3, 10, and 11. ‡ var. *auriculatum* in 2, 3, 4, 5, 7, 8, 10, 12, and 13.

ADDITIONAL SPECIES IN LIST

1. *Equisetum palustre* 1.
2. *Carex rostrata* 1.
3. *Lycopodium selago* +, *Carex dioica* 2, *Hylocomium splendens* 2.
4. *Lophozia ventricosa* 1.
6. *Mylia taylori* 1.
7. *Juncus effusus* 1, *Galium saxatile* +, *Polytrichum commune* +.
8. *Carex nigra* +.
9. *Empetrum nigrum* 3, *Dicranum scoparium* 1, *Pleurozium schreberi* 1, *Sphagnum fuscum* 3, *Calypogeia sphagnicola* +, *Cephalozia media* 1, *Mylia anomala* 2.
10. *Potamogeton polygonifolius* 2, *Utricularia minor* 1, *Cephalozia connivens* 1.
11. *Cephalozia macrostachya* +.

LOCALITIES

1. Kirkibost; 2. near Loch Meodal; 3. Loch nan Eilean; 4. Beinn a' Mhadaidh; 5. Uchd Mor; 6. Lochain Dubha; 7. Ben Suardal; 8. Loch Sligachan; 9. Loch Airigh na Saorach; 10. Sligachan; 11. Kyleakin; 12. Camasunary; 13, 14. Blà Bheinn; 15. Coire na Creiche.

TABLE 4.29

Class	OXYCOCCO-SPHAGNETEA						
Order	SPHAGNETALIA MAGELLANICI						
Alliance	**Erico-Sphagnion**						
Association	*Calluneto–Eriophoretum*						
	1	2	3	4	5		
Reference Number	B67	B68	B68	B68	B67		
	092	111	171	172	062		
Map Reference	657	446	222	222	756		
	113	708	417	417	212		
Altitude (feet)	400	900	1000	1000	1250		
Aspect (degrees)	270	.	180	180	.		
Slope (degrees)	3	.	2	3	.		
Cover (per cent)	100	100	100	100	100		
Plot area (square metres)	4	4	4	4	4	C	D
Calluna vulgaris	5	7	6	5	7	V	6.0
Empetrum nigrum	4	6	5	3	3	V	4.2
Erica tetralix	.	4	3	3	.	III	2.0
Vaccinium myrtillus	.	.	3	4	3	III	2.0
Molinia caerulea	3	3	2	2	2	V	2.4
Eriophorum angustifolium	4	3	4	3	3	V	3.4
E. vaginatum	7	7	8	8	7	V	7.4
Juncus squarrosus	3	.	2	1	2	IV	1.6
Trichophorum cespitosum	.	.	3	2	3	III	1.6
Polygala serpyllifolia	2	.	+	.	.	II	0.6
Potentilla erecta	3	.	3	.	2	III	1.6
Campylopus flexuosus	1	.	.	1	1	III	0.6
Dicranum scoparium	2	3	.	.	1	III	1.2
Hylocomium splendens	3	3	3	2	5	V	3.2
**Hypnum cupressiforme*	3	.	.	.	3	II	1.2
Pleurozium schreberi	2	3	2	2	1	V	2.0
Rhacomitrium lanuginosum	2	5	+	5	.	IV	2.6
Rhytidiadelphus loreus	.	4	3	1	3	IV	2.2
Sphagnum capillaceum	6	4	5	5	4	V	4.8
S. tenellum	4	.	3	4	.	III	2.2
Cladonia arbuscula	2	+	.	1	.	III	0.8
C. coccifera	3	.	.	.	1	II	0.8
C. uncialis	1	.	.	1	.	II	0.4
Total number of species (39)	24	16	20	18	22		

* var. *ericetorum* in 1 and 5. Mean number of species per relevé = 20.0.

ADDITIONAL SPECIES IN LIST

1. *Drosera rotundifolia* 1, *Leucobryum glaucum* 2, *Mylia taylori* 4, *Odontoschisma sphagni* 2, *Cladonia pyxidata* 3.
2. *Calypogeia muellerana* 1, *Cephalozia bicuspidata* +, *Diplophyllum albicans* 1.
3. *Erica cinerea* 2, *Carex echinata* 2, *Sphagnum papillosum* 3.
5. *Aulacomnium palustre* +, *Sphagnum fuscum* 2, *Lophozia incisa* 1, *Cladonia impexa* 1, *C. rangiformis* 1.

LOCALITIES

1. near Loch Meodal; 2. Coire Mhic Eachainn; 3, 4. Healaval Bheag; 5. Sgùrr na Coinnich.

TABLE 4.30

Class	MONTIO–CARDAMINETEA																	
Order	MONTIO–CARDAMINETALIA																	
Alliance	**Cardamino–Montion**																	
Association	*Philonoto–Saxifragetum stellaris*										*Koenigia islandica–Carex demissa nodum*					*Anthelia julacea banks*		
	1	2	3	4	5	6	7	8			9	10	11	12		13	14	
Reference number	B67 026	B67 123	B67 124	B67 021	B68 070	B68 106	B68 075	B68 072			B68 076	B68 034	B67 128	B67 133		B68 078	B67 058	
Map Reference	370 305	440 606	446 606	536 212	490 533	449 699	490 542	490 537			490 542	495 542	450 617	456 627		490 542	455 246	
Altitude (feet)	450	1200	1300	1900	1550	1550	2050	1800			2050	2250	1700	2000		2050	1800	
Aspect (degrees)	43	0	0	315	90	90	270	135			270	270	270	0		270	0	
Slope (degrees)	.	1	.	.	.	.	.	3			5	8	5	.		.	.	
Cover (per cent)	100	100	100	100	100	100	100	100			60	60	40	30		100	100	
Plot area (square metres)	4	4	4	4	4	4	4	4	C	D	4	4	4	4	D	4	4	D
Selaginella selaginoides	.	.	1	1	.	.	.	.	II	0.3	.	.	.	.		.	.	
Anthoxanthum odoratum	.	2	.	.	4	.	.	.	II	0.8	.	.	.	.		.	.	
Deschampsia cespitosa	.	4	3	.	3	4	3	.	IV	2.1	5	3	3	5	4.0	4	3	3.5
Festuca ovina	.	1	5	.	.	.	.	.	II	0.8	.	.	.	.		.	.	
F. rubra	3	.	2	.	5	4	.	.	III	1.8	.	.	.	.		.	.	
Poa subcaerulea	.	.	3	.	3	2	.	2	III	1.3	.	.	.	.		.	.	
Carex echinata	1	.	.	.	3	.	.	3	II	0.9	.	.	.	.		3	.	1.5
C. demissa	.	.	2	.	2	.	3	.	II	0.9	3	4	4	3	3.5	4	.	2.0
C. nigra	.	.	.	+	.	.	3	4	II	1.0	.	.	4	.		3	.	1.5
Juncus articulatus	.	.	.	.	1	.	.	3	II	0.5	.	.	.	.		.	.	
J. biglumis	.	.	.	.	.	.	+	1	II	0.3	3	5	2	.	2.5	.	.	
J. bulbosus	.	.	.	.	.	.	.	2	I	0.3	.	3	3	.	1.5	1	.	0.5
J. squarrosus	.	.	.	.	.	.	.	+	I	0.1	.	.	2	.	0.5	.	.	
J. triglumis	.	.	.	.	.	.	4	3	II	0.9	4	4	4	3	3.8	.	.	
Alchemilla xanthochlora	.	.	3	.	.	.	.	+	II	0.5	.	.	.	.		.	.	
Bellis perennis	.	.	2	.	+	.	.	.	II	0.4	.	.	.	.		.	.	
**Caltha palustris*	4	1	.	1	4	.	4	3	IV	2.1	.	.	.	.		.	.	
Cardamine flexuosa	.	1	1	.	4	3	.	2	IV	1.4	.	.	.	.		.	.	
Cerastium holosteoides	4	.	2	.	3	.	2	1	IV	1.5	.	.	.	.		.	1	0.5
Chrysosplenium oppositifolium	.	2	2	4	2	+	.	.	IV	1.4	.	.	.	.		.	.	
†*Cochlearia officinalis* agg.	.	.	.	.	.	.	3	.	I	0.4	.	1	.	.	0.3	.	.	
Epilobium alsinifolium	.	4	2	.	.	.	.	2	II	1.0	.	.	.	.		.	.	
E. anagallidifolium	.	.	3	.	2	4	.	3	III	1.5	.	.	.	.		.	.	
Euphrasia frigida	.	.	.	.	2	.	2	+	II	0.6	3	.	.	.	0.8	.	.	
Koenigia islandica	.	.	.	.	.	.	.	4	I	0.5	4	3	5	6	4.5	.	.	
Montia fontana* ssp. *fontana	6	6	5	6	7	4	.	5	V	4.9	.	.	.	.		.	.	
Pinguicula vulgaris	.	.	2	2	.	.	.	.	II	0.5	.	.	1	.	0.3	+	1	0.5

	1	2	3	4	5	6	7	8			9	10	11	12		13	14	
Prunella vulgaris	.	.	.	.	+	.	.	1	II	0.3	.	.	.	.		.	.	
Ranunculus acris	3	.	4	2	3	.	.	2	IV	1.8	.	3	.	.	0.8	2	.	1.0
R. flammula	.	.	.	.	3	3	.	.	II	0.8	.	.	.	.		1	.	0.5
Sagina procumbens	4	3	.	.	4	.	.	3	III	1.8	.	.	.	.		.	.	
S. saginoides	.	.	.	.	.	.	.	.			2	3	.	.	1.3	.	.	
Saxifraga stellaris	.	3	4	4	3	4	5	4	V	3.4	5	6	1	4	4.0	.	.	
Stellaria alsine	3	.	4	3	3	3	3	3	V	2.8	.	.	.	.		.	.	
Taraxacum officinale agg.	.	.	.	.	2	.	.	1	II	0.4	.	.	.	.		.	.	
Thalictrum alpinum	.	2	.	4	.	.	.	.	II	0.8	.	.	.	.		+	3	1.5
Acrocladium cuspidatum	4	2	4	3	3	.	1	.	IV	2.1	.	.	.	.		.	.	
A. sarmentosum	.	.	1	+	.	2	3	1	IV	1.0	5	4	5	.	3.5	5	.	2.5
Blindia acuta	.	2	.	.	.	.	.	.	I	0.3	6	5	6	8	6.3	.	.	
Bryum pseudotriquetrum	3	.	4	.	3	3	4	3	IV	2.5	.	.	.	.		.	.	
B. weigelii	.	.	.	+	4	5	.	3	III	1.6	.	.	.	.		.	.	
Cratoneuron filicinum	6	3	3	.	4	.	4	5	IV	3.1	.	.	.	.		.	.	
Dicranella palustris	.	4	4	5	+	5	4	5	V	3.5	.	3	.	.	0.8	.	.	
Drepanocladus exannulatus	.	.	.	.	.	7	3	+	II	1.4	.	.	.	.		.	.	
D. revolvens	.	.	.	2	.	.	.	1	I	0.4	.	.	3	.	0.8	.	.	
Mnium punctatum	.	.	1	.	3	.	.	.	II	0.5	.	.	.	.		.	.	
M. rugicum	.	.	1	.	.	.	.	3	II	0.5	.	.	.	.		.	.	
Oncophorus virens	.	.	.	.	.	.	2	+	II	0.4	.	.	.	.		.	.	
Philonotis fontana	8	8	8	7	7	6	7	9	V	7.5	.	4	.	.	1.0	.	2	1.0
‡*Sphagnum subsecundum*	.	.	.	3	+	.	+	1	III	0.8	3	.	.	.	0.8	5	2	3.5
Anthelia julacea	.	.	.	.	.	.	.	.			.	.	.	.		9	8	8.5
Chiloscyphus pallescens	.	5	3	2	+	.	.	.	III	1.4	.	.	.	.		.	.	
Marsupella aquatica	.	.	.	.	.	.	+	.	I		4	.	.	.	1.0	+	2	1.0
Scapania undulata	.	2	.	2	5	4	2	2	IV	2.1	3	8	2	3	4.0	+	2	1.0
Solenostoma cordifolium	.	7	.	4	+	.	4	4	IV	2.5	.	.	.	.		.	.	
Total number of species (89)	18	20	28	23	37	19	27	42			13	15	15	10		15	13	

Mean number of species per relevé = 28.8.
Total number of species in association = 80.

Mean number of species per relevé = 13.3.
Total number of species in *nodum* = 26.

Total number of species = 21.

* ssp. *minor* in 1, 2, 4, 5, 7, and 8. † ssp. *alpina* in 7 and 10. ‡ var. *auriculatum* in 4, 5, 7, 8, 9, 13, and 14.

ADDITIONAL SPECIES IN LIST

1. *Equisetum palustre* 1, *Trifolium repens* 1, *Mnium undulatum* 2, *Rhytidiadelphus squarrous* 2, *Sphagnum recurvum* 1, *Conocephalum conicum* 3.
2. *Pellia* sp. 2.
3. *Lotus corniculatus* 3.
4. *Geum rivale* 1, *Brachythecium plumosum* 5, *Cratoneuron commutatum* 1.
5. *Carex flacca* 2, *Viola riviniana* 2, *Cinclidium stygium* 3, *Sphagnum plumulosum* 1.
6. *Agrostis canina* 3, *Viola palustris* 1.
7. *Carex panicea* 1, *Acrocladium trifarium* +, *Scorpidium scorpioides* 5, *Riccardia pinguis* 1, *Scapania paludosa* 3, *Tritomaria polita* +.
8. *Festuca vivipara* 2, *Poa trivialis* 1, *Myosotis scorpioides* +, *Thymus drucei* 2, *Anomobryum filiforme* 1, *Pohlia wahlenbergii* var. *glacialis* 2.
11. *Carex dioica* 1.
12. *Deschampsia alpina* 2, *Luzula spicata* 3, *Rhacomitrium heterostichum* 3.
13. *Plantago maritima* 3.
14. *Saussurea alpina* 2, *Campylopus atrovirens* 1, *Polytrichum alpinum* 3, *Marsupella emarginata* 2.

LOCALITIES

1. Carbost; 2, 3. Beinn an Laoigh; 4. Blà Bheinn; 5. Bealach Beag; 6. Sgùrr Mor; 7, 8, 9, 10, 13. The Storr; 11, 12. Beinn Edra; 14. Coire na Creiche.

TABLE 4.31

Class	MONTIO–CARDAMINETEA													
Order	MONTIO–CARDAMINETALIA													
Alliance	**Cratoneurion commutati**													
Association	*Cratoneuron commutatum–Saxifraga aizoides nodum*					*Saxifragetum aizoidis*								
	1	2	3	4		5	6	7	8	9	10	11		
Reference Number	B68	B68	B67	B68		B67	B67	B67	B67	B68	B68	B68		
	090	091	007	232		089	016	018	019	237	239	109		
Map Reference	518	518	560	557		520	542	540	538	539	537	443		
	604	604	217	216		198	217	215	214	216	213	706		
Altitude (feet)	75	75	250	350		650	1100	1300	1400	1500	1600	1600		
Aspect (degrees)	0	0	0	0		225	45	45	0	315	0	45		
Slope (degrees)	85	85	90	80		70	60	70	70	75	75	70		
Cover (per cent)	100	100	100	100		100	100	100	100	100	100	75		
Plot area (square metres)	4	4	4	4	D	4	4	4	4	4	4	4	C	D
Asplenium viride	.	.	.	.		+	3	.	.	3	.	+	III	1.1
Cystopteris fragilis	.	.	.	.		.	3	3	.	3	2	2	IV	1.9
Selaginella selaginoides	.	3	.	.	0.8	2	+	2	3	3	3	3	V	2.4
Anthoxanthum odoratum	.	.	.	.		.	.	1	.	.	2	.	II	0.4
Deschampsia cespitosa	.	.	.	.		3	3	3	2	3	4	.	V	2.6
Festuca ovina	3	.	.	.	0.8	3	.	.	.	.	.	3	II	0.9
F. rubra	4	3	3	3	3.3	3	4	2	+	1	2	.	V	1.9
F. vivipara	.	2	.	1	0.8	.	.	.	1	.	3	3	III	1.0
Carex flacca	.	.	.	.		2	.	.	3	.	3	4	III	1.7
C. panicea	.	.	.	.		.	.	.	.	2	2	.	III	0.6
C. pulicaris	.	.	.	2	0.5	3	.	.	2	4	2	3	IV	2.0
Alchemilla alpina	.	.	.	.		1	4	.	4	1	.	.	III	1.4
A. glabra	.	.	.	.		2	3	2	3	3	4	3	V	2.9
Angelica sylvestris	.	2	.	.	0.5	.	2	.	.	2	4	2	III	1.4
Chrysosplenium oppositifolium	3	4	.	.	1.8	.	.	4	.	.	.	.	I	0.6
Crepis paludosa	2	3	.	.	1.3	.	.	.	.	.	2	.	I	0.3
Euphrasia officinalis agg.	.	3	.	.	0.8	.	.	.	.	.	1	2	II	0.4
Geum rivale	.	.	.	.		.	1	.	.	1	2	.	III	0.6
Hypericum pulchrum	.	.	1	2	0.8	2	.	.	.	.	.	.	I	0.3
Leontodon autumnalis	.	.	.	1	0.3	.	.	.	.	1	.	.	I	0.1
Oxyria digyna	.	.	.	.		.	1	+	.	1	3	.	III	0.9
Parnassia palustris	.	.	.	.		.	1	2	.	2	.	.	III	0.7
Pinguicula vulgaris	1	2	3	4	2.5	2	2	.	3	2	2	3	V	2.0
Ranunculus acris	.	.	.	.		1	2	3	1	3	3	.	V	1.9
Saussurea alpina	.	.	.	.		.	.	.	.	.	2	2	II	0.6
Saxifraga aizoides	4	5	5	6	5.0	7	8	8	7	8	8	7	V	7.6
S. oppositifolia	.	.	.	.		4	3	3	5	6	1	2	V	3.4

Sedum rosea	.	.	.	2	0.5	1	+	.	2	4	4	.	IV	1.7
Thalictrum alpinum	.	.	.	.		.	.	.	2	+	2	4	III	1.3
Thymus drucei	.	.	2	.	0.5	2	.	.	.	.	.	.	I	0.3
Trollius europaeus	.	.	.	.		.	.	.	1	.	3	.	II	0.6
Acrocladium cuspidatum	.	.	.	.		2	.	3	.	1	.	.	III	0.9
Amphidium mougeotii	.	.	.	.		.	2	.	.	.	4	.	II	0.9
Anoectangium aestivum	.	.	.	3	0.8	.	2	2	.	4	2	1	IV	1.6
Barbula fallax	.	.	.	.		3	.	.	.	.	1	.	II	0.6
Blindia acuta	.	.	2	3	1.3	3	.	3	3	3	5	3	V	2.9
Breutelia chrysocoma	.	.	1	1	0.5	.	.	.	5	.	.	.	I	0.7
Bryum pseudotriquetrum	.	1	3	2	1.5	1	2	.	.	4	1	3	IV	1.6
Campylium stellatum	.	.	.	4	1.0	.	.	4	.	.	.	.	I	0.6
Cratoneuron commutatum	9	9	9	8	8.8	4	.	2	.	1	.	1	III	1.1
Ctenidium molluscum	.	2	3	4	2.3	5	5	4	.	5	4	3	IV	3.7
Dichodontium pellucidum	.	.	1	+	0.3	.	.	.	.	.	.	.		
Ditrichum flexicaule	.	.	.	.		.	.	2	.	.	.	1	II	0.4
Drepanocladus revolvens	2	2	3	2	2.3	.	.	.	.	3	.	.	I	0.4
Fissidens adianthoides	.	.	.	.		.	.	.	.	.	3	2	II	0.7
F. cristatus	.	.	2	.	0.5	.	.	.	.	2	.	.	I	0.3
Gymnostomum aeruginosum	5	2	.	.	1.8	.	.	.	.	2	.	1	II	0.4
G. recurvirostrum	.	1	2	3	1.5	.	.	.	.	2	.	.	I	0.3
Mnium punctatum	.	.	2	.	0.5	.	.	2	.	.	1	.	II	0.4
Orthothecium rufescens	.	.	.	.		.	5	3	4	6	3	8	V	4.1
Tortella tortuosa	.	.	.	3	0.8	2	.	.	.	3	.	.	II	0.7
Conocephalum conicum	.	.	1	1	0.5	.	.	.	.	.	.	.		
Leiocolea muelleri	.	.	.	.		.	2	.	.	1	.	.	II	0.4
Pellia epiphylla	.	3	2	.	1.3	.	.	.	.	.	1	.	I	0.1
Plagiochila asplenioides	.	.	.	.		.	.	.	.	3	1	.	II	0.6
Plectocolea hyalina	.	.	.	1	0.3	.	.	.	.	.	1	.	I	0.1
Preissia quadrata	4	.	.	.	1.0	1	2	.	.	3	3	+	IV	1.4
Riccardia pinguis	3	3	1	1	2.0	1	2	.	.	1	4	1	IV	1.3
R. sinuata	1	.	.	.	0.3	.	.	.	.	.	1	.	I	0.1
Total number of species (89)	13	19	19	26		30	24	22	20	45	43	28		

Mean number of species per relevé = 19.3.
Total number of species in *nodum* = 43.

Mean number of species per relevé = 30.3.
Total number of species in association = 81.

ADDITIONAL SPECIES IN LIST

1. *Valeriana officinalis* 3.
2. *Rhinanthus minor* agg. 1, *Philonotis calcarea* 2.
3. *Scapania undulata* 2.
4. *Carex hostiana* 1, *Linum catharticum* +, *Dicranum scoparium* 1, *Solenostoma triste* +.
5. *Schoenus nigricans* 2, *Lotus corniculatus* 1, *Barbula ferruginascens* 2, *Eucladium verticillatum* 1, *Neckera crispa* 3.
7. *Cololejeunea calcarea* 1.
8. *Potentilla erecta* 1, *Viola riviniana* 2.
9. *Polystichum lonchitis* 3, *Anemone nemorosa* 3, *Filipendula ulmaria* 2, *Rumex acetosa* 4, *Succisa pratensis* 1, *Pohlia cruda* 1, *Scapania aspera* 2, *Solenostoma sphaerocarpoidea* 1, *Tritomaria quinquedentata* 1.
10. *Cochlearia officinalis* agg. 1, *Dicranella palustris* 1, *Philonotis fontana* 1, *Thuidium tamariscinum* 1, *Leiocolea bantriensis* 2.
11. *Carex lepidocarpa* 5, *Silene acaulis* 1.

LOCALITIES

1, 2. Lealt; 3, 4. Allt na Dunaiche; 5. S.W. spur of Blà Bheinn; 6, 7, 8, 9, 10. Coire Uaigneich, Blà Bheinn; 11. Sgùrr Mor.

TABLE 4.32

Class	MOLINIO–ARRHENATHERETEA
Order	MOLINIETALIA COERULEAE
Alliance	**Filipendulo–Petasition**
Association	*Juncus acutiflorus–Filipendula ulmaria*

	1	2	3	4	5	6	7	8	9	10	C	D
Reference Number	B67 137	B68 047	B68 028	B68 063	B68 035	B68 048	B68 353	B68 026	B68 360	B68 361		
Map Reference	505 646	505 646	500 535	493 486	375 660	505 646	578 086	502 523	514 545	514 545		
Altitude (feet)	250	250	1000	450	50	250	25	500	650	650		
Aspect (degrees)	.	.	90	.	270	.	.	50	90	90		
Slope (degrees)	.	.	12	.	3	4	.	10	5	2		
Cover (per cent)	100	100	100	100	100	100	100	100	100	100		
Plot area (square metres)	4	4	4	4	4	4	4	4	4	4		
Equisetum palustre	4	4	2	3	3	4	.	6	7	9	V	4.2
Thelypteris limbosperma	.	.	+	.	.	.	.	1	.	.	I	0.2
Agrostis canina	4	.	3	.	.	.	.	4	.	.	II	1.1
Anthoxanthum odoratum	.	6	.	4	3	6	5	4	3	3	IV	3.4
Cynosurus cristatus	.	3	.	4	2	4	.	3	.	.	III	1.6
Festuca rubra	.	.	.	.	.	.	5	6	.	.	I	1.1
F. vivipara	1	.	.	2	.	.	.	.	.	3	II	0.6
Holcus lanatus	2	2	2	3	3	3	4	5	4	.	V	2.8
Molinia caerulea	8	7	.	.	.	2	.	.	2	3	III	2.2
Carex echinata	3	2	3	.	.	2	3	3	4	.	IV	2.0
C. nigra	.	.	3	3	.	4	1	5	3	2	IV	2.1
C. panicea	.	.	.	2	.	.	2	.	.	1	II	0.5
C. pulicaris	.	3	.	.	.	2	.	3	1	2	III	1.1
Dactylorchis fuchsii	2	1	.	.	1	.	.	.	.	.	II	0.4
Eleocharis palustris	.	.	.	.	3	3	3	2	.	.	II	1.1
Eriophorum angustifolium	.	3	1	.	.	.	3	.	.	.	II	0.7
Juncus acutiflorus	.	3	8	7	8	6	7	7	5	2	V	5.3
J. articulatus	.	.	+	3	.	.	.	.	.	.	I	0.4
J. effusus	1	.	.	3	.	.	.	4	3	2	III	1.3
Luzula campestris	1	2	.	.	.	3	.	.	3	2	III	1.1
Angelica sylvestris	.	.	.	4	4	3	.	.	.	.	II	1.1
Bellis perennis	.	.	.	2	.	.	.	+	.	.	I	0.3
Caltha palustris	.	.	2	3	4	+	.	+	1	.	III	1.2
Cardamine pratensis	.	.	.	2	.	.	+	.	.	.	I	0.3
Cerastium holosteoides	.	.	.	1	.	1	.	3	.	.	II	0.5
Cirsium palustre	.	.	1	.	.	.	.	4	2	1	II	0.8
Crepis paludosa	.	+	.	.	.	2	.	.	.	.	I	0.3
Epilobium palustre	.	.	2	.	3	.	.	1	2	.	II	0.8
Euphrasia brevipila	.	2	.	1	.	4	1	.	.	2	III	1.0
Filipendula ulmaria	.	3	3	5	6	2	5	3	3	2	V	3.2
Galium palustre	.	.	.	3	2	.	1	2	.	.	II	0.8
G. saxatile	.	.	3	.	.	.	.	2	.	.	I	0.5

Lathyrus montanus	.	.	.	.	.	2	.	2	.	.	I	0.4
L. pratensis	.	2	.	.	3	.	.	+	.	.	II	0.6
Linum catharticum	.	2	.	.	.	.	.	.	.	1	I	0.3
Lotus corniculatus	.	.	.	.	.	1	2	.	.	.	I	0.3
Lychnis flos-cuculi	.	3	1	3	1	3	1	2	2	1	V	1.7
Menyanthes trifoliata	1	4	.	.	.	.	.	.	.	.	I	0.5
Myosotis scorpioides	.	+	.	.	2	.	2	2	.	.	II	0.7
Parnassia palustris	.	3	.	.	.	.	.	2	2	3	II	1.0
Pedicularis palustris	1	5	.	3	+	.	.	.	.	1	III	1.1
P. sylvatica	.	.	.	.	.	.	.	.	1	1	I	0.2
Plantago lanceolata	.	1	.	.	.	3	.	.	.	.	I	0.4
Potentilla erecta	4	.	4	3	.	3	2	3	2	2	IV	2.3
P. palustris	.	4	.	.	.	.	.	.	1	.	I	0.5
Prunella vulgaris	.	.	1	2	1	3	4	2	1	2	IV	1.6
Ranunculus repens	.	5	+	4	2	5	3	5	3	1	V	2.9
Rhinanthus minor ssp. *stenophyllus*	.	2	.	2	2	.	.	.	.	.	II	0.6
Rumex acetosa	.	.	4	.	3	.	.	4	.	.	II	1.1
Succisa pratensis	5	.	.	3	.	4	4	1	.	3	III	2.0
Trifolium pratense	2	2	2	.	3	2	.	.	.	.	III	1.1
T. repens	.	3	.	.	.	5	3	4	.	.	II	1.5
Trollius europaeus	.	2	.	.	.	4	.	.	2	2	II	1.0
Viccia cracca	.	+	.	.	.	3	.	.	.	.	I	0.4
Viola palustris	.	.	2	3	.	.	.	+	1	1	III	0.8
Acrocladium cuspidatum	.	5	3	3	3	4	2	3	3	1	V	2.7
Aulacomnium palustre	2	.	+	.	.	.	.	.	1	.	II	0.4
Campylium stellatum	.	3	.	.	.	.	2	.	.	1	II	0.5
Climacium dendroides	.	4	.	.	.	.	.	2	.	.	I	0.6
Hylocomium splendens	3	.	.	.	.	3	.	5	3	3	III	1.7
Mnium undulatum	.	.	1	.	.	2	2	.	.	.	II	0.5
Philonotis fontana	.	2	.	.	.	.	.	.	1	.	I	0.3
Pseudoscleropodium purum	3	.	.	.	.	4	.	.	1	.	II	0.8
Rhytidiadelphus squarrosus	2	5	3	.	3	5	2	3	4	3	V	3.0
Sphagnum palustre	.	.	4	.	.	.	.	.	2	.	I	0.6
S. plumulosum	2	2	2	.	.	.	.	.	.	.	II	0.6
S. recurvum	.	3	6	.	.	.	.	.	.	.	I	0.9
Thuidium tamariscinum	.	.	1	1	.	.	.	.	1	1	II	0.4
Lophocolea cuspidata	.	.	.	.	.	.	1	.	1	.	I	0.2
Pellia neesiana	.	.	.	+	.	+	3	.	.	.	II	0.5
Trichocolea tomentella	.	3	.	.	.	.	3	.	.	.	I	0.6
Total number of species (107)	25	39	31	34	26	38	33	39	34	33		

Mean number of species per relevé = 33.2

ADDITIONAL SPECIES IN LIST

1. *Salix aurita* 3, *Luzula multiflora* 2, *Narthecium ossifragum* 1, *Lotus pedunculatus* 2, *Pinguicula vulgaris* 1, *Calypogeia fissa* 2.
2. *Gymnadenia conopsea* 3, *Sphagnum subsecundum* var. *inundatum* +.
3. *Carex rostrata* 3, *Polygala serpyllifolia* +, *Polytrichum commune* 3.
4. *Lysimachia nemorum* 1, *Ranunculus flammula* 3, *Valeriana officinalis* 3, *Bryum pseudotriquetrum* 1, *Mnium rugicum* 1.
5. *Dactylis glomerata* 3, *Hypericum tetrapterum* 2, *Senecio aquaticus* 2.
6. *Arrhenatherum elatius* 4, *Deschampsia cespitosa* 3, *Mnium pseudopunctatum* +.
7. *Carex demissa* 1, *Iris pseudacorus* 2, *Hydrocotyle vulgaris* 3, *Drepanocladus revolvens* +, *Riccardia multifida* 1.
8. *Carex ovalis* 2, *Achillea ptarmica* 2.
9. *Cirsium heterophyllum* +, *Galium boreale* 1.
10. *Carex flacca* 3, *C. hostiana* +, *Hypericum pulchrum* 1, *Taraxacum officinale* agg. 1.

LOCALITIES

1, 2, 6. Loch Mealt; 3, 8. The Storr; 4. Loch Fada; 5. Totscore; 7. Rubha Sloc an Eòrna; 9, 10. near Tottrome.

TABLE 4.33

Class	MOLINIO–ARRHENATHERETEA													
Order	ARRHENATHERETALIA													
Alliance	Cynosurion cristati													
Association	*Centaureo–Cynosuretum*													

	1	2	3	4	5	6	7	8	9	10	11	12		
Reference Number	B69 006	B69 011	B69 008	B69 009	B69 007	B69 012	B69 013	B69 014	B69 015	B69 010	B69 016	B69 020		
Map Reference	643 242	518 137	662 223	698 117	662 223	518 137	648 232	648 232	645 235	644 245	643 243	495 667		
Altitude (feet)	30	100	50	50	50	100	30	30	30	50	50	300		
Aspect (degrees)	.	.	.	.	.	.	0	0	.	.	90	.		
Slope (degrees)	.	.	.	.	.	.	5	2	.	.	5	.		
Cover (per cent)	100	100	100	100	100	100	100	100	100	100	100	100		
Plot area (square metres)	4	4	4	4	4	4	4	4	4	4	4	4	C	D
Agrostis tenuis	.	.	.	.	.	.	.	.	.	.	3	4	I	0.6
Anthoxanthum odoratum	3	5	6	7	5	6	6	4	6	5	5	7	V	5.4
Cynosurus cristatus	8	7	7	5	8	8	6	7	8	6	7	5	V	6.8
Dactylis glomerata	3	4	.	.	.	.	.	.	.	.	.	.	I	0.6
Festuca rubra	3	6	4	3	4	4	7	6	4	7	6	6	V	5.0
Holcus lanatus	6	7	7	7	8	6	8	7	8	7	8	8	V	7.3
Lolium perenne	4	4	.	.	.	.	.	.	.	.	.	.	I	0.7
Poa pratensis	3	3	.	3	.	3	4	+	.	.	3	3	IV	2.0
Carex ovalis	.	.	4	.	1	.	.	.	1	.	.	.	II	0.5
Dactylorchis fuchsii	.	.	.	.	1	.	1	.	1	.	.	1	II	0.3
D. purpurella	1	1	.	.	.	.	.	1	4	+	1	.	III	0.8
Juncus effusus	.	.	.	.	.	.	.	.	.	.	3	3	II	0.5
Luzula campestris	.	.	1	2	1	.	3	3	3	3	3	3	IV	1.8
Platanthera chlorantha	.	+	.	1	.	.	.	2	1	.	.	.	II	0.4
Achillea millefolium	.	.	2	.	1	.	.	3	+	.	2	.	III	0.8
Alchemilla glabra	.	1	.	.	.	1	.	.	.	.	.	.	I	0.2
Anthriscus sylvestris	.	+	.	.	.	.	1	1	.	.	.	1	II	0.3
Bellis perennis	5	.	.	.	3	.	.	.	3	.	.	.	II	0.9
Centaurea nigra	3	5	5	6	4	4	5	6	5	4	4	4	V	4.6
Cerastium holosteoides	2	2	.	.	.	+	4	.	+	.	3	1	III	1.2
Chrysanthemum leucanthemum	3	4	6	3	4	5	4	5	4	3	4	3	V	4.0
C. segetum	.	.	.	.	.	.	.	.	.	.	3	3	I	0.5
Cirsium vulgare	1	.	.	.	.	.	+	.	1	.	.	.	II	0.3
Euphrasia brevipila	2	1	3	1	2	2	3	3	3	.	.	3	V	1.9
Filipendula ulmaria	.	.	+	.	.	.	.	1	.	4	.	.	II	0.5
Galium saxatile	.	.	.	+	.	.	.	+	.	.	3	3	II	0.7
Heracleum sphondylium	.	.	.	1	.	.	1	3	+	.	.	2	III	0.7
Hypochoeris radicata	.	2	1	2	2	3	2	1	3	3	.	.	IV	1.6
Lathyrus pratensis	.	.	.	3	.	1	.	4	1	2	.	3	III	1.2
Leontodon autumnalis	.	.	.	.	2	1	.	.	.	.	2	.	II	0.4
Lotus corniculatus	.	1	.	2	.	4	.	2	.	.	3	+	III	1.0
Plantago lanceolata	4	3	4	3	3	3	4	3	4	3	3	4	V	3.4
Potentilla erecta	.	1	.	.	.	1	.	.	.	.	3	3	II	0.7
Prunella vulgaris	+	.	.	3	1	.	.	.	1	.	+	.	III	0.6
Ranunculus repens	3	3	3	3	3	3	3	3	3	4	4	4	V	3.3
Rhinanthus minor* ssp. *stenophyllus	2	4	4	4	5	3	3	5	4	3	2	5	V	3.7
Rumex acetosa	.	4	.	3	.	3	+	3	2	.	4	3	IV	1.9
Senecia jacobea	2	+	3	1	3	2	3	3	3	2	.	3	V	2.2
Trifolium pratense	3	3	5	3	3	4	3	5	5	3	3	3	V	3.4
T. repens	6	3	3	4	4	3	4	3	4	4	4	5	V	3.9
Veronica chamaedrys	.	.	.	2	.	.	3	3	2	.	2	.	III	1.0
Vicia cracca	.	2	.	.	.	1	.	1	1	+	1	2	III	0.8
Acrocladium cuspidatum	.	.	2	.	.	1	.	.	.	4	.	.	II	0.6
Rhytidiadelphus squarrosus	.	+	1	2	3	2	4	+	3	.	1	.	IV	1.5
Thuidium tamariscinum	.	.	.	.	.	+	.	2	.	.	.	.	I	0.3
Total number of species (64)	24	29	20	27	22	26	26	32	31	23	29	30		

Mean number of species per relevé = 26.6.

ADDITIONAL SPECIES IN LIST

1. *Alopecurus pratensis* 3, *Phleum bertolonii* +, *Veronica filiformis* 3.
2. *Gymnadenia conopsea* 1, *Phleum pratensis* 3.
3. *Conopodium vulgare* 2.
4. *Carex flacca* 1, *Brachythecium rutabulum* +.
7. *Alchemilla xanthochlora* 1, *Festuca vivipara* +.
8. *Arrhenatherum elatius* 3, *Hylocomium splendens* 3.
9. *Potentilla anserina* 1.
10. *Carex echinata* 1, *C. panicea* 2, *Deschampsia cespitosa* 2, *Lychnis flos-cuculi* +.
12. *Angelica sylvestris* 1, *Equisetum sylvaticum* 3.

LOCALITIES

1, 10, 11. Corry; 2, 6. Elgol; 3, 5. Waterloo; 4. Camas Croise; 7, 8, 9. Broadford; 12. Staffi

TABLE 4.34

Class	MOLINIO–ARRHENATHERETEA
Order	ARRHENATHERETALIA
Alliance	**Cynosurion cristati**
Nodum	*Maritime grassland nodum*

	1	2	3	4	5		
Reference Number	B68	B68	B67	B68	B68		
	001	146	030	197	002		
Map Reference	409	132	320	222	410		
	743	475	345	612	743		
Altitude (feet)	75	100	300	30	50		
Aspect (degrees)	270	.	0	0	0		
Slope (degrees)	6	.	4	10	20		
Cover (per cent)	100	100	100	100	100		
Plot area (square metres)	4	4	4	4	4	C	D
Calluna vulgaris	3	2	2	.	.	III	1.4
Pteridium aquilinum	1	1	3	.	.	III	1.0
Agrostis stolonifera	4	5	5	4	4	V	4.4
Anthoxanthum odoratum	5	.	4	4	.	III	2.6
Arrhenatherum elatius	.	1	3	.	2	III	1.2
Cynosurus cristatus	5	4	3	.	.	III	2.4
Dactylis glomerata	3	3	4	4	7	V	4.2
Festuca rubra	7	5	6	6	5	V	5.8
F. vivipara	3	.	2	3	5	IV	2.6
Holcus lanatus	5	4	6	5	4	V	4.8
Sieglingia decumbens	4	4	2	.	.	III	2.0
Carex binervis	.	.	2	.	3	II	1.0
C. pulicaris	2	1	2	.	.	III	1.0
Angelica sylvestris	+	.	.	4	5	III	2.0
Bellis perennis	3	3	.	.	.	II	1.2
Euphrasia brevipila	3	3	+	.	.	III	1.4
Heracleum sphondylium	.	.	.	3	1	II	1.0
Hypericum pulchrum	.	+	.	.	2	II	0.6
Lathyrus montanus	1	.	1	.	.	II	0.4
L. pratensis	.	.	.	1	3	II	0.8
Leontodon autumnalis	4	2	.	.	2	III	1.6
Linum catharticum	.	3	.	3	.	II	1.2
Lotus corniculatus	3	3	+	4	.	IV	2.2
Plantago lanceolata	3	3	3	2	5	V	3.2
P. maritima	5	5	4	5	3	V	4.4
Polygala serpyllifolia	3	2	2	.	.	III	1.4
Potentilla erecta	3	3	4	.	2	IV	2.4
Primula vulgaris	.	.	.	2	3	II	1.0
Prunella vulgaris	3	2	1	2	.	IV	1.6
Ranunculus acris	+	2	.	.	.	II	0.6
Rhinanthus minor agg.	1	.	1	.	.	II	0.4
Rumex acetosa	2	.	.	.	3	II	1.0
Senecio vulgaris	.	2	.	+	2	III	1.0
Silene maritima	.	.	.	3	2	II	1.0
Thymus drucei	.	.	+	.	1	II	0.6
Trifolium pratense	2	.	.	4	.	II	1.2
T. repens	3	.	1	.	.	II	0.8
Viola riviniana	1	3	2	.	.	III	1.2
Ctenidium molluscum	.	1	2	.	.	II	0.8
**Hypnum cupressiforme*	2	.	2	.	.	II	0.8
Trichostomum crispulum	.	1	.	1	.	II	0.4
Frullania tamarisci	.	3	+	+	3	IV	1.6
Total number of species (65)	32	33	35	23	24		

* var. *ericetorum* in 3. Mean number of species per relevé = 29.4.

ADDITIONAL SPECIES IN LIST

1. *Carex pilulifera* 1, *Luzula campestris* 1, *Mnium undulatum* 1.
2. *Carex flacca* 3, *Hieracium pilosella* 1, *Plantago coronopus* 4, *Sedum anglicum* 4, *Campylopus flexuosus* 1, *Funaria attenuata* 1.
3. *Erica cinerea* 2, *Salix repens* ssp. *argentea* 2, *Luzula campestris* 2, *Galium saxatile* 1, *Veronica serpyllifolia* 1, *Hylocomium splendens* 2, *Pseudoscleropodium purum* 2.
4. *Anthyllis vulneraria* 2, *Armeria maritima* 4, *Centaurea nigra* 2, *Lophocolea bidentata* 1.
5. *Poa pratensis* 3, *Cerastium holosteoides* 1, *Sagina procumbens* +.

LOCALITIES

1, 5. Duntulm; 2. Neist Point; 3. Fiskavaig; 4. Trumpan.

TABLE 4.35

Class	ELYNO-SESLERIETEA													
Order	ELYNO-DRYADETALIA													
Alliance	**Kobresio-Dryadion**													
Association	*Dryas octopetala–Carex flacca*													
Facies	*Typicum*		*Flushed*			*Leached*				*Arctostaphylos*				
	1	2	3	4	5	6	7	8	9	10	11	12		
Reference Number	B68	B68	B67	B67	B67	B68	B68	B68	B68	B68	B68	B67		
	258	307	001	004	074	215	216	260	305	259	306	119		
Map Reference	611	617	611	612	594	584	584	584	619	611	617	611		
	201	197	202	198	200	187	187	187	196	201	197	201		
Altitude (feet)	75	400	100	250	100	100	75	75	450	75	400	75		
Aspect (degrees)	270	0	0	315	0	270	270	270	315	225	0	270		
Slope (degrees)	3	8	8	10	8	5	5	5	6	5	10	10		
Cover (per cent)	60	100	100	100	100	100	100	100	100	60	100	80		
Plot area (square metres)	4	4	4	4	4	4	4	4	4	4	4	4	C	D
Arctostaphylos uva-ursi	.	.	.	.	.	.	.	.	.	7	6	7	II	1.7
Betula pubescens	.	.	+	+	1	.	.	.	.	.	.	.	II	0.3
Calluna vulgaris	.	.	.	1	2	5	4	7	4	.	.	.	III	1.9
Dryas octopetala	8	9	7	7	7	7	8	5	8	5	6	.	V	6.4
Rubus saxatilis	2	.	1	.	.	.	.	.	.	1	.	3	II	0.6
Selaginella selaginoides	.	.	3	3	2	.	.	.	.	.	1	.	II	0.8
Agrostis canina	.	.	.	2	.	.	3	.	.	.	.	.	I	0.4
Anthoxanthum odoratum	.	.	3	3	.	.	3	2	2	.	.	4	III	1.4
Cynosurus cristatus	.	.	.	3	.	4	3	.	.	.	.	.	II	0.8
Festuca ovina	.	.	4	3	3	3	2	2	3	.	.	.	III	1.7
F. vivipara	4	2	4	2	4	.	2	3	2	2	3	4	V	2.7
Molinia caerulea	3	.	.	.	.	2	.	.	3	3	3	.	III	1.2
Sieglingia decumbens	3	.	.	.	.	4	4	4	2	2	3	.	III	1.8
Carex flacca	5	5	5	5	6	4	4	4	5	5	4	5	V	4.8
C. panicea	.	.	5	.	2	.	.	.	.	.	.	1	II	0.7
C. pulicaris	.	4	.	3	.	5	3	3	2	1	2	.	IV	1.9
Luzula campestris	.	.	.	.	.	.	2	.	2	.	.	1	II	0.4
Antennaria dioica	.	.	2	3	3	.	.	2	.	.	.	.	II	0.8
Bellis perennis	.	.	.	2	1	3	1	2	.	.	.	.	III	0.8
Centaurea nigra	.	.	.	.	.	.	.	.	.	1	.	3	I	0.3
Cerastium holosteoides	.	.	.	1	.	.	.	.	1	.	.	.	I	0.2
Euphrasia confusa	.	1	.	1	.	.	4	2	1	.	.	.	III	0.8
Hieracium pilosella	1	1	2	2	2	4	1	3	2	4	1	.	V	1.9
Hypericum pulchrum	.	.	+	.	2	.	.	.	.	1	1	1	III	0.5
Linum catharticum	4	4	.	1	.	4	3	2	4	4	3	.	IV	2.4
Lotus corniculatus	4	.	5	5	2	1	2	1	.	1	.	2	IV	1.9
Pinguicula vulgaris	.	.	3	2	3	.	.	.	.	.	.	.	II	0.7

Plantago lanceolata	.	.	2	3	2	3	2	3	.	.	.	.	III	1.3
P. maritima	3	2	2	1	2	.	5	3	.	2	.	2	IV	1.8
Polygala vulgaris	.	.	2	3	2	2	1	1	.	.	.	.	III	0.9
Potentilla erecta	.	1	1	4	2	1	+	3	3	.	2	.	IV	1.5
Prunella vulgaris	2	.	.	2	.	.	.	.	.	2	.	.	II	0.5
Succisa pratensis	.	.	.	2	2	.	.	.	1	.	3	.	II	0.7
Thymus drucei	4	3	5	2	3	4	3	1	4	3	3	3	V	3.2
Trifolium repens	.	.	.	2	.	.	+	.	.	.	.	.	I	0.3
Viola riviniana	.	.	+	3	.	2	3	4	2	1	2	2	IV	1.7
Breutelia chrysocoma	3	5	4	.	.	.	.	.	.	3	5	4	III	2.0
Ctenidium molluscum	5	5	4	5	5	3	3	1	4	4	5	5	V	4.1
Dicranum scoparium	.	.	.	2	.	3	1	2	.	1	.	.	II	0.8
Ditrichum flexicaule	3	.	2	5	3	.	.	2	.	1	.	1	III	1.4
Fissidens cristatus	.	.	.	.	.	2	.	.	.	.	2	2	II	0.5
Hylocomium brevirostre	.	4	.	1	.	.	3	.	2	1	.	.	III	0.9
H. splendens	.	2	2	5	.	3	.	4	5	.	3	3	IV	2.3
**Hypnum cupressiforme*	.	4	2	4	.	2	1	.	.	.	.	.	III	1.1
Neckera complanata	.	.	.	.	.	1	1	.	.	.	.	.	I	0.2
N. crispa	2	4	1	.	.	.	.	1	.	.	.	.	II	0.7
Pseudoscleropodium purum	.	3	.	.	.	.	.	2	4	4	3	.	III	1.3
Rhacomitrium lanuginosum	.	.	3	4	3	.	.	.	1	.	.	.	II	0.9
Rhytidiadelphus triquetrus	.	.	.	.	.	2	2	.	3	.	3	.	II	0.8
Thuidium tamariscinum	.	.	.	2	.	.	1	.	1	.	1	.	II	0.4
Tortella tortuosa	6	3	2	.	4	3	3	1	1	2	2	3	V	2.5
Frullania tamarisci	.	.	2	.	.	+	2	.	.	.	.	.	II	0.4
Scapania aspera	.	.	1	.	1	.	.	.	1	.	2	.	II	0.4
Total number of species (86)	19	19	36	43	28	26	32	31	29	25	26	22		

* var. *tectorum* in 2, 3, 4, 6, and 7. Mean number of species per relevé = 28.0.

ADDITIONAL SPECIES IN LIST

1. *Solidago virgaurea* 1, *Collema* sp. 2.
3. *Salix* sp. +, *Pteridium aquilinum* 2, *Carex nigra* 2, *Thalictrum alpinum* 2, *Acrocladium cuspidatum* +, *Entodon concinnus* +.
4. *Alchemilla xanthochlora* 2, *Anemone nemorosa* 1, *Filipendula ulmaria* 1, *Geum rivale* 1, *Gnaphalium sylvaticum* 1, *Lathyrus montanus* 1, *Campylium stellatum* 3.
5. *Festuca rubra* 3, *Schoenus nigricans* 2, *Saxifraga aizoides* 2.
6. *Leontodon autumnalis* 3, *Ranunculus acris* 1, *Taraxacum officinale* agg. 2.
8. *Erica cinerea* 5, *Campylium protensum* 1, *Rhytidiadelphus loreus* 2, *R. squarrosus* 1.
9. *Vaccinium myrtillus* 2, *Primula vulgaris* 3.
10. *Carex hostiana* 3.
11. *Polystichum aculeatum* 1, *Oxalis acetosella* 1.
12. *Encalypta streptocarpa* 1, *Orthotrichum anomalum* 1, *Pleurozium schreberi* 1.

LOCALITIES

1, 3, 10, 12. Coille Gaireallach; 2, 4, 5, 9, 11. Ben Suardal; 6, 7, 8. Camas Malag.

TABLE 4.36

Class	CARICETEA CURVULAE																			
Order	CARICETALIA CURVULAE																			
Alliance	**Arctostaphyleto–Cetrarion nivalis**																			
Association	*Cariceto–Rhacomitretum lanuginosi*															*Festuca ovina–Luzula spicata nodum*				
Facies	*Typicum*									*Cushion-herb*										
	1	2	3	4	5	6	7	8	9	10	11	12	13			14	15	16	17	
Reference Number	B68	B67	B68	B68	B67	B67	B68	B68	B68	B67	B68	B67	B68			B68	B67	B68	B68	
Map Reference	338	125	169	080	022	065	344	343	241	072	079	134	074			337	127	081	242	
	506	443	224	490	535	753	517	516	532	763	490	456	496			506	455	490	529	
	278	603	422	547	211	223	303	302	215	223	545	627	542			278	610	542	218	
Altitude (feet)	1500	1500	1600	1750	2000	2000	2200	2400	2500	2400	1850	2000	2300			1500	1600	2000	3000	
Aspect (degrees)	0	.	315	340	315	.	.	.	90	45	315	270	270			.	270	315	.	
Slope (degrees)	3	.	3	4	3	.	.	.	3	5	8	5	8			.	3	3	.	
Cover (per cent)	100	100	100	100	100	100	100	100	100	100	100	100	100			30	25	20	25	
Plot area (square metres)	4	4	4	4	4	4	4	4	4	4	4	4	4	C	D	4	4	4	4	D
Empetrum hermaphroditum	.	3	.	.	.	.	.	.	.	2	.	.	.	I	0.4	.	.	.	.	
Salix herbacea	2	4	2	3	.	4	.	.	3	3	3	4	4	IV	2.5	3	6	4	4	4.3
Vaccinium myrtillus	3	2	2	.	4	3	3	4	2	4	.	3	+	V	2.4	.	.	.	3	
V. vitis-idaea	.	.	4	.	.	2	.	1	.	2	.	.	.	II	0.7	.	2	.	.	0.5
Lycopodium alpinum	.	4	.	.	4	+	.	.	.	.	.	.	.	II	0.7	.	.	.	.	
L. selago	.	2	2	.	3	1	.	.	.	2	.	1	.	III	0.8	.	.	.	.	
Selaginella selaginoides	1	.	.	.	.	.	.	.	.	.	1	.	3	II	0.4	.	.	.	.	
Agrostis canina	.	.	3	.	.	.	.	.	4	.	.	.	.	I	0.5	.	2	.	.	0.5
A. tenuis	.	.	.	.	.	.	.	.	.	.	4	3	4	II	0.8	.	.	.	.	
Deschampsia flexuosa	2	2	3	2	4	2	3	2	4	.	.	.	.	IV	2.0	4	2	3	3	3.0
Festuca ovina	.	.	3	5	.	.	.	3	3	2	5	3	6	IV	2.3	6	5	6	6	5.8
F. vivipara	4	3	4	3	3	2	4	4	4	3	4	4	5	V	3.6	3	3	5	6	4.3
Nardus stricta	2	3	.	+	.	.	+	.	.	.	.	.	.	II	0.5	.	.	.	.	
Carex bigelowii	4	4	5	6	4	4	4	4	6	4	6	3	.	V	4.1	.	.	.	.	
C. pilulifera	.	4	3	.	1	1	1	2	3	.	.	.	.	III	1.2	+	.	.	.	0.3
Luzula spicata	.	.	.	.	.	.	.	.	.	.	.	.	.			2	3	2	+	2.0
L. sylvatica	.	.	.	.	.	.	1	.	1	.	.	.	.	I	0.2	.	.	.	.	
Alchemilla alpina	5	+	.	2	4	2	3	5	4	1	4	3	5	V	3.0	6	4	3	5	4.5
Antennaria dioica	.	.	.	.	2	2	.	.	.	.	.	2	.	II	0.5	+	.	.	.	0.3
Armeria maritima	.	.	.	.	.	.	.	.	.	5	.	.	3	I	0.6	.	.	.	.	
Cherleria sedoides	.	.	.	.	.	.	.	.	.	.	1	4	2	II	0.5	.	.	.	.	
Euphrasia officinalis agg.	1	.	.	.	.	.	.	.	.	.	.	.	2	I	0.2	2	.	.	.	0.5
Galium saxatile	3	2	3	5	2	4	4	4	2	2	3	4	3	V	3.2	3	3	.	1	1.8
Gnaphalium supinum	.	.	.	2	.	.	.	.	.	.	.	+	.	I	0.2	.	.	.	.	
Plantago maritima	.	.	.	.	.	.	.	.	.	.	.	.	1	I	0.1	1	.	.	.	0.3
Polygonum viviparum	.	.	.	.	.	.	.	.	.	2	4	5	4	II	1.2	1	.	.	.	0.3
Potentilla erecta	2	3	1	.	4	1	.	2	3	.	3	2	4	IV	1.9	.	.	4	.	1.0

Silene acaulis	.	.	.	.	.	.	.	.	.	.	2	3	2	II	0.5	.	.	.	.	
Thalictrum alpinum	.	.	.	.	.	.	.	.	.	.	2	.	1	I	0.2	.	.	.	.	
Thymus drucei	4	2	.	4	.	2	.	.	4	.	4	3	4	IV	2.1	3	.	4	3	2.5
Viola riviniana	1	1	2	1	.	.	.	1	2	.	2	2	.	IV	0.9	.	.	1	.	0.3
Andreaea alpina	.	.	1	.	.	.	.	.	1	.	1	.	.	II	0.2	.	2	2	1	1.3
Aulacomnium turgidum	.	.	.	.	.	.	.	.	.	.	2	.	3	I	0.4	.	.	.	.	.
Campylopus flexuosus	.	.	.	.	.	1	.	.	.	.	.	.	.	I	0.1	.	.	.	.	
Dicranum fuscescens	.	1	.	.	.	2	.	.	.	2	.	2	.	II	0.5	.	.	.	.	
D. scoparium	.	.	.	.	.	1	1	1	.	.	.	.	1	II	0.3	.	.	.	.	
Hylocomium splendens	.	.	.	.	.	.	.	1	.	.	+	.	.	I	0.2	.	.	.	.	
* *Hypnum cupressiforme*	4	.	.	.	.	.	1	.	.	.	.	1	.	II	0.5	.	.	.	.	
Oligotrichum hercynicum	.	.	.	.	.	.	.	.	.	.	.	.	.			2	3	+	4	2.5
Pleurozium schreberi	2	.	.	.	.	.	.	1	.	.	.	.	3	I	0.5	.	.	.	.	
Polytrichum alpinum	.	2	.	.	3	1	1	+	3	2	1	2	+	IV	1.3	.	1	.	1	0.5
P. piliferum	1	.	2	3	1	2	1	2	1	.	+	.	3	IV	1.3	1	2	.	3	1.5
Rhacomitrium fasciculare	.	.	+	.	.	.	.	.	3	.	.	.	4	II	0.6	.	.	.	.	
† *R. heterostichum*	.	.	.	.	.	.	.	.	1	.	.	1	.	I	0.2	.	3	2	.	1.3
R. lanuginosum	8	9	9	9	9	9	9	9	9	9	8	8	7	V	8.6	2	6	6	7	5.3
Rhytidiadelphus loreus	1	.	.	.	.	1	2	3	.	2	.	2	2	III	1.0	.	.	.	.	.
Diplophyllum albicans	.	.	+	.	1	.	.	.	.	.	.	1	.	II	0.2	.	.	.	.	
Nardia scalaris	1	.	.	1	.	.	1	.	.	.	.	.	.	II	0.2	.	.	1	.	0.3
Cetraria islandica	.	.	.	3	.	.	.	.	1	1	.	.	.	II	0.4	.	.	.	.	
Cladonia impexa	.	.	.	.	.	1	.	.	.	2	.	.	.	I	0.2	.	.	.	.	
C. rangiferina	.	.	.	.	.	.	.	.	.	1	.	1	.	I	0.2	.	.	.	.	
C. unicialis	1	5	+	.	2	2	1	1	2	3	.	3	1	V	1.7	.	2	.	.	0.5
Total number of species (70)	20	20	19	15	17	24	16	21	22	21	22	26	28			18	17	17	18	

Mean number of species per relevé = 20.8.
Total number of species in association = 58.

Mean number of species per relevé = 17.5.
Total number of species in *nodum* = 36.

* var. *ericetorum* in 1 and 7. var. *lacunosum* in 12. † var. *gracilescens* in 9, 15, and 16.

ADDITIONAL SPECIES IN LIST

2. *Rhacomitrium canescens* +.
5. *Polygala serpyllifolia* 2.
8. *Anthoxanthum odoratum* 2.
9. *Blechnum spicant* 2.
10. *Sphaerophorus globosus* 1.
11. *Alchemilla vestita* 3.
13. *Luzula campestris* 2, *Cerastium holosteoides* 2.
14. *Solidago virgaurea* +, *Succisa pratensis* 2.
15. *Anthelia juratzkana* +.
16. *Cerastium arcticum* +, *Koenigia islandica* +, *Anthelia julacea* +.
17. *Juncus trifidus* 5, *Conostomum tetragonum* 2, *Tetraplodon mnioides* +, *Stereocaulon vesuvianum* 3.

LOCALITIES

1, 14. Beinn Dearg; 2. Beinn Laoigh; 3. Healaval Bheag; 4, 11, 13, 16. The Storr; 5, 9, 17. Blà Bheinn; 6, 10. Sgùrr na Coinnich; 7, 8. Sgùrr Mhair; 12, 15. Beinn Edra.

TABLE 4.37

Class	CARICETEA CURVULAE																
Order	CARICETALIA CURVULAE																
Alliance	**Arctostaphyleto–Cetrarion nivalis**																
Association	*Rhacomitreto–Callunetum*												*Juniperus nana nodum*				
	1	2	3	4	5	6	7	8	9	10			11	12	13	14	
Reference Number	B68	B68	B67	B68	B68	B68	B68	B68	B67	B68			B68	B68	B68	B67	
	328	324	024	166	167	168	335	334	064	342			341	339	340	056	
Map Reference	576	524	552	216	216	225	505	505	753	520			515	514	515	451	
	012	183	210	429	429	423	284	285	222	285			280	272	273	248	
Altitude (feet)	500	600	1100	1150	1200	1200	1300	1350	1950	2000			1700	1900	2000	2200	
Aspect (degrees)	225	225	.	45	45	315	.	.	270	270			.	180	.	.	
Slope (degrees)	5	5	.	3	4	10	.	.	5	5			.	5	.	.	
Cover (per cent)	80	60	50	60	70	100	100	80	100	100			100	100	100	100	
Plot area (square metres)	4	4	4	4	4	4	4	4	4	4	C	D	4	4	4	4	D
Calluna vulgaris	7	8	7	7	7	8	7	8	7	6	V	7.2	5	3	3	.	2.8
Empetrum hermaphroditum	.	.	2	.	.	3	.	.	2	4	II	1.1	2	1	5	3	2.3
Erica cinerea	3	3	.	2	2	1	.	.	.	.	III	1.1	1	.	.	.	0.8
Juniperus communis ssp. *nana*	.	.	.	.	.	.	.	.	.	.			9	8	7	8	8.0
Salix herbacea	.	.	.	.	.	.	4	.	.	.	I	0.4	.	.	3	+	1.0
Vaccinium myrtillus	.	.	.	.	.	3	3	.	2	2	II	1.0	3	1	2	2	2.0
V. vitis-idaea	.	.	.	.	.	.	.	.	.	2	I	0.2	.	2	.	.	0.5
Lycopodium alpinum	.	.	.	.	.	.	.	.	.	.			.	.	1	2	0.8
L. selago	.	.	2	2	2	.	2	.	.	1	III	0.9	.	2	2	2	1.5
Agrostis canina	2	2	.	4	3	4	3	2	3	.	IV	2.3	.	.	.	.	
Deschampsia flexuosa	.	.	.	.	.	1	.	.	.	.	I	0.1	3	2	3	3	2.8
Festuca ovina	.	2	.	4	3	3	.	.	2	3	III	1.7	.	.	.	.	
F. vivipara	3	4	3	3	4	+	5	6	2	4	V	3.5	3	3	2	3	2.8
Molinia caerulea	3	2	.	.	.	.	.	.	.	.	I	0.5	.	.	.	.	
Nardus stricta	1	.	.	.	.	4	2	.	.	.	II	0.7	.	.	3	.	0.8
Carex bigelowii	.	.	3	3	4	.	4	3	2	3	IV	2.2	2	.	4	2	2.0
C. binervis	3	.	.	.	.	.	.	.	.	.	I	0.3	.	.	+	.	0.3
C. pilulifera	.	.	.	3	3	3	4	4	.	2	III	1.9	.	3	.	.	0.8
Trichophorum cespitosum	2	3	3	3	.	.	.	2	.	.	III	1.3	.	.	1	1	0.5
Alchemilla alpina	.	.	.	.	.	.	2	.	.	3	I	0.5	3	2	2	.	1.8
Antennaria dioica	1	2	3	2	2	.	3	3	3	.	IV	1.9	1	2	.	.	0.8
Euphrasia micrantha	1	3	.	1	1	1	.	2	.	.	III	0.9	1	.	.	.	0.3
Galium saxatile	.	.	.	.	.	3	1	.	.	3	II	0.7	.	.	3	.	0.8
Polygala serpyllifolia	.	.	.	2	.	+	.	2	.	.	II	0.5	1	.	.	.	0.3
Potentilla erecta	2	3	2	4	3	3	.	3	2	+	V	2.3	1	.	3	2	1.5
Solidago virgaurea	1	3	3	4	2	.	.	.	.	.	III	1.3	1	.	.	.	0.3
Succisa pratensis	1	.	.	.	2	.	3	2	.	.	II	0.8	.	1	.	.	0.3
Thymus drucei	.	.	.	.	2	.	3	2	.	.	II	0.7	4	1	.	.	1.3

Andreaea rothii	.	1	.	1	3	.	.	.	.	.	II	0.5	.	.	.	.	
Campylopus atrovirens	.	1	.	3	3	.	.	.	.	.	II	0.7	1	.	.	.	0.3
C. flexuosus	.	.	.	.	1	.	.	.	.	1	I	0.2	.	.	1	.	0.3
Dicranum scoparium	.	.	.	.	.	2	.	.	1	.	I	0.3	.	.	.	.	
Hylocomium splendens	.	.	.	.	.	3	+	.	3	.	II	0.7	.	.	3	.	0.8
**Hypnum cupressiforme*	4	.	.	2	3	2	4	2	.	.	III	1.7	3	2	2	1	2.0
Pleurozium schreberi	.	.	.	.	.	2	.	.	.	.	I	0.2	.	.	3	.	0.8
Polytrichum piliferum	2	.	.	.	.	1	2	2	.	2	III	0.9	1	.	1	.	0.5
Rhacomitrium fasciculare	.	1	.	4	5	.	.	.	.	.	II	1.0	.	.	.	.	
R. heterostichum	.	3	3	1	3	.	.	1	.	.	III	1.1	1	1	.	.	0.5
R. lanuginosum	8	7	9	8	8	8	8	7	8	8	V	7.1	5	3	5	7	5.0
Rhytidiadelphus loreus	.	.	.	.	.	2	.	.	3	.	I	0.5	.	.	4	.	1.0
Diplophyllum albicans	.	.	.	.	.	.	.	1	.	+	I	0.2	.	1	1	1	0.8
Gymnomitrion crenulatum	.	.	.	1	.	.	.	.	.	.	I	0.1	.	.	.	1	0.3
Nardia scalaris	.	.	.	.	.	.	2	1	.	1	II	0.4	.	.	.	.	
Cladonia arbuscula	2	2	.	.	2	.	2	1	1	.	III	1.0	.	1	2	.	0.8
C. rangiferina	.	.	.	.	.	.	.	.	3	1	I	0.4	.	3	1	.	1.0
C. subcervicornis	.	.	.	2	.	.	.	.	.	1	I	0.3	.	.	1	.	0.3
C. uncialis	4	3	2	2	3	1	4	2	1	3	V	2.5	2	3	3	2	2.5
Cornicularia aculeata	.	.	.	1	.	.	.	1	.	.	I	0.2	.	+	.	.	0.3
Sphaerophorus globusus	3	2	3	2	1	2	2	2	2	2	V	2.1	.	.	.	.	
Stereocaulon vesuvianum	.	2	.	1	.	.	.	.	.	.	I	0.3	.	.	.	.	
Total number of species (66)	21	20	14	26	28	23	24	22	19	22			22	21	20	18	

Mean number of species per relevé = 21.9.
Total number of species in association = 60.

Mean number of species per relevé = 20.3.
Total number of species in *nodum* = 45.

* var. *ericetorum* in 1, 4, 5, 6, 7, 8, 11, 12, and 13. var. *gracilescens* in 2, 4, 5, 8, 11, and 12.

ADDITIONAL SPECIES IN LIST

1. *Arctostaphylos uva-ursi* 5, *Salix repens* 1.
3. *Dactylorchis maculata* ssp. *ericetorum* +.
5. *Carex demissa* 2, *Leucorchis albida* +, *Sagina procumbens* 2, *Ochrolechia frigida* 1.
7. *Hieracium* sp. 2, *Marsupella emarginata* 1.
9. *Juncus squarrosus* 1, *Cetraria islandica* 1.
10. *Oligotrichum hercynicum* +.
11. *Viola riviniana*, 2.
13. *Polytrichum alpinum* 1.
14. *Anthelia julacea* 1, *Pleurozia purpurea* 2.

LOCALITIES

1. Aird of Sleat; 2. Camasunary; 3. Blà Bheinn; 4, 5, 6. Beinn a' Chapiull; 7, 8. Drium na Ruaige; 9. Sgùrr na Coinnich; 10, 12, 13. Beinn Dearg; 11. Bealach Mosgaraidh; 12. Coire na Creiche.

TABLE 4.38

	1	2	3	4	5	6	7	C	D	8	9	10	11	D
Class	CARICETEA CURVULAE													
Order	CARICETALIA CURVULAE													
Alliance	**Arctostaphyleto–Cetrarion nivalis**													
Association	*Rhacomitreto–Empetretum*									*Alchemilla alpina–Vaccinium myrtillus nodum*				
Reference Number	B68	B68	B68	B68	B68	B67	B67			B67	B67	B67	B67	
	108	163	164	345	246	069	070			035	059	055	071	
Map Reference	444	221	221	516	534	761	762			334	453	451	762	
	704	445	445	304	208	223	223			298	248	248	223	
Altitude (feet)	1400	1400	1400	2000	2200	2250	2300			800	1600	2100	2300	
Aspect (degrees)	45	0	0	0	0	315	45			0	45	315	315	
Slope (degrees)	15	5	10	8	5	5	15			45	30	40	30	
Cover (per cent)	100	100	100	100	100	100	100			100	100	100	100	
Plot area (square metres)	4	4	4	4	4	4	4	C	D	4	4	4	4	D
Empetrum hermaphroditum	5	5	6	8	6	6	8	V	6.3	.	.	+	.	0.3
Vaccinium myrtillus	5	3	6	4	4	3	4	V	4.1	5	6	6	7	6.0
V. vitis-idaea	.	.	.	.	.	1	2	II	0.4	.	.	.	1	0.3
Blechnum spicant	4	.	.	.	3	1	.	III	1.1	3	2	.	.	1.3
Hymenophyllum wilsonii	.	.	1	.	.	.	1	II	0.3	.	.	.	.	
Lycopodium alpinum	.	.	.	.	.	2	.	I	0.3	.	.	1	.	0.3
L. selago	.	2	3	.	4	3	2	IV	2.0	.	1	3	1	1.0
Selaginella selaginoides	.	1	1	.	.	.	.	II	0.3	1	.	.	.	0.3
Agrostis tenuis	.	3	3	.	.	.	.	II	0.9	.	.	.	.	
Deschampsia flexuosa	3	.	.	2	3	.	2	III	1.4	.	3	4	3	2.5
Festuca ovina	.	3	2	.	.	.	.	II	0.7	5	4	5	5	4.8
F. vivipara	4	2	4	4	4	3	3	V	3.4	2	2	4	3	2.8
Carex bigelowii	4	2	3	2	2	3	3	V	2.7	.	2	3	3	2.0
C. binervis	.	+	.	.	3	.	.	II	0.6	.	.	.	.	
C. pilulifera	.	3	3	.	+	.	.	III	1.0	.	.	.	.	
Luzula sylvatica	.	.	3	.	.	2	.	II	0.7	.	.	.	1	0.3
Alchemilla alpina	4	.	.	.	3	3	2	III	1.7	6	5	6	6	5.8
Armeria maritima	.	.	1	4	.	1	.	III	0.9	.	.	.	3	0.8
Galium saxatile	3	+	4	4	6	2	3	V	3.3	.	.	2	.	0.5
Hypericum pulchrum	1	1	.	.	.	.	.	II	0.3	.	.	.	.	
Plantago maritima	.	1	.	.	.	.	.	I	0.1	2	.	.	.	0.5
Potentilla erecta	3	.	3	.	3	.	.	III	1.3	3	3	.	.	1.5
Sedum rosea	2	.	2	.	.	.	1	III	0.7	.	.	.	.	
Solidago virgaurea	4	.	.	.	4	.	.	II	1.1	.	+	.	.	0.3
Succisa pratensis	.	.	.	.	1	.	.	I	0.1	1	.	.	.	0.3
Thymus drucei	3	4	.	.	2	.	.	III	1.3	.	.	.	.	
Viola riviniana	3	1	2	.	3	.	.	III	1.3	.	+	.	.	0.3
Andreaea alpina	.	.	.	.	2	.	.	I	0.3	.	.	1	.	0.3
Breutelia chrysocoma	5	4	5	.	.	.	.	III	2.0	4	.	.	.	1.0

Campylopus atrovirens	3	3	4	.	.	.	.	III	1.4	.	2	.	.	0.5
Dicranodontium uncinatum	.	.	.	.	.	2	2	II	0.6	.	.	.	.	
Dicranum fuscescens	.	.	.	.	2	.	.	I	0.3	.	2	+	.	0.8
D. scoparium	2	.	.	3	.	.	.	II	0.7	.	.	.	.	
Hylocomium splendens	.	.	3	1	1	3	.	III	1.1	3	.	.	3	1.5
**Hypnum cupressiforme*	2	.	.	.	.	.	2	II	0.6	2	3	.	.	1.3
Pleurozium schreberi	1	1	.	.	.	.	.	II	0.3	2	.	.	2	1.0
Polytrichum alpinum	.	2	2	2	2	3	.	IV	1.6	.	.	3	.	0.8
Rhacomitrium lanuginosum	9	9	8	7	8	8	7	V	8.0	8	8	8	8	6.0
Rhytidiadelphus loreus	.	.	5	3	.	4	4	III	2.3	2	.	.	.	0.5
Sphagnum plumulosum	.	.	3	.	.	.	.	I	0.4	1	.	.	.	0.3
†*S. subsecundum*	.	1	.	.	1	.	.	II	0.3	.	1	.	.	0.3
S. tenellum	.	.	.	.	.	2	2	II	0.6	.	.	.	.	
Tetraplodon mnioides	1	.	.	1	.	.	.	II	0.3	.	.	.	.	
Anastrepta orcadensis	.	.	.	2	.	2	1	III	0.7	.	.	.	.	
Anthelia julacea	.	1	.	1	1	.	1	III	0.6	.	.	.	.	
Bazzania pearsonii	.	.	.	1	.	.	1	II	0.3	.	.	.	.	
B. tricrenata	.	.	+	3	.	3	3	III	1.4	.	.	.	.	
Diplophyllum albicans	2	2	2	2	2	3	3	V	2.3	.	.	.	.	
Mylia taylori	.	.	3	1	.	3	2	III	1.3	.	.	.	.	
Nardia scalaris	.	1	.	.	.	.	.	I	0.1	.	1	.	.	0.3
Plagiochila carringtonii	.	.	.	1	.	2	2	III	0.7	.	.	.	.	
P. spinulosa	3	.	1	+	.	.	.	III	0.7	.	.	.	.	
Pleurozia purpurea	+	.	4	.	.	3	3	III	1.6	.	.	+	.	0.3
Ptilidium ciliare	.	.	.	.	.	1	.	I	0.1	.	.	.	1	0.3
Scapania gracilis	2	.	3	3	.	3	1	IV	1.7	.	.	.	.	
S. ornithopodioides	.	.	.	.	.	1	+	I	0.1	.	.	.	.	
Cladonia arbuscula	.	.	.	.	.	2	3	II	0.7	2	.	.	1	0.8
C. impexa	.	.	.	1	.	1	3	III	0.7	.	.	.	.	
C. uncialis	3	2	.	3	2	3	2	V	2.1	.	.	1	2	0.8
Total number of species (89)	31	30	32	28	27	35	28			21	18	17	16	

Mean number of species per relevé = 30.1.
Total number of species in association = 83.

Mean number of species per relevé = 18.0.
Total number of species in *nodum* = 43.

* var. *ericetorum* in 1, 7, 8, and 9. † var. *auriculatum* in 2, 5, and 9.

ADDITIONAL SPECIES IN LIST

1. *Erica cinerea* 4, *Thelypteris phegopteris* 2, *Polygala serpyllifolia* 2, *Veronica serpyllifolia* 1, *Polytrichum nanum* 1.
2. *Calluna vulgaris* 2, *Nardus stricta* 3, *Carex demissa* 2, *C. pulicaris* 1, *Marsupella emarginata* 2.
3. *Campylopus flexuosus* 1, *Dicranum majus* 1, *Thuidium tamariscinum* 1.
4. *Rumex acetosa* 3, *Silene acaulis* +, *Plagiothecium undulatum* 2, *Sphagnum capillaceum* 4.
5. *Trichophorum cespitosum* 1, *Cetraria islandica* 1.
6. *Juniperus communis* ssp. *nana* 1, *Salix herbacea* 1, *Pohlia nutans* 1, *Lophozia incisa* +, *Scapania nimbosa* 2.
8. *Thelypteris limbosperma* 2, *Anthoxanthum odoratum* 3, *Pinguicula vulgaris* 1, *Polytrichum piliferum* 2.
9. *Rubus saxatilis* +.
10. *Oligotrichum hercynicum* 2.

LOCALITIES

1. Sgùrr Mor; 2, 3. Healaval Mhor; 4. Glamaig; 5. Blà Bheinn; 6, 7, 11. Sgùrr na Coinnich; 8. Preshal More; 9, 10. Coire na Creiche.

TABLE 4.40‡

Class	NARDO–CALLUNETEA																												
Order	NARDETALIA																												
Alliance	Nardo–Galion saxatilis																												
Association	*Agrosto–Festucetum* (species-poor)										*Alchemilleto–Agrosto–Festucetum*								*Agrosto–Festucetum* (species-rich)								*Dwarf herb nodum*		
	1	2	3	4	5	6	7	8			9	10	11	12	13	14			15	16	17	18	19	20			21	22	
Reference Number	B67	B67	B67	B67	B67	B67	B68	B67			B67	B67	B68	B68	B68	B67			B67	B67	B68	B67	B67	B68			B67	B67	
	087	049	047	121	033	082	162	063			116	015	031	032	086	020			114	046	089	025	117	030			017	132	
Map Reference	513	424	625	433	355	533	222	756			517	542	496	499	485	536			516	613	517	560	517	496			542	456	
	190	256	212	617	300	193	446	212			406	217	536	540	550	212			137	202	604	202	406	536			217	618	
Altitude (feet)	30	200	500	750	750	750	1200	1300			800	1200	1400	1600	1450	1800			100	150	250	500	800	1300			1000	1750	
Aspect (degrees)	180	90	270	270	0	180	0	180			90	315	135	315	90	0			90	315	135	90	90	135			315	90	
Slope (degrees)	5	10	12	5	5	15	8	5			25	10	30	25	25	20			3	5	5	10	30	40			25	30	
Cover (per cent)	100	100	100	100	100	100	100	100			100	100	90	100	85	100			100	100	100	100	100	100			100	100	
Plot area (square metres)	4	4	4	4	4	4	4	4	C	D	4	4	4	4	4	4	C	D	4	4	4	4	4	4	C	D	4	4	D
Calluna vulgaris	.	3	3	.	3	3	1	.	IV	1.6	2	.	.	.	.	.	I	0.3	2	1	.	.	2	.	III	0.8	.	.	
Erica cinerea	.	.	.	.	.	.	.	.			.	.	.	.	.	.			.	.	+	.	.	+	II	0.3	.	.	
Vaccinium myrtillus	.	.	.	.	.	.	2	2	II	0.5	.	.	.	1	+	2	III	0.7	.	.	.	1	.	.	I	0.2	1	2	1.5
Blechnum spicant	.	.	.	.	.	.	2	.	I	0.3	.	.	.	.	.	5	I	0.8	.	.	.	.	3	1	II	0.7	.	.	
Pteridium aquilinum	.	.	1	.	1	.	.	.	II	0.3	.	.	.	.	.	.			.	1	.	.	.	.	I	0.2	.	.	
Selaginella selaginoides	.	.	.	.	.	.	.	.			3	1	.	3	2	.	IV	1.5	.	1	.	.	2	+	III	0.7	3	2	2.5
Agrostis canina	4	3	3	3	3	4	3	3	V	3.3	.	.	.	.	3	.	I	0.5	.	.	4	.	.	.	I	0.7	.	.	
A. tenuis	6	5	5	6	6	6	6	4	V	5.5	4	6	3	6	5	4	V	4.7	6	4	6	3	5	6	V	5.0	.	.	
Anthoxanthum odoratum	3	4	3	3	2	4	3	4	V	3.3	.	5	.	.	5	5	III	2.5	4	2	.	5	3	6	V	3.3	4	1	2.5
Cynosurus cristatus	.	.	.	.	.	.	.	.			.	.	.	.	.	.			3	.	4	1	.	.	III	1.3	.	.	
Deschampsia flexuosa	.	2	.	.	.	.	.	3	II	0.6	.	.	5	.	.	2	II	1.2	.	.	.	.	.	.			.	.	
Festuca ovina	4	2	3	7	5	4	6	5	V	4.5	5	4	3	5	7	2	V	4.3	6	6	7	5	6	7	V	6.2	4	3	3.5
F. rubra	2	.	.	.	.	.	.	2	II	0.5	.	.	.	.	.	.			.	.	5	2	4	4	IV	1.8	.	.	
F. vivipara	3	3	3	6	.	4	3	3	V	3.1	4	2	.	.	5	5	IV	2.7	4	2	4	.	4	.	IV	2.3	2	5	3.5
Holcus lanatus	2	.	.	.	.	.	.	.	I	0.3	2	2	.	.	.	.	II	0.7	.	.	.	.	3	.	I	0.5	.	.	
Nardus stricta	.	.	.	.	.	.	4	.	I	0.5	.	.	.	.	.	.			.	.	.	1	.	.	I	0.2	.	.	
Poa pratensis	.	.	.	.	.	.	.	.			.	.	3	.	.	.	I	0.5	.	2	.	.	.	3	II	0.8	.	.	
Carex binervis	.	.	.	.	3	2	.	.	II	0.6	.	.	.	.	.	.			1	3	.	2	.	3	IV	1.5	.	.	
C. flacca	.	.	.	.	.	.	2	.	I	0.3	.	1	.	.	.	.	I	0.2	.	2	.	.	.	.	I	0.3	3	.	1.5
C. ovalis	.	.	.	.	.	.	.	2	I	0.3	.	.	.	.	.	.			1	.	.	.	.	.	I	0.2	.	.	
C. panicea	.	.	1	.	.	.	.	.	I	0.1	.	.	.	.	.	.			.	.	.	.	.	.			.	.	
C. pilulifera	.	.	.	2	.	.	.	2	II	0.5	.	.	.	.	.	.			.	.	.	.	.	.			.	.	
C. pulicaris	.	.	1	.	.	.	3	.	II	0.5	3	2	.	.	.	.	II	0.8	3	2	2	3	3	.	V	2.2	2	.	1.0
Luzula campestris	2	.	.	.	.	.	.	2	II	0.5	.	2	.	2	2	.	III	1.0	.	.	1	.	.	.	I	0.2	1	.	0.5
L. multiflora	.	.	.	.	.	.	.	.			4	.	.	.	.	.	I	0.7	.	.	.	.	3	.	I	0.5	.	.	
L. sylvatica	.	.	.	.	.	.	.	.			.	.	.	1	3	.	II	0.7	.	.	.	2	.	.	I	0.3	.	.	
Achillea millefolium	.	.	1	.	.	.	.	.	I	0.1	2	.	.	3	.	2	II	1.2	.	.	.	.	.	.			.	.	
Alchemilla alpina	.	.	.	.	.	.	.	.			6	5	7	7	5	3	V	5.5	.	.	.	.	.	+	I	0.2	3	5	4.0
A. vestita	.	.	.	.	.	.	.	.			.	3	3	4	1	.	IV	1.8	.	.	.	.	.	.			2	.	1.0
A. xanthochlora	.	.	.	.	.	.	.	.			4	.	4	5	.	.	III	2.2	.	2	.	.	3	+	III	1.0	.	1	0.5
Angelica sylvestris	.	.	.	.	.	.	.	.			.	3	.	.	.	.	I	0.5	.	.	.	.	.	.			2	.	1.0
Antennaria dioica	.	.	.	.	.	1	.	.	I	0.1	.	.	.	.	.	.			.	2	.	+	.	.	II	0.5	.	.	
Bellis perennis	.	.	.	.	1	.	.	.	I	0.1	.	3	.	.	+	.	II	0.7	2	2	2	1	.	.	IV	1.2	3	.	1.5
Cerastium holosteoides	.	.	.	.	.	.	.	.			.	.	.	.	+	.	I		.	.	+	1	2	2	IV	1.0	.	.	
**Euphrasia officinalis* agg.	.	.	.	3	.	.	.	.	I	0.4	.	1	3	3	2	.	IV	1.5	2	.	3	.	1	4	IV	1.7	.	2	1.0
Filipendula ulmaria	.	.	.	.	.	.	.	.			1	3	.	.	.	.	II	0.7	.	1	.	.	2	.	II	0.5	1	.	0.5
Fragaria vesca	.	.	.	.	.	.	.	.			1	.	.	.	.	.	I	0.2	.	1	.	.	.	.	I	0.2	.	.	
Galium saxatile	2	2	1	4	3	3	4	4	V	2.9	.	.	3	4	3	5	IV	2.5	.	.	.	4	1	.	II	0.8	.	3	1.5
Hieracium pilosella	.	.	.	.	.	.	.	.			2	1	.	.	.	.	II	0.5	1	.	3	1	.	.	III	0.8	1	.	0.5
Hypericum pulchrum	.	.	.	.	.	.	.	.			2	.	.	.	.	.	I	0.3	.	.	1	.	1	+	II	0.5	.	1	0.5
Linum catharticum	.	.	.	.	.	.	.	.			.	.	.	.	.	.			3	1	4	.	3	.	IV	1.8	.	.	
Lotus corniculatus	.	.	2	.	.	.	.	.	I	0.3	4	.	.	.	.	.	I	0.7	4	3	4	.	6	5	V	3.7	.	.	
Oxalis acetosella	.	.	.	.	.	.	.	.			1	+	.	+	1	+	V	0.8	.	.	.	2	.	.	I	0.3	+	.	0.5
Parnassia palustris	.	.	.	.	.	.	.	.			.	.	+	3	.	.	II	0.7	.	1	.	.	1	.	II	0.3	2	.	1.0
Pedicularis sylvatica	.	2	.	.	.	3	.	.	II	0.6	.	.	.	.	.	.			.	.	.	.	.	.			.	.	
Pinguicula vulgaris	.	1	.	.	.	.	.	.	I		.	.	.	.	.	.			.	.	.	.	1	.	I	0 2	1	.	0.5

Polygala serpyllifolia	.	.	1	.	1	2	.	.	II	0.5	.	.	.	.	.	.			4	1	2	.	.	.	III	1.2	.	.	
Polygonum viviparum	.	.	.	.	.	.	.	.			.	.	.	.	.	.			.	2	.	.	.	.	I	0.3	2	+	1.5
Plantago lanceolata	.	1	2	.	1	.	.	.	II	0.5	1	1	.	.	.	.	II	0.3	3	2	3	.	2	.	IV	1.7	.	.	
P. maritima	.	.	.	.	.	.	.	.			.	.	.	.	.	.			.	.	2	.	2	.	II	0.7	.	.	
Potentilla erecta	1	2	2	5	3	2	4	2	V	2.6	3	.	.	3	.	3	III	1.5	4	3	3	2	3	3	V	3.0	3	3	3.0
Primula vulgaris	.	.	.	.	.	.	.	.			3	.	.	.	.	.	I	0.5	.	.	1	.	4	.	II	0.8	.	.	
Prunella vulgaris	.	.	.	.	.	.	1	.	I	0.1	3	.	3	4	3	.	IV	2.2	2	1	3	3	3	3	V	2.5	.	.	
Ranunculus acris	1	.	.	.	.	.	.	.	I	0.1	.	3	+	3	6	.	IV	2.2	.	2	.	2	3	3	IV	1.7	2	.	1.0
Rumex acetosa	.	.	2	.	.	.	.	.	I	0.3	2	2	+	3	+	.	V	1.5	.	3	.	.	3	3	III	1.5	2	.	1.0
Saxifraga aizoides	.	.	.	.	.	.	.	.			.	3	.	.	.	.	I	0.5	.	.	.	1	.	.	I	0.2	.	.	
Sedum rosea	.	.	.	.	.	.	.	.			.	+	.	.	.	.	I	0.2	.	.	.	+	.	.	I	0.2	1	.	0.5
Sibbaldia procumbens	.	.	.	.	.	.	.	.			.	.	.	.	.	.			.	.	.	.	.	.			3	4	3.5
Silene acaulis	.	.	.	.	.	.	.	.			.	.	.	.	.	.			.	.	.	.	.	.			6	4	5.0
S. maritima	.	.	.	.	.	.	.	.			.	.	.	.	.	.			.	.	2	.	1	.	II	0.5	.	.	
Succisa pratensis	.	.	.	.	.	.	.	.			1	.	.	.	.	.	I	0.2	.	.	.	.	3	.	I	0.5	1	.	0.5
Thymus drucei	.	.	2	.	.	.	2	.	II	0.5	4	4	3	4	4	.	V	3.2	3	2	3	3	5	4	V	3.3	2	4	3.0
Trifolium repens	3	.	.	2	.	.	.	.	II	0.6	1	.	.	.	.	.	I	0.2	.	.	2	.	2	.	II	0 7	.	.	
Veronica serpyllifolia	1	.	.	.	.	.	.	.	I	0.1	3	.	1	1	3	.	IV	1.3	.	.	.	.	.	+	I	0.2	.	.	
Viola riviniana	.	.	.	3	.	.	2	2	II	0.9	2	3	.	3	+	+	V	1.7	.	2	2	2	3	3	V	2.0	2	3	2.5
Breutelia chrysocoma	.	3	.	2	.	.	.	.	II	0.6	.	4	.	3	5	5	IV	2.8	4	.	.	2	3	1	IV	1.7	+	.	0.5
Ctenidium molluscum	.	.	.	.	.	.	.	.			.	6	.	.	.	.	I	1.0	2	3	3	3	2	.	V	2.2	5	.	2.5
Dicranum scoparium	.	.	2	3	2	2	1	2	IV	1.5	2	.	.	.	.	.	I	0.3	.	.	.	1	.	.	I	0.2	.	.	
Ditrichum flexicale	.	.	.	.	.	.	.	.			.	5	.	.	.	.	I	0.8	.	.	3	.	.	.	I	0.5	3	.	1.5
Hylocomium splendens	3	3	3	6	3	.	4	3	V	3.1	5	.	4	4	4	6	V	3.8	5	3	1	2	4	4	V	3.2	2	.	1.0
†***Hypnum cupressiforme***	.	1	.	4	2	2	.	3	IV	1.5	.	.	.	3	.	.	I	0.5	2	4	4	2	.	1	V	2.2	.	.	
Mnium hornum	.	.	.	.	.	.	.	.			.	.	.	+	.	.	I	0.2	.	.	.	1	.	.	I	0.2	.	.	
Pleurozium schreberi	.	4	3	3	1	3	.	3	IV	2.1	.	.	.	.	.	.			.	.	.	2	.	.	I	0.3	.	.	
Polytrichum alpinum	.	.	.	.	.	.	.	.			.	.	.	.	3	5	II	1.3	.	.	.	.	.	.			2	3	2.5
P. formosum	.	.	.	.	3	.	3	.	II	0.8	.	.	2	.	.	.	I	0.3	.	.	.	.	1	2	II	0.5	.	.	
P. piliferum	.	.	.	.	.	.	.	2	I	0.3	.	.	.	.	.	.			.	.	.	.	.	.			.	3	1.5
Pseudoscleropodium purum	.	.	.	1	.	.	.	.	I	0.1	4	.	.	.	.	.	I	0.7	2	3	3	.	4	1	V	2.2	.	1	0.5
Rhacomitrium lanuginosum	.	.	+	1	.	.	1	3	III	0.8	2	.	5	.	4	5	IV	2.7	1	3	.	.	5	2	IV	1.8	3	4	3.5
Rhytidiadelphus loreus	.	.	.	3	.	.	3	3	II	1.1	.	.	5	4	4	8	IV	3.5	.	3	.	.	.	2	II	0.8	.	.	
R. squarrosus	2	.	2	.	.	.	3	3	III	1.3	3	.	4	1	2	.	IV	1.7	.	.	.	2	2	5	III	1.5	.	.	
R. triquetrus	.	.	.	.	.	.	.	.			5	.	.	+	.	.	II	1.0	.	.	4	.	3	.	II	1.2	.	.	
Thuidium tamariscinum	.	.	.	3	1	.	1	.	II	0.6	+	.	.	4	1	4	IV	1.7	.	2	.	.	4	2	III	1.3	.	.	
Anastrepta orcadensis	.	.	.	.	.	.	.	.			.	.	.	1	.	3	II	0.7	.	.	.	.	.	.				.	
Diplophyllum albicans	.	.	.	.	.	.	.	.			.	.	.	1	1	3	III	0.8	.	.	.	.	.	.			.	1	0.5
Frullania tamarisci	.	.	.	.	.	.	.	.			2	.	.	2	2	.	III	1.0	2	.	2	.	3	2	IV	1.5	1	.	0.5
Ptilidium ciliare	.	.	.	.	.	.	.	.			.	.	.	2	.	.	I	0.3	.	.	.	.	.	2	I	0.3	.	2	1.0
Riccardia pinguis	.	.	.	.	.	.	.	.			.	.	.	.	.	.			1	.	.	.	.	.	I	0.2	.	.	
Cladonia arbuscula	.	.	.	.	.	.	.	.			.	.	.	.	.	.			.	.	1	1	.	1	III	0.5	.	.	
C. uncialis	.	.	.	.	.	.	.	1	I	0.1	.	.	.	.	.	.			.	.	.	.	.	.			.	1	0.5
Peltigera canina	1	.	.	.	.	.	.	.	I	0.1	.	.	1	1	.	.	II	0.3	.	.	.	.	.	1	I	0.2	.	.	
Total number of species (140)	15	19	22	22	18	15	25	24			36	30	22	42	38	26			27	37	37	33	45	36			39	28	
	Mean number of species per relevé = 20. Total number of species in association = 59.										Mean number of species per relevé = 32 3 Total number of species in association = 87.								Mean number of species per relevé = 35.8 Total number of species in association = 89.								Mean number of species per relevé = 33.5. Total number of species in *nodum* = 53.		

* Including *E. confusa*, *E. brevipila*, *E. micrantha* and *E. nemorosa*. † var. *ericetorum* in 2, 4, 5, 6, 8, and 16. var. *tectorum* in 12, 17, and 20.

ADDITIONAL SPECIES IN LIST

2. *Narthecium ossifragum* 2, *Trichophorum cespitosum* 2, *Leucobryum glaucum* 1.
7. *Molinia caerulea* 3, *Juncus effusus* +, *Sphagnum capillaceum* 2.
9. *Cirsium vulgare* +.
10. *Asplenium viride* +, *Oxyria digyna* +, *Taraxacum officinale* agg. 2.
11. *Alchemilla wichurae* 3.
12. *Isothecium myosuroides* var. *brachythecioides* 2, *Barbilophozia lycopodioides* 2, *Herberta straminea* 1, *Scapania aspera* 1, *Tritomaria quinquedentata* 2.
13. *Lycopodium selago* +, *Saxifraga hypnoides* 3, *Atrichum undulatum* 2, *Diphyscium foliosum* +, *Polytrichum urnigerum* 1, *Sphagnum tenellum* 1, *Nardia scalaris* 2.
14. *Sphagnum subsecundum* var. *auriculatum* 2, *Bazzania tricrenata* 1, *Scapania gracilis* +, *S. ornithopodioides* 3.
15. *Carex demissa* 2.
16. *Betula pubescens* 1, *Arrhenatherum elatius* 1.
17. *Sieglingia decumbens* 4, *Anthyllis vulneraria* 2, *Trifolium pratense* 1.
18. *Acrocladium cuspidatum* 1.
19. *Botrychium lunaria* 1, *Cirsium palustre* 3, *Epilobium montanum* 2, *Galium boreale* 1, *Peltigera apthosa* 1.
20. *Antitrichia curtipendula* 1.
21. *Deschampsia cespitosa* 3, *Geum rivale* 1, *Blindia acuta* 1, *Campylium stellatum* 2, *Fissidens cristatus* +.
22. *Vaccinium vitis-idaea* 2, *Cherleria sedoides* 1, *Rhacomitrium heterostichum* 1, *Marsupella alpina* +, *Cladonia coccifera* +.

LOCALITIES

1. Camasunary; 2. Coire na Creiche; 3, 16. Ben Suardal; 4. Corrie Amadal; 5. Preshal More; 6. Slat Bheinn; 7. Healaval Mhor; 8. Sgùrr na Coinnich; 9, 19. Ben Tianavaig; 10, 14, 21. Blà Bheinn; 11, 12, 20. The Storr; 13. Corrie Scamadal; 15. Elgol; 17. Lealt; 18. An Càrnach; 22. Beinn Edra.

‡ Table 4.39 can be found on p. 130.

TABLE 4.41

Class	NARDO-CALLUNETEA										
Order	NARDETALIA										
Alliance	**Nardo–Galion saxatilis**										
Association	*Nardo–Juncetum squarrosi*										
	1	2	3	4	5	6	7	8	9		
Reference Number	B67 130	B68 103	B68 073	B68 084	B68 170	B68 077	B67 126	B68 165	B68 104		
Map reference	455 616	445 690	492 538	488 548	225 421	490 542	443 603	220 445	445 690		
Altitude (feet)	1750	1650	2100	1650	1600	2050	1500	1500	1650		
Aspect (degrees)	270	135	270	315	.	270	.	.	135		
Slope (degrees)	3	10	5	5	.	5	.	.	5		
Cover (per cent)	100	100	100	100	100	100	100	100	100		
Plot area (square metres)	4	4	4	4	4	4	4	4	4	C	D
Calluna vulgaris	.	2	4	.	.	.	2	2	.	III	1.1
Empetrum nigrum	.	.	.	.	.	.	2	1	3	II	0.7
Vaccinum myrtillus	3	.	.	.	1	.	2	+	.	III	0.8
Lycopodium alpinum	3	.	.	.	.	.	3	.	+	II	0.8
L. selago	3	.	.	.	4	.	.	.	.	II	0.8
Selaginella selaginoides	.	.	2	2	.	.	.	.	.	II	0.4
Agrostis tenuis	3	5	3	.	3	.	.	.	.	III	1.6
Anthoxanthum odoratum	.	2	.	3	.	.	.	.	.	II	0.6
Deschampsia flexuosa	.	.	3	3	.	3	.	.	.	II	1.0
Festuca vivipara	.	4	5	4	2	.	.	.	2	III	1.9
Molinia caerulea	.	.	.	.	.	5	.	.	3	II	0.9
Nardus stricta	8	8	8	7	8	4	3	5	.	V	5.7
Carex binervis	.	3	4	.	.	.	.	.	.	II	0.8
C. echinata	.	2	.	.	.	3	.	.	4	II	1.0
C. panicea	.	3	.	.	.	.	1	.	2	II	0.7
C. pilulifera	2	2	3	1	.	.	.	.	.	III	0.9
Eriophorum angustifolium	.	.	.	.	.	.	.	2	4	II	0.7
Juncus kochii	.	2	.	.	.	.	.	.	2	II	0.4
J. squarrosus	2	5	6	7	7	8	8	8	8	V	6.6
Galium saxatile	3	+	3	4	1	4	3	4	3	V	2.9
Polygala serpyllifolia	1	+	2	.	.	.	.	.	1	III	0.6
Potentilla erecta	3	3	4	3	3	.	3	1	3	V	2.6
Thymus drucei	.	.	3	3	.	3	.	.	.	II	1.0
Viola palustris	.	3	.	.	.	.	.	.	2	II	0.6
V. riviniana	.	.	1	3	2	1	.	.	.	III	0.8
Hylocomium splendens	2	4	3	4	.	.	.	.	1	III	1.6
Polytrichum alpinum	4	.	.	2	2	3	4	1	.	IV	1.8
Rhacomitrium lanuginosum	2	.	6	.	8	+	8	3	.	IV	3.1
Rhytidiadelphus loreus	.	.	.	4	.	.	3	5	.	II	1.3
R. squarrosus	.	3	2	2	.	.	.	.	.	II	0.8
Sphagnum capillaceum	.	.	.	.	.	4	1	3	3	III	1.2
S. papillosum	.	3	.	.	3	8	4	7	7	III	3.6
S. plumulosum	.	.	.	.	2	3	.	2	.	II	0.8
Thuidium tamariscinum	.	3	.	3	.	.	.	.	.	II	0.7
Cladonia uncialis	.	.	.	.	1	.	4	.	.	II	0.6
Total number of species (65)	14	20	20	22	16	16	21	22	18		

Mean number of species per relevé = 18.8.

ADDITIONAL SPECIES IN LIST

1. *Festuca ovina* 3.
2. *Cerastium holosteoides* +.
3. *Alchemilla alpina* +, *Gentianella campestris* 1.
4. *Luzula campestris* 4, *Taraxacum officinale* agg. +, *Breutelia chrysocoma* +, *Ctenidium molluscum* +, *Pseudoscleropodium purum* 3, *Frullania tamarisci* +.
5. *Campylopus atrovirens* 2, *Sphagnum tenellum* 3.
6. *Carex curta* 3, *Calypogeia muellerana* 1, *Riccardia pinguis* 1.
7. *Eriophorum vaginatum* 2, *Pleurozium schreberi* 1, *Mylia taylori* 1, *Scapania gracilis* 1, *Cladonia arbuscula* 1.
8. *Luzula multiflora* 1, *L. sylvatica* 2, *Ranunculus flammula* 1, *Aulacomnium palustre* 4, *Campylopus flexuosus* 1, *Polytrichum commune* 2, *Anastrepta orcadensis* +, *Ptilidium ciliare* +.
9. *Pinguicula vulgaris* 1, *Sphagnum recurvum* 2.

LOCALITIES

1, 7. Beinn Edra; 2, 9. Sgùrr Mor; 3, 4, 6. The Storr; 5. Healaval Bheag; 8. Healaval Mhor.

TABLE 4.42

Class	NARDO–CALLUNETEA
Order	CALLUNO–ULICETALIA
Alliance	**Ericion cinereae**
Association	*Callunetum vulgaris*

	1	2	3	4	5	6	7	8		
Reference Number	B67 081	B67 031	B67 054	B68 054	B68 059	B68 115	B68 179	B67 073		
Map Reference	544 185	312 336	446 257	468 342	495 312	390 417	176 544	757 218		
Altitude (feet)	250	250	900	350	150	450	500	1600		
Aspect (degrees)	135	0	270	270	135	135	45	225		
Slope (degrees)	20	5	5	20	25	15	5	20		
Cover (per cent)	100	100	100	100	100	100	100	85		
Plot area (square metres)	4	4	4	4	4	4	4	4	C	D
Erica cinerea	3	.	2	5	6	4	6	7	V	4.1
Calluna vulgaris	8	9	8	9	8	8	8	8	V	8.3
Blechnum spicant	3	.	2	.	4	2	.	.	III	1.4
Agrostis canina	2	.	.	.	.	1	.	.	II	0.4
A. tenuis	3	.	3	3	3	3	3	.	IV	2.3
Deschampsia flexuosa	3	1	2	.	3	4	.	2	IV	1.9
Festuca ovina	.	.	.	.	.	2	2	2	II	0.8
Molinia caerulea	.	.	3	2	3	.	.	.	II	1.0
Carex binervis	.	.	1	3	3	4	5	.	IV	2.0
Trichophorum cespitosum	.	.	.	1	.	3	+	.	II	0.6
Galium saxatile	3	.	.	.	1	.	2	1	III	0.9
Lotus corniculatus	.	.	.	3	3	2	.	.	II	1.0
Polygala serpyllifolia	.	.	+	.	.	3	.	.	II	0.5
Potentilla erecta	3	3	2	2	4	4	4	2	V	3.0
Succisa pratensis	.	.	.	2	.	4	.	.	II	0.8
Viola riviniana	.	2	.	.	2	.	+	.	II	0.6
Breutelia chrysocoma	.	.	2	3	4	1	.	.	III	1.3
Dicranum scoparium	.	3	.	3	3	2	2	4	IV	2.1
****Hypnum cupressiforme***	5	3	4	5	4	5	4	2	V	4.0
Pleurozium schreberi	4	1	3	2	3	.	4	3	V	2.5
Rhacomitrium lanuginosum	.	.	1	3	.	.	.	2	II	0.8
Rhytidiadelphus loreus	.	.	3	1	3	2	.	3	III	1.5
Sphagnum capillaceum	.	.	4	+	.	.	.	.	II	0.6
Thuidium tamariscinum	4	2	.	.	3	.	2	.	III	1.4
Cladonia arbuscula	.	.	2	1	.	.	.	2	II	0.6
C. coccifera	.	.	.	.	.	1	.	2	II	0.4
C. uncialis	.	.	1	.	.	.	.	2	II	0.4
Total number of species (47)	11	11	20	21	19	23	16	17		

Mean number of species per relevé = 17.2.

* var. *ericetorum* in 1, 2, 3, 4, 5, 6, and 7.

ADDITIONAL SPECIES IN LIST

2. *Pteridium aquilinum* 2, *Lophocolea cuspidata* 2.
3. *Thelypteris limbosperma* 2, *Narthecium ossifragum* 2.
4. *Lycopodium selago* 2, *Festuca vivipara* 2, *Dactylorchis maculata* ssp. *ericetorum* +, *Antennaria dioica* 3.
5. *Hypericum pulchrum* 2, *Linum catharticum* +.
6. *Carex panicea* +, *Juncus squarrosus* 2, *Euphrasia micrantha* 1, *Pedicularis sylvatica* 1.
7. *Lycopodium clavatum* 4, *Pseudoscleropodium purum* 3.
8. *Vaccinium myrtillus* 1, *Cladonia crispata* +, *C. pyxidata* 1.

LOCALITIES

1. Slat Bheinn; 2. Fiskavaig; 3. Coire na Creiche; 4. Glen Varragill; 5. Loch Sligachan; 6. Beinn a' Mhadaidh; 7. Dunvegan Head; 8. Sgùrr na Coinnich.

TABLE 4.43

Class	NARDO–CALLUNETEA															
Order	CALLUNO–ULICETALIA															
Alliance	**Ericion cinerea**															
Association	*Calluna vulgaris–Sieglingia decumbens*												*Calluna vulgaris–Arctostaphylos uva-ursi nodum*			
	1	2	3	4	5	6	7	8	9	10			11	12	13	14	
Reference Number	B67	B68	B68	B68	B68	B68	B68	B68	B68	B68			B68	B68	B68	B68	
	139	182	183	184	185	186	195	196	261	262			312	331	189	188	
Map Reference	416	158	158	158	165	166	234	233	584	584			765	598	179	179	
	493	553	553	553	560	563	605	605	187	187			256	157	561	561	
Altitude (feet)	200	750	800	800	650	550	200	200	75	75			100	300	250	250	
Aspect (degrees)	180	270	180	100	270	270	225	180	270	270			180	180	180	180	
Slope (degrees)	5	25	30	20	5	5	3	5	10	10			30	25	5	5	
Cover (per cent)	100	100	100	100	100	100	100	100	100	100			100	100	100	100	
Plot area (square metres)	4	4	4	4	4	4	4	4	4	4	C	D	4	4	4	4	D
Arctostaphylos uva-ursi	.	.	.	.	.	.	.	.	.	.			5	7	6	4	5.5
Empetrum nigrum	.	.	.	1	.	.	2	+	.	.	II	0.4	1	4	.	.	1.3
Erica cinerea	2	5	5	.	4	6	5	6	7	8	V	4.8	5	4	7	4	5.0
Calluna vulgaris	7	8	7	8	8	8	8	7	8	7	V	7.6	8	7	6	5	6.5
Juniperus communis ssp. *nana*	.	.	.	.	.	.	.	.	.	.			.	.	6	8	3.5
Lonicera periclymenum	.	.	.	.	.	.	.	.	.	.			.	.	4	2	1.5
**Salix repens*	2	.	.	.	.	.	5	3	2	2	III	1.4	.	.	+	.	0.3
Blechnum spicant	.	4	3	3	.	2	+	.	.	.	III	1.3	.	.	1	.	0.3
Pteridium aquilinum	.	.	.	.	.	.	.	.	1	.	I	0.1	.	.	2	2	1.0
Agrostis canina	4	4	3	4	3	4	4	.	3	3	V	3.2	3	3	3	4	3.3
Anthoxanthum odoratum	5	.	4	3	3	4	4	3	2	.	IV	2.8	2	3	4	2	2.3
Deschampsia flexuosa	2	1	2	.	2	.	.	.	.	.	II	0.7	3	2	.	3	2.0
Festuca ovina	3	4	4	3	4	3	3	3	4	4	V	3.5	1	3	3	.	1.8
F. rubra	.	3	3	2	.	1	.	.	.	.	II	0.9	.	.	.	.	
F. vivipara	3	1	3	1	.	3	4	4	3	3	V	2.5	2	1	2	.	1.3
Holcus lanatus	.	3	2	2	.	.	.	.	.	.	II	0.7	.	.	3	.	0.8
Molinia caerulea	.	.	.	.	.	.	4	1	.	3	II	0.8	2	.	.	.	0.5
Sieglingia decumbens	2	4	4	4	4	3	2	3	4	3	V	3.3	3	4	3	.	2.5
Carex binervis	3	.	.	.	4	5	2	2	.	1	III	1.7	5	.	.	.	1.3
C. panicea	.	2	.	.	.	.	.	2	.	.	I	0.4	.	.	.	.	
C. pulicaris	.	3	3	3	3	3	3	3	2	3	V	2.6	2	.	.	.	0.5
†*Dactylorchis maculata*	2	.	.	.	.	.	1	1	.	.	II	0.4	.	.	.	.	
Luzula campestris	2	2	1	2	.	1	.	.	.	.	III	0.8	.	.	.	.	
Trichophorum cespitosum	2	.	.	.	.	.	1	.	.	.	I	0.3	2	.	.	.	0.5
Achillea millefolium	.	.	.	.	.	1	.	1	.	.	I	0.2	.	.	.	.	
Alchemilla xanthochlora	.	2	2	.	.	.	.	.	.	.	I	0.4	.	.	.	.	
Antennaria dioica	+	.	1	.	.	.	.	3	.	1	II	0.6	2	3	.	.	1.3
Anthyllis vulneraria	2	.	.	2	.	.	.	.	.	.	I	0.4	.	.	.	.	
Bellis perennis	.	.	.	.	.	.	2	.	.	.	I	0.2	.	.	.	.	
Carlina vulgaris	.	.	.	.	.	.	.	.	.	.			.	+	2	.	0.8
Cerastium holosteoides	.	.	2	1	.	.	.	.	.	.	I	0.3	.	.	.	.	
Euphrasia micrantha	.	3	2	2	1	2	3	2	2	.	IV	1.7	.	1	.	.	0.3
Galium saxatile	.	.	+	2	3	2	.	.	.	.	II	0.8	.	.	.	3	0.8
Hieracium pilosella	1	.	.	.	.	.	.	.	2	.	I	0.3	.	.	.	.	

Hypericum pulchrum	3	2	3	2	2	.	.	.	.	3	III	1.5	.	2	.	.	0.5
Lathyrus montanus	3	3	2	1	.	.	.	.	.	1	III	1.0	.	2	2	.	1.0
Leontodon autumnalis	.	.	.	+	+	.	1	.	.	.	II	0.3	.	.	.	.	
Linum catharticum	.	2	3	2	.	.	.	.	.	1	II	0.8	.	.	3	.	0.8
Lotus corniculatus	5	+	4	3	3	3	2	2	2	2	V	2.7	.	1	2	.	0.8
Lysimachia nemorum	.	1	1	.	.	.	.	.	.	.	I	0.2	.	.	.	.	
Pinguicula vulgaris	.	.	+	1	.	.	1	.	.	.	II	0.3	.	.	.	.	
Plantago lanceolata	.	.	3	1	+	.	2	2	2	4	IV	1.5	.	.	1	.	0.3
P. maritima	1	.	.	.	.	.	.	1	.	1	II	0.3	.	.	.	.	
Polygala serpyllifolia	1	.	.	1	1	.	.	.	1	1	III	0.5	.	.	.	.	
Potentilla erecta	4	4	3	4	5	4	2	4	4	.	V	3.4	1	.	1	3	1.3
Primula vulgaris	.	2	1	3	.	.	.	.	.	.	II	0.6	.	.	2	2	1.0
Prunella vulgaris	.	1	2	3	3	2	+	.	1	.	IV	1.3	.	.	2	.	0.5
Ranunculus acris	.	.	1	1	.	.	.	.	.	.	I	0.2	.	.	.	.	
Rhinanthus minor agg.	.	.	.	.	.	.	+	2	.	.	I	0.3	.	.	.	.	
Rumex acetosa	.	1	+	.	.	.	.	.	.	.	I	0.2	.	.	.	.	
Solidago virgaurea	.	2	+	.	.	.	.	.	.	.	I	0.3	.	2	2	.	1.0
Succisa pratensis	.	.	2	.	1	.	4	4	1	2	III	1.3	.	1	2	.	0.8
Taraxacum officinale agg.	1	.	.	+	.	.	.	.	.	.	I	0.2	.	.	1	.	0.3
Teucrium scorodonia	.	.	.	.	.	.	.	.	.	.			2	4	4	3	3.3
Thymus drucei	3	.	4	2	.	.	2	3	.	1	III	1.5	.	4	3	.	1.8
Trifolium repens	.	3	1	2	.	.	.	.	.	.	II	0.6	.	.	.	3	0.8
Viola riviniana	.	2	3	.	2	3	.	.	3	2	III	1.5	.	2	3	1	1.5
Breutelia chrysocoma	.	3	4	3	.	.	3	3	.	.	III	1.6	.	.	.	.	
Dicranum scoparium	2	3	3	.	1	1	.	1	.	.	III	1.1	.	1	.	2	0.8
Hylocomium splendens	2	4	.	2	2	2	2	3	5	5	V	2.7	.	.	.	.	
‡*Hypnum cupressiforme*	.	.	.	4	2	1	3	2	.	.	III	1.2	3	.	.	.	0.8
Mnium hornum	.	.	1	.	1	.	.	.	.	.	I	0.2	.	.	.	.	
Pleurozium schreberi	3	3	2	3	3	1	3	2	.	3	V	2.3	.	1	.	.	0.3
Pseudoscleropodium purum	.	.	.	.	1	.	3	4	.	.	II	0.8	.	.	.	2	0.5
Rhacomitrium lanuginosum	4	.	.	.	.	.	.	+	.	.	I	0.5	1	.	.	.	0.3
Rhytidiadelphus loreus	.	.	.	.	.	.	3	1	3	2	II	0.9	.	.	.	.	
R. triquetrus	.	4	4	5	.	.	.	.	2	.	II	1.5	.	.	.	1	0.3
Thuidium tamariscinum	.	2	.	1	2	.	.	2	.	.	II	0.7	.	1	.	1	0.5
Frullania fragilifolia	.	.	.	.	.	.	.	.	.	.			.	2	1	.	0.8
F. tamarisci	.	2	2	1	.	.	2	.	.	.	II	0.7	.	.	.	1	0.3
Total number of species (106)	32	39	43	43	29	23	38	37	22	26			21	22	33	20	

Mean number of species per relevé = 33.2.
Total number of species in association = 94.

Mean number of species per relevé = 24.0.
Total number of species in *nodum* = 52.

* ssp. *argentea* in 1, 7, 8, 9, and 10. † ssp. *ericetorum* in 1, 7, and 8. ‡ var. *ericetorum* in 5, 6, 7, 8, and 11. var. *tectorum* in 4.

ADDITIONAL SPECIES IN LIST

1. *Luzula multiflora* 1, *L. pilosa* 2, *Pyrola media* 3, *Peltigera apthosa* 1.
2. *Angelica sylvestris* +, *Filipendula ulmaria* 1, *Senecio vulgaris* 1, *Silene acaulis* 2, *Veronica officinalis* 2.
3. *Dryopteris filix-mas* 1, *Geum rivale* 1.
4. *Rubus saxatilis* 4, *Fragaria vesca* 2, *Galium boreale* 1, *Vicia sepium* 1, *Hylocomium brevirostre* 2.
5. *Carex demissa* 2, *Sagina procumbens* 1.
7. *Ulex europaeus* 2, *Vaccinium myrtillus* +, *Nardus stricta* 2, *Leucobryum glaucum* 3, *Scapania gracilis* 1.
8. *Juncus squarrosus* +, *Narthecium ossifragum* +, *Galium verum* +, *Gentianella campestris* 2, *Pedicularis sylvatica* 1.
10. *Carex flacca* 2, *Rhytidiadelphus squarrosus* 1.
11. *Campylopus flexuosus* 3, *Cornicularia aculeata* 1.
13. *Salix aurita* 2, *Agrostis stolonifera* 2, *Trichostomum crispulum* 3.

LOCALITIES

1. The Tote; 2, 3, 4, 5, 6, 13, 14. Dunvegan Head; 7, 8. Cnoc a' Chatha; 9, 10. Camas Malag; 11. Kyleakin; 12. Carn Dearg.

TABLE 4.44

Class	NARDO-CALLUNETEA							
Order	CALLUNO-ULICETALIA							
Alliance	**Myrtillion Boreale**							
Association	*Vaccineto–Callunetum hepaticosum*							
	1	2	3	4	5	6		
Reference Number	B68 005	B68 006	B68 233	B67 013	B68 120	B68 121		
Map Reference	413 762	414 761	553 215	552 214	494 531	494 531		
Altitude (feet)	150	150	450	500	1100	1100		
Aspect (degrees)	45	45	45	0	0	0		
Slope (degrees)	30	30	45	45	40	40		
Cover (per cent)	90	100	100	100	100	100		
Plot area (square metres)	4	4	4	4	4	4	C	D
Erica cinerea	2	2	.	.	4	3	IV	1.8
Calluna vulgaris	8	8	8	8	8	8	V	8.0
Lonicera periclymenum	1	+	–	–	–	–	II	0.3
Vaccinium myrtillus	.	3	4	3	4	4	V	3.0
Blechnum spicant	3	2	4	3	4	4	V	3.3
Dryopteris filix-mas	1	2	.	.	.	3	III	1.0
Hymenophyllum wilsonii	+	1	3	+	.	1	V	1.2
Thelypteris limbosperma	.	.	.	2	2	.	II	0.7
Agrostis tenuis	.	.	3	1	.	.	II	0.7
Deschampsia flexuosa	1	3	.	.	2	3	IV	1.5
Festuca vivipara	.	.	2	2	+	.	III	0.8
Molinia caerulea	.	.	3	4	.	.	II	1.2
Carex binervis	1	2	.	.	1	2	IV	1.0
**Dactylorchis maculata*	.	1	.	.	1	.	II	0.3
Luzula sylvatica	2	2	.	.	.	.	II	0.7
Trichophorum cespitosum	.	3	.	.	1	1	III	0.8
Euphrasia micrantha	+	.	1	.	.	.	II	0.3
Galium saxatile	.	.	.	2	3	2	III	1.2
Hypericum pulchrum	2	3	3	.	.	.	III	1.3
Pinguicula vulgaris	1	2	.	.	.	.	II	0.5
Potentilla erecta	3	3	4	2	3	3	V	3.0
Succisa pratensis	.	1	2	.	2	.	III	0.8
Viola riviniana	.	1	.	.	.	2	I	0.5
Breutelia chrysocoma	2	4	4	.	4	.	IV	2.3
Campylopus atrovirens	1	1	1	3	1	.	V	1.2
C. flexuosus	1	1	.	.	.	.	II	0.3
C. setifolius	.	.	2	.	1	.	II	0.5
Dicranum scoparium	2	.	.	3	1	.	III	1.0
D. majus	.	.	1	2	.	.	II	0.5

Dicranodontium uncinatum	.	.	2	.	.	+	II	0.5
Hookeria lucens	.	.	.	1	.	2	II	0.5
Hylocomium splendens	4	1	2	3	.	.	IV	1.7
H. umbratum	.	.	1	+	.	.	II	0.3
†***Hypnum cupressiforme***	1	1	1	2	2	3	V	1.7
Isothecium myosuroides	.	2	1	2	.	3	IV	1.3
Mnium hornum	1	.	.	.	1	.	II	0.3
Plagiothecium undulatum	3	2	1	.	1	.	IV	1.2
Pleurozium schreberi	2	.	1	.	3	.	III	1.0
Ptilium crista-castrensis	.	.	1	2	.	.	II	0.5
Rhacomitrium lanuginosum	1	2	5	4	7	7	V	4.3
Rhytidiadelphus loreus	2	1	3	3	3	4	V	2.7
Sphagnum capillaceum	3	2	2	3	4	2	V	2.7
S. plumulosum	2	3	.	5	.	2	IV	2.0
S. quinquefarium	3	.	2	.	2	3	IV	1.7
‡*S. subsecundum*	1	2	.	.	.	.	II	0.5
S. tenellum	2	4	1	2	.	.	IV	1.5
Thuidium delicatulum	.	.	.	.	2	3	II	0.8
T. tamariscinum	3	.	.	2	.	.	II	0.8
Trichostomum tenuirostre	.	.	1	.	.	2	II	0.5
Anastrepta orcadensis	+	.	2	2	1	1	V	1.2
Bazzania tricrenata	.	2	3	4	1	3	V	2.2
Calypogeia muellerana	.	1	.	.	1	.	II	0.3
Cephalozia bicuspidata	+	1	.	.	1	.	III	0.5
Diplophyllum albicans	4	5	3	2	2	4	V	3.3
Frullania tamarisci	.	.	.	2	1	.	II	0.5
Herberta adunca	5	3	4	6	4	3	V	4.2
Lejeunea patens	1	.	.	.	+	.	II	0.3
Lepidozia reptans	3	.	.	+	.	.	II	0.7
L. trichoclados	2	1	.	.	.	.	II	0.5
Mastigophora woodsii	.	.	4	6	.	1	III	1.8
Mylia taylori	3	2	2	4	3	.	V	2.3
Pellia epiphylla	+	.	.	.	.	1	II	0.3
Plagiochila spinulosa	3	3	3	4	3	3	V	3.2
Pleurozia purpurea	.	.	2	3	3	3	IV	1.8
Saccogyna viticulosa	2	3	.	.	.	.	II	0.8
Scapania gracilis	3	3	4	3	3	3	V	3.2
S. ornithopodioides	.	.	+	1	.	.	II	0.3
Total number of species (86)	46	45	40	42	40	36		

Mean number of species per relevé = 41.5.

* ssp. *ericetorum* in 2 and 5. † var. *ericetorum* in 1, 2, 3, 4, 5, and 6. ‡ var. *auriculatum* in 1 and 2.

ADDITIONAL SPECIES IN LIST

1. *Juniperus communis* ssp. *nana* +, *Pteridium aquilinum* 2, *Sphagnum robustum* 1, *Riccardia sinuata* 1.
2. *Sedum rosea* +, *Myurium hebridarum* 3, *Colura calyptrifolia* +, *Frullania germana* +, *Harpalejeunea ovata* 1.
3. *Cladonia uncialis* 2.
4. *Carex pulicaris* 2, *Hyocomium flagellare* +, *Barbilophozia barbata* +, *Herberta straminea* 3, *Lepidozia setacea* 1.
5. *Dryopteris borreri* 3, *Sphagnum fimbriatum* +.
6. *Rubus saxatilis* 1, *Carex pilulifera* 2, *Oxalis acetosella* 2, *Marsupella emarginata* 1.

LOCALITIES

1, 2. Meall Tuath; 3, 4. Blà Bheinn; 5, 6. Carn Liath.

TABLE 4.39

Class	SALICETEA HERBACEAE												
Order	DESCHAMPSIETO–MYRTILLETALIA												
Alliance	**Nardeto–Caricion bigelowii**												
Association	*Nardus stricta–Vaccinium myrtillus*												
Facies	*Typicum*									*Vaccinium-rich*			
	1	2	3	4	5	6	7	8	9	10	11		
Reference number	B68 336	B67 001A	B67 001B	B67 001C	B68 243	B68 244	B68 082	B68 083	B69 068	B67 067	B68 066		
Map reference	505 284	536 211	536 211	536 211	529 218	330 216	491 547	489 548	761 223	761 223	760 223		
Altitude (feet)	1800	1900	1900	1850	2900	2800	1850	2000	2250	2300	2300		
Aspect (degrees)	0	45	45	45	115	90	0	0	0	0	340		
Slope (degrees)	10	5	5	5	15	10	5	5	5	5	5		
Cover (per cent)	100	100	100	100	100	100	100	100	100	100	100		
Plot area (square metres)	4	4	4	4	4	4	4	4	4	4	4	C	D
Calluna vulgaris	1	2	+	.	.	.	2	3	.	.	.	III	0.8
Salix herbacea	.	.	.	.	.	.	.	.	.	3	3	I	0.5
Vaccinium myrtillus	.	2	3	3	4	3	3	2	4	8	7	V	3.5
Blechnum spicant	.	.	.	.	3	2	.	.	.	.	.	I	0.5
Lycopodium alpinum	4	2	3	2	.	4	2	2	.	2	3	V	2.2
L. selago	3	3	4	5	3	.	3	.	1	2	1	V	2.3
Agrostis tenuis	3	.	.	.	.	.	3	2	3	.	.	II	1.0
Festuca ovina	.	.	.	.	.	.	.	.	4	.	1	I	0.5
F. vivipara	.	.	.	.	.	3	4	.	2	2	2	III	1.2
Nardus stricta	8	9	8	7	9	8	9	8	6	4	4	V	7.3
Carex bigelowii	3	3	3	4	5	3	4	4	3	3	3	V	3.5
C. pilulifera	3	.	.	.	4	3	3	2	.	.	.	III	1.4
Luzula sylvatica	.	.	.	.	.	.	.	.	3	2	1	II	0.5
Alchemilla alpina	.	1	.	.	3	.	.	.	3	1	.	II	0.7
Galium saxatile	.	2	2	3	4	2	4	4	6	4	2	V	3.0
Polygala serpyllifolia	1	.	.	.	.	1	.	.	.	.	.	I	0.2
Potentilla erecta	3	1	+	3	3	4	.	4	2	2	3	V	2.4
Thymus drucei	.	2	.	.	.	.	4	.	.	.	.	I	0.5
Dicranum fuscescens	1	.	.	2	.	2	.	1	.	2	.	III	0.7
Hylocomium splendens	.	1	2	.	.	1	4	4	3	3	.	IV	1.6
Mnium hornum	.	.	.	.	.	.	2	.	2	.	.	I	0.4
Pleurozium schreberi	4	.	.	.	.	1	.	.	.	.	.	I	0.5
Polytrichum alpinum	.	2	3	3	.	.	3	.	3	5	4	IV	2.1
Rhacomitrium lanuginosum	5	6	5	7	5	3	3	5	.	4	5	V	4.4
Rhytidiadelphus loreus	2	4	3	3	.	.	4	3	8	4	4	V	3.2
Sphagnum palustre	.	.	1	.	.	.	.	.	1	.	1	I	0.3
Anastrepta orcadensis	.	.	.	.	.	.	.	.	2	3	3	II	0.7
Ptilidium ciliare	.	.	.	.	.	.	.	.	2	2	1	II	0.4
Cetraria islandica	2	3	2	3	4	3	2	2	.	1	.	V	2.0
Cladonia arbuscula	2	.	.	.	1	.	.	.	.	.	.	I	0.3
C. uncialis	3	2	3	2	3	2	+	1	.	2	2	V	1.9
Total number of species (54)	18	18	18	13	15	17	21	17	19	21	24		

Mean number of species per relevé = 18.3.

ADDITIONAL SPECIES IN LIST

1. *Trichophorum cespitosum* 4, *Succisa pratensis* 2.
2. *Polygonum viviparum* 1, *Sphagnum plumulosum* 2.
3. *Campylopus atrovirens* 2, *Rhytidiadelphus squarrosus* 3, *Anthelia julacea* 3.
5. *Molinia caerulea* 1, *Carex panicea* 2.
6. *Vaccinium vitis-idaea* 2.
7. *Viola riviniana* 2, *Breutelia chrysocoma* 3, *Sphagnum tenellum* 2
8. *Gnaphalium supinum* 4, *Hypnum cupressiforme* var. *ericetorum* 2.
9. *Deschampsia cespitosa* 5.
10. *Diplophyllum albicans* 1.
11. *Empetrum hermaphroditum* 2, *Polytrichum piliferum* 1, *Barbilophozia barbata* +, *Lophozia ventricosa*+*Mylia taylori* 1, *Scapania gracilis* 1.

LOCALITIES

1. Coire na Sgairde; 2, 3, 4. Coire Uaigneach; 5, 6. Blà Bheinn; 7, 8. The Storr; 9, 10, 11. Sgùrr na Coinnich.

TABLE 4.45

Class	BETULO–ADENOSTYLETEA
Order	ADENOSTYLETALIA
Alliance	**Dryoptero–Calamagrostidion purpureae**
Association	*Luzula sylvatica–Vaccinium myrtillus*

	1	2	3	4	5		
Reference Number	B67 106	B67 034	B68 122	B67 057	B68 240		
Map Reference	603 078	334 298	494 531	455 246	535 211		
Altitude (feet)	250	800	1100	1800	1700		
Aspect (degrees)	0	0	0	0	0		
Slope (degrees)	5	10	15	30	40		
Cover (per cent)	100	100	100	100	50		
Plot area (square metres)	2	4	4	4	4	C	D
Calluna vulgaris	4	3	3	.	.	III	2.0
Vaccinium myrtillus	6	5	5	5	5	V	5.2
Blechnum spicant	3	3	5	3	2	V	3.2
Dryopteris borreri	3	3	5	.	.	III	2.2
D. dilatata	4	.	3	.	.	II	1.4
D. filix-mas	3	2	3	.	.	III	1.6
Hymenophyllum wilsonii	3	+	.	.	.	II	0.8
Thelypteris dryopteris	2	.	.	1	.	II	0.6
T. limbosperma	4	6	5	.	.	III	3.0
T. phegopteris	3	1	.	.	.	II	0.8
Agrostis canina	1	.	4	.	4	III	1.8
Anthoxanthum odoratum	.	3	3	3	.	III	1.8
Deschampsia flexuosa	3	3	3	2	5	V	3.2
Festuca ovina	2	.	3	.	.	II	1.0
F. vivipara	.	.	.	2	4	II	1.2
Endymion non-scriptus	2	3	3	.	.	III	1.6
Luzula sylvatica	8	8	8	9	7	V	8.0
Alchemilla alpina	.	1	.	2	3	III	1.2
Cardamine flexuosa	.	+	2	.	.	II	0.6
Digitalis purpurea	.	.	1	.	1	II	0.4
Galium saxatile	.	2	4	3	3	IV	2.4
Hypericum pulchrum	.	2	1	.	.	II	0.6
Oxalis acetosella	3	3	2	3	2	V	2.6
Potentilla erecta	.	2	.	1	.	II	0.6
Viola riviniana	.	2	3	2	.	III	1.4
Breutelia chrysocoma	.	2	.	.	1	II	0.6
Dicranum scoparium	3	3	.	.	1	III	1.4
Hylocomium splendens	.	3	3	.	.	II	1.2
**Hypnum cupressiforme*	1	1	3	.	1	IV	1.2
Isothecium myosuroides	2	1	2	.	.	III	1.0
Mnium punctatum	.	2	1	.	.	II	0.6
Plagiothecium undulatum	2	3	.	.	.	II	1.0
Polytrichum formosum	3	.	1	.	2	III	1.2
Rhacomitrium lanuginosum	.	2	.	4	7	III	2.6
Rhytidiadelphus loreus	3	.	4	.	1	III	1.6
Sphagnum quinquefarium	3	.	3	.	.	II	1.2
†*S. subsecundum*	3	+	.	.	.	II	0.8
Thuidium delicatulum	3	.	2	.	.	II	1.0
T. tamariscinum	3	2	2	3	+	V	2.0
Diplophyllum albicans	2	.	.	.	2	II	0.8
Scapania gracilis	3	1	.	.	.	II	0.8
Total number of species (75)	41	35	34	16	26		

Mean number of species per relevé = 30.4. * var. *ericetorum* in 2 and 3. † var. *auriculatum* in 1 and 2.

ADDITIONAL SPECIES IN LIST

1. *Dryopteris aemula* 4, *Ajuga reptans* 2, *Anemone nemorosa* 3, *Hypericum androsaemum* 2, *Primula vulgaris* 3, *Dicranum majus* 3, *Hylocomium umbratum* 2, *Mnium hornum* 2, *Sphagnum fimbriatum* 3, *Lepidozia pearsonii* 2, *L. pinnata* 1, *Plagiochila spinulosa* 3, *Saccogyna viticulosa* 3.
2. *Luzula multiflora* 3, *Lotus corniculatus* 1, *Sedum rosea* 1, *Atrichum undulatum* 2, *Frullania tamarisci* 1.
3. *Erica cinerea* 1, *Carex binervis* 2, *Eurhynchium praelongum* var. *stokesii* 1, *Mnium undulatum* 1, *Pleurozium schreberi* 2, *Ptilium crista-castrensis* 2.
4. *Thalictrum alpinum* 2, *Thymus drucei* 2.
5. *Cryptogramma crispa* 4, *Dryopteris abbreviata* 4, *Lycopodium selago* 3, *Saxifraga hypnoides* 2, *S. stellaris* 3, *Rhacomitrium fasciculare* 5, *R. heterostichum* +, *Herberta adunca* 1.

LOCALITIES

1. Gillean Burn; 2. Preshal More; 3. Carn Liath; 4. Coire na Creiche; 5. Blà Bheinn.

TABLE 4.46

Class	BETULO-ADENOSTYLETEA								
Order	ADENOSTYLETALIA								
Alliance	**Mulgedion alpini**								
Association	*Luzula sylvatica–Silene dioica*								
	1	2	3	4	5	6	7		
Reference Number	B68	B68	B68	B68	B68	B67	B68		
	003	151	150	039	326A	109	187		
Map Reference	410	153	153	368	522	236	176		
	762	507	507	707	155	553	559		
Altitude (feet)	100	50	50	75	400	150	350		
Aspect (degrees)	315	0	0	0	315	0	0		
Slope (degrees)	40	5	10	30	10	10	60		
Cover (per cent)	80	100	100	100	100	100	100		
Plot area (square metres)	4	4	4	4	4	4	4	C	D
Calluna vulgaris	3	5	5	3	6	6	8	V	5.1
Empetrum nigrum	4	.	.	.	2	.	.	II	0.9
Erica cinerea	2	.	.	.	5	.	5	III	1.7
Juniperus communis ssp. *nana*	3	.	6	.	.	.	.	II	1.3
Populus tremula	.	.	.	.	4	3	.	II	1.0
Rubus saxatilis	.	.	.	.	1	3	3	III	1.0
Athyrium filix-femina	.	6	.	3	.	.	4	III	1.9
Dryopteris borreri	.	4	.	.	.	2	.	II	0.9
Polypodium vulgare	.	3	4	.	.	.	.	II	1.0
Thelypteris limbosperma	.	.	.	3	3	3	.	III	1.3
T. phegopteris	.	.	.	.	2	+	2	III	0.7
Agrostis tenuis	.	.	.	.	3	.	1	II	0.6
Arrhenatherum elatius	.	3	.	3	.	.	.	II	0.9
Deschampsia flexuosa	.	.	.	.	4	.	2	II	0.9
Festuca ovina	6	.	4	5	3	3	3	V	3.4
F. rubra	3	4	3	4	.	.	.	III	2.0
F. vivipara	.	.	.	.	3	.	1	II	0.6
Holcus lanatus	4	4	.	2	.	.	.	III	1.4
Carex binervis	.	.	.	.	2	.	3	II	0.7
C. pulicaris	2	.	.	.	3	.	4	III	1.3
Endymion non-scriptus	.	1	3	4	.	3	.	III	1.6
Luzula sylvatica	5	7	5	7	6	6	5	V	5.9
Orchis mascula	.	1	.	.	.	+	.	II	0.3
Angelica sylvestris	3	7	2	.	2	3	3	V	2.9
Armeria maritima	3	.	.	+	.	.	.	II	0.6
Centaurea nigra	.	3	1	.	.	.	.	II	0.6
Cirsium heterophyllum	.	.	.	.	3	3	.	II	0.9
Digitalis purpurea	.	.	.	3	.	.	3	II	0.9
Epilobium montanum	2	3	.	+	1	.	.	III	1.0
Filipendula ulmaria	.	4	4	.	4	.	4	III	2.3
Galium saxatile	.	.	.	.	2	2	.	II	0.6

Geum rivale	.	.	.	4	2	2	.	III	1.1
Hypericum pulchrum	1	.	.	2	1	1	3	IV	1.1
Lathyrus montanus	.	.	.	.	1	1	.	II	0.3
Lotus corniculatus	3	.	.	.	2	.	.	II	0.7
Plantago lanceolata	1	.	+	.	.	.	.	II	0.3
P. maritima	2	1	.	.	.	.	.	II	0.4
Polygala serpyllifolia	1	.	.	2	.	.	.	II	0.4
Potentilla erecta	3	1	.	.	3	.	3	III	1.4
Primula vulgaris	3	3	.	.	.	4	5	III	2.1
Prunella vulgaris	.	.	.	2	.	.	2	II	0.6
Rumex acetosa	3	4	4	3	3	3	.	V	2.9
Sedum rosea	7	5	5	5	5	4	.	V	4.4
Silene dioica	3	4	3	4	3	.	3	V	2.9
Solidago virgaurea	1	.	.	.	+	.	4	III	0.9
Succisa pratensis	.	.	.	4	3	.	.	II	1.0
Teucrium scorodonia	.	.	1	2	.	3	3	III	1.3
Thymus drucei	2	.	.	.	.	1	2	III	0.7
Valeriana officinalis	.	.	5	4	2	+	.	III	1.7
Veronica serpyllifolia	.	.	.	3	1	.	.	II	0.6
Viola riviniana	1	.	.	1	1	2	2	IV	1.0
Breutelia chrysocoma	.	.	.	.	3	3	2	III	1.1
Dicranum scoparium	.	.	3	3	.	.	.	II	0.9
Hylocomium brevirostre	.	.	.	.	4	1	.	II	0.7
H. splendens	.	.	.	.	3	.	3	II	0.9
**Hypnum cupressiforme*	.	.	+	.	.	4	.	II	0.7
Isothecium myosuroides	.	.	1	3	.	.	.	II	0.6
Mnium hornum	.	1	.	1	.	.	.	II	0.3
Pseudoscleropodium purum	.	.	2	3	1	.	.	III	0.9
Rhytidiadelphus squarrosus	.	.	.	2	.	1	.	II	0.4
R. triquetrus	.	.	1	.	4	2	.	III	1.0
Thuidium tamariscinum	.	.	4	.	2	2	4	III	1.7
Frullania tamarisci	.	.	.	2	2	2	3	III	1.3
Saccogyna viticulosa	.	1	.	.	.	3	.	II	0.6
Tritomaria quinquedentata	.	.	.	.	1	3	.	II	0.6
Total number of species (105)	27	24	24	35	54	43	31		

Mean number of species per relevé = 34.0.

* var. *resupinatum* in 3. † var. *ericetorum* in 6.

ADDITIONAL SPECIES IN LIST

1. *Carex flacca* 1, *Heracleum sphondylium* 3.
2. *Camptothecium sericeum* 1, *Fissidens taxifolius* 1.
3. *Asplenium adiantum–nigrum* +, *Lobaria pulmonaria* 2.
4. *Dryopteris aemula* 3, *D. filix-mas* 5, *Chamaenerion angustifolium* 4, *Crepis paludosa* 3, *Lathyrus pratensis* 3.
5. *Sorbus aucuparia* 3, *S. rupicola* 5, *Sieglingia decumbens* 3, *Alchemilla alpina* 1, *A. glabra* 4, *Anemone nemorosa* 2, *Fragaria vesca* 1, *Oxalis acetosella* 2, *Trollius europaeus* 3, *Vicia sylvatica* 4, *Ctenidium molluscum* 2, *Neckera crispa* 2, *Trichostomum brachydontium* 1, *Plagiochila asplenioides* 1.
6. *Blechnum spicant* 3, *Allium ursinum* +, *Antennaria dioica* 3, *Galium odoratum* 3, *Sanicula europaea* 3, *Vicia sepium* 1, *Plagiothecium undulatum* 2, *Pleurozium schreberi* 3, *Rhytidiadelphus loreus* 2, *Diplophyllum albicans* 1, *Plagiochila spinulosa* 3.
7. *Lonicera periclymenum* 3, *Salix aurita* 6, *Osmunda regalis* 5.

LOCALITIES

1. Meall Tuath; 2, 3. Meanish; 4. Camas Mor; 5. Carn Mor; 6. Lovaig Bay; 7. Dunvegan Head.

TABLE 4.47

Class	BETULO-ADENOSTYLETEA																		
Order	ADENOSTYLETALIA																		
Alliance	**Mulgedion alpini**																		
Association	*Betula pubescens–Cirsium heterophyllum*									*Sedum rosea–Alchemilla glabra*									
	1	2	3	4	5	6	7			8	9	10	11	12	13	14			
Reference number	B67	B68	B67	B67	B67	B68	B67			B67	B67	B67	B68	B68	B68	B67			
	029	096	077	003	104	061	108			102	104	118	235	110	085	135			
Map reference	370	381	567	611	603	406	373			552	547	517	542	442	485	450			
	330	609	201	211	077	322	363			214	216	406	215	708	550	608			
Altitude (feet)	100	50	100	150	200	300	300			600	650	800	1200	1300	1450	1500			
Aspect (degrees)	45	45	90	45	45	90	90			0	0	90	315	45	90	315			
Slope (degrees)	10	5	5	5	20	45	30			0	5	5	10	15	5	10			
Cover (per cent)	100	100	100	100	100	100	100			100	100	100	100	100	100	100			
Plot area (square metres)	16	4	16	4	16	4	8	C	D	4	4	4	4	4	4	4	C	D	
Betula pubescens **ssp.** ***odorata***	6	8	8	5	9	8	6	V	7.1	.	.	.	.	.	.	.			
Calluna vulgaris	.	.	.	.	.	1	.	I	0.1	.	2	.	.	.	.	.	I	0.3	
Corylus avellana	8	8	5	8	5	4	8	V	6.6	.	.	.	.	.	.	.			
Fraxinus excelsior	.	.	3	3	.	.	.	II	0.9	.	.	.	.	.	.	.			
Populus tremula	4	6	.	.	.	.	.	II	1.4	.	.	.	.	.	.	.			
Rubus saxatilis	.	.	.	3	.	.	.	I	0.4	.	4	.	3	.	.	.	II	1.0	
Salix atrocinerea	5	.	4	.	4	.	.	III	1.9	.	.	.	.	.	.	.			
Sorbus aucuparia	3	4	3	3	4	5	5	V	3.9	+	.	1	+	.	.	.	III	0.4	
Asplenium trichomanes	.	.	.	.	.	+	2	II	0.4	.	.	.	.	.	.	.			
A. viride	.	.	.	1	.	.	.	I	0.1	.	.	.	1	1	.	.	II	0.3	
Athyrium filix-femina	.	.	.	.	.	5	.	I	0.7	.	6	.	3	.	.	.	II	1.3	
Blechnum spicant	.	.	.	.	2	.	.	I	0.3	.	3	.	1	.	.	.	II	0.6	
Dryopteris borreri	.	3	3	2	.	.	6	III	2.0	3	.	3	5	.	.	.	III	1.6	
D. dilatata	2	.	.	.	.	.	.	I	0.3	.	.	4	.	.	.	.	I	0.6	
D. filix-mas	3	.	.	2	3	.	5	III	1.9	3	.	.	.	.	.	.	I	0.4	
Hymenophyllum wilsonii	.	.	1	.	.	4	.	II	0.7	.	.	.	2	.	.	.	I	0.3	
Polypodium vulgare	.	.	.	.	.	+	.	I	0.1	.	.	2	.	.	.	.	I	0.3	
Polystichum aculeatum	.	.	.	.	.	3	2	II	0.7	.	.	.	.	.	.	.			
Pteridium aquilinum	.	.	3	.	2	.	.	II	0.7	.	.	.	.	.	.	.			
Selaginella selaginoides	.	.	3	.	.	.	.	I	0.4	1	.	.	2	2	1	.	III	0.9	
Thelypteris limbosperma	.	.	4	.	2	.	.	II	0.9	3	.	.	5	.	.	.	II	1.1	
Anthoxanthum odoratum	.	4	4	.	.	.	3	III	1.6	3	3	4	3	.	.	.	III	1.9	
Arrhenatherum elatius	.	3	.	.	.	2	.	II	0.7	.	.	.	.	.	.	.			
Brachypodium sylvaticum	4	4	.	.	.	4	4	III	2.3	.	.	.	.	.	.	.			
Deschampsia cespitosa	4	5	3	6	7	5	.	V	4.3	5	4	5	4	5	3	6	V	4.6	
Festuca ovina	2	.	.	.	.	.	.	I	0.3	.	.	.	4	4	3	5	III	2.3	
F. vivipara	.	.	1	.	.	.	.	I	0.1	.	.	.	1	2	3	.	III	0.9	
Holcus lanatus	.	.	.	.	.	2	.	I	0.3	.	.	3	3	.	.	.	II	0.9	
Poa pratensis	.	.	2	3	.	.	.	II	0.7	.	3	.	.	.	.	.	I	0.4	
Allium ursinum	4	.	.	3	.	.	.	II	1.0	.	.	.	.	.	.	.			
Carex demissa	.	.	1	.	.	.	.	I	0.1	.	.	.	.	5	2	.	II	1.0	

C. flacca	.	2	.	.	.	.	.	I	0.3	.	.	.	.	3	.	.	I	0.4
C. nigra	.	3	.	.	1	.	.	II	0.6	.	2	.	.	.	.	.	I	0.3
C. pallescens	1	.	1	.	.	.	.	II	0.3	.	.	.	.	.	.	.		
C. panicea	.	2	.	.	2	.	.	II	0.6	.	2	.	.	.	.	.	I	0.3
C. pulicaris	.	3	.	2	.	.	.	II	0.7	2	+	.	3	.	.	.	III	0.9
Endymion non-scriptus	4	2	2	4	3	.	.	IV	2.1	.	3	.	2	.	.	.	II	0.7
Listera ovata	.	3	.	2	.	.	.	II	0.7	.	.	.	.	.	.	.		
Luzula sylvatica	.	3	.	.	.	7	4	III	2.0	4	4	7	4	4	3	3	V	4.1
Ajuga reptans	.	.	.	.	2	2	.	II	0.6	.	.	.	.	.	.	.		
Alchemilla alpina	.	.	.	.	.	.	.			+	1	1	3	.	2	.	IV	1.1
A. glabra	.	4	.	.	.	.	1	II	0.7	.	.	3	2	7	7	7	V	3.7
Anemone nemorosa	.	.	.	4	.	2	.	II	0.9	5	5	.	.	.	.	.	II	1.4
Angelica sylvestris	5	4	.	2	.	5	.	III	2.3	5	6	5	6	5	5	3	V	5.0
Caltha palustris	3	.	.	.	.	.	.	I	0.4	.	.	.	.	.	.	.		
Centaurea nigra	.	5	.	.	.	.	.	I	0.7	.	.	.	.	+	.	.	I	0.1
Chrysosplenium oppositifolium	3	.	.	.	.	.	3	II	0.9	.	.	.	.	+	2	.	II	0.4
Cirsium heterophyllum	5	5	6	4	5	5	4	V	4.9	4	3	.	3	.	.	.	III	1.4
Cochlearia officinalis agg.	.	.	.	.	.	.	.			.	.	.	.	4	4	3	III	1.6
Conopodium majus	4	.	3	.	.	.	2	III	1.3	.	.	.	.	.	.	.		
Crepis paludosa	.	.	4	4	.	3	.	III	1.6	4	.	.	2	.	.	1	III	1.0
Epilobium montanum	.	.	.	.	.	2	2	II	0.6	.	.	.	.	3	2	.	II	0.7
Filipendula ulmaria	7	7	5	6	6	5	5	V	5.9	4	5	5	4	3	3	4	V	4.0
Galium odoratum	3	.	.	2	.	.	3	III	1.1	.	.	.	.	.	.	.		
G. saxatile	.	.	.	.	.	.	.			.	.	2	3	.	.	.	II	0.7
Geranium robertianum	.	.	2	.	.	3	3	III	1.1	.	.	.	.	.	.	.		
Geum rivale	3	3	3	3	5	4	3	V	3.4	6	4	6	4	3	6	5	V	4.9
Heracleum sphondylium	2	.	.	3	.	.	.	II	0.7	.	+	.	.	.	.	.	I	0.1
Hieracium sp.	.	.	.	.	.	.	.			1	2	2	1	.	.	.	III	0.9
Hypericum pulchrum	.	.	.	1	.	.	.	I	0.1	1	3	3	3	.	.	.	III	1.4
Lathyrus montanus	.	.	.	.	.	1	.	I	0.1	.	.	1	.	.	.	.	I	0.1
Leontodon autumnalis	.	.	.	.	.	.	.			+	.	2	.	.	.	.	II	0.4
Lysimachia nemorum	.	.	2	.	2	.	.	II	0.6	2	.	.	.	.	.	.	I	0.3
Oxalis acetosella	2	.	3	.	3	.	2	III	1.4	.	.	1	.	.	.	.	I	0.1
Oxyria digyna	.	.	.	.	.	.	.			+	2	.	3	.	1	2	IV	1.3
Pinguicula vulgaris	.	2	1	.	.	.	.	II	0.4	1	2	.	.	1	1	.	III	0.7
Plantago lanceolata	.	.	.	.	.	.	.			2	.	3	.	.	.	.	II	0.7
Potentilla erecta	3	.	3	4	.	2	.	III	1.7	1	2	.	1	.	.	.	III	0.6
Primula vulgaris	3	.	3	4	4	3	3	V	2.9	1	1	2	2	.	.	.	III	0.9
Prunella vulgaris	.	.	.	.	1	.	.	I	0.1	.	.	.	1	.	.	.	I	0.1
Ranunculus acris	3	2	3	.	3	.	.	III	1.6	2	.	5	1	3	3	2	V	2.3
Rumex acetosa	3	.	.	.	.	.	1	II	0.6	3	3	3	3	3	5	3	V	3.3
Sanicula europaea	.	4	.	5	.	.	.	II	1.3	.	.	.	.	.	.	.		
Saussurea alpina	.	.	.	.	.	.	.			.	.	.	3	7	3	4	III	2.4
Saxifraga aizoides	.	.	.	.	.	.	.			2	4	4	5	.	2	.	IV	2.4
S. hypnoides	.	.	.	.	.	.	.			.	.	.	.	3	3	2	III	1.1
S. oppositifolia	.	.	.	.	.	.	.			.	.	.	1	.	1	.	II	0.3
Sedum rosea	.	.	.	.	.	.	.			.	5	3	7	5	5	4	V	4.1
Solidago virgaurea	.	.	.	.	.	3	.	I	0.4	.	2	1	2	1	1	.	IV	1.0
Succisa pratensis	.	3	.	.	.	3	.	II	0.9	2	1	3	4	.	.	.	III	1.4
Thymus drucei	.	.	.	.	.	+	.	I	0.1	.	2	4	.	1	2	.	III	1.3
Trollius europaeus	3	4	.	4	3	.	.	III	2.0	5	5	3	.	.	.	5	III	2.6
Valeriana officinalis	3	5	.	.	.	4	3	III	2.1	.	.	1	3	3	.	.	III	1.0

TABLE 4.47 (*cont.*)

Class	BETULO-ADENOSTYLETEA																		
Order	ADENOSTYLETALIA																		
Alliance	**Mulgedion alpini**																		
Association	*Betula pubescens–Cirsium heterophyllum*									*Sedum rosea–Alchemilla glabra*									
	1	2	3	4	5	6	7			8	9	10	11	12	13	14			
Reference number	B67	B68	B67	B67	B67	B68	B67			B67	B67	B67	B68	B68	B68	B67			
	029	096	077	003	104	061	108			012	014	118	235	110	085	135			
Map reference	370	381	567	611	603	406	373			552	547	517	542	442	485	450			
	330	609	201	211	077	322	363			214	216	406	215	708	550	608			
Altitude (feet)	100	50	100	150	200	300	300			600	650	800	1200	1300	1450	1500			
Aspect (degrees)	45	45	90	45	45	90	90			0	0	90	315	45	90	315			
Slope (degrees)	10	5	5	5	20	45	30			0	5	5	10	15	5	10			
Cover (per cent)	100	100	100	100	100	100	100			100	100	100	100	100	100	100			
Plot area (square metres)	16	4	16	4	16	4	8	C	D	4	4	4	4	4	4	4	C	D
Veronica serpyllifolia	.	.	1	.	.	.	.	I	0.1	.	.	1	.	.	.	.	I	0.1
Vicia sepium	.	.	.	.	.	3	3	II	0.9	.	.	.	.	.	.	.		
Viola riviniana	.	.	3	.	2	.	.	II	0.7	.	.	1	.	.	.	.	I	0.1
Acrocladium cuspidatum	.	.	4	.	.	.	.	I	0.6	3	+	.	.	4	4	.	III	1.7
Anoectangium aestivum	.	.	.	.	.	.	.			.	.	.	2	1	3	.	III	0.9
Blindia acuta	.	.	.	.	.	.	.			5	+	.	2	.	4	.	III	1.7
Breutelia chrysocoma	.	.	.	5	.	.	.	I	0.7	4	5	.	4	.	.	.	III	1.9
Bryum pseudotriquetrum	.	.	.	.	.	.	.			3	.	.	.	+	2	1	III	1.0
Cratoneuron commutatum	.	2	.	.	.	.	.	I	0.3	.	1	.	.	4	.	.	II	0.7
Ctenidium molluscum	.	4	2	5	.	.	.	III	1.6	3	5	2	2	4	4	2	V	3.1
Dicranum scoparium	.	.	.	.	2	.	.	I	0.3	.	+	.	.	.	.	.	I	0.1
D. majus	2	1	.	3	.	.	.	III	0.9	1	.	.	1	.	.	.	II	0.3
Distichium capillaceum	.	.	.	.	.	.	.			.	.	1	1	.	.	.	II	0.3
Ditrichum flexicaule	.	.	.	3	.	.	.	I	0.4	.	.	.	.	2	.	.	I	0.3
Drepanocladus uncinatus	.	.	.	.	.	.	.			2	2	.	.	.	1	.	III	0.7
Eurhynchium praelongum	3	.	.	.	.	3	3	III	1.3	.	.	.	.	.	.	.		
E. striatum	4	.	.	.	.	.	3	II	1.0	.	.	.	.	.	.	.		
Fissidens cristatus	.	1	.	.	.	2	.	II	0.4	.	.	.	.	.	.	.		
Hylocomium brevirostre	.	.	3	3	4	4	.	III	2.0	2	2	.	2	.	.	.	III	0.9
H. splendens	.	.	.	4	4	.	.	II	1.1	3	3	5	4	.	.	.	III	2.1
Isothecium myosuroides	.	.	.	2	1	.	.	II	0.4	.	.	.	.	.	.	.		
I. myurum	.	.	.	.	.	.	1	I	0.1	.	.	.	.	+	.	.	I	0.1
Leptodontium recurvifolium	.	.	.	.	.	.	.			.	2	.	.	1	.	.	II	0.4
Mnium hornum	.	.	.	.	1	.	.	I	0.1	.	.	.	+	.	.	.	I	0.1
M. punctatum	.	1	1	.	.	.	.	II	0.3	.	.	.	+	2	2	2	III	1.0
M. undulatum	3	3	.	2	2	2	1	V	1.9	.	.	1	.	.	.	.	I	0.1
Neckera crispa	.	.	.	3	.	.	.	I	0.4	.	.	.	3	.	.	.	I	0.4
Orthothecium rufescens	.	.	.	.	.	.	.			2	.	.	1	.	.	.	II	0.4
Philonotis fontana	.	.	.	.	.	.	.			.	.	.	.	3	3	.	II	0.9
Polytrichum formosum	.	.	.	3	2	.	.	II	0.7	.	.	1	.	.	.	.	I	0.1
Pseudoscleropodium purum	.	.	.	.	2	.	.	I	0.3	.	+	.	+	.	.	.	II	0.3

Rhacomitrium lanuginosum	.	.	.	.	.	.	.			.	.	2	4	.	.	2	III	1.1
Rhytidiadelphus loreus	5	.	3	.	.	.	.	II	1.1	.	.	+	.	.	.	.	III	0.1
R. triquetrus	5	5	6	3	3	5	3	V	4.3	3	3	5	3	.	.	5	IV	2.7
Thuidium delicatulum	3	.	3	2	.	4	.	III	1.7	.	.	.	.	.	.	.		
T. tamariscinum	4	.	3	4	.	3	3	IV	2.4	.	4	.	.	.	1	.	II	0.7
Tortella tortuosa	.	1	.	3	.	.	.	II	0.6	.	2	4	.	+	.	.	III	1.0
Trichostomum hibernicum	.	.	.	.	.	.	.			.	+	.	.	+	.	.	II	0.3
Frullania tamarisci	.	.	.	.	.	.	.			.	+	.	1	.	.	.	II	0.3
Herberta straminea	.	.	.	.	.	.	.			2	2	.	2	2	+	2	V	1.6
Leiocolea bantriensis	.	1	.	.	.	.	.	I	0.1	.	.	.	+	.	.	.	I	0.1
Mastigophora woodsii	.	.	.	.	.	.	.			.	2	.	1	.	.	.	II	0.4
Metzgeria hamata	.	+	.	.	.	.	.	I	0.1	2	2	.	.	.	.	.	II	0.6
Pellia epiphylla	.	.	.	.	.	.	.			3	.	.	+	.	.	.	II	0.6
**Plagiochila asplenioides*	2	.	1	.	.	+	2	III	0.9	.	.	.	1	.	.	1	II	0.3
Riccardia pinguis	.	.	.	.	.	.	.			2	2	.	.	.	1	.	III	0.7
Saccogyna viticulosa	.	1	.	1	.	+	.	III	0.4	.	.	.	.	.	.	.		
Peltigera canina	.	+	.	.	.	.	1	II	0.3	.	.	2	.	.	.	.	I	0.3
Total number of species (194)	41	44	46	43	35	41	32			50	57	56	69	47	44	26		

Mean number of species per relevé = 40.3.
Total number of species in association = 122.

* var. *major* in 1, 3, and 6.

Mean number of species per relevé = 49.8.
Total number of species in association = 156.

ADDITIONAL SPECIES IN LIST

1. *Galium aparine* 3, *Silene dioica* 4, *Stellaria holostea* 3.
2. *Juncus effusus* 2, *Orchis mascula* 2, *Rhinanthus minor* agg. 3, *Tussilago farfara* 4.
3. *Bellis perennis* 2, *Cardamine flexuosa* 2, *Digitalis purpurea* 1, *Atrichum undulatum* 3, *Fissidens taxifolius* 1, *Hookeria lucens* 2.
4. *Scapania aspera* 1.
5. *Ranunculus ficaria* 2, *Sphagnum fimbriatum* 1, *S. quinquefarium* 2.
6. *Lathyrus pratensis* +.
8. *Sphagnum plumulosum* 2, *S. subsecundum* var. *auriculatum* 2, *Conocephalum conicum* 1.
9. *Carex binervis* 1, *Campylium stellatum* 3, *Calypogeia muellerana* +, *Harpalejeunea ovata* +, *Plagiochila spinulosa* 1.
10. *Alchemilla xanthochlora* 2, *Draba incana* 2, *Fragaria vesca* 3, *Galium boreale* 4, *Linum catharticum* 1, *Sedum anglicum* 3, *Silene acaulis* 3, *Trifolium pratense* 3, *Bartramia pomiformis* 1, *Brachythecium plumosum* 1, *Camptothecium lutescens* 2, *Hypnum cupressiforme* var. *tectorum* 2, *Pleurozium schreberi* 1, *Metzgeria conjugata* 1.
11. *Vaccinium myrtillus* 2, *Polystichum lonchitis* 1, *Carex pilulifera* 1, *Bartramia ithyphylla* 1, *Ptilium crista-castrensis* 1, *Preissia quadrata* +, *Radula complanata* 1, *Solorina saccata* 1.
12. *Salix myrsinites* +, *Cystopteris fragilis* 3, *Chamaenerion angustifolium* +, *Rhinanthus borealis* 2, *Thalictrum alpinum* 3, *Fissidens adianthoides* 2, *Plagiobryum zierii* +, *Pohlia wahlenbergii* 1, *Trichostomum crispulum* +.
13. *Poa glauca* 2, *Euphrasia officinalis* agg. 1, *Saxifraga stellaris* 1, *Barbula fallax* 1, *Dicranella palustris* +, *Marsupella emarginata* 1, *Nardia scalaris* 1, *Riccardia sinuata* +.
14. *Bazzania tricrenata* 3, *Lophocolea cuspidata* 2, *Scapania gracilis* 1.

LOCALITIES

1. Loch Harport; 2. Camas Beag; 3. Faoilean; 4. Coille Gaireallach; 5. Gillean Burn; 6. Allt Coir' a' Ghobhainn; 7. Sumerdale River; 8, 9. Allt na Dunaiche; 10. Ben Tianavaig; 11. Coire Uaigneach; 12. Sgùrr Mor; 13. The Storr; 14. Corrie Amadal.

TABLE 4.48

Class	ALNETEA GLUTINOSAE
Order	ALNETALIA GLUTINOSAE
Alliance	**Alnion glutinosae**

	Alnus glutinosa woods
	1
Reference Number	B68 099
Grid Reference	490 674
Altitude (feet)	150
Aspect (degrees)	0
Slope (degrees)	10
Cover (per cent)	100
Plot area (square metres)	4

Alnus glutinosa	8	*Cirsium palustre*	+
		Galium palustre	4
Athyrium filix-femina	4	*Prunella vulgaris*	4
Dryopteris filix-mas	4	*Ranunculus acris*	5
		R. repens	4
Alopecurus geniculatus	3	*Stellaria alsine*	3
Anthoxanthum odoratum	4		
Deschampsia cespitosa	8	*Acrocladium cuspidatum*	3
Holcus lanatus	6	*Brachythecium rutabulum*	2
Poa trivialis	4	*Hookeria lucens*	1
		Mnium punctatum	2
Dactylorchis fuchsii	1		
Iris pseudacorus	+	*Lophocolea bidentata*	2
Juncus effusus	4	*Pellia epiphylla*	2
		Plagiochila asplenioides	1
Caltha palustris	3		
Cardamine flexuosa	+	Total number of species	29

Epiphytic bryophytes and lichens in *Alnus glutinosa* woods

	1	2	3
Reference Number	B68 100	B68 101	B68 102
Hypnum cupressiforme var. *resupinatum*	×	×	×
Ulota phyllantha	×	×	×
Frullania dilatata	×	×	×
Metzgeria fruticulosa	.	×	×
M. furcata	×	×	.
Parmelia glabratula	×	×	×
P. laevigata	×	×	×
P. physodes	×	×	×
P. saxatilis	×	×	×
Ramalina fastigiata	×	×	×
Usnea subfloridana	.	×	×
Total number of species (17)	9	14	13

ADDITIONAL SPECIES IN LIST

2. *Zygodon viridissimus* ×, *Lejeunea ulicina* ×, *Stenocybe pullatula* ×.
3. *Collema furfuraceum* ×, *Lecanora chlarotera* ×, *Pyrenula nitida* ×.

LOCALITY: Stenschall River, near Staffin.

TABLE 4.50‡

Class	QUERCETEA ROBORI–PETRAEAE
Order	QUERCETALIA ROBORI–PETRAEAE
Alliance	**Quercion robori–petraeae**
Association	*Oxalis acetosella–Rhytidiadelphus loreus*

	1	2	3	4	5	6	7	8	9	10	11	12	13	14	C	D
Reference Number	B68	B68	B68	B68	B68	B68	B68	B68	B 68	B68	B68	B68	B68	B68		
Map Reference	218 596 267	264 707 157	266 707 157	267 707 157	300 612 121	314 750 250	319 756 251	138 413 519	221 596 267	269 707 157	313 750 250	281 703 145	283 703 145	298 612 131		
Altitude (feet)	100	100	100	100	200	100	100	200	50	100	100	50	50	200		
Aspect (degrees)	.	225	225	225	0	0	0	45	0	225	0	45	45	0		
Slope (degrees)	0	5	5	3	5	2	5	5	5	5	5	10	5	20		
Cover (per cent)	100	100	100	100	100	100	100	100	100	100	100	100	100	100		
Plot area (square metres)	1	1	1	1	1	1	1	0.5	1	1	1	1	1	1	C	D
Sorbus aucuparia	.	.	.	1	.	1	1	.	3	2	1	.	3	1	III	0.9
Vaccinium myrtillus	.	.	.	.	4	4	3	.	.	4	.	5	5	6	III	2.2
Blechnum spicant	.	.	.	.	.	.	.	.	.	.	.	.	3	2	I	0.4
Hymenophyllum wilsonii	4	.	.	.	.	.	2	3	2	.	1	3	.	.	III	1.1
Anthoxanthum odoratum	.	.	.	.	2	2	.	.	.	.	3	.	.	.	II	0.5
Deschampsia flexuosa	4	4	4	5	3	3	.	3	4	6	3	5	3	5	V	3.7
Festuca vivipara	.	.	.	.	.	.	.	.	1	.	.	3	.	.	I	0.3
Endymion non-scriptus	2	3	.	.	.	.	.	.	.	.	.	.	2	.	II	0.5
Galium saxatile	.	.	.	2	3	3	.	.	.	2	.	2	.	.	II	0.9
Melampyrum pratense	.	.	.	.	.	.	.	.	.	.	.	.	1	2	I	0.2
Oxalis acetosella	3	4	4	2	3	2	2	2	2	3	5	3	3	.	V	2.7
Potentilla erecta	.	.	4	2	4	.	3	.	3	.	2	4	.	5	III	1.9
Breutelia chrysocoma	.	.	.	.	.	.	.	1	.	.	.	1	.	.	I	0.1
Dicranum majus	3	.	.	.	.	2	1	3	.	1	1	2	.	3	III	1.1
D. scoparium	.	.	1	.	.	.	3	.	1	.	2	.	1	.	II	0.6
Hylocomium brevirostre	4	7	8	7	5	4	8	7	2	7	3	5	5	2	V	5.3
H. splendens	8	5	3	4	3	2	3	2	6	5	5	6	5	3	V	4.3
H. umbratum	3	.	.	.	.	3	2	.	.	.	2	4	.	.	II	1.0
**Hypnum cupressiforme*	2	.	.	.	.	.	.	.	2	.	3	2	.	2	II	0.8
Isothecium myosuroides	1	3	.	3	2	.	.	3	3	1	.	.	3	.	III	1.4
Mnium hornum	.	.	.	.	.	.	.	2	1	.	1	.	1	.	II	0.4
Pleurozium schreberi	.	.	.	.	3	5	.	.	3	2	2	1	2	4	III	1.6
Polytrichum formosum	1	.	3	1	4	1	2	.	4	2	3	.	2	4	IV	1.9
Ptilium crista-castrensis	.	.	.	.	.	2	2	.	.	.	.	.	.	.	I	0.3
Rhytidiadelphus loreus	2	4	5	4	8	8	4	3	6	3	8	5	3	5	V	4.9
R. triquetrus	.	.	.	.	2	.	.	4	.	1	.	.	.	.	II	0.5
Thuidium delicatulum	4	6	4	5	3	5	2	4	7	5	2	3	4	3	V	4.1
T. tamariscinum	.	.	4	.	3	.	3	.	.	3	3	.	6	5	III	1.9
Bazzania trilobata	.	.	.	.	.	2	.	.	.	4	.	3	.	.	II	0.6
Diplophyllum albicans	.	.	.	.	.	.	.	.	.	.	1	.	.	1	I	0.1
Frullania tamarisci	1	.	.	.	1	.	.	.	.	3	.	.	1	.	II	0.4
Plagiochila spinulosa	3	.	.	2	.	1	.	.	.	.	1	.	.	.	II	0.5
Scapania gracilis	2	.	.	.	.	.	.	.	2	5	.	.	.	.	II	0.6
Total number of species (52)	16	8	13	12	16	17	18	14	17	18	20	19	20	23		

* var. *ericetorum* in 1, 11, 12, and 14. Mean number of species per relevé = 16.5.

ADDITIONAL SPECIES IN LIST

3. *Polypodium vulgare* agg. +, *Luzula multiflora* 1, *Sphagnum fimbriatum* 2.
7. *Lonicera periclymenum* 4, *Plagiothecium undulatum* 1.
8. *Geranium robertianum* 1, *Plagiochila asplenioides* 2, *Peltigera canina* 3.
12. *Eurhynchium striatum* 2, *Isothecium myurum* 2.
13. *Pteridium aquilinum* 2, *Pseudoscleropodium purum* 1.
14. *Betula pubescens* ssp. *odorata* 1, *Calluna vulgaris* 3, *Erica cinerea* 3, *Sphagnum capillaceum* 5, *S. quinquefarium* 3, *Calypogeia muellerana* 1, *Saccogyna viticulosa*.

LOCALITIES

1, 9. Near Allt Strollamus; 2, 3, 4, 10. E. side of Loch na Dal; 5, 14. Tokavaig; 6, 7, 11. Kyleakin; 8. Loch Eyre; 12, 13. W. side of Loch na Dal.

‡ Table 4.49 can be found overleaf.

TABLE 4.49

Class	QUERCETEA ROBORI–PETRAEAE																	
Order	QUERCETALIA ROBORI–PETRAEAE																	
Alliance	Quercion robori–petraeae																	
Association	*Betula pubescens–Vaccinium myrtillus*								*Corylus avellana–Oxalis acetosella*									
	1	2	3	4	5	6			7	8	9	10	11	12	13	14		
Reference Number	B68	B67	B67	B67	B67	B67			B67	B67	B67	B67	B67	B68	B68	B67		
Map Reference	317	097	040	096	100	120			098	101	105	041	078	320	137	102		
	750	625	709	640	598	612			613	602	603	703	567	762	413	603		
	250	126	153	121	199	123			118	198	081	145	201	251	519	201		
Altitude (feet)	100	200	100	200	200	200			250	200	100	50	200	150	200	150		
Aspect (degrees)	0	180	315	0	315	315			270	0	0	45	45	0	45	315		
Slope (degrees)	20	20	5	10	10	15			10	15	35	30	30	25	20	5		
Cover (per cent)	100	100	100	100	100	100			100	100	100	100	100	100	100	100		
Plot area (square metres)	16	16	4	16	16	4	C	D	16	16	16	16	16	16	16	4	C	D
Betula pubescens* ssp. *odorata	9	6	8	9	8	9	V	8.1	5	6	5	7	5	+	.	.	IV	3.6
Calluna vulgaris	5	3	+	3	5	3	V	3.3	1	.	.	2	.	.	.	.	II	0.4
Corylus avellana	+	.	2	.	.	3	III	1.0	9	9	8	9	9	8	9	.	V	7.6
Ilex aquifolium	+	3	.	.	.	.	II	0.7	.	.	.	.	.	.	.	.		
Lonicera periclymenum	.	3	.	.	.	1	II	0.7	.	.	.	.	.	.	.	.		
Quercus petraea	3	8	4	.	.	3	IV	3.0	.	3	2	.	.	.	.	.	II	0.6
Salix atrocinerea	.	.	.	4	.	2	II	1.0	.	.	.	3	.	.	3	.	II	0.8
S. caprea	.	.	.	3	2	.	II	0.8	.	.	.	.	.	.	.	.		
Sorbus aucuparia	4	3	3	4	3	3	V	3.3	3	.	3	4	3	4	.	.	IV	2.1
Vaccinium myrtillus	7	6	6	7	7	6	V	6.5	.	.	.	1	.	.	.	.	I	0.1
Athyrium filix-femina	.	1	.	.	.	2	II	0.5	.	.	2	.	3	3	2	.	III	1 3
Blechnum spicant	3	4	.	5	4	4	V	3.3	3	3	3	3	2	.	2	.	IV	2.0
Dryopteris aemula	2	.	.	.	.	.	I	0.3	.	.	.	.	+	.	.	.	I	0.1
D. borreri	.	.	.	.	.	.			.	.	.	.	4	.	4	.	II	1.0
D. dilatata	3	.	3	.	.	.	II	1.0	.	+	.	.	3	.	.	.	II	0.5
D. filix-mas	3	2	3	.	.	3	IV	1.8	2	2	3	3	3	.	.	.	IV	1.6
Hymenophyllum wilsonii	3	.	.	.	.	3	II	1.0	.	.	.	.	3	1	.	.	II	0.5
Polypodium vulgare	.	.	1	.	.	.	I	0.2	.	.	.	.	.	.	.	.	I	
Pteridium aquilinum	3	5	4	5	3	5	V	4.2	5	.	2	4	.	.	.	9	III	2.5
Thelypteris limbosperma	.	.	2	.	1	.	II	0.5	.	1	.	2	4	.	.	.	II	0.9
T. phegopteris	.	.	.	.	.	.			.	2	+	.	1	.	+	.	III	0.8
Agrostis canina	.	.	.	.	.	.			2	.	.	2	.	2	.	.	II	0.8
A. tenuis	4	.	.	.	4	.	II	1.3	.	.	.	.	.	.	.	.		
Anthoxanthum odoratum	4	3	3	3	3	4	V	3.3	5	3	5	6	.	6	3	3	V	3.9
Deschampsia cespitosa	.	.	.	.	.	.			.	5	5	4	6	4	7	6	V	4.6
D. flexuosa	5	4	5	4	4	5	V	4.5	4	.	.	.	.	.	.	.	I	0.5
Festuca vivipara	.	.	.	3	2	.	II	0.8	.	3	.	2	.	.	.	.	II	0.6
Holcus lanatus	3	.	.	.	.	.	I	0.5	.	.	.	4	.	1	.	.	II	0.6
Allium ursinum	.	.	.	.	.	.			1	.	.	.	.	.	4	.	II	0.6
Carex binervis	.	3	.	3	.	1	III	1.2	2	1	.	.	.	.	.	.	II	0.4
C. pallescens	.	.	1	.	1	.	II	0.3	+	2	1	3	.	.	.	1	IV	1.0
C. sylvatica	.	.	1	4	.	.	II	0.8	+	.	.	.	.	.	.	.	I	0.1
Endymion non-scriptus	.	3	3	.	3	3	IV	2.0	3	4	.	1	3	.	5	.	IV	2.0
Luzula campestris	.	.	.	2	.	.	I	0.3	.	1	.	1	.	.	.	.	II	0.3
L. multiflora	.	.	.	.	.	.			.	2	.	1	.	.	.	.	II	0.4
L. sylvatica	2	.	.	.	.	.	I	0.3	.	.	.	.	.	.	.	.		
Ajuga reptans	.	.	.	.	.	.			.	.	.	.	.	2	.	+	II	0.4
Anemone nemorosa	.	.	1	.	.	.	I	0.2	3	.	.	.	.	.	.	.	I	0.4
Caltha palustris	.	.	.	.	.	.			+	.	.	.	2	.	.	.	II	0.4
Cardamine flexuosa	.	.	.	.	.	.			.	.	.	.	1	1	.	.	II	0.3
Circaea intermedia	.	.	.	.	.	.			.	.	.	.	.	3	2	.	II	0.6
Conopodium majus	1	.	.	.	.	.	I	0.2	2	.	3	1	.	.	3	.	III	1.1
Digitalis purpurea	.	.	.	.	.	.			.	.	.	.	3	2	.	.	II	0.6
Filipendula ulmaria	.	.	.	.	.	.			.	3	3	.	1	2	.	3	IV	1.1
Galium saxatile	4	3	2	3	4	4	V	3.3	3	3	4	3	2	3	.	3	V	2.6
Geranium robertianum	.	.	.	.	.	.			.	3	.	.	.	5	4	3	III	1.9

Geum rivale	.	.	.	.	.	.			.	2	.	.	.	2	.	2	II	0.8
Lysimachia nemorum	.	.	1	.	.	.	I	0.2	.	2	3	.	2	1	3	.	IV	1.4
Melampyrum pratense	1	3	.	.	.	.	II	0.7	.	.	.	+	.	.	.	.	I	0.1
Oxalis acetosella	4	2	3	.	3	3	V	2.5	4	5	5	5	3	5	4	5	V	4.5
Polygala serpyllifolia	.	3	.	.	1	.	II	0.7	1	2	1	.	.	.	.	.	I	0.5
Potentilla erecta	3	4	3	4	3	5	V	3.7	3	3	4	4	4	.	.	3	IV	2.6
Primula vulgaris	.	.	2	.	.	.	I	0.3	5	5	5	5	3	4	4	.	V	3.9
Ranunculus acris	1	.	1	.	.	.	II	0.3	2	.	2	.	1	.	.	2	III	0.9
R. ficaria	.	.	.	.	.	.			.	2	.	.	2	.	.	1	II	0.6
Succisa pratensis	.	.	.	.	2	.	I	0.3	.	.	.	2	.	.	.	.	I	0.3
Veronia chamaedrys	.	.	.	.	.	.			.	.	.	1	.	1	.	.	II	0.3
V. serpyllifolia	.	1	.	.	.	.	I	0.2	.	.	.	1	.	.	.	1	II	0.1
Viola riviniana	2	.	2	.	.	.	II	0.7	3	3	4	2	2	1	4	2	V	2.6
Atrichum undulatum	.	.	.	.	.	.			.	1	1	.	.	.	.	.	II	0.3
Breutelia chrysocoma	.	.	2	.	.	.	I	0.3	1	.	.	.	.	.	.	.	I	0.1
Dicranodontium denudatum	1	.	1	.	.	.	II	0.3	.	.	.	.	1	.	.	.	I	0.1
Dicranum majus	1	3	4	.	.	5	IV	2.2	.	2	2	.	1	.	.	.	II	0.6
D. scoparium	.	3	3	.	2	.	III	1.3	.	.	.	.	.	.	.	.		
**Eurhynchium praelongum*	.	.	1	.	.	.	I	0.2	.	.	.	.	2	3	.	.	II	0.6
E. striatum	.	.	2	.	.	.	I	0.3	.	4	4	2	3	.	.	.	III	1.6
Heterocladium heteropterum	.	.	.	.	.	.			.	.	.	.	+	1	.	.	II	0.3
Hylocomium brevirostre	2	.	2	.	.	.	II	0.7	5	3	4	5	3	5	3	.	V	3.5
H. splendens	3	4	4	5	4	5	V	4.2	4	3	3	3	3	4	.	.	IV	2.5
H. umbratum	3	.	2	.	.	3	III	1.3	.	.	+	.	.	3	.	.	II	0.5
Hypnum callichroum	.	.	.	.	.	.			.	.	.	3	1	.	.	.	II	0.5
†*H. cupressiforme*	1	1	.	2	.	2	IV	1.2	.	3	1	.	3	1	.	.	III	1.0
Isothecium myosuroides	1	4	.	.	.	.	II	0.8	.	.	.	2	4	.	+	.	II	0.9
I. myurum	.	.	.	.	.	.			.	.	1	.	1	.	.	.	II	0.3
Leucobryum glaucum	.	1	1	.	.	+	III	0.5	.	.	.	1	.	.	.	.	I	0.1
Mnium hornum	2	.	3	.	.	2	III	1.2	1	.	1	.	1	2	.	.	III	0.6
M. undulatum	.	.	.	.	.	.			.	.	.	1	1	1	1	.	III	0.5
Plagiothecium sylvaticum	.	.	.	.	.	.			.	.	1	.	.	.	+	.	II	0.3
P. undulatum	1	3	2	.	2	3	V	1.8	1	.	.	.	1	2	.	.	II	0.5
Pleurozium schreberi	2	3	3	.	3	2	V	2.2	.	.	.	.	.	.	.	.		
Polytrichum formosum	2	4	3	.	1	3	V	2.2	.	2	.	.	2	2	.	.	II	0.8
Ptilium crista-castrensis	2	.	.	.	4	.	II	1.0	.	.	.	.	.	.	.	.		
Rhytidiadelphus loreus	4	4	3	.	3	1	V	2.5	3	3	.	5	6	4	.	.	IV	2.6
R. squarrosus	.	.	2	.	.	.	I	0.3	.	.	2	.	.	.	.	.	I	0.3
R. triquetrus	.	2	3	.	.	.	IV	0.8	.	+	2	2	.	.	5	.	III	1.3
Sphagnum fimbriatum	3	.	1	.	3	3	IV	1.7	.	.	.	3	.	.	.	.	I	0.4
S. quinquefarium	4	.	4	.	4	3	IV	2.5	.	.	.	2	.	.	.	.	I	0.3
Thuidium delicatulum	3	3	5	.	3	3	V	2.8	2	3	.	5	6	.	2	.	IV	2.3
T. tamariscinum	4	4	3	3	3	3	V	3.3	3	3	5	3	3	3	4	4	V	3.1
Bazzania trilobata	2	.	2	.	.	.	II	0.7	.	.	.	.	.	.	.	.		
Diplophyllum albicans	1	.	.	.	.	.	I	0.2	.	.	.	.	.	.	.	.		
Lepidozia reptans	1	.	.	.	.	1	II	0.3	.	.	.	.	.	.	.	.		
‡*Plagiochila asplenioides*	2	.	.	.	.	.	I	0.3	1	.	.	.	.	2	.	.	II	0.4
P. spinulosa	2	.	.	.	.	.	I	0.3	.	.	1	.	2	1	.	.	II	0.5
Saccogyna viticulosa	1	.	.	.	.	.	I	0.2	.	.	.	.	1	.	.	.	I	0.1
Scapania gracilis	1	2	3	3	.	2	V	1.8	.	.	.	.	3	.	1	.	II	0.5
S. nemorea	.	.	2	.	.	.	I	0.3	.	.	.	.	1	2	.	.	II	0.4
Peltigera canina	.	.	.	.	.	+	I	0.2	1	.	.	.	.	.	2	.	II	0.4
Total number of species (127)	54	36	52	20	31	38			36	40	40	44	56	39	26	16		

Mean number of species per relevé = 38.5.
Total number of species in association = 87.

Mean number of species per relevé = 40.1.
Total number of species in association = 106.

* var. *stokesii* in 12. † var. *ericetorum* in 1, 4, and 6. ‡ var. *major* in 1, 7, and 12.

ADDITIONAL SPECIES IN LIST

1. *Prunella vulgaris* 1, *Dicranella heteromalla* 1, *Calypogeia fissa* 1, *Cephalozia bicuspidata* 1, *Mylia taylori* 1.
2. *Teucrium scorodonia* 1.
3. *Hedera helix* 3, *Sanicula europaea* 2, *Hookeria lucens* 1, *Pseudoscleropodium purum* 1.
5. *Sphagnum capillaceum* 2.
7. *Carex remota* +.
8. *Polystichum aculeatum* +, *Ctenidium molluscum* 2.
9. *Dactylis glomerata* 2, *Galium odoratum* 1, *Fissidens taxifolius* 1, *Calypogeia arguta* 1.
10. *Carex panicea* 2, *Acrocladium cuspidatum* 2.
11. *Rubus fruticosus* agg. 1, *Mnium punctatum* 1, *Trichostomum tenuirostre* 1, *Adelanthus decipiens* +, *Frullania germana* 1, *F. tamarisci* 1, *Scapania umbrosa* 1.
12. *Prunus padus* 4, *Epilobium montanum* 1, *Galium aparine* 3.

LOCALITIES

1, 12. Kyleakin; 2. Ord; 3. E. side of Loch na Dal; 4. Coill a'Ghasgain; 5, 8, 14. Coille Gaireallach; 6, 7. Tokavaig; 9. Gillean Burn; 10. W. side of Loch na Dal; 11. Faoilean; 12. Loch Eyre.

TABLE 4.51

Class	QUERCETEA ROBORI–PETRAEAE														
Order	QUERCETALIA ROBORI–PETRAEAE														
Alliance	**Quercion robori–petraeae**														
Association	*Hymenophyllum wilsonii–Isothecium myosuroides*														
	1	2	3	4	5	6	7	8	9	10	11	12	13		
Reference Number	B68 139	B68 268	B68 276	B68 270	B68 272	B68 299	B68 316	B68 282	B68 280	B68 297	B68 315	B68 220	B68 222		
Map Reference	413 519	707 157	707 157	707 157	707 157	612 121	750 250	703 145	703 145	612 121	750 250	596 267	596 267		
Altitude (feet)	200	100	100	100	100	200	100	50	50	200	100	100	50		
Aspect (degrees)	45	225	225	225	225	0	0	45	45	0	0	0	0		
Slope (degrees)	80	70	70	80	60	70	80	90	70	80	80	50	45		
Cover (per cent)	100	100	100	100	100	100	100	100	100	100	100	100	100		
Plot area (square metres)	1	1	1	1	1	1	1	1	1	1	1	1	1	C	D
Hymenophyllum wilsonii	5	5	4	5	5	4	5	5	6	7	7	7	8	V	5.6
Deschampsia flexuosa	.	1	.	1	2	.	.	3	.	2	.	.	2	III	0.8
Campylopus flexuosus	.	.	.	.	.	.	.	2	.	1	.	.	.	I	0.2
Dicranum majus	.	3	.	.	1	.	.	3	.	.	.	.	.	II	0.5
D. scoparium	.	1	2	1	2	3	1	2	.	4	1	2	3	V	1.7
D. scottianum	.	.	.	2	.	+	.	.	.	.	.	.	3	II	0.5
**Hypnum cupressiforme*	.	3	5	3	4	1	2	.	.	2	1	2	3	IV	2.0
Isothecium myosuroides	7	8	7	6	5	8	5	7	8	5	5	6	3	V	6.2
Pleurozium schreberi	.	.	.	1	.	.	.	1	.	1	.	.	2	II	0.4
Polytrichum formosum	.	.	.	.	2	.	.	.	.	1	.	2	2	II	0.5
Rhacomitrium aciculare	1	.	.	2	.	.	.	.	.	.	.	.	.	I	0.2
Rhytidiadelphus loreus	.	.	.	.	.	1	1	2	2	1	1	.	.	III	0.6
Sphagnum quinquefarium	.	.	.	.	.	.	.	.	.	2	.	.	2	II	0.3
Thuidium delicatulum	3	.	.	.	.	.	2	4	.	1	.	.	.	II	0.8
T. tamariscinum	.	.	.	.	1	2	.	.	.	.	2	1	4	II	0.8
Adelanthus decipiens	.	.	5	3	1	.	.	.	.	.	.	.	.	II	0.7
Bazzania tricrenata	.	.	.	.	.	.	.	.	.	3	2	.	.	I	0.4
B. trilobata	.	.	.	.	2	2	.	.	.	.	.	.	.	I	0.3
Diplophyllum albicans	2	2	2	4	.	.	.	.	.	.	.	2	.	II	0.9
Frullania tamarisci	5	2	.	.	.	.	.	1	.	.	.	1	1	II	0.8
Lepidozia reptans	.	1	.	.	1	.	2	1	.	.	.	.	.	II	0.4
Plagiochila punctata	.	.	2	3	.	.	.	3	.	.	2	.	3	II	1.0
P. spinulosa	4	6	5	8	8	4	7	6	3	6	6	5	5	V	5.6
Saccogyna viticulosa	.	2	1	.	3	.	.	.	.	3	2	.	2	III	1.0
Scapania gracilis	3	4	4	.	2	5	3	4	3	5	4	4	.	V	3.4
Peltigera canina	4	.	.	.	.	.	.	.	.	.	.	.	1	I	0.4
Sticta fuliginosa	.	.	1	.	2	.	.	.	.	.	.	.	.	I	0.2
Total number of species (45)	14	13	12	12	16	11	9	16	7	16	11	12	17		

* var. *ericetorum* in 6, 7, 10, and 11. Mean number of species per relevé = 12.8.

ADDITIONAL SPECIES IN LIST

1. *Plagiothecium denticulatum* 2, *Rhacomitrium fasciculare* 1, *Lejeunea cavifolia* 1, *Metzgeria furcata* 1, *Nephromium laevigatum* 1.
2. *Scapania umbrosa* 1.
3. *Lobaria pulmonaria* 1.
5. *Hylocomium splendens* 1.
6. *Sticta sylvatica* 2.
8. *Festuca vivipara* 1, *Hylocomium brevirostre* 2.
9. *Galium saxatile* 2, *Cladonia* sp. 2.
10. *Sphaerophorus fragilis* 2.
12. *Oxalis acetosella* 1, *Frullania germana* 1.
13. *Mnium hornum* 1, *Mylia taylori* 3.

LOCALITIES

1. Loch Eyre; 2, 3, 4, 5. E. side Loch na Dal; 6, 10. Tokavaig; 7, 11. Kyleakin; 8, 9. W. side Loch na Dal; 12, 13. near Allt Strollamus.

TABLE 4.52

Class	QUERCETEA ROBORI–PETRAEAE
Order	QUERCETALIA ROBORI–PETRAEAE
Alliance	**Quercion robori–petraeae**
Association	*Open Boulder Association*

	1	2	3	4	5	6		
Reference number	B68	B68	B68	B68	B68	B68		
	219	271	273	274	275	279		
Map Reference	596	707	707	707	707	703		
	267	157	157	157	157	145		
Altitude (feet)	100	100	100	100	100	50		
Aspect (degrees)	315	225	225	225	225	45		
Slope (degrees)	70	60	80	75	80	60		
Cover (per cent)	60	50	60	70	70	70		
Plot area (square metres)	1	1	1	1	1	0.5	C	D
Dicranum scoparium	.	1	.	.	3	.	II	0.7
Grimmia hartmanii	4	5	1	.	.	.	III	1.7
Heterocladium heteropterum	6	3	7	7	6	6	V	5.8
Hyocomium flagellare	.	3	3	3	2	2	V	2.2
Hypnum callichroum	6	.	.	.	3	.	IV	1.5
Rhacomitrium aquaticum	3	6	5	3	4	7	V	4.7
R. fasciculare	.	4	6	.	.	.	II	1.7
Thuidium delicatulum	.	2	1	.	.	.	II	0.5
Trichostomum tenuirostre	3	.	.	3	2	4	IV	2.0
Diplophyllum albicans	3	4	1	3	3	4	V	3.0
Lejeunea patens	.	3	1	2	2	3	V	1.8
Marsupella emarginata	.	5	5	5	4	.	IV	3.2
Plagiochila spinulosa	.	.	.	1	1	.	II	0.3
Scapania gracilis	.	4	5	6	5	3	V	3.8
S. umbrosa	2	.	.	.	.	2	II	0.7
Total number of species (29)	11	12	12	14	14	11		

Mean number of species per relevé = 12.3.

ADDITIONAL SPECIES IN LIST

1. *Mnium punctatum* 3, *Plectocolea hyalina* 1, *Saccogyna viticulosa* +, *Scapania undulata* 4.
3. *Isothecium myosuroides* 2.
4. *Calypogeia fissa* 1, *Frullania tamarisci* 2, *Scapania nemorea* 1.
5. *Dicranum scottianum* 2, *Frullania germana* 3.
6. *Brachythecium plumosum* 1, *Aphanolejeunea microscopica* 3, *Plagiochila asplenioides* 3.

LOCALITIES

1. Near Allt Strollamus; 2, 3, 4, 5. E. side Loch na Dal; 6. W. side Loch na Dal.

TABLE 4.53

	Epiphytic bryophytes and lichens in the Betula–Vaccinium myrtillus Association						*Epiphytic bryophytes and lichens in the Corylus–Oxalis acetosella Association*						
	1	2	3	4	5	6	7	8	9	10	11	12	13
Reference number	B68 317	B67 097	B67 040	B67 096	B67 100	B67 120	B67 098	B67 101	B67 105	B67 041	B67 078	B68 320	B68 137
Hymenophyllum wilsonii	×	×	×	×	×	×	.	.	.	.	.	.	.
Camptothecium sericeum	.	.	.	.	.	.	×	.	.	.	×	.	×
Dicranum scoparium	×	×	×	×	×	×	×	×	.	.	.	.	.
Eurhynchium striatum	.	.	.	.	.	.	.	×	×	×	×	.	.
Hylocomium brevirostre	.	.	.	.	.	.	×	.	×	×	×	×	.
Hypnum cupressiforme var. *filiforme*	×	×	.	.	.	.	×	×	×	×	.	×	×
H. cupressiforme var. *resupinatum*	×	×	×	×	×	×	×	×	×	×	×	×	×
Isothecium myosuroides	×	×	×	×	×	×	×	×	×	×	×	×	×
I. myurum	.	.	.	.	.	.	.	.	.	×	.	.	×
Mnium hornum	×	.	×	.	.	×	.	.	×	.	×	.	.
Neckera complanata	.	.	.	.	.	.	×	×	.	×	.	×	.
Polytrichum formosum	×	×	×	.	.	×	.	×	.	.	.	.	.
Ulota bruchii	×	×	×	×	×	×	×	×	×	×	×	×	×
U. crispa	×	×	×	×	×	×	×	×	×	×	×	×	×
U. phyllantha	×	.	×	×	.	×	×	×	×	×	×	×	×
U. vittata	.	.	.	.	.	.	×	×	×	×	×	×	×
Aphanolejeunea microscopica	×	.	.	×	.	.	.	.	.	.	.	.	.
Frullania dilatata	.	.	×	×	.	.	×	×	×	×	×	×	×
F. germana	×	.	×	.	.	×	×	×	×	×	×	×	×
F. tamarisci	×	×	×	×	×	×	×	×	×	×	×	×	×
Lejeunea ulicina	×	.	×	×	.	×	×	×	×	×	.	×	×
Lepidozia reptans	×	.	×	×	×	×	.	.	.	.	.	.	.
Metzgeria furcata	.	.	.	.	.	.	×	×	×	×	×	×	×
Mylia cuneifolia	×	.	.	×	.	×	.	.	.	.	.	.	.
Plagiochila punctata	×	×	×	×	×	×	.	.	.	.	.	.	.
P. spinulosa	×	×	×	×	×	×	.	.	.	.	.	.	.
P. tridenticulata	×	.	.	×	.	.	.	.	.	.	.	.	.
Radula complanata	.	.	.	.	.	.	×	×	×	×	×	×	×
Scapania gracilis	×	×	×	×	×	×	.	.	.	.	.	.	.
Dimerella lutea	.	.	.	.	.	.	×	.	.	×	×	×	.
Leptogium burgessii	.	.	.	.	.	.	×	.	.	×	×	×	.
Lobaria laetevirens	×	×	×	×	.	×	×	.	.	×	.	×	.
L. pulmonaria	.	×	×	×	.	.	×	.	.	×	.	×	×
L. scrobiculata	.	.	.	.	.	.	×	.	.	.	.	×	.
Normandina pulchella	.	.	.	.	.	.	×	×	.	.	.	.	.
Pannaria pezizoides	.	.	.	.	.	.	×	.	×	×	.	×	×
P. rubiginosa	.	.	.	.	.	.	×	×	×	×	.	×	.
Parmeliella atlantica	.	.	.	.	.	.	×	×	.	×	.	×	.
P. plumbea	.	.	.	.	.	.	×	×	×	×	.	×	×
Pseudocyphellaria thouarsii	×	.	×	×	.	.	×	.	.	.	.	×	.
Pyrenula nitida	.	.	.	.	.	.	×	.	.	×	.	.	.
Sphaerophorus globosus	.	.	×	×	.	×	.	.	.	.	.	.	.
Sticta fuliginosa	×	.	×	×	.	.	×	×	×	×	×	×	×
S. limbata	.	.	.	.	.	.	×	.	×	×	.	×	.
S. sylvatica	×	.	×	×	.	.	×	.	×	×	×	×	×
Total number of species (60)	24	14	29	27	11	18	36	22	22	31	19	28	21

Mean number of species per stand = 20.5.   Mean number of species per stand = 25.6.

ADDITIONAL SPECIES IN LIST

3. *Adelanthus decipiens, Menegazzia terebrata, Parmelia crinita, P. laevigata, P. saxatilis, Usnea rubiginea.*
4. *Douinia ovata, Cetraria glauca, Pseudocyphellaria crocata, Usnea fragilescens.*
7. *Zygodon conoideus, Graphis scripta, Nephroma laevigatum, Thelotrema lepadinum.*
10. *Lecanora chlarotera, Parmeliella corallinoides.*
13. *Metzgeria fruticulosa.*

LOCALITIES: 1–13 as in Table 4.49.

TABLE 4.54

	Bryophytes of decaying logs in the Betula–Vaccinium myrtillus Association						*Bryophytes of decaying logs in Corylus–Oxalis acetosella Association*					
Reference Number	1 B68 317	2 B67 097	3 B67 040	4 B67 096	5 B67 100	6 B67 120	7 B67 098	8 B67 101	9 B67 105	10 B67 041	11 B67 078	12 B68 320
Dicranodontium denudatum	×	.	×	.	.	×	×	.	×	.	×	.
Dicranum scoparium	×	×	×	×	×	×	×	×	×	×	×	×
Hypnum cupressiforme	×	×	×	×	×	×	×	×	×	×	×	×
Isothecium myosuroides	×	×	×	×	×	×	×	×	×	×	×	×
Tetraphis pellucida	×	.	×	×	.	×	×	.	×	×	.	.
Blepharostoma trichophyllum	×	.	.	.	.	×	×	.	.	.	×	×
Cephalozia bicuspidata	×	×	×	×	×	×	×	×	×	×	×	×
C. connivens	×	.	×	.	.	×	×	.	.	.	.	.
C. media	×	.	.	.	.	×	×	.	.	.	.	.
Lepidozia pinnata	×	.	×	.	.	.	.	.	.	.	.	.
L. reptans	×	×	×	×	×	×	×	×	×	×	×	×
Lophocolea heterophylla	×	.	.	.	.	×	.	.	.	.	.	.
Lophozia incisa	×	.	×	×	.	×	×	.	×	×	×	×
L. ventricosa	×	×	×	×	×	×	×	×	×	×	.	×
Nowellia curvifolia	×	.	×	.	×	×	×	×	×	.	.	×
Plagiochila spinulosa	×	.	×	.	×	×	×	.	×	×	×	×
Riccardia latifrons	.	.	.	.	×	×	×	×	×	.	.	.
R. palmata	×	.	.	×	×	×	×	.	×	.	.	×
Scapania gracilis	×	×	×	×	×	×	×	.	×	×	×	×
S. umbrosa	×	.	×	.	.	×	×	.	×	×	×	×
Tritomaria exsecta	×	.	.	.	.	×	×	.	.	.	.	.
T. exsectiformis	×	.	×	.	.	.	.	.	.	.	.	.
Total number of species (22)	21	7	16	10	11	20	18	8	15	11	11	13

Mean number of species per stand = 14.2. Mean number of species per stand = 12.7

LOCALITIES: 1–12 as in Table 4.49.

TABLE 4.55

Class	QUERCO-FAGETEA
Order	FAGETALIA SYLVATICAE
Alliance	Fagion sylvaticae
Association	*Fraxinus excelsior–Brachypodium sylvaticum*

	1	2	3	4	5	C	D
Reference Number	B68	B67	B67	B67	B68		
	095	099	002	103	330		
Map Reference	393	613	609	607	575		
	643	118	211	202	200		
Altitude (feet)	100	300	100	100	100		
Aspect (degrees)	315	315	0	0	315		
Slope (degrees)	5	10	5	3	5		
Cover (per cent)	100	100	100	100	100		
Plot area (square metres)	16	16	16	16	4		
Betula pubescens ssp. *odorata*	.	3	4	+	.	III	1.6
Corylus avellana	4	8	8	9	8	V	7.4
Fraxinus excelsior	6	4	5	3	6	V	4.8
Sorbus aucuparia	3	3	3	.	.	III	1.8
Ulmus glabra	7	+	.	.	.	II	1.6
Viburnum opulus	.	.	3	2	.	II	1.0
Athyrium filix-femina	5	.	2	.	.	II	1.4
Blechnum spicant	.	2	2	.	.	II	0.8
Dryopteris filix-mas	5	2	3	2	.	IV	2.4
Pteridium aquilinum	.	1	.	.	3	II	0.8
Agrostis tenuis	3	3	3	3	2	V	2.8
Anthoxanthum odoratum	3	3	3	.	4	IV	2.6
Arrhenatherum elatius	3	.	1	.	3	II	1.4
Brachypodium sylvaticum	6	7	7	6	7	V	6.6
Dactylis glomerata	3	2	2	3	3	V	2.6
Deschampsia cespitosa	.	.	.	3	2	II	1.0
Allium ursinum	3	3	.	.	3	III	1.8
Carex sylvatica	.	1	.	3	.	II	0.8
Endymion non-scriptus	.	4	3	4	.	III	2.2
Anemone nemorosa	.	2	.	1	.	II	0.6
Bellis perennis	.	3	.	1	.	II	0.8
Cardamine flexuosa	+	+	.	.	1	III	0.6
Circaea intermedia	.	3	3	.	.	II	1.2
C. lutetiana	1	.	.	.	3	II	0.8
Conopodium majus	1	2	2	3	.	IV	1.6
Epilobium montanum	2	.	.	.	2	II	0.8
Filipendula ulmaria	7	3	3	3	6	V	4.4
Fragaria vesca	2	1	2	.	3	IV	1.6
Galium saxatile	.	.	2	2	.	II	0.8
Geranium robertianum	3	.	1	2	2	IV	1.6
Geum rivale	.	3	3	4	.	IV	2.0
Heracleum sphondylium	4	.	.	.	5	II	1.8
Lysimachia nemorum	4	1	4	2	.	IV	2.2
Oxalis acetosella	2	4	4	5	3	V	3.6
Potentilla erecta	.	2	.	1	.	II	0.6
Primula vulgaris	3	4	4	5	5	V	4.2
Prunella vulgaris	+	.	1	.	2	II	0.8
Ranunculus acris	2	1	.	.	.	II	0.6
Sanicula europaea	+	2	3	.	.	III	1.2
Vicia sepium	.	.	.	1	2	II	0.6
Viola riviniana	2	2	3	2	3	V	2.4
Ctenidium molluscum	.	1	5	2	5	IV	2.4
Eurhynchium praelongum	1	3	.	.	1	III	1.0
E. striatum	.	2	.	4	3	III	1.8
Fissidens taxifolius	.	+	.	1	.	II	0.4
Hylocomium brevirostre	+	2	.	4	5	IV	2.4
H. splendens	.	3	3	1	.	III	1.4
Isothecium myosuroides	.	.	2	1	.	II	0.6
I. myurum	4	.	3	.	1	III	1.6
Mnium undulatum	2	.	.	2	1	III	1.0
Rhytidiadelphus triquetrus	6	2	2	3	.	IV	2.6
Thuidium delicatulum	.	3	.	4	.	II	1.4
T. tamariscinum	2	3	2	1	2	V	2.0
**Plagiochila asplenioides*	.	.	.	1	2	II	0.6
Total number of species (95)	40	44	40	44	44		

* var. *major* in 4 and 5. Mean number of species per relevé = 42.4.

ADDITIONAL SPECIES IN LIST

1. *Angelica sylvestris* 4, *Chrysosplenium oppositifolium* 5, *Digitalis purpurea* 2, *Galium aparine* 1, *Silene dioica* 3, *Tussilago farfara* +, *Urtica dioica* 3.
2. *Prunus padus* 3, *Helictotrichon pratense* 1, *Glechoma hederacea* 2, *Rhytidiadelphus loreus* 2, *Lophocolea bidentata* 1.
3. *Lonicera periclymenum* +, *Gymnadenia conopsea* 1, *Listera ovata* 2, *Lathyrus montanus* 1, *Melampyrum pratense* 1, *Breutelia chrysocoma* 4, *Polytrichum formosum* 3.
4. *Thelypteris phegopteris* 1, *Ajuga reptans* 2, *Veronica chamaedrys* 3, *Atrichum undulatum* 1, *Fissidens cristatus* 1, *Pseudoscleropodium purum* 2, *Lejeunea cavifolia* 1, *Pellia epiphylla*, *Scapania aspera* 1.
5. *Rubus fruticosus* agg. 1, *Asplenium trichomanes* 1, *Senecio jacobea* 2, *Succisa pratensis* 2, *Anomodon viticulosus* 3, *Bryum capillare* 1, *Camptothecium sericeum* 3, *Rhytidiadelphus squarrosus* 2, *Thamnium alopecurum* 2, *Tortella tortuosa* 2, *Marchesinia mackaii* 2, *Metzgeria pubescens* 1, *Peltigera canina* 1.

LOCALITIES: 1. River Rha, Uig; 2. Tokavaig; 3, 4. Coille Gaireallach; 5. Torrin.

TABLE 4.56 LIMESTONE PAVEMENT COMMUNITIES

	1	2	3	4	5
Reference Number	B68 263	B68 302	B68 329	B68 303	B68 304
Map Reference	58– 18–	61– 12–	57– 20–	61– 19–	61– 19–
Altitude (feet)	100	300	100	500	500
Aspect (degrees)	270	270	225	315	315
Slope (degrees)	5	5	5	10	10
Plot area (square metres)	50	30	200	200	50
Species recorded mostly from saxicolous communities					
Asplenium adiantum-nigrum	.	×	.	×	.
A. ruta-muraria	×	.	×	×	.
A. trichomanes	×	×	×	×	×
A. viride	.	×	.	×	×
Camptothecium sericeum	×	.	×	×	×
Encalypta streptocarpa	.	×	×	×	.
Fissidens cristatus	×	×	×	×	×
Grimmia apocarpa	×	×	×	×	×
Neckera crispa	×	×	×	×	×
Orthotrichum anomalum	.	×	×	×	.
Tortella tortuosa	×	×	×	.	×
Trichostomum crispulum	×	.	.	×	.
Collema crispum	×	×	×	×	×
Species recorded mostly from grassland and dwarf-shrub communities					
Dryas octopetala	×	.	.	×	×
Rosa pimpinellifolia	×	.	×	×	.
Anthoxanthum odoratum	×	×	×	×	.
Arrhenatherum elatius	×	.	×	×	×
Festuca ovina	×	.	.	×	×
F. rubra	×	.	×	×	×
F. vivipara	×	×	×	×	×
Molinia caerulea	×	×	×	×	×
Sieglingia decumbens	×	×	.	×	.
Carex flacca	×	×	×	×	×
C. pulicaris	×	×	×	×	×
Antennaria dioica	×	.	×	×	×
Bellis perennis	×	×	×	×	.
Cirsium vulgare	×	.	×	×	.
Euphrasia confusa and *E. nemorosa*	×	×	×	×	.
Galium verum	×	.	×	.	.
Hieracium pilosella	×	×	×	×	×
Hypericum pulchrum	×	.	×	×	×
Linum catharticum	×	×	×	×	×
Lotus corniculatus	×	.	×	×	×
Plantago lanceolata	×	×	×	×	.
P. maritima	×	×	×	×	×
Polygala vulgaris	.	×	×	.	.
Polygonum viviparum	×	.	.	×	×
Potentilla erecta	×	.	×	×	×
Prunella vulgaris	×	.	×	×	.
Ranunculus repens	×	.	.	×	.
Succisa pratensis	.	×	×	×	×
Thymus drucei	×	×	×	×	×
Viola riviniana	×	×	×	×	×
Campylium protensum	×	.	×	.	.
Ditrichum flexicaule	.	×	×	×	×
Hylocomium splendens	×	×	.	×	×
**Hypnum cupressiforme*	.	×	×	×	×
Species recorded mostly from woodland communities					
Crataegus monogyna	×	.	×	×	.
Corylus avellana	.	.	×	×	×
Hedera helix	×	×	×	×	×
Salix aurita	×	×	.	×	.
Athyrium filix-femina	×	.	.	×	.
Dryopteris borreri	×	×	.	×	×
Phyllitis scolopendrium	×	×	×	×	×
Polystichum aculeatum	×	×	×	×	×
Pteridium aquilinum	.	.	×	×	×
Brachypodium sylvaticum	×	×	×	×	×
Allium ursinum	×	.	×	×	×
Endymion non-scriptus	.	.	×	×	×
Listera ovata	.	.	×	×	.
Anemone nemorosa	×	.	.	×	×
Epilobium montanum	.	.	×	×	.
Filipendula ulmaria	×	.	×	×	.
Hypericum androsaemum	×	.	×	.	.
Oxalis acetosella	.	.	×	×	×
Primula vulgaris	×	×	×	×	×
Sanicula europaea	×	.	×	×	×
Urtica dioica	×	.	.	×	.
Valeriana officinalis	×	.	×	×	×
Vicia sepium	×	×	×	×	.
Hylocomium brevirostre	×	×	×	×	.
Isothecium myurum	.	×	.	×	×
Mnium undulatum	.	×	×	×	×
Thamnium alopecurum	.	.	×	×	×
Thuidium tamariscinum	.	.	×	×	.
Plagiochila asplenioides	×	.	×	×	×
Other species					
Calluna vulgaris	×	×	.	×	.
Rubus saxatilis	×	×	×	×	×
Epipactis atrorubens	.	.	×	×	.
Fragaria vesca	.	.	×	×	.
Geranium robertianum	×	×	×	×	×
Leontodon autumnalis	×	×	×	.	.
Pinguicula vulgaris	×	.	.	×	.
Solidago virgaurea	.	×	×	.	.
Teucrium scorodonia	×	×	×	×	×
Ctenidium molluscum	×	×	×	×	×
Hypnum cupressiforme	×	.	.	×	×
†*Rhacomitrium lanuginosum*	×	.	.	×	×
Conocephalum conicum	×	×	.	×	.
Metzgeria pubescens	.	.	×	×	.
Scapania aspera	×	×	×	×	×
Total number of species (129)	69	52	85	95	63

* var. *ericetorum*. † var. *tectorum*.

Mean number of species per stand = 72.8.

ADDITIONAL SPECIES IN LIST

2. *Erica cinerea, Agrostis canina, Centaurea nigra, Tortula muralis, Frullania tamarisci.*
3. *Fraxinus excelsior, Salix repens, Festuca gigantea, Angelica sylvestris, Anthyllis vulneraria, Arabis hirsuta, Senecio jacobea, Anomodon viticulosus, Mnium longirostrum, Neckera complanata, Orthotrichum rupestre, Marchesinia mackaii, Porella laevigata, Protoblastenia rupestris.*
4. *Lonicera periclymenum, Sorbus aucuparia, Cystopteris fragilis, Cardamine pratensis, Cirsium heterophyllum, Geum rivale, Heracleum sphondylium, Stachys sylvatica, Acrocladium cuspidatum, Bryum capillare, Rhytidiadelphus triquetrus.*
5. *Arctostaphylos uva-ursi, Polypodium vulgare, Polystichum lonchitis, Myosotis discolor, Paris quadrifolia, Pseudoscleropodium purum, Gyalecta jenensis, Solorina saccata.*

LOCALITIES: 1. Camas Malag; 2. Tokavaig; 3. Torrin; 4, 5. Ben Suardal.

TABLE 4.57

	Hedwigia ciliata–Parmelia saxatilis	*Koenigia islandica* scree community	*Asplenium trichomanes–Fissidens cristatus*	*Puccinellia maritima–Ascophyllum nodosum*	*Puccinellia maritima–Festuca rubra*	*Juncus gerardii–Carex extensa*	*Armeria maritima–Grimmia maritima*	*Asplenium marinum–Grimmia maritima*	*Atriplex glabriuscula–Rumex crispus*	Brackish water communities	*Phragmites communis–Equisetum fluviatile*	*Schoenoplectus lacustris–Equisetum fluvatile*	*Carex rostrata–Menyanthes trifoliata*	*Littorella uniflora–Lobelia dortmanna*	*Potamogeton natans–Nymphaea alba nodum*	*Eriophorum angustifolium–Sphagnum cuspidatum*	*Carex lasiocarpa–Menyanthes trifoliata*	*Trichophorum cespitosum–Carex panicea*	*Molinia caerulea–Myrica gale*	*Sphagneto–Juncetum effusi*	*Carex–Sphagnum recurvum nodum*	*Carex rostrata–Aulacomnium palustre*	*Carex rostrata–Scorpidium scorpioides*	*Carex panicea–Campylium stellatum*	*Eriophorum latifolium–Carex hostiana*	*Schoenus nigricans*	*Carex–Saxifraga aizoides nodum*	*Trichophoreto–Callunetum*
Community Number	1	2	3	4	5	6	7	8	9	10	11	12	13	14	15	16	17	18	19	20	21	22	23	24	25	26	27	28
Antitrichia curtipendula (1)	II	.	.	.	.	.	.	.	.	.	.	.	.	.	.	.	.	.	.	.	.	.	.	.	.	.	.	.
Rhacomitrium aciculare (2)	+	.	.	.	.	.	.	.	.	.	.	.	.	.	.	.	.	.	.	.	.	.	.	.	.	.	.	.
Hypnum cupressiforme (3)	V	.	+	.	.	.	.	.	.	.	.	.	.	.	.	.	.	.	.	+	.	.	.	.	.	.	.	.
Glyphomitrium daviesii (4)	III	.	.	.	.	.	.	.	.	.	.	.	.	.	.	.	.	.	.	.	.	.	.	.	.	.	.	.
Grimmia trichophylla (5)	III	.	.	.	.	.	.	.	.	.	.	.	.	.	.	.	.	.	.	.	.	.	.	.	.	.	.	.
Hedwigia ciliata (6)	V	.	.	.	.	.	.	.	.	.	.	.	.	.	.	.	.	.	.	.	.	.	.	.	.	.	.	.
Parmelia omphalodes (7)	V	.	.	.	.	.	.	.	.	.	.	.	.	.	.	.	.	.	.	.	.	.	.	.	.	.	.	.
Parmelia saxatilis (8)	V	.	.	.	.	.	.	.	.	.	.	.	.	.	.	.	.	.	.	.	.	.	.	.	.	.	.	.
Lecanora dispersa (9)	V	.	.	.	.	.	.	.	.	.	.	.	.	.	.	.	.	.	.	.	.	.	.	.	.	.	.	.
Lecidia cyathoides (10)	III	.	.	.	.	.	.	.	.	.	.	.	.	.	.	.	.	.	.	.	.	.	.	.	.	.	.	.
Ochrolechia parella (11)	III	.	.	.	.	.	+	.	.	.	.	.	.	.	.	.	.	.	.	.	.	.	.	.	.	.	.	.
Parmelia glabratula (12)	II	.	.	.	.	.	+	.	.	.	.	.	.	.	.	.	.	.	.	.	.	.	.	.	.	.	.	.
Xanthoria parietina (13)	+	.	.	.	.	.	II	.	.	.	.	.	.	.	.	.	.	.	.	.	.	.	.	.	.	.	.	.
Aira praecox (14)	+	.	.	.	.	.	.	.	.	.	.	.	.	.	.	.	.	.	.	.	.	.	.	.	.	.	.	.
Ptychomitrium polyphyllum (15)	III	.	.	.	.	.	.	.	.	.	.	.	.	.	.	.	.	.	.	.	.	.	.	.	.	.	.	.
Rhacomitrium fasciculare (16)	V	.	.	.	.	.	.	.	.	.	.	.	.	.	.	.	.	.	.	.	.	.	.	.	.	.	.	.
Rhacomitrium heterostichum (17)	V	.	.	.	.	.	.	.	.	.	.	.	.	.	.	.	.	.	.	.	.	.	.	.	.	.	.	.
Rhacomitrium ellipticum (18)	+	II	.	.	.	.	.	.	.	.	.	.	.	.	.	.	.	.	.	.	.	.	.	.	.	.	.	.
Andreaea rothii (19)	+	II	.	.	.	.	.	.	.	.	.	.	.	.	.	.	.	.	.	.	.	.	.	.	.	.	.	.
Stereocaulon vesuvianum (20)	.	II	.	.	.	.	.	.	.	.	.	.	.	.	.	.	.	.	.	.	.	.	.	.	.	.	.	.
Polytrichum urnigerum (21)	.	II	.	.	.	.	.	.	.	.	.	.	.	.	.	.	.	.	.	.	.	.	.	.	.	.	.	.
Rhacomitrium canescens (22)	.	III	.	.	.	.	.	.	.	.	.	.	.	.	.	.	.	.	.	.	.	.	.	.	.	.	.	.
Sagina subulata (23)	.	IV	.	.	.	.	.	.	.	.	.	.	.	.	.	.	.	.	.	.	.	.	.	.	.	.	.	.
Cardaminopsis petraea (24)	.	V	.	.	.	.	.	.	.	.	.	.	.	.	.	.	.	.	.	.	.	.	.	.	.	.	.	.
Poa glauca (25)	.	III	.	.	.	.	.	.	.	.	.	.	.	.	.	.	.	.	.	.	.	.	.	.	.	.	.	.
Asplenium ruta-muraria (26)	.	.	III	.	.	.	.	+	.	.	.	.	.	.	.	.	.	.	.	.	.	.	.	.	.	.	.	.
Trichostomum crispulum (27)	.	.	III	.	.	.	.	.	.	.	.	.	.	.	.	.	.	.	.	.	.	.	.	.	.	.	.	.
Pohlia wahlenbergii (28)	.	.	+	.	.	.	.	.	.	.	.	.	.	.	.	.	.	.	.	.	.	.	.	.	.	.	.	.
Solorina saccata (29)	.	.	I	.	.	.	.	.	.	.	.	.	.	.	.	.	.	.	.	.	.	.	.	.	.	.	.	.
Distichium capillaceum (30)	.	.	+	.	.	.	.	.	.	.	.	.	.	.	.	.	.	.	.	.	.	.	.	.	.	.	.	.
Campylium protensum (31)	.	.	+	.	+	.	.	.	.	.	.	.	.	.	.	.	.	.	.	.	.	.	.	.	.	.	.	.
Camptothecium sericeum (32)	.	.	II	.	.	+	.	.	.	.	.	.	.	.	.	.	.	.	.	.	.	.	.	.	.	.	.	.
Collema sp. (33)	.	.	+	.	.	+	.	.	.	.	.	.	.	.	.	.	.	.	.	.	.	.	.	.	.	.	.	.
Neckera complanata (34)	.	.	I	.	.	.	.	.	.	.	.	.	.	.	.	.	.	.	.	.	.	.	.	.	.	.	.	.
Metzgeria pubescens (35)	.	.	+	.	.	.	.	.	.	.	.	.	.	.	.	.	.	.	.	.	.	.	.	.	.	.	.	.
Thamnium alopecurum (36)	.	.	II	.	.	.	.	.	.	.	.	.	.	.	.	.	.	.	.	.	.	.	.	.	.	.	.	.
Anomodon viticulosus (37)	.	.	+	.	.	.	.	.	.	.	.	.	.	.	.	.	.	.	.	.	.	.	.	.	.	.	.	.
Bryum capillare (38)	.	.	+	.	.	.	.	.	.	.	.	.	.	.	.	.	.	.	.	.	.	.	.	.	.	.	.	.
Lejeunea cavifolia (39)	.	.	II	.	.	.	.	.	.	.	.	.	.	.	.	.	.	.	.	.	.	.	.	.	.	.	.	.
Metzgeria furcata (40)	.	.	II	.	.	.	.	.	.	.	.	.	.	.	.	.	.	.	.	.	.	.	.	.	.	.	.	.
Sticta fuliginosa (41)	.	.	+	.	.	.	.	.	.	.	.	.	.	.	.	.	.	.	.	.	.	.	.	.	.	.	.	.
Amphidium mougeotii (42)	.	.	+	.	.	.	.	.	.	.	.	.	.	.	.	.	.	.	.	.	.	.	.	.	.	.	.	.
Pohlia cruda (43)	.	.	I	.	.	.	.	.	.	.	.	.	.	.	.	.	.	.	.	.	.	.	.	.	.	.	.	.
Cololejeunea calcarea (44)	.	.	I	.	.	.	.	.	.	.	.	.	.	.	.	.	.	.	.	.	.	.	.	.	.	.	.	.
Eucladium verticillatum (45)	.	.	I	.	.	.	.	.	.	.	.	.	.	.	.	.	.	.	.	.	.	.	.	.	.	.	.	.
Barbula ferruginascens (46)	.	.	+	.	.	.	.	.	.	.	.	.	.	.	.	.	.	.	.	.	.	.	.	.	.	.	.	.
Plagiochila asplenoides (47)	.	.	III	.	.	.	.	.	.	.	.	.	.	.	.	.	.	.	.	.	.	.	.	.	.	.	.	.
Asplenium trichomanes (48)	.	.	V	.	.	.	.	.	.	.	.	.	.	.	.	.	.	.	.	.	.	.	.	.	.	.	.	.
Asplenium viride (49)	.	.	III	.	.	.	.	.	.	.	.	.	.	.	.	.	.	.	.	.	.	.	.	.	.	.	.	.
Cystopteris fragilis (50)	.	.	III	.	.	.	.	.	.	.	.	.	.	.	.	.	.	.	.	.	.	.	.	.	.	.	.	.
Polystichum lonchitis (51)	.	.	I	.	.	.	.	.	.	.	.	.	.	.	.	.	.	.	.	.	.	.	.	.	.	.	.	.
Polystichum aculeatum (52)	.	.	II	.	.	.	.	.	.	.	.	.	.	.	.	.	.	.	.	.	.	.	.	.	.	.	.	.
Scapania aspera (53)	.	.	II	.	.	.	.	.	.	.	.	.	.	.	.	.	.	.	.	.	.	.	.	.	+	.	.	.
Fissidens cristatus (54)	.	.	V	.	.	.	.	.	.	.	.	.	.	.	.	.	.	.	.	.	.	.	.	.	.	.	.	.
Ascophyllum nodosum (55)		.	.	V	.	.	.	.	.	.	.	.	.	.	.	.	.	.	.	.	.	.	.	.	.	.	.	.

TABLE 4.57

	29 *Molinieto–Callunetum*	30 *Trichophoreto–Eriophoretum*	31 *Calluneto–Eriophoretum*	32 *Philonoto–Saxifragetum stellaris*	33 *Koenigia islandica–Carex demissa nodum*	34 *Cratoneuron commutatum–Saxifraga aizoides nodum*	35 *Saxifragetum aizoidis*	36 *Juncus acutiflorus–Filipendula ulmaria*	37 *Centaureo–Cynosuretum*	38 *Maritime grassland nodum*	39 *Lolium pereme–Plantago lanceolata*	40 *Dryas octopetala–Carex flacca*	41 *Cariceto–Rhacomitretum lanuginosi*	42 *Festuca ovina–Luzula spicata nodum*	43 *Rhacomitreto–Callunetum*	44 *Juniperus nana nodum*	45 *Rhacomitreto–Empetretum*	46 *Alchemilla alpina–Vaccinium myrtillus nodum*	47 *Nardus stricta–Vaccinium myrtillus*	48 *Agrosto–Festucetum* (species–poor)	49 *Alchemilleto–Agrosto–Festucetum*	50 *Agrosto–Festucetum* (species–rich)	51 *Nardo–Juncetum squarrosi*	52 *Callunetum vulgaris*	53 *Calluna vulgaris–Sieglingia decumbens*	54 *Calluna vulgaris–Arctostaphylos uva-ursi nodum*	55 *Vaccineto–Callunetum hepaticosum*	56 *Luzula sylvatica–Vaccinium myrtillus*	57 *Luzula sylvatica–Silene dioica*	58 *Betula pubescens–Cirsium heterophyllum*	59 *Sedum rosea–Alchemilla glabra*	60 *Betula pubescens–Vaccinium myrtillus*	61 *Corylus avellana–Oxalis acetosella*	62 *Oxalis acetosella–Rhytidiadelphus loreus*	63 *Hymenophyllum wilsonii–Isothecium myosuroides*	64 Open boulder association	65 *Fraxinus excelsior–Brachypodium sylvaticum*
(1)	.	.	.	.	.	.	.	.	.	.	.	.	.	.	.	.	.	.	.	.	.	.	.	.	.	.	.	.	.	.	.	.	.	.	.	.	.
(2)	.	.	.	.	.	.	.	.	.	.	.	.	.	.	.	.	.	.	.	.	.	.	.	.	.	.	.	.	.	.	.	.	.	.	+	.	.
(3)	.	.	.	.	.	.	.	.	.	.	.	.	.	.	.	.	.	.	.	.	.	.	.	.	.	.	.	.	.	.	.	.	.	.	III	.	.
(4)	.	.	.	.	.	.	.	.	.	.	.	.	.	.	.	.	.	.	.	.	.	.	.	.	.	.	.	.	.	.	.	.	.	.	.	.	.
(5)	.	.	.	.	.	.	.	.	.	.	.	.	.	.	.	.	.	.	.	.	.	.	.	.	.	.	.	.	.	.	.	.	.	.	.	.	.
(6)	.	.	.	.	.	.	.	.	.	.	.	.	.	.	.	.	.	.	.	.	.	.	.	.	.	.	.	.	.	.	.	.	.	.	.	.	.
(7)	.	.	.	.	.	.	.	.	.	.	.	.	.	.	.	.	.	.	.	.	.	.	.	.	.	.	.	.	.	.	.	.	.	.	.	.	.
(8)	.	.	.	.	.	.	.	.	.	.	.	.	.	.	.	.	.	.	.	.	.	.	.	.	.	.	.	.	.	.	.	.	.	.	.	.	.
(9)	.	.	.	.	.	.	.	.	.	.	.	.	.	.	.	.	.	.	.	.	.	.	.	.	.	.	.	.	.	.	.	.	.	.	.	.	.
(10)	.	.	.	.	.	.	.	.	.	.	.	.	.	.	.	.	.	.	.	.	.	.	.	.	.	.	.	.	.	.	.	.	.	.	.	.	.
(11)	.	.	.	.	.	.	.	.	.	.	.	.	.	.	.	.	.	.	.	.	.	.	.	.	.	.	.	.	.	.	.	.	.	.	.	.	.
(12)	.	.	.	.	.	.	.	.	.	.	.	.	.	.	.	.	.	.	.	.	.	.	.	.	.	.	.	.	.	.	.	.	.	.	.	.	.
(13)	.	.	.	.	.	.	.	.	.	.	.	.	.	.	.	.	.	.	.	.	.	.	.	.	.	.	.	.	.	.	.	.	.	.	.	.	.
(14)	.	.	.	.	.	.	.	.	.	.	+	.	.	.	.	.	.	.	.	.	.	.	.	.	.	.	.	.	.	.	.	.	.	.	.	.	.
(15)	.	.	.	.	.	.	.	.	.	.	.	.	.	.	.	.	.	.	.	.	.	.	.	.	.	.	.	.	.	.	.	.	.	.	.	.	.
(16)	.	.	.	.	.	.	.	.	.	.	.	.	II	.	II	.	.	.	.	.	.	.	.	.	.	.	.	+	.	.	.	.	.	.	+	.	.
(17)	.	.	.	.	+	.	.	.	.	.	.	.	I	III	III	.	.	.	.	.	.	.	.	.	.	.	.	+	.	.	.	.	.	.	.	.	.
(18)	.	.	.	.	.	.	.	.	.	.	.	.	.	.	.	.	.	.	.	.	.	.	.	.	.	.	.	.	.	.	.	.	.	.	.	.	.
(19)	.	.	.	.	.	.	.	.	.	.	.	.	.	.	II	.	.	.	.	.	.	.	.	.	.	.	.	.	.	.	.	.	.	.	.	.	.
(20)	.	.	.	.	.	.	.	.	.	.	.	.	.	+	I	.	.	.	.	.	.	.	.	.	.	.	.	.	.	.	+	.	.	.	.	.	.
(21)	.	.	.	.	.	.	.	.	.	.	+	.	.	.	.	.	.	.	.	.	+	.	.	.	.	.	.	.	.	.	.	.	.	.	.	.	.
(22)	.	.	.	.	.	.	.	.	.	.	.	.	+	.	.	.	.	.	.	.	.	.	.	.	.	.	.	.	.	.	.	.	.	.	.	.	.
(23)	.	.	.	.	.	.	.	.	.	.	.	.	.	.	.	.	.	.	.	.	.	.	.	.	.	.	.	+	.	.	.	.	.	.	.	.	.
(24)	.	.	.	.	.	.	.	.	.	.	.	.	.	.	.	.	.	.	.	.	.	.	.	.	.	.	.	.	.	.	.	.	.	.	.	.	.
(25)	.	.	.	.	.	.	.	.	.	.	.	.	.	.	.	.	.	.	.	.	.	.	.	.	.	.	.	.	.	.	.	.	.	.	.	.	.
(26)	.	.	.	.	.	.	.	.	.	.	.	.	.	.	.	.	.	.	.	.	.	.	.	.	.	.	.	.	.	.	.	.	.	.	.	.	.
(27)	.	.	.	.	.	.	.	.	.	II	.	.	.	.	.	.	.	.	.	.	.	.	.	.	.	+	.	.	.	.	+	.	.	.	.	.	.
(28)	.	.	.	.	.	.	.	.	.	.	.	.	.	.	.	.	.	.	.	.	.	.	.	.	.	.	.	.	.	.	+	.	.	.	.	.	.
(29)	.	.	.	.	.	.	.	.	.	.	.	.	.	.	.	.	.	.	.	.	.	.	.	.	.	.	.	.	.	.	+	.	.	.	.	.	.
(30)	.	.	.	.	.	.	.	.	.	.	.	.	.	.	.	.	.	.	.	.	.	.	.	.	.	.	.	.	.	.	II	.	.	.	.	.	.
(31)	.	.	.	.	.	.	.	.	.	.	.	+	.	.	.	.	.	.	.	.	.	.	.	.	.	.	.	.	.	.	.	.	.	.	.	.	.
(32)	.	.	.	.	.	.	.	.	.	.	.	.	.	.	.	.	.	.	.	.	.	.	.	.	.	.	.	.	+	.	.	.	.	.	.	.	.
(33)	.	.	.	.	.	.	.	.	.	.	.	+	.	.	.	.	.	.	.	.	.	.	.	.	.	.	.	.	.	.	.	.	.	.	.	+	.
(34)	.	.	.	.	.	.	.	.	.	.	.	I	.	.	.	.	.	.	.	.	.	.	.	.	.	.	.	.	.	.	.	.	.	.	.	.	.
(35)	.	.	.	.	.	.	.	.	.	.	.	.	.	.	.	.	.	.	.	.	.	.	.	.	.	.	.	.	.	.	.	.	.	.	.	.	.
(36)	.	.	.	.	.	.	.	.	.	.	.	.	.	.	.	.	.	.	.	.	.	.	.	.	.	.	.	.	.	.	.	.	.	.	.	.	+
(37)	.	.	.	.	.	.	.	.	.	.	.	.	.	.	.	.	.	.	.	.	.	.	.	.	.	.	.	.	.	.	.	.	.	.	.	.	I
(38)	.	.	.	.	.	.	.	.	.	.	+	.	.	.	.	.	.	.	.	.	.	.	.	.	.	.	.	.	.	.	.	.	.	.	.	.	+
(39)	.	.	.	.	.	.	.	.	.	.	.	.	.	.	.	.	.	.	.	.	.	.	.	.	.	.	.	.	.	.	.	.	.	.	+	.	+
(40)	.	.	.	.	.	.	.	.	.	.	.	.	.	.	.	.	.	.	.	.	.	.	.	.	.	.	.	.	.	.	.	.	.	.	+	.	.
(41)	.	.	.	.	.	.	.	.	.	.	.	.	.	.	.	.	.	.	.	.	.	.	.	.	.	.	.	.	.	.	.	.	.	.	+	.	.
(42)	.	.	.	.	.	.	II	.	.	.	.	.	.	.	.	.	.	.	.	.	.	.	.	.	.	.	.	.	.	.	.	.	.	.	.	.	.
(43)	.	.	.	.	.	.	+	.	.	.	.	.	.	.	.	.	.	.	.	.	.	.	.	.	.	.	.	.	.	.	.	.	.	.	.	.	.
(44)	.	.	.	.	.	.	+	.	.	.	.	.	.	.	.	.	.	.	.	.	.	.	.	.	.	.	.	.	.	.	.	.	.	.	.	.	.
(45)	.	.	.	.	.	.	+	.	.	.	.	.	.	.	.	.	.	.	.	.	.	.	.	.	.	.	.	.	.	.	.	.	.	.	.	.	.
(46)	.	.	.	.	.	.	+	.	.	.	.	.	.	.	.	.	.	.	.	.	.	.	.	.	.	.	.	.	.	.	.	.	.	.	.	.	.
(47)	.	.	.	.	.	.	II	.	.	.	.	.	.	.	.	.	.	.	.	.	.	.	.	.	.	.	.	.	+	I	I	.	.	+	.	+	.
(48)	.	.	.	.	.	.	.	.	.	.	.	.	.	.	.	.	.	.	.	.	.	.	.	.	.	.	.	.	.	II	.	.	.	.	.	.	.
(49)	.	.	.	.	.	.	III	.	.	.	.	.	.	.	.	.	.	.	.	.	+	.	.	.	.	.	.	.	.	I	II	.	.	.	.	.	+
(50)	.	.	.	.	.	.	IV	.	.	.	.	.	.	.	.	.	.	.	.	.	.	.	.	.	.	.	.	.	.	.	+	.	.	.	.	.	.
(51)	.	.	.	.	.	.	+	.	.	.	.	.	.	.	.	.	.	.	.	.	.	.	.	.	.	.	.	.	.	.	+	.	.	.	.	.	.
(52)	.	.	.	.	.	.	.	.	.	.	.	+	.	.	.	.	.	.	.	.	.	.	.	.	.	.	.	.	.	II	.	.	+	.	.	.	.
(53)	.	.	.	.	.	.	+	.	.	.	.	.	.	.	.	.	.	.	.	.	+	.	.	.	.	.	.	.	.	+	.	.	.	.	.	.	+
(54)	.	.	.	.	.	II	I	.	.	.	.	II	.	.	.	.	.	.	.	.	.	.	.	.	.	.	.	.	.	II	.	.	.	.	.	.	+
(55)	.	.	.	.	.	.	.	.	.	.	.	.	.	.	.	.	.	.	.	.	.	.	.	.	.	.	.	.	.	.	.	.	.	.	.	.	.

TABLE 4.57 *continued*

	Hedwigia ciliata–Parmelia saxatilis	*Koenigia islandica* scree community	*Asplenium trichomanes–Fissidens cristatus*	*Puccinellia maritima–Ascophyllum nodosum*	*Puccinellia maritima–Festuca rubra*	*Juncus gerardii–Carex extensa*	*Armeria maritima–Grimmia maritima*	*Asplenium marinum–Grimmia maritima*	*Atriplex glabriuscula–Rumex crispus*	Brackish water communities	*Phragmites communis–Equisetum fluviatile*	*Schoenoplectus lacustris–Equisetum fluviatile*	*Carex rostrata–Menyanthes trifoliata*	*Littorella uniflora–Lobelia dortmanna*	*Potamogeton natans–Nymphaea alba nodum*	*Eriophorum angustifolium–Sphagnum cuspidatum*	*Carex lasiocarpa–Menyanthes trifoliata*	*Trichophorum cespitosum–Carex panicea*	*Molinia caerulea–Myrica gale*	*Sphagneto–Juncetum effusi*	*Carex–Sphagnum recurvum nodum*	*Carex rostrata–Aulacomnium palustre*	*Carex rostrata–Scorpidium scorpioides*	*Carex panicea–Campylium stellatum*	*Eriophorum latifolium–Carex hostiana*	*Schoenus nigricans*	*Carex–Saxifraga aizoides nodum*	*Trichophoreto–Callunetum*
Community Number	1	2	3	4	5	6	7	8	9	10	11	12	13	14	15	16	17	18	19	20	21	22	23	24	25	26	27	28
Aster tripolium (56)	.	.	.	II	.	II	.	.	.	.	.	.	.	.	.	.	.	.	.	.	.	.	.	.	.	.	.	.
Puccinellia maritima (57)	.	.	.	V	V	+	.	.	.	.	.	.	.	.	.	.	.	.	.	.	.	.	.	.	.	.	.	.
Spergularia media (58)	.	.	.	II	I	I	.	.	.	.	.	.	.	.	.	.	.	.	.	.	.	.	.	.	.	.	.	.
Glaux maritima (59)	.	.	.	V	IV	V	.	.	III	IV	.	.	.	.	.	.	.	.	.	.	.	.	.	.	.	.	.	.
Triglochin maritima (60)	.	.	.	+	.	III	.	.	II	IV	.	.	.	.	.	.	.	.	.	.	.	.	.	.	.	.	.	.
Cochlearia officinalis agg. (61)	.	.	.	+	.	I	II	+	II	III	.	.	.	.	.	.	.	.	.	.	.	.	.	.	.	.	.	.
Armeria maritima (62)	.	.	.	V	V	V	V	IV	IV	+	.	.	.	.	.	.	.	.	.	.	.	.	.	.	.	.	III	.
Plantago maritima (63)	.	.	.	V	V	V	V	III	II	II	.	.	.	.	.	.	.	.	.	.	.	.	.	.	+	.	II	.
Festuca rubra (64)	II	.	.	.	V	V	V	IV	III	.	.	.	.	.	.	.	.	.	.	.	.	.	.	+	.	.	.	.
Leontodon autumnalis (65)	.	.	.	.	II	II	II	+	II	.	.	.	.	.	.	.	.	.	.	.	.	.	.	.	.	.	.	.
Grimmia maritima (66)	.	.	.	.	+	II	V	V	+	+	.	.	.	.	.	.	.	.	.	.	.	.	.	.	.	.	.	.
Trichostomum brachydontium (67)	.	.	.	.	II	.	II	V	+	.	.	.	.	.	.	.	.	.	.	.	.	.	.	.	.	.	.	.
Salicornia europaea (68)	.	.	.	.	+	.	.	.	+	.	.	.	.	.	.	.	.	.	.	.	.	.	.	.	.	.	.	.
Plantago coronopus (69)	.	.	.	.	II	II	II	.	+	.	.	.	.	.	.	.	.	.	.	.	.	.	.	.	.	.	.	.
Agrostis stolonifera (70)	.	.	.	.	.	V	I	+	III	V	.	.	.	.	.	.	+	.	.	.	.	.	.	.	.	.	.	.
Carex extensa (71)	.	.	.	.	.	III	.	.	.	.	.	.	.	.	.	.	.	.	.	.	.	.	.	.	.	.	.	.
Blysmus rufus (72)	.	.	.	.	.	III	.	.	.	+	.	.	.	.	.	.	.	.	.	.	.	.	.	.	.	.	.	.
Juncus gerardii (73)	.	.	.	.	.	V	.	.	II	IV	.	.	.	.	.	.	.	.	.	.	.	.	.	.	.	.	.	.
Amblystegium serpens (74)	.	.	.	.	.	I	.	.	+	.	.	.	.	.	.	.	.	.	.	.	.	.	.	.	.	.	.	.
Suaeda maritima (75)	.	.	.	.	.	+	.	.	+	.	.	.	.	.	.	.	.	.	.	.	.	.	.	.	.	.	.	.
Sagina maritima (76)	.	.	.	.	.	I	III	II	+	.	.	.	.	.	.	.	.	.	.	.	.	.	.	.	.	.	.	.
Ligusticum scoticum (77)	.	.	.	.	.	.	II	.	II	.	.	.	.	.	.	.	.	.	.	.	.	.	.	.	.	.	.	.
Rumex crispus var. *triangulatus* (78)	.	.	.	.	.	.	I	.	V	+	.	.	.	.	.	.	.	.	.	.	.	.	.	.	.	.	.	.
Anaptychia fusca (79)	.	.	.	.	.	.	III	.	.	.	.	.	.	.	.	.	.	.	.	.	.	.	.	.	.	.	.	.
Ramalina siliquosa (80)	.	.	.	.	.	.	III	+	.	.	.	.	.	.	.	.	.	.	.	.	.	.	.	.	.	.	.	.
Sedum anglicum (81)	III	.	.	.	.	.	II	+	.	.	.	.	.	.	.	.	.	.	.	.	.	.	.	.	.	.	.	.
Asplenium adiantum-nigrum (82)	.	.	+	.	.	.	.	II	.	.	.	.	.	.	.	.	.	.	.	.	.	.	.	.	.	.	.	.
Asplenium marinum (83)	.	.	.	.	.	.	.	V	.	.	.	.	.	.	.	.	.	.	.	.	.	.	.	.	.	.	.	.
Tripleurospermum maritimum (84)	.	.	.	.	.	.	.	II	IV	.	.	.	.	.	.	.	.	.	.	.	.	.	.	.	.	.	.	.
Atriplex glabriuscula (85)	.	.	.	.	.	.	.	.	V	.	.	.	.	.	.	.	.	.	.	.	.	.	.	.	.	.	.	.
Galium aparine (86)	.	.	.	.	.	.	.	.	V	.	.	.	.	.	.	.	.	.	.	.	.	.	.	.	.	.	.	.
Galium verum (87)	.	.	.	.	.	.	.	.	+	.	.	.	.	.	.	.	.	.	.	.	.	.	.	.	.	.	.	.
Agropyron repens (88)	.	.	.	.	.	.	.	.	II	.	.	.	.	.	.	.	.	.	.	.	.	.	.	.	.	.	.	.
Juncus bufonius (89)	.	.	.	.	.	.	.	.	III	II	.	.	.	.	.	.	.	.	.	.	.	.	.	.	.	.	.	.
Scirpus maritimus (90)	.	.	.	.	.	.	.	.	II	V	.	.	.	.	.	.	.	.	.	.	.	.	.	.	.	.	.	.
Stellaria media (91)	.	.	.	.	.	.	.	.	II	+	.	.	.	.	.	.	.	.	.	.	.	.	.	.	.	.	.	.
Sagina procumbens (92)	.	.	+	.	.	.	.	.	+	+	.	.	.	.	.	.	.	.	.	.	.	.	.	.	.	.	.	.
Potentilla anserina (93)	.	.	.	.	.	.	.	.	.	II	.	.	.	.	.	.	.	.	.	.	.	.	.	.	.	.	.	.
Drepanocladus aduncus (94)	.	.	.	.	.	.	.	.	.	III	.	.	.	.	.	.	.	.	.	.	.	.	.	.	.	.	.	.
Hydrocotyle vulgaris (95)	.	.	.	.	.	.	.	.	.	II	.	.	.	.	.	.	.	.	.	.	.	.	.	.	.	.	.	.
Iris pseudacorus (96)	.	.	.	.	.	.	.	.	.	II	.	.	.	.	.	.	.	.	.	.	.	+	.	.	.	.	.	.
Achillea ptarmica (97)	.	.	.	.	.	.	.	.	+	.	.	.	.	.	.	.	.	.	.	.	.	+	.	.	.	.	.	.
Caltha palustris (98)	.	.	.	.	.	.	.	.	.	III	.	.	.	.	.	.	.	.	.	.	.	III	II	.	.	.	.	.
Potentilla palustris (99)	.	.	.	.	.	.	.	.	.	+	II	I	II	.	.	.	III	+	.	.	.	V	III	.	.	.	.	.
Juncus articulatus (100)	.	.	.	.	.	.	.	.	+	IV	+	.	II	IV	.	.	I	+	.	.	+	III	II	V	III	.	III	.
Eleocharis palustris (101)	.	.	.	.	.	.	.	.	+	V	I	II	IV	III	.	.	.	.	+	.	.	II	+	II	I	I	.	.
Ranunculus flammula (102)	.	.	.	.	.	.	.	.	.	III	.	+	III	IV	.	.	III	+	.	.	.	V	III	II	I	.	III	.
Galium palustre (103)	.	.	.	.	.	.	.	.	.	III	.	+	.	.	.	.	III	.	.	.	.	IV	II	.	.	.	.	.
Phragmites communis (104)	.	.	.	.	.	.	.	.	.	V	V	.	+	.	.	.	.	.	.	.	.	.	+	.	.	+	.	.
Utricularia intermedia (105)	.	.	.	.	.	.	.	.	.	.	+	.	.	.	.	.	.	.	.	.	.	.	+	.	.	.	.	.
Equisetum fluviatile (106)	.	.	.	.	.	.	.	.	.	.	V	V	IV	II	IV	.	V	.	.	.	.	.	.	.	.	.	.	.
Juncus bulbosus (107)	.	.	.	.	.	.	.	.	.	.	II	II	.	IV	+	.	.	.	.	.	.	.	.	.	.	.	.	.
Potamogeton natans (108)	.	.	.	.	.	.	.	.	.	.	III	III	II	+	V	.	.	.	.	.	.	.	.	.	.	.	.	.
Nymphaea alba (109)	.	.	.	.	.	.	.	.	.	.	III	I	.	.	IV	.	.	.	.	.	.	.	.	.	.	.	.	.
Sparganium minimum (110)	.	.	.	.	.	.	.	.	.	.	+	.	.	.	+	.	I	.	.	.	.	.	.	.	.	.	.	.

TABLE 4.57 *continued*

	29 *Molinieto–Callunetum*	30 *Trichophoreto–Eriophoretum*	31 *Calluneto–Eriophoretum*	32 *Philonoto–Saxifragetum stellaris*	33 *Koenigia islandica–Carex demissa nodum*	34 *Cratoneuron commutatum–Saxifraga aizoides nodum*	35 *Saxifragetum aizoidis*	36 *Juncus acutiflorus–Filipendula ulmaria*	37 *Centaureo–Cynosuretum*	38 *Maritime grassland nodum*	39 *Lolium perenne–Plantago lanceolata*	40 *Dryas octopetala–Carex flacca*	41 *Cariceto–Rhacomitretum lanuginosi*	42 *Festuca ovina–Luzula spicata nodum*	43 *Rhacomitreto–Callunetum*	44 *Juniperus nana nodum*	45 *Rhacomitreto–Empetretum*	46 *Alchemilla alpina–Vaccinium myrtillus nodum*	47 *Nardus stricta–Vaccinium myrtillus*	48 *Agrosto–Festucetum* (species-poor)	49 *Alchemilleto–Agrosto–Festucetum*	50 *Agrosto–Festucetum* (species-rich)	51 *Nardo–Juncetum squarrosi*	52 *Callunetum vulgaris*	53 *Calluna vulgaris–Sieglingia decumbens*	54 *Calluna vulgaris–Arctostaphylos uva-ursi nodum*	55 *Vaccineto–Callunetum hepaticosum*	56 *Luzula sylvatica–Vaccinium myrtillus*	57 *Luzula sylvatica–Silene dioica*	58 *Betula pubescens–Cirsium heterophyllum*	59 *Sedum rosea–Alchemilla glabra*	60 *Betula pubescens–Vaccinium myrtillus*	61 *Corylus avellana–Oxalis acetosella*	62 *Oxalis acetosella–Rhytidiadelphus loreus*	63 *Hymenophyllum wilsonii–Isothecium myosuroides*	64 Open boulder association	65 *Fraxinus excelsior–Brachypodium sylvaticum*
(56)	.	.	.	.	.	.	.	.	.	.	.	.	.	.	.	.	.	.	.	.	.	.	.	.	.	.	.	.	.	.	.	.	.	.	.	.	.
(57)	.	.	.	.	.	.	.	.	.	.	.	.	.	.	.	.	.	.	.	.	.	.	.	.	.	.	.	.	.	.	.	.	.	.	.	.	.
(58)	.	.	.	.	.	.	.	.	.	.	.	.	.	.	.	.	.	.	.	.	.	.	.	.	.	.	.	.	.	.	.	.	.	.	.	.	.
(59)	.	.	.	.	.	.	.	.	.	.	.	.	.	.	.	.	.	.	.	.	.	.	.	.	.	.	.	.	.	.	.	.	.	.	.	.	.
(60)	.	.	.	.	.	.	.	.	.	.	.	.	.	.	.	.	.	.	.	.	.	.	.	.	.	.	.	.	.	.	.	.	.	.	.	.	.
(61)	.	.	.	I	II	.	+	.	.	.	.	.	.	.	.	.	.	.	.	.	.	.	.	.	.	.	.	.	.	.	III	.	.	.	.	.	.
(62)	.	.	.	.	.	.	.	.	.	+	.	.	I	.	.	.	.	.	.	.	.	.	.	.	.	.	.	.	II	.	.	.	.	.	.	.	.
(63)	.	.	.	.	.	.	.	.	.	V	+	IV	I	II	.	.	I	II	.	.	.	II	.	.	II	.	.	.	II	.	.	.	.	.	.	.	.
(64)	.	.	.	III	.	V	V	I	V	V	+	+	.	.	.	.	.	.	.	II	.	IV	.	.	II	.	.	.	III	.	I	.	.	.	.	.	.
(65)	.	.	.	.	.	II	I	.	II	III	+	+	.	.	.	.	.	.	.	.	.	.	.	.	II	.	.	.	.	.	.	.	.	.	.	.	.
(66)	.	.	.	.	.	.	.	.	.	.	.	.	.	.	.	.	.	.	.	.	.	.	.	.	.	.	.	.	.	.	.	.	.	.	.	.	.
(67)	.	.	.	.	.	.	.	.	.	.	.	.	.	.	.	.	.	.	.	.	.	.	.	.	.	.	.	.	+	.	.	.	.	.	.	.	.
(68)	.	.	.	.	.	.	.	.	.	.	.	.	.	.	.	.	.	.	.	.	.	.	.	.	.	.	.	.	.	.	.	.	.	.	.	.	.
(69)	.	.	.	.	.	.	.	.	.	+	.	.	.	.	.	.	.	.	.	.	.	.	.	.	.	.	.	.	.	.	.	.	.	.	.	.	.
(70)	.	.	.	.	.	.	.	.	.	V	II	.	.	.	.	.	.	.	.	.	.	.	.	.	.	+	.	.	.	.	.	.	.	.	.	.	.
(71)	.	.	.	.	.	.	.	.	.	.	.	.	.	.	.	.	.	.	.	.	.	.	.	.	.	.	.	.	.	.	.	.	.	.	.	.	.
(72)	.	.	.	.	.	.	.	.	.	.	.	.	.	.	.	.	.	.	.	.	.	.	.	.	.	.	.	.	.	.	.	.	.	.	.	.	.
(73)	.	.	.	.	.	.	.	.	.	.	.	.	.	.	.	.	.	.	.	.	.	.	.	.	.	.	.	.	.	.	.	.	.	.	.	.	.
(74)	.	.	.	.	.	.	.	.	.	.	.	.	.	.	.	.	.	.	.	.	.	.	.	.	.	.	.	.	.	.	.	.	.	.	.	.	.
(75)	.	.	.	.	.	.	.	.	.	.	.	.	.	.	.	.	.	.	.	.	.	.	.	.	.	.	.	.	.	.	.	.	.	.	.	.	.
(76)	.	.	.	.	.	.	.	.	.	.	.	.	.	.	.	.	.	.	.	.	.	.	.	.	.	.	.	.	.	.	.	.	.	.	.	.	.
(77)	.	.	.	.	.	.	.	.	.	.	.	.	.	.	.	.	.	.	.	.	.	.	.	.	.	.	.	.	.	.	.	.	.	.	.	.	.
(78)	.	.	.	.	.	.	.	.	.	.	.	.	.	.	.	.	.	.	.	.	.	.	.	.	.	.	.	.	.	.	.	.	.	.	.	.	.
(79)	.	.	.	.	.	.	.	.	.	.	.	.	.	.	.	.	.	.	.	.	.	.	.	.	.	.	.	.	.	.	.	.	.	.	.	.	.
(80)	.	.	.	.	.	.	.	.	.	+	.	.	.	.	.	.	.	.	.	.	.	.	.	.	.	.	.	.	.	.	.	.	.	.	.	.	.
(81)	.	.	.	.	.	.	.	.	.	.	.	.	.	.	.	.	.	.	.	.	.	.	.	.	.	.	.	.	.	.	+	.	.	.	.	.	.
(82)	.	.	.	.	.	.	.	.	.	.	.	.	.	.	.	.	.	.	.	.	.	.	.	.	.	.	.	.	+	.	.	.	.	.	.	.	.
(83)	.	.	.	.	.	.	.	.	.	.	.	.	.	.	.	.	.	.	.	.	.	.	.	.	.	.	.	.	.	.	.	.	.	.	.	.	.
(84)	.	.	.	.	.	.	.	.	.	.	.	.	.	.	.	.	.	.	.	.	.	.	.	.	.	.	.	.	.	.	.	.	.	.	.	.	.
(85)	.	.	.	.	.	.	.	.	.	.	.	.	.	.	.	.	.	.	.	.	.	.	.	.	.	.	.	.	.	+	.	.	+	.	.	.	+
(86)	.	.	.	.	.	.	.	.	.	.	.	.	.	.	.	.	.	.	.	.	.	.	.	.	.	.	.	.	.	.	.	.	.	.	.	.	.
(87)	.	.	.	.	.	.	.	.	.	.	.	.	.	.	.	.	.	.	.	.	.	.	.	.	+	.	.	.	.	.	.	.	.	.	.	.	.
(88)	.	.	.	.	.	.	.	.	.	.	+	.	.	.	.	.	.	.	.	.	.	.	.	.	.	.	.	.	.	.	.	.	.	.	.	.	.
(89)	.	.	.	.	.	.	.	.	.	.	.	.	.	.	.	.	.	.	.	.	.	.	.	.	.	.	.	.	.	.	.	.	.	.	.	.	.
(90)	.	.	.	.	.	.	.	.	.	.	.	.	.	.	.	.	.	.	.	.	.	.	.	.	.	.	.	.	.	.	.	.	.	.	.	.	.
(91)	.	.	.	.	.	.	.	.	.	.	.	.	.	.	.	.	.	.	.	.	.	.	.	.	.	.	.	.	.	.	.	.	.	.	.	.	.
(92)	.	.	.	.	.	.	.	.	.	+	II	.	.	.	.	.	.	.	.	.	.	.	.	.	+	.	.	.	.	.	.	.	.	.	.	.	.
(93)	.	.	.	.	.	.	.	.	+	.	+	.	.	.	.	.	.	.	.	.	.	.	.	.	.	.	.	.	.	.	.	.	.	.	.	.	.
(94)	.	.	.	.	.	.	.	.	.	.	.	.	.	.	.	.	.	.	.	.	.	.	.	.	.	.	.	.	.	.	.	.	.	.	.	.	.
(95)	.	.	.	.	.	.	.	+	.	.	.	.	.	.	.	.	.	.	.	.	.	.	.	.	.	.	.	.	.	.	.	.	.	.	.	.	.
(96)	.	.	.	.	.	.	.	+	.	.	.	.	.	.	.	.	.	.	.	.	.	.	.	.	.	.	.	.	.	.	.	.	.	.	.	.	.
(97)	.	.	.	.	.	.	.	+	.	.	.	.	.	.	.	.	.	.	.	.	.	.	.	.	.	.	.	.	.	.	.	.	.	.	.	.	.
(98)	.	.	.	IV	.	.	.	III	.	.	.	.	.	.	.	.	.	.	.	.	.	.	.	.	.	.	.	.	.	I	.	.	II	.	.	.	.
(99)	.	.	.	.	.	.	.	I	.	.	.	.	.	.	.	.	.	.	.	.	.	.	.	.	.	.	.	.	.	.	.	.	.	.	.	.	.
(100)	.	.	.	II	.	.	.	I	.	.	II	.	.	.	.	.	.	.	.	.	.	.	.	.	.	.	.	.	.	.	.	.	.	.	.	.	.
(101)	.	.	.	.	.	.	.	II	.	.	.	.	.	.	.	.	.	.	.	.	.	.	.	.	.	.	.	.	.	.	.	.	.	.	.	.	.
(102)	.	.	.	II	.	.	.	+	.	.	.	.	.	.	.	.	.	.	.	.	.	.	+	.	.	.	.	.	.	.	.	.	.	.	.	.	.
(103)	.	.	.	.	.	.	.	II	.	.	.	.	.	.	.	.	.	.	.	.	.	.	.	.	.	.	.	.	.	.	.	.	.	.	.	.	.
(104)	.	.	.	.	.	.	.	.	.	.	.	.	.	.	.	.	.	.	.	.	.	.	.	.	.	.	.	.	.	.	.	.	.	.	.	.	.
(105)	.	.	.	.	.	.	.	.	.	.	.	.	.	.	.	.	.	.	.	.	.	.	.	.	.	.	.	.	.	.	.	.	.	.	.	.	.
(106)	.	.	.	.	.	.	.	.	.	.	.	.	.	.	.	.	.	.	.	.	.	.	.	.	.	.	.	.	.	.	.	.	.	.	.	.	.
(107)	.	.	.	I	III	.	.	.	.	.	+	.	.	.	.	.	.	.	.	.	.	.	.	.	.	.	.	.	.	.	.	.	.	.	.	.	.
(108)	.	.	.	.	.	.	.	.	.	.	.	.	.	.	.	.	.	.	.	.	.	.	.	.	.	.	.	.	.	.	.	.	.	.	.	.	.
(109)	.	.	.	.	.	.	.	.	.	.	.	.	.	.	.	.	.	.	.	.	.	.	.	.	.	.	.	.	.	.	.	.	.	.	.	.	.
(110)	.	.	.	.	.	.	.	.	.	.	.	.	.	.	.	.	.	.	.	.	.	.	.	.	.	.	.	.	.	.	.	.	.	.	.	.	.

TABLE 4.57 *continued*

	Hedwigia ciliata–Parmelia saxatilis	*Koenigia islandica* scree community	*Asplenium trichomanes–Fissidens cristatus*	*Puccinellia maritima–Ascophyllum nodosum*	*Puccinellia maritima–Festuca rubra*	*Juncus gerardii–Carex extensa*	*Armeria maritima–Grimmia maritima*	*Asplenium marinum–Grimmia maritima*	*Atriplex glabriuscula–Rumex crispus*	Brackish water communities	*Phragmites communis–Equisetum fluviatile*	*Schoenoplectus lacustris–Equisetum fluviatile*	*Carex rostrata–Menyanthes trifoliata*	*Littorella uniflora–Lobelia dortmanna*	*Potamogeton natans–Nymphaea alba nodum*	*Eriophorum angustifolium–Sphagnum cuspidatum*	*Carex lasiocarpa–Menyanthes trifoliata*	*Trichophorum cespitosum–Carex panicea*	*Molinia caerulea–Myrica gale*	*Sphagneto–Juncetum effusi*	*Carex–Sphagnum recurvum nodum*	*Carex rostrata–Aulacomnium palustre*	*Carex rostrata–Scorpidium scorpioides*	*Carex panicea–Campylium stellatum*	*Eriophorum latifolium–Carex hostiana*	*Schoenus nigricans*	*Carex–Saxifraga aizoides nodum*	*Trichophoreto–Callunetum*
Community Number	1	2	3	4	5	6	7	8	9	10	11	12	13	14	15	16	17	18	19	20	21	22	23	24	25	26	27	28
Chara sp. (111)	.	.	.	.	.	.	.	.	.	.	+	.	.	.	II	.	.	.	.	.	.	.	.	.	+	.	.	.
Potamogeton gramineus (112)	.	.	.	.	.	.	.	.	.	.	+	.	.	+	.	.	.	.	.	.	.	.	.	.	.	.	.	.
Potamogeton coloratus (113)	.	.	.	.	.	.	.	.	.	.	+	.	.	+	.	.	.	.	.	.	.	.	.	.	.	.	.	.
Carex rostrata (114)	.	.	.	.	.	.	.	.	.	.	IV	IV	V	.	+	.	V	II	II	.	.	V	V	.	I	I	.	.
Potamogeton polygonifolius (115)	.	.	.	.	.	.	.	.	.	.	II	III	II	.	.	II	III	.	+	.	.	IV	III	+	III	III	.	.
Menyanthes trifoliata (116)	.	.	.	.	.	.	.	.	.	.	IV	III	V	.	+	IV	V	.	.	.	.	.	V	.	I	II	.	.
Utricularia minor (117)	.	.	.	.	.	.	.	.	.	.	I	I	.	.	.	II	+	.	.	.	.	.	III	.	II	III	.	.
Potamogeton perfoliatus (118)	.	.	.	.	.	.	.	.	.	.	.	+	+	.	III	.	.	.	.	.	.	.	.	.	.	.	.	.
Sparganium angustifolium (119)	.	.	.	.	.	.	.	.	.	.	.	+	.	.	IV	.	.	.	.	.	.	.	.	.	.	.	.	.
Eleogiton fluitans (120)	.	.	.	.	.	.	.	.	.	.	.	.	.	II	II	.	.	.	.	.	.	.	.	.	.	.	.	.
Myriophyllum alterniflorum (121)	.	.	.	.	.	.	.	.	.	.	.	+	.	II	IV	.	.	.	.	.	.	.	.	.	.	.	.	.
Schoenoplectus lacustris (122)	.	.	.	.	.	.	.	.	.	.	.	V	II	.	.	.	.	.	.	.	.	.	.	.	.	.	.	.
Eriocaulon septangulare (123)	.	.	.	.	.	.	.	.	.	.	.	.	II	+	.	.	+	.	.	.	.	.	.	.	.	.	.	.
Lobelia dortmanna (124)	.	.	.	.	.	.	.	.	.	.	.	.	II	V	.	.	.	.	.	.	.	.	.	.	.	.	.	.
Littorella uniflora (125)	.	.	.	.	.	.	.	.	.	.	.	.	.	V	.	.	.	.	.	.	.	.	.	.	.	.	.	.
Sphagnum magellanicum (126)	.	.	.	.	.	.	.	.	.	.	.	.	.	.	.	III	.	.	.	.	.	.	.	.	.	.	.	.
Rhynchospora alba (127)	.	.	.	.	.	.	.	.	.	.	.	.	.	.	.	IV	.	+	.	.	.	.	.	.	.	II	.	.
Carex pauciflora (128)	.	.	.	.	.	.	.	.	.	.	.	.	.	.	.	+	.	+	.	.	+	.	.	.	.	.	.	.
Gymnocolea inflata (129)	.	.	.	.	.	.	.	.	.	.	.	.	.	.	.	II	.	.	.	.	.	.	.	.	.	.	.	.
Sphagnum cuspidatum (130)	.	.	.	.	.	.	.	.	.	.	.	.	.	.	.	V	+	.	.	.	.	.	.	.	.	.	.	.
Eleocharis multicaulis (131)	.	.	.	.	.	.	.	.	.	.	.	.	.	.	.	II	+	+	.	.	.	.	.	.	.	.	.	.
Carex limosa (132)	.	.	.	.	.	.	.	.	.	.	.	.	.	.	.	II	V	+	.	.	.	.	II	.	+	.	.	.
Juncus kochii (133)	.	.	.	.	.	.	.	.	.	.	.	.	.	.	.	+	IV	+	+	.	III	II	II	III	III	I	.	.
Carex lasiocarpa (134)	.	.	.	.	.	.	.	.	.	.	.	.	.	.	.	.	V	.	.	.	.	.	.	.	.	.	.	.
Acrocladium giganteum (135)	.	.	.	.	.	.	.	.	.	.	.	.	.	.	.	.	I	.	.	.	.	+	+	.	.	.	.	.
Pedicularis palustris (136)	.	.	.	.	.	.	.	.	.	.	.	.	.	.	.	.	II	.	+	.	.	V	III	+	.	II	.	.
Aulacomnium palustre (137)	.	.	.	.	.	.	.	.	.	.	.	.	.	.	.	.	.	+	+	.	.	V	.	.	.	.	.	.
Equisetum palustre (138)	.	.	.	.	.	.	.	.	.	.	.	.	.	.	.	.	.	III	+	+	.	V	V	II	II	.	.	.
Sphagnum recurvum (139)	.	.	.	.	.	.	.	.	.	.	.	.	.	.	.	.	III	+	IV	V	V	V	II	.	.	.	.	.
Sphagnum subsecundum var. *inundatum* (140)	.	.	.	.	.	.	.	.	.	.	+	.	.	.	.	.	IV	III	I	.	II	II	III	.	II	III	.	.
Sphagnum subsecundum var. *auriculatum* (141)	.	.	.	.	.	.	.	.	.	.	.	.	.	.	.	IV	.	I	I	.	II	.	.	.	I	.	.	.
Sphagnum plumulosum (142)	.	.	.	.	.	.	.	.	.	.	.	.	.	.	.	II	.	III	III	.	IV	+	III	.	I	.	.	I
Myrica gale (143)	.	.	.	.	.	.	.	.	.	.	.	.	.	.	.	.	.	III	V	.	.	II	III	.	III	III	.	.
Sphagnum palustre (144)	.	.	.	.	.	.	.	.	.	.	.	.	.	.	.	IV	III	V	V	V	V	II	II	+	+		.	III
Carex echinata (145)	.	.	.	.	.	.	.	.	.	.	.	.	.	.	.	.	III	V	V	V	V	V	III	IV	III	IV	III	II
Carex panicea (146)	.	.	.	.	.	.	.	.	.	.	+	.	.	.	.	.	+	V	IV	I	II	+	V	V	V	V	V	II
Eriophorum angustifolium (147)	.	.	.	.	.	+	.	.	.	.	+	.	.	.	.	V	II	V	III	II	V	V	V	IV	I	III	II	IV
Molinia caerulea (148)	.	.	.	.	.	.	.	.	.	.	.	.	.	.	.	.	II	V	V	I	II	IV	II	+	III	III	II	III
Juncus squarrosus (149)	.	.	.	.	.	.	.	.	.	.	.	.	.	.	.	.	.	II	+	I	II	+	.	IV	.	.	.	IV
Deschampsia flexuosa (150)	.	.	.	.	.	.	.	.	.	.	.	.	.	.	.	.	.	II	II	III	II	+	.	.	.	.	.	+
Polygala serpyllifolia (151)	.	.	.	.	.	.	.	.	.	.	.	.	.	.	.	.	.	III	IV	V	II	.	.	+	.	.	.	.
Potentilla erecta (152)	.	.	.	.	.	.	.	.	.	.	.	.	.	.	.	.	+	V	V	V	II	+	III	V	I	I	.	V
Pinguicula vulgaris (153)	.	.	.	.	.	.	.	.	.	.	.	.	.	.	.	.	.	III	V	.	III	+	II	V	V	V	V	II
Drosera rotundifolia (154)	.	.	.	.	.	.	.	.	.	.	.	.	.	.	.	V	I	V	III	.	+	+	+	III	III	IV	.	II
Carex nigra (155)	.	.	.	.	.	.	.	.	.	II	.	III	.	II	.	.	V	II	+	IV	V	V	V	III	III	III	.	II
Juncus effusus (156)	.	.	.	.	.	.	.	.	.	.	.	.	.	I	.	.	.	.	II	V	.	III	.	+	.	.	.	+
Lophocolea bidentata (157)	.	.	.	.	.	.	.	.	.	.	.	.	.	.	.	.	.	.	.	IV	.	.	.	.	.	.	.	.
Polytrichum commune (158)	.	.	.	.	.	.	.	.	.	.	.	.	.	.	.	.	.	.	.	V	II	.	.	.	.	.	.	I
Cardamine pratensis (159)	.	.	.	.	.	.	.	.	.	.	.	.	.	.	.	.	.	.	.	+	III	.	.	.	.	.	.	.
Viola palustris (160)	.	.	.	.	.	.	.	.	.	II	.	.	.	.	.	.	+	.	.	III	II	II	+	.	.	.	.	.
Epilobium palustre (161)	.	.	.	.	.	.	.	.	.	+	.	.	.	.	.	.	.	.	.	+	.	III	+	.	.	.	.	.
Acrocladium cuspidatum (162)	.	.	.	.	.	.	.	.	.	+	.	.	.	.	.	.	.	.	.	+	.	V	+	+	+	.	.	.
Sphagnum squarrosum (163)	.	.	.	.	.	.	.	.	.	.	.	.	.	.	.	.	.	.	.	.	.	III	.	+	.	.	.	.
Carex curta (164)	.	.	.	.	.	.	.	.	.	.	.	.	.	.	.	.	+	.	.	.	.	III	.	.	+	.	.	.
Sphagnum warnstorfianum (165)	.	.	.	.	.	.	.	.	.	.	.	.	.	.	.	.	.	.	.	.	.	II	.	.	+	.	.	.

TABLE 4.57 *continued*

	29 *Molinieto–Callunetum*	30 *Trichophoreto–Eriophoretum*	31 *Calluneto–Eriophoretum*	32 *Philonoto–Saxifragetum stellaris*	33 *Koenigia islandica–Carex demissa nodum*	34 *Cratoneuron commutatum–Saxifraga aizoides nodum*	35 *Saxifragetum aizoidis*	36 *Juncus acutiflorus–Filipendula ulmaria*	37 *Centaureo–Cynosuretum*	38 *Maritime grassland nodum*	39 *Lolium perenne–Plantago lanceolata*	40 *Dryas octopetala–Carex flacca*	41 *Cariceto–Rhacomitretum lanuginosi*	42 *Festuca ovina–Luzula spicata nodum*	43 *Rhacomitreto–Callunetum*	44 *Juniperus nana nodum*	45 *Rhacomitreto–Empetretum*	46 *Alchemilla alpina–Vaccinium myrtillus nodum*	47 *Nardus stricta–Vaccinium myrtillus*	48 *Agrosto–Festucetum* (species-poor)	49 *Alchemilleto–Agrosto–Festucetum*	50 *Agrosto–Festucetum* (species-rich)	51 *Nardo–Juncetum squarrosi*	52 *Callunetum vulgaris*	53 *Calluna vulgaris–Sieglingia decumbens*	54 *Calluna vulgaris–Arctostaphylos uva-ursi nodum*	55 *Vaccineto–Callunetum hepaticosum*	56 *Luzula sylvatica–Vaccinium myrtillus*	57 *Luzula sylvatica–Silene dioica*	58 *Betula pubescens–Cirsium heterophyllum*	59 *Sedum rosea–Alchemilla glabra*	60 *Betula pubescens–Vaccinium myrtillus*	61 *Corylus avellana–Oxalis acetosella*	62 *Oxalis acetosella–Rhytidiadelphus loreus*	63 *Hymenophyllum wilsonii–Isothecium myosuroides*	64 Open boulder association	65 *Fraxinus excelsior–Brachypodium sylvaticum*
1)	.	.	.	.	.	.	.	.	.	.	.	.	.	.	.	.	.	.	.	.	.	.	.	.	.	.	.	.	.	.	.	.	.	.	.	.	.
2)	.	.	.	.	.	.	.	.	.	.	.	.	.	.	.	.	.	.	.	.	.	.	.	.	.	.	.	.	.	.	.	.	.	.	.	.	.
3)	.	.	.	.	.	.	.	.	.	.	.	.	.	.	.	.	.	.	.	.	.	.	.	.	.	.	.	.	.	.	.	.	.	.	.	.	.
4)	.	+	.	.	.	.	.	+	.	.	.	.	.	.	.	.	.	.	.	.	.	.	.	.	.	.	.	.	.	.	.	.	.	.	.	.	.
5)	.	+	.	.	.	.	.	I	.	.	.	.	.	.	.	.	.	.	.	.	.	.	.	.	.	.	.	.	.	.	.	.	.	.	.	.	.
6)	.	I	.	.	.	.	.	.	.	.	.	.	.	.	.	.	.	.	.	.	.	.	.	.	.	.	.	.	.	.	.	.	.	.	.	.	.
7)	.	+	.	.	.	.	.	.	.	.	.	.	.	.	.	.	.	.	.	.	.	.	.	.	.	.	.	.	.	.	.	.	.	.	.	.	.
8)	.	.	.	.	.	.	.	.	.	.	.	.	.	.	.	.	.	.	.	.	.	.	.	.	.	.	.	.	.	.	.	.	.	.	.	.	.
9)	.	.	.	.	.	.	.	.	.	.	.	.	.	.	.	.	.	.	.	.	.	.	.	.	.	.	.	.	.	.	.	.	.	.	.	.	.
0)	.	.	.	.	.	.	.	.	.	.	.	.	.	.	.	.	.	.	.	.	.	.	.	.	.	.	.	.	.	.	.	.	.	.	.	.	.
1)	.	.	.	.	.	.	.	.	.	.	.	.	.	.	.	.	.	.	.	.	.	.	.	.	.	.	.	.	.	.	.	.	.	.	.	.	.
2)	.	.	.	.	.	.	.	.	.	.	.	.	.	.	.	.	.	.	.	.	.	.	.	.	.	.	.	.	.	.	.	.	.	.	.	.	.
3)	.	.	.	.	.	.	.	.	.	.	.	.	.	.	.	.	.	.	.	.	.	.	.	.	.	.	.	.	.	.	.	.	.	.	.	.	.
4)	.	.	.	.	.	.	.	.	.	.	.	.	.	.	.	.	.	.	.	.	.	.	.	.	.	.	.	.	.	.	.	.	.	.	.	.	.
5)	.	.	.	.	.	.	.	.	.	.	.	.	.	.	.	.	.	.	.	.	.	.	.	.	.	.	.	.	.	.	.	.	.	.	.	.	.
6)	.	II	.	.	.	.	.	.	.	.	.	.	.	.	.	.	.	.	.	.	.	.	.	.	.	.	.	.	.	.	.	.	.	.	.	.	.
7)	.	III	.	.	.	.	.	.	.	.	.	.	.	.	.	.	.	.	.	.	.	.	.	.	.	.	.	.	.	.	.	.	.	.	.	.	.
8)	.	II	.	.	.	.	.	.	.	.	.	.	.	.	.	.	.	.	.	.	.	.	.	.	.	.	.	.	.	.	.	.	.	.	.	.	.
9)	.	II	.	.	.	.	.	.	.	.	.	.	.	.	.	.	.	.	.	.	.	.	.	.	.	.	.	.	.	.	.	.	.	.	.	.	.
0)	+	II	.	.	.	.	.	.	.	.	.	.	.	.	.	.	.	.	.	.	.	.	.	.	.	.	.	.	.	.	.	.	.	.	.	.	.
1)	.	.	.	.	.	.	.	.	.	.	.	.	.	.	.	.	.	.	.	.	.	.	.	.	.	.	.	.	.	.	.	.	.	.	.	.	.
2)	.	I	.	.	.	.	.	.	.	.	.	.	.	.	.	.	.	.	.	.	.	.	.	.	.	.	.	.	.	.	.	.	.	.	.	.	.
3)	.	.	.	.	.	.	.	.	.	.	.	.	.	.	.	.	.	.	.	.	.	.	II	.	.	.	.	.	.	.	.	.	.	.	.	.	.
4)	.	.	.	.	.	.	.	.	.	.	.	.	.	.	.	.	.	.	.	.	.	.	.	.	.	.	.	.	.	.	.	.	.	.	.	.	.
5)	.	.	.	.	.	.	.	.	.	.	.	.	.	.	.	.	.	.	.	.	.	.	.	.	.	.	.	.	.	.	.	.	.	.	.	.	.
6)	.	.	.	.	.	.	.	III	.	.	.	.	.	.	.	.	.	.	.	.	.	.	.	.	.	.	.	.	.	.	.	.	.	.	.	.	.
7)	.	I	+	.	.	.	.	II	.	.	.	.	.	.	.	.	.	.	.	.	.	.	+	.	.	.	.	.	.	.	.	.	.	.	.	.	.
8)	.	+	.	+	.	.	.	V	.	.	.	.	.	.	.	.	.	.	.	.	.	.	.	.	.	.	.	.	.	.	.	.	.	.	.	.	.
9)	II	.	.	+	.	.	.	I	.	.	.	.	.	.	.	.	.	.	.	.	.	.	+	.	.	.	.	.	.	.	.	.	.	.	.	.	.
0)	.	.	.	.	.	.	.	+	.	.	.	.	.	.	.	.	.	.	.	.	.	.	.	.	.	.	.	.	.	.	.	.	.	.	.	.	.
1)	.	IV	.	III	II	.	.	.	.	.	.	.	.	.	.	.	II	II	.	.	+	.	.	.	.	.	II	II	.	.	.	.	.	.	.	.	.
2)	I	I	.	+	.	.	.	II	.	.	.	.	.	.	.	.	I	II	+	.	.	.	II	.	.	.	IV	.	.	.	+	.	.	.	.	.	.
3)	I	V	.	.	.	.	.	.	.	.	.	.	.	.	.	.	.	.	.	.	.	.	.	.	.	.	.	.	.	.	.	.	.	.	.	.	.
4)	I	II	.	.	.	.	.	I	.	.	.	.	.	.	.	.	.	.	I	.	.	.	.	.	.	.	.	.	.	.	.	.	.	.	.	.	.
5)	I	III	+	III	.	.	.	IV	+	.	.	.	.	.	.	.	.	.	.	.	.	.	II	.	.	.	.	.	.	.	.	.	.	.	.	.	.
6)	+	.	.	+	.	.	III	II	+	.	.	II	.	.	.	.	.	.	+	I	.	.	II	+	I	.	.	.	.	II	I	.	+	.	.	.	.
7)	+	V	V	.	.	.	.	II	.	.	.	.	.	.	.	.	.	.	.	.	.	.	II	.	.	.	.	.	.	.	.	.	.	.	.	.	.
8)	V	V	V	.	.	.	.	III	.	.	.	III	.	.	I	.	.	.	+	+	.	.	II	II	II	II	II	.	.	.	.	.	.	.	.	.	.
9)	II	II	IV	I	II	.	.	.	.	.	.	.	+	.	+	.	.	.	.	.	.	.	V	+	+	.	.	.	.	.	.	.	.	.	.	.	.
0)	II	I	.	.	.	.	.	.	.	.	.	.	IV	V	I	V	III	IV	.	II	II	.	II	IV	IV	.	.	.	II	.	.	V	I	V	III	.	.
1)	III	III	II	.	.	.	.	+	.	III	.	.	.	.	II	II	+	.	I	II	.	III	III	II	II	.	.	.	II	.	.	II	I	.	.	.	.
2)	V	IV	III	.	.	.	+	IV	II	IV	.	IV	IV	II	V	IV	III	III	V	V	III	V	V	V	V	IV	V	II	III	III	III	V	IV	III	.	.	II
3)	+	II	.	II	II	V	V	+	.	.	.	II	.	.	.	.	.	+	.	I	.	I	+	.	.	.	II	.	.	II	III	.	.	.	.	.	.
4)	III	V	+	.	.	.	.	.	.	.	.	.	.	.	.	.	.	.	.	.	.	.	.	.	.	.	.	.	.	.	.	.	.	.	.	.	.
5)	.	+	.	II	II	.	.	IV	.	.	.	+	.	.	.	.	.	.	.	.	.	.	.	.	.	.	.	.	.	II	I	.	.	.	.	.	.
6)	.	+	.	.	.	.	.	III	III	.	.	.	.	.	.	.	.	.	.	+	.	.	.	.	.	.	.	.	.	+	.	.	.	.	.	.	.
7)	.	.	.	.	.	.	.	.	.	+	.	.	.	.	.	.	.	.	.	.	.	.	.	.	.	.	.	.	.	.	.	.	.	.	.	.	+
8)	.	+	.	.	.	.	.	+	.	.	.	.	.	.	.	.	.	.	.	.	.	.	+	.	.	.	.	.	.	.	.	.	.	.	.	.	.
9)	.	.	.	.	.	.	.	I	.	.	.	.	.	.	.	.	.	.	.	.	.	.	.	.	.	.	.	.	.	.	.	.	.	.	.	.	.
0)	.	.	.	+	.	.	.	III	.	.	.	.	.	.	.	.	.	.	.	.	.	.	II	.	.	.	.	.	.	.	.	.	.	.	.	.	.
1)	.	.	.	.	.	.	.	II	.	.	.	.	.	.	.	.	.	.	.	.	.	.	.	.	.	.	.	.	.	.	.	.	.	.	.	.	.
2)	.	.	.	IV	.	.	III	V	II	.	II	+	.	.	.	.	.	.	.	.	.	+	.	.	.	.	.	.	.	I	III	.	+	.	.	.	.
3)	.	.	.	.	.	.	.	.	.	.	.	.	.	.	.	.	.	.	.	.	.	.	.	.	.	.	.	.	.	.	.	.	.	.	.	.	.
4)	.	.	.	.	.	.	.	.	.	.	.	.	.	.	.	.	.	.	.	.	.	.	+	.	.	.	.	.	.	.	.	.	.	.	.	.	.
5)	.	.	.	.	.	.	.	.	.	.	.	.	.	.	.	.	.	.	.	.	.	.	.	.	.	.	.	.	.	.	.	.	.	.	.	.	.

TABLE 4.57 *continued*

	Hedwigia ciliata–Parmelia saxatilis	*Koenigia islandica* scree community	*Asplenium trichomanes–Fissidens cristatus*	*Puccinellia maritima–Ascophyllum nodosum*	*Puccinellia maritima–Festuca rubra*	*Juncus gerardii–Carex extensa*	*Armeria maritima–Grimmia maritima*	*Asplenium marinum–Grimmia maritima*	*Atriplex glabriuscula–Rumex crispus*	Brackish water communities	*Phragmites communis–Equisetum fluviatile*	*Schoenoplectus lacustris–Equisetum fluviatile*	*Carex rostrata–Menyanthes trifoliata*	*Littorella uniflora–Lobelia dortmanna*	*Potamogeton natans–Nymphaea alba nodum*	*Eriophorum angustifolium–Sphagnum cuspidatum*	*Carex lasiocarpa–Menyanthes trifoliata*	*Trichophorum cespitosum–Carex panicea*	*Molinia caerulea–Myrica gale*	*Sphagneto–Juncetum effusi*	*Carex–Sphagnum recurvum nodum*	*Carex rostrata–Aulacomnium palustre*	*Carex rostrata–Scorpidium scorpioides*	*Carex panicea–Campylium stellatum*	*Eriophorum latifolium–Carex hostiana*	*Schoenus nigricans*	*Carex–Saxifraga aizoides nodum*
Community Number	1	2	3	4	5	6	7	8	9	10	11	12	13	14	15	16	17	18	19	20	21	22	23	24	25	26	27
Chiloscyphus pallescens (166)	.	.	.	.	.	.	.	.	.	.	.	.	.	.	.	.	.	.	.	.	.	III	.	.	.	.	.
Pellia neesiana (167)	.	.	.	.	.	.	.	.	.	.	.	.	.	.	.	.	.	.	.	.	.	III	.	.	.	.	.
Myosotis scorpoides (168)	.	.	.	.	.	.	.	.	.	+	.	.	.	.	.	.	.	.	.	.	.	IV	.	.	.	.	.
Salix aurita (169)	.	.	.	.	.	.	.	.	.	.	.	.	.	.	.	.	.	.	II	.	.	+	.	.	.	.	.
Cirsium palustre (170)	.	.	.	.	.	.	.	.	.	.	.	.	.	.	.	.	.	.	+	+	.	II	+	.	.	.	.
Mnium pseudopunctatum (171)	.	.	.	.	.	.	.	.	.	.	.	.	.	.	.	.	.	.	.	.	.	III	+	.	.	.	.
Sphagnum teres (172)	.	.	.	.	.	.	.	.	.	.	.	.	.	.	.	.	.	.	.	.	.	III	+	.	.	.	.
Mentha aquatica (173)	.	.	.	.	.	.	.	.	.	.	.	.	.	.	.	.	+	.	.	.	.	III	II	.	.	.	.
Splachnum ampullaceum (174)	.	.	.	.	.	.	.	.	.	.	.	.	.	.	.	.	.	.	II	.	.	II	+	.	II	.	.
Mnium seligeri (175)	.	.	.	.	.	.	.	.	.	.	.	.	.	.	.	.	.	.	.	.	.	II	+	+	.	.	.
Sphagnum contortum (176)	.	.	.	.	.	.	.	.	.	.	.	.	.	.	.	.	.	.	+	.	.	II	III	.	II	I	.
Triglochin palustre (177)	.	.	.	.	.	.	.	.	.	.	.	.	.	.	.	.	I	.	+	.	.	+	II	+	III	.	.
Carex dioica (178)	.	.	.	.	.	.	.	.	.	.	.	.	.	.	.	.	+	.	+	.	.	II	III	II	IV	II	III
Bryum pseudotriquetrum (179)	.	.	.	.	.	.	.	.	.	.	.	.	.	.	.	.	.	.	.	.	.	II	II	II	II	.	III
Carex pulicaris (180)	.	.	I	.	.	.	.	.	.	.	.	.	.	.	.	.	.	II	III	.	.	+	II	III	III	I	IV
Campylium stellatum (181)	.	.	.	.	.	.	.	.	.	+	.	.	.	.	.	.	.	.	+	.	.	+	V	V	V	V	V
Riccardia pinguis (182)	.	.	.	.	.	.	.	.	.	+	.	.	.	.	.	.	.	II	.	.	.	.	+	II	III	I	V
Selaginella selaginoides (183)	.	.	I	.	.	.	.	.	.	.	.	.	.	.	.	.	.	III	.	.	+	.	+	V	IV	V	V
Carex demissa (184)	.	II	.	.	.	.	.	.	.	.	.	.	.	.	.	.	.	II	III	.	+	.	II	IV	V	.	V
Drepanocladus revolvens (185)	.	.	.	.	.	.	.	.	.	.	.	.	.	.	.	.	.	.	II	.	.	+	V	IV	III	II	V
Scorpidium scorpioides (186)	.	.	.	.	.	.	.	.	.	.	.	.	+	.	.	.	II	.	+	.	.	.	V	III	V	V	V
Carex hostiana (187)	.	.	.	.	.	.	.	.	.	.	.	.	.	.	.	.	.	+	.	.	.	.	II	II	V	II	II
Eleocharis quinqueflora (188)	.	.	.	.	.	.	.	.	.	.	.	.	.	.	.	.	.	.	.	.	.	.	III	IV	V	III	II
Euphrasia scottica (189)	.	.	.	.	.	.	.	.	.	.	.	.	.	.	.	.	.	II	.	.	.	.	+	III	III	.	V
Carex serotina (190)	.	.	.	.	.	+	.	.	.	.	.	.	.	.	.	.	.	.	.	.	.	.	II	.	.	.	.
Narthecium ossifragum (191)	.	.	.	.	.	.	.	.	.	.	.	.	.	.	.	IV	.	V	IV	.	.	.	+	II	III	III	II
Succisa pratensis (192)	.	.	.	.	.	.	.	.	.	.	.	.	.	.	.	.	+	III	.	+	.	III	II	+	IV	II	.
Breutelia chrysocoma (193)	.	.	+	.	.	.	.	.	.	.	.	.	.	.	.	.	.	III	II	.	IV	.	+	V	II	I	.
Calluna vulgaris (194)	.	.	.	.	.	.	.	.	.	.	.	.	.	.	.	.	.	IV	IV	.	+	.	.	+	II	I	.
Erica tetralix (195)	.	.	.	.	.	.	.	.	.	.	.	.	.	.	.	.	.	V	IV	.	+	.	.	IV	IV	III	.
Pinguicula lusitanica (196)	.	.	.	.	.	.	.	.	.	.	.	.	.	.	.	.	.	.	.	.	+	.	.	+	II	I	.
Riccardia sinuata (197)	.	.	.	.	.	.	.	.	.	.	.	.	.	.	.	.	.	.	.	.	.	.	.	+	.	.	+
Thalictrum alpinum (198)	.	.	.	.	.	.	.	.	.	.	.	.	.	.	.	.	.	.	.	.	.	.	.	+	I	.	IV
Fissidens adianthoides (199)	.	.	.	.	.	.	.	.	.	.	.	.	.	.	.	.	.	.	.	.	.	.	.	+	II	I	II
Blindia acuta (200)	.	.	.	.	.	.	.	.	.	.	.	.	.	.	.	.	.	.	.	.	.	.	.	III	IV	I	V
Carex flacca (201)	.	.	.	.	.	II	.	.	.	.	.	.	.	.	.	.	.	.	.	.	.	.	.	III	IV	I	V
Schoenus nigricans (202)	.	.	.	.	.	.	.	.	.	.	.	.	+	.	.	+	.	II	+	.	.	.	+	.	V	V	III
Drosera anglica (203)	.	.	.	.	.	.	.	.	.	.	.	.	.	.	.	V	.	+	.	.	.	.	+	.	III	V	II
Cinclidium stygium (204)	.	.	.	.	.	.	.	.	.	.	.	.	.	.	.	.	.	.	.	.	.	.	+	.	I	.	.
Philonotis calcarea (205)	.	.	.	.	.	.	.	.	.	.	.	.	.	.	.	.	.	.	.	.	.	.	+	.	+	.	.
Dactylorchis purpurella (206)	.	.	.	.	.	.	.	.	.	.	.	.	.	.	.	.	.	.	.	.	.	.	+	.	+	.	.
Platanthera bifolia (207)	.	.	.	.	.	.	.	.	.	.	.	.	.	.	.	.	.	.	.	.	.	.	+	.	+	.	.
Carex lepidocarpa (208)	.	.	.	.	.	.	.	.	.	.	.	.	.	.	.	.	.	.	.	.	.	.	.	.	I	I	II
Eriophorum latifolium (209)	.	.	.	.	.	.	.	.	.	.	.	.	.	.	.	.	.	.	.	.	.	.	.	.	V	II	.
Riccardia multifida (210)	.	.	.	.	.	.	.	.	.	.	.	.	.	.	.	.	.	.	.	.	.	.	.	.	+	.	.
Acrocladium trifarium (211)	.	.	.	.	.	.	.	.	.	.	.	.	.	.	.	.	.	.	.	.	.	.	.	.	I	.	.
Splachnum sphaericum (212)	.	.	.	.	.	.	.	.	.	.	.	.	.	.	.	.	.	.	.	.	.	.	.	.	+	.	.
Dactylorchis maculata ssp. *ericetorum* (213)	.	.	.	.	.	.	.	.	.	.	.	.	.	.	.	.	.	.	IV	.	.	.	.	.	.	.	.
Empetrum nigrum (214)	.	.	.	.	.	.	+	.	.	.	.	.	.	.	.	.	.	.	.	.	.	.	.	.	+	.	.
Rhacomitrium lanuginosum (215)	.	.	.	.	.	.	.	.	.	.	.	.	.	.	.	.	.	II	+	.	.	.	.	.	.	.	.
Hypnum cupressiforme var. *ericetorum* (216)	.	.	.	.	.	.	.	.	.	.	.	.	.	.	.	.	.	II	+	.	.	.	.	.	.	.	.
Trichophorum cespitosum (217)	.	.	.	.	.	.	.	.	.	.	.	.	.	.	.	.	.	V	.	.	.	.	+	.	.	.	.
Sphagnum tenellum (218)	.	.	.	.	.	.	.	.	.	.	.	.	.	.	.	.	.	II	.	.	.	.	.	.	.	.	.
Eriophorum vaginatum (219)	.	.	.	.	.	.	.	.	.	.	.	.	.	.	.	.	.	+	.	.	.	.	.	.	.	.	.
Campylopus flexuosus (220)	.	.	.	.	.	.	.	.	.	.	.	.	.	.	.	.	.	.	.	.	.	.	.	.	.	.	.

TABLE 4.57 *continued*

	29 *Molinieto–Callunetum*	30 *Trichophoreto–Eriophoretum*	31 *Calluneto–Eriophoretum*	32 *Philonoto–Saxifragetum stellaris*	33 *Koenigia islandica–Carex demissa nodum*	34 *Cratoneuron commutatum–Saxifraga aizoides nodum*	35 *Saxifragetum aizoidis*	36 *Juncus acutiflorus–Filipendula ulmaria*	37 *Centaureo–Cynosuretum*	38 *Maritime grassland nodum*	39 *Lolium perenne–Plantago lanceolata*	40 *Dryas octopetala–Carex flacca*	41 *Cariceto–Rhacomitretum lanuginosi*	42 *Festuca ovina–Luzula spicata nodum*	43 *Rhacomitreto–Callunetum*	44 *Juniperus nana nodum*	45 *Rhacomitreto–Empetretum*	46 *Alchemilla alpina–Vaccinium myrtillus nodum*	47 *Nardus stricta–Vaccinium myrtillus*	48 *Agrosto–Festucetum* (species-poor)	49 *Alchemilleto–Agrosto–Festucetum*	50 *Agrosto–Festucetum* (species-rich)	51 *Nardo–Juncetum squarrosi*	52 *Callunetum vulgaris*	53 *Calluna vulgaris–Sieglingia decumbens*	54 *Calluna vulgaris–Arctostaphylos uva-ursi nodum*	55 *Vaccineto–Callunetum hepaticosum*	56 *Luzula sylvatica–Vaccinium myrtillus*	57 *Luzula sylvatica–Silene dioica*	58 *Betula pubescens–Cirsium heterophyllum*	59 *Sedum rosea–Alchemilla glabra*	60 *Betula pubescens–Vaccinium myrtillus*	61 *Corylus avellana–Oxalis acetosella*	62 *Oxalis acetosella–Rhytidiadelphus loreus*	63 *Hymenophyllum wilsonii–Isothecium myosuroides*	64 Open boulder association	65 *Fraxinus excelsior–Brachypodium sylvaticum*
(66)	.	.	.	III	.	.	.	.	.	.	.	.	.	.	.	.	.	.	.	.	.	.	.	.	.	.	.	.	.	.	.	.	.	.	.	.	.
(67)	.	.	.	.	.	.	.	II	.	.	.	.	.	.	.	.	.	.	.	.	.	.	.	.	.	.	.	.	.	.	.	.	.	.	.	.	.
(68)	.	.	.	+	.	.	.	II	.	.	.	.	.	.	.	.	.	.	.	.	.	.	.	.	.	.	.	.	.	.	.	.	.	.	.	.	.
(69)	.	.	.	.	.	.	.	+	.	.	.	.	.	.	.	.	.	.	.	.	.	.	.	.	.	+	.	.	+	.	.	.	.	.	.	.	.
(70)	.	.	.	.	.	.	.	II	.	.	.	.	.	.	.	.	.	.	.	.	.	+	.	.	.	.	.	.	.	.	.	.	.	.	.	.	.
(71)	.	.	.	.	.	.	.	+	.	.	.	.	.	.	.	.	.	.	.	.	.	.	.	.	.	.	.	.	.	.	.	.	.	.	.	.	.
(72)	.	.	.	.	.	.	.	.	.	.	.	.	.	.	.	.	.	.	.	.	.	.	.	.	.	.	.	.	.	.	.	.	.	.	.	.	.
(73)	.	.	.	.	.	.	.	.	.	.	.	.	.	.	.	.	.	.	.	.	.	.	.	.	.	.	.	.	.	.	.	.	.	.	.	.	.
(74)	.	.	.	.	.	.	.	.	.	.	.	.	.	.	.	.	.	.	.	.	.	.	.	.	.	.	.	.	.	.	.	.	.	.	.	.	.
(75)	.	.	.	.	.	.	.	.	.	.	.	.	.	.	.	.	.	.	.	.	.	.	.	.	.	.	.	.	.	.	.	.	.	.	.	.	.
(76)	.	.	.	.	.	.	.	.	.	.	.	.	.	.	.	.	.	.	.	.	.	.	.	.	.	.	.	.	.	.	.	.	.	.	.	.	.
(77)	.	.	.	.	.	.	.	.	.	.	.	.	.	.	.	.	.	.	.	.	.	.	.	.	.	.	.	.	.	.	.	.	.	.	.	.	.
(78)	+	+	.	.	+	.	.	.	.	.	.	.	.	.	.	.	.	.	.	.	.	.	.	.	.	.	.	.	.	.	.	.	.	.	.	.	.
(79)	.	.	.	IV	.	IV	IV	+	.	.	.	.	.	.	.	.	.	.	.	.	.	.	.	.	.	.	.	.	.	.	III	.	.	.	.	.	.
(80)	.	.	.	.	.	II	IV	III	.	III	.	IV	III	II	.	.	+	.	.	II	V	V	.	.	V	II	+	.	III	II	III	.	.	.	.	.	.
(81)	.	.	.	.	.	II	I	II	.	.	.	+	.	.	.	.	.	.	.	.	.	.	.	.	.	.	.	.	.	.	+	.	.	.	.	.	.
(82)	.	.	.	+	.	V	IV	.	.	.	.	.	.	.	.	.	.	.	.	.	.	I	+	.	.	.	.	.	.	.	III	.	.	.	.	.	.
(83)	+	.	.	II	.	II	V	.	.	.	.	II	II	.	.	.	II	II	.	.	IV	I	II	.	.	.	.	.	.	I	III	.	.	.	.	.	.
(84)	.	.	.	II	V	.	.	+	.	.	.	.	.	.	+	.	+	.	.	.	.	+	.	.	+	.	.	.	.	I	II	.	.	.	.	.	.
(85)	.	.	.	I	II	V	I	+	.	.	.	.	.	.	.	.	.	.	.	.	.	.	.	.	.	.	.	.	.	.	.	.	.	.	.	.	.
(86)	.	.	.	+	.	.	.	.	.	.	.	.	.	.	.	.	.	.	.	.	.	.	.	.	.	.	.	.	.	.	.	.	.	.	.	.	.
(87)	.	.	.	.	.	+	.	+	.	.	.	+	.	.	.	.	.	.	.	.	.	.	.	.	.	.	.	.	.	.	.	.	.	.	.	.	.
(88)	.	.	.	.	.	.	.	.	.	.	.	.	.	.	.	.	.	.	.	.	.	.	.	.	.	.	.	.	.	.	.	.	.	.	.	.	.
(89)	.	.	.	.	.	.	.	.	.	.	.	.	.	.	.	.	.	.	.	.	.	.	.	.	.	.	.	.	.	.	.	.	.	.	.	.	.
(90)	.	.	.	.	.	.	.	.	.	.	.	.	.	.	.	.	.	.	.	.	.	.	.	.	.	.	.	.	.	.	.	.	.	.	.	.	.
(91)	V	V	.	.	.	.	.	+	.	.	.	.	.	.	.	.	.	.	.	+	.	.	.	+	+	.	.	.	.	.	.	.	.	.	.	.	.
(92)	II	.	.	.	.	.	+	III	.	.	.	II	.	+	.	II	I	II	+	.	I	I	.	II	III	III	III	.	II	II	III	I	I	.	.	.	+
(93)	II	II	.	.	.	III	I	.	.	.	.	III	.	.	.	.	III	II	+	I	IV	IV	+	III	III	.	IV	II	III	I	III	I	I	I	.	.	+
(94)	V	V	V	.	.	.	.	.	.	III	.	III	.	.	V	IV	+	.	III	IV	I	III	III	V	V	V	V	III	V	I	I	V	II	+	.	.	.
(95)	V	V	III	.	.	.	.	.	.	.	.	.	.	.	.	.	.	.	.	.	.	.	.	.	.	.	.	.	.	.	.	.	.	.	.	.	.
(96)	+	.	.	.	.	.	.	.	.	.	.	.	.	.	.	.	.	.	.	.	.	.	.	.	.	.	.	.	.	.	.	.	.	.	.	.	.
(97)	.	.	.	.	.	II	I	.	.	.	.	.	.	.	.	.	.	.	.	.	.	.	.	.	.	.	+	.	.	.	.	.	.	.	.	.	.
(98)	.	.	.	II	.	.	III	.	.	.	.	+	I	.	.	.	.	.	.	.	.	.	.	.	.	.	.	+	.	.	+	.	.	.	.	.	.
(99)	.	.	.	.	.	.	II	.	.	.	.	.	.	.	.	.	.	.	.	.	.	.	.	.	.	.	.	.	.	.	+	.	.	.	.	.	.
(100)	.	.	.	I	V	III	V	.	.	.	.	.	.	.	.	.	.	.	.	.	.	.	.	.	.	.	.	.	.	.	III	.	.	.	.	.	.
(101)	.	.	.	+	.	.	III	+	+	+	.	V	.	.	.	.	.	.	.	I	I	I	.	.	+	.	.	.	+	I	I	.	.	.	.	.	.
(102)	II	II	.	.	.	.	+	.	.	.	.	+	.	.	.	.	.	.	.	.	.	.	.	.	.	.	.	.	.	.	.	.	.	.	.	.	.
(103)	.	IV	.	.	.	.	.	.	.	.	.	.	.	.	.	.	.	.	.	.	.	.	.	.	.	.	.	.	.	.	.	.	.	.	.	.	.
(104)	.	.	.	+	.	.	.	.	.	.	.	.	.	.	.	.	.	.	.	.	.	.	.	.	.	.	.	.	.	.	.	.	.	.	.	.	.
(105)	.	.	.	.	.	+	.	.	.	.	.	.	.	.	.	.	.	.	.	.	.	.	.	.	.	.	.	.	.	.	.	.	.	.	.	.	.
(106)	.	.	.	.	.	.	.	.	II	.	.	.	.	.	.	.	.	.	.	.	.	.	.	.	.	.	.	.	.	.	.	.	.	.	.	.	.
(107)	.	.	.	.	.	.	.	.	.	.	.	.	.	.	.	.	.	.	.	.	.	.	.	.	.	.	.	.	.	.	.	.	.	.	.	.	.
(108)	.	.	.	.	.	.	+	.	.	.	.	.	.	.	.	.	.	.	.	.	.	.	.	.	.	.	.	.	.	.	.	.	.	.	.	.	.
(109)	.	.	.	.	.	.	.	.	.	.	.	.	.	.	.	.	.	.	.	.	.	.	.	.	.	.	.	.	.	.	.	.	.	.	.	.	.
(110)	.	.	.	.	.	.	.	+	.	.	.	.	.	.	.	.	.	.	.	.	.	.	.	.	.	.	.	.	.	.	.	.	.	.	.	.	.
(111)	.	.	.	+	.	.	.	.	.	.	.	.	.	.	.	.	.	.	.	.	.	.	.	.	.	.	.	.	.	.	.	.	.	.	.	.	.
(112)	+	.	.	.	.	.	.	.	.	.	.	.	.	.	.	.	.	.	.	.	.	.	.	.	.	.	.	.	.	.	.	.	.	.	.	.	.
(113)	II	.	.	.	.	.	.	.	.	II	.	.	.	.	+	.	.	.	.	.	.	.	.	+	II	.	II	.	.	.	.	.	.	.	.	.	.
(114)	II	+	V	.	.	.	.	.	.	.	.	.	.	.	.	.	.	.	.	.	.	.	II	.	II	III	.	.	II	.	.	.	.	.	.	.	.
(115)	IV	IV	IV	.	.	.	.	.	.	.	.	II	V	V	V	V	V	V	V	II	IV	IV	IV	II	I	II	V	III	.	.	III	.	.	.	.	.	.
(116)	II	II	II	.	.	.	.	.	.	.	.	.	I	.	III	V	II	III	+	III	.	I	.	V	III	II	V	IV	+	.	.	.	III	II	II	.	.
(117)	V	V	III	.	.	.	.	.	.	.	.	.	.	.	III	III	+	+	.	+	.	.	.	II	I	II	III	.	.	.	.	+	.	.	.	.	.
(118)	III	II	III	.	.	.	.	.	.	.	.	.	.	.	.	.	II	.	+	.	+	.	+	.	.	.	IV	.	.	.	.	.	.	.	.	.	.
(119)	II	IV	V	.	.	.	.	.	.	.	.	.	.	.	.	.	.	.	.	.	.	.	+	.	.	.	.	.	.	.	.	.	.	.	.	.	.
(120)	+	IV	III	.	.	.	.	.	.	+	.	.	I	.	I	II	.	+	.	.	.	.	+	.	.	+	II	.	.	.	.	.	.	.	I	.	.

TABLE 4.57 *continued*

Community Number	1 *Hedwigia ciliata–Parmelia saxatilis*	2 *Koenigia islandica* scree community	3 *Asplenium trichomanes–Fissidens cristatus*	4 *Puccinellia maritima–Ascophyllum nodosum*	5 *Puccinellia maritima–Festuca rubra*	6 *Juncus gerardii–Carex extensa*	7 *Armeria maritima–Grimmia maritima*	8 *Asplenium marinum–Grimmia maritima*	9 *Atriplex glabriuscula–Rumex crispus*	10 Brackish water communities	11 *Phragmites communis–Equisetum fluviatile*	12 *Schoenoplectus lacustris–Equisetum fluviatile*	13 *Carex rostrata–Menyanthes trifoliata*	14 *Littorella uniflora–Lobelia dortmanna*	15 *Potamogeton natans–Nymphaea alba nodum*	16 *Eriophorum angustifolium–Sphagnum cuspidatum*	17 *Carex lasiocarpa–Menyanthes trifoliata*	18 *Trichophorum cespitosum–Carex panicea*	19 *Molinia caerulea–Myrica gale*	20 *Sphagneto–Juncetum effusi*	21 *Carex–Sphagnum recurvum nodum*	22 *Carex rostrata–Aulacomnium palustre*	23 *Carex rostrata–Scorpidium scorpioides*	24 *Carex panicea–Campylium stellatum*	25 *Eriophorum latifolium–Carex hostiana*	26 *Schoenus nigricans*	27 *Carex–Saxifraga aizoides nodum*	28 [illegible]
Sphagnum papillosum (221)	.	.	.	.	.	.	.	.	.	.	.	.	.	.	.	.	.	.	.	.	.	.	.	.	.	.	.	[illegible]
Cladonia arbuscula (222)	.	.	.	.	.	.	.	.	.	.	.	.	.	.	.	.	.	.	.	.	.	.	.	.	.	.	.	[illegible]
Cladonia uncialis (223)	.	.	.	.	.	.	.	.	.	.	.	.	.	.	.	.	.	.	.	.	.	.	.	.	.	.	.	[illegible]
Odontoschisma sphagni (224)	.	.	.	.	.	.	.	.	.	.	.	.	.	.	.	.	.	+	.	.	.	.	.	.	.	.	.	[illegible]
Hylocomium splendens (225)	.	.	.	.	.	.	.	.	.	.	.	.	.	.	.	.	.	+	.	III	I	.	.	.	.	.	.	[illegible]
Pleurozium schreberi (226)	.	.	.	.	.	.	.	.	.	.	.	.	.	.	.	.	.	.	.	+	.	.	.	.	.	.	.	[illegible]
Dicranum scoparium (227)	+	.	.	.	.	.	.	.	.	.	.	.	.	.	.	.	.	+	.	.	.	.	.	.	.	.	.	[illegible]
Mylia taylori (228)	.	.	.	.	.	.	.	.	.	.	.	.	.	.	.	.	.	.	.	.	.	.	.	.	.	.	.	[illegible]
Rhytidiadelphus loreus (229)	.	.	.	.	.	.	.	.	.	.	.	.	.	.	.	.	.	+	.	.	.	.	.	.	.	.	.	I
Sphagnum capillaceum (230)	.	.	.	.	.	.	.	.	.	.	.	.	.	.	.	.	.	.	II	.	.	.	.	.	.	.	.	[illegible]
Cladonia impexa (231)	.	.	.	.	.	.	.	.	.	.	.	.	.	.	.	.	.	.	.	.	.	.	.	.	.	.	.	[illegible]
Erica cinerea (232)	.	.	.	.	.	.	.	.	.	.	.	.	.	.	.	.	.	.	.	.	.	.	.	.	.	.	.	[illegible]
Cladonia coccifera (233)	.	.	.	.	.	.	.	.	.	.	.	.	.	.	.	.	.	.	.	.	.	.	.	.	.	.	.	[illegible]
Cephalozia bicuspidata (234)	.	.	.	.	.	.	.	.	.	.	.	.	.	.	.	.	.	.	.	.	.	.	.	.	.	.	.	I
Diplophyllum albicans (235)	.	.	.	.	.	.	.	.	.	.	.	.	.	.	.	.	.	.	.	.	.	.	.	.	.	.	.	[illegible]
Sphagnum fuscum (236)	.	.	.	.	.	.	.	.	.	.	.	.	.	.	.	.	.	.	.	.	.	.	.	.	.	.	.	
Lophozia incisa (237)	.	.	.	.	.	.	.	.	.	.	.	.	.	.	.	.	.	.	.	.	.	.	.	.	.	.	.	[illegible]
Cladonia pyxidata (238)	.	.	.	.	.	.	.	.	.	.	.	.	.	.	.	.	.	.	.	.	.	.	.	.	.	.	.	[illegible]
Cladonia rangiformis (239)	.	.	.	.	.	.	.	.	.	.	.	.	.	.	.	.	.	.	.	.	.	.	.	.	.	.	.	[illegible]
Mylia anomala (240)	.	.	.	.	.	.	.	.	.	.	.	.	.	.	.	.	.	.	.	.	.	.	.	.	.	.	.	[illegible]
Lophozia ventricosa (241)	.	.	.	.	.	.	.	.	.	.	.	.	.	.	.	.	.	.	.	.	.	.	.	.	.	.	.	I
Lepidozia setacea (242)	.	.	.	.	.	.	.	.	.	.	.	.	.	.	.	.	.	.	.	.	.	.	.	.	.	.	.	I
Sphagnum rubellum (243)	.	.	.	.	.	.	.	.	.	.	.	.	.	.	.	.	.	IV	III	II	.	.	.	.	.	.	.	[illegible]
Sphagnum compactum (244)	.	.	.	.	.	.	.	.	.	.	.	.	.	.	.	.	.	IV	II	.	.	.	.	.	.	.	.	[illegible]
Pleurozia purpurea (245)	.	.	.	.	.	.	.	.	.	.	.	.	.	.	.	.	.	II	.	.	II	.	.	.	.	.	.	[illegible]
Pedicularis sylvatica (246)	.	.	.	.	.	.	.	.	.	.	.	.	.	.	.	.	.	II	+	.	.	.	.	III	.	.	.	[illegible]
Campylopus atrovirens (247)	.	.	.	.	.	.	.	.	.	.	.	.	.	.	.	.	.	III	.	.	.	.	.	.	.	.	.	[illegible]
Campylopus setifolius (248)	.	.	.	.	.	.	.	.	.	.	.	.	.	.	.	.	.	II	.	.	.	.	.	.	.	.	.	[illegible]
Campylopus shawii (249)	.	.	.	.	.	.	.	.	.	.	.	.	.	.	.	.	.	II	.	.	.	.	.	.	.	.	.	[illegible]
Sphagnum strictum (250)	.	.	.	.	.	.	.	.	.	.	.	.	.	.	.	.	.	+	.	.	.	.	.	.	.	.	.	[illegible]
Sphagnum imbricatum (251)	.	.	.	.	.	.	.	.	.	.	.	.	.	.	.	.	.	.	+	.	.	.	.	.	.	.	.	I
Dicranella heteromalla (252)	.	.	.	.	.	.	.	.	.	.	.	.	.	.	.	.	.	.	.	.	.	.	.	.	.	.	.	I
Juncus squarrosus (253)	.	.	.	.	.	.	.	.	.	.	.	.	.	.	.	.	.	II	+	I	II	+	.	IV	.	.	.	[illegible]
Cratoneuron filicinum (254)	.	.	.	.	.	+	.	.	.	.	.	.	.	.	.	.	.	.	.	.	.	.	.	.	+	.	.	
Stellaria alsine (255)	.	.	.	.	.	.	.	.	.	.	.	.	.	.	.	.	.	.	.	+	.	.	.	.	.	.	.	
Montia fontana ssp. *fontana* (256)	.	.	.	.	.	.	.	.	.	.	.	.	.	.	.	.	.	.	.	.	.	.	.	.	.	.	.	
Bryum weigelii (257)	.	.	.	.	.	.	.	.	.	.	.	.	.	.	.	.	.	.	.	.	.	.	.	.	.	.	.	
Mnium rugicum (258)	.	.	.	.	.	.	.	.	.	.	.	.	.	.	.	.	.	.	.	.	.	.	.	.	.	.	.	
Cardamine flexuosa (259)	.	.	.	.	.	.	.	.	.	.	.	.	.	.	.	.	.	.	.	.	.	.	.	.	.	.	.	
Epilobium anagallidifolium (260)	.	.	.	.	.	.	.	.	.	.	.	.	.	.	.	.	.	.	.	.	.	.	.	.	.	.	.	
Euphrasia frigida (261)	.	.	.	.	.	.	.	.	.	.	.	.	.	.	.	.	.	.	.	.	.	.	.	.	.	.	.	
Marsupella aquatica (262)	.	.	.	.	.	.	.	.	.	.	.	.	.	.	.	.	.	.	.	.	.	.	.	.	.	.	.	
Sagina saginoides (263)	.	.	.	.	.	.	.	.	.	.	.	.	.	.	.	.	.	.	.	.	.	.	.	.	.	.	.	
Juncus biglumis (264)	.	.	.	.	.	.	.	.	.	.	.	.	.	.	.	.	.	.	.	.	.	.	.	.	.	.	+	
Juncus triglumis (265)	.	.	.	.	.	.	.	.	.	.	.	.	.	.	.	.	.	.	.	.	.	.	.	.	.	.	III	
Saxifraga stellaris (266)	.	II	.	.	.	.	.	.	.	.	.	.	.	.	.	.	.	.	.	.	.	.	.	.	.	.	.	
Acrocladium sarmentosum (267)		.	.	.	.	.	.	.	.	.	.	.	.	.	.	.	.	+	.	.	.	.	.	.	I	.	.	
Koenigia islandica (268)	.	V	.	.	.	.	.	.	.	.	.	.	.	.	.	.	.	.	.	.	.	.	.	.	.	.	.	
Carex demissa (269)	.	II	.	.	.	.	.	.	.	.	.	.	.	.	.	.	.	II	III	.	+	.	II	IV	V	.	V	
Scapania undulata (270)	.	.	.	.	.	.	.	.	.	.	.	.	.	.	.	.	.	+	.	.	.	.	.	.	.	.	.	
Dicranella palustris (271)	.	.	.	.	.	.	.	.	.	.	.	.	.	.	.	.	.	.	.	.	.	+	.	.	.	.	.	
Ranunculus acris (272)	.	.	+	.	.	.	.	.	+	.	.	.	.	.	.	.	.	.	.	.	.	.	.	.	.	.	.	
Philonotis fontana (273)	.	.	.	.	.	.	.	.	.	.	.	.	.	.	.	.	.	.	.	.	.	.	.	.	.	.	.	
Deschampsia cespitosa (274)	.	.	.	.	.	.	.	.	.	.	.	.	.	.	.	.	.	.	.	.	.	.	.	.	.	.	.	
Pinguicula vulgaris (275)	.	.	.	.	.	.	.	.	.	.	.	.	.	.	.	.	.	III	V	.	III	+	II	V	V	V	V	I

TABLE 4.57 *continued*

	29 *Molinieto–Callunetum*	30 *Trichophoreto–Eriophoretum*	31 *Calluneto–Eriophoretum*	32 *Philonoto–Saxifragetum stellaris*	33 *Koenigia islandica–Carex demissa nodum*	34 *Cratoneuron commutatum–Saxifraga aizoides nodum*	35 *Saxifragetum aizoidis*	36 *Juncus acutiflorus–Filipendula ulmaria*	37 *Centaureo–Cynosuretum*	38 *Maritime grassland nodum*	39 *Lolium perenne–Plantago lanceolata*	40 *Dryas octopetala–Carex flacca*	41 *Cariceto–Rhacomitretum lanuginosi*	42 *Festuca ovina–Luzula spicata nodum*	43 *Rhacomitreto–Callunetum*	44 *Juniperus nana nodum*	45 *Rhacomitreto–Empetretum*	46 *Alchemilla alpina–Vaccinium myrtillus nodum*	47 *Nardus stricta–Vaccinium myrtillus*	48 *Agrosto–Festucetum* (species-poor)	49 *Alchemilleto–Agrosto–Festucetum*	50 *Agrosto–Festucetum* (species-rich)	51 *Nardo–Juncetum squarrosi*	52 *Callunetum vulgaris*	53 *Calluna vulgaris–Sieglingia decumbens*	54 *Calluna vulgaris–Arctostaphylos uva-ursi nodum*	55 *Vaccineto–Callunetum hepaticosum*	56 *Luzula sylvatica–Vaccinium myrtillus*	57 *Luzula sylvatica–Silene dioica*	58 *Betula pubescens–Cirsium heterophyllum*	59 *Sedum rosea–Alchemilla glabra*	60 *Betula pubescens–Vaccinium myrtillus*	61 *Corylus avellana–Oxalis acetosella*	62 *Oxalis acetosella–Rhytidiadelphus loreus*	63 *Hymenophyllum wilsonii–Isothecium myosuroides*	64 Open boulder association	65 *Fraxinus excelsior–Brachypodium sylvaticum*
221)	II	V	+	.	.	.	.	.	.	.	.	.	.	.	.	.	.	.	.	.	.	.	III	.	.	.	.	.	.	.	.	.	.	.	.	.	.
222)	II	II	III	.	.	.	.	.	.	.	.	.	.	.	III	III	II	III	I	.	.	III	+	II	.	.	.	.	.	.	.	.	.	.	.	.	.
223)	III	III	II	.	.	.	.	.	.	.	.	.	V	II	V	V	V	III	V	I	.	.	II	II	.	.	+	.	.	.	.	.	.	.	.	.	.
224)	+	II	+	.	.	.	.	.	.	.	.	.	.	.	.	.	.	.	.	.	.	.	.	.	.	.	.	.	.	.	.	.	.	.	.	.	.
225)	II	+	V	.	.	.	.	III	+	+	+	IV	I	.	II	II	III	III	IV	V	V	V	III	.	V	.	IV	II	II	II	III	V	IV	V	+	.	III
226)	+	+	V	.	.	.	.	.	.	.	.	+	I	.	I	II	II	III	I	IV	.	I	+	V	V	II	III	+	+	.	+	V	.	IV	II	.	.
227)	+	+	III	.	.	+	.	.	.	.	.	II	II	.	I	.	I	III	.	IV	I	I	.	IV	III	III	III	III	II	I	I	III	.	II	V	II	.
228)	+	+	+	.	.	.	.	.	.	.	.	.	.	.	.	.	.	III	+	.	.	.	+	.	II	IV	V	V	.	.	.	+	.	.	+	.	.
229)	+	.	IV	.	.	.	.	.	.	.	.	+	III	.	I	II	III	II	V	II	IV	III	II	III	II	.	V	III	+	II	III	V	IV	V	III	.	+
230)	III	.	V	.	.	.	.	.	.	.	.	.	.	.	.	.	+	.	.	+	.	.	III	II	.	.	V	.	.	.	.	+	.	+	.	.	.
231)	II	.	+	.	.	.	.	.	.	.	.	.	.	.	.	.	III	.	.	.	.	.	.	.	.	.	.	.	.	.	.	.	.	.	.	.	.
232)	II	.	+	.	.	.	.	.	.	+	.	+	.	.	III	II	.	+	.	.	.	II	.	V	V	.	IV	+	III	.	.	.	.	+	.	.	.
233)	.	.	II	.	.	.	.	.	.	.	.	.	.	.	.	.	.	.	.	.	.	.	.	II	.	V	.	.	.	.	.	.	.	.	.	.	.
234)	.	I	+	.	.	.	.	.	.	.	.	.	.	.	.	.	.	.	.	.	.	.	.	.	.	.	III	.	.	.	.	+	.	.	.	.	.
235)	.	I	+	.	.	.	.	.	.	.	.	.	II	.	I	IV	.	V	+	.	.	III	.	.	.	II	V	.	+	.	.	I	.	I	II	V	.
236)	.	+	+	.	.	.	.	.	.	.	.	.	.	.	.	.	.	.	.	.	.	.	.	.	.	.	.	.	.	.	.	.	.	.	.	.	.
237)	.	.	+	.	.	.	.	.	.	.	.	.	.	.	.	.	+	.	.	.	.	.	.	.	.	.	.	.	.	.	.	.	.	.	.	.	.
238)	.	.	+	.	.	.	.	.	.	.	.	.	.	.	.	.	.	.	.	.	.	.	.	+	.	.	.	.	.	.	.	.	.	.	.	.	.
239)	.	.	+	.	.	.	.	.	.	.	.	.	.	.	.	.	.	.	.	.	.	.	.	.	.	.	.	.	.	.	.	.	.	.	.	.	.
240)	.	+	.	.	.	.	.	.	.	.	.	.	.	.	.	.	.	.	.	.	.	.	.	.	.	.	.	.	.	.	.	.	.	.	.	.	.
241)	.	+	.	.	.	.	.	.	.	.	.	.	.	.	.	.	.	.	+	.	.	.	.	.	.	.	.	.	.	.	.	.	.	.	.	.	.
242)	.	I	.	.	.	.	.	.	.	.	.	.	.	.	.	.	.	.	.	.	.	.	.	.	.	.	+	.	.	.	.	.	.	.	.	.	.
243)	.	V	.	.	.	.	.	.	.	.	.	.	.	.	.	.	.	.	.	.	.	.	.	.	.	.	.	.	.	.	.	.	.	.	.	.	.
244)	III	V	.	.	.	.	.	.	.	.	.	.	.	.	.	.	.	.	.	.	.	.	.	.	.	.	.	.	.	.	.	.	.	.	.	.	.
245)	IV	V	.	.	.	.	.	.	.	.	.	.	.	.	.	+	III	II	.	.	.	.	.	.	.	.	IV	.	.	.	.	.	.	.	.	.	.
246)	IV	II	.	.	.	.	.	I	.	.	.	.	.	.	.	.	.	.	.	II	.	.	.	+	+	.	.	.	.	.	.	.	.	.	.	.	.
247)	III	IV	.	.	.	.	.	.	.	.	.	.	.	.	II	II	III	II	+	.	.	.	+	.	III	.	V	.	.	.	.	.	.	.	.	.	.
248)	+	I	.	.	.	.	.	.	.	.	.	.	.	.	.	.	.	.	.	.	.	.	.	.	.	.	II	.	.	.	.	.	.	.	.	.	.
249)	+	I	.	.	.	.	.	.	.	.	.	.	.	.	.	.	.	.	.	.	.	.	.	.	.	.	.	.	.	.	.	.	.	.	.	.	.
250)	III	I	.	.	.	.	.	.	.	.	.	.	.	.	.	.	.	.	.	.	.	.	.	.	.	.	.	.	.	.	.	.	.	.	.	.	.
251)	II	II	.	.	.	.	.	.	.	.	.	.	.	.	.	.	.	.	.	.	.	.	.	.	.	.	.	.	.	.	.	.	.	.	.	.	.
252)	.	.	.	.	.	.	.	.	.	.	.	.	.	.	.	.	.	.	.	.	.	.	.	.	.	.	.	.	.	.	.	+	.	.	.	.	.
253)	II	II	IV	I	II	.	.	.	.	.	.	.	.	.	+	.	.	.	.	.	.	.	V	+	+	.	.	.	.	.	.	.	.	.	.	.	.
254)	.	.	.	IV	.	.	.	.	.	.	.	.	.	.	.	.	.	.	.	.	.	.	.	.	.	.	.	.	.	.	.	.	.	.	.	.	.
255)	.	.	.	V	.	.	.	.	.	.	.	.	.	.	.	.	.	.	.	.	.	.	.	.	.	.	.	.	.	.	.	.	.	.	.	.	.
256)	.	.	.	V	.	.	.	.	.	.	.	.	.	.	.	.	.	.	.	.	.	.	.	.	.	.	.	.	.	.	.	.	.	.	.	.	.
257)	.	.	.	III	.	.	.	.	.	.	.	.	.	.	.	.	.	.	.	.	.	.	.	.	.	.	.	.	.	.	.	.	.	.	.	.	.
258)	.	.	.	II	.	.	.	+	.	.	.	.	.	.	.	.	.	.	.	.	.	.	.	.	.	.	.	.	.	.	.	.	.	.	.	.	.
259)	.	.	.	V	.	.	.	.	.	.	.	.	.	.	.	.	.	.	.	.	.	.	.	.	.	.	.	II	.	+	.	.	II	.	.	.	III
260)	.	.	.	III	.	.	.	.	.	.	.	.	.	.	.	.	.	.	.	.	.	.	.	.	.	.	.	.	.	.	.	.	.	.	.	.	.
261)	.	.	.	II	II	.	.	.	.	.	.	.	.	.	.	.	.	.	.	.	.	.	.	.	.	.	.	.	.	.	.	.	.	.	.	.	.
262)	.	.	.	I	II	.	.	.	.	.	.	.	.	.	.	.	.	.	.	.	.	.	.	.	.	.	.	.	.	.	.	.	.	.	.	.	.
263)	.	.	.	.	III	.	.	.	.	.	.	.	.	.	.	.	.	.	.	.	.	.	.	.	.	.	.	.	.	.	.	.	.	.	.	.	.
264)	.	.	.	I	IV	.	.	.	.	.	.	.	.	.	.	.	.	.	.	.	.	.	.	.	.	.	.	.	.	.	.	.	.	.	.	.	.
265)	.	.	.	II	V	.	.	.	.	.	.	.	.	.	.	.	.	.	.	.	.	.	.	.	.	.	.	.	.	.	.	.	.	.	.	.	.
266)	.	.	.	V	V	.	.	.	.	.	.	.	.	.	.	.	.	.	.	.	.	.	.	.	.	.	.	.	.	.	+	.	.	.	.	.	.
267)	.	.	.	IV	IV	.	.	.	.	.	.	.	.	.	.	.	.	.	.	.	.	.	.	.	.	.	.	.	.	.	.	.	.	.	.	.	.
268)	.	.	.	I	V	.	.	.	.	.	.	.	.	+	.	.	.	.	.	.	.	.	.	.	.	.	.	.	.	.	.	.	.	.	.	.	.
269)	.	.	.	II	V	.	.	+	.	.	.	.	.	.	+	.	+	.	.	.	.	+	.	.	+	.	.	.	.	I	II	.	.	.	.	.	.
270)	.	.	.	IV	V	+	.	.	.	.	.	.	.	.	.	.	.	.	.	.	.	.	.	.	.	.	.	.	.	.	.	.	.	.	.	+	.
271)	.	.	.	V	II	.	+	.	.	.	.	.	.	.	.	.	.	.	.	.	.	.	.	.	.	.	.	.	.	.	+	.	.	.	.	.	.
272)	.	.	.	IV	II	.	V	.	.	II	.	+	.	.	.	.	.	.	.	I	IV	IV	.	.	I	.	.	.	.	III	V	II	III	.	.	.	II
273)	.	.	.	V	II	.	+	I	.	.	.	.	.	.	.	.	.	.	.	.	.	.	.	.	.	.	.	.	.	.	II	.	.	.	.	.	.
274)	.	.	.	IV	V	.	V	+	+	.	.	.	.	.	.	.	.	.	+	.	.	.	.	.	.	.	.	.	.	V	V	.	V	.	.	.	II
275)	+	II	.	II	II	V	V	+	.	.	.	II	.	.	.	.	.	+	.	I	.	I	+	.	.	.	II	.	.	II	III	.	.	.	.	.	.

TABLE 4.57 *continued*

Community Number	1 *Hedwigia ciliata–Parmelia saxatilis*	2 *Koenigia islandica* scree community	3 *Asplenium trichomanes–Fissidens cristatus*	4 *Puccinellia maritima–Ascophyllum nodosum*	5 *Puccinellia maritima–Festuca rubra*	6 *Juncus gerardii–Carex extensa*	7 *Armeria maritima–Grimmia maritima*	8 *Asplenium marinum–Grimmia maritima*	9 *Atriplex glabriuscula–Rumex crispus*	10 Brackish water communities	11 *Phragmites communis–Equisetum fluviatile*	12 *Schoenoplectus lacustris–Equisetum fluviatile*	13 *Carex rostrata–Menyanthes trifoliata*	14 *Littorella uniflora–Lobelia dortmanna*	15 *Potamogeton natans–Nymphaea alba nodum*	16 *Eriophorum angustifolium–Sphagnum cuspidatum*	17 *Carex lasiocarpa–Menyanthes trifoliata*	18 *Trichophorum cespitosum–Carex panicea*	19 *Molinia caerulea–Myrica gale*	20 *Sphagneto–Juncetum effusi*	21 *Carex–Sphagnum recurvum nodum*	22 *Carex rostrata–Aulacomnium palustre*	23 *Carex rostrata–Scorpidium scorpioides*	24 *Carex panicea–Campylium stellatum*	25 *Eriophorum latifolium–Carex hostiana*	26 *Schoenus nigricans*	27 *Carex–Saxifraga aizoides nodum*	28 *Trichophoreto–Callunetum*
Bryum pseudotriquetrum (276)	.	.	.	.	.	.	.	.	.	.	.	.	.	.	.	.	.	.	.	.	.	II	II	II	II	.	III	.
Riccardia pinguis (277)	.	.	.	.	.	.	.	.	.	+	.	.	.	.	.	.	.	II	.	.	.	.	+	II	III	I	V	.
Selaginella selaginoides (278)	.	.	I	.	.	.	.	.	.	.	.	.	.	.	.	.	.	III	.	.	+	.	+	V	IV	V	V	.
Mnium punctatum (279)	.	.	+	.	.	.	.	.	.	.	.	.	.	.	.	.	.	.	.	.	.	.	.	II	.	.	.	.
Cratoneuron commutatum (280)	.	.	.	.	.	.	.	.	.	.	.	.	.	.	.	.	.	.	.	.	.	.	.	.	I	.	IV	.
Saxifraga aizoides (281)	.	.	.	.	.	.	.	.	.	.	.	.	.	.	.	.	.	.	.	.	.	.	.	.	.	.	V	
Conocephalum conicum (282)	.	.	II	.	.	.	.	.	.	.	.	.	.	.	.	.	.	.	.	.	.	.	.	.	.	.	.	.
Euphrasia officinalis agg. (283)	.	.	.	.	II	.	.	+	.	.	.	.	.	.	.	.	.	.	.	.	.	.	.	.	.	.	.	.
Sedum rosea (284)	.	.	.	.	.	.	.	+	+	.	.	.	.	.	.	.	.	.	.	.	.	.	.	.	.	.	.	.
Anoectangium aestivum (285)	.	.	I	.	.	.	.	.	.	.	.	.	.	.	.	.	.	.	.	.	.	.	.	.	.	.	.	.
Chrysosplenium oppositifolium (286)	.	.	II	.	.	.	.	.	.	.	.	.	.	.	.	.	.	.	.	.	.	.	.	.	.	.	.	.
Pellia epiphylla (287)	.	.	I	.	.	.	.	.	.	.	.	.	.	.	.	.	.	.	.	.	.	.	.	.	II	I	.	.
Preissia quadrata (288)	.	.	II	.	.	.	.	.	.	.	.	.	.	.	.	.	.	.	.	.	.	.	.	.	.	.	.	.
Gymnostomum aeruginosum (289)	.	.	+	.	.	.	.	.	.	.	.	.	.	.	.	.	.	.	.	.	.	.	.	.	.	.	.	.
Plectocolea hyalina (290)	.	.	.	.	.	.	.	.	.	.	.	.	.	.	.	.	.	.	.	.	.	.	.	.	.	.	.	.
Crepis paludosa (291)	.	.	+	.	.	.	.	.	.	.	.	.	.	.	.	.	.	.	.	.	.	.	.	.	.	.	.	.
Hypericum pulchrum (292)	.	.	+	.	.	.	.	.	.	.	.	.	.	.	.	.	.	.	+	.	.	.	.	.	I	.	II	.
Carex pulicaris (293)	.	.	I	.	.	.	.	.	.	.	.	.	.	.	.	.	.	II	III	.	.	+	II	III	III	I	IV	.
Festuca rubra (294)	II	.	.	.	V	V	V	IV	III	.	.	.	.	.	.	.	.	.	.	.	.	.	.	+	.	.	III	.
Festuca vivipara (295)	.	V	.	.	.	.	.	.	.	.	.	.	.	.	.	.	.	.	II	I	III	.	.	.	.	.	V	+
Angelica sylvestris (296)	.	.	.	.	.	.	.	.	.	.	.	.	.	.	.	.	.	.	.	.	.	.	.	.	.	.	.	.
Leontodon autumnalis (297)	.	.	.	.	II	II	II	+	II	.	.	.	.	.	.	.	.	.	.	.	.	.	.	.	.	.	.	.
Ctenidium molluscum (298)	.	.	III	.	.	.	.	.	.	.	.	.	.	.	.	.	.	.	.	.	.	.	.	III	II	.	III	.
Fissidens cristatus (299)	.	.	V	.	.	.	.	.	.	.	.	.	.	.	.	.	.	.	.	.	.	.	.	.	.	.	.	.
Tortella tortuosa (300)	.	.	III	.	.	.	.	.	.	.	.	.	.	.	.	.	.	.	.	.	.	.	.	.	I	.	.	.
Asplenium viride (301)	.	.	III	.	.	.	.	.	.	.	.	.	.	.	.	.	.	.	.	.	.	.	.	.	.	.	.	.
Oxyria digyna (302)	.	II	.	.	.	.	.	.	.	.	.	.	.	.	.	.	.	.	.	.	.	.	.	.	.	.	.	.
Cystopteris fragilis (303)	.	.	III	.	.	.	.	.	.	.	.	.	.	.	.	.	.	.	.	.	.	.	.	.	.	.	.	.
Barbula fallax (304)	.	.	.	.	.	.	.	.	.	.	.	.	.	.	.	.	.	.	.	.	.	.	.	.	+	.	.	.
Leiocolea muelleri (305)	.	.	+	.	.	.	.	.	.	.	.	.	.	.	.	.	.	.	.	.	.	.	.	.	.	.	.	.
Orthothecium rufescens (306)	.	.	II	.	.	.	.	.	.	.	.	.	.	.	.	.	.	.	.	.	.	.	.	.	+	.	.	.
Saxifraga oppositifolia (307)	.	.	+	.	.	.	.	.	.	.	.	.	.	.	.	.	.	.	.	.	.	.	.	.	.	.	.	.
Alchemilla glabra (308)	.	.	.	.	.	.	.	.	.	.	.	.	.	.	.	.	.	.	.	.	.	.	.	.	.	.	.	.
Parnassia palustris (309)	.	.	.	.	.	.	.	.	.	.	.	.	.	.	.	.	.	.	.	+	.	+	.	+	.	.	+	.
Filipendula ulmaria (310)	.	.	.	.	.	.	.	.	.	.	.	.	.	.	.	.	.	.	.	.	.	III	.	.	.	.	.	.
Thuidium tamariscinum (311)	.	.	.	.	.	.	.	.	.	.	.	.	.	.	.	.	.	.	.	III	.	.	.	+	.	.	.	.
Rumex acetosa (312)	.	.	.	.	.	.	.	.	+	.	.	.	.	.	.	.	.	.	.	II	.	III	.	.	.	.	.	.
Lotus corniculatus (313)	.	.	.	.	.	.	+	.	.	.	.	.	.	.	.	.	.	.	.	.	.	.	.	.	.	.	+	.
Carex flacca (314)	.	.	.	.	.	II	.	.	.	.	.	.	.	.	.	.	.	.	.	.	.	.	.	III	IV	I	V	.
Acrocladium cuspidatum (315)	.	.	.	.	.	.	.	.	.	+	.	.	.	.	.	.	.	.	.	+	.	V	+	+	+	.	.	.
Anthoxanthum odoratum (316)	.	.	.	.	.	.	.	.	.	.	.	.	.	.	.	.	.	.	.	III	II	.	.	II	.	.	.	.
Hylocomium splendens (317)	.	.	.	.	.	.	.	.	.	.	.	.	.	.	.	.	.	+	.	III	I	.	.	.	.	.	.	+
Lychnis flos-cuculi (318)	.	.	.	.	.	.	.	.	.	.	.	.	.	.	.	.	.	.	.	.	.	IV	.	.	.	.	.	.
Juncus acutiflorus (319)	.	.	.	.	.	.	.	.	.	.	.	.	.	.	.	.	.	.	.	.	.	III	.	.	.	.	.	.
Trichocolea tomentella (320)	.	.	.	.	.	.	.	.	.	.	.	.	.	.	.	.	.	.	.	.	.	+	.	.	.	.	.	.
Lophocolea cuspidata (321)	.	.	.	.	.	.	.	.	.	.	.	.	.	.	.	.	.	.	.	.	.	+	.	.	.	.	.	.
Senecio aquaticus (322)	.	.	.	.	.	.	.	.	.	.	.	.	.	.	.	.	.	.	.	.	.	+	.	.	.	.	.	.
Dactylorchis fuchsii (323)	.	.	.	.	.	.	.	.	.	.	.	.	.	.	.	.	.	.	.	.	.	.	.	.	.	.	.	.
Vicia cracca (324)	.	.	.	.	.	.	.	.	.	.	.	.	.	.	.	.	.	.	.	.	.	.	.	.	.	.	.	.
Gymnadenia conopsea (325)	.	.	.	.	.	.	.	.	.	.	.	.	.	.	.	.	.	.	.	.	.	.	.	.	.	.	.	.
Dactylis glomerata (326)	.	.	.	.	.	.	.	.	.	.	.	.	.	.	.	.	.	.	.	.	.	.	.	.	.	.	.	.
Rhinanthus minor agg. (327)	.	.	.	.	.	.	.	.	.	.	.	.	.	.	.	.	.	.	.	.	.	II	.	+	.	.	.	.
Lathyrus pratensis (328)	.	.	.	.	.	.	.	.	.	.	.	.	.	.	.	.	.	.	.	.	.	.	.	.	.	.	.	.
Arrhenatherum elatius (329)	.	.	II	.	.	.	.	.	.	.	.	.	.	.	.	.	.	.	.	.	.	.	.	.	.	.	.	.
Trifolium pratense (330)	.	.	.	.	.	.	.	.	.	.	.	.	.	.	.	.	.	.	.	.	.	.	.	.	.	.	.	.

TABLE 4.57 *continued*

	29 *Molinieto-Callunetum*	30 *Trichophoreto-Eriophoretum*	31 *Calluneto-Eriophoretum*	32 *Philonoto-Saxifragetum stellaris*	33 *Koenigia islandica-Carex demissa nodum*	34 *Cratoneuron commutatum-Saxifraga aizoides nodum*	35 *Saxifragetum aizoidis*	36 *Juncus acutiflorus-Filipendula ulmaria*	37 *Centaureo-Cynosuretum*	38 *Maritime grassland nodum*	39 *Lolium perenne-Plantago lanceolata*	40 *Dryas octopetala-Carex flacca*	41 *Cariceto-Rhacomitretum lanuginosi*	42 *Festuca ovina-Luzula spicata nodum*	43 *Rhacomitreto-Callunetum*	44 *Juniperus nana nodum*	45 *Rhacomitreto-Empetretum*	46 *Alchemilla alpina-Vaccinium myrtillus nodum*	47 *Nardus stricta-Vaccinium myrtillus*	48 *Agrosto-Festucetum* (species-poor)	49 *Alchemilleto-Agrosto-Festucetum*	50 *Agrosto-Festucetum* (species-rich)	51 *Nardo-Juncetum squarrosi*	52 *Callunetum vulgaris*	53 *Calluna vulgaris-Sieglingia decumbens*	54 *Calluna vulgaris-Arctostaphylos uva-ursi nodum*	55 *Vaccineto-Callunetum hepaticosum*	56 *Luzula sylvatica-Vaccinium myrtillus*	57 *Luzula sylvatica-Silene dioica*	58 *Betula pubescens-Cirsium heterophyllum*	59 *Sedum rosea-Alchemilla glabra*	60 *Betula pubescens-Vaccinium myrtillus*	61 *Corylus avellana-Oxalis acetosella*	62 *Oxalis acetosella-Rhytidiadelphus loreus*	63 *Hymenophyllum wilsonii-Isothecium myosuroides*	64 Open boulder association	65 *Fraxinus excelsior-Brachypodium sylvaticum*
76)	.	.	.	IV	.	IV	IV	+	.	.	.	.	.	.	.	.	.	.	.	.	.	.	.	.	.	.	.	.	.	.	III	.	.	.	.	.	.
77)	.	.	.	+	.	V	IV	.	.	.	.	.	.	.	.	.	.	.	.	.	.	I	+	.	.	.	.	.	.	.	III	.	.	.	.	.	.
78)	+	.	.	II	.	II	V	.	.	.	.	II	II	.	.	.	II	II	.	.	IV	I	II	.	.	.	.	.	.	I	III	.	.	.	.	.	.
79)	.	.	.	II	.	II	II	.	.	.	.	.	.	.	.	.	.	.	.	.	.	.	.	.	.	.	.	II	.	II	III	.	+	.	.	+	.
80)	.	.	.	+	.	V	III	.	.	.	.	.	.	.	.	.	.	.	.	.	.	.	.	.	.	.	.	.	.	I	II	.	.	.	.	.	.
81)	.	.	.	.	.	V	V	.	.	.	.	+	.	.	.	.	.	.	.	.	I	I	.	.	.	.	.	.	.	.	IV	.	.	.	.	.	.
82)	.	.	.	+	.	III	.	.	.	.	.	.	.	.	.	.	.	.	.	.	.	.	.	.	.	.	.	.	.	.	+	.	.	.	.	.	.
83)	.	.	.	.	.	II	II	.	.	.	.	.	I	II	.	.	.	.	.	I	IV	IV	.	.	.	.	.	.	.	.	+	.	.	.	.	.	.
84)	.	.	.	.	.	II	IV	.	.	.	.	.	.	.	.	.	III	.	.	.	I	.	.	.	.	.	+	+	V	.	V	.	.	.	.	.	.
85)	.	.	.	.	.	II	IV	.	.	.	.	.	.	.	.	.	.	.	.	.	.	.	.	.	.	.	.	.	.	.	III	.	.	.	.	.	.
86)	.	.	.	.	.	III	I	.	.	.	.	.	.	.	.	.	.	.	.	.	.	.	.	.	.	.	.	.	.	II	II	.	.	.	.	.	+
87)	.	.	.	.	.	III	I	.	.	.	.	.	.	.	.	.	.	.	.	.	.	.	.	.	.	.	II	.	.	.	II	.	.	.	.	.	.
88)	.	.	.	.	.	II	IV	.	.	.	.	.	.	.	.	.	.	.	.	.	.	.	.	.	.	.	.	.	.	.	+	.	.	.	.	.	.
89)	.	.	.	.	.	III	II	.	.	.	.	.	.	.	.	.	.	.	.	.	.	.	.	.	.	.	.	.	.	.	.	.	.	.	.	.	.
90)	.	.	.	.	.	II	I	.	.	.	.	.	.	.	.	.	.	.	.	.	.	.	.	.	.	.	.	.	.	.	.	.	.	.	.	+	.
91)	.	.	.	.	.	III	I	I	.	.	.	.	.	.	.	.	.	.	.	.	.	.	.	.	.	.	.	.	+	III	III	.	.	.	.	.	.
92)	.	.	.	.	.	III	I	+	.	II	.	III	.	.	.	.	II	.	.	.	.	II	.	+	III	II	III	II	IV	I	III	.	.	.	.	.	.
93)	.	.	.	.	.	II	IV	III	V	III	.	IV	III	II	.	.	+	.	.	II	V	V	.	.	V	II	+	.	III	II	III	.	.	.	.	.	.
94)	.	.	.	III	.	V	V	I	+	V	.	+	.	.	.	.	.	.	.	II	.	IV	.	.	II	.	.	.	III	.	.	.	.	.	.	.	.
95)	.	.	.	+	.	III	III	II	+	IV	.	V	V	V	V	V	V	V	III	V	IV	IV	III	+	V	IV	III	II	II	I	III	II	II	I	+	.	.
96)	.	.	.	.	.	II	III	II	II	III	.	.	.	.	.	.	.	.	.	.	I	.	.	.	+	.	.	.	V	III	V	.	.	.	.	.	+
97)	.	.	.	.	.	II	I	.	.	III	+	+	.	.	.	.	.	.	.	.	.	.	.	.	II	.	.	.	.	.	.	.	.	.	.	.	.
98)	.	.	.	.	.	IV	IV	.	.	II	.	V	.	.	.	.	.	.	.	.	I	V	+	.	.	.	.	.	+	III	V	.	+	.	.	.	IV
99)	.	.	.	.	.	II	I	.	.	.	.	II	.	.	.	.	.	.	.	.	.	.	.	.	.	.	.	.	.	II	.	.	.	.	.	.	+
00)	.	.	.	.	.	II	II	.	.	.	.	V	.	.	.	.	.	.	.	.	.	.	.	.	.	.	.	.	.	II	III	.	.	.	.	.	+
01)	.	.	.	.	.	.	III	.	.	.	.	.	.	.	.	.	.	.	.	.	+	.	.	.	.	.	.	.	.	I	II	.	.	.	.	.	.
02)	.	.	.	.	.	.	III	.	.	.	.	.	.	.	.	.	.	.	.	.	+	.	.	.	.	.	.	.	.	.	IV	.	.	.	.	.	.
03)	.	.	.	.	.	.	IV	.	.	.	.	.	.	.	.	.	.	.	.	.	.	.	.	.	.	.	.	.	.	.	+	.	.	.	.	.	.
04)	.	.	.	.	.	.	II	.	.	.	.	.	.	.	.	.	.	.	.	.	.	.	.	.	.	.	.	.	.	.	+	.	.	.	.	.	.
05)	.	.	.	.	.	.	III	.	.	.	.	.	.	.	.	.	.	.	.	.	.	.	.	.	.	.	.	.	.	.	.	.	.	.	.	.	.
06)	.	.	.	.	.	.	V	.	.	.	.	.	.	.	.	.	.	.	.	.	.	.	.	.	.	.	.	.	.	.	II	.	.	.	.	.	.
07)	.	.	.	.	.	.	V	.	.	.	.	.	.	.	.	.	.	.	.	.	.	.	.	.	.	.	.	.	.	.	II	.	.	.	.	.	.
08)	.	.	.	.	.	.	V	.	+	.	.	.	.	.	.	.	.	.	.	.	.	.	.	.	.	.	.	.	+	II	V	.	.	.	.	.	.
09)	.	.	.	.	.	.	III	II	.	.	.	.	.	.	.	.	.	.	.	.	II	II	.	.	.	.	.	.	.	.	.	.	.	.	.	.	.
10)	.	.	.	.	.	.	+	V	II	.	.	+	.	.	.	.	.	.	.	.	II	II	.	.	+	.	.	.	.	V	V	.	IV	.	.	.	II
11)	+	.	.	.	.	.	+	II	I	.	.	II	.	.	.	.	+	.	.	II	IV	III	II	III	II	II	II	V	III	IV	II	V	V	III	II	.	V
12)	.	.	.	.	.	.	+	II	IV	II	.	.	.	.	.	.	+	.	.	I	V	III	.	.	I	.	.	.	V	II	V	.	.	.	.	.	.
13)	.	.	.	+	.	.	+	I	III	IV	.	IV	.	.	.	.	.	.	.	I	V	V	II	.	V	III	.	+	II	.	.	.	.	.	.	.	.
14)	.	.	.	+	.	.	III	+	+	+	.	V	.	.	.	.	.	.	.	I	I	.	.	.	+	.	.	.	+	I	I	.	.	.	.	.	.
15)	.	.	.	IV	.	.	III	V	II	.	II	+	.	.	.	.	.	.	.	.	.	+	.	.	.	.	.	.	.	I	III	+	.	.	.	.	.
16)	.	.	.	II	.	.	II	IV	V	III	II	III	+	.	.	.	.	+	.	V	III	V	II	.	IV	V	.	III	.	III	III	V	V	II	.	.	IV
17)	II	+	V	.	.	.	.	III	+	+	+	IV	I	.	II	II	III	III	IV	V	V	V	III	.	V	.	IV	II	II	II	III	V	IV	V	+	.	III
18)	.	.	.	.	.	.	.	V	+	.	.	.	.	.	.	.	.	.	.	.	.	.	.	.	.	.	.	.	.	.	.	.	.	.	.	.	.
19)	.	.	.	.	.	.	.	V	.	.	.	.	.	.	.	.	.	.	.	.	.	.	.	.	.	.	.	.	.	.	.	.	.	.	.	.	.
20)	.	.	.	.	.	.	.	I	.	.	.	.	.	.	.	.	.	.	.	.	.	.	.	.	.	.	.	.	.	.	.	.	.	.	.	.	.
21)	.	.	.	.	.	.	.	I	.	.	.	.	.	.	.	.	.	.	.	.	.	.	.	+	.	.	.	.	.	.	+	.	.	.	.	.	.
22)	.	.	.	.	.	.	.	II	.	.	.	.	.	.	.	.	.	.	.	.	.	.	.	.	.	.	.	.	.	.	.	.	.	.	.	.	.
23)	.	.	.	.	.	.	.	II	II	.	.	.	.	.	.	.	.	.	.	.	.	.	.	.	.	.	.	.	.	.	.	.	.	.	.	.	.
24)	.	.	.	.	.	.	.	I	III	.	.	.	.	.	.	.	.	.	.	.	.	.	.	.	.	.	.	.	.	.	.	.	.	.	.	.	.
25)	.	.	.	.	.	.	.	+	+	.	.	.	.	.	.	.	.	.	.	.	.	.	.	.	.	.	.	.	.	.	.	.	.	.	.	.	+
26)	.	.	.	.	.	.	.	I	I	V	.	.	.	.	.	.	.	.	.	.	.	.	.	.	I	.	.	.	.	+	.	.	.	.	.	.	.
27)	.	.	.	.	.	+	.	II	V	II	.	.	.	.	.	.	.	.	.	.	.	.	.	.	.	.	.	.	.	.	.	.	.	.	.	.	.
28)	.	.	.	.	.	.	.	II	III	II	.	.	.	.	.	.	.	.	.	.	.	.	.	.	.	.	.	.	+	+	.	.	.	.	.	.	.
29)	.	.	.	.	.	.	.	+	+	III	.	.	.	.	.	.	.	.	.	.	.	+	.	.	.	.	.	.	II	II	.	.	.	.	.	.	II
30)	.	.	.	.	.	.	.	III	V	II	.	.	.	.	.	.	.	.	.	.	.	+	.	.	.	.	.	.	.	+	.	.	.	.	.	.	.

TABLE 4.57 *continued*

Community Number	1 *Hedwigia ciliata–Parmelia saxatilis*	2 *Koenigia islandica* scree community	3 *Asplenium trichomanes–Fissidens cristatus*	4 *Puccinellia maritima–Ascophyllum nodosum*	5 *Puccinellia maritima–Festuca rubra*	6 *Juncus gerardii–Carex extensa*	7 *Armeria maritima–Grimmia maritima*	8 *Asplenium marinum–Grimmia maritima*	9 *Atriplex glabriuscula–Rumex crispus*	10 Brackish water communities	11 *Phragmites communis–Equisetum fluviatile*	12 *Schoenoplectus lacustris–Equisetum fluviatile*	13 *Carex rostrata–Menyanthes trifoliata*	14 *Littorella uniflora–Lobelia dortmanna*	15 *Potamogeton natans–Nymphaea alba nodum*	16 *Eriophorum angustifolium–Sphagnum cuspidatum*	17 *Carex lasiocarpa–Menyanthes trifoliata*	18 *Trichophorum cespitosum–Carex panicea*	19 *Molinia caerulea–Myrica gale*	20 *Sphagneto–Juncetum effusi*	21 *Carex–Sphagnum recurvum nodum*	22 *Carex rostrata–Aulacomnium palustre*	23 *Carex rostrata–Scorpidium scorpioides*	24 *Carex panicea–Campylium stellatum*	25 *Eriophorum latifolium–Carex hostiana*	26 *Schoenus nigricans*	27 *Carex–Saxifraga aizoides nodum*	28 *Trichophoreto–Callunetum*
Holcus lanatus (331)	.	.	.	.	.	.	.	.	II	.	.	.	.	.	.	.	.	.	.	.	.	III	.	.	.	.	.	.
Ranunculus repens (332)	.	.	.	.	.	.	.	.	.	.	.	.	.	.	.	.	.	.	.	.	.	.	.	.	.	.	.	.
Euphrasia brevipila (333)	.	.	.	.	.	.	.	.	.	.	.	.	.	.	.	.	.	.	.	.	.	.	.	.	.	.	.	.
Rhytidiadelphus squarrosus (334)	.	.	.	.	.	.	.	.	.	.	.	.	.	.	.	.	.	.	.	IV	.	II	.	.	.	.	.	.
Pseudoscleropodium purum (335)	.	.	.	.	.	.	.	.	.	.	.	.	.	.	.	.	.	.	.	+	.	.	.	.	+	.	.	.
Lathyrus montanus (336)	.	.	.	.	.	.	.	.	.	.	.	.	.	.	.	.	.	.	.	.	.	.	.	.	.	.	.	.
Luzula campestris (337)	.	.	.	.	.	.	.	.	.	.	.	.	.	.	.	.	.	.	.	III	.	.	.	.	.	.	.	.
Cerastium holosteoides (338)	.	III	.	.	.	.	.	.	.	.	.	.	.	.	.	.	.	.	.	.	.	.	.	.	.	.	.	.
Trifolium repens (339)	.	.	.	.	.	.	.	.	.	.	.	.	.	.	.	.	.	.	.	.	.	.	.	.	.	.	.	.
Plantago lanceolata (340)	.	.	.	.	II	.	.	.	.	.	.	.	.	.	.	.	.	.	.	.	.	.	.	.	.	.	.	.
Prunella vulgaris (341)	.	.	+	.	.	.	.	.	.	.	.	.	.	.	.	.	.	.	.	.	.	.	.	+	+	.	.	.
Bellis perennis (342)	.	.	+	.	.	.	.	.	.	.	.	.	.	.	.	.	.	.	.	.	.	.	.	.	.	.	.	.
Cynosurus cristatus (343)	.	.	.	.	.	.	.	.	.	.	.	.	.	.	.	.	.	.	.	.	.	.	.	+	.	.	.	.
Carex ovalis (344)	.	.	.	.	.	.	.	.	.	.	.	.	.	.	.	.	.	.	.	+	.	.	.	.	.	.	.	.
Taraxacum officinale agg. (345)	.	.	.	.	.	.	.	.	.	.	.	.	.	.	.	.	.	.	.	.	.	.	.	II	.	.	.	.
Ceratodon purpureus (346)	.	.	.	.	.	.	.	.	.	.	.	.	.	.	.	.	.	.	.	.	.	.	.	.	.	.	.	.
Poa annua (347)	.	.	.	.	.	.	.	.	.	.	.	.	.	.	.	.	.	.	.	.	.	.	.	.	.	.	.	.
Plantago major (348)	.	.	.	.	.	.	.	.	+	.	.	.	.	.	.	.	.	.	.	.	.	.	.	.	.	.	.	.
Lolium perenne (349)	.	.	.	.	.	.	.	.	+	.	.	.	.	.	.	.	.	.	.	.	.	.	.	.	.	.	.	.
Achillea millefolium (350)	.	.	.	.	.	.	.	.	.	.	.	.	.	.	.	.	.	.	.	.	.	.	.	.	.	.	.	.
Brachythecium rutabulum (351)	.	.	.	.	.	.	.	.	.	.	.	.	.	.	.	.	.	.	.	.	.	.	.	.	.	.	.	.
Equisetum sylvaticum (352)	.	.	.	.	.	.	.	.	.	.	.	.	.	.	.	.	.	.	.	.	.	.	.	.	.	.	.	.
Cirsium vulgare (353)	.	.	.	.	.	.	.	.	.	.	.	.	.	.	.	.	.	.	.	.	.	.	.	.	.	.	.	.
Anthriscus sylvestris (354)	.	.	.	.	.	.	.	.	.	.	.	.	.	.	.	.	.	.	.	.	.	.	.	.	.	.	.	.
Veronica chamaedrys (355)	.	.	.	.	.	.	.	.	.	.	.	.	.	.	.	.	.	.	.	.	.	.	.	.	.	.	.	.
Hypochoeris radicata (356)	.	.	.	.	.	.	.	.	.	.	.	.	.	.	.	.	.	.	.	.	.	.	.	.	.	.	.	.
Chrysanthemum leucanthemum (357)	.	.	.	.	.	.	.	.	.	.	.	.	.	.	.	.	.	.	.	.	.	.	.	.	.	.	.	.
Senecio jacobea (358)	.	.	.	.	.	.	.	.	+	.	.	.	.	.	.	.	.	.	.	.	.	.	.	.	.	.	.	.
Poa pratensis (359)	.	.	.	.	.	.	.	.	.	.	.	.	.	.	.	.	.	.	.	.	.	.	.	.	.	.	.	.
Centaurea nigra (360)	.	.	.	.	.	.	.	.	.	.	.	.	.	.	.	.	.	.	.	.	.	.	.	.	.	.	.	.
Heracleum sphondylium (361)	.	.	.	.	.	.	.	.	.	.	.	.	.	.	.	.	.	.	.	.	.	.	.	.	.	.	.	.
Senecio vulgaris (362)	.	.	.	.	+	.	.	.	.	.	.	.	.	.	.	.	.	.	.	.	.	.	.	.	.	.	.	.
Silene maritima (363)	.	.	.	.	.	.	.	.	+	.	.	.	.	.	.	.	.	.	.	.	.	.	.	.	.	.	.	.
Agrostis stolonifera (364)	.	.	.	.	.	V	I	+	III	V	.	.	.	.	.	.	+	.	.	.	.	.	.	.	.	.	.	.
Plantago maritima (365)	.	.	.	V	V	V	V	III	II	II	.	.	.	.	.	.	.	.	.	.	.	.	.	.	+	.	II	.
Viola riviniana (366)	.	II	II	.	.	.	.	.	.	.	.	.	.	.	.	.	.	.	.	.	.	.	.	+	.	.	+	.
Thymus drucei (367)	.	V	.	.	.	.	II	.	.	.	.	.	.	.	.	.	.	.	.	.	.	.	.	.	.	.	III	.
Calluna vulgaris (368)	.	.	.	.	.	.	.	.	.	.	.	.	.	.	.	.	.	IV	IV	.	+	.	.	+	II	I	.	V
Hieraceum pilosella (369)	.	.	.	.	.	.	.	.	.	.	.	.	.	.	.	.	.	.	.	.	.	.	.	.	.	.	.	.
Sieglingia decumbens (370)	.	.	.	.	.	.	.	.	.	.	.	.	.	.	.	.	.	.	.	.	.	.	.	.	.	.	.	.
Linum catharticum (371)	.	.	III	.	.	.	.	.	.	.	.	.	.	.	.	.	.	.	.	.	.	.	.	.	+	.	.	.
Dryas octopetala (372)	.	.	.	.	.	.	.	.	.	.	.	.	.	.	.	.	.	.	.	.	.	.	.	.	.	.	+	.
Euphrasia confusa (373)	.	.	.	.	.	.	.	.	.	.	.	.	.	.	.	.	.	.	.	.	.	.	.	.	.	.	.	.
Polygala vulgaris (374)	.	.	.	.	.	.	.	.	.	.	.	.	.	.	.	.	.	.	.	.	.	.	.	.	.	.	.	.
Hypnum cupressiforme var. *tectorum* (375)	.	.	.	.	.	.	.	.	.	.	.	.	.	.	.	.	.	.	.	.	.	.	.	.	.	.	.	.
Ditrichum flexicaule (376)	.	.	+	.	.	.	.	.	.	.	.	.	.	.	.	.	.	.	.	.	.	.	.	.	.	.	.	.
Neckera crispa (377)	.	.	I	.	.	.	.	.	.	.	.	.	.	.	.	.	.	.	.	.	.	.	.	.	.	.	.	.
Agrostis canina (378)	.	V	.	.	.	.	.	.	.	.	.	.	.	.	.	.	.	.	.	II	.	II	.	.	.	.	.	I
Festuca ovina (379)	.	.	V	.	.	.	.	.	.	.	.	.	.	.	.	.	.	.	.	II	.	.	.	.	III	.	III	.
Rhacomitrium lanuginosum (380)	+	II	.	.	.	.	.	.	.	.	.	.	.	.	.	.	.	II	+	.	.	.	.	.	.	.	.	IV
Vaccinium myrtillus (381)	.	.	.	.	.	.	.	.	.	.	.	.	.	.	.	.	.	+	.	.	.	.	.	.	.	.	.	II
Galium saxatile (382)	.	II	.	.	.	.	.	.	.	.	.	.	.	.	.	.	.	.	II	V	.	+	.	.	.	.	.	.
Hypnum cupressiforme var. *ericetorum* (383)	.	.	.	.	.	.	.	.	.	.	.	.	.	.	.	.	.	II	+	.	.	.	.	.	.	.	.	II
Lycopodium selago (384)	.	.	.	.	.	.	.	.	.	.	.	.	.	.	.	.	.	.	+	.	.	.	.	.	.	.	.	I
Nardus stricta (385)	.	.	.	.	.	.	.	.	.	.	.	.	.	.	.	.	.	.	.	.	+	.	.	.	.	.	.	.

TABLE 4.57 *continued*

	29 *Molinieto–Callunetum*	30 *Trichophoreto–Eriophoretum*	31 *Calluneto–Eriophoretum*	32 *Philonoto–Saxifragetum stellaris*	33 *Koenigia islandica–Carex demissa nodum*	34 *Cratoneuron commutatum–Saxifraga aizoides nodum*	35 *Saxifragetum aizoidis*	36 *Juncus acutiflorus–Filipendula ulmaria*	37 *Centaureo–Cynosuretum*	38 *Maritime grassland nodum*	39 *Lolium perenne–Plantago lanceolata*	40 *Dryas octopetala–Carex flacca*	41 *Cariceto–Rhacomitretum lanuginosi*	42 *Festuca ovina–Luzula spicata nodum*	43 *Rhacomitreto–Callunetum*	44 *Juniperus nana nodum*	45 *Rhacomitreto–Empetretum*	46 *Alchemilla alpina–Vaccinium myrtillus nodum*	47 *Nardus stricta–Vaccinium myrtillus*	48 *Agrosto–Festucetum* (species-poor)	49 *Alchemilleto–Agrosto–Festucetum*	50 *Agrosto–Festucetum* (species-rich)	51 *Nardo–Juncetum squarrosi*	52 *Callunetum vulgaris*	53 *Calluna vulgaris–Sieglingia decumbens*	54 *Calluna vulgaris–Arctostaphylos uva-ursi nodum*	55 *Vaccineto–Callunetum hepaticosum*	56 *Luzula sylvatica–Vaccinium myrtillus*	57 *Luzula sylvatica–Silene dioica*	58 *Betula pubescens–Cirsium heterophyllum*	59 *Sedum rosea–Alchemilla glabra*	60 *Betula pubescens–Vaccinium myrtillus*	61 *Corylus avellana–Oxalis acetosella*	62 *Oxalis acetosella–Rhytidiadelphus loreus*	63 *Hymenophyllum wilsonii–Isothecium myosuroides*	64 Open boulder association	65 *Fraxinus excelsior–Brachypodium sylvaticum*
331)	.	.	.	.	.	.	.	V	V	V	.	.	.	.	.	.	.	.	.	I	II	I	.	.	II	I	.	III	.	I	II	I	II	.	.	.	.
332)	.	.	.	.	.	.	.	V	V	.	IV	.	.	.	.	.	.	.	.	.	.	.	.	.	.	.	.	.	.	.	.	.	.	.	.	.	.
333)	.	.	.	.	.	.	.	III	IV	III	II	.	.	.	.	.	.	.	.	.	.	.	.	.	.	.	.	.	.	.	.	.	.	.	.	.	.
334)	.	.	.	+	.	.	.	V	.	.	+	+	.	.	.	.	.	.	.	III	IV	III	II	.	+	.	.	.	II	.	.	I	I	.	.	.	+
335)	.	.	.	.	.	.	.	II	.	+	+	III	.	.	.	.	.	.	.	I	I	V	+	+	II	II	.	.	III	II	I	+	.	+	.	.	+
336)	.	.	.	.	.	.	.	I	IV	II	.	+	.	.	.	.	.	.	.	.	.	.	.	.	III	III	.	.	II	I	I	.	.	.	.	.	+
337)	.	.	.	.	.	.	.	III	III	+	.	II	+	.	.	.	.	.	+	II	III	I	+	.	III	.	.	.	.	.	.	I	II	.	.	.	.
338)	.	.	.	IV	.	.	.	II	V	+	III	I	+	.	.	.	.	.	.	.	I	IV	+	.	I	.	.	.	.	.	.	.	.	.	.	.	.
339)	.	.	.	+	.	.	.	II	V	II	IV	I	.	.	.	.	.	.	.	II	I	II	.	.	II	II	.	.	.	.	.	.	.	.	.	.	.
340)	.	.	.	.	.	.	.	I	III	V	IV	III	.	.	.	.	.	.	.	II	II	IV	.	.	IV	II	.	.	II	.	II	.	.	.	.	.	.
341)	.	.	.	II	.	.	.	IV	II	IV	III	II	.	.	.	.	.	.	.	I	IV	V	.	.	IV	II	.	.	II	I	I	+	.	.	.	.	II
342)	.	.	.	II	.	.	.	I	V	II	V	III	.	.	.	.	.	.	.	.	I	IV	.	.	I	.	.	.	.	+	.	.	.	.	.	.	II
343)	.	.	.	.	.	.	.	III	II	III	II	II	.	.	.	.	.	.	.	.	.	III	.	.	.	.	.	.	.	.	.	.	.	.	.	.	.
344)	.	.	.	.	.	.	.	+	.	.	II	.	.	.	.	.	.	.	.	I	.	I	.	.	.	.	.	.	.	.	.	.	.	.	.	.	.
345)	.	.	.	II	.	.	.	+	.	.	II	+	.	.	.	.	.	.	.	.	+	.	+	.	I	II	.	.	.	.	.	.	.	.	.	.	.
346)	.	.	.	.	.	.	.	.	.	.	III	.	.	.	.	.	.	.	.	.	.	.	.	.	.	.	.	.	.	.	.	.	.	.	.	.	.
347)	.	.	.	.	.	.	.	.	.	.	IV	.	.	.	.	.	.	.	.	.	.	.	.	.	.	.	.	.	.	.	.	.	.	.	.	.	.
348)	.	.	.	.	.	.	.	.	.	.	V	.	.	.	.	.	.	.	.	.	.	.	.	.	.	.	.	.	.	.	.	.	.	.	.	.	.
349)	.	.	.	.	.	.	.	.	I	.	V	.	.	.	.	.	.	.	.	.	.	.	.	.	.	.	.	.	.	.	.	.	.	.	.	.	.
350)	.	.	.	.	.	.	.	.	III	.	II	.	.	.	.	.	.	.	.	I	II	.	.	.	I	.	.	.	.	.	.	.	.	.	.	.	.
351)	.	.	.	.	.	.	.	.	+	.	II	.	.	.	.	.	.	.	.	.	.	.	.	.	.	.	.	.	.	.	.	.	.	.	.	.	.
352)	.	.	.	.	.	.	.	.	+	.	.	.	.	.	.	.	.	.	.	.	.	.	.	.	.	.	.	.	.	.	.	.	.	.	.	.	.
353)	.	.	.	.	.	.	.	.	I	.	.	.	.	.	.	.	.	.	.	.	+	.	.	.	.	.	.	.	.	.	.	.	.	.	.	.	.
354)	.	.	.	.	.	.	.	.	II	.	.	.	.	.	.	.	.	.	.	.	.	.	.	.	.	.	.	.	.	.	.	.	.	.	.	.	.
355)	.	.	.	.	.	.	.	.	III	.	.	.	.	.	.	.	.	.	.	.	.	.	.	.	.	.	.	.	.	.	.	.	II	.	.	.	+
356)	.	.	.	.	.	.	.	.	IV	.	.	.	.	.	.	.	.	.	.	.	.	.	.	.	.	.	.	.	.	.	.	.	.	.	.	.	.
357)	.	.	.	.	.	.	.	.	V	.	.	.	.	.	.	.	.	.	.	.	.	.	.	.	.	.	.	.	.	.	.	.	.	.	.	.	.
358)	.	.	.	.	.	.	.	.	V	.	.	.	.	.	.	.	.	.	.	.	.	.	.	.	.	.	.	.	.	.	.	.	.	.	.	.	+
359)	.	.	.	.	.	.	.	.	IV	+	.	.	.	.	.	.	.	.	.	.	I	II	.	.	.	.	.	.	.	II	I	.	.	.	.	.	.
360)	.	.	.	.	.	.	.	.	V	+	.	I	.	.	.	.	.	.	.	.	.	.	.	.	.	.	.	.	II	I	I	.	.	.	.	.	.
361)	.	.	.	.	.	.	.	.	III	II	.	.	.	.	.	.	.	.	.	.	.	.	.	.	.	.	.	.	+	II	I	.	.	.	.	.	II
362)	.	.	.	.	.	.	.	.	.	III	.	.	.	.	.	.	.	.	.	.	.	.	.	.	+	.	.	.	.	.	.	.	.	.	.	.	.
363)	.	.	.	.	.	.	.	.	.	II	.	.	.	.	.	.	.	.	.	.	.	II	.	.	.	.	.	.	.	.	.	.	.	.	.	.	.
364)	.	.	.	.	.	.	.	.	.	V	II	.	.	.	.	.	.	.	.	.	.	.	.	.	.	+	.	.	.	.	.	.	.	.	.	.	.
365)	.	.	.	.	.	.	.	.	.	V	+	IV	I	II	.	.	I	II	.	.	.	II	.	.	II	.	.	.	II	.	.	.	.	.	.	.	.
366)	.	.	.	+	.	.	+	.	.	III	+	IV	IV	II	.	+	III	II	+	II	V	V	III	II	III	IV	I	III	IV	II	I	II	V	.	.	.	V
367)	.	.	.	+	.	II	I	.	.	II	II	V	IV	IV	II	III	III	.	I	II	V	V	II	.	III	III		+	III	I	III	.	.	.	.	.	.
368)	V	V	V	.	.	.	.	.	.	III	.	III	.	.	V	IV	+	.	III	IV	I	III	III	V	V	V	V	III	V	I	I	V	II	+	.	.	.
369)	.	.	.	.	.	.	.	.	.	+	+	V	.	.	.	.	.	.	.	.	II	III	.	.	I	.	.	.	.	.	.	.	.	.	.	.	.
370)	.	.	.	.	.	.	.	.	.	III	.	III	.	.	.	.	.	.	.	.	.	+	.	.	V	IV	.	.	+	.	.	.	.	.	.	.	.
371)	.	.	.	.	.	+	I	.	.	II	.	IV	.	.	.	.	.	.	.	.	.	I	.	+	II	II	.	.	.	.	+	.	.	.	.	.	.
372)	.	.	.	.	.	.	.	.	.	.	.	V	.	.	.	.	.	.	.	.	.	.	.	.	.	.	.	.	.	.	.	.	.	.	.	.	.
373)	.	.	.	.	.	.	.	.	.	.	.	III	.	.	.	.	.	.	.	.	.	.	.	.	.	.	.	.	.	.	.	.	.	.	.	.	.
374)	.	.	.	.	.	.	.	.	.	.	.	III	.	.	.	.	.	.	.	.	.	.	.	.	.	.	.	.	.	.	.	.	.	.	.	.	.
375)	.	.	.	.	.	.	.	.	.	.	.	III	.	.	.	.	.	.	.	.	I	II	.	.	.	.	.	.	.	.	+	.	.	.	.	.	.
376)	.	.	.	.	.	.	II	.	.	.	.	III	.	.	.	.	.	.	.	.	I	I	.	.	.	.	.	.	.	I	I	.	.	.	.	.	.
377)	.	.	.	.	.	.	+	.	.	.	.	II	.	.	.	.	.	.	.	.	.	.	.	.	.	.	.	.	+	I	I	.	.	.	.	.	.
378)	.	.	.	+	.	.	.	II	.	.	.	I	I	II	IV	.	.	.	.	V	I	I	.	II	V	V	.	III	.	.	.	.	II	.	.	.	.
379)	.	.	.	II	.	.	II	.	.	.	.	III	IV	V	III	.	II	V	I	V	V	V	+	II	V	IV	.	II	V	I	III	.	.	.	.	.	.
380)	IV	IV	IV	.	.	.	.	.	.	.	.	II	V	V	V	V	V	V	V	II	IV	IV	IV	II	I	II	V	III	.	.	III	.	.	.	.	.	.
381)	.	.	III	.	.	.	.	.	.	.	.	+	V	II	II	V	V	V	V	II	III	I	III	+	+	.	V	V	.	.	+	V	I	III	.	.	.
382)	.	+	.	.	.	.	.	I	II	+	.	.	V	IV	II	II	V	II	V	V	IV	II	V	III	II	II	III	IV	II	.	II	V	V	II	+	.	II
383)	II	II	.	.	.	.	.	.	.	II	.	.	I	.	III	V	II	III	+	III	.	I	.	V	III	II	V	IV	+	.	.	+	III	II	II	.	.
384)	+	+	.	.	.	.	.	.	.	.	.	.	III	.	III	IV	IV	IV	V	.	+	.	II	+	.	.	.	+	.	.	.	.	.	.	.	.	.
385)	.	I	.	.	.	.	.	.	.	.	.	.	II	.	II	II	+	.	V	I	.	I	V	.	+	.	.	.	.	.	.	.	.	.	.	.	.

TABLE 4.57 *continued*

Community Number	1 *Hedwigia ciliata–Parmelia saxatilis*	2 *Koenigia islandica* scree community	3 *Asplenium trichomanes–Fissidens cristatus*	4 *Puccinellia maritima–Ascophyllum nodosum*	5 *Puccinellia maritima–Festuca rubra*	6 *Juncus gerardii–Carex extensa*	7 *Armeria maritima–Grimmia maritima*	8 *Asplenium marinum–Grimmia maritima*	9 *Atriplex glabriuscula–Rumex crispus*	10 Brackish water communities	11 *Phragmites communis–Equisetum fluviatile*	12 *Schoenoplectus lacustris–Equisetum fluviatile*	13 *Carex rostrata–Menyanthes trifoliata*	14 *Littorella uniflora–Lobelia dortmanna*	15 *Potamogeton natans–Nymphaea alba nodum*	16 *Eriophorum angustifolium–Sphagnum cuspidatum*	17 *Carex lasiocarpa–Menyanthes trifoliata*	18 *Trichophorum cespitosum–Carex panicea*	19 *Molinia caerulea–Myrica gale*	20 *Sphagneto–Juncetum effusi*	21 *Carex–Sphagnum recurvum nodum*	22 *Carex rostrata–Aulacomnium palustre*	23 *Carex rostrata–Scorpidium scorpioides*	24 *Carex panicea–Campylium stellatum*	25 *Eriophorum latifolium–Carex hostiana*	26 *Schoenus nigricans*	27 *Carex–Saxifraga aizoides nodum*	28 *Trichophoreto–Callunetum*
Alchemilla alpina (386)	.	V	.	.	.	.	.	.	.	.	.	.	.	.	.	.	.	.	.	.	.	.	.	.	.	.	.	.
Deschampsia flexuosa (387)	.	.	.	.	.	.	.	.	.	.	.	.	.	.	.	.	.	II	III	III	II	+	.	.	.	.	.	+
Cladonia uncialis (388)	.	.	.	.	.	.	.	.	.	.	.	.	.	.	.	.	.	.	.	.	.	.	.	.	.	.	.	III
Empetrum hermaphroditum (389)	.	.	.	.	.	.	.	.	.	.	.	.	.	.	.	.	.	.	.	.	.	.	.	.	.	.	.	.
Polytrichum alpinum (390)	.	.	.	.	.	.	.	.	.	.	.	.	.	.	.	.	.	.	.	.	.	.	.	.	.	.	.	.
Vaccinium vitis-idaea (391)	.	.	.	.	.	.	.	.	.	.	.	.	.	.	.	.	.	.	.	.	.	.	.	.	.	.	.	+
Salix herbacea (392)	.	.	.	.	.	.	.	.	.	.	.	.	.	.	.	.	.	.	.	.	.	.	.	.	.	.	.	.
Polytrichum piliferum (393)	.	.	.	.	.	.	.	.	.	.	.	.	.	.	.	.	.	.	.	.	.	.	.	.	.	.	.	.
Diplophyllum albicans (394)	.	.	.	.	.	.	.	.	.	.	.	.	.	.	.	.	.	.	.	.	.	.	.	.	.	.	.	II
Carex bigelowii (395)	.	.	.	.	.	.	.	.	.	.	.	.	.	.	.	.	.	.	.	.	.	.	.	.	.	.	.	.
Cladonia rangiferina (396)	.	.	.	.	.	.	.	.	.	.	.	.	.	.	.	.	.	.	.	.	.	.	.	.	.	.	.	.
Rhacomitrium heterostichum (397)	V	.	.	.	.	.	.	.	.	.	.	.	.	.	.	.	.	.	.	.	.	.	.	.	.	.	.	.
Sphaerophorus globosus (398)	.	.	.	.	.	.	.	.	.	.	.	.	.	.	.	.	.	.	.	.	.	.	.	.	.	.	.	.
Nardia salaris (399)	.	II	.	.	.	.	.	.	.	.	.	.	.	.	.	.	.	.	.	.	.	.	.	.	.	.	.	.
Cetraria islandica (400)	.	.	.	.	.	.	.	.	.	.	.	.	.	.	.	.	.	.	.	.	.	.	.	.	.	.	.	.
Gnaphalium supinum (401)	.	.	.	.	.	.	.	.	.	.	.	.	.	.	.	.	.	.	.	.	.	.	.	.	.	.	.	.
Cherleria sedoides (402)	.	II	.	.	.	.	.	.	.	.	.	.	.	.	.	.	.	.	.	.	.	.	.	.	.	.	.	.
Silene acaulis (403)	.	III	.	.	.	.	.	.	.	.	.	.	.	.	.	.	.	.	.	.	.	.	.	.	.	.	.	.
Andreaea alpina (404)	.	.	.	.	.	.	.	.	.	.	.	.	.	.	.	.	.	.	.	.	.	.	.	.	.	.	.	.
Polygonum viviparum (405)	.	.	.	.	.	.	.	.	.	.	.	.	.	.	.	.	.	.	.	.	.	.	.	.	.	.	.	.
Luzula spicata (406)	.	III	.	.	.	.	.	.	.	.	.	.	.	.	.	.	.	.	.	.	.	.	.	.	.	.	.	.
Oligotrichum hercynicum (407)	.	V	.	.	.	.	.	.	.	.	.	.	.	.	.	.	.	.	.	.	.	.	.	.	.	.	.	.
Cornicularia aculeata (408)	.	.	.	.	.	.	.	.	.	.	.	.	.	.	.	.	.	.	.	.	.	.	.	.	.	.	.	.
Cladonia subcervicornis (409)	II	.	.	.	.	.	.	.	.	.	.	.	.	.	.	.	.	.	.	.	.	.	.	.	.	.	.	.
Gymnomitrion crenulatum (410)	+	.	.	.	.	.	.	.	.	.	.	.	.	.	.	.	.	.	.	.	.	.	.	.	.	.	.	.
Carex pilulifera (411)	.	.	.	.	.	.	.	.	.	.	.	.	.	.	.	.	.	.	.	.	.	.	.	.	.	.	.	.
Cladonia arbuscula (412)	.	.	.	.	.	.	.	.	.	.	.	.	.	.	.	.	.	.	.	.	.	.	.	.	.	.	.	II
Campylopus atrovirens (413)	.	.	.	.	.	.	.	.	.	.	.	.	.	.	.	.	.	III	.	.	.	.	.	.	.	.	.	III
Lycopodium alpinum (414)	.	.	.	.	.	.	.	.	.	.	.	.	.	.	.	.	.	.	.	.	.	.	.	.	.	.	.	.
Anthelia julacea (415)	.	.	.	.	.	.	.	.	.	.	.	.	.	.	.	.	.	.	.	.	.	.	.	.	.	.	+	.
Pleurozia purpurea (416)	.	.	.	.	.	.	.	.	.	.	.	.	.	.	.	.	.	II	.	.	II	.	.	.	.	.	.	II
Juniperus communis ssp. *nana* (417)	.	.	.	.	.	.	.	.	.	.	.	.	.	.	.	.	.	.	.	.	.	.	.	.	.	.	.	.
Tetraplodon mnioides (418)	.	.	.	.	.	.	.	.	.	.	.	.	.	.	.	.	.	.	.	.	+	.	.	.	.	.	.	+
Pohlia nutans (419)	.	.	.	.	.	.	.	.	.	.	.	.	.	.	.	.	.	.	.	.	.	.	.	.	.	.	.	+
Plagiochila carringtonii (420)	.	.	.	.	.	.	.	.	.	.	.	.	.	.	.	.	.	.	.	.	.	.	.	.	.	.	.	.
Dicranum fuscescens (421)	.	.	.	.	.	.	.	.	.	.	.	.	.	.	.	.	.	.	.	.	.	.	.	.	.	.	.	.
Ptilidium ciliare (422)	.	.	.	.	.	.	.	.	.	.	.	.	.	.	.	.	.	.	.	.	.	.	.	.	.	.	.	.
Blechnum spicant (423)	.	.	.	.	.	.	.	.	.	.	.	.	.	.	.	.	.	.	II	.	.	.	.	.	.	.	.	.
Breutelia chrysocoma (424)	.	.	+	.	.	.	.	.	.	.	.	.	.	.	.	.	.	III	II	.	+	.	+	V	II	I	.	III
Agrostis tenuis (425)	.	.	.	.	.	.	.	.	.	.	.	.	.	.	.	.	.	.	.	.	.	.	.	.	.	.	.	.
Veronica serpyllifolia (426)	.	.	.	.	.	.	.	.	.	.	.	.	.	.	.	.	.	.	.	.	.	.	.	.	.	.	.	.
Euphrasia officinalis agg. (427)	.	.	.	.	II	.	.	+	.	.	.	.	.	.	.	.	.	.	.	.	.	.	.	.	.	.	.	.
Alchemilla vestita (428)	.	.	.	.	.	.	.	.	.	.	.	.	.	.	.	.	.	.	.	.	.	.	.	.	.	.	.	.
Oxalis acetosella (429)	.	.	III	.	.	.	.	.	.	.	.	.	.	.	.	.	.	.	.	.	.	.	.	.	.	.	.	.
Fragaria vesca (430)	.	.	I	.	.	.	.	.	.	.	.	.	.	.	.	.	.	.	.	.	.	.	.	.	.	.	.	.
Peltigera apthosa (431)	.	.	.	.	.	.	.	.	.	.	.	.	.	.	.	.	.	.	.	.	.	.	.	.	.	.	.	.
Alchemilla xanthochlora (432)	.	.	.	.	.	.	.	.	.	.	.	.	.	.	.	.	.	.	.	.	.	.	.	.	.	.	.	.
Galium boreale (433)	.	.	.	.	.	.	.	.	.	.	.	.	.	.	.	.	.	.	.	.	.	.	.	.	.	.	.	.
Anthyllis vulneraria (434)	.	.	.	.	.	.	.	.	.	.	.	.	.	.	.	.	.	.	.	.	.	.	.	.	.	.	.	.
Frullania tamarisci (435)	III	.	I	.	.	.	.	.	.	.	.	.	.	.	.	.	.	.	.	.	.	.	.	.	.	.	.	.
Carex binervis (436)	.	.	.	.	.	.	.	.	.	.	.	.	.	.	.	.	.	.	.	.	.	.	.	.	.	.	.	.
Euphrasia micrantha (437)	.	.	.	.	.	.	.	.	.	.	.	.	.	.	.	.	.	.	.	.	.	.	.	.	.	.	.	.
Calypogeia muellerana (438)	.	.	.	.	.	.	.	.	.	.	.	.	.	.	.	.	.	.	.	.	.	.	.	.	.	.	.	.
Arctostaphylos uva-ursi (439)	.	.	.	.	.	.	.	.	.	.	.	.	.	.	.	.	.	.	.	.	.	.	.	.	.	.	.	.
Salix repens (440)	.	.	.	.	.	.	.	.	.	.	.	.	.	.	.	.	.	.	.	.	.	.	.	.	.	.	.	.

TABLE 4.57 *continued*

	29 *Molinieto–Callunetum*	30 *Trichophoreto–Eriophoretum*	31 *Calluneto–Eriophoretum*	32 *Philonoto–Saxifragetum stellaris*	33 *Koenigia islandica–Carex demissa nodum*	34 *Cratoneuron commutatum–Saxifraga aizoides nodum*	35 *Saxifragetum aizoidis*	36 *Juncus acutiflorus–Filipendula ulmaria*	37 *Centaureo–Cynosuretum*	38 *Maritime grassland nodum*	39 *Lolium perenne–Plantago lanceolata*	40 *Dryas octopetala–Carex flacca*	41 *Cariceto–Rhacomitretum lanuginosi*	42 *Festuca ovina–Luzula spicata nodum*	43 *Rhacomitreto–Callunetum*	44 *Juniperus nana nodum*	45 *Rhacomitreto–Empetretum*	46 *Alchemilla alpina–Vaccinium myrtillus nodum*	47 *Nardus stricta–Vaccinium myrtillus*	48 *Agrosto–Festucetum* (species-poor)	49 *Alchemilleto–Agrosto–Festucetum*	50 *Agrosto–Festucetum* (species-rich)	51 *Nardo–Juncetum squarrosi*	52 *Callunetum vulgaris*	53 *Calluna vulgaris–Sieglingia decumbens*	54 *Calluna vulgaris–Arctostaphylos uva-ursi nodum*	55 *Vaccineto–Callunetum hepaticosum*	56 *Luzula sylvatica–Vaccinium myrtillus*	57 *Luzula sylvatica–Silene dioica*	58 *Betula pubescens–Cirsium heterophyllum*	59 *Sedum rosea–Alchemilla glabra*	60 *Betula pubescens–Vaccinium myrtillus*	61 *Corylus avellana–Oxalis acetosella*	62 *Oxalis acetosella–Rhytidiadelphus loreus*	63 *Hymenophyllum wilsonii–Isothecium myosuroides*	64 Open boulder association	65 *Fraxinus excelsior–Brachypodium sylvaticum*
386)	.	.	.	.	.	.	III	.	.	.	.	.	V	V	I	IV	III	V	II	.	V	I	+	.	.	.	.	III	+	.	IV	.	.	.	.	.	.
387)	II	I	.	.	.	.	.	.	.	.	.	.	IV	V	+	V	III	IV	.	II	II	.	II	IV	IV	.	.	.	II	.	.	V	I	V	III	.	.
388)	III	III	II	.	.	.	.	.	.	.	.	.	V	II	V	V	V	III	V	I	.	.	II	II	.	.	+	.	.	.	.	.	.	.	.	.	.
389)	.	.	.	.	.	.	.	.	.	.	.	.	I	.	II	V	V	II	+	.	.	.	.	.	.	.	.	.	.	.	.	.	.	.	.	.	.
390)	.	.	.	.	.	.	.	.	.	.	.	.	IV	II	.	+	IV	II	IV	.	II	.	IV	.	.	.	.	.	.	.	.	.	.	.	.	.	.
391)	.	.	.	.	.	.	.	.	.	.	.	.	II	II	I	II	II	II	+	.	.	.	.	.	.	.	.	.	.	.	.	.	.	.	.	.	.
392)	.	.	.	.	.	.	.	.	.	.	.	.	IV	V	I	III	+	.	I	.	.	.	.	.	.	.	.	.	.	.	.	.	.	.	.	.	.
393)	.	.	.	.	.	.	.	.	.	.	.	.	IV	IV	III	II	.	+	+	II	.	.	.	.	.	.	.	.	.	.	.	.	.	.	.	.	.
394)	.	I	+	.	.	.	.	.	.	.	.	.	II	.	I	IV	.	V	+	.	.	III	.	.	.	II	V	.	+	.	.	I	.	I	II	V	.
395)	.	.	.	.	.	.	.	.	.	.	.	.	V	.	IV	IV	.	.	V	.	.	.	+	.	.	.	.	.	.	.	.	.	.	.	.	.	.
396)	.	.	.	.	.	.	.	.	.	.	.	.	I	.	I	III	.	.	.	.	.	.	.	.	.	.	.	.	.	.	.	.	.	.	.	.	.
397)	.	.	.	.	+	.	.	.	.	.	.	.	I	III	III	.	.	.	.	.	.	.	.	.	.	.	.	+	.	.	.	.	.	.	.	.	.
398)	.	.	.	.	.	.	.	.	.	.	.	.	+	.	V	.	.	.	.	.	.	.	.	.	.	.	.	.	.	.	.	.	.	.	.	.	.
399)	.	.	.	.	.	.	.	.	.	.	.	.	III	.	II	.	I	II	.	.	+	.	.	.	.	.	.	.	.	.	+	.	.	.	.	.	.
400)	.	.	.	.	.	.	.	.	.	.	.	.	II	.	+	.	+	.	V	.	.	.	.	.	.	.	.	.	.	.	.	.	.	.	.	.	.
401)	.	.	.	.	.	.	.	.	.	.	.	.	I	.	.	.	.	.	+	.	.	.	.	.	.	.	.	.	.	.	.	.	.	.	.	.	.
402)	.	.	.	.	.	.	.	.	.	.	.	.	II	.	.	.	.	.	.	.	.	.	.	.	.	.	.	.	.	.	.	.	.	.	.	.	.
403)	.	.	.	.	.	.	+	.	.	.	.	.	II	.	.	.	+	.	.	.	.	.	.	.	+	.	.	.	.	.	+	.	.	.	.	.	.
404)	.	.	.	.	.	.	.	.	.	.	.	.	II	IV	.	.	I	II	.	.	.	.	.	.	.	.	.	.	.	.	.	.	.	.	.	.	.
405)	.	.	.	.	.	.	.	.	.	.	.	.	II	II	.	.	.	.	+	.	.	I	.	.	.	.	.	.	.	.	.	.	.	.	.	.	.
406)	.	.	.	.	+	.	.	.	.	.	.	.	.	V	.	.	.	.	.	.	.	.	.	.	.	.	.	.	.	.	.	.	.	.	.	.	.
407)	.	.	.	.	.	.	.	.	.	.	.	.	.	V	+	.	.	+	.	.	.	.	.	.	.	.	.	.	.	.	.	.	.	.	.	.	.
408)	.	.	.	.	.	.	.	.	.	.	.	.	.	.	I	II	.	.	.	.	.	.	.	.	.	.	+	.	.	.	.	.	.	.	.	.	.
409)	.	.	.	.	.	.	.	.	.	.	.	.	.	.	I	II	.	.	.	.	.	.	.	.	.	.	.	.	.	.	.	.	.	.	.	.	.
410)	.	.	.	.	.	.	.	.	.	.	.	.	.	.	I	II	.	.	.	.	.	.	.	.	.	.	.	.	.	.	.	.	.	.	.	.	.
411)	.	.	.	.	.	.	.	.	.	+	.	.	.	.	III	II	III	.	III	II	.	.	III	.	.	.	+	.	.	.	+	.	.	.	.	.	.
412)	II	II	III	.	.	.	.	.	.	.	.	.	.	.	III	III	II	III	I	.	.	III	+	II	.	.	.	.	.	.	.	.	.	.	.	.	.
413)	III	IV	.	.	.	.	.	.	.	.	.	.	.	.	II	II	III	II	+	.	.	.	+	.	III	.	V	.	.	.	.	.	.	.	.	.	.
414)	.	.	.	.	.	.	.	.	.	.	.	.	II	.	.	III	I	II	V	.	.	.	II	.	.	.	.	.	.	.	.	.	.	.	.	.	.
415)	.	.	.	.	.	.	.	.	.	.	.	.	.	.	.	+	III	.	+	.	.	.	.	.	.	.	.	.	.	.	.	.	.	.	.	.	.
416)	IV	V	.	.	.	.	.	.	.	.	.	.	.	.	.	+	III	II	.	.	.	.	.	.	.	.	IV	.	.	.	.	.	.	.	.	.	.
417)	.	.	.	.	.	.	.	.	.	.	.	.	.	.	.	V	+	.	.	.	.	.	.	.	.	.	.	.	.	.	.	.	.	.	.	.	.
418)	.	.	.	.	.	.	.	.	.	.	.	.	.	+	.	.	II	.	.	.	.	.	.	.	.	.	.	.	.	.	.	.	.	.	.	.	.
419)	.	.	.	.	.	.	.	.	.	.	.	.	.	.	.	.	+	.	.	.	.	.	.	.	.	.	.	.	.	.	.	.	.	.	.	.	.
420)	.	.	.	.	.	.	.	.	.	.	.	.	.	.	.	.	III	.	.	.	.	.	.	.	.	.	.	.	.	.	.	.	.	.	.	.	.
421)	.	.	.	.	.	.	.	.	.	.	.	.	II	.	.	.	I	III	III	.	.	.	.	.	.	.	.	.	.	.	.	.	.	.	.	.	.
422)	.	.	.	.	.	.	.	.	.	.	.	.	.	.	.	.	I	II	II	.	I	I	+	.	.	.	.	.	.	.	.	.	.	.	.	.	.
423)	.	+	.	.	.	.	.	.	.	.	.	.	+	.	.	.	III	III	I	I	I	II	III	.	III	II	V	V	+	I	II	V	IV	I	.	.	II
424)	II	II	.	.	.	III	I	.	.	.	.	III	.	.	.	.	III	II	+	II	IV	IV	+	III	III	.	IV	II	III	I	III	I	I	I	.	.	+
425)	.	.	.	.	.	.	.	.	I	.	II	.	II	.	.	.	II	.	II	V	V	V	III	IV	.	.	II	.	II	.	.	II	.	.	.	.	V
426)	.	.	.	.	.	.	.	.	.	+	.	.	.	.	.	.	+	.	.	I	IV	I	.	.	.	.	.	.	II	I	I	I	II	.	.	.	.
427)	.	.	.	.	.	II	II	.	.	.	.	.	I	II	.	.	.	.	.	I	IV	IV	.	.	.	.	.	.	.	.	+	.	.	.	.	.	.
428)	.	.	.	.	.	.	.	.	.	.	.	.	+	.	.	.	.	.	.	.	IV	.	.	.	.	.	.	.	.	.	.	.	.	.	.	.	.
429)	.	.	.	.	.	.	.	.	.	.	.	+	.	.	.	.	.	.	.	.	V	I	.	.	.	.	I	V	+	III	I	V	V	V	+	.	V
430)	.	.	.	.	.	.	.	.	.	.	.	.	.	.	.	.	.	.	.	.	I	I	.	.	+	.	.	.	+	.	+	.	.	.	.	.	IV
431)	.	.	.	.	.	.	.	.	.	.	.	.	.	.	.	.	.	.	.	.	+	.	.	.	+	.	.	.	.	.	.	.	.	.	.	.	.
432)	.	.	.	II	.	.	.	.	+	.	.	+	.	.	.	.	.	.	.	.	III	III	.	.	II	III	.	.	.	.	+	.	.	.	.	.	.
433)	.	.	.	.	.	.	.	+	.	.	.	.	.	.	.	.	.	.	.	.	.	+	.	.	+	.	.	.	.	.	+	.	.	.	.	.	.
434)	.	.	.	.	.	.	.	.	.	+	.	.	.	.	.	.	.	.	.	.	.	+	.	.	I	.	.	.	.	.	.	.	.	.	.	.	.
435)	.	.	.	.	.	.	.	.	.	IV	.	.	.	.	.	.	.	.	.	.	III	IV	+	.	II	II	II	+	III	.	II	.	+	II	II	+	.
436)	.	.	.	.	.	.	.	.	.	II	.	.	.	.	I	II	II	.	.	II	.	IV	II	IV	III	II	IV	+	II	.	+	III	II	.	.	.	.
437)	.	.	.	.	.	.	.	.	.	.	.	.	.	III	II	.	.	.	.	.	.	.	.	+	IV	II	II	.	.	.	.	.	.	.	.	.	.
438)	.	.	+	.	.	.	.	.	.	.	.	.	.	.	.	.	.	.	.	.	.	.	+	.	.	II	.	.	.	.	+	.	.	+	.	.	.
439)	.	.	.	.	.	.	.	.	.	.	.	II	.	.	+	.	.	.	.	.	.	.	.	.	.	V	.	.	.	.	.	.	.	.	.	.	.
440)	.	.	.	.	.	.	.	.	.	+	.	.	.	.	+	.	.	.	.	.	.	.	.	.	III	II	.	.	.	.	.	.	.	.	.	.	.

TABLE 4.57 *continued*

	1 *Hedwigia ciliata–Parmelia saxatilis*	2 *Koenigia islandica* scree community	3 *Asplenium trichomanes–Fissidens cristatus*	4 *Puccinellia maritima–Ascophyllum nodosum*	5 *Puccinellia maritima–Festuca rubra*	6 *Juncus gerardii–Carex extensa*	7 *Armeria maritima–Grimmia maritima*	8 *Asplenium marinum–Grimmia maritima*	9 *Atriplex glabriuscula–Rumex crispus*	10 Brackish water communities	11 *Phragmites communis–Equisetum fluviatile*	12 *Schoenoplectus lacustris–Equisetum fluviatile*	13 *Carex rostrata–Menyanthes trifoliata*	14 *Littorella uniflora–Lobelia dortmanna*	15 *Potamogeton natans–Nymphaea alba nodum*	16 *Eriophorum angustifolium–Sphagnum cuspidatum*	17 *Carex lasiocarpa–Menyanthes trifoliata*	18 *Trichophorum cespitosum–Carex panicea*	19 *Molinia caerulea–Myrica gale*	20 *Sphagneto–Juncetum effusi*	21 *Carex–Sphagnum recurvum nodum*	22 *Carex rostrata–Aulacomnium palustre*	23 *Carex rostrata–Scorpidium scorpioides*	24 *Carex panicea–Campylium stellatum*	25 *Eriophorum latifolium–Carex hostiana*	26 *Schoenus nigricans*	27 *Carex–Saxifraga aizoides nodum*	28 *Trichophoreto–Callunetum*
Gentianella campestris (441)	.	.	.	.	.	.	.	.	.	.	.	.	.	.	.	.	.	.	.	.	.	.	.	.	.	.	.	.
Mylia taylori (442)	.	.	.	.	.	.	.	.	.	.	.	.	.	.	.	.	.	.	.	.	.	.	.	.	.	.	.	II
Frullania fragilifolia (443)	.	.	.	.	.	.	.	.	.	.	.	.	.	.	.	.	.	.	.	.	.	.	.	.	.	.	.	.
Carlina vulgaris (444)	.	.	.	.	.	.	.	.	.	.	.	.	.	.	.	.	.	.	.	.	.	.	.	.	.	.	.	.
Teucrium scorodonium (445)	.	.	.	.	.	.	.	.	.	.	.	.	.	.	.	.	.	.	.	.	.	.	.	.	.	.	.	.
Lonicera periclymenum (446)	.	.	.	.	.	.	.	.	.	.	.	.	.	.	.	.	.	.	.	.	.	.	.	.	.	.	.	.
Hookeria lucens (447)	.	.	.	.	.	.	.	.	.	.	.	.	.	.	.	.	.	.	.	.	.	.	.	.	.	.	.	.
Barbilophozia barbata (448)	.	.	.	.	.	.	.	.	.	.	.	.	.	.	.	.	.	.	.	.	.	.	.	.	.	.	.	.
Sphagnum plumulosum (449)	.	.	.	.	.	.	.	.	.	.	.	.	.	.	.	II	.	III	III	.	IV	+	III	.	I	.	.	I
Anastrepta orcadensis (450)	.	.	.	.	.	.	.	.	.	.	.	.	.	.	.	.	.	.	.	.	.	.	.	.	.	.	.	.
Sphagnum capillaceum (451)	.	.	.	.	.	.	.	.	.	.	.	.	.	.	.	.	.	.	II	.	.	.	.	.	.	.	.	III
Sphagnum tenellum (452)	.	.	.	.	.	.	.	.	.	.	.	.	.	.	.	.	.	II	.	.	.	.	.	.	.	.	.	.
Scapania ornithopodioides (453)	.	.	.	.	.	.	.	.	.	.	.	.	.	.	.	.	.	.	.	.	.	.	.	.	.	.	.	.
Bazzania tricrenata (454)	.	.	.	.	.	.	.	.	.	.	.	.	.	.	.	.	.	.	.	.	.	.	.	.	.	.	.	.
Mastigophora woodsii (455)	.	.	.	.	.	.	.	.	.	.	.	.	.	.	.	.	.	.	.	.	.	.	.	.	.	.	.	.
Harpalejeunea ovata (456)	.	.	.	.	.	.	.	.	.	.	.	.	.	.	.	.	.	.	.	.	.	.	.	.	.	.	.	.
Lepidozia reptans (457)	.	.	.	.	.	.	.	.	.	.	.	.	.	.	.	.	.	.	.	.	.	.	.	.	.	.	.	.
Hyocomium flagellare (458)	.	.	.	.	.	.	.	.	.	.	.	.	.	.	.	.	.	.	.	.	.	.	.	.	.	.	.	.
Lejeunea patens (459)	.	.	.	.	.	.	.	.	.	.	.	.	.	.	.	.	.	.	.	.	.	.	.	.	.	.	.	.
Trichostomum tenuirostre (460)	.	.	.	.	.	.	.	.	.	.	.	.	.	.	.	.	.	.	.	.	.	.	.	.	.	.	.	.
Herberta adunca (461)	.	.	.	.	.	.	.	.	.	.	.	.	.	.	.	.	.	.	.	.	.	.	.	.	.	.	.	.
Ptilium crista-castrensis (462)	.	.	.	.	.	.	.	.	.	.	.	.	.	.	.	.	.	.	.	.	.	.	.	.	.	.	.	.
Scapania gracilis (463)	III	.	.	.	.	.	.	.	.	.	.	.	.	.	.	.	.	.	.	.	.	.	.	.	.	.	.	I
Isothecium myosuroides (464)	III	.	.	.	.	.	.	.	.	.	.	.	.	.	.	.	.	.	.	.	.	.	.	.	.	.	.	.
Thuidium delicatulum (465)	.	.	.	.	.	.	.	.	.	.	.	.	.	.	.	.	.	.	.	.	.	.	.	.	.	.	.	.
Sphagnum quinquefarium (466)	.	.	.	.	.	.	.	.	.	.	.	.	.	.	.	.	.	.	.	.	.	.	.	.	.	.	.	.
Dicranum majus (467)	.	.	.	.	.	.	.	.	.	.	.	.	.	.	.	.	.	.	.	.	.	.	.	.	.	.	.	.
Hymenophyllum wilsonii (468)	.	.	+	.	.	.	.	.	.	.	.	.	.	.	.	.	.	.	.	.	.	.	.	.	.	.	.	.
Sphagnum fimbriatum (469)	.	.	.	.	.	.	.	.	.	.	.	.	.	.	.	.	.	.	.	.	.	.	.	.	.	.	.	.
Saccogyna viticulosa (470)	.	.	+	.	.	.	.	.	.	.	.	.	.	.	.	.	.	.	.	.	.	.	.	.	.	.	.	.
Plagiochila spinulosa (471)	.	.	+	.	.	.	.	.	.	.	.	.	.	.	.	.	.	.	.	.	.	.	.	.	.	.	.	.
Plagiothecium undulatum (472)	.	.	.	.	.	.	.	.	.	.	.	.	.	.	.	.	.	.	.	+	.	.	.	.	.	.	.	.
Mnium hornum (473)	.	.	.	.	.	.	.	.	.	.	.	.	.	.	.	.	.	.	.	.	.	.	.	.	.	.	.	.
Thelypteris limbosperma (474)	.	.	.	.	.	.	.	.	.	.	.	.	.	.	.	.	.	.	.	.	.	.	.	.	.	.	.	.
Dryopteris filix-mas (475)	.	.	.	.	.	.	.	.	.	.	.	.	.	.	.	.	.	.	.	.	.	.	.	.	.	.	.	.
Luzula sylvatica (476)	.	.	.	.	.	.	.	.	.	.	.	.	.	.	.	.	.	.	.	.	.	.	.	.	.	.	.	+
Dryopteris borreri (477)	.	.	.	.	.	.	.	.	.	.	.	.	.	.	.	.	.	.	.	.	.	.	.	.	.	.	.	.
Luzula multiflora (478)	.	.	.	.	.	.	.	.	.	.	.	.	.	.	.	.	.	.	.	.	.	II	.	.	.	.	.	.
Thelypteris phegopteris (479)	.	.	.	.	.	.	.	.	.	.	.	.	.	.	.	.	.	.	.	.	.	.	.	.	.	.	.	.
Dryopteris aemula (480)	.	.	.	.	.	.	.	.	.	.	.	.	.	.	.	.	.	.	.	.	.	.	.	.	.	.	.	.
Dryopteris dilatata (481)	.	.	.	.	.	.	.	.	.	.	.	.	.	.	.	.	.	.	.	.	.	.	.	.	.	.	.	.
Ajuga reptans (482)	.	.	.	.	.	.	.	.	.	.	.	.	.	.	.	.	.	.	.	.	.	.	.	.	.	.	.	.
Digitalis purpurea (483)	.	.	.	.	.	.	.	.	.	.	.	.	.	.	.	.	.	.	.	.	.	.	.	.	.	.	.	.
Primula vulgaris (484)	.	.	+	.	.	.	.	.	.	.	.	.	.	.	.	.	.	.	.	.	.	.	.	.	.	.	.	.
Endymion non-scriptus (485)	.	.	.	.	.	.	.	.	.	.	.	.	.	.	.	.	.	.	.	.	.	.	.	.	.	.	.	.
Hylocomium brevirostre (486)	.	.	.	.	.	.	.	.	.	.	.	.	.	.	.	.	.	.	.	.	.	.	.	.	.	.	.	.
Polypodium vulgare (487)	.	.	+	.	.	.	.	+	.	.	.	.	.	.	.	.	.	.	.	.	.	.	.	.	.	.	.	.
Anemone nemorosa (488)	.	.	+	.	.	.	.	.	.	.	.	.	.	.	.	.	.	.	.	.	.	.	.	.	.	.	.	.
Athyrium filix-femina (489)	.	.	.	.	.	.	.	.	.	.	.	.	.	.	.	.	.	.	.	.	.	.	.	.	.	.	.	.
Sorbus aucuparia (490)	.	.	.	.	.	.	.	.	.	.	.	.	.	.	.	.	.	.	.	.	.	.	.	.	.	.	.	.
Rhytidiadelphus triquetrus (491)	.	.	+	.	.	.	.	.	.	.	.	.	.	.	.	.	.	.	.	.	.	.	.	.	.	.	.	.
Geum rivale (492)	.	.	.	.	.	.	.	.	.	.	.	.	.	.	.	.	.	.	.	.	.	.	.	.	.	.	.	.
Ctenidium molluscum (493)	.	.	III	.	.	.	.	.	.	.	.	.	.	.	.	.	.	.	.	.	.	.	.	III	II	.	III	.
Rumex acetosa (494)	.	.	.	.	.	.	.	.	+	.	.	.	.	.	.	.	.	.	.	II	.	III	.	.	.	.	.	.
Solidago virgaurea (495)	.	.	.	.	.	.	.	.	.	.	.	.	.	.	.	.	.	.	.	.	.	.	.	.	.	.	.	.

TABLE 4.57 *continued*

	29 *Molinieto–Callunetum*	30 *Trichophoreto–Eriophoretum*	31 *Calluneto–Eriophoretum*	32 *Philonoto–Saxifragetum stellaris*	33 *Koenigia islandica–Carex demissa nodum*	34 *Cratoneuron commutatum–Saxifraga aizoides nodum*	35 *Saxifragetum aizoidis*	36 *Juncus acutiflorus–Filipendula ulmaria*	37 *Centaureo–Cynosuretum*	38 *Maritime grassland nodum*	39 *Lolium perenne–Plantago lanceolata*	40 *Dryas octopetala–Carex flacca*	41 *Cariceto–Rhacomitretum lanuginosi*	42 *Festuca ovina–Luzula spicata nodum*	43 *Rhacomitreto–Callunetum*	44 *Juniperus nana nodum*	45 *Rhacomitreto–Empetretum*	46 *Alchemilla alpina–Vaccinium myrtillus nodum*	47 *Nardus stricta–Vaccinium myrtillus*	48 *Agrosto–Festucetum* (species-poor)	49 *Alchemilleto–Agrosto–Festucetum*	50 *Agrosto–Festucetum* (species-rich)	51 *Nardo–Juncetum squarrosi*	52 *Callunetum vulgaris*	53 *Calluna vulgaris–Sieglingia decumbens*	54 *Calluna vulgaris–Arctostaphylos uva-ursi nodum*	55 *Vaccineto–Callunetum hepaticosum*	56 *Luzula sylvatica–Vaccinium myrtillus*	57 *Luzula sylvatica–Silene dioica*	58 *Betula pubescens–Cirsium heterophyllum*	59 *Sedum rosea–Alchemilla glabra*	60 *Betula pubescens–Vaccinium myrtillus*	61 *Corylus avellana–Oxalis acetosella*	62 *Oxalis acetosella–Rhytidiadelphus loreus*	63 *Hymenophyllum wilsonii–Isothecium myosuroides*	64 Open boulder association	65 *Fraxinus excelsior–Brachypodium sylvaticum*
441)	.	.	.	.	.	.	.	.	.	.	.	.	.	.	.	.	.	.	.	.	.	.	+	.	+	.	.	.	.	.	.	.	.	.	.	.	.
442)	+	+	.	.	.	.	.	.	.	.	.	.	.	.	.	.	.	III	+	.	.	.	+	.	II	IV	V	V	.	.	.	+	.	.	+	.	.
443)	.	.	.	.	.	.	.	.	.	.	.	.	.	.	.	.	.	.	.	.	.	.	.	.	.	III	.	.	.	.	.	.	.	.	.	.	.
444)	.	.	.	.	.	.	.	.	.	.	.	.	.	.	.	.	.	.	.	.	.	.	.	.	.	III	.	.	.	.	.	.	.	.	.	.	.
445)	.	.	.	.	.	.	.	.	.	.	.	.	.	.	.	.	.	.	.	.	.	.	.	.	.	V	.	.	III	.	.	+	.	.	.	.	.
446)	.	.	.	.	.	.	.	.	.	.	.	.	.	.	.	.	.	.	.	.	.	.	.	.	.	III	II	.	+	.	.	II	.	+	.	.	+
447)	.	.	.	.	.	.	.	.	.	.	.	.	.	.	.	.	.	.	.	.	.	.	.	.	.	.	II	.	.	+	.	+	.	.	.	.	.
448)	.	.	.	.	.	.	.	.	.	.	.	.	.	.	.	.	.	.	+	.	.	.	.	.	.	.	+	.	.	.	.	.	.	.	.	.	.
449)	II	I	.	+	.	.	.	II	.	.	.	.	.	.	.	.	I	II	+	.	.	.	II	.	.	.	IV	.	.	.	+	.	.	.	.	.	.
450)	.	.	.	.	.	.	.	.	.	.	.	.	.	.	.	.	III	.	II	.	.	.	+	.	.	.	V	.	.	.	.	.	.	.	.	.	.
451)	III	.	V	.	.	.	.	.	.	.	.	.	.	.	.	.	+	.	.	+	.	.	III	II	.	.	V	.	.	.	.	+	.	+	.	.	.
452)	II	III	II	III	.	.	.	.	.	.	.	.	.	.	.	.	II	.	+	.	.	.	+	.	.	.	IV	.	.	.	.	.	.	.	.	.	.
453)	.	.	.	.	.	.	.	.	.	.	.	.	.	.	.	.	I	.	.	.	+	.	.	.	.	.	II	.	.	.	.	.	.	.	.	.	.
454)	.	.	.	.	.	.	.	.	.	.	.	.	.	.	.	.	III	.	.	.	+	.	.	.	.	.	V	.	.	.	+	.	.	.	I	.	.
455)	.	.	.	.	.	.	.	.	.	.	.	.	.	.	.	.	.	.	.	.	.	.	.	.	.	.	III	.	.	.	II	.	.	.	.	.	.
456)	.	.	.	.	.	.	.	.	.	.	.	.	.	.	.	.	.	.	.	.	.	.	.	.	.	.	+	.	.	.	+	.	.	.	.	.	.
457)	.	.	.	.	.	.	.	.	.	.	.	.	.	.	.	.	.	.	.	.	.	.	.	.	.	.	II	.	.	.	.	II	.	.	II	.	.
458)	.	.	.	.	.	.	.	.	.	.	.	.	.	.	.	.	.	.	.	.	.	.	.	.	.	.	+	.	.	.	.	.	.	.	V	.	.
459)	.	.	.	.	.	.	.	.	.	.	.	.	.	.	.	.	.	.	.	.	.	.	.	.	.	.	II	.	.	.	.	.	.	.	V	.	.
460)	.	.	.	.	.	.	.	.	.	.	.	.	.	.	.	.	.	.	.	.	.	.	.	.	.	.	II	.	.	.	.	+	.	.	IV	.	.
461)	.	.	.	.	.	.	.	.	.	.	.	.	.	.	.	.	.	.	.	.	.	.	.	.	.	.	V	+	.	.	.	.	.	.	.	.	.
462)	.	.	.	.	.	.	.	.	.	.	.	.	.	.	.	.	.	.	.	.	.	.	.	.	.	.	II	+	.	.	+	II	.	+	.	.	.
463)	.	.	.	.	.	.	.	.	.	.	.	.	.	.	.	.	IV	.	+	.	+	.	+	.	+	.	V	II	.	.	+	V	II	II	V	V	.
464)	.	.	.	.	.	.	.	.	.	.	.	.	.	.	.	.	.	.	.	.	.	.	.	.	.	.	IV	III	.	II	.	II	II	III	V	+	II
465)	.	.	.	.	.	.	.	.	.	.	.	.	.	.	.	.	.	.	.	.	.	.	.	.	.	.	II	II	.	III	.	V	IV	V	II	II	II
466)	.	.	.	.	.	.	.	.	.	.	.	.	.	.	.	.	.	.	.	.	.	.	.	.	.	.	IV	II	.	+	.	IV	I	+	II	.	.
467)	.	.	.	.	.	.	.	.	.	.	.	.	.	.	.	.	+	.	.	.	.	.	.	.	.	.	II	+	.	III	II	IV	II	III	II	.	.
468)	.	.	.	.	.	.	.	.	.	.	.	.	.	.	.	.	II	.	.	.	.	.	.	.	.	.	V	II	.	II	I	II	III	III	V	.	.
469)	.	.	.	.	.	.	.	.	.	.	.	.	.	.	.	.	.	.	.	.	.	.	.	.	.	.	+	+	.	+	.	IV	I	+	.	.	.
470)	.	.	.	.	.	.	.	.	.	.	.	.	.	.	.	.	.	.	.	.	.	.	.	.	.	.	III	+	+	III	.	I	I	+	III	+	.
471)	.	.	.	.	.	.	.	.	.	.	.	.	.	.	.	.	III	.	.	.	.	.	.	.	.	.	IV	+	+	.	+	I	II	II	V	II	.
472)	+	.	.	.	.	.	.	.	.	.	.	.	.	.	.	.	+	.	.	.	.	.	.	.	.	.	IV	II	+	.	.	V	II	+	.	.	.
473)	.	.	.	.	.	.	.	.	.	.	.	.	.	.	.	.	.	I	.	.	I	I	.	.	I	.	II	+	II	I	I	III	III	II	+	.	.
474)	.	.	.	.	.	.	.	I	.	.	.	.	.	.	.	.	.	+	.	.	.	.	.	+	.	.	II	III	III	II	II	II	II	.	.	.	.
475)	.	.	.	.	.	.	.	.	.	.	.	.	.	.	.	.	.	.	.	.	.	.	.	.	+	.	III	III	+	III	I	IV	IV	.	.	.	IV
476)	.	.	.	.	.	.	.	.	.	.	.	.	I	.	.	.	II	II	II	.	II	I	.	.	.	.	II	V	V	III	V	I	.	.	.	.	.
477)	.	.	.	.	.	.	.	.	.	.	.	.	.	.	.	.	.	.	.	.	.	.	.	.	.	.	+	III	II	III	III	.	II	.	.	.	.
478)	.	.	.	.	.	.	.	+	.	.	.	.	.	.	.	.	.	.	.	.	I	I	+	.	+	.	.	+	III	.	.	.	II	+	.	.	.
479)	.	.	.	.	.	.	.	.	.	.	.	.	.	.	.	.	+	.	.	.	.	.	.	.	.	.	.	II	III	.	.	.	III	.	.	.	+
480)	.	.	.	.	.	.	.	.	.	.	.	.	.	.	.	.	.	.	.	.	.	.	.	.	.	.	.	+	+	.	.	I	I	.	.	.	.
481)	.	.	.	.	.	.	.	.	.	.	.	.	.	.	.	.	.	.	.	.	.	.	.	.	.	.	.	III	.	I	I	II	II	.	.	.	.
482)	.	.	.	.	.	.	.	.	.	.	.	.	.	.	.	.	.	.	.	.	.	.	.	.	.	.	.	+	.	II	.	.	II	.	.	.	+
483)	.	.	.	.	.	.	.	.	.	.	.	.	.	.	.	.	.	.	.	.	.	.	.	.	.	.	.	II	II	+	.	.	II	.	.	.	+
484)	.	.	.	.	.	.	.	.	.	II	.	+	.	.	.	.	.	.	.	.	I	II	.	.	II	III	.	+	III	V	III	I	V	.	.	.	V
485)	.	.	.	.	.	.	.	.	.	.	.	.	.	.	.	.	.	.	.	.	.	.	.	.	.	.	.	III	III	IV	II	IV	IV	II	.	.	III
486)	.	.	.	.	.	.	.	.	.	.	.	III	.	.	.	.	.	.	.	.	.	.	.	.	+	.	.	.	II	III	III	II	V	V	+	.	IV
487)	.	.	.	.	.	.	.	.	.	.	.	.	.	.	.	.	.	.	.	.	.	.	.	.	.	.	.	.	II	I	I	I	I	+	.	.	.
488)	.	.	.	.	.	.	+	.	.	.	.	+	.	.	.	.	.	.	.	.	.	.	.	.	.	.	.	.	+	II	II	I	I	.	.	.	II
489)	.	.	.	.	.	.	.	.	.	.	.	.	.	.	.	.	.	.	.	.	.	.	.	.	.	.	.	.	III	I	II	II	III	.	.	.	II
490)	.	.	.	.	.	.	.	.	.	.	.	.	.	.	.	.	.	.	.	.	.	.	.	.	.	.	.	.	+	V	III	V	IV	III	.	.	III
491)	.	.	.	.	.	.	.	.	.	.	.	II	.	.	.	.	.	.	.	.	II	II	.	.	II	II	.	.	III	V	IV	IV	III	II	.	.	IV
492)	.	.	.	+	.	.	III	.	.	.	.	+	.	.	.	.	.	.	.	.	.	.	.	.	+	.	.	.	III	V	V	.	II	.	.	.	IV
493)	.	.	.	.	.	IV	IV	.	.	II	.	V	.	.	.	.	.	.	.	.	I	V	+	.	.	.	.	.	+	III	V	.	+	.	.	.	IV
494)	.	.	.	.	.	.	+	II	IV	II	.	.	.	.	.	.	.	.	.	I	V	III	.	.	I	.	.	.	V	II	V	.	.	.	.	.	.
495)	.	.	.	.	.	.	.	.	.	.	.	+	.	+	III	II	II	II	.	.	.	.	.	.	I	III	.	.	III	I	IV	.	.	.	.	.	.

TABLE 4.57 *continued*

	1 *Hedwigia ciliata–Parmelia saxatilis*	2 *Koenigia islandica* scree community	3 *Asplenium trichomanes–Fissidens cristatus*	5 *Puccinellia maritima–Festuca rubra*	4 *Puccinellia maritima–Ascophyllum nodosum*	6 *Juncus gerardii–Carex extensa*	7 *Armeria maritima–Grimmia maritima*	8 *Asplenium marinum–Grimmia maritima*	9 *Atriplex glabriuscula–Rumex crispus*	10 Brackish water communities	11 *Phragmites communis–Equisetum fluviatile*	12 *Schoenoplectus lacustris–Equisetum fluviatile*	13 *Carex rostrata–Menyanthes trifoliata*	14 *Littorella uniflora–Lobelia dortmanna*	15 *Potamogeton natans–Nymphaea alba nodum*	16 *Eriophorum angustifolium–Sphagnum cuspidatum*	17 *Carex lasiocarpa–Menyanthes trifoliata*	18 *Trichophorum cespitosum–Carex panicea*	19 *Molinia caerulea–Myrica gale*	20 *Sphagneto–Juncetum effusi*	21 *Carex–Sphagnum recurvum nodum*	22 *Carex rostrata–Aulacomnium palustre*	23 *Carex rostrata–Scorpidium scorpioides*	24 *Carex panicea–Campylium stellatum*	25 *Eriophorum latifolium–Carex hostiana*	26 *Schoenus nigricans*	27 *Carex–Saxifraga aizoides nodum*	28 *Trichophoreto–Callunetum*
Angelica sylvestris (496)	.	.	.	.	.	.	.	.	.	.	.	.	.	.	.	.	.	.	.	.	.	.	.	.	.	.	.	.
Alchemilla glabra (497)	.	.	.	.	.	.	.	.	.	.	.	.	.	.	.	.	.	.	.	.	.	.	.	.	.	.	.	.
Valeriana officinalis (498)	.	.	.	.	.	.	.	.	.	.	.	.	.	.	.	.	.	.	.	.	.	+	.	.	.	.	.	.
Epilobium montanum (499)	.	.	II	.	.	.	.	.	.	.	.	.	.	.	.	.	.	.	.	.	.	.	.	.	.	.	.	.
Trollius europaeus (500)	.	.	.	.	.	.	.	.	.	.	.	.	.	.	.	.	.	.	.	.	.	.	.	.	.	.	.	.
Cirsium heterophyllum (501)	.	.	.	.	.	.	.	.	.	.	.	.	.	.	.	.	.	.	.	.	.	.	.	.	.	.	.	.
Sedum rosea (502)	.	.	.	.	.	.	.	+	+	.	.	.	.	.	.	.	.	.	.	.	.	.	.	.	.	.	.	.
Chamaenerion angustifolium (503)	.	.	.	.	.	.	.	.	.	.	.	.	.	.	.	.	.	.	.	.	.	.	.	.	.	.	.	.
Lobaria pulmonaria (504)	.	.	.	.	.	.	.	.	.	.	.	.	.	.	.	.	.	.	.	.	.	.	.	.	.	.	.	.
Tritomaria quinquedentata (505)	.	.	+	.	.	.	.	.	.	.	.	.	.	.	.	.	.	.	.	.	.	.	.	.	.	.	.	.
Rubus saxatilis (506)	.	.	.	.	.	.	.	.	.	.	.	.	.	.	.	.	.	.	.	.	.	.	.	.	.	.	.	.
Populus tremula (507)	.	.	.	.	.	.	.	.	.	.	.	.	.	.	.	.	.	.	.	.	.	.	.	.	.	.	.	.
Orchis mascula (508)	.	.	.	.	.	.	.	.	.	.	.	.	.	.	.	.	.	.	.	.	.	.	.	.	.	.	.	.
Galium odoratum (509)	.	.	.	.	.	.	.	.	.	.	.	.	.	.	.	.	.	.	.	.	.	.	.	.	.	.	.	.
Fissidens taxifolius (510)	.	.	.	.	.	.	.	.	.	.	.	.	.	.	.	.	.	.	.	.	.	.	.	.	.	.	.	.
Allium ursinum (511)	.	.	I	.	.	.	.	.	.	.	.	.	.	.	.	.	.	.	.	.	.	.	.	.	.	.	.	.
Sanicula europaea (512)	.	.	.	.	.	.	.	.	.	.	.	.	.	.	.	.	.	.	.	.	.	.	.	.	.	.	.	.
Silene dioica (513)	.	.	.	.	.	.	.	.	.	.	.	.	.	.	.	.	.	.	.	.	.	.	.	.	.	.	.	.
Vicia sepium (514)	.	.	.	.	.	.	.	.	.	.	.	.	.	.	.	.	.	.	.	.	.	.	.	.	.	.	.	.
Brachypodium sylvaticum (515)	.	.	.	.	.	.	.	.	.	.	.	.	.	.	.	.	.	.	.	.	.	.	.	.	.	.	.	.
Tussilago farfara (516)	.	.	.	.	.	.	.	.	.	.	.	.	.	.	.	.	.	.	.	.	.	.	.	.	.	.	.	.
Listera ovata (517)	.	.	.	.	.	.	.	.	.	.	.	.	.	.	.	.	.	.	.	.	.	.	.	.	.	.	.	.
Fraxinus excelsior (518)	.	.	.	.	.	.	.	.	.	.	.	.	.	.	.	.	.	.	.	.	.	.	.	.	.	.	.	.
Geranium robertianum (519)	.	.	III	.	.	.	.	.	.	.	.	.	.	.	.	.	.	.	.	.	.	.	.	.	.	.	.	.
Betula pubescens (520)	.	.	.	.	.	.	.	.	.	.	.	.	.	.	.	.	.	.	.	.	.	.	.	.	.	.	.	.
Conopodium majus (521)	.	.	.	.	.	.	.	.	.	.	.	.	.	.	.	.	.	.	.	.	.	.	.	.	.	.	.	.
Eurhynchium praelongum (522)	.	.	.	.	.	.	.	.	.	.	.	.	.	.	.	.	.	.	.	+	.	.	.	.	.	.	.	.
Corylus avellana (523)	.	.	.	.	.	.	.	.	.	.	.	.	.	.	.	.	.	.	.	.	.	.	.	.	.	.	.	.
Plagiochila asplenoides var. *major* (524)	.	.	.	.	.	.	.	.	.	.	.	.	.	.	.	.	.	.	.	.	.	.	.	.	.	.	.	.
Eurhynchium striatum (525)	.	.	.	.	.	.	.	.	.	.	.	.	.	.	.	.	.	.	.	.	.	.	.	.	.	.	.	.
Salix atrocinerea (526)	.	.	.	.	.	.	.	.	.	.	.	.	.	.	.	.	.	.	.	.	.	.	.	.	.	.	.	.
Carex pallescens (527)	.	.	.	.	.	.	.	.	.	.	.	.	.	.	.	.	.	.	.	.	.	.	.	.	.	.	.	.
Ranunculus ficaria (528)	.	.	.	.	.	.	.	.	.	.	.	.	.	.	.	.	.	.	.	.	.	.	.	.	.	.	.	.
Isothecium myurum (529)	.	.	.	.	.	.	.	.	.	.	.	.	.	.	.	.	.	.	.	.	.	.	.	.	.	.	.	.
Leiocolea bantriensis (530)	.	.	.	.	.	.	.	.	.	.	.	.	.	.	.	.	.	.	.	.	.	.	.	.	+	.	.	.
Metzgeria hamata (531)	.	.	+	.	.	.	.	.	.	.	.	.	.	.	.	.	.	.	.	.	.	.	.	.	.	.	.	.
Mnium undulatum (532)	.	.	.	.	.	.	.	.	.	.	.	.	.	.	.	.	.	.	.	.	.	.	.	.	+	.	.	.
Filipendula ulmaria (533)	.	.	.	.	.	.	.	.	.	.	.	.	.	.	.	.	.	.	.	.	.	III	.	.	.	.	.	.
Deschampsia cespitosa (534)	.	.	.	.	.	.	.	.	.	.	.	.	.	.	.	.	.	.	.	.	.	.	.	+	.	.	.	.
Lysimachia nemorum (535)	.	.	.	.	.	.	.	.	.	.	.	.	.	.	.	.	.	.	.	.	.	.	.	.	.	.	.	.
Ranunculus acris (536)	.	.	+	.	.	.	.	.	+	.	.	.	.	.	.	.	.	.	.	.	.	.	.	III	.	.	.	.
Anoectangium aestivum (537)	.	.	I	.	.	.	.	.	.	.	.	.	.	.	.	.	.	.	.	.	.	.	.	.	.	.	.	.
Herberta straminea (538)	.	.	.	.	.	.	.	.	.	.	.	.	.	.	.	.	.	.	.	.	.	.	.	.	.	.	.	.
Oxyria digyna (539)	.	II	.	.	.	.	.	.	.	.	.	.	.	.	.	.	.	.	.	.	.	.	.	.	.	.	.	.
Saxifraga hypnoides (540)	.	II	.	.	.	.	.	.	.	.	.	.	.	.	.	.	.	.	.	.	.	.	.	.	.	.	.	.
Drepanocladus uncinatus (541)	.	.	.	.	.	.	.	.	.	.	.	.	.	.	.	.	.	.	.	.	.	.	.	.	.	.	.	.
Saussurea alpina (542)	.	.	.	.	.	.	.	.	.	.	.	.	.	.	.	.	.	.	.	.	.	.	.	.	.	.	.	.
Brachythecium plumosum (543)	.	.	.	.	.	.	.	.	.	.	.	.	.	.	.	.	.	.	.	.	.	.	.	.	.	.	.	.
Scapania gracilis (544)	III	.	.	.	.	.	.	.	.	.	.	.	.	.	.	.	.	.	.	.	.	.	.	.	.	.	.	I
Peltigera canina (545)	.	.	.	.	.	.	.	.	.	.	.	.	.	.	.	.	.	.	.	+	.	.	.	.	.	.	.	.
Polytrichum formosum (546)	.	.	.	.	.	.	.	.	.	.	.	.	.	.	.	.	.	.	.	.	.	.	.	.	.	.	.	.
Pteridium aquilinum (547)	.	.	.	.	.	.	.	.	.	.	.	.	.	.	.	.	.	.	.	.	.	.	.	.	.	.	.	.
Hylocomium umbratum (548)	.	.	.	.	.	.	.	.	.	.	.	.	.	.	.	.	.	.	.	.	.	.	.	.	.	.	.	.
Melampyrum pratense (549)	.	.	.	.	.	.	.	.	.	.	.	.	.	.	.	.	.	.	.	.	.	.	.	.	.	.	.	+
Bazzania trilobata (550)	.	.	.	.	.	.	.	.	.	.	.	.	.	.	.	.	.	.	.	.	.	.	.	.	.	.	.	.

TABLE 4.57 *continued*

	29 *Molinieto-Callunetum*	30 *Trichophoreto-Eriophoretum*	31 *Calluneto-Eriophoretum*	32 *Philonoto-Saxifragetum stellaris*	33 *Koenigia islandica-Carex demissa nodum*	34 *Cratoneuron commutatum-Saxifraga aizoides nodum*	35 *Saxifragetum aizoidis*	36 *Juncus acutiflorus-Filipendula ulmaria*	37 *Centaureo-Cynosuretum*	38 *Maritime grassland nodum*	39 *Lolium perenne-Plantago lanceolata*	40 *Dryas octopetala-Carex flacca*	41 *Cariceto-Rhacomitretum lanuginosi*	42 *Festuca ovina-Luzula spicata nodum*	43 *Rhacomitreto-Callunetum*	44 *Juniperus nana nodum*	45 *Rhacomitreto-Empetretum*	46 *Alchemilla alpina-Vaccinium myrtillus nodum*	47 *Nardus stricta-Vaccinium myrtillus*	48 *Agrosto-Festucetum* (species-poor)	49 *Alchemilleto-Agrosto-Festucetum*	50 *Agrosto-Festucetum* (species-rich)	51 *Nardo-Juncetum squarrosi*	52 *Callunetum vulgaris*	53 *Calluna vulgaris-Sieglingia decumbens*	54 *Calluna vulgaris-Arctostaphylos uva-ursi nodum*	55 *Vaccineto-Callunetum hepaticosum*	56 *Luzula sylvatica-Vaccinium myrtillus*	57 *Luzula sylvatica-Silene dioica*	58 *Betula pubescens-Cirsium heterophyllum*	59 *Sedum rosea-Alchemilla glabra*	60 *Betula pubescens-Vaccinium myrtillus*	61 *Corylus avellana-Oxalis acetosella*	62 *Oxalis acetosella-Rhytidiadelphus loreus*	63 *Hymenophyllum wilsonii-Isothecium myosuroides*	64 Open boulder association	65 *Fraxinus excelsior-Brachypodium sylvaticum*
(496)	.	.	.	.	.	II	III	II	+	III	.	.	.	.	.	.	.	.	.	.	I	.	.	.	+	.	.	.	V	III	V	.	.	.	.	.	.
(497)	.	.	.	.	.	.	V	.	I	.	.	.	.	.	.	.	.	.	.	.	.	.	.	.	.	.	.	.	+	II	V	.	.	.	.	.	.
(498)	.	.	.	.	.	+	.	+	.	.	.	.	.	.	.	.	.	.	.	.	.	.	.	.	.	.	.	.	III	III	III	.	.	.	.	.	.
(499)	.	.	.	.	.	.	.	.	.	.	.	.	.	.	.	.	.	.	.	.	.	+	.	.	.	.	.	.	III	II	II	.	+	.	.	.	II
(500)	.	.	.	.	.	.	II	II	.	.	.	.	.	.	.	.	.	.	.	.	.	.	.	.	.	.	.	.	+	III	III	.	.	.	.	.	.
(501)	.	.	.	.	.	.	.	+	.	.	.	.	.	.	.	.	.	.	.	.	.	.	.	.	.	.	.	.	II	V	III	.	.	.	.	.	.
(502)	.	.	.	.	.	II	IV	.	.	.	.	.	.	.	.	.	III	.	.	.	I	I	.	.	.	.	+	+	V	.	V	.	.	.	.	.	.
(503)	.	.	.	.	.	.	.	.	.	.	.	.	.	.	.	.	.	.	.	.	.	.	.	.	.	.	.	.	+	.	+	.	.	.	.	.	.
(504)	.	.	.	.	.	.	.	.	.	.	.	.	.	.	.	.	.	.	.	.	.	.	.	.	.	.	.	.	+	.	.	.	.	.	+	.	.
(505)	.	.	.	.	.	.	+	.	.	.	.	.	.	.	.	.	.	.	.	.	+	.	.	.	.	.	.	.	II	.	.	.	.	.	.	.	.
(506)	.	.	.	.	.	.	.	.	.	.	.	II	.	.	.	.	.	I	.	.	.	.	.	.	+	.	+	.	III	II	.	.	.	.	.	.	.
(507)	.	.	.	.	.	.	.	.	.	.	.	.	.	.	.	.	.	.	.	.	.	.	.	.	.	.	.	.	II	II	.	.	.	.	.	.	.
(508)	.	.	.	.	.	.	.	.	.	.	.	.	.	.	.	.	.	.	.	.	.	.	.	.	.	.	.	.	II	+	.	.	.	.	.	.	.
(509)	.	.	.	.	.	.	.	.	.	.	.	.	.	.	.	.	.	.	.	.	.	.	.	.	.	.	.	.	+	III	.	.	+	.	.	.	.
(510)	.	.	.	.	.	.	.	.	.	.	.	.	.	.	.	.	.	.	.	.	.	.	.	.	.	.	.	.	+	+	.	.	+	.	.	.	II
(511)	.	.	.	.	.	.	.	.	.	.	.	.	.	.	.	.	.	.	.	.	.	.	.	.	.	.	.	.	+	II	.	.	II	.	.	.	III
(512)	.	.	.	.	.	.	.	.	.	.	.	.	.	.	.	.	.	.	.	.	.	.	.	.	.	.	.	.	+	II	.	+	.	.	.	.	III
(513)	.	.	.	.	.	.	.	.	.	.	.	.	.	.	.	.	.	.	.	.	.	.	.	.	.	.	.	.	V	+	.	.	.	.	.	.	+
(514)	.	.	.	.	.	.	.	.	.	.	.	.	.	.	.	.	.	.	.	.	.	.	.	.	+	.	.	.	+	II	.	.	.	.	.	.	II
(515)	.	.	.	.	.	.	.	.	.	.	.	.	.	.	.	.	.	.	.	.	.	.	.	.	.	.	.	.	.	III	.	.	.	.	.	.	V
(516)	.	.	.	.	.	.	.	.	.	.	.	.	.	.	.	.	.	.	.	.	.	.	.	.	.	.	.	.	.	+	.	.	.	.	.	.	+
(517)	.	.	.	.	.	.	.	.	.	.	.	.	.	.	.	.	.	.	.	.	.	.	.	.	.	.	.	.	.	II	.	.	.	.	.	.	+
(518)	.	.	.	.	.	.	.	.	.	.	.	.	.	.	.	.	.	.	.	.	.	.	.	.	.	.	.	.	.	II	.	.	.	.	.	.	V
(519)	.	.	.	.	.	.	.	.	.	.	.	.	.	.	.	.	.	.	.	.	.	.	.	.	.	.	.	.	.	III	.	.	III	+	.	.	IV
(520)	.	.	.	.	.	.	.	.	.	.	.	II	.	.	.	.	.	.	.	.	.	+	.	.	.	.	.	.	.	V	.	V	IV	+	.	.	III
(521)	.	.	.	.	.	.	.	.	+	.	.	.	.	.	.	.	.	.	.	.	.	.	.	.	.	.	.	.	.	III	.	I	III	.	.	.	IV
(522)	.	.	.	.	.	.	.	.	.	.	+	.	.	.	.	.	.	.	.	.	.	.	.	.	.	.	.	.	.	III	.	I	.	.	.	.	III
(523)	.	.	.	.	.	.	.	.	.	.	.	.	.	.	.	.	.	.	.	.	.	.	.	.	.	.	.	.	.	V	.	III	V	.	.	.	V
(524)	.	.	.	.	.	.	.	.	.	.	.	.	.	.	.	.	.	.	.	.	.	.	.	.	.	.	.	.	.	III	.	I	II	.	.	.	II
(525)	.	.	.	.	.	.	.	.	.	.	.	.	.	.	.	.	.	.	.	.	.	.	.	.	.	.	.	.	.	II	.	I	III	+	.	.	III
(526)	.	.	.	.	.	.	.	.	.	.	.	.	.	.	.	.	.	.	.	.	.	.	.	.	.	.	.	.	.	III	.	II	II	.	.	.	.
(527)	.	.	.	.	.	.	.	.	.	.	.	.	.	.	.	.	.	.	.	.	.	.	.	.	.	.	.	.	.	II	.	II	IV	.	.	.	.
(528)	.	.	.	.	.	.	.	.	.	.	.	.	.	.	.	.	.	.	.	.	.	.	.	.	.	.	.	.	.	+	.	.	II	.	.	.	.
(529)	.	.	.	.	.	.	.	.	.	.	.	.	.	.	.	.	.	.	.	.	.	.	.	.	.	.	.	.	.	I	I	.	II	+	.	.	III
(530)	.	.	.	.	.	.	+	.	.	.	.	.	.	.	.	.	.	.	.	.	.	.	.	.	.	.	.	.	.	I	I	.	.	.	.	.	.
(531)	.	.	.	.	.	.	.	.	.	.	.	.	.	.	.	.	.	.	.	.	.	.	.	.	.	.	.	.	.	I	II	.	.	.	.	.	.
(532)	.	.	.	+	.	.	.	II	.	+	.	.	.	.	.	.	.	.	.	.	.	.	.	.	.	.	.	+	.	V	I	.	III	.	.	.	III
(533)	.	.	.	.	.	.	I	V	II	.	.	+	.	.	.	.	.	.	.	.	II	II	.	.	+	.	.	.	.	V	V	.	IV	.	.	.	II
(534)	.	.	.	IV	V	.	V	+	+	.	.	.	.	.	.	.	.	.	+	.	.	.	.	.	.	.	.	.	.	V	V	.	V	.	.	.	II
(535)	.	.	.	.	.	.	.	+	.	.	.	.	.	.	.	.	.	.	.	.	.	.	.	.	+	.	.	.	.	II	I	I	IV	.	.	.	IV
(536)	.	.	.	IV	II	.	V	.	.	II	.	.	.	.	.	.	.	.	.	I	IV	IV	.	.	I	.	.	.	.	III	V	II	III	.	.	.	.
(537)	.	.	.	.	.	II	IV	.	.	.	.	.	.	.	.	.	.	.	.	.	.	.	.	.	.	.	.	.	.	.	III	.	.	.	.	.	.
(538)	.	.	.	.	.	.	.	.	.	.	.	.	.	.	.	.	.	.	.	.	.	+	.	.	.	.	+	.	.	.	V	.	.	.	.	.	.
(539)	.	.	.	.	.	.	III	.	.	.	.	.	.	.	.	.	.	.	.	.	+	.	.	.	.	.	.	.	.	.	IV	.	.	.	.	.	.
(540)	.	.	.	.	.	.	.	.	.	.	.	.	.	.	.	.	.	.	.	.	+	.	.	.	.	.	.	+	.	.	III	.	.	.	.	.	.
(541)	.	.	.	.	.	.	.	.	.	.	.	.	.	.	.	.	.	.	.	.	.	.	.	.	.	.	.	.	.	.	III	.	.	.	.	.	.
(542)	.	.	.	.	.	.	II	.	.	.	.	.	.	.	.	.	.	.	.	.	.	.	.	.	.	.	.	.	.	.	III	.	.	.	.	.	.
(543)	.	.	.	+	.	.	.	.	.	.	.	.	.	.	.	.	.	.	.	.	.	.	.	.	.	.	.	.	.	.	+	.	.	.	.	+	.
(544)	.	.	.	.	.	.	.	.	.	.	.	.	.	.	.	.	IV	.	+	.	+	.	+	.	+	.	V	II	.	.	+	V	II	II	V	V	.
(545)	.	.	.	.	.	.	.	.	.	.	.	.	.	.	.	.	.	.	.	I	II	I	.	.	.	.	.	.	.	II	I	I	II	+	I	.	+
(546)	.	.	.	.	.	.	.	.	.	.	.	.	.	.	.	.	.	.	.	.	II	I	II	.	.	.	.	III	.	II	I	V	II	I	II	.	+
(547)	.	.	.	.	.	.	.	.	.	III	.	+	.	.	.	.	.	.	.	II	.	III	.	+	I	III	+	.	.	II	.	V	III	+	.	.	II
(548)	.	.	.	.	.	.	.	.	.	.	.	.	.	.	.	.	.	.	.	.	.	.	.	.	.	.	II	+	.	.	.	III	II	II	.	.	.
(549)	+	.	.	.	.	.	.	.	.	.	.	.	.	.	.	.	.	.	.	.	.	.	.	.	.	.	.	.	.	.	.	II	I	I	.	.	+
(550)	.	.	.	.	.	.	.	.	.	.	.	.	.	.	.	.	.	.	.	.	.	.	.	.	.	.	.	.	.	.	.	II	.	II	I	.	.

TABLE 4.57 *continued*

	1 *Hedwigia ciliata–Parmelia saxatilis*	2 *Koenigia islandica* scree community	3 *Asplenium trichomanes–Fissidens cristatus*	4 *Puccinellia maritima–Ascophyllum nodosum*	5 *Puccinellia maritima–Festuca rubra*	6 *Juncus gerardii–Carex extensa*	7 *Armeria maritima–Grimmia maritima*	8 *Asplenium marinum–Grimmia maritima*	9 *Atriplex glabriuscula–Rumex crispus*	10 Brackish water communities	11 *Phragmites communis–Equisetum fluviatile*	12 *Schoenoplectus lacustris–Equisetum fluviatile*	13 *Carex rostrata–Menyanthes trifoliata*	14 *Littorella uniflora–Lobelia dortmanna*	15 *Potamogeton natans–Nymphaea alba nodum*	16 *Eriophorum angustifolium–Sphagnum cuspidatum*	17 *Carex lasiocarpa–Menyanthes trifoliata*	18 *Trichophorum cespitosum–Carex panicea*	19 *Molinia caerulea–Myrica gale*	20 *Sphagneto–Juncetum effusi*	21 *Carex–Sphagnum recurvum nodum*	22 *Carex rostrata–Aulacomnium palustre*	23 *Carex rostrata–Scorpidium scorpioides*	24 *Carex panicea–Campylium stellatum*	25 *Eriophorum latifolium–Carex hostiana*	26 *Schoenus nigricans*	27 *Carex–Saxifraga aizoides nodum*	28 *Trichophoreto–Callunetum*
Calypogeia fissa (551)	.	.	.	.	.	.	.	.	.	.	.	.	.	.	.	.	.	.	.	.	.	.	.	.	.	.	.	.
Leucobryum glaucum (552)	.	.	.	.	.	.	.	.	.	.	.	.	.	.	.	.	.	.	.	.	.	.	.	.	.	.	.	.
Carex sylvatica (553)	.	.	.	.	.	.	.	.	.	.	.	.	.	.	.	.	.	.	.	.	.	.	.	.	.	.	.	.
Quercus petraea (554)	.	.	.	.	.	.	.	.	.	.	.	.	.	.	.	.	.	.	.	.	.	.	.	.	.	.	.	.
Dicranodontium denudatum (555)	.	.	.	.	.	.	.	.	.	.	.	.	.	.	.	.	.	.	.	.	.	.	.	.	.	.	.	.
Prunus padus (556)	.	.	.	.	.	.	.	.	.	.	.	.	.	.	.	.	.	.	.	.	.	.	.	.	.	.	.	.
Atrichum undulatum (557)	.	.	.	.	.	.	.	.	.	.	.	.	.	.	.	.	.	.	.	.	.	.	.	.	.	.	.	.
Circaea intermedia (558)	.	.	.	.	.	.	.	.	.	.	.	.	.	.	.	.	.	.	.	.	.	.	.	.	.	.	.	.
Rubus fruticosus agg. (559)	.	.	.	.	.	.	.	.	.	.	.	.	.	.	.	.	.	.	.	.	.	.	.	.	.	.	.	.
Adelanthus decipiens (560)	.	.	.	.	.	.	.	.	.	.	.	.	.	.	.	.	.	.	.	.	.	.	.	.	.	.	.	.
Frullania germana (561)	III	.	.	.	.	+	.	.	.	.	.	.	.	.	.	.	.	.	.	.	.	.	.	.	.	.	.	.
Scapania umbrosa (562)	.	.	.	.	.	.	.	.	.	.	.	.	.	.	.	.	.	.	.	.	.	.	.	.	.	.	.	.
Hypnum callichroum (563)	.	.	.	.	.	.	.	.	.	.	.	.	.	.	.	.	.	.	.	.	.	.	.	.	.	.	.	.
Heterocladium heteropterum (564)	.	.	+	.	.	.	.	.	.	.	.	.	.	.	.	.	.	.	.	.	.	.	.	.	.	.	.	.
Dicranum scottianum (565)	.	.	.	.	.	.	.	.	.	.	.	.	.	.	.	.	.	.	.	.	.	.	.	.	.	.	.	.
Grimmia hartmanii (566)	.	.	.	.	.	.	.	.	.	.	.	.	.	.	.	.	.	.	.	.	.	.	.	.	.	.	.	.
Rhacomitrium aquaticum (567)	.	.	.	.	.	.	.	.	.	.	.	.	.	.	.	.	.	.	.	.	.	.	.	.	.	.	.	.
Marsupella emarginata (568)	.	.	.	.	.	.	.	.	.	.	.	.	.	.	.	.	.	+	.	.	.	.	.	.	.	.	.	.

ADDITIONAL SPECIES IN COMMUNITY

1. *Grimmia ovalis* I, *Hedwigia integrifolia* I, *Pterogonium gracile* I, *Ulota americana* II, *Ulota phyllantha* I, *Caloplaca ferruginea* I, *Ochrolechia tartarea* II, *Umbilicaria pustulata* I, *Umbilicaria torrefacta* I; **2.** *Sibbaldia procumbens* II; **3.** *Phyllitis scolopendrium* II, *Isopterygium pulchellum* I, *Rhynchostegiella tenella* I, *Pellia endiviifolia* I, *Porella platyphylla* I, *Radula aquilegia* I, *Radula lindbergiana* I, *Gyalecta jenensis* II, *Lobaria scrobiculata* I, *Protoblastenia rupestris* I; **5.** *Daucus carota* I; **6.** *Carex distans* I, *Carex scandinavica* II, *Eleocharis uniglumis* I; **7.** *Cerastium atrovirens* I, *Ramalina curnowii* I, *Verrucaria maura* I; **8.** *Bryum alpinum* I; **9.** *Equisetum arvense* II, *Agropyron junceiforme* I, *Carex otrubae* I, *Lycopus europaeus* II, *Myosotis discolor* I, *Polygonum persicaria* I, *Scutellaria galericulata* I, *Sonchus arvensis* I, *Pottia heimii* I; **12.** *Glyceria fluitans* I, *Potamogeton lucens* I; **14.** *Baldellia ranunculoides* II, *Isoetes lacustris* I, *Nitella* sp. I; **15.** *Callitriche stagnalis* I; **16.** *Sphagnum pulchrum* II, *Cladopodiella fluitans* I; **17.** *Carex diandra* I, *Drepanocladus fluitans* II; **18.** *Scapania irrigua* I; **19.** *Anagallis tenella* I, *Drosera intermedia* I; **20.** *Sphagnum girgensohnii* II; **22.** *Acrocladium cordifolium* I, *Acrocladium stramineum* I, *Dicranum bonjeani* I; **23.** *Dactylorchis incarnata* I; **27.** *Gymnostomum recurvirostrum* II; **28.** *Campylopus brevipilus* I, *Campylopus introflexus* I, *Nowellia curvifolia* I, *Odontoschisma denudatum* I, *Cladonia digitata* I, *Cladonia floerkiana* I, *Icmadophila ericetorum* I; **29.** *Sphagnum molle* I; **30.** *Calypogeia sphagnicola* I, *Cephalozia connivens* I, *Cephalozia macrostachya* I, *Riccardia latifrons* I; **32.** *Poa subcaerulea* I, *Poa trivialis* I, *Epilobium alsinifolium* II, *Anomobryum filiforme* I, *Drepanocladus exannulatus* II, *Onchophorus virens* II, *Pohlia wahlenbergii* var. *glacialis* I, *Scapania paludosa* I, *Tritomaria polita* I; **33.** *Deschampsia alpina* II; **34.** *Dichodontium pellucidum* II, *Solenostoma triste* II; **35.** *Solenostoma sphaerocarpoidea* I;

TABLE 4.57 *continued*

	29 *Molinieto–Callunetum*	30 *Trichophoreto–Eriophoretum*	31 *Calluneto–Eriophoretum*	32 *Philonoto–Saxifragetum stellaris*	33 *Koenigia islandica–Carex demissa nodum*	34 *Cratoneuron commutatum–Saxifraga aizoides nodum*	35 *Saxifragetum aizoidis*	36 *Juncus acutiflorus–Filipendula ulmaria*	37 *Centaureo–Cynosuretum*	38 *Maritime grassland nodum*	39 *Lolium perenne–Plantago lanceolata*	40 *Dryas octopetala–Carex flacca*	41 *Cariceto–Rhacomitretum lanuginosi*	42 *Festuca ovina–Luzula spicata nodum*	43 *Rhacomitreto–Callunetum*	44 *Juniperus nana nodum*	45 *Rhacomitreto–Empetretum*	46 *Alchemilla alpina–Vaccinium myrtillus nodum*	47 *Nardus stricta–Vaccinium myrtillus*	48 *Agrosto–Festucetum* (species-poor)	49 *Alchemilleto–Agrosto–Festucetum*	50 *Agrosto–Festucetum* (species-rich)	51 *Nardo–Juncetum squarrosi*	52 *Callunetum vulgaris*	53 *Calluna vulgaris–Sieglingia decumbens*	54 *Calluna vulgaris–Arctostaphylos uva-ursi nodum*	55 *Vaccineto–Callunetum hepaticosum*	56 *Luzula sylvatica–Vaccinium myrtillus*	57 *Luzula sylvatica–Silene dioica*	58 *Betula pubescens–Cirsium heterophyllum*	59 *Sedum rosea–Alchemilla glabra*	60 *Betula pubescens–Vaccinium myrtillus*	61 *Corylus avellana–Oxalis acetosella*	62 *Oxalis acetosella–Rhytidiadelphus loreus*	63 *Hymenophyllum wilsonii–Isothecium myosuroides*	64 Open boulder association	65 *Fraxinus excelsior–Brachypodium sylvaticum*
551)	.	.	.	.	.	.	.	+	.	.	.	.	.	.	.	.	.	.	.	.	.	.	.	.	.	.	.	.	.	.	.	+	.	.	.	+	.
552)	+	II	.	.	.	.	.	.	.	.	.	.	.	.	.	.	.	.	.	+	.	.	.	.	+	.	.	.	.	.	.	III	.	.	.	.	.
553)	.	.	.	.	.	.	.	.	.	.	.	.	.	.	.	.	.	.	.	.	.	.	.	.	.	.	.	.	.	.	.	II	I	.	.	.	II
554)	.	.	.	.	.	.	.	.	.	.	.	.	.	.	.	.	.	.	.	.	.	.	.	.	.	.	.	.	.	.	.	VI	II	.	.	.	.
555)	.	.	.	.	.	.	.	.	.	.	.	.	.	.	.	.	.	.	.	.	.	.	.	.	.	.	.	.	.	.	.	II	I	.	.	.	.
556)	.	.	.	.	.	.	.	.	.	.	.	.	.	.	.	.	.	.	.	.	.	.	.	.	.	.	.	.	.	.	.	.	+	.	.	.	+
557)	.	.	.	.	.	.	.	.	.	.	.	.	.	.	.	.	.	.	.	.	+	.	.	.	.	.	.	+	.	+	.	.	II	.	.	.	+
558)	.	.	.	.	.	.	.	.	.	.	.	.	.	.	.	.	.	.	.	.	.	.	.	.	.	.	.	.	.	.	.	.	II	.	.	.	II
559)	.	.	.	.	.	.	.	.	.	.	.	.	.	.	.	.	.	.	.	.	.	.	.	.	.	.	.	.	.	.	.	.	+	.	.	.	+
560)	.	.	.	.	.	.	.	.	.	.	.	.	.	.	.	.	.	.	.	.	.	.	.	.	.	.	.	.	.	.	.	.	+	.	II	.	.
561)	.	.	.	.	.	.	.	.	.	.	.	.	.	.	.	.	.	.	.	.	.	.	.	.	.	.	+	.	.	.	.	.	+	.	+	+	.
562)	.	.	.	.	.	.	.	.	.	.	.	.	.	.	.	.	.	.	.	.	.	.	.	.	.	.	.	.	.	.	.	.	+	.	+	II	.
563)	.	.	.	.	.	.	.	.	.	.	.	.	.	.	.	.	.	.	.	.	.	.	.	.	.	.	.	.	.	.	.	.	II	.	.	IV	.
564)	.	.	.	.	.	.	.	.	.	.	.	.	.	.	.	.	.	.	.	.	.	.	.	.	.	.	.	.	.	.	.	.	II	.	.	V	.
565)	.	.	.	.	.	.	.	.	.	.	.	.	.	.	.	.	.	.	.	.	.	.	.	.	.	.	.	.	.	.	.	.	.	.	II	+	.
566)	.	.	.	.	.	.	.	.	.	.	.	.	.	.	.	.	.	.	.	.	.	.	.	.	.	.	.	.	.	.	.	.	.	.	.	III	.
567)	.	.	.	.	.	.	.	.	.	.	.	.	.	.	.	.	.	.	.	.	.	.	.	.	.	.	.	.	.	.	.	.	.	.	.	V	.
568)	.	.	.	.	.	.	.	.	.	.	.	.	.	.	+	.	+	.	.	.	.	.	.	.	.	.	+	.	.	.	+	.	.	.	.	IV	.

36. *Hypericum tetrapterum* I, *Lotus pedunculatus* I, *Climaceum dendroides* I; **37.** *Alopecurus pratensis* I, *Phleum bertolonii* I, *Phleum pratense* I, *Platanthera chlorantha* II, *Chrysanthemum segetum* I, *Veronica filiformis* I; **38.** *Funaria attenuata* I; **39.** *Alopecurus geniculatus* I, *Juncus tenuis* I, *Polygonum aviculare* I, *Rumex acetosella* II, *Rumex obtusifolius* II, *Veronica agrestis* I, *Archidium alternifolium* I, *Barbula unguiculata* I, *Bryum bicolor* II, *Bryum pallens* I; **40.** *Gnaphalium sylvaticum* I, *Encalypta streptocarpa* I, *Entodon concinnus* I, *Orthotrichum anomalum* I; **41.** *Aulacomnium turgidum* I, *Hypnum cupressiforme* var. *lacunosum* I; **42.** *Juncus trifidus* II, *Cerastium arcticum* II, *Conostomum tetragonum* II, *Anthelia juratzkana* II; **43.** *Leucorchis albida* I, *Ochrolechia frigida* I; **45.** *Dicranodontium uncinatum* II, *Polytrichum nanum* I, *Scapania nimbosa* I, *Bazzania pearsonii* II; **49.** *Botrychium lunaria* I, *Alchemilla wichurae* I, *Diphyscium foliosum* I, *Isothecium myosuroides* var. *brachythecioides* I, *Barbilophozia lycopodioides* I; **52.** *Lycopodium clavatum* I, *Cladonia crispata* I; **53.** *Luzula pilosa* I, *Pyrola media* I, *Ulex europaeus* I, *Veronica officinalis* I, **55.** *Myurium hebridarum* I, *Sphagnum robustum* I, *Colura calyptrifolia* I, *Lepidozia trichoclados* I; **56.** *Cryptogramma crispa* I, *Dryopteris abbreviata* I, *Thelypteris dryopteris* II, *Hypericum androsaemum* I, *Eurynchium praelongum* var. *stokesii* I, *Lepidozia pearsonii* I, *Lepidozia pinnata* I; **58.** *Stellaria holostea* I; **59.** *Salix myrsinites* I, *Draba incana* I, *Rhinanthus borealis* I, *Bartramia ithyphylla* I, *Bartramia pomiformis* I, *Camptothecium lutescens* I, *Leptodontium recurvifolium* II, *Plagiobryum zierii* I, *Trichostomum hibernicum* II, *Metzgeria conjugata* I, *Radula complanata* I; **60.** *Hedera helix* I, *Ilex aquifolium* II, *Salix caprea* II; **61.** *Carex remota* I, *Plagiothecium sylvaticum* II, *Calypogeia arguta* I; **62.** *Plagiothecium denticulatum* I, *Plagiochila punctata* I, *Nephromium laevigatum* I, *Sphaerophorus fragilis* I, *Sticta sylvatica* I; **64.** *Aphanolejeunea microscopica* I, *Scapania nemorea* I; **65.** *Ulmus glabra* II, *Viburnum opulus* II, *Helictotrichon pratense* I, *Glechoma hederacea* I, *Marchesinia mackaii* I.

5

THE DISTRIBUTION AND ECOLOGY OF THE FLORA AND VEGETATION

1. GENERAL CONSIDERATIONS

The rich and varied flora of the Isle of Skye is integrated into the wide variety of plant communities described in Chapter 4. The present distribution of these communities appears to be largely a result of three major interacting environmental variables – (*a*) climate, (*b*) geology, topography, and soils, and (*c*) land use. All three of these factors vary greatly within the comparatively small area of Skye, as described in Chapter 3.

The present climate of Skye is extremely oceanic. It is characterised by a narrow temperature range, high winds, and an excess of precipitation over evapotranspiration. Due to the island's relatively northerly position, the average annual temperature (15.5 °F, 8.6 °C) is rather low, resulting in an overall cool, moist climate.

These climatic factors combine with the geology and topography of the island in controlling the characteristics of the soils. Due to the precipitation excess the soils are readily leached, except where flushed from areas of adjacent basic rocks. Where topographical conditions prevent adequate drainage, the soils tend to be water-logged, and peat formation frequently occurs. Due to the humid climate, peat development is widespread in hollows and on relatively flat ground, and thus bog vegetation is the predominant vegetational type in these areas.

The interaction of the climate with the geology and topography in turn influences the land use within the island. Due to the nature of the underlying rocks, the distribution and extent of leached or water-logged soils, and the rugged topography of Skye, man's habitations and croftings are generally confined to small areas of low ground with relatively fertile soils near the coast. Climatic factors such as exposure to strong winds and the low average temperatures restrict the range of crops that can be grown profitably on the island. However, the better-drained dwarf-shrub heath and grassland communities of the uplands are used extensively as hill pasture, and evidence will be presented to indicate that these communities have been derived largely from former woodland as a result of felling, grazing, and burning. In contrast, the alpine zone, with its more severe climate and correspondingly shorter growing season supports communities which approach 'natural' vegetation more closely than any other vegetation type in Britain today.

The extreme oceanicity of the regional climate, the varied geology and topography, and the differences in land use provide the three major interacting factors in the ecosystem which determine the occurrence, relative abundance, and distribution of the various plant communities in the different parts of the island. This chapter attempts an ecological synthesis of the phytosociological data presented in Chapter 4, in order to discuss the observed vegetational pattern in relation to the possible ecological factors influencing it.

Fig. 5 lists the principal plant communities occurring on Skye today. The classification adopted differs somewhat from the systematic phytosociological order used in Chapter 4. It is based partially on the physiognomy and life-forms of the dominant species, and partially on the ecology of the communities and their habitats. However, as is apparent from Fig. 5, this ecological and physiognomical grouping corresponds closely in practice to the higher phytosociological units of Chapter 4. Fig. 5 indicates the altitudinal range, so far as it is known, and the spatial distribution within the Isle of Skye of each vegetational type considered.

Six geographical regions have been delimited within the island on the basis of the topography and the solid geology (see Figs. 2, 3). The regions are as follows:

1. *Sleat.* The boundary between regions 1 and 2 is drawn along the A851 road from Loch na Dal to Broadford. The boundary between regions 1 and 3 is drawn through Glen Suardal from Broadford to

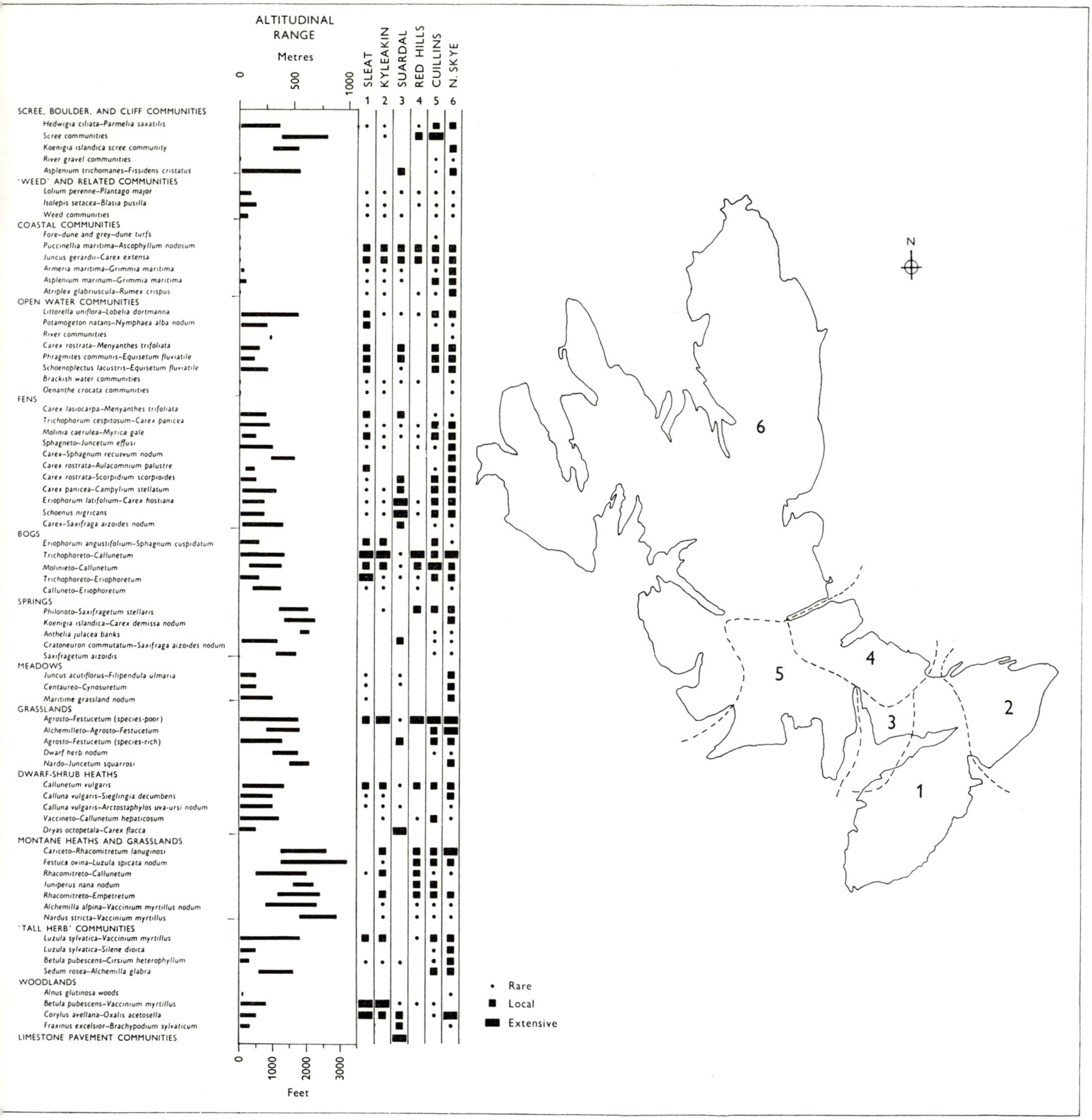

Figure 5. Present distribution of the principal vegetational types in the six regions of Skye. The nomenclature of the vegetational types follows Chapter 4, and the terms rare, local, and extensive are defined in Chapter 5.

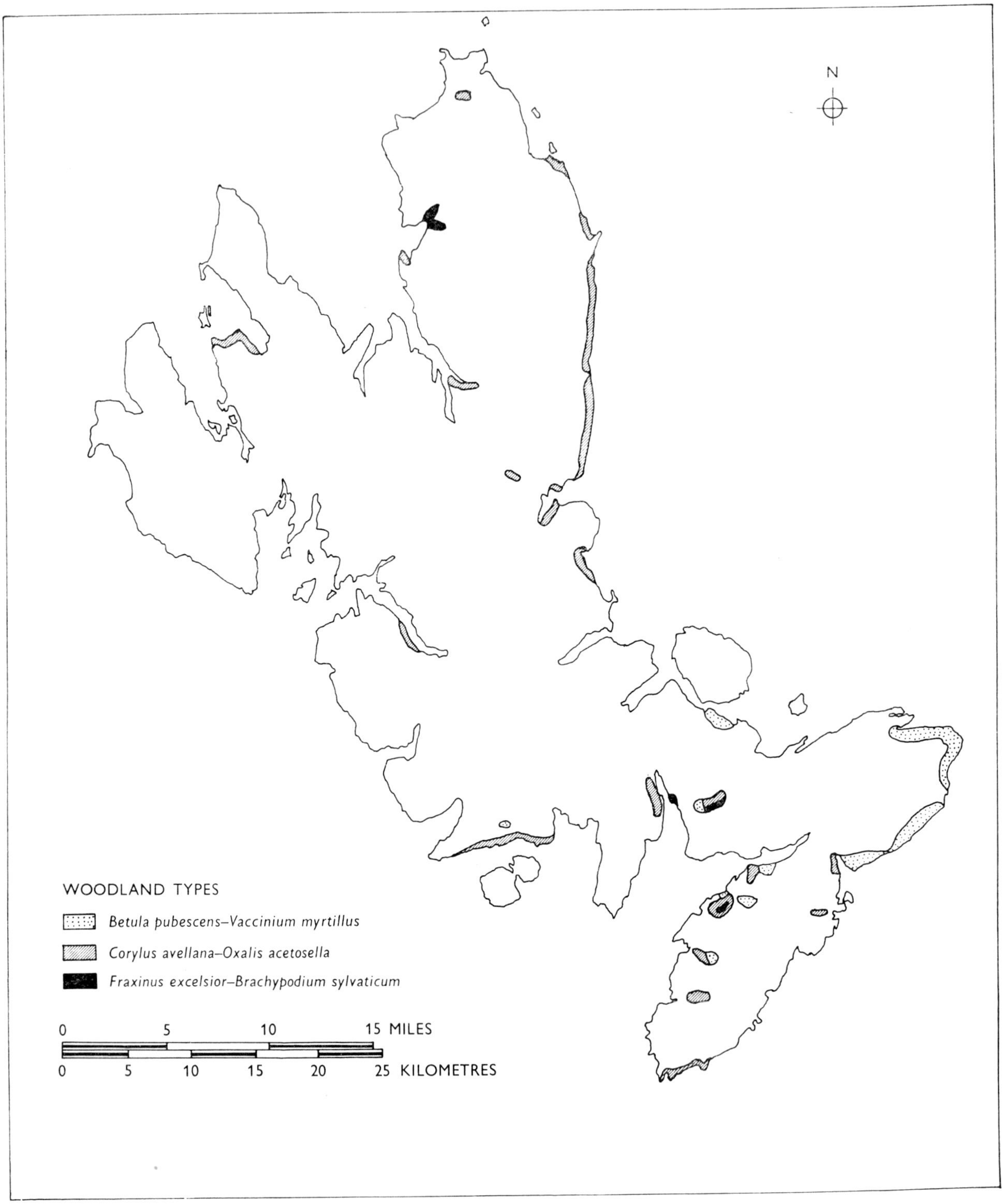

Figure 6. Present distribution of the three principal woodland types on the Isle of Skye.

Eilean Heast, and across Loch Eishort, to exclude the limestones at Ord.

2. *Kyleakin.*

3. *Suardal.* This area includes Ben Suardal, Loch Cill Chriosd, and Torrin, and extends southwards to include Rubha Suisnish, and the limestones at Ord in the Sleat.

4. *Red Hills.* The boundary between regions 4 and 3 is drawn from Loch Slapin, through Strath Suardal to Broadford. A line is drawn from Loch Sligachan through Glen Sligachan to include Lord MacDonald's Forest and Marsco, and turning eastwards to include Glas Bheinn Mhor and Strath Mor.

5. *Cuillins.* This region comprises the main mountain range delimited by Glens Drynoch, Brittle, and Sligachan, and also includes Blà Bheinn and the Elgol Peninsula.

6. *Northern Skye.*

The known distribution of the various plant communities in each of these regions is shown on Fig. 5. The extent of each community in a region is indicated by one of three symbols, which are explained in the figure. The terms that the symbols represent – extensive, local, and rare – depend on the nature of the vegetational type, and they are used here only for comparing the relative abundance of similar vegetational types. Thus an extensive occurrence of spring communities covers a much smaller area of ground than does a limited occurrence of bog in the same region. Although the descriptive method is qualitative and subjective, it appears that certain communities have distinct geographical distributions within the island, the possible causes for which are discussed below.

2. THE WOODLAND ZONE

I. WOODLANDS

The climatic forest limit or potential tree-line is a convenient datum in considering the natural vegetational zonation in any mountainous region. The woodland zone is here defined as the ground and the associated flora and vegetation lying below the potential tree-line. In Scandinavia, where ideas on altitudinal zonation of vegetation were initially developed, there is still an abundance of woodland and scrub on the lower mountain slopes. This is in contrast with the typical treeless landscape of the British uplands. Any attempt at the reconstruction of the former woodland extent on Skye, both altitudinally and geographically, must draw on fragmentary, and often indirect evidence based on the distribution of (*a*) present woodlands, (*b*) scattered trees and shrubs, and (*c*) buried tree stumps.

The present distribution of woodlands on Skye is shown in Fig. 6. All the known areas of woodland of one hectare or more are mapped, except for plantations. There is a concentration of woodland of both the *Betula pubescens–Vaccinium myrtillus* and *Corylus avellana–Oxalis acetosella* types in the Sleat and Kyleakin regions. Woodland is sparse in northern Skye, the majority being coastal *Corylus avellana* scrub developed on steep talus slopes below the sea-cliffs. The highest altitude to which any of the Skye woodlands ascends today is 800 feet (245 m). These woods seldom, if ever, show a natural upper limit. Nearly all these woodland fragments are found in areas either protected, to some degree, from grazing animals, or immune from bog development, due to their occurrence on steep, well-drained and often boulder-strewn slopes.

The occurrence of scattered trees throughout the island indicates a former more widespread tree cover on Skye. Occasional trees of *Betula pubescens* ssp. *odorata*, *Corylus avellana*, *Salix aurita*, *S. caprea*, *S. cinerea* ssp. *atrocinerea*, and *Sorbus aucuparia*, and more rarely *Ilex aquifolium*, *Populus tremula*, *Prunus padus*, and *Quercus petraea* occur on inaccessible ledges in many of the low-lying sheltered ravines throughout the island, in steep block-litters, and on ungrazed islands in inland lochs, for example in Loch nan Eilean, Loch Coruisk, and Lochain Dubha.

Further evidence for the former extent of woodland on Skye comes from the occurrence of tree stumps (mainly birch and willow) buried by peat. The distribution of these stumps within the island is very disjunct, but their frequency closely parallels the present woodland distribution, with the densest concentration being found in the Sleat and Kyleakin regions. Pine stumps are conspicuously absent, except for a small area near Kyleakin. Wood remains are extremely rare in the extensive and often deep peat-cuttings in northern Skye, and those that have been found tend to be in low-lying, sheltered areas.

At the natural tree line in Scandinavia today, there is frequently a well-marked zone of sub-alpine scrub between the forest and the alpine zones (Dahl, 1956; Löve, 1970; Nordhagen, 1943; Rune, 1965). As with the lowland woodlands, sub-alpine scrub on Skye is very fragmentary, consisting of small stands of birch, willow, and juniper scrub, from which little evidence can be gained about the former tree line. Occasional bushes of birch, rowan, *Salix aurita*, *S. caprea*, and *S. repens* can be found, however, on inaccessible inland cliff ledges between 1200 and

1300 feet (365–400 m), as, for example, at The Quirang and in Coire Uaigneach, Blà Bheinn. There are only a few known bushes of the more montane *Salix myrsinites* and *S. phylicifolia* on Skye, growing on moist, basic cliffs with 'tall herbs' at 1400 feet (425 m). *Juniperus communis* ssp. *nana* occurs locally on several sea-cliffs and on dry, inland cliffs up to at least 1000 feet (305 m), and as a high-level plant of wind-exposed summit ground between 1700 and 2200 feet (520–675 m). The delimitation of a sub-alpine zone on Skye is thus extremely difficult, as it is elsewhere in Scotland (Poore & McVean, 1957). The situation is further confused by the prominence of birch in woods at low altitudes.

Although there can be little doubt that sub-alpine scrub was once more widespread on Skye and elsewhere in Scotland (McVean & Ratcliffe, 1962), the present evidence only permits the distinction of a 'woodland zone', which includes both the forest zone and the sub-alpine zone of the Scandinavian ecologists.

From the above evidence it can be concluded that woodland was once more widespread on Skye. Some indication of its former nature and extent may be gained from the composition and distribution of the remaining fragments. The Sleat and Kyleakin regions were probably the most densely wooded, although sheltered areas in northern Skye, and the lower slopes of the Cuillins and the Red Hills probably supported woodland, perhaps of a rather open character. Juniper and willow scrub may have occurred at higher altitudes, perhaps up to at least 425 m, as well as on much of the lower ground in northern Skye that is occupied today by 'tall herb' meadows.

The reduction in woodland cover may be attributed to two main causes. Soil degradation and peat formation on flat and gently sloping ground during the Flandrian would have limited tree growth in many areas, and human deforestation, either directly by clear-felling, or indirectly by burning and grazing, would have reduced the tree cover on the steeper, better-drained sites. The only published pollen diagrams prepared from Flandrian deposits on Skye are from the Trotternish Peninsula (Vasari & Vasari, 1968), and these diagrams suggest that in that region rather open birch-hazel woodlands were predominant and that closed woodland was never widespread. Similar palynological data are required from the other regions of Skye to provide a basis for the reconstruction of the Flandrian distribution and character of the woodlands over the island, which today are only represented by fragmentary stands.

The causes of the past and present distribution of woodland on Skye may be sought in regional differences in environmental factors. The chief of these is climate, which has complex and multi-factorial effects on tree growth (see Pears, 1967; Spence, 1960). A certain summer warmth, which can be expressed either in terms of the number of days with a mean temperature maximum above 5.6 °C (42 °F) (Manley, 1952) or 10 °C (50 °F) (Köppen, 1923; Spence, 1960), or as accumulated temperatures (Gregory, 1954), is generally considered essential for tree growth. Although most of lowland Skye lies within a temperature regime apparently suitable for tree growth, well-developed woodland seems to be restricted, and appears to have been so in the past, to the Sleat and Kyleakin regions, presumably for other climatic reasons.

Within areas of suitable temperature regime, exposure to wind may become an important factor controlling tree growth, especially in a highly oceanic region such as Skye (see Spence, 1960). It is probable that the broad distribution of woodlands on the island in the past was largely controlled by wind exposure, until this natural pattern was altered, to some degree, by man.

Although there are very few comparative quantitative meteorological data from the different regions of Skye (see Chapter 3), qualitative differences can be deduced from the distribution and performance of various plants; for example, an analysis of the representation of the different phytogeographical groups of Atlantic bryophytes, as defined by Ratcliffe (1968), in the six regions of Skye (Table 5.1), suggests that the Sleat Peninsula is the mildest region, for it supports the highest number of Southern–Atlantic species on Skye.

It is perhaps significant that many of the members of the Southern–Atlantic group have a world distribution centered upon warm oceanic, or even tropical regions (Greig-Smith, 1950; Ratcliffe, 1968), and yet reach their northernmost known localities in or near the Sleat Peninsula. These include *Acrobolbus wilsonii*, *Adelanthus decipiens* (see Fig. 8 in Ratcliffe, 1968), *Hymenophyllum tunbridgense*, *Jubula hutchinsiae*, *Lejeunea mandonii*, and *Radula carringtonii*. The climatic mildness of the Sleat is further indicated by the earlier maturation of crops there (Murray, 1966). Although the effects of past woodland treatment cannot entirely be ignored, the mild climate of the Sleat is probably an important factor responsible for the greater development, both past and present, of woodland in that region.

TABLE 5.1. *Distribution of Atlantic bryophytes in the six geographical regions on Skye*

Phytogeographical groups (after Ratcliffe, 1968)	Geographical regions on Skye: Sleat	Kyleakin	Suardal	Red Hills	Cuillins	Northern Skye	Skye Total	British Total
Southern-Atlantic	7	1	1	1	4	1	8	27
Mediterranean-Atlantic	1	0	0	0	2	4	4	42
Northern-Atlantic	8	13	6	12	14	14	19	25
Widespread-Atlantic	19	18	9	14	20	16	21	24
Sub-Atlantic	30	26	23	24	29	33	39	45
Western British	25	23	15	17	24	20	28	35
Total number of taxa	90	81	54	68	93	88	119	198

There are six distinct woodland types occurring on Skye today. These are the *Alnus glutinosa* woods, and the *Betula pubescens–Vaccinium myrtillus*, *Corylus avellana–Oxalis acetosella*, *Luzula sylvatica–Vaccinium myrtillus*, *Betula pubescens–Cirsium heterophyllum*, and *Fraxinus excelsior–Brachypodium sylvaticum* Associations. The dominant tree species occur in several of these communities, and as a result the woodland types are distinguished largely on the basis of the floristic composition of the herb and ground layers (see Table 4.57). These floristic differences are described in Chapter 4, and they can be ascribed to variations in soil factors resulting from geology and topography and in grazing pressures. The most widespread woodland types on Skye are the *Betula pubescens–Vaccinium myrtillus* and *Corylus avellana–Oxalis acetosella* Associations (see Figs. 5, 6), the other types being restricted at present to a few stands only, due either to a rarity of suitable habitats or to a high degree of biotic interference.

Although none of the Skye woods appear to be completely 'natural', that is undisturbed by man, the frequent occurrence of a luxuriant growth of drought-sensitive bryophytes and pteridophytes on boulders within the woods may indicate some continuity of tree cover during their history (see Ratcliffe, 1968). It is possible that much of the birch and hazel on Skye is serally related to oak, elm and, perhaps, ash, but in the absence of historical data, the matter is unresolved.

Only one woodland type on Skye, namely the *Alnus glutinosa* type, occurs on damp, water-logged soils, either on flushed slopes or along stream-sides. All the other woodland types favour moist but well-drained soils. A marked gradient in the base-status of the woodland soils appears to represent an important ecological factor in the differentiation of the woodland types (see also Klötzli, 1970; Tittensor & Steele, 1971). The *Fraxinus excelsior–Brachypodium sylvaticum* woods are very rare on Skye (Fig. 5), being restricted to rendzinas or deep brown earths of high pH (5.5–6.4) developed over either Jurassic or Durness limestones. It is probable that the areal extent of this woodland type has been much reduced by selective felling in the past (McVean, 1964). The *Corylus avellana–Oxalis acetosella* Association, which is the most abundant woodland type on Skye today, occurs on the more fertile brown earth soils (pH range 5.1–6.0) that are frequently flushed by irrigation, and are developed over basalt, gabbro, limestone, and, more rarely, sandstone. All the *Corylus avellana* woods are browsed and grazed, to some degree, by wild and domestic animals. The importance of this biotic factor in influencing the floristic character of the herb layer and the associated tall shrubs is strikingly demonstrated by the differences between the herb and shrub floras of grazed areas and of areas protected, in some way, from intensive grazing and browsing, for example on inaccessible ledges in ravines or on steep, block-strewn ground. The ungrazed stands are characterised by an abundance of 'tall herbs', such as *Angelica sylvestris*, *Cirsium heterophyllum*, *Crepis paludosa*, *Filipendula ulmaria*, and *Geum rivale* (*Betula pubescens–Cirsium heterophyllum* Association). This community would probably be more widespread on Skye in the absence of intense grazing and browsing, as it is in parts of Scandinavia today.

On poorer soils, such as humus podsols or acidic brown earths (pH range 3.7–4.9) developed over granite or sandstone, in the Sleat, Kyleakin, and Red Hills regions (Fig. 5 and Fig. 6), the prominent woodland type is the *Betula pubescens–Vaccinium myrtillus* Association. As with the *Corylus avellana–Oxalis acetosella* woods of richer soils, the present structure and composition of the herb layer in the birch woods is largely controlled by animal grazing and browsing. On acidic, steep slopes and ravine ledges that are largely ungrazed *Luzula sylvatica* and *Vaccinium myrtillus* are prominent, with an abundance of the pteridophytes *Blechnum spicant*, *Dryopteris aemula*, *D. borreri*, *D. dilatata*, and *Thelypteris dryopteris* (*Luzula sylvatica–Vaccinium myrtillus* Association). It is probable that the Skye birch woods would have such a herb layer in the absence of intensive grazing. The shrubs *Ilex aquifolium* and *Lonicera periclymenum*, and the tree *Sorbus aucuparia* would probably be more frequent in such woods. Ungrazed acidic deciduous woods are extremely rare in Britain as a whole, but fragments still persist in steep, blocky ground in western Ireland (for example at Slish Wood, Co. Sligo, Uragh Wood, Co. Kerry, and Cromaglan, Co. Kerry), south-west England (for example at Black Tor Copse and Wistman's Wood, Devon), north Wales (for example at Ceunant Llennyrch, Merioneth, and on the north side of Llyn Padarn, Caernarvonshire), and western Scotland (for example on the south side of Loch Assynt, Sutherland, and along the coast south of Tarbert, Kintyre), and on wooded islands in western Scotland (McVean, 1958*b*; Tittensor & Steele, 1971) and western Ireland (Webb & Glanville, 1962).

2. DWARF-SHRUB HEATHS AND GRASSLANDS

Although it is probable that many of the better drained slopes on Skye once supported woodland or scrub to an altitude of at least 800 feet (245 m), with sub-alpine scrub extending to a greater altitude, the predominant vegetation types on well drained soils within the potential woodland zone today are grasslands and dwarf-shrub heaths (Fig. 5). The whole complex of grasslands and heaths which lies within the former forest zone appears to have resulted largely from deforestation, and to be maintained today by a combination of burning, grazing, and trampling (see King & Nicholson, 1964; Nicholson, 1970; Ratcliffe, 1959). The ecological factors influencing the balance between grassland and heath are not so clear, however, and the possible factors are discussed below.

Most of the woodland remnants on Skye have a predominantly grassy and mossy herb and ground vegetation closely resembling the Agrosto–Festucetum grasslands in floristic composition (see Table 4.57). As discussed above, these surviving woodland fragments have been greatly modified by browsing, grazing, and trampling, and it is likely that deforestation today would lead directly to the formation of grasslands. This is unlikely to have been the case, however, when the woodlands were less severely modified. Clearance of ungrazed acidic woodlands, such as those described above, would probably result in the development of dwarf-shrub heath, with an abundance of *Vaccinium myrtillus*. This would probably be rapidly invaded by *Calluna vulgaris* in the absence of grazing, forming a mixed *Calluna–Vaccinium* vegetation, such as occurs today in hill regions with a low biotic pressure, for example on the Rhinog Mountains in Merioneth, north Wales. In contrast, clearance of 'tall herb' woodlands on richer soils would probably result in the direct replacement of woodland by species-rich grasslands. McVean & Ratcliffe (1962) comment that during the early nineteenth century, which was the main period of deforestation in the Scottish Highlands, the grazing pressures were lower than today, and that many woodlands would have been naturally replaced by dwarf-shrub heaths rather than by grasslands.

Within what appears to be edaphically, topographically, and climatically uniform ground, there is frequently a mosaic of grassland and heath within a comparatively small area. Ratcliffe (1959) has presented detailed evidence to demonstrate that, in north Wales, the balance between dwarf-shrub heaths and grasslands is largely biotically controlled: the conversion of heaths to grasslands is a function of overall grazing intensity, combined with intensive and prolonged burning and selective grazing preferences between communities and between species within communities. Such vegetational mosaics therefore probably reflect uneven biotic pressures and differing land-use histories. Evidence similar to that described by Ratcliffe (1959) and Edgell (1971) for north Wales exists on Skye. The survival of dwarf-shrub dominated vegetation in situations naturally protected from grazing animals, and perhaps also from fire, can be seen over the island. The vegetation of most acidic cliff ledges up to at least 1700 feet (520 m) consists predominantly of *Calluna vulgaris* and *Vaccinium myrtillus*, in contrast to the adjacent grassland slopes. Luxuriant growths of these species occur on the inaccessible tops of large detached blocks, often with seedlings of *Betula pubescens* and *Sorbus aucuparia*. Good examples may be seen below Carn Liath, on the south-west slopes of Gars-Bheinn, and in parts of the Red Hills. Similarly ungrazed and unburnt islands in lochs (for example at Loch Fada, Loch Airigh na Saorach, and Loch an Dubha in Glen Sligachan) and in rivers (for example in the River Sligachan and the Abhainn Camas Fhionnairidh) are densely heather clad, often with some birch and rowan trees, in contrast to the Agrosto–Festucetum grasslands of the grazed loch margins and river banks. Reduction of biotic pressures by fencing the various dwarf-shrub and grassland communities gives further evidence for their seral relationships. The changes observable in Forestry Commission enclosures, where there is complete protection from burning and grazing, show fairly rapid revertence from grassland to dwarf-shrub heath. The changes appear to depend on the degree of modification prior to fencing, for if the dwarf shrubs have been completely eradicated, there is merely an increase in luxuriance and changes in the proportionate abundance of the dominant grasses. On dry rather acidic sites *Agrostis* spp. tend to increase at the expense of *Festuca ovina*, whereas on better soils there is not only an increase in the more succulent grasses, especially of *Festuca rubra* and *Deschampsia cespitosa*, but there are reductions in the species diversity and in the abundance of several herbs, for example *Thymus drucei* and *Trifolium repens*. Such changes are strikingly shown by the differences between unfenced and fenced species-rich grasslands on the north-east facing slopes below An Càrnach. Welch & Rawes (1966) report similar changes following fencing in comparable vegetation types in the northern Pennines within a period of six years. Recovery of *Calluna vulgaris* in fenced areas on Skye depends on its survival in the grassland communities. Grazed-down remnants regain their former stature, but there appears to be little fresh seedling establishment, thereby limiting its recovery to former dominance on the less strongly modified sites. Harris (1939) demonstrated a substantial increase in the vigour of *Calluna* and *Vaccinium myrtillus* in Agrosto–Festucetum grasslands in Cwm Aran on Cader Idris, north Wales, following two years enclosure.

The Agrosto–Festucetum grasslands and the closely related Nardo–Juncetum squarrosi Association form a complex of closely related communities of broadly similar structure and floristic composition with several constant species in common. There are, however, some consistent differences in their floristic composition, mainly in the herbs and bryophytes, as described in Chapter 4 (see also Table 4.57). These floristic differences appear to reflect variations in soil moisture and soil basicity (see Edgell, 1971; Ratcliffe, 1959). The two major grassland types are clearly differentiated ecologically by soil moisture conditions, for the Nardo–Juncetum squarrosi Association is restricted to damp podsols or shallow peats that are often gleyed, whereas the Agrosto–Festucetum grasslands occur on well-drained podsols or brown earths.

Within the Agrosto–Festucetum grassland complex, the widespread species-poor association is seemingly differentiated from the other types by a lower soil base-status, for it occurs on skeletal brown earths or podsols of low pH (4.4–5.1). It is the most widespread grassland type on Skye today (Fig. 5). Heddle & Ogg (1936) have shown in their work on Scottish hill-pastures that species-poor grasslands such as the Agrosto–Festucetum type can be converted artifically to species-rich turf merely by diverting the natural flow of stream water to irrigate the soils of the species-poor stands, suggesting that soil fertility is a principal differentiating factor. The factors differentiating the *Alchemilla*-rich association from the species-rich association are less clear, however, for they frequently occur on rather similar soil types (well drained brown earths, with a pH range of 5.2–5.4 and 5.0–6.4, respectively). The *Alchemilla* grasslands tend to occur on soils with a slightly lower soil fertility than the species-rich type, for *Alchemilla* turf is entirely absent from the richest limestone soils on Skye. Where the two grassland types do occur together, for example on the eastern slopes on the Trotternish ridge, the species-rich stands frequently favour the more intensely irrigated areas, suggesting that soil fertility and irrigation may be important differentiating factors.

There is a similar edaphic differentiation within the dwarf-shrub communities. The widespread Callunetum vulgaris and *Calluna vulgaris–Sieglingia decumbens* Associations are restricted to the well-drained soils, whereas the Vaccineto–Callunetum hepaticosum stands favour moist, peaty soils. The vegetational endpoint of this soil-moisture gradient on gentle slopes is Trichophoreto–Callunetum or Molinieto–Callunetum bog. The major ecological factor distinguishing the two *Calluna vulgaris* heaths of drier soils appears to be soil basicity. Callunetum vulgaris occurs on iron-humus podsols of low pH (3.8–4.7) and is thus widespread on Skye (Fig. 5). The *Calluna vulgaris–Sieglingia decumbens* Association and the related *Calluna vulgaris–Arctostaphylos uva-ursi nodum* favour more fertile brown earths of a rather higher pH (4.9–6.1) and often occur in coastal areas where there may be some nutrient enrichment from sea-spray. These communities are rather rare on Skye (Fig. 5), considering the relative abundance of base-rich soils. Their rarity may result, however, from the fact that sites with fertile soils are grazed

TABLE 5.2

1. 'SPECIES-POOR SERIES'

Community	Soil type	Soil pH	Rock type	Altitudinal range (feet)	Mean no. of species per relevé
Luzula sylvatica–Vaccinium myrtillus	Raw humus	3.8–4.3	Granite, sandstone, gabbro	50–1700	30
Betula pubescens–Vaccinium myrtillus	Humus, podsols or brown earths	3.7–4.9	Granite, sandstone	50–800	38
Callunetum vulgaris	Iron-humus podsols	3.8–4.7	Granite, sandstone, gabbro, basalt	100–1600	17
Agrosto–Festucetum (species-poor)	Podsols or skeletal brown earths	4.4–5.1	Granite, sandstone, gabbro, basalt	30–1750	20

2. 'SPECIES-RICH SERIES'

Community	Soil type	Soil pH	Rock type	Altitudinal range (feet)	Mean no. of species per relevé
'Tall herb' communities	Irrigated brown earths	5.5–6.9	Basalt, limestone, gabbro	50–1600	45
Corylus avellana–Oxalis acetosella	Irrigated brown earths	5.1–6.0	Basalt, limestone, gabbro, sandstone	50–500	40
Calluna vulgaris–Sieglingia decumbens	Brown earths	4.9–6.1	Basalt, limestone	75–1000	33
Agrosto–Festucetum (species-rich and Alchemilleto–)	Brown earths	5.0–6.4	Basalt, limestone	25–1800	34

selectively by wild and domestic animals, and as a result the communities are some of the first to undergo modification. Some of the stands of these communities in northern Skye are at present being replaced by species-rich *Agrostis–Festuca* grasslands as a result of burning combined with grazing, and it is now virtually impossible to estimate how widespread the associations were in the past.

There is a general correlation on Skye between the areal extent of grasslands on base-rich soils, and the number and quality of the sheep they support, for there is a selective grazing of the more nutritious swards. On many of the rich grassy slopes in the Trotternish Peninsula, the grazing has been so intense that extensive low-altitude screes have resulted. By their instinctive preference for the richer grasslands, sheep tend to accentuate any edaphically controlled differences in the original vegetation, and they may even produce vegetational differences where none existed before. This has occurred on hills with mixtures of base-rich and base-deficient rocks that have been more heavily stocked with sheep than adjacent hills composed solely of acidic rocks. The vegetation of both rock types in the first area then show a greater modification than that of the second. Glamaig, with its mixture of basic and acidic rocks, provides an interesting comparison with the nearby granitic Red Hills. Agrosto–Festucetum grassland predominates on the lower slopes of Glamaig, and Callunetum vulgaris is virtually absent (except on ungrazed cliff-ledges), even on the poorest soils, whereas Callunetum is frequent on similar poor soils on the slopes of the adjacent Red Hills.

Table 5.2 summarises the inferred relationships between the grasslands, dwarf-shrub heaths, and woodlands occurring on well-drained soils on Skye, in terms of two parallel vegetational series. The different internal levels within a series appear to be controlled biotically, whereas the two series are apparently differentiated throughout by soil base-status. The consistently higher pH values for the grassland soils compared with the soils of the corresponding dwarf-shrub heaths may result from the more rapid biological turnover in the grasslands, whereas there is a slow decomposition and rapid accumulation of *Calluna* litter in the dwarf-shrub communities (cf. Cormack & Gimingham, 1964).

The altitudinal range of the anthropogenic grasslands and dwarf-shrub heaths suggests that they are derived not only from low-altitude woodlands but also from sub-alpine scrub communities. Remnants of these communities are now restricted to inaccessible cliff habitats, either as scattered bushes, or as *Sedum rosea–Alchemilla glabra* 'tall herb' communities. The floristic consistency of the derived grasslands throughout their altitudinal range further emphasises the difficulties of delimiting a sub-alpine zone on Skye.

Unlike the Agrosto–Festucetum grasslands, the

Nardo–Juncetum squarrosi Association extends above the potential tree and shrub limit to an altitude of 2100 feet (645 m) in northern Skye (Fig. 5). The association shows little floristic modification at high altitudes, except for a general reduction in vegetative growth and inflorescence production (see Pearsall, 1950; Welch, 1966). The abundance of *Juncus squarrosus* in the vegetation may be largely a reflection of the recent history of land use, for as Welch (1966) has shown, it is never a constituent of climax vegetation, as its seedling establishment is largely dependent on burning, grazing, treading, and erosion. Harris (1939) demonstrated that *Juncus squarrosus* rapidly decreased in abundance if sheep were excluded from upland grasslands. Selective sheep grazing and trampling may be responsible for the dominance of *Juncus squarrosus* in some stands. Selective grazing can allow the rush to establish itself as small circular colonies on gentle slopes or as dense communities on gentler ill-drained sites where it has a slight competitive advantage over other species (Kershaw & Tallis, 1958).

The Vaccineto–Callunetum hepaticosum Association of steep north- or east-facing blocky slopes is an extremely rare community on Skye today (Fig. 5), presumably due to the destruction of the dwarf-shrub component by burning and grazing (see Ratcliffe, 1968). Some idea of its former extent is given by the scattered occurrence of fragmentary hepatic-rich stands on steep rock ledges in ravines, on cliffs, and in block litters protected, to some degree, from burning and grazing. The community was probably locally common on Skye in areas of suitable topography and microclimate, but it has diminished in abundance with the replacement of dwarf-shrub vegetation by grassland. Many steep hill-sides on Skye support Callunetum vulgaris communities with a moss carpet and only a few leafy hepatics present. Several of these stands may be derived from Vaccineto–Callunetum hepaticosum following burning on steep north- or east-facing slopes. *Calluna vulgaris* may regenerate successfully, but recolonisation by liverworts is slow, and often a moss carpet develops of common species such as *Hypnum cupressiforme* var. *ericetorum*, *Pleurozium schreberi*, and *Rhacomitrium lanuginosum* and with hepatics such as *Diplophyllum albicans* and *Frullania tamarisci*.

One of the striking features of the woodland zone is the abundance of bracken, *Pteridium aquilinum*. The species occurs in quantity up to 1000 feet (305 m), and locally even to 1200 feet (365 m), corresponding roughly with the potential forest limits. Many of the open birch woods have luxuriant growths of *Pteridium*, and this is probably its natural habitat on Skye. Although in places the dense stands of bracken may be relics of former woodland, it easily invades both species-poor and species-rich Agrosto–Festucetum grasslands, and can produce pure, dense stands. All stages of bracken invasion can be seen on Skye up to a complete replacement of the grasses by dominant, tall (2–3 m high) *Pteridium* with only a dense layer of litter below. The most bracken-infested slopes on Skye are in the Trotternish Peninsula and in Strath Suardal, and they are all in areas where replacement of dwarf-shrub heath by grassland is most complete. Growth and spread of bracken can also be encouraged by heather burning, and stands of bracken may even replace Callunetum vulgaris directly, for example on the badly burnt lower-slopes of Slat Bheinn. *Pteridium* cannot tolerate waterlogged soils, and as a result, on the eastern slopes of the southern end of the Trotternish ridge, extensive and dense stands of *Pteridium* may be interrupted only by *Trichophorum cespitosum–Carex panicea*, *Molinia caerulea–Myrica gale*, or Sphagneto–Juncetum effusi mire communities which form an unfavourable habitat for the fern.

In general, the present distribution and geographical extent of grassland and dwarf-shrub heaths within the woodland zone on Skye appear to have developed in response to biotic influences over the past few centuries, particularly since the introduction of sheep onto the island in the latter half of the nineteenth century. Sheep grazing and associated management practices are an integral part of the ecosystem, affecting not only the spatial patterns and the floristic composition and dynamics of the vegetation, but also the nature of soil and slope development. Much of the evidence for biotically-induced vegetational differentiation is indirect and circumstantial, and it is often difficult to separate it from evidence for differentiation due to edaphic controls. Soil, vegetation, and land use together form an ecological entity on Skye, and it does not appear desirable, or indeed possible, to place them in a hierarchy of relative ecological importance.

Within the woodland zone there are, however, several inland sites supporting dwarf-shrub heaths that are subjected to severe wind exposure. Such areas frequently have shallow, skeletal soils and are thus unlikely to have ever supported closed woodland. Dry, wind-exposed, low-lying rock knolls, generally of sandstone, granite, or gabbro, are the characteristic habitat of the Rhacomitreto–Callunetum

Association, growing on shallow ranker soils. Although primarily a montane community (Fig. 5) it descends to 500 feet (152 m) in the woodland zone on Skye, as it does elsewhere in the north-west Highlands (McVean & Ratcliffe, 1962). It is, however, a rare community in the lowlands, perhaps reflecting the high biotic pressures to which the woodland zone is subjected, for dwarf prostrate *Calluna vulgaris* is markedly less resistant to burning and grazing than is the taller heather shrub. *Dryas octopetala–Carex flacca* heaths are restricted on Skye to the Durness limestone outcrops in the Suardal area (Fig. 5), and they occur on shallow, rendzina-like soils developed directly over the limestone. The history and status of this community is not clear, for although it is heavily grazed by sheep and, to some degree, by rabbits, it is unlikely to be entirely anthropogenic in view of its floristic affinities to 'natural' montane communities. Some of the limestone areas that presently support the *Dryas* heaths may once have supported open hazel scrub, or even *Fraxinus excelsior–Brachypodium sylvaticum woodland*, such as occurs today at Coille Gaireallach in Strath Suardal. There is accumulating evidence from palynological and archaeological studies to suggest that some deciduous woodland may have occurred in parts of the extensive limestone pavements of the Burren in western Ireland (Ivimey-Cook & Proctor, 1966*b*) and of the Craven Pennines (Pigott & Pigott, 1963). There are no ecological reasons to suggest that this was not also the case for Skye limestone pavements, although there are at present no relevant palynological data. It is perhaps significant that although many of the species that occur in the *Dryas* heaths at Suardal are generally associated with treeless vegetation, several of them are tolerant of some shade. For example, *Dryas octopetala* and *Polystichum lonchitis* can occur in small openings in sub-alpine birch woods in Swedish Lappland and in spruce forests in the Öst-Tirol, whereas *Rubus saxatilis* and *Thalictrum alpinum* are found quite commonly in birch woods in Swedish Lappland. *Arctostaphylos uva-ursi* and *Galium boreale* are frequent components of pine forests in Minnesota, U.S.A. In contrast to the Suardal stands, the *Dryas* heaths at Camas Malag occur on very exposed rocky sites by the coast, and these areas may well have been permanently treeless in the Flandrian.

3. OTHER ANTHROPOGENIC COMMUNITIES WITHIN THE WOODLAND ZONE

There are several other plant communities on Skye that appear to be largely anthropogenic, but in contrast to the dwarf-shrub heaths and the grassland discussed above, they do not occupy such extensive areas of the island. Although the *Lolium perenne–Plantago major* Association and the *Isolepis setacea–Blasia pusilla* communities occur in virtually all the regions on Skye (Fig. 5), they are rather restricted in their areal extent, being found in artificial man-made habitats such as roadsides, trampled paths, and derelict ground. Communities of 'weed' species such as *Capsella bursa-pastoris*, *Polygonum aviculare*, *P. persicaria*, *Spergula arvensis*, and *Stellaria media* are widespread but extremely local (Fig. 5), occurring on open waste ground around disused crofts and derelict buildings. The Centaureo–Cynosuretum Association, on the other hand, is locally frequent in the lowlying, fertile areas of northern Skye, the Sleat, and Strath Suardal (Fig. 5). The community is maintained by man as an enclosed hay-meadow community within the crofting townships, and it is thus entirely anthropogenic. It is mown annually, and the soil fertility is maintained largely by manuring.

The *Juncus acutiflorus–Filipendula ulmaria* Association is closely related floristically and ecologically to the Centaureo–Cynosuretum Association (see Table 4.57). They have similar distributions within Skye (Fig. 5), but, as discussed in Chapter 4, they appear to differ in their soil moisture requirements and their management by man. The 'rushy' meadows of the *Juncus acutiflorus–Filipendula ulmaria* Association are a characteristic community of damp, fertile meadows and of streamsides in much of northern Skye. The community occurs more locally in the Sleat and near Torrin. The rich assemblage of 'tall herbs' has obvious floristic affinities with the natural *Betula pubescens–Cirsium heterophyllum* communities of ungrazed woods and lowland basic cliff-ledges (see Table 4.57). The meadow soils are rather similar to to the woodland soils, being fertile and periodically irrigated brown earths of moderately high pH. Several of the meadow sites tend to be rather wet resulting in some gleyed soils in areas of impeded drainage. It is highly probable that these meadows are biotically derived from willow, alder, and birch dominated 'tall-herb' communities (see Pigott, 1956; Sjörs, 1954). Occasional, rather stunted, trees of birch and alder persist in some of the northern Skye meadows, and *Salix aurita*, *S. repens*, and *S. viminalis* can be locally frequent in this community along streams. *Salix caprea*, *S. nigricans*, and *S. pentandra* also occur, but they are rather rare. Some of the stands may have developed in sites of damp fields that were once cultivated but which are now derelict.

Most of the low-level screes of the Red Hills and of the eastern slopes of the Trotternish basalt ridge are probably the indirect result of grazing, trampling, and burning, and they can thus be regarded as largely anthropogenic. Repeated burning, trampling, and intensive and prolonged over-grazing on steep slopes (generally of 30° or more) can result in the loss of a continuous vegetational cover, leading to soil erosion and gullying (see Edgell, 1971; McVean & Lockie, 1969). In some areas there may be direct transitions from dwarf-shrub heath to eroding soil and bare scree, whereas in other areas in the Red Hills a variety of stages in heath degradation can be seen, dependent on the nature of the scree material and the intensity of biotic pressure. The stages can be Agrosto–Festucetum grasslands, open *Festuca ovina* turf with abundant *Galium saxatile*, *Sedum anglicum*, and *Polytrichum piliferum*, and bare and eroding scree littered with burned and dead *Calluna* remains. Gully erosion is particularly prevalent on the basalt slopes, where the deep soils overlying weathered bedrock offer little resistance to erosive agents once the vegetational cover is lost. In both Trotternish and the Red Hills the screes often have a brown tint due to exposure of the skeletal brown soil, and erosion faces commonly separate the adjacent stable ground from the screes. In these instances the screes consist of the larger angular fragments that were once part of the stable soil cover, but that have been exposed by loss of soil and fine material, and are thus liable to downward gravitational movements. The degree of stability is influenced by the size and shape of the rock fragments, by soil drainage and gravitational processes, and by biotic disturbance. Extensive scree formation or reactivation are likely to have accompanied deforestation, and in some existing woods, such as the birch wood below Creag Strollamus in the Red Hills, heavy grazing and trampling by sheep has so reduced the field layer that much of the ground is already loose, bare scree and eroding soil; when the trees die, only bare scree will remain.

4. BOGS AND FENS

Bogs and fens are the most widespread and extensive natural communities at present within the potential woodland zone on Skye, occurring wherever there is some impeded drainage. There is evidence from buried tree remains to suggest that some of the bogs occupy sites that once supported woodland. In contrast, however, many of the fens occur in permanently waterlogged areas, for example as marginal reedswamps, around lochs as 'mud-bottom' communities within fens, or in strongly soligenous soaks. These areas are unlikely ever to have been forested. Within the Coille Gaireallach wood in Strath Suardal there are small stands of the *Carex panicea–Campylium stellatum*, *Eriophorum latifolium–Carex hostiana*, and *Schoenus nigricans* rich-fen communities, suggesting that these types of rich-fen may occupy natural openings. The shallowness of the aerobic layer above the permanently waterlogged subsoil is probably important in inhibiting the growth of trees and shrubs in such areas (see Sjörs, 1950*b*). The effects of trampling and grazing may also be important in maintaining the openness of the *Eriophorum latifolium–Carex hostiana* flush Association and the related high-altitude *Carex–Saxifraga aizoides nodum*.

Human activities greatly influence the bogs on Skye, through drainage, peat cutting, burning, and, to some extent, animal grazing and trampling. When disturbance of Trichophoreto–Eriophoretum bogs results in a lowering of the water-table, *Calluna vulgaris* and *Trichophorum cespitosum* increase at the expense of *Sphagnum* spp., especially *S. fuscum*, *S. imbricatum*, *S. magellanicum*, *S. papillosum*, and *S. rubellum*. If grazing and burning are also involved, herbaceous plants increase, whereas *Calluna vulgaris* and *Myrica gale* are gradually eliminated. Although the vegetation may eventually recover after a single fire, repeated burning at short intervals rapidly causes a drastic and apparently irreversible change in the floristic composition of the bog, resulting in the dominance of *Trichophorum cespitosum*, often with conspicuous hummocks of *Rhacomitrium lanuginosum*.

Burning of Trichophoreto–Callunetum bogs on shallow peat generally results in a discontinuous vegetational cover. *Trichophorum cespitosum* becomes more tussocky in its growth, leaving bare or lichen-encrusted areas between tussocks. Later stages of degradation involve the complete breakdown of the peat to give a sparsely vegetated mixture of greasy, black humus and peat, with loose stones and gravel. The frequent development of a surface algal crust renders the peat impermeable, thereby increasing the run-off, and encouraging sheet erosion (McVean & Lockie, 1969). Extreme examples of this form of bog degradation can be seen in Glen Arroch and in parts of the Red Hills.

'Hagging' or gullying is a further form of peat erosion, and on Skye it is particularly prevalent on the high-level plateau Calluneto–Eriophoretum bogs in the Trotternish Peninsula. Drainage streams cut back into the peat from the edges of the bog, and subsequent water, wind, and frost erosion cause gullying, often down to the underlying mineral soil. As soon as bare peat is exposed, it will rapidly break down unless it is rapidly colonised by plants. The eroded peat is washed down the slopes below, and the site of its deposition is generally marked by a vigorous growth of *Nardus stricta* and other grasses. In some areas *Carex–Sphagnum recurvum* mires occur within the peat haggs. *Juncus squarrosus* is locally frequent, or even dominant, in places on some of the plateau bogs on Skye, and it has evidently replaced *Eriophorum vaginatum* as the dominant plant on some of the drier bogs. The striking dominance of *Molinia caerulea* in the Molinieto–Callunetum Association, especially on the lower slopes of the Cuillins, may also reflect human interference. Increased flowering of *Molinia caerulea* after burning has been demonstrated to be due to higher temperature at the growing apices resulting from removal of the insulating litter layer (Ratcliffe, 1964).

In contrast, fens tend to be less affected by human interference than bogs, as they are more difficult to burn and their water regime is usually less readily altered. By comparison with Scandinavian fens (Nordhagen, 1927, 1943; Persson, 1961), willows such as *Salix arbuscula*, *S. lanata*, *S. lapponum*, *S. myrsinites*, and *S. phylicifolia* are likely to have been formerly prominent in several of the rich- and intermediate-fens on Skye. The *Salix lapponum–Carex inflata* (*C. rostrata*)–*Sphagnum warnstorfianum* Sociation described by Nordhagen (1943) is clearly related floristically to the Skye *Carex rostrata–Aulacomnium palustre* Association, as is the Salicetum myrsinitis caricetosum Sociation (Nordhagen, 1943) to the *Carex panicea–Campylium stellatum* Association. The absence of willows in the Scottish fens is probably a result of intensive grazing by domestic animals (see Poore, 1955*c*), for such populations of these willows as do occur are now mainly confined to inaccessible cliff habitats. In some respects *Myrica gale* is the life-form counterpart of the willows, and in some stands of *Molinia caerulea–Myrica gale* fens, occasional plants of *Salix aurita* can be found. The dominance of *Juncus effusus* in the Sphagneto–Juncetum effusi poor-fen community probably results from grazing, the influence of intensive treading, and manuring by domestic animals.

There is some variation in the regional distribution of the mire communities on Skye (Fig. 5). Bog communities are rare as a whole in the limestone areas of Suardal, presumably because of the lack of suitable habitats there. Trichophoreto–Callunetum bog is the most extensive and widespread bog type on the island today, perhaps as a result of extensive human interference by drainage, peat cutting, and burning of the lowland bogs. In contrast to its abundance in other areas, this bog type is rather local in the Cuillin Hills, its place on the shallow disturbed peats on the lower slopes of the Cuillins being taken by Molinieto–Callunetum bog. *Molinia caerulea* may be favoured in this region by the frequent irrigation by mildly basic water in these bogs. Trichophoreto–Eriophoretum bog is rather rare and local (Fig. 5) in all the regions on Skye except in the Sleat Peninsula, where undisturbed bogs are common in the more remote areas. Calluneto–Eriophoretum bog is restricted to flat or gently sloping ground at moderate altitudes, and it is absent from the Cuillin region, probably as a result of the steep topography.

Trichophorum cespitosum–Carex panicea, *Molinia caerulea–Myrica gale*, and Sphagneto–Juncetum effusi poor-fen communities occur widely but rather locally throughout the island (Fig. 5) in suitable soligenous sites, but only in northern Skye and in the Cuillins do these communities become prominent, presumably because of the more basic rocks in these areas. The *Carex–Sphagnum recurvum nodum* is extremely rare on Skye (Fig. 5), being restricted to soligenous soaks within high-altitude plateau bogs, which only occur in northern Skye. *Carex rostrata–Aulacomnium palustre* intermediate-fen communities, and the frequently associated *Carex lasiocarpa–Menyanthes trifoliata* community of water-logged hollows within the fen stands, tend to occur as marginal communities around lowland lochs. Their distribution on Skye (Fig. 5) tends to follow that of suitable lochs, and it thus closely parallels the distribution of aquatic reed-swamp communities, such as the *Phragmites communis–Equisetum fluviatile* and *Carex rostrata–Menyanthes trifoliata* Associations.

Although several of the rich-fen communities (Tofieldietalia) occur in nearly all the regions on Skye (Fig. 5), the *Carex rostrata–Scorpidium scorpioides*, *Carex panicea–Campylium stellatum*, *Eriophorum latifolium–Carex hostiana*, and *Schoenus nigricans* Associations are rare in all the regions except northern Skye, the Cuillins, and Suardal. This geographical pattern, with the main distribution centred on the basic rocks of northern Skye (basalt), Cuillins (gabbro and peridotite), and Suardal (limestone), reflects an important direction of variation within the mire vegetation complex on Skye, namely the bog/poor-fen/rich-fen gradient of Sjörs (1948, 1950*b*). The gradual floristic gradient from *Sphagnum*-dominated bogs, through poor-fens and intermediate-fens, to

TABLE 5.3

	pH	K_{corr} (µmhos)	Calcium content (milligrams/litre)	Number of readings
Bogs (Oxycocco–Sphagnetea)	3.6–4.8	20–47 (33)	0.1–0.6 (0.3)	17
Poor-fens (Caricion canescentis-fuscae)	4.4–5.9	81–150 (108)	0.2–2.0 (0.9)	15
Intermediate-fens (Sphagno–Tomenthypnion)	4.8–5.3	110–137 (121)	2.2–2.5 (2.3)	5
Rich-fens (Tofieldietalia)	5.2–7.2	96–400 (220)	0.3–14.8 (5.9)	26

Figures in parentheses are mean values.

rich-fens dominated by sedges and 'brown mosses', appears to reflect a chemical gradient of decreasing acidity, increasing specific conductivity (K_{corr}), and increasing calcium concentration of the mire waters. The mean and the range of the values for these parameters in all the bog, poor-fen, intermediate-fen, and rich-fen waters analysed from Skye are summarised in Table 5.3.

There is a broad correlation between the floristic trends and the chemical data (see Sjörs, 1950*a*), although there is an overlap of some of the measured properties of the water chemistry of the main mire types. Such overlap suggests that in some poor-fen communities the rates of water-flow and nutrient recycling may be more important factors than the actual mineral content of the water at any one time (Malmer, 1962). There is little overlap between the values for pH, specific conductivity, and calcium concentration of waters from bogs and fens, respectively. This sharp chemical distinction corresponds to the *mineralbodenwassergrenze* of Thunmark (1940).

The height of the water table and seasonal fluctuations in level appear to be a second principal direction of variation in influencing the mire vegetation. This is clearly an important factor in the ecological differentiation of wet 'mud-bottom' communities (Scheuchzerietalia) with a scattered bryophyte cover in the ground layer, from the carpet, lawn, and hummock communities of the Caricetalia fuscae, Tofieldietalia, and Oxycocco–Sphagnetea, all of which have a more or less continuous moss layer. The differentiation between these communities appears to depend, for example, on the aeration of the substratum which is influenced by the different water-table levels. The differentiation between open-water communities of the Magnocaricion (*Carex rostrata–Menyanthes trifoliata* Association) and of the Scheuchzerietalia also appears to be partly related to water table differences.

A third direction of floristic variation appears to be related to altitude and exposure, with some communities, for example the *Carex–Sphagnum recurvum* and the *Carex–Saxifraga aizoides noda*, being restricted to higher altitudes. Possible additional ecological factors acting within the main directions of variation that may be important in differentiating between related mire communities, such as peat depth, peat type, slope, aspect, biotic influences, and rate and extent of water flow have been discussed, where relevant, in Chapter 4.

5. FRESHWATER LOCHS

The floristic composition of the Skye freshwater lochs appears to be related to the surrounding solid-rock geology, presumably acting through the media of water chemistry and substrate. The known occurrence of all aquatic and semi-aquatic macrophytes in a variety of lochs on Skye of roughly comparable dimensions and morphometry are shown in Fig. 7. Data on the water chemistry of the lochs are also presented. The lochs are arranged along a gradient of floristic richness, with the lochs supporting the lowest number of macrophytes grouped on the left. The chemical data show a broad correlation between the sequential arrangement of lochs by floristic richness and certain features of the water chemistry. Besides describing the approximate limits of the tolerance ranges for individual species, the chemical data show a fairly close correlation with the general floristic trends. Values for specific conductivity, pH, and calcium and magnesium concentrations are highest in the lochs supporting the greatest number of aquatic species. Conversely the lowest values for these chemical features are found in the floristically poor lochs such as Loch Airigh na Saorach, Lochan nan Dubhrachan, and Lochain Dubha. These lochs are all situated within the Torridonian sandstones of the Sleat Peninsula, whereas lochs occurring on gabbro or basalt tend to

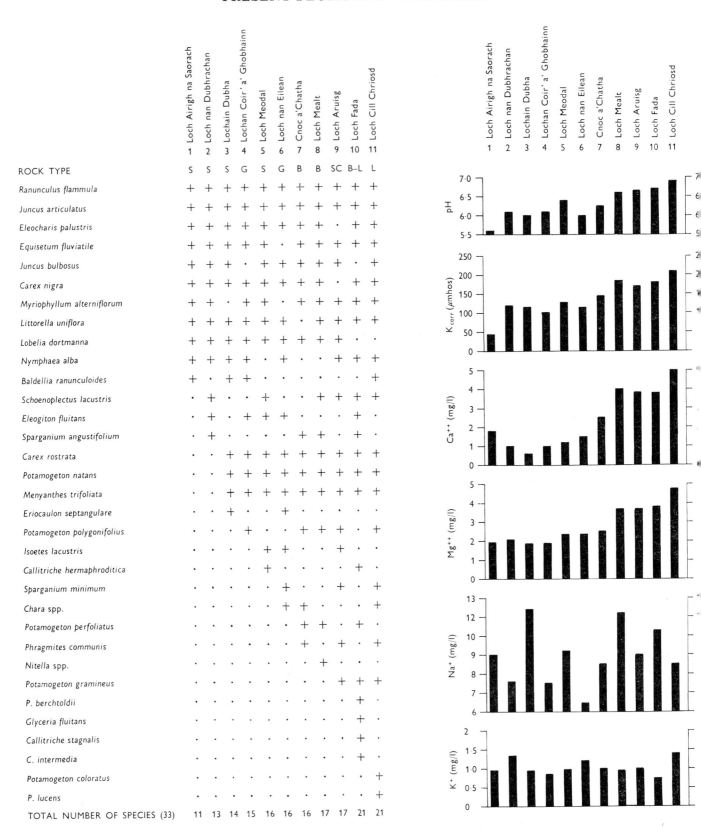

	1 Loch Airigh na Saorach	2 Loch nan Dubhrachan	3 Lochain Dubha	4 Lochan Coir' a' Ghobhainn	5 Loch Meodal	6 Loch nan Eilean	7 Cnoc a'Chatha	8 Loch Mealt	9 Loch Aruisg	10 Loch Fada	11 Loch Cill Chriosd
ROCK TYPE	S	S	S	G	S	G	B	B	SC	B–L	L
Ranunculus flammula	+	+	+	+	+	+	+	+	+	+	+
Juncus articulatus	+	+	+	+	+	+	+	+	+	+	+
Eleocharis palustris	+	+	+	+	+	+	+	+	·	+	+
Equisetum fluviatile	+	+	+	+	+	·	+	+	+	+	+
Juncus bulbosus	+	+	+	·	+	+	+	+	+	·	+
Carex nigra	+	+	+	+	+	+	+	+	·	+	+
Myriophyllum alterniflorum	+	+	·	+	+	·	+	+	+	+	+
Littorella uniflora	+	+	+	+	+	+	·	+	+	+	+
Lobelia dortmanna	+	+	+	+	+	+	+	+	+	·	·
Nymphaea alba	+	+	+	+	·	+	·	·	+	+	+
Baldellia ranunculoides	+	·	+	+	·	·	·	·	·	·	+
Schoenoplectus lacustris	·	+	·	·	+	·	·	+	+	+	+
Eleogiton fluitans	·	+	·	+	+	+	·	·	·	+	·
Sparganium angustifolium	·	+	·	·	·	·	+	+	·	+	·
Carex rostrata	·	·	+	+	+	+	+	+	+	+	+
Potamogeton natans	·	·	+	+	+	+	+	+	+	+	+
Menyanthes trifoliata	·	·	+	+	+	+	+	+	+	+	+
Eriocaulon septangulare	·	·	+	·	·	+	·	·	·	·	·
Potamogeton polygonifolius	·	·	·	+	·	·	+	+	+	·	+
Isoetes lacustris	·	·	·	·	+	+	·	·	+	·	·
Callitriche hermaphroditica	·	·	·	·	+	·	·	·	·	+	·
Sparganium minimum	·	·	·	·	·	+	·	·	+	·	+
Chara spp.	·	·	·	·	·	+	+	·	·	·	+
Potamogeton perfoliatus	·	·	·	·	·	·	+	+	·	+	·
Phragmites communis	·	·	·	·	·	·	+	·	+	·	+
Nitella spp.	·	·	·	·	·	·	·	+	·	·	·
Potamogeton gramineus	·	·	·	·	·	·	·	·	+	+	+
P. berchtoldii	·	·	·	·	·	·	·	·	·	+	·
Glyceria fluitans	·	·	·	·	·	·	·	·	·	+	·
Callitriche stagnalis	·	·	·	·	·	·	·	·	·	+	·
C. intermedia	·	·	·	·	·	·	·	·	·	+	·
Potamogeton coloratus	·	·	·	·	·	·	·	·	·	·	+
P. lucens	·	·	·	·	·	·	·	·	·	·	+
TOTAL NUMBER OF SPECIES (33)	11	13	14	15	16	16	16	17	17	21	21

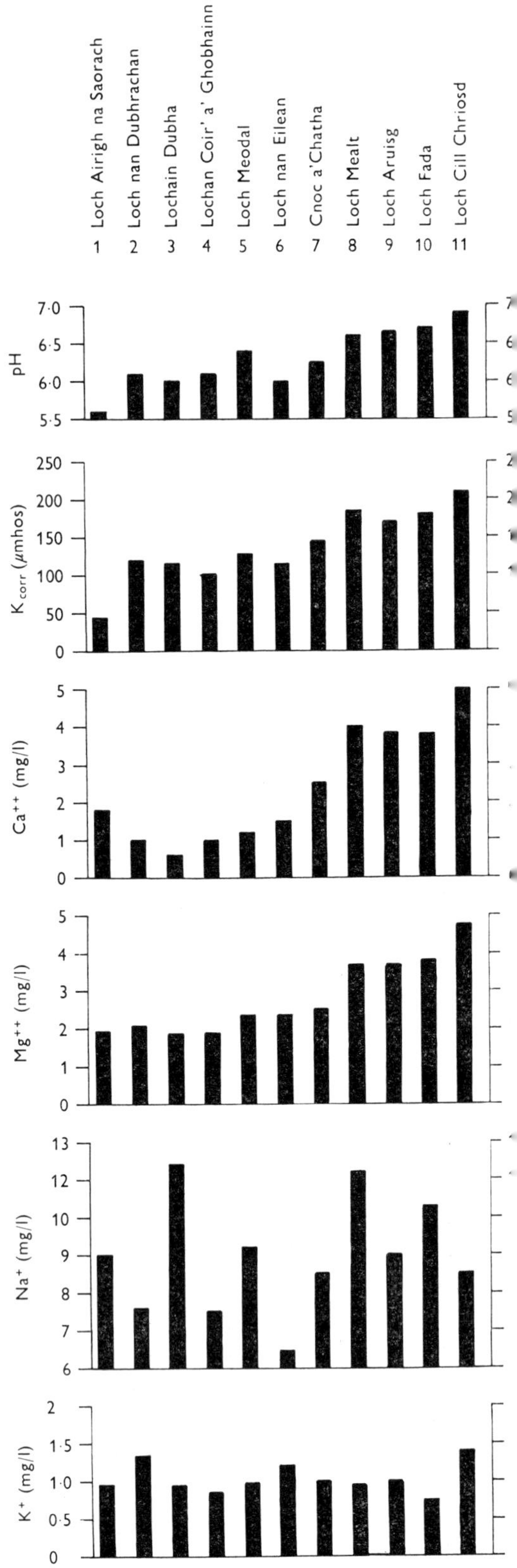

Key to rock types: S = Sandstone, G = Gabbro, B = Basalt, SC = Schist, L = Limestone.

Figure 7. Present distribution of aquatic vascular plants in eleven freshwater lochs situated in different geological surroundings on Skye, and water chemical data for the same lochs.

have both a richer flora and slightly richer water. The floristically richest lochs are situated on Moine schist (Loch Aruisg), basalt and Jurassic limestone (Loch Fada), or Durness limestone (Loch Cill Chriosd). Sodium and potassium concentrations show no obvious correlations with the floristic or geological gradients, and they are probably an expression of the exposure of the lochs to sea-spray (see Gorham, 1958; Holden, 1961).

A striking feature of the results presented on Fig. 7 is that many species occur in the majority of the lochs examined despite the marked chemical differences between the various lochs. This group includes *Nymphaea alba*, *Littorella uniflora*, *Myriophyllum alterniflorum*, *Potamogeton natans*, and *Lobelia dortmanna*, although there is a slight tendency for the latter species to be absent from the richest sites. Several of these species are considered to be ubiquitous in relation to water basicity elsewhere in Scotland by Spence (1967), in Wales by Seddon (1967), in Sweden by Lundh (1951), and in Denmark by Iversen (1929). Besides their wide chemical tolerance, some of these species probably have a high competitive ability related to their life form. For example, *Littorella uniflora* is a stoloniferous, rosette plant, forming dense mats in shallow water. The absence of some of these species, for example *Lobelia dortmanna*, from the floristically richest lochs may result from competition from other more luxuriant species (see Lundh, 1951; Seddon, 1965). The wide ecological tolerances of these species serve to emphasise their limited value as indicators of past limnological conditions (cf. Vasari & Vasari, 1968).

There is a small group of species that are restricted on Skye to lochs with waters of high specific conductivity (150 μmhos or more), high calcium and magnesium concentrations (4 and 3 milligrams/litre), and pH values greater than 6.5. These species include *Glyceria fluitans*, *Potamogeton coloratus*, *P. gramineus*, and *P. lucens*. *P. lucens* appears to be consistently restricted to calcareous waters elsewhere in Scotland (Spence, 1967), in Wales (Seddon, 1967), and in Sweden (Lohammar, 1965; Lundh, 1951), suggesting its potential value as an indicator species in palaeoecological studies.

The factors that appear to influence the spatial distribution of the various aquatic communities within the lochs are complex, for exposure to waves, nature of substrate, aspect, and water depth all appear to be important (see Spence, 1964, 1967). The possible inter-relationships of the *Carex rostrata–Menyanthes trifoliata*, *Littorella uniflora–Lobelia dortmanna*, *Phragmites communis–Equisetum fluviatile*, *Schoenoplectus lacustris–Equisetum fluviatile*, and *Potamogeton natans–Nymphaea alba* communities to these environmental factors have been discussed in Chapter 4, and are illustrated, to some degree, in Figs. 13, 15, 17, and 19.

The *Littorella uniflora–Lobelia dortmanna* Association is the most widely distributed aquatic community on Skye (Fig. 5), occurring on wave-exposed stony and sandy margins of many lowland and upland lochs in all the six regions. In contrast, the *Potamogeton natans–Nymphaea alba nodum* is rather rare and local (Fig. 5), as it is only known in small lochans or in sheltered bays of the larger lowland lochs in the Sleat, in northern Skye, and in the Cuillin valleys. Reedswamp communities occur more widely, but they tend to be restricted to moderately sheltered sites in the Sleat, Strath Suardal, the Cuillins, and northern Skye.

6. INLAND CLIFFS, LIMESTONE PAVEMENTS, AND ROCK OUTCROPS

Steep inland cliffs, screes, and rock outcrops are likely to have provided open treeless habitats within the woodland zone during the Flandrian (see Pigott & Walters, 1954). Although occasional trees of birch and *Sorbus aucuparia* occur on some rock-ledges, the greater part of the lowland crags remained treeless. The screes and block litters below the cliffs may have supported open woodland, as occurs today in suitable habitats in northern Scandinavia (Lundqvist, 1968). There are several impressive inland crags, many of which support interesting floras, especially the basic basaltic and limestone cliffs. Although the main localities for mountain plants on Skye are cliffs above 1000 feet (305 m), several low-lying inland cliffs such as those at Preshal More, An t Sròn near Camasunary, and Ben Tianavaig, also support interesting montane taxa.

On some of the larger basic lowland cliffs, fragmentary stands of 'tall herb' dominated vegetation are found, resembling in floristic composition the field layer of the *Betula pubescens–Cirsium heterophyllum* woods, with *Angelica sylvestris*, *Cirsium heterophyllum*, *Crepis paludosa*, *Filipendula ulmaria*, *Geum rivale*, *Luzula sylvatica*, *Orchis mascula*, *Trollius europaeus*, and *Valeriana officinalis*. These stands are restricted to broad, stable ledges that are inaccessible to grazing animals, and where a deep, periodically flushed, nitrifying soil has accumulated. Several woody species may occur on these larger ledges, including *Betula pubescens* ssp. *odorata*, *Juniperus communis* ssp.

nana, *Lonicera periclymenum*, *Populus tremula*, *Prunus padus*, *Ribes spicatum*, *Rubus idaeus*, *R. saxatilis*, *Salix aurita*, *S. caprea*, *S. cinerea*, *S. repens*, *Sorbus aucuparia*, and *S. rupicola*.

Low-lying cliffs and rock outcrops also provide habitats, free from both intense competition and grazing, for several interesting vascular plants and bryophytes. Many of these species grow on rather thin, immature soils consisting of mixtures of humus and downwashed mineral particles that have accumulated in shallow crevices or on small rock-ledges. Shaded mildly basic cliffs, generally of north or east aspect, invariably support *Alchemilla alpina*, *Antennaria dioica*, *Festuca vivipara*, *Hymenophyllum wilsonii*, *Lathyrus montanus*, *Plantago maritima*, *Poa nemoralis*, *Saxifraga hypnoides* (also a scree coloniser), *Sedum rosea*, *Silene maritima*, *Solidago virgaurea*, *Amphidium mougeotii*, *Frullania germana*, *Glyphomitrium daviesii*, *Harpalejeunea ovata*, *Lejeunea cavifolia*, and *Metzgeria conjugata*. Shaded rock-crevices provide habitats for the ferns *Asplenium trichomanes*, *Cystopteris fragilis*, and, more rarely, *Polystichum aculeatum*. These ferns frequently grow with *Anoectangium aestivum*, *Preissia quadrata*, *Tortella tortuosa*, *Trichostomum crispulum*, and *Tritomaria quinquedentata*. *Anthyllis vulneraria*, *Arctostaphylos uva-ursi*, *Galium boreale*, *Antitrichia curtipendula*, *Camptothecium lutescens*, *C. sericeum*, *Frullania fragilifolia*, *Grimmia apocarpa*, *G. trichophylla*, *Orthotrichum anomalum*, *Neckera complanata*, *Tortula subulata*, and *Placopsis gellida* favour fairly dry, sun-exposed rocks, generally of south or west aspect. *Saxifraga oppositifolia*, *Silene acaulis*, and *Ptychomitrium polyphyllum* are most frequent on areas of dry, crumbling rocks, but *Silene acaulis* can also occur on steep banks below cliffs and as a coloniser of open, earthy screes with *Alchemilla alpina*, *Botrychium lunaria*, and *Saxifraga hypnoides*. Periodically irrigated, lightly shaded, basic rock-faces are the characteristic habitat for *Rhacomitrium ellipticum* on Skye, whereas in inland localities on Skye, *Glyphomitrium daviesii* appears to favour irrigated detached rocks in block litters. Although it occurs occasionally on dry, south-facing cliffs, *Asplenium adiantum-nigrum* is most frequent amidst blocks below the cliffs.

Besides the species mentioned above, there is a group of cliff plants that are rather local and rare in lowland Skye, occurring in widely scattered stations, or even, in extreme cases, having only one or two known localities on the island. The montane plants *Oxyria digyna*, *Dryas octopetala*, and *Thalictrum alpinum* have scattered localities on one or two ledges on basalt or dolerite rock-outcrops. *Saxifraga aizoides* is similarly extremely rare on such cliffs, being restricted to strongly calcareous, damp cliff-faces. *Dryas octopetala*, *Saxifraga aizoides*, and *Thalictrum alpinum* occur more abundantly on the low-lying Durness limestones of the Ben Suardal area. *Asplenium viride* and *Polystichum lonchitis* are rather local ferns of shaded, basic rock-crevices as are the bryophytes *Barbula ferruginascens*, *Cololejeunea calcarea*, *Distichium capillaceum*, *Hypnum callichroum*, *Metzgeria hamata*, *M. pubescens*, *Mnium marginatum*, *Neckera crispa*, *Orthothecium rufescens*, and *Pohlia cruda*, and the lichens *Gyalecta jenensis* and *Solorina saccata*. Dry, frequently crumbling, basaltic cliffs provide specialised habitats for several rather local species on Skye, including *Arabidopsis thaliana*, *Cardaminopsis petraea*, *Carlina vulgaris*, *Crepis capillaris* (var. *glandulosa*), *Draba incana*, *Orobanche alba*, *Poa glauca*, *Vicia orobus*, *Amphidium lapponicum*, *Grimmia apocarpa* var. *homodictyon*, *G. decipiens* var. *decipiens*, *G. decipiens* var. *robusta*, *G. funalis*, *G. orbicularis*, *G. stricta*, *G. torquata*, *Orthotrichum rupestre*, and *Reboulia hemisphaerica*.

The Durness limestone pavements support a rich and ecologically diverse flora (see Table 4.56) with plants characteristic of saxicolous, grassland, dwarf-shrub, and woodland communities. As discussed previously, it is not known whether the limestone pavements were treeless during the Flandrian, or whether they supported open hazel scrub or even ashwoods. Some exposed sites, such as the coastal pavements at Camas Malag, are likely to have been virtually treeless for much of the Flandrian. Besides providing the sole habitat for the *Dryas octopetala–Carex flacca* heaths on Skye, the Durness limestone supports several species that appear, at present, to be restricted on Skye to this geological formation. They include *Calamogrostis epigejos*, *Epipactis atrorubens*, *E. helleborine*, *Melica nutans*, *Amblystegiella sprucei*, *Campylium chrysophyllum*, *Campylopus subulatus*, *Gymnostomum recurvirostrum* var. *insigne*, *Leiocolea turbinata*, *Scapania compacta*, *Seligeria acutifolia* var. *longiseta*, *Trichostomum crispulum* var. *brevifolium*, and *Collema crispum*.

Several of the low-lying basalt cliffs support a rich and varied *Hieracium* flora, including *H. anglicum*, *H. argenteum*, *H. caledonicum*, *H. chloranthum* Pugsl., *H. euprepes*, *H. langwellense* F. J. Hanb., *H. nitidum* Backh., *H. orimeles* F. J. Hanb. ex. W. R. Linton, *H. petrocharis* (E. F. Linton) W. R. Linton, *H. rubiginosum* F. J. Hanb., *H. shoolbredii* E. S. Marshall, *H. subrude* (Arv.-Touv) Arv.-Touv, and *H. uiginskyense*. There is also a characteristic hawkweed flora of the Durness limestone outcrops on Skye, including *H. ampliatum* (W. R. Linton) A. Ley, *H. anglicum*, *H.*

duriceps F. J. Hanb., *H. euprepes*, *H. pictorum* E. F. Linton, *H. recticulatum*, *H. rhomboides* (Sternström) Johans., *H. shoolbredii*, and the phytogeographically interesting endemics *H. cravoniense*, *H. cymbifolium*, and *H. langwellense*.

There are several impressive cliffs formed of extensive outcrops of Jurassic limestone on Skye, especially along the coast, for example at Rubha na h-Airde Glaise near Portree, at Bearreraig Bay east of The Storr, by the Lealt Waterfall, and in the Elgol Peninsula. The east- and south-facing cliffs between Rubha na h-Airde Glaise and Bearreraig Bay are mostly rather dry, and support a flora with southern affinities, including *Arabis hirsuta*, *Arrhenatherum elatius*, *Asplenium ruta-muraria*, *Geranium lucidum*, *G. robertianum*, *Hieracium iricum*, *Hedera helix*, *Helictotrichon pratense*, *Torilis japonica*, *Trifolium dubium* *Anomodon viticulosus*, *Camptothecium lutescens*, *Ctenidium molluscum*, *Ditrichum flexicaule*, *Encalypta streptocarpa*, *Neckera complanata*, *Orthotrichum rupestre*, *Porella platyphylla*, *Rhynchostegiella tenella*, *Tortula intermedia*, and *T. muralis*. Shaded, damp or even dripping crevices and rocks provide habitats for *Phyllitis scolopendrium* and *Polystichum aculeatum*, and for a wide variety of bryophytes including *Cololejeunea calcarea*, *Cratoneuron commutatum*, *Dicranella subulata*, *Eucladium verticillatum*, *Gymnostomum aeruginosum*, *G. calcareum*, *G. recurvirostrum*, *Preissia quadrata*, *Solenostoma pumilum*, *S. sphaerocarpoidea*, and *S. triste*. On sheltered, moist ledges and steep, flushed areas, 'tall herb' vegetation predominates, with *Allium ursinum*, *Angelica sylvestris*, *Brachypodium sylvaticum*, *Caltha palustris*, *Carex laevigata*, *C. pallescens*, *Crepis paludosa*, *Equisetum telmateia*, *Eupatorium cannabinum*, *Geum rivale*, *Hypericum androsaemum*, *H. tetrapterum*, *Petasites hybridus*, *Silene dioica*, *Tussilago farfara*, and *Valeriana officinalis*. Other species of interest that occur on the Jurassic limestone cliffs in the Elgol Peninsula or near Broadford include *Agrimonia eupatoria*, *Hieracium pictorum*, *H. shoolbredii*, *Lapsana communis*, *Oenanthe crocata*, *Polypodium interjectum*, *Populus tremula*, *Scrophularia nodosa*, *Sedum rosea*, *Leiocolea badensis*, *L. muelleri*, *Marchesinia mackaii*, *Metzgeria pubescens*, and *Philonotis calcarea*.

A striking feature of the flora of many of the inland, low-lying cliffs and rock outcrops on Skye is the occurrence together of species of markedly contrasting phytogeographical affinities (see Chapter 6). For example, the Arctic–Alpines *Saxifraga oppositifolia*, *Sedum rosea*, and *Silene acaulis* grow on the same crag as the Southern Continental species *Arabis hirsuta*, *Carlina vulgaris*, *Galium verum*, and *Trichostomum crispulum*. This phytogeographical diversity is a feature of many lowland cliff floras, both in Britain (see Table 1 in Pigott & Walters, 1954) and in Scandinavia (see Lid, 1958; Lundqvist, 1968; Nordhagen, 1943).

7. COASTAL COMMUNITIES

Within the potential woodland zone on Skye, there is a consistent geographical pattern in the present distribution of woodlands, dwarf-shrub heaths, grasslands, mires, and inland cliff communities, with some associations centred on the poorer, acidic soils of the granite and sandstone regions, whereas others are largely restricted to the richer soils of the basalt and/or limestone areas. Soils developed on gabbro tend to occupy an intermediate position between these two broad groups. Similarly the freshwater lochs show a floristic pattern that apparently reflects differences in the surrounding geology. In contrast the coastal communities on Skye tend to be more uniformly distributed around the island (see Fig. 5), and they show little dependence on the rock type. In extreme coastal habitats it is probable that ecological factors such as exposure and salinity are of such overriding importance in influencing the floristic composition and structure and the vegetational zonation of the saltmarshes, sea-cliffs, and maritime grasslands, that factors such as soil base-status tend to be of less importance than in inland habitats (Malloch, 1971). In view of their exposure, high salinity, and overall instability, it is unlikely that these coastal habitats could have ever supported woodland, although some fragments of coastal scrub, generally dominated by *Corylus avellana*, persist on steep, talus slopes below some of the larger sea-cliffs.

The larger basalt sea-cliffs in northern Skye are up to 1000 feet (305 m) high. The cliff-top vegetation is generally a species-rich maritime grassland differing from inland grasslands in the dominance of *Agrostis stolonifera*, *Dactylis glomerata*, *Holcus lanatus*, and *Festuca rubra*. This grassland type occurs as a narrow zone between the typically rather low-grown species-rich *Calluna vulgaris–Sieglingia decumbens* heath and the open cliff-edge communities. *Alchemilla alpina*, *Anthyllis vulneraria*, *Plantago maritima*, *Rubus saxatilis*, *Saxifraga hypnoides*, *Silene acaulis*, and *S. maritima* frequently occur in these open, rather unstable, cliff-edge situations. The flora and vegetation of the upper cliff-ledges and rock crevices of the larger sea-cliffs are rather similar to those of inland basalt cliffs, for the large, stable and periodically irrigated ledges generally support communities dominated by 'tall herbs' (*Luzula sylvatica–Silene dioica* Association). This coastal association differs from the inland lowland stands in the greater abundance of *Calluna vulgaris*, *Sedum rosea*, and *Silene dioica*. Some of the cliffs support some trees and shrubs, mainly *Juniperus communis* ssp. *nana*, *Lonicera periclymenum*, *Populus tremula*, *Sorbus aucuparia* and, more rarely, *S. rupicola*. *Vicia sylvatica* appears to be restricted on Skye to coastal cliff-ledges. Several montane plants occur on smaller ledges and in crevices on the basic sea-cliffs. These include *Alchemilla alpina*, *Antennaria dioica*, *Draba incana*, *Galium boreale*, *Rubus saxatilis*, *Saxifraga hypnoides*, *S. oppositifolia*, *Silene acaulis*, *Anoectangium aestivum*, *Distichium capillaceum*, *Grimmia apocarpa* var. *homodictyon*, and *G. funalis*. More local components on the basic sea-cliffs include *Cardaminopsis petraea*, *Dryas octopetala*, *Oxyria digyna*, *Thalictrum alpinum*, and *Grimmia torquata*. Similar mixed assemblages of lowland, coastal, and inland montane species on sea-cliffs in western Norway have been described by Nordhagen (1922) and Skogen (1965).

The influence of sea-spray becomes increasingly important at lower levels on the larger sea-cliffs, resulting in the characteristic cliff-ledge community of moderately exposed sites dominated by *Armeria maritima* with several associated halophytes (*Armeria maritima–Grimmia maritima* Association), including *Ligusticum scoticum*. This association appears to be largely indifferent to rock type on Skye, as does the *Asplenium marinum–Grimmia maritima* Association of more sheltered recesses and overhangs on coastal cliffs.

Possible ecological factors influencing the floristic composition of the *Atriplex glabriuscula–Rumex crispus* shingle-beach communities include the age, stability, and substrate of the beach (see Scott, 1963*a*). The Skye data are too limited, however, to provide a basis for discussion of the influence of such factors in the stands examined.

Variations in salinity appear to be important ecological factors in the differentiation of the various saltmarsh communities on Skye. Observations on the sodium chloride content of soils from the three principal saltmarsh communities on Skye indicate that it decreases in the order *Puccinellia maritima–Ascophyllum nodosum* Subassociation, *Puccinellia maritima–Festuca rubra* Subassociation, and *Carex extensa–Juncus gerardii* Association. The soil data closely follow the observed vegetational zonation (cf. Tyler, 1971). The first community characterises the lowest areas in the saltmarshes, which are most frequently submerged by the sea (at least 8 hours a day); the second community invariably occurs as a transitional zone between the lower and upper saltmarshes; and the third community is restricted to the uppermost areas. Further factors influencing the saltmarsh vegetation on Skye may include drainage, fluctuations in water table, grazing, exposure, and physical features of the substrate, in particular the particle size.

An important floristic feature of several of the coastal habitats on Skye is the occurrence of many so-called 'weed' species in apparently natural habitats. Species such as *Plantago lanceolata* and *Senecio vulgaris* are relatively common in maritime grasslands and dwarf-shrub heaths. *Galium aparine*, *Rumex crispus*, and *Stellaria media* occur frequently in shingle beach communities. *Agropyron repens*, *Equisetum arvense*, *Plantago major*, *Polygonum aviculare*, *P. persicaria*, *Sagina procumbens*, and *Sonchus arvensis* are also recorded from shingle beaches on Skye. The fore-dune community at Glenbrittle provides an apparently natural habitat for *Sonchus asper*. Ledges on sea-cliffs support *Chamaenerion angustifolium*, *Lapsana communis*, *Plantago lanceolata*, and *Urtica dioica*. Similar weed species occur in coastal habitats in western Norway (see Nordhagen, 1922; Skogen, 1965).

The significance of such coastal environments as providing suitable open habitats for several of these weed species has been discussed by Nordhagen (1940) who regards drift-line communities as ancient and wholly natural habitats, from which common ruderal species may well have spread into man-made habitats (see also Faegri, 1963). There is the possibility of ecotypic differentiation between the plants occuring in natural, coastal habitats and in artificial, man-made areas, for several of these 'weedy' species are extremely variable in morphology. The basis for this variation has not been investigated, but it may well be genotypic rather than phenotypic (Lövkvist, 1962).

There are, however, some species on Skye that are only known to occur in artificial, man-made habitats. These include *Brassica napus*, *B. rapa*, *Capsella bursa-pastoris*, *Chenopodium album*, *Rumex obtusifolius*, *Sinapsis alba*, and *Spergula arvensis*, and the recent introductions *Juncus tenuis* and *Matricaria matricarioides*. Some species on Skye are only known in anthropogenic meadow communities or by streams within crofting townships, for example *Aegopodium podagraria*, *Anthriscus sylvestris*, *Astrantia major*, *Chrysanthemum leucanthemum*, *C. segetum*, *C. vulgare*, *Cicerbita macrophylla*, *Myrrhis odorata*, *Peuce-*

danum ostruthium, *Salix alba*, *S. fragilis*, *S. pentandra*, *S. purpurea*, and *S. viminalis*. While some of those species such as *Astrantia major*, *Cicerbita macrophylla*, and *Peucedanum ostruthium* are known introductions, it is difficult to assess the status of several other of these plants in view of their frequent associations with man and his settlements (Bradshaw, 1962). Many of the willow species in this group are widely planted as osiers, and *Aegopodium podagraria* and *Chrysanthemum vulgare* are commonly cultivated as medicinal herbs. Clapham (1953) has discussed this problem in detail, and he points out that in Scandinavia and central Europe plants like *Aegopodium podagraria*, *Anthriscus sylvestris*, *Chrysanthemum vulgare*, and *Tussilago farfara* occur in apparently natural woodland and coastal communities, and that there may be no reason to doubt their native status in Britain. Many of the meadow and weedy species that are only known on Skye today in anthropogenic habitats may well have once occurred in 'tall herb' woodlands or in coastal shingle-beach or fore-dune communities, since several of the species are vigorously growing perennials, often with a strong capacity for vegetative spread and with demands for nitrophilous soils. Because of their biology, they could readily have become prominent in man-made habitats, and they may also have attracted man's attention as potential food plants or medicinal herbs, and they may thus have been introduced more widely.

3. THE ALPINE ZONE

I. INTRODUCTION

The alpine zone is here defined as the ground and its associated flora and vegetation lying above the potential altitudinal limits of forest and tall scrub. On Skye it is generally represented by ground above 1500 feet (460 m). During the Flandrian, especially in the so-called 'climatic optimum', the potential tree-line was probably higher than 1500 feet (460 m) but undoubtedly much of the ground above 2000 feet (610 m) has been treeless during the last 10000 years. The alpine zone on Skye is broadly equivalent to the low alpine zone or dwarf-shrub belt delimited by ecologists in Scandinavia (Dahl, 1956; Nordhagen, 1927, 1943), and by Poore & McVean (1957) in Scotland. However, small areas of the alpine zone on Skye, such as the *Festuca ovina–Luzula spicata nodum*, could be assigned floristically to the Scandinavian middle alpine zone or grass-heath belt, in that they lack dwarf-shrubs. Such a zonal division would result in an arbitrary separation between closely related communities, and hence the more general term 'alpine zone' is preferred.

The climate of the alpine zone is more severe than in the woodland zone, with lower temperatures, greater precipitation, more frequent cloud cover, stronger winds, greater frequency of frosts, and more prolonged snow-lie, although the relations of these features to local topography are often complex (see Chapter 3). As a result of this climatic severity and short growing season associated with the generally more rugged topography, the alpine zone as a whole is subjected to a lower biotic pressure than the woodland zone, and as a result many of the alpine or montane communities on Skye can be regarded as 'semi-natural' or even 'natural' in their floristic composition and structure.

The known occurrence of all the montane vascular plants and bryophytes in the various hill regions of Skye are shown in Table 5.4. The term 'montane plant' is used here to refer to plants that belong essentially to the alpine zone, but not necessarily to a definite phytogeographical group such as the Arctic–Alpine Element. A montane plant is one which, on Skye, generally occurs most abundantly above 1000 feet (310 m), although many are also recorded from lower altitudes. Species are grouped on Table 5.4 in terms of their *lowest* known altitudinal locality, and they are listed alphabetically within each altitudinal group.

Although montane vegetation in the strict sense is absent from the Sleat and the Suardal regions, several montane plants are found near sea-level in these regions, occurring either in open gravel communities or on coastal rocks and sea-cliffs. To altitudinal descent of montane plants to near sea-level in north-west Scotland is well known (see McVean & Ratcliffe, 1962) and although not all species reach sea-level, the majority occur at consistently lower levels on Skye and elsewhere in north-west Scotland than in the southern and eastern parts of their Scottish range. A similar trend is discernable in the present distribution patterns of several montane plants in Scandinavia and the Faeröes (Dahl, 1951).

The altitudinal descent of montane plants and, to some degree, of alpine vegetation, for example the Rhacomitreto–Callunetum Association, in north-west Scotland, is considered to result from the combined influences of the decreasing temperature gradient from south to north, and the increasing oceanicity from east to west (McVean & Ratcliffe, 1962). It is perhaps significant that the maximum summer temperatures in the Scottish Highlands fall

TABLE 5.4

DISTRIBUTION OF MONTANE PLANTS IN THE ISLE OF SKYE

Lower limit (feet)	VASCULAR PLANTS	LOCALITIES											
		1	2	3	4	5	6	7	8	9	10	11	12
	Arabis alpina	+	.	.	.	.	.	.	.	.	.	.	.
	Cerastium arcticum	+	.	.	.	+	.	.	.	.	.	.	.
	Deschampsia alpina	+	+	.	.	+	+	.	.	.	.	.	.
	Draba norvegica	+	.	.	.	.	.	.	.	.	.	.	.
2000	*Juncus trifidus*	+	+	.	.	.	.	.	.	.	.	.	.
	Dryopteris abbreviata	+	+	.	.	.	.	.	.	.	.	.	.
	Euphrasia frigida	+	.	.	.	+	.	+	.	.	.	.	.
	Gnaphalium supinum	+	.	.	.	+	+	.	.	.	.	.	.
	Juncus biglumis	.	.	.	.	+	+	+	+	.	.	.	.
	J. triglumis	+	.	.	.	+	+	+	+	.	.	.	.
	?*Loiseleuria procumbens*	+	.	.	.	.	.	.	.	.	.	.	.
	Luzula spicata	+	+	+	+	+	+	.	.	.	.	.	.
	Poa alpina	+	.	.	.	+	.	.	.	.	.	.	.
	Sagina saginoides	.	.	.	.	+	+	+	.	.	.	.	.
	Salix herbacea	+	+	+	+	+	+	+	+	.	+	.	.
	Saxifraga nivalis	+	.	.	.	+	+	+	.	.	.	.	.
1500	*Sibbaldia procumbens*	.	+	.	.	.	+	.	.	.	.	.	.
	Alchemilla wichurae	.	.	.	.	+	.	.	.	.	.	.	.
	Carex bigelowii	+	+	+	+	+	+	+	+	.	+	.	.
	Cryptogramma crispa	+	+	+	.	+	.	.	.	+	.	.	.
	Empetrum hermaphroditum	+	+	+	+	+	+	+	+	.	.	.	.
	Epilobium alsinifolium	+	+	.	.	+	+	+	+	.	.	.	.
	E. anagallidifolium	.	.	.	.	+	+	+	+	.	.	.	.
	Koenigia islandica	.	.	.	.	+	+	.	.	.	.	.	.
	Poa balfourii	.	.	.	.	+	+	+	+	.	.	.	.
	P. glauca	+	.	.	.	+	+	+	+	+	.	.	.
	Rhinanthus borealis	.	.	.	.	+	.	+	+	.	.	.	.
	Salix myrsinites	.	.	.	.	.	.	.	+	.	.	.	.
	Saussurea alpina	+	+	.	.	+	+	+	+	.	+	.	.
	Tofieldia pusilla	+	.	.	.	.	.	.	.	.	.	.	.
1000	*Veronica serpyllifolia* ssp. *humifusa*	.	.	.	.	.	.	+	.	.	.	.	.
	Cochlearia officinalis ssp. *alpina*	+	+	.	.	+	+	+	+	+	.	.	.
	Lycopodium alpinum	+	+	+	+	+	+	+	+	.	.	.	.
	?*Orthilia secunda*	+	.	.	.	.	.	.	.	.	.	.	.
500	*Saxifraga stellaris*	+	+	+	+	+	+	+	+	.	+	.	.
	Alchemilla alpina	+	+	+	+	+	+	+	+	+	.	+	.
	Arctostaphylos uva-ursi	+	+	+	+	.	.	+	.	.	.	+	+
	Asplenium viride	.	+	.	+	+	+	+	+	.	.	+	+
	Cardaminopsis petraea	+	+	+	.	+	+	+	+	+	.	.	.
	Cherleria sedoides	.	.	.	.	+	+	+	.	.	.	.	.
	Draba incana	.	+	.	.	+	+	+	+	+	.	.	.
	Dryas octopetala	.	+	.	.	.	.	.	.	+	.	+	.
	Festuca vivipara	+	+	+	+	+	+	+	+	+	+	+	+
	Galium boreale	+	+	+	.	+	+	+	+	+	+	+	.
	Juniperus communis ssp. *nana*	+	+	+	+	.	+	.	.	+	+	.	+
	Lycopodium selago	+	+	+	+	+	+	+	+	+	+	+	+
	Oxyria digyna	+	+	+	+	+	+	+	+	+	+	.	.
	Polygonum viviparum	+	+	.	+	+	+	+	+	+	.	+	.
	Polystichum lonchitis	.	+	.	.	+	.	+	+	.	.	+	.
	Rubus saxatilis	+	+	+	+	+	+	+	+	+	+	+	+
	Saxifraga aizoides	.	+	.	.	+	+	+	+	.	.	+	.
	S. hypnoides	+	+	.	.	+	+	+	+	+	+	.	.
	S. oppositifolia	+	+	.	.	+	+	+	+	+	.	.	.
	Sedum rosea	+	+	.	+	+	+	+	+	+	+	.	+
	Silene acaulis	+	+	.	.	+	+	+	+	+	.	.	.
0	*Thalictrum alpinum*	+	+	.	+	+	+	+	+	+	+	+	.
	Total number of species (56)	40	34	16	17	43	38	37	41	19	13	12	7

TABLE 5.4 *continued*

Lower limit (feet)	BRYOPHYTES	LOCALITIES 1	2	3	4	5	6	7	8	9	10	11	12
	Arctoa fulvella	.	+	.	.	.	.	.	.	.	.	.	.
	Conostomum tetragonum	.	+	.	.	.	.	.	.	.	.	.	.
	Dicranum falcatum	.	.	+	.	.	.	.	.	.	.	.	.
	Hylocomium pyrenaicum	.	.	.	.	+	.	.	.	.	.	.	.
	Oncophorus virens	.	.	.	.	+	.	.	.	.	.	.	.
	Pohlia wahlenbergii var. *glacialis*	.	.	.	.	+	.	.	.	.	.	.	.
	Scapania nimbosa	.	.	.	+	.	.	.	.	.	.	.	.
	S. paludosa	.	.	.	.	+	.	.	.	.	.	.	.
2000	*Tritomaria polita*	.	.	.	.	+	.	.	.	.	.	.	.
	Anomobryum concinnatum	.	.	.	.	+	.	.	.	.	.	.	.
	Aulacomnium turgidum	.	.	.	.	+	.	.	.	.	.	.	.
	Barbilophozia lycopodioides	.	.	.	.	+	.	+	.	.	.	.	.
	Bazzania pearsonii	+	.	+	+	.	.	.	.	.	.	.	.
	Bryum weigelii	.	+	.	.	+	.	+	+	.	.	.	.
	Dicranoweisia crispula	.	.	.	.	+	.	+	.	.	.	.	.
	Dicranum starkei	.	+	.	.	.	.	.	.	.	.	.	.
	Ditrichum lineare	+	.	+	.	+	.	.	.	.	.	.	.
	D. zonatum	+	.	+	.	.	.	.	.	.	.	.	.
	Encalypta rhabdocarpa	.	.	.	.	+	.	+	.	.	.	.	.
	Gymnomitrion corallioides	+	.	.	.	.	.	.	.	.	.	.	.
	Lophozia obtusa	.	.	.	.	+	.	.	.	.	.	.	.
	Pohlia polymorpha	.	.	.	.	+	.	.	.	.	.	.	.
	Pterygynandrum filiforme	.	.	.	.	+	.	.	.	.	.	.	.
	?*Rhacomitrium microcarpon*	.	.	.	.	+	.	.	.	.	.	.	.
	Scapania gymnostomophila	.	.	.	.	+	.	+	.	.	.	.	.
	S. calcicola	.	.	.	.	+	.	+	.	.	.	.	.
1500	*S. uliginosa*	.	.	+	.	.	.	.	.	.	.	.	.
	Amphidium lapponicum	.	.	.	.	+	+	+	+	+	.	.	.
	Anthelia juratzkana	.	+	.	.	+	+	+	.	.	.	.	.
	Encalypta ciliata	.	+	.	.	+	.	+	.	.	.	.	.
	Marsupella alpina	.	+	.	.	.	+	.	.	.	.	.	.
	M. stableri	+	+	+	.	+	.	.	.	.	.	.	.
	Plagiobryum zierii	+	+	.	+	+	+	+	+	.	.	.	.
	Plagiochila carringtonii	+	+	+	+	.	.	.	.	.	.	.	.
	Plagiopus oederi	.	+	.	.	.	.	.	.	.	.	.	.
	Plagiothecium denticulatum var. *obtusifolium*	.	.	.	.	+	+	.	+	.	.	.	.
	Pohlia ludwigii var. *latifolia*	+	.	.	.	.	.	.	.	.	.	.	.
1000	*Solenostoma oblongifolium*	.	+	.	.	+	.	+	.	.	.	.	.
	Andreaea alpina	+	+	+	+	+	+	+	+	+	+	.	.
	Bartramia ithyphylla	+	+	.	+	+	.	+	+	+	.	.	.
	Bryum dixonii	+	.	.	.	.	.	.	.	.	.	.	.
	Dicranum blytii	.	+	.	.	+	.	.	.	.	.	.	.
	Eremonotus myriocarpus	+	+	.	+	+	.	+	.	.	.	.	.
	Grimmia doniana	+	+	+	.	.	.	.	.	.	.	.	.
	G. torquata	.	+	.	.	+	.	+	+	+	.	.	.
	Gymnomitrion concinnatum	+	+	+	.	+	+	.	.	.	.	.	.
	G. obtusum	+	+	+	.	+	.	+	.	.	.	.	.
	Herberta straminea	+	+	.	.	+	+	+	+	.	.	.	.
	Leiocolea heterocolpos	.	+	.	.	.	.	.	.	.	.	.	.
	Leptodontium recurvifolium	.	+	.	.	+	.	.	+	.	.	.	.
	Marsupella adusta	.	+	.	.	.	.	.	.	.	.	.	.
	Mastigophora woodsii	+	+	+	.	+	.	+	.	.	.	.	.
	Mnium orthorhynchum	.	+	.	.	+	.	+	+	.	.	.	.
	Plectocolea subelliptica	.	+	.	.	+	.	.	.	.	.	.	.
	Polytrichum alpinum	+	+	+	+	+	+	+	+	.	+	.	.
	Scapania ornithopodioides	+	+	+	+	.	.	.	.	.	.	.	.
500	*Tetraplodon angustatus*	+	+	.	.	.	.	.	.	.	.	.	.
	Acrocladium sarmentosum	+	+	+	+	+	+	+	+	+	+	.	+
	A. trifarium	+	+	.	.	+	.	.	.	.	.	.	.
	Anastrepta orcadensis	+	+	+	+	+	+	.	.	.	+	+	+

TABLE 5.4 *continued*

Lower limit (feet)	BRYOPHYTES	LOCALITIES 1	2	3	4	5	6	7	8	9	10	11	12
	Anoectangium aestivum	+	+	+	+	+	+	+	+	+	+	.	+
	Antitrichia curtipendula	+	+	.	+	+	+	+	+	+	.	+	.
	Barbula ferruginascens	+	+	.	.	+	+	+	+	+	+	.	.
	B. icmadophila	.	.	.	.	+	.	+	.	.	.	.	.
	Dicranodontium uncinatum	.	+	+	+	.	.	.	.	.	.	.	+
	Distichium capillaceum	.	+	.	+	+	.	+	+	+	.	.	+
	Entodon concinnus	.	.	.	.	+	.	.	.	+	.	+	.
	Grimmia apocarpa var. *homodictyon*	.	.	.	.	+	.	+	+	+	.	.	.
	G. funalis	+	+	.	.	+	.	+	+	+	+	.	+
	G. ovalis	+	.	.	.	+	.	.	.	.	.	.	.
	G. patens	+	+	.	.	.	.	.	+	.	.	.	.
	G. stricta	.	+	.	.	+	+	+	+	+	.	+	+
	Gymnomitrion crenulatum	+	+	+	+	+	.	+	+	.	+	.	.
	Herberta adunca	+	+	+	+	+	.	+	.	.	.	+	+
	Isothecium myosuroides var. *brachythecioides*	.	+	.	.	+	.	+	+	.	.	.	.
	Marsupella sphacelata	+	+	+	.	+	+	.	.	.	.	.	.
	Mnium marginatum	+	+	.	.	+	.	+	+	+	+	+	.
	M. stellare	.	+	.	.	+	.	+	+	.	.	+	+
	Orthothecium intricatum	.	+	.	.	+	.	+	+	.	.	+	+
	O. rufescens	.	+	.	.	.	.	.	+	.	.	+	.
	Pohlia cruda	+	+	.	+	+	+	+	+	+	.	.	.
	P. elongata	+	+	.	+	+	+	.	+	.	+	+	.
	Radula lindbergiana	+	+	.	.	+	.	.	+	.	.	.	+
0	*Rhacomitrium ellipticum*	+	+	.	+	+	+	+	+	+	+	.	.
	Total number of species (84)	37	53	21	20	62	19	37	30	16	11	10	11
	Total number of vascular plants and bryophytes (140)	77	87	37	37	105	57	74	71	35	24	22	18

? = not seen recently.

LOCALITIES

1. Cuillins including Glamaig; 2. Blà Bheinn; 3. Red Hills; 4. Kyleakin Hills; 5. The Storr; 6. Beinn Edra; 7. The Quirang; 8. Sgùrr Mor; 9. Ben Tianavaig; 10. Macleod's Tables; 11. Ben Suardal; 12. Sleat Peninsula.

sharply towards the north-west and with proximity to the sea. This trend of decreasing summer warmth may largely account for the gradual altitudinal descent of montane plants in highly oceanic regions (cf. Dahl, 1951). However, it is also evident that many montane plants are absent or extremely rare at low levels, probably not because of their intolerance to high summer temperatures, but because they cannot withstand the intensity of competition from tall-shrubs and trees. The severe winds in north-west Scotland may thus be an important factor in influencing montane plant distribution in that it helps to maintain favourable treeless habitats close to sea-level. As several montane vascular plants can be grown successfully in lowland gardens in southern Britain, the lower natural limits of these species are more likely to be controlled by competition rather than by temperature directly (Ratcliffe, 1968).

2. SUMMIT VEGETATION

The predominant communities of level or gently sloping ground above 1500 feet (460 m) on Skye, are chionophobous grass and dwarf-shrub heaths (Caricetea curvulae) and chionophilous snow-patches (Salicetea herbaceae). Of the chionophobous communities present on Skye, the most widespread and abundant is Cariceto–Rhacomitretum lanuginosi heath (Fig. 5). It is local on the Kyleakin hills, the Red Hills, and the Cuillins, but it is extensive on the flat and gentle sloping summit ground in northern Skye. *Festuca ovina–Luzula spicata* 'fell-field' communities are rare on the Kyleakin hills, but they are locally frequent in extremely wind-exposed sites in the Red Hills, the Cuillins, and northern Skye. This regional pattern (Fig. 5) may reflect the generally more exposed nature of the western part of the island, as discussed in the previous section on the woodland zone. Rhacomitreto–Callunetum communities are local in the Red Hills and in the Kyleakin region (Fig. 5) but they are rare in the Cuillins and northern Skye, whereas communities dominated by prostrate *Juniperus communis* ssp. *nana* are restricted on Skye to ground above 1700 feet (520 m) in the Red Hills and the Cuillins (Fig. 3). The reasons for this geographical pattern are not clear, but as both dwarf-shrub communities are particularly sensitive to burning, and, to some degree, grazing, their present distribution within Skye may reflect differences in land use practice. Rhacomitreto–Empetretum communities of summit block detritus, steep but stabilised block screes, and acidic cliff-ledges are widely but locally distributed in all the hill regions on Skye (Fig. 5). The *Alchemilla alpina–Vaccinium myrtillus nodum* is equally widespread but rare in the alpine zone on Skye.

Snow-patch communities of the *Nardus stricta–Vaccinium myrtillus* Association are widely distributed within Skye, but they are always rather rare (Fig. 5). The spatial distributions between the chionophilous and the chionophobous communities are largely a result of differences in the duration of snow-lie. The duration of snow-lie depends not only on the regional macro-climate, but also on local factors, such as the extent of snow-gathering ground, altitude, topography, and the degree of shelter from wind and sun. Although there is some floristic and vegetational variation in the chionophobous communities on Skye associated with differences in altitude and exposure, such as the decreasing prominence of dwarf-shrubs with increasing altitude and/or exposure, much of the wind-exposed summit vegetation on Skye is extremely uniform in its floristic composition and structure. There are only some minor differences in the geographical distribution of these communities on the island (Fig. 5), despite the marked geological differences between the Red Hills, the Kyleakin region, the Cuillins, and northern Skye. In general, leaching predominates in montane areas, except where the soils are periodically flushed. As a result the soils of the various summit communities are rather similar rankers or shallow podsols of low pH (3.8–4.8), irrespective of the underlying rock. The abundance of basiphilous herbs, such as *Cherleria sedoides*, *Polygonum viviparum*, *Silene acaulis*, and *Thalictrum alpinum*, in the 'cushion-herb' facies of the Cariceto–Rhacomitretum lanuginosi heath in northern Skye may reflect slightly more fertile soils developed over basalts.

Summit vegetation is also diversified by differences in soil drainage. In areas of impeded drainage, there is often some development of raw humus and thin peats, and at such sites there is an increased abundance of hygrophilous species in the vegetation, such as *Juncus squarrosus*, *Nardus stricta*, and *Trichophorum cespitosum*. Wherever drainage water emerges at the ground surface as springs, rills, streams, or flushes there is a marked vegetational change. The bryophyte-dominated Philonoto–Saxifragetum stellaris springs of base-poor waters (pH 5.0–6.2, specific conductivity 80–106 μmhos, calcium concentration 0.1–1.0 milligrams/litre, magnesium concentration 0.8–1.7 milligrams/litre) occur widely but locally in all the hill regions on Skye (Fig. 5). Such springs are quite extensive in northern Skye, where the alternation of hard impermeable olivine-basalt lava flows and softer permeable amygdaloidal slag results in a local abundance of springs and seepage areas. In contrast, the *Cratoneuron commutatum–Saxifraga aizoides* springs are restricted to limestone or highly calcareous basalt outcrops with drainage water of high pH (6.8–7.4), high specific conductivity (208–500 μmhos), and high calcium and magnesium concentrations (7.6–9.6 and 8.3–17.1 milligrams/litre respectively). On Skye these two main types of montane springs appear to be clearly differentiated, both floristically and ecologically.

The restriction of the *Koenigia islandica–Carex demissa* flush communities to the Trottenish summit area appears inexplicable in terms of chemical factors, in view of the low base-status of the water (pH 5.8–6.1, specific conductivity 95–97 μmhos, calcium concentration 0.1–0.2 milligrams/litre, magnesium concentration 0.5–1.0 milligrams/litre). The ecological factors that differentiate the *Anthelia julacea*-dominated springs from the commoner Philonoto–Saxifragetum stellaris Association are similarly not clear, but irrigation by snow-meltwater, water temperature, and the rate of water-movement may all be important.

Montane grasslands on slopes below the summits tend to be similar in floristic composition to the Agrosto–Festucetum grasslands of the woodland zone. Stands of these grasslands at altitudes above about 1500 feet (460 m) differ slightly from their lowland counterparts in the occurrence of montane species such as *Alchemilla alpina*, *Cherleria sedoides*, *Galium boreale*, *Oxyria digyna*, *Polygonum viviparum*, *Saxifraga hypnoides*, *Silene acaulis*, *Barbilophozia lycopodioides*, *Isothecium myosuroides* var. *brachythecioides*, and *Peltigera apthosa*. The geographical distribution of the three principal Agrosto–Festucetum grasslands in the alpine zone is similar to that found in the woodland zone, reflecting, to some degree, the differing edaphic conditions within Skye. The Dwarf herb *nodum* is virtually restricted to the alpine zone, and its distribution on Skye is centred on the rich, flushed soils in Coire Uaigneach, Blà Bheinn, and at high altitudes in Trotternish.

Under the cool, moist climate of the alpine zone, surface leaching is the most prominent pedogenic process, and in combination with the widespread occurrence of base-poor rocks, it is responsible for the general prevalance of infertile soils. The associated tendency for the development of raw acid humus and thin peat is equally widespread. Even in areas of base-rich rocks, leaching is frequently so prominent, especially on freely draining sites, that the fertile base-rich soils are restricted to areas where leaching is counteracted, to some degree, by flushing processes. The high nutrient status of the soils can be maintained either by irrigation by water which is strongly charged with dissolved solutes removed from rocks and other soils by leaching (wet flushing *sensu* Dahl, 1956) or by mechanical enrichment due to the downwash of mineral particles by gravity or frost movements from unstable rock outcrops (dry flushing *sensu* Dahl, 1956). Montane communities that are largely dependent on flushing by irrigation include the *Carex–Saxifraga aizoides nodum* and the Alchemilleto–Agrosto–Festucetum grasslands. In general, both irrigation and mechanical enrichment tend to be active in the same area, for example on steep cliff-faces with Saxifragetum aizoidis banks and *Sedum rosea–Alchemilla glabra* ledge communities, and on steep grazed slopes below cliffs with Agrosto–Festucetum (species-rich) grasslands and the related Dwarf herb *nodum*. The varying intensity of these two flushing processes within an area of uniform parent rock can result in striking vegetational patterns, for example the Alchemilleto–Agrosto–Festucetum and Agrosto–Festucetum (species-rich) grasslands below the cliffs at The Storr, and the *Luzula sylvatica–Vaccinium myrtillus* and *Sedum rosea–Alchemilla glabra* ledge communities on Blà Bheinn.

Solifluction phenomena occur above about 2000 feet (610 m) on all the main hill regions on Skye, but they are generally rather rare. Well developed earth hummocks between 15 and 30 cm high and 40 and 120 cm in diameter, with a closed vegetational cover and a mineral soil centre, occur within Cariceto–Rhacomitretum lanuginosi summit heaths on flat and gentle sloping areas (1–5°) on some summit plateaux above 2000 feet (610 m), such as The Storr and Beinn Edra. Similar features are described from Snowdonia in north Wales by Ball & Goodier (1970). A widely accepted mode of formation (Lundqvist, 1962) is that if there is local microtopographical variation in the ground and the vegetation, the thicker vegetation will give greater protection from frosts. Surrounding ground will thus freeze first, and, following this, ice penetrating beneath the unfrozen area will force it upwards to initiate the formation of a hummock. In some areas where the ground begins to slope more steeply (5° or more), the hummocks elongate and frequently become confluent to form parallel ridges running down the slope. Particularly fine examples of this can be seen near the summit of The Storr. These ridges of elongated hummocks appear to correspond to the 'stripe hummocks' described by Lundqvist (1962) in Scandinavia, and to the small unsorted stripes described by Ball & Goodier (1970) in north Wales.

Hillside terraces running across the slope (5–18°) occur widely, but locally, on many of the Skye hills. The terraces are tongue-shaped or lobed with their curved fronts orientated downslope, and with continuous turf-banked lobes. In some areas, for example on Beinn Dearg in Lord MacDonald's Forest, and on The Storr, the banks of the terraces are actively curling over to envelop the surface humus and vegetation, especially where the soils have a high clay content (cf. Dahl, 1956; Warren Wilson, 1952). These morphological features appear to correspond to the 'turf-banked lobes' described by Ball & Goodier (1970) from north Wales. Occasional stone-banked lobes occur on slopes in the Red Hills, but as the frontal stone banks are moss and lichen covered there is no reason to suggest that they are actively moving at present (cf. Ball & Goodier, 1970). Movement of the turf-banked lobes is active, however, and it appears to occur mainly in the spring and early summer when snow meltwater saturates the surface soil and causes it to flow over the deeper, still frozen, subsoil (amorphous solifluction *sensu* Dahl, 1956). Terraces on the basalt summit plateau of The Storr at 2100 feet (686 m) have at times become so charged with water that when a spring thaw coincides with heavy rain, the terraces have burst and formed small mud-flows. In some localities it is difficult, however, to disentangle the possible influences on their formation of gelifluction (*sensu* Ball & Goodier, 1970), frost-creep, and treading by animals. Although treading by animals may play a part in the formation of some terraced slopes, it is improbable that this could produce the lobate forms within the alpine zone on Skye. The relationship between turf-banked and stone-banked lobes on Skye is not clear, but there is a tendency for turf-banked lobes to occur on slopes lacking large stones and boulders (cf. Galloway, 1961).

Many of the terrace flats are barren of vegetation, and the bare ground frequently exhibits structured cryoturbation phenomena, such as up-ended rock-slabs, small sorted stone-polygons, and sorted stone-stripes. Similar structured features can also be found on level or gentle sloping areas of many of the more exposed summits within areas of open 'fell-field' vegetation, for example on Blà Bheinn, Sgùrr na Banachdich, and The Storr. The small stone-polygons generally consist of a central area of mud associated with small rock detritus, surrounded by polygonal boundaries of larger stones. The diameter of these features is between 1 and 3 feet (0.3–1 m). The stone-stripes are rather small in size, with a distance of 18 to 30 inches (45–75 cm) between stripes. The stone-stripes contain exposed bare stones of 10 to 30 cm in size, but the depth to which sorting extends is quite shallow, of the order of 15 to 25 cm. On the summit plateau to the north-west of The Storr there is a wide range of cryoturbation patterns with well-defined stone-polygons, elongated oval polygons, sinuous sorted stone-stripes, and well-developed sorted stone-stripes. Although it is generally believed that polygons become stripes 'as soon as the surface acquires an appreciable slope' (Pearsall, 1950), observations on The Storr summit suggest that the relationships between slope and stone patterns at this site are not so simple. Although there can be little doubt that cryoturbation or structured solifluction is the result of winter frost activities, the actual mechanism of formation of these structured solifluction features is not clear. Observations on the distribution of stone-polygons and stone-stripes on Skye and elsewhere in north-west Scotland suggest that the water content of the soil may be important. Possibly, saturation of the soil in winter followed by the formation of ice may aid the penetration of frost, as ice is a better conductor of heat than snow or aerated soils. In spring, the soils of these open areas may become so saturated with water after snow thaw and heavy rain, that small mud flows may occur. This gelifluction may assist downslope orientation of the frost-heaved stones. Caine (1963) has suggested that preferential water flow in the summer may also aid in the development and maintenance of stone-stripe patterns in the Lake District.

Soil instability, resulting from active gelifluction and cryoturbation, has important effects on summit vegetation, both mechanically and chemically. Many plants are unable to grow where the root systems are constantly subjected to the physical stresses of soil movement, whereas others may benefit from the soil disturbance by the replenishment of nutrients otherwise lost by leaching. Solifluction features also influence vegetation through forming microtopographical and thus microclimatic differences of soil moisture, snow-lie, and exposure. It is of interest that the present climate in the alpine zone of Skye is able to produce patterned ground in suitable sites at the highest altitudes, and that active sorted stone-stripes and terraces can form on slopes at altitudes as low as 1500 feet (460 m).

Screes are rare in the Kyleakin hills, local in the Red Hills, and extremely common in the Cuillins (Fig. 5). The extent of screes is a function both of land use practices and of local geology. The former is important in terms of the loss of vegetational cover as a result of grazing, trampling, and burning. The latter is important in terms of influencing the rates of physical weathering, and the topography. The steep backwalls of the Cuillin corries are inherently unstable, resulting in the constant accretion of freshly shattered rock to the extensive scree-strewn slopes, whereas the topographically more subdued slopes of the Red Hills and the Kyleakin hills are less unstable, and there is little evidence to indicate addition of material as a result of contemporary frost-shattering and other weathering processes. Fine-grained basalt screes supporting *Koenigia islandica* scree communities are naturally restricted to the basalts of northern Skye, and they are only found on the steep eastern slopes of the Trotternish basalt escarpment, up to an altitude of 1750 feet (535 m). These screes probably result from both the loss of vegetational cover by grazing and trampling, especially at low altitudes, and from continual addition of rock debris from the inherently unstable basalt cliffs nearby.

3. CLIFF VEGETATION

Although several of the montane plants listed in Table 5.4 grow in some of the montane communities described in Chapter 4, for example *Alchemilla alpina*, *Carex bigelowii*, *Cherleria sedoides*, *Gnaphalium supinum*, *Lycopodium alpinum*, *Salix herbacea*, *Sibbaldia procumbens*, *Silene acaulis*, and *Aulacomnium turgidum* in summit heaths and montane grasslands, *Cerastium arcticum*, *Deschampsia alpina*, *Luzula spicata*, and *Anthelia juratzkana* in 'fell-field' stands, and *Epilobium alsinifolium*, *E. anagallidifolium*, *Juncus biglumis*, *J. triglumis*, *Koenigia islandica*, *Saxifraga stellaris*, *Bryum weigelii*, *Oncophorus virens*, and *Scapania paludosa* in montane springs and flushes, there are many species that are restricted on Skye to open rock habitats, with little or no associated vegetation, and often to basic substrata in areas protected, in some way, from grazing. Basic cliffs, especially those at high altitudes, are thus the principal habitats for the rarer montane species on Skye. Many of these species in association with lowland and indifferent species from the heterogeneous complex of cliff vegetation, ranging from 'tall herb' communities of broad, stable ledges to the chomophytic types belonging to unstable rock-face habitats.

The granite and sandstone cliffs of the Red Hills and the Kyleakin hills are floristically dull and rather uniform, with the larger north-facing ledges supporting stands of the *Luzula sylvatica–Vaccinium myrtillus* Association, and at higher altitudes (above 1700 feet, 520 m) the Rhacomitreto–Empetretum communities, with *Carex bigelowii*, *Empetrum hermaphroditum*, *Juncus trifidus*, *Lycopodium selago*, and *Salix herbacea*. Notable plants recorded from the Red Hills include *Cryptogramma crispa*, *Juniperus communis* ssp. *nana*, *Luzula spicata*, *Dicranum falcatum*, *Ditrichum lineare*, *Marsupella stableri*, and *Scapania uliginosa*. *S. nimbosa* is restricted on Skye to the Kyleakin hills. The extensive gabbro outcrops in the Cuillins, on Blà Bheinn, and on Glamaig are comparatively poor floristically, for despite the basic character of the rock, its great resistance to weathering does not produce strongly basic soils. *Arabis alpina* has its sole British locality on ledges high in one of the northern Cuillin corries. Nearby on cliffs near Sgùrr nan Gillean, *Draba norvegica* has its only known station on Skye, and *Cerastium arcticum* has one of its two known Skye localities there. *Saxifraga nivalis* and *Poa alpina* also occur in the northern corries of the Cuillins, and they are otherwise restricted on Skye to the Trotternish Peninsula. *Tofieldia pusilla* has its only Skye locality in flushes near Sgùrr nan Eag. The main vegetation of the cliff-ledges in the Cuillins is Empetreto–Rhacomitretum stands, with *Alchemilla alpina*, *Antennaria dioica*, *Solidago virgaurea*, and *Andreaea alpina*. *Cardaminopsis petraea*, *Oxyria digyna*, and *Rubus saxatilis* are locally frequent on small ledges and crevices, and in earthy screes. *Saussurea alpina*, *Saxifraga oppositifolia*, *Sedum rosea*, *Silene acaulis*, *Thalictrum alpinum*, *Anoectangium aestivum*, *Mnium marginatum*, *Plagiobryum zierii*, and *Pohlia cruda* have scattered occurrences on basic outcrops in several of the corries. The higher summits and screes support *Cryptogramma crispa*, *Deschampsia alpina*, *Dryopteris abbreviata*, *Juniperus communis* ssp. *nana*, *Juncus trifidus*, *Ditrichum lineare*, *D. zonatum*, *Grimmia doniana*, *G. ovalis*, *G. patens*, *Gymnomitrion concinnatum*, *G. crenulatum*, *G. obtusum*, *Marsupella alpina*, and *M. stableri*. *Arctoa fulvella*, *Bryum dixonii*, *Conostomum tetragonum*, *Dicranum starkei*, *Gymnomitrion corallioides*, *Marsupella adusta*, *Pohlia ludwigii* var. *latifolia*, and *Tetraplodon angustatus* are confined on Skye to the Cuillins or Blà Bheinn.

The rich flora and luxuriant vegetation of the extensive, north-east-facing cliffs of metamorphosed Jurassic limestones in Coire Uaigneach on Blà Bheinn contrast markedly with the rather sparse vegetational cover of the nearby gabbro cliffs. The larger, more stable and periodically irrigated ledges on the limestone cliffs support *Sedum rosea–Alchemilla glabra* 'tall herb' communities with a local abundance of *Cochlearia officinalis* ssp. *alpina*, *Oxyria digyna*, *Rubus saxatilis*, *Saxifraga hypnoides*, and *Trollius europaeus*. More local species on these ledges include *Saussurea alpina*, *Leptodontium recurvifolium*, *Trichostomum hibernicum*, *Herberta straminea*, and *Mastigophora woodsii*. Saxifragetum aizoidis banks occur on the steep, often near-vertical, cliff-faces, with *Saxifraga aizoides*, *S. oppositifolia*, *Thalictrum alpinum*, and *Orthothecium rufescens*. *Cochlearia officinalis* ssp. *alpina*, *Saxifraga aizoides*, *S. hypnoides*, and *Thalictrum alpinum* grow equally well, often with *Saxifraga stellaris*, in stony flushes and by rills, and they are often more plentiful in these situations than on the main cliffs. Occasional rather dwarfed individuals of the taller growing species, such as *Saussurea alpina*, can be found in rocky ground away from the cliffs, but only the smaller species, such as *Thalictrum alpinum*, are able to flourish in areas unprotected from sheep.

Sheltered north-facing crevices and recesses on the main cliffs of Coire Uaigneach support the montane facies of the *Asplenium trichomanes–Fissidens cristatus* Association, with the ferns *Asplenium viride*, *Cystopteris fragilis*, and *Polystichum lonchitis* growing amidst the bryophytes *Anoectangium aestivum*, *Distichium capillaceum*, *Isopterygium pulchellum*, *Mnium marginatum*, *M. orthorhynchum*, *M. stellare*, *Pohlia cruda*, and *Leiocolea heterocolpos*. Besides the larger ledge and crevice habitats, the cliffs provide a wide range of specialised rock microhabitats such as small open ledges, pockets, crevices, and steep slabs – all habitats where gravity restricts soil development to early stages. Due to the aspect of the cliffs, the open rock-face habitats in Coire Uaigneach are generally rather shaded and moist, and they support a characteristic but heterogeneous assemblage of rupestral species, including *Cardaminopsis petraea*, *Saxifraga oppositifolia*, *Barbula ferruginascens*, *Bartramia hallerana*, *B. ithyphylla*, *Dicranum blyttii*, *D. starkei*, *Encalypta ciliata*, *Grimmia apocarpa*, *G. stricta*, *Isothecium myosuroides* var. *brachythecioides*, *Neckera crispa*, *Orthothecium intricatum*, *Plagiopus oederi*, *Pohlia elongata*, *Rhacomitrium ellipticum*, *Seligeria doniana*, *S. pusilla*, *Anthelia juratzkana*, *Cololejeunea calcarea*, *Colura calyptrifolia*, *Eremonotus myriocarpus*, *Harpalejeunea ovata*, *Marsupella adusta*, *M. alpina*, *M. stableri*, *Metzgeria hamata*, *Plectocolea subelliptica*, *Radula lindbergiana*, *Scapania aequiloba*, *S. aspera*, *Solenostoma oblongifolium* (K. Müll.) K. Müll., *Gyalecta jenensis*, and *Solorina saccata*. The Jurassic limestone cliffs are the sole locality for *Hieracium lingulatum* Backh. ex Hook. & Arnott. on Skye. This is one of the two members of the Section Subalpina within the genus *Hieracium* known to occur on Skye, the other species being the British endemic *H. petrocharis* which occurs on a low-lying basalt cliff in northern Skye. Despite the altitude reached by the Cuillins and nearby hills, no species of the Section Alpina have been found on Skye (Kenneth & Stirling, 1970). Other hawkweeds of note found on Blà Bheinn include *H. pictorum* and *H. piligerum* (Pugsl.) P. D. Sell & C. West.

The richest area for montane plants on Skye is the extensive basalt escarpment in the Trotternish Peninsula, especially The Storr and The Quirang, although Beinn Edra and Sgùrr Mor also support several interesting species not known, at present, elsewhere in Trotternish (Table 5.4). All the basalt areas in Trotternish are rather similar topographically, and they provide a wide range of open habitats, with extensive and rather unstable outcrops of basalt, in parts strongly calcareous, of varying aspect and shelter, block litters and screes, gullies, and montane grasslands on the steep slopes below the cliffs. Many of the cliffs and rock outcrops are unstable and rapidly weather to produce a fine-grained reddish lithosol. The larger, more stable cliffs generally of north or east aspect support *Sedum rosea–Alchemilla glabra* 'tall herb' ledge communities, *Asplenium trichomanes–Fissidens cristatus* fern-rich communities in shaded crevices and recesses, and, more rarely, Saxifragetum aizoidis banks on steep, irrigated cliffs. *Alchemilla glabra*, *Cystopteris fragilis*, *Cochlearia officinalis* ssp. *alpina*, *Oxyria digyna*, *Rubus saxatilis*, *Saxifraga hypnoides*, *S. oppositifolia*, *Sedum rosea*, *Thalictrum alpinum*, *Anoectangium aestivum*, *Bartramia ithyphylla*, *Distichium capillaceum*, *Isopterygium pulchellum*, *Mnium marginatum*, *M. orthorhynchum*, *M. stellare*, *Pohlia cruda*, and *Herberta straminea* are locally abundant in these communities on the Trotternish cliffs, as they are in Coire Uaigneach. However, *Asplenium viride*, *Polystichum lonchitis*, *Saussurea alpina*, and *Saxifraga aizoides* are markedly rarer on the basalt cliffs than in comparable communities on the limestone cliffs in Coire Uaigneach.

The *Sedum rosea–Alchemilla glabra*, *Asplenium trichomanes–Fissidens cristatus* (montane facies), and Saxifragetum aizoidis communities are restricted on Skye to the high altitude basic cliffs of Trotternish and of Blà Bheinn (Fig. 5), reflecting the specific edaphic and climatic requirements of these communities.

Although many of the cliffs and rock outcrops in Trotternish are north- or east-facing, there are some dry, sun-exposed south-facing crags. These support a characteristic, but rather diverse, flora, including *Antennaria dioica*, *Anthyllis vulneraria*, *Arabis hirsuta*, *Cardaminopsis petraea*, *Draba incana*, *Poa balfourii*, *P. glauca*, *Saxifraga oppositifolia*, *Silene acaulis*, *Amphidium lapponicum*, *Antitrichia curtipendula*, *Encalypta ciliata*, *E. rhabdocarpa*, *Grimmia apocarpa*, *G. decipiens* var. *robusta*, *G. funalis*, *G. stricta*, *G. torquata*, *Orthotrichum rupestre*, *Pterogonium gracile*, *Tortula subulata*, *Gymnomitrion concinnatum*, *Preissia quadrata*, *Reboulia hemisphaerica*, and *Scapania aspera*. More local and restricted species of this habitat include *Dryas octopetala* (recorded from near Beinn Edra), *Barbula icmadophila*, *Grimmia apocarpa* var. *homodictyon*, *Anthelia juratzkana*, *Porella cordeana*, *Anomobryum concinnatum*, *Pterygynadrum filiforme*, and *Targionia hypophylla* (not seen recently). The last three are only known on Skye at The Storr.

Damp rocks or bare soil on shaded cliffs and in gullies, generally of north or east aspect, also support a rich assemblage of montane plants, including *Luzula spicata*, *Oxyria digyna*, *Poa alpina*, *Rhinanthus borealis*, *Saxifraga hypnoides*, *S. stellaris*, *Sedum rosea*, *Barbula ferruginascens*, *Ditrichum lineare*, *Grimmia patens*, *Hypnum callichroum*, *Leptodontium recurvifolium*, *Neckera crispa*, *Orthothecium intricatum*, *Plagiobryum zierii*, *Plagiothecium denticulatum* var. *obtusifolium*, *Pohlia elongata*, *P. polymorpha*, *P. rothii*, *Cololejeunea calcarea*, *Colura calyptrifolia*, *Eremonotus myriocarpus*, *Harpalejeunea ovata*, *Marsupella funckii*, *Plectocolea subelliptica*, *Porella laevigata*, *P. cordeana*, *Scapania calcicola*, *S. gymnostomophila*, *Solenstoma oblongifolium*, *Gyalecta jenensis*, and *Solorina saccata*. The few known colonies of *Saxifraga nivalis* on Skye are restricted to shaded, rather mossy, crevices and small overhangs on the basalt cliffs, with one station in the Cuillins. The saxifrage colonies generally consist of a few rather small plants only. The trio of coastal species, *Plantago maritima*, *Armeria maritima*, and *Silene maritima*, are locally frequent on several of the basalt cliffs. *Plantago maritima* is the most widespread and it is abundant in a range of habitats, such as moist cliff-ledges, earthy screes, gullies, flushes, and summit heaths. Whereas this species favours rather moist sites, *Silene maritima* appears to favour dry, basic rocks and it often grows with *Cardaminopsis petraea*, *Draba incana*, and *Galium boreale*. *Armeria maritima* is curiously patchy in its inland distribution on Skye, but it occurs on several Trotternish cliffs, often on rocks that are slightly enriched by irrigation. On damper cliffs and rock slabs that are frequently irrigated, *Cochleria officinalis* ssp. *alpina*, *Epilobium alsinifolium*, and *Saxifraga stellaris* are prominent, with *Andreaea* spp., *Blindia acuta*, *Rhacomitrium ellipticum* and, more rarely, *Seligeria recurvata*. The highest set of cliffs in Trotternish is the north-east-facing buttress that drops vertically from the summit of The Storr into the sheltered, upper part of Coire Scamadal. On these high cliffs, there are several interesting species including *Saxifraga nivalis*, *Aulacomnium turgidum*, and *Hylocomium pyrenaicum*. *Cerastium arcticum* grows nearby in open summit 'fell-field' communities. Several of the basalt cliffs support interesting *Hieracium* floras. Species recently recorded at The Quirang include *H. anglicum*, *H. argenteum*, *H. euprepes*, and the British endemic *H. langwellense*.

Several interesting montane plants occur in habitats away from the main Trotternish cliffs. The species-rich grasslands developed on well-drained soils on the steep slopes below the cliffs support an abundance of *Alchemilla alpina*, with *A. wichurae* (restricted to The Storr), *Botrychium lunaria*, *Cherleria sedoides*, *Sibbaldia procumbens*, *Silene acaulis*, *Thalictrum alpinum*, and *Polygonum viviparum*. The last-named species is inexplicably rare on the basalt, occurring in rather small quantity in the species-rich grasslands adjoining the cliffs, on rather wet, open ledges, and in summit heaths. The grasslands are rich in bryophytes, including the montane species *Aulacomnium turgidum*, *Entodon concinnus*, *Isothecium myosuroides* var. *brachythecioides*, *Barbilophozia lycopodioides*, and *Lophozia obtusa*. Fine-grained basalt screes are relatively common on steep slopes below the cliffs, either in areas that are naturally unstable or in areas that are over-grazed by sheep and rabbits. These screes support several interesting species, including *Cardaminopsis petraea*, *Koenigia islandica*, *Luzula spicata*, *Poa glauca*, *Sagina saginoides*, and *Saxifrage hypnoides*. Areas of block litters, such as at Carn Liath and at The Storr, provide specialised habitats for *Cryptogramma crispa*, *Hymenophyllum wilsonii*, *Antitrichia curtipendula*, *Dicranoweisia crispula*, *Dicranum blyttii*, *Glyphomitrium daviesii*, *Grimmia apocarpa* var. *homodictyon*, *G. decipiens* var. *robusta*, *G. ovalis*, *G. patens*, *Pohlia polymorpha*, *Pterogonium gracile*, *Ptychomitrium polyphyllum*, *Ulota americana*, *Gymnomitrion crenulatum*, and *G. obtusum*.

Species of interest that occur at The Quirang, but which are not known at The Storr, include *Veronica serpyllifolia* ssp. *humifusa*, *Seligeria pusilla*, *Haplomitrium hookeri*, *Porella thuja*, and *Scapania aequiloba*. *Salix myrsinites* and *Orthothecium rufescens* are only known at Sgùrr Mor, whereas *Marsupella alpina* has its sole Trotternish station on Beinn Edra.

4. THE MONTANE FLORA

The richness of the montane flora at a single locality in Scotland, as assessed in terms of numbers of species, appears to be largely a result of two factors – altitude and geology. As montane species requiring base-rich soils far outnumber the calcifuge and indifferent species in the present Scottish montane flora (see Ferreira, 1959), the floristically rich areas are those with extensive outcrops of basic, calcareous rocks. All such localities tend to have some acidic rocks and poor soils in addition, so that they also support a proportion of the calcifuge and indifferent elements of the montane flora. On mountains where both basic and non-basic rocks occur together, the richness of the montane flora generally depends on the range of altitude, so that the highest mountains usually support the largest number of montane species. Many of the rarer species appear to require conditions generally associated with high altitudes, such as prolonged snow-lie, whereas some dwarf shrubs evidently have an upper altitudinal limit. Besides needing base-rich soils at high altitudes, the majority of Scottish mountain plants cannot compete successfully in a dense, closed vegetation, and they thus require open conditions; others require protection from the heavy sheep and deer grazing to which many of the Scottish hills are now subjected. The last two requirements are largely satisfied on steep, cliff-faces. Moreover, even on basic rocks, leaching and accumulation of acid humus are so active that base-rich soils are only maintained on irrigated or unstable, rocky ground. The richest localities for montane plants are thus those where basic rocks occur as steep, unstable outcrops at a range of altitudes, but particularly at high levels.

The importance of high altitudes for many mountain plants on Skye is shown by the relatively poor montane flora of the low-lying limestones of Ben Suardal (Table 5.4), although some species such as *Dryas octopetala*, *Polygonum viviparum*, and *Saxifraga aizoides* grow there in some abundance. The importance of basic rock-outcrops coupled with high altitudes is also shown by the greater number of montane species recorded from the Cuillins and Blà Bheinn compared with those from the nearby granite Red Hills of comparable extent and altitude. The importance of soil-nutrient enrichment by flushing, either by irrigation or by downwash of mineral particles from unstable rock outcrops, is clearly shown by the floristic richness of BenTianavaig (1352 feet, 412 m) with its extensive, unstable, landslipped east-facing scarp, in comparison with the poor flora of the Macleod's Tables, despite the comparable size, altitude, and rock type. The east-facing basalt scarp of the Trotternish Peninsula and, to a lesser degree, the limestone cliffs of Coire Uaigneach on Blà Bheinn appear to fulfil the requirements for montane plants more than any other localities on Skye, and they are thus the floristically richest areas (Table 5.4).

There is now considerable evidence from Quaternary palaeobotanical studies to indicate the former occurrence during Devensian (Weichselian) times of several of the montane species listed on Table 5.4 in areas outside their present distributional range (see Conolly & Dahl, 1970; Godwin, 1956; Tralau, 1963). The gradual restriction of a once more widespread montane flora to high ground and specialised habitats is generally regarded as a direct or indirect result of climatic changes during Flandrian times. Although the mountain flora of Britain can be regarded as being 'relict', each species will have a different critical threshold to environmental changes, and there will thus be all degrees of disjunction or 'relictness' (see Holmquist, 1962), resulting in widely different distributional patterns.

An important factor in the distribution and survival of montane plants is the ability of the various species to maintain their populations and to spread both vegetatively and by seed. Within the present montane flora of Skye, there is a group of species which occurs in most localities where conditions seem suitable, including low-lying inland cliffs and coastal habitats. This group includes *Alchemilla alpina*, *Galium boreale*, *Lycopodium selago*, *Saxifraga hypnoides*, *S. oppositifolia*, *Sedum rosea*, and *Silene acaulis*. Discontinuities in their present distributions can often be explained in terms of a lack of suitable habitats, whereas the occasional absence of some of these species from likely localities may be attributed to the element of chance that must always influence plant dispersal. It is perhaps significant that many of the species that have a wide altitudinal range occur widely in suitable habitats on Skye and in Britain as a whole. Many of them are evidently able to spread vegetatively or by seed, although their effective dispersal range may often be rather small. Their occurrences on open river gravels, on recently colonised rock falls, and in abandoned quarries, illustrate their potential reproductive and dispersal capacities.

In contrast, the rarest species on Skye are generally confined to high levels (see Table 5.4). The absence of several of these species from many apparently suitable habitats may largely be a matter of chance, for either the species were never able to colonise these localities, or else they have died out in these areas due to competition, climatic change (Dahl, 1951; Conolly, 1961; Conolly & Dahl, 1970), or disease (Patton, 1923), and they have been subsequently unable to recolonise lost ground. This can result in a strikingly disjunct distribution, either on a local scale within Skye, or on a broader, national scale. Plants such as *Arabis alpina*, *Cerastium arcticum*, *Deschampsia alpina*, *Draba norvegica*, *Poa alpina*, *Salix myrsinites*, *Saxifraga nivalis*, and *Tofieldia pusilla* are now restricted on Skye to a few scattered stations, or even to single localities, and they evidently exist under sub-optimal conditions today. Their present reproductive powers suffice to maintain their remaining small populations. Some of these species, such as *Salix myrsinites* and *Tofieldia pusilla*, are locally frequent elsewhere in the Scottish Highlands and set good seed in some localities. Others, including *Draba norvegica* and *Saxifraga nivalis*, are nowhere plentiful in Britain, and their rarity may be due partly to a poor capacity for spread, even under optimal conditions. Indeed, some of these relict colonies appear to be declining in quantity on Skye. The recently discovered colony of two bushes of *Salix myrsinites* has a poor, stunted growth with small leaves and many dead twigs. The willow has a generally unhealthy look compared with many of the bushes of larger populations of *S. myrsinites* at, for example, Inchnadamph in west Sutherland, Loch Einich in Aberdeenshire, and Caenlochan Glen in Angus. Similarly the absence of recent records of *Loiseleuria procumbens* and *Orthilia secunda* from the Cuillins may represent recent extinctions of small, relict populations.

A further factor determining the distribution of

montane plants is climate. The connection between the occurrence of mountain plants and a cool climate is implicit, but Dahl (1951), Conolly (1961), and Conolly & Dahl (1970) have considered this general correlation in detail for Scandinavia and the British Isles. They suggest the importance of a critical maximum summer temperature as a limiting factor. Since the critical temperature is not the same for all species, different species will have different lower altitudinal limits in the same area. The varying altitudinal ranges of the Skye species (see Table 5.4) may well be due to this effect, for species confined to high levels may not be able to survive under the relatively higher temperatures tolerated by the species which descend to near sea-level. The lower altitudinal limits presented in Table 5.4 may not represent a strict sequence of critical temperatures but only indicate a general trend. The two extreme groups, those restricted to altitudes above 2000 feet (610 m) and those occurring at or near sea level on Skye, show some differentiation with regard to maximum summer temperatures when compared with Conolly & Dahl's (1970) figures of limiting isotherms for British montane species in the Scottish Highlands. The limiting isotherms are 21 or 22 °C for the species restricted to altitudes above 2000 feet (610 m) on Skye, and between 22 and 24/25 °C for the species occurring at or near sea-level on Skye. However, when Dahl's temperature classes and distribution maps for Scandinavian montane plants are compared with the distribution of the same species in Skye, certain discrepancies are apparent. For example, *Saxifraga stellaris*, *Sedum rosea*, and *Silene acaulis* ('limiting' temperatures in Fennoscandia 25 °C; Dahl, 1951) are some of the commonest montane plants on Skye, whereas *Arabis alpina* ('limiting' temperature 26 °C), *Saxifraga nivalis* (27 °C), *Salix myrsinites* (28/29 °C), and *Tofieldia pusilla* (29 °C) are among the rarest.

Some of these species may be too rare today on Skye due to historical factors, to indicate their true lower altitudinal limits. Such boundaries are, however, fairly well defined for more widespread plants, like *Carex bigelowii*, *Oxyria digyna*, *Salix herbacea*, *Saxifraga hypnoides*, *Sedum rosea*, and *Thalictrum alpinum*. The lower limits of these six species all show a gradual altitudinal descent with increasing distance northwards in Britain, and this trend is consistent with the concept of limiting maximum summer temperatures, although the indirect effects of humidity cannot be ruled out as possible additional factors. It is difficult to distinguish warmth-sensitive species from those which require prolonged snow-cover or a low winter temperature, for such plants are all naturally confined to high altitudes. The physiological significance of prolonged snow-lie may also differ between species, and an apparent dependence on this factor may be merely coincidental in some species. In many instances the significance of prolonged snow-lie may be related to the protection the snow gives to the plant from extremes of winter cold, whereas in other cases snow may be important in maintaining moist and open habitats.

There is, however, a small group of species whose present restricted distributions on Skye appear to be explicable in terms of the limited availability of suitable but rather specialised habitats. There appear to be very few outcrops of igneous rocks on Skye that contain enough lime for exacting calcicolous species such as *Dryas octopetala*. Elsewhere in Scotland, this species has a preference for dry, and often sun-exposed sites, but most of the high-lying calcareous rocks on Skye tend to be rather moist and shaded. *Koenigia islandica* is inexplicably restricted in Britain to basalt areas, namely the Isles of Skye and Mull. In Scotland and in Scandinavia the moss *Pohlia wahlenbergii* var. *glacialis* luxuriates in springs fed by water whose temperature is consistently less than 4 °C (Dahl, 1956; McVean & Ratcliffe, 1962). Such springs are generally restricted to the neighbourhood of late snow-beds, and are thus extremely rare on Skye. This lack of habitat may be responsible for the very restricted distribution of the moss on the island.

Disjunct distributions of the kind shown by many of the montane plants on Skye present, to some extent, an inscrutable problem, for one has to explain not so much why a plant grows where it does, as why it is missing from so many other places that are apparently equally suitable. When all the obvious possibilities have been considered, the distribution of many species remains inadequately explained in terms of gross environmental factors. Montane plants in Britain are at the limits of their range, and thus have a scattered distribution. Such limits are necessarily mobile over long periods of time – either extending or retreating – and it follows that the flora of any area must therefore have a number of rare species, since conditions are usually marginal for at least some species. The relative slowness with which most plants appear or disappear under gradually changing conditions ensures that only a small proportion of the available habitats holds any species at its limits of range, but the actual place where the plant becomes established, or survives, may depend largely on chance.

4. PLANT INDICATORS OF SOIL

In phytosociological studies the soils of the various vegetational units are often ignored, whereas in detailed ecological investigations the influences of soil type and its chemical and physical characteristics upon the vegetation frequently form the basis of the work. In this study, with its emphasis on vegetational description, only limited observations on the associated soils have been made. Indications of the soil types, the range of soil pH, and the nature of the underlying rocks have been given in the descriptions of the plant communities in Chapter 4. The possible role of soil factors in the ecological differentiation of the various communities has been considered in the present chapter.

The ranges of pH values of the soils and mire and spring waters examined for each of the more abundant vegetational types are presented in Fig. 8. Within each nodum the pH values are reasonably constant with a general range of variation of less than one pH unit, but there is considerable overlap of the pH values of different noda. There are insufficient pH determinations from Skye to draw curves for each nodum as Braun-Blanquet (1951) and Gjaerevoll (1956) have done, but comparisons of the pH values for various closely related noda within the mires and springs, the grasslands, the dwarf-shrub heaths, the 'tall herb' communities, and the woodlands, show in some cases significant differences in soil or water pH between noda.

The relation between soil type and soil pH on Skye is shown in Table 5.5.

TABLE 5.5

Soil Type	pH range	Number of readings
Blanket peats and raw humus	3.6–4.5	22
Podsols within the Woodland Zone	3.7–5.1	20
Alpine podsols	4.0–4.8	5
Brown earths	5.0–6.9	55
Calcareous rendzinas	5.6–7.2	12
Alpine rankers	3.8–4.8	17
Skeletal and solifluction soils	4.0–4.5	4
Peaty gleys and flushed peats	4.3–5.9	29
Fen peats, lake muds, and marls	5.2–7.2	26

As the vegetation and soil type are closely related, the distribution map of the various vegetational types in the six regions on Skye (Fig. 5) reflects, to a large degree, the general distribution of soil types on the island. Blanket peats, podsols, peaty gleys, and flushed peats are widespread throughout Skye, whereas alpine rankers and skeletal and solifluction soils are restricted to high altitudes. Brown earths are largely centred on the basalt, gabbro, and limestone areas. Although brown earths can be found on granite and sandstone, they are generally on slopes that are periodically flushed. Rendzinas are confined to the limestones on Skye, and they support either *Dryas octopetala–Carex flacca* heath or *Fraxinus excelsior–Brachypodium sylvaticum* woodlands.

In the field it is clear that there is some floristic differentiation between the various rock types on Skye. For example, some species are restricted to limestone soils and outcrops, whereas several species occur in the basalt, gabbro, and limestone areas, and yet avoid the acidic rocks entirely. The existence on Skye of such a distinction between the flora of the limestones and of the basic igneous rocks is of particular interest. There is increasing evidence from experimental autecological studies that, although calcium has long been regarded as the most significant ion, acting directly or indirectly, for 'calcicoles', there are some species that grow equally well when magnesium replaces calcium as the predominant cation. The important distinction between calciphilous species that are restricted to calcium-rich soils, and basiphilous species that are restricted to base-rich soils where the predominant cation may be calcium, magnesium, or even sodium, has been discussed in detail by Ferreira (1963).

The available calcium status of a soil depends largely on the ease with which calcium is released from the parent rock (Ferreira, 1959). Calcium is most readily available to plants when it is present as calcium carbonate. Although some igneous rocks have a high calcium content, the calcium is often in the form of silicates, chiefly plagioclase felspars such as labradorite, and it is thus largely unavailable to the plants, with the result that the local flora and vegetation is rather similar to that of non-calcareous sandstones or granites. Although there is considerable variation in the chemical composition of the basalts and related igneous rocks on Skye, magnesium and calcium tend to occur together in the ratio of 1:1 to 1:3 (Anderson & Dunham, 1966).

To illustrate the edaphic preferences of many of the species on Skye, the vascular flora has been grouped into eight categories, on the basis of field observations of species abundance in relation to soil type and parent rock. It should be emphasised that

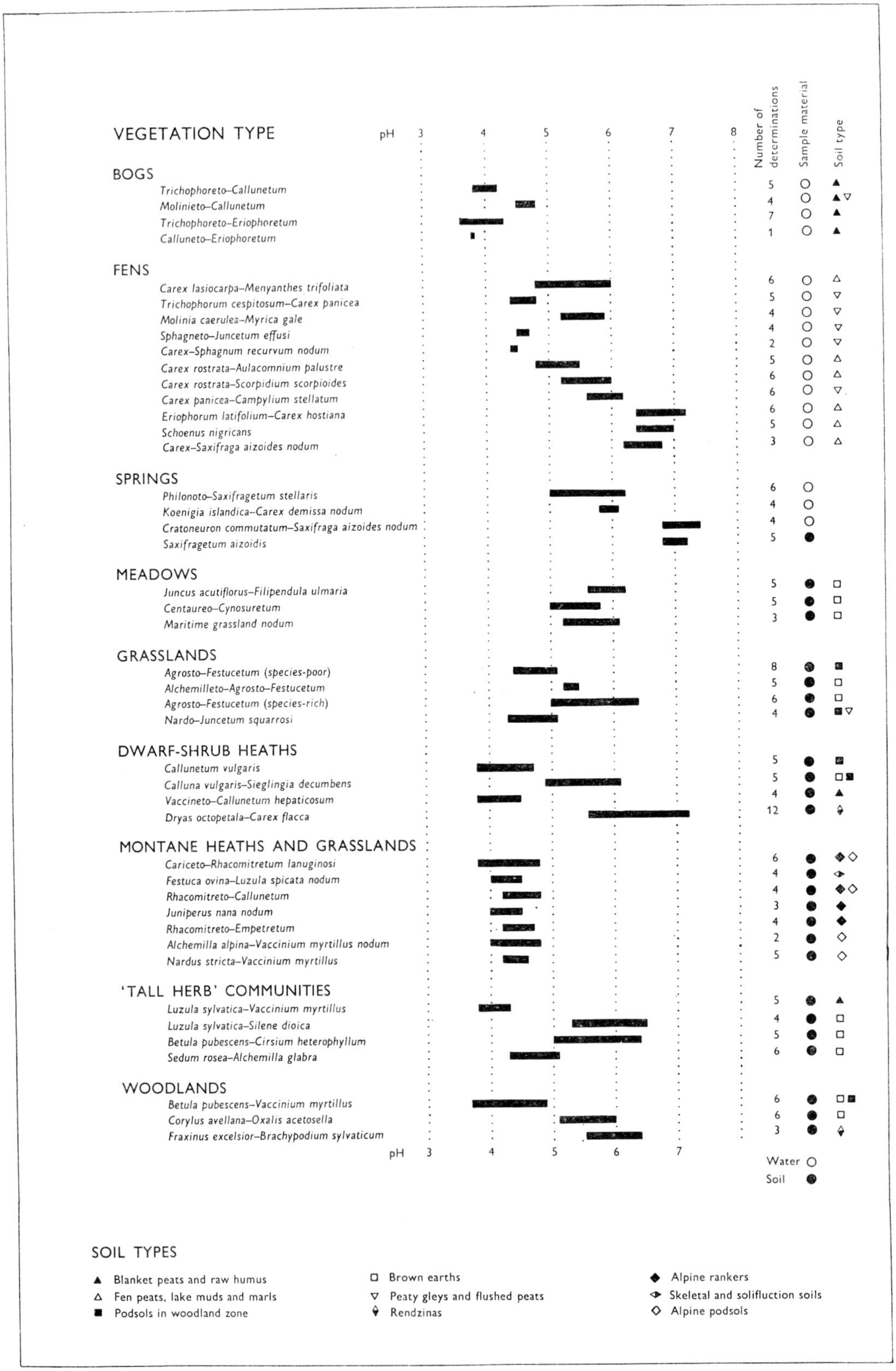

Figure 8. The range of pH values for soils or water from the principal vegetational types on Skye. The number of determinations, the material sampled, and the soil type are also shown.

the observations are restricted to Skye since some species, such as *Sibbaldia procumbens*, *Equisetum hyemale*, *Melica nutans*, and *Vaccinium vitis-idaea*, show edaphic preferences on Skye which differ from those elsewhere in Scotland. The species listed in Tables 5.6–5.10 have been mostly recorded in the vegetational analyses. Although the method is subjective, it gives an indication of the edaphic differentiation of the present flora and it provides a background for considering the edaphic features of the Late-Devensian flora, and it should be regarded as a first step in examining edaphic differentiation within the Skye flora. The groups are as follows:

1. *Calcifuges* (Table 5.6).* These are species that are largely restricted on Skye to iron or humus podsols, alpine rankers, acidic peats (wet or dry), and soils with raw humus, generally with a soil pH of less than 4.5. Although the physical properties of the soils may be important in influencing root growth, the fact that none of the mire species grow on calcareous peats of similar, though not identical, physical properties, suggests that the soil chemistry may also be significant.

2. *Calciphiles* (Table 5.7). These are species that are exclusive to, or strongly selective for, soils developed on limestone, with a pH greater than 6.0. This list corresponds closely to McVean & Ratcliffe's (1962) group of 'exacting calcicoles' that characterises soils of high exchangeable calcium content (>300 milligrams/100 grams soil) and high pH (>6.0). Several of these species appear to have a specific need for calcium, and will not grow on other base-rich substrata (Ferreira, 1963).

The diversity of the physical characteristics of the soils, such as moisture and texture, on which *Dryas octopetala*, *Saxifraga aizoides*, and *S. oppositifolia* occur, suggests that, within limits, it is the chemical, rather than the physical, properties of the soil which are important. Similarly, species such as *Arabis hirsuta*, *Asplenium viride*, *Epipactis atrorubens*, and *Polystichum lonchitis* that are restricted to dry well-drained soils appear to be intolerant of waterlogging, and scarcely, if ever, occur on acid soils with similar physical properties, suggesting again that the chemical characteristics are important.

3. *Basiphiles* (Table 5.8). These are species that are confined to base-rich soils, generally brown earths with a pH range of 5.0–6.0, developed on limestone, basalt, or gabbro. Many species are included here that are characteristic of communities dependent on flushing, for example the 'tall herbs' *Angelica sylvestris*, *Cirsium heterophyllum*, *Crepis paludosa*, *Trollius europaeus*, and *Valeriana officinalis*, and the rich-fen species *Carex hostiana*, *Eleocharis quinqueflora*, and *Eriophorum latifolium*. Some rare montane plants, such as *Arabis alpina*, *Cerastium arcticum*, *Draba norvegica*, *Koenigia islandica*, and *Saxifraga nivalis*, are included here, in view of their restriction to basic rocks at high altitudes in the Cuillins or in Trotternish. Many of the species in this group are recorded from serpentine rocks in Scotland by Proctor & Woodell (1971) and Spence (1957), and in western Norway by Knaben (1950).

4. *Indifferents* (Table 5.9). This group includes species that grow on a wide range of soil and rock types, and that appear to be indifferent to soil acidity and calcium status. Some of the species only occur sparingly on soils at one or other end of the soil basicity series, and their optimum soil conditions are denoted on Table 5.9 by A (acid soils) and B (basic soils).

5. *Species that avoid the poorest soils* (Table 5.10). These are species that have a wide edaphic tolerance on Skye, but which avoid the poorest soils, especially acid peats and mor humus of low pH (<4.5). Many of the species included in this group have their optimum occurrence in basiphilous vegetation.

6. *Coastal species* (unlisted). These are forty-eight species restricted to coastal habitats on Skye, either in salt marshes, sand dunes, sea-cliffs, or shingle beaches.

7. *Aquatic species* (unlisted). These are forty-six species restricted to open freshwater habitats on Skye.

8. *Not classified* (unlisted). The remaining 188 vascular plants known at present on Skye are included in this group. The majority are associated with artificial man-made habitats or restricted to single localities, for which there is little or no information concerning their soil preferences.

A striking feature of these tables is the very large number of species with wide edaphic tolerances on Skye. These species have limited value as reliable indicators of soil conditions on the island. Several of the indifferent species would be regarded as indicative of base-rich soils elsewhere in their range.

* Tables 5.6 to 5.9 are on pp. 205–6.

For example, *Silene acaulis* is a strict basiphile in its southernmost British localities in north Wales and Lakeland, but in the Cairngorms and the north-west Highlands, it is a prominent component of summit vegetation growing on alpine rankers of low pH and low base content. Similarly, *Cherleria sedoides* and the montane form of *Armeria maritima* are largely indifferent to soil base-status and often occur with *Silene acaulis* in summit heaths on the poorest rocks, including quartzite, in the north-west Highlands. This is in contrast to their restriction to moderately rich soils in central Scotland. A similar trend occurs in some bryophytes. For example, *Aulacomnium turgidum*, *Hylocomium pyrenaicum*, and *Hypnum hamulosum*, are restricted to base-rich sites in central Scotland, but they are rather indifferent in the north-west Highlands. All these species can occur in closed vegetation on poor soils, so that their wide edaphic tolerances are probably not an effect of differences in competition, as discussed by Ferreira (1959; cf. Bamberg & Major, 1968; Tansley, 1917). In contrast, *Cardaminopsis petraea* occurs in open vegetation on a range of rock types, but it is only found in closed vegetation on Skye on basic rocks.

Some mire plants show a similar variation in their edaphic tolerance within their British range, for example *Schoenus nigricans*, *Utricularia vulgaris* agg., *U. minor*, *Campylium stellatum*, and *Scorpidium scorpioides*. On Skye, and elsewhere in north-west Scotland, these species occasionally occur in poor-fens, or even in bogs, in contrast to their restriction to rich-fens in southern Britain. Similarly, if European ranges are considered, *Eriophorum angustifolium*, *Molinia caerulea*, and *Narthecium ossifragum* are reported to be exclusive to fen communities in southern Sweden (Malmer, 1962), in contrast to their British ecology.

Juncus squarrosus and *Nardus stricta* are generally regarded as plants of acidic, base-deficient soils (see Jefferies & Willis, 1964), but on Skye and elsewhere in Scotland (McVean & Ratcliffe, 1962) both species occur on a wide range of soil types, and they are often associated with irrigation effects. Similarly, several species of *Carex*, for example *C. demissa* (cf. Clymo, 1962), *C. echinata*, *C. nigra*, and *C. rostrata*, and of *Juncus*, such as *J. acutiflorus*, *J. effusus*, and *J. kochii*, have a wide edaphic tolerance on Skye and they occur frequently, or even dominate, in a range of mire types. Despite their prominence in these communities, they have no value as differential species (see Table 4.57), and the vegetation has to be characterised in terms of subsidiary species, especially bryophytes. Similarly, the grasses *Festuca ovina*, *F. vivipara*, and *Agrostis* spp. show a wide edaphic tolerance, although *A. canina* and *A. stolonifera* tend to avoid the poorest soils (cf. Clarkson, 1965).

Some species show a restriction to basic substrata on Skye, and elsewhere in north-west Scotland, whereas in southern and eastern Britain they appear to be largely indifferent to soil type, for example *Equisetum telmateia* and *Phyllitis scolopendrium*. In contrast, species such as *Dryas octopetala*, *Epipactis atrorubens*, and *Saxifraga oppositifolia* appear to be calciphilous throughout their British range. Many of the calcifuge species on Skye are equally consistent in their soil preferences in Britain.

Many members of the Ericaceae show wide edaphic tolerances on Skye, for example *Arctostaphylos uva-ursi*, *Calluna vulgaris*, *Erica cinerea*, *E. tetralix*, and *Vaccinium myrtillus*. Much has been written about the calcifuge habit of *Calluna vulgaris*, and it has been suggested (cf. Webb, 1947) that when *Calluna* occurs on basic rocks it is rooted in pockets of raw humus (as it is in some of the *Dryas* heaths on Skye). *Calluna* is, however, a frequent component of some 'tall herb' communities on irrigated, basic rocks on Skye, and in the *Calluna vulgaris–Sieglingia decumbens* heaths there are intimate mixtures of *Calluna*, *Erica cinerea*, and basiphilous herbs such as *Galium boreale*, *Gentianella campestris*, and *Rubus saxatilis*. In these communities there are no signs that *Calluna* is rooted in leached pockets. Similarly *Erica tetralix* is locally frequent in areas adjoining rich-fens and flushes, for example in the *Eriophorum latifolium–Carex hostiana* Association, where there are no indications of local acidification. *Vaccinium myrtillus* occurs sparingly in some species-rich grasslands, whereas *Arctostaphylos uva-ursi* is locally dominant in *Dryas* heaths, and on limestone pavements. *Empetrum nigrum* occurs occasionally on limestone soils, but it often tends to be rather chlorotic.

The occurrence of interesting mixed communities of calcifuges, calciphiles, and basiphiles may, in some instances, be the result of sudden changes in soil conditions within a small area. For example, on Camas Malag, *Dryas octopetala* is abundant in a moss mat of *Dicranum scoparium*, *Hylocomium splendens*, *Rhacomitrium lanuginosum*, and other common calcifuge species. The mosses grow on the leached surface layer (pH range 4.9–5.4), whereas the *Dryas* is rooted into the cracks in the underlying limestone (pH range 6.2–7.2). Variations in soil pH values of over two pH units can be found in such communities over vertical distances of less than 10 cm.

Possible causes of the differences in edaphic tolerances within the geographical range of a species have not been extensively investigated. Beyond the general correlation already discussed, it can only be assumed that different climatic areas may produce physiological adaptations in some species (cf. Mooney & Billings, 1961), or that genotypic variation may produce locally adapted races, such as has been shown to occur on a local scale in relation to differences in soil nutrient levels (Bradshaw, McNeilly & Gregory, 1965; Snaydon & Bradshaw, 1961), or on a large scale in relation to soil types (Proctor, 1971).

TABLE 5.6. *Calcifuges*

Blechnum spicant	*Euphrasia micrantha*
Carex binervis	*Gnaphalium supinum*
C. curta	*Hymenophyllum tunbridgense*
C. pauciflora	*H. wilsonii*
C. pilulifera	*Ilex aquifolium*
Cryptogramma crispa	*Juncus trifidus*
Dactylorchis maculata ssp. *ericetorum*	*Listera cordata*
Deschampsia flexuosa	*Lycopodium alpinum*
D. setacea	*L. clavatum*
Digitalis purpurea	*L. selago*
Dryopteris abbreviata	*Melampyrum pratense*
D. aemula	*Pedicularis sylvatica*
D. borreri	*Rhynchospora alba*
D. dilatata	*Rumex acetosella*
Empetrum hermaphroditum	*Thelypteris dryopteris*
Eriophorum vaginatum	*T. limbosperma*
	Vaccinium vitis-idaea

TABLE 5.7. *Calciphiles*

Arabis hirsuta	*H. pubescens*
Asplenium ruta-muraria	*Melica nutans*
A. viride	*Ophioglossum vulgatum*
Carex caryophyllea	*Paris quadrifolia*
C. lepidocarpa	*Phyllitis scolopendrium*
Cystopteris fragilis	*Polystichum lonchitis*
Dryas octopetala	*Rosa pimpinellifolia*
Epipactis atrorubens	*Salix myrsinites*
E. helleborine	*Saxifraga aizoides*
Euphrasia confusa	*S. oppositifolia*
Geranium lucidum	*Torilis japonica*
Helictotrichon pratense	

TABLE 5.8. *Basiphiles*

Alchemilla filicaulis	*Gentianella campestris*
A. glabra	*Geranium robertianum*
A. vestita	*Geum rivale*
A. wichurae	*Heracleum sphondylium*
A. xanthochlora	*Hieracium pilosella*
Agrimonia eupatoria	*Juncus articulatus*
Allium ursinum	*J. biglumis*
Angelica sylvestris	*J. triglumis*
Anthyllis vulneraria	*Koenigia islandica*
Arabidopsis thaliana	*Linum catharticum*
Arabis alpina	*Listera ovata*
Arrhenatherum elatius	*Mercurialis perennis*
Asplenium adiantum-nigrum	*Orchis mascula*
A. trichomanes	*Oxyria digyna*
Bellis perennis	*Parnassia palustris*
Botrychium lunaria	*Pedicularis palustris*
Brachypodium sylvaticum	*Petasites hybridus*
Briza media	*Poa alpina*
Campanula rotundifolia	*P. glauca*
Cardamine flexuosa	*Polygala vulgaris*
C. hirsuta	*Polygonum viviparum*
Carex diandra	*Polypodium interjectum*
C. dioica	*Polystichum aculeatum*
C. flacca	*Primula vulgaris*
C. hostiana	*Prunella vulgaris*
C. laevigata	*Prunus padus*
C. pulicaris	*Ranunculus acris*
Carlina vulgaris	*R. ficaria*
Cerastium arcticum	*Rhinanthus borealis*
*Chamaenerion angustifolium**	*Ribes spicatum*
Chrysosplenium oppositifolium	*Rubus saxatilis*
Circaea intermedia	*Sagina nodosa*
C. lutetiana	*S. saginoides*
Cirsium heterophyllum	*S. subulata*
C. vulgare	*Salix phylicifolia*
Coeloglossum viride	*Sanicula europaea*
Crataegus monogyna	*Saussurea alpina*
Crepis paludosa	*Saxifraga hypnoides*
Dactylis glomerata	*S. nivalis*
Dactylorchis incarnata	*Sedum rosea*
D. purpurella	*Selaginella selaginoides*
Draba incana	*Sibbaldia procumbens*
D. norvegica	*Silene maritima*†
Eleocharis quinqueflora	*Sorbus rupicola*
Epilobium montanum	*Thalictrum alpinum*
Equisetum hyemale	*T. minus*
E. telmateia	*Tofieldia pusilla*
E. variegatum	*Trifolium pratense*
Eriophorum latifolium	*Trollius europaeus*
Eupatorium cannabinum	*Tussilago farfara*
Euphrasia scottica	*Ulmus glabra*
Festuca gigantea	*Valeriana officinalis*
Filipendula ulmaria	*Veronica chamaedrys*
Fragaria vesca	*V. officinalis*
Fraxinus excelsior	*Viburnum opulus*
Galium boreale	*Vicia orobus*
G. odoratum	*V. sepium*
G. verum	*V. sylvatica*

* In 'natural' habitats. † In inland habitats.

TABLE 5.9. *Indifferents*

Agrostis tenuis (?A)	*Hypericum androsaemum*
Alchemilla alpina	*H. pulchrum*
Antennaria dioica	*Juncus squarrosus* (A)
*Armeria maritima**	*Juniperus communis* ssp. *nana*
Arctostaphylos uva-ursi	*Lonicera periclymenum*
Betula pubescens (A)	*Luzula spicata*
Calluna vulgaris (A)	*L. sylvatica* (A)
Cardaminopsis petraea	*Menyanthes trifoliata*
Carex bigelowii (A)	*Molinia caerulea*
C. echinata	*Myrica gale*
C. lasiocarpa	*Nardus stricta* (A)
C. limosa	*Narthecium ossifragum*
C. nigra	*Osmunda regalis*
C. rostrata	*Pinguicula vulgaris*
Cherleria sedoides	*Plantago maritima**
Deschampsia alpina	*Polygala serpyllifolia*
D. cespitosa (B)	*Polypodium vulgare*
Drosera anglica	*Potamogeton polygonifolius*
D. rotundifolia	*Potentilla erecta* (A)
Dryopteris filix-mas (A)	*Quercus petraea*
Eleocharis multicaulis (A)	*Salix herbacea*
E. palustris	*Saxifraga stellaris*
Empetrum nigrum (A)	*Silene acaulis*
Endymion non-scriptus	*Solidago virgaurea*
Erica cinerea (A)	*Sorbus aucuparia*
E. tetralix (A)	*Teucrium scorodonia*
Eriophorum angustifolium (A)	*Trichophorum cespitosum* (A)
Euphrasia frigida	*Utricularia vulgaris* agg.
Festuca ovina	*U. minor*
F. vivipara	*Vaccinium myrtillus* (A)
Galium saxatile (A)	

* In inland habitats.

TABLE 5.10. *Species that avoid the poorest soils*

Achillea millefolium	*Lythrum salicaria*
A. ptarmica	*Mentha aquatica*
Agrostis canina	*Montia fontana*
A. stolonifera	*Myosotis caespitosa*
Ajuga reptans	*M. discolor*
Alnus glutinosa	*M. secunda*
Alopecurus geniculatus	*M. scorpioides*
A. pratensis	*Odontites verna*
Anagallis tenella	*Orobanche alba*
Anemone nemorosa	*Oxalis acetosella*
Anthoxanthum odoratum	*Phleum bertolonii*
Anthriscus sylvestris	*P. pratensis*
Athyrium filix-femina	*Phragmites communis*
Caltha palustris	*Pinguicula lusitanica*
Cardamine pratensis	*Plantago lanceolata*
Carex demissa	*P. major*
C. ovalis	*Platanthera bifolia*
C. pallescens	*P. chlorantha*
C. panicea	*Poa nemoralis* (inc. *P. balfourii*)
C. remota	*P. pratensis*
C. sylvatica	*P. subcaerulea*
Centaurea nigra	*P. trivialis*
Cerastium holosteoides	*Populus tremula*
Chrysanthemum leucanthemum	*Potentilla palustris*
Cirsium palustre	*Pteridium aquilinum*
Cochlearia officinalis agg.	*Pyrola media*
Conopodium majus	*Ranunculus bulbosus*
Corylus avellana	*R. repens*
Cynosurus cristatus	*Rhinanthus minor* agg.
Dactylorchis fuchsii	*Rubus idaeus*
Drosera intermedia	*Rumex acetosa*
Dryopteris carthusiana	*R. longifolius*
Epilobium alsinifolium	*Sagina procumbens*
E. anagallidifolium	*Salix aurita*
E. obscurum	*S. caprea*
E. palustre	*S. cinerea*
Equisetum palustre	*S. pentandra*
E. sylvaticum	*S. purpurea*
Euphrasia brevipila	*S. repens*
E. nemorosa	*S. viminalis*
Festuca pratensis	*Schoenus nigricans*
F. rubra	*Scrophularia nodosa*
Galium palustre	*Senecio aquatica*
Gymnadenia conopsea	*S. jacobea*
Hedera helix	*Sieglingia decumbens*
Holcus lanatus	*Silene dioica*
Hydrocotyle vulgaris	*Stachys palustris*
Hypericum tetrapterum	*S. sylvatica*
Iris pseudacorus	*Stellaria alsine*
Juncus acutiflorus	*S. holostea*
J. effusus	*Succisa pratensis*
J. kochii	*Taraxacum officinale* agg.
Lathyrus montanus	*Thymus drucei*
L. pratensis	*Trifolium medium*
Leontodon autumnalis	*T. repens*
Leucorchis albida	*Ulex europaeus*
Lotus corniculatus	*Veronica serpyllifolia*
L. pedunculatus	*V. serpyllifolia* ssp. *humifusa*
Luzula campestris	*V. scutellata*
L. multiflora	*Vicia cracca*
L. pilosa	*Viola palustris*
Lychnis flos-cuculi	*V. riviniana*
Lysimachia nemorum	

6

THE PHYTOGEOGRAPHY

1. THE FLORA

The first botanical records from the Isle of Skye were made by the Reverend J. Lightfoot when he visited the island in 1772. Since then, many botanists have visited Skye, and the flora is now relatively well known. Nevertheless, after 200 years of botanical exploration, new species continue to be added to the island's floral list. Perhaps the most notable recent discovery on Skye was that of *Koenigia islandica*, which was first recorded for the British Isles from The Storr in 1950 (see Raven, 1952).

Despite continuing botanical interest in Skye, little has been published about its rich and diverse flora. A detailed vascular plant flora is now being prepared by Mrs C. W. Murray and the author, and work on a bryophyte flora is also in progress. At present the lichen flora, especially the microlichens, is not well known, and the algal and fungal floras have apparently not been studied at all. At the end of 1970 the known Skye flora consisted of 547 native species of flowering plants (excluding members of the genera *Hieracium* and *Taraxacum*, and of the subgenus *Rubus* within the genus *Rubus*), with 43 introduced species, 42 species of pteridophytes, 370 mosses, 181 hepatics, and 154 lichens.

The present flora of Skye includes several interesting and rare species of both phanerogams and cryptogams many of which have diverse distributional patterns today. A classification has been attempted of the present vascular plant flora of Skye into phytogeographical or floristic elements to illustrate its geographical affinities and to compare them with those of the past flora. The term *floristic element* is used, as proposed by Cain (1947), to refer to groups of species that have similar geographical distributions at the present day within the area under consideration. It is not used in the wider sense of Dansereau (1957) to refer to a group of species which have not only a common distributional area but also a common origin and migratory, and even evolutionary, history. The only modern phytogeographical account of the British phanerogam flora is that by Matthews (1937, 1955), but in that account only about 45% of the present British flora is considered in detail, in particular the montane and northern taxa. The only phytogeographical analysis of the British bryophyte flora is that by Ratcliffe (1968), but his account is restricted to Atlantic species.

A phytogeographical classification of as many members of the present Skye flora as possible was considered desirable. Only the vascular plant and bryophyte floras of Skye are sufficiently well known to permit such a classification. Tables 6.1–6.12 present the phytogeographical classification of the vascular plant flora. The sparsity of reliable distributional data for the British bryophyte flora prevents a similar detailed classification of the Skye bryophytes, but bryophytes and lichens that appear to have distributional patterns analogous to those of vascular plants are referred to in the text.

In any phytogeographical survey, although it is possible to arrange some species into distinctive groups or elements according to their present distribution, no two species have exactly the same geographical scatter or continuity of distribution within their total range. There is frequently such a wide variation of geographical distribution within a group, that links between any two related groups can often be found, and it may thus be difficult to classify some taxa. The problem is basically one of the description and delimitation of a multidimensional continuum, to which there is often no single solution. Geographical groupings into floristic elements must therefore be thought of as convenient approximations or reference points that describe easily detectable clusters within the distributional continuum, and should not be regarded as representing real discontinuities.

If data on plant distributions are quantified, as by presence and absence records within specific geographical units, they can be subjected to classification techniques such as association analysis or cluster analysis, thereby producing an objectively derived grouping of species with the greatest similarities in geographical distribution (floristic elements). Proctor

(1964, 1967) has analysed the distribution of liverworts in Britain in this way, using the Watsonian vice-counties as the basic geographical unit. Holloway & Jardine (1968) and Holloway (1969) have analysed faunal distributions within the large Indo–Australian area in an analogous way to derive areas of similar faunas (faunal centres), and groups of organisms with similar geographical distributions (faunal elements).

Such a rigorous approach has not been attempted here, for two main reasons. Firstly the basis for the phytogeographical classification is the total European distribution of each species, and this is, at present, so imperfectly known for many taxa that a numerical analysis would have a spurious objectivity. Secondly, the main purpose is not geographical classification *per se*, but to provide a convenient arrangement of species which can be applied to a consideration of the past flora. Moreover, taxonomic confusion and changes hinder still further any approach to finality in any geographical classification.

The present vascular plant flora of Skye has been divided subjectively into a number of floristic elements defined by their total present geographical distribution within Europe, rather than within the British Isles alone. Although many species have distribution patterns in Britain that match, on a small scale, their distribution in mainland Europe, there are several species that have distributions that do not parallel their broader European pattern, for example *Saxifraga hypnoides* (see Jäger, 1968), and *Geocalyx graveolens* (see Birks *et al.*, 1969*b*).

The floristic elements adopted here are similar in part to those used by Matthews (1937, 1955) to characterise the British flora, and in part to those used by Hultén (1950) to characterise the Scandinavian flora. Data on the distribution of the species concerned have been drawn from a variety of sources, the major ones for the vascular plants being Faegri (1960), Hultén (1950, 1958, 1964), Lye (1967*b*), Matthews (1937, 1955), Meusel, Jäger & Weinart (1965), Oberdorfer (1970), Rodriquez (1966), and Roisin (1969). Distributional data for bryophytes have been obtained from the accounts by Arnell (1956), Herzog (1926), Lye (1967*b*), Nyholm (1954–69), Podpera (1954), Ratcliffe (1968), and Störmer (1969).

Several phytogeographers have proposed boundaries to define specific floristic provinces within Europe, and in the case of the Atlantic province there is a fair measure of agreement between the boundaries suggested by Braun-Blanquet (1923), Troll (1925), Faegri (1960), and Roisin (1969). Suggestions about the delimitation of a Sub-Atlantic province, and the subdivision of both the Atlantic and Sub-Atlantic provinces show much greater divergence of opinion. In general the geographical divisions of Europe proposed by Troll (1925), and adopted by Faegri (1960) and Ratcliffe (1968) have been followed. Species of restricted or markedly disjunct distributions are particularly difficult to classify, but they have been assigned, as far as possible, to the most appropriate floristic element, to avoid a large residual heterogenous group of unclassified species. Geographical criteria alone have been used as far as possible, but in a few instances ecological criteria have proved useful. While the classification presented here cannot be regarded as final, it is hoped that the arrangement adopted will not be unduly sensitive to the inevitable changes in knowledge of species distributions within Europe.

The following floristic elements have been distinguished within the present Skye flora.

1. ATLANTIC ELEMENT (= Oceanic Elements, Matthews, 1937; = Eu-Atlantic Elements, Troll, 1925 and Roisin, 1969)

This floristic element (Table 6.1)* consists of species with a western distribution in Europe that are confined to the strictly Atlantic coastal region extending from western Norway to Portugal and south-west Spain (see Fig. 1 in Ratcliffe, 1968). There may be a few scattered occurrences to the east and/or south of this region. This floristic province corresponds to Troll's (1925), Faegri's (1960), and Roisin's (1969) Eu-Atlantic floristic region, and to Braun-Blanquet's (1923) *Domaine Atlantique*. This large element of fifty-three species can be conveniently subdivided into smaller groups on the basis of latitudinal distribution within the Atlantic zone.

a. *Southern Atlantic* (Ratcliffe, 1968). This group contains species found mainly in southern and western parts of the British Isles, western France, the Iberian Peninsula, and often extending to Macaronesia and the Tropics. Very few of the species in this group are known in Scandinavia. There are only eleven phanerogams on Skye with this distributional pattern (Table 6.1), including *Carex extensa*, *C. laevigata*, *Euphrasia occidentalis*, *Hypericum androsaemum*, *Pinguicula lusitanica*, *Polygonum raii*, *Sagina*

* Tables 6.1 to 6.1 are on pp. 215–18.

maritima, and *Scrophularia aquatica*. The group is mainly composed of cryptogams, which include the pteridophytes *Dryopteris aemula* and *Hymenophyllum tunbridgense*, the moss *Sematophyllum novae-caesareae*, and the liverworts *Acrobolbus wilsonii*, *Adelanthus decipiens*, *Lejeunea mandonii*, *Jubula hutchinsiae*, *Marchesinia mackaii*, and *Radula carringtonii*. All these hepatics belong to the rather broad 'Macaronesian–Tropical' element in the British liverwort flora distinguished by Greig-Smith (1950). The lichen *Sticta canariensis*, which appears to have a comparable distribution, may also be included in this group. As discussed in Chapter 5 this group is largely restricted on Skye to the Sleat Peninsula in the south.

b. *Northern Atlantic* (Ratcliffe, 1968). This group consists of six species (Table 6.1) found mainly in northern Britain and extending northwards to the Faeröes and/or western Norway. All the species in this group are found in Scandinavia, and they are generally not known in mainland Europe south of the Baltic. This group (Table 6.1) includes the circumpolar coastal plant *Honkenya peploides*, and other coastal plants such as *Atriplex glabriuscula*, *Blysmus rufus*, and *Elymus arenarius*. There are also several large leafy liverworts on Skye with a Northern Atlantic distribution within Europe, such as *Bazzania pearsonii*, *Herberta adunca*, *H. straminea*, *Mastigophora woodsii*, *Plagiochila carringtonii*, *Pleurozia purpurea*, *Scapania nimbosa*, and *S. ornithopodioides*. Several of these have scattered occurrences in northern or tropical montane regions such as Alaska, Himalaya, Hawaii, and Yunnan, and they correspond to the Disjunct–Temperate, Boreal–Tropical, and American elements of Greig-Smith (1950). Other interesting components of this group include *Bryum riparium*, *Cephaloziella pearsonii*, *Gymnomitrion crenulatum*, *Rhabdoweisia crenulata*, and *Sphagnum strictum*.

c. *Widespread Atlantic* (Ratcliffe, 1968). This group consists of thirty-five species that are widely distributed throughout the Atlantic zone of Europe, extending from western Norway and the Faeröes to the Iberian Peninsula and Macaronesia. Several species (Table 6.1) occurring on Skye have such a distributional pattern in Europe, and they occur in a range of habitats on the island. For example, woodland species in this group include *Endymion nonscriptus* and *Hymenophyllum wilsonii*, with the bryophytes *Dicranum scottianum*, *Lepidozia pinnata*, *Mylia cuneifolia*, *Plagiochila punctata*, *Saccogyna viticulosa*, and *Ulota vittata*. Several bryophyte species within this geographical group favour shaded, humid habitats, for example in ravines and by waterfalls, and these include *Aphanolejeunea microscopica*, *Colura calyptrifolia*, *Drepanolejeunea hamatifolia*, *Fissidens curnowii*, *Harpalejeunea ovata*, *Lophocolea fragrans*, *Metzgeria hamata*, *Plagiochila tridenticulata*, and *Radula aquilegia*. Many of the hepatics belong to Greig-Smith's (1950) 'Macaronesian–Tropical' element. The lichen *Sticta dufourii* appears to belong to this group (see distribution map in Jørgensen, 1969).

Species of this group occurring in dwarf-shrub heaths include *Carex binervis*, *Erica cinerea*, *Thymus drucei*, and *Ulex europeus*. *Deschampsia setacea*, *Erica tetralix*, *Juncus kockii*, *Myrica gale*, *Narthecium ossifragum*, and *Pedicularis sylvatica* ssp. *hibernica* (Skogen, 1966; Webb, 1956) are members of this floristic group that occur in damp, mire habitats. *Eleogiton fluitans* is an aquatic component, whereas *Agropyron junceiforme*, *Ammophila arenaria*, *Armeria maritima*, *Asplenium marinum*, *Cakile maritima*, *Cerastium atrovirens*, *Salsola kali*, and *Tripleurospermum maritimum* are some of the coastal species in this group. *Sedum anglicum* and *Vicia orobus* are rupestral species, as are the bryophytes *Frullania germana*, *Glyphomitrium daviesii*, and *Hedwigia integrifolia*. *Normandina pulchella*, *Pseudocyphellaria crocata*, *P. thouarsii*, *Ramalina curnowii*, and *Sticta limbata* are lichens with comparable European distributions.

d. *Mediterranean–Atlantic* (Ratcliffe, 1968). This group contains species centred on southern Britain and south-western Europe, but extending eastwards into coastal Mediterranean regions. It is poorly represented in the Skye flora, with only one phanerogam, *Catapodium marinum* (Table 6.1), and four bryophytes, *Campylopus polytrichoides*, *Porella thuja*, *Targionia hypophylla*, and *Trichostomum brachydontium* var. *littorale*.

2. SUB-ATLANTIC ELEMENT (Ratcliffe, 1968)

This large floristic element (Table 6.2) consists of 116 species that are widely distributed in the Atlantic province of Europe, but unlike the Atlantic Element, this group is well represented in parts of central Europe and frequently occurs in southern Fennoscandia. Some of the species in this element are found quite widely around the Mediterranean, and a few reach Asia Minor. Many of the species included in the Sub-Atlantic Element are classed as Atlantic species by continental phytogeographers, but many of the species are widespread in the British Isles and show little or no western bias. The element is tentatively divided into three groups on the basis of latitudinal distribution within Europe.

a. *Southern Sub-Atlantic.* This group of eight species (Table 6.2) contains species that occur within the Sub-Atlantic region of Europe, but which are absent from Fennoscandia, or occur in the extreme southern part only. The group is ecologically heterogeneous with species of mire habitats (*Anagallis tenella*, *Juncus acutiflorus*), meadows (*Euphrasia nemorosa*, *Juncus acutiflorus*), and coastal habitats (*Carex distans*, *C. otrubae*). The only bryophytes on Skye with comparable European distributions are *Campylostelium saxicola*, *Funaria attenuata*, *Leptodontium flexifolium*, and *Orthotrichum pulchellum*.

b. *Northern Sub-Atlantic.* This small group of six species (Table 6.2) has a distribution pattern centred on north-west Europe, and it is absent or extremely rare in more southerly areas such as the Iberian Peninsula, and the Mediterranean. It contains three aquatic plants (*Isoetes lacustris*, *Littorella uniflora*, *Sparganium angustifolium*), one mire plant (*Rhynchospora alba*), one montane plant (*Saxifraga hypnoides*), and one species of dwarf-shrub heaths and acidic grasslands (*Carex pilulifera*). Several Skye bryophytes appear to have comparable distribution patterns, including *Dicranodontium uncinatum*, *Grimmia maritima*, *Rhacomitrium ellipticum*, *Ulota phyllantha*, *Anastrepta orcadensis*, and *Douinia ovata* (see Table 4 in Ratcliffe, 1968).

c. *Widespread Sub-Atlantic.* This large group of 102 species (Table 6.2) occurs widely throughout western Europe. It is difficult in some cases to decide whether to assign a species that occurs rather rarely in southern Scandinavia to this group or to the Southern Sub-Atlantic group. Table 6.2 indicates those species classed in this group that have southern affinities, and which are rather rare and local in southern Scandinavia. Plants from a wide range of habitats occur in this group. *Blechnum spicant*, *Carex sylvatica*, *Corylus avellana*, *Ilex aquifolium*, *Quercus petraea*, and *Sanicula europea* are woodland species. *Alchemilla xanthochlora*, *Bellis perennis*, *Hypochaeris radicata*, *Luzula campestris*, *Polygala vulgaris*, and *Trifolium dubium* are typically grassland species. Plants of dwarf-shrub communities include *Euphrasia micrantha*, *Sarothamnus scoparius*, and *Sieglingia decumbens*. Mire plants are well represented, with, for example, *Carex hostiana*, *Drosera anglica*, *D. intermedia*, *D.* × *obovata*, *Potamogeton polygonifolius*, *Schoenus nigricans*, and *Trichophorum cespitosum*. There are several meadow species including *Centaurea nigra*, *Heracleum sphondylium*, *Hypericum tetrapterum*, *Lotus pedunculatus*, and *Senecio aquaticus*. Coastal species on Skye in this group include *Plantago coronopus*, *Spergularia media*, and *Thalictrum minus*. Aquatic species are well represented, with, for example, *Baldellia ranunculoides*, *Callitriche intermedia*, *Isoetes echinospora*, *Myriophyllum alterniflorum*, and *Potamogeton coloratus*. There is also a small group of rupestral ferns, including *Asplenium adiantum-nigrum*, *Phyllitis scolopendrium*, *Polystichum aculeatum*, and *Polypodium interjectum*.

There are many bryophytes on Skye with a widespread Sub-Atlantic distribution within Europe (see Ratcliffe, 1968). These include *Breutelia chrysocoma*, *Campylopus atrovirens*, *C. brevipilus*, *C. flexuosus*, *Fontinalis squarrosa*, *Funaria obtusa*, *Heterocladium heteropterum*, *Hookeria lucens*, *Hyocomium flagellare*, *Pterogonium gracile*, *Ptychomitrium polyphyllum*, *Lejeunea patens*, *Odontoschisma sphagni*, *Plagiochila spinulosa*, *Porella laevigata*, and *Scapania gracilis*. Lichens occurring on Skye with comparable 'Sub-Atlantic' distributions in Europe include *Lobaria amplissima*, *L. laetevirens*, *Nephroma laevigatum*, *Pannaria rubiginosa*, *Parmeliellia plumbea*, and *Sticta fuliginosa*.

3. CONTINENTAL ELEMENT (Matthews, 1937) This floristic element (Table 6.3) consists of 120 species with a rather eastern distribution in Europe, with their headquarters in central Europe, and often extending eastwards into Russia and Asia. This geographical area corresponds to the *Domaine Médio-Européen* of Braun-Blanquet (1923). A sharp distinction between the Continental and the Sub-Atlantic Elements is rather difficult to define, and some of the species in these elements may appear to other phytogeographers to be misplaced.

The Continental Element is divided into three groups (Table 6.3) on the basis of latitudinal distribution with mainland Europe.

a. *Southern Continental* (Matthews, 1937). This small group of eighteen species (Table 6.3) is found mainly in central and southern Europe, extending into the Mediterranean region, and even into north Africa and south-west Asia. The species in this group do not extend further north than southern Scandinavia. None of the species in this group play a prominent role in the vegetational cover on Skye, being rather rare or local species restricted either to dry, south-facing limestone slopes or basic rock outcrops

(*Arabidopsis thaliania*, *Arabis hirsuta*, *Carlina vulgaris*, *Galium verum*, *Ophioglossum vulgatum*, *Orobanche alba*, *Primula veris*, *Torilis japonica*), coastal habitats, (*Lycopus europaeus*, *Salicornia europaea*, *Samolus valerandi*, *Spergularia marina*, *Suaeda maritima*), or to man-made habitats (*Anagallis minima*, *Arctium minus*, *Capsella bursa-pastoris*, *Galium mollugo*, *Veronica polita*). Bryophytes occurring on Skye that appear to have a comparable European distribution include the rupestral species *Anomodon viticulosus*, *Grimmia orbicularis*, *Gymnostomum calcareum*, *Rhynchostegiella tenella*, *Scapania compacta*, *Tortula intermedia*, and *Trichostomum crispulum*, and the 'weedy' species *Archidium alternifolium*, *Barbula hornsuchiana*, *Ephemerum serratum* var. *serratum*, and *Riccia beyrichiana*.

b. *Northern Continental* (Matthews, 1937). This group contains seventy three members of the Skye flora (Table 6.3) with distributions centred mainly on northern and central Europe (*Domaine circumboréal – Domaine médio-européen*; Braun-Blanquet, 1923), and often extending north to the Arctic Circle. In southern Europe they are largely found in subalpine situations. This group is well represented on Skye in a range of habitats. The 'tall herbs' *Alchemilla glabra*, *Crepis paludosa*, *Filipendula ulmaria*, *Rumex acetosa*, and *Vicia sylvatica* belong to this group, as do the following woodland and scrub species: *Betula pendula*, *B. pubescens* ssp. *odorata*, *Melica nutans*, *Populus tremula*, *Prunus padus*, *Ribes spicatum*, *Salix caprea*, *S. nigricans*, *S. pentandra*, *Sorbus aucuparia*, *Thelypteris dryopteris*, and *T. phegopteris*. The woodland moss *Ptilium crista-castrensis* has a comparable 'boreal' European distribution. Species of mire habitats are well represented in this group and include *Carex curta*, *C. diandra*, *C. lasiocarpa*, *C. limosa*, *C. pauciflora*, *Drosera rotundifolia*, *Eleocharis quinqueflora*, *Eriophorum latifolium*, *Menyanthes trifoliata*, *Pedicularis palustris*, *Potentilla palustris*, *Urticularia intermedia*, *U. minor*, and *U. vulgaris*. *Sphagnum girgensohnii*, *S. robustum*, and *S. warnstorfianum* appear to belong to this floristic group. There are several species in this group that frequently occur in grasslands or dwarf-shrub heaths, and these include *Alchemilla vestita*, *Antennaria dioica*, *Coeloglossum viride*, *Galium boreale*, *Gentianella campestris*, *Listera cordata*, *Lycopodium clavatum*, *Pyrola media*, *Rubus saxatilis*, *Vaccinium myrtillus*, and *V. vitis-idaea*. Aquatic species are well represented, with *Callitriche hermaphroditica*, *Carex vesicaria*, *Potamogeton alpinus*, *P. gramineus*, *P. perfoliatus*, *P. praelongus*, and *Subularia aquatica*. *Glaux maritima* is the only coastal species in this group, although on Skye *Scutellaria galericulata* is restricted to coastal shingle habitats. Bryophytes of note in this group occurring on Skye include *Cynodontium strumiferum*, *Leiocolea heterocolpos*, *Lophozia obtusa*, and *Nardia geoscyphus*.

c. *Widespread Continental* (= Continental Element, Matthews, 1937). This group (Table 6.3) contains species that are widely distributed throughout central and eastern Europe, but that become rare in Scandinavia and in the Mediterranean area. It is represented by only twenty-nine species in the Skye flora. Several of the species in the group favour dry basic habitats, for example *Agrimonia eupatoria*, *Briza media*, *Mycelis muralis*, and *Trifolium campestre*. A large proportion of the species in this group occur most frequently on Skye in anthropogenic communities, for example *Artemisia vulgaris*, *Cynosurus cristatus*, *Erodium cicutarium*, *Inula helenium*, *Phleum bertolonii*, *Rumex longifolius*, and *Sherardia arvensis*. Bryophytes with comparable European distributions occurring on Skye include the rupestral species *Antitrichia curtipendula*, *Encalypta streptocarpa*, and *Orthotrichum rupestre*, the epiphytes *Cryphaea heteromalla*, *Orthotrichum diaphanum*, and *Tortula laevipila*, and the 'waste-ground' species *Fossombronia incurva*, *Lunularia cruciata*, and *Pottia truncata*.

4. NORTHERN–MONTANE ELEMENT (Matthews, 1937)

This element (Table 6.4) consists of fourteen species with distributions centred on northern Europe where they occur in the woodland or the sub-alpine zones. They also occur in central and southern Europe, but they are restricted there to sub-alpine or montane habitats. They are generally absent from the lowlands of central Europe. This element is closely related to the Arctic–Alpine and the Northern Continental Elements, but it differs largely in its altitudinal distribution. The species in this element occur in a range of habitats on Skye: *Cirsium heterophyllum*, *Cochlearia officinalis* ssp. *alpina*, *Salix phylicifolia*, and *Trollius europaeus* occur in 'tall herb' communities; *Alchemilla filicaulis*, *Arctostaphylos uva-ursi*, *Empetrum nigrum*, *Leucorchis albida*, and *Lycopodium selago* in grasslands and dwarf-shrub heaths; and *Carex dioica*, *Equisetum variegatum*, *Eriophorum angustifolium*, and *E. vaginatum* in mire habitats.

Several members of the Skye bryophyte flora have comparable distribution patterns in Europe, for example *Polytrichum alpinum* and *Barbilophozia lycopodioides* in grassland communities, and *Acrocladium trifarium* and *Cinclidium stygium* in mire habitats. The coprophilous moss *Tetraplodon angustatus* has a specialised microhabitat within dwarf-shrub heath communities. There are several cryptogams of montane cliff habitats within this floristic element, for example the fern *Asplenium viride*, and the bryophytes *Anoectangium aestivum*, *Bartramia ithyphylla*, *Dicranum blyttii*, *Grimmia ovalis*, *Hypnum callichroum*, *Orthothecium intricatum*, *Plagiopus oederi*, *Pohlia elongata*, and *Eremonotus myriocarpus*. Similarly *Acrocladium sarmentosum*, *Bryum weigelii*, *Anthelia julacea*, *Hygrobiella laxifolia*, *Nardia compressa*, *Scapania paludosa*, and *S. uliginosa* are characteristic of montane spring and stream-side habitats.

5. ARCTIC–SUBARCTIC ELEMENT (Matthews, 1937)

This element (Table 6.5) consists of fourteen species with European distributions restricted to the British Isles and northern Europe. Many of the species occur north of the Arctic Circle, and extend into arctic or subarctic regions of North America. The element is moderately well represented in the present Skye flora by species largely restricted to montane habitats. These include *Alchemilla wichurae*, *Cerastium arcticum*, *Deschampsia alpina*, *Draba norvegica*, *Euphrasia frigida*, *E. scottica*, *Festuca vivipara*, *Koenigia islandica*, *Poa subcaerulea*, *Rhinanthus borealis*, *Andreaea alpina*, and *Solenostoma oblongifolium*. *Bryum dixonii* has its only non-British station in Norway, and it is therefore placed in this floristic element. A few species occur in lowland habitats including the coastal species *Carex scandinavica*, *Ligusticum scoticum*, and *Mertensia maritima*, and the chasmophyte *Sorbus rupicola*. Several of the non-endemic members of the Skye *Hieracium* flora are only known outside Britain in Scandinavia, Iceland, or the Faeröes. These include *Hieracium anglicum*, *H. argenteum*, *H. caledonicum*, *H. euprepes*, *H. iricum*, *H. pictorum*, *H. reticulatum*, *H. rhomboides*, *H. rubiginosum*, *H. sparsifolium*, *H. stenopholodium* (Dahlst.) Omang, and *H. strictiforme*.

6. ARCTIC–ALPINE ELEMENT (Matthews, 1937)

This element (Table 6.6) consists of thirty-nine species with distributions centred on arctic and subarctic areas of northern Europe, but unlike the previous element, the species also occur at high altitudes in central Europe. It is well represented in the modern Skye flora, with *Alchemilla alpina*, *Carex bigelowii*, *Empetrum hermaphroditum*, *Epilobium alsinifolium*, *E. anagallidifolium*, *Gnaphalium supinum*, *Juniperus communis* ssp. *nana*, *Luzula spicata*, *Lycopodium alpinum*, *Oxyria digyna*, *Polygonum viviparum*, *Salix herbacea*, *Saxifraga aizoides*, *S. oppositifolia*, *S. stellaris*, *Sedum rosea*, *Silene acaulis*, and *Thalictrum alpinum*. More restricted species on Skye include *Arabis alpina*, *Cardaminopsis petraea*, *Cryptogramma crispa*, *Draba incana*, *Dryas octopetala*, *Dryopteris abbreviata*, *Juncus trifidus*, *J. triglumis*, *Loiseleuria procumbens*, *Poa alpina*, *P. glauca*, *Polystichum lonchitis*, *Sagina saginoides*, *Salix myrsinites*, *Saussurea alpina*, *Saxifraga nivalis*, *Sibbaldia procumbens*, *Tofieldia pusilla*, and *Veronica serpyllifolia* ssp. *humifusa*.

There are several bryophytes in this floristic element, including *Anthelia juratzkana*, *Aulacomnium turgidum*, *Barbula icmadophila*, *Conostomum tetragonum*, *Dicranoweisia crispula*, *Dicranum starkei*, *Ditrichum zonatum*, *Grimmia torquata*, *Gymnomitrion corallioides*, *Hylocomium pyrenaicum*, *Oncophorus virens*, *Orthothecium rufescens*, and *Scapania gymnostomophila*. As discussed in Chapter 5, several of these Arctic–Alpine species, both phanerogam and cryptogam, descend to near sea-level on Skye (see Table 5.4) and elsewhere in north-west Scotland.

7. ALPINE ELEMENT (Matthews, 1937)

This element consists of species that occur in Britain, but which are otherwise restricted to montane areas in central Europe and which are absent from northern Europe and arctic regions. The element is poorly represented in the British flora as a whole, and the only representative on Skye (Table 6.7) appears to be the montane plant *Cherleria sedoides*.

8. WIDESPREAD SPECIES

This is the largest floristic group within the present Skye flora, and contains 229 species (Table 6.8). The species in this group have widespread and nearly continuous distributions in Europe, and they belong to the General European, European, and Northern Hemisphere Elements distinguished by Matthews (1937). Many of the species in this group have present ranges that encompass several floristic provinces (*sensu* Good, 1964), and are more or less cosmopolitan in their world distribution. Although the group is of limited phytogeographical interest, many of the species within it are ecologically important and form a prominent component of the present vegetation of Skye. Such species include *Agrostis canina*, *A. tenuis*, *Calluna vulgaris*, *Carex rostrata*, *Festuca ovina*, *Nardus stricta*, *Phragmites communis*, and *Pteridium aquilinum*.

Many of the species included in this group are extremely common and widespread on Skye, and frequently show a broad ecological amplitude. There are, however, some species within this group that are very rare or local on Skye, for example *Eleocharis uniglumis*, *Epipactis atrorubens*, *E. helleborine*, *Hippuris vulgaris*, *Lythrum salicaria*, *Paris quadrifolia*, and *Viburnum opulus*.

9. NORTH AMERICAN ELEMENT

(Matthews, 1955)

This element consists of native species with a wider distributional area in North America than in Europe. It is a small element within the total British flora, and its only representatives on Skye (Table 6.9) are *Eriocaulon septangulare* and the hepatic *Plectocolea paroica*. The introduced species *Juncus tenuis* would belong here, but it is classed with the other introduced plants.

10. ENDEMIC ELEMENT

This element (Table 6.10) comprises species not known to occur outside the British Isles. It is a small element in the British flora, and within the Skye flora it contains only *Cochlearia danica*. There are in addition nineteen species of *Hieracium* and five moss taxa that do not appear to have been recorded from outside the British Isles. It is not comparable to the other floristic elements distinguished, for the different endemics have different distribution patterns within the British Isles. Their affinities to a particular element can only be determined by comparing their British distributions with those of non-endemic species, and by considering their taxonomic relationships.

Amongst the British endemic *Hieracium* taxa which occur on Skye, nine species (*H. chloranthum*, *H. ebudicum* Pugsl., *H. lingulatum*, *H. nitidum*, *H. petrocharis*, *H. piligerum*, *H. shoolbredii*, *H. subhirtum* (F. J. Hanb.) Pugsl., *H. uistense* (Pugsl.) P. D. Sell & C. West) are restricted to the Hebrides and the Scottish mainland, and two others (*H. hebridense* Pugsl., *H. langwellense*) also occur in western Ireland. Of the other endemic species occurring on Skye, the most interesting is probably *H. cymbifolium*, with its distribution centred on the Carboniferous limestones of Derbyshire, Staffordshire, and the northern Pennines, which has a recently discovered outlier on the Durness limestone on Skye, and on the Jurassic limestones on Raasay.

Four of the British endemic moss taxa have strikingly Atlantic distributions within the British Isles. The distributions of *Campylopus shawii*, *Leptodontium recurvifolium*, and *Trichostomum hibernicum* resemble those of the Northern Atlantic group within Britain, whereas *Fissidens celticus* has affinities with the Southern Atlantic group (Ratcliffe, 1968). The remaining endemic taxon, *Grimmia apocarpa* var. *homodictyon*, occurs locally on dry basic-rock outcrops in the Scottish Highlands, with a southern outlier by Maize Beck, Teesdale, and thus it has affinities with either the Arctic–Alpine or the Arctic–Subarctic elements.

11. INTRODUCED SPECIES

This group of forty-three species (Table 6.11) within the Skye flora is extremely heterogeneous, and it contains species that are considered by Clapham *et al.* (1962) to be introduced into the British Isles, or that are considered by the author to be likely introductions to the Isle of Skye although they are native in other areas of Britain (for example *Alisma lanceolatum*, *Fagus sylvatica*, *Hippophaë rhamnoides*, *Sorbus aria*). Several floristic elements are represented within the group, with, for example, species of North American range (*Juncus tenuis*, *Mimulus guttatus*, *Montia sibirica*, *Symphoricarpos rivularis*), of Southern Continental Europe range (*Aesculus hippocastanum*, *Castanea sativa*), of Southern Hemisphere origin (*Crocosmia* × *crocosmiflora*, *Epilobium nerterioides*, *Fuchsia magellanica*, *Mimulus luteus*), and of Mediterranean range (*Barbarea intermedia*). Many of the species in this group occur either as planted trees in townships or around crofts, or as 'weeds' in fields and meadows.

12. UNCLASSIFIED SPECIES

Two species in the Skye flora, *Dactylorchis purpurella* and *Poa balfourii*, (Table 6.12) are unclassified because of a lack of reliable distributional data within Europe.

The percentage representation of each floristic element within the total native vascular plant flora of Skye is shown in Table 6.13, which summarises the phytogeographical affinities of the present flora. One of the striking features of the present flora of Skye is that representatives of contrasting phytogeographical groups such as the Arctic–Alpine, Arctic–Subarctic, Southern Continental, Southern Atlantic, and Mediterranean Atlantic Elements occur together within a relatively small area, or even within the same locality. This phytogeographical diversity may reflect, in part, the wide range of habitats and rock types that occur within the island. The equable oceanic climate is probably also of considerable importance in influencing the great floristic diversity, for presumably the temperature extremes must lie within the physiological tolerances of both the Northern and Southern species. The summers are presumably never too warm for Northern–Montane, Arctic–Subarctic, and Arctic–Alpine species, and conversely the winters are never too cold for the Mediterranean Atlantic, Southern Atlantic, and Southern Continental species. Within the regional climatic picture, there will also be important microclimatic gradients, and it is perhaps a significant feature that many of the Southern Continental species represented in the Skye flora are restricted within the island to dry, lowlying south-facing slopes or rock outcrops (see Lundqvist, 1968), whereas many of the Arctic–Subarctic and Arctic–Alpine species are restricted to high altitude sites, or to shaded north-facing slopes at moderate elevations.

2. THE VEGETATION

The present plant communities of Skye have a striking diversity of geographical affinities. Several communities have a widespread distribution, similar to that of the widespread species which comprise a large fraction of the present flora (Table 6.8), and they occur, with little variation, throughout most of Europe. Such widespread communities include the *Lolium perenne–Plantago major*, *Isolepis setacea–Blasia pusilla*, *Schoenoplectus lacustris–Phragmites communis*, Agrosto–Festucetum grasslands, *Potamogeton natans–Nymphaea alba*, and *Fraxinus excelsior–Brachypodium sylvaticum* noda.

The geographical affinities of most of the plant communities are, however, either Northern or Arctic–Alpine on the one hand or Atlantic or Sub-Atlantic on the other.

Associations occurring on Skye with an apparently similar distribution in Europe to the Northern–Montane floristic element include the *Eriophorum latifolium–Carex hostiana*, *Carex rostrata–Aulacomnium palustre*, *Carex rostrata–Scorpidium scorpioides*, and *Carex panicea–Campylium stellatum* Associations of mire habitats. The 'tall herb' communities (*Betula pubescens–Cirsium heterophyllum* and *Sedum rosea–Alchemilla glabra* Associations) also appear to have Northern–Montane affinities. The Philonoto–Saxifragetum stellaris, *Cratoneuron commutatum–Saxifraga aizoides*, *Carex–Saxifraga aizoides*, and Saxifragetum aizoidis noda appear to have an Arctic–Alpine distribution in Europe. There are seven communities that appear to be Arctic–Subarctic in geographical range. These are the *Koenigia islandica–Carex demissa*, *Anthelia julacea* banks, *Nardus stricta–Vaccinium myrtillus*, Cariceto–Rhacomitretum lanuginosi, Rhacomitreto–Callunetum, *Festuca ovina–Luzula spicata*, and Rhacomitreto–Empetretum noda. The last four of these have some Atlantic affinities in their distribution.

Many of the Skye communities are markedly Atlantic in their European distribution. Communities with a widespread Atlantic distribution occurring in western Norway, western Britain, and the western fringe of the European mainland include the Puccinellietum maritimae, *Armeria maritima–Grimmia maritima*, *Asplenium marinum–Grimmia maritima*, *Trichophorum cespitosum–Carex panicea*, Callunetum vulgaris, *Calluna vulgaris–Sieglingia decumbens*, Nardo–Juncetum squarrosi, *Luzula sylvatica–Vaccinium myrtillus*, *Betula pubescens–Vaccinium myrtillus*, and *Corylus avellana–Oxalis acetosella* Associations. The communities dominated by bryophytes and lichens that occur on decaying logs, on trees, and on boulders in the woodlands on Skye probably also have widespread Atlantic distributions. In contrast there is a group of communities that appear to occur only in western Britain, western Norway, and/or the Faeröes and thus resemble the Northern Atlantic floristic group in their ranges. These communities include the *Atriplex glabriscula–Rumex crispus*, *Luzula sylvatica–Silene dioica*, *Molinia caerulea–Myrica gale*, Molinieto–Callunetum, and *Nardus stricta–Vaccinium myrtillus* Associations. The only communities on Skye that appear to have Southern Atlantic affinities are the coastal *Juncus gerardii–Carex extensa* Association, and the *Oenanthe crocata* stands of streamsides.

There is a small group of associations that appears, on present information, to be restricted to the British Isles, and all these communities have a markedly Atlantic distribution within Britain. They are the Trichophoreto–Eriophoretum, Centaureo–Cynosuretum, *Juniperus nana*, and Vaccineto–Callunetum hepaticosum Associations. It is possible that these communities may occur in the Faeröes or in western Norway, but they do not appear to have been recorded. It is interesting to note that the British endemic mosses *Campylopus shawii*, *Leptodontium recurvifolium*, and *Trichostomum hibernicum* have a similar Atlantic distribution within the British Isles.

Despite the geographical diversity of the vegetation of Skye, there are many similarities to the vegetation of other western areas, with a comparable altitudinal zonation and physiognomy of vegetation, in the Scottish Highlands (McVean & Ratcliffe, 1962) and, to some extent, in Norway. The principal differences between the vegetation of the Scottish Highlands and Norway have been discussed in detail by McVean & Ratcliffe (1962), and by Poore & McVean (1957). Briefly they can be attributed to the following features of the Scottish environment.

1. The greater oceanicity of the Scottish climate, including exposure to Atlantic gales, is reflected in several ways by Scottish vegetation. The lower altitudinal limit of tree growth in western Scotland may result from the prevalence of high winds along the west coast, for tree growth is evidently limited by wind rather than by low temperatures. There is a greater prominence of bryophytes, pteridophytes, and Atlantic phanerogams in Scottish vegetation, and indeed several Scottish communities are dominated by bryophytes or ferns. In contrast the characteristic Scandinavian lichen-heath of the alpine zone is extremely rare in the Scottish Highlands, and it is centred on the most continental areas. The high rainfall and atmospheric humidity of Scotland results in the predominance of peaty and leached soils, and in the widespread development of blanket-bog.

2. The higher summer and winter temperatures in Scotland are reflected by the variability of snow-lie in the Scottish mountains. The generally colder climate of Scandinavia may be a contributory factor in the greater prominence and diversity of montane plants there.

3. The more intensive land use and grazing pressures in Scotland have resulted in a paucity of natural woodland, sub-alpine scrub and 'tall herb' vegetation, and a corresponding abundance of anthropogenic grasslands and dwarf-shrub heaths.

3. COMPARISON WITH OTHER AREAS

Although the Skye flora is now comparatively well known, at least for the vascular plants and bryophytes, there are some species recently recorded from the nearby but smaller Inner Hebridean islands of Rhum and Raasay, which might be expected to occur on Skye but which have not been found growing there. The Rhum flora contains the Arctic–Subarctic species *Arenaria norvegica* ssp. *norvegica* and *Oedipodium griffithianum*, and the Southern Atlantic *Spergularia rupicola*, all of which could occur on Skye.

Ajuga pyramidalis is a Northern–Montane species surprisingly absent from Skye, which has several stations on Rhum, and so are the mosses *Drepanocladus vernicosus* and *Hypnum hamulosum*. Other striking absentees from Skye occurring on Rhum include *Asplenium septentrionale*, *Equisetum pratense*, *Oenanthe lachenalii*, *Potamogeton filiformis*, *P. pectinatus*, *Pyrola minor*, *Rhynchospora fusca*, *Thlaspi alpestre*, *Rhodobryum roseum*, and the three Rhum endemic *Euphrasia* species, *E. eurycarpa*, *E. heslop-harrisonii*, and *E. rhumica* (data from Eggeling, 1965). There are several species of note that have recently been recorded from the Island of Raasay to the east of Skye (Fig. 1) which are curiously absent from Skye. These include *Lycopodium annotinum* (also on Scalpay), *Neottia nidus-avis*, *Potamogeton filiformis*, *Pyrola minor*, and *Typha angustifolia* (Murray, 1970).

Outside Scotland, the Faeröes have the strongest affinities in flora and vegetation to Skye. This is not surprising considering the insular character of the Faeröes, similar geology and topography, and oceanic climate. There is no modern phytosociological description of the Faeröes, but the accounts by Böcher (1937, 1940), Hansen (1967), and Ostenfeld (1908) suggest the occurrence of many communities similar to those on Skye. The flora is naturally of a more northern character, with several species occurring on the Faeröes that are not known at present on Skye. These include *Cerastium cerastoides*, *Juncus balticus*, *Luzula arcuata*, *Sagina intermedia*, *Saxifraga rivularis*, *Sedum villosum*, *Hygrohypnum smithii*, *Polytrichum norvegicum*, *Pseudoleskea patens*, *Marsupella sparsifolia*, *Odontoschisma elongatum*, *Cladonia ecmocyna*, and *Solorina crocea*. Other Faeröes species not known in Scotland at present include *Angelica archangelica* L., *Carex lyngbei* Hornem., *Epilobium lactiflorum* Hausskn., *Papaver radicatum* Rottb., *Ranunculus glacialis*, and *Salix glauca* L. There are, however, some occurrences in the Faeröes, which are surprising in view of their present British distributions. These include *Saxifraga rosacea*, *Sphagnum balticum*, *Weissia tortilis*, and *Porella thuja* (data from Hansen, 1966, 1968; Jensen, 1901; Lange, 1963).

TABLE 6.1. *Atlantic Element*

a. Southern Atlantic	
Carex extensa	*Mecanopsis cambrica*
C. laevigata	*Pinguicula lusitanica*
Dryopteris aemula	*Polygonum raii*
Euphrasia occidentalis	*Sagina maritima*
Hymenophyllum tunbridgense	*Scrophularia aquatica*
Hypericum androsaemum	
b. Northern Atlantic	
Atriplex glabriuscula	*Euphrasia confusa*
Blysmus rufus	*E. curta*
Elymus arenarius	*Honkenya peploides*
c. Widespread Atlantic	
Agropyron junceiforme	*Cochlearia danica*
Ammophila arenaria	*C. officinalis* ssp. *officinalis*
Armeria maritima	*Corydalis claviculata*
Asplenium marinum	*Deschampsia setacea*
Cakile maritima	*Digitalis purpurea*
Carex arenaria	*Eleogiton fluitans*
C. binervis	*Endymion non-scriptus*
Cerastium atrovirens	*Erica cinerea*

TABLE 6.1 *continued*

E. tetralix	*Scirpus maritimus*
Hymenophyllum wilsonii	*S. tabernaemontani*
Juncus kochii	*Sedum anglicum*
Myrica gale	*Silene maritima*
Narthecium ossifragum	*Thymus drucei*
Pedicularis sylvatica ssp. *hibernica*	*Triglochin maritima*
Plantago maritima	*Tripleurospermum maritimum*
Puccinellia maritima	*Ulex europeus*
Salsola kali	*Vicia orobus*
	Zostera marina
d. Mediterranean Atlantic	
Catapodium marinum	

TABLE 6.2. *Sub-Atlantic Element*

a. Southern Sub-Atlantic	
Anagallis tenella	*Euphrasia nemorosa*
Carex distans	*Juncus acutiflorus*
C. otrubae	*Lepidium heterophyllum*
Equisetum telmateia	*Zerna ramosa*
b. Northern Sub-Atlantic	
Carex pilulifera	*Rhynchospora alba*
Isoetes lacustris	*Saxifraga hypnoides*
Littorella uniflora	*Sparganium angustifolium*
c. Widespread Sub-Atlantic (s = with southern affinities)	
Aira caryophyllea (s)	*Glyceria declinata* (s)
A. praecox	*Hedera helix* (s)
Ajuga reptans (s)	*Heracleum sphondylium*
Alchemilla xanthochlora	*Hydrocotyle vulgaris* (s)
Allium ursinum	*Hypericum humifusum*
Anthyllis vulneraria	*H. pulchrum*
Aphanes microcarpa	*H. tetrapterum*
Asplenium adiantum-nigrum	*Hypochaeris radicata*
Baldellia ranunculoides (s)	*Ilex aquifolium* (s)
Bellis perennis	*Isoetes echinospora*
Blechnum spicant	*Juncus bulbosus*
Bromus sterilis	*J. squarrosus*
Callitriche intermedia	*Lathyrus montanus*
Cardamine flexuosa	*Leontodon taraxacoides*
C. hirsuta	*Lonicera periclymenum*
Carex flacca	*Lotus pedunculatus*
C. hostiana	*Luzula campestris*
C. pulicaris	*L. sylvatica*
C. remota	*Lysimachia nemorum*
C. sylvatica	*Mercurialis perennis* (s)
Centaurea nigra	*Montia fontana*
Centaurium erythraea (s)	*Myosotis discolor*
Chrysosplenium oppositifolium	*Myriophyllum alterniflorum*
Circaea intermedia	*Nymphaea alba*
Cladium mariscus (s)	*Oenanthe crocata*
Conopodium majus	*Osmunda regalis* (s)
Corylus avellana	*Pedicularis sylvatica* spp. *sylvatica*
Crepis capillaris	*Phyllitis scolopendrium* (s)
Drosera anglica	*Plantago coronopus* (s)
D. intermedia	*Polygala serpyllifolia*
D. × *obovata*	*P. vulgaris*
Dryopteris borreri	*Polystichum aculeatum*
Eleocharis multicaulis	*Polypodium interjectum*
Epilobium obscurum	*Potamogeton coloratus*
Euphrasia micrantha	*P. polygonifolius*
Fraxinus excelsior	*Potentilla sterilis*
Galium saxatile	*Primula vulgaris* (s)
Geranium lucidum	

TABLE 6.2 *continued*

Quercus petraea	*Senecio aquaticus*
Ranunculus hederaceus	*S. sylvaticus*
Rosa canina	*Sieglingia decumbens*
R. pimpinellifolia	*Spergularia media*
Rumex conglomeratus	*Stachys arvensis*
R. obtusifolius	*Taraxacum laevigatum*
Sagina apetala (s)	*T. palustre*
S. subulata	*Teucrium scorodonia* (s)
Salix cinerea	*Thalictrum minus* (s)
Sambucus nigra	*Thelypteris limbosperma*
Sanicula europaea	*Trichophorum cespitosum*
Sarothamnus scoparius (s)	*Trifolium dubium* (s)
Schoenus nigricans	*Veronica agrestis*
Scutellaria minor	*Vulpia bromoides*

TABLE 6.3. *Continental Element*

a. Southern Continental	
Anagallis minima	*Ophioglossum vulgatum*
Arabidopsis thaliana	*Orobanche alba*
Arabis hirsuta	*Primula veris*
Arctium minus	*Salicornia europaea*
Capsella bursa-pastoris	*Samolus valerandi*
Carlina vulgaris	*Spergularia marina*
Galium mollugo	*Suaeda maritima*
G. verum	*Torilis japonica*
Lycopus europaeus	*Veronica polita*
b. Northern Continental	*Parnassia palustris*
Alchemilla glabra	*Pedicularis palustris*
A. vestita	*Pinguicula vulgaris*
Antennaria dioica	*Polygonum bistorta*
Betula pendula	*Populus tremula*
B. pubescens ssp. *odorata*	*Potamogeton alpinus*
Botrychium lunaria	*P. gramineus*
Calamagrostis epigejos	*P. perfoliatus*
Callitriche hermaphroditica	*P. praelongus*
Carex curta	*Potentilla palustris*
C. diandra	*P. reptans*
C. lasiocarpa	*Prunus padus*
C. limosa	*Pyrola media*
C. ovalis	*Ramischia secunda*
C. pauciflora	*Ribes spicatum*
C. serotina	*Rosa villosa*
C. vesicaria	*Rubus saxatilis*
Coeloglossum viride	*Rumex acetosa*
Crepis paludosa	*Sagina nodosa*
Drosera rotundifolia	*Salix aurita*
Eleocharis quinqueflora	*S. caprea*
Epilobium palustre	*S. nigricans*
Eriophorum latifolium	*S. pentandra*
Filipendula ulmaria	*Scutellaria galericulata*
Galeopsis bifida	*Solidago virgaurea*
Galium boreale	*Sorbus aucuparia*
G. uliginosum	*Sparganium minimum*
Gentianella campestris	*Subularia aquatica*
Glaux maritima	*Taraxacum spectabile*
Lamium moluccellifolium	*Thelypteris dryopteris*
Listera cordata	*T. phegopteris*
Luzula pilosa	*Utricularia intermedia*
Lycopodium clavatum	*U. minor*
Melampyrum pratense	*U. vulgaris*
Melica nutans	*Vaccinium myrtillus*
Menyanthes trifoliata	*V. vitis-idaea*
Myosotis caespitosa	*Vicia sylvatica*
M. secunda	*Viola palustris*

TABLE 6.3 *continued*

c. Widespread Continental (s = with southern affinities)

Adoxa moschatellina	*Erodium cicutarium* (s)
Agrimonia eupatoria	*Euphrasia brevipila*
Artemisia vulgaris	*Gymnadenia conopsea*
Berula erecta (s)	*Inula helenium*
Briza media	*Iris pseudacorus* (s)
Carex demissa	*Mycelis muralis*
C. lepidocarpa	*Phleum bertolonii*
C. paniculata	*Ranunculus trichophyllus*
Cephalanthera longifolia	*Rumex longifolius*
Circaea lutetiana (s)	*Sherardia arvensis*
Cynosuras cristatus	*Trifolium campestre* (s)
Dactylorchis incarnata	*Trisetum flavescens*
Epilobium parviflorum (s)	*Typha latifolia*
Equisetum hyemale	*Veronica montana*
E. sylvaticum	

TABLE 6.4. *Northern–Montane Element*

Alchemilla filicaulis	*Equisetum variegatum*
Arctostaphylos uva-ursi	*Eriophorum angustifolium*
Asplenium viride	*E. vaginatum*
Carex dioica	*Leucorchis albida*
Cirsium heterophyllum	*Lycopodium selago*
Cochlearia officinalis ssp. *alpina*	*Salix phylicifolia*
Empetrum nigrum	*Trollius europaeus*

TABLE 6.5. *Arctic–Subarctic Element*

Alchemilla wichurae	*Festuca vivipara*
Carex scandinavica	*Koenigia islandica*
Cerastium arcticum	*Ligusticum scoticum*
Deschampsia alpina	*Mertensia maritima*
Draba norvegica	*Poa subcaerulea*
Euphrasia frigida	*Rhinanthus borealis*
E. scottica	*Sorbus rupicola*

TABLE 6.6. *Arctic–Alpine Element*

Alchemilla alpina	*P. glauca*
Arabis alpina	*Polygonum viviparum*
Cardaminopsis petraea	*Polystichum lonchitis*
Carex bigelowii	*Sagina saginoides*
Cryptogramma crispa	*Salix herbacea*
Draba incana	*S. myrsinites*
Dryas octopetala	*Saussurea alpina*
Dryopteris abbreviata	*Saxifraga aizoides*
Empetrum hermaphroditum	*S. nivalis*
Epilobium alsinifolium	*S. oppositifolia*
E. anagallidifolium	*S. stellaris*
Gnaphalium supinum	*Sedum rosea*
Juncus biglumis	*Selaginella selaginoides*
J. trifidus	*Sibbaldia procumbens*
J. triglumis	*Silene acaulis*
Juniperus communis ssp. *nana*	*Thalictrum alpinum*
Loiseleuria procumbens	*Tofieldia pusilla*
Luzula spicata	*Veronica serpyllifolia* ssp. *humifusa*
Lycopodium alpinum	
Oxyria digyna	
Poa alpina	

TABLE 6.7. *Alpine Element*

Cherleria sedoides

TABLE 6.8. *Widespread Species*

Achillea millefolium	*Eleocharis palustris*
A. ptarmica	*E. uniglumis*
Agropyron caninum	*Epilobium montanum*
A. repens	*Epipactis atrorubens*
Agrostis canina	*E. helleborine*
A. stolonifera	*Equisetum arvense*
A. tenuis	*E. fluviatile*
Alnus glutinosa	*E. palustre*
Alopecurus geniculatus	*Erophila verna*
A. pratensis	*Eupatorium cannabinum*
Anagallis arvensis	*Euphorbia helioscopia*
Anchusa arvensis	*E. peplus*
Anemone nemorosa	*Festuca arundinacea*
Angelica sylvestris	*F. gigantea*
Anthoxanthum odoratum	*F. ovina*
Anthriscus sylvestris	*F. pratensis*
Arenaria serpyllifolia	*F. rubra*
Arrhenatherum elatius	*Fragaria vesca*
Asplenium ruta-muraria	*Fumaria officinalis*
A. trichomanes	*Galeopsis tetrahit*
Aster tripolium	*Galium aparine*
Athyrium filix-femina	*G. odoratum*
Atriplex hastata	*G. palustre*
A. patula	*Geranium dissectum*
Barbarea vulgaris	*G. molle*
Betonica officinalis	*G. robertianum*
Brachypodium sylvaticum	*Geum rivale*
Bromus mollis	*G. urbanum*
Callitriche stagnalis	*Glechoma hederacea*
Calluna vulgaris	*Glyceria fluitans*
Caltha palustris	*Gnaphalium sylvaticum*
Calystegia sepium	*G. uliginosum*
Campanula rotundifolia	*Helictotrichon pratense*
Cardamine pratensis	*H. pubescens*
Carex caryophyllea	*Hieracium pilosella*
C. echinata	*Hippuris vulgaris*
C. nigra	*Holcus lanatus*
C. pallescens	*H. mollis*
C. panicea	*Isolepis setacea*
C. rostrata	*Juncus articulatus*
Catabrosa aquatica	*J. bufonius*
Cerastium glomeratum	*J. conglomeratus*
C. holosteoides	*J. effusus*
Chamaenerion angustifolium	*J. gerardii*
Chenopodium album	*Koeleria cristata*
Chrysanthemum leucanthemum	*Lamium album*
C. vulgare	*L. purpureum*
Cirsium arvense	*Lapsana communis*
C. palustre	*Lathyrus pratensis*
C. vulgare	*Lemna minor*
Convolvulus arvensis	*Leontodon autumnalis*
Crataegus monogyna	*L. hispidus*
Cystopteris fragilis	*Linum catharticum*
Dactylis glomerata	*Listera ovata*
Dactylorchis fuchsii	*Lolium perenne*
D. maculata ssp. *ericetorum*	*Lotus corniculatus*
Daucus carota	*Luzula multiflora*
Deschampsia cespitosa	*Lychnis flos-cuculi*
D. flexuosa	*Lythrum salicaria*
Dryopteris carthusiana	*Medicago lupulina*
D. dilatata	*Mentha aquatica*
D. filix-mas	*M. arvensis*

TABLE 6.8 *continued*

Molinia caerulea	*S. purpurea*
Myosotis arvensis	*S. repens*
M. scorpioides	*S. triandra*
Myriophyllum spicatum	*S. viminalis*
Nardus stricta	*Schoenoplectus lacustris*
Nuphar lutea	*Scrophularia nodosa*
Odontites verna	*Sedum acre*
Orchis mascula	*Senecio jacobea*
Oxalis acetosella	*S. vulgaris*
Paris quadrifolia	*Silene dioica*
Petasites hybridus	*S. vulgaris*
Phalaris arundinacea	*Sinapis arvensis*
Phleum pratensis	*Solanum dulcamara*
Phragmites communis	*Sonchus arvensis*
Plantago lanceolata	*S. asper*
P. major	*Sparganium emersum*
Platanthera bifolia	*S. erectum*
P. chlorantha	*Spergula arvensis*
Poa annua	*Stachys palustris*
P. nemoralis	*S. sylvatica*
P. pratensis	*Stellaria alsine*
P. trivialis	*S. graminea*
Polygonum amphibium	*S. holostea*
P. aviculare	*S. media*
P. convolvulus	*Succisa pratensis*
P. hydropiper	*Symphytum officinale*
P. persicaria	*Taraxacum officinale*
Polypodium vulgare	*Thlaspi arvensis*
Potamogeton lucens	*Trifolium medium*
P. natans	*T. pratense*
Potentilla anserina	*T. repens*
P. erecta	*Triglochin palustris*
Prunella vulgaris	*Tussilago farfara*
Prunus spinosa	*Ulmus glabra*
Pteridium aquilinum	*Urtica dioica*
Quercus robur	*U. urens*
Ranunculus acris	*Valeriana officinalis*
R. bulbosus	*Valerianella locusta*
R. ficaria	*Veronica arvensis*
R. flammula	*V. beccabunga*
R. repens	*V. chamaedrys*
Rhinanthus minor agg.	*V. officinalis*
Ribes uva-crispa	*V. scutellata*
Rorippa microphylla	*V. serpyllifolia*
R. nasturtium-aquaticum	*Viburnum opulus*
Rubus fruticosus agg.	*Vicia cracca*
R. idaeus	*V. hirsuta*
Rumex acetosella	*V. sepium*
R. crispus	*Viola arvensis*
Ruppia maritima	*V. canina*
Sagina procumbens	*V. riviniana*
Salix alba	*V. tricolor*
S. fragilis	

TABLE 6.9. *North American Element*

Eriocaulon septangulare

TABLE 6.10. *Endemic Species*

Cochlearia scotica

TABLE 6.11. *Introduced Species*

Acer pseudoplatanus	*Galanthus nivalis*
Aegopodium podagraria	*Hippophaë rhamnoides*
Aesculus hippocastanum	*Humulus lupulus*
Alisma lanceolatum	*Juncus tenuis*
Astrantia major	*Laburnum anagyroides*
Barbarea intermedia	*Matricaria matricarioides*
Brassica napus	*Mimulus guttatus*
B. rapa	*M. luteus*
Bromus lepidus	*Montia sibirica*
Calystegia sepium ssp. *pulchra*	*Myrrhis odorata*
C. sepium ssp. *sylvatica*	*Papaver dubium*
Castanea sativa	*Peucedanum ostruthium*
Centranthus ruber	*Polygonum cuspidatum*
Chrysanthemum parthenium	*Rhododendron ponticum*
C. segetum	*Sinapsis alba*
Cicerbita macrophylla	*Sorbus aria*
Cotoneaster microphyllus	*Symphoricarpos rivularis*
Crocosmia × *crocosmiflora*	*Tilia* × *europea*
Cymbalaria muralis	*Veronica filiformis*
Epilobium nerterioides	*V. persica*
Fagus sylvatica	*Vinca minor*
Fuchsia magellanica	

TABLE 6.12. *Unclassified Species*

Dactylorchis purpurella *Poa balfourii*

TABLE 6.13. *Percentage representation of floristic elements in the native vascular plant flora of the Isle of Skye*

Floristic Element	Total number of species	Percentage of total native flora
1. Atlantic		
(*a*) Southern Atlantic	11	1.8
(*b*) Northern Atlantic	6	1.0
(*c*) Widespread Atlantic	35	5.9
(*d*) Mediterranean Atlantic	1	0.2
Total	53	8.9
2. Sub-Atlantic		
(*a*) Southern Sub-Atlantic	8	1.4
(*b*) Northern Sub-Atlantic	6	1.0
(*c*) Widespread Sub-Atlantic	102	17.3
Total	116	19.7
3. Continental		
(*a*) Southern Continental	18	3.1
(*b*) Northern Continental	73	12.4
(*c*) Widespread Continental	29	4.9
Total	120	20.4
4. Northern–Montane	14	2.4
5. Arctic–Subarctic	14	2.4
6. Arctic–Alpine	39	6.6
7. Alpine	1	0.2
8. Widespread species	229	38.7
9. North American	1	0.2
10. Endemic	1	0.2
11. Unclassified species	2	0.3

PART III

THE PALAEOECOLOGICAL INVESTIGATIONS

7

POLLEN ANALYTICAL AND STRATIGRAPHICAL METHODS

1. SAMPLING TECHNIQUES

The sediment depth and lithology at the five sites investigated were determined by a series of trial borings with a modified Hiller sampler (Thomas, 1964) with Lichtwardt (1952) extension rods. Samples for pollen analysis were obtained from cores collected during the period of 1966 to 1968, with a hand-operated stationary piston corer (Livingstone, 1955*a*; Rowley & Dahl, 1956; Vallentyne, 1955) in core tubes of 3.2 cm inner diameter and 1.23 m length, using Lichwardt extension rods. Samples for radiocarbon dating were subsequently obtained from larger diameter cores (5.3 cm) using a square-rod piston sampler (Wright, 1967*b*).

Field methods throughout followed those described by Wright, Livingstone & Cushing (1965). Core tubes were sealed and labelled in the field, and stored wet in a cold-room at 5 °C until required. The cores were extruded in the laboratory where the sediment lithology could be examined and described in detail, and samples taken for pollen analysis. At some sites, where the recovery of dry, compact sediments was incomplete with the usual 1 m drive, a 0.5 m drive was used to ensure complete core recovery. Nearly continuous sets of core segments were obtained from single boreholes at all the sites studied.

The vertical interval of sampling for pollen analysis was determined partly by lithological and stratigraphical considerations and partly by the suspected rates of accumulation of the various sediment types. The vertical interval between samples never exceeded 10 cm, and the vertical thickness of each sample was 1 cm or less.

2. SEDIMENT DESCRIPTION AND NOMENCLATURE

The system proposed by Troels-Smith (1955) was adopted with slight modifications as an objective and comprehensive method for the field description of fresh-water sediments. The degree of darkness (nig), stratification (strf), elasticity (elas), and dryness (sicc), and the relative proportions of the various component elements were noted and scored on a 5-point scale. Sediment colour, including any changes on exposure to air, and the nature of the contacts between each lithological unit were also recorded. An additional physical property, the degree of softness, was noted on a 4-part scale from very soft to very firm. As softness is related to the water content of the sediment, this scale is a subdivision of Troels-Smith's categories *siccitas* 1 and 2. The degree of humicity (humo) was estimated from the supernatant colour of the samples after brief boiling in 10% sodium hydroxide solution.

The following additional tests were made on the sediments. The degree of calcareousness (calc) was estimated from the sediment reaction to cold 10% hydrochloric acid. Loss on ignition was determined by combustion at 550 °C for 12 hours of samples previously dried at 105 °C. The ignition loss reasonably reflects the organic carbon content, except in argillaceous sediments, where it greatly overestimates the carbon content (Mackereth, 1966). To characterise the sediments further, the coarse fraction after alkali-maceration was examined microscopically, the residual components were identified, and the relative proportions were estimated visually and scored on a 5-point scale (abundant, frequent, occasional, rare, absent). The level of abundance assigned to a given component depended on its relative density compared not only with all other components in the sediment under examination but also with the same component in all other sediment samples studied. A simple water-mount of each untreated sample was also examined prior to chemical treatment. These relatively simple methods permit the recognition of minor lithological features that may be undetected in a visual examination of the sediments.

Nomenclature of sediment types largely follows the classification of Troels-Smith (1955) with certain exceptions. No attempt at naming organic, limnic sediments has been made, for as Grosse-Brauckmann (1961) has discussed, there is a considerable confusion about the use of terms 'dy', 'gyttja', and 'sapropel'. The non-commital term '*mud*' is favoured here to signify a Quaternary sediment with a high content of organic matter consisting largely of the elements *Limus detrituosus* and *Detritus granosus*.

3. SAMPLE PREPARATION

Sediment samples were prepared for pollen analysis by the standard concentration procedure summarised below.

1. Boiling with 10% sodium hydroxide for 5 minutes in a water bath;
2. Decanting to remove sand, and sieving to remove coarse organic detritus;
3. Treatment with cold 10% hydrochloric acid to remove carbonates;
4. Treatment with 40% hydrofluoric acid for up to 1 hour at boiling point, or 12–15 hours at room temperature, to remove silicates;
5. Treatment with hot 10% hydrochloric acid for 20 minutes to remove colloidal silicates and silicofluorides;
6. Treatment with hot 10% nitric acid for 2 minutes, when necessary, to remove pyrites (see Vallentyne, 1963);
7. Acetolysis at 95 °C in a water bath for 1 minute in a mixture of acetic anhydride (nine parts) and concentrated sulphuric acid (one part);
8. Neutralisation and staining with safranin; and
9. Mounting in glycerine jelly.

Care was taken to prepare slides of thickness between 15 and 25 μm, to avoid excessive compression and resultant changes in grain size (Cushing, 1961). The advantages of silicone oil as a mounting medium were not fully realised when this investigation was started. The use of silicone oil for routine analysis is, however, conditional on the availability of pollen reference material also mounted in silicone oil.

4. POLLEN ANALYSIS

All pollen and spores were counted using a Leitz Laborlux microscope at a magnification of ×400, using ×8 Periplan oculars, a ×40 apochromatic objective (numerical aperture (N.A.) = 0.95), and an achromatic–aplanatic condenser (N.A. = 1.25). Critical examinations and identifications were made with an apochromatic oil-immersion objective (×90; effective N.A. = 1.32). The same objective, but with the condenser immersed, was used when the highest resolution was required. For measurements of grain size, an ocular micrometer scale was used, with one division = 1.3 μm at a magnification of ×1000. All size measurements were made as soon as possible after preparation to avoid any changes in pollen size due to swelling (see Andersen, 1960).

An integral number of slides from each level was counted, to avoid any errors associated with non-random pollen distributions (Brookes & Thomas, 1967). Traverses were spaced at regular intervals of 500 μm across the whole slide. Copies of the tabulated pollen counts have been deposited at the National Lending Library, Boston Spa, Yorkshire, U.K. as Supplementary Publication No. SUP 90002 (16 pp. 1 microfiche). The primary data are thus available for different statistical treatments and handling.

5. CHOICE OF POLLEN SUM

In the absence of an independent parameter, it is necessary to express the observed pollen and spore frequencies on a relative scale. The frequencies can be expressed as percentages of a pollen sum, which should only include pollen and spore types derived from taxa with broadly similar physiognomy or ecological tolerances at the present day. Each extant pollen and spore type may represent

(i) taxa only known at present to grow on well-drained soils,
(ii) taxa which may grow at present on well-drained as well as on waterlogged soils, and
(iii) taxa only known at present to grow on waterlogged soils.

The frequencies of all determinable pollen and spore types of extant vascular plants of groups (i) and (ii) are expressed as percentages of the sum (ΣP) of all such types. No corrections were applied for the effects of different pollen productivities (cf. Faegri & Iversen, 1964). Pollen and spores of vascular plants that are considered to have grown locally within the site of deposition are excluded from the basic sum. As the sediments examined in this study are entirely limnic, the open water of the lake is regarded as the site of deposition, and hence the pollen and spores of all obligate submerged, floating, and emergent aquatic plants (group iii) are excluded from ΣP. The choice of the pollen sum (ΣP) is based on the principle of inclusion within the calculation base of all members of the 'universe', which is here taken to be the atmospheric rain of pollen grains and spores of extant vascular plants (Cushing, 1963; Wright & Patten, 1963). The exclusion of wind-disseminated spores of terrestrial thallophytes and bryophytes from ΣP is largely due to lack of knowledge of these spore types.

The frequencies of categories not included in ΣP, namely pollen and spores of obligate aquatic taxa, *Sphagnum* spores, indeterminable pollen and spore types,* unknown types, and pre-Quaternary microfossils are expressed separately on the basis advocated by Faegri (1966), Faegri & Iversen (1964), and Faegri & Ottestad (1948). These authors emphasise that any pollen or spore category excluded from the main sum (ΣP) must be included in the sum from which its percentages are calculated, for example aquatic pollen and spore frequencies are expressed as percentages of ΣP + Σ Aquatics. In the absence of a more meaningful parameter, the frequencies of the algae *Pediastrum* and *Botryococcus*, and of hystrichosphaerids and dinoflagellates are presented as percentages of ΣP + Σ Algae, and the frequencies of fungal remains as percentages of ΣP + Σ Fungal remains.

6. FORMAT OF POLLEN DIAGRAMS†

The basic results are presented as pollen diagrams (Plates 1–5) with a uniform format to permit ease of comparison. On the extreme left, the radiocarbon dates obtained from the profile in question are given in radiocarbon years before present (B.P.). The lengths of the different core segments from which the samples for pollen analysis and radiocarbon dating were taken are shown to the left of the lithological column. The sediment lithology is represented diagrammatically by the symbols proposed by Troels-Smith (1955). The density of the symbols illustrates the relative proportions of the various component elements in the sediments; the symbols are explained at the base of each diagram. A summary or total diagram follows in which are shown the relative pollen frequencies of the four broad physiognomic categories: trees (*Alnus*, *Betula* undiff., *Corylus avellana*, *Pinus*, *Populus tremula*, *Prunus* cf. *P. padus*, *Quercus*, *Sorbus aucuparia*, *S.* cf. *S. rupicola*, *Ulmus*), shrubs (*Betula* cf. *B. nana*, *Ephedra distachya* type, *E. fragilis* type, *Hippophaë rhamnoides*, *Juniperus communis*, *Salix* undiff., *Salix* cf. *S. herbacea*, *Viburnum opulus*), dwarf shrubs (*Calluna vulgaris*, *Empetrum* cf. *E. nigrum*, Ericaceae undiff., *Rubus saxatilis*), and herbs (including pteridophytes). Individual silhouette curves for all the pollen and spore types identified are then presented in order of stratigraphic occurrence within the four categories. All the curves are drawn to a standard scale. The black curves indicate percentages directly from the scales at the bottom of the diagram; the unshaded curves are exaggerated ten times. The occurrences of pollen and spore types that were observed either during the preparation of the sample or during scanning of the prepared slides but that were not recorded during the routine analysis are indicated on the pollen diagrams by a +. To the right of the curves, the number of pollen grains and spores in the basic sum (ΣP), and the number of pollen and spore types in the sum (Σ Taxa) for each sample are shown. Pollen and spore types excluded from the main sum are then given, and grouped with the categories of obligate aquatics, *Sphagnum*, indeterminable pollen and spores, unknown types, pre-Quaternary microfossils, algae, and fungal remains. At the extreme right the local and regional pollen assemblage zones are shown, with a depth scale.

In Chapter 14 ecological and stratigraphical groupings and recalculation of the primary data have been carried out in order to illustrate particular points and to test specific hypotheses. The basis of each calculation is indicated in the text and on the special pollen diagrams. All the calculations are derived from the primary data presented in Plates 1–5.

* An exception to this procedure is made at Loch Cill Chriosd (see p. 265) because of the high frequencies of indeterminable pollen there.

† Located inside back cover.

8

POLLEN AND SPORE IDENTIFICATIONS

As palaeoecologists seek increasingly more detailed information from pollen-analytical data, there is a growing necessity for the determination of pollen and spores to the lowest possible taxonomic level. The improvement in optical equipment, the compilation of extensive pollen reference collections, and advances in pollen morphological knowledge permit the recognition of types that were once regarded as indistinguishable. It is important, however, to describe and define the identified types, to permit the reader not only to benefit from the observations, but also to judge the reliability and accuracy of the determinations.

Short descriptions of the less common pollen and spore types identified in this study are presented, together with their known taxonomic limits. Pollen morphological terminology follows the system proposed by Iversen & Troels-Smith (1950), and for convenience the abbreviations suggested by those authors are used. The abbreviations are listed in Table 8.1. In addition, the term *perf* is used as an abbreviation for perforations or holes of the tectum that are distinctly smaller in diameter than the distance between the perforations, and *perf-D* for their diameter. The term *semi-tec* is used as an abbreviation for a semi-tectate structure (Faegri & Iversen, 1964), occurring in grains whose tectum is perforated by holes that are larger in diameter than the distance between the holes. Use of the terms micro-ret, micro-bac, and micro-ech follows the definitions presented by Beug (1961). In the case of spores, the morphological terminology of Erdtman, Berglund & Praglowski (1961) is used. No attempt has been made to present a complete description of each pollen or spore type, but only those features that are considered characteristic and diagnostic of each type are given. These observations are based on all the available reference material, but when published accounts or keys for particular taxa have been used, these are quoted. Most of the reference material was prepared by acetolysis, stained with safranin, and mounted in glycerine jelly. In view of the problems of size changes of pollen and spores mounted in this medium (see Andersen, 1960; Cushing, 1961; Erdtman & Praglowski, 1959), only large size differences in the reference material have been considered reliable. Size statistical methods have only been used in particularly critical cases, where the morphological differences between the pollen or spores of different species appear to be rather slight.

The reference material used in this study is primarily derived from the collection of over 9000 slides in the Sub-Department of Quaternary Research, University of Cambridge (see Andrew, 1970), but in some cases it has been supplemented by material at the Geological Survey of Denmark in Copenhagen and at the Limnological Research Center, University of Minnesota.

All the fossil preparations that have been counted and examined have been retained, and the positions of the interesting or difficult fossil pollen and spore types are marked on the slides. The co-ordinates relating to all these fossil grains and spores for the micrometer stage of Leitz Laborlux microscope No. 589992 are on file at the Sub-Department of Quaternary Research, University of Cambridge. Co-ordinates of reference points on the slides are also on file, as these can be used for the calibration of vernier scales on other microscopes (Pierce, 1959; Traverse, 1958). This documentation has been useful in the checking of all determinations made during the course of the investigations, for it has been possible to examine all the finds of a particular pollen type at the same time, thereby giving a higher degree of consistency and reliability than might otherwise be possible.

As pollen and spores can be transported considerable distances from their source, there is a finite probability that pollen or spores of *any* plant in the world may be encountered. Although the identifications are based entirely on morphological criteria, the latter are sometimes not sufficiently precise to distinguish the pollen and spores of taxa of the present indigenous British flora from those occurring elsewhere. Where such uncertainties occur the pollen or spore type is assigned to a native British taxon. A

TABLE 8.1. *Abbreviations used for pollen morphological terms and parameters (from Iversen & Troels-Smith, 1950)*

aeq	aequator, aequatoriales	inter P	interporium, interporia
anl	annulus, annuli, annulate	l	limes
bac	baculum, bacula, baculate	lac	lacuna, lacunae, lacunate
C	colpus, colpi	Lg	longitudinal length
C3	tricolpate	Lt	transverse length
C3P3	tricolporate	lum	lumen, lumina
C peri	pericolpate	M	measurement
C stp	stephanocolpate	med	median
C syn	syncolpate	mg	margo
C P peri	pericolporate	P	porus, pori
C P stp	stephanocolporate	P1	monoporate
cav	cavea, cavate	P3	triporate
cla	clava, clavae, clavate	P peri	periporate
col	columella, columellae	P stp	stephanoporate
cost	costa, costae	pol	pole
D	diameter	polar	polar area
ech	echinus, echini, echinate	prol	prolate
ekt	ektexine	psi	psilate
end	endexine	ret	reticulum, reticulate
ex	exine	rug	rugulatus, rugulate
Fen	fenestrate	sca	scabrate
foc	focus level (0–5)*	subsph	subsphaeroidal
fov	foveolate	str	striate
gem	gemma, gemmae, gemmate	tec	tectum, tectate
gran	granula, granulae, granulate	tr C	transverse colpus, transverse colpi
I	index, indices	val	valla, vallae
inap	inaperturate	ver	verruca, verrucae, verrucate
intec	intectate	vest	vestibulum
inter C	intercolpium, intercolpia		
C-Lg	length of meridional colpi	(P,l-P,l)-M	distance between two adjacent pori
col-D	diameter of columellae	P-Lg	meridional diameter of porus
ekt-M	thickness of ektexine	P-Lt	equatorial diameter of porus
end-M	thickness of endexine	P-M	diameter of porus
ex-M	thickness of exine	polar-I	polar area index (polar-M/Lt, +)
lum-D	diameter of lumina	sculp-alt	height of sculpturing elements
Cα1–4	colpus form	Pα1–4	porus form
Cβ1–3	colpus delimitation	Pαa–d	porus shape
Cγ1–3	colpus structure	Pβ1–3	porus delimitation
Σ	number of apertures	Pγ1–3	porus structure

*See plate X in Iversen & Troels-Smith (1950).

further assumption made is that the fossil flora is similar taxonomically to the present flora, and thus that the fossil pollen and spores can be compared and identified with pollen and spores of present-day taxa.

Intraspecific variation can be an important factor in limiting the separation of closely allied taxa on pollen morphological criteria, and thus the number of independent collections of each taxon examined is relevant to the reliability of the determination. Throughout these notes, therefore, the number of collections examined (coll.) is given in parentheses, after the name of the taxon, and in the case of large families within which the pollen morphological variation is small, the number of species studied is also noted.

The nomenclature and the order in which the families, genera, and species are placed follow Clapham *et al.* (1962), unless otherwise stated.

1. CONVENTIONS

The degree of certainty in the determination of plant fossils should be clearly defined, so that equal weight in interpretation is not given to both certain (i.e. beyond reasonable doubt) and doubtful identifications. Throughout this work, a standardised set of conventions is used, and the following examples serve for explanation:

Gramineae	Family determination certain, types or subgroups undetermined or indeterminable.
Thalictrum	Genus determination certain, types or subgroups undetermined or indeterminable.

Plantago lanceolata	Species determination certain.
Sedum cf. *S. rosea*	Genus determination certain, species identification less certain because of imperfect preservation of fossil grain or spore, inadequate reference material, or close morphological similarity of the grain or spore with those of other taxa. In each case, the reason is explained in the notes on the determination.
Plantago major/ P. media	One fossil type present; only two taxa are considered probable alternatives, but further distinctions are not possible on the basis of pollen or spore morphology alone. In view of their modern ecology and/or distribution, the occurrence of both taxa is considered equally likely.
Angelica type	One fossil type present, three or more taxa are possible alternatives, but further distinctions are not possible on the basis of pollen or spore morphology alone. The selection of the taxon name is based on modern ecological and/or phytogeographical criteria. The notes on the determination list all the known possibilities.
Rosaceae undifferentiated (undiff.)	Family determination certain, some morphological types distinguished and presented separately. Curve represents fossil grains or spores that were not or could not be separated beyond family level.
Stellaria undiff.	Genus determination certain, some morphological types distinguished and presented separately. Curve represents fossil grains or spores that were not or could not be separated beyond genus level.

2. PTERIDOPHYTA

Lycopodiaceae

Lycopodium. The spore morphology of the five British species of *Lycopodium* is summarised in Table 8.2. (See also Erdtman *et al.* 1961.)

Two fossil spores were referred to *Lycopodium clavatum*, four to *L. annotinum*, forty-four to *L. alpinum*, and a very large number to *L. selago*.

TABLE 8.2. *Morphological characteristics of modern spores of* Lycopodium *species*

Species	Sculpture	No. of lum on med of distal face	lum-D (μm)	No. of muri on equator	Spore shape	No. of coll. examined
Lycopodium selago	coarsely rug-fov	.	.	.	hexangular	3
L. inundatum	irregular rug	.	.	.	sub-triang.	3
L. annotinum	ret	5–6	5–7.5	20–24	sub-triang.	4
L. clavatum	ret	9–11	2.5–3	35–41	sub-triang.	4
L. alpinum	ret	5–8	4–5	27–33	sub-triang.	4

TABLE 8.3. *Measurements of modern microspores of* Isoetes lacustris *and* I. echinospora

Species	Locality	Mean size (μm)	Standard deviation (μm)	Total no. of spores measured
Isoetes lacustris	Co. Sligo, Ireland	33.81	±1.83	100
I. lacustris	Westmorland, England	33.56	±1.69	100
I. lacustris	North Wales	33.89	±1.77	100
I. lacustris	South Jutland, Denmark	33.99	±2.34	100
	Total	33.85	±1.93	400
I. echinospora	Cumberland, England	24.41	±2.06	100
I. echinospora	Western Norway	24.10	±1.77	100
I. echinospora	North Wales	24.74	±2.23	100
	Total	24.41	±2.04	300

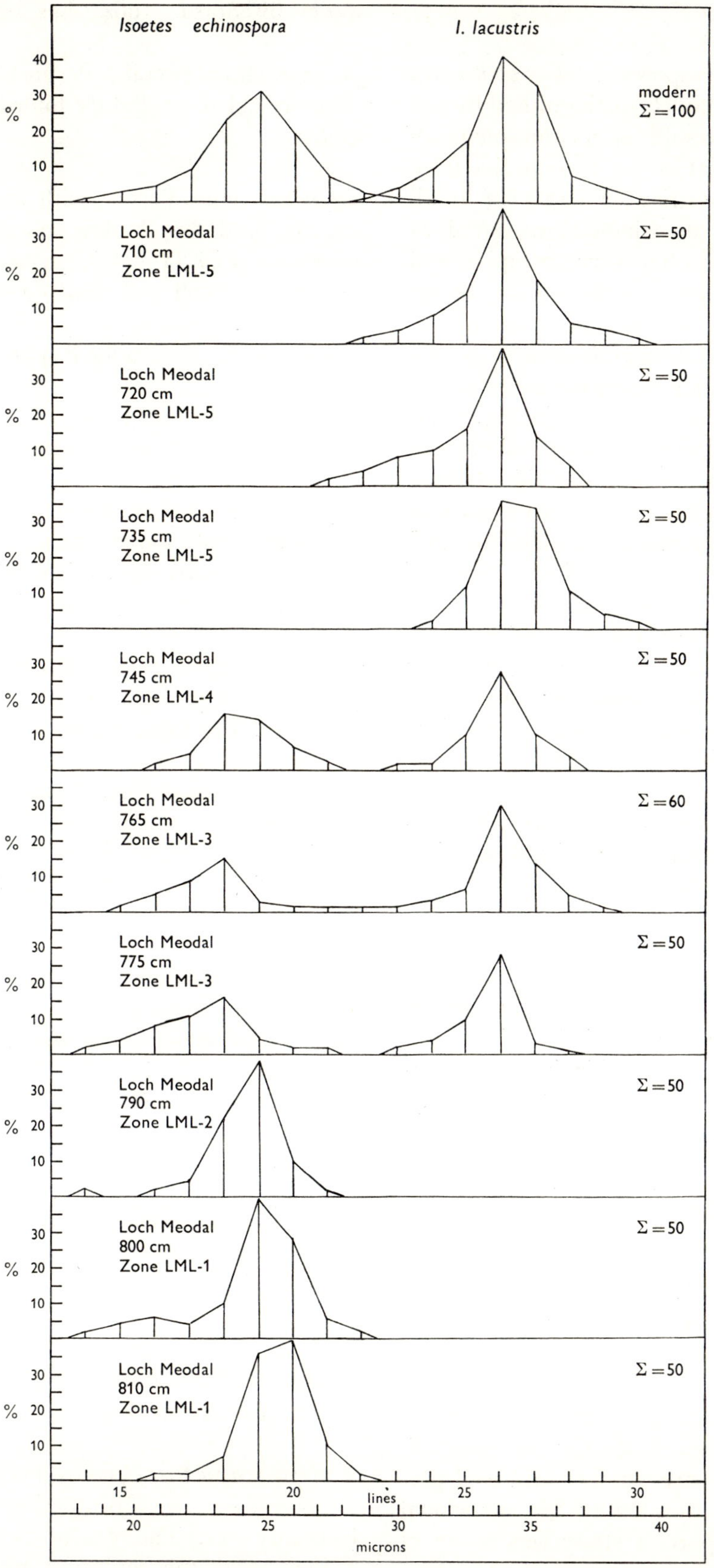

Figure 9. Size–frequency distribution curves of modern and fossil microscopes of *Isoetes*. The number of spores measured is also shown.

Isoetaceae

Isoetes. The monolete microspores of *Isoetes echinospora* and *I. lacustris* can be effectively distinguished by size (see Andersen, 1961). Results of measurements of modern reference material of the two species from various localities are summarised in Table 8.3. In all these measurements only the exine was measured, as the loose, thin perine was often very crumpled and folded. The longest diameter parallel to the furrow was measured to an accuracy of one ocular micrometer division (1.3 μm) at a magnification of $\times 900$.

Summation size-frequency curves for the reference material of the two species are shown in Fig. 9. As there is little overlap in the size range of modern microspores of the two species, individual fossil microspores can be referred to one or other species on the basis of size with a high degree of confidence (cf. Godwin, 1956). At Loch Meodal the number of fossil microspores was large enough, however, to permit size-frequency analysis. The result of measurements of fossil microspores from nine stratigraphic levels are also shown in Fig. 9, and they support the specific distinctions made during routine counting.

Osmundaceae

Osmunda regalis (4 coll.). Trilete, sculptural elements fused into ret or rug pattern on the distal face (see Andersen, 1961). Sixteen fossil spores.

Polypodiaceae

The reference material examined comprises the following genera: *Pteridium, Cryptogramma, Anogramma, Adiantum, Blechnum, Phyllitis, Asplenium* (7 spp.), *Ceterach, Cystopteris* (3 spp.), *Woodsia* (2 spp.), *Dryopteris* (9 spp.), *Polystichum* (3 spp.), *Thelypteris* (5 spp.), and *Polypodium* (3 spp.).

Pteridium aquilinum (5 coll.). Trilete, psi when perine absent.

Cryptogramma crispa (5 coll.). Trilete, ver; ver diminishing in size towards the triradiate scar, magna. See Seddon (1962).

All the other British genera in this family (except *Adiantum* and *Anogramma*) have monolete spores, the determination of which is usually only possible when the perine or exospore is intact and well preserved. In an attempt to identify the occasional intact fossil monolete spore, a study was made of the spore morphology of the present British taxa. The morphological account of Fennoscandian fern spores by Sorsa (1964) has been of limited use.

Blechnum spicant (3 coll.). Perine very thin (<0.5 μm), often wrinkled or slightly folded, psi. Twenty fossil spores.

Asplenium type, Perine with sparse ech (sculp-alt, <2 μm) and few shallow folds. Includes *Asplenium adiantum-nigrum* (1 coll.), *A. obovatum* (1 coll.), *A. trichomanes* (2 coll.), *A. viride* (2 coll.), *A. ruta-muraria* (1 coll.), *A. septentrionale* (2 coll.), and *Ceterach officinarum* (2 coll.). Seven fossil spores.

Athyrium filix-femina (3 coll.). Perine thin (<0.5 μm), smooth or faintly ver or rug-sca. Three fossil spores.

Athyrium alpestre type. Perine with few shallow folds (<3 μm deep), loosely attached to exine, sca-psi. Includes *Athyrium alpestre* (3 coll.), *Woodsia ilvensis* (2 coll.), and *W. alpina* (3 coll.). Ten fossil spores.

Cystopteris fragilis (4 coll.). Perine with prominent ech (sculp-alt, + 5–7 μm, and 5–7 μm apart), psi or micro-ret. Ten fossil spores.

Dryopteris filix-mas type. Perine distinctly folded (*ca.* 5 μm deep), psi or micro-ret. Includes *Dryopteris filix-mas* (2 coll.), *D. borreri* (1 coll.), *D. abbreviata* (1 coll.), *D. villarii* (1 coll.), *D. aemula* (2 coll.), *Thelypteris limbosperma* (2 coll.), and *T. robertiana* (2 coll.).

Dryopteris carthusiana type. Like *Dryopteris filix-mas* type, except densely ech (sculp-alt, + 2–3 μm). Includes *Dryopteris carthusiana* (2 coll.), *D. dilatata* (3 coll.), *D. assimilis* (1 coll.), *D. cristata* (1 coll.), and *Cystopteris dickieana* (1 coll.). Two fossil spores.

Polystichum type. Perine densely ech (sculp-alt, + <4 μm), barely folded. Includes *Polystichum setiferum* (2 coll.), *P. aculeatum* (2 coll.), *P. lonchitis* (2 coll.), *Asplenium marinum* (1 coll.), and *Phyllitis scolopendrium* (2 coll.). Four fossil spores.

Thelypteris phegopteris (2 coll.). Perine thin, with discontinuous folds (up to 5 μm deep), psi; M, + 50–60 μm. Twenty fossil spores.

Thelypteris dryopteris (3 coll.). Perine saccate, ret (lum-D, + <2 μm), or if the perine is lacking the exine is faintly ver. The ver are low and angular in outline, and the sculpture may be described as areolate.

Polypodium. Perine absent; ex-M, + 3–5 μm; ver. Includes *Polypodium vulgare* (2 coll.), *P. interjectum* (1 coll.), and *P. australe* (1 coll.).

Polypodiaceae undiff. All monolete, psi spores with perine absent or poorly preserved are included in this category. Such spores may belong to species of any of the following genera: *Blechnum, Phyllitis, Asplenium, Ceterach, Athyrium, Cystopteris, Woodsia, Dryopteris, Polystichum*, and *Thelypteris* (including *T. dryopteris* p.p.).

3. GYMNOSPERMAE

Cupressaceae

Juniperus communis. Pollina inap or P1, intec, gem, subsph, minuta–media. A very variable grain, commonly split in two in fossil condition (see Bertsch, 1961), with much variation in the density of gem (see the scanning electron micrographs by Pilcher, 1968 and Reyre, 1968). In intact grains a small circular pore can sometimes be seen. No distinction appears possible between the pollen of *Juniperus communis* ssp. *communis* (6 coll.) and of *J. communis* ssp. *nana* (3 coll.).

Ephedraceae

Accounts of the pollen morphology of the family have been published by Steeves & Barghoorn (1959) and Welten (1957). Within the present European taxa, two pollen morphological types can be distinguished (see Beug, 1957, 1961).

Ephedra fragilis type. Furrows (not true colpi) unbranched; equivalent to pollen types C and D of Steeves & Barghoorn (1959). Includes *Ephedra fragilis* ssp. *fragilis* Desf. (2 coll.), *E. fragilis* ssp. *campylopoda* (C. A. Meyer) Ascherson & Graebner (1 coll.), *E. strobilacea* Bunge (1 coll.), and *E. alata* Decaisne (1 coll.), as well as several American species (see Cushing, 1963; Janssen, 1967*a*). Pollen morphological distinctions have been made within this type on the basis of grain size, number of ridges, and structural features (Florin, 1969; Welten, 1957), but the available reference material is too variable to apply such distinctions to the eighteen fossil grains found.

Ephedra distachya type. Furrows branched, with lateral branches extending up the meridional ridges; equivalent to pollen type A of Steeves & Barghoorn (1959). Includes *Ephedra distachya* ssp. *distachya* L. (2 coll.), *E. distachya* ssp. *helvetica* (C. A. Meyer) Ascherson & Graebner (1 coll.), *E. major* ssp. *major* Host. (3 coll.) (syn. *E. nebrodensis* Tineo ex Guss.), and *E. major* ssp. *procera* (Fischer & C. A. Meyer) Markgraf (1 coll.). One fossil grain.

4. ANGIOSPERMAE

Ranunculaceae

The reference material examined comprises the following genera: *Caltha, Trollius, Helleborus* (2 spp.), *Aconitum, Actaea, Anemone* (2 spp.), *Clematis, Ranunculus* (22 spp.), *Aquilegia*, and *Thalictrum* (3 spp.).

Caltha type. Pollina C3, Cγ2, tec with fine col, sca with regularly and rather densely arranged micro-ech, minuta. Includes *Caltha palustris* ssp. *palustris* (5 coll.), *C. palustris* ssp. *minor* (2 coll.), *Aquilegia vulgaris* (2 coll.), and *Aconitum anglicum* p.p. (1 coll.).

Trollius europaeus (6 coll.). Pollina C3, Cα2a, Cβ2a, Cγ2, tec, col distinct at polar, col intra-str, str-rug, val distinct but very fine, minuta. One fossil grain.

Anemone type. Pollina C3 or C peri (CΣ4–6), Cγ2, tec with homogeneous isodiametric coarse col (col-D, + *ca.* 1 μm) and numerous fine perf, sca. See Huynh (1970). Includes *Anemone nemorosa* (3 coll.), *A. pulsatilla* (3 coll.), and *Actaea spicata* (5 coll.). One fossil grain.

Ranunculus acris type. (*Ranunculus acer* type of Andersen, 1961). Pollina C3 or C peri (CΣ4–12), Cγ2, tec with col of two orders, with fine col usually fused arranged around each of the coarse col (col-D, + > 1.5 μm), sca or ver, polar I medium-small. Includes *Ranunculus acris* (3 coll.), *R. repens* (3 coll.), *R. bulbosus* (3 coll.), *R. sardous* (2 coll.), *R. parviflorus* (2 coll.), *R. auricomus* (2 coll.), *R. lingua* (3 coll.), *R. ficaria* (4 coll.), and *Clematis vitalba* (3 coll.).

Ranunculus trichophyllus type (Andersen, 1961). Pollina as in *Ranunculus acris* type, except fine col evenly distributed. Includes *Ranunculus flammula* (4 coll.), *R. reptans* (4 coll.), *R. ophioglossifolius* (2 coll.), *R. sceleratus* (3 coll.), *R. hederaceus* (3 coll.), *R. omiophyllus* (1 coll.), *R. tripartitus* (1 coll.), *R. fluitans* (1 coll.), *R. circinatus* (1 coll.), *R. trichophyllus* (2 coll.), *R. aquatilis* (3 coll.), *R. peltatus* (2 coll.), and *R. baudotii* (2 coll.).

Thalictrum (3 spp., 21 coll.). Pollina P peri, PΣ4–12, Pβ1a–Pβ2, Pγ2, tec, col (incertae) – col intrabac, ord; psi with minute ech, minuta. The reference material is very variable, and no specific determinations appear possible.

Nymphaeaceae

Nymphaea. Two subspecies of *Nymphaea alba* are recognised in Britain, ssp. *alba* (2 coll.) and ssp. *occidentalis* (2 coll.). The taxonomic status of the latter taxon is not clear (Heslop-Harrison, 1955). The problems of pollen morphology within the genus have been discussed by Godwin (1959), who also considered the distinction between the pollen of the European species *Nymphaea candida* C. Presl. in J. & C. Presl. (2 coll.) and *N. alba* s.l. On the basis of these distinctions, the Skye fossil grains do not appear to represent *N. candida*.

Nuphar (2 spp., 5 coll.). Watts (1959) has commented on variation in the density and form of echini in the pollen of *Nuphar*, and has tentatively referred fossil pollen on the basis of sparse, slender echini to *N. pumila*. He notes, however, that the fossil material is somewhat intermediate in character. Heslop-Harrison (1953), in discussing *N.* × *spennerana*, concludes that this taxon is probably of hybrid origin between *N. lutea* and *N. pumila*. The occurrence of hybridisation thus limits any reliable specific determination made on the basis of pollen alone.

Violaceae

Viola (12 spp., 23 coll.). Pollina C3, Cα3, tec; col-D, ± < 0.5 μm; psi; ex-M, ± *ca.* 1 μm; subsph, media. One grain in surface sample.

Polygalaceae

Polygala (4 spp., 11 coll.). Pollina C P stp (CΣ8–12) or Fen, polar with ± isodiametric lac, psi. One fossil grain.

Hypericaceae

Hypericum pulchrum type. Pollina C3 or C3P3, Cα3 a-Cα3c, cost C marked, semi-tec, micro-ret; lum-D, ± < 1 μm; lum-D = muri width, prol-subsph, minuta. See H. H. Birks (1969). Includes *Hypericum pulchrum* (3 coll.), *H. tetrapterum* p.p. (3 coll.), and *H. montanum* (1 coll.). Three fossil grains.

Cistaceae

Helianthemum chamaecistus type. (*H. nummularium* type of Iversen, 1944 and Erdtman *et al.*, 1961). Pollina C3P3, Cβ2, Pαb, Pβ1a–Pβ2, polar-I < 0.25, col intra-ret, tec, perf numerous, str-rug, str moderately distinct, prol (Lg/Lt, ± 1.4–1.6), media. Includes *Helianthemum chamaecistus* (6 coll.) and *H. appeninum* (4 coll.). Two fossil grains.

Caryophyllaceae

An account of the pollen morphology of the British representatives of this family was prepared during this work. The accounts by Andersen (1961), Chanda (1962), Faegri & Iversen (1964), and Fredskild (1967) have also been useful. The reference material examined comprises the following genera: *Silene* (10 spp.), *Lychnis* (3 spp.), *Dianthus* (3 spp.), *Saponaria*, *Cerastium* (10 spp.), *Myosoton*, *Stellaria* (8 spp.), *Moenchia*, *Sagina* (7 spp.), *Minuartia* (3 spp.), *Cherleria*, *Honkenya*, *Moehringia*, *Arenaria* (4 spp.), *Spergula*, *Spergularia* (4 spp.), *Corrigiola*, *Herniaria*, *Illecebrum*, and *Scleranthus* (2 spp.).

Silene dioica type. (*Melandrium* of Andersen, 1961; see also Chanda, 1962). Pollina P peri (PΣ20–30), anl not diffuse, col intra-ret, perf-D *ca.* 0.5–1.0 μm. See scanning electron micrographs by Roland (1969). Includes *Silene dioica* (5 coll.), *S. alba* (3 coll.), *S. conica* (3 coll.), and *S. noctiflora* (2 coll.). Seven fossil grains.

Silene maritima type. Pollina P peri (PΣ20–30), anl not diffuse, perf-D < 0.5 μm, perf distinct but scattered, sca or ech; M, ± 32–45 μm. Includes *Silene vulgaris* (4 coll.), *S. maritima* (6 coll.), *S. gallica* (1 coll.), *S. otites* (3 coll.), and *S. nutans* (3 coll.). Nine fossil grains.

Silene cf. *S. acaulis* (9 coll.). Pollina P peri (PΣ20–30), anl distinct and broad, col intra-bac or partially intra-ret, perf distinct but scattered, sca or ech rather distinct; M, ± 23–32 μm. Nineteen fossil grains.

Lychnis flos-cuculi (3 coll.). Pollina P peri (PΣ20–35); P–M, ± > 3 μm; anl not diffuse, perf distinct but scattered, sca. Rather similar grains are found in *Lychnis alpina* (3 coll.) and *L. viscaria* (4 coll.), but the pollen of *L. flos-cuculi* can be distinguished by P–M, ± ⩾ (P,l–P,l)–M. One fossil grain.

Cerastium alpinum type. Pollina P peri (PΣ20–36), anl diffuse (Pβ3a), col heterogeneous, col finest and densest around P and ± fused with anl, coarse col unevenly scattered in inter P, perf very numerous and dense, sca; M, ± 35–45 μm. Includes *Cerastium cerastoides* (2 coll.), *C. arvense* (5 coll.), *C. alpinum* (4 coll.), *C. arcticum* (3 coll.), and *C. nigrescens* (1 coll.). Sixteen fossil grains.

Cerastium cf. *C. holosteoides* (2 coll.). Pollina as in

TABLE 8.4. *Measurements of modern pollen of* Lotus *species*

Species	Locality	Mean size (Lg) (μm)	Standard deviation (μm)	Total number of grains measured
Lotus corniculatus	Isle of Skye, Scotland	18.45	±1.61	100
L. corniculatus	Teesdale, England	19.02	±1.36	100
L. corniculatus	Norfolk, England	19.05	±1.32	100
L. corniculatus	Suffolk, England	19.28	±1.28	100
	Total	18.95	±1.43	400
L. pedunculatus	Cumberland, England	13.98	±1.45	100
L. pedunculatus	Norfolk, England	13.00	±1.34	100
L. pedunculatus	Argyll, Scotland	13.05	±1.39	100
	Total	13.34	±1.46	300
L. tenuis	Zealand, Denmark	13.61	±1.77	100
L. tenuis	Cambridgeshire, England	12.29	±1.32	50
L. tenuis	Kent, England	13.94	±1.44	100
	Total	13.48	±1.67	250
L. angustissimus	Penzance, England	13.59	±1.72	100
L. angustissimus	Cornwall, England	12.77	±1.59	50
	Total	13.31	±1.72	150
L. hispidus	Penzance, England	13.10	±0.98	50
L. hispidus	Cornwall, England	13.08	±1.13	50
	Total	13.09	±1.05	100

Cerastium alpinum type, except distinctly ech. Two fossil grains.

Stellaria undiff. Pollina P peri (PΣ12–15), anl rather diffuse (Pβ3a), col heterogeneous, col finest and densest around P and ± fused with anl, coarse col unevenly scattered in inter P, perf numerous and dense, sca; M, + 20–32 μm. See Erdtman (1968). Includes *Stellaria nemorum* (2 coll.), *S. media* (3 coll.), *S. neglecta* (1 coll.), *S. graminea* (5 coll.), and *S. alsine* (3 coll.). Twenty fossil grains.

Stellaria holostea (6 coll.). Pollina P peri (PΣ12), col heterogeneous, col coarse in inter P, col very fine around P; the P in depressions, the inter P forming a pentagonal pattern of ridges, perf numerous and dense, sca-ech, sca elements *ca.* 0.5 μm. See Andersen (1961), Erdtman *et al.* (1961), and Faegri & Iversen (1964). Twelve fossil grains.

Sagina. Pollina P peri (PΣ25–40); P–M, + <2 μm; perf numerous and rather dense, sca. See Andersen (1961) and Faegri & Iversen (1964). Includes *Sagina apetala* (2 coll.), *S. ciliata* (1 coll.), *S. maritima* (1 coll.), *S. procumbens* (3 coll.), *S. saginoides* (3 coll.), *S. subulata* (1 coll.), and *S. nodosa* (2 coll.). The reference material is too limited to permit separations within the genus. Fourteen fossil grains.

Arenaria type. Pollina P peri (PΣ12–30), anl distinct, perf numerous and dense, sca indistinct; M, + 28–32 μm. Includes *Minuartia verna* (4 coll.), *M. hybrida* (2 coll.), *M. stricta* (1 coll.), *Cherleria sedoides* (4 coll.), *Honkenya peploides* (2 coll.), *Moehringia trinervia* (2 coll.), *Arenaria serpyllifolia* (3 coll.), *A. leptoclados* (1 coll.), *A. ciliata* (3 coll.), *A. norvegica* (5 coll.), *Moenchia erecta* (1 coll.), *Cerastium glomeratum* (2 coll.), *C. atrovirens* (2 coll.), *C. pumilum* (1 coll.), and *C. semidecandrum* (5 coll.). Nine fossil grains.

Spergula arvensis (6 coll.). Pollina C peri (CΣ4–12), tec, numerous perf, psi-sca, ± micro-ech. One fossil grain.

Papilionaceae

An unpublished key to the pollen of this family by Faegri (1956), and the account by Andersen (1961) have been useful. The reference material examined comprises the following genera: *Genista* (3 spp.), *Ulex* (3 spp.), *Sarothamnus*, *Ononis* (3 spp.), *Medicago* (5 spp.), *Trifolium* (19 spp.), *Anthyllis*, *Lotus* (5 spp.), *Astragalus* (3 spp.), *Oxytropis* (2 spp.), *Ornithopus* (2 spp.), *Hippocrepis*, *Onobrychis*, *Vicia* (11 spp.), and *Lathyrus* (8 spp.).

Trifolium (47 coll.). Pollina C3P3, P usually distinct, Pαb–Pαc, cost C present, tec, col distinct, ret (rarely

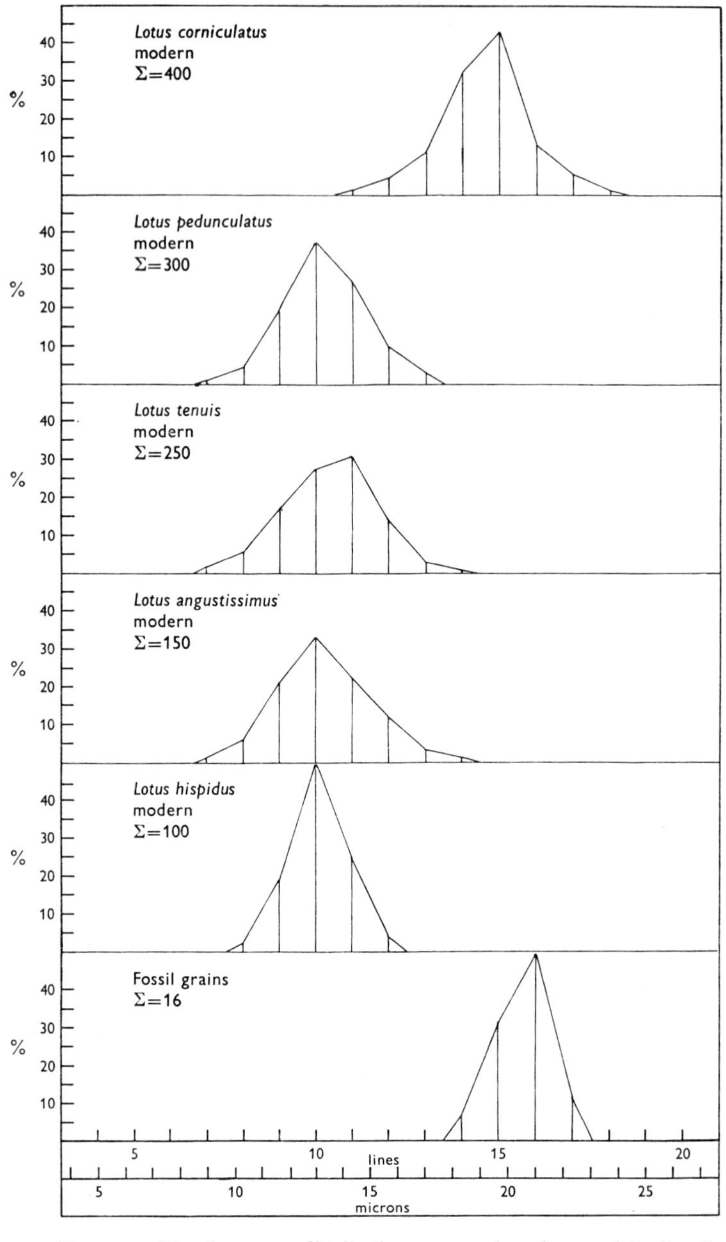

Figure 10. Size–frequency distribution curves of modern and fossil pollen of *Lotus*. The number of pollen grains measured is also shown.

fov); lum-D, + > 1 μm; Lg/Lt, + > 1.3; M, + 25–35 μm. One fossil grain.

Trifolium cf. *T. repens* (7 coll.). Pollina C3P3, Cβ3, P moderately distinct, Pαc, tec, ret, fov on polar; lum-D, + < 1 μm; ex-M, + > 1 μm; Lg/Lt, + > 1.3; M, + 20–25 μm. One fossil grain.

Lotus cf. *L. corniculatus* (4 coll.). Pollina C3P3, Pαc, tec, psi, P-Lg 5–10% Lg, polar-I > 0.4; ex-M, + < 1 μm; Lg/Lt, + > 1.3; M, + 16–22 μm. Rather similar grains occur in *Hippocrepis comosa* (3 coll.; P-Lg 20% Lg) and *Ornithopus perpusillus* (3 coll.; P-Lg 15% Lg) but distinctions have been made on the basis of P-Lg measurements (see Andersen, 1961). Tentative specific determinations of the sixteen fossil grains found have been made on the basis of Lg, + measurements. Results of pollen size measurements of modern reference material of the five British species of *Lotus* from various localities are summarised in Table 8.4. Measurements were made to an accuracy of one ocular micrometer division (1.3 μm) at a magnification of 900 ×. Summation size–frequency curves for the reference material of the five species are shown in Fig. 10. The sixteen fossil grains found have Lg, + between 18.2 and 21.1 μm, with a mean of 20.27 μm (s = 0.85 μm). By comparison with the measurements of the reference material, the fossil grains are tentatively referred to *L. corniculatus*.

cf. *Oxytropis*. Pollina C3P3, Cβ3, P distinct, Pαc, tec, col incertus, fov on inter C, fov-psi on polar; ex-M, + < 1 μm; M, + > 35 μm. The rather limited reference material (*Oxytropis campestris* 2 coll., *O. halleri* 2 coll.), coupled with the difficulties of specific identity of the modern British *Oxytropis* populations necessitate a tentative determination. One fossil grain.

Vicia/Lathyrus. (Andersen, 1961; *Vicia* type of Faegri & Iversen, 1964.) Pollina C3P3, P very distinct, Pβ3b, cost C thick, tec, ret; lum-D, + > 1 μm; ex-M, + *ca.* 1.5 μm; prol, media. Includes *Vicia* (11 spp., 31 coll.) and *Lathyrus* (8 spp., 18 coll.). Twelve fossil grains.

Rosaceae

Pollen identifications were aided by the pollen morphological accounts of the family by Andersen (1961), Faegri & Iversen (1964), and Reitsma (1966) The reference material examined comprises the following genera: *Filipendula* (2 spp.), *Rubus* (8 spp.), *Potentilla* (11 spp.), *Sibbaldia*, *Fragaria*, *Geum* (2 spp.), *Dryas*, *Agrimonia* (2 spp.), *Alchemilla* (8 spp.), *Aphanes* (2 spp.), *Sanguisorba*, *Poterium*, *Rosa* (14 spp.), *Prunus* (3 spp.), *Cotoneaster*, *Crataegus* (2 spp.), *Sorbus* (12 spp.), and *Malus*.

Filipendula. No distinction appears possible between the pollen of *Filipendula ulmaria* (6 coll.), and *F. vulgaris* (4 coll.). See Berglund (1966*a*).

Rubus saxatilis (3 coll.). Pollina C3, Cα3c–Cα3f, cost C moderate, tec perf, psi or very faintly rug; ex-M, + < 1.5 μm; polar-I small, minuta. The pollen of *R. arcticus* (2 coll.) is rather similar, but polar-I medium (see Andersen, 1961; Krog, 1954). Six fossil grains.

Potentilla type. Pollina C3 or C3P3, Cγ3, tec, rug-str, val distinct and rather coarse, minuta-media. Includes *Potentilla* (11 spp., 40 coll.), *Fragaria vesca* (6 coll.), and *Sibbaldia procumbens* (4 coll.).

Geum (2 spp., 7 coll.). Pollina C3 or C3P3, Cα4, tr C, tec, rug-str, val distinct and rather coarse, val usually parallel to C, prol; M, + 26–29 μm. Two fossil grains.

Dryas octopetala (13 coll.). Pollina C3 or C3P3, Cα3c–Cα3f, tec, rug-str, vermiculate, val short and branched, and rather coarse; ex-M, + < 1.5 μm; M, + < 28 μm. See Florin (1969). Three fossil grains.

Alchemilla (8 spp., 13 coll.). Pollina C3 or C3P3, Cα3c, cost C distinct, tec, col distinct (especially in inter C), psi (rarely str), equatorial limb semi-angular; ex-M, + > 2 μm; ekt-M > end-M, minuta. Twenty six fossil grains.

Prunus cf. *P. padus* (5 coll.). Pollina C3 or C3P3, Cα3d–Cα3e, cost C distinct, tec, rug-str, val distinct but delicate, val frequently branched in inter C; ex-M, + > 1.5 μm; end-M ⩾ ekt-M, subsph; M, + < 28 μm. Differs from pollen of *Prunus avium* (3 coll.) and *P. spinosa* (3 coll.) in val structure, ex-M, and M. See Praglowski (1962). Nine fossil grains.

Sorbus aucuparia (5 coll.). Pollina C3 or C3P3, Cα3h, cost C indistinct, tec, rug-str, val rather delicate but distinct; ex-M, + > 1.5 μm; end-M ⩾ ekt-M; M, + 22–27 μm. See Praglowski (1962) and scanning electron micrographs by Pilcher (1968).

Sorbus cf. *S. rupicola* (2 coll.). Pollina C3 or C3P3, Cα3c–Cα3f, cost C indistinct, tec, rug, val indistinct; ex-M, + > 1.5 μm; end-M = ekt-M; M, + 29–34 μm. Differs from pollen of *Sorbus aria* (4 coll.) in val structure and form of C, but rather similar grains occur in the related taxa *S. porrigentiformis* (1 coll.) and *S. lancastriensis* (1 coll.). In view of their present restricted geographical range the latter two species are considered unlikely to have occurred on Skye. The possibility must be considered, however, that the Late-Devensian and early Flandrian *S. rupicola* populations were not genetically identical with the present-day taxon. Four fossil grains.

Crassulaceae

Sedum cf. *S. rosea* (6 coll.). Pollina C3P3, Cα2b, Cβ2a, Cγ1, Pαb, tec, col incertus, str, val straight, forming intercrossing str (see interference-contrast micrographs by Sorsa, 1968); ex-M, + *ca.* 1–1.5 μm; polar-I small; M, + 18–21 μm. Rather similar grains occur in *Sedum villosum* (4 coll.) and *S. anglicum*

(3 coll.) but M, + 23–25 μm, whereas *S. telephium* (6 coll.), *S. acre* (3 coll.), and *S. forsteranum* (2 coll.) differ slightly in val structure. Ten fossil grains.

cf. *Sedum*. Pollina C3P3, Cβ2a, Cγ1, Pαb, tec, col incertus, psi to faintly rug-str, val very indistinct; ex-M, + 1 μm; polar-I small; M, + 20–23 μm. Due to the poor preservation of the sculptural features of the four fossil grains found at Lochan Coir' a' Ghobhainn, they are only tentatively referred to *Sedum*.

Saxifragaceae

The pollen morphology of all the native British members of the family represented in the available reference material is summarised in Table 8.5. The accounts by Faegri & Iversen (1964) and Fredskild (1967) have been useful. Since this work was completed, Ferguson & Webb (1970) have published a valuable account of the pollen morphology of the genus *Saxifraga* as a whole, with scanning electron micrographs of the pollen of some of the British species. Four fossil grains of *Saxifraga nivalis*, thirty-five fossil grains of *S. stellaris*, fifty-one fossil grains of *S. hypnoides*, nineteen fossil grains of *S. aizoides*, and twenty-four fossil grains of *S. oppositifolia* were found.

Droseraceae

Drosera cf. *D. intermedia*. In the pollen tetrads of *Drosera intermedia* (7 coll.) the ech are small (sculp alt, + < 2 μm) and rather uniform in shape and size, whereas the ech are markedly heterogeneous and of two size classes in the pollen tetrads of *D. rotundifolia* (6 coll.) and *D. anglica* (5 coll.). See Andersen (1961), Beug (1961), and Chanda (1965*a*). One fossil tetrad.

Elaeagnaceae

Hippophaë rhamnoides (3 coll.). Pollina C3P3, Cα1a, Pα3, tec, psi-sca, polar-I < 0.25, subsph, media. See Erdtman *et al.* (1961). One fossil grain.

Onagraceae (16 spp., 34 coll.)

Epilobium type. Pollina P3, Pα4, P-vest > 8 μm, magna. Includes *Epilobium* (11 spp., 19 coll.) and *Chamaenerion angustifolium* (4 coll.). Twenty fossil grains.

Callitrichaceae

Callitriche (4 spp., 4 coll.). Pollina inap or C3, intec, cla-bac with tendency to fuse into ret, ex-M, + < 1 μm, minuta. Two fossil grains.

Umbelliferae

A key to the pollen types within the family was prepared during this work. Cerceau's pollen morphological account (1959) is of limited use. The reference material examined comprises the following genera: *Sanicula*, *Eryngium* (2 spp.), *Chaerophyllum*, *Anthriscus* (2 spp.), *Scandix*, *Myrrhis*, *Torilis* (3 spp.), *Conium*, *Bupleurum* (3 spp.), *Trinia*, *Apium* (3 spp.), *Petroselinum* *Sison*, *Cicuta*, *Carum* (2 spp.), *Conopodium*, *Pimpinella* (2 spp.), *Sium*, *Berula*, *Crithmum*, *Seseli*, *Oenanthe* (7 spp.), *Silaum*, *Meum*, *Selinum*, *Ligusticum*, *Angelica*, *Peucedanum* (2 spp.), *Pastinaca*, *Heracleum*, and *Daucus*.

Sanicula europaea (4 coll.). Pollina C3P3, tr C, tec, psi-sca, C-Lg > 60% Lg; ex-M (pol), + > 2 μm; Lg/Lt, + 2.0–2.3; Lg 24–30 μm, irregular-shaped grain. One fossil grain.

Conopodium type. Pollina C3P3, tr C, tec, psi-sca, C-Lg 30–60% Lg; ex-M (pol), + > 2 μm; Lt/Lg, + *ca.* 2; Lg 22–28 μm, blunt poles. Includes *Conopodium majus* (3 coll.), *Anthriscus sylvestris* (4 coll.), and *Pimpinella major* p.p. (1 coll.). Three fossil grains.

Heracleum sphondylium (4 coll.). Pollina C3P3, tr C, tec; col-D, + 1–1.5 μm; sca, C-Lg 30–50% Lg; ex-M (pol), + > 2.5 μm; Lg/Lt, + 2–2.4; Lg > 32 μm, blunt poles. Eleven fossil grains.

Angelica type. Pollina C3P3, tr C, tec, psi-sca, C-Lg > 60% Lg; ex-M (pol), + > 2 μm; Lg/Lt, + 1.7–2.2; Lg 22–30 μm, blunt poles. Includes *Angelica sylvestris* (4 coll.), *Carum verticillatum* (2 coll.), *Meum athamanticum* (2 coll.), *Selinum carvifolia* (2 coll.), *Peucedanum officinale* (1 coll.), *Ligusticum scoticum* (4 coll.), and *Silaum silaus* (2 coll.).

Euphorbiaceae

Mercurialis perennis (3 coll.). Pollina C3P3, tr C, Cα4, semi-tec; col-D, + *ca.* 1 μm; ret-cla; lum-D, + *ca.* 1 μm; ex-M, + > 2 μm; ekt-M > end-M, subsph, media. The sculptural elements of this grain may be isolated (thin cla or bac) or partially fused at the extreme top (foc 1) to form a ret. Rather similar grains are found in *Mercurialis annua* (3 coll.; grain smaller and sculptural elements not fused at all; see Grüger, 1968) and *Viburnum lantana* (5 coll.; col-D, + > 1.5 μm, sculptural elements partially fused into ret). One fossil grain.

TABLE 8.5. *Morphological characteristics of modern pollen of the Saxifragaceae*

Species	Pollen type	Colpus structure	Sculpture and structure	Exine structure and thickness	M, +	No. of coll. examined
Saxifraga nivalis	C3	Cα2–Cα3a, Cβ 2a–Cβ3a, Cγ1	micro-ret, lum-D < 1.0 μm, lum ± circular, lum D < muri breadth; semi-tec col incertus. In some grains psi, tec perf	< 1.5 μm ekt-M = end M	19–23 μm	4
S. stellaris	C3	Cα3, Cβ2a–Cβ3a, Cγ1–Cγ2	micro-ret, lum D *ca.* 1 μm, lum irregular and angular; lum-D > muri breadth; semi-tec, col distinct; col-D, + < 0.5 μm	< 1.5 μm ekt-M = end-M	17–20 μm	6
S. hirculus	C3	Cα2, Cβ2a, Cγ2–Cγ3	sca ± rug-str; tec, col uniform, col-D, + ca. 1 μm	< 1.5 μm ekt-M > end-M	29–33 μm	2
S. spathularis	C3	Cα2, Cβ2a, Cγ2–Cγ3	sca ± rug-str; tec, col uniform; col-D, + *ca.* 1 μm	< 1.5 μm ekt-M > end-M	23–26 μm	1
S. hirsuta	C3	Cα2, Cβ2a, Cγ2–Cγ3	sca ± rug-str; tec, col uniform; col-D, + *ca.* 1 μm	> 1.5 μm ekt-M > end-M	23–26 μm	2
S. tridactylites	C3	Cα2, Cβ2a, Cγ2	sca ± rug-str; tec, col uniform; col-D, + *ca.* 1 μm	< 1.5 μm ekt-M > end-M	16–20 μm	2
S. granulata	C3	Cα2, Cβ2a, Cγ2–Cγ3, ± cost-C	sca; tec, col uniform; col-D, + < 1 μm	< 1.5 μm ekt-M > end-M	21–25 μm	4
S. cernua	C3 or C peri	Cα2, Cβ2a, Cγ2–Cγ3	sca ± rug-str; tec, col uniform; col-D, + ⩾ 1 μm	> 1.5 μm ekt-M > end-M	29–32 μm	1
S. rivularis	C3	Cα2, Cβ2a, Cγ2	sca ± rug-str; tec, col uniform; col-D, + ⩾ 1 μm	> 1.5 μm ekt-M > end-M	30–34 μm	3
S. cespitosa	C3 or C peri	Cα2, Cβ2a, Cγ2–Cγ3	sca ± micro-ech; tec, col uniform; col-D, + *ca.* 1 μm	> 1.5 μm ekt-M > end-M	27–31 μm	4
S. hypnoides	C3 or C peri	Cα2, Cβ2a, Cγ2–Cγ3	sca ± micro-ech; tec, col uniform; col-D, + > 1.5 μm	> 1.5 μm ekt-M > end-M	26–29 μm	4
S. aizoides	C3	Cα2, Cβ2a, Cγ2	rug-str, val coarse and discontinuous, often tr to C on two of inter C; tec, col not coincident with val	> 1.5 μm ekt-M > end-M	25–27 μm	6
S. oppositifolia	C3	Cα2–Cα3, Cβ2a, Cγ2	str, val delicate but distinct, often parallel to C on two of inter C; tec, col not coincident with val	< 1.5 μm ekt-M ⩾ end-M	24–26 μm	5
Chrysosplenium oppositifolium	C3	Cα2–Cα3, Cβ2, Cγ1	micro-ret, lum ± isodiametric, lum-D 0.5 μm; intec, col incertus. Polar tec perf	< 1.5 μm ekt-M = end-M	12–15 μm	3
C. alternifolium	C3	Cα2–Cα3, Cβ2, Cγ1	micro-ret, lum ± isodiametric, lum-D < 0.5 μm; intec, col incertus. Polar tec perf	< 1.5 μm ekt-M = end-M	12–15 μm	2

TABLE 8.6. *Morphological characteristics of modern pollen of* Oxyria digyna *and* Rumex *species*

Species	Pollen type	Pore structure	Sculpture and structure	Shape of lum or perf	Polar-I	M, +	No. of coll. examined
Oxyria digyna	C3P3 or C P peri	Pα1–Pα2, Pαa–Pαb (cost P moderate)	micro-ret, semi-tec; col distinct; col-D, + > 0.5 µm; lum-D > col-D. (Some grains psi or sca, tec perf, col distinct)	isodiametric, rounded	medium–small	18–28 µm	8
Rumex acetosella	C3P3 or C P peri	Pα2, Pαa (cost P moderate-thin)	micro-ret, semi-tec; col distinct; col-D, + < 0.5 µm; lum-D ≥ col-D	irregular, angular	small	18–22 µm	6
R. tenuifolius	C3P3 or C P peri	Pα2, Pαa (cost P moderate-thin)	micro-ret, semi-tec; col distinct; col-D, + < 0.5 µm; lum-D ≥ col-D	isodiametric, rounded	small	15–20 µm	2
R. acetosa	C3P3 or C P peri	Pα2, Pαb (cost P moderate-thin)	micro-ret, semi-tec; col distinct; col-D, + < 0.5 µm; lum-D ≥ col-D	irregular, angular	medium–large	15–20 µm	4
R. hydrolapathum	C3P3 or C P peri	Pα1–Pα4, Pαb (cost P moderate)	psi, tec perf; col distinct; col-D, + < 0.5 µm; col-D > perf-D	isodiametric	small	42–46 µm	4
R. aquaticus	C3P3 or C P peri	Pα1–Pα4, Pαb–Pαc (cost P moderate)	psi, tec perf; col distinct; col-D, + < 0.5 µm; col-D > perf D	isodiametric, rounded	small	38–45 µm	1
R. longifolius	C3P3 or C P peri	Pα1–Pα4, Pαb–Pαc (cost P moderate)	psi, tec perf; col distinct; col-D, + < 0.5 µm; col-D > perf-D	isodiametric	small	26–30 µm	3
R. crispus	C3P3 or C P peri	Pα1–Pα2, Pαa–Pαc (cost P thick)	psi, tec perf; col distinct; col-D, + < 0.5 µm; col-D ≥ perf-D	isodiametric, rounded	small	26–30 µm	3
R. obtusifolius	C3P3 or C P peri	Pα4, Pαc (cost P moderate)	psi, tec perf; col distinct; col-D, + < 0.5 µm; col-D > perf-D	irregular, angular	small	25–30 µm	2
R. pulcher	C3P3 or C P peri	Pα2–Pα4, Pαb–Pαc (cost P moderate)	micro-ret, semi-tec; col distinct; col-D, + < 0.5 µm; lum-D ≥ col-D	isodiametric, rounded	small	26–30 µm	4
R. sanguineus	C3P3 or C P peri	Pα1–Pα4, Pαc (cost P thin)	psi, tec perf; col distinct; col-D, + < 0.5 µm; col-D = perf-D	isodiametric, rounded	small	25–30 µm	1
R. conglomeratus	C3P3 or C P peri	Pα4, Pαb–Pαc (cost P moderate)	micro-ret, semi-tec, (some grains psi, tec perf); col distinct; col-D, + < 0.5 µm; col-D > perf-D (lum-D)	isodiametric, rounded	small	23–28 µm	2
R. rupestris	C3P3	Pα1–Pα4, Pαb (cost P moderate)	psi, tec perf; col distinct; col-D, + < 0.5 µm; col-D = perf-D	isodiametric	small	25–30 µm	1
R. palustris	C3P3 or C P peri	Pα2, Pαb–Pαc (cost P moderate)	psi, tec perf; col distinct; col-D, + < 0.5 µm; col-D < perf-D	isodiametric, rounded	small	26–32 µm	2
R. maritimus	C3P3 or C P peri	Pα2, Pαc (cost P moderate)	psi, tec perf, (some grains micro-ret, semi-tec); col distinct; col-D, + *ca.* 0.5 µm; col-D ≥ perf-D (lum-D)	isodiametric, rounded	small	25–30 µm	2

Polygonaceae

Koenigia islandica (3 coll.). Pollina P peri (PΣ12–14), Pα2, Pαa–Pαc, Pβ2, Pγ1; P-Lg, + 3 μm; P-Lt, + 1 μm or less; tec, ech; sculp-alt, + 0.5–1 μm; subsph, minuta. See Hafsten (1958) and Hedberg (1946). Rather similar grains are found in *Sagittaria sagittifolia* (4 coll.; Pαb, Pβ1, media). Three fossil grains.

Polygonum viviparum/P. bistorta. Pollina C3P3, Pαc, Pβ1–Pβ2, tec, col heterogeneous and branched, col coarsest towards pol, perf scattered, psi-sca or fov; ex-M(pol), + 3–4 μm; ex-M(aeq), + 2–3 μm; Lg/Lt, + >1.2; M, + >30 μm. See Florin (1969) and Hedberg (1946). Includes *Polygonum viviparum* (6 coll.) and *P. bistorta* (6 coll.). Twenty-one fossil grains.

Rumex and *Oxyria*. The morphology of the pollen of the native British members of these genera represented in the available reference material is summarised in Table 8.6. Two fossil grains were found of *Rumex crispus* type (includes *Rumex longifolius*, *R. crispus*, *R. obtusifolius*, *R. sanguineus*, *R. conglomeratus* p.p., *R. rupestris*, *R. palustris*, and *R. maritimus* p.p.), as well as a very large number of fossil grains of *Oxyria digyna* and *Rumex acetosa*.

Urticaceae

Urtica. Pollina P3, intec, sca (gran inord); ex-M, + <1 μm; subsph, minuta. P protrude slightly with thin cost P. Includes *Urtica urens* (2 coll.) and *U. dioica* (3 coll.). Specific determinations are only possible with phase contrast optics (see Andersen, 1961; Krog, 1954). Rather similar grains are found in *Parietaria diffusa* (3 coll.) but they differ in P structure.

Betulaceae

Betula cf. *B. nana*. The problems of distinguishing the pollen of *Betula nana* from the pollen of the tree species of *Betula* in a form suitable for statistical pollen analysis are discussed by Berglund & Digerfeldt (1970) and Birks (1968). Throughout the present work measurements of grain diameter and of grain diameter: pore depth have been made on all fossil *Betula* grains encountered during routine analysis (Σ = 5246 grains), except for a small number (Σ = 192, 3.6% of the total) that were too badly deteriorated (mainly crumpled and corroded) to permit such measurements. Fossil grains of *Betula* cf. *B. nana* have been distinguished on the basis of both grain size and pore depth (see Birks, 1968). *Betula* undiff. includes all other grains referable to the genus.

Corylaceae

Corylus avellana. Although all the fossil grains encountered appear to fall within the range of morphological variation of the modern reference material of *Corylus avellana* (8 coll.; small endopore and ± rugulate sculpturing with a few scattered micro-ech – see Praglowski (1962), the scanning electron micrographs by Pilcher (1968), and the electron micrographs of carbon replicas by Bradley (1958)), the possibility that some of the fossil grains originate from *Myrica gale* (10 coll.) cannot be entirely excluded on morphological criteria alone, especially if the fossil grains are deteriorated in some way, particularly as a result of exine degradation and/or corrosion.

Salicaceae

Populus tremula (5 coll.). Pollina inap, intec, sca-ret; ex-M, + <1.5 μm; subsph. Ekt is often broken into irregular patches or groups of granules by small rifts (see Müller-Stoll, 1956). Gran-D varies from *ca.* 0.5 μm to less than 0.1 μm, and is thus close to the resolution limits of visible-light microscopy. Gran are irregularly spaced, but are usually closely crowded. Gran may be pointed (micro-ech) or rounded (micro-bac), and may be either isolated and distinct, or partially fused together to form small irregular patches of tec, or even a rough ret. See electron micrographs by Rowley & Erdtman (1967).

Salix cf. *S. herbacea* (4 coll.). Pollina C3, semi-tec, col incertus, ret, distinct mg; lum-D, + >1 μm; muri with irregular thickenings, minuta. See Faegri (1953), Faegri & Iversen (1964), and Florin (1969). This is a variable pollen type, and only tentative determinations appear possible until more is known of the pollen morphological variation within the genus.

Salix undiff. Several morphologically distinct pollen types are recognisable in the fossil material, but the available reference material (18 spp., 35 coll.) is too limited and too variable to allow further determination.

Ericaceae (20 spp., 98 coll.)

No distinctions, other than *Calluna vulgaris* (7 coll., irregular tetrad, short C, often CΣ4 per single grain, ver; see Beug, 1961 and Oldfield, 1959), were made within this rather heterogeneous group. The pollen category Ericaceae undiff. may thus include tetrads of several taxa within the Ericaceae, plus *Pyrola minor* (2 coll.), *P. media* (1 coll.), *P. rotundifolia* (4 coll.), and *Moneses uniflora* (4 coll.) of the Pyrolaceae, and even poorly preserved tetrads from taxa within the Empetraceae. In well preserved material (for example in the modern pollen rain studies) *Vaccinium* type pollen (Andersen, 1961; Fredskild, 1967; Menke, 1963) was distinguished by polar-I medium, psi, media. Includes *Andromeda polifolia* p.p. (6 coll.), *Vaccinium vitis-idaea* (4 coll.), *V. myrtillus* (5 coll.), *V. uliginosum* (4 coll.), *V. oxycoccus* (6 coll.), *V. microcarpon* (1 coll.), *Pyrola media* p.p. (1 coll.), and *Pyrola minor* p.p. (2 coll.).

Empetraceae

Empetrum cf. *E. nigrum*. Tetrads of *Empetrum* can generally be distinguished in well-preserved fossil material by the short and irregular C, the absence of cost C, the sca sculpture, and end-M > ekt-M (see Beug, 1961, and Oldfield, 1959). Specific distinctions between the tetrads of the diploid *Empetrum nigrum* and of the tetraploid *E. hermaphroditum* require size statistics (see Andersen, 1961; Beug, 1957; Faegri, 1945; Jessen, 1949). For the available reference material tetrads of *E. nigrum* (6 coll., 50 tetrads each) have a size range of 24.7–36.4 μm, with a mean of 28.30 μm ($s = 3.73$ μm), whereas tetrads of *E. hermaphroditum* (5 coll., 50 tetrads each) have a size range of 29.9–46.8 μm (mean = 40.32 μm; $s = 3.82$ μm). Although all the fossil tetrads encountered that could be measured ($\Sigma = 1479$ tetrads) were less than 36.4 μm in greatest diameter, they can only be tentatively referred to *E. nigrum* s.s. because of the considerable overlap in tetrad size within the modern reference material.

Plumbaginaceae

Armeria maritima. Twenty seven fossil grains of both the 'A' and 'B' morphological types (see Erdtman *et al.*, 1961; Iversen, 1940; Praglowski & Erdtman, 1969) were found in the ratio of 1:3.5. *Armeria maritima* (7 coll.) is the most likely taxon concerned, although *Limonium* (4 spp., 13 coll.) cannot be disregarded on pollen morphological criteria.

Primulaceae (16 spp., 43 coll.)

Primula. Pollina C stp (CΣ4–10), semi-tec, ret, polar-I large. Includes *Primula veris* (3 coll.), *P. elatior* (3 coll.), and *P. vulgaris* (2 coll.). Three grains in surface samples.

Scrophulariaceae (55 spp., 123 coll.)

Veronica (16 spp., 39 coll.). Pollina C3, Cβ2a, tec, psi; col-D, + 0.5–1 μm; polar-I medium; ex-M, + > 1.5 μm; subsph, media. Rather similar grains are found in *Euphrasia* (8 spp., 15 coll.) and *Rhinanthus* (2 spp., 5 coll.), but they differ from *Veronica* in polar-I, ex-M, +, and col-D, +. See Andersen (1961). Two fossil grains.

Pedicularis (2 spp., 6 coll.). Pollina C syn (CΣ2), C fused in a ring, Cγ1, tec perf, col incertus, psi, subsph, minuta-media. See Beug (1961). One fossil grain.

Melampyrum (4 spp., 12 coll.). Pollina C3, Cα1a, Cβ2, Cγ1, tec, col incertus in inter C, psi, polar-I small, subsph, rather octangular in equatorial view, minuta. See Faegri & Iversen (1964). Twenty-eight fossil grains.

Labiatae (46 spp., 110 coll.)

Thymus type. (*Mentha* type of Andersen, 1961, and Faegri & Iversen, 1964). Pollina C stp (CΣ6), semi-tec, ret, polar-I medium, subsph, media. Includes *Mentha* (5 spp., 7 coll.), *Lycopus europaeus* (3 coll.), *Origanum vulgare* (2 coll.), *Thymus* (3 spp., 8 coll.), *Calamintha* (3 spp., 3 coll.), *Acinos arvensis* (2 coll.), and *Clinopodium vulgare* (3 coll.). Twenty-nine fossil grains.

Plantaginaceae

The accounts of the pollen morphology of the family by Andersen (1961) and Faegri & Iversen (1964) have been valuable. Table 8.7 summarises the major distinctions of pollen morphology of the British species as seen in the available reference material (see also Bassett & Crompton, 1968, and electron micrographs of carbon replicas by Bradley, 1958).

Plantago major/*P. media*. Pollen of *Plantago major* and *P. media* are not readily distinguishable from each other in fossil condition, but all those fossil grains that were determinable are referred to *Plantago major*.

Plantago lanceolata. The occurrence of annulate and operculate pollen within the *Plantago maritima* complex in northern and central Europe, Greenland, and North America (Andersen, 1961) necessitates the analysis of pore numbers to effectively separate pollen of *P. lanceolata* from annulate pollen

TABLE 8.7. *Morphological characteristics of modern polle n of* Littorella uniflora *and* Plantago *species*

Species	Pore number	Pore delimitation and structure	Verrucae	Scabrate elements	M, +	No. of coll. examined
Plantago major	(4)5–8(9)	Pβ1a; Pγ2	distinct	indistinct or absent; psi	19–25	5
P. media	(4)5–7(8)	Pβ1a, rarely Pβ2; Pγ2	very distinct and coarse	distinct	18–26	9
P. lanceolata	(7)8–12(14)	Pβ3b; Pγ3	± diffuse–distinct	very distinct; micro-ech	12–28	5
P. maritima	(3)5–8(9)	Pβ2; Pγ2	± diffuse–absent	very distinct; micro-ech	22–29	12
P. coronopus	(4)5–8(9)	Pβ3b; Pγ3, rarely Pγ2	distinct–diffuse	minute	23–28	3
Littorella uniflora	(6)7–14(15)	Pβ2, rarely Pβ1a or Pβ3; Pγ2	distinct–diffuse	indistinct or absent	29–36	6

of taxa within the *P. maritima* complex (for example *P. alpina* L., *P. serpentina* All.). In Fig. 11 the frequency distributions of pore numbers for modern reference material of *P. lanceolata* (9 coll., 100 grains each; Andersen, 1961) are compared with the pore numbers of the twenty-two fossil annulate *Plantago* grains found. The fossil grains have a mean pore number of 9.95 (s = 0.84 pores; range = 8–12 pores), and they clearly fall within the observed range of modern *P. lanceolata* pollen, to which they are thus referred.

Plantago maritima s.s. 188 fossil grains of *Plantago maritima* were recorded during routine analysis. They have a mean pore number of 6.15 (s = 0.69 pores; range = 4–9 pores). By comparison with the pore numbers of pollen of modern reference material (Fig. 11 and Andersen, 1961), all the fossil grains can be referred to the north European taxon *P. maritima* L. So far, all plants examined from coastal and inland populations in the British Isles (12 coll.) have pollen with non-annulate pores. Further reference material is required, however, in view of the old records of *P. alpina* and *P. serpentina* growing in the Scottish Highlands (White, 1869; see also Gregor, 1939). No reliable pollen morphological differences are discernable in plants from inland and coastal habitats in Britain, because of the clinal variation within the British populations (Gregor, 1938).

Campanulaceae

Campanula type. Pollina P3 or P stp (PΣ4), ech; sculp-alt, + *ca.* 1 μm; ex-M, + < 2 μm; subsph, media. Includes *Campanula* (5 spp., 15 coll.), *Legousia hybrida* (2 coll.), and *Phyteuma* (2 spp., 6 coll.). Rather similar grains are found in *Jasione montana* (6 coll.; sculp-alt, + < 1 μm; M, + 18–25 μm) and *Wahlenbergia hederacea* (4 coll.; sculp-alt, + < 1 μm; M, + 16–23 μm). See Birks & Ransom (1969). Four fossil grains.

Rubiaceae

Pollina C stp (CΣ6–10), tec, psi-sca, minuta. Includes *Sherardia arvensis* (3 coll.), *Asperula cynanchica* (3 coll.), *Galium* (13 spp., 29 coll.), and *Rubia peregrina* (2 coll.).

Caprifoliaceae

Viburnum opulus (4 coll.). Pollina C3P3, Cβ3a, ± tr C, cost C moderate, PαC, semi-tec; col-D, + > 1.5 μm; ret; lum-D, + > 1.5 μm, homobrochate; ex-M, + > 1.5 μm; ekt-M *ca.* = end-M, subsph, media. Rather similar grains are found in *Viburnum lantana* (5 coll.; col only partially fused into ret). One fossil grain.

Valerianaceae

Valeriana officinalis (3 coll.). Pollen of *Valeriana officinalis* differs from pollen of *V. dioica* (3 coll.) in sculp-alt, + 0.5–1.5 μm, rather than 2.0–2.5 μm in *V. dioica*. See Wagenitz (1956). Thirteen fossil grains.

Compositae (101 spp., 239 coll.)

The pollen morphology of the family has been considered by Stix (1960) and Erdtman *et al.* (1961).

Ambrosia type. Pollina C3P3, Cβ2b, tec; col-D, + < 0.5 μm; ech; sculp-alt, + > 1–2 μm; polar-I very

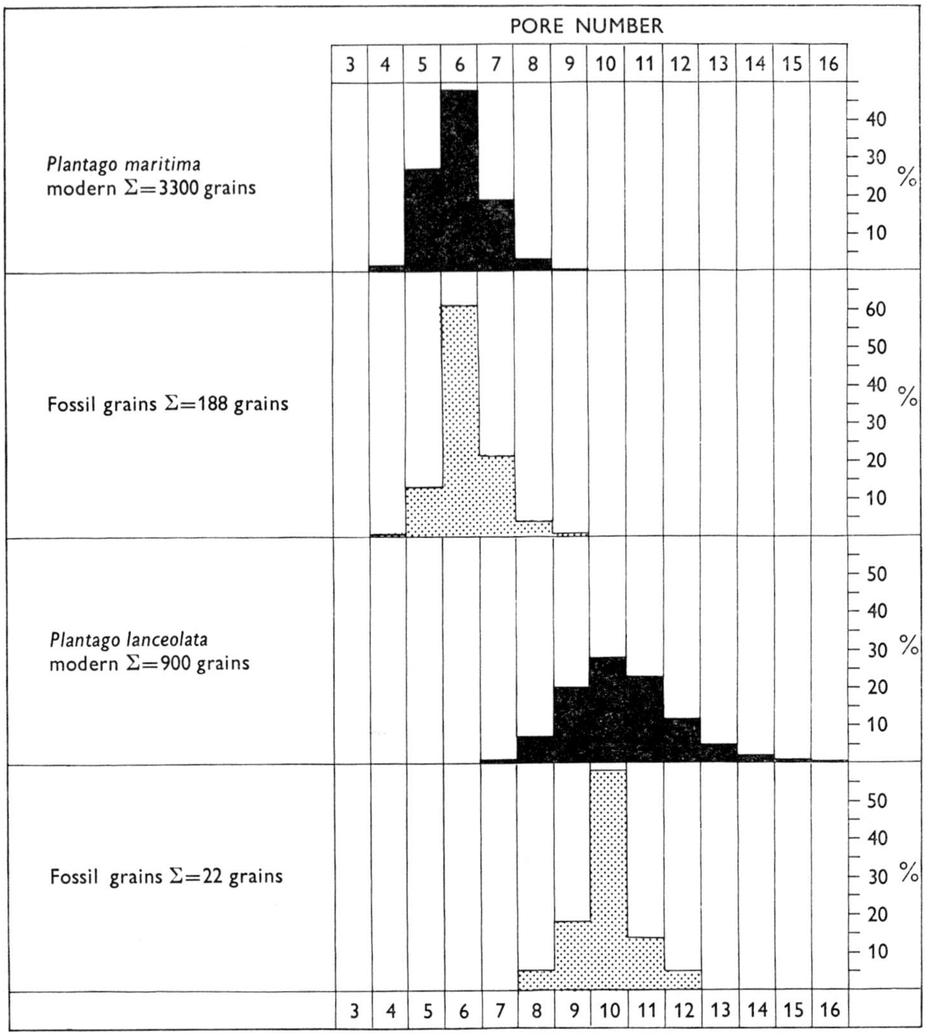

Figure 11. Pore number–frequency distribution in modern pollen of *Plantago maritima* and *P. lanceolata* (black) and of fossil pollen (shaded). The number of pollen grains examined is also shown.

large, subsph, minuta. See Cushing (1963). Includes *Ambrosia* L. (9 spp., 18 coll.), *Franseria* Cav. (8 spp., 11 coll.), and *Iva axillaris* Pursh (2 coll.). Rather similar grains are found in *Iva xanthifolia* Nutt. (3 coll.; polar-I medium), *I. dealbata* Gray (1 coll.; polar-I medium), *I. ciliata* Willd. (3 coll.; col-D, + >1 μm), *I. frutescens* L. (4 coll.; col-D, + >1 μm), *I. imbricata* Walt. (3 coll.; col-D, + >1 μm). *I. angustifolia* (1 coll.; col-D, + >1 μm), *I. microcephala* Nutt. (1 coll.; col-D, + >1 μm), and *Xanthium* (4 spp., 5 coll.; sculp-alt, + <1 μm, cav). One fossil grain.

Antennaria type. Pollina C3P3, tec, ech; sculp-alt, + <2 μm; ex-M, + <4 μm, subsph, media. Includes *Gnaphalium* (5 spp., 10 coll.), *Filago* (3 spp., 4 coll.), and *Antennaria dioica* (2 coll.). Thirteen fossil grains.

Achillea type. Pollina C3P3, tec, ech; sculp-alt, + >3 μm; ex-M, + >3 μm; col coarse and often branched, subsph, minuta-media. Includes *Anthemis* (2 spp., 3 coll.), *Chamaemelum nobile* (1 coll.), *Achillea* (2 spp., 8 coll.), *Otanthus maritimus* (2 coll.), *Tripleurospermum maritimum* (3 coll.), *Matricaria recutita* (2 coll.), and *Chrysanthemum* (4 spp., 8 coll.). Two fossil grains.

Artemisia cf. *A. norvegica*. Pollen of *Artemisia norvegica* (8 coll.) differs from pollen of all other European species of *Artemisia* so far examined (22 spp., 30 coll.) in the reference collections at Cambridge and Copenhagen in their larger and more prominent ech (sculp-alt 0.6–0.9 μm), thicker ex (ex-M, + >3.5 μm), and larger grain size (M, + 24–28 μm). See Erdtman *et al.* (1961). There is, however, considerable variation in grain morphology within the rather limited reference material examined, and not all grains of modern *A. norvegica* are so markedly ech, and are thus indistinguishable from pollen of other *Artemisia* species. In view of this variation, it is felt to be advisable at this stage to keep the specific determinations of the fossil grains tentative until more is known of the systematic variation in pollen morphology within the genus.

Cirsium/Carduus. Pollina C3P3, tec, ech; sculp-alt, + > 5 μm; ex-M, + > 5 μm; subsph, media-magna. Includes *Carduus* (3 spp., 7 coll.) and *Cirsium* (8 spp., 20 coll.). Eighteen fossil grains.

Saussurea alpina (9 coll.). Pollina C3P3, tec, col heterogeneous and of irregular shape; col-D, + > 2 μm; ech; sculp-alt, + 1–3 μm; ex-M, + > 6 μm; subsph; M, + 35–45 μm. See Seddon (1962). Rather similar grains are found in *Carlina vulgaris* (3 coll.; col homogeneous; col-D, + < 2 μm; sculp-alt, + < 1 μm), *Serratula tinctoria* (3 coll.; sculp-alt, + > 2 μm), and *Arctium* (2 spp., 6 coll.; M, + 30–34 μm).

Solidago type. Pollina C3P3, tec, ech; sculp-alt, + 2–3 μm; ex-M, + 3–4 μm; subsph, media. Includes *Senecio* (10 spp., 17 coll.), *Tussilago farfara* (3 coll.), *Petasites hybridus* (2 coll.), *Inula* (3 spp., 3 coll.), *Pulicaria* (2 spp., 3 coll.), *Solidago virgaurea* (4 coll.), *Aster* (2 spp., 7 coll.), *Erigeron* (2 spp., 6 coll.), *Bellis perennis* (4 coll.), and *Eupatorium cannabinum* (2 coll.).

Liguliflorae. Pollina Fen, ech. Includes *Cichorium intybus* (3 coll.), *Lapsana communis* (3 coll.), *Hypochoeris* (3 spp., 5 coll.), *Leontodon* (3 spp., 8 coll.), *Picris* (2 spp., 3 coll.), *Tragopogon pratensis* (3 coll.), *Lactuca* (3 spp., 5 coll), *Mycelis muralis* (2 coll.), *Sonchus* (4 spp., 9 coll.), *Cicerbita alpina* (4 coll.), *Hieracium* (2 spp., 4 coll.), *Crepis* (5 spp., 10 coll.), and *Taraxacum* (4 spp., 6 coll.).

Alismataceae

The major distinctions in pollen morphology of the British species within the family are summarised in Table 8.8. See also Andersen (1961). Two fossil grains were referred to *Sagittaria sagittifolia*.

Potamogetonaceae

Potamogeton type. Pollina inap, semi-tec, col ± distinct, ret; lum-D, + *ca.* 1 μm; lum angular in shape, minuta-media. Includes *Potamogeton* (subgenus *Potamogeton;* 18 spp., 25 coll.), *Groenlandia densa* (2 coll.), and *Triglochin* (2 spp., 6 coll.). Reliable determinations of *Triglochin* pollen only appear possible with phase contrast optics (see Beug, 1961; Faegri & Iversen, 1964).

Potamogeton (Subgenus *Coleogeton*). Pollina inap, intec, cla-bac, gran scattered, forming indistinct ret; lum-D, + < 1 μm; lum round in shape, subsph, minuta-media. See Beug (1961) and Faegri & Iversen (1964). Includes *Potamogeton filiformis* (1 coll.) and *P. pectinatus* (3 coll.). Thirty-two fossil grains.

Sparganiaceae

Sparganium type. Pollina P1, ret, subsph, media. See Beug (1961). Includes *Typha angustifolia* (2 coll.), monads of *T. latifolia* (3 coll.), and *Sparganium* (4 spp., 12 coll.). There is considerable variation within the rather limited reference material examined, and no reliable separation of *Typha* pollen from *Sparganium* pollen appears possible (see Andersen, 1961).

Sparganium cf. *S. minimum* (3 coll.). Pollina P1, ret, heterobrochate, muri markedly thicker than in other taxa; lum-D, + 1–3 μm; subsph, media. Ten fossil grains.

Cyperaceae (96 spp., 169 coll.)

The pollen morphological account of this family by Faegri & Iversen (1964) has been useful. In general the Cyperaceae grains were badly crumpled in the fossil material, and only a small percentage (generally < 10% or less) were well enough preserved to permit further determination. Three morphological types were observed in the fossil material, but no attempt has been made to separate them quantitatively.

Carex type (Faegri & Iversen, 1964). Pollina inap or P1, tec, perf with 3–6 lac, lac usually circular; M, + 26–38 μm. Includes *Eriophorum* (4 spp., 9 coll.), *Scirpus sylvaticus* (2 coll.), *Trichophorum cespitosum* (2 coll.), *Kobresia simpliciuscula* (2 coll.), and all species of *Carex* examined (64 spp., 105 coll.) except *C. hirta* (3 coll.). The distinctions between *Carex* and *Eriophorum* pollen (see Faegri & Iversen, 1964) do not appear possible in the reference material examined (cf. Fredskild, 1967). This pollen type occurs in all the pollen zones at all the sites examined.

Schoenoplectus type (Faegri & Iversen, 1964). Pollina inap or P1, tec, perf with 3–5 lac. Length of lac > 40% Lg; M, + 40–55 μm. Includes *Schoenoplectus americanus* (1 coll.), *S. lacustris* (4 coll.), *S. tabernaemontani* (2 coll.), *Holoschoenus vulgaris* (3 coll.), *Eleocharis palustris*

TABLE 8.8. *Morphological characteristics of modern pollen of the Alismataceae*

Species	Pollen type	Pore number	Pore form and delimitation	Structure and sculpture	Grain shape	P-M, +	M, +	No. of coll. examined
Baldellia ranunculoides	P peri	9–14	Pαb, Pβ2	tec; sca, col in inter P arranged into micro-ret	polyhedric–rounded	2–3 μm	22–26 μm	2
Luronium natans	P peri	12–18	Pαb, Pβ3a	tec; sca ± micro-ech, col heterogeneous, coarse in inter P, with tendency to form irregular ret, fine col forming indistinct anl	polyhedric	2.5–4 μm	23–25 μm	2
Alisma plantago-aquatica	P peri	10–15	Pαb, Pβ3a –Pβ3b	tec; sca, col in inter P arranged into micro-ret; lum-D, + < 0.5 μm; fine col forming broad and usually distinct anl	polyhedric	3–4 μm	22–26 μm	2
A. lanceolatum	P peri	10–15	Pαb, Pβ2–Pβ3a	tec; sca, col irregularly scattered, col in inter P tend to form indistinct ret, fine col forming diffuse, broad anl	polyhedric	3–4 μm	25–30 μm	2
Damasonium alisma	P peri	8–13	Pαb, Pβ2	tec; sca, col evenly distributed, with some tendency to form micro-ret in inter P	polyhedric–rounded	3–4 μm	28–32 μm	2
Sagittaria sagittifolia	P peri	8–12	Pαb, Pβ1	tec; ech; sculp-alt, + *ca.* 1 μm; col evenly distributed	rounded	3–4 μm	25–28 μm	4

(3 coll.), and *E. parvula* (1 coll.). This pollen type occurs rather rarely at all the sites examined, and only in pollen zones LML-5, LF-6, LM-7, LCC-7, and LCG-5.

Eleocharis type. (*Schoenus* type of Faegri & Iversen, 1964). Pollina inap or P1, tec, perf with 3–5 lac. Length of lac >40% Lg; M, + 22–37 μm. Includes *Eleocharis acicularis* (3 coll.), *E. quinqueflora* (3 coll.), *E. multicaulis* (1 coll.), *E. uniglumis* (1 coll.), *E. austriaca* (1 coll.), *Blysmus rufus* (1 coll.), *B. compressus* (1 coll.), *Schoenoplectus triquetrus* (1 coll.), *Isolepis cernua* (1 coll.), *Eleogiton fluitans* (1 coll.), *Cyperus fuscus* (1 coll.), *C. longus* (2 coll.), *Schoenus nigricans* (3 coll.), *S. ferrugineus* (1 coll.), and *Rhynchospora fusca* (3 coll.). Grains of this pollen type are very rare at all the sites, and are only found in pollen zones LML-5, LF-6, LM-7, LCC-7, and LCG-5.

5. UNIDENTIFIED TYPES

Unknown

The unknown category comprises those spores and pollen grains that are preserved well enough to allow recognition of their essential morphological features, but that cannot be assigned with confidence to any known taxon below the rank of order. Many of the unknown types are probably derived from unfamiliar, extant or extinct taxa not represented in the reference collections, but some may represent immature or aberrant grains of familiar taxa. Each unknown grain can be classified as a distinct type that can be identified when it occurs again. Table 8.9 summarises the occurrence of these unknown types at the five sites investigated.

TABLE 8.9. *Occurrence of unknown pollen and spore types*

Site	Number of unknown pollen grains and spores	Number of unknown morphological types
Loch Meodal	3	3
Loch Fada	5	5
Loch Mealt	3	3
Loch Cill Chriosd	14	6
Lochan Coir' a' Ghobhainn	7	4
Total at five sites	32 grains	13 discrete types

Indeterminable

Pollen grains and spores may be indeterminable because their essential morphological features are in some way indiscernible, preventing their confident assignment to any pollen or spore type, known or unknown. Unlike the grains or spores that are classed as unknown, indeterminable grains cannot be differentiated into distinct pollen or spore types. Pollen grains or spores may be indeterminable for several reasons, and they can be grouped accordingly.

(i) *Indeterminable: concealed.* Concealed grains are those whose critical morphological features are obscured, in some way, by organic or inorganic debris (see Neves & Sullivan, 1964) that surrounds or adheres to them. Grains that cannot be turned to a suitable orientation for critical examination are also included in this class. This class corresponds to the *a.i.l.* (*ad indeterminable latitans*) group of Fredskild (1967) and Jørgensen (1963).

(ii) *Indeterminable: deteriorated.* Deteriorated pollen grains are those whose exines have undergone changes so great that the essential morphological features of structure, sculpture, or apertures cannot be resolved with any confidence. At least four distinct types of pollen deterioration can be recognised in the fossil material examined (see also H. J. B. Birks, 1970; Cushing, 1964*b*, 1967*b*).

(a) *Corrosion.* Corroded grains are those whose exines are affected by a distinctive pitting or etching. The corroded areas tend to be randomly scattered on pollen grain or spore surface, and typically the corrosion only appears to affect the ektexine, or the outer layer of a spore wall. Corrosion must normally be severe, with most of the ektexine or spore wall destroyed, before the grain or spore becomes indeterminable. Slight corrosion of apertures may, however, result in serious identification problems, for example in distinguishing between *Betula* and *Corylus* pollen. Typically corroded pollen grains are illustrated by Elsik (1966, Plate 1; 1968, Plate 1; 1971) and by Havinga (1964, Plate 2; 1967, Figures 1, 2; 1971).

(b) *Degradation.* Degraded grains are those whose structural and sculptural features cannot be resolved. The entire exine is generally affected by this condition, and most degraded grains are indeterminable. In extreme cases (as in the lower samples at Loch Cill Chriosd), the pollen wall may appear completely amorphous, so that it becomes increasingly difficult to distinguish such grains from other organic particles with any degree of confidence, thereby introducing a degree of subjectivity into the numerical analysis. A structural rearrangement of the pollen wall appears to occur in degradation, for structural elements frequently seem to be partially fused, but without any noticeable loss of pollen wall substance (cf. corrosion). The reaction of exines to staining appears to be affected, to some degree, by degradation (cf. Stanley, 1966), but this point is largely unexplored.

(c) *Breakage.* Broken grains are those that are fragmented, or whose exines are badly broken, crushed, or ruptured.

(d) *Crumpling.* Crumpled grains are those that are badly folded, wrinkled, twisted, or collapsed. This group corresponds to the *a.i.p.* (*ad indeterminabile plicatum*) class of Fredskild (1967) and Jørgensen (1963) whereas their *a.i.d.* (*ad indeterminabile destructum*) category appears to include the broken, degraded, and corroded groups.

In practice these four types of pollen deterioration are not mutually exclusive, and any one grain or spore may be affected by two or more kinds of deterioration. During routine analysis such grains or spores were only recorded as indeterminable: deteriorated, but a note of the kind or kinds of exine deterioration present was made.

The problems of pollen and spore identification become most critical when preservation is poor, as discussed by Cushing (1967*b*). In such cases, the reliability of the pollen counts may be less than for samples where the preservation is good. It is therefore essential to indicate the reliability of the pollen counts, both within a single stratigraphical section and between sections. This is most readily done by recording the three major categories of unidentified types, namely unknown, indeterminable: concealed, and indeterminable: deteriorated. This has been done in all the routine analyses from Loch Meodal, Loch Fada, Loch Cill Chriosd, and Lochan Coir' a' Ghobhainn. Indeterminable grains and unknown types are the residue of problems of identification that the pollen analyst should continually strive to reduce, and the documentation and inclusion of the frequencies of these types of unidentified pollen in the results of the analyses give some measure of the analyst's success and of the degree and extent of pollen deterioration in the samples examined.

9

THE VEGETATION AND STRATIGRAPHY OF THE INVESTIGATED SITES

The Isle of Skye is readily divisible into six geographic and topographic units (see Fig. 5), each with a range of differing soil types. Each region supports a distinctive flora and a variety of different plant communities which appear to be related to its geology and soils, as discussed in Chapters 4 and 5. The correspondence between the distribution of the modern flora and vegetation and the geological and edaphic conditions suggests that similar geological controls may have existed during Late-Devensian time. The Isle of Skye includes several freshwater lochs containing sediments, and these provide suitable sites for the application of pollen analysis as a palaeoecological tool for the reconstruction of the past flora and vegetation within a specific geographical area.

The selection of sites for sampling and subsequent study was designed to test the hypothesis that the Late-Devensian flora and vegetation were highly diverse on a small scale within Skye, and to discover whether the variations in the pollen assemblages could be related to the local geological and edaphic conditions. A further criterion of the site selection was that a minimum number of sites should yield a maximum amount of pertinent information.

The principal aim of the palaeoecological investigations was to study the spatial variation and differentiation in the flora and vegetation in regions of differing physical conditions at specific points in time during the Late-Devensian and early Flandrian, in order to study the relationships between the plant cover and the physical aspects of the landscape, and thus to investigate the controls imposed by geology, soil types, and other ecological factors on the pattern of the Late-Devensian flora and vegetation. A secondary aim was to study the temporal changes in the Late-Devensian flora and vegetation by stratigraphical observations at specific points in space, and to consider the possible causes and mechanisms of such changes. The study of spatial variation requires the detailed sampling and comparative study of sediments of about the same age from sites in the main geological and topographical regions on Skye. Ideally the sediments should represent intervals of time sufficiently short that regional environmental changes are minimal. The study of temporal variation requires detailed sampling and stratigraphical study at sites chosen for their close relationships in space and time to geomorphic, glacial, and other environmental events. Careful and independent time control is essential for both types of study, but the site selection may necessarily differ.

Possible sites for study were selected in each of the six geological and topographical regions on the Isle of Skye (Fig. 5). Since the project was primarily concerned with detecting vegetational differentiation between areas, sites of comparable basin size (cf. Maher, 1963; Tauber, 1965), morphometry, and catchment area were chosen as far as possible, but in the absence of a boat, corings were limited to lochs with marginal fens, thereby restricting the number of suitable sites. After trial borings in a large number of fens, five sites of medium size were chosen for detailed study. The position of these sites in relation to the six geological and topographical regions is shown in Fig. 12. The figure also shows the location of Loch Cuithir, a site studied by Vasari & Vasari (1968), and of An Sgùman, a site on the western slopes of the Cuillins that has been briefly examined and where the pollen stratigraphy is relevant to temporal changes in the landscape. Details of each of five principal sites are included in the relevant sections of this chapter, but some comments on their general distribution are appropriate here.

Two sites (Loch Mealt and Loch Fada) in the exposed basaltic Trotternish Peninsula were selected for study. Both sites lie within a similar geological complex of basalts, dolerite sills, and underlying Jurassic rocks. The two sites were chosen to permit comparisons to be made between sites of differing topographical settings within the same geological formations. Loch Fada is surrounded by steep,

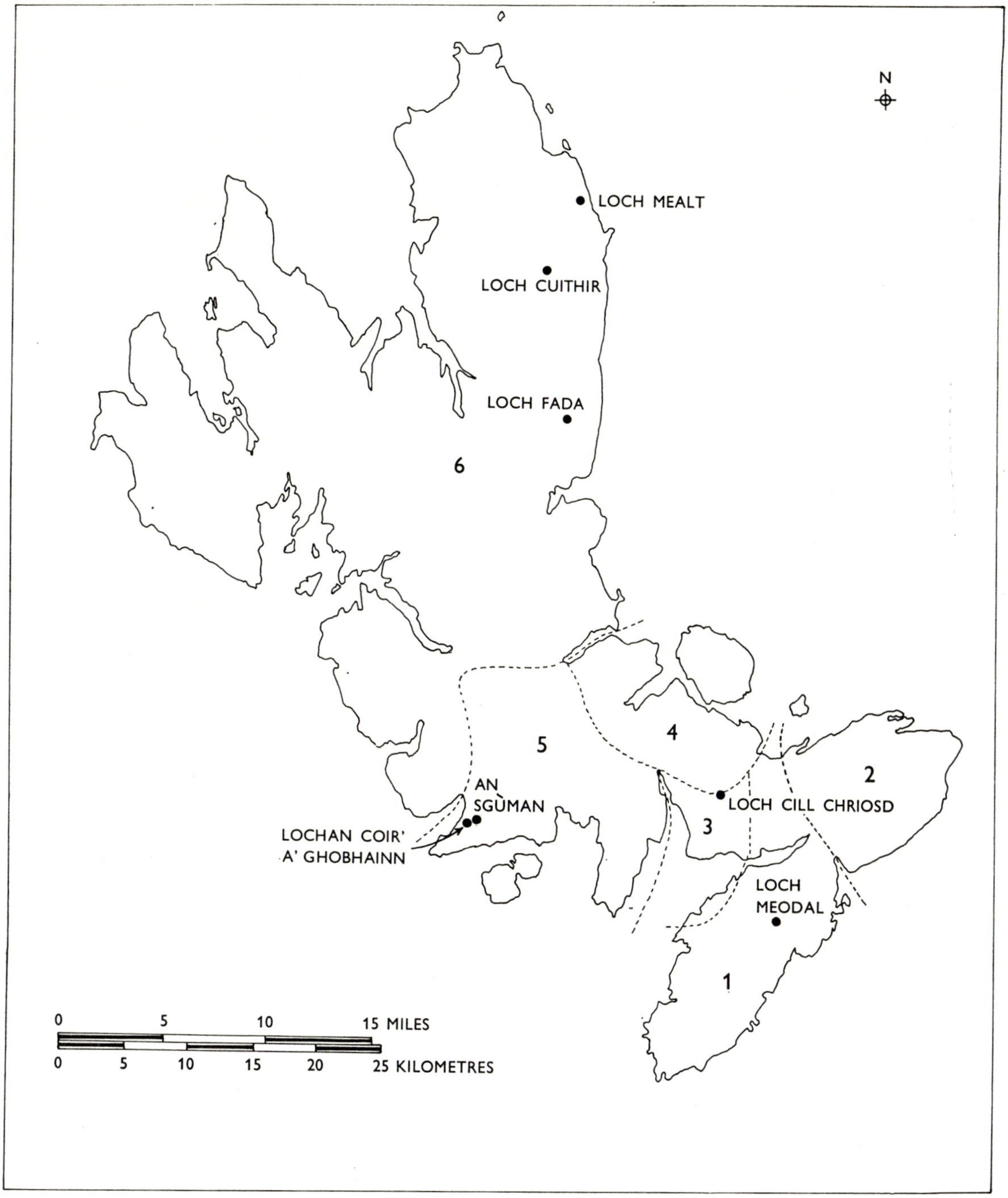

Figure 12. Index map of the Isle of Skye, showing location of sites that have been examined palynologically by the author or by Vasari & Vasari (1968) in relation to the six geological and topographical regions of the island.

rocky slopes, whereas the immediate surroundings of Loch Mealt are gentler and topographically more subdued. Loch Cill Chriosd, which lies on the contact between the Durness limestones and the granite of the Red Hills, was selected as one of the few suitable sites in either the limestone region of Ben Suardal (Region 3 on Fig. 5), and on the granites of the Red Hills (Region 4 on Fig. 5). No suitable sites could be found in the Kyleakin region (Fig. 5). It is considered, however, the floristic and vegetational history discernable at Loch Meodal in the Sleat Peninsula (Region 1 in Fig. 5) may be similar to that of the Kyleakin area in view of the rather similar geology and topography, and the present flora and vegetation of the two regions. Lochan Coir' a' Ghobhainn was chosen as a representative low-lying site in the Cuillin region. To investigate the stratigraphic relationships of the most recent phase of corrie glaciation in this region, an additional site at An Sgùman, which overlies the youngest glacial drift and thus lies within the limits of this glaciation, was cored and its pollen stratigraphy briefly examined for comparison with the nearby Lochan Coir' a' Ghobhainn that lies outside the margin of the drift and thus presumably beyond the limits of this glacial episode.

The altitude of the five principal sites studied ranges from 65 feet (20 m) to 450 feet (135 m) Ordnance Datum (O.D.). The altitudinal range of the sites was not considered to be sufficiently large to be a critical ecological factor in influencing the floristic and vegetational patterns. The five main sites studied are regarded as adequate initial representatives of the major geological and thus the ecological regions on Skye today.

The attractiveness of many of the sites on Skye for studies of floristic and vegetational history is enhanced by the phytogeographically diverse and ecologically distinctive plant assemblages that occur near the sites today. The presence of such a flora and vegetation poses questions, the solution of which can be aided by pollen analysis. Moreover the existence of a rich flora in the area promises a wealth of information as the record of that flora is traced back in time.

In the site descriptions, a brief resumé of the surrounding vegetation is given, in an attempt to place the sites into their present ecological contexts. Where relevés are available for the specific areas described, the relevant list and table numbers are given in brackets. The table numbers are in italic, and refer to Tables 4.1–4.56 in Chapter 4.

1. LOCH MEODAL

I. LOCATION AND VEGETATION

Loch Meodal is situated 16 km south of Broadford and 8 km north-north-east of Ardavasar in the Sleat Peninsula (Fig. 12) at 5°5′W, 57°8′N (National Grid Reference 18/656112). It lies in a gently sloping basin at 350 feet (105 m) O.D. within an area of rugged topography of Torridonian sandstone and Lewisian gneiss rock knolls protruding amidst the extensive peat-covered flat ground. The loch (Fig. 13) is fed by several streams flowing from the north and west, and is drained by a large outflow stream flowing into Knock Bay 2.5 km to the south-east.

The surrounding vegetation (Fig. 13) is a mosaic of mire communities, varying floristically in relation to slope, peat depth, and soligenous influences (see Fig. 4). In the wetter hollows between the rocky knolls Trichophoreto–Eriophoretum bog predominates. Trichophoreto–Callunetum bog characterises the shallower peat on the gently sloping rock knolls. Stream courses are marked by dense *Molinia caerulea–Myrica gale* mires, and steep, well-drained sandstone and gneiss outcrops support Callunetum vulgaris heath or the biotically derived Agrosto–Festucetum (species-poor) grassland. Notable plants in the area include the mire plants *Carex pauciflora*, *Drosera anglica*, and *Sphagnum imbricatum*.

There are extensive areas of *Betula pubescens–Vaccinium myrtillus* woodland on both the north- and south-facing slopes above the Ord River 1.5 km north-west of the loch. Further west between Ord and Tokavaig, *Betula pubescens–Vaccinium myrtillus* (6; *4.49*), *Corylus avellana–Oxalis acetosella* (7; *4.49*) and, more rarely, *Fraxinus excelsior–Brachypodium sylvaticum* (2; *4.55*) woods from an extensive woodland mosaic on the quartzites, sandstones, and Durness limestones. *Betula pubescens* ssp. *odorata* and *Corylus avellana* are the dominant trees in these woods, whereas *Fraxinus excelsior*, *Prunus padus*, *Quercus petraea*, *Salix cinerea*, *Sorbus aucuparia*, and *Ulmus glabra* are rarer components. The floors of these woods are boulder strewn, and they support a luxuriant bryophyte flora (p. 68) including the southern liverwort *Adelanthus decipiens*. Wooded ravines at Ord provide the northernmost known station for *Hymenophyllum tunbridgense*, and for several rare and local bryophytes (see p. 69). The strong representation of this 'Macaronesian–Tropical' element (*sensu* Greig-Smith, 1950) reflects the sheltered and equable climate of the Sleat area (see Chapter 5). Wooded fragments occur nearer Loch Meodal in the gorge of the outflow stream, consisting of *Betula pubescens* ssp. *odorata*, *Populus tremula*, *Quercus petraea*, and *Sorbus aucuparia*. It is probable that the area near the loch was once more extensively forested prior to the widespread development of bog.

The flora and vegetation of the loch is rather poor (Figs. 7, 13) with *Carex rostrata–Menyanthes trifoliata* (Magnocaricion) communities (8; *4.14*) favouring rather organic substrata in shallow water at the north end, merging into *Schoenoplectus lacustris–Equisetum fluviatile* stands (8; *4.13*) in deeper water. Along the exposed stony shores of the eastern side of the loch *Littorella uniflora–Lobelia dortmanna* (10;

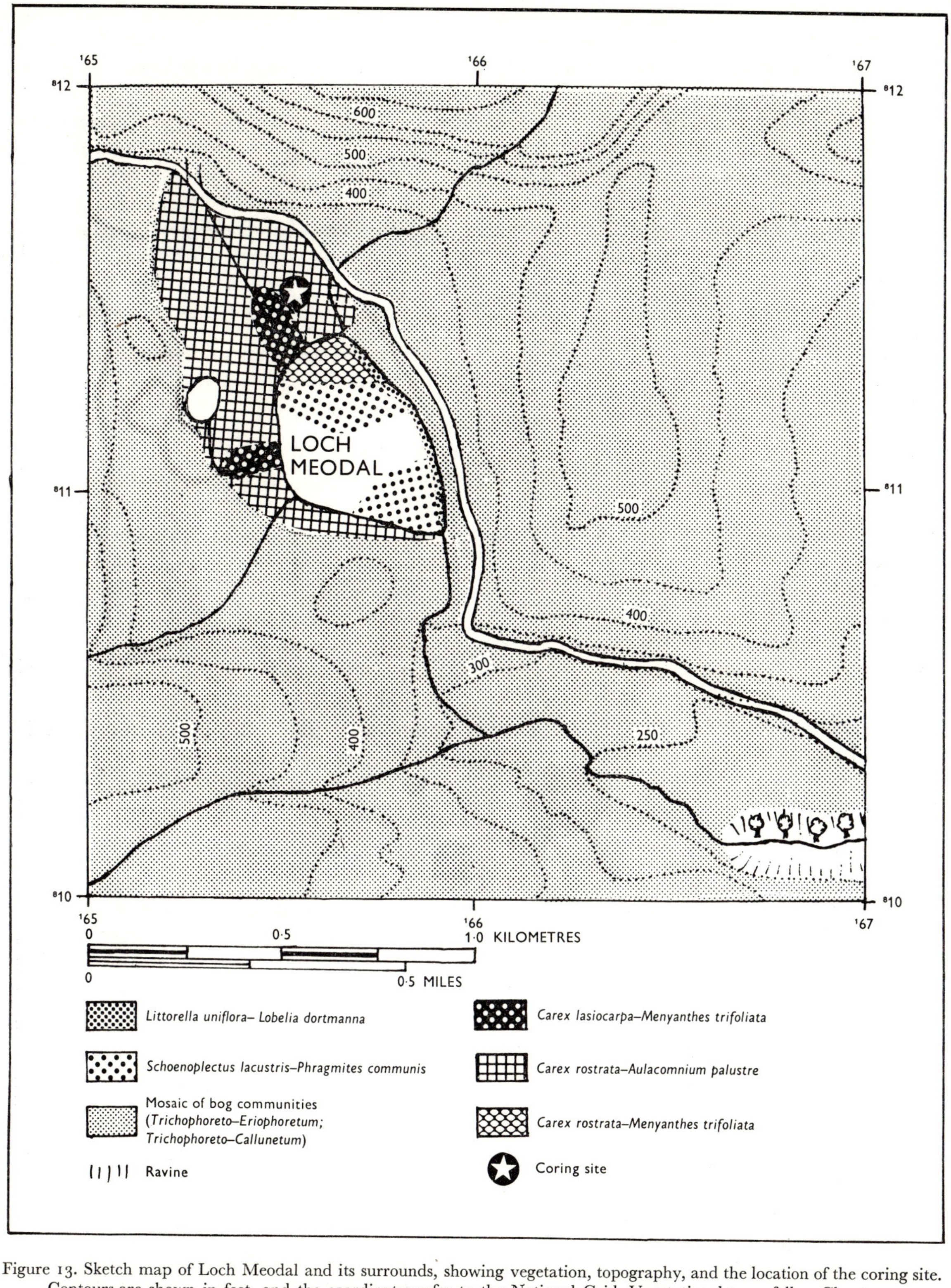

Figure 13. Sketch map of Loch Meodal and its surrounds, showing vegetation, topography, and the location of the coring site. Contours are shown in feet, and the coordinates refer to the National Grid. Vegetational types follow Chapter 4.

4.10) communities occur, with *Isoetes lacustris*, grading into *Schoenoplectus lacustris* stands, with prominent *Eleocharis palustris* towards the outflow stream (11; *4.10*). At the northern end an extensive fen has developed. The principal vegetation type of the fen is *Carex rostrata–Aulacomnium palustre* intermediate-fen communities (5; *4.22*). Occasional soligenous sites support *Carex rostrata–Scorpidium scorpioides* rich-fens (5; *4.23*). In water logged hollows within the fen, fine stands of *Carex lasiocarpa–Menyanthes trifoliata* 'mud-bottom' communities occur with *Carex limosa* and *Sparganium minimum* (3, 4; *4.18*). Further notable species of the loch and fen include *Callitriche hermaphroditica*, *Carex curta*, *C. dioica*, *Utricularia intermedia*, *U. minor*, *Sphagnum squarrosum*, and *S. warnstorfianum*. Details of the chemistry of the loch water are given on Fig. 7.

2. SEDIMENT STRATIGRAPHY

A series of trial borings on a north-west to south-east transect across the fen was made in 1966, and the core used for pollen analysis was taken at the point having the thickest sequence of deposits. The location of the coring sites is shown on Fig. 13. A description is given below of the sediment lithology of the relevant levels in the cores used for pollen analysis; abbreviations follow Troels-Smith (1955). Sediment depths are measured from the fen surface.

700–740 cm	Fine detritus mud, dark brown, darkens slightly on exposure to air. Very soft, nig 3, strf 0, elas 2, sicc 1, calc 0; humo 2; $Ld^2 3$, Dg 1, Dh +. Lower boundary sharp.
740–750 cm	Sandy fine detritus mud, dark brown mottled with sand grains, darkens slightly on exposure to air. Firm, nig 3, strf 0, elas 1, sicc 2, calc 0; humo 2; Ga 2, $Ld^2 1$, Gs 1, Dg +, Gg +. Lower boundary sharp.
750–780 cm	Fine detritus mud, dark brown, darkens slightly on exposure to air. Firm, nig 3, strf 0, elas 1, sicc 2, calc 0; humo 2; $Ld^2 3$, Ga 1, Dh +, Dg +. Lower boundary sharp.
780–790 cm	Silty fine detritus mud, grey-brown, darkens on exposure to air. Firm, nig 2, strf 0, elas 1, sicc 2, calc 0; humo 1; Ag 2, $Ld^2 1$, Ga 1. Lower boundary gradual over 2 cm.
790–810 cm	Fine sand and silt, grey-brown, pales on drying. Very firm, nig 1, strf 0, elas 0, sicc 3, calc 0; Ag 2, Ga 2. Lower boundary very gradual.
810–815 cm	Sand and silt, pale grey-brown, turns pale brown on exposure to air. Very firm, nig 1–2, strf 0, elas 0, sicc 3, calc 0; Ag 2, Ga 1, Gs 1. Lower boundary gradual over 1 cm.
815–820+ cm	Sand and gravel, pale grey-brown, stained with iron. Very firm, nig 1–2, strf 0, elas 0, sicc 3, calc 0; Gg 3, Gs 1. Base not seen.

The detailed sediment stratigraphy, based on microscopic examination, and the loss on ignition curve are shown in Fig. 14.

3. POLLEN STRATIGRAPHY

For convenience the sediments between 700 and 815 cm at Loch Meodal are divided into five biostratigraphic intervals, based upon the composition of the pollen and spore content, as shown in the pollen diagram (Plate 1). These local pollen zones are numbered and defined from the base upwards, and prefixed by the site designation 'LML'. The pollen zones defined here are intended to apply only to this pollen diagram. The total number of determinable pollen and spores included in ΣP per sample ranges from 231 to 536, with a mean of 378 and a median of 364. The local pollen zones are briefly defined as follows. All percentages quoted are based on ΣP.

LML-1 787.5–815 cm. This is the lowest zone recorded in the sediments. It is characterised by abundant herb pollen, with Gramineae pollen dominant, with values of 25% or more. *Rumex acetosa* pollen attains values of 4% or more. Pollen of *Artemisia* cf. *A. norvegica*, Liguliflorae, *Ranunculus acris* type, and *Thalictrum*, and spores of *Botrychium lunaria*, *Lycopodium selago*, and *Selaginella selaginoides* are consistently present in low amounts. Pollen of dwarf shrubs is prominent, with values up to 15%.

LML-2 777.5–787.5 cm. Characterised by abundant herb pollen, with Gramineae dominant (20% or more). *Rumex acetosa*, *Ranunculus acris* type, *Artemisia* cf. *A. norvegica*, *Thalictrum*, and *Selaginella selaginoides* values are as in zone LML-1. *Lycopodium selago* spores are absent. *Juniperus communis* pollen is prominent with frequences of 10% or more.

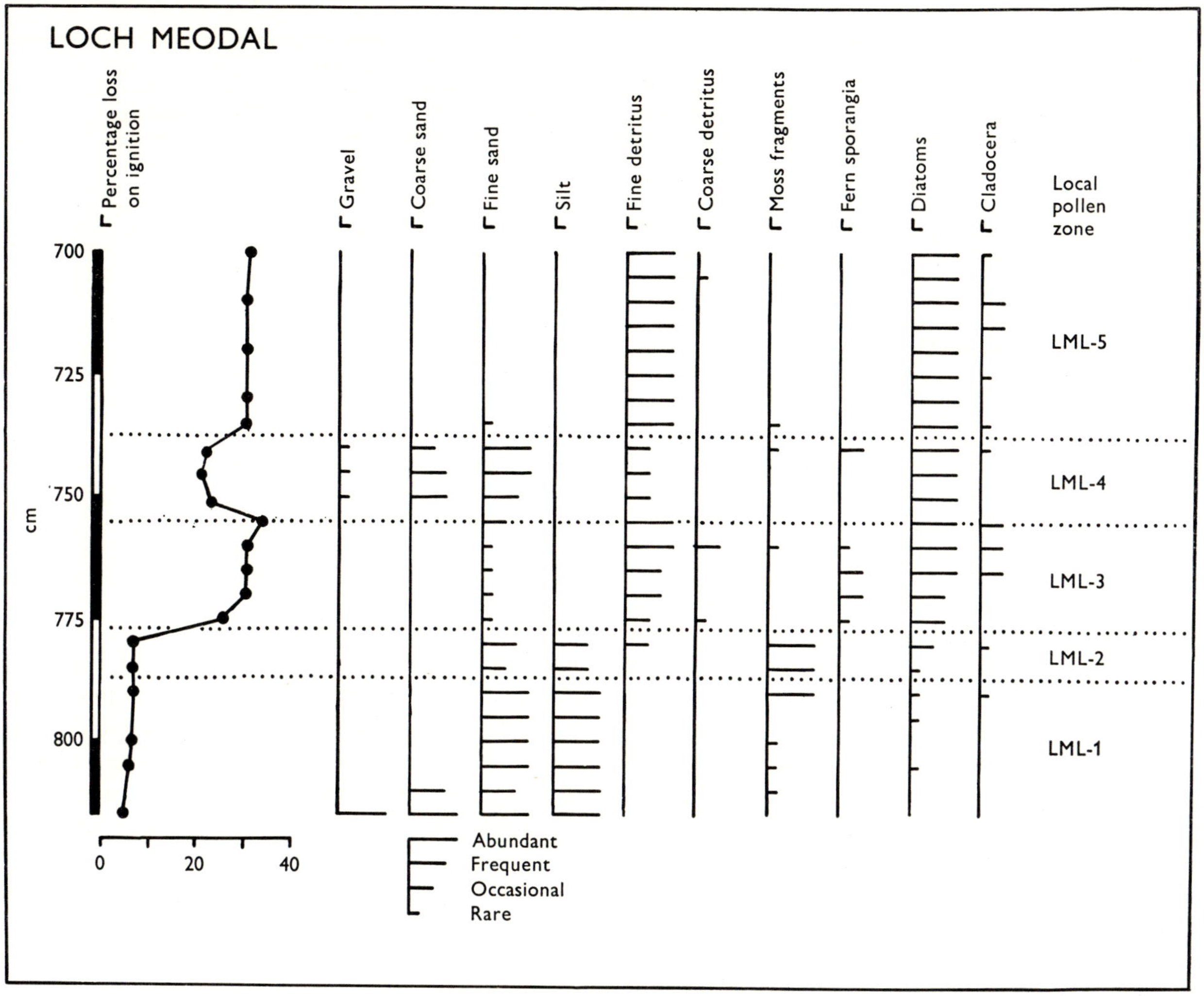

Figure 14. Sediment stratigraphy at Loch Meodal in relation to the local pollen zones, based on microscopic examination of the sediments and of residues following alkali maceration, and the percentage loss on ignition curve.

Dwarf-shrub pollen values are lower than in zone LML-1.

LML-3 755–777·5 cm. Characterised by increased arboreal pollen values, with *Betula* undiff. pollen attaining values of 25% or more. *Salix* pollen frequencies are 5% or more, and *Populus tremula* pollen is consistently present in low amounts. Shrub and dwarf-shrub pollen values are lower than in the underlying zones, as are the pollen frequencies of many herbaceous taxa. *Filipendula*, *Melampyrum*, and *Valeriana officinalis* pollen occur consistently in low amounts. *Thelypteris dryopteris* spores attain values of 2% or more throughout the zone.

LML-4 737·5–755 cm. Characterised by abundant herb pollen, with Gramineae pollen dominant, with values up to 30%. *Rumex acetosa*, *Ranunculus acris* type, and *Thalictrum* pollen attain values comparable to those in zones LML-1 and LML-2. *Betula* cf. *B. nana* pollen is prominent with frequencies of 8% or more. *Juniperus communis* pollen values are low throughout, and *Betula* undiff. pollen percentages are lower than in zones LML-3 and LML-5. *Artemisia* undiff. and *Thymus* type pollen are consistently present in low amounts.

LML-5 737·5 cm upwards. Characterised by abundant arboreal pollen, with *Betula* undiff. and *Corylus avellana* pollen frequencies of 15% or more. *Sorbus aucuparia* and *Populus tremula* pollen occur in low amounts in the zone. *Salix* pollen frequencies decrease

TABLE 9.1

	Type of remains	Local pollen zone LML-1	LML-2	LML-3	LML-4	LML-5
Betula nana	fr	+	.	.	+	.
B. pubescens	fr	.	.	+	+	+
Carex rostrata	fr	.	.	+	.	.
Juncus articulatus/J. acutiflorus	s	.	.	+	.	+
Juncus undiff.	s	.	.	.	.	+
Drepanocladus	lvs	.	+	.	.	.
Hylocomium splendens	lvs	+	+	+	.	.
Polytrichum juniperinum	lvs	+	+	.	.	.
Rhacomitrium undiff.	lvs	+	+	+	+	+
R. fasciculare	lvs	+	+	.	.	.
R. lanuginosum	lvs	+	+	.	.	.
Bosmina cf. *B. coregoni**	h	.	.	+	+	+
Cristatella mucedo	st	+	.	+	.	.

(fr = fruit; h = head-shield; lvs = leaves; s = seed; st = statoblast).
* Criteria for specific identifications follow Goulden & Frey (1963).

throughout the zone. *Juniperus communis* and *Betula* cf. *B. nana* pollen values are low throughout. Rubiaceae, *Melampyrum*, and *Urtica* pollen, and *Pteridium aquilinum* spores are consistently present in this zone. *Isoetes lacustris* microspores are prominent, with values of 10% or more. The upper boundary of this zone is not defined.

The indeterminable: deteriorated pollen category at Loch Meodal (Plate 1) attains values of 2 to 5% in zones LML-1 and LML-2, and in some samples in zone LML-4, whereas the values in zones LML-3 and LML-5 are consistently 1% or less. Of the four classes of pollen deterioration discussed in Chapter 8, exine degradation accounted for 66% of all the pollen deterioration in the profile, with exine corrosion prominent in the fine detritus muds of zones LML-3 and LML-5. The distribution and occurrence of indeterminable: deteriorated pollen appear to be related to the sediment lithology, with the highest frequencies in the silts and sands below 780 cm. In contrast, the indeterminable: concealed category shows little variation within the profile, with low values throughout (cf. H. J. B. Birks, 1970; Cushing, 1964*b*, 1967*b*). No microfossils of undoubted pre-Quaternary age were found in the Loch Meodal sediments.

4. MACROFOSSILS

Macrofossils identified from the residues after sample-preparation are listed in Table 9.1. The occurrences in the local pollen zones are indicated in the table.

5. RADIOCARBON DATE

Radiocarbon assay by the University of Cambridge Radiocarbon Laboratory of a sample of fine detritus mud ($Ld^2 3$, Dg 1, Dh +) from 725 to 730 cm depth (zone LML-5) in an adjacent large diameter (5.3 cm) core and correlated with the main pollen sequence (Plate 1) by sediment lithology and pollen stratigraphy, gave an age determination of 9482 ± 150 radiocarbon years B.P. (Q-961; Switsur & West, 1972).

2. LOCH FADA

1. LOCATION AND VEGETATION

Loch Fada lies 6 km north of Portree and 5 km south of The Storr in The Trotternish Peninsula (Fig. 12) at 6° 12′ W, 57° 27′ N (National Grid Reference 18/494494). The loch (Fig. 15) is at an altitude of 450 feet (135 m) O.D. in a steep-sided rock basin formed within a strongly westerly dipping complex of the Great Estuarine Series (Jurassic) and olivine-basalt and dolerite sills. The extensive Trotternish basalt scarp, with its impressive cliffs and landslip features, lies less than 1 km to the west. The loch is fed by several streams rising in the higher ground to the west and south, and it is drained by the large outflow stream flowing into Loch Leathan to the north. The water-level of Loch Fada was slightly raised in 1952 by the construction of a dam at the outflow of Loch Leathan.

The surrounding vegetation is a complex of mires, meadows, and grasslands. On the flat and gently

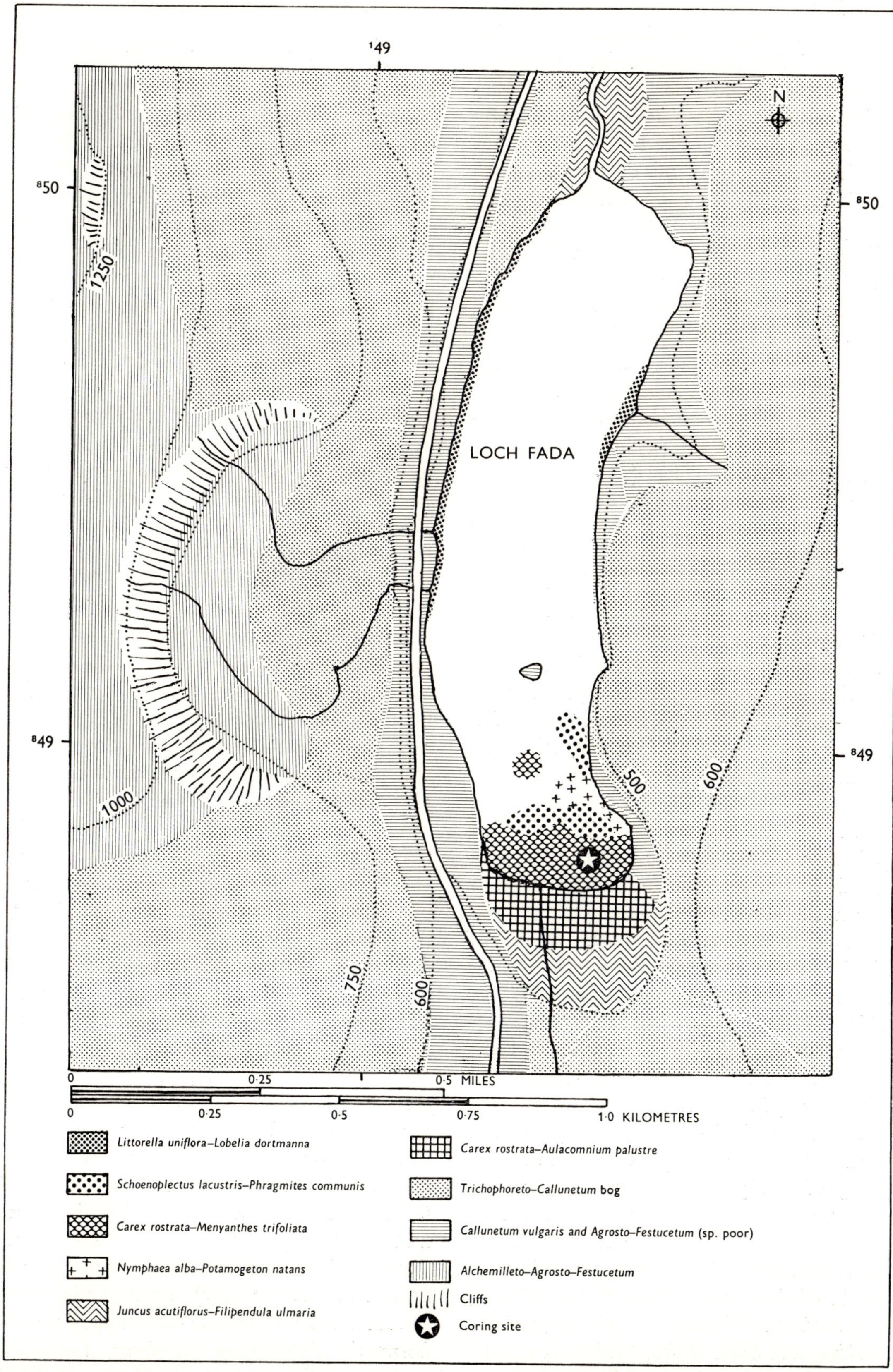

Figure 15. Sketch map of Loch Fada and its surrounds, showing vegetation, topography, and the location of the coring site. Contours are shown in feet, and the coordinates refer to the National Grid. Vegetational types follow Chapter 4.

sloping ground to the east of Loch Fada, Trichophoreto–Callunetum bog predominates, often with abundant *Rhacomitrium lanuginosum*. In soligenous areas along streams and near rock outcrops *Trichophorum cespitosum–Carex panicea* stands are locally frequent. On steeper, better drained sites Callunetum vulgaris heath occurs locally on dry rock knolls, but in parts it is heavily sheep-grazed to Agrosto–Festucetum (species-poor) grassland, often with dense *Pteridium aquilinum*. The steeper basalt slopes to the west of Loch Fada are primarily covered by Agrosto–Festucetum grasslands, but in wetter flushed sites *Juncus acutiflorus–Filipendula ulmaria* communities occur, with *Lychnis flos-cuculi* and *Parnassia palustris*. Nearer the basalt cliffs, Alchemilleto–Agrosto–Festucetum grasslands become increasingly prominent. The basalt cliffs nearest to Loch Fada (Fig. 15) outcrop between 800 and 1000 feet (245–305 m) and they support an interesting and diverse flora. On the damper, north-facing crags, 'tall herb' ledges occur with *Alchemilla glabra*, *Cirsium heterophyllum*, *Luzula sylvatica*, *Orchis mascula*, *Sedum rosea*, *Trollius europaeus*, and *Valeriana officinalis*. On drier rock outcrops *Saxifraga oppositifolia* is locally frequent, with *Asplenium viride*, *Draba incana*, *Galium boreale*, *Rubus saxatilis*, *Antitrichia curtipendula*, and *Barbula icmadophila*. More widespread species on the cliffs include *Alchemilla alpina*, *Cystopteris fragilis*, *Saxifraga hypnoides*, *Selaginella selaginoides*, *Silene acaulis*, and *S. maritima*. In a damp, steep, north-east-facing gully there is a small colony of *Poa glauca* and *P. balfourii*, with *Epilobium alsinifolium*, *Oxyria digyna*, and *Saxifraga stellaris*. The cliff flora as a whole is similar to, but not as rich as, that of The Storr to the north (see Chapter 5).

The loch is only 2.5 km west of the Sound of Raasay. The impressive sea-cliffs between Bearreraig Bay and Rubha na h-Airde Glaise provide extensive outcrops of Jurassic limestones, overlain by columnar-jointed basalts. The only woodland near Loch Fada occurs on the sheltered limestone under-cliff of the sea-cliffs. Dense *Corylus avellana* scrub occurs with some *Populus tremula*, *Salix cinerea*, *Sorbus aucuparia*, and *Ulmus glabra*. The understorey is dominated by *Athyrium filix-femina*, *Dryopteris borreri*, and *Brachypodium sylvaticum*. Flushed species-rich grasslands occur on the talus slopes below, whilst wet-soaks support an abundance of *Equisetum telmateia* with *Caltha palustris*, *Cirsium heterophyllum*, *Crepis paludosa*, *Eupatorium cannabinum*, *Filipendula ulmaria*, *Geum rivale*, *Petasites hybridus*, and *Silene dioica*. Sheltered coastal gorges support a local abundance of *Phyllitis scolopendrium*, with *Anomodon viticulosus* and *Cololejeunea calcarea*. *Cratoneuron commutatum* tufa-springs occur rarely.

The close juxtaposition of northern–montane, arctic–alpine, southern, atlantic, and continental species within the same regional climate near Loch Fada is of phytogeographical and ecological interest, and it poses questions which pollen analysis can aid in answering. This floristic diversity also serves to emphasise the wide range of habitats around the site. It is likely that tree growth would occur at low altitudes near the site wherever there is some shelter from the strong westerly winds and where bog development is prevented.

A list of the aquatic plants and a brief vegetational account of Loch Fada is given by Vasari & Vasari (1968). The distribution of the communities is shown in Fig. 15. Along the exposed western and eastern stony shores, stands of *Littorella uniflora–Lobelia dortmanna* communities occur, with small areas of *Potamogeton natans* and *P. perfoliatus* in deeper water. At the southern end there is a complex of *Schoenoplectus lacustris–Equisetum fluviatile*, *Potamogeton natans–Nymphaea alba*, and Magnocaricion communities, grading into intermediate- and rich-fens. The vegetational pattern is obscured by an area of Magnocaricion swamp outside the *Schoenoplectus lacustris* and floating-leaf stands. It is probably a floating peat-raft that became detached following the rise in water-level. Fragmentary *Potamogeton natans–Nymphaea alba*, stands occur, with *Myriophyllum alterniflorum*, *Potamogeton perfoliatus*, and *Sparganium augustifolium* (5; *4.11*), and in shallower water *Schoenoplectus lacustris* predominates (10; *4.13*). In water of 15–30 cm depth there are extensive areas of *Carex rostrata–Menyanthes trifoliata* communities (6; *4.14*) and in drier areas to the south a complex of fen types occurs. *Carex rostrata–Aulacomnium palustre* intermediate-fen is widespread, with *Acrocladium stramineum*, *Mnium pseudopunctatum*, *Sphagnum squarrosum*, *S. teres*, and *S. warnstorfianum* (4; *4.22*), grading into *Juncus acutiflorus–Filipendula ulmaria* communities with many 'tall herbs' (4; *4.32*) on silty alluvial soils around the inflow. In wetter areas within the fen 'mud-bottom' communities are local with *Carex curta*, *C. diandra*, *C. lasiocarpa*, *C. limosa*, and *Acrocladium giganteum* (6; *4.18*) and in strongly soligenous sites *Carex rostrata–Scorpidium scorpioides* rich-fens occur with *Carex lepidocarpa* and *C. serotina* (6; *4.23*). Further notable species of the loch and fen include *Callitriche hermaphroditica*, *C. intermedia*, *Potamogeton gramineus*, *Veronica scutellata*, and *Acrocladium sarmentosum*. Details of the chemistry of the loch water are given in Fig. 7.

2. SEDIMENT STRATIGRAPHY

A series of probings on a west–east transect across the fen was made in 1966, and the core used for pollen analysis was taken at the point having the thickest sequence of deposits. The location of the coring site is shown on Fig. 15. A description is given below of the sediment lithology of the relevant levels in the cores used for pollen analysis; abbreviations follow Troels-Smith (1955). Sediment depths are measured from the fen surface.

420–450 cm — Fine detritus mud, dark brown, quickly darkens on exposure to air. Soft, nig 3, strf 0, elas 3, sicc 2, calc 0; humo 2; $Ld^2 3$, Dg 1, Dh +, Ga +. *Melosira arenaria* Moore var. *hungarica* Pantocsek abundant. Lower boundary gradual over 1 cm.

450–510 cm — Silty fine detritus mud, dark brown, quickly darkens on exposure to air. Firm, nig 3, strf 0, elas 2, sicc 2, calc 0; humo 2; $Ld^2 2$, Ag 2, Dg +, Dh +, Ga +. Lower boundary gradual over 1 cm.

510–540 cm — Fine detritus mud with fine sand, dark brown, quickly darkens on exposure to air. Soft, nig 3, strf 0, elas 3, sicc 2, calc 0; humo 2; $Ld^2 2$, Ga 1, Dg 1, Dh +. Vivianite present. Lower boundary gradual over 3 cm.

540–565 cm — Silty mud with fine sand, blue-grey, browns slightly on exposure to air. Firm, nig 1–2, strf 0, elas 2, sicc 2, calc 0; humo 2; Ag 2, $Ld^2 1$, Ga 1. Lower boundary sharp.

565–580 cm — Silt and fine sand, blue-grey, turns pink-brown on exposure to air. Firm, nig 2, strf 0, elas 1, sicc 2, calc 1; Ag 2, Ga 2. Lower boundary gradual over 1 cm.

580–600 cm — Silty mud with fine sand, grey-brown, darkens slightly on exposure to air. Firm, nig 2, strf 0, elas 2, sicc 2, calc 0; humo 1; Dg 1, $Ld^2 1$, Ag 1, Ga 1, Dh +. Lower boundary gradual over 1 cm.

600–618 cm — Silt and fine sand, with tendency for fine sand to occur in thin laminae, pale grey, no colour change on exposure to air. Very firm, nig 1, strf 2, elas 2, sicc 3, calc 1; Ag 2, Ga 2, Ld^2 +. Lower boundary sharp.

618–620 cm — Bryophyte layer, dark brown, no change on exposure to air. Very firm nig 3, strf 3–4, elas 2, sicc 3, calc 0; humo 3; Tb 2, Ag 1, Ga 1, Dg +, Dh +. Lower boundary sharp.

620–660+ cm — Silt and fine sand, dark grey, no colour change on exposure to air. Very firm, nig 1–2, strf 0, elas 0, sicc 3, calc 1–2; Ag 2, Ga 2. Base not seen.

The detailed sediment stratigraphy based on microscopic examination, and the loss on ignition curve, are shown in Fig. 16.

3. POLLEN STRATIGRAPHY

For convenience the sediments between 420 and 660 cm at Loch Fada are divided into six biostratigraphic intervals, based upon the composition of the pollen and spore content, as shown in the pollen diagram (Plate 2). These local pollen zones are numbered and defined from the base upwards, and prefixed by the site designation 'LF'. The pollen zones defined here are intended to apply only to this pollen diagram. The total number of determinable pollen and spores included in ΣP per sample ranges from 69 to 400, with a mean of 233 and a median of 248. A detailed pollen diagram for the sequence 613–627 cm has been presented elsewhere (H. J. B. Birks, 1970). The local pollen zones are briefly defined as follows. All percentages quoted are based on ΣP.

LF-1 — 622.5–660 cm. This is the lowest zone recorded in the sediments at Loch Fada, and it is characterised by abundant herb pollen, with Cyperaceae pollen dominant, attaining values of 40% or more. *Lycopodium selago* spore frequencies are 5% or more. *Artemisia* cf. *A. norvegica* and *Salix* cf. *S. herbacea* pollen are consistently present in low amounts. The values of *Juniperus communis* pollen, of dwarf-shrub pollen, and of Polypodiaceae undiff. spores are low in this and the overlying zone. Pre-Quaternary microfossils occur in moderate frequencies (10% or more) in this and the succeeding zone.

LF-2 — 577.5–622.5 cm. Characterised by abundant herb pollen, with Gramineae pollen dominant, attaining values of 35% or more. *Rumex acetosa* pollen values are 5% or more. The pollen of Cruciferae, Liguliflorae, *Ranunculus acris* type, *Solidago* type, and *Thalictrum*, and

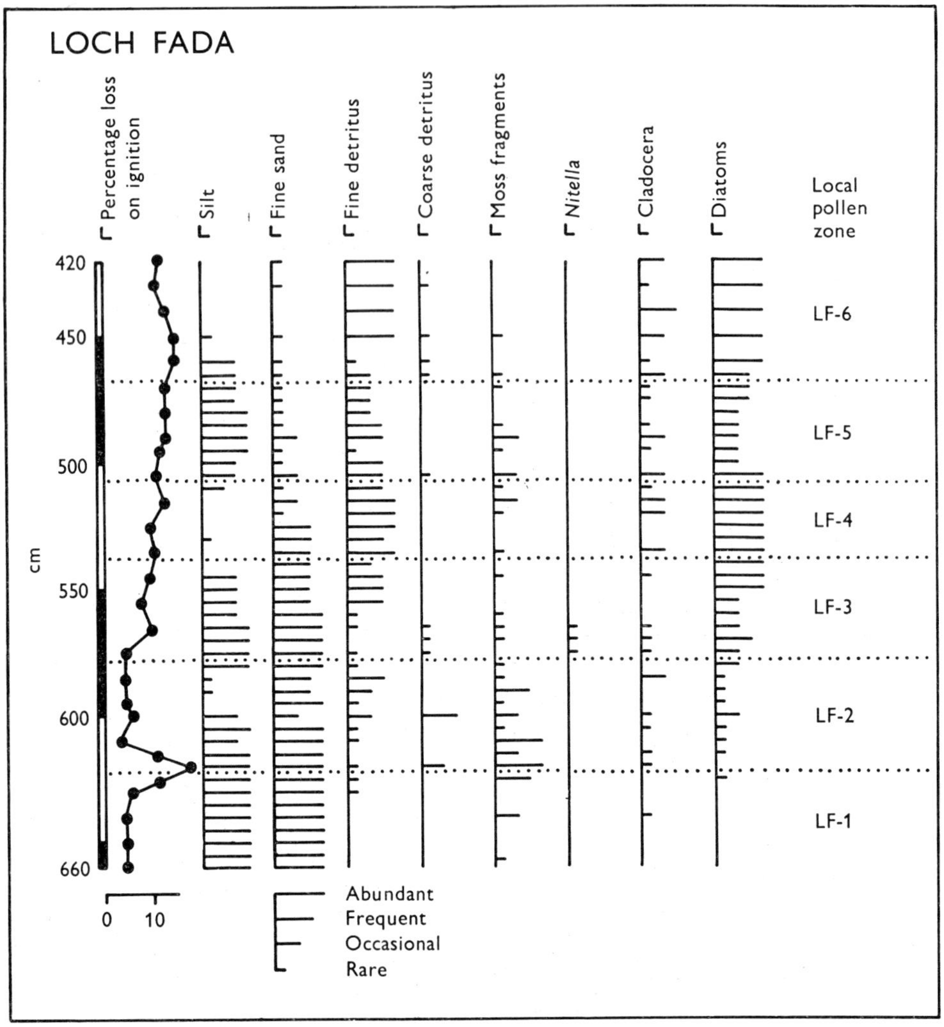

Figure 16. Sediment stratigraphy at Loch Fada in relation to the local pollen zones, based on microscopic examination of the sediments and of residues following alkali maceration, and the percentage loss on ignition curve.

spores of *Selaginella selaginoides* are consistently present in low frequencies. Pollen of *Cerastium alpinum* type and *Saussurea alpina* are more abundant in this zone than in any other at Loch Fada. There is a wide range of additional pollen types of herbaceous taxa in the zone. Pollen of dwarf shrubs have low values throughout. Pollen of aquatics appear in abundance in the upper part of the zone.

LF-3 537·5–577·5 cm. Characterised by abundant herb pollen, with Gramineae pollen dominant (25% or more). *Ranunculus acris* type, *Rumex acetosa*, and *Thalictrum* pollen values are as in zone LF-2, but those of Cruciferae, Liguliflorae, *Selaginella selaginoides*, and *Solidago* type are lower than in zone LF-2. *Juniperus communis* pollen frequencies are 7·5% or more, and *Populus tremula* pollen is present in low frequencies. Polypodiaceae undiff. spore values attain 5% or more. *Betula* undiff. pollen values are 5% or less. Dwarf-shrub pollen values are low throughout. There is a wide range of pollen types of aquatic taxa.

LF-4 507·5–537·5 cm. Characterised by abundant herb pollen, with Gramineae dominant. *Rumex acetosa* pollen values are as in zone LF-3 but those of Polypodiaceae undiff., *Ranunculus acris* type, and *Thalictrum* are lower than in zone LF-3. *Filipendula* pollen is present with frequencies of 5% or more. *Betula* undiff. pollen attains values of 10% or more. *Urtica* pollen, and *Sphagnum* and *Thelypteris dryopteris* spores are present in low but consistent amounts. Dwarf-shrub pollen values are low throughout.

LF-5 467·5–507·5 cm. Characterised by abundant

herb pollen, with Gramineae pollen dominant with values of 20% or more. Tree pollen values are lower than in zone LF-4, but the frequencies of *Betula* cf. *B. nana* pollen rise to 10% or more. There is a slight increase in the values of Cruciferae, *Ranunculus acris* type, and *Thalictrum* pollen in this zone. *Artemisia* undiff. pollen is consistently present in low amounts. Dwarf-shrub pollen values are low throughout.

LF-6 467.5 cm upwards. Characterised by increasing values of arboreal pollen, with both *Betula* undiff. and *Corylus avellana* pollen attaining frequencies of 15% or more. *Populus tremula* and *Sorbus aucuparia* pollen are consistently present in low amounts. *Filipendula* pollen is present with values of 5% or more, and *Urtica* and *Cirsium/Carduus* pollen are consistently present. Dwarf-shrub pollen values are low throughout the zone. The upper boundary of the zone is not defined.

The minerogenic sediments (silts and fine sands) of zones LF-1 and LF-2 contain up to 13% pre-Quaternary microfossils and up to 11% indeterminable: deteriorated pollen and spores (Plate 2). Exine degradation (*sensu* H. J. B. Birks, 1970; Cushing. 1964*b*, 1967*b*) accounts for 71% of the indeterminable category in these two zones, and pollen breakage 22%. The pre-Quaternary microfossil category includes spores and pollen of undoubted pre-Quaternary age, as described by Couper (1958) from the Great Estuarine Series (Jurassic) on Skye. The following types were tentatively identified by comparison with Couper's description and illustrations:

Abietineapollenites microalatus R. Potonie
Abietineapollenites minimus Couper
Appendicisporites Weyland & Krieger
Araucariacites australis Cookson
Brachyphyllum mamillare Bronge
Cicatricosisporites brevilaesuratus Couper
Cicatricosisporites undiff. R. Potonie & Gelletich
Cingulatisporites dubius Couper
Cingulatisporites foveolatus Couper
Cingulatisporites rigidus Couper
Classopollis torosus (Reissinger) Couper
Cyathidites minor Couper
Foveotriletes microreticulatus Couper
Gleicheniidites senonicus Ross
Lygodiosporites perverrucatus Couper
Monosulcites minimus Couper
Monosulcites undiff. Cookson *ex* Couper
Perinopollenites elatoides Couper
Pilosisporites brevipapillosus Couper
Pteruchipollenites thomasii Couper

In addition the following pollen and spore types, possible of Tertiary age, were present:

cf. *Engelhardtia*
Pistillipollenites macgregorii Rouse
Sigmopollis hispidus Hedlund
Tetrapollis Pflug
Trudopollis Pflug
(See Hedlund, 1965; Manum, 1962; Rouse & Srivastava, 1970.)

A further five unknown types were found with obvious morphological affinities with pre-Quaternary microfossils, but they could not be matched with any previously described fossil taxa. Dinoflagellates, hystrichosphaerids, and a variety of other microfossils were also present in the samples containing Jurassic pollen and spores. The following tentative determinations were made from the illustrations and descriptions in Harland (1968), Rossignol (1961), and Wall (1967):

Hystrichosphaera bentori Rossignol
Hystrichosphaera bulloidea Deflandre & Cookson
Hystrichosphaera furcata (Ehrenberg) Wetzel
Hystrichosphaera membranacea (Rossignol) Wall
Hystrichosphaera mirabilis Rossignol
cf. *Leptodinium* Klement
Lingulodium Wall
Operculodinium centrocarpum (Deflandre & Cookson) Wall
Operculodinium giganteum Wall
Peridinium Ehrenberg

Evitt & Davidson (1964), Wall & Dale (1967, 1968*a*) and Wall, Guillard & Dale (1967), have shown that many hystrichosphaerids are modern dinoflagellate resting cysts, and they are thus not necessarily indicative of redeposition from older, pre-Quaternary sediments (cf. Iversen, 1936, 1942). However, the close stratigraphical association of hystrichosphaerids and Jurassic spores and pollen in zones LF-1 and LF-2, and the absence of hystrichosphaerids from sediments lacking equivocal pre-Quaternary microfossils in zones LF-3, LF-4, LF-5, and LF-6 suggests that they are redeposited and thus they did not live in the loch at the time of deposition (cf. Churchill & Sarjeant, 1963; Varma, 1964). The same reasoning can be applied to the occurrence of several other

TABLE 9.2

	Type of remains	Local pollen zone					
		LF-1	LF-2	LF-3	LF-4	LF-5	LF-6
Betula nana	fr	.	.	+	.	+	+
B. pubescens	fr	.	.	.	.	.	+
cf. *Ceratophyllum*	sp	.	.	.	.	+	+
Equisetum	sh	.	.	.	.	.	+
Juncus articulatus/J. acutiflorus	s	+	+	+	+	+	+
J. effusus/J. conglomeratus	s	.	.	.	.	.	+
Salix herbacea	lvs	+	+	.	.	.	.
Acrocladium cuspidatum	lvs	.	+	+	+	+	+
A. sarmentosum	lvs	.	+	.	.	.	.
Andreaea rupestris	lvs	+	.	.	.	.	.
Antitrichia curtipendula	lvs	+	+	+	.	+	+
Aulacomnium palustre	lvs	.	.	.	.	.	+
Brachythecium	lvs	.	.	.	.	.	+
Bryum	lvs	.	+	.	.	.	.
Campylium stellatum	lvs	+	.	.	.	.	.
Cratoneuron commutatum	lvs	.	+	.	+	+	.
Dichodontium pellucidum	lvs	+	+	.	.	.	.
Distichium capillaceum	lvs	.	+	.	.	.	.
Drepanocladus exannulatus	lvs	+	+	.	.	.	.
D. revolvens	lvs	.	+	.	.	.	.
Eurhynchium	lvs	.	.	.	+	.	.
Hylocomium splendens	lvs	+	+	+	+	+	.
Mnium orthorhynchum	lvs	.	.	.	.	+	.
M. pseudopunctatum	lvs	.	.	.	.	.	+
Plagiothecium undulatum	lvs	.	.	.	+	.	.
Pleurozium schreberi	lvs	.	+	.	+	+	.
Pohlia cf. *P. wahlenbergii*	lvs	.	+	.	.	.	.
Polytrichum alpinum	lvs	+	.	.	.	.	.
Rhacomitrium undiff.	lvs	+	+	+	.	.	.
R. fasciculare	lvs	+	+	.	.	+	.
R. lanuginosum	lvs	+	+	+	.	.	.
Rhytidiadelphus squarrosus	lvs	.	+	.	.	.	.
Sphagnum	lvs	+	.	.	.	+	.
Nitella	oos	.	.	+	.	.	.
Bosmina longirostris	h	.	+	+	+	+	+
Cristatella mucedo	st	.	.	+	+	+	+
Daphnia	ep	.	.	+	+	+	+
Plumatella	st	.	.	+	.	.	.

(ep = ephippia; fr = fruit; h = head-shield; lvs = leaves; oos = oospores; s = seed; sh = sheath; sp = spines; st = statoblast.)

distinctive microfossils of unknown affinities in zones LF-1 and LF-2, for example *Crassosphaera* (Cookson & Manum, 1960), *Leiosphaerida telmatica*, and *Micrhystridium penkridgensis* (Sarjeant & Strachan, 1968). All these microfossils are grouped with the pollen and spores of pre-Quaternary age and affinities into a single category, here termed pre-Quaternary microfossils. The frequencies of this category are expressed on Plate 2 as a percentage of the pollen sum (ΣP) plus the pre-Quaternary category.

4. MACROFOSSILS

Macrofossils identified from the residues after sample preparation are listed in Table 9.2. The occurrences in the local pollen zones are indicated in the table.

The following additional macrofossils were recorded by Vasari & Vasari (1968). The relationships of these to the present local pollen stratigraphy are tentative.

	Type of remains	Local pollen zone
Carex echinata	fr	? LF-2; LF-3 or LF-4.
Montia fontana ssp. *fontana*	s	? LF-3 or LF-4.
Myriophyllum alterniflorum	fr	? LF-3 or LF-4.
Potamogeton sp.	fst	? LF-5.
Vaccinium myrtillus	s	? LF-2.
Cratoneuron filicinum	lvs	? LF-6.
Mnium cf. *M. longirostrum*	lvs	? LF-6.

(fr = fruit; fst = fruitstone; lvs = leaves; s = seed).

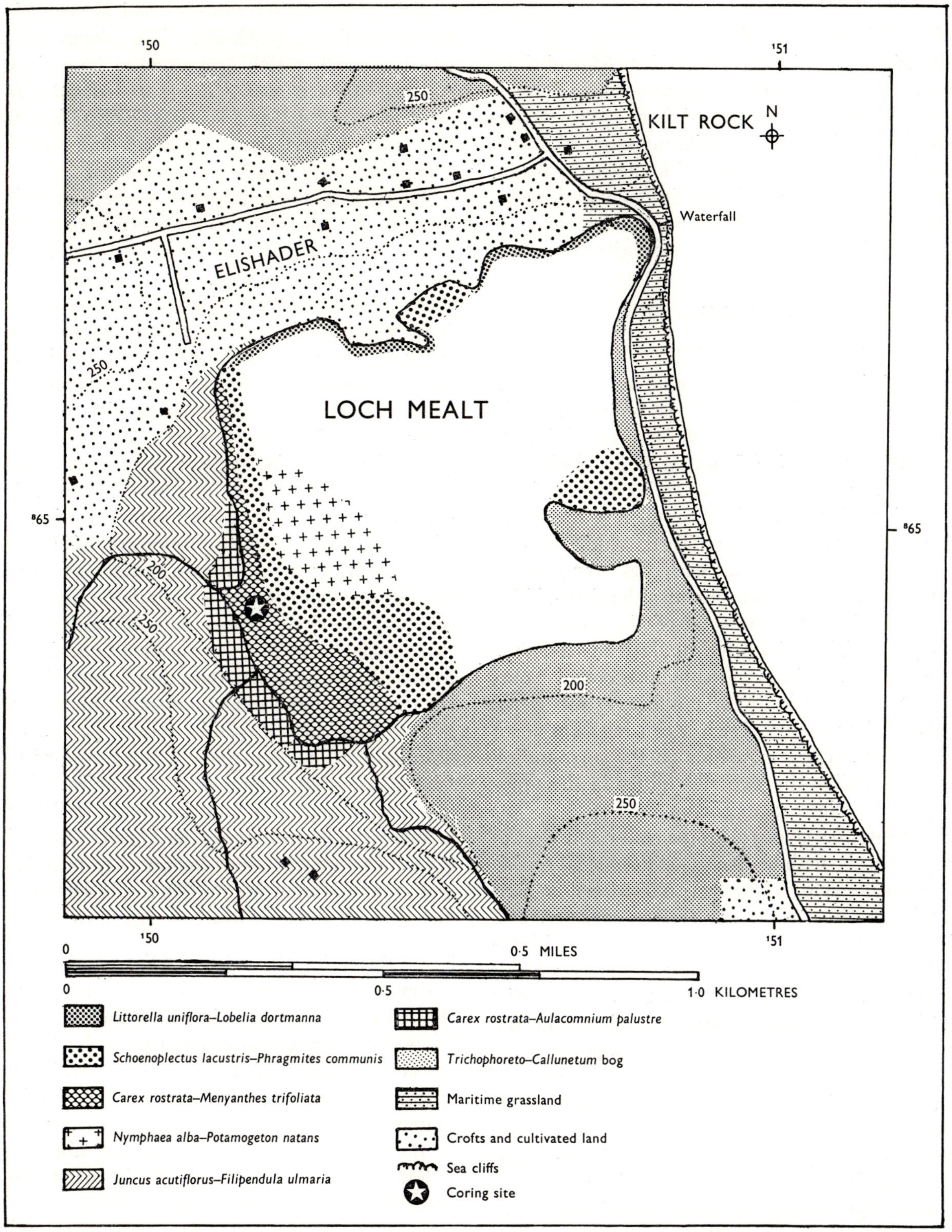

Figure 17. Sketch map of Loch Mealt and its surrounds, showing vegetation, topography, and the location of the coring site. Contours are shown in feet, and the coordinates refer to the National Grid. Vegetational types follow Chapter 4.

5. RADIOCARBON DATE

Radiocarbon assay by the University of Cambridge Radiocarbon Laboratory of a sample of fine detritus mud ($Ld^2 3$, Dg 1, Dh +, Ga +) from 440 to 450 cm depth (Zone LF-6) in an adjacent large diameter (5.3 cm) core and correlated with the main pollen sequence (Plate 2) by sediment lithology and pollen stratigraphy gave an age determination of 7500 ± 120 radiocarbon years B.P. (Q-960; Switsur & West, 1972).

3. LOCH MEALT

1. LOCATION AND VEGETATION

Loch Mealt is situated on the top of an exposed sea-cliff 20 km north of Portree and 3.5 km south-south-east of Staffin in the Trotternish Peninsula (Fig. 12) at 6°8′W, 57°36′N (National Grid Reference 18/505650). It lies in a gently sloping rock-basin at 170 feet (51 m) O.D. within a complex of the Great Estuarine Series (Jurassic) and Tertiary dolerite sills. The steep Trotternish basalt scarp lies over 5 km to the west, and the notable botanical locality of The Quirang is 6.5 km north-west of the loch. Loch Mealt (Fig. 17) is fed by three small streams from the south and west, and is drained by a spectacular out-flow that drops vertically for 170 feet (51 m) over a dolerite sill into the sea. Loch Mealt is 14 km north of Loch Fada (Fig. 12). Although the surrounding geology is similar the two sites differ in the topo-graphy of their immediate surrounds.

The vegetation (Fig. 17) to the south and west of Loch Mealt is mainly *Juncus acutiflorus–Filipendula ulmaria* meadows developed on moist, well-aerated soils with *Lathyrus montanus*, *Trollius europaeus*, and *Vicia cracca* (6; *4.32*). On small areas of steep, block-strewn ground low-grown *Corylus avellana* or *Betula pubescens* ssp. *odorata* scrub persists, with *Angelica sylvestris* and *Filipendula ulmaria* prominent in the understorey. Much of the ground to the north of the loch is crofted at present, although extensive areas of heavily cut Trichophoreto–Callunetum bog occur in waterlogged hollows. Sphagneto–Juncetum effusi mires occur locally along streamsides. Sheep-grazed maritime grasslands predominate to the east of the loch, with *Agrostis stolonifera*, *Armeria maritima*, *Festuca rubra*, and *Plantago maritima*. Well-developed stands of *Luzula sylvatica–Silene dioica* communities occur on inaccessible ledges on the basalt sea-cliffs nearby with *Rumex acetosa*, *Sedum rosea*, *Trollius europaeus*, and *Valeriana officinalis*. Nearby at the base of the cliffs at Rubha Garbhaig there is an interesting area of scrubby birch–hazel–rowan wood developed on a north-east-facing block-litter. The blocks within the wood support a rich cryptogamic flora, including *Hymenophyllum wilsonii*, *Hylocomium brevirostre*, *Hypnum callichroum*, *Aphanolejeunea microscopica*, *Colura calyptrifolia*, *Harpalejeunea ovata*, and *Plagiochila tridenticulata*, suggesting locally sheltered conditions.

There is a sparse aquatic vegetation (Fig. 17) around the northern and eastern shores of Loch Mealt, with *Littorella uniflora–Lobelia dortmanna* stands on gravel in shallow water (3; *4.10*), and occasional *Schoenoplectus lacustris* reedswamps occurring in small bays. There is extensive fen and reedswamp develop-ment on the more sheltered western and southern shores. At the outer edge of the fen, there is a narrow strip of floating-leaved aquatics with *Myriophyllum alterniflorum*, *Potamogeton natans*, *P. perfoliatus*, and *Sparganium angustifolium* (4; *4.11*) bordering the extensive *Schoenoplectus lacustris–Equisetum fluviatile* stands (9; *4.13*). In shallower water there is a narrow fringe of *Carex rostrata–Menyanthes trifoliata* com-munities (1, 3; *4.14*), merging rather abruptly into the *Carex rostrata–Aulacomnium palustre* intermediate-fen (2, 3; *4.22*) with *Carex dioica*, *Pedicularis palustris*, *Acrocladium cordifolium*, *A. stramineum*, *Mnium pseudo-punctatum*, *Sphagnum contortum*, and *S. teres*. Within the fen there is a large soligenous soak supporting *Carex rostrata–Scorpidium scorpioides* stands (4; *4.23*) with abundant *Menyanthes trifoliata*, associated with *Carex serotina*, *Eleocharis quinqueflora*, *Acrocladium giganteum*, and *Cinclidium stygium*. In drier areas, *Molinia caerulea* is increasingly prominent with *Salix aurita* (1, 2; *4.32*), which merges on shallow silty peat into the *Juncus acutiflorus* meadows (6; *4.32*). Details of the chemistry of the loch water are given in Fig. 7.

2. SEDIMENT STRATIGRAPHY

A stratigraphic section on a west–east transect across the fen was constructed in 1966, and the core used for pollen analysis was taken at the point having the thickest sequence of deposits. The location of the coring site is shown on Fig. 17. A description is given below of the sediment lithology of the relevant levels in the cores used for pollen analysis; abbreviations follow Troels-Smith (1955). Sediment depths are measured from the fen surface.

350–420 cm	Fine detritus mud, pale greenish-brown, darkens slightly on ex-posure to air. Soft, nig 1–2, strf 0, elas 3, sicc 2, calc 0; humo 1; $Ld^1 3$, Dg 1, Ga +, [test.moll. +]. Lower boundary gradual over 3 cm.

420–460 cm Silty fine detritus mud, dark brown, pales on exposure to air. Firm, nig 3, strf 0, elas 2, sicc 2, calc 0; humo 1; $Ld^1 2$, Ag 1, Ga 1, Dh +. Lower boundary gradual over 1 cm.

460–565 cm Humified fine detritus mud, very dark brown, rapidly darkens on exposure to air. Soft, nig 4, strf 0, elas 3, sicc 2, calc 0; humo 2–3; $Ld^3 3$, Dg 1, Dh +, Tb +, Ga +. Vivianite present. Lower boundary sharp.

565–600 cm Silty fine detritus mud, grey-brown, iron stained, darkens on exposure to air. Firm, nig 1, strf 0, elas 1, sicc 2, calc 0; humo 3; Ag 3, $Ld^3 1$, Dg +. Vivianite present. Lower boundary gradual over 1 cm.

600–650+ cm Silt, blue-grey, no colour change on exposure to air. Very firm, nig 1, strf 0, elas 0, sicc 3, calc 1–2; Ag 4. Base not seen.

The detailed sediment stratigraphy, based on microscopic examination, and the loss on ignition curve are shown in Fig. 18. Subsequent corings in 1967 and 1968 with a mechanised rig have revealed a further sequence of silts and silty muds resting on bedrock at 12.25 m depth. Preliminary pollen analyses indicate that the strata are polleniferous throughout. The age and possible significance of the deeper sequence must await radiocarbon dating and detailed pollen analyses.

3. POLLEN STRATIGRAPHY

For convenience the sediments between 350 and 650 cm at Loch Mealt are divided into seven biostratigraphic intervals, based upon the composition of the pollen and spore content, as shown in the pollen diagram (Plate 3). These local pollen zones are numbered and defined from the base upwards, and prefixed by the site designation 'LM'. The pollen zones defined here are intended to apply only to this diagram. The total number of determinable pollen and spores included in ΣP per sample ranges from 86 to 410, with a mean of 224 and a median of 234. The local pollen zones are briefly defined as follows. All percentages quoted are based on ΣP.

LM-1 632.5–650 cm. This is the lowest zone recorded in the sediments examined at Loch Mealt and it is characterised by abundant herb pollen, with Cyperaceae pollen dominant attaining values of 40% or more. *Lycopodium selago* spores have values of 5% or more. Shrub and dwarf-shrub pollen frequencies are both less than 10%, and tree pollen frequencies are extremely low.

LM-2 572.5–632.5 cm. Characterised by abundant herb pollen, with Gramineae pollen dominant, attaining values of at least 30%. *Rumex acetosa* pollen frequencies are 5% or more, and pollen of *Ranunculus acris* type and *Thalictrum*, and spores of *Botrychium lunaria* and *Selaginella selaginoides* are consistently present. There is a wide range of pollen types of herbaceous taxa. Pollen values of trees, shrubs, and dwarf shrubs are low throughout this zone.

LM-3 545–572.5 cm. Characterised by abundant herb pollen, with Gramineae pollen dominant, attaining values of 30% or more. *Rumex acetosa*, *Thalictrum*, and *Ranunculus acris* type pollen frequencies are as in zone LM-2, but *Selaginella selaginoides* spore percentages are lower than in zone LM-2. *Juniperus communis* pollen attains values of 7.5% or more and Polypodiaceae undiff. spore values are 5% or more. Pollen frequencies of aquatic taxa increase throughout the zone.

LM-4 485–545 cm. Characterised by abundant herb pollen, with Gramineae pollen dominant with values of 30% or more. *Rumex acetosa* and *Ranunculus acris* type pollen values are slightly lower than in zone LM-3. *Betula* undiff. pollen frequencies are 8% or more throughout, and dwarf-shrub pollen values increase in the upper part of the zone. *Filipendula*, *Plantago major/P. media*, and *Urtica* pollen occur consistently in the zone, the former taxon being present with pollen frequencies of 5% or more. Pollen and spores of aquatic taxa are abundant in the zone.

LM-5 435–485 cm. Characterised by abundant herb pollen, with Gramineae pollen dominant. *Rumex acetosa* pollen values are 5% or more. Tree pollen frequencies are low (3% or less). *Betula* cf. *B. nana* pollen attains values of 8% or more, and dwarf-shrub pollen frequencies are at least 10%.

LM-6 400–435 cm. Characterised by abundant herb pollen, with Gramineae pollen dominant. *Juniperus communis* pollen values are between 5% and 10%, and *Betula* cf. *B. nana*

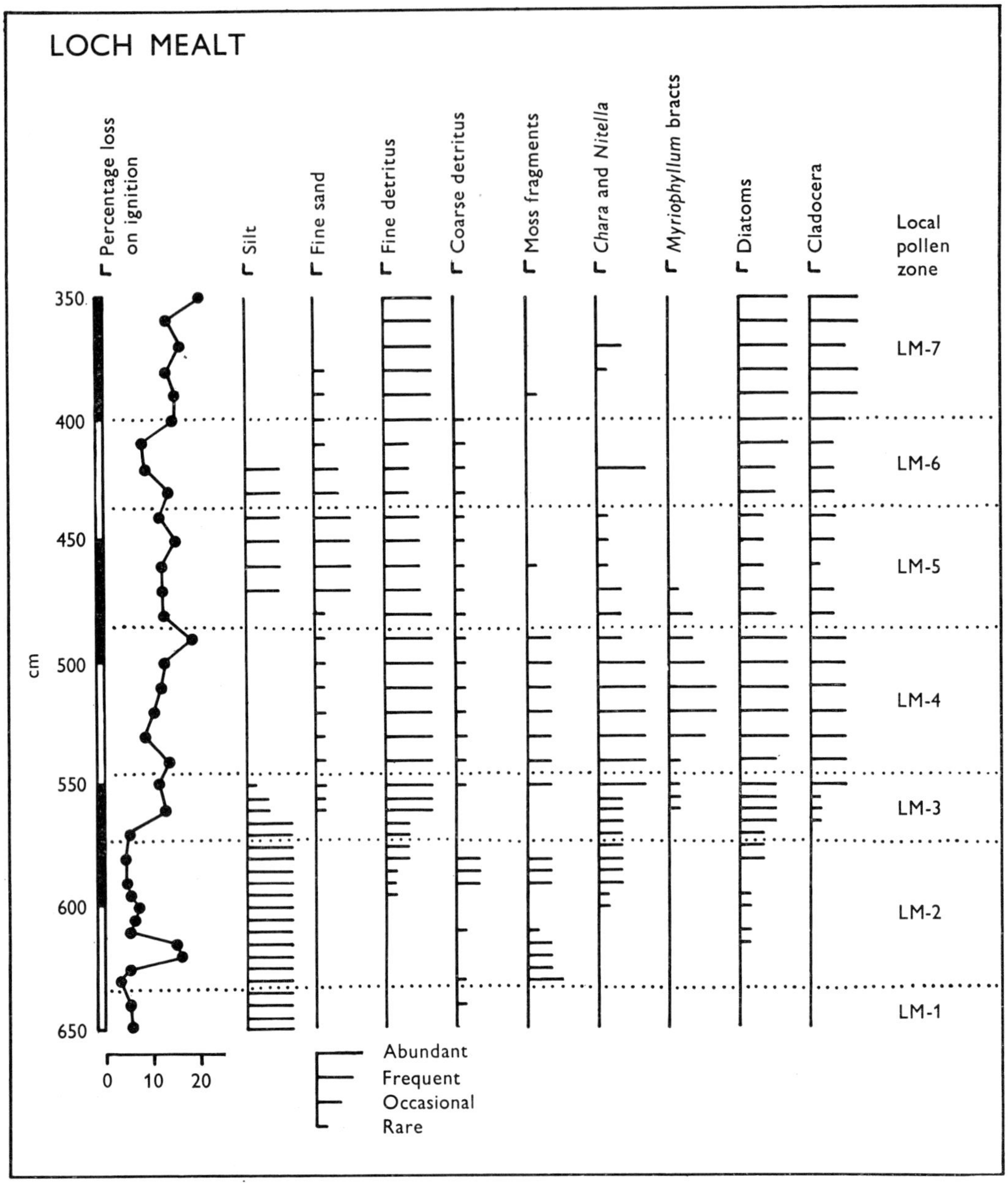

Figure 18. Sediment stratigraphy at Loch Mealt in relation to the local pollen zones, based on microscopic examination of the sediments and of residues following alkali maceration, and the percentage loss on ignition curve.

pollen values are low (2% or less). Dwarf-shrub pollen values are lower than in zone LM-5.

LM-7 400 cm upwards. Characterised by increasing values of arboreal pollen (10–40%), with *Betula* undiff. and *Corylus avellana* both attaining values of 10% or more. Values of *Salix* pollen also increase, reaching 13%. Dwarf-shrub and herb pollen values decrease accordingly, but *Filipendula* pollen is prominent with frequencies of 10% or more. *Heracleum sphondylium* and *Urtica* pollen are consistently present in low amounts. The upper boundary of this zone is not defined.

4. MACROFOSSILS

Macrofossils identified from the residues after sample preparation are listed in Table 9.3. Their occurrences in the local pollen zones are indicated in the table.

TABLE 9.3

	Type of remains	Local pollen zone						
		LM-1	LM-2	LM-3	LM-4	LM-5	LM-6	LM-7
Carex	fr	.	.	.	+	.	.	+
Betula pubescens	fr	.	.	.	.	.	.	+
Equisetum	sh	.	.	.	+	.	.	.
Myriophyllum	br	.	.	+	+	.	.	.
Salix herbacea	lvs	+	+	.	.	.	.	.
Acrocladium giganteum	lvs	.	.	.	+	.	.	.
Barbula icmadophila	lvs	.	+	.	.	.	.	.
Brachythecium	lvs	.	.	.	+	.	.	.
Bryum	lvs	.	+	.	+	.	.	.
Campylium stellatum	lvs	+	.	.	+	.	.	.
Dichodontium pellucidum	lvs	.	.	.	.	+	.	.
Drepanocladus revolvens	lvs	.	.	.	+	.	.	.
Hylocomium splendens	lvs	+	+	.	+	+	+	+
Hypnum cupressiforme	lvs	.	.	.	+	.	.	.
Polytrichum alpinum	lvs	+	.	.	.	.	.	.
Rhacomitrium undiff.	lvs	+	+	.	+	+	+	.
R. fasciculare	lvs	+	+	+	+	.	.	.
R. lanuginosum	lvs	+	+	.	.	.	.	.
Sphagnum undiff.	lvs	.	+	.	.	.	.	.
S. palustre	lvs	.	.	.	+	.	.	.
Thuidium cf. *T. delicatulum*	lvs	.	+	.	+	.	.	.
Tortula	lvs	.	.	.	+	.	.	.
Chara	oos	.	.	+	+	.	.	.
Nitella	oos	.	+	+	+	+	+	+
Chironomidae	hc	.	.	+	+	.	+	+
Daphnia	ep	.	.	+	+	+	+	+
Cristatella mucedo	st	.	+	.	+	+	+	+
Plumatella	st	.	.	+	+	+	+	+

(br = bracts; ep = ephippia; fr = fruit; hc = head capsule; lvs = leaves; oos = oospores; sh = sheath; st = statoblast.)

4. LOCH CILL CHRIOSD

I. LOCATION AND VEGETATION

Loch Cill Chriosd is situated 4 km south-west of Broadford and 3 km east of Loch Slapin in Strath Suardal (Fig. 12) at 5°58′W, 57°12′N (National Grid Reference 18/605203). It lies in a steep-sided basin at 65 feet (20 m) O.D. on the contact between the Durness limestone to the south and east, and the granite and granophyre of the Beinn na Caillich range to the north and west (Fig. 19). The granite slopes are steep and rise to 2400 feet (735 m). The limestone ground to the south is gentler, rising to 922 feet (380 m) on Ben Suardal. The contact between the granite and the limestone is irregular, for in the south there is a smaller granite intrusion at Beinn an Dubhaich (see Fig. 19). The loch is fed by several streams draining from both rock types, those from the north and west descending over 1500 feet (460 m) from the Beinn na Caillich range. The main stream from the south runs through a limestone ravine in Coille Gaireallach, and a subsidiary stream is spring-fed on Ben Suardal. The loch is drained by a large outflow stream, flowing northwards into Broadford Bay.

The lower south-facing granite slopes of Beinn na Caillich support heavily-grazed Agrosto–Festucetum (species-poor) grassland, often with abundant *Pteridium aquilinum*. Small areas of Callunetum vulgaris heath persist in less heavily grazed, blocky areas. Trichophoreto–Callunetum bog occurs widely but locally in flatter, wetter sites. On ground above 1500 feet (460 m) there are extensive granitic screes colonised in part by *Cryptogramma crispa* and *Lycopodium selago*. On wind-exposed summit ground above 2000 feet (610 m) there is a mosaic of Cariceto–Rhacomitretum lanuginosi heath, *Festuca ovina–Luzula spicata* 'fell-field', and *Juniperus communis* ssp. *nana* scrub, and in more sheltered areas, chionophilous *Nardus stricta–Vaccinium myrtillus* communities occur. Notable species of these montane communities include *Alchemilla alpina*, *Antennaria dioica*, *Carex bigelowii*, *Lycopodium alpinum*, *Salix herbacea*, and *Dicranum falcatum*. Small areas of Philonoto–Saxifragetum stellaris springs occur with *Acrocladium sarmentosum* and *Scapania uliginosa*. In the north-facing

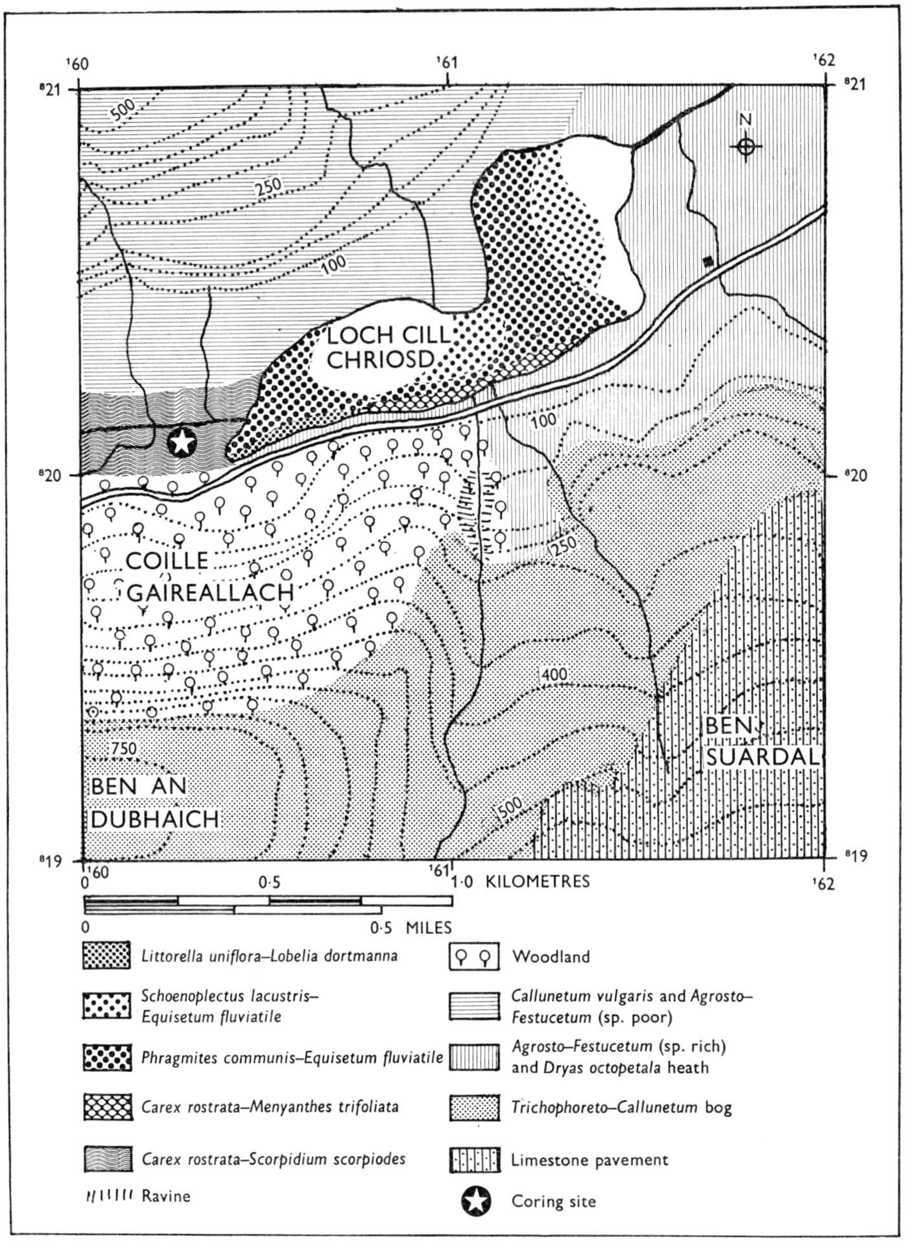

Figure 19. Sketch map of Loch Cill Chriosd and its surrounds, showing vegetation, topography, and the location of the coring site. Contours are shown in feet, and the coordinates refer to the National Grid. Vegetational types follow Chapter 4.

Coire Seamraig and Coire Reidh, fragments of Vaccineto–Callunetum hepaticosum occur on steep, block-strewn ground with *Hymenophyllum wilsonii* and a rich assemblage of leafy hepatics (see p. 65). Rhacomitreto–Empetretum stands characterise the few cliff-ledges.

Near the loch the floor of Strath Suardal is damp meadowland grazed by cattle, but nearer Broadford, where the influence of the limestone is reduced, Trichophoreto–Callunetum bog is extensive, with smaller areas of Sphagneto–Juncetum effusi and *Molinia caerulea–Myrica gale* stands.

Coille Gaireallach is an extensive area of wood to the south of Loch Cill Chriosd. It is primarily a *Corylus avellana–Oxalis acetosella* wood (8; *4.49*) with a floristically rich herbaceous understorey developed over limestone drift soils. Around outcrops of limestone pavement there are small areas of *Fraxinus excelsior–Brachypodium sylvaticum* (3, 4; *4.55*) woodland. Within Coille Gaireallach there are well developed 'tall herb' communities on ungrazed ledges in the steep limestone gorge (4; *4.47*) with *Cirsium heterophyllum*, *Crepis paludosa*, *Filipendula ulmaria* *Galium odoratum*, *Heracleum sphondylium*, *Listera ovata*, *Rubus saxatilis*, *Sanicula europaea*, and *Trollius europaeus*. In crevices of the limestone ravine walls *Asplenium trichomanes–Fissidens cristatus* stands occur (9; *4.4*) with *Asplenium viride*, *Cystopteris fragilis*, and *Orthothecium rufescens*. Additional interesting plants occurring in the wood and gorge include *Arctostaphylos uva-ursi*, *Galium boreale*, *Melica nutans*, *Phyllitis scolopendrium*, *Polystichum lonchitis*, *Prunus padus*, *Viburnum opulus*, *Amblystegiella sprucei*, *Antitrichia curtipendula* (on hazel trees), *Seligeria acutifolia* var. *longiseta*, *Cololejeunea calcarea*, and *Solorina saccata*.

On moving southwards from the limestone to the granite of Beinn an Dubhaich, there is a sharp and marked change to *Betula pubescens–Vaccinium myrtillus* woodland (5; *4.49*) with *Sorbus aucuparia*, and an understorey dominated by *Vaccinium myrtillus* and *Calluna vulgaris*, with *Deschampsia flexuosa*, *Blechnum spicant*, and *Potentilla erecta*.

There are a few treeless limestone outcrops within the wood that support small areas of *Dryas octopetala–Carex flacca* heath with *Plantago maritima*, *Saxifraga aizoides*, *Selaginella selaginoides*, and *Thalictrum alpinum*. More extensive areas of *Dryas octopetala* heath occur above the wood on Ben Suardal (Table 4.35). Here there is a mosaic of open limestone pavement (Table 4.56), *Dryas* heath, and grazed Agrosto–Festucetum (species-rich) grasslands on drift soils. Notable plants in these communities include *Alchemilla alpina*, *Antennaria dioica*, *Arctostaphylos uva-ursi*, *Botrychium lunaria*, *Epipactis atrorubens*, *Ophioglossum vulgatum*, *Paris quadrifolia*, *Polygonum viviparum*, and *Metzgeria pubescens*. *Cratoneuron commutatum* springs occur locally, grading into open *Eriophorum latifolium–Carex hostiana* gravel flushes with *Carex lepidocarpa*, *Eleocharis quinqueflora*, *Euphrasia scottica*, and *Cinclidium stygium* (2, 19; *4.25*). In non-wooded areas on the Beinn an Dubhaich granite Trichophoreto–Callunetum bog is widespread, with *Campylopus atrovirens* var. *falcatus*, *C. setifolius*, *C. shawii*, and *Sphagnum strictum* locally frequent in mildly soligenous sites.

Loch Cill Chriosd supports a rich and varied aquatic flora (Figs. 7, 19). On the stony loch margins there are stands of *Littorella uniflora* communities (7; *4.10*) with *Baldellia ranunculoides*, *Myriophyllum alterniflorum*, *Potamogeton coloratus*, *P. gramineus*, *P. natans*, and *Chara delicatula*. *Carex rostrata–Menyanthes trifoliata* (7; *4.14*) stands form a marginal reedswamp in shallow water on deep organic muds. Small areas of 'mud-bottom' communities occur locally, with *Carex lasiocarpa*, *C. limosa*, *C. rostrata*, *Sparganium minimum*, *Acrocladium giganteum*, and *Scorpidium scorpioides*. In water of 30 cm or more depth extensive beds of *Phragmites communis* occur (1, 2, 3; *4.13*) with *Nymphaea alba*, whilst stands of *Schoenoplectus lacustris* with *Potamogeton lucens* (11, 13; *4.13*) form an outer zone in deeper water. Details of the chemistry of the loch water are given in Fig. 7.

There is extensive fen development around the main inflow at the western end of the loch. It consists largely of *Carex rostrata–Scorpidium scorpioides* rich-fen (7; *4.23*) with *Carex dioica* and *Sphagnum contortum*. Soligenous soaks receiving drainage water from the limestone are dominated by *Schoenus nigricans* (13, 14; *4.25*) with *Drosera anglica*, *Eleocharis quinqueflora*, and *Eriophorum latifolium*. At the south edge of the fen there is a floristically rich area of calcareous turf hummocks within open mud and gravel (11; *4.25*) kept open by cattle trampling (see p. 46).

2. SEDIMENT STRATIGRAPHY

A series of trial borings on a north–south transect across the fen was made in 1967, and the core used for pollen analysis was taken at the point having the thickest sequence of deposits. The location of the coring site is shown on Fig. 19. A description is given below of the sediment lithology of the relevant levels in the cores used for pollen analysis; abbreviations follow Troels-Smith (1955). Sediment depths are measured from the fen surface.

345–400 cm	Slightly fibrous fine detritus mud, dark brown, darkens rapidly on exposure to air. Soft, nig 3, strf 0, elas 3, sicc 2, calc 0; humo 3; $Ld^2$3, Dg 1, Dh +. *Najas flexilis* seeds frequent. Lower boundary sharp.
400–430 cm	Silty fine detritus mud with fine sand, grey, darkens slightly on exposure to air. Soft, nig 1–2, strf 0, elas 1, sicc 2, calc 3–4; humo 2; Ag 2, Ga 2, Ld^2 +, Dg +. Lower boundary sharp.
430–432 cm	Coarse sand, brownish-grey, reddens on drying. Very firm nig 1, strf 1, elas 0, sicc 3, calc 4; Gs 4, Ga +. Lower boundary sharp.
432–441 cm	Silty fine detritus mud with fine sand, medium grey, darkens on

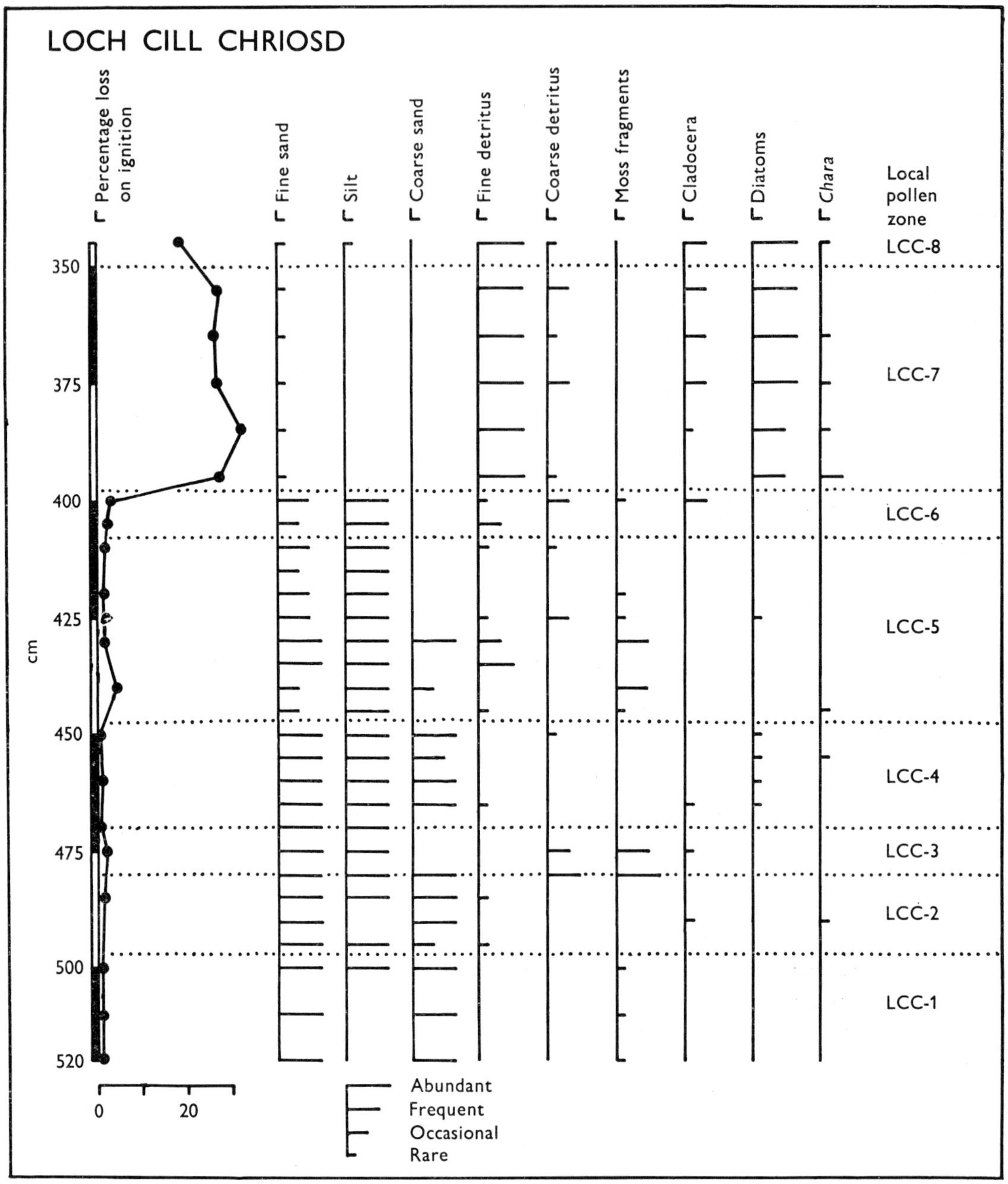

Figure 20. Sediment stratigraphy at Loch Cill Chriosd in relation to the local pollen zones, based on microscopic examination of the sediments and of residues following alkali maceration, and the percentage loss on ignition curve.

exposure to air. Soft, nig 2, strf 0, elas 1, sicc 2, calc 3; humo 2; Ag 2, Ga 2, Ld^2 +, Dg +, [test. moll. +]. Lower boundary sharp.

441–443 cm — Coarse sand, brownish-grey, reddens on drying. Very firm, nig 1, strf 1, elas 0, sicc 3, calc 1; Gs 4. Lower boundary sharp.

443–453 cm — Silt, grey, no colour change on exposure to air. Firm, nig 1, strf 0, elas 0, sicc 2–3, calc 3; Ag 4, Ga +, Gs +, [test. moll. +]. Lower boundary gradual over 4 cm.

453–498 cm — Sandy silt interbedded and interlaminated with coarse sand laminae at 460–462 cm (brownish-grey, reddens on drying, very firm, nig 1, strf 1, elas 0, sicc 3, calc; Gs 4) and 489–491 cm (brownish-grey, reddens on drying, very firm, nig 1, strf 1, elas 0, sicc 3, calc 1; Gs 4), grey, no colour change on exposure to air. Firm, nig 1, strf 0–1, elas 0, sicc 2, calc 3–4; Ag 2, Ga 2, Lc+, Gs +, [test. moll. +]. Lower boundary gradual over 3 cm.

498–516 cm Coarse sand and silt, grey brown, reddens on drying. Very firm, nig 1, strf 0, elas 1, sicc 3, calc 4; Ag 2, Ga 1, Gs 1, [test. moll. +]. Lower boundary sharp.

516–520+ cm Coarse sand, pale brown, no change on exposure to air, reddens on drying. Very firm, nig 2, strf 0, elas 1, sicc 3, calc 4; Gs 4, Ga +. Base not seen.

The detailed sediment stratigraphy, based on microscopic examination, and the loss on ignition curve are shown in Fig. 20.

3. POLLEN STRATIGRAPHY

In contrast to the pollen diagrams from the other sites the pollen sum (ΣP) at Loch Cill Chriosd includes the indeterminable pollen categories (indet: deteriorated, and indet:concealed). The basal sediments contain large quantities (75% or more) of pollen and spores so badly deteriorated that reliable identifications are impossible. As Cushing (1967*a*, 1967*b*) has discussed, it cannot be presumed that all pollen and spore types deteriorate in constant proportion to their numbers, and the inclusion of this category in the pollen sum thus serves to emphasise that the percentages of the determinable pollen and spore types are minimal estimates only. At all the other sites investigated the frequencies of the indeterminable categories are low (< 10%), and they are thus excluded from the main pollen sum.

For convenience the sediments between 395 and 520 cm at Loch Cill Chriosd are divided into eight biostratigraphic intervals, based upon the composition of the pollen and spore content, as shown in the pollen diagram (Plate 4). These local pollen zones are numbered and defined from the base upwards, and prefixed by the site designation 'LCC'. The pollen zones defined here are intended to apply only to this pollen diagram. The total number of pollen and spores (determinable and indeterminable) included in ΣP per sample ranges from 99 to 798, with a mean of 328 and a median of 251. The local pollen zones are briefly defined as follows. All percentages quoted are based on ΣP.

LCC-1 497.5–520 cm. This is the lowest zone recorded in the sediments at Loch Cill Chriosd, and it is characterised by high frequences of indeterminable:deteriorated pollen and spores. Of all the indeterminable:deteriorated grains counted in the zone, 88% were indeterminable because of exine degradation (*sensu* H. J. B. Birks, 1970; Cushing, 1964*b*, 1967*b*). Subjective judgement during the analyses of the samples suggested that the majority of the indeterminable grains were in fact Cyperaceae pollen too badly degraded to permit reliable identification. The 'true' percentages (that is the percentages that would be observed if pollen deterioration was negligible) of Cyperaceae pollen may well be higher than is shown.

LCC-2 480–497.5 cm. Characterised by abundant herb pollen, with Cyperaceae pollen dominant with values of 20% or more. *Lycopodium selago* spores attain values of 6% or more, and Ericaceae undiff. pollen frequencies are at least 10%. Spores of *Botrychium lunaria* and *Selaginella selaginoides*, and pollen of *Salix* cf. *S. herbacea* are consistently present in low amounts. There is a wide range of pollen types of herbaceous taxa in the zone. Pollen of trees and shrubs have low values throughout. Pollen of aquatic taxa is virtually absent. Indeterminable pollen values are 10% or less.

LCC-3 470–480 cm. Characterised by abundant herb pollen, with Gramineae pollen dominant (20% or more). *Rumex acetosa* pollen occurs with frequencies of 3% or more, whilst Cyperaceae, Ericaceae undiff., and *Lycopodium selago* values are lower than in zone LCC-2, with frequencies of 20% or less, 10% or less, and 5% or less respectively. *Juniperus communis* pollen values exceed 20%. *Filipendula* pollen occurs consistently in low amounts in this and the succeeding zone. The zone is richer in pollen and spore types than the preceding zone. Pollen of aquatic taxa is poorly represented.

LCC-4 447.5–470 cm. Characterised by abundant herb pollen, with Gramineae pollen dominant, attaining values of 30% or more. *Betula* undiff. pollen frequencies are between 7.5% and 10%, and *Rumex acetosa* pollen occurs with values of 3% or more.

TABLE 9.4

	Type of remains	Local pollen zone							
		LCC-1	LCC-2	LCC-3	LCC-4	LCC-5	LCC-6	LCC-7	LCC-8
Betula pubescens	fr	.	.	.	.	.	.	+	+
Equisetum	sh	.	.	.	.	.	.	+	+
Najas flexilis	s	.	.	.	.	.	.	+	+
Salix herbacea	lvs	.	+	.	.	+	.	.	.
Acrocladium giganteum	lvs	.	.	.	.	.	+	+	.
Ctenidium molluscum	lvs	.	.	.	.	.	+	.	.
Hylocomium splendens	lvs	.	+	.	.	+	.	.	.
Polytrichum alpinum	lvs	.	+	.	.	.	.	.	.
Rhacomitrium undiff.	lvs	+	+	.	.	+	.	.	.
R. fasciculare	lvs	.	.	.	.	+	.	.	.
R. lanuginosum	lvs	.	+	.	.	+	.	.	.
Scorpidium scorpioides	lvs	.	.	.	.	.	.	+	.
Chara	oos	.	.	+	+	+	+	+	+
Cristatella mucedo	st	.	.	.	.	.	.	+	+
Daphnia	ep	.	.	+	+	.	+	+	+
Plumatella	st	.	.	.	.	.	.	+	.

(ep = ephippia; fr = fruit; lvs = leaves; oos = oospores; s = seed; sh = sheath; st = statoblast.)

Betula cf. *B. nana* pollen values are low. Pollen percentages of dwarf shrubs and other shrubs are also low.

LCC-5 407.5–447.5 cm. Characterised by abundant herb pollen, with Cyperaceae pollen dominant (20% or more). Pollen of Ericaceae undiff. and *Empetrum* cf. *E. nigrum*, and spores of *Lycopodium selago* are prominent with frequencies of 5% or more. *Salix* cf. *S. herbacea* and Cruciferae pollen are consistently present in low percentages, whereas *Selaginella selaginoides* spore values are variable, but generally exceed 5%. *Alchemilla*, *Artemisia* cf. *A. norvegica*, and *Artemisia* undiff. pollen, and *Botrychium lunaria* and *Cryptogramma crispa* spores are consistently present in low frequencies.

LCC-6 397.5–407.5 cm. Characterised by abundant herb pollen, with Gramineae pollen dominant, with values of 20% or more. *Juniperus communis* pollen is also prominent, with frequencies of 10% or more. *Filipendula* pollen and *Thelypteris dryopteris* spores are consistently present in low amounts. Polypodiaceae undiff. spores have values of 10% or more. Dwarf-shrub pollen values are lower than in zone LCC-5.

LCC-7 350–397.5 cm. Characterised by abundant arboreal pollen, with values of at least 20% of both *Betula* undiff. and *Corylus avellana* pollen. *Sorbus aucuparia*, *Populus tremula*, and *Filipendula* pollen, and *Polypodium* and *Pteridium aquilinum* spores occur consistently as low percentages. Polypodiaceae undiff. spores have values of 5% or more. Shrub and dwarf-shrub pollen values are low throughout. Herb pollen types are less frequent than in other zones, but *Caltha* type, *Plantago lanceolata*, *P. major*/*P. media*, and *Ranunculus acris* type pollen are consistently present in low percentages.

LCC-8 350 cm upwards. Not examined in detail, but the lower boundary is drawn where *Corylus avellana* pollen values exceed those of *Betula* undiff. pollen.

The minerogenic sediments (silts, fine sands, and coarse sands) of zones LCC-1, LCC-2, LCC-3, LCC-4, and LCC-5 contain up to 57.6% hystrichosphaerids. *Operculodinium centrocarpum* is the commonest taxon present, with some *Hystrichosphaera furcata*, *H. bulloidea*, *H. membranacea*, and *H. mirabilis*. In contrast to the sediments at Loch Fada that contain both hystrichosphaerids and pre-Quaternary pollen grains and spores, no pollen or spores of undoubted pre-Quaternary age were found in the sediments examined at Loch Cill Chriosd. There is thus no reason to regard the hystrichosphaerid assemblage at Loch Cill Chriosd as being redeposited from pre-Quaternary sediments. Comparable assemblages have been described recently from Flandrian marine deposits at Borth Bog, Wales (Harland, 1968) and at Woodgrange, Co. Down in Northern Ireland (Downie & Singh, 1969).

4. MACROFOSSILS

Macrofossils identified from the residues after sample preparation are listed in Table 9.4. Their occurrences in the local pollen zones are indicated in the table.

5. RADIOCARBON DATE

Radiocarbon assay by the University of Cambridge Radiocarbon Laboratory of a sample of fine detritus mud ($Ld^2 3$, Dg 1, Dh +) from 395 to 400 cm depth (Zone LCC-6/LCC-7) in an adjacent large diameter (5.3 cm) core and correlated with the main pollen sequence (Plate 4) by sediment lithology and pollen stratigraphy gave an age determination of 9655 ± 150 radiocarbon years B.P. (Q-959; Switsur & West, 1972).

5. LOCHAN COIR' A' GHOBHAINN

1. LOCATION AND VEGETATION

Lochan Coir' a' Ghobhainn is situated 3 km south-east of Glenbrittle House and 4 km south-west of the summit (3309 feet, 1010 m) of Sgùrr Sgumain on the lower south-west slopes of the Cuillin Hills (Fig. 12) at 6°18′W, 57°11′N (National Grid Reference 18/417183). There is a group of three small lochans lying within an area of subdued hummocky moraines at an altitude of 275 feet (82 m) O.D. The lochan studied (Fig. 21) is the middle one of the three. The underlying rocks are olivine-dolerite sills, and there is an outcrop of ultra-basic peridotite 1.8 km to the east of the lochan at An Sgùman. The gabbro of the Cuillins occurs 2 km to the north-east of the lochan. The lochan is fed by a sluggish stream rising in the higher ground in the north-east, and is drained by a small stream flowing into Loch Brittle.

The surrounding vegetation is predominantly Molinieto–Callunetum bog occurring from sea-level to about 1000 feet (305 m) with *Campylopus atrovirens* var. *falcatus*, *C. schwarzii*, *C. shawii*, *Pleurozia purpurea*, *Sphagnum imbricatum*, *S. molle*, and *S. strictum* as notable components. On drier, gabbro knolls Trichophoreto–Callunetum bog occurs locally, grading into Callunetum vulgaris heath on steep, well-drained slopes. In the few waterlogged hollows Trichophoreto–Eriophoretum bog is found, and one such area on the slopes of Sgùrr Dearg has a well-developed aligned pattern of bog pools, with *Carex limosa* and *Sphagnum magellanicum*. Stream courses are marked either by dense *Molinia caerulea–Myrica gale* stands or by open *Eriophorum latifolium–Carex hostiana* gravel flushes (8; *4.25*) with *Drosera anglica*, *Eleocharis quinqueflora*, *Pinguicula lusitanica*, and *Schoenus nigricans*. Below the peridotite outcrop of An Sgùman there is an extensive flush dominated by *Schoenus nigricans* and *Phragmites communis*, with *Acrocladium trifarium*, *Scorpidium scorpioides*, *Sphagnum contortum*, and *S. warnstorfianum*. This is the site referred to as An Sgùman where the pollen stratigraphy has been examined briefly. The outcrop itself is dry, and supports a sparse but interesting flora, which includes *Antennaria dioica*, *Gentianella campestris*, *Glyphomitrium daviesii*, *Grimmia decipiens* var. *decipiens*, *G. decipiens* var. *robusta*, *G. funalis*, *G. ovalis*, *G. patens*, *Rhacomitrium ellipticum*, and *Ulota hutchinsiae*.

In steep blocky areas where bog development is prevented and grazing animals are excluded, small fragments of woodland occur locally at low altitudes. For example, rather stunted *Betula pubescens* ssp. *odorata*, *Corylus avellana*, *Ilex aquifolium*, *Quercus petraea*, and *Sorbus aucuparia* occur in a block litter at 750 feet (225 m) below Sgùrr nan Eag. *Luzula sylvatica* and *Vaccinium myrtillus* dominate the understorey. On and between the blocks *Hymenophyllum wilsonii*, *Thelypteris phegopteris*, *Dicranum scottianum*, *Frullania germana* (also on trees), and *Plagiochila spinulosa* are of interest, as is the epiphyte *Ulota vittata*. More extensive wooded areas persist on and under the steep sea-cliffs above Soay Sound, for example between Ulfhart Point and An Leac. Birch and hazel dominate, with *Ilex aquifolium*, *Populus tremula*, *Prunus padus*, *Quercus petraea*, *Salix aurita*, *Sorbus aucuparia*, and *Ulmus glabra*. The floor of the woods are steep and blocky with a herb-rich understorey approaching the *Corylus avellana–Oxalis acetosella* Association. Species of interest in these woods include *Dryopteris aemula*, *Polystichum aculeatum*, *Grimmia hartmanii*, *Harpanthus scutatus*, *Hylocomium brevirostre*, *Hypnum callichroum*, and *Plagiochila punctata*. Several deeply cut wooded ravines along the coast support a rich cryptogamic flora including *Hymenophyllum wilsonii*, *Aphanolejeunea microscopica*, *Cephaloziella pearsonii*, *Drepanolejeunea hamatifolia*, *Harpalejeunea ovata*, *Herberta adunca*, *Marchesinia mackaii*, *Trichostomum hibernicum*, and *Sticta dufourii*. Inaccessible ledges on the sea-cliffs are habitats for *Agrimonia eupatoria*, *Hypericum androsaemum*, *Juniperus communis* ssp. *nana*, *Osmunda regalis*, and *Vicia sylvatica*. *Asplenium marinum* communities occur in sheltered overhangs at the base of the low sea-cliffs.

Although the low-lying areas around Lochan Coir' a' Ghobhainn are largely treeless today, the occurrence of small woodland fragments on steep broken ground suggests that woodland may once have been more widespread prior to the spread of

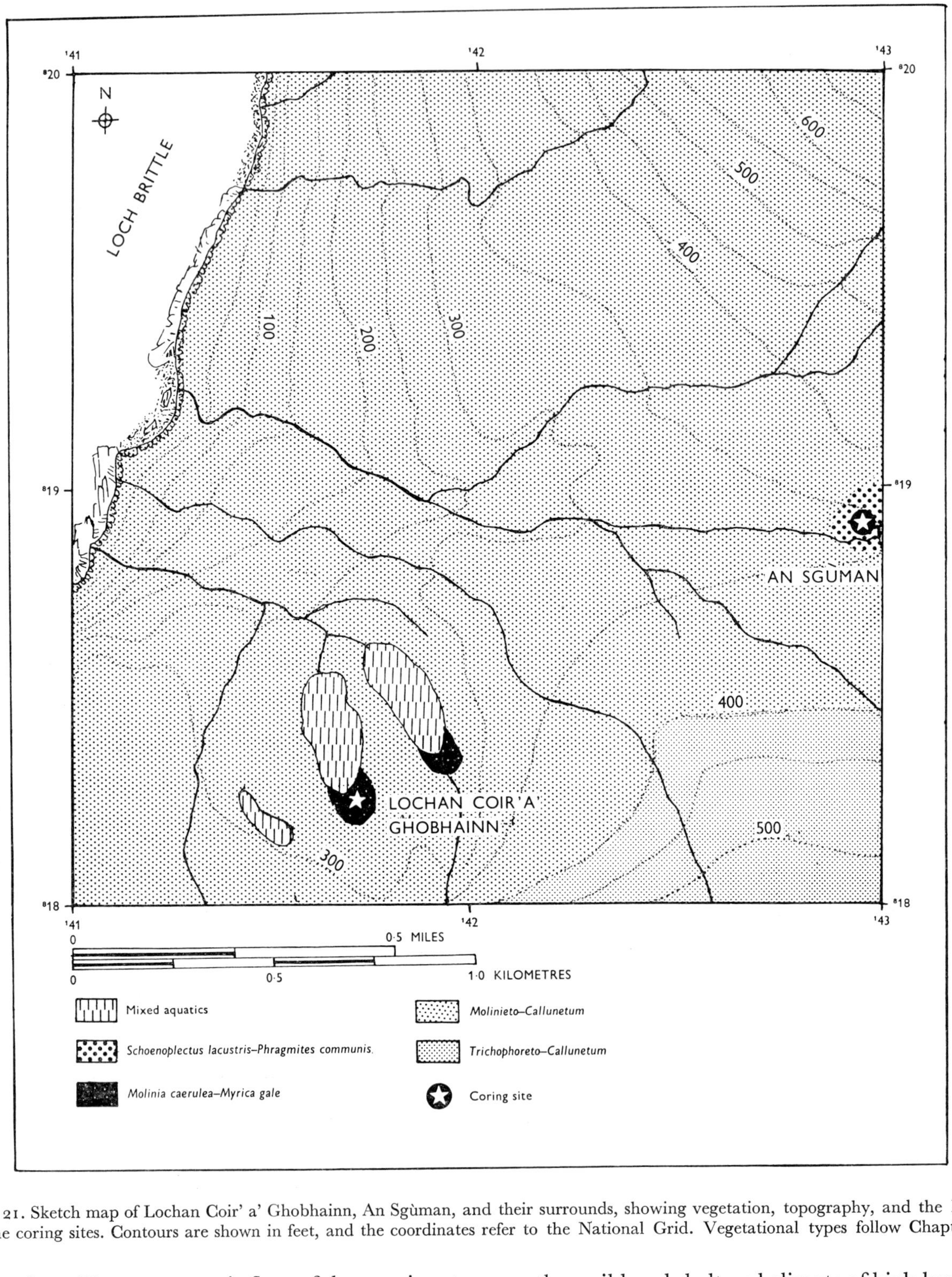

Figure 21. Sketch map of Lochan Coir' a' Ghobhainn, An Sgùman, and their surrounds, showing vegetation, topography, and the location of the coring sites. Contours are shown in feet, and the coordinates refer to the National Grid. Vegetational types follow Chapter 4.

blanket-bog. The cryptogamic flora of the area is not as rich in 'Macaronesian–Tropical' species (*sensu* Greig-Smith, 1950) as the Sleat Peninsula, but the occurrence of several such taxa near Lochan Coir' a' Ghobhainn suggests that the low ground experiences a rather mild and sheltered climate of high humidity and equable temperatures (Ratcliffe, 1968).

On the higher ground above 1000 feet (305 m) there are extensive and rather unstable screes, bare gabbro cliffs, and deeply cut corries with steep backwalls leading to the summit ridge. Few plants grow on the unstable screes, but in the more stable areas there is some vegetational cover, with scattered plants of *Alchemilla alpina*, *Cardaminopsis petraea*, *Lycopodium selago*, *Oxyria digyna*, *Saxifraga stellaris*, *Sedum rosea*, *Vaccinium myrtillus*, *Antitrichia curtipendula*, *Grimmia doniana*, *Polytrichum alpinum*, *Rhacomitrium fasciculare*, and *R. lanuginosum*. There is a sparse plant cover on the cliffs and in the corries. Occasionally ledges support some 'tall herbs', for example *Geum rivale*, *Polygonum viviparum*, *Saussurea alpina*, *Sedum rosea*, *Thalictrum alpinum*, and *Trollius europaeus*, with *Cystopteris fragilis* and *Selaginella selaginoides*. *Saxifraga oppositifolia* occurs on drier outcrops in several corries, and *Arabis alpina*, *Cerastium arcticum*, and *Draba norvegica* are notable species with single Cuillin stations in the northern corries. *Tofieldia pusilla* has its sole Skye locality near Sgùrr nan Eag. The wind-exposed ridges and cols above the corries support Cariceto–Rhacomitretum lanuginosi heath, *Juniperus communis* ssp. *nana* scrub, and *Festuca ovina–Luzula spicata* 'fell-field' communities, with *Alchemilla alpina*, *Armeria maritima*, *Carex bigelowii*, *Deschampsia alpina*, *Gnaphalium supinum*, *Juncus trifidus*, *Luzula spicata*, *Plantago maritima*, and *Salix herbacea*. Notable bryophytes of the higher ground include *Acrocladium sarmentosum*, *Bryum dixonii*, *Ditrichum lineare*, and *Gymnomitrion corallioides*.

Lochan Coir' a' Ghobhainn is rather shallow (less than 2 m depth of water in the centre) and it supports almost continuous *Carex rostrata–Menyanthes trifoliata* stands (2; *4.14*) with *Nymphaea alba* ssp. *occidentalis*. Around the exposed rocky shores *Littorella uniflora–Lobelia dortmanna* communities occur with *Baldellia ranunculoides* (8; *4.10*). At the southern end of the lochan, a *Molinia caerulea–Myrica gale* fen (5; *4.20*) has developed along the sluggish inflow.

2. SEDIMENT STRATIGRAPHY

A series of trial borings on a north–south transect through the *Molinia caerulea–Myrica gale* fen at the southern end of the lochan was made in 1968, and the core used for pollen analysis was taken at the point having the thickest sequence of deposits. The location of the coring site is shown in Fig. 21. A description is given below of the sediment lithology of the relevant levels in the cores used for pollen analysis; abbreviations follow Troels-Smith (1955). Sediment depths are measured from the fen surface.

300–322.5 cm	Slightly fibrous fine detritus mud, medium-brown, darkens on exposure to air. Firm, nig 2, strf 0, elas 2, sicc 2, calc 0; humo 2; Dg 2, $Ld^2$2, Dg +. Lower boundary sharp.
322.5–326 cm	Diatomite, pale whitish-grey, pales on drying. Firm, nig 0–1, strf 0, elas 2, sicc 2, calc 0; Lso 4, Ld^2 +, Dg +. Lower boundary sharp.
326–337 cm	Slightly fibrous fine detritus mud, medium-brown, darkens slightly on exposure to air. Firm, nig 2, strf 0, elas 2, sicc 2–3, calc 0; humo 3; Dg 2, $Ld^2$2, Dh +, Ag +. Lower boundary sharp.
337–356 cm	Silty mud with detritus, fine sand, and stones, grey-brown, no colour change on exposure to air. Firm, nig 2, strf 0, elas 1, sicc 2–3, calc 0; humo 2–3; Ag 2, $Ld^2$1, Ga 1, Gs +, Gg +, Tb +, Dh +. Lower boundary gradual over 3 cm.
356–362.5 cm	Silty fine detritus mud, dark brown, darkens on exposure to air. Firm, nig 3, strf 0, elas 2, sicc 2, calc 0; humo 3; $Ld^2$2–3, Ag 1, Dg 1, Dh +, Tb +. Lower boundary sharp.
362.5–383 cm	Silty diatomaceous fine detritus mud, green-grey, pales on exposure to air. Soft, nig 1–2, strf 1, elas 1–2, sicc 2, calc 0; humo 1; $Ld^2$2, Lso 2, Dg +, Dh +, Ag +, Ga +. Lower boundary gradual over 3 cm.
383–391 + cm	Silt and fine sand, pale grey, no colour change on exposure to air. Very firm, nig 1, strf 1, elas 1, sicc 3, calc 0; Ag 3, Ga 1, Dg +, Gs +. Base not seen.

The detailed sediment stratigraphy, based on microscopic examination, and the loss on ignition curve are shown in Fig. 22.

3. POLLEN STRATIGRAPHY

For convenience the sediments between 300 and 390 cm at Lochan Coir' a' Ghobhainn are divided into five biostratigraphic intervals, based upon the composition of the pollen and spore content, as shown in the pollen diagram (Plate 5). These local pollen zones are numbered and defined from the base upwards, and prefixed by the site designation 'LCG'. The pollen zones defined here are intended

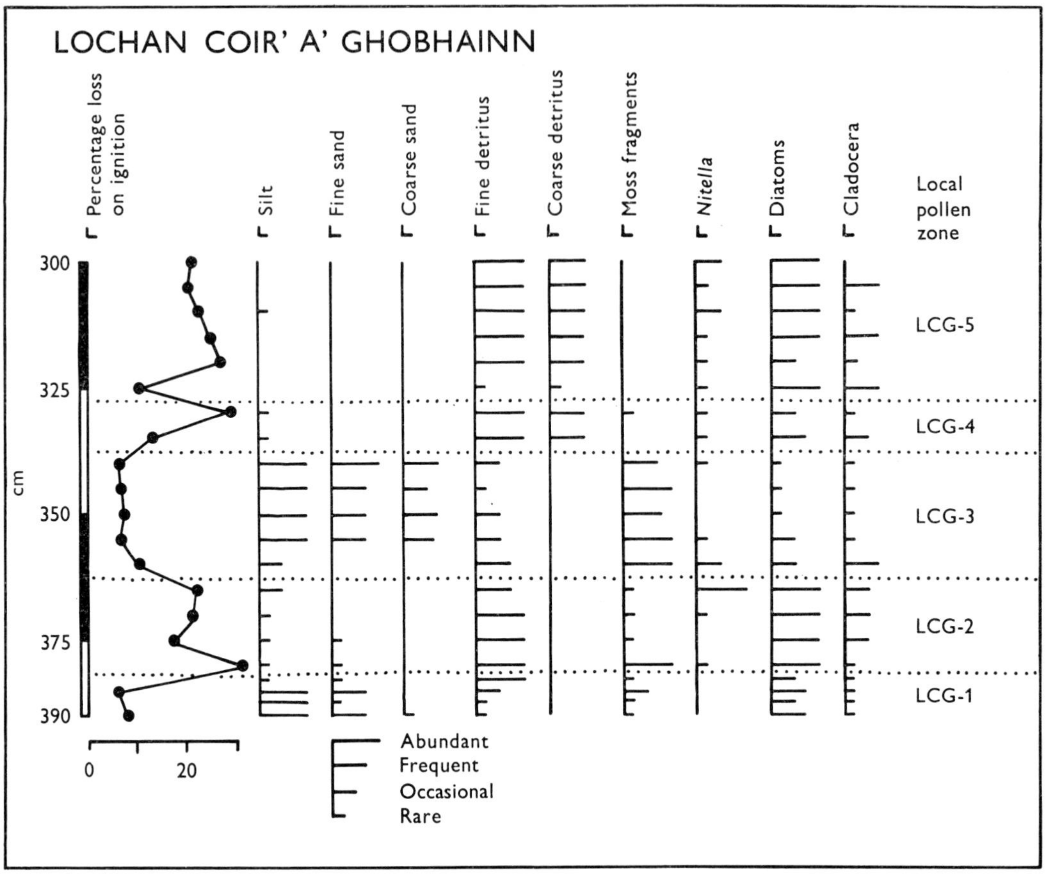

Figure 22. Sediment stratigraphy at Lochan Coir' a' Ghobhainn in relation to the local pollen zones, based on microscopic examination of the sediments and of residues following alkali maceration, and the percentage loss on ignition curve.

to apply only to this pollen diagram. The total number of determinable pollen and spores included in ΣP per sample ranges from 299 to 1848, with a mean of 1036 and a median of 1006. The local pollen zones are briefly defined as follows. All percentages quoted are based on ΣP.

LCG-1 381.25–390 cm. This is the lowest zone recorded in the sediments at Lochan Coir' a' Ghobhainn, and it is characterised by abundant herb pollen with Cyperaceae pollen dominant, with values of 20% or more. *Oxyria digyna* pollen is particularly prominent, with values of 10% or more. *Lycopodium selago* spores attain values of 10% or more. Pollen of trees, shrubs, dwarf shrubs, and obligate aquatic taxa are all rare with low frequencies. *Artemisia* cf. *A. norvegica*, *Artemisia* undiff., Caryophyllaceae, Cruciferae, cf. *Sedum*, and *Silene maritima* type pollen occur consistently in low frequencies.

LCG-2 362.5–381.25 cm. Characterised by abundant herb pollen with Cyperaceae pollen dominant, with values of 30% or more. Tree, shrub, and dwarf-shrub pollen frequencies are all 10% or less. *Lycopodium selago* spores attain values of 6% or more throughout, and there is a wide range oi pollen of herbaceous taxa present in the zone.

LCG-3 337.5–362.5 cm. Characterised by abundant dwarf-shrub pollen with Ericaceae undiff. tetrads dominant, with values of 30% or more. *Empetrum* cf. *E. nigrum* pollen is present with values of 5 to 10%. Tree and shrub pollen frequencies are low throughout, and herb pollen percentages are lower than in zone LCG-2. *Lycopodium selago* spores have frequencies of 5% or more, and *Salix* cf. *S. herbacea* pollen is consistently present. Caryophyllaceae undiff. pollen and *Selaginella selaginoides* microspores attain values of 2% or more throughout, and

TABLE 9.5

	Type of remains	Local pollen zone				
		LCG-1	LCG-2	LCG-3	LCG-4	LCG-5
Carex undiff.	fr	.	.	+	.	.
C. rostrata	fr	.	.	.	.	+
Isoetes lacustris	ms	.	.	.	+	.
Juncus articulatus/J. acutiflorus	s	.	.	.	+	+
Myriophyllum alterniflorum	s	.	+	.	+	.
Ranunculus (subgenus *Batrachium*)	ach	.	+	.	.	.
Salix herbacea	lvs	+	+	+	.	.
Selaginella selaginoides	ms	.	+	+	.	.
Acrocladium sarmentosum	lvs	.	+	.	.	.
Antitrichia curtipendula	lvs	.	+	+	.	.
Bryum	lvs	.	+	.	.	.
Drepanocladus	lvs	.	+	+	.	.
Hylocomium splendens	lvs	+	+	+	.	.
Polytrichum alpinum	lvs	+	+	+	.	.
Rhacomitrium undiff.	lvs	+	+	+	+	.
R. lanuginosum	lvs	.	.	+	.	.
Sphagnum	lvs	.	+	.	.	.
Nitella	oos	.	+	+	+	+
Bosmina longirostris	h	.	+	+	+	+
Daphnia	ep	.	+	+	+	+

(ach = achene; ep = ephippia; fr = fruit; h = head-shield; lvs = leaves; ms = megaspore; s = seed.)

Liguliflorae, *Sagina*, and *Succisa pratensis* pollen occur consistently in low amounts.

LCG-4 327.5–337.5 cm. Characterised by abundant herb pollen with Gramineae pollen dominant, attaining values of 20% or more. *Rumex acetosa* pollen occurs with frequencies of 4% or more. *Juniperus communis* pollen is prominent with values of 10% or more. Pollen of trees, other shrubs, and dwarf shrubs have low frequencies throughout. Polypodiaceae undiff. spores attain values of up to 10%. *Myriophyllum alterniflorum* pollen is present in high amounts, with a range of pollen and spore types of other aquatic taxa.

LCG-5 337.5 cm upwards. Characterised by abundant arboreal pollen with values of 20% or more of *Betula* undiff. pollen and 10% or more of *Corylus avellana* pollen. Pollen of *Sorbus aucuparia*, *Populus tremula*, and *Prunus* cf. *P. padus* are consistently present in low amounts, but pollen of other deciduous trees is virtually absent. Shrub and dwarf-shrub pollen types attain low values. Values of herb pollen types are lower than in the other zones, but pollen of *Filipendula*, *Plantago maritima*, *Ranunculus acris* type, and *Urtica* are consistently present in low amounts. Polypodiaceae undiff. spores attain values of 5–10%. The upper boundary of the zone is not defined.

Because fungal remains are prominent constituents of some of the sediments analysed at Lochan Coir' a' Ghobhainn, the relative abundances of the fungal hyphal fragments (largely septate ascomycete hyphae) and of fungal spores in the sediments were recorded during the pollen analyses. The frequencies of all fungal remains found (hyphal fragments + spores) are expressed as percentages of $\Sigma P + \Sigma$ Fungal Remains on Plate 5. The ratio of fungal spores to fungal hyphae is also shown. Cushing (1964*b*) and H. J. B. Birks (1970) have presented evidence to suggest that fungal spores are characteristic, in part at least, of autochthonous sediments, as the spores are largely wind-dispersed and they are presumably deposited directly with the pollen into the site of deposition. An abundance of ascomycete fungal hyphae may, however, be suggestive of allochtonous sediments in which there is an incorporation of terrestrial material such as soil, peat, or humus into the site of deposition. In general fungal hyphal fragments are rare in the majority of *limnic* sediments examined, with the exception of inwashed layers of plant detritus (H. J. B. Birks, 1970; Cushing, 1964*b*) and litter horizons representing the surface accumulation of litter on buried ice masses prior to the ice block melting to form a lake basin (Cushing,

1963, 1967*a*; Florin & Wright, 1969). At Lochan Coir' a' Ghobhainn there are high frequencies (15–20%) of fungal remains (predominantly hyphal fragments) in the detrital silts of zone LCG-3, and low frequencies (3–6%) of fungal remains (mainly fungal spores) in the fine detritus muds and diatomites of zones LCG-4 and LCG-5. Moderately high frequencies of both fungal spores and fungal hyphae occur in the silty muds of zones LCG-1 and LCG-2.

The values of indeterminable: deteriorated pollen are low throughout the profile, but the highest frequencies (up to 8%) are in zone LCG-3. Exine corrosion accounted for 52% of the indeterminable category in this zone, and breakage and crumpling 22% and 18% respectively. No undoubted pre-Quaternary microfossils were found in the Lochan Coir' a' Ghobhainn sediments.

4. MACROFOSSILS

Macrofossils identified from the residues after sample preparation are listed in Table 9.5. Their occurrences in the local pollen zones are indicated in the table.

5. RADIOCARBON DATES

Four radiocarbon dates have been obtained from different levels in the core sampled for pollen analysis. The datings obtained at the University of Cambridge Radiocarbon Laboratory are as follows (see Switsur & West, 1972).

Sample depth (cm) and local pollen zone	Laboratory number	Sediment type dated	Radiocarbon date (years B.P.)
315–317.5 (LCG-5)	Q-958	Fine detritus mud ($Ld^2$2, Dg 2, Dh +)	8650 ± 110
335–337.5 (LCG-4)	Q-957	Fine detritus mud ($Ld^2$2, Dg 2, Dh +, Ag +)	9420 ± 150
362.5–365 (LCG-2)	Q-956	Diatomaceous fine detritus mud ($Ld^2$2, Lso 2, Dg +, Dh +, Ag +, Ga +)	9691 ± 150
380–382.5 (LCG-1/LCG-2)	Q-955	Diatomaceous fine detritus mud ($Ld^2$2, Lso 2, Dg +, Dh +, Ag +, Ga +)	10254 ± 220

10

ZONATION OF THE POLLEN DIAGRAMS

It is often desirable to divide each pollen diagram into smaller units for ease in (*a*) the description and (*b*) the discussion and comparison of pollen sequences. The most useful unit of subdivision of the vertical dimension of a pollen diagram is the *pollen zone*, here defined as a body of sediment with a consistent and homogeneous fossil pollen and spore content that is distinguished from adjacent sediment bodies by differences in the kind and frequencies of its contained fossil pollen grains and spores. A number of pollen zones have been delimited and defined for each of the five stratigraphic sequences investigated (see Chapter 9), and these are termed *local pollen zones*. These local zones are based on the observed changes in the frequencies of a range of pollen and spore types, determinable and indeterminable. Although they are useful in describing the features of the pollen diagrams at each site, the local zones are of limited use in discussion and comparison between sites because of the varying criteria adopted in their delimitation.

There are, however, overall similarities in the pollen and spore composition of many of the local pollen zones at the different sites on Skye, thus permitting an attempt to define a series of *regional pollen zones* and to map their distribution in space and time. To be of regional value and to permit discussion and comparison between sites, the regional zones are defined only on the basis of observable and significant changes in the frequencies of the more widespread pollen and spore components in the fossil spectra. In practice, the local zones tend to be subdivisions of the regional system, although there are some local zones with characteristic and distinctive fossil pollen assemblages that are, at present, only known at single sites, and are thus of no regional significance.

Palaeontologists and stratigraphers have recently formulated a revised Code of Stratigraphic Nomenclature (American Commission on Stratigraphic Nomenclature, 1961; Geological Society of London, 1967, 1969). Although the problems of Quaternary pollen stratigraphy were not specifically considered when the Code was written, the definitions and recommendations of the Code apply clearly and precisely to the usage and nomenclature of pollen zones, as discussed by Cushing (1964*a*).

As defined above, a pollen zone, whether it is of local or regional character, is a *biostratigraphic unit* which is 'a body of rock strata characterised by its content of fossils contemporaneous with the deposition of the strata' (Amer. Comm., Article 19). As Quaternary pollen zones are rarely, if ever, characterised by the unique occurrence of one or more pollen grain or spore types, of the various types of units or *zones* in biostratigraphic classification that are distinguished by the Stratigraphical Code, a pollen zone as defined above corresponds most closely to the category of the *assemblage zone* (see Cushing, 1964*a*). An assemblage zone is defined by the Code as 'a body of strata characterized by a certain assemblage of fossils without regard to their ranges; it receives its name from one or more of these fossils' (Amer. Comm., Article 21; Geol. Soc., 1969, Section 11, subsection A, paragraph ii).

Article 21(a) of the Amer. Comm. amplifies the nature of the assemblage zone (see also Teichert, 1958). 'The bases for recognizing assemblage zones includes variations in the fossil taxa, in abundance of specimens, or in both. Such variations are usually in response to environment though evolutionary change may be a factor. The assemblage zone may indicate ecologic facies or age or both. It is, however, primarily a grouping of strata according to directly observable fossil content. Assemblage zones may be based on all the fossils or only on specific kinds.'

Article 21(b) of the Amer. Comm. further states that 'the assemblage zone is usually named from one or more taxa particularly prominent or diagnostic of the assemblage, although name-givers need not be confined to the zone or found in every part of it.'

The regional pollen assemblage zones used in this study are named, defined, and described in accordance with the Code of Stratigraphic Nomenclature (see Cushing, 1967*a*). The present scheme is based upon a subjective comparison of all the pollen diagrams now available for the Isle of Skye. The zones are named after taxa whose pollen grains or spores are characteristically more abundant in a given zone than in those above or below it. If a choice in the naming of a zone is possible, preference is usually, but not necessarily, given to a combination of names of taxa that are believed to have some ecological or sociological association. The regional pollen assemblage zones are divided into assemblage subzones for further convenience, but, as permitted by the Code, not all intervals within an assemblage zone need be given subzone names (Amer. Comm., Article 20(e)). As required by the Code each assemblage zone is defined at a specific type locality and section.

In view of the limited number of sites investigated, the assemblage zones described here must be regarded as tentative, and the names proposed are informal (in the sense of the Code). To emphasise the informal nature of these zones, the initial letter of the term 'zone' is not capitalised in accordance with the Code (Amer. Comm., Article 24(d)).

For the sake of brevity in discussion the word 'assemblage' is often omitted from the zonal and subzonal names, but it should be emphasised that, although the names of the zone or subzone are suggestive of their fossil composition, it is a group of taxa, rather than one or two taxa, that gives the pollen zones their character, and that the zones are defined by the accompanying description.

The zones are described from oldest to youngest, as they appear in the sediments examined. Throughout the descriptions the pollen percentages quoted are based on a sum of total determinable pollen (ΣP). The known geographical extent of the regional assemblage zones is based on all the published pollen diagrams in Great Britain and Ireland.

Although the pollen zone boundaries were initially located by inspection, chi-square tests of homogeneity (Mosimann, 1965) were made between all contiguous pairs of samples in the five sequences examined to provide some form of objective division of the biostratigraphical data for comparison with the initial subjective division (cf. Dale & Walker, 1970; Kershaw, 1970). Chi-square tests of homogeneity were used as a means of testing the hypothesis that adjacent levels are similar in their pollen composition. Chi-squares were calculated using the computer program CHIPOLL (H. J. B. Birks, unpublished). Any deviations from this hypothesis would suggest that significant differences in pollen composition exist between those levels, thereby providing a means of locating the points of significant difference in pollen frequencies between levels in a fixed stratigraphical sequence. The frequencies of all pollen and spore types included within the basic pollen sum (ΣP) that have values of 5% or more in at least one spectrum were used for the computation of the chi-square values. The chi-square values and the appropriate significance levels for each pair of levels at all the sites studied are plotted in stratigraphical order on Fig. 23, with the local and regional pollen zones. In general the positions of the highest chi-square values, corresponding to the greatest heterogeneity between adjacent levels, closely coincide with the upper and lower boundaries of the pollen zones that were initially located by inspection. This provides independent confirmation that the initial positionings of the zone boundaries were the most appropriate in terms of the observed fluctuations in pollen and spore frequencies. It should be noted, however, that the chi-square tests also indicate statistically significant differences between adjacent levels that do not coincide with the initially selected zone boundaries, especially at Loch Cill Chriosd and Lochan Coir' a' Ghobhainn. Many of these levels of statistical heterogeneity do not, however, appear appropriate for the purpose of delimiting upper or lower boundaries of pollen assemblage zones. The demonstration of such heterogeneity within the zones is, however, of considerable interest, the causes of which are matters for interpretation and for further study.

As Dale & Walker (1970) have discussed, the value of a numerical analysis of pollen stratigraphical data is not so much in the production of zonation schemes that are considered to be more 'meaningful' than subjectively derived divisions, but rather that they focus attention on the definition and consistent application of particular criteria for the delimitation of pollen zone boundaries.

1. *LYCOPODIUM*–CYPERACEAE ASSEMBLAGE ZONE

Type locality and section: Lochan Coir' a' Ghobhainn (Plate 5). Zone LCG-2 and zone LCG-3 (337·5–381.25 cm).

Description: Nonarboreal pollen (N.A.P.) is 85% or more of total pollen, with Cyperaceae and Gramineae pollen prominent. Cyperaceae pollen values consistently exceed Gramineae pollen percentages with values of 30% or more. *Lycopodium selago* spores attain values of 5% or more throughout. Ericaceae undiff. pollen may be relatively important. *Athyrium alpestre* type and *Cryptogramma crispa* spores are exclusive, and

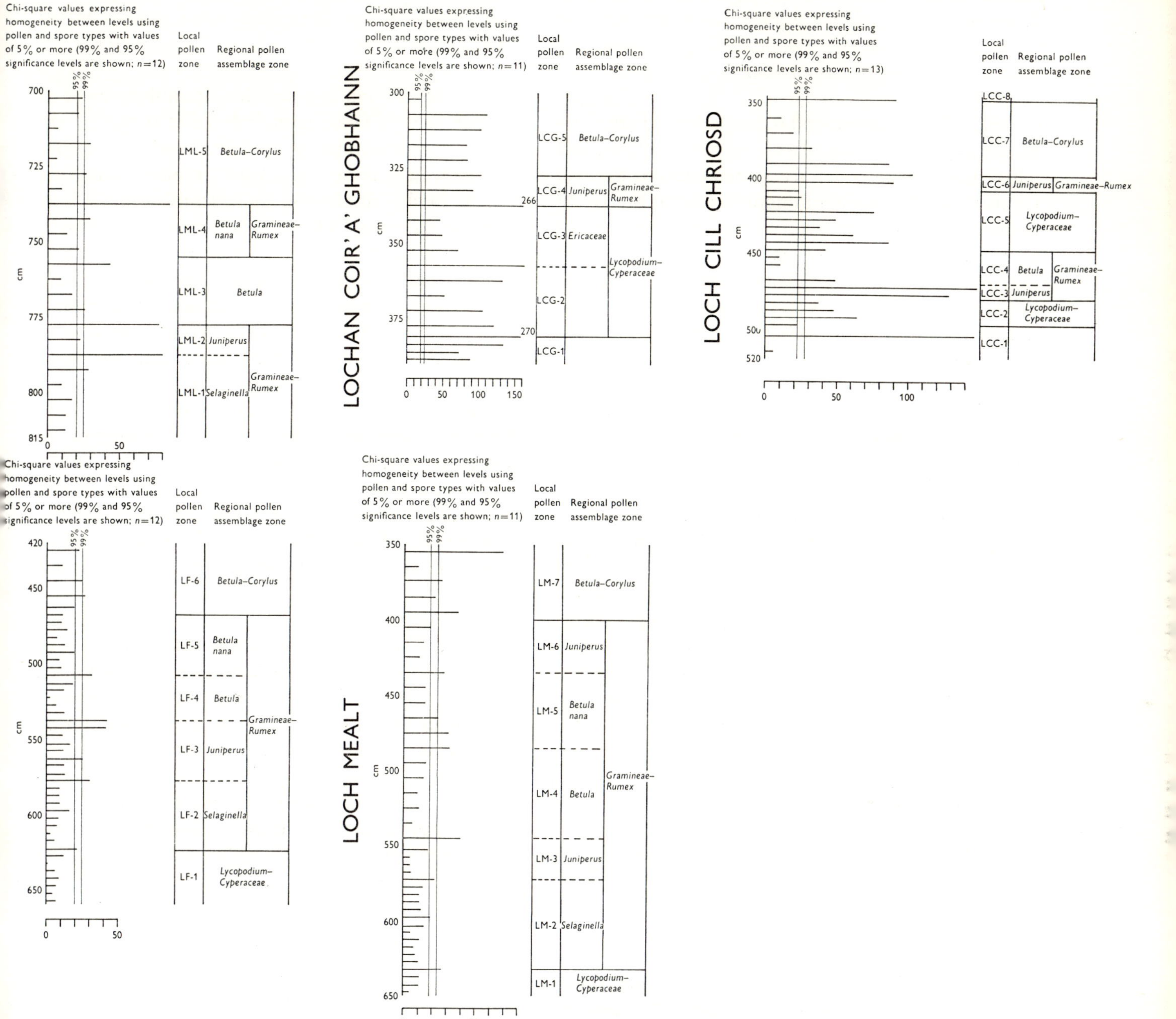

Figure 23. Chi-square values between all contiguous pairs of samples in the five pollen stratigraphical sequences based on all pollen and spore types included in ΣP with values of 5% or more. The 95 and 99% significance levels, the local pollen zones, and the regional pollen assemblage zones are also shown. Abbreviations: n = number of degrees of freedom.

Antennaria type, *Artemisia* cf. *A. norvegica*, *Salix* cf. *S. herbacea*, and *Saxifraga stellaris* pollen are selective to the zone. *Oxyria digyna* pollen values are low (less than 2%) throughout the zone.

Contacts: The upper boundary is placed where *Lycopodium selago* spore values decrease to 1% or less, and where Gramineae pollen frequencies exceed those of Cyperaceae. The zone commonly occurs as the lowest polleniferous sediment overlying glacial drift, except at Loch Cill Chriosd where it occurs intercalated within the Gramineae–*Rumex* zone. The lower boundary at this site is placed where there is an abrupt rise of *Lycopodium selago* spore and Cyperaceae pollen values.

Subdivisions: The following subzone is recognized:

Ericaceae assemblage subzone: The subzone is only known at Lochan Coir' a' Ghobhainn where it occurs for 25 cm in the upper part of the assemblage zone (zone LCG-3). Ericaceae undiff. is the dominant pollen type with values of 30% or more, and Cyperaceae pollen values are depressed to 25% or less. *Empetrum* cf. *E. nigrum* pollen occurs in values of 10% or less, and a wide range of pollen types occurs in low frequencies. The lower boundary of the subzone is placed where pollen of Ericaceae undiff. increases to more than 20%; the upper boundary is as for the *Lycopodium*–Cyperaceae zone.

Other occurrences: The assemblage zone also occurs at the following sites on the Isle of Skye:

Loch Fada	(Plate 2)	Zone LF-1	(35.5 cm thick)
Loch Mealt	(Plate 3)	Zone LM-1	(17.5 cm thick)
Loch Cill Chriosd	(Plate 4)	Zone LCC-2	(17.5 cm thick)
		Zone LCC-5	(40 cm thick)

As defined broadly above the assemblage zone can also be recognised in Late-Devensian sediments near Loch Assynt, Sutherland (H. J. B. Birks, unpublished data), at Loch Dungeon, Kirkcudbrightshire (zone LD-1a; H. H. Birks, 1969, 1972), at Blea Tarn, Westmorland (phases 1–3; Pennington, 1970; Tutin, 1969; zone BTA; Pennington & Lishman, 1971), and at Llyn Dwythwch and Nant Ffrancon, Caernarvonshire (zones I and III; Seddon, 1962). The pollen assemblage recorded at Loch Droma, Ross and Cromarty (Kirk & Godwin, 1963) is broadly similar to this assemblage zone, but it differs in the extremely high values (50% or more) of *Empetrum* pollen. The complete absence of any Ericaceae pollen in the published diagram is striking, and indeed anomalous in view of the convincing macrofossil evidence for abundant local chionophilous vegetation.

Age and extent: The base of the assemblage zone at Lochan Coir' a' Ghobhainn is dated at 10254 ± 220 (Q-955) radiocarbon years B.P., and the upper boundary at 9420 ± 150 (Q-956) radiocarbon years B.P. At Loch Cill Chriosd the assemblage zone is at least 9655 ± 150 (Q-959) radiocarbon years old. There is a radiocarbon date of 12810 ± 155 radiocarbon years B.P. (Q-457) from Loch Droma, and Pennington & Lishman (1971) correlated their local pollen zone BTA at Blea Tarn, Westmorland with 'period A' of the Late-Devensian that has been radiocarbon dated at Blelham Bog, Lancashire between 13450 ± 200 (I-3596) and 14330 ± 230 (Q-758) radiocarbon years B.P. (Pennington & Bonny, 1970; Buckley & Willis, 1970).

The full geographical extent of the zone is unknown, but it is likely to be found more widely in the Scottish Highlands, the Southern Uplands and in Lakeland. It is strikingly absent from sites in lowland Britain.

Remarks: The zone is associated with sediments of distinctive lithology, being fine-grained, unstratified silts of low organic content (<5% loss on ignition), often with thin organic bands with a characteristic macrofossil assemblage that includes *Salix herbacea*, *Hylocomium splendens*, *Polytrichum alpinum*, *Rhacomitrium* spp., and *R. lanuginosum*. All the Cyperaceae pollen grains found in this assemblage zone that are well enough preserved to allow further determination are identified as *Carex* type.

2. GRAMINEAE–*RUMEX* ASSEMBLAGE ZONE

Type locality and section: Loch Fada (Plate 2). Zones LF-2 to LF-5 (467.5–622.5 cm).

Description: N.A.P. is more than 70% throughout the zone. Gramineae is the dominant pollen type with values of 30% or more, and Cyperaceae pollen values are consistently lower than the Gramineae pollen frequencies. *Rumex acetosa* pollen attains values of 3% or more throughout the zone, and pollen of *Ranunculus acris* type, Rosaceae undiff., and *Thalictrum* is consistently present in low frequencies. *Empetrum* cf. *E. nigrum*, Ericaceae undiff., and *Salix* pollen values are generally less than 10%. Pollen of

Alchemilla, *Cerastium alpinum* type, *Lotus* cf. *L. corniculatus*, *Plantago major*/*P. media*, *Potentilla* type, *Ranunculus acris* type, *Saussurea alpina*, *Saxifraga aizoides*, *S. oppositifolia*, and *S. hypnoides*, and spores of *Botrychium lunaria* and *Selaginella selaginoides* are selective, and pollen of *Polygala*, *Saxifraga nivalis*, and *Sedum* cf. *S. rosea* are exclusive to the zone. *Lycopodium selago* spore frequencies are low throughout the zone (1% or less). The assemblage is floristically rich with 96 pollen and spore types recorded in 85 samples with a mean of 24.3 types per sample.

Contacts: The lower boundary is placed where Gramineae pollen values exceed those of Cyperaceae, and where *Rumex acetosa* pollen rises to 3% or more; at the upper boundary arboreal pollen (largely *Betula* undiff. and/or *Corylus avellana*) values increase to 30% or more.

Subdivisions: The following subzones are recognised:

Selaginella selaginoides assemblage subzone (Zone LF-2): Gramineae pollen values are high throughout with frequencies of 30% or more. *Rumex acetosa* pollen is present with values of 5% or more. *Selaginella selaginoides* microspores consistently occur with values of 2% or more. Cruciferae, *Ranunculus acris* type, and *Thalictrum* pollen, and *Botrychium lunaria* spores are consistently present in low frequencies. There is a variety of Compositae and Caryophyllaceae pollen types present in the subzone, including Liguliflorae, *Saussurea alpina*, *Solidago* type, *Cerastium alpinum* type, and *Arenaria* type. There is a wide variety of other herb pollen types present. *Betula* undiff., *Betula* cf. *B. nana*, and *Juniperus communis* pollen values are all less than 5% each, and pollen of dwarf shrubs have frequencies of less than 10%. The lower boundary is placed where Gramineae pollen values exceed those of Cyperaceae, and where the frequencies of *Lycopodium selago* spores decrease to 1% or less. The upper boundary is drawn where *Juniperus communis* pollen values rise to 7.5% or more.

Juniperus communis assemblage subzone (Zone LF-3): *Juniperus communis* pollen values are 7.5% or more, but *Betula* undiff. and *Betula* cf. *B. nana* pollen are infrequent with values of 5% or less. *Salix* pollen frequencies are generally 5% or more. Pollen of dwarf shrubs have frequencies of less than 10%. Herb pollen values are slightly lower than in the *Selaginella* subzone. Polypodiaceae undiff. spores often attain values of 10% or more. The lower boundary is placed where *Juniperus communis* pollen values increase to 7.5% or more, whereas the upper boundary is placed where *Betula* undiff. pollen values increase to 7.5% or more.

Betula assemblage subzone (Zone LF-4): *Betula* undiff. pollen values are between 7.5% and 15% *Betula* cf. *B. nana* pollen frequencies are less than 5%. *Juniperus communis* pollen values are rather variable, being between 5% and 10%. Pollen of *Populus tremula*, *Filipendula*, *Plantago major*/*P. media*, and *Urtica* are characteristic of but not exclusive to the subzone. The frequencies of pollen of *Rumex acetosa*, *Ranunculus acris* type, and *Thalictrum* are somewhat lower than in the other subzones within the assemblage zone. The lower boundary is placed where *Betula* undiff. pollen percentages increase to 7.5% or more, whereas the upper boundary is placed where arboreal pollen values fall to 10% or less.

Betula nana assemblage subzone (Zone LF-5): *Betula* cf. *B. nana* pollen values are 7.5% or more, whereas *Betula* undiff. and *Juniperus communis* pollen are infrequent with values of 5% or less. *Artemisia* undiff. pollen is consistently present in low amounts. The lower boundary is placed where *Betula* cf. *B. nana* pollen values rise to 7.5% or more, and the upper boundary is placed where arboreal pollen (mainly *Betula* undiff. and *Corylus avellana*) values rise to 20% or more.

Other occurrences: The assemblage zone with its four subzones also occurs at Loch Mealt (Zones LM-2 to LM-6; Plate 3) where it is 232.5 cm thick. The zone and some of the subzones are also present, but not so extensively, at the following sites on the Isle of Skye:

Loch Meodal (Plate 1)	Zones LML-1, 2	(37.5 cm thick)
	Zone LML-4	(17.5 cm thick)
Loch Cill Chriosd (Plate 4)	Zones LCC-3, 4	(32.5 cm thick)
	Zone LCC-6	(10 cm thick)
Lochan Coir' a' Ghobhainn (Plate 5)	Zone LCG-4	(12.5 cm thick)
Loch Cuithir (Vasari & Vasari, 1968)	Zones III-IV, IV	(75 cm thick)

As defined broadly above the assemblage zone and its subzones can be recognised in many Late-Devensian pollen diagrams in northern and western Britain, and in western Norway, for example zone II at Llyn Dwythwch and Nant Ffrancon, Caernarvonshire (Seddon, 1962), zones I, I–II, II, II–III, and III at Elan Valley, Cardiganshire (Moore, 1970), zones I–III at Moss Lake, Liverpool (Godwin, 1959), zone III at Malham Tarn, Yorkshire (Pigott & Pigott, 1963), zones I and III Skelsmergh Tarn and Kentmere A, Westmorland (Walker, 1955), zones I and III at Helton Tarn and Witherslack Hall,

Westmorland (Smith, 1958), zones I and III, zones 1–4i and 6–7, and zones Ba, Bb, Be, and Bf at Blelham Bog, Lancashire (Evans, 1970; Pennington, 1970; Pennington & Bonny, 1970), zones C1–C8 in the Cumberland lowland (Walker, 1966), zone II at Bradford Kaims and Longlee Moor, Northumberland (Bartley, 1966), zones 1a–1c at Tadcaster, Yorkshire (Bartley, 1962), zones II, III, and IVa at Ballaugh, Isle of Man (Mitchell, 1958), zones I, II, and III at Corstorphine, Edinburgh (Newey, 1970), zones LI–LIII at Culhorn Mains and Little Lochans, Wigtownshire (Moar 1969*a*), zones LI–LIII at Yesnaby, Orkney (Moar, 1969*b*), zone II at Loch Mahaick, Perthshire (Donner, 1958), the Gramineae–*Salix* assemblage zone in the Galloway Hills, south-west Scotland (H. H. Birks, 1972), zone II and zones I–III at Drymen, Stirlingshire (Donner, 1957; Vasari & Vasari, 1968), zones I–III at Loch of Park and Loch Kinord, Aberdeenshire (Vasari & Vasari, 1968), periods A–C and transitions 1 and 2 at Loch Sionascaig, Ross and Cromarty (Pennington & Lishman, 1971), zones I and II at Roddans Port, Co. Down (Morrison & Stephens, 1965), zones II and III at Cannons Lough, Co. Derry (Smith, 1961), zones I and II at Lecale, Co. Down (Singh, 1970), zones 1 and 2 at Lough Goller and Gortalecka, Co. Clare (Watts, 1963), zones I and III at Lista, south-west Norway (Hafsten, 1963), and zones B1, B2, and B3 at Blomöy, western Norway (Mangerud, 1970).

Related assemblages, but differing in their higher frequencies of *Artemisia* undiff. and *Helianthemum* pollen and lower *Rumex* pollen values, occur in Late-Devensian deposits in southern and eastern Britain (Godwin, 1968; Suggate & West, 1959).

Age and extent: The absolute age of the zone on Skye is unknown, but there are radiocarbon dates of 9655 ± 150 (Q-959) and 9420 ± 150 (Q-957) radiocarbon years B.P. for the *Juniperus communis* assemblage subzone at Loch Cill Chriosd (Zone LCC-6) and at Lochan Coir' a' Ghobhainn (Zone LCG-4) respectively. Elsewhere in Britain it generally occurs between about 10000 and 14300 radiocarbon years B.P. (see Godwin & Willis, 1959; Morrison & Stephens, 1965; Pennington & Bonny, 1970) and in western Norway it occurs from about 9300 to 12000 radiocarbon years B.P. (Mangerud, 1970).

The geographical extent of the zone is generally northern and western in Britain, and is probably more widespread in Scotland than the present data indicate.

3. *BETULA* ASSEMBLAGE ZONE

Type locality and section: Loch Meodal (Plate 1). Zone LML-3 (755–777.5 cm).

Description: Arboreal pollen (A.P.) is more than 30% in the zone with *Betula* undiff. pollen values exceeding 25%. *Corylus avellana* and *Pinus* pollen values are less than 10% and *Populus tremula* pollen is present in low but consistent frequencies. Pollen of other deciduous trees are virtually absent. Shrub and dwarf-shrub pollen values are low, and Gramineae and Cyperaceae are the most important N.A.P. types. *Filipendula* and *Melampyrum* pollen are characteristic of the zone. Polypodiaceae undiff. spores attain values of 15% or more.

Contacts: The lower boundary is placed where *Betula* undiff. pollen values exceed 10% and where *Juniperus communis* pollen values fall to 5% or less; the upper boundary is drawn where *Betula* undiff. pollen values fall to 15% or less, and where N.A.P. frequencies rise to 80%.

Other occurrences: On the Isle of Skye the assemblage zone is only known at Loch Meodal, but comparable assemblages occur widely but rather locally in western Britain, for example in low lying sites in north Wales (Seddon, 1962), around Morecambe Bay (zone II at Haweswater, Lancashire, and Helton Tarn and Witherslack Hall, Westmorland; Oldfield, 1960; Smith, 1958), in the southern part of Lakeland (zone II, zones Bc–Bd, and zones 4ii and 5 at Blelham Bog, Lancashire; Evans, 1970; Pennington & Bonny, 1970; Pennington, 1970; 38–60 cm at Windermere 1; Godwin, 1960; zone II at Skelsmergh Tarn and Kentmere A, Westmorland; Walker, 1955), in Yorkshire (zone II at Tadcaster; Bartley, 1962), and in south-west Ireland (zone 2 at Long Range, Co. Kerry; Watts, 1963). Related assemblages, but differing in higher frequencies of *Pinus* pollen, occur in southern England (Godwin, 1968; Suggate & West, 1959), southern Scandinavia, and central Europe.

Age and extent: The absolute age of the zone on Skye is unknown but it is at least 9500 radiocarbon years B.P. old. Elsewhere in Britain it has been dated between about 10800 and 12500 radiocarbon years B.P.; for example at Helton Tarn, Westmorland there is a date of 10760 ± 140 radiocarbon years B.P. (Q-92; Godwin & Willis, 1959), at Low Wray

Bay, Windermere there is a date of 11878 ± 120 radiocarbon years B.P. (Q-284; Godwin & Willis, 1959; Godwin, 1960), and at Blelham Tarn there are dates ranging from 11450 ± 180 to 12460 ± 190 radiocarbon years B.P. for the upper and lower boundaries of the zone (I-3595 and I-3591 respectively; Pennington & Bonny, 1970; Buckley & Willis, 1970).

The assemblage zone is only known in areas that have a relatively mild oceanic climate today. It is probably more widespread in parts of western Scotland, northern England, and north Wales than the present data indicate. Its occurrence on the Isle of Skye is its northernmost known locality.

Remarks: The high *Betula* undiff. pollen values in the zone are accompanied by macrofossils of *Betula pubescens* s.l. at Loch Meodal, as they are at other sites in Britain.

4. *BETULA–CORYLUS* ASSEMBLAGE ZONE

Type locality and section: Loch Cill Chriosd (Plate 4). Zone LCC-7 (350–397.5 cm).

Description: A.P. is more than 30% in the zone, with *Betula* undiff. and *Corylus* avellana pollen values exceeding 15% each. *Pinus* pollen frequencies are low (10% or less), and *Populus tremula* and *Sorbus aucuparia* pollen are consistently present in very low amounts. Pollen of other deciduous trees (*Alnus, Quercus, Ulmus*) are sparsely represented. *Salix* pollen can attain values of up to 15%, and *Betula* cf. *B. nana* and *Juniperus communis* pollen frequencies are 5% or less. Pollen frequencies of dwarf shrubs are low (5% or less), and herb pollen values are lower than in other assemblage zones. *Filipendula, Melampyrum,* and *Urtica* pollen occur consistently in the zone and are characteristic of this zone and the *Betula* assemblage zone at some sites on Skye. Pollen of *Plantago major/P. media, Potentilla* type, and *Ranunculus acris* type are also consistently present. *Anemone* type, *Conopodium* type, *Geum, Heracleum sphondylium,* Liliaceae, *Sanicula europaea, Sorbus* cf. *S. rupicola,* and *Trollius europaeus* pollen, and *Osmunda regalis* and *Pteridium aquilinum* spores are exclusive to the zone. Polypodiaceae undiff. spores attain values of 5% or more throughout.

Contacts: The lower boundary is placed where *Betula* undiff. and *Corylus avellana* pollen values exceed 10%. The upper boundary is tentatively drawn where *Corylus avellana* pollen values exceed those of *Betula* undiff., and where *Quercus* and *Ulmus* pollen frequencies become continuous.

Other occurrences: The assemblage zone also occurs at the following sites on the Isle of Skye:

Loch Meodal (Plate 1)	Zone LML-5	(at least 37.5 cm thick)
Loch Fada (Plate 2)	Zone LF-6	(at least 47.5 cm thick)
Loch Mealt (Plate 3)	Zone LM-7	(at least 50 cm thick)
Lochan Coir' a' Ghobhainn (Plate 5)	Zone LCG-5	(at least 37.5 cm thick)
Loch Cuithir (Vasari & Vasari, 1968)	Zone V	(65 cm thick)

Comparable pollen assemblages can be commonly recognised in pollen diagrams from sites in northern and western Britain, for example in the Galloway Hills of south-west Scotland (*Betula–Corylus/Myrica* assemblage zone; H. H. Birks, 1969, 1972), in the central and eastern Highlands (H. H. Birks, 1969, 1970), in the Cumberland lowland (Cumbrian zones C9 and C10; Walker, 1966), in Northumberland (zones IV and V; Bartley, 1966), in the Morecambe area (zone IV–V; Oldfield, 1960; Smith, 1958), and the lower Tees basin (zones I–IV; Bellamy, Bradshaw, Millington & Simmons, 1966). The zone occurs as far south as Bagmere, Cheshire (zone IV–V; Birks, 1965), Cwm Idwal, Caernarvonshire (zones IV–V; Godwin, 1955), and Gortalecka, Co. Clare (Watts, 1963). A similar assemblage occurs at Blomöy in the Bergen district of western Norway (zone B5; Mangerud, 1970). In southern England a related pollen assemblage occurs, but with higher *Pinus* and decreased *Betula* pollen values (Godwin, 1940, 1968).

Age and extent: Available radiocarbon dates place the age of the beginning of this zone on Skye between about 8800 and 9500 radiocarbon years B.P. The upper boundary is not dated. Elsewhere in Britain the zone has been dated between 9000 and 10000 radiocarbon years B.P.; for example at Scaleby Moss, Cumberland (Godwin, Walker & Willis, 1957) there are relevant dates ranging from 10160 ± 193 B.P. (Q-152) to 8816 ± 192 B.P. (Q-162), and at Red Moss, Lancashire (Hibbert, Switsur & West, 1971) there are dates ranging from 9798 ± 200 B.P. (Q-924) to 8790 ± 170 B.P. (Q-920). There is a radiocarbon date of 9340 ± 160 radiocarbon years B.P. (T-623) for the beginning of a comparable assemblage zone in western Norway (zone B5; Mangerud, 1970).

High frequencies of both *Betula* undiff. and *Corylus avellana* pollen, associated with very low pollen frequencies of other deciduous trees are strikingly characteristic of many sites in northern and western Britain, especially in Scotland (see H. H. Birks, 1969).

5. ADVANTAGES IN THE USE OF POLLEN ASSEMBLAGE ZONES

In the division of stratigraphical sequences and the time they represent there are several types of subdivision (see Miller, 1965; Størmer, 1966) based on concepts of time, climate, biostratigraphy, soils, lithology, and landforms (see Mangerud, 1970; West, 1968). Quaternary pollen stratigraphy is a palaeontological technique, and as such its subdivisions are logically based on biostratigraphic criteria. It is to this end that the application of the Code of Stratigraphic Nomenclature to Quaternary pollen stratigraphy has definite advantages over the more traditional procedures of assigning numerals, or a combination of numbers and letters, to pollen zones (see Cushing, 1963, 1964*a*).

The designation of pollen zones by names, rather than by numerals or letters, provides greater flexibility in use. As zones are traced from one study area to another or as further strata are examined, new zones may appear and established zones may disappear. Named zones can thus be inserted or deleted accordingly, without disrupting the sequence. Duplication of zonal designations is avoided, as the Code provides that a name once formally proposed is 'pre-empted from use as the name of any other formal unit in the same category' (Article 3). The spatial and temporal extension of a named pollen zone is subject to question and reinterpretation, but under the Code a zone name cannot validly be duplicated for a different zone at another type locality or area. Named zones are particularly valuable in examples of the stratigraphic phenomenon termed 'revertence' by von Post (1946), where the pollen stratigraphy suggests a succession from one pollen assemblage to another and back to the first. An additional advantage of applying names to pollen assemblage zones is that the zone names immediately suggest the composition of the pollen spectra, thus facilitating ease of discussion and precise comparison of pollen spectra and pollen diagrams.

The second, and more important benefit that the Code provides is that it encourages the precise recognition, description, and characterisation of the pollen zones on the basis of the observations alone, without any preconceptions of past climate or time significance (Cushing 1964*a*). Assemblage zones are biostratigraphic units that are defined solely on the observable contained fossils without any reference to the sediment lithology, to the inferred environmental and climatic conditions, or to the assumed time equivalence (see Hedberg, 1961; Teichert, 1958). Although the zones are highly discontinuous laterally, they can be recognised over a geographical and stratigraphic interval of sufficient magnitude to make them useful for purposes of biostratigraphic comparisons between sites. They carry no ecological, temporal, or climatic implications, and the use of the Code of Stratigraphic Nomenclature emphasises this point. Many pollen zonation schemes, although initially based on basic biostratigraphic evidence and criteria (for example Godwin, 1940; Jessen, 1935), have come to acquire inferred ecological, temporal, or climatic connotations. As there is an intuitive relationship between fossil pollen spectra and past vegetation near the site of deposition, it is tempting to consider a pollen zone directly as a kind of fossil plant community. As there is undoubtedly some relationship between regional vegetation and regional climate, pollen zones similarly tend to acquire climatic implications. As marked vegetational and climatic changes within an area are likely to be synchronous or nearly so, pollen zone boundaries are frequently regarded as synchronous stratigraphic horizons throughout their geographical extent; the pollen zone thereby is assumed to represent a unit of time stratigraphy. There is a further tendency to equate biostratigraphical units with lithological units without any evidence for such a correlation, leading to such illogicalities as 'Zone III. Lake clay, pollen not preserved' (Bartley, 1966, p. 145) and 'Zone III. Silty clays or sands poor in pollen' (Donner, 1957, p. 231).

The application of a standard, pre-determined scheme of pollen zones with their implied connotations of climatic, ecological, and temporal significance to the subdivision of primary data obtained from a variety of sites in differing climatic and physiognomic settings over broad areas can lead to generalisations based on subjective inferences, and it may result in a circularity of argument in interpretation. When information is limited, confusion of the concepts of time, climate, and ecological succession with the observable biostratigraphic data presented in pollen diagrams may result in the extension and correlation of pollen zones far beyond the limits imposed by the evidence itself. It is only after careful interpretation of fossil pollen spectra in terms of past flora and vegetation that the role of environmental factors such as soil, hydroseral changes, human influences, and climate can be logically considered. If, after a thorough comparison with modern ecological processes and situations, there are grounds to invoke climatic determinism in influencing the vegetational succession, pollen zones can then be used for the purpose of correlation between profiles within the defined study area.

As discussed by Faegri (1963) and Smith (1965) there is increasing realisation that plants react individually to environmental changes in differing ecological settings, and that differences in rates of plant migration and soil development should be considered more fully in interpreting vegetational changes. Indeed Iversen (1960) and Walker (1966) have questioned whether any climatic significance can be attached to several of the pollen zone boundaries in the Flandrian. It is highly probable that a single set of pollen zones, such as the traditional British scheme of zone I to zone VIII (Godwin, 1940, 1956), cannot both efficiently and meaningfully subdivide all the pollen sequences and yet maintain a position in time established by either radiocarbon dating or regional climatic events.

There are now several striking demonstrations of the asynchroneity of well-marked vegetational changes within the Flandrian in north-west Europe, indicating that if these changes are used to delimit pollen zones then these zones cannot be regarded as reliable time stratigraphic units. Examples in northern Europe include the initial expansion of *Betula* pollen at the opening of the Flandrian in Scandinavia (Donner, 1966), the first expansion of *Corylus avellana* pollen in Scandinavia (Hafsten, 1969, 1970), the first consistent occurrence of *Picea abies* pollen in Scandinavia (Aario, 1965; Aartolahti, 1966; Moe, 1970), the appearance of *Tilia cordata* pollen in Finland (Aartolahti, 1967; Alhonen, 1968), and the expansion of *Alnus glutinosa* pollen in north-west Europe (Hibbert *et al.*, 1971). These examples serve to emphasise the importance of testing the synchroneity of zonal systems elsewhere in Europe by radiocarbon dating, rather than assuming their synchroneity in discussing vegetational and historical concepts such as 'regional parallelism' over broad areas.

Pollen analysis cannot make its full potential contribution to the elucidation of floristic and vegetational history so long as unjustified inferences or hypotheses are allowed to distort the primary data. To take the fullest advantage of both the stratigraphical and palaeoecological value of pollen analytical data, the stratigraphic units used in the description, discussion, and comparison of the data should be defined in a way that excludes any temporal, ecological, or climatic implications. The approach adopted here has thus been to subdivide the pollen diagram in as objective a way as possible, and to study subsequently the spatial and temporal distribution of the resulting biostratigraphic units. The ecological interpretation of such zones in terms of past flora, vegetation, and thus environment is greatly aided by investigations of modern pollen rain in relation to extant vegetation. These studies are discussed in Chapter 11.

11

THE RELATION OF MODERN POLLEN SPECTRA TO VEGETATION IN SCOTLAND

The ecological interpretation of pollen diagrams in terms of past flora and vegetation has long been recognised as a complex problem, requiring not only a thorough knowledge of the present-day ecology and sociology of the taxa involved, but also information on the relationships between modern pollen rain and the vegetation from which it is derived. The representation of any taxon in a pollen spectrum depends on many interacting factors, including its pollen production and phenology, its frequency within the vegetation, the structure of the community in which it occurs, its mode of pollen dispersal, and the processes of pollen deposition, sedimentation, and preservation within the sedimentary environment. The interactions of these factors are sufficiently complex (see Davis, 1968; Tauber, 1965, 1967) that few authors other than Livingstone & Estes (1967) and Livingstone (1968) have attempted any quantitative reconstructions of past vegetation. A factual basis for the interpretation of pollen diagrams can, to some degree, be provided by a study of modern pollen spectra in relation to present-day vegetation (Davis, 1967*a*; Wright, 1967*a*). Such information can be used in two distinct ways (see Janssen, 1970).

From the relation between the pollen percentages of different taxa in modern spectra and the percentages of the same taxa in the surrounding vegetation, 'correction factors' or R-values can be computed for the different components of the pollen rain (Davis, 1963; Faegri, 1947; Fagerlind, 1952; Iversen, 1947). This has been done in Denmark (Andersen, 1967, 1970; Faegri & Iversen, 1964), in Belgium (Heim, 1970), in Nova Scotia (Livingstone, 1968), in Vermont (Davis & Goodlett, 1960), in Greenland (Iversen, 1952–3), in Minnesota (Janssen, 1967*b*), in New Jersey (Comanor, 1968), and in Japan (Tsukada, 1958). The theoretical composition of the former vegetation can then be inferred by assuming that the contemporary R-values for each taxon are applicable to the fossil pollen spectra. There are, however, many problems in the computation and use of such R-values (see Davis, 1969; Faegri, 1966; Lichti-Federovich & Ritchie, 1965). The most serious drawback is that the areal extent of the vegetation contributing pollen to a particular sample site is not known with any certainty, and it is thus impossible to delimit accurately the size of vegetational plot to be sampled. Moreover, the R-value for a given taxon depends on its abundance in a particular community and on its vegetational environment, as demonstrated by Janssen (1967*b*), who has shown significant variations in R-values for the same tree taxa occurring in different forest types in Minnesota. A similar variation in R-values for the same tree taxa within a relatively small area has also been shown by Comanor (1968). Contemporary R-values cannot therefore be confidently applied to fossil pollen frequencies, in view of possible past variations in pollen production and pollen sedimentation, and of changes in the vegetational environment and community structure with time. Although R-values have been used in the interpretation of fossil pollen frequencies (for example Davis, 1963, 1965; Livingstone, 1968) the quantitative significance of the conclusions is open to question.

A second approach, and the one followed here, is to attempt to characterise a range of modern vegetation types by means of contemporary pollen spectra, and then to compare the modern spectra with fossil pollen assemblages (Davis, 1967*a*; Lichti-Federovich & Ritchie, 1965, 1968; McAndrews, 1966, 1967; Wright, McAndrews & van Zeist, 1967). If similar pollen assemblages can be recognised in a stratigraphic sequence of fossil pollen, the past changes in vegetation over time can be interpreted in terms of present vegetational differences in space. Any marked similarities that exist between the modern and the fossil spectra can thus provide, if used with caution, an objective basis for the reconstruction of the past vegetation (Wright, 1967*a*). Besides comparing modern and fossil pollen percentages, the occurrence of pollen and spore types of 'indicator species', here defined as morphologically distinctive pollen and spores of taxa of narrow ecological or sociological amplitudes today that are characteristic or diagnostic of particular present-day plant communities, in fossil assemblages provide a further basis for the interpretation and reconstruction of past vegetation from fossil spectra (see Janssen, 1967*a*, 1970). If no match can be made with the fossil spectra, then either modern analogues should be sought elsewhere, or it may be concluded that the vegetation of a particular time interval represented by the fossil pollen spectra has no modern counterpart. The success at the reconstruction and sophisticated interpretations of vegetational history through the use of surface samples in north-western Minnesota by McAndrews (1966, 1967) and by Janssen (1967*a*), in New Mexico by Bent & Wright (1963), in south-western Yukon by Rampton (1971), in western Iran by Wright *et al.* (1967), in Germany by Menke (1963, 1969), and in Greenland by Fredskild (1967), have demonstrated the value of this approach.

Few such studies have been carried out in Europe, possibly due to the assumption that the modern vegetation is so disturbed that such an approach would be of little value in considering past vegetation (Wright, 1971). Although this is largely true for many lowland regions in Britain, there is a wide range of natural or semi-natural communities occurring both on the Isle of Skye (see Chapters 4 and 5) and elsewhere in Scotland (McVean & Ratcliffe, 1962), especially in the alpine zone. As there are floristic affinities between the Late-Devensian pollen flora of Skye and the present Scottish mountain flora, a survey of surface pollen spectra of Scottish mountain vegetation was undertaken in a search for modern vegetational analogues to the fossil pollen spectra.

1. METHODS

Plots of uniform floristic composition and structure of at least 25 square metres in area were selected in the field from a wide range of natural and semi-natural communities in northern Britain. The plot locations and site characteristics are listed in Table 11.1. All the species present within the plot were recorded, and their combined cover and abundance were estimated and scored on the 10-point Domin scale (see Chapter 4). From these plots samples were collected for pollen analysis. The majority of the samples were moss polsters (commonly *Rhacomitrium lanuginosum* or *Sphagnum* spp.), but in a few localities where no satisfactory polsters could be found, plant detritus or surface soil was collected. All samples were collected from ground level. Each sample was composed of 6 to 10 subsamples of about 3 to 5 cm^2 surface area from within the plot to minimise any local over-representation by included anthers etc. These subsamples were amalgamated and treated as a single sample for preparation and analysis. The samples were collected in polythene bags and stored in a cold-room at 5 °C until required.

In the laboratory each sample was stirred vigorously in distilled water in a 1 litre beaker, and subsequently sieved to remove coarse plant detritus and sand. After centrifugation the samples were prepared for microscopic examination by the standard procedures outlined in Chapter 7. Several pollen types, for example *Geranium* and *Primula*, that have not been identified in the fossil material were encountered in the spectra from the modern samples and these pollen types are described in Chapter 8. Pollen and spore preservation in all the samples was good, as shown by the low (<4.6%) indeterminable category (Plate 6).

The pollen and spore frequencies are expressed in a variety of ways, and are presented as histograms in Plate 6 and Fig. 24. In Plate 6 the frequencies of all determinable local pollen and spore types are expressed as percentages relative to the sum (ΣP) of all such types. Local pollen and spore types are here defined as pollen and spores indistinguishable morphologically from the pollen and spore types of the taxa occurring within or in close proximity to the vegetational plot. The total number of pollen and spores included in this sum ranges from 232 to 1249, with a mean of 495 and a median of 445. If a taxon shows an unexpectedly high value in a certain spectrum its frequency is calculated in the normal manner, but the pollen and spore frequencies of the other taxa in the spectrum are expressed as a percentage of the pollen sum excluding that taxon (Wright & Patten, 1963). In the present study *Alchemilla*, *Calluna vulgaris*, *Dryopteris carthusiana* type, *Dryopteris filix-mas* type, *Plantago lanceolata*, *Potentilla* type, Rubiaceae, and *Trollius europaeus* pollen and spores are excluded from the pollen sum for certain spectra. Unknown and indeterminable types, and spores of Sphagnaceae are excluded from ΣP throughout, and are expressed as percentages of $\Sigma P + \Sigma$ Unknown and $\Sigma P + \Sigma$ *Sphagnum* spores, respectively. The frequencies of pollen and spores of taxa not represented in or near a given vegetational

TABLE 11.1. *Locations and site details of vegetational plots studied in the surface sample survey*
(The plots are listed here in the same order as the samples and the pollen spectra on Plate 6)

Plot and Sample Number	National Grid Reference	Aspect (degrees)	Altitude (feet)	Slope (degrees)	Locality
35	18/607202	0	100	5	Coille Gaireallach, Skye
36	18/703145	45	50	20	Loch na Dal, Skye
31	18/567201	45	200	15	Faoilean, Skye
34	18/602198	0	200	10	Coille Gaireallach, Skye
13	18/611211	45	100	2	Coille Gaireallach, Skye
19	18/372333	45	50	15	Loch Harport, Skye
30	18/567201	45	200	5	Faoilean, Skye
3	35/903278	225	850	5	Wynch Bridge, Teesdale
32	18/640121	0	200	15	Coill a'Ghasgain, Skye
33	18/598199	315	100	12	Coille Gaireallach, Skye
4	35/887284	45	1000	5	High Force, Teesdale
2	35/890280	45	1150	10	Holwick, Teesdale
24	18/451248	315	2000	5	Coire na Creiche, Skye
48	29/170115	90	1950	2	Cul Mor, West Ross
29A	18/613202	315	150	5	Ben Suardal, Skye
37	18/517406	90	800	25	Ben Tianavaig, Skye
15	18/542217	315	1200	5	Blà Bheinn, Skye
18	18/542217	315	1000	5	Blà Bheinn, Skye
14	18/552214	0	500	10	Allt na Dunaich, Skye
38	18/517406	90	800	5	Ben Tianavaig, Skye
45	18/450608	315	1500	20	Corrie Amadal, Skye
50	28/284864	0	2300	20	Glen Douchary, West Ross
56	27/434866	45	2800	25	Moy Corrie, Invernesshire
49	28/280863	0	2250	60	Glen Douchary, West Ross
58	37/255742	0	2500	10	Corrie Fee, Angus
57	27/438886	90	2790	20	Corrie Ardair, Invernesshire
1	18/537212	45	1900	5	Blà Bheinn, Skye
27	18/760223	315	2250	10	Sgùrr na Coinnich, Skye
9	36/162158	45	2400	5	White Coomb, Moffat
44	18/456627	270	2100	2	Beinn Edra, Skye
26	18/753223	.	2000	0	Sgùrr na Coinnich, Skye
40	18/443603	.	1500	0	Beinn Laoigh, Skye
41	18/450617	270	1500	5	Beinn Edra, Skye
42	18/456613	30	1600	5	Beinn Edra, Skye
43	18/455619	0	2000	5	Beinn Edra, Skye
47	29/1--0--	315	2300	5	Cul Mor, West Ross
51	28/2--8--	0	2850	2	West Ross

plot are not plotted on Plate 6, and their frequencies are instead presented in Fig. 24 as percentages of $\Sigma P + \Sigma$ Non-local pollen. These non-local pollen and spore types are considered to represent, in part at least, the regional component (*sensu* Janssen, 1966) and the extraregional component (*sensu* McAndrews, 1967) of the pollen rain. In Fig. 24, the relationships between arboreal pollen (A.P.) and nonarboreal pollen (N.A.P.), and between locally and non-locally derived pollen and spores are shown as percentages of $\Sigma P + \Sigma$ Non-local Pollen.

The modern pollen spectra are grouped on Plate 6 according to the vegetation of the plots from which the samples were collected. Four main vegetation types are distinguished here: alpine summit vegetation (Caricetea curvulae, Salicetea herbaceae); sub-alpine grasslands, 'tall herb' communities, and *Salix* scrub (Mulgedion alpini, Nardo–Galion saxatilis); *Betula pubescens* woodlands (Mulgedion alpini, Quercetea robori–petraeae); and *Corylus avellana* woodlands (Mulgedion alpini, Quercetea robori–petraeae). Nomenclature of vegetation types follows Chapter 4 and McVean & Ratcliffe (1962), unless otherwise stated. Within each main type, the spectra are arranged according to the phytosociological affinities of the vegetation of the relevant plot so that surface pollen spectra from floristically and sociologically similar plots are grouped together. Within each association or *nodum* the spectra are arranged in

in surface pollen spectra

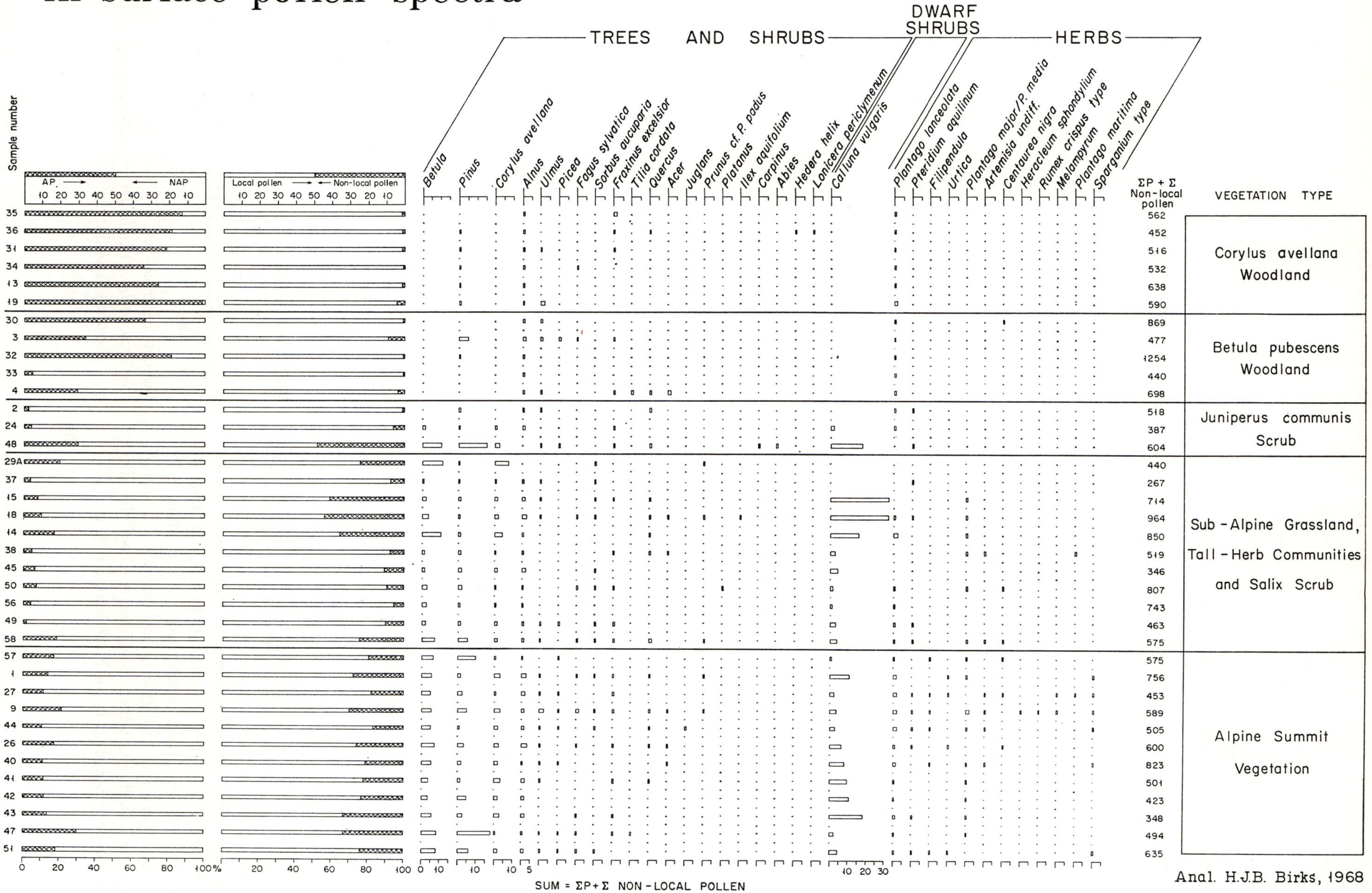

Figure 24. Pollen diagram of non-local pollen and spore types only, in the surface pollen spectra. Scale at base gives percentages for the histograms. Values are expressed as percentages of $\Sigma P + \Sigma$ Non-local pollen. All histograms are plotted to the same scale. Abbreviations: anal. = analysed, A.P. = arboreal pollen, N.A.P. = nonarboreal pollen, P = pollen, undiff. = undifferentiated.

relation to either the altitude of the plot sampled or in relation to general trends in the frequencies of a particularly diagnostic or prominent pollen or spore type. In addition to the four main vegetation types, the pollen spectra from plots of *Juniperus communis*-dominated vegetation (2, 24, 48) are grouped here, for the purposes of discussion, into a separate vegetational unit, although, on phytosociological criteria, samples 24 and 48 (*Juniperus nana nodum*) strictly belong to the Caricetea curvulae (summit vegetation).

On Plate 6 the pollen and spore types are grouped into four broad physiognomic categories of trees (*Betula*, *Corylus avellana*, *Populus tremula*, *Prunus* cf. *P. padus*, *Sorbus aucuparia*), shrubs (*Juniperus communis*, *Salix*), dwarf shrubs (*Calluna vulgaris*, *Empetrum*, *Rubus saxatilis*, *Vaccinium* type), and herbs (including pteridophytes), and individual histograms for all the pollen and spore types identified and included within the basic pollen sum are presented in order of occurrence from the bottom to the top of the diagram within the four physiognomic categories. All the histograms are drawn to a standard scale. To the right of the histograms on Plate 6 the number of pollen grains and spores in the basic sum (ΣP) and the number of pollen and spore types in the sum (Σ Taxa) for each spectrum are shown. Unidentified (indeterminable and unknown) types and *Sphagnum* spores are excluded from the sum, and their frequencies are shown at the extreme right of Plate 6, along with details of the vegetational types from which the spectra are derived. For comparison, the spectra of non-local pollen and spores in the samples examined (Fig. 24) are arranged in the same vertical order as on Plate 6 and within the same four broad vegetational categories.

The vegetational data for the plots examined are presented in Plate 7 and the plots are arranged in the same vertical sequence as the surface pollen spectra. Bryophytes and lichens, although of considerable floristic and vegetational value, have been omitted from the diagram as they are of little importance in terms of relationships between modern pollen spectra and vegetation. The Domin values for cover and abundance of the vascular plants have been transformed to a linear scale (Bannister, 1966) to depict the species' cover and abundance within the plots. The relationships between the Domin scale and the transformed means are shown in Table 11.2. The histograms are drawn to the same scale throughout, which is drawn to half the size of the percentage scales of Plate 6 and Fig. 24.

TABLE 11.2. *Relationships between the Domin scale of cover and abundance and the transformed mean cover-abundance (from Bannister, 1966)*

Domin Number	+	1	2	3	4	5	6	7	8	9	10
Percentage mean cover-abundance value	+	2.5	5	10	30	35	45	55	68	86	100

Taxa with indistinguishable pollen grains or spores are bracketed together on Plate 7, for example *Salix* spp. and *Alchemilla* spp. When more than one stratum is present in the vegetation, the cover and abundance of each layer are estimated separately, and as a result the total cover for each plot (Plate 7) may exceed 100%. The vascular plants that occur within the plots examined, but whose pollen grains were not found in the analyses, are grouped together at the extreme right of Plate 7.

Although the methods of pollen sampling and vegetational description are rather crude, they are considered to be the most practicable in view of the time available and the remoteness of much of the vegetation examined. For a survey such as this, the use of moss polsters has advantages over more refined quantitative pollen trapping techniques. Moss polsters contain several years pollen accumulation, thus giving an integrated picture of the pollen deposition. Only the percentage pollen frequency can be determined, but this is adequate for a primary survey (Wright, 1967*a*, 1968).

2. POLLEN SPECTRA FROM MONTANE SUMMIT VEGETATION

Samples for pollen analysis were collected from the four principal types of montane summit-heaths and related snow-patch communities that occur in the alpine zone above 1500 feet (460 m) in north-west Scotland today. The vegetational types examined are as follows:

Caricetea curvulae	
Cariceto–Rhacomitretum lanuginosi Association	Nos. 9, 26, 40, 44
Festuca ovina–Luzula spicata nodum	Nos. 41, 42, 43, 47, 51
Salicetea herbaceae	
Nardus stricta–Vaccinium myrtillus Association	Nos. 1, 17

Cryptogrammeto–Athyrietum chionophilum Association (McVean & Ratcliffe, 1962) No. 57

All these communities, except the Cryptogrammeto–Athyrietum chionophilum Association occur on the Isle of Skye today, and their floristic composition, ecology, and inter-relationships have been discussed in Chapters 4 and 5. Cariceto–Rhacomitretum lanuginosi summit heaths and *Festuca ovina–Luzula spicata* communities of 'fell-fields' favour wind-exposed summit plateaux, whereas *Nardus stricta–Vaccinium myrtillus* snow-patch communities are restricted to areas of prolonged snow-lie in sheltered gullies and corries. Cryptogrammeto–Athyrietum chionophilum communities occur widely but rather locally above 2500 feet (765 m) in the Scottish Highlands (McVean & Ratcliffe, 1962) and in Scandinavia (Dahl, 1956; Gjaerevoll, 1950, 1956; Nordhagen, 1927, 1943). This association favours stabilised block-screes, often in gullies, and throughout its range it appears to be entirely dependent on prolonged snow-lie, perhaps for protection against winter frost (Nordhagen, 1943). This restriction of *Cryptogramma crispa* to chionophilous vegetation in the Scottish Highlands and Scandinavia is in contrast to its remarkable abundance on screes, outcrops of acidic rock, and even on stone walls in north Wales, Lakeland, and the Southern Uplands.

The classificatory position of the Cryptogrammeto-Athyrietum chionophilum is rather debatable, for Nordhagen (1943) and Gjaerevoll (1950, 1956) have grouped it in the class Salicetea herbaceae, but Dahl (1956) and McVean & Ratcliffe (1962) have referred it to the class Betulo–Adenostyletea. Despite these classificatory uncertainties the association is one of the most characteristic chionophilous communities in Scotland, and its absence from Skye at present probably reflects the variable and short length of snow-lie on the island (see Chapter 3).

Although the four communities examined are varied in both their floristic composition and their present ecology, the main feature they share is the low cover of vascular plants (Plate 7) as the result either of dominance by mosses, especially of *Rhacomitrium lanuginosum* (for example plots 9, 26, 40), or of extreme openness of the vegetation (for example plots 42, 43, 47, 51). *Alchemilla alpina*, *Carex bigelowii*, *Festuca ovina* agg. (including *F. vivipara*), *Galium saxatile*, *Lycopodium selago*, and *Potentilla erecta* occur in 75% or more of the plots examined. *Cherleria sedoides*, *Empetrum nigrum* agg., *Gnaphalium supinum*, *Lycopodium alpinum*, *Polygonum viviparum*, *Salix herbacea*, and *Sibbaldia procumbens* occur more rarely, and *Artemisia norvegica*, *Deschampsia alpina*, *Juncus trifidus*, *Koenigia islandica*, and *Luzula spicata* are rare but characteristic components of the plots from 'fell-fields'.

The most striking feature of the pollen spectra from these communities (Plate 6) is the dominance of Cyperaceae pollen throughout (30–50.5%), despite the low cover-abundance (30% or less) of *Carex bigelowii* in the plots. Similar high representation of sedge pollen in modern spectra from related communities are found in Greenland (Fredskild, 1967), and in Low-Arctic Canada (Lichti-Federovich & Ritchie 1968; Ritchie & Lichti-Federovich, 1967), suggesting that high Cyperaceae pollen frequencies in spectra need not always indicate the local presence of reedswamps (cf. Rampton, 1971; Welten, 1950). The values of Gramineae pollen are surprisingly low in these spectra in view of the prominence of *Deschampsia flexuosa*, *Festuca ovina* agg., and *Nardus stricta* in several of the plots. However, the poor representation of grasses in these spectra is naturally exaggerated by the predominance of viviparous species such as *Festuca vivipara* in alpine communities, and by the poor flowering of, for example, *Nardus stricta* when it occurs in snow-patch communities. Despite their low cover-abundance values (30% or less), *Lycopodium selago* and *L. alpinum* have consistent spore percentages between 2.8 and 18.6% each, indicating a good representation in modern spectra. A similar feature was reported in south-west Greenland by Iversen (1945). *Galium saxatile* (Rubiaceae pollen), *Potentilla erecta* (*Potentilla* type pollen), and *Thymus drucei* (*Thymus* type pollen) are similarly well represented in the pollen spectra with values up to 11% despite their low cover in the vegetational plots. In contrast, members of the Juncaceae are not represented at all in the modern spectra, no doubt because of the poor preservation of Juncaceae pollen (cf. Fredskild, 1970). *Alchemilla alpina*, *Cherleria sedoides* (*Arenaria* type pollen), *Gnaphalium supinum* (*Antennaria* type pollen), and *Vaccinium myrtillus* (*Vaccinium* type pollen) are consistently poorly represented (0.2–4.3%) in the pollen spectra in relation to their high cover-abundance in the plots (up to 45%). *Artemisia norvegica*, *Cryptogramma crispa*, *Polygonum viviparum*, and *Saxifraga stellaris* are only represented in the pollen spectra, with values of up to 9.5%, when the plants are locally present in the plots. The low values of *Artemisia* cf. *A. norvegica* pollen are not unexpected in view of the shy flowering of the plants in the two known Scottish localities.

Pollen of Cruciferae, Liguliflorae, *Ranunculus acris* type, *Rumex acetosa*, *Saxifraga hypnoides*, *Succisa pratensis*, and *Solidago* type, and spores of Polypodiaceae undiff., *Polypodium*, *Selaginella selaginoides*, and *Sphagnum* occur with low but consistent percentages in the spectra, but although the plants occur nearby they are all absent from the actual plots examined. Several of these taxa appear to have a high pollen production and effective dispersal, for when they do occur in the vegetation, for example *Rumex acetosa* and *Saxifraga hypnoides*, high pollen percentages are frequently noted. However, this is not the case with Liguliflorae, *Polypodium vulgare*, and *Succisa pratensis* pollen or spores, for in samples 37 and 38 low pollen and spore frequencies occur despite the local presence of these taxa in the plots. It is possible that effects of differential pollen preservation are important here, for pollen of Liguliflorae and *Succisa pratensis* and spores of *Polypodium* appear to be markedly resistant to corrosion and degradation, and are thus frequently characteristic of pollen spectra from soils (Havinga, 1963). No explanation can be offered for the occurrence of *Salix* pollen (most of which is not *S. herbacea*) and *Empetrum* pollen in small amounts (0.2–3.3%) in all the spectra, despite their absence from several plots. Both taxa are known to have a poor pollen representation in modern spectra elsewhere (Firbas, 1934; Iversen, 1945; Menke, 1963; Srodon, 1960; Welten, 1950), but there is some evidence that, although *Empetrum nigrum* and *E. hermaphroditum* have low pollen productions, their pollen is more effectively dispersed than that of many Ericaceae species (other than *Calluna vulgaris*) (Fredskild, 1967; Iversen, 1945). This might be expected in view of the floral biology and wind pollination of *Empetrum*.

Three samples (41, 42, and 43) were analysed from plots where *Koenigia islandica* attained cover values of 30% or more. *Koenigia islandica* pollen was only found in one spectrum (3.1% in sample 42). It is perhaps significant that this was a silt sample rather than a moss polster, suggesting that *Koenigia* pollen is rarely, if ever, dispersed into the atmosphere but is trapped by water movement into silts within the wet stony rills in which it grows. The incorporation of its pollen into lake sediments may therefore be by stream inwash of silts rather than by direct aerial dispersal. Highly variable percentages of *Koenigia* pollen occur in modern spectra in Spitsbergen (Srodon, 1960).

Montane summit vegetation appears to produce modern pollen spectra that are characteristic and distinctive of this broad vegetational type. In contrast to all the other spectra produced by the other vegetational types examined in this survey, spectra from summit vegetation are characterised by the dominance of Cyperaceae pollen, and by the consistent occurrence of spores of *Lycopodium selago* and *L. alpinum* with frequencies of 3% or more. *Antennaria* type and *Saxifraga stellaris* pollen occur more rarely but they are virtually exclusive to spectra from summit vegetation. It does not appear possible, however, to distinguish all the vegetation types on the basis of the pollen or spore composition alone, except by the occurrence of pollen or spores of rare taxa of narrow ecological and sociological amplitude ('indicator species' *sensu* Janssen, 1970), such as *Artemisia norvegica*, *Koenigia islandica*, and *Sagina* in spectra from some of the 'fell-field' plots, and *Cryptogramma crispa* and *Athyrium alpestre* in the Cryptogrammeto–Athyrietum chionophilum spectra. The percentages of *Lycopodium selago* and *L. alpinum* spores are consistently higher in spectra from chionophilous vegetation than in spectra from chionophobous stands, whereas the frequencies of Rubiaceae pollen and, to some extent, of *Potentilla* type are higher in spectra from the Cariceto–Rhacomitretum lanuginosi community than in spectra from the other vegetation types examined. That such a clear distinction is not possible on the basis of pollen alone is not surprising in view of the general floristic similarity of the communities, for the floristic differentiation between them at the present is largely based on species of poor pollen representation, such as *Luzula spicata* and *Juncus trifidus*, or on bryophytes and lichens that make no contribution to the pollen or spore assemblage, such as *Rhacomitrium lanuginosum* and *Cetraria islandica* (see Chapter 4 and Table 4.57).

3. POLLEN SPECTRA FROM SUB-ALPINE GRASSLANDS, 'TALL HERB' COMMUNITIES, AND *SALIX* SCRUB

Samples for pollen analysis were collected from the five principal sub-alpine communities that occur below 2000 feet (610 m) in north-west Scotland today. The vegetational types examined are as follows:

Mulgedion alpini	
Sedum rosea–Alchemilla glabra Association	Nos. 14, 38, 45
Salix lapponum–Luzula sylvatica nodum. (McVean & Ratcliffe, 1962)	Nos. 49, 58
Species-rich Deschampsietum cespitosae alpinum Association. (McVean & Ratcliffe, 1962)	Nos. 50, 56
Nardo–Galion saxatilis	
Agrosto–Festucetum (Alchemilleto- and species-rich Associations)	Nos. 15, 29A, 37
Dwarf herb *nodum*	No. 18

Sedum rosea–Alchemilla glabra, Alchemilleto–Agrosto–Festucetum, Agrosto–Festucetum (species-rich) grasslands, and Dwarf herb communities all occur on the Isle of Skye today (see Chapters 4 and 5). They are clearly floristically and edaphically related, and all favour intermittently flushed brown-earth soils. The main ecological differentiation appears to be that *Sedum rosea–Alchemilla glabra* stands with many 'tall herbs' are restricted to inaccessible ungrazed cliff-ledges, whereas the Agrosto–Festucetum and the related Dwarf herb communities commonly occur on the grazed slopes below the cliffs. Species-rich Deschampsietum cespitosae grasslands occur locally throughout the Scottish Highlands (McVean & Ratcliffe, 1962), but they are surprisingly absent from Skye. The community generally favours north- and east-facing steep slopes between 1600 and 3000 feet (490–920 m). This association is also a biotically-produced community derived from 'tall herb' stands, and it owes its existence to grazing by sheep and deer. The two plots analysed both occur on grazed slopes below precipitous cliffs, the ledges of which support 'tall herb' and *Salix lapponum* communities. Many 'tall herbs', for example *Angelica sylvestris*, *Rumex acetosa*, *Sedum rosea*, may occur as sparse, dwarfed plants in the grassland, where *Deschampsia cespitosa* has clearly increased at their expense. The differentiating ecological factors between the Deschampsietum cespitosae and the Dwarf herb communities are not clear, but differences in both irrigation and snow-cover appear to be important (McVean & Ratcliffe, 1962). Similar communities occur locally in Scandinavia in comparable ecological situations (Nordhagen, 1927, 1943).

Salix lapponum–Luzula sylvatica communities do not occur on Skye today and they are rather rare in Scotland, generally occurring as fragmentary stands restricted to north- and east-facing ungrazed cliff-ledges between 2000 and 3000 feet (610–920 m). Two extensive stands were examined, one in Clova dominated by *Salix lanata* (58), and one in west Ross dominated by *S. lapponum* (49). The stands have several species in common with 'tall herb' communities, for example *Alchemilla glabra*, *Luzula sylvatica*, *Rumex acetosa*, and *Saussurea alpina*. The Scottish association is clearly related to the more extensive and characteristic sub-alpine and low-alpine willow scrub of Scandinavia (Dahl, 1956; Nordhagen, 1927, 1943). The differentiation in Scotland between willow- and 'tall herb'-dominated ledges is not clear, but it may largely be influenced by historical factors, although there is often a tendency for the 'tall herb' communities to occur on the richer sites.

It is clear that the communities examined are all closely related, and represent the principal sub-alpine communities of basic soils and their biotic derivatives occurring in Scotland today. Species occurring in 75% or more of the plots are *Alchemilla alpina*, *Anthoxanthum odoratum*, *Deschampsia cespitosa*, *Potentilla erecta*, *Ranunculus acris*, and *Viola riviniana*. There is a local abundance of 'tall herbs' in the plots with, for example, *Cirsium heterophyllum*, *Crepis paludosa*, *Filipendula ulmaria*, *Geum rivale*, *Saussurea alpina*, and *Trollius europaeus*, and a general absence of many of the characteristic summit heath species.

All the pollen spectra from these communities are characterised by a dominance of Gramineae pollen (26–61%; Plate 6), no doubt because of the prolific production of the dominant grasses *Deschampsia cespitosa* and *Anthoxanthum odoratum* (see Pohl, 1937). A similar predominance of grass pollen in modern spectra from comparable communities occurs in the Alps (Lüdi & Vareschi, 1936), in Greenland (Fredskild, 1967), and in the Pennines (Pigott, 1958). This is in contrast to the rather poor representation of grasses in the modern spectra from summit vegetation. *Rumex acetosa* appears to have a good pollen representation in modern spectra from these communities, with values between 3.0 and 6.8% despite a low cover-abundance in the plots (5–35%). *Rumex acetosa* is reported by Pohl (1937) to have a vast pollen production, estimated at 400 million grains per plant. Similarly *Filipendula ulmaria*, *Potentilla erecta* (*Potentilla* type pollen), *Ranunculus acris* (*Ranunculus acris* type pollen), *Saxifraga hypnoides*, *Selaginella selaginoides* (cf. Welten,

1950), and *Thalictrum alpinum* are well represented in the pollen spectra with values up to 15.2% although they are all of minor significance in the vegetation. Over-representation of a similar magnitude for some of these taxa, or related ones, is discernable in the data of Bartley (1967), Fredskild (1967), and Heim-Thomas (1969).

In contrast to the pollen spectra from summit vegetation, *Galium saxatile* (Rubiaceae pollen) and *Thymus drucei* (*Thymus* type pollen) do not attain such high pollen values in spectra from grasslands and 'tall herb' communities, although the species are of similar abundance in the plots from both types of vegetation. This may result from the greater absolute pollen production in the sub-alpine communities especially by grasses, tending to depress, on a percentage basis, the pollen values of minor components. Such a situation serves to emphasise the extreme caution that is required in computing meaningful 'correction-factors' (see Fagerlind, 1952).

Salix lanata and *S. lapponum* are grossly under-represented in the spectra with pollen values between 0.7 and 2.5% and cover-abundance in the plots of 45 to 68%. Poor representation of willows in modern pollen spectra has been well demonstrated in Lappland (Firbas, 1934; Van der Hammen, 1951), Greenland (Iversen, 1945), North America (Janssen, 1966), Belgium (Heim, 1970), and the Alps (Welten, 1950). Similarly *Vaccinium myrtillus* (*Vaccinium* type pollen) is poorly represented, as are the 'tall herbs' *Angelica sylvestris* (*Angelica* type pollen), *Cirsium heterophyllum* (*Cirsium*/*Carduus* pollen), *Crepis paludosa* (Liguliflorae pollen), *Geum rivale*, *Sedum rosea*, *Trollius europaeus*, and *Valeriana officinalis*, all with pollen values of less than 4.6% and cover-abundance values in the plots of up to 45%. *Alchemilla alpina*, *A. glabra*, *Anemone nemorosa*, *Primula vulgaris*, *Succisa pratensis*, and *Viola riviniana* are also poorly represented, as the result of either apomixis, cleistogamy, or low pollen production.

There are several taxa that are not represented at all in the modern spectra, despite their occurrence in the vegetation plots. The absence of pollen of *Luzula sylvatica* is accounted for by poor preservation, but the absence, even of single grains, of *Euphrasia officinalis* agg. (mainly *E. brevipila*), *Linum catharticum*, *Oxalis acetosella*, *Parnassia palustris*, *Pinguicula vulgaris*, *Polygala serpyllifolia*, and *Sedum anglicum*, probably indicates a very low pollen production and poor dispersal. *Linum catharticum* is known to have a low pollen production of only about 20000 grains per plant (Faegri & Iversen, 1964).

Armeria maritima, *Cerastium alpinum* (*C. alpinum* type pollen), *Lotus corniculatus*, *Oxyria digyna*, *Polygonum viviparum*, *Rubus saxatilis*, *Saxifraga stellaris*, and *Silene acaulis* are represented with low values in the pollen spectra only when they are locally present in the plots. Occasionally, grains of *Saxifraga aizoides* and *S. oppositifolia* occur in samples from plots where the plants are absent, perhaps because the pollen is washed onto cliff ledges from nearby Saxifragetum aizoidis banks. Similarly, some taxa of summit vegetation such as *Artemisia norvegica* and *Lycopodium* spp. are represented by scattered grains or spores in the spectra. These grains are probably washed down from the summit ground by seepage of ground water and flushing of the cliffs below, on the ledges of which the samples in question were collected. Although ferns have a limited occurrence in the vegetation plots, their spores attain values of up to 16.9%. Rather curiously there is little correlation between the occurrence of fern spores and the corresponding plants, for example *Thelypteris dryopteris* spores occur in spectra 14, 15, 18, 29A, and 56, yet the plant is only present in plot 58.

The sub-alpine 'tall-herb'- and willow-dominated communities and the biotically derived grassland communities produce distinctive modern pollen assemblages, with a dominance of pollen of Gramineae (26% or more) and consistent occurrence of pollen of *Rumex acetosa*, *Ranunculus acris* type, and *Thalictrum* with individual values between 1.4 and 7.2%. Pollen of 'tall herbs' such as *Angelica sylvestris* (*Angelica* type), *Filipendula ulmaria*, and *Trollius europaeus* occur more abundantly in modern spectra from these communities than in any other samples examined in this study. Similarly, the pollen of the herbs *Alchemilla*, *Saxifraga aizoides*, *S. hypnoides*, and *S. oppositifolia*, and the spores of the dwarf pteridophytes *Botrychium lunaria* and *Selaginella selaginoides* are most prominent in modern spectra from sub-alpine communities (see also Welten, 1950). Pollen of *Cerastium alpinum*, *Saussurea alpina*, *Sedum rosea*, and *Veronica* are exclusive to modern spectra from sub-alpine communities. Because of the poor pollen representation of many of the phytosociologically characteristic and differential species in the communities examined, it does not appear possible, however, to characterise consistently the different associations within the alliance Mulgedion alpini on the basis of their contemporary pollen spectra, or indeed to distinguish them from the biotically derived grasslands of the alliance Nardo–Galion saxatilis on the basis of pollen alone.

4. POLLEN SPECTRA FROM *JUNIPERUS COMMUNIS* SCRUB

Juniperus communis occurs in a range of growth-forms and communities in northern Britain today, and to provide a basis for interpreting the possible significance of its fossil pollen frequencies in the sediments examined from Skye, surface samples were collected from a selection of these juniper-dominated communities.

On Skye and elsewhere in north-west Scotland extreme prostrate forms of *Juniperus communis* ssp. *nana* occur in a distinctive low-alpine community (*Juniperus nana nodum* in the class Caricetea curvulae – see Chapter 4), between 1000 and 2000 feet (305–610 m) on level or gently sloping wind-exposed knolls (McVean & Ratcliffe, 1962). Sample 48 comes from one such stand on Cul Mor, west Ross. It is a strikingly chionophobous community that grades into chionophilous *Vaccinium myrtillus* or Callunetum communities in more sheltered hollows. The juniper bushes rarely flower in these communities. *Juniperus communis* ssp. *nana* is extremely sensitive to burning (McVean, 1961*b*), and occurs on most of the undisturbed wooded islands in lochs in the western Highlands (McVean, 1958*b*), and as scattered bushes on ungrazed cliff-ledges, descending to sea-level on the Isle of Skye. In Scandinavia prostrate juniper occurs at higher altitudes in the low-alpine zone, but there it is restricted to mildly chionophilous communities, often with *Betula nana*, where the snow melts by early June (Dahl, 1956; Gjaerevoll & Bringer, 1965; Nordhagen, 1927, 1943). In continental climates the younger branches are killed by frost, wind, and ice-abrasion, unless protected by some snow-cover (see Hedberg, Mårtensson & Rudberg, 1952), but in the more oceanic climate of western Scotland juniper does not appear to be so dependent on prolonged snow-lie.

Patches of flowering juniper scrub dominated by small bushes intermediate in growth-form between *Juniperus communis* ssp. *nana* and *J. communis* ssp. *communis* occur locally in Scotland, for example at Bettyhill in Sutherland, and in Lakeland (Ratcliffe, 1960). In leaf characters these colonies more closely resemble ssp. *communis*, to which they are referred here. The taxonomy of these northern populations requires investigation. In floristic composition the stands have affinities with the *Juniperus nana* community, and sample 24 was collected from such an intermediate stand.

In the eastern Highlands and in northern England tall, dense *Juniperus communis* ssp. *communis* thickets occur locally between 1000 and 1800 feet (305–550 m), often with a fern-rich understorey (*Juniperus–Thelypteris nodum*; McVean & Ratcliffe, 1962). Fragmentary stands also occur on islands in north-west Scotland (McVean, 1958*b*), suggesting that the community may once have been more widespread. One of the finest surviving examples is at Holwick Scars, Teesdale (Pigott, 1956), where sample 2 was collected. Related communities with tall juniper, but lacking many of the ferns, occur in the Scandinavian sub-alpine zone, favouring the drier, poorer soils, whereas willows such as *Salix lapponum* thrive on wetter, richer sites, especially in areas that are irrigated by snow meltwater (Nordhagen, 1927, 1943).

Mixed birch–juniper woods are very rare in Britain today, but good examples are known near High Force in Teesdale (Pigott, 1956) where sample 4 was collected, and on Morrone near Braemar (McVean & Ratcliffe, 1962). Similar communities occur more widely in open 'heathy' birchwoods in Scandinavia (Hämet-Ahti, 1963; Nordhagen, 1927).

There is considerable variation in the representation of *Juniperus communis* pollen in the modern spectra (Plate 6): 2.5% in sample 48, 36.9% in sample 24, 49.2% in sample 2, and 7.1% in sample 4.

Plot 4 is dominated by *Betula pubescens* ssp. *odorata* but with a juniper-rich understorey, and its pollen spectrum is thus grouped with the other spectra from birch woodlands. Plot 48 comes from a well developed stand of the *Juniperus nana nodum* and it is thus strictly referable on floristic criteria to the alpine summit-heath communities of the class Caricetea curvulae (see Chapter 4). It is of interest that its pollen spectrum, with 54% Cyperaceae pollen and 1.6% *Lycopodium selago* spores, so closely resembles the modern pollen assemblages produced by other communities within the Caricetea curvulae.

The representation of *Juniperus communis* pollen in modern spectra appears to be influenced not only by the abundance of the plant in the vegetation, but by its growth-form, flowering, and ecology (Iversen, 1954). In Scotland prostrate juniper is poorly represented (plot 48) because of its shy flowering in exposed habitats, whereas intermediate, well-grown bushes (plot 24) are moderately well represented in the pollen spectra. High pollen values in modern spectra are, however, only produced by tall, dense scrub (plot 2). In mixed birch–juniper woods *Juniperus* pollen values appear to be reduced, partly because of the reduced flowering of juniper in shade and partly because of the high pollen production of birch, which tends, on a percentage basis, to suppress the representation of the understorey species. Vasari & Vasari (1968) present similar pollen data for juniper communities in northern Finland, with between 1 and 5% *Juniperus* pollen in mixed birch–alder–juniper woods, and up to 45% in open *Juniperus*-dominated fens. Iversen (1954) records low pollen frequencies (3%) in surface muds from 'a valley in Greenland in which *Juniperus* is frequent, but dwarfed'.

These four pollen spectra from northern Britain support the views of Iversen (1954) on the significance of changes in juniper frequencies in pollen diagrams. More data would have been desirable but were not obtained, as well-developed stands of juniper scrub are so scarce in Britain at present.

Among the other pollen types in the spectra from this vegetational type *Empetrum* spp. and *Vaccinium myrtillus* are again poorly represented. The ferns *Thelypteris dryopteris* and *T. limbosperma* are also under-represented, with only 0.9% spore frequencies, despite cover-abundance values of up to 45%.

5. POLLEN SPECTRA FROM *BETULA PUBESCENS* WOODLANDS

Surface samples for pollen analysis were collected from the two principal types of woodland in northern and western Britain that are dominated by *Betula pubescens* ssp. *odorata* today. The woodland types examined are as follows:

Mulgedion alpini
Betula pubescens–Cirsium heterophyllum Association — Nos. 3, 30

Quercion robori–petraeae
Betula pubescens–Vaccinium myrtillus Association — Nos. 4, 32, 33

Although the two woodland types are similar in terms of the dominant trees and shrubs, they differ considerably in their understorey species and in their ecological requirements (see Chapters 4 and 5). In the *Betula pubescens–Vaccinium myrtillus* Association, *Vaccinium myrtillus* is a prominent component of the forest floor, with *Deschampsia flexuosa*, *Galium saxatile*, *Oxalis acetosella*, *Potentilla erecta*, and ferns. On steep and sheltered north- and east-facing slopes, bryophytes become prominent, both on boulders and on the floor of the woods. The *Betula pubescens–Vaccinium myrtillus* Association typically occurs on either acidic podsols or brown earth soils.

In contrast, the *Betula pubescens–Cirsium heterophyllum* Association has an abundance of 'tall herbs' in the understorey, for example *Cirsium heterophyllum*, *Crepis paludosa*, *Filipendula ulmaria*, *Geum rivale*, and *Trollius europaeus*. This woodland type occurs on fertile, irrigated brown earths, but it is always restricted to areas that are protected in some way from grazing animals. Typical ecological situations are broad ledges in inaccessible rocky ravines, or on steep blocky slopes.

Extensive stands of such woods are now rare in Britain, and only two examples were examined (samples 3 and 30), one near Wynch Bridge, Teesdale (Pigott, 1956) and one on the Isle of Skye. As discussed in Chapters 4 and 5, comparable woods are common in sub-alpine situations in Scandinavia today, and probably were once more widespread in northern Britain.

In studying the relationship between modern pollen spectra and vegetation in woodlands, it is necessary to consider how large a wooded area is contributing to the local pollen rain. Andersen (1967, 1970) has shown in a detailed study of Draved Forest in Denmark that pollen percentages of a given tree species decrease strongly between 20 and 30 m away from dense stands of the species within the forest, and that there is a close correlation between the pollen frequencies and basal area of the trees within a 30 m radius of the pollen sample. In the time available for the present study, measurements were not possible of basal area or of relative density, frequency, and dominance, and hence of importance value (Janssen, 1966, 1967*b*; Wright *et al.*, 1967) or importance percentage (McAndrews, 1966). Instead the canopy cover of the various trees was estimated on the Domin scale within a plot of 625 square metres.

All the spectra from the woods are dominated by *Betula* pollen, with values from 26.3 to 80.7% (Plate 6). There are significant correlation coefficients (r = 0.87 and 0.97, respectively) between the local pollen percentages in surface samples and the canopy cover for both *Betula pubescens* and *Corylus avellana* in the woods examined (Fig. 25), similar to the correlations found by Andersen (1967, 1970) between local tree pollen percentages and basal areas. The calculated regression line, the regression equation, the correlation coefficient (r) and the number of samples (N) upon which the regression line is based are shown on Fig. 25. Tree-birches have long been recognised as being well-represented in modern pollen spectra (Bastin, 1964; Faegri &

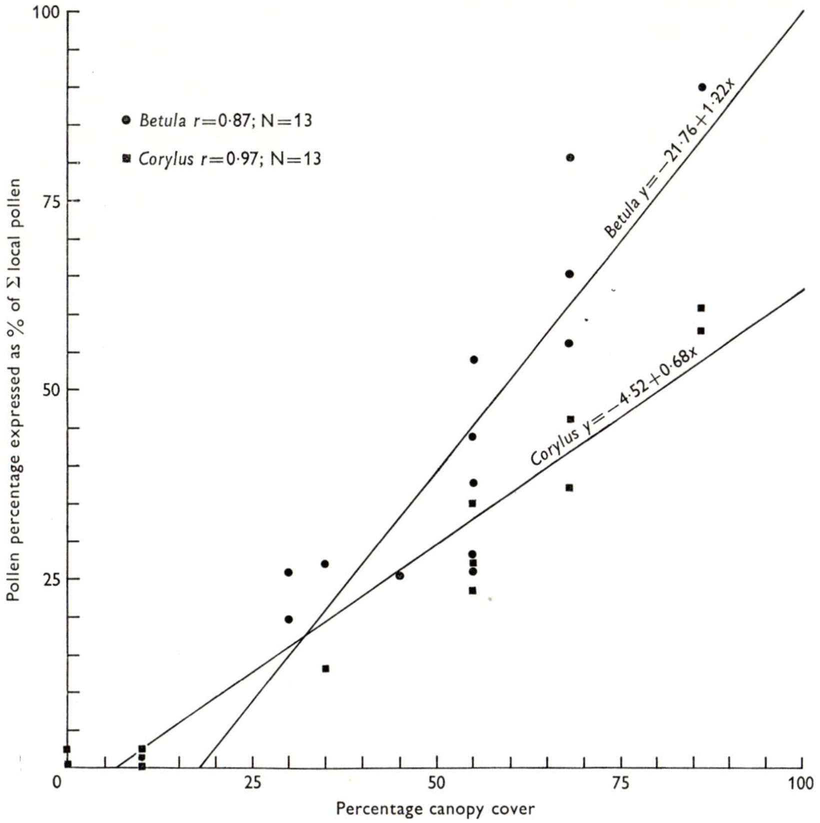

Figure 25. Relationship of percentages of *Betula* and *Corylus* pollen in surface samples to percentage crown cover. Calculated regression lines are shown. Abbreviations: r = correlation coefficient, N = number of observations.

Iversen, 1964; Heim, 1962, 1970; Jonassen, 1950; McAndrews, 1966). In contrast the associated trees and shrubs *Salix cinerea* ssp. *atrocinerea* and *Sorbus aucuparia* are poorly represented, with 0.1–1.4%, and 0.1–0.2% pollen frequencies respectively, despite a canopy cover of up to 30%. Sample 4 is from a wood with *Juniperus communis* as a prominent understorey species (30% cover and abundance) below High Force in Teesdale. The wood is rather open and blocky, with abundant ferns, especially *Dryopteris borreri*, *D. dilatata*, *Thelypteris dryopteris*, *T. limbosperma*, and *T. phegopteris* (Plate 7). *Juniperus communis* pollen values are only 7.1%, and the significance of this is discussed above. *Dryopteris filix-mas* type and *D. carthusiana* type (includes *D. dilatata*) spore percentages are high, as they are in spectrum 30. Both samples are from woodland plots with abundant ferns. In general, however, fern spore percentages are rather variable in these woodland spectra, as they are in the surface pollen data of Bastin (1964), Firbas (1934), and Heim (1962, 1970).

Although there are considerable floristic differences between the two *Betula*-dominated woodland types examined (Plate 7), there are only minor differences in the composition of their pollen spectra (Plate 6). *Vaccinium myrtillus*, although an important understorey species in some stands (Plate 7), is represented by low pollen values between 0.2 and 4.6% in the spectra. A similar under-representation of *V. myrtillus* in woodland spectra was noted by Heim (1962, 1970). Similarly the prominent and characteristic 'tall herbs' in plots 3 and 30, for example *Angelica sylvestris* (*Angelica* type pollen), *Cirsium heterophyllum* (*Cirsium/Carduus* pollen), *Crepis paludosa* (Liguliflorae pollen), *Filipendula ulmaria*, *Geum rivale*, and *Trollius europaeus*, are represented by low pollen values (0.1–6.3%). Many of these 'tall herbs', for example *Cirsium heterophyllum*, *Crepis paludosa*, *Trollius europaeus*, and *Valeriana officinalis*, are also poorly represented in other spectra from plots where the plants grow (for example plots 14, 29A, and 38), but the representation of *Filipendula ulmaria* in spectra from the 'tall herbs' woods (mean percentage = 2.85%) contrasts with its poorer pollen representation (1.76%) in treeless sub-alpine 'tall herb' communities, although the species is of comparable abundance in both vegetational types. This is probably due to the reduced flowering of *Filipendula* in sub-alpine habitats in contrast to its prolific flowering in lowland 'tall herb' woodlands. *Filipendula ulmaria* generally has a high pollen representation in lowland, wooded localities (Andersen, 1970; Heim-Thomas, 1969).

As in other spectra, several taxa, although present in the plots, are rarely if ever, represented in the pollen spectra, for example *Oxalis acetosella* and *Viola riviniana*. The absence of *Pteridium aquilinum* spores in any of the woodland spectra examined is very striking, in view of its high cover-abundance (10–35%) in the plots studied. *Pteridium aquilinum* appears to sporulate rather rarely in shaded, woodland habitats, in contrast to its prolific fruiting in some open treeless habitats (Andersen 1970; Heim 1970; Janssen 1967*a*). There is a group of plants that are only represented in the pollen spectra with low values when they are present in the plots, for example *Campanula latifolia* (*Campanula* type pollen) and *Prunus padus*.

As the overall pollen representation of the understorey species is poor, the characterisation of the different woodland types on the basis of their modern pollen spectra is thus rather difficult. However, within the spectra from the birch woodlands examined, pollen of the 'tall herb' species such as *Filipendula ulmaria*, *Cirsium heterophyllum*, *Geum rivale*, and *Trollius europaeus* are virtually exclusive to the modern spectra from stands of the *Betula pubescens–Cirsium heterophyllum* Association, thus permitting some characterisation of the woodlands on the basis of pollen composition. In contrast the percentages of fern spores (Polypodiaceae undiff., *Dryopteris filix-mas* type, and *Blechumn spicant*) tend to be consistently greater in spectra from the *Betula pubescens–Vaccinium myrtillus* woods than in spectra from the woods with abundant 'tall herbs'. A further distinguishing feature is that the spectra from the 'tall herb' woods are markedly richer in pollen and spore types than are the spectra from grazed *Betula pubescens–Vaccinium myrtillus* woods. Forty-one pollen and spore types are recorded in the two spectra (3, 30) from the 'tall herb' stands with a total local pollen sum of 647, whereas thirty-three pollen and spore types are recorded in the three spectra (4, 32, 33) from the grazed woods, although the total number of pollen and spores counted in these spectra is considerably greater ($\Sigma P = 2359$).

6. POLLEN SPECTRA FROM *CORYLUS AVELLANA–BETULA PUBESCENS* WOODLANDS

Mixed woodlands dominated by *Corylus avellana* and *Betula pubescens* are locally frequent today on the Isle of Skye (see Fig. 6) and elsewhere in northern and western Britain. Surface samples for pollen analysis were collected from the two principal types of mixed hazel–birch woods occurring on Skye. The two types of woodland examined are as follows:

Mulgedion alpini	
Betula pubescens–Cirsium heterophyllum Association	Nos. 13, 19
Quercion robori–petraeae	
Corylus avellana–Oxalis acetosella Association	Nos. 31, 34, 35, 36

Although these two woodland types are similar in terms of the dominant canopy trees and shrubs, they differ considerably in their understorey species and in their ecological requirements. In the *Corylus avellana–Oxalis acetosella* Association, the understorey is characterised by an abundance of *Conopodium majus*, *Endymion non-scriptus*, *Oxalis acetosella*, *Potentilla erecta*, and *Primula vulgaris*. The *Betula pubescens–Cirsium heterophyllum* stands have abundant 'tall herbs' in the understorey, such as *Cirsium heterophyllum*, *Filipendula ulmaria*, *Heracleum sphondylium*, and *Silene dioica*. The community occurs on steep, rocky ground in areas that are generally inaccessible to grazing animals. Both these woodland types occur on fertile, brown earth soils. The striking floristic differences between them appear, however, to result primarily from differences in the degree of grazing and other biotic pressure (see Chapters 4 and 5).

All the pollen spectra from the woods are dominated by *Betula* and *Corylus avellana* pollen, with values of 25.4–54.3%, and 13.3–61.3% respectively (Plate 6). The relations between the canopy cover of *Betula pubescens* and *Corylus avellana* and the corresponding pollen percentages are shown in Fig. 25. It is clear that hazel and birch are both well represented in these pollen spectra, although birch has a slightly higher representation (cover percentage/pollen percentage = 0.82) than does hazel (1.48). Their high representation is expected in view of their high pollen production, estimated by Pohl (1937) as being between 4 and 6 million pollen grains per inflorescence. A comparable representation of *Corylus* in modern pollen spectra is reported by Heim

(1970). The high representation of *Corylus avellana* in these spectra is in contrast to the findings of Firbas (1934) and Jonassen (1950), who reported values of between 1 and 13% in spectra close to dense hazel scrub. However, their samples were from woods where hazel is growing as an understorey species. In such situations hazel is reported to flower sparingly (Andersen, 1970; Iversen, 1960; Jonassen, 1950).

Salix spp. and *Sorbus aucuparia* are poorly represented in the spectra with pollen values of 0.2–1.9% and a canopy cover up to 30%, with the exception of 7.1% *Salix* pollen in spectrum 19, as are the characteristic 'tall herb' species of plots 13 and 19, with the exception of 2.8% *Heracleum sphondylium* and 4.3% *Filipendula* pollen in spectrum 19. Similarly the prominent understorey species of the *Corylus avellana–Oxalis acetosella* woods, such as *Conopodium majus* (*Conopodium* type pollen), *Endymion non-scriptus* (Liliaceae pollen), and *Galium saxatile* (Rubiaceae pollen), are poorly represented (0.2–0.9%) and *Chrysosplenium oppositifolium, Digitalis purpurea, Listera ovata, Lysimachia nemorum, Oxalis acetosella, Primula vulgaris,* and *Viola riviniana* are not represented at all in the pollen spectra (cf. Andersen, 1970; Bastin, 1964; Heim, 1970). *Anemone nemorosa, Sanicula europaea,* and *Rubus saxatilis* are represented by low pollen values (0.2–1.0%), but only in spectra from plots in which they occur (cf. Andersen, 1970). Fern spore percentages are variable, with high values (31.8%) of *Dryopteris filix-mas* type spores in spectrum 31, associated with abundant *Dryopteris borreri* and *Thelypteris limbosperma* (spores of both these ferns are of the *Dryopteris filix-mas* type – see Chapter 8) in the plot (cf. Andersen, 1970; Heim 1962). On the other hand *Thelypteris dryopteris* spores attain 9.8% in spectrum 19, but the fern is not present in the corresponding plot. Similarly, *Rumex acetosa* pollen occurs in low frequencies (0.2–0.8%) in the spectra, although the plant is not present in the plots.

As in the modern spectra from the birch woods, pollen of understorey species is poorly represented, and thus the two woodland types are difficult to distinguish on pollen criteria alone. There is a similar poor representation of understorey species in pollen spectra from woodlands in Belgium (Bastin, 1964; Heim, 1962, 1970; Mullenders, 1962), in Denmark (Andersen, 1970), in Holland (Hartman, 1968), and in Minnesota (Janssen, 1966). The principal difference between the pollen spectra from the two types of mixed birch–hazel woodland is the occurrence of pollen of 'tall herbs', such as *Angelica* type, *Cirsium/Carduus*, *Filipendula*, and *Heracleum sphondylium*, and the somewhat higher values of *Salix* pollen in the spectra from the *Betula pubescens–Cirsium heterophyllum* stands, whereas in spectra from the *Corylus avellana–Oxalis acetosella* woods, pollen of many of the 'tall herbs' are absent, or if present, the pollen frequencies are markedly lower than in spectra from 'tall herb' stands. The percentages of fern spores (Polypodiaceae undiff., *Dryopteris filix-mas* type, *D. carthusiana* type, and *Blechnum spicant*) tend to be higher in the spectra from the grazed woodlands than in spectra from the 'tall herb' stands. As in the pollen spectra from the birch woods, there is a greater diversity of pollen and spore types in spectra from the woods rich in 'tall herbs' than in spectra from the grazed woodlands. Thirty-nine pollen and spore types are recorded in the two spectra (13, 19) from the 'tall herb' woods with a total pollen sum of 1192 grains whereas thirty-five pollen and spore types are present in the four spectra (31, 34, 35, 36) from the *Corylus avellana–Oxalis acetosella* woods, despite the fact that the total number of pollen and spores counted in these spectra is considerably greater ($\Sigma P = 2031$).

7. NON-LOCAL POLLEN AND SPORES

All the spectra examined contained pollen and spores derived from taxa not recorded in or near the vegetational plots. The frequencies of these types are shown in Fig. 24. Such non-local pollen and spores may be regionally or extraregionally derived. Regional pollen and spores are here defined as pollen and spores indistinguishable morphologically from the pollen and spore types of taxa occurring today within the broad geographical area of the study, in this case the Isle of Skye and north-west Scotland, whereas extraregional pollen and spores are derived from taxa that are not known to occur in the broad geographical area of the study. The processes of pollen transport of the regional component are complex, for as the majority of the regional pollen is derived from woodland species it probably originates, in part at least, from pollen initially dispersed through the woodland canopy and into the canopy air currents above the woodlands, whereas its sedimentation may largely result from impact with raindrops (Tauber, 1965). Processes of long-distance transport of extraregional pollen and spores have been investigated by Hirst, Stedman & Hurst (1967), and appear to be largely influenced by turbulence in the upper atmosphere (cf. Christie & Ritchie, 1969).

These complex processes of pollen dispersal and sedimentation are in contrast to the rather simpler dispersal processes of the local and extra-local pollen components (Janssen, 1966; Turner, 1964) that comprise the majority of the pollen and spores in the spectra examined. In wooded areas, the local and extra-local components of anemophilous tree species are probably largely accounted for by dispersal through the trunk-space (Janssen, 1966; Tauber, 1965, 1967), as well as by rain deposition of pollen caught on twigs and leaves in the crown layer during the flowering season, and by anthers, inflorescences, and catkins falling to the ground (see Andersen, 1970).

In the spectra from treeless vegetation (summit heaths and sub-alpine grasslands and 'tall herb' communities) the frequencies of non-locally derived pollen are markedly higher (means of 24.4% and 22.8% of total pollen, respectively) than in the woodland spectra (mean = 2.1%). Pollen of *Alnus*, *Betula*, *Calluna vulgaris*, *Corylus avellana*, *Pinus*, *Plantago lanceolata*, and *Urtica*, and the spores of *Pteridium aquilinum* occur consistently in the spectra from treeless areas. All the tree and shrub types have a high pollen production (Pohl, 1937), and they have been shown by other workers to have an effective dispersal (Dyakowska, 1937; Heim, 1962; Janssen, 1966). Many of these pollen types occur often in surface spectra from treeless areas (Aario, 1940; Bartley, 1967; Lichti-Federovich & Ritchie, 1968; Rampton, 1971; Ritchie & Lichti-Federovich, 1967; Srodon, 1960; Terasmae, 1967). Although *Calluna vulgaris* is nominally an entomophilous species, large amounts of its pollen are liberated into the atmosphere late in its flowering season (Pohl, 1937), and its pollen is well dispersed (H. H. Birks, 1969; Jonassen, 1950). It is probable that *Urtica dioica* and *Pteridium aquilinum* have a high pollen and spore production, and judging from the low weight of *Urtica* pollen (Dyakowska & Zurzycki, 1959) its pollen is likely to have a low settling velocity and thus an effective dispersal.

Rarer and more scattered pollen types in the modern spectra include *Abies*, *Acer*, *Artemisia* undiff., *Carpinus*, *Fagus sylvatica*, *Fraxinus excelsior*, *Juglans*, *Picea*, *Platanus*, *Quercus*, *Sparganium* type, *Tilia cordata*, and *Ulmus*. Some of these taxa, for example *Abies*, *Acer*, *Fagus*, *Fraxinus*, *Picea*, and *Ulmus*, have been shown to have a low pollen production and/or a poor pollen dispersal and hence a low representation in modern spectra (Erdtman, 1969; Heim, 1962, 1970; Janssen, 1966; McAndrews, 1966; Pohl, 1937; Tsukada, 1958). *Tilia cordata* is reported to have a moderately high pollen production (Pohl, 1937), but its entomophilous nature may limit the dispersal of its pollen (Hyde & Williams, 1945). The scattered and infrequent occurrence of these grains in the surface spectra may largely represent long-distance or extraregional dispersal in the upper atmosphere as many of these pollen types are derived from taxa not known to occur today in the broad geographical area of study. In contrast, *Pinus* and *Betula* pollen occur consistently in the surface spectra from treeless communities in Scotland, and they can be regarded as part of the regional pollen component (*sensu* Janssen, 1966) that is characteristic of the broad geographical area of north-west Scotland, in that their pollen frequencies vary little from one spectrum to another in samples collected within the same geographical region.

Artemisia pollen often occurs in modern spectra from areas some distance from suitable sources, for example in Greenland (Fredskild, 1967), and in Sweden (Erdtman, 1969), as does *Sparganium* type pollen in spectra from areas where suitable habitats for either *Sparganium* or *Typha* spp. are absent, for example in western Iran (Wright *et al.*, 1967).

In the pollen spectra from the woodlands occasional grains of *Alnus*, *Fagus sylvatica*, *Fraxinus excelsior*, *Hedera helix*, *Lonicera periclymenum*, *Picea*, *Pinus*, *Plantago lanceolata*, *Quercus*, and *Ulmus* occur. *Hedera* and *Lonicera* pollen probably originate from plants within the wood that were not noted in the vegetational survey. The occurrence of pollen of several trees not known to occur within the woods must represent long-distance pollen dispersal into the woods, as was found in woodland studies by Andersen (1967, 1970), Bastin (1964), Hartman (1968), Heim (1962, 1970), Janssen (1966), and Mullenders (1962). Occasional grains of *Plantago lanceolata* also occur in woodland spectra elsewhere (Andersen, 1970; Bastin, 1964; Heim, 1962, 1970; Jonassen, 1950). Andersen (1970) suggests that the pollen of species not occurring locally in a forest is carried over the canopy by turbulent air flow, and is mixed in the canopy where it is caught by filtration. Subsequent rain washing results in its deposition onto the forest floor.

There is an interesting relationship between the percentages of locally derived pollen, the A.P./N.A.P. ratio, and the vegetation type. In alpine summit heaths and snow-bed communities with a low cover of vascular plants and a low local production of pollen and spores, there is a high repre-

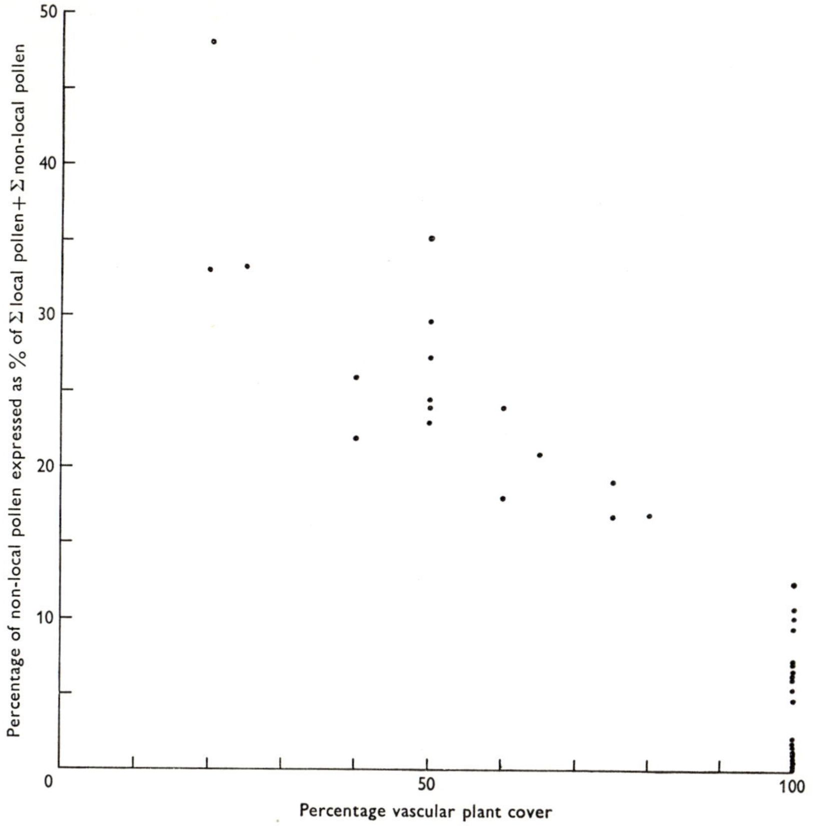

Figure 26. Relationship of non-local pollen percentages in surface samples to percentage total vascular plant cover in the sample plots.

sentation of non-local derived pollen (17–33%; mean percentage = 28.4%). The majority of this (Fig. 24) is tree pollen, giving a percentage A.P. between 11 and 30% of total pollen (mean = 15.7%). In the closed grassland communities of the sub-alpine zone there is a higher local pollen production, the relative contribution of the non-local component is thus reduced (5.6–44%; mean = 21.8%) and the percentage A.P. falls to between 3.6 and 20% (mean = 10.1%). In the woodland spectra the non-local component is greatly reduced, because of the extremely high pollen production by the trees growing locally. The relation of non-local pollen percentages to vascular plant cover in the plots examined is shown in Fig. 26.

The spectra as a whole show a variation in A.P. values from high percentages in the woodlands, reduced A.P. values in the sub-alpine grasslands, and increased A.P. percentages in montane summit communities. This may largely be the result of variations in the relative representation of the non-local component and it is not a true indication of the balance between forested and treeless communities. Rather similar results were found by Aario (1940) in Finnish Lappland (see Fig. 28 in Berglund, 1966*a*) with about 45% A.P. in treeless areas and 80% A.P. in forested regions. On an absolute basis the A.P. frequencies (as number of grains per 50 mg of air-dried soil sample) were 69 in treeless areas, and 1520 to 1951 in woodland. A similar absolute range is reported by Ritchie & Lichti-Federovich (1967) in a transect from forest to tundra in Canada. Such artefacts arise from the use of relative rather than absolute values and they serve to emphasise the extreme caution required in interpreting vegetational changes on the basis of A.P./N.A.P. proportions (see Livingstone, 1955*b*; cf. Walker, 1966).

8. PROBLEMS IN THE COMPARISON OF MODERN AND FOSSIL POLLEN SPECTRA

Pollen and spore percentages for selected taxa in the thirty-seven surface samples analysed are summarised in Table 11.3. The data from these surface samples show recognisable and consistent relationships between the pollen percentages and vegetation. Before applying the data obtained from this survey

TABLE 11.3. *Summary of selected pollen and spore percentages in surface samples*

Community	Sample No.	Corylus	Betula	Juniperus	Salix	Gramineae	Cyperaceae	Rumex acetosa	Filipendula	Ranunculus acris type	Thalictrum	Lycopodium selago
Corylus avellana–	31, 34, 35, 36	25.6–61.3	25.6–54.3	0	0.2–1.3	4.3–15.2	1.8–7.6	0.2–0.8	0.2–0.6	0.4–0.9	0	0
Oxalis acetosella		37.7	40.1	0	0.5	8.5	3.4	0.3	0.4	0.5	0	0
Betula pubescens–Cirsium	13, 19	13.3–46.2	25.4–27	0	1.9–7.1	7.1–8.7	3.0–3.2	0.2–1.1	1.6–4.3	0.5–1.8	0.2	0
heterophyllum (with *Corylus*)		30.7	26.2	0	0.7	7.8	3.1	0.5	3.1	1.1	0.1	0
Betula pubescens–Cirsium	3, 30	1.2–1.4	26–65	0–0.7	0.3–1.4	7.8–30.3	1.5–11.5	0.2–0.5	0.2–6.2	1.5–2.5	0–0.2	0
heterophyllum (without *Corylus*)		1.5	61.7	0.2	0.8	18.1	5.7	0.3	2.6	2.6	0.09	0
Betula pubescens–Vaccinium	4, 32, 33	0.2–2.5	28–81	0–7.1	0.1–0.5	10.9–42	1.2–3.9	0–0.4	0–0.3	0–0.9	0	0
myrtillus		0.6	61.0	2.0	0.1	21.7	2.7	0.1	0.08	0.2	0	0
Juniperus communis scrub	2, 24, 48	0	0–1.6	2.5–49	0–0.6	25.1–39	1.0–54.1	0–0.8	0	0–1.0	0–0.3	0–1.6
		0	0.7	34.7	0.2	31.7	24.8	0.4	0	0.2	0.08	0.4
Agrosto–Festucetum and	15, 18, 29A, 37	0	0	0–0.2	0–0.7	31.8–46.6	12.8–17.1	3.0–3.6	0.5–1.2	1.4–5.2	0.9–2.4	0–0.5
Dwarf herb *nodum*		0	0	0.06	0.1	37.1	14.9	3.2	0.6	3.3	1.6	0.1
Deschampsietum cespitosae	50, 56	0	0	0.4–0.9	0.1–0.4	48.9–61.0	20.1–21.7	4.0–4.7	0.1–0.6	1.4–4.4	1.3–1.5	0–0.7
		0	0	0.6	0.2	55.1	20.9	4.3	0.3	2.3	1.4	0.14
Sedum rosea–Alchemilla	14, 38, 45	0	0	0–0.3	0.2–1.0	26.2–44.8	8.3–13.0	3.5–6.8	2.7–5.8	2.5–3.5	0.4–1.9	0–1.0
glabra		0	0	0.12	0.4	37.1	11.2	4.8	3.9	3.1	0.9	0.2
Salix lapponum–Luzula	49, 58	0	0	0.5	0.7–2.5	34.7–61.3	8.7–9.9	3.9–5.3	0.5	2.8–7.2	0.7–2.2	1.8–2.2
sylvatica		0	0	0.4	1.6	48.2	9.3	4.5	0.4	4.9	1.2	2.0
Cryptogrammeto–	57	0	0	0.4	0.2	45.8	28.0	0.6	0	0.4	0.2	3.2
Athyrietum chionophilum		0	0	0.4	0.2	45.8	28.0	0.6	0	0.4	0.2	3.2
Nardus stricta–	1, 27	0	0	0	0.2–0.3	14.8–30.1	29.4–38.3	0.2–0.8	0	0.3–1.5	0	14.6–14.8
Vaccinium myrtillus		0	0	0	0.2	23.9	34.6	0.4	0	0.9	0	14.6
Cariceto–Rhacomitretum	9, 26, 40, 44	0	0	0–0.5	0.5–3.4	20.4–38.9	29.8–45.4	0–1.9	0	0.4–1.4	0–0.7	3.1–14.2
lanuginosi		0	0	0.25	1.4	24.0	36.9	0.4	0	1.0	0.2	7.2
Festuca ovina–Luzula	41, 42, 43, 47,	0	0	0–0.6	0.6–1.2	18.9–26.1	44.4–50.5	0–0.5	0	0.2–2.1	0.4–1.2	2.8–4.1
spicata	51	0	0	0.28	0.91	20.7	48.0	0.2	0	0.9	0.7	2.9

Upper figures are range of percentages; lower figures are mean percentages.
All percentages are based on sum of all determinable local pollen (with selected exclusions).

to the interpretation of the fossil pollen diagrams, it is necessary, however, to consider the limitations and validity of this comparative method, in view of the fact that this type of study has not been attempted before in Britain.

Although the number of samples analysed is rather small, the samples are considered to represent the principal range of montane and woodland vegetation types occurring in north-west Scotland today. Much of the vegetation has been disturbed, to some degree, by man through burning and by grazing animals, but it is likely that these communities produce characteristic pollen spectra that are probably similar to those from relatively undisturbed vegetation. It is not possible, however, to say that a distinct community *always* produces a distinct pollen spectrum. This hypothesis cannot be adequately tested at present because the modern pollen rain of much of the vegetation of upland Britain has yet to be examined.

Another important limitation on the method as used here is that any comparisons attempted are between modern pollen spectra derived from moss polsters or surface soils, and fossil spectra deposited in open water. There are, at present, no comparative data either supporting or invalidating such comparisons. A study of recent pollen spectra in surface lake muds in Scotland, similar to those of Lichti-Federovich and Ritchie (1968) and McAndrews (1966, 1967) in North America is regarded as an imperative field for investigation. There is increasing evidence for the important role of water transport in the influx of pollen into lakes in areas of rugged relief (R. M. Peck, unpublished data; Ingram *et al.*, 1959). A comparative programme of surface samples, detailed vegetational surveys, and pollen trapping in lakes of varying catchment and basin size is required before the relationships between pollen spectra and surrounding vegetation can be more fully understood. Studies should also be made of variability of pollen spectra from surface muds within a single basin of deposition as a basis for assessing variabilities in pollen spectra between basins (see Davis, Brewster & Sutherland, 1969).

In theory it should be possible for a particular pollen assemblage (expressed in relative frequencies) to be derived from two or more quite different vegetation types. Species with a very low pollen representation constitute 'blind spots' (*sensu* Davis, 1963) or 'silent areas' in the vegetation that are barely registered in the pollen spectra. Communities that differ greatly in the extent of such 'silent areas', but that are similar in other respects, could then be expected to produce similar relative pollen percentages (Davis, 1963; Fagerlind, 1952). To some degree the summit heath and snow-bed communities fall in this type, with a varying vegetational prominence of species not contributing to the pollen spectra, for example *Rhacomitrium lanuginosum*, *Luzula spicata*, and *Juncus trifidus*.

A further problem is the difficulty of evaluating the significance of the variation in pollen percentages between samples. For example, large variations in pollen percentages from taxa with a high pollen production may represent smaller differences in terms of vegetational composition than small variations in pollen percentages of taxa with a low pollen production. In general, however, the differences in pollen percentages in samples collected from different communities are greater than the differences in pollen percentages in samples collected from the same community as shown by chi-square tests of homogeneity (Mosimann, 1965; see also Heim, 1971). In attempting any comparisons between modern and fossil pollen assemblages, the variations in fossil pollen percentages from level to level and from site to site within the same pollen assemblage zone raise further difficulties. Averaging fossil spectra should be avoided, as trends may exist within an assemblage zone. These various problems are inherent in any attempt to compare fossil pollen spectra with modern pollen spectra. More extensive studies of modern and fossil pollen spectra and the application of statistical methods for data analysis and comparison may ultimately provide some solution. At present it is preferable only to attempt comparisons with the fossil pollen assemblages on a rather broad basis, and not to seek an exact match between specific modern and fossil spectra (cf. Ogden, 1969).

Despite these limitations and problems, the use of modern surface samples as a comparative means for finding modern vegetational analogues for former vegetation is the soundest basis currently available for the interpretation of pollen diagrams in terms of past vegetation. If there is a close match between the modern and the fossil spectra then a vegetational reconstruction can be made with some confidence. On the other hand when a close match is not found, and the deduction is made that the past vegetation has no modern counterpart – as can occur when the flora and vegetation developed under edaphic, climatic, or successional conditions not existing today – some vegetational reconstruction can still be attempted from the data on surface samples. The available palaeofloristic data provide information as to the species formerly present and, from the surface pollen spectra, it is possible to assess the modern pollen representation of those species. Comparison between the modern values and the fossil percentages can then provide a crude estimate of the relative abundance of the species in the former vegetation. The application of the modern surface sample data to the interpretation of the fossil pollen assemblages from the Isle of Skye is discussed in Part IV.

PART IV

THE LATE-DEVENSIAN FLORA AND VEGETATION OF THE ISLE OF SKYE

12

THE LATE-DEVENSIAN FLORA

1. INTRODUCTION

As in the study of the present plant cover of a given area, there are two possible approaches to the interpretation of pollen diagrams from an area. The *floristic approach* is concerned with the distribution in space and time of taxa considered as individuals, and the basic unit of study is generally the species. The *vegetational approach* is concerned with the spatial and temporal distribution of aggregates of species, and the basic unit of study is the plant community. Both approaches are useful in ecology and in palaeoecology, and each has its own advantages and limitations.

The reconstruction of either past flora or past vegetation from a pollen-stratigraphical record presents many difficulties. The compilation of a comprehensive list of taxa present in the past flora of an area is severely limited by the incompleteness of the fossil pollen record. Many of the plant species that are present in the flora and vegetation at any one time produce and disperse such small amounts of pollen or spores that there is a very low probability of finding a single grain of any of them. Studies of modern pollen spectra (see Chapter 11) show that many taxa are not represented in the pollen rain. Furthermore the limitations of present pollen morphological knowledge coupled with the problems of pollen deterioration in sediments often make identifications impossible to the low taxonomic level that is necessary for a thorough floristic analysis. It is here that the study of plant macrofossils – that is, plant parts other than pollen and microspores – is most valuable, for it increases the chance of determination of fossil remains to the species level. After the recovery and identification of numerous macrofossils and the counting of many thousands of pollen grains, the floral list will still contain several gaps, particularly in taxonomic groups such as the Gramineae whose pollen grains, although extremely numerous in Quaternary sediments, are closely similar in morphology and are thus nearly all indistinguishable, and whose floral parts and seeds are apparently rarely preserved.

All the sediments examined on Skye, although providing floristically rich fossil pollen and spore assemblages, are poor in their macrofossil content. The sediments are fine-grained limnic deposits formed in open water, and such sediments frequently contain few macrofossils, in contrast to the rich assemblages of seeds, fruits, and leaves recorded from coarse limnic muds and from fluviatile sediments.

Besides the limitations imposed by the processes of fossilisation and indentification and by the scope of the present investigation, a further limitation in the palaeofloristic data from Skye is an incomplete knowledge of the stratigraphic range and spatial distribution of several of the pollen and spore types identified. The pollen counts were made at different times, and for that reason the analyses are of varying degrees of detail. For example at Loch Mealt (analysed in 1966 and 1967) no morphological separation of Caryophyllaceae pollen or of many of the spores of the Polypodiaceae was attempted. Thus the absence of a pollen or spore type from one diagram that is present in another may only mean that the type was not determined, and not that it was absent from the site analysed earlier.

The advantages of the floristic approach in palaeoecology are similar to those in ecology. A floristic analysis of a given region is, like pollen analysis, concerned with the total composition of the plant cover in that region, rather than with the way the species are distributed or segregated within that region (Cushing, 1963). However, the floristic information derived from a pollen spectrum is not confined to a clearly defined region. The area of integration of the pollen rain is bounded not by the limits set by the investigator but by the tenuous limits of probability that influence the processes of pollen dispersal. Despite the many limitations of the fossil pollen record, a comparison of the affinities of the fossil pollen rain to present-day plant distributions is valuable in throwing light on the phytogeographical affinities of the past flora.

In this chapter the stratigraphic sequences from the five sites studied on Skye are regarded as being of comparable age, and they are equated with the Late-Devensian Substage and Subage and the early part of the Flandrian Stage and Age. The bases of these correlations are discussed in Chapter 13.

2. THE FOSSIL FLORA

1. THE POLLEN FLORA

In compiling the Late-Devensian flora of the Isle of Skye, all the fossil plant remains, either pollen, spores, or macrofossils found in the *Betula–Corylus*, *Betula*, Gramineae–*Rumex*, and *Lycopodium*–Cyperaceae assemblage zones at the five sites examined are considered together and listed in Table 12.1. The Table indicates whether each taxon has been identified from pollen, from macrofossils, or from both. Records of taxa that are represented by a single pollen grain or spore at the site in question are shown in parentheses. Taxa identified from macrofossils at Loch Fada by Vasari & Vasari (1968) are also included. The majority of the taxa are identified to varying taxonomic ranks on the basis of pollen or spore occurrences, giving a total of 144 taxa, of which 130 are determined to genus, species group, or species. A further twenty taxa are identified from macrofossils, fifteen of which are not known as pollen or spores in the fossil flora. The total vascular flora represented in the Late-Devensian sediments on Skye is thus 159 taxa. As the majority of the records comprising the fossil flora are based on pollen or spore determinations, the flora is here termed '*the pollen flora*'. Records that are based on macrofossil remains are indicated in the discussion by an asterisk (*). The distribution of the fossils in terms of the five sites examined is shown in Table 12.1. The distribution of the fossils in terms of the local and regional pollen zones at each site is indicated, in the case of microfossils, on the pollen diagram (Plates 1–5), and, in the case of macrofossils, in Tables 9.1 to 9.5 in Chapter 9. The nomenclature and the order in which the families, genera, and species are placed in Table 12.1 follow Clapham *et al.* (1962).

2. PHYTOGEOGRAPHY OF THE POLLEN FLORA

The Late-Devensian pollen flora is subdivided into a number of floristic elements defined on the basis of the present geographical distribution of the taxa involved (see Chapter 6) in order to compare the phytogeographical affinities of the Late-Devensian pollen flora with the affinities of the present-day flora of Skye. Of the floristic elements delimited and discussed in Chapter 6, the following elements are represented within the Late-Devensian pollen flora.

(i) *Atlantic Element.* Four pollen types occur in the Late-Devensian pollen flora that are derived from taxa with a Widespread Atlantic distribution today. They are:

Armeria maritima, *Plantago maritima*, *Silene maritima* type, *Thymus* type.

No pollen types of taxa of the Southern Atlantic, Mediterranean Atlantic, or Northern Atlantic groups are represented in the pollen flora.

(ii) *Sub-Atlantic Element.* There are eighteen pollen and spore types in the Late-Devensian pollen flora that represent taxa with Sub-Atlantic distributions today. Four of these types are referable to taxa in the Northern Sub-Atlantic group. They are:

*Isoetes lacustris**, *Littorella uniflora*, *Najas flexilis**, *Saxifraga hypnoides*.

The remainder are derived from taxa with a Widespread Sub-Atlantic distribution today, with the following types:

Blechnum spicant, *Conopodium* type, *Corylus avellana*, *Drosera* cf. *D. intermedia*, *Heracleum sphondylium*, *Hypericum pulchrum* type, *Isoetes echinospora*, *Mercurialis perennis*, *Montia fontana**, *Myriophyllum alterniflorum**, *Nymphaea alba*, *Osmunda regalis*, *Polygala*, *Sanicula europaea*.

There are no pollen or spore types of taxa of the Southern Sub-Atlantic group in the pollen flora.

(iii) *Continental Element.* This floristic element is well represented in the Late-Devensian pollen flora with twenty three pollen and spore types derived from taxa with markedly Continental ranges today. The majority of them belong to the Northern Continental group, but there are five representatives of the Southern Continental group and one member of the Widespread Continental group.

The following pollen and spore types are assigned to the Southern Continental group:

Ephedra distachya type, *E. fragilis* type, *Helianthemum chamaecistus* type, *Ophioglossum vulgatum*, *Sagittaria sagittifolia*.

The following types are referred to the Northern Continental group:

Antennaria type, *Betula pubescens**, *Betula* undiff., *Botrychium lunaria*, *Filipendula*, *Lycopodium clavatum*, *Melampyrum*, *Menyanthes trifoliata*, *Populus tremula*, *Prunus* cf. *P. padus*, *Rubus saxatilis*, *Rumex acetosa*, *Sorbus aucuparia*, *Sparganium* cf. *S. minimum*, *Thelypteris dryopteris*, *T. phegopteris*, *Vaccinium myrtillus**.

TABLE 12.1. *The Late-Devensian flora of the Isle of Skye*

	Type of fossil remains	Loch Meodal	Loch Fada	Loch Mealt	Loch Cill Chriosd	Lochan Coir' a' Ghobhainn
Lycopodiaceae						
Lycopodium selago	s	+	+	+	+	+
Lycopodium annotinum	s	.	(+)	(+)	(+)	(+)
Lycopodium clavatum	s	.	(+)	(+)	.	.
Lycopodium alpinum	s	+	+	.	+	+
Lycopodium undiff.	s	.	.	.	.	+
Selaginellaceae						
Selaginella selaginoides	s, ms	+	+	+	+	+*
Isoetaceae						
Isoetes lacustris	s, ms	+	.	+	(+)	+*
Isoetes echinospora	s	+	.	.	.	.
Equisetaceae						
Equisetum	s, sh	+	+*	+*	+*	+
Osmundaceae						
Osmunda regalis	s	+	.	.	+	+
Polypodiaceae						
Pteridium aquilinum	s	+	.	.	+	.
Cryptogramma crispa	s	(+)	.	.	+	+
Blechnum spicant	s	+	.	.	(+)	+
Asplenium type	s	.	.	.	+	.
Athyrium filix-femina	s	.	.	.	+	.
Athyrium alpestre type	s	.	.	.	+	+
Cystopteris fragilis	s	.	+	.	+	.
Dryopteris filix-mas type	s	+	.	.	+	+
Dryopteris carthusiana type	s	+	.	.	.	.
Polystichum type	s	.	.	.	+	.
Thelypteris phegopteris	s	+	.	.	+	.
Thelypteris dryopteris	s	+	+	.	+	+
Polypodium	s	+	+	+	+	+
Polypodiaceae undiff.	s	+	+	+	+	+
Ophioglossaceae						
Botrychium lunaria	s	+	+	+	+	+
Ophioglossum vulgatum	s	.	+	+	.	.
Pinaceae						
Pinus	p	+	+	+	+	+
Cupressaceae						
Juniperus communis	p	+	+	+	+	+
Ephedraceae						
Ephedra fragilis type	p	(+)	+	.	+	+
Ephedra distachya type	p	.	.	.	(+)	.
Ranunculaceae						
Caltha type	p	(+)	+	.	+	+
Trollius europaeus	p	.	.	.	(+)	.
Anemone type	p	.	.	.	(+)	.
Ranunculus acris type	p	+	+	+	+	+
Ranunculus trichophyllus type	p	+	+	+	+	+
Ranunculus subgenus *Batrachium*	ach	.	.	.	.	+
Thalictrum	p	+	+	+	+	+
Nymphaeaceae						
Nymphaea alba	p	+	+	.	+	.
Nuphar	p	+	+	(+)	+	.
Ceratophyllaceae						
cf. *Ceratophyllum*	sp	.	+	.	.	.
Cruciferae	p	+	+	+	+	+
Polygalaceae						
Polygala	p	.	.	(+)	.	.
Hypericaceae						
Hypericum pulchrum type	p	.	.	.	+	.
Cistaceae						
Helianthemum chamaecistus type	p	.	.	.	+	.
Caryophyllaceae						
Silene dioica type	p	.	+	.	+	+
Silene maritima type	p	.	.	.	.	+

TABLE 12.1 *continued*

	Type of fossil remains	Loch Meodal	Loch Fada	Loch Mealt	Loch Cill Chriosd	Lochan Coir' a' Ghobhainn
Caryophyllaceae *continued*						
Silene cf. *S. acaulis*	p	.	+	.	+	+
Lychnis flos-cuculi	p	.	.	.	(+)	.
Cerastium alpinum type	p	(+)	+	.	+	+
Cerastium cf. *C. holosteoides*	p	.	+	.	.	.
Stellaria holostea	p	.	+	.	+	+
Stellaria undiff.	p	.	(+)	.	+	+
Sagina	p	.	+	(+)	+	+
Arenaria type	p	.	+	.	+	+
Spergula arvensis	p	.	.	+	.	.
Caryophyllaceae undiff.	p	+	+	+	+	+
Portulaceae						
Montia fontana ssp. *fontana*	sd	.	+	.	.	.
Chenopodiaceae	p	+	+	+	+	+
Papilionaceae						
Trifolium cf. *T. repens*	p	.	.	.	(+)	.
Trifolium undiff.	p	.	(+)	.	.	.
Lotus cf. *L. corniculatus*	p	.	+	.	.	+
cf. *Oxytropis*	p	.	.	.	(+)	.
Vicia/Lathyrus	p	.	+	+	(+)	+
Papilionaceae undiff.	p	+	(+)	.	+	+
Rosaceae						
Filipendula	p	+	+	+	+	+
Rubus saxatilis	p	.	+	.	+	+
Potentilla type	p	+	+	+	+	+
Geum	p	.	.	.	+	.
Dryas octopetala	p	.	(+)	.	+	.
Alchemilla	p	.	+	.	+	+
Prunus cf. *P. padus*	p	.	.	.	(+)	+
Sorbus aucuparia	p	+	+	.	+	.
Sorbus cf. *S. rupicola*	p	.	.	.	+	.
Rosaceae undiff.	p	+	+	+	+	+
Crassulaceae						
Sedum cf. *S. rosea*	p	.	+	+	(+)	.
cf. *Sedum*	p	.	.	.	.	+
Saxifragaceae						
Saxifraga nivalis	p	.	+	+	.	.
Saxifraga stellaris	p	.	+	+	+	+
Saxifraga hypnoides	p	.	+	+	+	+
Saxifraga aizoides	p	(+)	+	.	+	.
Saxifraga oppositifolia	p	.	+	+	+	.
Droseraceae						
Drosera cf. *D. intermedia*	p	.	.	.	(+)	.
Elaeagnaceae						
Hippophaë rhamnoides	p	.	.	.	.	(+)
Onagraceae						
Epilobium type	p	+	+	+	+	+
Haloragaceae						
Myriophyllum spicatum	p	.	.	+	+	.
Myriophyllum alterniflorum	p, fr	+	+*	+	+	+
Myriophyllum undiff.	br	.	+	.	.	.
Callitrichaceae						
Callitriche	p	.	+	.	.	.
Umbelliferae						
Sanicula europaea	p	.	.	.	(+)	.
Conopodium type	p	.	.	.	(+)	.
Angelica type	p	+	+	+	+	+
Heracleum sphondylium	p	.	+	+	.	.
Umbelliferae undiff.	p	.	.	.	(+)	+
Euphorbiaceae						
Mercurialis perennis	p	.	.	.	(+)	.
Polygonaceae						
Koenigia islandica	p	.	.	+	.	.
Polygonum viviparum/P. bistorta	p	.	.	+	+	+

TABLE 12.1 *continued*

	Type of fossil remains	Loch Meodal	Loch Fada	Loch Mealt	Loch Cill Chriosd	Lochan Coir' a' Ghobhainn
Polygonaceae *continued*						
Rumex acetosa	p	+	+	+	+	+
Rumex crispus type	p	.	.	.	(+)	(+)
Oxyria digyna	p	.	+	.	+	+
Urticaceae						
Urtica	p	+	+	+	+	+
Ulmaceae						
Ulmus	p	+	+	.	+	+
Betulaceae						
Betula pubescens	fr	+	+	+	+	.
Betula nana	fr	+	+	.	.	.
Betula cf. *B. nana*	p	+	+	+	+	+
Betula undiff.	p	+	+	+	+	+
Alnus	p	+	(+)	+	+	(+)
Corylaceae						
Corylus avellana	p	+	+	+	+	+
Quercus	p	+	(+)	+	+	+
Salicaceae						
Populus tremula	p	+	+	.	+	+
Salix herbacea	lvs	.	+	+	+	+
Salix cf. *S. herbacea*	p	.	+	.	+	+
Salix undiff.	p	+	+	+	+	+
Ericaceae						
Calluna vulgaris	p	.	.	.	+	+
Vaccinium myrtillus	sd	.	+	.	.	.
Ericaceae undiff.	p	+	+	+	+	+
Empetraceae						
Empetrum cf. *E. nigrum*	p	+	+	+	+	+
Plumbaginaceae						
Armeria maritima	p	.	.	.	+	+
Menyanthaceae						
Menyanthes trifoliata	p	.	(+)	(+)	.	.
Scrophulariaceae						
Veronica	p	.	.	.	.	+
Pedicularis	p	(+)	.	.	.	.
Melampyrum	p	+	.	+	.	.
Labiatae						
Thymus type	p	+	+	+	+	+
Plantaginaceae						
Plantago major/P. media	p	+	+	+	+	+
Plantago lanceolata	p	+	+	.	+	+
Plantago maritima	p	+	+	+	+	+
Littorella uniflora	p	+	+	+	+	+
Campanulaceae						
Campanula type	p	.	(+)	+	(+)	.
Rubiaceae	p	+	+	+	+	+
Caprifoliaceae						
Viburnum opulus	p	(+)	.	.	.	.
Valerianaceae						
Valeriana officinalis	p	+	+	+	(+)	.
Dipsacaceae						
Succisa pratensis	p	+	+	(+)	+	+
Compositae						
Ambrosia type	p	.	.	(+)	.	.
Antennaria type	p	.	(+)	.	+	+
Solidago type	p	+	+	+	+	+
Achillea type	p	.	.	.	(+)	(+)
Artemisia cf. *A. norvegica*	p	+	+	+	+	+
Artemisia undiff.	p	+	+	+	+	+
Cirsium/Carduus	p	.	+	+	(+)	+
Saussurea alpina	p	+	+	+	+	+
Liguliflorae	p	+	+	+	+	+
Alismataceae						
Sagittaria sagittifolia	p	.	.	.	+	.

TABLE 12.1 *continued*

	Type of fossil remains	Loch Meodal	Loch Fada	Loch Mealt	Loch Cill Chriosd	Lochan Coir' a' Ghobhainn
Potamogetonaceae						
Potamogeton type	p	+	+	+	+	+
Potamogeton subgenus *Coleogeton*	p	+	+	+	+	+
Potamogeton undiff.	fst	.	+	.	.	.
Najadaceae						
Najas flexilis	sd	.	.	.	+	.
Liliaceae	p	.	.	(+)	.	.
Juncaceae						
Juncus effusus/J. conglomeratus	sd	.	+	.	.	.
Juncus articulatus/J. acutiflorus	sd	+	+	.	.	.
Juncus undiff.	sd	+	.	.	.	.
Sparganiaceae						
Sparganium type	p	+	+	+	+	+
Sparganium cf. *S. minimum*	p	+	+	.	+	+
Cyperaceae						
Carex type	p	+	+	+	+	+
Carex rostrata	fr	+	.	.	.	+
Carex echinata	fr	.	+	.	.	.
Carex undiff.	fr	.	.	+	.	+
Schoenoplectus type	p	+	+	+	+	+
Eleocharis type	p	+	+	+	+	+
Cyperaceae	p	+	+	+	+	+
Gramineae	p	+	+	+	+	+

Abbreviations: ach = achene; br = bract; fr = fruit; fst = fruitstone; lvs = leaves; ms = megaspore; p = pollen; s = spore; sd = seed; sh = sheath; sp = spine.
(+) One pollen grain or spore only at the particular site;
+ More than one pollen grain or spore at the particular site;
* Macrofossils present as well as pollen or spores.

The only representative of the Widespread Continental group in the pollen flora is *Ranunculus trichophyllus* type.

(iv) *Northern–Montane Element.* Five pollen and spore types in the Late-Devensian pollen flora are derived from taxa with a Northern-Montane distribution today. They are:

Empetrum cf. *E. nigrum*, *Lycopodium annotinum*, *L. selago*, *Potamogeton* (*Coleogeton*), *Trollius europaeus.*

(v) *Arctic–Subarctic Element.* This element is represented by the following four pollen types in the Late-Devensian pollen flora:

Artemisia cf. *A. norvegica*, *Cerastium alpinum* type, *Koenigia islandica*, *Sorbus* cf. *S. rupicola.*

(vi) *Arctic–Alpine Element.* The Arctic-Alpine Element is well represented in the Late-Devensian pollen flora with the following twenty pollen and spore types:

Athyrium alpestre type, *Betula nana**, *Betula* cf. *B. nana*, *Cryptogramma crispa*, *Dryas octopetala*, *Juniperus communis*, *Lycopodium alpinum*, *Oxyria digyna*, *Polygonum viviparum/P. bistorta*, *Salix herbacea**, *Salix* cf. *S. herbacea*, *Saussurea alpina*, *Saxifraga aizoides*, *S. nivalis*, *S. oppositifolia*, *S. stellaris*, *Sedum* cf. *S. rosea*, *Selaginella selaginoides**, *Silene* cf. *S. acaulis*, *Thalictrum.*

(vii) *Arctic–Alpine/Alpine Element.* A single pollen grain at Loch Cill Chriosd was tentatively referred to the genus *Oxytropis*. It may be derived from either *O. halleri* (an Alpine species today with stations in the Alps, Pyrenees, and Carpathians, and a single locality in eastern Albania) or from *O. campestris* (an Arctic–Alpine species today). The fossil grain is assigned to this transitional floristic element.

(viii) *Widespread Species.* This is the largest floristic element represented with the Late-Devensian pollen flora with forty-two pollen and spore types derived from taxa with widespread ranges at the present day. The following types are included in this element:

Achillea type, *Alnus*, *Anemone* type, *Angelica* type, *Athyrium filix-femina*, *Calluna vulgaris*, *Caltha* type, *Campanula* type, *Carex echinata**, *C. rostrata**, *Cerastium* cf. *C. holosteoides*, cf. *Ceratophyllum**, *Cystopteris fragilis*, *Dryopteris carthusiana* type, *D. filix-mas* type, *Eleocharis* type, *Equisetum**, *Geum*, *Juncus articulatus/J. acutiflorus**,

*Juncus effusus/J. conglomeratus**, *Lotus* cf. *L. corniculatus*, *Lychnis flos-cuculi*, *Myriophyllum spicatum*, *Nuphar*, *Plantago lanceolata*, *Plantago major/P. media*, *Polypodium*, *Pteridium aquilinum*, *Ranunculus acris* type, *Rumex crispus* type, *Schoenoplectus* type, *Silene dioica* type, *Spergula arvensis*, *Stellaria holostea*, *Stellaria* undiff., *Succisa pratensis*, *Trifolium* cf. *T. repens*, *Ulmus*, *Urtica*, *Valeriana officinalis*, *Veronica*, *Viburnum opulus*.

(ix) *North American Element. Ambrosia* type is the only pollen type in the pollen flora that is assigned to this floristic element.

(x) *Unclassified*. This is the second largest group within the Late-Devensian pollen flora, and it is composed of forty pollen and spore types whose determinations are not sufficiently precise to allow their assignment to any of the floristic elements. The pollen and spore types included are the following:

Alchemilla, *Arenaria* type, *Artemisia* undiff., *Asplenium* type, *Callitriche*, *Carex* undiff.*, *Carex* type, Caryophyllaceae undiff., Chenopodiaceae, *Cirsium/Carduus*, Cruciferae, Cyperaceae undiff., *Epilobium* type, Ericaceae undiff., Gramineae, *Juncus* undiff.*, Liguliflorae, Liliaceae, *Lycopodium* undiff., *Myriophyllum* undiff.*, Papilionaceae undiff., *Pedicularis*, *Pinus*, Polypodiaceae undiff., *Polystichum* type, *Potamogeton* type, *Potamogeton* undiff., *Potentilla* type, *Quercus*, *Ranunculus* (*Batrachium*)*, Rosaceae undiff., Rubiaceae, *Sagina*, *Salix* undiff., cf. *Sedum*, *Solidago* type, *Sparganium* type, *Trifolium* undiff., Umbelliferae undiff., *Vicia/Lathyrus*.

(xi) *Introduced Species*. The single pollen grain of *Hippophaë rhamnoides* at Lochan Coir' a' Ghobhainn is derived from a species whose occurrence on Skye today on modern phytogeographical criteria is considered unlikely to be native. The taxon is classified as an Introduced Species in Chapter 6, and the pollen grain is classed accordingly.

The percentage representation of each floristic element within the total Late-Devensian pollen flora is shown in Table 12.2. The representation of the same floristic elements within the present native flora of Skye is also given in Table 12.2. Nearly all the floristic elements of the present flora of Skye are represented in the fossil pollen flora in roughly comparable proportions, although the Atlantic and Sub-Atlantic Elements are rather poorly represented, and the Arctic–Alpine Element is more prominent in the Late-Devensian pollen flora than in the present flora of the island. The principal difference between the fossil pollen flora and the modern flora is the large unclassified category (25%) in the pollen flora in comparison with the low unclassified element (0.3%) in the present flora. This is due largely to the taxonomic limitations in the identifications of the fossil pollen grains and spores. To obtain a more meaningful comparison between the past and present floras, it is necessary to compare the fossil pollen flora not with the modern flora in terms of species but in terms of pollen and spore types. For this comparison all the members of the present native flora of Skye have been grouped on the basis of the author's present pollen morphological knowledge into as many identifiable pollen and spore types as possible. As a result of this grouping, the 589 species in the present flora are represented by 204 identifiable pollen and spore types. This modern pollen flora has been classified into floristic elements in the same way as the fossil pollen flora, and the comparison of the percentage

TABLE 12.2. *Comparison of the percentage of floristic elements in the Late-Devensian flora and the present vascular plant flora of Skye*

Floristic Element	Late Devensian Flora: Total	Late Devensian Flora: Percentage	Modern Flora: Total	Modern Flora: Percentage
1. Atlantic				
(*a*) Southern Atlantic	0	0	11	1.8
(*b*) Northern Atlantic	0	0	6	1.0
(*c*) Widespread Atlantic	4	2.5	35	5.9
(*d*) Mediterranean Atlantic	0	0	1	0.2
Total	4	2.5	53	8.9
2. Sub-Atlantic				
(*a*) Southern Sub-Atlantic	0	0	8	1.4
(*b*) Northern Sub-Atlantic	4	2.5	6	1.0
(*c*) Widespread Sub-Atlantic	14	8.8	102	17.3
Total	18	11.3	116	19.7
3. Continental				
(*a*) Southern Continental	5	3.1	18	3.1
(*b*) Northern Continental	17	10.7	73	12.4
(*c*) Widespread Continental	1	0.6	29	4.9
Total	23	14.4	120	20.4
4. Northern–Montane	5	3.1	14	2.4
5. Arctic–Subarctic	4	2.5	14	2.4
6. Arctic–Alpine	20	12.6	39	6.6
7. Arctic–Alpine/Alpine	1	0.6	0	0
8. Alpine	0	0	1	0.2
9. Widespread Species	42	26.0	229	38.7
10. North American	1	0.6	1	0.2
11. Endemic	0	0	1	0.2
12. Unclassified	40	25.0	2	0.3
13. Introduced	1	0.6	.	.
	159		589	

TABLE 12.3. *Comparison of the percentage representation of floristic elements in the Late-pollen flora (excluding macrofossils) and the modern pollen flora of Skye*

Floristic Element	Late-Devensian Flora Total	Late-Devensian Flora Percentage	Modern Flora Total	Modern Flora Percentage
1. Atlantic				
(*a*) Southern Atlantic	0	0	3	1.5
(*b*) Northern Atlantic	0	0	1	0.5
(*c*) Widespread Atlantic	4	2.8	12	5.8
(*d*) Mediterranean Atlantic	0	0	0	0
Total	4	2.8	16	7.8
2. Sub-Atlantic				
(*a*) Southern Sub-Atlantic	0	0	0	0
(*b*) Northern Sub-Atlantic	3	2.1	3	1.5
(*c*) Widespread Sub-Atlantic	13	9.0	29	14.1
Total	16	11.1	32	15.5
3. Continental				
(*a*) Southern Continental	5	3.4	5	2.4
(*b*) Northern Continental	15	10.4	22	10.7
(*c*) Widespread Continental	1	0.7	4	1.9
Total	23	14.5	31	15.1
4. Northern–Montane	5	3.4	4	1.9
5. Arctic–Subarctic	4	2.8	4	1.9
6. Arctic–Alpine	18	12.4	18	8.8
7. Arctic–Alpine/Alpine	1	0.7	0	0
8. Alpine	0	0	0	0
9. Widespread Species	37	25.7	56	27.2
10. North American	1	0.7	1	0.5
11. Endemic	0	0	0	0
12. Unclassified	37	25.7	43	21.0
13. Introduced	1	0.7	.	.
	144		205	

representation of the floristic elements in the two pollen floras is shown in Table 12.3. The fifteen records in the Late-Devensian flora based on macrofossils are excluded from the fossil pollen flora in Table 12.3.

When the modern and fossil floras are compared on a similar basis, several interesting features are discernible. The Atlantic Element and, to some degree, the Sub-Atlantic Element are less prominent in the Late-Devensian pollen flora than they are in modern pollen flora, whereas the Continental and Widespread Elements are equally represented in both pollen floras. The Arctic–Alpine Element and, to some degree, the Northern–Montane and Arctic–Subarctic Elements are numerically more important components of the fossil pollen flora than of the modern pollen flora with a total representation of 18.6% of Arctic–Alpine, Arctic–Subarctic, and

TABLE 12.4. *Contribution of floristic elements to the Late-Devensian pollen flora and pollen rain of Skye*

Floristic Element	Percentage of total pollen flora	Percentage of total pollen rain
1. Atlantic		
(*a*) Southern Atlantic	0	0
(*b*) Northern Atlantic	0	0
(*c*) Widespread Atlantic	2.8	0.39
(*d*) Mediterranean Atlantic	0	0
Total	2.8	0.39
2. Sub-Atlantic		
(*a*) Southern Sub-Atlantic	0	0
(*b*) Northern Sub-Atlantic	2.1	1.11
(*c*) Widespread Sub-Atlantic	9.0	7.17
Total	11.1	8.27
3. Continental		
(*a*) Southern Continental	3.4	0.04
(*b*) Northern Continental	10.4	9.90
(*c*) Widespread Continental	0.7	0.22
Total	14.5	10.17
4. Northern–Montane	3.4	5.17
5. Arctic–Subarctic	2.8	0.22
6. Arctic–Alpine	12.4	14.46
7. Arctic–Alpine/Alpine	0.7	0.002
8. Alpine	0	0
9. Widespread Species	25.7	3.45
10. North American	0.7	0.002
11. Endemic	0	0
12. Unclassified	25.7	57.87
13. Introduced	0.7	0.002

Northern Montane Elements in the Late-Devensian pollen flora compared with 12.6% in the present pollen flora.

The most interesting feature of the Late-Devensian pollen flora is the diversity of its present phytogeographical affinities. This observation is reinforced by an appraisal of the relative contributions of the different floristic elements to the total Late-Devensian pollen rain. In Table 12.4 the sum of the number of pollen grains and spores of the various types assigned to each floristic element is expressed as a percentage of the total number of pollen grains and spores counted in all the samples at all the sites examined.

If the Late-Devensian pollen flora and pollen rain are regarded as representative, in some degree, of the composition of the actual Late-Devensian flora of Skye, it is strongly suggestive that the past flora was as diverse in its phytogeographical affinities as the present flora of Skye. This inference is of considerable interest, for it is difficult to reconcile this view with the notion that the varied geographical affinities of a modern flora of an area are the result of a long history of successive migrations of plant populations with different origins. If the latter view is correct, the initial flora of a newly deglaciated landscape would not be expected to be as complex and as diverse, in terms of its present geographical affinities, as the modern flora on which those affinities are based. Several hypotheses can be advanced to explain the diverse composition of the pollen flora, and these are presented and discussed in section 3 of this chapter (p. 314).

3. FLORISTIC COMPARISONS WITHIN SKYE

When a comparison is made between the fossil pollen and the modern pollen flora of Skye, it is notable that 90% of the fossil pollen and spore types are represented by taxa in the present flora of the island. With such a high proportion of the Late-Devensian pollen flora represented in the present flora, it is possible to subdivide the fossil pollen flora on the basis of the past and present distributions of the taxa concerned *within* the island in order to discover if there is any evidence for distributional changes in the Skye flora since Late-Devensian times. Four groups can be recognised:

(i) *Widespread Species.* This is the largest group (61% of the total pollen flora) and it is composed of ninety-six pollen and spore types derived from taxa with widespread distributions today on the Isle of Skye. The group includes a few species of wide distribution on Skye, for example *Pteridium aquilinum*, *Rumex acetosa*, and *Sorbus aucuparia*, but most of its members are pollen or spore types that were not or could not be subdivided to generic or specific rank, for example Cruciferae, Gramineae, and *Salix* undiff.

The following fossil types are included:

Achillea type, *Alnus*, *Anemone* type, *Angelica* type, *Armeria maritima*, *Artemisia* undiff., *Athyrium filix-femina*, *Betula pubescens**, *Betula* undiff., *Blechnum spicant*, *Calluna vulgaris*, *Caltha* type, *Carex echinata**, *C. rostrata**, *Carex* type, *Carex* undiff.*, Caryophyllaceae undiff., *Cerastium* cf. *C. holosteoides*, Chenopodiaceae, *Cirsium/Carduus*, *Conopodium* type, *Corylus avellana*, Cruciferae, Cyperaceae, *Dryopteris carthusiana* type, *D. filix-mas* type, *Eleocharis* type, *Empetrum* cf. *E. nigrum*, *Epilobium* type, *Equisetum**, Ericaceae undiff., *Filipendula*, *Geum*, Gramineae, *Heracleum sphondylium*, *Hypericum pulchrum* type, *Juncus articulatus/J. acutiflorus**, *Juncus effusus/J. conglomeratus**, *Juncus* undiff.*, Liguliflorae, Liliaceae, *Littorella uniflora*, *Lotus* cf. *L. corniculatus*, *Lychnis flos-cuculi*, *Lycopodium selago*, *Lycopodium* undiff., *Melampyrum*, *Menyanthes trifoliata*, *Montia fontana**, *Myriophyllum alterniflorum*, *Myriophyllum* undiff.*, Papilionaceae undiff., *Pedicularis*, *Plantago lanceolata*, *Plantago major/P. media*, *P. maritima*, *Polygala*, Polypodiaceae undiff., *Polypodium*, *Potamogeton* type, *Potamogeton* undiff.*, *Potentilla* type, *Pteridium aquilinum*, *Quercus*, *Ranunculus acris* type, *R. trichophyllus* type, Rosaceae undiff., Rubiaceae, *Rumex acetosa*, *R. crispus* type, *Sagina*, *Salix* undiff., *Sanicula europaea*, *Schoenoplectus* type, cf. *Sedum*, *Selaginella selaginoides*, *Silene dioica* type, *S. maritima* type, *Solidago* type, *Sorbus aucuparia*, *Spergula arvensis*, *Stellaria holostea*, *Stellaria* undiff., *Succisa pratensis*, *Thelypteris dryopteris*, *T. phegopteris*, *Thymus* type, *Trifolium* cf. *T. repens*, *Trifolium* undiff., *Ulmus*, Umbelliferae undiff., *Urtica*, *Vaccinium myrtillus**, *Valeriana officinalis*, *Veronica*, *Vicia/Lathyrus*.

The group consists largely of pollen and spore types of taxa of broad present phytogeographical and/or ecological affinities, but there are some species of narrower geographical range, for example *Armeria maritima* and *Plantago maritima* (Widespread Atlantic), *Blechnum spicant* and *Montia fontana** (Widespread Sub-Atlantic), *Littorella uniflora* (Northern Sub-Atlantic), *Menyanthes trifoliata* and *Thelypteris dryopteris* (Northern Continental), and *Empetrum* cf. *E. nigrum* and *Lycopodium selago* (Northern–Montane).

(ii) *Local species.* This group consists of twenty-four pollen and spore types (15% of the total pollen flora) derived from taxa with local and rather restricted distributions on Skye today, and which occur in a few regions of the island only, or in extreme cases, such as *Koenigia islandica*, in a single region. None of the fossil records are, however, from sites outside the present distribution on Skye (cf. group iii).

The following fossil types are included:

Alchemilla, *Antennaria* type, *Arenaria* type, *Asplenium* type, *Callitriche*, *Cystopteris fragilis*, *Drosera* cf. *D. intermedia*, *Dryas octopetala*, *Juniperus communis*, *Koenigia islandica*, *Oxyria digyna*, *Polygonum viviparum/P. bistorta*, *Polystichum* type, *Populus tremula*, *Prunus* cf. *P. padus*, *Rubus saxatilis*, *Salix herbacea**, *Salix* cf. *S. herbacea*, *Saxifraga hypnoides*, *S. nivalis*, *S. stellaris*, *Silene* cf. *acaulis*, *Sorbus* cf. *S. rupicola*, *Trollius europaeus*.

The group consists largely of taxa of Northern–Montane, Arctic–Alpine, and Arctic–Subarctic affinities. The majority of the taxa are montane plants on Skye today, and several of them appear to have rather specialised edaphic requirements, for example *Dryas octopetala* and *Saxifraga nivalis* (see Chapter 5).

(iii) *Disjunct species.* This group contains twenty-three pollen and spore types (14% of the total pollen flora) derived from taxa that have local and restricted distributions on Skye today, but in contrast to the previous group, there are fossil occurrences from sites in regions where the taxa in question are not known to occur at the present day.

The following fossil types are included:

Botrychium lunaria, *Campanula* type, *Cerastium alpinum* type, *Cryptogramma crispa*, *Isoetes echinospora*, *I. lacustris**, *Lycopodium alpinum*, *L. clavatum*, *Mercurialis perennis*, *Myriophyllum spicatum*, *Nuphar*, *Nymphaea alba*, *Ophioglossum vulgatum*, *Osmunda regalis*, *Ranunculus* (*Batrachium*)*, *Saussurea alpina*, *Saxifraga aizoides*, *S. oppositifolia*, *Sedum* cf. *S. rosea*, *Sparganium* type, *Sparganium* cf. *S. minimum*, *Thalictrum*, *Viburnum opulus*.

This group of taxa is notable in the diversity of both its present geographical affinities and its modern ecological tolerances. Species of the Sub-Atlantic Element include the aquatics *Isoetes lacustris** (Northern Sub-Atlantic), *I. echinospora* (Widespread Sub-Atlantic) and *Nymphaea alba* (Widespread Sub-Atlantic), the woodland herb *Mercurialis perennis* (Widespread Sub-Atlantic), and the ferm *Osmunda regalis* (Widespread Sub-Atlantic), whereas the dwarf pteridophytes *Botrychium lunaria*, *Lycopodium clavatum*, and *Ophioglossum vulgatum* belong to the Continental Element. The Arctic–Alpine Element is well represented in this group with the montane plants *Cryptogramma crispa*, *Saussurea alpina*, *Saxifraga aizoides*, *S. oppositifolia*, and *Sedum* cf. *S. rosea*. *Myriophyllum spicatum* and *Viburnum opulus* are both species with a Widespread geographical range but which are rare and disjunct on Skye today.

(iv) *Species not known on Skye today*. This is the smallest group (10% of the total pollen flora) and comprises sixteen pollen and spore types derived from taxa that are presently not known to occur on the Isle of Skye. It is represented by:

Ambrosia type, *Artemisia* cf. *A. norvegica*, *Athyrium alpestre* type, *Betula nana**, *Betula* cf. *B. nana*, cf. *Ceratophyllum**, *Ephedra distachya* type, *E. fragilis* type, *Helianthemum chamaecistus* type, *Hippophaë rhamnoides*, *Lycopodium annotinum*, *Najas flexilis**, cf. *Oxytropis*, *Pinus*, *Potamogeton* (*Coleogeton*), *Sagittaria sagittifolia*.

This group is diverse in its present-day phytogeography and its ecology, with aquatic taxa such as cf. *Ceratophyllum* (Widespread with southern affinities) *Najas flexilis* (Northern Sub-Atlantic), *Potamogeton* (*Coleogeton*) (Northern–Montane), and *Sagittaria sagittifolia* (Southern Continental). There are montane taxa such as *Athyrium alpestre* type, *Betula nana*, and cf. *Oxytropis* with Arctic–Alpine affinities, and *Artemisia* cf. *A. norvegica* with an Arctic–Subarctic distribution today. *Helianthemum chamaecistus* type is a lowland grassland taxon of Southern Continental affinities, whereas *Ambrosia* type, *Ephedra distachya* type, and *E. fragilis* type are not native members of the present British flora. They have North American, Southern Continental, and Southern Continental ranges respectively today. Although *Hippophaë rhamnoides* occurs on Skye today, it is not considered native on the island (see Chapter 6), and it is classified accordingly in this group.

From a palaeofloristic viewpoint the occurrence in the Late-Devensian pollen flora of 66% of all the modern pollen and spore types that are currently represented in the Skye flora is of interest. It is not surprising that absentees from the Late-Devensian pollen flora include species that, although widespread on the island today, are virtually restricted to woodland communities, such as *Fraxinus excelsior*, *Hedera helix*, *Ilex aquifolium*, and *Lonicera periclymenum*. There is, however, a group of more unexpected absentees from the Late-Devensian pollen flora in view of their present ecology and/or wide distribution within Skye. This group includes *Anthyllis vulneraria*, *Arctostaphylos uva-ursi*, *Digitalis purpurea*, *Empetrum hermaphroditum*, *Euphrasia* spp., *Lobelia dortmanna*, *Parnassia palustris*, *Pinguicula vulgaris*, *Tofieldia pusilla*, *Utricularia*, ssp., and *Viola* spp. In studies of modern pollen rain, many of these taxa have been shown to be poorly represented in pollen spectra, or not represented at all, despite their presence in the nearby vegetation (see Chapter 11). Their absence in the Late-Devensian pollen flora may not, therefore, be indicative of their absence from the flora of Skye in Late-Devensian times.

4. FLORISTIC COMPARISONS WITH OTHER AREAS

There are very few detailed Late-Devensian pollen floras available for comparison from other areas within Great Britain, although there are well-documented macrofossil floras of Late-Devensian age from Ireland (Jessen, 1949; Mitchell, 1954), from the Isle of Man (Dickson, Dickson & Mitchell, 1970), and from other parts of England (Godwin, 1956). The Late-Devensian pollen flora from Skye is therefore compared with the comprehensive Late-Weichselian (Late-Devensian) pollen floras from Denmark (Iversen, 1954) and from southern Sweden (Berglund 1966*a*). It should be emphasised that the chances of deposition, preservation, and identification of the fossil types will vary considerably from site to site and from area to area, and the pollen floras are too heterogeneous for any detailed comparisons. Various features of interest emerge, however, from a general comparison between the Skye and Scandinavian pollen floras. Of the 144 fossil pollen and spore types represented in the Skye list, eighty-four of them (58%) occur in the Danish lists and 64% of them occur in the Swedish lists. A comparable percentage is obtained in a comparison between the Skye lists and Anderson's (1961) lists for Early Weichselian deposits in Denmark. There are two principal groups of pollen and spore types that occur in the Skye lists but that are absent from the Scandinavian fossil pollen floras. Taxa of Arctic–Subarctic and Arctic–Alpine affinities are more prominent in the Skye list, with *Artemisia* cf. *A. norvegica*, *Athyrium alpestre* type, *Cryptogramma crispa*, and *Saxifraga nivalis* not recorded from the Scandinavian sites. *Blechnum spicant*, *Conopodium* type, *Drosera* cf. *D. intermedia*, *Hypericum pulchrum* type, *Mercurialis perennis*, *Osmunda regalis*, and *Saxifraga hypnoides* form part of the sizeable Sub-Atlantic Element within the Skye fossil pollen flora, but none of these types are recorded in the Late-Weichselian pollen floras in Scandinavia. More surprising absentees in the Scandinavian floras include *Sagittaria sagittifolia*, *Stellaria holostea*, *Succisa pratensis*, and *Viburnum opulus*, all of which occur in the Skye pollen flora and in several other Late-Devensian floras from sites elsewhere in Britain. It is perhaps significant that, in the case of *Sagittaria sagittifolia*, *Stellaria holostea*, and *Succisa pratensis*, these species have rather western and/or southern distributions in Scandinavia today (Faegri, 1960; Hultén, 1950).

There are several absentees in the Late-Devensian pollen flora of Skye of pollen types that are frequently recorded in sediments of correlative age in southern Britain and Scandinavia. *Alisma plantago-aquatica*, *Centaurea scabiosa*, *Jasione* type, *Myriophyllum verticillatum*, *Pastinaca sativa*, *Polemonium caeruleum*, *Polygonum amphibium*, *Poterium sanguisorba*, *Rumex acetosella*, s.l., *Sanguisorba officinalis*, and *Valeriana dioica* are frequent pollen types in Late-Devensian sediments elsewhere in Britain. Pollen of *Artemisia* undiff., *Campanula* type, and *Helianthemum chamaecistus* type are rather rare in the Skye sediments in contrast to their relatively high frequencies in Late-Devensian sediments in southern Britain. Some of the absentees from the Skye pollen flora are not unexpected in view of the present distributions in Scotland of many of the taxa concerned. The virtual absence of *Polemonium caeruleum* pollen from Late-Devensian sediments in Scotland (the only grain so far known is at Loch of Park, Aberdeenshire in zone Ib; Vasari & Vasari, 1968) is of particular interest in view of the species' present distribution that is centred on the Carboniferous limestones of the Pennines and with a single station in the Cheviots (Pigott, 1958).

5. THE MOSS FLORA

Macroscopic fossil remains of thirty-eight moss taxa have been recovered and identified from the Late-Devensian sediments on Skye (see Table 12.5). In addition *Sphagnum* spores were found at every site examined. This is a very low fraction (10.3%) of the total modern moss flora of the island (370 taxa). Despite the rich hepatic flora occurring on Skye today (181 taxa), no fossil remains of liverworts have been found in the Skye sediments. The thirty-eight mosses all occur on Skye at present, and the vast majority are widespread species occurring in a range of habitats throughout the island, for example *Acrocladium cuspidatum*, *Dichodontium pellucidum*, *Drepanocladus revolvens*, *Hylocomium splendens*, and *Rhacomitrium* spp.

Andreaea rupestris is a rather local montane species on Skye today, occurring on cliff faces and boulders of a variety of rock types (basalt, gabbro, granite, sandstone, and gneiss). It does not appear to have been previously recorded from Late-Devensian sediments. *Barbula icmadophila*, *Distichium capillaceum*, and *Mnium orthorhynchum* are all local montane species on Skye today, being restricted to basic rock outcrops in Trotternish, the Cuillins, or Ben Suardal. *Distichium capillaceum* and *Mnium orthorhynchum* favour shaded crevices in calcareous or, at least, strongly basic rocks on Skye, and they have several stations along the Trotternish basalt ridge and on the Jurassic limestones on Blà Bheinn. *Barbula icmadophila* is a very rare species today both on Skye and in Britain as a whole. It is restricted in Britain to dry and crumbling, mildly basic-rock outcrops and open turf near The Storr and The Quirang on Skye, on Ben Lawers, Perthshire, and in Glencoynedale, Cumberland. The Quirang is its *locus classicus* in Britain, where it was first recorded as a British species by H. N. Dixon in 1893. It favours open, rather unstable habitats, and, although it is unknown in fruit in Britain at present, it is abundant on an artificial basalt cutting formed in 1952 near Loch Leathan, east of The Storr, where it grows with the introduced *Epilobium nerterioides* and the non-fruiting moss *Gymnostomum calcareum*. *Barbula icmadophila* has an Arctic–Alpine range today, occurring on open river-gravel

TABLE 12.5. *The Late-Devensian moss flora of the Isle of Skye*

	Loch Meodal	Loch Fada	Loch Mealt	Loch Cill Chriosd	Lochan Coir' a' Gho-bhainn
Acrocladium cuspidatum	.	+	.	.	.
Acrocladium giganteum	.	.	+	+	.
Acrocladium sarmentosum	.	+	.	.	+
Andreaea rupestris	.	+	.	.	.
Antitrichia curtipendula	.	+	.	.	.
Aulacomnium palustre	.	+	.	.	.
Barbula icmadophila	.	.	+	.	.
Brachythecium	.	+	+	.	.
Bryum	.	+	+	.	+
Campylium stellatum	.	+	+	.	.
Cratoneuron commutatum	.	+	.	.	.
Cratoneuron filicinum	.	+	.	.	.
Ctenidium molluscum	.	.	.	+	.
Dichodontium pellucidum	.	+	+	.	.
Distichium capillaceum	.	+	.	.	.
Drepanocladus exannulatus	.	+	.	.	.
Drepanocladus revolvens	.	+	+	.	.
Drepanocladus undiff.	+	.	.	.	.
Eurhynchium	.	+	.	.	.
Hylocomium splendens	+	+	+	+	+
Hypnum cupressiforme	.	.	+	.	.
Mnium cf. *M. longirostrum*	.	+	.	.	.
Mnium orthorhynchum	.	+	.	.	.
Mnium pseudopunctatum	.	+	.	.	.
Plagiothecium undulatum	.	+	.	.	.
Pleurozium schreberi	.	+	.	.	.
Pohlia cf. *P. wahlenbergii*	.	+	.	.	.
Polytrichum alpinum	.	+	+	+	+
Polytrichum juniperinum	+	.	.	.	.
Rhacomitrium fasciculare	+	+	+	+	.
Rhacomitrium lanuginosum	+	+	+	+	+
Rhacomitrium undiff.	+	+	+	+	+
Rhytidiadelphus squarrosus	.	+	.	.	.
Scorpidium scorpioides	.	.	.	+	.
Sphagnum palustre	.	.	+	.	.
Sphagnum undiff.	.	+	+	.	.
Thuidium cf. *T. delicatulum*	.	.	+	.	.
Tortula	.	.	+	.	.

and wet rocks in Scandinavia (Nyholm, 1956), on glacial outwash gravels in south-west Iceland (Persson, 1964) and in the Yukon (H. J. B. Birks, unpublished data), and on bare solifluction soil, in open 'fell-fields', and in rock crevices in Peary Land, north Greenland (Holmen, 1960) and on Ellesmere Island (Schuster, Steere & Thomson, 1959).

The Late-Devensian moss flora of Skye consists largely of taxa with a widespread distribution in Europe today, although there are some species with an Arctic–Alpine range today (*Barbula icmadophila*, *Distichium capillaceum*, *Mnium orthorhynchum*) and some with a rather Sub-Atlantic distribution in Europe (*Plagiothecium undulatum*, *Rhacomitrium lanuginosum*, *Thuidium* cf. *T. delicatulum*). The fossil moss flora is not as diverse in its present phytogeographical affinities, however, as the pollen flora.

3. SIGNIFICANCE OF THE POLLEN FLORA

As discussed above, the most striking features of the Late-Devensian pollen flora of Skye are its considerable ecological and phytogeographical diversity and the fact that such a high proportion (90%) of the taxa represented by the pollen flora occur on Skye today. There is, however, some palynological evidence for changes in the distribution of twenty-four per cent of the pollen flora, either distributional changes within the island (14%) or changes on a larger scale within Scotland (8.1%) or even within Europe (1.9%). Before considering the possible causes of such changes in distribution, it is pertinent to discuss how reliable the Late-Devensian pollen flora is as a record of the flora growing on Skye during Late-Devensian times, and to assess whether the observed changes in distribution of pollen or spore types represent real changes in the distribution of the taxa concerned.

Three hypotheses can be advanced to explain the diverse composition of the Late-Devensian pollen flora and the occurrence of pollen and spores of taxa not currently known in the present flora of Skye. One hypothesis proposes that the Late-Devensian pollen flora is contaminated by secondary pollen that is reworked and redeposited from pollen-bearing sediments of pre-Late-Devensian age, and thus that part of the pollen flora may not represent the actual flora living near the site of deposition (Andersen, 1961; Iversen, 1936, 1942). Although several microfossils of undoubted pre-Quaternary age occur in the sediments at Loch Fada (particularly in zones LF-1 and LF-2), indicating that reworking and redeposition of pollen and spores has occurred, there is no evidence at this site to suggest that secondarily redeposited pollen of Quaternary taxa are a significant component of the pollen flora (H. J. B. Birks, 1970). This hypothesis cannot therefore account for the floristic diversity at Loch Fada, nor for the similarities of the pollen floras at the other sites. In the absence of evidence to the contrary, this hypothesis is accordingly rejected.

A second hypothesis attempts to reconcile the diversity of the pollen flora by proposing that all or a part of the pollen flora is blown from sources that are considerable distances away, and thus it may have no relationship to the flora or vegetation immediately surrounding the site of deposition. At present there are two possible ways to test the hypothesis of long-distance transport, and both of these yield negative evidence only. One way is to demonstrate in the same stratigraphical position the presence of macrofossils of the taxa whose pollen or spores are suspected of being wind-transported over great distances. The second possibility is to demonstrate a significant variation in the amount of pollen or spores of the suspected taxa in correlative sediments nearby. If such a variation occurs without a corresponding fluctuation in the other pollen percentages (or if it occurs when measured as absolute pollen influx), and if the distance between the sediment samples is small in comparison with the postulated distance of pollen transport, the variation may be assumed to be due to local changes in the source. A similar argument can be applied to variation in pollen percentages within a stratigraphical sequence at a single site. Unfortunately, however, no limits can be set at present on the amount of variation that can be allowed before the hypothesis of long-distance transport can be confidently rejected. An additional but less satisfactory approach to the problem of long-distance transport requires a knowledge of the present-day pollen production and dispersal, and hence the pollen representation of the taxa in question. Such knowledge can be obtained most readily from studies of modern pollen rain. It is considered that if a taxon has a low pollen production and/or poor dispersal, and thus a low representation in modern pollen spectra, it is unlikely that its pollen will be dispersed over great distances, whereas there is a greater probability that the pollen of a taxon with a high pollen production, an effective pollen dispersal, and a high representation will be dispersed over long distances. In many instances there is inadequate knowledge of the pollen representation of the taxa in question in a variety of modern ecological settings. In some cases there is so much variation in the representation of a particular taxon that the attempt to decide whether a particular pollen or spore type in a fossil assemblage reflects the occurrence of that taxon near the site in question, or whether it results from long-distance transport and bears no relationship to the local flora and vegetation, involves a considerable degree of subjectivity.

There is, however, convincing evidence for the long-distance transport of pollen of *Pinus* and of other trees such as *Alnus*, *Quercus*, and *Ulmus* (see Chapter 11 and references therein), of *Ephedra* (Maher, 1964; Salmi, 1969), and of *Ambrosia* (Bassett & Terasmae, 1962) at the present day. Eighteen grains of *Ephedra fragilis* type and one of *E. distachya* type have been found in the Late-Devensian sediments on Skye, adding to the now numerous records of these distinctive pollen types from Late-Devensian deposits elsewhere in Britain and in western Europe. The wide dispersal of *Ephedra* pollen is strikingly exemplified by its occurrence in peats on Tristan da Cunha and on Gough Island, where the nearest likely source of such pollen is South America, some 1500 miles (2400 km) west of the islands (Hafsten, 1960). In considering the records of *Ephedra* pollen in Late-Wisconsin deposits in Minnesota, Michigan, and Wisconsin, Maher (1964) demonstrated that long range transport of *Ephedra* pollen can occur over distances of up to 750 miles (1200 km) at the present day under special meteorological conditions. Similarly King & Kapp (1963) report grains of *Ephedra* in modern spectra in eastern Ontario 1300 miles (2080 km) north-east of the present range of the genus in the south-western United States. Salmi (1969) has recently reported the pollen of *Ephedra* along with pollen of *Fagopyrum*, *Magnolia*, and *Zea*, in 'red snow' that fell in southern Finland in April 1965. Such snow appears to have been derived under particular meteorological conditions from a source area of red dust north of the Black Sea and Asov Sea between the Caucasus and Crimea (see also Lundqvist & Bengtsson, 1970). Bortenschlager (1967) analysed the pollen content of firn samples from an Austrian glacier. In an 8 m ice profile that probably represents the years 1944 to 1951, twenty-six grains of *Ephedra* were recorded, all in samples with a high dust content. Observations on dust incidence using meteorological test-balloons indicate that high altitude air currents can frequently carry dust from arid regions (for example in North Africa) to central and western Europe. None of Bortenschlager's grains were of the local alpine *Ephedra distachya* type, but they most closely resembled pollen of the North African and Mediterranean taxa *E. altissima* Desp. and *E. alata* (belonging to the morphological types of *E. strobilacea* type and *E. fragilis* type; see Welten, 1957). Bortenschlager suggests on the basis of this evidence that fossil grains of these types may be due to long-distance transport from North Africa.

In contrast to these observations, Welten (1957) showed in the Swiss Alps that on the basis of surface pollen samples *Ephedra distachya* is poorly represented in the pollen rain, and that 0.5 to 1.0% *Ephedra* pollen (expressed as a percentage of total pollen) indicates the local presence of *Ephedra* bushes. From these observations, Welten (1957, p. 35) states: '*An einer reichlichen Verbreitung von Ephedra nördlich der Alpen und einer sporadischen Verbreitung bis hinauf nach Südskandinavien wahrend der letzten Glazial und Spätglazialzeit ist heute nicht zu zweifeln.*'

It is difficult to reconcile these two conflicting sets of observations, but it is striking that in Late-Devensian and early Flandrian deposits in Denmark the ratio of *Ephedra distachya* type pollen to *E. fragilis* type (including *E. strobilacea* type of Welten, 1957) is 4.8:1 (data from Iversen, 1954; Jørgensen, 1963; Krog, 1954, 1959), whereas in Sweden and Norway the ratio is 1:1.4 (data from Appendix to Berglund, 1966*a*; Danielsen, 1970; Florin, 1969; Hafsten, 1956, 1963; Mangerud, 1970) and in Scotland the ratio is 1:3.1 (unpublished data of R. Andrew and H. H. Birks, and Moar, 1969*a*, 1969*b*). It is possible that *E. distachya* occurred widely in northern and central Europe in the Late-Weichselian (Late-Devensian) (see Fig. 2 in Iversen, 1964) and persisted for part of the Flandrian in areas such as the Great Alvar on the Island of Öland, as proposed by Iversen (1954) (cf. Königsson, 1968). There is little evidence, however, to suggest that *Ephedra distachya* occurred in Britain during Late-Devensian or Flandrian times (cf. Godwin, 1956). It is now restricted in north-west Europe to coastal dunes between the Loire estuary and south Finisterre in France, where it occurs with such plants as *Corynephorus canescens*, *Dianthus gallicus* Pers., *Helichrysum stoechas* (L.) DC., *Herniaria ciliolata*, *Silene conica*, *S. otites*, and *Pleurochaete squarrosa* (Géhu & Petit, 1965). The scattered occurrences of *Ephedra distachya* pollen in Flandrian deposits in Finisterre (Van Zeist, 1964) may reflect a long history of the species in the area.

In contrast, the former occurrence of the Mediterranean *Ephedra fragilis* as far north as Skye in Late-Devensian times is considered highly improbable in view of its present distribution in Europe (see Fig. 1 in Welten, 1957). The grains encountered in the Skye sediments almost certainly represent long-distance transport. The majority of the American species produce pollen of the *E. fragilis* type (Steeves & Barghoorn, 1959), and it is quite possible that the Scottish grains are derived by long-distance transport from North America rather than from southern and central Europe or North Africa.

The hypothesis of long-distance transport for *Ephedra* pollen is strengthened by the find of one pollen grain of *Ambrosia* type at Loch Mealt (zone LM-1), as all the possible genera that could contribute this pollen type to the pollen rain (*Ambrosia*, *Franseria*, and *Iva* p.p.) are exclusively North American in their present native ranges. Bassett & Terasmae (1962) have demonstrated the consistent presence of *Ambrosia* type pollen in modern spectra in eastern Canada at least 375 miles (600 km) north of the nearest occurrence of the genus in Canada, and Ritchie & Lichti-Federovich (1967) and Terasmae (1967) report *Ambrosia* type pollen in surface spectra as far north as 74°41′ in northern Canada some 1500 miles (2400 km) north of its present range. In view of the long-distance dispersal of *Ambrosia* type pollen at the present day and the fact that the occurrence of plants of *Ambrosia* or related genera on Skye in Late-Devensian times is highly unlikely for phytogeographical reasons, the hypothesis of long-distance pollen transport is advanced to explain the single grain of *Ambrosia* type in the Skye pollen flora. It is possible that some of the unknown pollen and spore types encountered during the analyses (see Chapter 8) may be similarly derived from non-British taxa whose pollen or spore morphology is unfamiliar to me. The occasional grains of *Alnus*, *Pinus*, *Quercus*, and *Ulmus* in the Late-Devensian sediments on Skye may result from either contamination in sampling (this is considered unlikely in view of the coring and sampling methods) or from long-distance transport. Although these trees were almost certainly absent from Skye in Late-Devensian times, they appear to have been locally abundant in the Flandrian (H. J. B. Birks, unpublished data; Vasari & Vasari, 1968).

The single grain of *Hippophaë rhamnoides* at Lochan Coir' a' Ghobhainn is of note in view of the fact that although *Hippophaë* occurs on Skye today, it is not considered to be native in its northern localities in Britain (Clapham *et al.*, 1962). *Hippophaë* appears to be a poor pollen producer today (Firbas, 1934) and consistent pollen values between 1 and 5% are considered by Danielsen (1970) to be indicative of local stands of *Hippophaë*. Scattered grains in the absence of the characteristic stellate leaf and stem hairs cannot, however, be regarded as indisputable evidence that this shrub ever grew near the site in question (Faegri, 1943; Hafsten, 1966).

Of the remainder of the pollen flora, some pollen and spore types can be considered members of the Skye flora in the Late-Devensian by the application of the criteria discussed above. Thus *Betula pubescens*, *B. nana*, *Salix herbacea*, *Selaginella selaginoides*, and a number of aquatic taxa are known as macrofossils (Table 12.1). The percentages of *Artemisia* cf. *A. norvegica*, *Empetrum* cf. *E. nigrum*, Ericaceae undiff., *Filipendula*, *Juniperus communis*, *Ranunculus acris* type,

Rumex acetosa, and *Thalictrum* pollen, and of *Lycopodium selago* spores are sufficiently variable, both from site to site and from zone to zone in a single stratigraphic sequence, to suggest that the presence of these taxa near the sites was highly likely in Late-Devensian times. Similarly *Corylus avellana* must have been present at least in the *Betula–Corylus* zone, and the presence of members of the Gramineae and Cyperaceae is scarcely in question. The high frequencies of pollen and spores of aquatic taxa are likely to indicate the local presence of the taxa concerned, although it should be noted that occasional grains of *Sparganium* type were found in modern pollen spectra from areas some distance from suitable pollen sources (see Chapter 11). In view of the low pollen representation of many herbaceous taxa in modern spectra, it is highly likely that the pollen of *Koenigia islandica*, *Rubus saxatilis*, *Saxifraga aizoides*, *S. nivalis*, *S. oppositifolia*, *S. stellaris*, *Sedum* cf. *S. rosea*, and *Silene* cf. *S. acaulis* and spores of *Cryptogramma crispa* imply the presence of the relevant taxa in the flora near the site of deposition. The presence of most of the rest of the types that occur sporadically in small percentages in the pollen flora and the pollen rain is open to some doubt if they are considered individually. With the exception of the Southern Continental, the North American, and the Introduced Elements, however, most of the floristic elements in the pollen flora are so large, either in terms of the number of types (Table 12.2) or in their total contribution to the pollen (Table 12.4) or both, that it is difficult to explain them all by the hypothesis of long-distance transport.

A third hypothesis accepts the ecological and phytogeographical diversity of the Late-Devensian pollen flora as indicative of the character of the Late-Devensian flora on Skye. The diverse composition of the fossil pollen flora on Skye is not without parallels elsewhere, for example a mixture of floristic elements (arctic–alpine, arctic–subarctic, boreal, continental, steppe) is regarded as characteristic of Late-Weichselian floras elsewhere in north-west Europe (Berglund, 1966*a*; Godwin, 1956; Iversen, 1954; Lang, 1952). Similarly in the Great Lakes Region of the United States the Late-Wisconsin pollen flora is characterised by its floristic heterogeneity with arctic–alpine, boreal, deciduous, and prairie elements all well represented (Cushing, 1963, 1965; H. J. B. Birks, unpublished data). In discussing the Late-Weichselian pollen record in Denmark and in reconstructing the environment it indicates, Iversen (1954) treats each taxon individually and recognises that taxa which today are widely separated geographically and ecologically apparently existed side-by-side under the special climatic, edaphic, seral, and light conditions of Late-Weichselian time. It is perhaps significant that of the modern pollen diagrams that are available from other areas in western Britain, and elsewhere in north-west Europe none shows a Late-Devensian pollen flora that is appreciably less diverse than that of the present study.

The third hypothesis is therefore the one preferred here, combined with the hypothesis of long-distance transport for pollen of certain taxa. The following pollen types are considered to have probably been blown to the sites from outside the Isle of Skye during Late-Devensian times: *Alnus*, *Ambrosia* type, *Ephedra distachya* type, *Ephedra fragilis* type, *Hippophaë rhamnoides*, *Pinus*, *Quercus*, and *Ulmus*. The following group consists of pollen or spore types that may or may not have been blown in from outside the island: *Achillea* type, *Lycopodium annotinum*, *Lycopodium clavatum*, *Rumex crispus* type, and *Viburnum opulus*. The criteria used in making these decisions include the number of pollen grains or spores found in the Late-Devensian sediments, the stratigraphical variation in frequencies between sites and within profiles, the present-day representation of these taxa in modern pollen spectra, and the present distribution of the taxa concerned. The remainder of the pollen and spore types in the Late-Devensian pollen flora are considered to indicate the presence of the relevant taxa on the Isle of Skye in Late-Devensian times, although an unknown fraction of the pollen grains and spores of these taxa may also have been blown in from outside the island.

4. CAUSES OF FLORISTIC CHANGE

I. THE MONTANE FLORA

The interest of phytogeographers has been focused on the history of the British mountain flora since the classic essay of Edward Forbes in 1846 on *The Fauna and Flora of the British Isles*. Much attention has been given to the former occurrence of northern and montane taxa in areas south of their present range during Devensian times. There is now an impressive body of evidence to indicate the former occurrence of several such plants in southern England (Conolly & Dahl, 1970). There is, however, little information concerning the history of mountain plants in areas where they still occur today, with the exception of the studies of Godwin (1955) and Seddon (1962) in

Snowdonia. Donner's (1962) pollen diagrams from Breadalbane in central Scotland are not detailed enough to provide much floristic information concerning the history of montane plants in that area. Similarly, although there is a high concentration of modern pollen diagrams from Lakeland prepared by Pennington (1964, 1970), Walker (1955, 1965) and others, the results are too limited in their floristic content to provide much information pertinent to the history of the montane flora in that area.

The modern and Late-Devensian floras on Skye contain many northern and montane taxa (see Chapters 5 and 6). Nearly all the members of the present montane flora of the island (Table 5.4) with distinctive pollen or spore types occur in the fossil pollen flora, and in the case of the majority of the taxa involved there is no evidence for changes in their distribution within the island since the Late-Devensian, for example *Dryas octopetala*, *Koenigia islandica*, *Oxyria digyna*, *Rubus saxatilis*, *Saxifraga hypnoides*, *S. nivalis*, *S. stellaris*, and *Silene acaulis*. Species that are curiously rare and localised on Skye at present, for example *Dryas octopetala*, *Koenigia islandica*, and *Saxifraga nivalis*, appear to have been similarly rare and restricted in their distribution in Late-Devensian times, whereas pollen and spores of the more widespread species at present, for example *Lycopodium selago*, *Saxifraga hypnoides*, and *Silene acaulis*, occur in sediments at several of the sites investigated. Many of these more widespread taxa have a wide altitudinal range today (see Table 5.4 and Chapter 5), and are found from near sea level to 3000 feet (920 m) on Skye. They appear to be able to spread and colonise new habitats (see Chapter 5).

There is, however, pollen evidence to suggest changes in the distribution of at least eight montane taxa within the island since Late-Devensian times. The records of pollen of *Cerastium alpinum* type, *Saussurea alpina*, *Saxifraga aizoides*, and *Thalictrum* (?*T. alpinum*), and spores of *Cryptogramma crispa* and *Lycopodium alpinum* at Loch Meodal suggest the occurrence of these plants in the Sleat Peninsula during Late-Devensian times, where none of these taxa occur today. It should be noted, however, that *Cerastium alpinum* type, *Cryptogramma crispa*, and *Saxifraga aizoides* are represented by only one grain or spore each at Loch Meodal, and that *Lycopodium alpinum* and *Saussurea alpina* are represented by two spores and three grains respectively. It is possible, therefore, that these isolated grains and spores are blown in from elsewhere in the island, and thus that they do not reflect the occurrence of the plants in the Sleat. If the taxa did occur near the site, their subsequent extinction is readily explicable in view of their present-day requirements for high altitudes and/or open basic-rock outcrops. Bog and woodland are now widespread in the Sleat (see Fig. 5), and, as there is no ground above 1000 feet (305 m), there is an absence of suitable refugia for the more demanding montane plants in this area. In the pollen diagram from Loch Meodal (Plate 1) many of the montane taxa disappear from the pollen record during the *Betula* zone (zone LML-3), suggesting that closed communities and woodland developed earlier here than elsewhere on Skye.

The absence of *Saussurea alpina*, *Saxifraga oppositifolia*, and *Sedum rosea* from the limestones of Ben Suardal today is curious in view of the occurrence of their pollen in Late-Devensian sediments at Loch Cill Chriosd (Plate 4). Although much of Ben Suardal is wooded at present (see Fig. 19) many montane plants occur there today, including *Alchemilla alpina*, *Dryas octopetala*, *Rubus saxatilis*, and *Saxifraga aizoides*. Both *Saxifraga oppositifolia* and *Sedum rosea* descend to near sea-level elsewhere on Skye (Table 5.4), so a present-day climatic restriction is unlikely. Their absence from Ben Suardal must therefore be explained in terms of extinction due to woodland development in the Flandrian, and their subsequent inability to recolonise lost ground. As *Saussurea alpina* does not descend, as far as is known, on Skye below 1200 feet (365 m), its absence from Ben Suardal (922 feet, 280 m) may be explicable as a climatic restriction (Dahl, 1951).

Cerastium alpinum type pollen occurs in Late-Devensian sediments at Loch Cill Chriosd, Loch Fada, and Lochan Coir' a' Ghobhainn, as well as at Loch Meodal. It is unfortunately impossible to be certain what taxon or taxa are concerned, but tentative determinations on the basis of pore number frequencies and grain size (see Fredskild, 1967) suggest that *Cerastium arcticum* may have been involved. *Cerastium arcticum* is restricted at present on Skye to high altitude gabbro rock-ledges near Sgùrr nan Gillean and to a small area of summit 'fell-field' near The Storr (see Chapter 5). It may well have been more widespread on Skye in Late-Devensian times, as it is today on the basalts of the Faeröes (Hansen, 1966). In Scotland today it appears to be rather indifferent to substrate, occurring on quartzites on Conival in Sutherland and on Ruadh-stac Mor in the Kinlochewe Forest of west Ross, on Moine granulites and schists on Beinn Dearg, west Ross, on Lewisian gneiss in the Letterewe Forest, west Ross, and on Dalradian schists and limestones near Ben Alder, Inverness-shire. It occurs in a variety of habitats in Scotland, for example in 'fell-field' and summit stoney-detritus, on rock ledges, and in fine-grained screes, that are generally at high altitudes (2500–3500 feet, 765–1070 m). Its ecology at the sole British locality south of the Scottish Highlands in Snowdonia is strikingly different from any of its Scottish stations, being in an open spring community at a comparatively low altitude (1950 feet, 637 m). In Scandinavia, Gjaerevoll (1956) and Nordhagen (1943) record *C. arcticum* from high-altitude moist chionophilous communities developed on basic soils (alliances Oppositifolio–Oxyrion and Ranunculeto–Oxyrion respectively), growing with, for example, *Epilobium anagallidifolium*, *Oxyria digyna*, *Ranunculus acris*, *Saxifraga aizoides*, *S. oppositifolia*, and *Sagina saginoides*. Its requirements for high altitudes and its indifference to habitat and substrate suggest that its present distribution in Scotland may be climatically determined, for example by an intolerance of summer warmth (Dahl, 1951; Conolly & Dahl, 1970) or a need for a certain winter cold. If so, its reduction in range since Late-Devensian times on Skye could be regarded as an effect of climatic change. It is perhaps significant that its pollen is found until the close of the Late-Devensian at the sites near large mountain ranges (Lochan Coir' a' Ghobhainn, zone LCG-3; Loch Cill Chriosd, zone LCC-5), but it disappears from the stratigraphic record in the *Juniperus* subzones of the Gramineae–*Rumex* zone at Loch Fada (zone LF-3) and at Loch Meodal (zone LML-2).

The abundance of *Artemisia* cf. *A. norvegica* and *Betula* cf. *B. nana* pollen and of *Athyrium alpestre* type spores in the Late-Devensian pollen rain on Skye, coupled with macrofossils of *Betula nana* provide further evidence for distributional changes in the Skye flora since Late-Devensian times, as none of these taxa are known to occur on the island today. Although only one grain of cf. *Oxytropis* was found (zone LCC-2), it probably reflects the local presence of a member of the genus on Skye at that time, but the single spores of *Lycopodium annotinum* at four sites cannot be regarded as irrefutable evidence for the former occurrence of this plant on Skye, in view of its high spore production and representation in modern spectra (Iversen, 1945).

Fruits and/or pollen of *Betula nana* occur in Late-Devensian sediments at all the sites examined, and they extend into the *Betula–Corylus* zone. Vasari & Vasari (1968) record macrofossils of *B. nana* at Loch Cuithir in northern Skye (see Fig. 12) in zone VIIb (Late Flandrian). *Betula nana* in Britain today is exclusively a 'peat-alpine', occurring with other dwarf shrubs in blanket-bogs between 1000 and 2800 feet (305–855 m) in the eastern and central Highlands and with a recently discovered southern outlier on Widdybank Fell in Teesdale. It was extremely widespread in Britain during the Devensian (see Map 1 in Tralau, 1963 and Fig. 9 in Conolly & Dahl, 1970), suggesting that it once grew on mineral soil in this country, as it does in Scandinavia, Iceland, and Greenland today. It also occurred in the Faeröes in early Flandrian times, but it is not known to grow there today (Johansen, 1968). In Scandinavia *B. nana* shows a wide ecological amplitude, for besides occurring as a prominent component in sub-alpine and low-alpine Oxycocco–Empetrion hermaphroditi bogs (Nordhagen, 1936, 1943; Sonesson, 1970) and in a variety of fen communities (Dahl, 1956; Persson, 1961), it also occurs in several sub-alpine and low-alpine communities on mineral soil. It is intolerant of dense shade, but it can occur in rather open heathy birchwoods in the sub-alpine zone. At higher altitude it can dominate in both mildly chionophilous and mildly chionophobous dwarf-shrub communities (Dahl, 1956; Gjaerevoll & Bringer, 1965; Nordhagen, 1943) on a range of stable soils, but it tends to favour well-drained, acidic sites. It commonly occurs in a complex mosaic with *Juniperus communis* spp. *nana*, *Salix glauca*, *S. lanata*, and *S. lapponum* in a transitional zone with winter snow protection, early spring melt, and a rather long vegetative period. The branches of the shrubs are protected from wind- and ice-abrasion in the winter by snow cover both in mire and in terrestrial sites (see Sonesson, 1969). Juniper and dwarf birch tend to favour the drier, acidic soils, whereas the willows dominate on wetter and richer sites. *Betula nana* also occurs in *Dryas*-heath with *Salix reticulata*, *Carex atrata*, *C. rupestris*, and *Cassiope tetragona* (L.) D. Don, for example at Åbisko, Swedish Lappland.

Its restriction over much of Britain since Late-Devensian times may result partly from direct climatic effects, and partly from a restriction of habitat due to woodland development in the Flandrian. Its restriction to bogs in Britain today is surprising, in view of its broad ecological tolerances in Scandinavia, but there is the possibility suggested by Poore & McVean (1957) of ecotypic differentiation in the British populations. Similarly the preference of *Chamaepericlymenum suecicum* and *Rubus chamaemorus* for bogs in Britain today, again largely centred on the central and eastern Highlands, contrasts with their present ecology and habitat preferences in Scandinavia (see Birks & Ransom, 1969), and suggests that ecotypic differentiation may also have occurred.

Judging by the abundance of *Artemisia* cf. *A. norvegica* pollen at all the sites investigated on Skye, *Artemisia norvegica* must have been locally frequent on the island during Late-Devensian times. Its pollen persists to the beginning of the *Betula–Corylus* zone at Loch Cill Chriosd (zone LCC-6) and at Lochan Coir' a' Ghobhainn (zone LCG-3). It is a plant that could still be growing on Skye today, for there is an abundance of suitable habitats on the wind-exposed summit ridges of the Cuillins and the Red Hills. In Britain *Artemisia norvegica* is at present only known in two Scottish localities, both in west Ross. In both these stations it is locally frequent in open *Juncus trifidus–Festuca ovina* 'fell-field' communities between 2400 and 2800 feet (710–855 m). The communities are very similar in floristic composition and ecology to the Skye *Luzula spicata–Festuca ovina nodum* (see Chapter 4 and Table 4.35). The Scottish plants have been termed variety *scotica* by Hultén (1954), and they are said to differ from the Norwegian and northern Ural plants in their size, flower pubescence, leaf-shape, and the number of capitula. In Norway it is reported to grow on a range of acidic and basic rocks in open 'fell-field', scree, and gravel communities (Faegri, personal communication; Gjaerevoll, 1963; Ryvarden & Kaland, 1968). Its pollen has only been recently tentatively distinguished from other *Artemisia* species, but it has been recorded from Late-Devensian deposits at Loch Dungeon, Kirkcudbrightshire (H. H. Birks, 1972), near Loch Assynt, Sutherland (H. J. B. Birks, unpublished data), at Loch Droma, west Ross (R. Andrew, unpublished data), and at Elan Valley, Cardiganshire (Moore, 1970). Lundqvist (1967) records it from Weichselian deposits in central Sweden. Its present restriction to exposed high-altitude sites in Scotland may be a result of direct climatic effects. In view of their broadly similar history on Skye it is interesting that *Artemisia norvegica* and *Cerastium arcticum* have a similar maximum summer temperature isotherm of 22 °C in Scandinavia today (Dahl, 1951).

The ten spores of *Athyrium alpestre* type in Late-Devensian sediments at Lochan Coir' a' Ghobhainn and Loch Cill Chriosd could be derived from *Athyrium alpestre*, *Woodsia alpina*, or *W. ilvensis*. In view of their present-day ecology and distribution the most likely taxon is *Athyrium alpestre*, although *Woodsia alpina* has been doubtfully recorded from The Quirang.* There do not appear to be any suitable localities for either species of *Woodsia* on Skye today in view of their habitat preferences elsewhere in Britain. *Athyrium alpestre* is restricted in Britain to the Scottish Highlands at present, and its distribution is centred on the central and eastern Highlands. It generally occurs above 2000 feet (610 m) in areas of block-scree with prolonged snow-lie, often with *Cryptogramma crispa* (Cryptogrammeto–Athyrietum chionophilum Association; see McVean & Ratcliffe, 1962 and Chapter 11), and, more rarely, on ungrazed cliff-ledges with other ferns (for example *Dryopteris abbreviata*, *D. assimilis*, *D. dilatata*, *Thelypteris limbosperma*) and with *Salix lapponum* and *S. lanata*. It appears to be consistently associated with prolonged snow-lie in Britain, Scandinavia, and the Alps, probably as a protection from winter frost. Its absence from Skye today may be explicable in terms of the short and rather variable winter snow-lie, even at high altitudes (see Chapters 3 and 4).

A tentative determination was made of a single grain at Loch Cill Chriosd (zone LCC-2) to the genus *Oxytropis*. Neither British species occurs on Skye today, although it is possible that *O. halleri* may grow on the very extensive and precipitous basalt sea-cliffs in north Skye, for it grows in similar habitats on basic sea-cliffs in Sutherland, Caithness, and east Ross. It also occurs on inland cliffs above 2000 feet (610 m) on Ben Vrackie and on Ben Chonzie in Perthshire, and in species-rich turf on Ben Sgulaird in Argyll. There is also an old record from the Mull of Galloway. *O. campestris* is rarer in Scotland, however, being restricted to dry, highly calcareous crags in Glen Clova, Angus and on Ben-y-Gloe, Perthshire. There is also a population of *Oxytropis* on Dun Ban near the Mull of Kintyre growing with *Dryas octopetala*, *Saxifraga oppositifolia*, and *Sedum rosea*, whose specific identity is in doubt due to variation in the flower colour (cf. *Astragalus alpinus*). Both species grow in a variety of habitats in the Alps and (in the case of *O. campestris*) in Scandinavia, for example on open glacial gravels, river gravels, sub-alpine and alpine grasslands, and chionophobous *Dryas*-heaths. Either species of *Oxytropis* could have grown on the Suardal limestones on Skye in Late-Devensian times, and its extinction could be due to climatic change, woodland development, or grazing.

As discussed above, the single spores of *Lycopodium*

* The specimen cannot be traced, but it is almost certainly incorrect.

annotinum in the sediments at Loch Fada (zone LF-4), Loch Cill Chriosd (zone LCC-3), Loch Mealt (zone LM-7), and Lochan Coir' a' Ghobhainn (zone LCG-3) are not conclusive proof of the former occurrence of this species on Skye today in view of its present distribution and ecology in Britain. In the Scottish Highlands it favours dwarf-shrub heaths, block screes, and grasslands on acid to mildly basic soils, generally above 1000 feet (305 m), although Clapham *et al.* (1962) record it as low as 150 feet (46 m). It is generally a local plant, with its present British headquarters in the central Highlands, but with occasional scattered stations in north-west Scotland, including two recently discovered localities in the Inner Hebrides (Isle of Raasay and on Scalpay). In its southernmost British locality in Lakeland it grows in some abundance in biotically derived Nardetum grassland. In Scandinavia and central Europe it also occurs in rather open coniferous and birch woodland. Its spores have been widely recorded from Late-Devensian sediments in north and central Wales (Seddon, 1962; Moore, 1970), northern England (Bartley, 1962, 1966; Dickson *et al.*, 1970; Franks & Pennington, 1961; Godwin, 1959; Walker, 1966), and Scotland (H. H. Birks, 1969), and from Flandrian deposits in northern England (Pigott & Pigott, 1963) and Scotland (H. H. Birks, 1969, 1970; Moar, 1969*b*).

2. AQUATIC PLANTS

Although the present distribution of several aquatic plants on Skye may be inadequately known, especially of inconspicuous, submerged species, the pollen and macrofossil evidence suggests that several taxa have become restricted in their range on the island since Late-Devensian times. The trophic state of a lake during its interglacial development reflects to a large degree the state of the soils in its drainage basin (Andersen, 1966). At the close of a glaciation the upland soils are unleached and base-rich (Andersen, 1969), and the lake water is nutrient-rich and supports a rich aquatic flora. As the interglacial sequence proceeds, the surrounding soils become progressively leached, often with the development of bog, and the lakes become increasingly oligotrophic. This parallel series of soil and lake changes has been demonstrated from the Eemian (Ipswichian) and Harreskovian (? Cromerian) interglacials in Denmark by Andersen (1964, 1966). During the Flandrian interglacial man has played an increasingly important role in influencing the landscape, especially through forest clearance and agriculture. Such effects accelerate soil erosion and nutrient run-off and thus lead to an increase in lake eutrophication. The interglacial lake sequence is thus reversed, and as a result many lakes in Britain appear to be eutrophic today, for example Blelham Tarn, Lancashire (Evans, 1970), Esthwaite Water, Lancashire (Goulden, 1964; Round, 1961), and Loch of Park, Aberdeenshire (Vasari & Vasari, 1968), which were oligotrophic earlier in their history before the intervention of man.

There are several aquatic species on Skye whose distribution does not appear to have been affected by changes in the lochs since Late-Devensian times. These include *Equisetum* (possibly *E. fluviatile*), *Littorella uniflora*, *Menyanthes trifoliata*, and *Myriophyllum alterniflorum*, all of which are species of wide ecological tolerances on Skye today (see Chapter 5 and Fig. 7), and elsewhere in Scotland (Spence, 1966, 1967). There is, however, evidence for a restriction in range of several more base-demanding aquatic species such as cf. *Ceratophyllum*, *Myriophyllum spicatum*, and *Potamogeton* (*Coleogeton* – either *P. filiformis* or *P. pectinatus*). It should be noted that the fossil records of *Ceratophyllum* from Loch Fada (zone LF-6) are tentative, for they are based on the occurrence of narrow, elongated (*ca.* 40 μm long), thick walled, and sharply pointed marginal leaf-spines (see Plate 39 in Wasylikowa, 1964 and Fig. 4 in Mamakowa, 1968). It is possible that other submerged hydrophytes produce similar leaf spines, thus necessitating a tentative determination. No fruits were found, so no specific designation is possible. Neither species is known on Skye at the present day, but *C. demersum* occurs in its northernmost known British station on the Isle of Rona near Skye. It is possible that *C. demersum* may yet be found growing on Skye in, for example, Loch Cill Chriosd, for it appears to be restricted to calcareous, or at least base-rich lochs in Scotland today (Spence, 1967). Its present distribution extends to 69 °N in Scandinavia (Julin & Luther, 1959) where it appears to have an ecological tolerance similar to that in Scotland. Fossil leaf-spines and fruits of *Ceratophyllum* have been recorded from several Late-Devensian and early Flandrian deposits in Britain and in Ireland (Godwin, 1956; Jessen, 1949; Vasari & Vasari, 1968).

Neither British member of the subgenus *Coleogeton* (*Potamogeton filiformis* and *P. pectinatus*) are known to occur on Skye today, although they both occur elsewhere in the Hebrides. *P. filiformis* has recently been recorded from the nearby Isle of Raasay (Murray,

1970). Both species can occur in brackish habitats such as coastal lagoons, growing on lime-rich sandy silt with *Myriophyllum alterniflorum*, *Chara* spp., and *Najas flexilis*, for example at Loch Hallam in South Uist. They also occur in inland base-rich lochs. Schoof-van Pelt & Westhoff (1969) describe an interesting *Potamogeton filiformis–Chara* community from lakes in the calcareous coastal margin of Co. Galway and from Lough Ree in Co. Roscommon, where *P. filiformis* is associated with *Myriophyllum alterniflorum*, *M. spicatum*, *Najas flexilis*, *Potamogeton gramineus*, *P. coloratus*, *P. pusillus*, *P. berchtoldii*, *P. natans*, *Chara* spp., and *Littorella uniflora* (cf. *Potamogeton filiformis–Chara* association; Spence, 1964).

Myriophyllum spicatum is restricted at present on Skye to two highly eutrophic and polluted lochs in northern Skye, but it is absent from Loch Fada, Loch Mealt, and Loch Cill Chriosd where its pollen in Late-Devensian sediments suggest its former presence at these sites. It is likely that the extinction of all these base-demanding aquatic taxa since Late-Devensian and early Flandrian times from the lochs examined on Skye is a result of the increased oligotrophy of the loch water following soil leaching and bog development during the Flandrian, as was discussed by Vasari & Vasari (1968) at Loch Fada. Only a few of the Skye lochs appear to have been influenced by recent eutrophication processes. In the present study these are Loch Cill Chriosd, Loch Mealt and, to a lesser degree, Loch Fada. However several of the aquatic taxa do not appear to have been able to recolonise the sites that they once occupied in the Late-Devensian.

A similar restriction in the range of *Ceratophyllum demersum* is known in Scandinavia and elsewhere in Britain. Samuelsson (1934) interpreted this as a result of nutrient impoverishment of lake waters in its northern localities, but Godwin (1956) cites it as an example of restriction possibly due to climatic change. It is difficult, however, to conceive of climatic factors acting in the Flandrian that could restrict a thermophilous species such as this whose range was apparently well established in Late-Devensian and early Flandrian times.

There are some distributional changes which cannot be readily explained in such a way, for example microspores of *Isoetes lacustris* were found in sediments at four of the sites investigated, and yet the plant only persists in one of them, namely Loch Meodal. Similarly, *I. echinospora* has apparently disappeared from Loch Meodal, for it has only one known Skye station at present near Dunvegan. *Sparganium* cf. *S. minimum* pollen occurs at Loch Fada and Lochan Coir' a' Ghobhainn but the plant is not known at these sites today, although it still occurs at Loch Cill Chriosd and Loch Meodal where its pollen was also found in the Late-Devensian sediments. The above are all species characteristic of acidic or neutral lochs, but *Isoetes* spp. can occasionally occur in richer waters (Seddon, 1965, 1967). *Sparganium minimum* tends to favour highly organic substrata in shallow water, for example in communities of the Caricion lasiocarpae and the Phragmition, whilst *Isoetes* spp. commonly occur on stony loch bottoms where there is little competition from other hydrophytes. The restriction in the distribution of *Isoetes* on Skye may reflect changes in the physical character of the loch bottom, for the deposition of organic mud in the Flandrian would tend to eliminate *Isoetes* from its former Late-Devensian sites. On the other hand *Isoetes* may be grossly under-recorded at the present day, due to problems of sampling submerged aquatics.

The Late-Devensian occurrences of pollen of *Sagittaria sagittifolia* at Loch Cill Chriosd (zones LCC-2 and LCC-5) are of interest for this species is not regarded as a native Scottish plant today (Clapham *et al.*, 1962). Although it is primarily a stream and riverside plant, it occurs in shallow reedswamps around the Cheshire meres. Its pollen is also known from Late-Devensian sediments at Oulton Moss, Cumberland (Walker, 1966). In view of its present Scandinavian distribution its occurrence in western Scotland today would be in no way as surprising as some of the recent discoveries of Mediterranean–Atlantic and Southern–Atlantic bryophytes and pteridophytes in western Scotland.

Seeds of *Naias flexilis* occur abundantly in early Flandrian deposits (zone LCC-7) at Loch Cill Chriosd. Although it has several Hebridean localities today, it is not known to occur on Skye at present, but it could easily have been overlooked. According to Backman (1948) it occurs in a wide range of water depths (20–600 cm) and it is indifferent to substrate. It grows best in shallow water, but is apparently restricted to deeper water by competition with larger hydrophytes. Being a submerged annual species, it has a high seed production, in contrast to the majoriy of perennial aquatics that rarely flower, and maintain themselves by vegetative growth. It is a circumpolar species that appears to have been more widely distributed in Europe in the Flandrian (see Map 194 in Hultén, 1958). Its seeds are locally frequent in several Late-Devensian and Flandrian sites in Scotland (H. H. Birks, 1970; Durno, 1958; Vasari & Vasari, 1968). Although its present restriction is commonly regarded as resulting from a climatic deterioration (Godwin, 1956), its distribution and ecology in Scotland today suggest that other factors may be important, for example increased competition due to lake shallowing and hydroseral development.

The present restriction of *Nymphaea alba* (both subspecies) to occasional lochs on Skye is inexplicable in view of its apparently wider extent in the Late-Devensian as judged by its pollen at Loch Cill Chriosd, Loch Fada, and Loch Meodal. Under-recording cannot be invoked in this case. *Nuphar lutea* is also inexplicably rare on Skye today, being restricted to one peaty lochan in northern Skye. Although no specific identifications appear possible on the basis of pollen alone (see Chapter 8) pollen of the genus occurs in the sediments at Loch Fada, Loch Mealt, Loch Meodal, and Loch Cill Chriosd suggesting that the genus occurred in all these lochs in Late-Devensian times. Both *Nuphar* and *Nymphaea* have a wide ecological tolerance in terms of water depth and lake chemistry at the present day, and no reasons can be advanced to explain their present restricted occurrence on Skye.

3. OTHER TAXA

There is a variety of pollen and spore types of several taxa of lowland terrestrial habitats in Late-Devensian sediments at sites in regions of Skye where the taxa do not occur today. Although there is some doubt as to whether some of the taxa grew locally, for example *Campanula* type and *Helianthemum chamaecistus* type, due to the small number of grains found, it is likely that some, if not all, of these taxa did indeed grow outside their present range on Skye. The occurrence of spores of *Ophioglossum vulgatum* at Loch Mealt (zone LM-7) and at Loch Fada (zones LF-5 and LF-6), of *Botrychium lunaria* at all the sites examined, of pollen of *Campanula* type at Loch Cill Chriosd (zone LCC-7), Loch Fada (zone LF-2), and Loch Mealt (zone LM-2), of *Mercurialis perennis* at Loch Cill Chriosd (zone LCC-3), and of *Helianthemum chamaecistus* type at Loch Cill Chriosd (zones LCC-5 and LCC-6) is of considerable floristic interest in view of the present restricted distributions of these taxa on Skye today, and in the case of *Helianthemum*, absence from the island. Although only two pollen grains of *Helianthemum* were found, they are likely to have been locally produced, for Proctor & Lambert (1961) have demonstrated the poor representation of the genus in pollen spectra at the present day. Although some of these taxa will ascend to over 2000 feet (610 m) they are not primarily mountain plants today. It is likely that with the spread of woodland during the Flandrian, associated with soil deterioration and bog development in the lowlands, treeless grassland communities on base-rich soils would have become greatly restricted in areal extent, except in exposed, coastal areas and on shallow limestone soils on steep slopes (Pigott & Walters, 1954). The present restriction on Skye of *Ophioglossum vulgatum* to a single station near Ben Suardal and of *Campanula rotundifolia* to a small area in the Sleat Peninsula may be a result of such factors.

The present restriction of *Helianthemum chamaecistus* in Scotland to well-drained sandy soils of rather low base status in the eastern Highlands and to the limestones on Lismore in Loch Linnhe in the western Highlands is unaccountable in terms of its possible Late-Devensian occurrence on the Isle of Skye, coupled with records of its pollen in Late-Devensian sediments in west Ross (Pennington & Lishman, 1971) and in the Orkneys (Moar, 1969*b*) (both areas are outside its present Scottish range). This serves to emphasise the element of chance that underlies all plant distributions. Similarly, it is difficult to understand what factors could lead to the present restriction of *Mercurialis perennis* on Skye to a single wooded ravine near Loch Bracadale in northern Skye when the limestone pavements of Ben Suardal would seem to have provided an ideal habitat for its survival there since Late-Devensian times.

Spores of *Osmunda regalis* occur in the *Betula–Corylus* zone at Lochan Coir' a' Ghobhainn, Loch Meodal, and Loch Cill Chriosd. Although *Osmunda* does not occur around the shores of these lochs or in the marginal reedswamps of any of these sites today, it occurs in all the main regions on Skye. It is a rather local plant on Skye at present, but with a wide ecological amplitude occurring, for example, on inaccessible ledges by waterfalls, on sheltered ledges on sea-cliffs, in sea-caves, by streams, in mesotrophic mires, and by loch shores. Elsewhere in Britain it also grows in *Phragmites* reedswamps, by rivers, and in wet woods. Although it is widely distributed throughout Britain, it is a lowland plant with its present headquarters in western Ireland. It is markedly southern in its distribution in Scandinavia today and the occurrence of its spores in early Flandrian deposits on Skye contrasts with the first appearance of spores in southern Scandinavia in the late Boreal (Berglund, 1966*b*; Hafsten, 1956). Its local distribution on Skye probably results from its sensitivity and susceptibility to grazing and burning, thereby restricting it to areas protected in some way.

It is difficult to decide whether the single spores of *Lycopodium clavatum* in the sediments at Loch Fada (zone LF-2) and at Loch Mealt (zone LM-5) reflect the local presence of the species near these sites in Late-Devensian times. At present it is restricted on Skye to two areas of unburnt Callunetum vulgaris in the north-western part of the island and to a small area of mixed dwarf-shrub heath in the Sleat Peninsula. Elsewhere in Britain it grows to 2000 feet (610 m) in a range of acidic dwarf-shrub heaths and grasslands, and appears to avoid mire habitats. It often favours rather dry, south-facing slopes and its present restriction on Skye may result from its sensitivity to burning, to which such communities are particularly susceptible, in contrast to the damper, north-facing stands of the Callunetum vulgaris and Vaccineto–Callunetum Associations (see Chapter 4).

It should be emphasised that owing to the limited specific determinatons imposed by pollen morphology, the available floristic evidence is restricted to only a small proportion of the likely Late-Devensian flora. It is highly probable in view of their present restricted range on Skye that there have been distributional changes of, for example, *Arabis alpina*, *Draba norvegica*, *Salix myrsinites*, and *S. phylicifolia*, but unfortunately there is no direct fossil evidence. Many plants within the same floristic elements on Skye appear to have reacted individually to environmental changes, and not in collective units such as communities or floristic elements (cf. Faegri, 1963). This observation draws attention to the need for increased knowledge about present ecotypes, their environmental tolerance, and the degree to which they are in equilibrium with their present environment. It is clear that many factors have been involved in influencing the present Skye flora since Late-Devensian times, and it is evident that in the case of the species within the montane flora for which the fossil pollen record provides abundant evidence, no one single ecological factor, such as maximum summer temperature, can adequately explain both the extinction and presence of certain mountain plants on Skye (cf. Conolly, 1961; Conolly & Dahl, 1970; Dahl, 1951, 1963). Effects of competition, forest development, soil deterioration and bog development, grazing, recent land-use, climatic changes, genetical variability, and ecotypic differentiation (see Andersen, 1961) all appear to have been important factors in influencing the observed floristic changes within the Isle of Skye since Late-Devensian times.

13

THE LATE-DEVENSIAN VEGETATION

1. APPROACHES TO THE RECONSTRUCTION OF PAST VEGETATION

Pollen analysis provides information relevant to the reconstruction not only of the past flora but also of the past vegetation of an area. This is in the form of the numerical data resulting from the counts of the various pollen and spore types present in a stratigraphical series of sediment samples. Some functional relationship is presumed to exist between the number of pollen grains of a particular taxon deposited in the sediment and the abundance of that taxon in the vegetation surrounding the site of deposition (Davis, 1963; Fagerlind, 1952). The function is undoubtedly complex and contains a large number of independent variables including the physiological factors affecting the flowering and pollen production of the individual plant, the abundance and frequency of the taxon within the vegetation, the structure of the community in which it occurs, the mode of pollen dispersal, the meteorological factors influencing pollen transportation, and the physical, chemical, and biological conditions that control pollen sedimentation and preservation at the site of deposition. It is generally considered, however, that the frequency of the pollen of a given taxon is roughly proportional to the abundance of the taxon in the surrounding vegetation, and that gross changes in the numbers of pollen grains and spores (usually expressed as relative frequencies) in a sediment can often be interpreted as indicating corresponding changes in the composition of the vegetation. Because pollen spectra give no direct information about the spatial and temporal composition or distribution of the plant communities that comprise the vegetation of an area, an inferential approach is required to reconstruct the past vegetation. Some of the difficulties inherent in such an approach can, however, be reduced by a thorough knowledge of modern plant communities and the pollen rain that they produce. The consideration of past flora and vegetation is an essential stage in a palaeoecological study, for it is only after a thorough reconstruction of the past landscape, of which the flora and vegetation were an integral, and often a dominant part, that the role and interplay of environmental factors within that landscape – the ecosystem or biogeocoenose – can be inferred from the observed evidence of the sediments and their contained fossils. It is at this stage that notions of past climate can be logically considered.

One approach to the problem of the interpretation of fossil pollen spectra in terms of past vegetation is to compare the fossil assemblages with contemporary pollen spectra from known extant vegetation types (see Chapter 11). If similarities in pollen content and pollen proportions exist between the modern and the fossil spectra, it may be concluded that a similar vegetation produced the fossil assemblage, thereby providing some basis for the reconstruction of past vegetation in terms of modern analogues (McAndrews, 1966). Some qualifications to this approach are, however, needed. A comparison between fossil pollen spectra and modern spectra from the same site of deposition is moderately simple as it only involves a comparison in time rather than one in both time and space. However, the past and present spectra from one site are rarely, if ever, comparable in terms of their pollen content and proportions, thereby posing the question – what type of plant community or range of communities does the fossil spectrum resemble? Present day analogues are therefore sought elsewhere, thereby introducing a transfer in space as well as in time. The simplest situation is one in which the fossil spectrum can be matched in terms of pollen content and proportion with modern spectra which (*a*) are distinctive from all other contemporary spectra, (*b*) refer to a characteristic and homogeneous plant community, and (*c*) are derived from comparable sites of deposition in topographically similar areas (Oldfield, 1970).

If no modern pollen spectra can be found that are comparable with the fossil spectra, the conclusion is drawn that the past vegetation represented by the fossil spectra has no known modern counterpart. The hypothesis chosen to explain the diversity of the

Late-Devensian pollen flora interpreted it as representative of a complex flora of Late-Devensian age. This hypothesis has the corollary that the plant communities present on Skye in Late-Devensian times may have harboured associations of species that were different from any found today. The concept of the 'climax' (Clements, 1936) as a fixed association of plants towards which vegetational change converges under constant climate appears to have little practical utility in the interpretation of pollen diagrams, which frequently illustrate constantly changing combinations and proportions of different taxa. Of greater use is the individualistic concept of vegetation (Gleason, 1939) which recognises the uniqueness of plant communities in space and time, and stresses the behavioural rather than the floristic classification of communities. As it seems highly likely that the combination of edaphic, climatic, and biotic conditions during Late-Devensian times differed from any combination known today, it may be misleading to assume that the same plant association necessarily existed then as at present (Iversen, 1964; Lang, 1967) if the individualistic concept of vegetation is accepted as a working hypothesis.

In some instances the fossil pollen spectra may not only be dissimilar from present day pollen spectra but they may be indicative of more than one plant community. Just as present vegetation is rarely, if ever, a uniform homogeneous cover, it is likely that in Late-Devensian times there was a complex mosaic of plant communities. Each community would have its own floristic composition, structure, and pattern, and each would be associated with a particular habitat and differentiated from each other by factors of topography, soil type, climate, drainage, snow-cover, etc. As the fossil pollen assemblage may represent an integrated pollen rain derived from several plant communities within the area reflected by the pollen rain, comparison with modern spectra from single uniform vegetational types may not be profitable. Further problems and limitations in the comparison of modern and fossil pollen spectra have been discussed in Chapter 11.

A second approach to the reconstruction of the past vegetation from fossil pollen spectra involves application of the known ecological preferences and tolerances of the individual taxa concerned. The assumption is generally made in Quaternary palaeoecology that the morphology and physiology of the present species have not changed significantly since at least the time of the last glaciation (cf. Firbas, 1949). If this assumption is justified, and it is difficult to see how it can be tested and evaluated, then the ecological requirements of the species concerned should be the same today as they were in Late-Devensian times. Many plant species today contain a great number of ecotypes, each with slightly different ecological tolerances. As the distinction between ecotypes cannot be made from fossil evidence, care must therefore be taken in any attempt at the reconstruction of past vegetation that argues from present-day ecological observations and geographical ranges, for it is the ecotype rather than the morphological species that is the basic ecological unit within a plant community. Furthermore, the present ecological tolerances of some species may be broader in the absence of competition than they are in its presence, whereas deficiencies in the habitat requirements of particular species may have been compensated by other environmental factors that do not now operate at the same intensity within the present geographical range of the species (Faegri in Lang, 1967). The latter possibility is a great problem in the interpretation of Late-Devensian pollen assemblages, since it is highly probable that both climate and soil were radically different from present conditions, but that it is exactly these differences that are of the greatest interest to the palaeoecologist. It is therefore essential to consider the 'species' in its broadest ecological sense to embrace a range of ecotypes from a variety of regions within the present geographical range of the species (Iversen, 1964) and, if possible, to base any palaeoecological conclusions on several taxa within the fossil assemblage and not on any single taxon (Andersen, 1961; Iversen, 1954, 1964; cf. Brown, 1971).

The attempt to group the Late-Devensian pollen types into communities that presumably existed at or near the site of deposition is further hindered by the broad ecological amplitude of many of the taxa involved. The abundant pollen types of Gramineae, Cyperaceae, *Salix*, and Ericaceae undiff., all of which must have been present in the Late-Devensian vegetation and which together form the bulk of the pollen rain, can be found today in a wide variety of communities and habitats ranging from lowland mires to montane summit-heaths. From the pollen spectra alone, no deductions can be made about which habitats were the most important sites for each of these taxa. For information about the communities and the habitats present, one must consider the minor components of the pollen rain and attempt to find taxa whose present environmental and sociological amplitudes are sufficiently restricted ('indicator species') that some inferences can be made about the composition of the past vegetation.

The ultimate but still remote desideratum in Quaternary palaeoecology is the compilation of quantitative data on the production of pollen by individual species throughout their present range, on pollen dispersal and sedimentation, on lake sedimentation and pollen accumulation rates, and on the environmental parameters that control the flowering distribution, and ecology of the species. Then one might be in a position to analyse and to interpret the fossil record of individual taxa through a stratigraphical sequence, in terms of interactions between species, and possibly to infer past changes in the environment.

It is, however, impossible to proceed along these lines at present, because the pertinent palynological and autecological data are lacking. Much of our knowledge about the ecology of particular species comes, not from experimental autecological studies, but from studies of the floristics of whole vegetational types accompanied by observations on environmental parameters. A study of modern plant communities may be as informative about the ecological requirements of individual species as a detailed autecological investigation. One limitation on the use of modern autecological data is that the competition factor may not be considered. The use of groups of taxa that have similar ecological and sociological tolerances today rather than the reliance on a single 'indicator species' may be more valuable in reconstructions of past communities, for, as the fossil record is traced back in time, the problem of ecotypic differentiation becomes more and more acute. There is likely to be less chance that such differentiation has occurred in a group of taxa than in a single taxon. An arrangement of the species composition of the major plant communities on Skye into taxa with similar sociological amplitudes today (Table 4.57) thus provides a useful frame of reference for the reconstruction of past vegetation (see Janssen, 1967*a*, 1970).

A third approach to the reconstruction of past communities from the fossil pollen record involves the use of quantitative models. If an assemblage of fossils consistently occurs in a series of samples within and between stratigraphic sequences, interspecific associations or 'recurrent groups' can be derived statistically from the observed fossil data using some coefficient of similarity (Fager, 1957). Such an approach has been used in the reconstruction of past communities from fossil assemblages of marine invertebrates (Fox, 1968; Johnson, 1962; Valentine & Mallory, 1965; Valentine & Peddicord, 1967), of microplankton (Brideaux, 1971), and of Permian pollen and spores (Clapham, 1970*a*, 1970*b*). In these instances, however, the unit of study, namely the fossil assemblage, is assumed to be closely related in space to the death assemblage or thanatocoenose, and thus to the life assemblage or biocoenose (Lawrence, 1968), whereas in Quaternary pollen analysis much of the pollen and spore rain that enters the site of deposition and thereby forms the death and subsequently the fossil assemblage is derived from an indefinable source area and life assemblage. There is thus no simple spatial relationship between a fossil pollen assemblage and the life assemblage of plants that produced it. Recurrent groups of fossil pollen and spores can only, therefore, refer to 'associations' in time, whereas the Quaternary palaeoecologist is concerned with the association of taxa both in time and in space. Although such quantitative approaches may be valuable in particular Quaternary palaeoecological problems, they do not appear to be applicable to the present study.

The approaches adopted here to the problems of the interpretation of the pollen record from Skye in terms of past vegetation are based in part on the comparative approach using the modern surface sample data derived from a range of montane communities today (see Chapter 11), and in part on the use of indicator species and stratigraphically related taxa both within a profile and between profiles. Some idea of the former abundance of the taxa concerned can be gained from comparisons between the representation of the taxa in modern pollen assemblages and the observed pollen percentages in the fossil spectra. Comparisons between the fossil assemblage treated as a whole with modern pollen spectra can provide some idea of the past vegetation, in broad physiognomical terms at least, whereas the use of indicator species can permit more precise interpretations of the fossil assemblages in terms of particular plant associations. At best these approaches provide a rather imperfect picture of the former vegetation of Skye during Late-Devensian times, and it should be emphasised that the reconstructions and interpretations presented are subject to the qualifications, limitations, and assumptions indicated above.

2. INFERRED VEGETATIONAL HISTORY AT LOCH MEODAL

I. GRAMINEAE–*RUMEX* ASSEMBLAGE ZONE (zones LML-1 and LML-2)

The low values (2.9–6.9%) of arboreal pollen (*Betula* undiff. and *Pinus*) throughout the Gramineae–*Rumex* zone (Plate 1) indicate that the landscape was virtually treeless at this time. The tree pollen present in the sediments probably resulted from long-distance transport. By analogy with modern plant communities and recent pollen spectra, the fossil pollen assemblages recorded in this and the overlying zones represent at least three vegetational and habitat types, as there are a wide variety and abundance of pollen and spores of taxa that are today characteristic of montane shrub and dwarf-shrub heaths and acid woodlands, of species-rich grasslands and willow scrub, and of aquatic communities. The simplest hypothesis to explain this admixture of ecological elements proposes that there was a mosaic of vegetational types around the site. Such a mosaic may have been controlled and maintained by differences in topography, soil type, and moisture, just as the present mosaic of plant communities near the loch appears to be (see Chapter 9 and Fig. 13). Dwarf-shrub heaths may have been widespread on the poor, acidic soils around the site, and the species-rich grasslands with willows may have been locally frequent on the richer, flushed soils, such as on irrigated slopes and along stream courses. The aquatic communities would have been restricted to permanently waterlogged and submerged habitats.

Although the relative frequencies of Ericaceae pollen are rather low in this zone (4.3–11%), they probably reflect quite extensive stands of dwarf-shrubs, considering the poor pollen representation of many members of the Ericaceae in modern pollen spectra (see Chapter 11). Associated species in the dwarf-shrub communities may have included *Betula nana* (pollen and macrofossils), *Empetrum nigrum*, *Juniperus communis*, *Cryptogramma crispa*, and *Lycopodium selago*, with members of the Cyperaceae and Gramineae, and the mosses *Hylocomium splendens*, *Polytrichum juniperinum*, *Rhacomitrium* spp., and *Sphagnum*. This assemblage is closely similar, both in floristic composition and, as far as can be assessed from relative pollen frequencies, in species abundance, to the Phyllodoco–Vaccinetum myrtilli and the Hylocomieto–Betuletum nanae Associations within the order Deschampsieto–Myrtilletalia (Dahl, 1956; Nordhagen, 1943). These communities occur today in the low-alpine zone in Scandinavia in oligotrophic chionophilous or seasonally wet sites on stable soils that are frequently podsolised. Related communities occur locally in areas of prolonged snow-lie in Scotland today but in contrast to the Scandinavian communities, the Scottish communities, including the Skye stands of the *Nardus stricta–Vaccinium myrtillus* snow-patch Association (Table 4.38), lack *Betula nana* (McVean & Ratcliffe, 1962). The surface sample data presented in Chapter 11 and Plate 6 are based solely on British vegetation and they do not therefore provide any information on the relative representation of *B. nana* in the modern pollen rain when it grows in such communities. Analyses by H. H. Birks (1969) of surface samples from bog communities in the central Highlands in which *B. nana* is a prominent component indicate that the plant has a moderately good pollen representation. The modern representation data presented by Iversen (1945) and Fredskild (1967) from a range of communities containing *B. nana* in Greenland are comparable to the Scottish results. The presumed local presence of *B. nana* at Loch Meodal at this time is supported by the occurrence of macrofossils in zones LML-1 and LML-4.

Juniperus communis was probably present in the dwarf-shrub communities around Loch Meodal during the time of zone LML-1, perhaps restricted to sheltered habitats, although its low pollen frequencies may reflect the widespread occurrence of the prostrate but poorly flowering *Juniperus communis* ssp. *nana*, such as occurs in either extremely chionophobous or extremely chionophilous situations today (see Chapter 11). The low but consistent values of *Artemisia* cf. *A. norvegica* pollen in this zone suggest that small areas of open 'fell-field' occurred nearby, probably on extremely wind-exposed rock-knolls with little or no winter snow cover.

Communities dominated by grasses and *Salix* spp. and with a wide variety of associated species appear to have been locally prominent during the time of zone LML-1, perhaps favouring the more fertile and irrigated deep brown earth soils along the stream courses. *Salix* spp. (not *S. herbacea*) were probably frequent, for despite the low pollen values in this zone (0.9–4.0%), they undoubtedly reflect the local occurrence of willows (see Chapter 11). The relative frequencies of *Rumex acetosa*, *Ranunculus acris* type, and *Thalictrum* pollen, and of Polypodiaceae undiff. (including *Dryopteris filix-mas* type and *Thelypteris phegopteris*), *Selaginella selaginoides*, and *Botrychium lunaria* spores suggest that these taxa were prominent in the local vegetation. They may have been associates of *Salix* on the damp, fertile sites, although the dwarf pteridophytes may have favoured slightly more open sites of reduced competition. The low but consistent values of *Epilobium* type, *Plantago maritima*, *Potentilla* type, *Saussurea alpina*, *Succisa pratensis*, and *Thymus* type pollen are suggestive of the local occurrence of these taxa at this time, along with members of the Caryophyllaceae, Cruciferae, Liguliflorae, and Papilionaceae. These taxa may have been associates of either the *Salix*-dominated communities or the dwarf-shrub communities, as many of them occur in a wide range of montane vegetational types today, and there are no obvious stratigraphical features to suggest particular associations. These willow-dominated communities may have resembled in floristic composition the *Salix lapponum* communities that occur in Scotland today (McVean & Ratcliffe, 1962 and Chapter 11) and the Norwegian sub-alpine and low-alpine association Rumiceto–Salicetum lapponae (Dahl, 1956) and related Scandinavian communities (Nordhagen, 1927, 1943). The present restriction of the Scottish *Salix* stands to ungrazed cliff-ledges limits any palaeoecological deductions being drawn from their present Scottish ecology. In Scandinavia, however, the community commonly occurs in a mosaic of shrubs on non-calcareous soils in the sub-alpine and low-alpine regions (Du Rietz, 1950) in a transitional zone of short snow-lie (Gjaerevoll & Bringer, 1965). In such situations today, juniper and dwarf birch favour the drier, poorer soils whereas the willows thrive on the wetter and richer sites, often in areas where the soil is flushed by snow melt-water. In general terms, the fossil assemblage of dry-land taxa in zone LML-1 is thus interpreted as representing a vegetation similar to the characteristic shrub-dominated mosaic of communities of the sub-alpine and low-alpine zones in Scandinavia today.

The high inorganic content of the sediments in zones LML-1 and LML-2 implies a discontinuous vegetational cover within the catchment area of the loch, resulting in soil erosion and minerogenic deposition in the loch. Occasional bands of interstratified terrestrial mosses, especially in zone LML-2 (Fig. 14), possibly result from inwashing of soil from the slopes around similar to that described from Loch Fada (H. J. B. Birks, 1970). Wave erosion of the loch margins may also have contributed to the minerogenic deposition, for the local aquatic flora and vegetation appears to have been rather sparse at this time. The fossil assemblage of aquatic taxa includes spores of *Isoetes echinospora*, pollen of *Myriophyllum alterniflorum*, *Nymphaea*, *Potamogeton* type, *Potamogeton* (*Coleogeton*), and *Sparganium* type, and the algae *Botryococcus* and *Pediastrum*. The assemblage suggests that the loch was moderately eutrophic. Although *Isoetes echinospora* is primarily a species of oligotrophic lakes today, it appears to have a wide chemical tolerance (Seddon, 1965; cf. Lang, 1955, 1967). Little is known about the ecology of the two algae recorded but they tend to avoid the poorest waters (Salmi, 1963; Whiteside, 1965) and are commonly planktonic, but in shallow water *Pediastrum* may also occur as an epiphyte on aquatic macrophytes (Lund, 1961).

The *Juniperus* assemblage subzone (zone LML-2) is generally similar to the previous subzone (zone LML-1) in its pollen content and relative percentages, except for the increased frequencies of *Juniperus communis* pollen (9.6–14%) and, to some degree, of *Betula* undiff. pollen, and an absence of *Lycopodium selago* spores. The high values of *Juniperus* pollen are interpreted here as reflecting improved flowering of juniper, rather than an increased number of bushes (see Chapter 11), perhaps as a result of reduced snow-lie in the growing season. The willow- and grass-dominated communities appear to have changed little in this subzone, although *Angelica* type, *Cerastium alpinum* type, and *Saxifraga aizoides* pollen are recorded for the first time. Some or all of these taxa may have been growing locally in these communities.

The overall vegetation of the region during the time of the Gramineae–*Rumex* zone at Loch Meodal is thus visualised as a mosaic of sub-alpine and low-alpine shrub communities similar in floristic composition to those occurring on mildly basic soils above the tree-line in Scandinavia today, and differentiated ecologically by habitat factors such as topography, soil basicity, irrigation, and snow-cover.

2. *BETULA* ASSEMBLAGE ZONE (zone LML-3)

The high percentages of *Betula* undiff. pollen associated with macrofossils of *Betula pubescens* in this zone are interpreted as reflecting the development of birch woodland near the site. It is not possible to distinguish the two subspecies of *B. pubescens* on the basis of the macrofossils, but the majority of the pollen found in the sediments of this zone falls within the size range of modern *B. pubescens* ssp. *odorata* pollen (Birks, 1968). This subspecies is the predominant taxon of northern and western Britain today.

It is difficult to evaluate the role of *Populus tremula* in the local vegetation at this time from the low pollen percentages found in this zone. Lichti-Federovich & Ritchie (1965) report high values of pollen of *P. tremuloides* Michx. in atmospheric samples in Canada, and low values in recent limnic sediments. This disparity has been ascribed to the poor preservation of *Populus* pollen in sediments (Sangster & Dale, 1961, 1964). In north-west Europe there is little evidence to suggest that *P. tremula* has a high pollen production (Heim, 1970; Mullenders, 1962). There are also no indications to suggest that *Populus* pollen is particularly susceptible to exine corrosion (see Cushing, 1967*b*). The suggestion presented by Cushing that exine thinning and crumpling may limit its determination in fossil sediments seems a more realistic explanation for the low *Populus* pollen values in surface samples, Jørgensen (1963) has demonstrated that differences in *Populus* pollen frequencies in similar samples are primarily due to excessive crumpling, and that this can occur as a result of different chemical treatments in sediment preparation. The low values of *Populus tremula* pollen in this zone at Loch Meodal may therefore be suggestive of the local presence of the tree, perhaps in openings within the birch woods. Aspen is a light demanding tree, and on Skye today it is generally restricted to steep talus slopes, ungrazed ledges on cliffs, or in ravines below 1200 feet (365 m). It occurs on a range of rock types, but generally avoids the Durness limestone. In Scandinavia it ascends to the sub-alpine zone, but it is frequently dwarfed and sterile there (Selander, 1950).

The decreased frequencies of *Betula* cf. *B. nana* and *Juniperus communis* pollen in zone LML-3 indicates that woodland development may have occurred on the base-poor, well-drained sites, perhaps in sheltered areas, thereby shading out these shrubs. There is no change in the percentages of *Salix* pollen, suggesting that there was probably little, if any, reduction in the areal extent of the willow-dominated communities. The consistent occurrence, with moderate percentages, of pollen of Ericaceae, *Betula* cf. *B. nana*, *Potentilla* type, *Melampyrum*, and Rubiaceae, of spores of *Blechnum spicant*, *Dryopteris filix-mas* type, *Polypodium*, *Thelypteris dryopteris*, and *T. phegopteris*, and of remains of the moss *Hylocomium splendens* in this zone may reflect, in part at least, the composition of the woodland understorey. The fossil assemblage is broadly similar to modern pollen spectra from birch woodlands occurring in the Sleat Peninsula today (see Chapter 11 and Plate 6), although *Betula nana* does not grow in such communities either on Skye or anywhere in Scotland today. The occurrence of *B. nana* confers floristic affinities with the modern subalpine birch forests of acid soils in Scandinavia described by Du Rietz (1950), Hämet-Ahti (1963), Leach & Polunin (1932), and Nordhagen (1927, 1943). However, the fossil assemblage differs from the modern Scandinavian counterparts (for example the subalpine *Empetrum* type; Hämet-Ahti, 1963) in its abundance of ferns, perhaps reffecting more oceanic conditions. Sub-alpine birch woods rich in ferns occur in western Scandinavia today (Hämet-Ahti, 1953; Knaben, 1950), but they frequently lack *Betula nana*. The occurrence of fern sporangia in the sediments of this zone is further indication of the abundance of pteridophytes in the vegetation at this time.

Little change in floristic composition appears to have occurred in the *Salix*-dominated communities of the damp, rich sites in this zone. Pollen of *Filipendula* (probably *Filipendula ulmaria*), *Valeriana officinalis*, and *Viburnum opulus* are first recorded in this zone, and in view of their modern ecological and sociological preferences, they may well have occurred in these communities. There is an absence of pollen and spores of several montane taxa in this and the succeeding zones, such as *Artemisia* cf. *A. norvegica*, *Cerastium alpinum* type, *Saussurea alpina*, *Saxifraga aizoides*, and *Selaginella selaginoides*. The majority of these taxa do not occur today in the Sleat, and possible causes for their extinction are discussed in Chapter 12. The reduced relative frequencies of *Rumex acetosa*, *Ranunculus acris* type, Gramineae, and *Thalictrum* pollen may be artefacts resulting from an increased absolute pollen production by the communities on the poor soils, rather than from a real decrease in their contribution to the total pollen rain. If this explanation is correct, one would expect the percentages of *Salix* pollen to be similarly depressed. This is not the case, however, but in the absence of measurements of pollen influx (pollen accumulation per unit area per unit time) the problem remains unresolved. The occurrence of pollen of *Plantago lanceolata* and *Plantago major*/*P. media* in this zone suggest that grassland communities lacking trees and shrubs must have persisted locally to provide habitats for these shade-intolerant herbs.

The high organic content of the sediments in this zone (Fig. 14), and the low silt and sand content suggest that there was little influx of mineral material into the loch, thereby indicating soil stability and a stable landscape within the catchment. Macrofossils of *Carex rostrata* and *Juncus articulatus/J. acutiflorus* indicate that some marginal reed-swamp development occurred, perhaps with *Equisetum*. This would also result in some stabilisation around the shores of the loch. Pollen and spores of aquatic taxa in this zone include *Isoetes echinospora*, *I. lacustris*, *Littorella uniflora*, *Nymphaea*, *Potamogeton* type, *Ranunculus trichophyllus* type, and *Sparganium* type. This assemblage is similar to the present flora of the loch (Fig. 7) and it suggests that the water was oligotrophic at the time of zone LML-3. *Botryococcus*, *Pediastrum*, and a variety of diatoms are moderately abundant in this zone, but in the absence of specific determinations, little can be deduced from these fossils about the palaeolimnology of the loch. The interpretation of the oligotrophic status of the loch is supported, however, by the occurrence of the planktonic cladoceran *Bosmina* cf. *B. coregonii* in this and the succeeding zones, as it is considered by Goulden (1964) and Goulden and Frey (1963) to be indicative of rather base-poor waters today.

3. *BETULA NANA* ASSEMBLAGE SUBZONE OF THE GRAMINEAE–*RUMEX* ZONE (zone LML-4)

The inwash of fine and coarse sand and gravel into the loch throughout the time of deposition of the *Betula nana* assemblage subzone (zone LML-4), with a corresponding decrease in the percentage organic content of the sediments (Fig. 14), implies that soil erosion occurred locally, and that there was therefore an incomplete vegetational cover in the catchment area. The pollen assemblage, with tree pollen values considerably lower than in the previous zone, reflects a revertence, to some extent, towards a treeless low-alpine shrub-dominated vegetation. The assemblage differs, however, from the assemblages recorded from zones LML-1 and LML-2 in the high frequencies (6.1–10%) of *Betula* cf. *B. nana* pollen, and in the absence of pollen and spores of several montane and northern taxa such as *Artemisia* cf. *A. norvegica*, *Lycopodium selago*, and *Selaginella selaginoides*. *Rumex acetosa*, *Ranunculus acris* type, Cruciferae, and *Thalictrum* pollen attain relative values comparable to those in zones LML-1 and LML-2.

The vegetational picture is thus one of reduced woodland cover and increased landscape instability. The reduction in the woodland cover may have resulted in the increased expression in the pollen rain of understorey species such as *Betula nana*, whose local presence in this zone is confirmed by macrofossils, and to the development of *Betula nana* heath (Leach & Polunin, 1932; Nordhagen, 1936). *Juniperus communis* pollen values are very low in this zone, indicating that this shrub may have been virtually eliminated from the area by competition with trees in the preceeding *Betula* zone, and that it was apparently unable to recolonise lost ground. Despite the low percentages of *Betula* undiff. pollen (5.9–6.7%), tree birches may have persisted locally, as evidenced by the presence of macrofossils of *Betula pubescens* in this zone. Sheltered ravines and south-facing slopes may have provided suitable microhabitats for its survival.

There are few indications of changes in the floristic composition of the grassland willow-dominated communities in this zone, except for increased relative frequencies of Gramineae, *Rumex acetosa*, *Thalictrum*, and *Ranunculus acris* type pollen. *Filipendula* and *Valeriana officinalis* pollen are virtually absent, however, suggesting a reduction in the abundance of these taxa in the zone. *Artemisia* undiff. pollen attains low but consistent percentages in the zone, but in view of the high production and wide dispersal of *Artemisia* pollen (Bent and Wright, 1963; Maher, 1963), it is difficult to assess whether the low pollen frequencies at Loch Meodal imply the local presence of the genus. *Artemisia* species (other than *A. norvegica*) appear to have been extremely rare on Skye in Late-Devensian times, as they are today, in contrast to assemblages of correlative age further south and east where pollen values of 10% or more are frequently found (Godwin, 1968; Iversen, 1954; Lang, 1952; Van der Hammen, 1951). The genus is generally xerophilous in Europe today (Andersen, 1961; Iversen, 1954), and it is possible that suitable habitats with dry, well-drained soils were extremely limited in north-west Scotland in the Late-Devensian, due to prolonged snow-lie and high soil-moisture. Despite the marked changes in sediment lithology in this zone there is little evidence for any changes in the flora of the loch, except for the first occurrence of *Nuphar* and *Sparganium* cf. *S. minimum* pollen. Neither of these two taxa are indicative of any changes in the trophic status of the loch, as they can occur in a wide variety of lake types in Scotland today.

4. *BETULA–CORYLUS* ASSEMBLAGE ZONE (zone LML-5)

The *Betula–Corylus* zone is characterised by tree pollen values of 36% or more, consisting primarily of *Betula* undiff. and *Corylus avellana* pollen, and of low consistent percentages of *Pinus*, *Populus tremula*, and *Sorbus aucuparia* pollen. It is difficult to decide whether the *Pinus* pollen values (4.5–8.2%) imply the local presence of pine, or whether they result from long-distance transport of pollen. The isolated grains of *Alnus*, *Quercus*, and *Ulmus* in this zone are interpreted, however, as the result of long-distance dispersal. The high percentage of tree pollen is considered to reflect the extensive development of woodland in the environs of the site. *Corylus avellana* pollen expands rather rapidly after its first appearance at the opening of the zone and there is a reciprocal fall in *Salix* pollen values. This may indicate that hazel colonised the richer sites that were formerly occupied by willows and 'tall herbs' whereas birch-dominated woodland developed on the poorer soils. *Populus tremula* and *Sorbus aucuparia* have a wide edaphic tolerance at the present day, and they could have occurred in either woodland type during the time of this zone. Comparisons between the percentages of *Corylus* pollen in this zone and in modern spectra from hazel-dominated woods on Skye, suggest that hazel was the dominant canopy species in these woods, and that it was not growing as an understorey shrub (see Chapter 11). The low but consistent frequencies of *Angelica* type, *Caltha* type, *Filipendula*, *Succisa pratensis*, and *Urtica* pollen suggest that the relevant taxa may have occurred in the hazel woods, as *Angelica sylvestris*, *Caltha palustris*, *Filipendula ulmaria*, *Succisa pratensis* and *Urtica dioica* all occur today in wooded 'tall herb' communities on Skye (see Tables 4.47 and 4.57). The understorey in the birch woods was probably rather similar to that of the woods that developed in zone LML-3, except that in the present zone *Betula* cf. *B. nana* and *Juniperus communis* pollen are virtually absent. Pollen of Ericaceae, *Melampyrum*, *Potentilla* type, and Rubiaceae, and spores of *Blechum spicant*, *Dryopteris filix-mas* type, *D. carthusiana* type, *Polypodium*, *Thelypteris dryopteris*, and *T. phegopteris* probably reflect the floristic character of understorey of the birch woods. Such an assemblage is very similar to the present birch woodlands that occur in the Sleat Peninsula today (Tables 4.45 and 4.49).

Betula undiff. and *Corylus avellana* pollen attain their maximum values in the zone between 725 and 730 cm depth. Virtually no pollen or spores of shade-intolerant taxa occur above these levels, suggesting that the woodland cover was virtually continuous around the site, thereby considerably restricting any treeless habitats. It is of interest that *Populus tremula* pollen attains its highest values in the lower part of this zone that is characterised by rapidly rising tree pollen values.

Organic muds accumulated in the loch throughout the zone. The absence of any coarse minerogenic material in the sediments (Fig. 14) reflects the overall stability of the landscape concomitant with the development of woodland within the catchment area of the loch. The aquatic assemblage as a whole indicates that, as in the previous zone, the loch water was base poor. The high values of *Isoetes lacustris* microspores suggest that there were extensive beds of *Isoetes* in the loch, probably on silty substrata and associated with *Littorella uniflora*. The consistent occurrence of pollen of *Nymphaea*, *Nuphar*, *Potamogeton* type, *Ranunculus trichophyllus* type, *Sparganium* type, and *Sparganium* cf. *S. minimum*, of spores of *Equisetum*, and of seeds of *Juncus articulatus*/*J. acutiflorus* suggests that communities of macrophytes occurred locally on organic substrata, perhaps in sheltered inlets, and that marginal fen communities were beginning to form around the shore. The fossil assemblage of aquatic taxa is similar, but not identical, to the present aquatic flora of the loch (Fig. 7).

Osmunda regalis spores are recorded for the first time in the zone. As discussed in Chapter 12, it has a wide ecological tolerance today. It may, therefore, have grown locally around the loch, as it does today around the nearby Loch Gauscavaig, or in the wetter woodland communities.

3. INFERRED VEGETATIONAL HISTORY AT LOCH FADA

I. *LYCOPODIUM*–CYPERACEAE ASSEMBLAGE ZONE (zone LF-1)

The extremely high values of herb pollen in this zone at Loch Fada (Plate 2) indicate that the landscape at the time of this zone was treeless and virtually shrubless. The inorganic nature of the sediments throughout the zone (silts and fine sands) is likely to have resulted from inwashing following soil erosion and instability on the slopes around the loch, suggesting that there was an incomplete vegetational cover. Comparisons of the fossil spectra of this zone with the modern pollen spectra from Scotland (Plate 6 and Table 11.3) indicate a close resemblance between the fossil spectra and modern spectra from low-alpine summit-heath communities (Caricetea curvulae) and from snow-patch and snow-bed communities (Salicetea herbaceae). It is difficult to distinguish these two broad vegetation types on the basis of pollen spectra alone (Chapter 11 and Table 11.3), but the absence of spores of the pteridophytes *Cryptogramma crispa* and *Athyrium alpestre*, and the very low relative frequencies of Ericaceae pollen in the fossil assemblage from Loch Fada suggest that chionophilous vegetation was not common near the site. The consistent occurrence of

Artemisia cf. *A. norvegica* pollen in moderate frequencies in this zone provides strong indications for the presence of chionophobous vegetation, as *A. norvegica* is exclusive to the *Juncus trifidus–Festuca ovina nodum* in Scotland today (McVean & Ratcliffe, 1962). This community and the related *Festuca ovina–Luzula spicata nodum* (Chapter 4 and Table 4.36) are the characteristic vegetation types of wind-blasted open 'fell-field' habitats at high altitudes in north-west Scotland today. The abundance of moss fragments of *Rhacomitrium* spp. (mainly *R. lanuginosum*) in the sediments of this and the succeeding zone (Fig. 16) may indicate the dominance of *Rhacomitrium* heath near the site at this time. *Rhacomitrium* heath (Cariceto–Rhacomitretum lanuginosi Association) is also a markedly chionophobous community at the present day on Skye and elsewhere in north-west Scotland (see Chapter 4).

The abundance of pollen of Cyperaceae and Gramineae, of spores of *Lycopodium selago*, of leaves and pollen of *Salix herbacea*, and of moss fragments of *Hylocomium splendens*, *Polytrichum alpinum*, and *Rhacomitrium* spp. suggest that these taxa were prominent components of the vegetation. The occurrence of *Antennaria* type, *Artemisia* cf. *A. norvegica*, Cruciferae, *Oxyria digyna*, *Ranunculus acris* type, *Rumex acetosa*, *Sagina*, *Saussurea alpina*, *Saxifraga hypnoides*, *S. stellaris*, *Silene* cf. *S. acaulis*, *Solidago* type, and *Thalictrum* pollen, of *Botrychium lunaria* and *Selaginella selaginoides* spores, and of the mosses *Andreaea rupestris* and *Antitrichia curtipendula* in this zone may also indicate their presence locally.

By reference to modern montane communities in Scotland, the vegetation around Loch Fada at the time of this zone can thus be visualised as an extensive *Rhacomitrium* heath with grasses and *Carex* spp., *Lycopodium selago*, *Salix herbacea*, *Antennaria dioica* (or *Gnaphalium supinum*), *Hylocomium splendens*, and *Polytrichum alpinum*. Small areas of wind-blasted 'fell-field' may have occurred locally with *Artemisia norvegica*. A species-rich heath may have occurred in suitable habitats, with *Botrychium lunaria*, *Ranunculus acris*, *Saxifraga hypnoides*, *Selaginella selaginoides*, *Silene acaulis*, *Solidago virgaurea*, *Thalictrum alpinum*, and *Antitrichia curtipendula* (cf. Polygoneto–Rhacomitretum lanuginosi Association; McVean & Ratcliffe, 1962; see also Böcher, 1937). Unstable basalt screes may have provided suitable habitats for *Oxyria digyna*, *Sagina*, members of the Cruciferae, and *Andreaea rupestris* (see Basalt Scree Communities, Table 4.2). Montane spring communities with *Saxifraga stellaris*, *S. hypnoides*, and the hygrophilous mosses *Dichodontium pellucidum* and *Drepanocladus exannulatus* may have occurred locally around spring-heads (cf. Philonoto–Saxifragetum stellaris Association; Table 4.30).

In general the overall vegetation may have been very similar to the mosaic of community types that occurs above 2000 feet (610 m) on the summit ground of The Storr today. In Scandinavian terminology, the vegetation was of mid- or low-alpine character in floristic composition and physiognomy. There are, however, some indications that communities with 'tall herbs' may have occurred during the time of this zone as there is pollen of *Angelica* type, *Rumex acetosa*, *Saxifraga aizoides*, and *Saussurea alpina*, and spores of Polypodiaceae undiff. Grass-dominated swards rich in 'tall herbs' could have occurred locally on deep, fertile soils in sheltered irrigated sites, for example along streams and in rocky gullies. With the exception of occasional grains of *Myriophyllum alterniflorum* and *Potamogeton* type, and scattered colonies of *Botryococcus* and *Pediastrum*, the loch appears to have supported few biota at this time.

2. GRAMINEAE–*RUMEX* ASSEMBLAGE ZONE (zones LF-2 to LF-5)

The Gramineae–*Rumex* zone at Loch Fada (Plate 2) differs markedly from the previous pollen zone in its pollen and spore composition, being dominated throughout by pollen of Gramineae, and with a wide variety of pollen and spore types that are absent from the *Lycopodium*–Cyperaceae zone. Several of the characteristic pollen and spore types of the *Lycopodium*–Cyperaceae zone are extremely rare or absent in this zone, for example *Lycopodium selago*, *Artemisia* cf. *A. norvegica*, *Salix* cf. *S. herbacea*, and *Saxifraga stellaris*.

There is a thin but conspicuous layer of high organic content (Fig. 16) rich in bryophyte remains interstratified into the silts and sands of zone LF-2, 2.5 cm above the lower boundary of the Gramineae–*Rumex* zone. A detailed pollen diagram for the interval 613 to 627 cm and an interpretation of the origin of this bryophyte layer has been presented elsewhere (H. J. B. Birks, 1970), but a brief summary is given here as it provides valuable information about the type of vegetation present around Loch Fada at this time. There is a group of microfossils characteristic of the bryophyte layer including *Caltha* type, *Epilobium* type, *Sagina*, *Saxifraga stellaris*, *Stellaria* undiff., and *Succisa pratensis*, abundant fungal hyphae, fungal fruit bodies of the genus *Microthyrium* (see Godwin & Andrew, 1951) and testaceous rhizopods, a high proportion of indeterminable: corroded and deteriorated: corroded pollen, and remains of the bryophytes *Acrocladium sarmentosum*, *A. cuspidatum*, *Bryum*, *Dichodontium pellucidum*, *Drepanocladus exannulatus*, *Pohlia* cf. *P. wahlenbergii*, and *Rhytidiadelphus squarrosus* (see Fig. 2 in H. J. B. Birks, 1970). Although some of these bryophyte taxa can occur in marginal fen and lakeside communities today, the majority are characteristically terrestrial species, suggesting that the bryophyte layer represents material washed into the loch from the surrounding slopes. The micro- and macro-fossil assemblage suggests a derivation from the distinctive oligotrophic bryophyte-dominated montane spring community Philonoto–Saxifragetum stellaris (Table 4.30, and McVean & Ratcliffe, 1962), with the occurrence of pollen of the association constants *Saxifraga stellaris* and *Stellaria alsine* (*Stellaria* undiff. pollen). A modern pollen spectrum from such a community resembles the fossil spectra in its pollen content and pollen proportions.

The bryophyte layer is thus interpreted as being derived from such a spring community, and it probably represents detached masses of the bryophyte carpet that were dislodged by seasonal flooding, washed into the loch, and incorporated into the accumulating silts. The bryophyte mass may have brought into the loch its associated soil fungal hyphae, microfauna, and pollen spectra, thereby introducing into the sediments pollen that had been previously exposed to aerial oxidation and microbial attack. Such oxidative processes have been shown experimentally to lead to exine corrosion similar to that found in the bryophyte layer (Elsik, 1966; Havinga, 1964, 1967). The high proportions (50–60%) of indeterminable: corroded pollen in this layer contrasts with the preponderance of indeterminable: degraded pollen (71%) in the minerogenic silts of the rest of zones LF-1 and LF-2.

Comparisons of the fossil pollen spectra of the *Selaginella* subzone of the Gramineae–*Rumex* zone (zone LF-2) with modern spectra (Plate 6 and Table 11.3) suggest that sub-alpine species-rich grasslands and 'tall herb' communities, dominated by prolific pollen producers such as *Deschampsia cespitosa*, were probably the principal vegetation types near Loch Fada during the time of this sub-zone. The inorganic nature of the sediments indicates that soil erosion and instability were frequent, however, suggesting that the vegetational cover was far from continuous. The rich floristic assemblage recorded in the subzone suggests that at least two contrasting vegetational types were common.

The high frequencies of pollen of *Ranunculus acris* type, Cruciferae, *Thalictrum*, and *Solidago* type, and of spores of *Selaginella selaginoides*, and the less frequent occurrences with low percentages of *Saussurea alpina*, *Lotus* cf. *L. corniculatus*, *Saxifraga oppositifolia*, *S. hypnoides*, *Cerastium alpinum* type, *Arenaria* type, *Silene* cf. *S. acaulis*, and *Campanula* type pollen, of *Botrychium lunaria* spores, and of the mosses *Antitrichia curtipendula*, *Distichium capillaceum*, *Hylocomium splendens*, and *Rhacomitrium* spp. may reflect the floristic composition of an open, low-growing species-rich turf. *Betula nana* and *Empetrum nigrum* may also have occurred locally. The pollen taxa that are indicative of a species-rich turf occur in similar proportions as in surface samples from the low-alpine Dwarf herb *nodum* (Plate 6), described from the Scottish Highlands by McVean & Ratcliffe (1962). This community is rather rare on Skye today, but small stands occur at high altitudes (above 2000 feet, 610 m) in Trotternish and on Blà Bheinn (see Table 4.40 and Chapter 4). The *nodum* typically occurs on steep, well-drained, brown earths soils, that are periodically flushed by mineral downwash from unstable rock outcrops. The stands generally experience moderate snow cover in the winter, with rapid melting in early spring. Comparable communities occur widely on basic rocks in Scandinavia, for example the *Potentilla crantzii–Polygonum viviparum* Association within the low-alpine Potentilleto–Polygonion vivipari Alliance (Nordhagen, 1927, 1936).

On more stable, wetter and deeper soils, such as along stream banks and in hollows, 'tall herb' communities may have been present. Judging by their percentages in this subzone, *Salix*, *Rumex acetosa*, *Saussurea alpina*, and ferns may have been prominent components. Pollen of *Angelica* type, *Epilobium* type, Liguliflorae, *Rubus saxatilis*, and *Sedum* cf. *S. rosea* may also originate from such communities, for *Angelica sylvestris*, *Epilobium montanum* and *Chamaenerion angustifolium*, *Crepis paludosa*, *Rubus saxatilis*, and *Sedum rosea* occur with high constancy and fidelity in sub-alpine and low-alpine 'tall herb' communities (Adenostyletalia) on Skye today (Tables 4.47, 4.57) and in Scandinavia (Nordhagen, 1927, 1936, 1943). The mosses *Acrocladium cuspidatum*, *Hylocomium splendens*, and *Rhytidiadelphus squarrosus* may have been associates in this community. 'Tall herb' communities occur locally on ungrazed, base-rich cliff ledges above about 1000 feet (305 m) in Trotternish today.

The occasional grains of *Artemisia* cf. *A. norvegica* and spores of *Lycopodium alpinum* and *L. selago* in this subzone suggest that small areas of open 'fell-field' may have persisted on particularly exposed sites, such as low-lying rock-knolls or on summit plateaux.

The moderate frequencies of *Myriophyllum alterniflorum* and *Potamogeton* type pollen, the scattered grains of *Nymphaea* and *Sparganium* cf. *S. minimum*, and the occurrence of diatoms, *Pediastrum*, *Botryococcus*, and a variety of cladocera indicate that the loch became increasingly productive during the time of this subzone in contrast to its low biological content in the previous zone. The presence of the cladoceran *Bosmina longirostris* suggests that the loch was both eutrophic (Goulden, 1964; Goulden & Frey, 1963) and deep (Megard, 1964, 1967).

The *Juniperus* subzone (zone LF-3) appears to reflect a phase of more continuous vegetational cover and increased soil stability. Growth of shrubs, such as *Juniperus communis*, *Salix*, and *Betula nana*, suggest that conditions were less extreme than in previous zones. Judging by their representation in modern pollen spectra, the frequencies of *Juniperus communis* and *Salix* pollen in this subzone indicate that these shrubs were probably quite frequent at this time. In view of their present ecological tolerances, they may have occurred in different communities and on soils of differing moistures. The scattered grains of *Populus tremula* in the subzone suggest that this tree was present locally, and despite its rather low pollen frequencies *Betula nana* must have occurred nearby, as its macrofossils occur in the sediments of this subzone. It is difficult to decide whether the low percentages of *Betula* undiff. pollen reflect local tree development in particularly favourable sites, or whether they are the result of long-distance pollen transport. The consistency of the *Betula* undiff. pollen curve at Loch Fada and in the correlative subzone at the nearby Loch Mealt (Plate 3) discourages the notion of long-distance dispersal.

The 'tall herb' communities that were discussed in the consideration of the previous subzone show little change during the time of the *Juniperus* subzone, although the relative frequencies of *Salix* pollen are slightly reduced, and pollen of *Filipendula*, *Stellaria holostea*, and *Urtica* are recorded for the first time towards the end of the subzone. The fossil assemblage closely resembles the *Salix lapponum–Filipendula ulmaria* sub-alpine communities described from Norway by Nordhagen (1927, 1943). The species-rich turf communities were probably reduced in areal extent during *Juniperus* subzone time by the development of juniper scrub and by greater soil stability. This may explain the reduction in the relative frequencies of *Botrychium lunaria* and *Selaginella selaginoides*. Both these dwarf pteridophytes favour rather open turf on Skye today, as they appear to be intolerant of competition from tall-growing herbs and grasses. Pollen of *Alchemilla*, *Dryas octopetala*, *Plantago major*/*P. media*, *Plantago maritima*, *Potentilla* type, and *Thymus* type are first recorded from this subzone. It is probable that these pollen are derived from taxa that occurred in the species-rich turf, as many of these taxa favour open, grassland communities today (see Table 4.57). The occurrence of pollen of *Plantago major*/*P. media* is of interest, as *Plantago major* primarily occurs today on Skye in heavily trampled anthropogenic habitats (*Lolium perenne–Plantago major* Association; Table 4.5) although it is also known in one stand of coastal shingle-beach vegetation (see Chapter 5), whereas *P. media* is not known to occur in north-west Scotland at the present-day. The moderately high frequencies of this pollen type in Late-Devensian sediments at Loch Fada and at the other sites examined imply the local presence of one or other or both of these taxa on Skye during Late-Devensian times. The pollen of these two species are not readily distinguishable from each other in fossil spectra (Chapter 8), but all the fossil grains that were determinable at Loch Fada and at the other sites on Skye were referred to *P. major*. The single grain of *Saxifraga nivalis* in the *Juniperus* subzone may originate from the species-rich turf community, for although it is primarily a plant of shaded base-rich rock-crevices on Skye and elsewhere in the Scottish Highlands, the Southern Uplands, Lakeland, the northern Pennines, and north Wales, it can occasionally occur in open species-rich grassland on steep, flushed slopes, for example on Creag Mhor and Ben Lawers in Perthshire and in the Ben Alder range in west Inverness. Increased competition and/or climatic changes may have been responsible for the apparent disappearance of several montane taxa during this subzone. Pollen of *Artemisia* cf. *A. norvegica*, *Cerastium alpinum* type, and *Silene* cf. *S. acaulis*, although present in moderate frequencies in the *Selaginella* subzone, are absent from the *Juniperus* subzone and the overlying subzones.

The first continuous curves of *Empetrum* cf. *E. nigrum* and Ericaceae pollen and the first appearance of *Sphagnum* spores occur in the *Juniperus* subzone. They may all be indicative of the onset of soil deterioration and leaching around Loch Fada. Similar changes in soil conditions during Late-Weichselian (Late-Devensian) times are discussed by Berglund (1966*a*), Berglund & Malmer (1971), and Iversen (1954).

In contrast to the previous subzone, the loch appears to have supported a diverse flora and fauna in this subzone. Pollen of *Myriophyllum alterniflorum*,

Potamogeton type, *Nymphaea*, *Sparganium* type, *Callitriche*, *Ranunculus trichophyllus* type, *Littorella uniflora*, and *Potamogeton* (*Coleogeton*), oospores of *Nitella*, abundant *Pediastrum*, *Botryococcus*, and diatoms, statoblasts of the bryozoa *Cristatella mucedo* and *Plumatella*, and remains of cladocera including *Daphnia* and *Bosmina longirostris* give some indication of the aquatic organisms that lived in the loch at this time. The majority of these taxa are indifferent to lake trophic status and water chemistry today (see Fig. 7), but *Potamogeton* (*Coleogeton*–either *P. filiformis* or *P. pectinatus*) and *Bosmina longirostris* suggest that the loch water was base-rich. The absence of any extensive development of aquatic plant communities at Loch Fada at this time compared with the picture at the nearby Loch Mealt (Plate 3) may result from the steep topography of Loch Fada, rather than the low basicity of the water or an unfavourable climate.

The *Betula* subzone (zone LF-4) differs primarily from the previous subzone in the increased relative frequencies of *Betula* undiff. pollen (7.7–9.4%). The higher percentages may reflect the local development of copses of tree birches in favourable, sheltered habitats such as rocky gullies and south-facing slopes as occurs today in parts of southern Greenland and Iceland (Anderson *et al.*, 1966; Böcher, 1954; Hansen, 1930). The predominant vegetation types at the time of this subzone were probably the same as in the previous subzone, with juniper scrub, 'tall herb' communities, and species-rich grassland. Although the vegetation was probably low-alpine or sub-alpine in its floristic composition and physiognomy, it is likely that factors such as wind-exposure may have limited tree growth rather than low temperature. Pollen of *Filipendula* and *Urtica* occur in this subzone, and both *Filipendula ulmaria* and *Urtica dioica* are considered to be thermophilous species (Iversen, 1954). Although *F. ulmaria* occurs in the low-alpine zone in Scandinavia today, it is rare and usually sterile above the sub-alpine zone (Nordhagen, 1943; Selander, 1950). *Populus tremula* and *Sorbus aucuparia* may also have been present locally. The percentages of *Pinus* pollen in the Gramineae–*Rumex* zone and the other zones at Loch Fada are so consistently low that they are almost certainly the result of long-distance transport, using the criteria proposed in Chapter 12.

The 'tall herb' communities do not appear to have changed to any extent in this subzone, although pollen of *Cirsium*/*Carduus*, *Silene dioica* type, *Valeriana officinalis*, and *Vicia*/*Lathyrus*, and spores of *Thelypteris dryopteris* occur for the first time. *Thelypteris dryopteris* may have occurred in these communities, but by analogy with its present ecology it would have favoured the poorer soils. The species-rich turf communities appear, however, to have been further reduced in areal extent, as indicated by the decreased contributions of Gramineae, Cruciferae, *Ranunculus acris* type, and *Thalictrum* pollen to the total pollen rain. This restriction may have resulted either from further development of shrub-dominated vegetation or from further soil acidification in the less intensely flushed sites. Leaching and soil acidification would encourage the development of dwarf-shrub heaths. The pollen of *Empetrum* cf. *E. nigrum*, Ericaceae, and Rubiaceae, the spores of *Lycopodium annotinum*, *L. selago*, and *Polypodium*, and remains of the mosses *Plagiothecium undulatum*, *Pleurozium schreberi*, and *Sphagnum* in this subzone may reflect the occurrence of such heaths. There is little evidence to suggest any such change in the flora or fauna of the loch during the *Betula* subzone.

The *Betula nana* subzone (zone LF-5) is interpreted as reflecting a revertence to a predominantly shrub vegetation and to conditions of incomplete vegetational cover, resulting in soil erosion and the deposition of silt and fine sand in the loch. Such tree growth as occurred during the time of the previous subzone was reduced, whereas *Betula nana* clearly expanded. The high relative frequencies of *Betula* cf. *B. nana* pollen (7.1–11.8%) in this subzone are accompanied by macrofossils of *B. nana* in the sediments. There are no changes in the relative frequencies of *Salix* undiff. pollen, but the values of *Juniperus communis* pollen are slightly reduced. The reduction in the relative frequencies of *Juniperus* pollen may result from an absolute increase of other components of the pollen sum tending to suppress, on a percentage basis, the juniper pollen values rather than reflecting a real change in the influx of *Juniperus communis* pollen into the site at this time.

As *Betula nana* only occurs in bog habitats today in Britain, no obvious modern analogues exist within the British Isles. *Betula nana* occurs in a variety of habitats and vegetational types in Scandinavia today, but unfortunately there are no relevant surface sample data. Any reconstruction of the vegetation represented by the pollen assemblages of this subzone must therefore be extremely tentative. As discussed in Chapter 12, the present ecology of *B. nana* and *Juniperus communis* in sub-alpine and low-alpine vegetation in Scandinavia is rather similar. It is therefore difficult to understand what environmental factors could result in an expansion of *Betula nana*, but not of

Juniperus communis, as appears to have occurred during the time of the *Betula nana* subzone. There is no evidence to indicate that *Juniperus* had become restricted due to extensive development of woodland (cf. zones LML-3 and LML-4 at Loch Meodal). Judging from the published relevés, *Betula nana* appears to tolerate and flower in a wider range of conditions of exposure, snow-cover (see Fig. 23 in Nordhagen, 1927), altitude, and soil type in Scandinavia than does *Juniperus communis*. Its wide ecological tolerance may result from the marked adaptability of its shoot system, varying from large bushes 1 m or more in height to the low-growing prostrate form of exposed sites (Leach & Polunin, 1932). *Betula nana* has a shorter reproductive cycle than does juniper, and its seedlings can colonise a wider range of soil types than juniper seedlings can. It is therefore likely that under conditions of deteriorating climate, *Betula nana* may have a selective advantage over *Juniperus communis*. From the fossil assemblage at Loch Fada, it is not clear what environmental factors may have been operative at the time of the *Betula nana* subzone, but evidence from correlative zones at other sites suggests that an increase in snow-lie and a lowering of temperature may have occurred at this time. It is possible that *Betula nana*-dominated snow beds (cf. Hylocomieto–Betuletum nanae and Ptilidieto–Betuletum nanae Associations; Dahl, 1956) were widespread in Trotternish at the time of this subzone. *Juniperus communis* is intolerant of long snow-cover in Scandinavia today (Nordhagen, 1943). The landscape may thus have been of a low-alpine character (Hansen, 1930; Nordhagen, 1943). However, an increase in exposure associated with a lowering of temperature could also have favoured an expansion of *Betula nana* at the expense of *Juniperus communis*, considering the wide ecological tolerance of *B. nana* in Scandinavia today. There is no way to decide from the available evidence which of these hypotheses is the correct one.

The increase in the relative frequencies of *Ranunculus acris* type, Cruciferae, and *Thalictrum* pollen suggest that the species-rich turf communities may have expanded during the time of the *Betula nana* subzone, perhaps as a result of soil instability on steep slopes. The occasional grains of *Cerastium* cf. *C. holosteoides* in this subzone are of interest, in view of the present ecology of this taxon on Skye. The spores of *Cystopteris fragilis* in this subzone may have originated from the nearby basalt cliffs, or from areas of large basalt blocks. Remains of the saxicolous moss *Mnium orthorhynchum* also occur in this subzone. Spores of *Ophioglossum vulgatum* occur consistently in this subzone. The open species-rich turf communities may have provided an ideal habitat for this dwarf pteridophyte. Remains of *Mnium pseudopunctatum* are also recorded from this subzone. This moss grows today in the marginal-fen communities at the south end of the loch, but it also occurs in the rather unusual habitat of moist, flushed cliff-ledges at The Storr. The low frequencies of *Artemisia* undiff. pollen in this subzone do not necessarily imply the local presence of the genus at this time. There is little evidence to suggest that there were any changes in the aquatic flora of the loch during the time of the *Betula nana* subzone, despite the marked changes in sediment lithology and composition.

3. *BETULA–CORYLUS* ASSEMBLAGE ZONE (zone LF-6)

This zone is characterised by tree pollen values between 10.5 and 38.8%. These values are interpreted as reflecting the local development of birch and hazel scrub (see Chapter 11, Table 11.3, and Plate 6). The presence of *Betula pubescens* at this time is confirmed by the occurrence of its macrofossils in the sediments. The relative tree pollen frequencies in this zone are lower than in the correlative zone at Loch Meodal (zone LML-5), suggesting that woodland development may not have been as extensive in Trotternish as it was in the Sleat. A similar differentiation exists between the two regions today (see Figs. 5, 6), as discussed in Chapter 5. The relative values of *Corylus avellana* pollen are slightly higher than the values of *Betula* undiff. pollen at Loch Fada, whereas at Loch Meodal the reverse is the case. The apparent success of hazel in the Trotternish area may have been a result either of its tolerance to wind-exposure, or, more likely, of the favourable fertile, basic soils of the basalt. *Populus tremula* and *Sorbus aucuparia* appear to have been present locally. *Salix* undiff. pollen shows little change in the relative frequencies from the previous zone, whereas *Betula* cf. *B. nana* and *Juniperus communis* pollen values decline gradually throughout the zone. Willow thickets with 'tall herbs' may have persisted in sites that were too wet for tree growth. Grass- and 'tall herb'-dominated communities appear to have been frequent throughout the time of this zone, although the stands may not have been as rich in species composition as they were during the time of the Gramineae–*Rumex* zone. Pollen of *Angelica* type, *Cirsium*/*Carduus*, *Filipendula*, *Valeriana officinalis*, and *Vicia*/*Lathyrus* occur consistently, and *Heracleum sphondylium* and *Trifolium* pollen are first recorded from this zone. The relevant taxa are likely to have grown together in ungrazed 'tall herb' communities during the time of this zone, just as they do today in suitable localities in northern Skye (see Tables 4.47, 4.57).

The low content of silt and fine sand in the sediments of this zone (Fig. 16) suggests that there was little soil erosion and instability within the catchment area, indicating that there was a continuous vegetational cover on the slopes around the loch. A rich and diverse assemblage of fossil remains of aquatic and wetland taxa are recorded in this zone, including leaf spines of cf. *Ceratophyllum*, seeds of *Juncus articulatus/J. acutiflorus* and *Juncus effusus/J. conglomeratus*, sheaths of *Equisetum*, head-shields of *Bosmina longirostris*, and an abundance of the diatom *Melosira arenaria* var. *hungarica*. The occurrence of *Ceratophyllum* and of *Bosmina longirostris* suggests that the loch was moderately base-rich at this time, as it is today (see Fig. 7).

4. PRE-QUATERNARY MICROFOSSILS, POLLEN PRESERVATION, AND SEDIMENT LITHOLOGY

The minerogenic sediments of zones LF-1 and LF-2 contain up to 13% pre-Quaternary microfossils and up to 11% indeterminable: deteriorated pollen (Plate 2). As discussed in Chapter 9, exine degradation (*sensu* Cushing, 1964*b*, 1967*b*; H. J. B. Birks, 1970) accounts for 71% of the indeterminable category in these two zones, and pollen breakage 22%. The category of pre-Quaternary microfossils consists primarily of pollen and spores of Jurassic age (see p. 255), but also some pollen and spores of Tertiary age, and a variety of dinoflagellates, hystrichosphaerids, and acritarchs. The frequencies of pre-Quaternary microfossils and of indeterminable: deteriorated pollen are low in zones LF-3, LF-4, and LF-6, but they are slightly higher in the silty muds of zone LF-5. There is thus a close correspondence between the sediment lithology, the frequencies of indeterminable: deteriorated pollen, and the occurrence of pre-Quaternary microfossils, with high values of indeterminable and pre-Quaternary types tending to occur in minerogenic sediments.

Iversen (1936) first drew attention to the association of pre-Quaternary microfossils with minerogenic sediments. The relationship of poorly preserved pollen, whether it be primary or secondary, with minerogenic sediments has been noted by several workers. Iversen (1942) comments that poorly preserved pollen with a 'fused' appearance, evidently similar to the degraded type, is characteristic of till samples, and Heinonen (1957) reports that pollen in till is often broken, crumpled, and worn thin. Cushing (1964*b*, 1967*b*) has demonstrated that spectra containing a high proportion of pre-Quaternary microfossils largely contain degraded pollen, and that pollen with degraded exines most commonly occur in minerogenic sediments. Experimental work on pollen deterioration has largely concentrated on corrosion, microbial, and oxidative effects (Elsik, 1966, 1971; Havinga, 1964, 1967, 1971; Sangster & Dale, 1961, 1964), and there appears to have been little work on mechanical effects (Faegri, 1971). Pollen breakage and exine degradation may result from mechanical damage due to physical abrasion and compression. It is perhaps significant that R. M. Peck (unpublished data) has found that modern pollen entering lakes by stream transport is often poorly preserved, and that the major forms of deterioration are breakage and exine degradation.

The occurrence of pre-Quaternary microfossils in moderately high frequencies in zones LF-1 and LF-2 suggests that reworking and redeposition of pollen and spores from earlier deposits may have been important during the deposition of the silts and fine sands of zones LF-1 and LF-2. While it is clear that the Jurassic and Tertiary pollen and spore types in these zones are secondarily derived, what fraction of the remainder of the total fossil assemblage, both determinable and indeterminable, is also secondarily derived is unknown. It does not appear possible to distinguish qualitatively or quantitatively the primary and secondary components of the pollen assemblage that occurs in the minerogenic sediments at Loch Fada on the basis of the kind and extent of pollen deterioration alone. The most likely sources for the silts and fine sands, and therefore for the secondary microfossils, in the sediments of zones LF-1 and LF-2 are the till fragments and the more extensive head and landslip deposits that occur around the loch. These deposits are locally rich in fragments of Tertiary lignite and of Jurassic coal, sandstone, and shale. No unoxidised samples of these drifts have been found, and it has not therefore been possible to apply a quantitative subtraction method to estimate the proportions of the primary and secondary components in the pollen assemblage (cf. Iversen, 1936, 1942; Suggate & West, 1959). It is possible that the high frequencies of broken and degraded pollen in the minerogenic sediments may have resulted merely from physical damage of primary pollen incurred during stream transportation into the loch (cf. Faegri, 1971), rather than from several cycles of redeposition. Processes of pollen deterioration and sedimentation are so variable and so little understood that more information, both experimental and observational, is needed before the full significance of the various forms of pollen deterioration in fossil spectra can be interpreted.

4. INFERRED VEGETATIONAL HISTORY AT LOCH MEALT

The pollen stratigraphy at Loch Mealt (Plate 3) has the same general characteristics as that at the nearby Loch Fada, and as a result the same pollen assemblage zones can be recognized at the two sites. To avoid repetition, only the salient and contrasting features of the pollen stratigraphy at Loch Mealt will be discussed and interpreted here.

1. *LYCOPODIUM*–CYPERACEAE ASSEMBLAGE ZONE (zone LM-1)

The pollen spectra (Plate 3) and the nature of the sediments (Fig. 18) in this zone suggest a phase of widespread chionophobous low-alpine *Rhacomitrium*-heath, of unstable soils, and of incomplete vegetational cover. The heath communities appear to have been rather species-rich with *Salix herbacea*, *Ranunculus acris* type, *Botrychium lunaria*, *Selaginella selaginoides*, *Hylocomium splendens*, *Polytrichum alpinum*, and *Rhacomitrium* spp. Pollen of *Artemisia* cf. *A. norvegica* suggest that areas of open, wind-blasted 'fell-field' may have occurred locally. The relative frequencies of *Betula* cf. *B. nana* and Ericaceae pollen imply the local presence of these taxa, perhaps in small shrub-dominated snow-patches in sheltered hollows. The loch appears to have been virtually devoid of aquatic macrophytes at the time of this zone.

2. GRAMINEAE–*RUMEX* ASSEMBLAGE ZONE (zones LM-2 to LM-6)

The pollen assemblage recorded in this zone suggests that a mosaic of vegetational types rather comparable to that described from Loch Fada may have also existed around Loch Mealt at the time of this zone. The *Selaginella* subzone (zone LM-2) is interpreted as reflecting a widespread rather open, low-alpine or sub-alpine species-rich grassland, perhaps favouring well-drained soils, whereas in wetter situations 'tall herb' communities with *Rumex acetosa*, *Saussurea alpina*, other members of the Compositae, and ferns may have occurred locally, perhaps with some *Salix*. A wide variety of pollen and spore types of taxa that occur today in open montane grassland communities are recorded in this subzone, including *Botrychium lunaria*, *Campanula* type, *Plantago maritima*, *Polygala*, *Polygonum viviparum/P. bistorta*, *Potentilla* type, *Ranunculus acris* type, Rubiaceae, *Saxifraga hypnoides*, *S. oppositifolia*, *Selaginella selaginoides*, *Solidago* type, *Succisa pratensis*, and *Thalictrum*. The moss *Barbula icmadophila* may have grown either in this community or on dry rock outcrops, as it does today at The Quirang and The Storr. The occasional grains of *Artemisia* cf. *A. norvegica* suggest that open 'fell-field' areas may have persisted locally, perhaps in particularly exposed sites or at high altitudes. The occurrence of several grains of *Koenigia islandica* at 585 cm and 590 cm, associated with pollen of *Sagina* and with high values of Cyperaceae pollen suggests that open gravel flush communities, perhaps similar to the present *Carex demissa–Koenigia islandica nodum* (see Chapter 4 and Table 4.30), occurred within the catchment of the site. As discussed in Chapter 11 the absence of *Koenigia islandica* pollen in moss polsters collected near stands of this community on Beinn Edra, and the abundance of *Koenigia islandica* pollen in the wet silts of one such flush suggest that pollen spectra from these *Koenigia* communities may be incorporated into lake sediments by inwashing of silts and clays, rather than by direct aerial dispersal. The occurrence of coarse organic detritus and of terrestrial moss fragments in the sediments at the level of the *Koenigia* pollen in Loch Mealt lends support to this hypothesis. The loch appears to have become increasingly productive during the time of this subzone, with fossil remains of *Myriophyllum alterniflorum*, *M. spicatum*, *Potamogeton* type, *Isoetes lacustris*, *Littorella uniflora*, *Sparganium* type, *Potamogeton* (*Coleogeton*), *Nitella*, *Botryococcus*, *Pediastrum*, and diatoms.

Juniperus communis, although poorly represented in the pollen spectra of zone LM-2, was probably locally frequent in the vegetation at the time of the *Juniperus* subzone (zone LM-3), as its pollen frequencies attain values of 5% or more. The other shrubs present, *Salix* and *Betula nana*, may also have been frequent components of the vegetation. The expansion of *Juniperus communis* at this time may indicate a general climatic amelioration (Iversen, 1954). The other communities appear similar to those that may have occurred during the time of the *Selaginella* subzone, although the low content of silt and fine sand in the sediments (Fig. 18) suggest that there was less soil erosion, and, perhaps, a more continuous vegetational cover during *Juniperus* subzone times than formerly.

The occurrence of pollen of *Spergula arvensis* in this subzone is of interest, as the plant is exclusively a species of man-made artificial habitats on Skye today. However, it is recorded from 'natural' communities in Iceland growing with *Koenigia islandica* on open, moist gravels and silt (Thoroddsen, 1914). The increasing frequencies of *Myriophyllum alterniflorum* and *M. spicatum* pollen in this subzone, associated with abundant macrofossils of *Myriophyllum* and oospores of *Chara* and *Nitella* suggest that extensive beds of submerged aquatics may have developed at this time in the gently sloping and rather shallow inlets on the western shore of the loch near the coring site (cf. Loch Fada). The aquatic flora and fauna were clearly diverse, with abundant macrophytes, algae, Chironomidae, Cladocera, and Bryozoa, the latter probably occurring on the submerged macrophytes.

As discussed in the interpretation of the pollen stratigraphy at Loch Fada, it is difficult to assess the significance of the slightly higher relative frequencies of *Betula* undiff. pollen that characterise the *Betula* subzone (LM-4). It is possible that they are the result of some tree growth near the site in particularly sheltered and favourable localities. In contrast to the stratigraphy at Loch Fada, the values of *Juniperus communis* pollen decrease in this subzone at Loch Mealt. The causes of this decrease are not clear. Communities with 'tall herbs' appear to have been quite widespread during the time of this subzone, as they are today around the site (see Fig. 17 and Chapter 5). Pollen of *Angelica* type, *Cirsium/Carduus*, *Filipendula*, *Sedum* cf. *S. rosea*, *Urtica*, *Valeriana officinalis*, and *Vicia/Lathyrus* as well as pollen of the commoner taxa previously recorded in zones LM-2 and LM-3 are present in the *Betula* subzone. All these taxa occur today in 'tall herb' communities in northern Skye (see Tables 4.47 and 4.57). Pollen of *Thalictrum*, *Ranunculus acris* type, *Potentilla* type, *Rubiaceae*, and *Plantago major/P. media*, and spores of *Botrychium lunaria* and *Selaginella selaginoides* in this subzone suggest that open grassland communities were widespread at this time, but they do not appear to have been as rich in species as at Loch Fada. The absence from the Loch Mealt sediments of pollen of many of the more exacting basiphilous herbs which are present in correlative zones at Loch Fada, and the higher frequencies of *Empetrum* cf. *E. nigrum* and Ericaceae pollen at Loch Mealt suggest that soil leaching and acidification may have occurred more widely near Loch Mealt. The immediate surroundings of Loch Mealt are gentler and topographically more subdued than those of Loch Fada, and it is therefore probable that at Loch Mealt pedogenic processes of nutrient enrichment by flushing, either wet or dry (*sensu* Dahl, 1956), could not counteract the effects of leaching, whereas at Loch Fada the steep slopes and the continual addition of mineral material from unstable rock outcrops would have maintained a high soil fertility. A similar differentiation in the surrounding vegetation of the two sites can be seen today, with widespread bog communities near Loch Mealt (Fig. 17) in contrast to the grassland communities on the steep, well-drained sites around Loch Fada (Fig. 15).

Besides the extensive development of aquatic vegetation in the loch at this time, marginal fen communities appear to have been present, as remains of *Acrocladium giganteum*, *Bryum*, *Campylium stellatum*, *Drepanocladus revolvens*, and *Sphagnum palustre* occur in this subzone. This bryophyte assemblage suggests floristic affinities with present-day communities of either the Sphagno–Tomenthypnion or the Eriophorion latifoliae Alliances (see Chapter 4 and Table 4.57).

Whatever tree growth that occurred during the time of the *Betula* subzone appears to have been reduced during the time of the succeeding *Betula nana* subzone (zone LM-5). The inwash and deposition of silt and fine sand suggests that the soils were unstable, perhaps as a result of incomplete vegetational cover. Such soil disturbances may have resulted in nutrient enrichment in the grassland communities, for the relative frequencies of pollen and spores of several basiphilous taxa attain values in this subzone, comparable to those recorded in the *Juniperus* and *Selaginella* subzones, but considerably higher than the values noted in the previous *Betula* subzone. Pollen and spores in this group include *Botrychium lunaria*, *Polygonum viviparum/P. bistorta*, and *Saxifraga oppositifolia*, and, to some degree, *Ranunculus acris* type, *Selaginella selaginoides*, and *Thalictrum*. The single grain of *Saxifraga nivalis* recorded in this subzone may indicate the local presence of this species, perhaps occurring in the open turf communities, as at Loch Fada. On more stable, and possibly more acid soils, heath communities with *Betula nana*, *Juniperus communis*, *Empetrum nigrum*, and members of the Ericaceae may have been locally frequent. 'Tall herb' communities appear to have persisted throughout the time of the *Betula nana* subzone, although they may have been less rich in species and with a reduced cover of willows at this time. The decrease in frequencies of *Myriophyllum* pollen and of other aquatic organisms in this subzone may have resulted from shallowing of the bays by sediment deposition, thereby restricting the number of suitable habitats for submerged aquatics near the coring site. As little is known about the factors that influence the flowering of aquatic macrophytes and their pollen representation in modern situations, any interpretation of the observed Late-Devensian changes at Loch Mealt can only be tentative.

There are very few vegetational changes discernable in the pollen stratigraphy of the succeeding *Juniperus* subzone (zone LM-6), except for an apparent change in shrub dominance. The cessation of extensive minerogenic sedimentation in the loch occurs during the time of this subzone, suggesting a more stable landscape and a more continuous vegetational cover than in the previous *Betula nana* subzone. As discussed in the interpretation of the *Betula nana* subzone at Loch Fada, it is difficult, with our present knowledge of the ecology of the two shrubs, to explain these changes in shrub dominance, assuming that the observed changes in relative pollen frequency reflect changes in plant abundance. In view of the present-day ecology of juniper and its modern pollen representation (see Chapter 11), it is likely that the pollen stratigraphy of this subzone reflects a transitional phase prior to the development of open woodland in the succeeding zone.

3. *BETULA–CORYLUS* ASSEMBLAGE ZONE (zone LM-7)

The increased relative frequencies of *Betula* undiff. and *Corylus avellana* pollen in this zone (zone LM-7) at Loch Mealt are interpreted as reflecting the development of woodland near the site. The local presence of *Betula pubescens* is indicated by macrofossils in this zone. The tree pollen percentages are similar to those in the correlative zone at Loch Fada, but they are considerably lower than those found at Loch Meodal (Plate 1) or Loch Cill Chriosd (Plate 4). In view of the occurrence of their pollen in this zone at other sites on Skye, it is likely that *Populus tremula* and *Sorbus aucuparia* were present near Loch Mealt. However, the pollen types were not distinguished during the analyses of samples from this site. It is possible that the continuous record of Rosaceae undiff. pollen in this zone at Loch Mealt may consist largely of pollen of *Sorbus aucuparia*. The rather low percentages of tree pollen in this zone suggest that, as at Loch Fada, woodland was not extensive at this time, and was probably restricted to sheltered localities. Such woodland that did occur appears to have developed largely at the expense of the grassland and heath communities of the well-drained sites rather than at the expense of the 'tall herb' and willow communities, judging by the observed changes in pollen percentages. Pollen of *Potentilla* type and *Melampyrum*, and spores of *Polypodium* and *Lycopodium annotinum* in this zone may have been derived from the field layer of the woods. Several 'tall herbs', whose pollen are frequent in this zone, may have also occurred in these woods. The abundance of pollen of *Salix*, *Filipendula*, *Heracleum sphondylium*, and *Urtica*, and of spores of Polypodiaceae undiff. in this zone suggest that 'tall herb' communities may have been locally frequent, for example on sites that were too wet or too exposed to allow tree growth. It is possible that 'tall herb' communities may also have occurred in the drier parts of the marginal fen on the western shore of the loch, as they do today.

The loch appears to have supported a rich aquatic flora and fauna at the time of this zone. *Potamogeton* type is the principal pollen type present, although pollen of *Littorella uniflora*, *Menyanthes trifoliata*, *Potamogeton* (*Coleogeton*), and *Sparganium* type are also present. Algal remains are abundant, with large numbers of *Botryococcus* and *Pediastrum* colonies, abundant diatoms, and occasional oospores of *Nitella*. The fossil assemblage is similar, but not identical, to the present aquatic flora of the loch (Fig. 7), suggesting that the trophic status at the time of this zone may have been similar to the present status of Loch Mealt.

5. INFERRED VEGETATIONAL HISTORY AT LOCH CILL CHRIOSD

Loch Cill Chriosd lies on the contact between the granites of the Beinn na Caillich range to the north and the Durness limestones of Ben Suardal to the south (Fig. 19). It is likely that the sediments and their contained pollen and spore assemblages are derived from both of these contrasting areas. The sediment lithology (Fig. 20 and Plate 4) supports this hypothesis as several layers of coarse non-calcareous sand are intercalated within calcareous silts and fine detritus muds. In attempting to reconstruct the past vegetation from the fossil assemblages recorded in the sediments at Loch Cill Chriosd, it is necessary to distinguish between the two areas.

Zone LCC-1 (Plate 4) is characterised by high frequencies of indeterminable: deteriorated pollen and spores. As discussed in Chapter 9, exine degradation and pollen breakage accounts for 88% of the indeterminable category in this zone, and the majority of the indeterminable grains may have been Cyperaceae pollen that were too poorly preserved to permit reliable determinations. The high frequencies of degraded pollen on this zone and, to a lesser extent, at the 430 cm level in zone LCC-5, are associated with the presence of coarse sand (0.6–2 mm diameter) in the sediments. Pollen degradation and breakage in these samples may have resulted from physical abrasion and mechanical damage, either during pollen transportation in the inflowing streams or during diagenesis. Little can be deduced about the vegetation that existed near the site at the time of zone LCC-1 except that the composition and the frequencies of the determinable pollen and spores in the zone indicate open, herbaceous vegetation that was probably similar to that represented by the pollen assemblage of the succeeding zone.

I. *LYCOPODIUM*–CYPERACEAE ASSEMBLAGE ZONE (zone LCC-2)

Comparisons of the fossil pollen spectra in the *Lycopodium*–Cyperaceae zone at Loch Cill Chriosd with modern pollen spectra from Scotland (Plate 6 and Table 11.3) suggest that the principal vegetational type represented by the fossil assemblage was similar in floristic composition to the low-alpine snow-bed Cryptogrammeto–Athyrietum chionophilum Association (McVean & Ratcliffe, 1962) and to communities of the Cryptogrammo–Athyrion alpestris Alliance (Gjaerevoll, 1950, 1956; Nordhagen, 1936, 1943) as spores of the indicator taxa *Cryptogramma crispa* and *Athyrium alpestre* (type) are consistently present. The community today is restricted in Scotland to bouldery areas with prolonged snow-lie above 1500 feet (765 m), and it is possible that this community was widespread during the time of this zone in the snow-covered block screes below the corries of Beinn na Cailleach. It is likely, in view of the terminal moraine features in Coire Beithe, that small corrie glaciers were present at this time. Besides *Athyrium alpestre* and *Cryptogramma crispa*, possible associated taxa in this community whose fossil remains occur in this zone include *Empetrum nigrum*, *Hylocomium splendens*, *Lycopodium selago*, *Polytrichum alpinum*, *Rhacomitrium* spp., *Salix herbacea*, and members of the Cyperaceae, Gramineae, and Ericaceae. The scattered grains of *Saxifraga stellaris* and *Caltha* type suggest that montane spring communities (Cardamino–Montion Alliance) may have occurred locally, perhaps in areas fed by snow meltwater, as both *Saxifraga stellaris* and *Caltha palustris* are characteristic of such communities today (see Tables 4.30, 4.57).

A wide variety of pollen and spore types of taxa that are characteristic today of calcareous or, at least, base-rich soils, is recorded, and it is likely that the fossil assemblage reflects, to some degree, the composition of the vegetation of the north-facing limestone slopes. The assemblage as a whole suggests that a species-rich open grass-dominated turf was widespread, with small areas of flush communities on moist gravels. Pollen of *Alchemilla*, *Cerastium alpinum* type, *Oxyria digyna*, cf. *Oxytropis*, *Plantago maritima*, *Polygonum viviparum*/*P. bistorta*, *Potentilla* type, *Rubus saxatilis*, *Rumex acetosa*, *Saussurea alpina*, *Saxifraga hypnoides*, *S. oppositifolia*, *Silene* cf. *S. acaulis*, *Solidago* type, *Thalictrum*, and *Thymus* type, and spores of *Asplenium* type, *Botrychium lunaria*, *Cystopteris fragilis*, *Polystichum* type, and *Selaginella selaginoides* may be derived from taxa growing in the species-rich turf, as many of these taxa are characteristic today of montane grassland and dwarf-herb communities. Taxa such as *Saxifraga aizoides* and *Selaginella selaginoides*, whose pollen and spores are consistently present, may have favoured rather moister sites, as they do today in the Saxifragetum aizoidis Association and *Carex–Saxifraga aizoides nodum* (see Chapter 4, Table 4.57, and McVean & Ratcliffe, 1962). The pollen of *Armeria maritimia* in this zone suggests that this species occurred locally, perhaps in the open gravel flush communities with *Saxifraga aizoides*, as it does today in Teesdale, or in the species-rich turf. The fossil assemblage suggests that the vegetation on the limestone near the site at this time had affinities with the low-alpine Dwarf herb *nodum* (Chapter 4 and McVean & Ratcliffe, 1962), such as occurs today on intermittently irrigated slopes on the Dalradian limestones in the Ben Alder range in west Inverness. There are, however, also some similarities between the fossil assemblage and present day communities of calcareous cliff-faces, such as those described by Nordhagen (1943) from Sikilsdalen in the alliance Kobresio–Dryadion, and to communities of the mildly chionophilous alliance Potentilleto–Polygonion vivipari (Nordhagen, 1927, 1936). The Scottish Dwarf herb *nodum* has affinities with the latter alliance (McVean & Ratcliffe, 1962). The fossil assemblage has further affinities with present-day communities of calcareous montane scree and rock-debris, such as occurs below Craig Maud in Glen Clova, Angus and near Inchnadamph, west Sutherland (alliance Arenarion norvegicae; Nordhagen, 1936, 1954), and with *Dryas octopetala* 'fell-field' communities and *Saxifraga oppositifolia* 'barrens' such as occur in the Arctic today (Elkington, 1965; McVean, 1955; Polunin, 1945).

It is likely that a complex mosaic of communities occurred on the limestone slopes at the time of this zone, such as persists today on a small scale on Ben Suardal. In view of the aspect, the communities were probably influenced, to some degree, by prolonged snow-lie. Several of the species whose pollen is present in this zone are characteristic of the chionophilous alliances of calcareous soils in Scandinavia today (alliances Reticulato–Poion alpinae, Oppositifolio–Oxyrion, and Ranunculo–Poion alpinae; Gjaerevoll, 1956). *Juniperus communis* pollen is consistently present in this zone, suggesting the local occurrence of the plant, probably as the prostrate *J. communis* ssp. *nana*. It may have occurred on either rock type, but the flowering bushes were probably restricted to particularly favourable and sheltered areas with a moderate snow-cover. In contrast to the pollen assemblages recorded at Loch Meodal and at the sites in Trotternish, pollen of *Betula* cf. *B. nana* is not a prominent component of any of the pollen spectra at Loch Cill Chriosd.

The high (up to 57.6%) but rather variable frequencies of hystrichosphaerids in the sediments of this and the succeeding zones (LCC-3, LCC-4, and, to some extent, LCC-5) are of interest. The assemblage consists primarily of *Operculodinium centrocarpum*, with some *Hystrichosphaera furcata*, *H. bulloidea*, *H. membranacea*, and *H. mirabilis*, and it is characteristic of marine conditions today (Downie & Singh, 1969; Harland, 1968). One hypothesis to explain the occurrence of these hystrichosphaerids in Late-Devensian sediments is to propose that they are reworked and redeposited from older marine strata (Iversen, 1936, 1942). However, the absence of any pollen and spores of undoubted pre-Quaternary age in this sequence (cf. Loch Fada) and the demonstration that many hystrichosphaerids represent resting cysts of extant members of the Dinophyceae (Evitt & Davidson, 1964; Wall & Dale, 1967, 1968*a*, 1968*b*) are presumptive evidence that the hystrichosphaerids are not secondarily derived, and this hypothesis is accordingly rejected.

A second hypothesis to explain the fossil assemblage accepts the hystrichosphaerids as being primary in origin, with the corollary that the sediments of zones LCC-1, LCC-2, LCC-3, LCC-4, and possibly of LCC-5 are marine in origin. The occurrence of pollen of *Sparganium* type, *Sagittaria sagittifolia*, *Myriophyllum alterniflorum*, and *Ranunculus trichophyllus* type in these zones apparently contradicts this hypothesis, as the taxa concerned are generally regarded as being characteristic of freshwater conditions today. Similarly the algae *Pediastrum* and *Botryococcus* are usually considered to be genera of freshwater today (Cookson, 1953) although there are instances where they have been recorded from marine sediments (Evitt, 1963; Erdtman, 1969). The Flandrian pollen diagram prepared from Hallarums Mose in south-east Sweden by Berglund (1964) is of interest in that it shows high frequencies of *Pediastrum* colonies in marine fine-detritus muds and clays containing abundant marine and brackish-water diatoms, seeds of *Ruppia*, fossil leaves of *Zostera marina*, and high values of hystrichosphaerids. The frequencies of pollen of obligate freshwater aquatic taxa in these zones at Loch Cill Chriosd are not sufficiently high or continuous to provide irrefutible evidence for the existence of freshwater conditions throughout the time of these zones. It is highly probable that the site was influenced to some degree, by seawater, as the present altitude of the site is 20 m O.D. and that of the Late-Devensian sediments is 16 m O.D. There is independent geomorphic evidence to indicate a sea-level in Late-Devensian times of at least 30 m on Skye and elsewhere in western Scotland (Donner, 1959; Kirk, Rice & Synge, 1966; McCann, 1966). In view of this high sea-level in Late-Devensian times, it is likely that the Broadford River, which is the principal outflow of Loch Cill Chriosd today, was under tidal influence, and that parts of the present floodplain of the river may have been submerged by the sea. Periodic marine incursions, similar to those described by Berglund (1964) for south-eastern Sweden, may have occurred during the time of zones LCC-1, LCC-2, LCC-3, LCC-4, and LCC-5, thereby introducing marine fossils into the sediments of the loch. This hypothesis does not account for the parallelism between the curves for Hystrichosphaerids, *Pediastrum*, and *Botryoccus*, which remains unexplained.

2. GRAMINEAE–*RUMEX* ASSEMBLAGE ZONE (zones LCC-3 and LCC-4)

The decrease in relative frequencies of Cyperaceae and Ericaceae undiff. pollen and of *Lycopodium selago* spores in this assemblage zone, coupled with the absence of pollen and spores of many of the taxa characteristic of snow-bed vegetation today which occur consistently in the preceding zone, suggests that there was considerable reduction, if not disappearance, of the snow-fields on the slopes of Beinn na Caillich during the time of this zone. The pollen assemblage indicates that there was an extension of species-rich grassland communities, with increased frequencies of many of the pollen types present in the previous zone. *Antennaria* type, *Ranunculus acris* type, and *Sagina* pollen are recorded for the first time in this zone. These grains may have been derived from taxa in the grassland communities. It is possible that the frequencies of *Artemisia* undiff. pollen in this and the succeeding zone (LCC-5) indicate the local presence of the genus at this time, perhaps growing in open, well-drained limestone turf. As its low pollen values in many Late-Devensian assemblages in western Britain have been ascribed to the rarity of this xerophilous genus in the west at this time, as a result of soil moisture and snow-cover, it is of interest that some of the highest values of *Artemisia* pollen recorded from Late-Devensian sediments in western Britain occur in sites in the limestone district of the Burren, Co. Clare (Watts, 1963).

The *Juniperus* assemblage subzone (zone LCC-3) with *Juniperus* pollen frequencies of 10.8% or more is interpreted as reflecting the expansion or increased flowering of juniper, probably as a result of reduced snow-cover. In contrast to the correlative zones at the sites in Trotternish, 'tall-herb'-dominated vegetation appears to have been rather rare near Loch Cill Chriosd, for although *Cirsium/Carduus*, *Filipendula*, *Mercurialis perennis*, *Rumex acetosa*, *Salix* undiff., *Saussurea alpina*, *Sedum* cf. *S. rosea*, *Stellaria holostea*, and *Urtica* pollen are present in this subzone, their relative frequencies are very low. 'Tall herb' communities today favour moist and deep, fertile brown earth soils (see Chapters 4 and 5), and they are presently restricted on Ben Suardal to the sheltered, humid gorge in Coille Gaireallach (see Chapter 9). This contrasts with the widespread occurrence of 'tall herbs' on the moist basalt soils in Trotternish today. It is probable that a comparable floristic differentiation also existed between the two areas in Late-Devensian times, influenced primarily by differences in soil moisture.

The increased frequencies of *Betula* undiff. pollen in the *Betula* assemblage subzone (zone LCC-4) may reflect the development of small birch copses in sheltered localities in Strath Suardal, but the possibility of long-distance pollen dispersal cannot be discounted. The pollen assemblage as a whole suggests that species-rich grassland communities were widespread throughout the time of the subzone. The inorganic nature of the sediments in this subzone suggests that soil instability and soil erosion were widespread. However, the origins of the sediments are not clear, and the high inorganic content may result from deposition in marine conditions rather than from extensive inwashing of terrestrial material.

3. *LYCOPODIUM*–CYPERACEAE ASSEMBLAGE ZONE (zone LCC-5)

The pollen assemblage of this zone appears to reflect a revertence to the fern-rich low-alpine snow-bed vegetation that was present during the time of zone LCC-2, as the pollen assemblages of the two zones are very similar, with high relative frequencies of Cyperaceae and Ericaceae undiff. pollen and of *Lycopodium selago* spores, and a low but consistent occurrence of *Athyrium alpestre* type, *Cryptogramma crispa*, and *Lycopodium alpinum* spores, of *Salix herbacea* leaves and pollen, and of *Hylocomium splendens*, *Rhacomitrium fasciculare*, and *R. lanuginosum*. It is possible that the ferns *Blechnum spicant*, *Dryopteris filix-mas*, and *Polypodium*, the spores of which all occur in this zone, also grew in the snow-bed communities, as they are recorded from stands of the Cryptogrammeto–Athyrietum chionophilum Association in Scotland today (McVean & Ratcliffe, 1962). Pollen identified as that of *Empetrum* cf. *E. nigrum* also appears in moderate frequencies in this zone, but as the pollen of Ericaceae undiff. and of *Empetrum* are similar in morphology, the parallelism of their pollen curves in this zone suggests some difficulties in identification. *Artemisia* cf. *A. norvegica* pollen attains moderate values throughout the zone. The species may have been frequent in open, granite screes with little or no winter snow-cover. The occurrence of montane spring communities (Cardamino–Montion) during the time of this zone is suggested by the presence of *Caltha* type, *Epilobium* type, *Saxifraga stellaris*, and *Stellaria* undiff. pollen; *Caltha palustris*, *Epilobium alsinifolium* and *E. anagallidifolium*, *Saxifraga stellaris*, and *Stellaria alsine* are characteristic of montane spring communities on Skye today (see Table 4.30 and 4.57).

The redevelopment of snow-beds, as evidenced by the occurrence of chionophilous vegetation, on Beinn na Caillich was probably associated with the youngest phase of corrie glaciation restricted to the high corries of the Cuillins, Blà Bheinn, and the Red Hills. The coarse sand layers in the lithology may reflect inwashing of granite debris by meltwater or by amorphous solifluction processes.

The vegetation on the Durness limestone at the time of this zone appears to have been a species-rich open turf, rather similar in floristic composition to that reconstructed from the fossil assemblage of zone LCC-2. *Arenaria* type, *Dryas octopetala*, *Helianthemum chamaecistus* type, *Hypericum pulchrum* type, and *Plant-*

ago major/P. media pollen are additional pollen types in zone LCC-5. In view of their present ecological preferences, the taxa concerned may all have grown in the open turf communities. A mosaic of communities was probably present on the limestone, differentiated by factors of exposure and soil moisture. *Artemisia* and *Helianthemum chamaecistus* may have favoured the dry, well-drained sites, whereas *Saxifraga aizoides* and *Selaginella selaginoides* may have grown together on moist gravel in open flush communities. Low-growing herbs such as *Alchemilla*, *Cerastium alpinum*, *Hypericum pulchrum*, *Plantago maritima*, *Polygonum viviparum*, *Sagina*, *Silene acaulis*, *Succisa pratensis*, *Thalictrum*, and *Thymus drucei* may have grown with *Dryas octopetala* in a community closely similar in floristic composition to the present *Dryas*-heaths of Ben Suardal (Table 4.35). Scattered 'tall herbs' and ferns may have persisted locally, probably in moist sheltered areas on deep soils, as scattered grains of *Angelica* type, *Filipendula*, *Saussurea alpina*, *Silene dioica* type, *Stellaria holostea*, *Urtica*, and *Vicia/Lathyrus*, and spores of *Asplenium* type, *Cystopteris fragilis*, and *Dryopteris filix-mas* type occur throughout the zone. *Juniperus communis* appears to have occurred locally, perhaps restricted to sheltered but dry habitats.

4. GRAMINEAE–*RUMEX* ASSEMBLAGE ZONE (zone LCC-6)

The *Juniperus* subzone of the Gramineae–*Rumex* zone (LCC-6) appears to reflect a vegetation broadly similar to that postulated to have occurred during the time of zone LCC-3. Chionophilous communities appear to have become increasingly more restricted during the time of this subzone, as deduced from the decreasing relative frequencies of Cyperaceae and Ericaceae undiff. pollen, and of *Lycopodium selago*, *L. alpinum*, and *Cryptogramma crispa* spores. The relative frequencies of *Juniperus communis* pollen (12.4–13%) suggest that the shrub may have been frequent and flowering profusely, perhaps in association with a variety of ferns, as spores of *Athyrium filix-femina*, *Dryopteris filix-mas* type, *Polypodium*, *Thelypteris dryopteris*, and *T. phegopteris* are recorded with moderate frequencies in this subzone. Such an assemblage resembles the sub-alpine *Juniperus–Thelypteris nodum* described by McVean & Ratcliffe (1962). The apparent success of *Juniperus* scrub at this time may have been a result of decreased snow-cover (see Chapter 11).

The increased values of *Betula* undiff. pollen and the appearance of *Populus tremula* pollen in this zone suggest that some tree growth occurred at this time. The marked lithological change at 400 cm (Fig. 20) from silty mud with sand of low organic content to fine detritus mud with a loss-on-ignition of 25% or more suggests the development of a closed, continuous vegetational cover in the catchment area, thereby reducing the influx into the loch of coarse minerogenic material following soil instability and erosion. It is perhaps significant that pollen types of several montane taxa, such as *Artemisia* cf. *A. norvegica*, *Cerastium alpinum* type, *Oxyria digyna*, *Saxifraga oppositifolia*, *Saussurea alpina*, and *Silene* cf. *S. acaulis*, disappear from the fossil record before or in this subzone. If the absence of their pollen is indicative of the absence of plants, their apparent local extinction during the time of this zone may reflect their intolerance of competition in closed communities, treeless or wooded, although climatic effects may also have been important. None of these taxa occur near the site today. Species-rich grassland communities were probably locally frequent, as pollen of *Alchemilla*, *Dryas octopetala*, *Helianthemum chamaecistus* type, *Plantago major/P. media*, *Plantago maritima*, *Ranunculus acris* type, *Saxifraga hypnoides*, and *Thalictrum*, and spores of *Botrychium lunaria* and *Selaginella selaginoides* occur in this zone. 'Tall herb' communities may have occurred sparingly, judging by the low frequencies of *Angelica* type, *Filipendula*, *Rumex acetosa*, *Saussurea alpina*, and *Urtica* pollen. The loch appears to have supported a richer and more diverse assemblage of aquatic taxa in this zone than in any other of the zones. Pollen of *Littorella uniflora*, *Myriophyllum alterniflorum*, *M. spicatum*, *Potamogeton* type, and *Sparganium* type, frequent remains of Cladocera including *Daphnia*, oospores of *Chara*, abundant diatom frustules, and a range of other algae indicate the variety of aquatic biota present in the loch at the time of this zone.

5. *BETULA–CORYLUS* ASSEMBLAGE ZONE (zone LCC-7)

The *Betula–Corylus* zone is interpreted as reflecting the extensive development of woodland in Strath Suardal, as the relative frequencies of tree pollen reach 70% of the total pollen sum. These values are comparable to those in the correlative zone at Loch Meodal (Plate 1) but they are higher than those recorded at the sites in Trotternish. *Betula pubescens* was present locally, as shown by the occurrence of its macrofossils. Woodland probably occurred on both the slopes of Ben Suardal (as it does today; see Fig. 19) and on the south-facing granite slopes of Beinn na Caillich which presently support anthropogenic grasslands and dwarf-shrub heaths. The low frequencies of *Populus tremula*, *Prunus* cf. *P. padus*, *Sorbus aucaparia*, and *Sorbus* cf. *S. rupicola* pollen in this zone probably reflect the local occurrence of these shade-intolerant trees, as they are poorly represented in modern pollen spectra (see Chapter 11). The low frequencies of *Alnus*, *Pinus*, *Quercus*, and *Ulmus* pollen in the zone are attributed to long-distance pollen transport. The shade-intolerant shrubs *Betula nana* and *Juniperus communis* appear to have become increasingly rare during the time of this zone, whereas the low but consistent frequencies of *Salix* undiff. pollen probably reflect the occurrence of willow thickets either in wet sites within the woods, or in the marginal fens.

The consistent occurrence of pollen of *Calluna vulgaris*, Ericaceae undiff., and *Potentilla* type, and of spores of *Polypodium*, *Pteridium aquilinum*, and *Thelypteris dryopteris* in this zone suggests that these taxa may have been frequent components of the woodland flora. Judging by their present sociological tolerances (see Table 4.57) they were probably part of the field layer of the acidic birchwoods that developed on the granite slopes of Beinn na Caillich and of Beinn na Dubraich (cf. *Betula pubescens–Vaccinium myrtillus* Association; Table 4.49), perhaps with *Sorbus aucuparia* and *Populus tremula* as associated trees. The presence of *Anemone* type, *Angelica* type, *Conopodium* type, *Filipendula*, *Geum*, *Ranunculus acris* type, *Rumex acetosa*, *Sanicula europaea*, *Trollius europaeus*, *Urtica*, and *Valeriana officinalis* pollen, and of *Thelypteris phegopteris* spores in this zone may reflect the floristic character of the hazel-dominated woods that were probably widespread on the richer and deeper soils. *Betula pubescens*, *Populus tremula*, *Prunus padus*, *Sorbus aucuparia*, and *Sorbus rupicola* may also have been present in these woods. *Sorbus rupicola* does not occur on the Durness limestone at Ben Suardal today, but it has small colonies on vertical basalt cliffs at Càrn Mor, Elgol, on Jurassic limestones along the Drinan coast on the eastern side of the Elgol Peninsula, and on dry peridotite cliffs at Càrn Dearg just to the south of Coille Gaireallach. It occurs on Durness limestone cliffs at Kishorn in west Ross and at Inchnadamph in west Sutherland. The fossil assemblage is strikingly similar in floristic composition to the 'tall herb' communities that occur on ungrazed ledges in the ravine at Coille Gaireallach (Tables 4.47 and 4.57).

The occasional records of *Arenaria* type, *Campanula* type, *Dryas octopetala*, *Hypericum pulchrum* type, *Plantago lanceolata*, *Plantago major/P. media*, *Plantago maritima*, *Polygonum viviparum/P. bistorta*, *Saxifraga aizoides*, *S. hypnoides*, and *Trifolium* cf. *T. repens* pollen, and of *Botrychium lunaria* and *Selaginella selaginoides* spores in this zone suggest that non-wooded areas persisted locally to provide habitats for these shade-intolerant herbs and dwarf pteridophytes. Such habitats may have been in exposed sites or around rock outcrops with soils too shallow for tree growth. *Dryas octopetala* heath (Table 4.35) still persists in such areas today. It is extremely difficult to evaluate the frequency or the magnitude of such areas from relative pollen frequencies, because the absolute pollen production of woodland stands is considerably greater than that of treeless herbaceous communities. Pollen diagrams from sites in the sub-alpine zone at Åbisko in Swedish Lappland (Sonesson, 1968) show only scattered occurrences of pollen and spores of montane taxa throughout the sequence, in contrast to the probable abundance of such taxa in the vegetation. Such examples serve to illustrate the caution that is required in reconstructing the floristic and vegetational history of presumed 'refugia' from palynological data at, for example, Cwm Idwal (Godwin, 1955), upper Teesdale (Pigott, 1956), and the Craven Pennines (Pigott & Pigott, 1963).

Loch Cill Chriosd appears to have supported a rich aquatic flora at the time of this zone. All the pollen types of aquatic taxa that were present in the previous zone are also present in zone LCC-7, along with pollen of *Menyanthes trifoliata*, *Nuphar*, *Nymphaea*, *Potamogeton* (*Coleogeton*), and *Sparganium* cf. *S. minimum*, and spores of *Isoetes lacustris*. Seeds of *Najas flexilis* are frequent in the sediments of this zone. The fossil assemblage of aquatic macrophytes resembles the present aquatic flora of the loch (see Fig. 7), but *Isoetes lacustris*, *Myriophyllum spicatum*, *Najas flexilis*, *Nuphar*, and *Potamogeton* (*Coleogeton*) are not known to occur there today. The fossil assemblage suggests that the water of the loch was base-rich and clear. Reed-swamp and rich-fen communities appear to have developed at this time, perhaps at the western end of the loch where there is currently an extensive rich-fen, as there are remains of the mosses *Acrocladium giganteum* and *Scorpidium scorpioides*, and pollen of *Drosera* cf. *D. intermedia*, *Lychnis flos-cuculi*, *Menyanthes trifoliata*, and *Sparganium* cf. *S. minimum*. *Osmunda regalis* may have been a notable component of these fens.

6. INFERRED VEGETATIONAL HISTORY AT LOCHAN COIR' A' GHOBHAINN

I. POLLEN ZONE LCG-I

The basal pollen spectra at Lochan Coir' a' Ghobhainn (zone LCG-1; Plate 5) differ from all the other pollen spectra at this or at any other of the sites examined on Skye in the high relative frequencies of *Oxyria digyna* pollen (6.9–16.6%) associated with high values of *Lycopodium selago* spores. Pollen of *Artemisia* cf. *A. norvegica*, *Artemisia* undiff., *Betula* cf. *B. nana*, Caryophyllaceae undiff., Chenopodiaceae, Cruciferae, *Empetrum* cf. *E. nigrum*, Liguliflorae, *Ranunculus acris* type, *Rumex acetosa*, *Salix* cf. *S. herbacea*, *Salix* undiff., *Saxifraga stellaris*, and *Thalictrum*, and spores of *Cryptogramma crispa* and *Equisetum* occur consistently with moderate frequencies in this basal zone. There are also occasional grains of *Alchemilla*, *Cerastium alpinum* type, *Rubus saxatilis*, *Sagina*, cf. *Sedum*, *Silene* cf. *S. acaulis*, *Silene maritima* type, and *Stellaria* undiff., and remains of *Hylocomium splendens*, *Polytrichum alpinum*, and *Rhacomitrium* spp. Percentages of pollen of trees, shrubs, and dwarf shrubs are low throughout. The low organic content and the abundance of silt and fine sand in the sediments (Fig. 22) suggest that the vegetation on the slopes around the lochan was very open and that the soils were unstable.

The fossil assemblage closely resembles in floristic composition the rather heterogeneous pioneer floras that occur today on young glacial gravels in Norway (Faegri, 1933), Sweden (Stork, 1963), and south-east Iceland (Persson, 1964). Species such as *Oxyria digyna*, *Lycopodium selago*, *Cardaminopsis petraea*, *Empetrum nigrum*, *Leontodon autumnalis*, *Ranunculus acris*, *Rumex acetosa*, *Salix herbacea*, *Saxifraga stellaris*, *Equisetum arvense*, *Alchemilla alpina*, *Cerastium alpinum*, *Rubus saxatilis*, *Sagina saginoides*, *Sedum annuum* L., *Silene acaulis*, *Stellaria graminea*, *Polytrichum alpinum*, and *Rhacomitrium canescens* are prominent components of the pioneer flora today on glacial gravels up to 20 years old in the Josteldalsbre in Norway (Faegri, 1933). *Oxyria digyna* is particularly characteristic of open rather moist gravels and silts, and it is one of the most prominent pioneer species on bare river gravels and on recent rock-falls on Skye today as it is throughout its range in the Arctic and in the Alps. The basal pollen zone at Lochan Coir' a' Ghobhainn is thus interpreted as reflecting the initial colonisation of the glacial moraines and associated outwash deposits, within which the lochan lies, that were deposited as ice retreated from the lower slopes of the Cuillins.

2. *LYCOPODIUM*–CYPERACEAE ASSEMBLAGE ZONE (zones LCG-2 and LCG-3)

Comparisons between the fossil spectra of zone LCG-2 and the modern pollen spectra from Scotland (Plate 6 and Table 11.3) suggest that the vegetation present during the time of the zone was a mosaic of low-alpine or mid-alpine chionophilous and chionophobous vegetation types that were presumably differentiated ecologically by factors of slope, aspect, and exposure. The consistent occurrence of spores of *Athyrium alpestre* type, *Blechnum spicant*, *Cryptogramma crispa*, *Dryopteris filix-mas* type, *Lycopodium alpinum*, and *Thelypteris dryopteris* in this zone suggests, by analogy with modern communities, that the snow-bed Cryptogrammeto–Athyrietum chionophilum Association (McVean & Ratcliffe, 1962) may have occurred at this time on the steep, block-strewn slopes below the corries with moderate snow-cover in the winter and spring. As discussed in Chapter 11, this community does not occur on Skye today, perhaps as a result of the short and irregular snow-cover. The high values of Ericaceae undiff. pollen in this zone suggests that members of this family, for example *Vaccinium myrtillus*, were prominent components of the nearby vegetation.

The occurrence in this zone of pollen of *Alchemilla*, *Arenaria* type, *Armeria maritima*, *Cerastium alpinum* type, *Lotus* cf. *L. corniculatus*, *Plantago maritima*, *Polygonum viviparum*/*P. bistorta*, *Ranunculus acris* type, *Rumex acetosa*, *Saussurea alpina*, *Saxifraga hypnoides*, *Silene* cf. *S. acaulis*, *Solidago* type, *Thalictrum*, and *Thymus* type, of spores of *Botrychium lunaria* and *Selaginella selaginoides*, and of abundant remains of the mosses *Antitrichia curtipendula*, *Hylocomium splendens*, *Polytrichum alpinum* and *Rhacomitrium* spp. suggest that a species-rich *Rhacomitrium*-heath, perhaps similar to the Polygoneto–Rhacomitretum lanuginosi Association (McVean & Ratcliffe, 1962), occurred widely. Such a fossil assemblage could also be interpreted as reflecting species-rich grassland communities, as it is at Loch Fada, but as Cyperaceae pollen and *Lycopodium selago* spores are so prominent in this zone, the reconstruction proposed here in terms of low-alpine chionophobous vegetation (Caricetea curvulae) is preferred. The present habitat preferences of the Polygoneto–Rhacomitretum lanuginosi Association in north-west Scotland are wind-exposed, flat or gently sloping summit areas, generally on base-rich rocks. The pollen of *Antennaria* type, *Betula* cf. *B. nana*, *Empetrum* cf. *E. nigrum*, *Potentilla* type, Rubiaceae, and *Salix* cf. *S. herbacea*, and of spores of *Lycopodium selago* in this zone may have originated from either the chionophilous or the chionophobous communities, as all the taxa concerned have a wide ecological tolerance today. The scattered grains of *Artemisia* cf. *A. norvegica* suggest that the plant occurred locally, perhaps in open scree communities or in wind-blasted 'fell-field' habitats. The presence of montane spring communities during the time of this zone is suggested by the occurrence of *Caltha* type, *Epilobium* type, *Saxifraga stellaris*, and *Stellaria* type pollen and of *Acrocladium sarmentosum* and *Bryum* macrofossils, as all these taxa are characteristic of montane spring communities on Skye today (Cardamino–Montion Alliance; Tables 4.30, 4.57).

The low frequencies of *Betula* undiff., *Sorbus aucuparia*, *Prunus* cf. *P. padus*, and *Juniperus communis* pollen in this zone suggest that occasional trees and shrubs may have grown nearby, presumably in particularly favourable and sheltered localities such as on south-facing slopes and in rocky gorges. The scattered grains of *Angelica* type, *Cirsium/Carduus*, *Filipendula*, *Stellaria holostea*, and *Urtica* indicate that 'tall herbs' occurred sparingly, perhaps associated with the limited tree and shrub growth. It is an interesting analogy that birch copses with willows and 'tall herbs' occur today in particularly sheltered sites only 1 km away from the Skatafell glacier in south-east Iceland (Persson, 1964) and 5 km from the large Drangajökull ice-cap in north-west Iceland (Anderson *et al.*, 1966).

Despite the overall low-alpine character of the vegetation at the time of zone LCG-2 the low inorganic content of the sediments in the lochan (Fig. 22) suggests that the vegetation cover was moderately continuous and that the soils were generally stable, at least at low altitudes. The deposition of diatomite suggests that the shallow lochan was rather productive, with abundant diatom blooms. The fossil assemblage of aquatic macrophytes (*Myriophyllum alterniflorum*, *Potamogeton* type, *Ranunculus trichophyllus* type, *Sparganium* type, and *Sparganium* cf. *S. minimum* pollen), of algae (*Botryococcus*, *Nitella*, and *Pediastrum*), and of cladocera (*Bosmina longirostris* and *Daphnia*) suggests that the lochan was moderately eutrophic at the time of the zone.

The deposition of silt, fine sand, coarse sand, and angular gabbro debris up to 9 mm in diameter in the lochan during the time of the Ericaceae subzone (zone LCG-3) effectively eliminated almost all aquatic macrophytes and algae from the lochan. As the sediment shows no signs of being water-sorted, it is interpreted here as representing a solifluction deposit, in view of the angular fragments and the frequent occurrence of thin contorted lenses of leaf debris within the deposit. Mass movement of debris occurs today in arctic and alpine regions as the result of amorphous solifluction or gelifluction processes (*sensu* Ball & Goodier, 1970), in which water-saturated debris is moved down-slope during seasonal thaws (Jahns, 1967).

This is in contrast to the mechanical sorting and rearrangement of debris *in situ* by structured solifluction or cryoturbation. Amorphous solifluction does not appear to require permanently frozen ground, or severe winter frosts, but merely a high ground-water-table, abundant snow in the winter and spring, and a long melting period. During the period of snow-melting in the spring and summer, the soils become water-saturated, particularly on slopes below melting snow-beds (Dahl, 1956; Hedberg *et al.*, 1952; Troll, 1944). Amorphous solifluction is characteristic of arctic or alpine areas with an oceanic climate today. Buried humus layers are frequent in such solifluction lobes (see Fig. 32 in Dahl, 1956; Warren Wilson, 1952), and these may be preserved as thin contorted organic laminae rich in plant detritus within coarse inorganic debris, such as are found in the sediments of the Ericaceae subzone. The laminae in zone LCG-3 contain leaves of *Salix herbacea*, megaspores of *Selaginella selaginoides*, abundant moss fragments (Fig. 22), and high frequencies of fungal hyphae (Plate 5).

In view of the proposed origin of the sediments of zone LCG-3 involving amorphous solifluction and down-slope movement of soil, it is possible that these sediments may contain redeposited pollen and spores that were preserved in the soil and humus that has developed during the time of zone LCG-2. There are few differences in the pollen composition of the sediments of the two zones, except for the very high relative frequencies of Ericaceae undiff. pollen (up to 40%) and the increased percentages of indeterminable: deteriorated pollen in the Ericaceae subzone. Pollen identified as *Empetrum* cf. *E. nigrum* also occurs with moderate frequencies (3.5–11.2%) in the subzone, but as the pollen of the two taxa are similar, the reciprocal character of their curves suggests some difficulties in identification. Pollen of *Armeria maritima*, Caryophyllaceae undiff., Liguliflorae, *Saussurea alpina*, *Succisa pratensis*, and, to some degree, *Solidago* type, and spores of *Selaginella selaginoides* attain higher relative frequencies in this subzone than in the previous one. All members of the Ericaceae (other than *Calluna vulgaris*) that occur in montane communities today in Scotland appear to have a very low modern pollen representation (Plate 6). The high values of Ericaceae undiff. tetrads in this subzone therefore create a problem in the interpretation and the reconstruction of the past vegetation.

The most likely hypothesis proposes that the Ericaceae undiff. tetrads are not primary in origin, but that they have been redeposited from soil and humus formed, in part at least, during the time of the previous subzone. High tetrad frequencies are commonly found in pollen spectra from soils, possibly as a result of differential pollen preservation (Havinga, 1963). The high frequencies of indeterminable: deteriorated pollen (primarily exine corrosion (52% of the total indeterminable category)), with some breakage (22%) and crumpling (18%) in the Ericaceae subzone may result from aerial oxidation, microbial attack, and mechanical damage in redeposition. The increased relative frequencies of *Armeria maritima*, Caryophyllaceae undiff., Liguliflorae, *Saussurea alpina*, and *Succisa pratensis* pollen, and of *Selaginella selaginoides* spores in this subzone similarly may not result from changes in the abundance of these taxa in the vegetation, but from the incorporation of redeposited pollen and spores. All these pollen and spore types are large and robust and they are generally identifiable even after considerable exine deterioration. They often occur with high frequencies in Flandrian soil profiles (Havinga, 1963), perhaps because of their great resistance to destruction. The abundance of ascomycete fungal hyphae in the sediments of the subzone provides further support for the hypothesis that terrestrial material such as soil and humus has been incorporated into the silts and sands of the Ericaceae subzone (see p. 271; Cushing, 1964*b*; H. J. B. Birks, 1970).

The vegetation present during the time of the Ericaceae subzone was probably rather similar to that proposed for zone LCG-2, but with more widespread snow-beds and considerable soil instability. Communities influenced by prolonged and extensive snow-lie, for example in the alpine alliances Herbaceon, Polytrichion norvegici (Gjaerevoll, 1950, 1956), and Cassiopeto–Salicion herbaceae (Dahl, 1956) may have occurred quite widely, especially in sheltered hollows at high altitudes. These alliances comprise oligotrophic snow-bed communities on seasonally moist solifluction soils, and the cover of vascular plants is usually rather low. Bryophytes such as *Anthelia julacea*, *Dicranum starkei*, *Gymnomitrion concinnatum*, *Marsupella varians*, *Pleuroclada albescens*, and *Polytrichum norvegicum* are characteristic. Humus layers buried by amorphous solifluction are frequent (Dahl, 1956). Due to the low vascular-plant cover, such communities would contribute little to the pollen rain. Permanently wet solifluction soils in the low-, mid-, and high-alpine zones similarly support little vegetation today (Ranunculeto–Oxyrion digynae and Stellario–Oxyrion Alliances; Dahl, 1956; Gjaerevoll, 1956), and even the ubiquitous *Salix herbacea* shows reduced vitality in such conditions. Species that are able to tolerate such adverse conditions, for example *Carex lachenalii*, *Cerastium cerastioides*, *Deschampsia alpina*, *Epilobium anagallidifolium*, *Juncus trifidus*, *Oxyria digyna*, *Polygonum viviparum*, *Sagina saginoides*, and *Veronica alpina* (Gjaerevoll, 1956), may produce so little pollen, due to their reduced flowering, that they would make little contribution in the pollen spectra. The occasional grains of *Antennaria* type, *Epilobium* type, *Oxyria digyna*, *Polygonum viviparum/P. bistorta*, *Sagina*, *Stellaria* undiff., and *Veronica* in the Ericaceae subzone may be derived from taxa growing in such habitats. The pollen of *Antennaria* type may be derived, in part at least, from *Gnaphalium supinum*, a species resistant to solifluction (Dahl, 1956) and of high constancy in the alliance Herbaceon (see Table 16 in Gjaerevoll, 1956), whereas *Polygonum viviparum*, *Sagina*, *Epilobium*, *Oxyria digyna*, *Stellaria*, and *Veronica* may have been present in wet irrigated and rather silty areas (cf. alliance Stellario–Oxyrion, see Table 29 in Gjaerevoll, 1956).

This phase of snow-bed expansion and amorphous solifluction was probably associated with the last phase of corrie glaciation in the Cuillins. This phase is marked, for example, by small arcuate block moraines at 1500 feet (460 m) below Coire Lagan, and by glacial-outwash fans extending to about 450 feet (140 m) at An Sgùman and Lòn Ban. Corings and preliminary pollen analyses of basal organic deposits at An Sgùman show that the oldest pollen spectra present there belong to the *Betula–Corylus* zone. The An Sgùman sediments overlie outwash of the youngest corrie glaciation whereas Lochan Coir' a' Ghobhainn lies well outside the margin of the youngest drift, and thus presumably beyond the limits of this glacial phase. The biostratigraphical and geomorphic relationships of the two sites suggest, therefore, that the glacial phase predates the time of the *Betula–Corylus* zone, and it is tentatively correlated with the Ericaceae subzone of the *Lycopodium*–Cyperaceae zone.

There are very low frequencies of pollen of trees, shrubs, and aquatic taxa in this subzone. It is of general palaeoecological interest that although the pollen spectra of the Ericaceae subzone provide little direct information relevant to the reconstruction of the vegetation present at the time of the subzone, a picture of the landscape at that time, including the vegetation, emerges when lithological evidence is also considered.

3. GRAMINEAE–*RUMEX* ASSEMBLAGE ZONE (zone LCG-4)

The *Juniperus* subzone of the Gramineae–*Rumex* zone (zone LCG-4) appears to reflect a transitional stage in the vegetational development from the treeless, alpine landscape described above to the wooded sub-alpine conditions of the succeeding zone. It is closely similar to zone LCC-6 at Loch Cill Chriosd. Chionophilous communities appear to have become increasingly more restricted during the time of the *Juniperus* subzone, as suggested by the decreasing frequencies of Cyperaceae and Ericaceae undiff. pollen, and of *Lycopodium selago*, *L. alpinum*, *Cryptogramma crispa*, and *Athyrium alpestre* type spores. The high relative frequencies of *Juniperus communis* pollen (11.9–12.9%) suggest that the shrub was moderately frequent and was flowering profusely, perhaps as a result of the decreased snow-cover and greater soil stability during the time of this subzone. Concomitant with the expansion of *Juniperus* pollen in the sediments is a marked change in the sediment lithology (Fig. 22): the silt and sand content drops abruptly and the organic content and the relative abundance of fine and coarse detritus increase sharply. The simplest explanation for these lithological changes is a cessation in the supply of minerogenic material resulting from greater soil stability at this time. The shrub may have been associated with a variety of ferns, as spores of *Dryopteris filix-mas* type, *Polypodium*, *Thelypteris dryopteris*, and Polypodiaceae undiff. occur in moderate amounts in this subzone (cf. the sub-alpine *Juniperus–Thelypteris nodum;* McVean & Ratcliffe, 1962). The increasing frequencies of *Betula* undiff. pollen and the low but consistent values of *Populus tremula*, *Prunus* cf. *P. padus*, and *Sorbus aucuparia* pollen suggest that some tree growth occurred locally at this time. The assemblage of pollen of herbaceous taxa recorded in this subzone suggests that species-rich grassland communities were common at this time. The occurrence of pollen of *Alchemilla*, *Armeria maritima*, *Plantago maritima*, *Ranunculus acris* type, *Saxifraga hypnoides*, and *Thalictrum* suggests floristic affinities, with the Dwarf herb *nodum* (McVean & Ratcliffe 1962), whereas pollen of *Filipendula*, *Rumex acetosa*, *Saussurea alpina*, and *Urtica* confer affinities with 'tall herb' communities of the Adenostyletalia (see Tables 4.47, 4.57). Perhaps the grasslands occurred on the drier, more exposed sites, whereas the 'tall herb' stands were restricted to the moist, irrigated and sheltered areas.

The lochan appears to have supported an abundance of aquatic taxa at this time. The high frequencies of *Myriophyllum alterniflorum* pollen in this sub-zone are accompanied by abundant seeds. Pollen of other aquatic macrophytes are present, including *Littorella uniflora*, *Potamogeton* type, and *Ranunculus trichophyllus* type, along with seeds of *Juncus articulatus*/*J. acutiflorus*, oospores of *Nitella*, and megaspores of *Isoetes lacustris*, *Pediastrum*, *Botryococcus*, and diatoms are abundant, and cladoceran remains, including *Bosmina longirostris* and *Daphnia*, are frequent. The assemblage suggests that the lochan was moderately eutrophic during the time of this subzone, perhaps as a result of minerogenic deposition, soil disturbance, and associated mineral recycling during the time of the previous subzone.

4. *BETULA–CORYLUS* ASSEMBLAGE ZONE (zone LCG-5)

Pollen of trees attain values between 26 and 47% in this zone, suggesting the local development of woodland on the lower slopes of the Cuillins. *Betula* undiff. pollen percentages increase near the lower boundary of the zone, whereas *Corylus avellana* pollen does not attain high values until later in the zone. This pattern contrasts with the pollen stratigraphy of the correlative zones at other sites on Skye. The causes for this difference are not known. *Populus tremula*, *Prunus padus*, and *Sorbus aucuparia* were probably present nearby, judging by the low frequencies of their pollen in this zone. The assemblage as a whole suggests that a rather open sub-alpine birch-dominated wood occurred nearby, with *Corylus avellana*, *Populus tremula*, *Prunus padus*, and *Sorbus aucuparia*. The high frequencies of Polypodiaceae undiff. spores, and the presence of *Blechnum spicant*, *Dryopteris filix-mas* type, *Polypodium*, and *Thelypteris dryopteris* spores suggest that ferns may have been prominent components of the understorey. Some 'tall herbs' may have occurred locally in the woods, perhaps in moist, fertile sites, as pollen of *Angelica* type, *Cirsium*/*Carduus*, *Filipendula*, *Rumex acetosa*, and *Urtica* are present in low amounts (cf. *Betula pubescens–Cirsium heterophyllum* Association; Table 4.47). Shrub and dwarf-shrub communities may have occurred in exposed localities, as the values of *Juniperus communis* and Ericaceae undiff. pollen are moderately high. They may also have occurred in openings within the woodland. The consistent occurrence of pollen of *Lotus* cf. *L. corniculatus*, *Plantago lanceolata*, *Plantago major/P. media*, *P. maritima*, *Ranunculus acris* type, and *Thalictrum* in this zone, associated with moderate frequencies of Gramineae pollen (11.6–24%), suggests that grassland communities also persisted. The fossil assemblage is rather similar to the floristic composition of the Maritime grassland *nodum* that occurs on Skye today (Table 4.34), differing only from the modern *nodum* in the presence of *Plantago major* or *P. media*. This feature of the Late-Devensian vegetation is discussed below (p. 381). It is possible that the grasslands present during the time of the *Betula-Corylus* zone were restricted to exposed coastal areas, as the Maritime grassland *nodum* is today.

The consistent frequencies of *Calluna vulgaris* pollen and of *Sphagnum* spores in the zone may reflect the beginnings of local bog development on the slopes nearby. The lochan appears to have supported an aquatic flora comparable to the one it supports today with abundant *Carex rostrata*, *Juncus articulatus/J. acutiflorus*, and *Littorella uniflora* (Fig. 7). Pollen of *Potamogeton* (*Coleogeton*) is present, however, in the *Betula–Corylus* zone, but neither *Potamogeton filiformis* nor *P. pectinatus* occur in the lochan today.

7. COMPARISONS AND CORRELATIONS WITHIN SKYE

There are two other diagrams from the Isle of Skye available for comparison with the pollen diagrams discussed above. These are from Loch Fada and from Loch Cuithir (Vasari & Vasari, 1968). In contrast to the diagram from Loch Fada presented here (Plate 2), the diagram published for this site by Vasari & Vasari extends from the Late-Devensian to the present day. The precise location of their coring site in the fen at the south end of Loch Fada is unknown, but as the boring was relatively deep, penetrating 6 metres of sediment without reaching bedrock, it was probably close to the present sampling site (Fig. 15). The Late-Devensian and early Flandrian pollen spectra in the Vasari & Vasari diagram are based on rather low pollen sums, ranging from 5 to 100 total pollen, and on rather widely spaced samples. Only a small number of pollen and spore types appear to have been determined to a low taxonomic level, and several types that have a distinctive stratigraphy in the author's diagram (Plate 2), such as *Filipendula*, *Lycopodium selago*, and *Thelypteris dryopteris*, are not distinguished. Detailed comparisons between the two diagrams from Loch Fada are somewhat difficult, although the diagrams resemble each other in their general pollen stratigraphy. The *Betula–Corylus* assemblage zone can be recognised in the Vasari & Vasari diagram, between 505 cm and about 460 cm, corresponding in part to their pollen zones IV and V. The underlying sediments and pollen spectra in their diagram are clearly referable to the Gramineae–*Rumex* assemblage zone. The *Juniperus* subzone can be distinguished between 520 cm and 550 cm, and the *Selaginella* subzone can be tentatively recognised (mainly by the very low values of tree, shrub, and dwarf-shrub pollen) between 550 cm and 600 cm, corresponding in part to their pollen zones III and III–IV. In contrast to the author's diagram, the frequencies of *Selaginella selaginoides* spores in this subzone are very low. The *Betula nana* subzone cannot be distinguished in the Vasari & Vasari diagram, since no separation of *B. nana* pollen was attempted. The *Lycopodium*–Cyperaceae assemblage zone is not represented at all, perhaps because the boring did not extend deep enough. Several quantitative differences exist between the two diagrams from Loch Fada. For example, the frequencies of *Thalictrum*, *Ranunculus*, and Cruciferae pollen are very low in the Vasari & Vasari diagram, compared with their values in Plate 2, whereas the percentages of *Betula* pollen in the Vasari & Vasari diagram are consistently higher than the total values of *Betula* undiff. and *Betula* cf. *B. nana* pollen in Plate 2. The reasons for these differences are not known.

Loch Cuithir lies 6 km south-south-west of Loch Mealt and 11 km north of Loch Fada on the eastern slopes of the Trotternish basalt ridge (Fig. 12). The pollen diagram published by Vasari & Vasari (1968) from Cuithir can be matched in rather broad terms with the diagrams presented here from Loch Mealt (Plate 3) and Loch Fada (Plate 2). However, in the Loch Cuithir diagram only the *Betula–Corylus* assemblage zone and the *Juniperus* subzone of the Gramineae–*Rumex* assemblage zone can be recognised (at 355–420 cm and 420–495 cm, respectively). The general correspondence of the diagrams from the three sites in Trotternish suggests that the pollen stratigraphical changes recognisable in them are the result of changes in regional vegetation, and are thus likely to be time-correlative.

The pollen stratigraphy at Loch Meodal (Plate 1) corresponds closely to that at Loch Fada and at Loch Mealt, and it differs only in the absence of the *Lycopodium*–Cyperaceae assemblage zone and in the high relative frequencies of *Betula* undiff. pollen. The

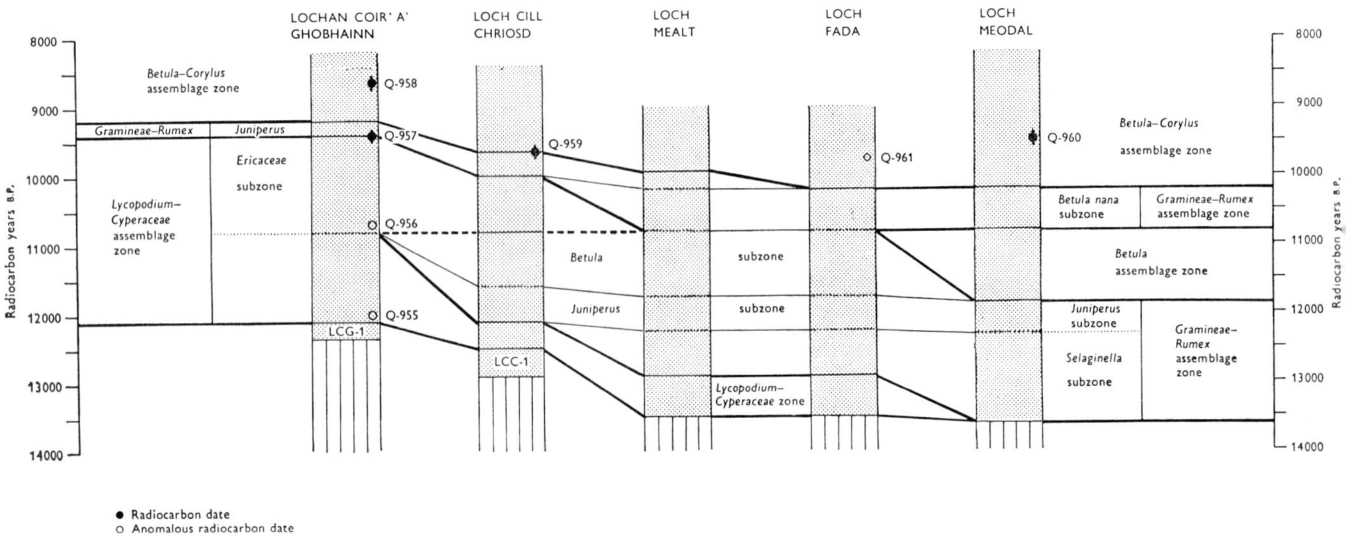

Figure 27. Correlation chart of Late-Devensian and early Flandrian pollen zones on the Isle of Skye. Radiocarbon dates are shown by solid circles; the vertical line indicates the reported single standard deviation. Anomalous radiocarbon dates are shown by open circles, and they are plotted by stratigraphic position, not age.

samples with high values of *Betula* undiff. pollen are distinguished at Loch Meodal as a separate *Betula* pollen assemblage zone. Comparisons with the pollen diagram from Loch Cill Chriosd (Plate 4) and Lochan Coir' a' Ghobhainn (Plate 5) are more difficult, however, for although similar pollen assemblage zones and subzones occur at all the sites on Skye, their stratigraphical occurrence at Loch Cill Chriosd and Lochan Coir' a' Ghobhainn differs from the pollen sequences at the sites in Trotternish and the Sleat.

At Lochan Coir' a' Ghobhainn (Plate 5) the pollen stratigraphy consist of a lower *Lycopodium*–Cyperaceae assemblage zone and an upper *Betula–Corylus* assemblage zone separated by a stratigraphically thin *Juniperus* subzone of the Gramineae–*Rumex* zone. This contrasts markedly with the observed pollen stratigraphy of sites in Trotternish, where the *Lycopodium*–Cyperaceae assemblage zone is separated stratigraphically from the *Betula–Corylus* zone by a considerable thickness of sediment with a contained pollen and spore assemblage referable to the Gramineae–*Rumex* assemblage zone. The basal pollen spectra at Lochan Coir' a' Ghobhainn (local pollen zone LCG-1) differ from all other pollen spectra so far examined on Skye, and although the zone is extremely characteristic and distinctive, it is only known at this site.

The pollen diagram from Loch Cill Chriosd (Plate 4) has some features in common with the diagram from the sites in Trotternish and some features in common with Lochan Coir' a' Ghobhainn. The *Lycopodium*–Cyperaceae assemblage zone occurs twice in the sequence examined, once near the base of the profile, as at Loch Fada and Loch Mealt, and once just below the lower boundary of the *Betula–Corylus* assemblage zone, as at Lochan Coir' a' Ghobhainn. The two *Lycopodium*–Cyperaceae zones are separated by the *Juniperus* and the *Betula* subzones of the Gramineae–*Rumex* assemblage zone. More detailed comparisons of the pollen diagrams from the Isle of Skye require the pollen zone boundaries to be correlated in time.

In view of the observed differences in the pollen stratigraphy between sites, it is clear that pollen stratigraphy cannot be used here as a means of time-correlation between the sites, except in small uniform areas such as Trotternish. The various pollen assemblage zones and subzones that were defined in Chapter 10 and discussed in this chapter for the five sites investigated can be ordered stratigraphically and geographically and correlated in time by means of radiocarbon dates. A correlation chart for these zones is shown in Fig. 27. The available radiocarbon dates from Loch Meodal, Loch Cill Chriosd, and Lochan Coir' a' Ghobhainn are plotted as solid circles with the reported standard deviations marked as vertical lines. When they are not dated directly, the ages of the zone boundaries have been estimated by linear interpolation or extrapolation on graphs of sediment depth plotted against radiocarbon age, with the upper surface of the sediment taken as zero radiocarbon years B.P. The upper and lower boundaries of the assemblage zones at each site are denoted by a solid line, whereas the boundaries of the assemblage subzones within an assemblage zone at each site are shown by a dotted line. Where the same assemblage zone or subzone occurs at two or more sites, the boundaries of that zone or subzone are connected between sites by a solid line, whereas related but not identical pollen assemblages are joined by a dashed line.

The date from Loch Fada (7500 ± 120 radiocarbon years B.P.; Q-961) is considerably younger than the other radiocarbon dates obtained from the *Betula–Corylus* zone on Skye, and it is therefore considered unreliable for the purposes of time correlation. In the absence of an absolute chronology at Loch Fada, the age of the upper and lower boundaries of the *Betula nana* subzone at this site are assumed to be the same age as those at Loch Meodal, and the ages of the boundaries of the other zones and subzones at Loch Fada are obtained by linear extrapolation from these points. No radiocarbon dates are available from Loch Mealt, but the similarities of the pollen stratigraphy at this site to that at Loch Fada suggest that the zone boundaries at Loch Mealt can be assumed, with some confidence, to be the same age as the equivalent pollen zone boundaries at Loch Fada. In addition to the radiocarbon date at Loch Fada (Q-961), the lower two dates at Lochan Coir' a' Ghobhainn (Q-955 and Q-956) are also considered to be too young. The causes of these apparently young ages are not clear, but the difficulties in pretreatment of the sample from Loch Fada (Switsur & West, 1972) and the possibilities of contamination by infiltration of humus-rich ground-water through the shallow deposits at Lochan Coir' a' Ghobhainn may be important. The latter possibility is particularly relevant in view of the extremely soligenous nature of much of the peat on the lower slopes of the Cuillins today (see Chapters 4 and 5). Contamination of a sample with a true radiocarbon age of about 11 000 radiocarbon years B.P. with less than 2% contemporary carbon would result in an apparent radiocarbon age of 9000 radiocarbon years B.P. (Olsson, 1968).

Clearly the time interval represented by some of the pollen assemblage zones and subzones (Fig. 27) may be smaller than the present precision of radiocarbon dating of a variety of organic limnic sediments, which may be no better than 1500 radiocarbon years (Broecker, 1965; Odgen, 1967). Because of the low precision of individual dates, the number of available datings and of pollen diagrams from Skye is fewer than is desired for reliable time-stratigraphical control. In view of the low organic content of many of the Late-Devensian sediments on Skye, it is virtually impossible, however, to obtain radiocarbon dates for several of the zone boundaries. Few conclusions can therefore be drawn about the variation in age of the pollen zone boundaries with geographical position within Skye. If the supposed pollen zone equivalence and the time-correlation of the zone boundaries are correct, then the most striking features of the correlation chart (Fig. 27) are that the age of the upper boundary of the *Lycopodium*–Cyperaceae assemblage zone is clearly younger at Lochan Coir' a' Ghobhainn and Loch Cill Chriosd than at Loch Fada and Loch Mealt, and that the age of the lower boundary of the *Betula–Corylus* assemblage zone is similarly not isochronous throughout Skye. A possible explanation for these differences in the age and duration of the pollen zones on Skye is that the environmental changes that are presumably reflected by the observed changes in pollen stratigraphy were sufficiently gradual to allow local factors such as edaphic and topographic differences between the sites to influence, to some degree, the rate of vegetational change and the succession of plant communities. The significance of these features will be discussed more fully in Chapter 14 in considering the vegetational differentiation within Skye during Late-Devensian times.

8. COMPARISONS AND CORRELATIONS WITH POLLEN DIAGRAMS FROM OTHER AREAS

Comparisons of the four pollen assemblage zones delimited on the Isle of Skye with pollen assemblages described from elsewhere in the British Isles were presented in Chapter 10 when discussing the known geographical extent of each of the assemblage zones. The correlation in time of these and related pollen assemblage zones throughout the British Isles has not been attempted in detail, although such a study would be of value in considering the variability in age of pollen zone boundaries with geographical position within the British Isles.

The lower boundary of the *Betula–Corylus* assemblage zone appears to represent in vegetational terms 'the beginning of the spread of thermophilous and deciduous trees' on Skye, and, by definition, this boundary must be regarded as the transition between

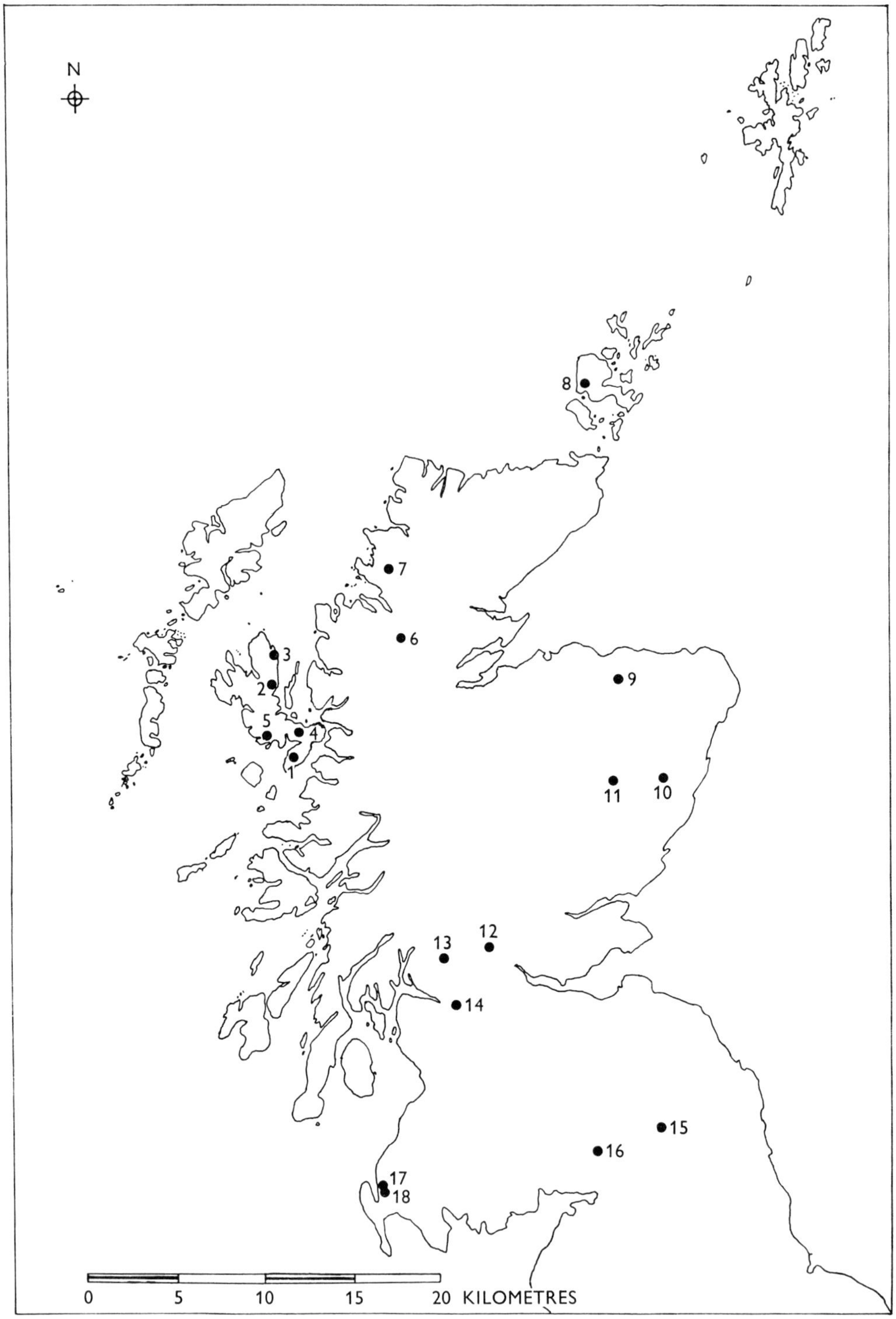

Figure 28. Index map of sites in Scotland from which Late-Devensian pollen diagrams have been published. Listed below for each numbered locality is the name of the site, its county, the authors, and the year of publication.

1. Loch Meodal, Inverness-shire (H. J. B. Birks, 1969)
2. Loch Fada, Inverness-shire (H. J. B. Birks, 1969)
3. Loch Mealt, Inverness-shire (H. J. B. Birks, 1969)
4. Loch Cill Chriosd, Inverness-shire (H. J. B. Birks, 1969)
5. Lochan Coir' a' Ghobhainn, Inverness-shire (H. J. B. Birks, 1969)
6. Loch Droma, Ross and Cromarty (Kirk & Godwin, 1963)
7. Loch Sionascaig, Ross and Cromarty (Pennington & Lishmann, 1971)
8. Yesnaby, Orkney (Moar, 1969*b*)
9. Garral Hill, Banffshire (Donner, 1957)
10. Loch of Park, Aberdeenshire (Vasari & Vasari, 1968)
11. Loch Kinord, Aberdeenshire (Vasari & Vasari, 1968)
12. Loch Mahaick, Perthshire (Donner, 1958)
13. Dryman, Stirlingshire (Donner, 1957; Vasari & Vasari, 1968)
14. Garscadden Mains, Lanarkshire (Donner, 1957)
15. Corstorphine, Midlothian (Newey, 1970)
16. Bigholm Burn, Dumfriesshire (Moar, 1969*a*)
17. Little Lochans, Wigtownshire (Moar, 1969*a*)
18. Culhorn Mains, Wigtownshire (Moar, 1969*a*)

the Flandrian and Devensian Stages and Ages (Shotton & West, 1969; West, 1967). As can be seen in the correlation chart (Fig. 27) this pollen-analytical level is markedly metasynchronous, however, within the comparatively small area of the Isle of Skye (cf. Donner, 1966). The lower boundary of the zone at Loch Meodal, Loch Fada, and Loch Mealt occurs at about 10000 to 10200 radiocarbon years B.P. This is broadly similar to radiocarbon dates obtained for the opening of the Flandrian elsewhere in the British Isles (Godwin, 1960; Hibbert *et al.*, 1971) and in western Europe (Berglund, 1966*a*; Kubitzki, 1961; Nilsson, 1964). The underlying pollen assemblage zones are, in the absence of any evidence for stratigraphic discontinuities, referable to the Late-Devensian Substage and Subage as defined in Chapter 2 and by Shotton & West (1969).

There is a change in pollen stratigraphy at about 10800 radiocarbon years B.P. at all the sites examined on Skye (Fig. 27), and this pollen stratigraphical change is correlated in time with the close of the Allerød interstadial. This event is generally between 10800 and 11000 radiocarbon years B.P. elsewhere in Britain (Godwin & Willis, 1959) and in Scandinavia (Berglund, 1966*a*; Iversen, 1953; Tauber, 1970). The period of time on Skye between about 10200 and 10800 radiocarbon years B.P. can be correlated with 'period C' or 'post-interstadial' of Pennington & Lishman (1971) and the 'Younger *Dryas* stadial' (Iversen, 1953; Mangerud, 1970). The beginning of the *Betula* assemblage zone at Loch Meodal and of the *Betula* subzone of the Gramineae–*Rumex* zone at Loch Mealt, Loch Fada, and Loch Cill Chriosd occurs between 11600 and 11850 radiocarbon years B.P. This is roughly similar in age to the opening of the 'Allerød interstadial', as defined by the observed rise in relative frequencies of tree pollen in Denmark and southern Sweden where it has been radiocarbon dated between 11800 and 12100 radiocarbon years B.P. (Berglund, 1966*a*; Iversen, 1953; Tauber, 1970). In the British Isles there is evidence from a variety of sources and from several sites to suggest that so-called 'interstadial conditions', as inferred from fossil assemblages and lithological evidence, began at about 12800 radiocarbon years B.P. (Coope, 1970; Pennington & Bonny, 1970; Pennington and Lishman, 1971). The only pollen stratigraphical evidence on Skye for any vegetational changes occurring at about this time is the transition from the *Lycopodium*–Cyperaceae assemblage zone to the Gramineae–*Rumex* zone at Loch Fada and Loch Mealt (Fig. 27). Until more radiocarbon dates are obtained from these sites and further sites are examined in detail both on Skye and elsewhere in Scotland, all correlations must be necessarily tentative.

There are relatively few Late-Devensian pollen diagrams prepared from sites in Scotland available for comparison with the diagrams from the Isle of Skye. Loch Droma in Ross and Cromarty (Kirk & Godwin, 1963) is the nearest site to the Isle of Skye (Fig. 28) from which a Late-Devensian pollen diagram has been published. It is an important site, and although the Late-Devensian pollen stratigraphy is incomplete, there is a radiocarbon date of 12810 ± 155 radiocarbon years B.P. (Q-457) from a thin organic band interstratified within fine-grained silts. The silts yielded a rich and diverse macrofossil assemblage, especially of bryophytes. To facilitate comparison, the pollen analyses by Miss R. Andrew have been recalculated and presented in a comparable way (Fig. 29) to the Skye data. The high percentages of *Lycopodium selago* and *L. alpinum* spores, and Cyperaceae pollen values exceeding Gramineae pollen percentages suggest correlation with the *Lycopodium*–Cyperaceae assemblage zone. However, the pollen spectra above 55 cm at Loch Droma contain extremely high values of *Empetrum* pollen (16.7–65.8%), and thus they do not resemble any of the pollen assemblages recorded on Skye. If the difficulties in the identification and consistent separation of tetrads of *Empetrum* from those of Ericaceae undiff. that were mentioned above in discussing the Ericaceae subzone at Lochan Coir' a' Ghobhainn are considered, it is possible that the high frequencies of Ericaceae undiff. tetrads at the latter site may largely consist of *Empetrum*. If this were the case, the pollen assemblages at the two sites would be very similar. Other features in common are the high values of Liguliflorae and *Saussurea alpina* pollen and of *Selaginella selaginoides* spores. However, the radiocarbon data at Loch Droma is considerably older than the suggested age of the Ericaceae subzone on Skye (Fig. 27). Problems in the age determination of the Loch Droma sediments are discussed by Kirk & Godwin (1963). Comparisons and correlations of the Loch Droma pollen diagram with other published diagrams in Scotland are equally difficult, however, as no other spectra have been published that have up to 65.8% *Empetrum* pollen and 29% *Lycopodium selago* spores, although Pennington & Lishman (1971, p. 310) state that 'there is a strong correlation between the pollen diagram for Loch Droma and that for Loch Sionascaig'.

LOCH DROMA, ROSS AND CROMARTY

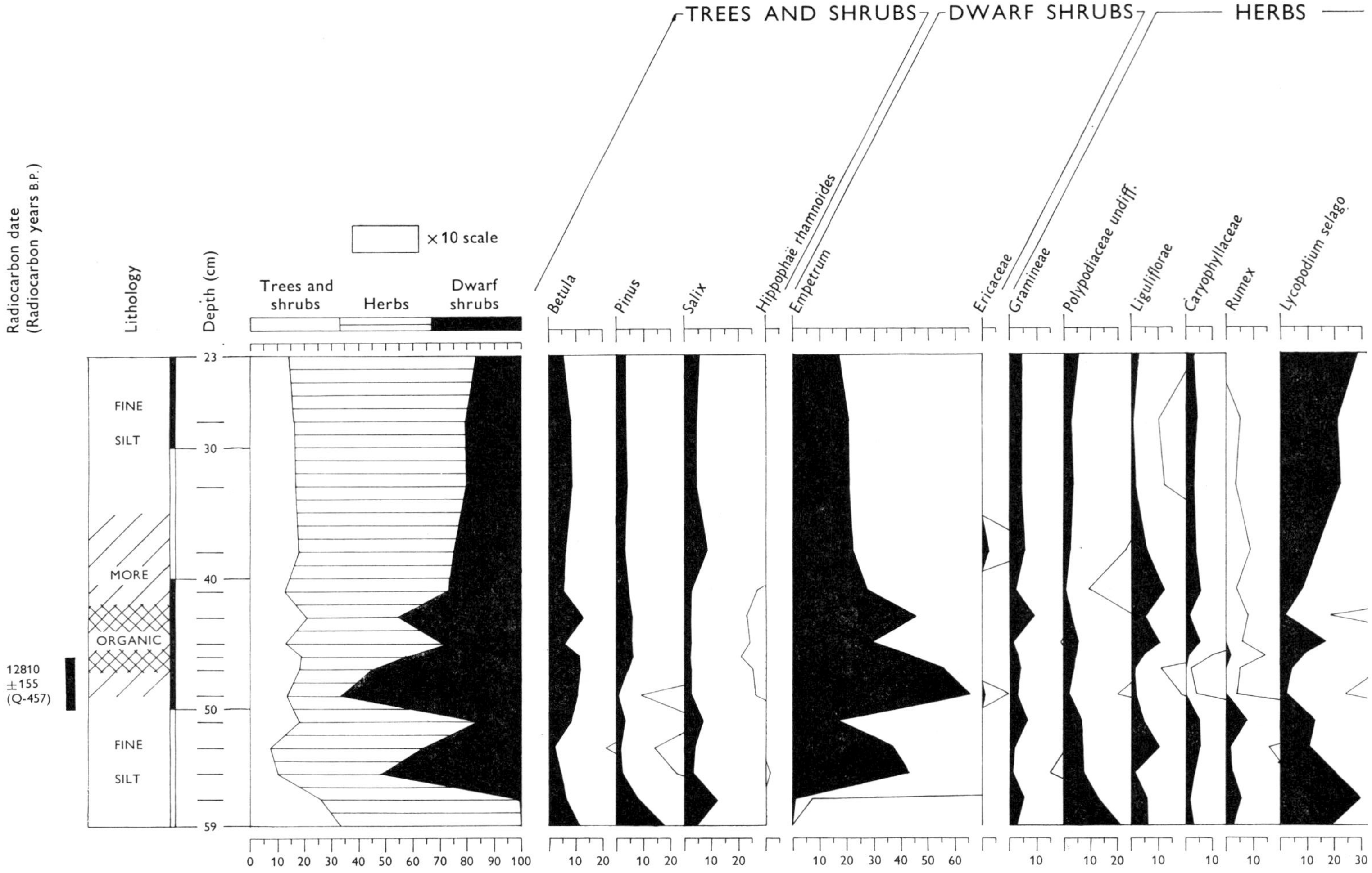

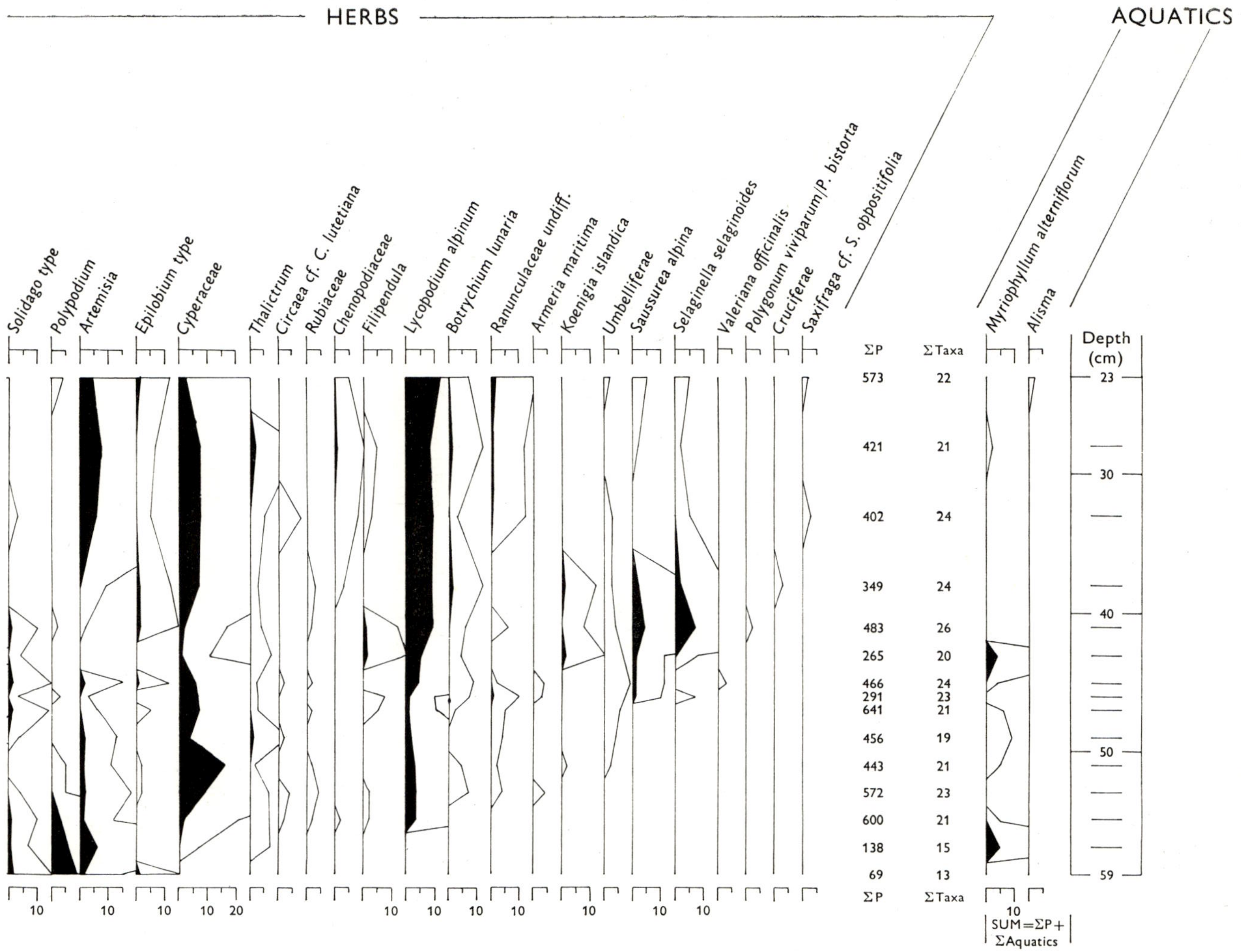

Anal. R. Andrew, 1959

Figure 29. Pollen diagram from Loch Droma, Ross and Cromarty. Redrawn from Kirk & Godwin (1963) and calculated as percentages of the sum of pollen grains and sporesof all extant vascular plants excluding obligate aquatic taxa. Scale at base of diagram gives percentages for black silhouettes; unshaded silhouettes are exaggerated 10× scale. All curves are plotted to the same scale. Abbreviations: anal. = analysed, P = pollen, undiff. = undifferentiated.

Pennington & Lishman (1971) have published a detailed pollen diagram from Loch Sionascaig in Ross and Cromarty (Fig. 28). It is similar in general pollen stratigraphy to the diagrams from Loch Fada and Loch Mealt on Skye, with a well marked Gramineae–*Rumex* assemblage zone with low relative frequencies of *Betula* and other tree pollen types throughout. The assemblage zone comprises their periods A–C and transitions 1 and 2. Although the spectra below 590 cm in period A have some similarities with the *Lycopodium*–Cyperaceae zone, they differ in their high frequencies of *Rumex* pollen. The assemblage subzones within the Gramineae–*Rumex* zone are more difficult to compare, and no direct equivalents of the Skye subzones are suggested here, although the same general components and trends are discernible within the zone as represented on the Loch Sionascaig diagram. The spectra in this zone differ, however, from the spectra from the Trotternish sites in their high relative frequencies of *Empetrum* pollen and Filicales (Polypodiaceae undiff.) spores and the low percentages of *Filipendula*, *Ranunculus*, and *Thalictrum* pollen, and of *Selaginella selaginoides* spores. These differences may be related to local edaphic conditions.

Comparisons with the pollen diagrams of Donner (1957, 1958) from sites in the central and western Highlands (Fig. 28) are difficult because the Late-Devensian pollen stratigraphy is incomplete at Donner's sites. The pollen spectra from Garral Hill, Banffshire in the eastern Highlands (Fig. 28) are referable to the Gramineae–*Rumex* zone, but the *Empetrum* pollen percentages are rather higher than in any of the spectra on Skye. There are radiocarbon dates for this profile ranging from 10808 ± 230 (Q-104) to 11888 ± 225 (Q-101) radiocarbon years B.P. (Godwin & Willis, 1959). Vasari & Vasari (1968) have also published pollen diagrams that cover Late-Devensian times from two sites in Aberdeenshire (Fig. 28). The pollen spectra in their pollen zones I, II, and III generally resemble the Gramineae–*Rumex* assemblage zone, with the *Betula* and *Juniperus* subzones being particularly pronounced. Like the Garral Hill diagram, the Aberdeenshire pollen diagrams differ from the Skye spectra in their high frequencies of *Empetrum* pollen (particularly at Loch Kinord) and of *Artemisia* pollen.

The Late-Devensian pollen diagram from Yesnaby on the Mainland of the Orkney Islands (Fig. 28; Moar, 1969*b*) closely resembles the diagrams from Loch Fada and Loch Mealt in the low values of tree pollen throughout and the dominance of Gramineae pollen. Differences exist, however, between the Orkney diagram and those from Skye, particularly in the very low frequencies of *Juniperus* pollen throughout and the rather high percentages of *Empetrum* pollen in zone LII of Moar's diagram.

There are several published Late-Devensian pollen diagrams from sites in southern Scotland (Fig. 28; Moar, 1969*a*; Newey, 1970). The diagram from Corstorphine near Edinburgh (Newey, 1970) is generally similar to the Gramineae–*Rumex* zone, with some of the spectra (particularly in Newey's zone II) referable to the *Betula* subzone. The diagrams from Culhorn Mains and Little Lochans, Wigtownshire (Moar, 1969*a*) are rather similar to the Corstorphine diagram, and are referable to the Gramineae–*Rumex* assemblage zone. The complex lithostratigraphy at Bigholm Burn, Dumfriess-shire discourages any attempt at comparison or correlation, although radiocarbon dates of 11820 ± 180 (Q-694), 11580 ± 180 (Q-694), and 10820 ± 170 (Q-695) radiocarbon years B.P. have been obtained from the basal and included peat layers at this profile.

There are three detailed pollen diagrams from sites in western Norway at latitudes slightly further north than Scotland (58–61 ° N). The diagram from Jaeren (Chanda, 1965*b*) is generally similar in pollen stratigraphy to the diagram from Loch Meodal, with a well-marked *Betula* assemblage zone extending from about 10800 to 12800 radiocarbon years B.P. No *Juniperus* pollen is present in the Jaeren diagram, in contrast to Loch Meodal. The diagram from Lista in southern Norway (Hafsten, 1963) is rather similar to the Jaeren diagram, with a *Betula* zone date at about 11500 radiocarbon years B.P. The diagram prepared by Mangerud (1970) from Blomöy in western Norway is closely comparable to the diagrams from Loch Fada and Loch Mealt with a Gramineae–*Rumex* assemblage zone (zones B1–B3) dated from 12070 ± 180 (T-672) to 9340 ± 160 (T-623) radiocarbon years B.P., and a *Betula–Corylus* zone (zone B5) with a lower boundary of 9340 ± 160 (T-623) radiocarbon years B.P. The chief differences from the Skye diagrams are the high relative frequencies of *Salix* and Cyperaceae pollen and the low values of *Juniperus* pollen.

As discussed in Chapter 10, the Gramineae–*Rumex* assemblage zone and some of its subzones can also be recognised in Late-Devensian pollen diagrams from sites in northern England, north Wales, and Ireland, and it has been dated in these areas between about 10000 and 14300 radiocarbon years B.P. Similarly the *Betula–Corylus* assemblage zone occurs widely at sites in northern and western Britain, occurring as far south as Cheshire, Caernarvonshire, and Co. Clare. The lower boundary of this zone has been dated between 9000 and 10000 radiocarbon years B.P. The *Lycopodium*–Cyperaceae assemblage zone is more restricted in its known geographical extent, as it is only known in montane areas of western Scotland, the Lake District, and north Wales. It is particularly well-developed at Llyn Dwythwch and Nant Ffrancon, Caernarvonshire (Seddon, 1962). The *Betula* assemblage zone is similarly rather restricted in its known occurrences in Britain, occurring locally at low lying sites in north Wales, northern England, and south-west Ireland, and as discussed in Chapter 10, it is only known in areas that have a relatively mild oceanic climate today. It also has a restricted time-stratigraphical range, from about 10800 to 12500 radiocarbon years B.P.

Pollen diagram from sites in southern England (Godwin, 1968; Suggate & West, 1959) and from the adjacent European mainland (Behre, 1966; Berglund 1966*a*; Iversen, 1954; Krog, 1954; Van der Hammen, 1951) show few similarities to the group of diagrams from the Isle of Skye and elsewhere in northern and western Britain that were discussed above. Although the same major pollen types are present in all the diagrams, their distribution and relative abundance are quite different at the southern and eastern sites. The pollen zones present on Skye and elsewhere in the north and west of Britain cannot be found further south. It appears that the differences between the vegetation of southern and eastern Britain and northern and western Britain were at least as pronounced in Late-Devensian times as they are at the present day. Detailed pollen diagrams with radiocarbon dates from sites in intermediate areas must be available, however, before the spatial and temporal relationships of the southern pollen zones to the northern zones can be clarified.

14

THE LATE-DEVENSIAN LANDSCAPE

1. INTRODUCTION

The third level of interpretation of pollen stratigraphical data is the reconstruction of the past landscape and thus the conditions under which the past flora and vegetation lived. The reconstruction of the landscape, including its topography and the organisms that populated it, is generally the ultimate desideratum of Quaternary palaeoecological studies. It can only be attempted after all the accumulated observations and analyses of chronologically and stratigraphically correlated biota and lithologies have been assembled into a coherent picture of past conditions. Inferences about the interactions of the biotic and abiotic components of the landscape and about the influence of environmental factors within that landscape – the ecosystem – can then be attempted.

Due to the limitations of the fossil record and the restricted scope of the investigation, the reconstruction of the Late-Devensian landscape of the Isle of Skye is necessarily incomplete, and it is strongly biassed towards the past vegetation or phytocoenose and its relations to the geological and edaphical conditions within the ecosystem. One of the aims of the study was the testing of the hypothesis that the Late-Devensian flora and vegetation were diverse on a small scale within Skye, just as the present flora and vegetation of the island are today. Consideration of this hypothesis requires the study of the spatial distribution of the past flora and vegetation within the landscape at particular points in time, in order to discover whether the observed variations in the fossil pollen assemblages and hence the past plant cover can be related to physical conditions of the landscape. This approach therefore investigates the controls imposed by the abiotic components of the landscape on the pattern and distribution of the Late-Devensian flora and vegetation at any one time.

A second aim was to study the temporal changes in the Late-Devensian flora and vegetation at specific points in space, in order to discover the possible causes and mechanisms of such changes. In view of these two aims, the discussion of the Late-Devensian landscape presented in this chapter will therefore consider the spatial and temporal aspects separately. There is independent geomorphological evidence of landscape development during Late-Devensian times and a brief description of the topographical and physiographical processes that appear to have occurred is presented first, as it is possible that changes in topography and landscape development influenced the temporal and spatial distribution of the flora and vegetation and its fossil record on Skye.

It is only after discussion of these aspects of the past landscape that the role of climate in the landscape can be considered. As past climate cannot be measured directly, its reconstruction must depend entirely on inference from observations of the fossil record dating from the time period of interest. The formulation of any climatic model has thus been delayed until all the observations have been synthesised into a coherent picture of the past landscape. When the palaeolandscape of Skye has been reconstructed from the observed evidence of the sediments and their contained fossils, the interplay of forces within that landscape can be inferred. It is at this stage of reasoning that notions of past climate can be logically considered. As the biotic component is the most complex part of any landscape or ecosystem, its detailed reconstruction in space and in time is essential, for it can provide, by careful inference, information about the abiotic component, including climate. Such inferences are based on the present environmental tolerances of the taxa and the communities concerned, and the assumption is made, as in the reconstruction of the past vegetation, that the ecological tolerances have not changed significantly since at least the time of the last glaciation.

2. TOPOGRAPHICAL AND PHYSIOGRAPHICAL PROCESSES

There are very few observations and interpretations of the glacial history of the Isle of Skye. Forbes (1845) and Harker (1901) emphasised the importance of corrie glaciation centred on the Cuillins in the glacial history of the island, and more recently Charlesworth (1956) and Sissons (1967*a*) have suggested local ice-cap development in the Cuillins and Red Hills, with isolated corrie glaciation in the Trotternish Peninsula. Although Charlesworth and Sissons equated this glacial episode with the Highland Readvance stade, there are differing views amongst glacial geologists and geomorphologists as to the areal magnitude and geographical extent of the Highland Readvance in northern Scotland (Kirk *et al.*, 1966; Sissons, 1967*b*; Sugden, 1970).

It was thus necessary to attempt to reconstruct the glacial history of Skye, for glaciation is considered to be the predominant geomorphological process acting during the time of the Devensian. The following features were noted and mapped in the field on a scale of 1:63360 (H. J. B. Birks, unpublished data).

- (i) lodgement till
- (ii) ablation till
- (iii) terminal and lateral moraine features
- (iv) corries
- (v) nivation hollows and protalus ramparts
- (vi) erratics
- (vii) eskers and kames
- (viii) glacial striae
- (ix) outwash gravels
- (x) rock weathering
- (xi) block fields
- (xii) periglacial features
- (xiii) raised shoreline features

Many other features preserved in the present topography of Skye remain to be studied. An account of the glacial history of the island has been prepared on the basis of this field mapping, but only the salient features are discussed here. The recent glacial history of the island appears to be as follows:

1. Along the west coast of Scotland, including the Isle of Skye, glacial striae, erratics, and the occurrence of pockets of weathered till indicate that Skye and the other islands in the Inner Hebrides were once covered by ice from the Scottish mainland. The age of this glaciation is not known.

2. There followed a phase (? interglacial) during which extensive rock weathering, both chemical and mechanical, occurred. In the Sleat, Elgol, and Trotternish Peninsulas thicknesses of up to 50 feet (17 m) of weathered rock and 'tors' can be found. Highly shattered bedrock outcrops occur on the low tops of the hills, the slopes of which are covered by a mixture of shattered local rock and weathered till. On steeper ground thicknesses of up to 20 feet (7 m) of angular head have been found overlying 15 feet (5 m) of weathered, rotten gabbro bedrock. Whatever the age of these weathering processes, it is likely that these areas have not been overridden by ice since the time that the weathering occurred. In none of the sections examined was there any evidence of fresh ablation or lodgement till overlying weathered bedrock. In the centre of the island there is, however, abundant geomorphological evidence to suggest more recent glaciation.

3. An ice-cap was developed around the Cuillins and the Red Hills that fed large valley glaciers in Glen Varragill, Glen Drynoch, Glen Sligachan, Loch Sligachan, Strath Mor, and Strath Beag, as well as in several small valleys in the Red Hills. The decay of these valley glaciers resulted in the deposition of extensive areas of a characteristic hummocky ablation till overlying lodgement till delimited by well developed arcuate end-moraine features at Glen Varragill, Glen Drynoch, the Braes, Ob Apoldoire, and near Loch Eishort. The restricted occurrence of fresh hummocky till in central Skye supports the view of a limited recent glaciation there, whereas the absence of fresh kame or morainic features near Broadford suggests that there was no fusion of local Cuillin ice with ice from the mainland extending out of Loch Alsh or Loch Carron. However, the massive ablation till and kame features in Glen Arroch suggests that a small ice lobe may have crossed from Glenmore and Glenelg at Kyle Rhea to halt at the watershed in Glen Arroch, and to discharge meltwater through the gorge of Abhainn Lusa, thereby forming the outwash terraces between Breakish and Kyleakin.

The western and southern corries in the Cuillins, for example Coire Lagan, Coire na Banachdich, and Coir 'a Ghrunnda, appear to have supported more restricted glaciers during this phase. The limits of this glaciation are marked by distinctive arcuate terminal moraine and outwash features. Lochan Coir' a' Ghobhainn lies within the ablation till of this phase.

The only evidence available at present for the possible age of this Cuillin glaciation comes from the occurrence of deposits of Late-Devensian age in several lochs within the morainic limits of the glaciation. The pollen succession at Lochan Coir' a' Ghobhainn appears to record the local colonisation of the moraines around the site, suggesting that there may be little difference in age between the ice retreat and the basal sediments in the lochan. If this is so, this glaciation must therefore have occurred before

12500 radiocarbon years B.P. (Fig. 27). The association of the Glen Arroch glacial outwash gravels with a high sea-level (90–110 feet, 27–33 m) at Kyleakin and Breakish provides indirect evidence for the age of this glacial phase. According to the shoreline relation diagram presented by Synge & Stephens (1966), the association of a sea-level at this height in relation to the 30-feet (9 m) isobase of the main Flandrian shoreline suggests that the Glen Arroch glacier can be correlated with either the Strath Broom/Garve or the Loch Broom/Fortrose moraines. The age of these moraines is not known, but they must predate the deposits at Loch Droma dated to 12810 ± 155 radiocarbon years B.P. (Kirk *et al.*, 1966). They may thus be tentatively correlated with the Perth Readvance glaciation that culminated about 12000 radiocarbon years B.P. (Sissons, 1967*a*, 1967*b*).

4. There is geomorphological evidence in the corries of the Cuillins, of Blà Bheinn, and of some of the Red Hills to indicate the redevelopment of small corrie glaciers subsequent to the main Cuillin glaciation. This phase is marked by small arcuate block moraines at 1000 feet (305 m) or above, inside which are abundant hummocky moraines, often littered with angular boulders. Pollen stratigraphical results at Lochan Coir' a' Ghobhainn and at An Sgùman suggests that this phase occurred some time before 9500 radiocarbon years B.P. and after 10800 radiocarbon years B.P. This glacial phase can thus be time-correlated with the Loch Lomond or Highland Readvance of 10300 to 10800 radiocarbon years B.P. (Sissons, 1967*b*). The palynological and lithostratigraphical succession at Lochan Coir' a' Ghobhainn suggests that snow-beds were extensive at this time, and that amorphous solifluction or gelifluction processes occurred at altitudes as low as 275 feet (82 m). Snow-beds may also have developed in the Red Hills at this time, as suggested by the pollen sequence at Loch Cill Chriosd. Many of the rather shallow, perched corrie-like features in the Red Hills, for example Coire na h'Airidhe on the north side of Glamaig, are interpreted as being nivation hollows ringed by protalus ramparts. They probably developed as small snow patches in shallow concavities, and subsequent enlargement by freeze-thaw processes, associated with a climatic deterioration, would result in their deepening, and in the presence of permanent snow-beds.

Several corrie-like features are discernible on the eastern flanks of the Trotternish basalt, ridge, for example Coire Scamadal to the north of The Storr, and Coire Cuithir. Morainic features only occur at Cuithir, suggesting the former occupation by ice. The other hollows are interpreted as representing nivation hollows. Nivation processes may have enlarged pre-existing depressions formed by landslipping.

Before about 12000 radiocarbon years B.P. sediments of low organic content, mainly silts and fine sands, accumulated in all the lochs examined (Fig. 30). As discussed in Chapter 13 the high inorganic content of the sediments suggests that there was little continuous vegetational cover either in or around the lochs at this time, thereby leading to soil erosion, slope instability, and inwashing of minerogenic material. If the temporal relationships suggested above between the basal sediments at Lochan Coir' a' Ghobhainn and the retreat stages of the ice that formed the basin now occupied by the lochan are correct, it is probable that the sediments that predate 12500 radiocarbon years B.P. at Loch Fada, Loch Mealt, Loch Meodal, and Loch Cill Chriosd (Fig. 27) accumulated at the same time as the melting of the large valley-glacier complex that had developed out from the Cuillins and the Red Hills. Geomorphological evidence suggests that the ice extended at least as far north as Eas na Coille in Glen Varragill about 12 km south of Loch Fada. As Lochan Coir' a' Ghobhainn is the only site in Fig. 27 that overlies the drift of this glacial phase, the young age of the basal sediments is not therefore surprising. This phase of deglaciation and ice wastage in central Skye must have been one of considerable landscape instability. The abundance and form of the ablation-till hummocks and the extent of fluvio-glacial outwash deposits in central Skye suggest that the ice downwasted primarily by stagnation and disintegration rather than by an orderly retreat of the ice margin. The instability of the landscape at this time would have resulted from the continual shifting of meltwater streams, the deposition and redeposition of outwash sands and gravels such as at the northern end of Glen Varragill, the continual erosion by glacial meltwater forming deeply cut gorges, and the melting of buried ice. The magnitude of the latter process is open to speculation but the probable amount of ice present in the area under consideration suggests that it may have been an important factor.

A feature closely related to the development of the landscape at this time is the movement of the ground water-table. During and immediately after the ice wastage the water table may have been essentially at ground level. Lowering of the water table by surface drainage may have been slow, however, until the

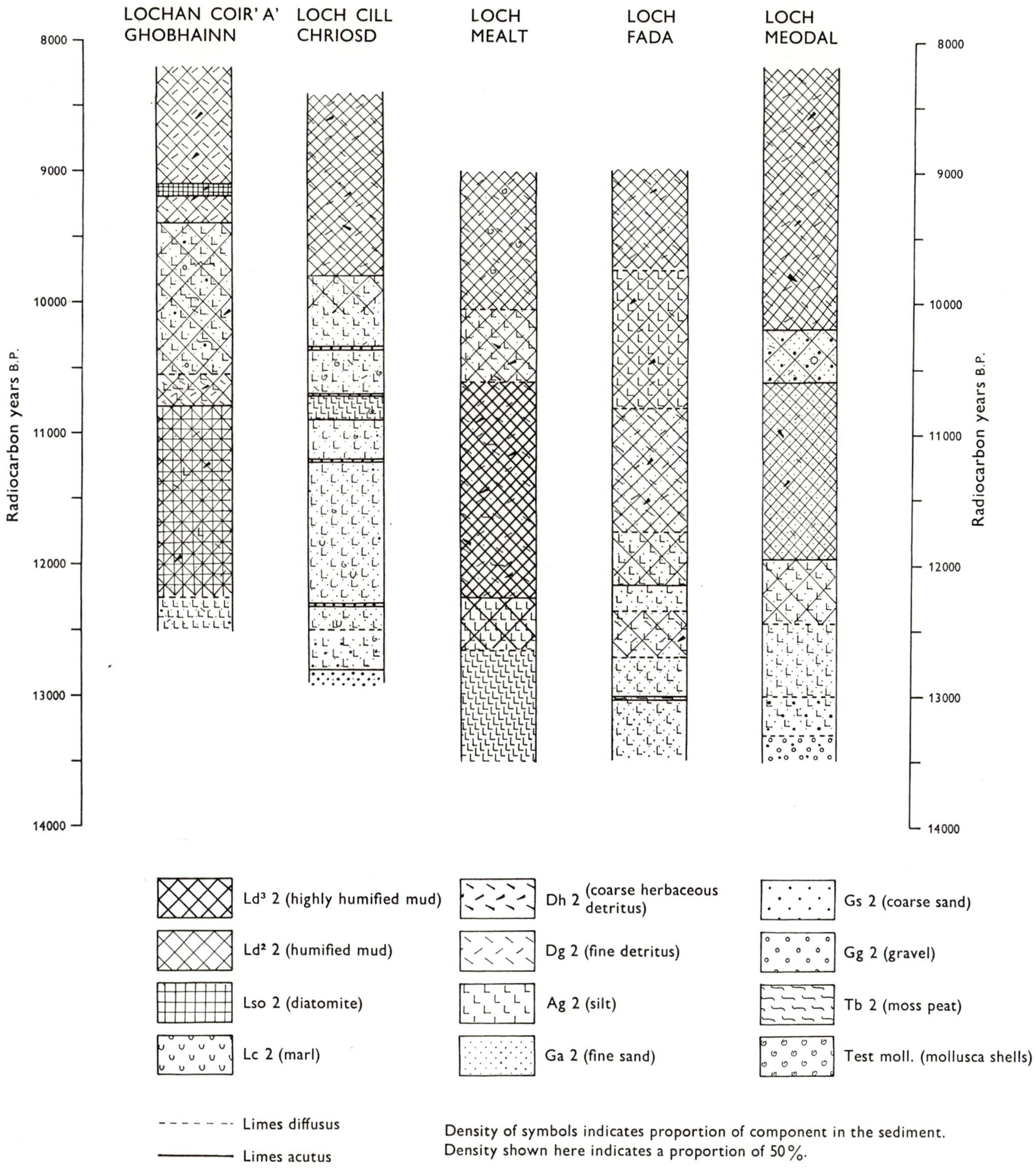

Figure 30. Comparison of sediment lithologies at the five sites examined, based on the correlation chart (Fig. 27) and the sediment lithologies described in Chapter 9. Symbols for sediment types follow Troels-Smith (1955) and they are explained on the diagram.

present stream patterns had developed by down-cutting and erosion within the landscape. Melting of any buried ice masses may have had an important effect on the water regime, because of the volume reduction and changes in drainage following melting. It is likely that the water table remained close to the soil surface, at least in low-lying areas, for some time after the melting away of surface ice in central Skye.

Organic muds began to accumulate at about 12 200 radiocarbon years B.P. at Loch Mealt and at 11 900 B.P. at Loch Meodal (Fig. 30). Diatomaceous muds started to accumulate at about the same time in Lochan Coir' a' Ghobhainn. Organic muds, but with a high inorganic content, began to form slightly later at Loch Fada, at about 11 750 B.P. There was little accumulation of organic sediments at Loch Cill Chriosd prior to 10 000 B.P., but the origins of the minerogenic sediments at this site are not clear (see Chapter 13). The increased organic content of the sediments that accumulated between about 12 000 and 10 800 radiocarbon years B.P., coupled with a decreased influx of silt and fine sand (Figs. 14, 16, 18, and 22), is interpreted as reflecting decreased soil erosion, greater landscape stability, and increased organic productivity in the lochs at this time. It is probable that little, if any, ice wastage was occurring at this time in the lowlands of Skye.

At about 10 800 radiocarbon years B.P. there is a revertence to sediments of high inorganic content at all the sites examined on Skye (Fig. 30). The sediments at Loch Fada and Loch Mealt contain little coarse-grained minerogenic material, whereas at Loch Meodal there is abundant fine and coarse sand and some gravel in the sediments that accumulate at this time. At Lochan Coir' a' Ghobhainn the deposits that formed at this time contain large angular rock fragments, as well as silts and sands. These deposits appear to have resulted from amorphous solifluction processes, as discussed in Chapter 13. This widespread and virtually synchronous phase of minerogenic deposition on Skye appears to be related temporally to a vegetational revertence to open, treeless communities, resulting in a generally unstable landscape between about 10 800 and 10 200 years B.P., with local corrie glaciation in the Cuillins, Blà Bheinn, and in parts of the Red Hills, and extensive snow-bed development elsewhere. The sparse vegetational cover, associated with soil erosion and abundant meltwater would have resulted in rapid run-off, frequent flooding, and deposition of coarse debris on low ground. Material transported by wind could not be demonstrated in significant quantities in the sediments. It is possible that many of the larger alluvial fans that are common where upland streams debouch onto valley floors were formed or, at least, were greatly augmented at this time.

In spite of the deposition of minerogenic material in the lochs at this time, there do not seem to have been many changes in the loch biota (except at Lochan Coir' a' Ghobhainn), suggesting that the mineral material is largely related to changes in the landscape around the lochs rather than to changes in the physical conditions within the lochs. The abundance and nature of the inorganic material deposited at this time may be related to the local geology and topography around the site as well as to the intensity of the erosional processes. For example, the high inorganic content of the Late-Devensian sediments at Loch Fada compared with those at Loch Mealt may be a result of the topographical differences around the sites rather than a result of different degrees of erosion.

At about 10 200 radiocarbon years B.P. the deposition of mineral material in the lochs ceased at Loch Meodal and Loch Mealt, whereas it continued at Loch Fada and Loch Cill Chriosd to about 9800 B.P. and at Lochan Coir' a' Ghobhainn to about 9400 B.P. Fine detritus muds of high organic content accumulated in the lochs since these times, and there is no indication in the sediment lithology of the physical conditions of the soils within the catchment areas of the lochs. It is perhaps significant that if the correlations presented in Fig. 27 between the pollen zone boundaries at the sites examined are correct then the lithological changes at each site (Fig. 30) are not isochronous within Skye, suggesting that lithostratigraphical correlations within the Late-Devensian may not be a suitable means of time-correlation (cf. Bartley, 1966; Donner, 1957). Changes in pollen stratigraphy and in sediment lithology are generally, but not precisely, related in time, and the lack of synchroneity in the pollen stratigraphy is similarly reflected in the sediment lithology.

The rate of sediment accumulation during the Late Devensian differs from one site to another. The rate appears to be two to three times more rapid at Loch Fada and Loch Mealt than at the other sites. This difference is probably related to the surrounding geology and to varying rates of erosion near the sites, with a rapid rate of weathering in the basalt regions compared with the comparatively slow weathering of gabbro, granite, and sandstone.

Besides the inwashing of inorganic material, there appears to have been considerable erosion of surface soil and of humus at various times during the Late-Devensian on Skye. This is shown by the frequent occurrence of remains of terrestrial bryophytes and of fungal hyphae incorporated into the limnic sediments. The origin of the well-marked bryophyte layer at Loch Fada is discussed in detail in Chapter 13. In general, bryophyte remains are most frequent in the minerogenic sediments on Skye, suggesting that they are largely derived by inwashing.

There are no indications in the present landscape of Skye to suggest that permafrost occurred at all widely on the island. Fossil frost wedges and involutions are extremely rare on Skye, as they are in much of western Scotland (see Fig. 89 in Sissons, 1967*a*). Unambiguous geological evidence for other periglacial processes occurring at this time is lacking.

The most striking geomorphological features of the Trotternish Peninsula are the extensive landslips, for example at The Quirang and at The Storr. The mechanisms of these slips are discussed by Andersen & Dunham (1966) and they are interpreted as being rotational slip features. They consider (p. 195) that 'the earliest post-glacial period (Pollen Zone I) was apparently wet and one of extensive solifluction. In Skye this was probably the period of landslipping immediately following the retreat of the Highland ice. Pollen Zone II with a drier, milder climate (Allerød) left no recognizable deposits on Skye.' Apart from the error in equating Pollen Zone I with the earliest post-glacial period, there is evidence at Loch Fada that sediments of at least 13500 radiocarbon years B.P. occur in a basin within one of the landslip features. This indicates that the landslipping that formed this basin occurred prior to this time. It is not possible on the available evidence to suggest any further age for the landslipping, and it is likely that it does not represent any single synchronous physiographical process. It is possible that the silt and fine sand in the Late-Devensian sediments at Loch Fada may have resulted not only from soil erosion within the catchment area but also from landslipping on the slopes above the loch.

It is probable that the sea-level around Skye was considerably higher during Late-Devensian times than at present, as evidenced by the raised shoreline features at Kyleakin and Breakish and by the possible marine transgressions reflected in the sediments at Loch Cill Chriosd. If there was a Late-Devensian sea-level of 30 m or more higher than the present level, the distribution of land and sea around the island would have differed from the present situation. For example, much of Strath Suardal, Strath Mor, and Glen Brittle would have been submerged by the sea. The land would have been draining to a marine base-level somewhat higher than at present, and this may have influenced the down-cutting of streams and rivers.

The landscape during the Late-Devensian appears to have been one of considerable instability with extensive soil erosion and inwashing of material. The present evidence, including the available radiocarbon dates and the correlation of the pollen diagrams, suggests that changes in the landscape were occurring at the time that the sediments, including pollen and spores, were accumulating in the lochs examined. There was a phase of extensive deglaciation prior to about 12000 radiocarbon years B.P., and a comparatively short and restricted phase of corrie glaciation centred on the Cuillins between about 10800 and 10000 years B.P., associated with the development of snow-beds in the Red Hills. Other physiographic processes occurring during Late-Devensian times appear to have been amorphous solifluction, land- and sea-level changes associated with isostatic recovery of the land and eustatic changes in sea-level, and possible landslipping in the basalt areas in Trotternish. The physiographical setting was thus probably rather similar to that of the present day, but with greater surface instability and shallower soils. Controls imposed by the solid geology on the topography and on pedogenic processes will have also been important in influencing the environment of the Late-Devensian flora and vegetation.

3. SPATIAL AND TEMPORAL DIFFERENTIATION OF FLORA AND VEGETATION

A generalised comparison of the inferred vegetational history at the five sites investigated on the Isle of Skye is given in Fig. 31. It is based on the correlation chart presented in Fig. 27 and on the vegetational reconstructions proposed for each site in Chapter 13. Although several problems remain unresolved in the reconstruction of the past vegetation, the gross physiognomy and floristic affinities of the vegetation from which each major assemblage zone was derived is scarcely in doubt. As discussed in Chapters 4 and 5 there is today considerable differentiation in the flora and vegetation of Skye, largely as a result of differences in geology, soils, topography, and climate. The five sites chosen for pollen analysis were selected as being representative of the principal geological

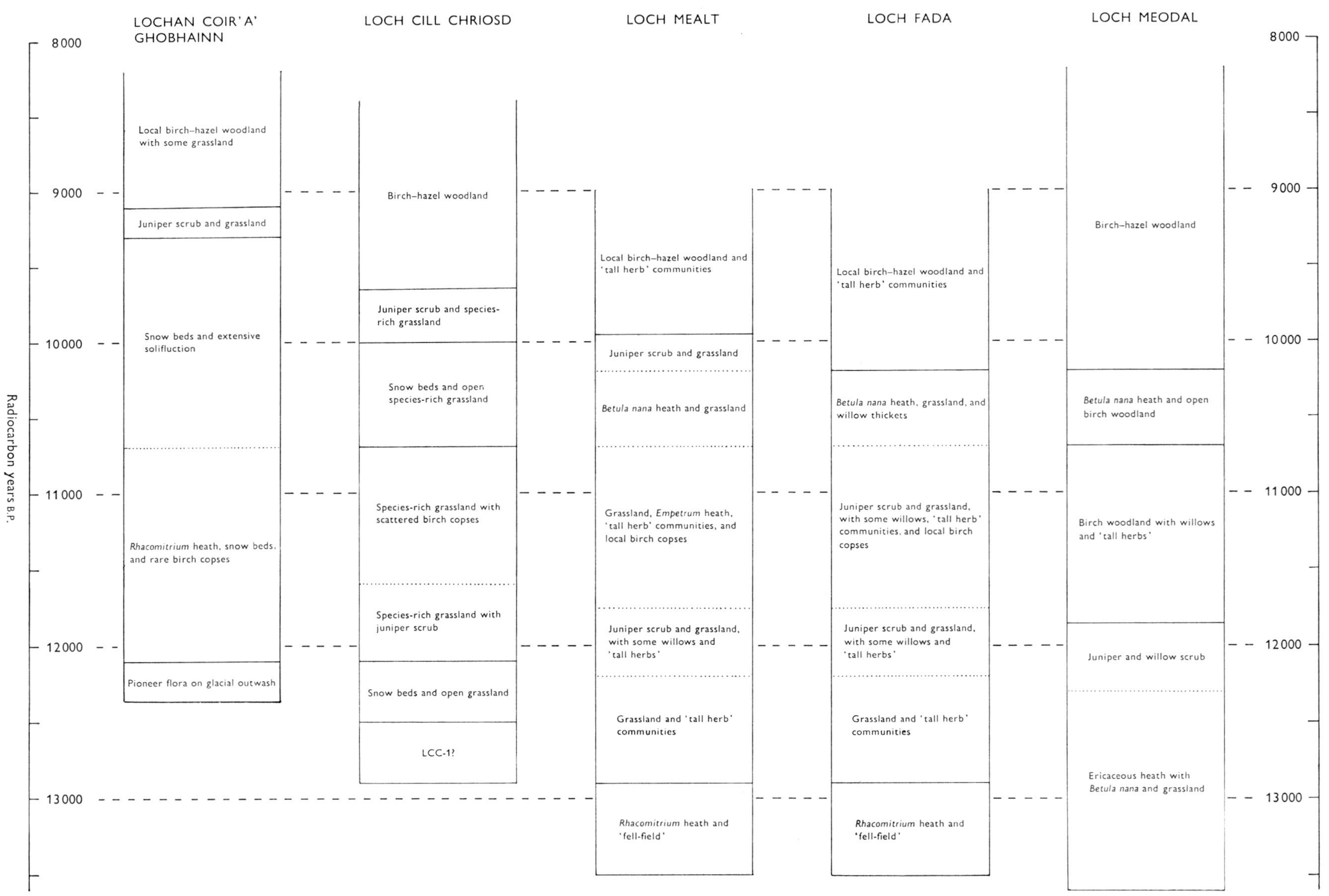

Figure 31. Generalised comparison of the inferred vegetational history at the five sites investigated, based on the correlation chart (Fig. 27) and on the vegetational reconstructions presented in Chapter 13.

and vegetational regions within the island today (Fig. 12), in order to study the vegetational diversity within Skye during Late-Devensian times. A cursory examination of the five pollen diagrams (Plates 1–5) reveals several significant differences in the pollen stratigraphy and the fossil assemblages between sites. Such differences may result from the varying contribution of the local and regional components of the pollen rain at each site, and thus they may bear no direct relation to the surrounding vegetation. The sites studied are of roughly comparable size and morphometry, and any effects of differential pollen transport and sedimentation are therefore minimised. The consistency of the pollen record within each site, both in terms of floristic composition and relative percentages, is suggestive that significant variations in the fossil pollen assemblages reflect variations in the past vegetation.

To aid in the discussion of vegetational differentiation on Skye during Late-Devensian times, the pollen stratigraphical data for the five sites studied are summarised in Figs. 32 and 33. The pollen frequencies, based on the sum of all determinable pollen and spores of non-aquatic taxa (ΣP), are presented in terms of nine broad groups of pollen and spore types. The groups are based on the present ecological and sociological preferences of the taxa concerned (derived largely from Table 4.57). The percentages of pollen and spores of all taxa within a group are summed for each stratigraphical level to give a total relative frequency of that group. The nine groups are

1. *Woodland.* Includes *Anemone* type, *Athyrium filix-femina*, *Betula* undiff., *Conopodium* type, *Corylus avellana*, *Melampyrum*, *Mercurialis perennis*, *Polypodium*, *Populus tremula*, *Prunus* cf. *P. padus*, *Pteridium aquilinum*, *Sanicula europaea*, *Sorbus aucuparia*, *Sorbus* cf. *S. rupicola*, *Thelypteris dryopteris*, *T. phegopteris*, and *Viburnum opulus*.

2. *Grassland.* Includes *Alchemilla*, *Arenaria* type, *Armeria maritima*, *Artemisia* undiff., *Botrychium lunaria*, *Campanula* type, *Cerastium alpinum* type, *Cerastium* cf. *C. holosteoides*, *Dryas octopetala*, *Helianthemum chamaecistus* type, *Hypericum pulchrum* type, *Lotus* cf. *L. corniculatus*, *Ophioglossum vulgatum*, cf. *Oxytropis*, *Plantago lanceolata*, *Plantago major*/*P. media*, *P. maritima*, *Polygala*, *Polygonum viviparum*/*P. bistorta*, *Potentilla* type, *Ranunculus acris* type, *Saxifraga aizoides*, *S. hypnoides*, *S. nivalis*, *S. oppositifolia*, *Selaginella selaginoides*, *Silene* cf. *S. acaulis*, *Thalictrum*, *Trifolium* undiff., and *Trifolium* cf. *T. repens*.

3. *Tall Herbs.* Includes *Angelica* type, *Cirsium*/*Carduus*, *Filipendula*, *Geum*, *Heracleum sphondylium*, *Lychnis flos-cuculi*, *Rubus saxatilis*, *Rumex acetosa*, *Salix* undiff., *Saussurea alpina*, *Sedum* cf. *S. rosea*, *Silene dioica* type, *Stellaria holostea*, *Trollius europaeus*, *Urtica*, *Valeriana officinalis*, and *Vicia*/*Lathyrus*.

4. *Juniper scrub.* Includes *Juniperus communis*.

5. *Shrub heath.* Includes *Betula* cf. *B. nana*, *Calluna vulgaris*, *Empetrum* cf. *E. nigrum*, Ericaceae undiff., *Lycopodium annotinum*, and *L. clavatum*.

6. *Chionophilous taxa.* Includes *Athyrium alpestre* type, *Cryptogramma crispa*, and *Lycopodium alpinum*.

7. *Chionophobous taxa.* Includes *Artemisia* cf. *A. norvegica*.

8. *Montane heaths* (either chionophilous or chionophobous). Includes *Lycopodium selago* and *Salix* cf. *S. herbacea*.

9. *Springs.* Include *Caltha* type, *Epilobium* type, *Koenigia islandica*, *Saxifraga stellaris*, and *Stellaria* undiff.

A common vertical scale of radiocarbon years B.P. is used throughout, based on the correlation chart (Fig. 27). The order of sites is the same as in Fig. 27, and the sample levels at each site are distributed through each pollen zone at distances proportional to their initial intervals at the point of sampling. The pollen assemblage zones are also shown. A constant scale is used within each group, but no attempt is made to keep the scales uniform for different groups, as the curves in Figs. 32 and 33 are intended to permit comparisons between sites, not between groups.

Woodland development on Skye before about 10000 radiocarbon years B.P. (Fig. 32) appears to have been restricted to the Sleat Peninsula (Loch Meodal), but scattered copses, primarily of birch, may have occurred elsewhere on the island, presumably in particularly favourable and sheltered sites. In the early Flandrian (*ca.* 9000 radiocarbon years B.P.) hazel and birch woods appear to have been most extensive in the Sleat (Loch Meodal) and in Strath Suardal (Loch Cill Chriosd), but more limited in their areal extent in Trotternish (Loch Fada and Loch Mealt) and the Cuillins. Despite the necessary caution in interpreting relative pollen percentages, the observed variations in the frequencies of pollen of woodland taxa are regarded as indicative of the former woodland pattern. The extent of the former

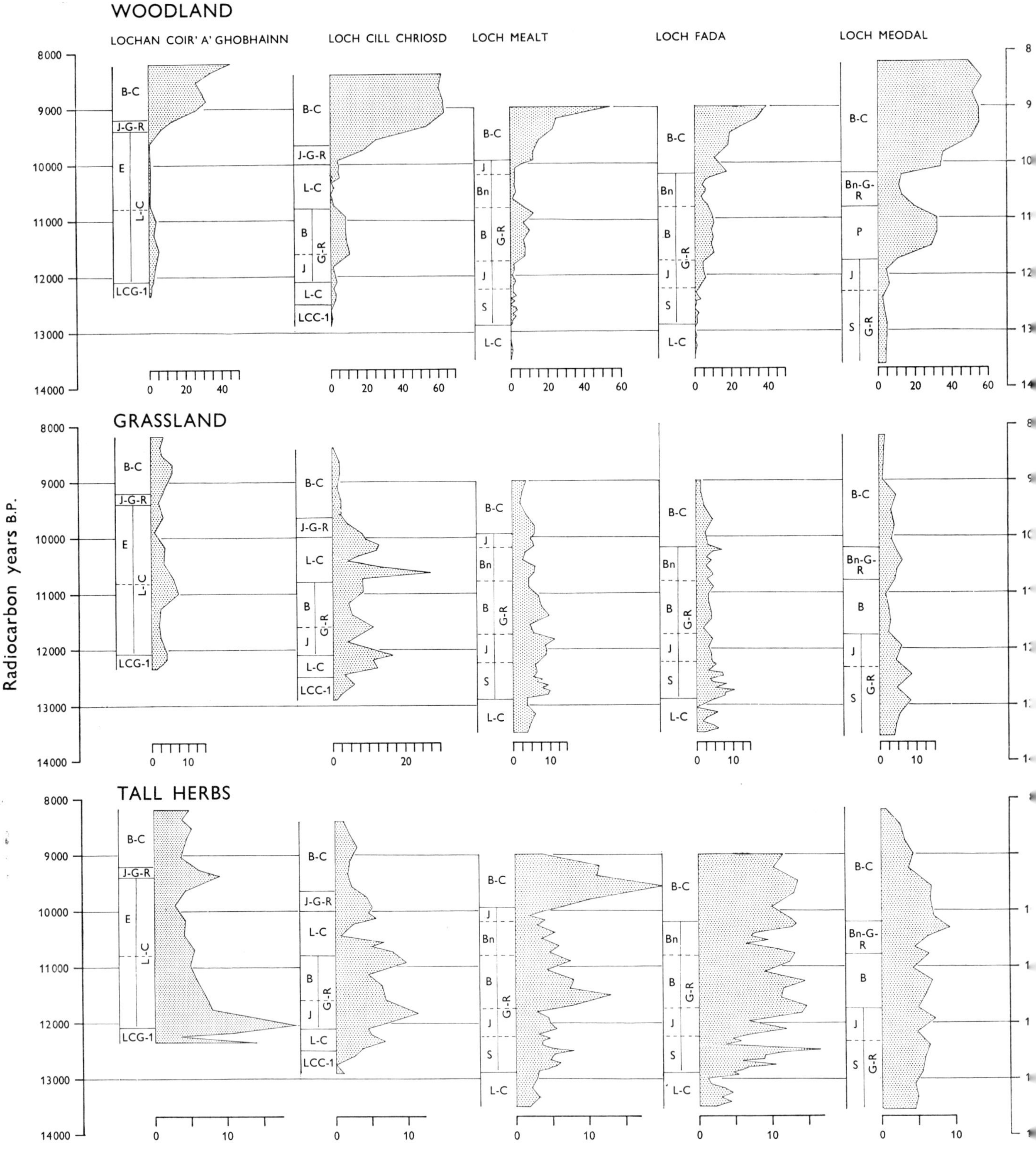

Figure 32. For legend see facing page.

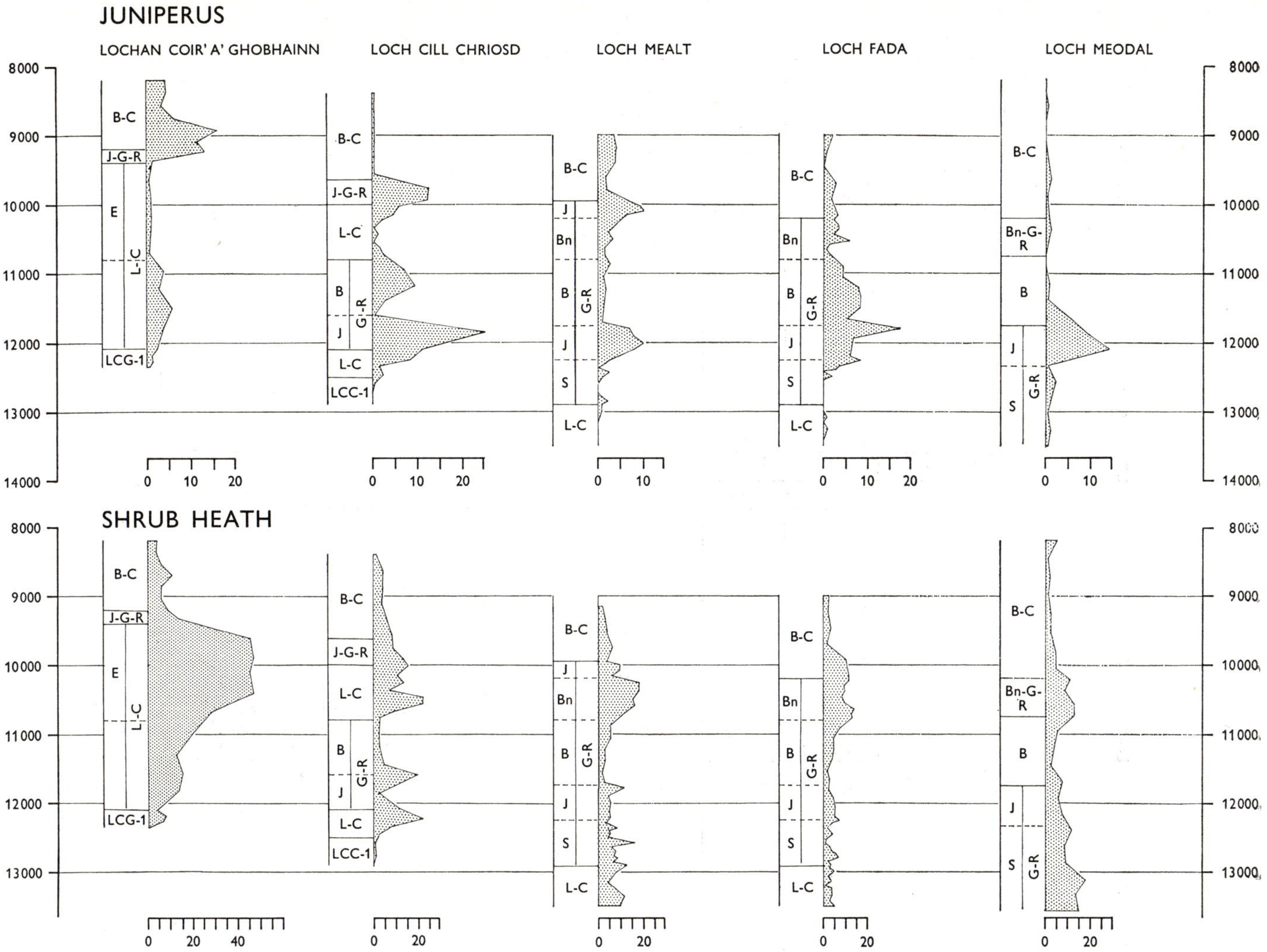

Figure 32. Summation curves for five groups of pollen and spore types based on the present ecological preferences of the taxa concerned at the five sites investigated. The groups are defined in Chapter 14 and are expressed as percentages of total determinable pollen and spores, excluding obligate aquatic taxa. A constant vertical scale of radiocarbon years B.P. is used, based on the correlation chart in Fig. 27, and the sample levels are distributed within each pollen zone at distances proportional to their initial intervals of sampling. Scale at base of each curve gives percentages for shaded silhouette. The pollen assemblage zones are also shown. Abbreviations: *B* = *Betula*, *Bn* = *Betula nana*, *C* = Cyperaceae, *E* = Ericaceae, *G* = Gramineae, *J* = *Juniperus*, *L* = *Lycopodium*, *R* = *Rumex*, *S* = *Selaginella*.

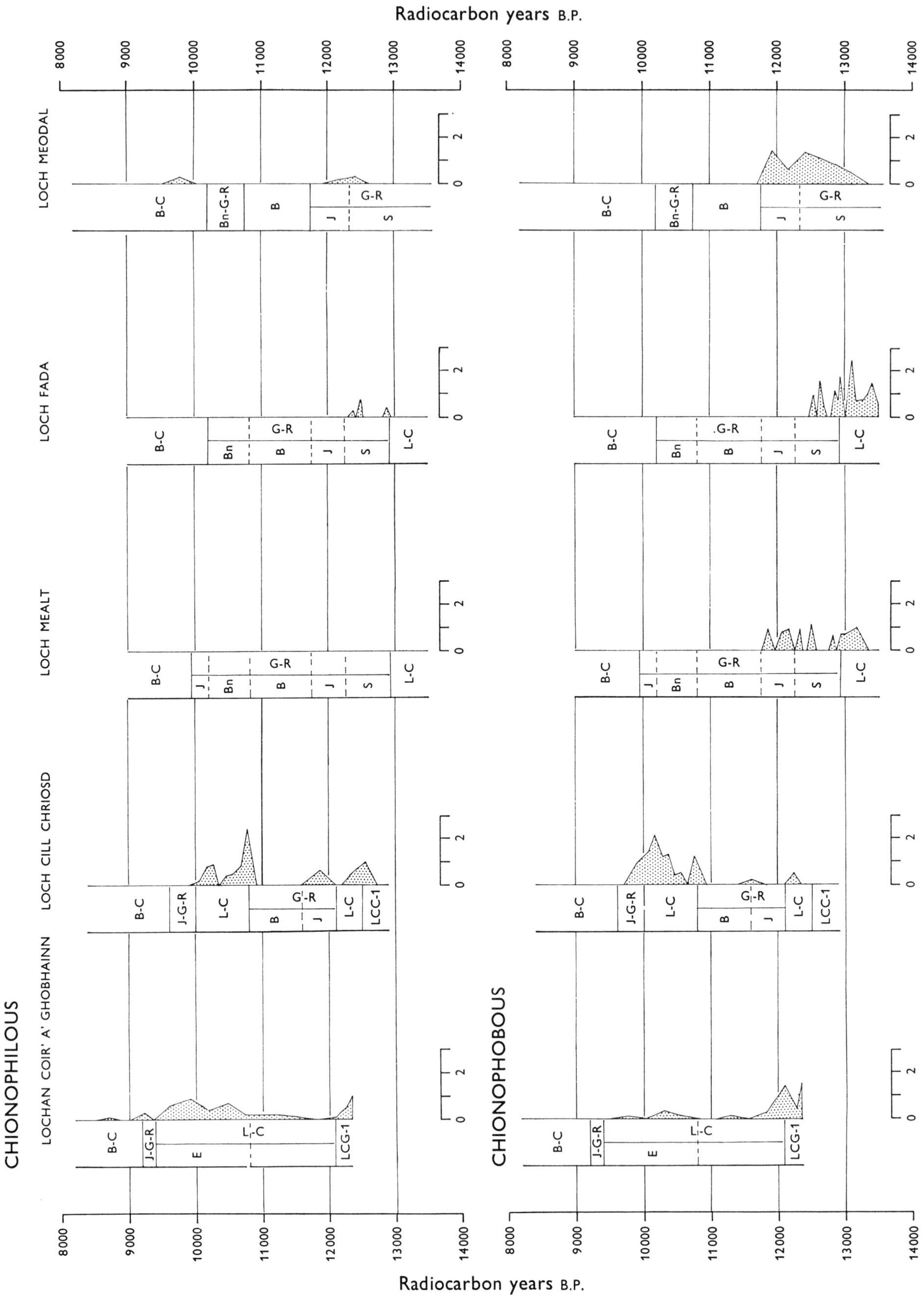

CHIONOPHILOUS
CHIONOPHOBOUS
LOCHAN COIR' A' GHOBHAINN
LOCH CILL CHRIOSD
LOCH MEALT
LOCH FADA
LOCH MEODAL
Radiocarbon years B.P.

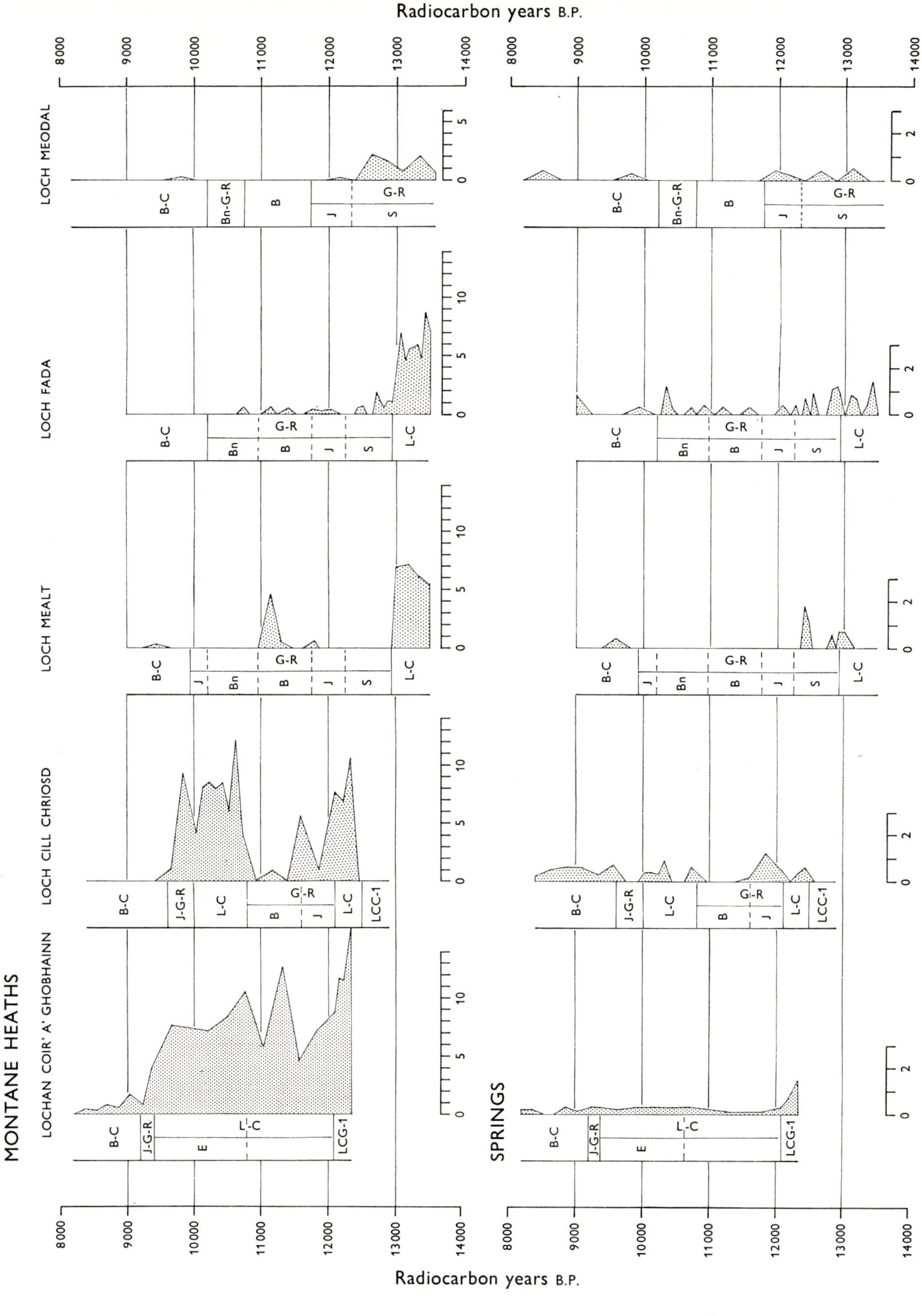

Figure 33. Summation curves for four groups of pollen and spore types based on the present ecological preferences of the taxa concerned. See Chapter 14 and caption to Figure 32 for further explanation and abbreviations.

woodland appears to have been similar to the present distribution of woodland on Skye (Fig. 6 and Chapter 5), suggesting that conditions for woodland development about 10000 years ago were more favourable in the southern part of the island than in the northern and western parts. The present pattern of woodland distribution on Skye appears to result largely from climatic gradients within the island, and the existence of a comparable vegetational pattern in the past is suggestive that similar climatic gradients and controls existed then, with the Sleat Peninsula experiencing a milder, less exposed climate than elsewhere on the island.

Sparsity of tree pollen is characteristic of many Late-Devensian pollen diagrams from sites in northern and western Britain (see Fig. 9 in Seddon, 1962; Smith, 1965), in contrast to the higher percentages of both birch and pine pollen at sites in southern England and on the European mainland. Imposed on this general pattern there are, however, scattered instances where the birch pollen frequencies and the occurrence of macrofossils imply the local development of woodland in the north and west, for example around Morecambe Bay (Oldfield, 1960; Smith, 1958), in the southern part of Lakeland (Evans, 1970; Pennington, 1970; Walker, 1955), in south-west Ireland (Watts, 1963), and in the Sleat Peninsula of Skye. In view of the mild oceanic climate that these areas experience today, the local development of woodland in particularly sheltered sites is not surprising, and it emphasises the importance of local climatic factors in influencing vegetational diversity. The conclusion of Donner (1957) that Scotland north of the Forth–Clyde line lay beyond the limit of tree birches in the Late-Devensian is now untenable.

The comparatively poor success of birch and hazel in the Trotternish Peninsula in the Late-Devensian and the early Flandrian is probably a result of wind exposure limiting tree growth in the northern part of the island to lowlying sheltered areas. *Populus tremula* and *Sorbus aucuparia* are more tolerant of exposure than either birch or hazel, and it is of interest that there are no significant differences in their relative pollen frequencies between the sites where their pollen have been identified. However, the pollen values are so low, presumably because of their poor pollen representation, that it is difficult to assess their real role in the past vegetation of Skye. Both *Populus tremula* and *Sorbus aucuparia* are typically pioneer, light-demanding trees whose pollen occur consistently at the transition from treeless vegetation to birch or mixed birch–hazel woodland, but usually after the characteristic expansion of *Juniperus communis* pollen (Berglund, 1966*a*; Iversen, 1954, 1960). Their ecological roles are thus rather transitory and they appear to be influenced by the availability of habitats rather than by specific edaphic preferences.

Low-alpine or mid-alpine chionophilous vegetation (Fig. 33) appears to have been primarily restricted during Late-Devensian times to the Red Hills (Loch Cill Chriosd) and the Cuillins (Lochan Coir' a' Ghobhainn). The restriction of corrie glaciation during the Late-Devensian to these montane areas may reflect the more prolonged snow-lie there. The former occurrence of alpine chionophilous and chionophobous vegetation and of montane heaths near Lochan Coir' a' Ghobhainn (Fig. 33) at the same time (about 11300 radiocarbon years B.P.) as the development of woodland in the Sleat (Fig. 32), demonstrates the considerable vegetational diversity that must have existed within Skye at this time. This diversity was presumably a result of the strong climatic and topographic gradients acting within the island.

The extension or redevelopment of snow-bed vegetation, the onset of amorphous solifluction, and the development of small corrie glaciers in the Cuillins and the Red Hills between about 10800 and 10000 radiocarbon years ago contrasts with the occurrence of mildly chionophilous dwarf-birch vegetation elsewhere in the island at this time. The persistence of low-alpine and mid-alpine chionophilous vegetation and of amorphous solifluction processes up to about 9500 radiocarbon years B.P. at Lochan Coir' a' Ghobhainn (Fig. 33) contrasts with the development of birch and hazel woods in the Sleat, Trotternish, and Strath Suardal at this time (Fig. 32). Presumably the environmental changes that are reflected by the observed changes in pollen stratigraphy either occurred at different times at different places within the island, or, more probably, the environmental changes were sufficiently gradual to allow local factors such as edaphic, climatic, and topographic differences between the regions to influence, to some degree, the rate of vegetational change and the succession of plant communities.

The observed differences between sites in frequencies of pollen of the grassland group, the 'tall herb' group, and the shrub heath group (Fig. 32) provide further evidence to indicate the differentiation of vegetation within Skye during Late-Devensian and early Flandrian times. This differentiation appears to have been largely the result of edaphic differences between regions rather than being climatically controlled.

The high frequencies of pollen of 'tall herbs' and *Salix* (other than *Salix herbacea*) at Loch Fada and Loch Mealt (Fig. 32) suggest that communities with 'tall herbs' and willows were more widespread in the Trotternish region than elsewhere in the island during the Late-Devensian. Such communities today require deep, moist soils that are base-rich, well aerated, and frequently irrigated. These edaphic conditions are frequent in the basalt regions today, as shown by the abundance of lowland 'tall herb' meadows (*Juncus acutiflorus–Filipendula ulmaria* Association; Table 4.32 and Fig. 5) in northern Skye and by the frequent, but local, occurrence of stands of the *Sedum rosea–Alchemilla glabra* Association (Table 4.47 and Fig. 5) on ungrazed cliff-ledges above 1000 feet (305 m) on the Trotternish cliffs. The former abundance of comparable communities in this area in the Late-Devensian suggests that suitable edaphic conditions also existed in the past. The limestone soils on Ben Suardal today, although highly basic, are probably too dry and well-drained to permit the extensive development of 'tall herb' communities. The largest stand of 'tall herbs' on the Durness limestones in this area today occurs on the shaded moist ledges in the wooded gorge in Coille Gaireallach (see Chapter 9, p. 263). The soils developed over gabbro, granite, and sandstone are probably not basic enough today to support any abundance of 'tall herbs'. The low Late-Devensian values of pollen of 'tall herbs' at Loch Meodal (sandstone) and Lochan Coir' a' Ghobhainn (gabbro) and the moderately high frequencies at Loch Cill Chriosd suggest that a comparable vegetational pattern existed in the past. This pattern may have been largely controlled by edaphic differences between the regions.

The extremely rich floristic composition of the Late-Devensian grassland communities on the Durness limestones of Ben Suardal (as recorded at Loch Cill Chriosd) contrasts with the rather species-poor assemblage of comparable age that existed on the Torridonian sandstones around Loch Meodal. The equivalent grassland communities on the basalts around the two sites in Trotternish appear to have been rather intermediate in their floristic richness. A comparable floristic series exists on Skye today within the Agrosto–Festucetum grasslands in the three areas, with the species-poor, the *Alchemilla*-rich, and the species-rich associations largely reflecting an edaphic gradient of increasing basicity (Chapters 4 and 5). The existence of a similar floristic series in the Late-Devensian suggests that comparable edaphic gradients also existed at that time.

Dwarf-shrub heaths, dominated by *Empetrum* spp. and with members of the Ericaceae, do not appear to have been a prominent vegetational type on Skye during Late-Devensian times, with the possible exception of before about 12000 radiocarbon years B.P. at Loch Meodal. The very high frequencies of Ericaceae undiff. tetrads between about 9500 and 10800 radiocarbon years B.P. at Lochan Coir' a' Ghobhainn are interpreted in Chapter 13 as resulting from redeposition following solifluction and inwashing of mineral soils rather than reflecting dominant dwarf-shrub heaths. The apparent rarity of dwarf-shrub heaths on Skye in the Late-Devensian may have been a result of the generally high base-status of the soils in Trotternish (basalt), Suardal (limestone), and the Cuillins (gabbro). There is, however, an interesting differentiation between the two sites in Trotternish. The moderately high frequencies of *Empetrum* cf. *E. nigrum* and Ericaceae pollen, associated with scattered grains of several calcifuge species and the absence of pollen of many of the more exacting basiphilous herbs at Loch Mealt in zones LM-5 and LM-6 suggest that dwarf-shrub heaths may have developed quite extensively on the topographically subdued surrounds of the site, probably as a result of soil leaching and acidification. In contrast at the nearby Loch Fada, the *Empetrum* cf. *E. nigrum* and Ericaceae pollen values do not attain such high values at this time. Presumably the steep, unstable slopes and the continual addition of mineral material from unstable rock outcrops were able to maintain a higher soil fertility and to counteract the processes of leaching and surface acidification. Comparable vegetational and edaphic differences are observable around the two sites today, with the extensive development of bog and acidic grassland on the flat and gently sloping ground near Loch Mealt contrasting with the *Alchemilla*-rich grasslands on the steep slopes near Loch Fada.

There are few modern analogues on Skye for the shrub-dominated communities that appear to have been prominent during the time of the *Juniperus* and *Betula nana* subzones. Both shrubs are largely indifferent to soil type today, and the development, or at least the flowering, of these shrubs is probably controlled by particular conditions of exposure, shade, competition, and snow-lie rather than by local differences in soil. There is little significant variation between the sites in the observed frequencies of pollen of these shrubs. It is of interest that juniper scrub (Fig. 32) appears to have flourished at about the same time at different sites on Skye before 11000

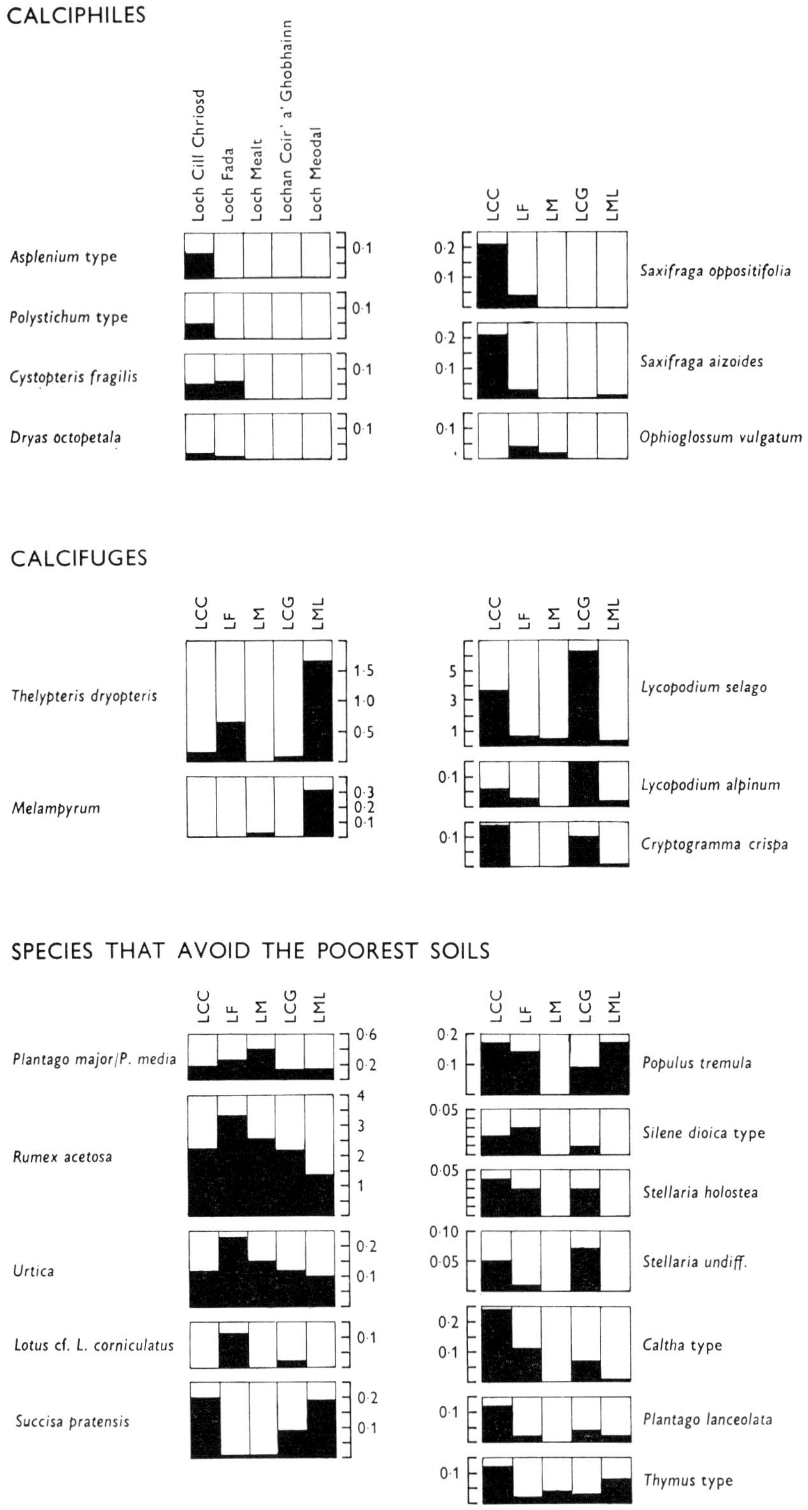
CALCIPHILES
Loch Cill Chriosd
Loch Fada
Loch Mealt
Lochan Coir' a' Ghobhainn
Loch Meodal
LCC
LF
LM
LCG
LML
Asplenium type
Polystichum type
Cystopteris fragilis
Dryas octopetala
Saxifraga oppositifolia
Saxifraga aizoides
Ophioglossum vulgatum
CALCIFUGES
Thelypteris dryopteris
Melampyrum
Lycopodium selago
Lycopodium alpinum
Cryptogramma crispa
SPECIES THAT AVOID THE POOREST SOILS
Plantago major/P. media
Rumex acetosa
Urtica
Lotus cf. L. corniculatus
Succisa pratensis
Populus tremula
Silene dioica type
Stellaria holostea
Stellaria undiff.
Caltha type
Plantago lanceolata
Thymus type

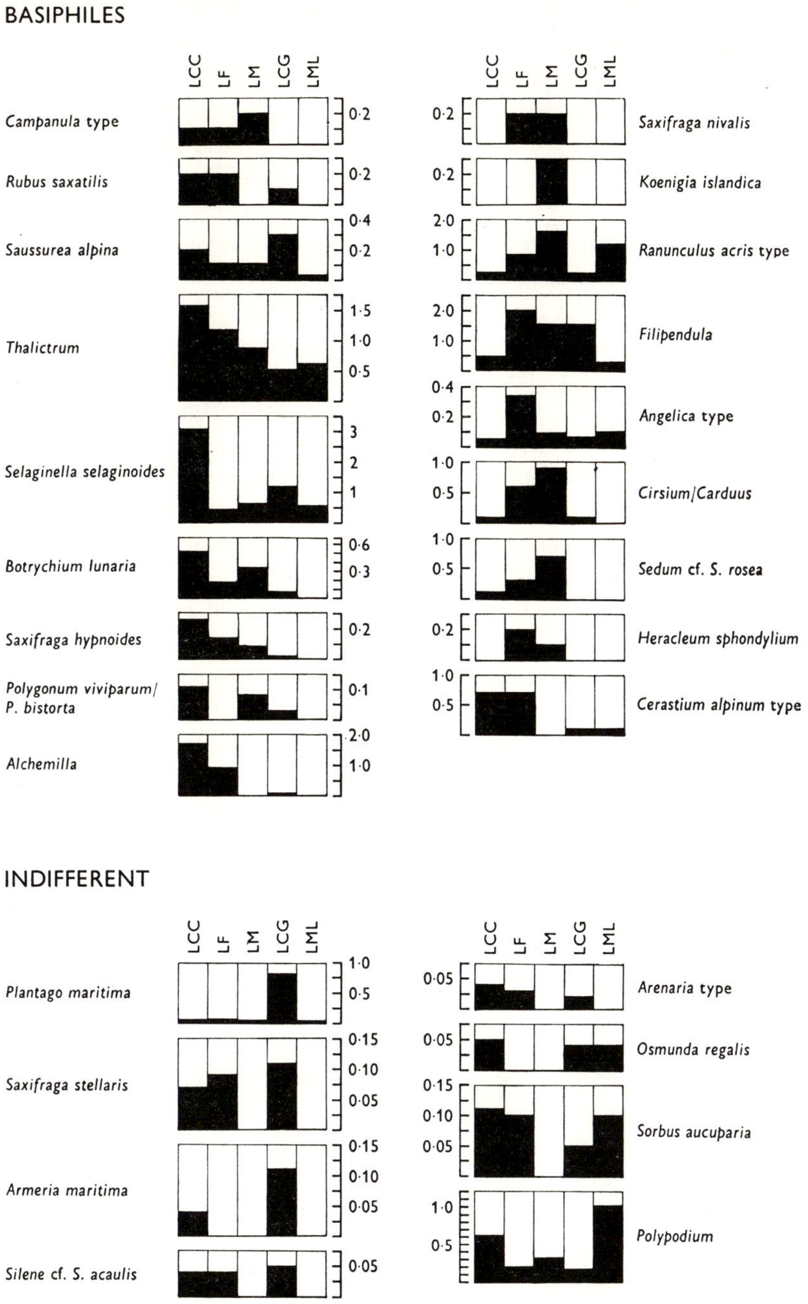

Figure 34. Relative frequencies for pollen and spore types of taxa that occur in the present edaphic categories defined in Chapter 5, expressed as a percentage of the total number of determinable pollen and spores, excluding obligate aquatic taxa. Pollen totals: Loch Cill Chriosd 8433; Loch Fada 10504; Loch Mealt 9215; Lochan Coir' a' Ghobhainn 21 757; Loch Meodal 9074.

radiocarbon years B.P., but at different times after 10000 radiocarbon years B.P. It always appears to have predominated in a short-lived (300–500 radiocarbon years) transitional stage from treeless to wooded vegetation.

Montane spring communities (Cardamino–Montion) occur widely but rather locally throughout Skye today (Fig. 5), and they appear to be indifferent to rock type, although they avoid the limestones. It is interesting that comparable communities appear to have occurred, with little temporal variation, in the Cuillins, the Red Hills, and Trotternish in the Late-Devensian (Fig. 33). In contrast, spring communities with *Koenigia islandica* are inexplicably restricted to the Trotternish Peninsula today. They appear to have been similarly restricted in Late-Devensian times, but in view of their undoubtedly poor representation in the pollen rain (see Chapter 11), little can be deduced from their absence from the fossil record.

In Chapter 5 all the species in the present vascular plant flora of Skye are grouped into eight categories on the basis of their present soil preferences. The principal directions of variation are between those species that are centred on limestone soils (calciphiles, Table 5.7), those species that occur on a range of basic soils developed over basalt, gabbro, and limestone (basiphiles, Table 5.8), and those species that only occur on acidic soils (calcifuges, Table 5.6). There are two intermediate groups of indifferent species (Table 5.9) and of species that avoid the poorest soils (Table 5.10). The coastal, aquatic, and unclassified categories are not considered here.

In order to demonstrate whether a similar edaphic differentiation existed within the Late-Devensian flora of Skye, the relative frequencies of pollen and spore types of taxa that occur in the present edaphic categories are presented in Fig. 34. The relative frequencies of each type at each site are expressed as a percentage of the total number of determinable pollen and spores included in ΣP at each site. As all the pollen analyses are from limnic sediments deposited in basins of roughly similar size, local over-representation of particular taxa is unlikely, and the relative frequencies are thus comparable between sites. No attempt is made to keep the scales uniform for different taxa, for the histograms in Fig. 34 are intended to compare frequencies between sites, not between taxa (cf. the pollen diagrams). The pollen and spore types are grouped in the same way as their modern taxonomic counterparts into the five edaphic categories, and the sites are arranged along the geological series of limestone–basalt–gabbro–sandstone namely Loch Cill Chriosd, L. Fada, L. Mealt, Lochan Coir' a' Ghobhainn, and Loch Meodal.

There is a small group of calciphilous taxa (Fig. 34), such as *Asplenium* type and *Polystichum* type, whose spores are restricted in their Late-Devensian occurrences to the limestones around Loch Cill Chriosd, whereas there is a larger group of pollen and spore types, including *Cystopteris fragilis*, *Dryas octopetala*, *Saxifraga aizoides*, and *S. oppositifolia*, with their greatest frequencies at Loch Cill Chriosd, but with low values at Loch Fada and Loch Mealt. This Late-Devensian pattern corresponds closely to the present distribution of the calciphilous group on Skye, with their headquarters centred on the Durness limestones of Ben Suardal and with scattered occurrences on calcareous basalt cliffs in the Trotternish Peninsula. The former occurrence of *Ophioglossum vulgatum* spores at Loch Fada and Loch Mealt contrasts with the present restriction of the species on Skye to the limestones near Ben Suardal.

The Late-Devensian frequencies of pollen and spores of calcifuge species (Fig. 34) does not correspond so closely with the present distribution of the taxa concerned. Pollen of *Melampyrum* (? *M. pratense* or *M. sylvaticum*) and spores of *Thelypteris dryopteris* have their highest Late-Devensian frequencies at Loch Meodal in the Sleat, just as these taxa have their present Skye headquarters on the acid soils of this region. In contrast, however, the past frequencies of spores of *Cryptogramma crispa*, *Lycopodium alpinum*, and *L. selago* are highest at Loch Cill Chriosd and Lochan Coir' a' Ghobhainn. Although all these taxa are strictly calcifuge in their edaphic tolerances today, they are also montane plants on Skye. It is therefore of interest that the highest frequencies of their spores in the Late-Devensian are at the two sites receiving pollen and spores, in part at least, from high ground, namely the Cuillins (Lochan Coir' a' Ghobhainn) and the Red Hills (Loch Cill Chriosd).

Basiphilous species occur on limestone, basalt, and gabbro on Skye today. The frequencies of pollen and spores of basiphilous taxa in the Late-Devensian (Fig. 34) form four groups. There is a small group of taxa whose pollen frequencies vary little from one site to another, but they are restricted to sites on limestone, basalt, or gabbro. This group includes *Campanula* type, *Rubus saxatilis*, and *Saussurea alpina*. There is a large group of taxa that have their highest pollen and spore frequencies at Loch Cill Chriosd and lower values at the other sites. Some of the types in this group (*Alchemilla*, *Botrychium lunaria*, *Polygonum vivi-*

parum/P. bistorta, and *Saxifraga hypnoides*) do not occur at Loch Meodal, whereas *Selaginella selaginoides* and *Thalictrum* occur there with low relative frequencies. There is a small group of pollen types whose Late-Devensian occurrences are restricted to the basalts of Loch Fada and Loch Mealt (*Koenigia islandica* and *Saxifraga nivalis*). There is a group of pollen types that, although they are present at all the sites, attain their maximum frequencies at Loch Fada or Loch Mealt rather than at Loch Cill Chriosd. This group consists of *Angelica* type, *Cirsium/Carduus*, *Filipendula*, *Heracleum sphondylium*, *Ranunculus acris* type, and *Sedum* cf. *S. rosea*. This group consists predominantly of pollen of 'tall herbs'. Communities of 'tall herbs' appear to have been most abundant in Trotternish at this time (Fig. 32).

There is a small group of indifferent species within the Late-Devensian pollen flora (Fig. 34). As expected the frequencies of these taxa vary little between sites, for example *Arenaria* type, *Osmunda regalis*, *Plantago maritima*, *Saxifraga stellaris*, *Silene* cf. *S. acaulis*, and *Sorbus aucuparia*. The pollen of *Armeria maritima* is curiously restricted in its Late-Devensian occurrence on Skye, in contrast to the widespread distribution of the plant on the island today. The high values of *Armeria maritima* pollen at Lochan Coir' a' Ghobhainn are paralleled by the high frequencies of *Plantago maritima* at this site. This may result from the proximity of the site to the sea, and to the development of maritime grassland communities (see Chapter 13). The high frequencies of *Polypodium* spores at Loch Meodal may reflect the more sheltered climate in the Sleat as well as particularly favourable edaphic conditions.

The pollen of taxa that avoid the poorest soils on Skye today (Fig. 34) show a widespread distribution in the Late-Devensian, but they generally have their highest values at the basalt sites of Loch Fada and Loch Mealt (for example *Lotus* cf. *L. corniculatus*, *Plantago major/P. media*, *Rumex acetosa*, and *Urtica*). The pollen values of *Populus tremula*, *Silene dioica* type, *Stellaria holostea*, *Stellaria* undiff., and *Thymus* type vary little from one site to another, and they are thus similar in their Late-Devensian pollen frequencies to the indifferent category. In contrast to many of the more demanding basiphilous species, pollen of taxa in this group occur in moderate frequencies at Loch Meodal.

The former occurrence in low amounts of pollen of some basiphilous and even calciphilous species at Loch Meodal is interesting in view of the present geology, soils, and flora around the site today. Pollen of these taxa occur mainly in zone LML-1 (Plate 1) prior to the development of *Juniperus communis* scrub in the succeeding zone. An analogous situation occurs today on recently deglaciated terrain, where calciphilous and basiphilous species occur on open, young, slightly basic drift in contrast to the older woody vegetation on leached, humus-rich soils (Faegri, 1933; Persson, 1964).

It is of considerable palaeoecological interest that a strongly marked edaphic differentiation appears to have existed within Skye during Late-Devensian times, and that the differentiation was comparable to the present pattern on Skye. It is suggestive that much of the floristic and vegetational differentiation within the Late-Devensian landscape was edaphically controlled, and that the soils at this time were far from uniform. It is also suggestive that the present distribution of some of the more exacting species on Skye may reflect particular edaphic requirements rather than historical changes. The complexity of the many interacting factors that have been discussed in Chapter 12 emphasises the danger of invoking any single factor to interpret the present distribution of any single taxon within Skye.

In considering the temporal variations in vegetation during the Late-Devensian on Skye, the main features of interest discernible from Figs. 32 and 33 are the different rates of vegetational change at each of the sites investigated. For example, the rate at which herbaceous and shrub communities were replaced by trees at about 10200 radiocarbon years B.P. appears to have varied from site to site. At Loch Meodal the transition was rapid, the new balance being established in about 150 radiocarbon years. At Loch Cill Chriosd the same vegetational change appears to have taken about 400 radiocarbon years, whereas at Loch Fada, Loch Mealt, and Lochan Coir' a' Ghobhainn the change, once initiated, was hardly completed in 700 radiocarbon years. These differences may have been related to the availability of suitable soils, to topographical and climatic differences, or to the proximity to seed sources.

These different rates of changes at about 10200 radiocarbon years B.P. are apparently real, as they cannot be entirely due to differences in sampling intervals. At Loch Meodal and Loch Cill Chriosd pollen stratigraphical changes are usually fairly rapid and clearly defined, at Loch Fada and Loch Mealt they are less so, although in general they are still well marked, whereas at Lochan Coir' a' Ghobhainn a particular pollen stratigraphical change frequently covers a longer period of time than at other sites. As a corollary, the changes are usually less well defined, and a number of otherwise apparently independent changes necessarily overlap in time. This may be a factor in causing the high statistical heterogeneity in the spectra at this site (Fig. 23 and Chapter 10). The differences in rates of stratigraphical changes between sites may be a result of differences in the relative contributions of the local and regional components of the pollen rain at each site; the more restricted an area from which most of the pollen is derived, the more sharply would a vegetational change be reflected. Sites receiving a larger regional component, on the other hand, would be expected to show rather gradual changes. In view of the size and morphometry of the various sites, there seems to be no reason for supposing that Loch Meodal and Loch Cill Chriosd should have been more influenced in this way than Loch Fada or Loch Mealt. It is more likely, however, that differences in soils, regional topography, and exposure may have determined the rates of vegetational changes.

A feature of similarity between the sites is the consistent increase in pollen frequencies of *Juniperus communis* at all the sites at about 12250 radiocarbon years B.P., and of *Betula* undiff. pollen values at all the sites at about 11800 radiocarbon years B.P. These synchronous pollen stratigraphical and presumably vegetational changes imply a lack of competition between these plants at these times. Environmental conditions must have been within the ecological tolerances of the taxa and the plants must have been readily available for colonisation either from outside the area or from isolated stands within Skye. Competition between woody plants does not appear to have been an important ecological factor until about 10000 radiocarbon years B.P. when *Corylus avellana* pollen first appears in significant amounts.

Prior to about 12250 radiocarbon years B.P. the vegetation throughout Skye appears to have been predominantly herbaceous. It seems likely that between 13500 and 12300 radiocarbon years B.P. there was an incomplete vegetational cover and that the vegetation was susceptible to rapid and rather ephemeral changes induced by topographical and physiographical changes. Such physical changes within the landscape were probably relatively frequent during the initial phases of landscape evolution following the retreat and melting of the main Cuillin ice mass from central Skye.

Between about 12300 and 11800 radiocarbon years B.P. the development of juniper scrub and of small wooded areas suggests some stabilisation of the landscape. By about 11000 radiocarbon years B.P. the frequencies of tree pollen begin to decrease, however, and the vegetational patterns that had taken between 500 and 900 radiocarbon years to achieve and that had been maintained for a rather shorter period appear to have taken only 150 to 200 radiocarbon years to disrupt. At all the sites on Skye this transition is characterised by a decrease in values of tree pollen and a marked increase in the pollen of herbs, dwarf-shrubs and shrubs. As discussed above there is independent evidence for lithological and geomorphological changes at this time. The pollen and spore types contributing to this increase vary from site to site and from time to time, but Gramineae, Cyperaceae, and *Betula* cf. *B. nana* predominate. This sequence of vegetational changes appears to have lasted for different periods of time at different sites, from about 600 radiocarbon years at Loch Meodal, Loch Fada, and Loch Mealt, to about 800 at Loch Cill Chriosd, and about 1200 radiocarbon years at Lochan Coir' a' Ghobhainn. The levels in the pollen stratigraphy from which these periods are assessed are more or less arbitrarily determined because the changes from one assemblage zone to another are rarely sharply defined. However, it is suggestive that the rates and duration of vegetational change were different in different localities on Skye during the Late-Devensian.

The subsequent expansion of tree pollen and presumably of trees began at different times at different sites. This expansion appears to have consisted almost entirely of *Betula*, with some *Populus tremula* and *Sorbus aucuparia*. The different rates at which birch pollen increased are discussed above. The early stages of this expansion are often accompanied by a marked increase in the frequency of *Juniperus* pollen (for example at Loch Cill Chriosd and Loch Mealt). This juniper phase appears to have been rather shortlived, however, suggesting that trees were able to occupy areas that were initially colonised by *Juniperus*. The shrub would thus be shaded out (see Chapter 11 and Plate 6). The continued presence of pollen of *Juniperus* and of a variety of shade-intolerant herbs in consistent frequencies after 10000 radiocarbon years B.P. indicate that the woodland cover at this time was not continuous. *Corylus avellana* appears to have attained considerable importance in the vegetation on Skye at about this time, but the first significant increase in its pollen frequencies occurs at different times at different sites, for example at about 10000 radiocarbon years B.P. at Loch Meodal, at about 9500 radiocarbon years B.P. at Loch Cill Chriosd, at about 9000 radiocarbon years

B.P. at Loch Fada and Loch Mealt, and at 8650 radiocarbon years B.P. at Lochan Coir' a' Ghobhainn.

Discussion has centred on the differences in the times and rates of stratigraphical and vegetational changes during the Late-Devensian at the various sites on Skye. The apparent lack of synchroneity and the differences in the rates of change at each site may reflect the importance of local habitat conditions such as slope, aspect, soil type, and exposure in influencing the response of vegetation to environmental changes. As Smith (1965) has discussed, during an environmental change (generally involving climate) conditions may become favourable for a particular species or vegetational type in one area before they do so in another nearby locality, whereas in other areas conditions may never become critical enough to initiate a change in the vegetation. The effects of any environmental change will always depend on whether or not the change crosses the critical *threshold* of a particular vegetational type. The concept of vegetational *inertia* to environmental change (Smith, 1965) is also important in considering rates and times of vegetational change. An environmental change in one area may result in conditions favourable for a new, immigrant species, whereas in another ecological setting the same environmental change may only produce conditions that are just above the critical physiological and ecological thresholds for the existence and survival of that species, and then perhaps only in particularly favourable micro-habitats. In such a situation the presence of the existing vegetation might well act as a barrier to invasion and thus provide resistance or inertia to a rapid vegetational change.

The general sequences of inferred vegetational changes appear to have been roughly parallel, if not strictly synchronous, from site to site on Skye (Figs. 27, 31), and there are some major trends during Late-Devensian times that are exhibited by the flora, the vegetation, and the landscape as a whole. It is these trends that require a general explanation, and the possible causes of these trends are discussed in the next section.

4. CAUSES OF VEGETATIONAL CHANGE

In the discussion of floristic and vegetational history and differentiation at the five sites studied, it is apparent that a wide range of species and communities were present on Skye in Late-Devensian and early Flandrian times. Despite this marked vegetational diversity, there is discernible a consistent sequence (Fig. 31) that appears to reflect a progressive stabilisation of the landscape, culminating in the local development of birch woodland at about 11 800 radiocarbon years B.P. in the so-called Allerød interstadial. The varying extent of this woodland at each site provides evidence for the vegetational differentiation that existed on Skye at this time.

This unidirectional sequence of increasing landscape stability is interrupted at about 10800 radiocarbon years B.P. by a phase of soil instability, solifluction, and corrie glaciation and, to some degree, of vegetational revertence. The occurrence of a series of roughly synchronous changes at all the sites examined is reflected in the sediment lithology, and by different species and communities in a variety of ecological and topographical settings, and implies that the changes at about this time are unlikely to reflect local events, but rather that they are expressions of a widespread vegetational and geomorphological response to a change in a major environmental factor within the Late-Devensian landscape. The most likely environmental factors that can have such widespread effects in different ecosystems are changes in regional climate. It is highly probable that this phase of landscape instability and vegetational revertence reflects a climatic deterioration. Such a climatic shift may have been a decreased mean temperature leading to an increased snow-lie and a higher incidence of frosts. This would result in snow-bed development and local corrie glaciation on high ground. Other climatic changes, such as changes in precipitation and in wind velocity, may also have been important, but the available evidence is not critical enough to permit detailed palaeoclimatic reconstructions.

In view of the similarities between modern montane communities and the vegetational types inferred from the fossil pollen sequences prior to 10800 radiocarbon years B.P. and the present altitudinal range of such communities (cf. Plates 6, and 7), it is highly probable that the vegetational succession recorded in the pollen profiles was changing in response to an ameliorating climate, with a succession from low- or mid-alpine communities, through sub-alpine shrub communities, to local birchwood development (see Fig. 31). As temperature is one of the most important single variables that influences the altitudinal distribution of modern plant communities, it is reasonable to infer that the past succession of vegetational types was the result of an increase in temperature. The temperature depression implied by the former occurrence of low-alpine vegetation at or near sea-level on Skye is of the order of 4 or 5 °C, assuming a lapse rate of 1 °F (0.56 °C) for every 270 feet (82 m) (see Chapter 3). Factors such as exposure to wind may also be important in influencing the altitudinal zonation today, so this temperature depression may be an over-estimate.

It is not possible to deduce whether the rate of temperature increase was gradual and step-wise, thereby controlling the rate of vegetational change, or whether it was sudden and the vegetation showed a lag in its response to climatic change. Such a lag can result from differing rates of soil development (Faegri, 1963), coupled with problems of migration, plant dispersal, and seedling establishment of new species (Iversen, 1960; Smith, 1965). Studies on the vegetational succession on recently deposited glacial moraines (Faegri, 1933; Persson, 1964) show that under constant climatic conditions, the time taken for the development of birch scrub on bare moraine is of the order of 200 to 250 years, and that soil development must reach a critical stage of stability and humus content before trees can colonise. Such a time lag will be considerably longer, however, if there are no suitable seed sources in the immediate vicinity.

A quantitative estimate of the climatic variables involved from the palaeobotanical data requires not only a thorough floristic and vegetational reconstruction, but a detailed knowledge of the ecological requirements and climatic tolerances, both of the taxa represented and of the communities present. Such an approach assumes that the physiology of the present morphological species has not changed significantly since the Late-Devensian (see Chapter 13). Even if this assumption is justified, the lack of detailed autecological information concerning the relevant taxa clearly limits any accurate estimate of past climate. Much climatic inference has been made on the relationship of present geographical ranges of species to selected climatic parameters, for example by Brown (1971), Conolly & Dahl (1970), and Dahl (1951). A causal relationship between climate and species distribution is assumed, even though experimental evidence on the climatic requirements and tolerances of individual species is rarely, if ever, available. Brockmann-Jerosch (1913) pointed out that standard meteorological data often show little correlation with the distribution of vegetation types and plant species, especially when a single parameter such as mean, maximum, or minimum temperatures, is tested as the possible controlling factor. His insistence on the significance of 'climatic character' as a whole rather than of any single readily measurable climatic factor is an indication of the complexity of the problem. Too little is understood of the relationships between organisms and climate to permit the precise quantitative evaluation of the climate and of the magnitude of its changes in Late-Devensian times on Skye. Only a few tentative generalisations appear possible.

Thus the picture of climatic events during the Late-Devensian on Skye appears to be of progressive amelioration from about 13 500 to 10 800 radiocarbon years B.P., perhaps with a temperature rise of 4 to 5 °C. The presence of *Betula pubescens* at about 11 800 radiocarbon years B.P. implies that the mean July temperature at that time was at least 12 °C (Iversen, 1954), whereas the consistent records of *Littorella uniflora* pollen at this time is suggestive of mean July temperatures of 14 °C or more (Andersen, 1961; Samuelsson, 1934). This is about the same as the present July values for lowland Skye (see Chapter 3).

There was a short-lived but marked deterioration in climate at about 10800 radiocarbon years B.P. with a decrease in temperature and an increased snow-lie. Manley (1964) has estimated, on the basis of the extent of lowering of the snowline for corrie glaciation, that mean summer temperatures in north-west Britain were lowered by about 4 or 5 °C at this time. There was a return to more favourable conditions at the beginning of the *Betula–Corylus* zone at about 10000 radiocarbon years B.P. None of the plants or vegetational types recorded in this zone indicate a climate different in any way to the present climate of Skye, and it is therefore likely that the climate after 10000 radiocarbon years B.P. was rather similar to that of today. The possibility exists, however, that the climate of Late-Devensian times on Skye was radically different from that of today in that the annual, seasonal, and even diurnal distribution of temperature, precipitation, and wind velocity may have been different from the present, although the annual means of these parameters need not have differed greatly from present values. Testing this hypothesis will only be possible when more is learned about the climatic requirements and the ecological interactions of the species involved and when methods of estimating past climate in terrestrial situations have been developed that do not merely argue from present distributional ranges of plants and animals. Oxygen-isotope studies of freshwater sediments of Late-Weichselian and Flandrian age, such as have been made in Germany (Lang, 1970), may thus provide an important insight into past climatic changes.

The principal determinants of vegetational change during the Late-Devensian on Skye appear to have been climatic changes of small magnitude that crossed the critical thresholds of both communities and individual species. Imposed on the general climatically controlled vegetational sequence on Skye are local factors operating at each site and influencing more local vegetational changes. The most marked effects are edaphic changes such as leaching and acidification favouring the spread of *Empetrum* at Loch Mealt (cf. Berglund & Malmer, 1971). Such edaphic changes during the Late-Devensian may also be reflected by changes in the trophic status of the lochs, for example at Loch Meodal. Varying intensities of competition may also have been important, especially in influencing the former occurrence of taxa that are today restricted to open habitats with low competition.

5. PROBLEMS IN THE RECONSTRUCTION

Five critical problems concerned with the interpretation of the floristic, vegetational, and ecological history of the Isle of Skye in Late-Devensian times remain largely unsolved. The first concerns the floristic composition of the fossil assemblages recorded in the Late-Devensian. The former abundance of *Betula nana* in the Late-Devensian vegetation of Skye is inexplicable in terms of its present ecology in Britain. This problem is discussed in Chapter 12, where the possibility of ecotypic variation is suggested. The occurrence of pollen of *Plantago major/P. media* and of several other ruderal taxa such as *Artemisia* undiff. and Chenopodiaceae in significant amounts also creates a problem in the proposed vegetational reconstructions presented above, as none of these taxa occur in modern montane communities in Scotland today. Perhaps their occurrence in the Late-Devensian was a result of large herbivorous mammals grazing in the species-rich and sub-alpine grasslands and 'tall herb' communities that existed during the time of the Gramineae–*Rumex* zone. The present evidence does not support this or any alternative hypothesis.

The second problem concerns the virtual absence of *Corylus avellana* pollen and presumably of *Corylus avellana* plants before about 10000 radiocarbon years B.P. on the Isle of Skye. The species today tolerates a wide variety of soil types in Scotland, but it generally favours those which are basic and moderately damp rather than those that are perennially waterlogged. Hazel is intolerant of shade, although less so than birch, but it flowers and fruits profusely in the absence of an overtopping canopy. It is generally regarded as a 'thermophilous' species today, in view of its present geographical range in Scandinavia. It extends to 68°N in Norway but only to 63°N in eastern Sweden. In the northern part of its range it flowers progressively later at higher latitudes, suggesting a strict temperature control (Hultén, 1950). It seems likely that spring temperatures consistently above 2 °C must be reached to enable the successful flowering and fruit development of hazel (Walker, 1966). These climatic conditions lie broadly in the present climatic regime, within the 15 °C mean July daily maximum isotherm in north-west Europe. Hafsten (1956) has suggested that a June–September mean temperature of 10.5 °C may be a significant climatic limit for *Corylus*. On Skye, the present value for the mean July maximum temperature is 18.3 °C in the lowlands and for the June–September mean is 14.8 °C (see Chapter 3).

If the reconstruction of the Late-Devensian landscape of Skye, including its climate, presented above is valid, it seems inconceivable that conditions were not suitable for the germination, growth, and flowering of *Corylus avellana*, especially during the period 11800 to 10800 radiocarbon years B.P., in view of the present climatic and ecological tolerances of the species. To postulate limiting biotic factors, such as the presence of blights or rusts, merely shifts the problem to another organism. The argument that hazel was delayed in reaching areas as far north as Skye is also unsatisfactory (cf. Faegri, 1963). There is no evidence to suggest the occurrence of *Corylus* anywhere in Britain prior to about 10000 radiocarbon years B.P., and yet its pollen appears in significant amounts at sites throughout northern and western Britain at about the same time (Hibbert *et al.*, 1971), implying a rapid migration and spread of the species. In view of this apparently rapid spread in the early part of the Flandrian, it is difficult to conceive of what environmental factors could have limited its expansion in the Late-Devensian other than climate. It is possible that the climate during Late-Devensian times was radically different from any known today in some respect critical to hazel but not to birch. For example, the spring and summer temperatures in the Late-Devensian may have been as high as at present but with a greater minimum and maximum temperature range and a higher incidence of spring frosts than exists today anywhere within the range of *Corylus avellana*. Such a climatic regime may have favoured birch and other trees and shrubs, and yet it may have failed to reach some critical threshold necessary for the establishment and survival of hazel. Testing this hypothesis may be possible when more is known about the climatic requirements of the species involved, and when studies have been made near the western and southern limits of the Devensian glaciations. Until then, the problem remains unresolved.

The third problem, closely related to the preceding one, is concerned with age of the lower boundary of the *Betula–Corylus* assemblage zone and with the varying rates of expansion of *Betula* undiff. and *Corylus avellana* pollen. The opening of the zone occurs at differrent times at different places on Skye (Fig. 27), ranging from 10200 radiocarbon years B.P. at Loch Meodal and Loch Fada, to 9200 radiocarbon years B.P. at Lochan Coir' a' Ghobhainn. The first significant increases in *Corylus* and *Betula* undiff. pollen values are also metasynchronous within Skye, occurring at about 10000 radiocarbon years B.P. at Loch Meodal, at 9650 radiocarbon years B.P. at Loch Cill-Chriosd, and between 9200 and 8650 radiocarbon years B.P. at Lochan Coir' a' Ghobhainn. The hypothesis of different migration rates within an area as small as Skye cannot explain these differences of 1000 radiocarbon years or more. If the environmental reconstruction for the opening of the *Betula–Corylus* zone is correct, namely that there was a widespread climatic amelioration at about 10000 radiocarbon years B.P., the apparent metasynchroneity of the lower boundary of the zone is unexpected. It suggests that either the chronology is in error, that the environmental reconstruction is incorrect, or that some unknown factor was operative that inhibited the establishment and development of *Betula* and *Corylus* in some areas after they had expanded in other areas on Skye. Perhaps the climatic changes that are presumed to have occurred at about this time were sufficiently gradual to allow local environmental factors such as edaphic, topographic, microclimatic, or competitive factors to influence the rate of vegetational change and the expansion of *Betula* and *Corylus avellana* at this time. Like the preceding problem, this one remains unsolved at present.

The fourth problem is to explain the pollen stratigraphical changes that occur in the pollen diagrams between 13500 and 11800 radiocarbon years B.P. Because neither the vegetation nor the prevailing climate of this time are well understood, any interpretation of fluctuations in the pollen stratigraphy must remain speculative. As discussed above, the stratigraphical changes are interpreted as reflecting a vegetational succession responding to a climatic amelioration and resulting in a progressive stabilisation of the Late-Devensian landscape. The nature of the climatic change is uncertain, but it probably involved either an increase in temperature or a decrease in wind exposure, or a seasonal redistribution of either or both of these climatic parameters. It is not possible to decide from the available evidence whether the climatic change was gradual, coinciding in time with the pollen zone boundaries at about 12900, 12250, and 11800 radiocarbon years B.P. (Fig. 27) and thus reaching critical thresholds for vegetational change at these times, or whether there was a single climatic change at about 12900 radiocarbon years B.P. and the pollen stratigraphical changes record a progressive vegetational succession in response to this change.

The opening of the *Juniperus* subzone at about 12250 radiocarbon years B.P. is marked by significant increases in the relative frequencies of pollen of aquatic taxa at all the sites except Loch Cill Chriosd. Although aquatic plant development is undoubtedly a local vegetational change within the site of deposition, the fact that it occurred not only in isolated basins but throughout the island at this time suggests that it was a response to a widespread environmental change. As both aquatic plants and *Juniperus communis* are considered by Iversen (1954, 1964) to be particularly sensitive indicators of climatic change, the pollen stratigraphical changes occurring at this time may reflect a sharp increase in temperature. However *Betula* undiff. pollen does not show any significant increase in its frequencies until about 11800 radiocarbon years B.P. How much of this delay is due to the migration rate and spread of tree birches under favourable climatic conditions, and how much of it is due to competition with other woody species is unknown. Evidence from fossil coleopteran remains in Late-Devensian sediments (Coope, 1970) suggest that the course and magnitude of climatic changes, particularly of temperature, at this time may have been markedly greater than has been supposed from palaeobotanical evidence. Until methods of estimating past climate have been developed that are not based solely on changes in animal or plant populations, the problem of climatic changes on Skye before 11800 radiocarbon years B.P. must remain unresolved (cf. Lang, 1970).

The fifth problem is closely related to the preceding one and it concerns the pollen stratigraphy and inferred vegetational history between about 11 800 and 12 500 radiocarbon years B.P., the time of the so-called Bølling interstadial and the Bølling–Allerød stadial (Older *Dryas* period *sensu* Iversen, 1954) recorded from Denmark, Holland, and Germany (Iversen, 1942, 1954; Lang, 1952; Müller, 1953; Tauber, 1970; Van der Hammen, 1951; Van der Hammen *et al.*, 1967). Although the pollen stratigraphy appears to extend to about 13 600 radiocarbon years B.P. (Fig. 27), thus covering the interval of time of the Bølling interstadial and Bølling–Allerød stadial in north-west Europe, there is no indication of any pollen stratigraphical or environmental changes that could be equated with the interstadial or stadial. The present interpretation of the pollen stratigraphy suggests that there was a progressive unidirectional vegetational succession from low-alpine or mid-alpine communities to sub-alpine juniper scrub, presumably in response to a climatic amelioration starting at about 12 800 radiocarbon years B.P. corresponding to the transition between the *Lycopodium*–Cyperaceae and the Gramineae–*Rumex* zones. The *Juniperus* subzone begins consistently on Skye between 12 100 and 12 300 radiocarbon years B.P., at about the time of the Bølling interstadial in Denmark (Tauber, 1970). If the proposed model of the vegetation at this time is correct, a climatic deterioration such as is presumed to have occurred at the time of the Bølling–Allerød stadial would have resulted in an expansion of low-alpine vegetation and a recession of sub-alpine juniper and grassland communities, at least at the sites in Trotternish and the Sleat. The pollen stratigraphy should thus record an increase in Cyperaceae pollen and *Lycopodium selago* spores and a corresponding decrease in *Juniperus communis*, Gramineae, and *Rumex acetosa* pollen, and in pollen and spores of a variety of herbaceous taxa. No such pollen stratigraphical changes can be detected in any of the pollen diagrams from Skye or from elsewhere in Scotland. There is thus no evidence for any vegetational or climatic recession between about 12 800 radiocarbon years B.P. and the opening of the Allerød interstadial *s.s.* at 11 800 radiocarbon years B.P.

This conclusion contradicts the widespread assumption that such a climatic oscillation must have occurred in Scotland (Jardine, 1968; Penny, 1964; Vasari & Vasari, 1968). At least three alternative explanations can be proposed as working hypotheses.

1. A climatic oscillation occurred in Denmark, Holland, and Germany but it was local in its areal extent and in its effects on vegetation, and did not extend to north-west Scotland. It thus might not have had any marked effects on the vegetation and hence the pollen rain in Scotland at this time.

2. A climatic oscillation occurred in Scotland but it was either too brief or of insufficient amplitude to cross any critical vegetational threshold, and thus it did not affect the vegetation at this time to any extent recognisable at the current level of interpretations of the observed pollen stratigraphy. Alternatively the climatic oscillation may have only influenced parameters such as the precipitation–evaporation ratio, to which the vegetation in Scotland and its pollen rain at this time were relatively insensitive. It is also possible that a climatic change at the time of the Bølling is recorded in the Skye pollen stratigraphy but that it has been misinterpreted here as minor fluctuations of no regional significance. If this is so, then future examination of further sites on Skye and from adjacent areas should reveal the same fluctuations consistently. Testing of this hypothesis must come either from palaeoclimatic evidence other than pollen stratigraphy or it must await improved techniques for interpreting environmental changes from pollen analytical data.

3. The pollen stratigraphy itself is inadequately known. It is considered, in the case of the Isle of Skye at least, that the number of pollen profiles and their position in space and time is sufficiently adequate to make the absence of any critical pollen stratigraphical changes at this time significant. However, the proposed chronology and zone correlations may be in error, or perhaps the interval of sampling at each site is too great to reveal the expected changes in pollen stratigraphy. It is considered unlikely, however, that any significant stratigraphical changes would be missed in *all* the profiles in view of the fact that the stratigraphical resolution for each level at some sites is less than 100 radiocarbon years.

The pollen stratigraphy for the time interval from 10 500 to 14 300 radiocarbon years B.P. at Blelham Bog, Lancashire (Pennington & Bonny, 1970) also shows no stratigraphical fluctuations at the time of the Bølling–Allerød stadial in Denmark, either in terms of relative pollen percentages or as absolute pollen influx. There is similarly little pollen stratigraphical evidence for any such oscillation in the pollen diagrams from Loch Sionascaig in Ross and Cromarty (Pennington & Lishmann, 1971) or from Jaeren in south-west Norway (Chanda, 1965*b*) where the available radiocarbon dates indicate that the profiles represent the time span in question. This is strongly suggestive that the vegetational and climatic histories of western Britain and western Norway differed from those of Denmark, Holland, and Germany, with a short-term climatic oscillation registered in the pollen stratigraphy from the latter areas only. Many more detailed pollen diagrams with associated radiocarbon dates must be analysed, however, before the regional differentiation of the Late-Devensian environment can be confidently reconstructed.

PART V

CONCLUSIONS

15

GENERAL CONCLUSIONS

The present study was conceived as a test of the applicability of pollen analysis as a method for reconstructing the landscape of the Isle of Skye during Late-Devensian times, including its flora, vegetation, and climate. A second aim was to study the spatial arrangement of the flora and vegetation within the Late-Devensian landscape as a means of testing the hypothesis that the plant cover of the island was as diversified at that time as it is at present. The project attempted to discover whether the spatial variation in fossil pollen asesmblages, and thus in the past flora and vegetation, could be related to the contrasting geological conditions within the island. This aspect of the project was concerned with the relationships between the plant cover and the physical aspects of the landscape, and with the controls imposed by geology, soil types, and topography on the spatial differentiation of the Late-Devensian flora and vegetation. A further aim was to study the temporal changes in the Late-Devensian flora and vegetation by observations on pollen stratigraphical changes, and to consider the possible causes and mechanisms of such changes.

Pollen analytical data by their very nature can only provide information pertaining to the past flora and vegetation. There is, however, a tendency to regard palynological data as direct evidence of past climate and of sediment age, as well as of flora and vegetation. If it is to be successful as a method in Quaternary palaeoecology, pollen analysis must be able to supply data and permit inferences that are independent of other means of inquiry. The present study has attempted such an independence.

The project has involved several stages. First, a phytosociological survey was made of the present vegetation of Skye (Chapter 4) to provide a basis on which to consider the role of environmental factors in influencing the spatial distribution and floristic composition of the present vegetation, and to provide background knowledge of the present ecological and sociological tolerances of individual species within the present flora of the island. The principal directions of variation, such as edaphic, topographical, climatic, and biotic factors, that appear to influence the present floristic and vegetational differentiation within the island were then considered (Chapter 5). A phytogeographical analysis of the present vascular plant flora was attempted (Chapter 6) to provide a basis for considering the geographical affinities of the Late-Devensian flora (Chapter 12).

The selection of sites for pollen analytical study (Chapter 9) was based on the present ecological variation within the island, to permit a comparison between the floristic and vegetational differentiation in the past and present. The palynological data obtained from analysis of the cores (Chapter 7) were simplified by classifying them into a series of biostratigraphic units, termed pollen assemblage zones (Chapter 10). A study of modern pollen rain in a range of vegetation types in Scotland was made (Chapter 11) to provide a basis for the subsequent interpretation of the fossil pollen assemblages.

With this background knowledge of the present flora, vegetation, and pollen rain of the Isle of Skye, an attempt was made to reconstruct the Late-Devensian vegetational history at each site independently (Chapter 13) by means of comparisons with modern pollen assemblages and from the occurrence of pollen and spores of 'indicator species'. The basis for the identification of many of these pollen types was described in Chapter 8. The Late-Devensian flora was also considered (Chapter 12), both as a single unit for analysis of its phytogeographical affinities, and as smaller regional units for considering floristic changes between regions within the island. The pollen assemblage zones were ordered stratigraphically and geographically within Skye and correlated in time by radiocarbon dates (Chapter 13), and comparisons and correlations made with other regions.

Although there are several important differences in the pollen assemblages at each site, a consistent vegetational succession within the interval of time studied is discernible. The rates and directions of this succession appear to be primarily controlled by climatic changes (Chapter 14), and some rather tentative reconstructions of the Late-Devensian climate were attempted. The spatial variations of the flora and vegetation within the Late-Devensian landscape were also considered, and the causes of this variation appear to have been differences in soils, climate, and topography. Several problems in the reconstruction remain unsolved, and these were discussed in Chapter 14. The Late-Devensian flora and vegetation of Skye appear to have been as diverse, both ecologically and geographically, as their modern counterparts. The vegetational and floristic diversity that appears to have existed on Skye at this time is readily interpretable in terms of the same broad ecological factors that influence the present flora and vegetation of the island.

It is of considerable interest that pollen analysis can distinguish such differences, for it demonstrates the sensitivity of the method in detecting past vegetational patterns and its value as a tool in Quaternary palaeoecology. It is remarkable that such differences are detectable, in view of the inadequacy of the fossil pollen record, both in providing information about species presence, and in our ignorance of the area of vegetation that pollen spectra reflect. A pollen diagram cannot be regarded as a direct record of either the past flora or vegetation, for although it contains indications of both, it is different from either. Just as present floristic and vegetational units can be mapped, pollen spectra can also be ordered in space, but they are a totally different kind of mappable unit. A pollen spectrum exists only at a single minute point in space – the area of sediment surface sampled within the basin of deposition – compared with the area occupied by a plant community of a floristic element. The spectrum owes its character, however, not to the minute area in which it is found, but to the undefined area of vegetation that contributes pollen to it. It is the mappable lateral variation as well as the stratigraphical variation of a series of pollen spectra that provides the strength of the method as a palaeoecological technique.

Two features of ecological interest arise from the present study. Firstly, it is notable that such a well-marked spatial differentiation in the Late-Devensian flora and vegetation, developed largely in response to habitat factors, was present in an area so far north and apparently so soon after the close of the last glaciation. Secondly, the apparent juxtaposition and mixture of species for which there are no longer modern analogues, and the extreme flexibility of response of individual plant species to changing conditions in the environment are of ecological interest, and they merit detailed consideration as phenomena that would not be readily predicted from observations of present-day ecosystems. Palaeoecological studies can thus contribute ideas and historical perspectives to modern ecological theory and concepts, such as the nature of vegetation in terms of the individuality and uniqueness of the plant community, not only in space but also in time.

An attempt was made to consider the possible role of external factors, in particular climatic factors, in influencing the direction and rate of vegetational change during Late-Devensian times. Although the probable importance of climate as a determining factor can be recognised qualitatively, no reliable quantitative estimates of the climatic parameters of the rate and magnitude of the changes involved can be made. Climatic reconstructions from biological evidence are notoriously difficult, and as emphasised in Chapter 14 palaeoclimatologists need to develop methods of estimating past climate that do not only depend on arguments concerning the present distribution of plants and animals in relation to broad regional climatic parameters.

An important conclusion that emerges from this study is that, in the handling of the palynological data, the subdivision and zonation of the pollen diagrams must be approached with care. In this project the striking differences in the pollen assemblages from site to site emphasise the desirability of considering each sequence independently, until some means of time-correlation is available. In north-west Europe the classical pollen zones I, II, and III of the Late-Weichselian (Late-Devensian) have been applied to totally different pollen assemblages in widely differing ecological and topographical areas. These zones, with their connotations of time-correlation and climatic equivalence, have been applied to pollen diagrams, not only throughout Europe, but also in eastern Africa and south America. Correlations of pollen zones and inferred environmental history do not appear to be easy even within the small area of Great Britain. The claim of Van der Hammen & Vogel (1966) that 'the sum of C-14 dates and pollen data has proved that the subdivisions of the Late-glacial are based on world-wide and perfectly synchronous climatic changes and fluctuations' is a dubious and hazardous assumption. Such an approach prejudges both the interpretation of the palynological sequence in terms of the observable data and the correlation of the deposits in time. The power of Quaternary pollen analysis lies in the wide scope of inferences permitted by comparison of its results with modern examples, but to allow generalisations based on inference to be substituted for objectively determined data is to invite confusion and to foster a circularity of approach.

In order to refine the reconstruction of vegetational and environmental history of the Isle of Skye during Late-Devensian times, more detailed and more extensive data are required on the relationships of modern pollen rain to vegetation, particularly in communities that do not occur in Scotland today. Modern pollen spectra are considered to provide the most valuable link in the interpretation of fossil pollen assemblages in terms of modern vegetational analogues. Processes of pollen dispersal, sedimentation, and preservation also need to be studied in a range of ecological and topographical settings, and further attention should be given to pollen morphological problems, in an attempt to permit more detailed determinations of fossil grains of potential 'indicator species'. Such a study requires not only improved microscopy, but an enlarged pollen reference collection. The determination of absolute pollen influx values rather than relative pollen percentages in the Late-Devensian sediments on Skye may aid in the resolution of some of the problems encountered in the vegetational reconstructions. The measurement of pollen influx in terms of the number of grains deposited per unit area per unit time has been made for a sequence of lake deposits in the eastern United States by Davis (1967*b*) and subsequently by other American workers, and for a profile of Late-Devensian sediments in north-west England by Pennington & Bonny (1970). Such studies are of value in the assessment of changes in pollen influx, avoiding the restraints imposed by the expression of the pollen frequencies on a relative percentage basis.

Besides developments in the methodology of pollen analysis, a more detailed reconstruction of the past vegetation from pollen stratigraphical data will require methods which permit more detailed comparisons to be made between modern and fossil pollen spectra and the further use of 'indicator species'. The principal limitation in the interpretation of the pollen stratigraphy in terms of environmental history is the lack of knowledge of the modern ecological tolerances of many of the taxa concerned. At present, the geographical location of modern pollen assemblages and hence of modern vegetation types that are analogous to the fossil assemblages gives a generalised idea of past environmental conditions. To carry the palaeoecological inferences to a more precise level, the critical factors influencing the abundance and performance of the taxa in question will need to be identified and interpreted.

The individualistic concept of vegetation focuses attention on the environmental tolerance of the individual species that constitute the vegetation. Autecological studies of at least the major dominants of the vegetation are invaluable for the Quaternary palaeoecologist who attempts to reconstruct past environments from a fragmentary fossil assemblage. Each extension of knowledge about the ecology of the life history of species whose presence in a palaeoflora can be demonstrated limits the possible range of environmental conditions at the time and place where the plant occurred. Fossil pollen spectra could provide a record of changing proportions of plant communities, but if they are to be interpreted, knowledge of the population biology and dynamics of the species concerned is required.

The Skye project has co-ordinated modern ecological observations and Quaternary palaeoecological investigations in an attempt to reconstruct the flora, vegetation, and landscape of the Isle of Skye during Late-Devensian times. Palaeoecology and ecology cannot be divorced, for the interpretation of the former is entirely dependent on modern ecological observations through the principal of methodological uniformitarianism. The success of this project may be assessed by the degree to which it has aided in the redefinition and re-evaluation of the problems and approaches within the temporal and geographical extent of the study and by the extent to which it has demonstrated the interdependence of modern ecology and Quaternary palaeoecology.

BIBLIOGRAPHY AND INDEX

BIBLIOGRAPHY

Aario, L. (1940). Waldgrenzen und subrezenten Pollenspektren in Petsamo, Lappland. *Ann. Acad. Sci. Fenn.* A, **54** (8), 1–120.

Aario, R. (1965). Die Fichtenverhäufigung im Lichte von C^{14}-bestimmungen und die Altersverhaltnisse der Finnischen Pollenzonen. *C. R. Soc. Geol. Fin.* **37**, 215–31.

Aartolahti, T. (1966). Über die Einwanderung und die Verhäufigung der Fichte in Finnland. *Annls. bot. fenn.* **3**, 368–79.

Aartolahti, T. (1967). Zur Rationellen *Tilia*-pollengrenze (To) in Finnland. *Fennia*, **97**, 1–30.

Aletsee, L. (1967). Begriffliche und floristische Grundlagen zu einer pflanzengeographischen Analyse der europäischen Regenwassermoorstandorte. *Beitr. Biol. Pflanzen*, **43**, 117–60, 161–283.

Alhonen, P. (1968). Radiocarbon ages from the bottom deposit of Lake Sarkkilanjarri, south-western Finland. *Bull. Geol. Soc. Finland*, **40**, 65–70.

Allorge, P. (1921–22). Les associations végétales du Vexin Français. *Revue gén. bot.* **33–4**.

American Commission on Stratigraphic Nomenclature (1961). Code of stratigraphic nomenclature. *Amer. Assoc. Petroleum Geologists Bull.* **45**, 645–55.

Andersen, S. Th. (1960). Silicone oil as a mounting medium for pollen grains. *Danm. geol. Unders.* Ser. IV, **4**, (1), 24 pp.

Andersen, S. Th. (1961). Vegetation and its environment in Denmark in the Early Weichselian Glacial. *Danm. geol. Unders.* Ser. II, **75**, 175 pp.

Andersen, S. Th. (1964). Interglacial plant successions in the light of environmental changes. *Rep. VIth Int. Quat. Congr.* **2**, 359–68.

Andersen, S. Th. (1966). Interglacial vegetational succession and lake development in Denmark. *Palaeobotanist*, **15**, 117–27.

Andersen, S. Th. (1967). Tree pollen rain in a mixed deciduous forest in South Jutland (Denmark). *Rev. Palaeobotan. Palynol.* **3**, 267–75.

Andersen, S. Th. (1969). Interglacial vegetation and soil development. *Medd. dansk. geol. Foren.* **19**, 90–102.

Andersen, S. Th. (1970). The relative pollen productivity and pollen representation of North European trees, and correction factors for tree pollen spectra. *Danm. geol. Unders.* Ser. II, **96**, 99 pp.

Anderson, D. J. (1965). Classification and ordination in vegetation science: controversy over a non-existent problem? *J. Ecol.* **53**, 521–6.

Anderson, D. J., Cooke, R. C., Elkington, T. T. & Read, D. J. (1966). Studies on structure in plant communities II. The structure of some dwarf-heath and birch-copse communities in Skjaldfannardalur, North-West Iceland. *J. Ecol.* **54**, 781–93.

Anderson, F. W. & Dunham, K. C. (1966). *The Geology of North Skye.* Memoir Geological Survey. Edinburgh.

Andrew, R. (1970). The Cambridge Pollen Reference Collection. In *Studies in the Vegetational History of the British Isles* (ed. by D. Walker & R. G. West). Cambridge.

Annual Average Rainfall Map (1967). *Average annual rainfall map for the period 1916–1950 for Great Britain (North).* H.M.S.O. London.

Armstrong, W. & Boatman, D. J. (1967). Some field observations relating the growth of bog plants to conditions of soil aeration. *J. Ecol.* **55**, 101–10.

Arnell, S. (1956). *Illustrated Moss Flora of Fennoscandia.* 1. *Hepaticae.* Lund.

Asprey, G. F. (1947). The vegetation of the islands of Canna and Sanday, Inverness-shire. *J. Ecol.* **34**, 182–93.

Backman, A. L. (1948). *Naias flexilis* in Europa während der Quartarzeit. *Acta bot. fenn.* **43**, 1–44.

Balátová-Tuláčková, E. (1963) Zur Systematik der europaischen Phragmitetea. *Preslia*, **55**, 118–22.

Balátová-Tuláčková, E. (1968). Grundwasserganglinien und Weisengesellschaften. *Acta sc. nat. Brno*, **2** (2), 37 pp.

Ball, D. F. & Goodier, R. (1970). Morphology and distribution of features resulting from frost-action in Snowdonia. *Field Studies*, **3**, 193–218.

Bamberg, S. A. & Major, J. (1968). Ecology of the vegetation and soils associated with calcareous parent materials in three alpine regions of Montana. *Ecol. Monogr.* **38**, 127–67.

Bannister, P. (1966). The use of subjective estimates of cover-abundance as the basis for ordination. *J. Ecol.* **54**, 665–74.

Barclay-Estrup, P. & Gimingham, C. H. (1969). The description and interpretation of cyclical processes in a heath community. 1. Vegetational change in relation to the *Calluna* cycle. *J. Ecol.* **57**, 737–58.

Barkman, J. J. (1958). *Phytosociology and Ecology of Cryptogamic Epiphytes.* Essen.

Bartley, D. D. (1962). The stratigraphy and pollen analysis of lake deposits near Tadcaster, Yorkshire. *New Phytol.* **61**, 277–87.

BIBLIOGRAPHY

Bartley, D. D. (1966). Pollen analysis of some lake deposits near Bamburgh in Northumberland. *New Phytol.* **65**, 141–56.

Bartley, D. D. (1967). Pollen analysis of surface samples of vegetation from arctic Quebec. *Pollen Spores* **9**, 101–6.

Bassett, I. J. & Terasmae, J. (1962). Ragweeds, *Ambrosia* species, in Canada and their history in Postglacial time. *Can. J. Bot.* **40**, 141–50.

Bassett, I. J. & Crompton, C. W. (1968). Pollen morphology and chromosome numbers of the family Plantaginaceae in North America. *Can. J. Bot.* **46**, 349–61.

Bastin, B. (1964). Recherches sur les relations entre la vegetation actuelle et le spectre pollinique recent dans la foret de Soignes (Belgique). *Agricultura,* **12**, 341–73.

Beeftink, W. G. (1965). *De Zoutvegetatie van ZW-Nederland Beschouwd in Europees Verband.* Wageningen.

Beeftink, W. G. (1968). Die Systematik der Europäischen Salzpflanzengesellschaffen. In *Pflanzensoziologische Systematik* (ed. by R. Tüxen). The Hague.

Behre, K-E. (1966). Untersuchungen zur spätglazialen und frühpostglazialen Vegetationsgeschichte Ostfrieslands. *Eiszeit u. Gegenw.* **17**, 69–84.

Bellamy, D. J., Bradshaw, M. E., Millington, G. R. & Simmons, I. G. (1966). Two Quaternary deposits in the lower Tees basin. *New Phytol.* **65**, 429–42.

Bent, A. M. & Wright, H. E. (1963). Pollen analysis of surface materials and lake sediments from the Chuska Mountains, New Mexico. *Bull. geol. soc. Amer.* **74**, 491–500.

Berglund, B. E. (1963). Vegetation på ön Senoren III. Havsstrandvegetationen. *Bot. Notiser,* **116**, 305–22.

Berglund, B. E. (1964). The Post-glacial shore displacement in Eastern Blekinge, South-Eastern Sweden. *Sver. geol. Unders.* Ser. C, Årb. **59** (5), 47 pp.

Berglund, B. E. (1966*a*). Late-Quaternary Vegetation in Eastern Blekinge, South-Eastern Sweden. I. Late-glacial time. *Op. bot. Soc. bot. Lund,* **12** (1), 180 pp.

Berglund, B. E. (1966*b*). Late Quaternary vegetation in Eastern Blekinge, South-eastern Sweden. II. Post-glacial time. *Op. bot. Soc. bot. Lund,* **12** (2), 190 pp.

Berglund, B. E. & Digerfeldt, G. (1970). A palaeoecological study of the Late-glacial lake at Torreberga, Scania, South Sweden. *Oikos,* **21**, 98–128.

Berglund, B. E. & Malmer, N. (1971). Soil conditions and late-glacial stratigraphy. *Geol. Fören. Förh. Stock.* **93**, 575–86.

Berset, J. (1969). *Paturages, Prairies et Marais Montagnards et Subalpins des Préalpes Fribourgeoises.* Fribourg.

Bertsch, A. (1961). Untersuchungen an rezenten und fossilen Pollen von *Juniperus. Flora,* **150**, 503–10.

Beug, H-J. (1957). Untersuchungen zur spätglazialen und frühpostglazialen Floren- und Vegetationsgeschichte einiger Mittelgebirge. *Flora,* **145**, 167–211.

Beug, H-J. (1961). *Leitfaden der Pollenbestimmung.* Stuttgart.

Birks, H. H. (1969). *Studies in the vegetational history of Scotland.* Ph.D. dissertation, University of Cambridge.

Birks, H. H. (1970). Studies in the vegetational history of Scotland I. A pollen diagram from Abernethy Forest, Inverness-shire. *J. Ecol.* **58**, 827–46.

Birks, H. H. (1972). Studies in the vegetational history of Scotland II. Two pollen diagrams from the Galloway Hills, Kirkcudbrightshire. *J. Ecol.* **60**, 183–217.

Birks, H. J. B. (1965). Late-glacial deposits at Bagmere, Cheshire and Chat Moss, Lancashire. *New Phytol.* **64**, 270–85.

Birks, H. J. B. (1968). The identification of *Betula nana* pollen. *New Phytol.* **67**, 309–14.

Birks, H. J. B. (1969). *The Late-Weichselian and Present Vegetation of the Isle of Skye.* Ph.D. dissertation, University of Cambridge.

Birks, H. J. B. (1970). Inwashed pollen spectra at Loch Fada, Isle of Skye. *New Phytol.* **69**, 807–20.

Birks, H. J. B., Birks, H. H. & Ratcliffe, D. A. (1969*a*). Mountain plants on Slieve League, Co. Donegal. *Ir. Nat. J.* **16**, 203–4.

Birks, H. J. B., Birks, H. H. & Ratcliffe, D. A. (1969*b*). *Geocalyx graveolens* (Schrad.) Nees in Kerry, a hepatic new to Ireland. *Ir. Nat. J.* **16**, 204–5.

Birks, H. J. B. & Ransom, M. E. (1969). An interglacial peat at Fugla Ness, Shetland. *New Phytol.* **68**, 777–96.

Birse, E. L. & Robertson, J. S. (1967) Vegetation. In *The Soils of the Country round Haddington and Eyemouth.* Mem. Soil Survey. Edinburgh.

Birse, E. M. (1958). Ecological studies of growth-form in bryophytes. III. The relationships between the growth-form of mosses and ground-water supply. *J. Ecol.* **46**, 9–27.

Boatman, D. J. (1960). The relationships of some bog communities in Western Galway. *Proc. R. Ir. Acad.* B, **61**, 141–66.

Boatman, D. J. (1961). Vegetation and peat characteristics of blanket bogs in County Kerry. *J. Ecol.* **49**, 507–17.

Boatman, D. J. & Armstrong, D. (1968). A bog type in North-West Sutherland. *J. Ecol.* **56**, 129–41.

Böcher, T. W. (1937). Nogle studier over Faeröernes alpine vegetation. *Bot. Tidsskr.* **44**, 154–201.

Böcher, T. W. (1940). Studies on the plant-geography of the North Atlantic heath formation. I. The heaths of the Faroes. *K. danske Vidensk. Selsk., Biol. Medd.* **15** (3), 64 pp.

Böcher, T. W. (1943). Studies on the plant-geography of the North Atlantic heath formation. II. Danish dwarf-shrub communities in relation to those of Northern Europe. *K. danske Vidensk. Selsk., Biol. Skr.* **2** (7), 129 pp.

Böcher, T. W. (1954). Oceanic and Continental Vegetational Complexes in Southwest Greenland. *Meddr. Grønland,* **148** (1), 336 pp.

Bortenschlager, S. (1967). Pollenanalytische Ergebnisse einer Firnprofiluntersuchung am Kesselwandferner (3240 m), Ötztal, Tirol. *Grana Palynol.* **7** (1), 259–74.

Bradley, D. E. (1958). The study of pollen grain surfaces in the electron microscope. *New Phytol.* **57**, 226–9.
Bradshaw, A. D., McNeilly, T. S. & Gregory, R. P. G. (1965). Industrialization, evolution and the development of heavy metal tolerance in plants. In *Ecology and the Industrial Society* (ed. by G. T. Goodman, R. W. Edwards & J. M. Lambert). Oxford.
Bradshaw, M. E. (1962). The distribution and status of five species of the *Alchemilla vulgaris* L. aggregate in Upper Teesdale. *J. Ecol.* **50**, 681–706.
Braun, W. (1968). Die Kalkflachmoore und ihre Wichtigsten Kontaktgesellschaften im Bayerischen Alpenvorland. *Dissertationes Botanicae*, **1**, 134 pp.
Braun-Blanquet, J. (1923). *L'Origine et le développment des flores dans le Massif Central de la France avec aperçu sur les migrations des flores de l'Europe Sub-occidentale.* Paris and Zurich.
Braun-Blanquet, J. (1948). *La végétation alpine des Pyrénées orientales.* Barcelona.
Braun-Blanquet, J. (1948–50). Übersicht der Pflanzengesellschaften Rätiens. *Vegetatio*, **1**, 29–41; 129–46; 285–316; **2**, 20–37; 214–37; 241–60.
Braun-Blanquet, J. (1951). *Pflanzensoziologie; Grundzüge der Vegetationskunde.* Vienna.
Braun-Blanquet, J. (1966–67). Vegetationsskizen aus dem Baskenland mit Ausblicken auf das Weitere Ibero-Atlantikum. *Vegetatio*, **13**, 117–47; **14**, 1–126.
Braun-Blanquet, J. & Tüxen, R. (1952). Irische Pflanzen gesellschaften. *Veröff. geobot. Inst. Zurich*, **25**, 224–415.
Brideaux, W. W. (1971). Recurrent species groupings in fossil microplankton assemblages. *Palaeogeogr., Palaeoclimatol., Palaeoecol.* **9**, 101–22.
Brockmann-Jerosch, H. (1913). Der Einfluss des Klimacharakters auf die Verbreitung der Pflanzen und Pflanzengesellschaften. *Engler's Bot. Jb.* **49**, 19–43.
Broecker, W. S. (1965). Isotope geochemistry and the Pleistocene climatic record. In *The Quaternary of the United States* (ed. by H. E. Wright & D. G. Frey). Princeton.
Brooks, D. & Thomas, K. W. (1967). The distribution of pollen grains on microscope slides. 1. The nonrandomness of the distribution. *Pollen Spores* **9**, 621–9.
Brown, A. P. (1971). The *Empetrum* pollen record as a climatic indicator in the Late Weichselian and Early Flandrian of the British Isles. *New Phytol.* **70**, 841–9.
Buckley, J. D. & Willis, E. H. (1970). Isotopes' Radiocarbon Measurements VIII. *Radiocarbon*, **12**, 87–129.
Burrichter, E. (1969). Das Zwillbrocker Venn, Westmünsterland, in moor- und vegetationskundlicher Sicht. *Abhand, aus dem Landes. für Naturkunde zu Münster in Westfalen* **31**, 1–60.
Cain, S. A. (1947). Characteristics of natural areas and factors in their development. *Ecol. Monogr.* **17**, 185–200.
Caine, T. N. (1963). The origin of sorted-stripes in the Lake District, Northern England. *Geogr. Annlr.* A, **45**, 172–9.
Cerceau, M-T. (1959). Cle de determination d'Ombelliferes de France et d'Afrique du Nord d'après leurs grains de pollen. *Pollen Spores* **1**, 145–90.
Ceška, A. (1966). Estimation of the mean floristic similarity between and within sets of vegetational relevés. *Folia Geobot. Phytotax.* **1**, 93–100.
Chanda, S. (1962). On the pollen morphology of some Scandinavian Caryophyllaceae. *Grana Palynol.* **3** (3), 67–89.
Chanda, S. (1965*a*). The pollen morphology of Droseraceae with special reference to taxonomy. *Pollen Spores* **7**, 509–28.
Chanda, S. (1965*b*). The history of vegetation of Brøndmyra, a late-glacial and early post-glacial deposit in Jaeren, South Norway. *Årbok Univ. Bergen* Nr. 1, 17 pp.
Charlesworth, J. K. (1956). The Late-glacial History of the Highlands and Islands of Scotland. *Trans. R. Soc. Edinb.* **62**, 769–928.
Christie, A. D. & Ritchie, J. C. (1969). On the use of isentropic trajectories in the study of pollen transports. *Natur. can.* **96**, 531–49.
Churchill, D. M. & Sarjeant, W. A. S. (1963). Freshwater microplankton from Flandrian (Holocene) peats of Southwestern Australia. *Grana Palynol.* **3** (3), 29–53.
Clapham, A. R. (1953). Human factors contributing to a change in our flora: the former ecological status of certain hedgerow species. In *The Changing Flora of Britain* (ed. by J. E. Lousley). Arbroath.
Clapham, A. R., Tutin, T. G. & Warburg, E. F. (1962). *Flora of the British Isles.* Cambridge.
Clapham, W. B. (1970*a*). Nature and paleogeography of Middle Permian floras of Oklahoma as inferred from their pollen record. *J. Geol.* **78**, 153–71.
Clapham, W. B. (1970*b*). Evolution of Upper Permian terrestrial floras in Oklahoma as determined from pollen and spores. *North Am. Paleont. Convention*, Chicago, 1969 Proc., E, 411–27.
Clark, S. C. (1968). The structure of some *Ulex galii* heaths in Eastern Ireland. *Proc. R. Ir. Acad.* B, **66**, 43–51.
Clarkson, D. T. (1965). Calcium uptake by calcicole and calcifuge species in the genus *Agrostis* L. *J. Ecol.* **53**, 427–36.
Clements, F. E. (1936). Nature and structure of the climax. *J. Ecol.* **24**, 252–84.
Climatological Atlas of the British Isles (1952). Meteorological Office, London.
Clough, C. T. & Harker, A. (1904). *The Geology of West Central Skye.* Memoir Geological Survey, London.
Clymo, R. S. (1962). An experimental approach to part of the calcicole problem. *J. Ecol.* **50**, 707–31.
Comanor, P. L. (1968). Forest vegetation and the Pollen Spectrum: an examination of the usefulness of the R value. *Bull. New Jersey Acad. Sci.* **13**, 7–19.
Conolly, A. P. (1961). Some climatic and edaphic indications from the Late-glacial flora. *Proc. Linn. Soc. Lond.* **172**, 56–62.

Conolly, A. P. & Dahl, E. (1970). Maximum summer temperature in relation to the modern and Quaternary distributions of certain arctic-montane species in the British Isles. In *Studies in the Vegetational History of the British Isles* (ed. D. Walker & R. G. West). Cambridge.

Cookson, I. C. (1953). Records of the occurrence of *Botryococcus braunii, Pediastrum* and the Hystrichosphaeridea in Cainozoic deposits of Australia. *Melbourne Nat. Mus. Mem.* **18**, 107–23.

Cookson, I. C. & Manum, S. (1960). On *Crassosphaera*, a new genus of microfossils from Mesozoic and Tertiary deposits. *Nytt Mag. Bot.* **8**, 5–9.

Coombe, D. E. & White, F. (1951). Notes on calcicolous communities and peat formation in Norwegian Lappland. *J. Ecol.* **39**, 33–62.

Coombe, D. E. & Frost, L. C. (1956). The heaths of the Cornish serpentine. *J. Ecol.* **44**, 226–56.

Coope, G. R. (1970). Climatic interpretations of Late Weichselian coleoptera from the British Isles. *Rev. Géogr. Phys. et Géol. Dynam.* **12**, 149–55.

Cormack, E. & Gimingham, C. H. (1964). Litter production by *Calluna vulgaris* (L.) Hull. *J. Ecol.* **52**, 285–97.

Couper, R. A. (1958). British Mesozoic microspores and pollen grains. A systematic and stratigraphic study. *Palaeontographica* B, **103**, 75–179.

Cushing, E. J. (1961). Size increase in pollen grains mounted in thin slides. *Pollen Spores*, **3**, 265–74.

Cushing, E. J. (1963). *Late-Wisconsin pollen stratigraphy in east-central Minnesota.* Ph.D. thesis, University of Minnesota.

Cushing, E. J. (1964*a*). Application of the Code of Stratigraphic Nomenclature to Pollen Stratigraphy. Unpublished manuscript.

Cushing, E. J. (1964*b*). Redeposited pollen in Late-Wisconsin pollen spectra from east-central Minnesota. *Am. J. Sci.* **262**, 1075–88.

Cushing, E. J. (1965). Problems in the Quaternary phytogeography of the Great Lakes Region. In *The Quaternary of the United States* (ed. by H. E. Wright & D. G. Frey). Princeton.

Cushing, E. J. (1967*a*). Late-Wisconsin pollen stratigraphy and the glacial sequence in Minnesota. In *Quaternary Paleoecology* (ed. by E. J. Cushing & H. E. Wright). New Haven and London.

Cushing, E. J. (1967*b*). Evidence for differential pollen preservation in Late Quaternary sediments in Minnesota. *Rev. Palaeobotan. Palynol.* **4**, 87–101.

Dahl, E. (1951). On the relation between summer temperature and the distribution of alpine vascular plants in the lowlands of Scandinavia. *Oikos*, **3**, 22–52.

Dahl, E. (1956). Rondane. Mountain vegetation in South Norway and its relation to the environment. *Skr. norske Vidensk.-Akad. I. Mat.-Nat.* No. 3, 374 pp.

Dahl, E. (1963). On the heat exchange of a wet vegetation surface and the ecology of *Koenigia islandica*. *Oikos*, **14**, 190–211.

Dahl, E. & Hadač, E. (1941). Strandgesellschaften der Insel Ostøy im Oslofjord. *Nytt Mag. Natur.* B, **82**, 251–312.

Dahl, E. & Hadač, E. (1949). Homogeneity of plant communities. *Studia bot. Čechosl.* **10**, 159–76.

Dale, M. B. & Walker, D. (1970). Information analysis of pollen diagrams 1. *Pollen Spores*, **12**, 21–37.

Danielsen, A. (1970). Pollen-analytical late Quaternary studies in the Ra district of Østfold, South-east Norway. *Årb. Univ. Bergen.* Nr. 14, 146 pp.

Dansereau, P. (1957). *Biogeography. An ecological perspective.* New York.

Davis, M. B. (1963). On the theory of pollen analysis. *Am. J. Sci.* **261**, 897–912.

Davis, M. B. (1965). Phytogeography and palynology of North-eastern United States. In *The Quaternary of the United States* (ed. by H. E. Wright & D. G. Frey). Princeton.

Davis, M. B. (1967*a*). Late-glacial climate in Northern United States: A comparison of New England and the Great Lakes Region. In *Quaternary Paleoecology* (ed. by E. J. Cushing & H. E. Wright). New Haven & London.

Davis, M. B. (1967*b*). Pollen accumulation rates at Rogers Lake, Connecticut during Late- and Post-glacial time. *Rev. Palaeobotan. Palynol.* **2**, 219–30.

Davis, M. B. (1968). Pollen grains in lake sediments: redeposition caused by seasonal water circulation. *Science*, **162**, 796–9.

Davis, M. B. (1969). Palynology and environmental history during the Quaternary Period. *Amer. Sci.* **57**, 317–32.

Davis, M. B. & Goodlett, J. C. (1960). Comparison of the present vegetation with pollen spectra in surface samples from Brownington Pond, Vermont. *Ecology* **41**, 346–57.

Davis, R. B., Brewster, L. A. & Sutherland, J. (1969). Variation in pollen spectra within lakes. *Pollen Spores* **11**, 557–71.

Den Hartog, C. & Segal, S. (1964). A new classification of the water-plant communities. *Acta bot. neerl.* **13**, 367–93.

Dickinson, D. H., Pearson, M. C. & Webb, D. A. (1964). Some microhabitats of The Burren, their micro-environments and vegetation. *Proc. R. Ir. Acad.* B, **63**, 291–302.

Dickson, C. A., Dickson, J. H. & Mitchell, G. F. (1970). The Late-Weichselian flora of the Isle of Man. *Phil. Trans. R. Soc.* B, **258**, 31–79.

Donner, J. J. (1957). The geology and vegetation of Late-glacial retreat stages in Scotland. *Trans. R. Soc. Edinb.* **63**, 221–64.

Donner, J. J. (1958). Loch Mahaick, a late-glacial site in Perthshire. *New Phytol.* **57**, 183–6.

Donner, J. J. (1959). The Late- and Post-glacial raised beaches in Scotland. *Ann. Acad. Sci. Fenn.* A, III Geol–Geog. **53**, 1–25.

Donner, J. J. (1962). On the Post-glacial history of the Grampian Highlands of Scotland. *Commentat. biol.* **24**, (6), 1–29.

Donner, J. J. (1966). The Late-glacial and early Post-glacial pollen stratigraphy of southern and eastern Finland. *Commentat. biol.* **29** (9), 1–24.

Downie, C. & Singh, G. (1969). Dinoflagellate cysts from estuarine and raised beach deposits at Woodgrange, Co. Down, N. Ireland. *Grana Palynol.* **9** (1–3), 124–32.

Du Rietz, G. E. (1930). Classification and nomenclature of vegetation. *Svensk bot. Tidskr.* **24**, 489–503.

Du Rietz, G. E. (1949). Huvudenheter och Huvudgränser i Svensk Myrvegetation. *Svensk bot. Tidskr.* **43**, 274–309.

Du Rietz, G. E. (1950). Phytogeographical Excursion to the surroundings of Lake Torneträsk in Torne Lappmark (Northern Sweden). *Excursion Guide* VIIth Int. Bot. Congress, Stockholm.

Du Rietz, G. E. (1954). Die Mineralbodenwasserzeigergrenze als Grundlage einer Natürlichen Zweigliederung der Nord- und Mitteleuropäischen Moore. *Vegetatio*, **5–6**, 571–85.

Durno, S. E. (1958). Identification of fossil fruits of *Naias flexilis* in Scotland. *Trans. Proc. bot. soc. Edinb.* **37**, 222–3.

Duvigneaud, P. (1949). Classification phytosociologique des tourbières de l'Europe. *Bull. Soc. r. Bot. Belg.* **81**, 58–129.

Dyakowska, J. (1937). Researches on the rapidity of the falling down of pollen of some trees. *Bull. Acad. pol. Sci. Lett.* B, **1**, 155–68.

Dyakowska, J. & Zurzycki, J. (1959). Gravimetric studies on pollen. *Bull. Acad. pol. Sci. Biol.* **7**, 11–16.

Eddy, A., Welch, D. & Rawes, M. (1969). The Vegetation of the Moor House National Nature Reserve in the Northern Pennines, England. *Vegetatio*, **16**, 239–84.

Edgell, M. C. R. (1969). Vegetation of an upland ecosystem: Cader Idris, Merionethshire. *J. Ecol.* **57**, 335–59.

Edgell, M. C. R. (1971). A preliminary study of some environmental variables in an upland ecosystem: Cader Idris, Merionethshire. *J. Ecol.* **59**, 189–201.

Eggeling, W. J. (1965). Check list of the plants of Rhum, Inner Hebrides (V.C. 104, North Ebudes). *Trans. Proc. bot. soc. Edinb.* **40**, 20–59; 60–99.

Elkington, T. T. (1965). Studies on the variation of the genus *Dryas* in Greenland. *Meddr. Grønland* **178** (1), 56 pp.

Elsik, W. C. (1966). Biologic degradation of fossil pollen grains and spores. *Micropaleontology* **12**, 515–18.

Elsik, W. C. (1968). Palynology of a Paleocene Rockdale Lignite, Milam County, Texas. 1. Morphology and Taxonomy. *Pollen Spores* **10**, 263–314.

Elsik, W. C. (1971). Microbial degradation of sporopollenin. In *Sporopollenin* (ed. by J. Brooks, P. R. Grant, M. D. Muir, P. van Gijzel & G. Shaw). London and New York.

Engelskjön, T. (1970). Flora of Nord-Fuglöy, Troms. *Astarte* **3**, 63–82.

Erdtman, G. (1968). On the exine of *Stellaria crassipes* Hult. *Grana Palynol.* **8** (2–3), 271–6.

Erdtman, G. (1969). *Handbook of Palynology*. Copenhagen and New York.

Erdtman, G., Berglund, B. E. & Praglowski, J. R. (1961). *An Introduction to a Scandinavian Pollen Flora*. Stockholm.

Erdtman, G. & Praglowski, J. R. (1959). Six notes on pollen morphology and pollen morphological techniques. *Bot. Notiser* **112**, 175–84.

Evans, G. H. (1970). Pollen and diatom analysis of late-Quaternary deposits in the Blelham Basin, North Lancashire. *New Phytol.* **69**, 821–74.

Evitt, W. R. (1963). Occurrence of freshwater alga *Pediastrum* in Cretaceous marine sediments. *Am. J. Sci.* **261**, 890–3.

Evitt, W. R. & Davidson, S. E. (1964). Dinoflagellate Studies. 1. Dinoflagellate cysts and thecae. *Stanford Univ. Publ. Geol.* **10**, 1–12.

Faegri, K. (1933). Über die Langenvegetation einiger Gletscher des Jostedalsbre und die dadurch bedingten Pflanzensukzessionen. *Årbok. Mus. Bergen* Nr. 7, 255 pp.

Faegri, K. (1943). Studies on the Pleistocene of Western Norway. III. Bømlo. *Årbok Mus. Bergen* Nr. 8, 100 pp.

Faegri, K. (1945). A pollen diagram from the sub-alpine region of Central South Norway. *Norsk geol. Tidsskr.* **25**, 99–126.

Faegri, K. (1947). Heterodoske tanker om pollen analysen. *Geol. Fören. Förh. Stock.* **69**, 55–66.

Faegri, K. (1953). On the periglacial flora of Jaeren. *Norsk geogr. Tidsskr.* **14**, 61–76.

Faegri, K. (1956). Palynological studies of N.W. European Papilionaceae. Unpublished manuscript.

Faegri, K. (1960). *Maps of distribution of Norwegian vascular plants.* 1. *Coast Plants.* Oslo.

Faegri, K. (1963). Problems of immigration and dispersal of the Scandinavian flora. In *North Atlantic Biota and their history* (ed. by A. Löve & D. Löve). Oxford.

Faegri, K. (1966). Some problems of representativity in pollen analysis. *Palaeobotanist* **15**, 135–40.

Faegri, K. (1971). The preservation of sporopollenin membranes under natural conditions. In *Sporopollenin* (ed. by J. Brooks, P. R. Grant, M. D. Muir, P. van Gijzel & G. Shaw). London and New York.

Faegri, K. & Iversen, J. (1964). *Textbook of Pollen Analysis.* Copenhagen and Oxford.

Faegri, K. & Ottestad, P. (1948). Statistical problems in pollen analysis. *Årbok. Univ. Bergen* Nr. 3, 28 pp.

Fager, E. W. (1957). Determination and analysis of recurrent groups. *Ecology* **30**, 586–95.

Fagerlind, F. (1952). The real signification of pollen diagrams. *Bot. Notiser* **105**, 185–224.

Fairbairn, W. A. (1968). Climatic zonation in the British Isles. *Forestry* **41**, 117–30.

Ferguson, I. K. & Webb, D. A. (1970). Pollen morphology in the genus *Saxifraga* and its taxonomic significance. *Bot. J. Linn. Soc.* **63**, 295–311.

Ferreira, R. E. C. (1959). Scottish mountain vegetation in relation to geology. *Trans. Proc. bot. soc. Edinb.* **37**, 229–50.

Ferreira, R. E. C. (1963). Some distinctions between calciphilous and basiphilous plants. *Trans. Proc. bot. soc. Edinb.* **89**, 399–413.

Firbas, F. (1934). Über die Bestimmung der Walddichte und der Vegetation Waldloser Gebiete mit Hilfe der Pollenanalyse. *Planta* **22**, 109–45.

Firbas, F. (1949). *Spät- und nacheiszeitliche Waldgeschichte Mitteleuropas nördlich der Alpen* 1. Jena.

Fitzpatrick, E. A. (1964). The soils of Scotland. In *The Vegetation of Scotland* (ed. by J. H. Burnett). Edinburgh.

Florin, M-B. (1969). Late-glacial and Pre-boreal vegetation in Central Sweden. 1. Records of pollen species. *Svensk bot. Tidskr.* **63**, 143–87.

Florin, M-B. & Wright, H. E. (1969). Diatom evidence for the persistence of stagnant glacial ice in Minnesota. *Bull. geol. soc. Amer.* **80**, 695–704.

Forbes, J. D. (1845). Notes on the topography and geology of the Cuchullin Hills in Skye, and on traces of ancient glaciers which they present. *Edinb. New Phil. J.* **40**, 76–99.

Fox, W. T. (1968). Quantitative paleoecologic reconstruction of fossil communities in the Richmond Group. *J. Geol.* **76**, 613–40.

Franks, J. W. & Pennington, W. (1961). The Late-glacial and Post-glacial deposits of the Esthwaite Basin, North Lancashire. *New Phytol.* **60**, 27–42.

Fransson, S. (1963). Myrvegetation vid Rörvattenån i Nordvästra Jämtland. *Svensk bot. Tidskr.* **57**, 283–332.

Fredskild, B. (1967). Palaeobotanical investigations at Sermermuit, Jakobshavn, West Greenland, *Meddr. Grønland*, **178** (4), 54 pp.

Fredskild, B. (1970). Palynological Part. In *The Urus* (*Bos primigenius* Bojanus) *and Neolithic Domesticated Cattle* (*Bos taurus domesticus* Linné) *in Denmark* by M. Degerbøl & B. Fredskild. *K. danske Vidensk. Selsk., Biol. Skr.* **17** (1), 1–234.

Galloway, R. F. (1961). Solifluction in Scotland. *Scott. geogr. Mag.* **77**, 75–87.

Gams, H. (1941). Über neue Beiträge zur Vegetationssystematik unter besonderer Berücksichtigung des floristischen Systems von Braun-Blanquet. *Bot. Arch.* **42**, 201–38.

Géhu, J. M. (1961). Les groupments végétaux du bassin de la Sambre, Française. *Vegetatio*, **10**, 69–148, 161–208, 257–372.

Géhu, J. M. (1964*a*). L'excursion dans le nord et l'ouest de la France de la Société Internationale de phytosociologie. *Vegetatio*, **12**, 1–95.

Géhu, J. M. (1964*b*). Sur la végétation halophile des Falaises Bretonnes. *Revue gén. bot.*, **71**, 73–8.

Géhu, J. M. & Géhu, J. (1969). Les associations végétales des dunes mobiles et des bordures de plages de la côte Atlantique Française. *Vegetatio*, **18**, 122–66.

Géhu, J. M. & Petit, M. (1965). Notes sur la végétation de dunes littorales de Charente et de Vendee. *Bull. Soc. bot. Nord Fr.* **18**, 69–88.

Geological Society of London (1967). Report of the Stratigraphical Code Sub-Committee. *Proc. Geol. Soc. Lond.* **1638**, 75–87.

Geological Society of London (1969). Recommendations on stratigraphical usage. *Proc. Geol. Soc. Lond.* **1656**, 139–66.

Gibb, D. C. (1957). The free-living forms of *Ascophyllum nodosum* (L.) Lejol. *J. Ecol.* **45**, 49–83.

Gillham, M. E. (1957). Coastal vegetation of Mull and Iona in relation to salinity and soil reaction. *J. Ecol.* **45**, 757–78.

Gilmour, J. S. L. & Walters, S. M. (1963). Philosophy and Classification. In *Vistas in Botany*, IV (ed. by W. B. Turrill). London.

Gimingham, C. H. (1961). North European heath communities: a 'network of variation'. *J. Ecol.* **49**, 655–94.

Gimingham, C. H. (1964*a*). Maritime and submaritime communities. In *The Vegetation of Scotland* (ed. by J. H. Burnett). Edinburgh.

Gimingham, C. H. (1964*b*). Dwarf Shrub Heaths. In *The Vegetation of Scotland* (ed. by J. H. Burnett). Edinburgh.

Gimingham, C. H. (1969). The interpretation of variation in North-European dwarf-shrub heath communities. *Vegetatio* **17**, 89–108.

Gittins, R. (1965). Multivariate approaches to a limestone grassland community. III. A comparative study of ordination and association-analysis. *J. Ecol.* **53**, 411–25.

Gjaerevoll, O. (1950). The snow-bed vegetation in the surroundings of Lake Torneträsk, Swedish Lappland. *Svensk bot. Tidskr.* **44**, 387–440.

Gjaerevoll, O. (1956). The Plant Communities of the Scandinavian Alpine Snow-beds. *K. norske Vidensk. Selsk. Forh.* Nr. 1., 405 pp.

Gjaerevoll, O. (1963). Survival of plants on nunataks in Norway during the Pleistocene glaciation. In *North Atlantic Biota and their History* (ed. by A. Löve & D. Löve). Oxford.

Gjaerevoll, O. & Bringer, K-G. (1965). Plant cover of the alpine regions. In *The Plant Cover of Sweden. Acta Phytogeogr. suec.* **50**, 314 pp.

Gleason, H. A. (1939). The individualistic concept of the plant association. *Amer. Midl. Nat.* **21**, 92–108.

Godwin, H. (1940). Pollen analysis and forest history of England and Wales. *New Phytol.* **39**, 370–400.

Godwin, H. (1955). Vegetational history at Cwm Idwal: A Welsh plant refuge. *Svensk bot. Tidskr.* **49**, 35–43.

Godwin, H. (1956). *The History of the British Flora.* Cambridge.

Godwin, H. (1959). Studies of the Post-glacial history of British vegetation. XIV. Late-glacial deposits at Moss Lake, Liverpool. *Phil. Trans. R. Soc.* B, **242**, 127–49.

Godwin, H. (1960). Radiocarbon dating and Quaternary history in Britain. *Proc. R. Soc.* B, **153**, 287–320.

Godwin, H. (1968). Studies of the Post-glacial history of British vegetation. XV. Organic deposits at Old Buckenham Mere, Norfolk. *New Phytol.* **67**, 95–107.

Godwin, H. & Andrew, R. (1951). A fungal fruit-body common in Post-glacial peat deposits. *New Phytol.* **50**, 179–83.

Godwin, H., Walker, D. & Willis, E. H. (1957). Radiocarbon dating and post-glacial vegetational history: Scaleby Moss. *Proc. R. Soc.* B, **147**, 352–66.

Godwin, H. & Willis, E. H. (1959). Radiocarbon dating of the Late-glacial Period in Britain. *Proc. R. Soc.* B, **150**, 199–215.

Good, R. (1964). *The geography of the flowering plants.* London.

Goodall, D. W. (1954). Objective methods for the classification of vegetation. III. An essay in the use of factor analysis. *Aust. J. Bot.* **2**, 304–24.

Goodall, D. W. (1963). The continuum and the individualistic association. *Vegetatio* **11**, 297–316.

Goodall, D. W. (1970). Statistical plant ecology. *Ann. Rev. Ecol. Syst.* **1**, 99–124.

Gorham, E. (1958). The influence and importance of daily weather conditions on the supply of chloride, sulphate and other ions to freshwater from atmospheric precipitation. *Phil. Trans. R. Soc.* B, **241**, 147–78.

Görs, S. (1964). Beiträge zur Kenntnis basiphiler Flachmoorgesellschaften (Tofieldietalia Prsg. apud Oberd. 49) 2. Teil: Das Mehlprimel- Kopfbinsen-Mor [Primulo-Schoenetum ferruginei Oberd. (57) 62]. *Veröff d. Landesstelle f. Naturschutz u. Landschaftspflege Baden-Württemberg*, **32**, 7–42.

Gould, S. J. (1965). Is Uniformitarianism Necessary? *Am. J. Sci.* **263**, 223–8.

Goulden, C. E. (1964). The history of the Cladoceran fauna of Esthwaite Water (England) and its limnological importance. *Arch. Hydrobiol.*, **60**, 1–52.

Goulden, C. E. & Frey, D. G. (1963). The occurrence and significance of lateral head pores in the genus *Bosmina* (Cladocera). *Int. Revue ges. Hydrobiol.* **48**, 513–22.

Green, F. H. W. (1959). Four years' experience in attempting to standardize measurements of potential evapo-transpiration in the British Isles and the ecological significance of the results. *Int. Union Geodesy and Geophysics*, **48**, 92–100.

Green, F. H. W. (1964). A map of annual average potential water deficit in the British Isles. *J. appl. Ecol.* **1**, 151, 158.

Gregor, J. W. (1938). Experimental Taxonomy. II. Initial population differentiation in *Plantago maritima* L. of Britain. *New Phytol.* **37**, 15–49.

Gregor, J. W. (1939). Experimental Taxonomy. IV. Population differentiation in North American and European sea plantains allied to *Plantago maritima* L. *New Phytol.* **38**, 293–322.

Gregory, S. (1954). Accumulated temperature maps of the British Isles. *Trans. Inst. Br. Geogr.* **20**, 59–73.

Greig-Smith, P. (1950). Evidence from hepatics on the history of the British flora. *J. Ecol.* **38**, 320–44.

Greig-Smith, P. (1964). *Quantitative Plant Ecology*. London.

Grime, J. P. (1963). Factors determining the occurrence of calcifuge species on shallow soils over calcareous substrata. *J. Ecol.* **51**, 375–90.

Grosse-Brauckmann, G. (1961). Zur terminologie organischer sediments. *Geol. Jb.* **79**, 117–44.

Grubb, P. J., Green, H. E. & Merrifield, R. C. J. (1969). The ecology of chalk heath: its relevance to the calcicole-calcifuge and soil acidification problems. *J. Ecol.* **57**, 175–212.

Grüger, J. (1968). Untersuchungen zur spätglazialen und frühpostglazialen Vegetationsentwicklung der Südalpen im Umkreis des Gardasees. *Bot. Jb.* **88**, 163–99.

Haapasaari, M. (1966). The genus *Gymnomitrion* Corda in Finland. *Ann. Univ. Turku.* A. II, **36**, 211–35.

Hadač, E. (1970). Sea-shore communities of Reykjanes Peninsula, S.W. Iceland (Plant communities of Reykjanes Peninsula, Part 2). *Folia Geobot. phytotax.* **5**, 133–44.

Hadač, E. (1971). The vegetation of springs, lakes and 'flags' of Reykjanes Peninsula, S.W. Iceland (Plant Communities of Reykjanes Peninsula, Part 3). *Folia Geobot. Phytotax.* **6**, 29–41.

Hadač, E. & Vaňa, J. (1967). Plant communities of mires in the western part of the Krkonose Mountains, Czechoslovakia. *Folia Geobot. Phytotax.* **2**, 213–54.

Hafsten, U. (1956). Pollen-analytic investigations on the late Quaternary development in the inner Oslofjord area. *Årbok. Univ. Bergen* Nr. 8, 161 pp.

Hafsten, U. (1958). Finds of subfossil pollen of *Koenigia islandica* from Scandinavia. *Bot. Notiser*, **111**, 333–5.

Hafsten, U. (1960). Pleistocene development of vegetation and climate in Tristan da Cunha and Gough Island. *Årbok, Univ. Bergen* Nr. 20, 48 pp.

Hafsten, U. (1963). A late-glacial pollen profile from Lista, South Norway. *Grana Palynol.* **4** (2), 326–37.

Hafsten, U. (1966). Den senkvartaere forekomst av tindved (*Hippophaë rhamnoides* L.) i Sør-Norge. *Blyttia* **24**, 196–215.

Hafsten, U. (1969). A proposal for a synchronous subdivision of the Late Pleistocene Period having global and universal applicability. *Nytt Mag. Bot.* **16**, 1–13.

Hafsten, U. (1970). A sub-division of the late Pleistocene period on a synchronous basis, intended for global and universal usage. *Palaeogeogr., Palaeoclimatol., Palaeoecol.* **7**, 279–96.

Hallberg, H. P. (1971). Vegetation auf den Schalenablagerungen in Bohuslän, Schweden. *Acta Phytogeogr. suec.* **56**, 136 pp.

Hämet-Ahti, L. (1963). Zonation of the mountain birch forests in northernmost Fennoscandia. *Ann. bot. Soc. 'Vanamo'* **34** (4), 127 pp.

Hansen, H. M. (1930). Studies on the vegetation of Iceland. In *The Botany of Iceland*, **3** (1), 186 pp. Copenhagen.
Hansen, K. (1966). Vascular plants in the Faeroes. *Dansk bot. Ark.* **24** (3), 141 pp.
Hansen, K. (1967). Edaphic conditions of vegetation types in the Faeroes. *Oikos* **18**, 217–32.
Hansen, K. (1968). Lichens in the Faeroes. *Bot. Tidsskr.* **63**, 305–18.
Harker, A. (1901). Ice-erosion in the Cuillin Hills, Skye. *Trans. R. Soc. Edinb.* **40**, 221–52.
Harker, A. (1904). *The Tertiary Igneous Rocks of Skye.* Memoir Geological Survey. London.
Harland, R. (1968). A microplankton assemblage from the Post-Pleistocene of Wales. *Grana Palynol.* **8** (2–3), 536–54.
Harris, T. M. (1939). Notes on a fencing experiment. *J. Ecol.* **27**, 383.
Harrison, C. M. (1970). The phytosociology of certain English heathland communities. *J. Ecol.* **58**, 573–89.
Hartman, A. A. (1968). A study on pollen dispersal and sedimentation in the Western part of the Netherlands. *Acta bot. neerl.* **17**, 506–49.
Havinga, A. J. (1963). A palynological investigation of soil profiles developed in coversand. *Meded. Landb-Hoogesch. Wageningen* **63** (1), 93 pp.
Havinga, A. J. (1964). Investigation into the differential corrosion susceptibility of pollen and spores. *Pollen Spores* **6**, 621–35.
Havinga, A. J. (1967). Palynology and pollen presentation. *Rev. Palaeobotan. Palynol.* **2**, 81–98.
Havinga, A. J. (1971). An experimental investigation into the decay of pollen and spores in various soil types. In *Sporopollenin* (ed. by J. Brooks, P. R. Grant, M. D. Muir, P. van Gijzel & G. Shaw). London and New York.
Haynes, V. M. (1968). The influence of glacial erosion and rock structure on corries in Scotland. *Geogr. Annlr.* A, **50**, 221–34.
Hedberg, H. D. (1961). Stratigraphic classification and terminology. Statement of principles. *Int. Geol. Congr.* **21** (25), 1–38.
Hedberg, O. (1946). Pollen morphology in the genus *Polygonum* L. *s. lat.* and its taxonomical significance. *Svensk bot. Tidskr.* **40**, 371–404.
Hedberg, O., Mårtensson, O. & Rudberg, S. (1952), Botanical investigations in the Pältsa region of northernmost Sweden. *Bot. Notiser* (Suppl.), **3** (2), 209 pp.
Heddle, R. G. & Ogg, W. G. (1936). Irrigation experiments on a Scottish hill pasture. *J. Ecol.* **24**, 220–31.
Hedlund, R. W. (1965). *Sigmopollis hispidus* Gen. et sp. nov. from Miocene sediments, Elko County, Nevada. *Pollen Spores* **7**, 89–92.
Heim, J. (1962). Recherches sur les relations entre la végétation actuelle et le spectre pollinque récent dans les Ardennes Belges. *Bull. Soc. r. Bot. Belg.* **96**, 5–92.
Heim, J. (1970). *Les relations entre les spectres pollinques recents et la végétation actuelle en Europe Occidentale.* Louvain.
Heim, J. (1971). Étude statistique sur la validité des spectres polliniques provenant d'échantillons de mousses. *Lejeunia* **58**, 34 pp.
Heim-Thomas, D. (1969). Étude palynologique du Marais de Vance (Belgique). *Acta Geogr. Lovan,* **7**, 113–39.
Heinonen, L. (1957). Studies on the microfossils in the tills of the North European Glaciation. *Ann. Acad. Sci. Fenn.* A, **52** (3), 1–92.
Herzog, T. (1926). *Geographie der Moose.* Jena.
Heslop-Harrison, Y. (1953). *Nuphar intermedia* Ladeb., a presumed relict hybrid in Britain. *Watsonia,* **3**, 7–25.
Heslop-Harrison, Y. (1955). *Nymphaea* L. em. Sm. *J. Ecol.,* **43**, 719–34.
Hibbert, F. A., Switsur, V. R. & West, R. G. (1971). Radiocarbon dating of Flandrian pollen zones at Red Moss, Lancashire. *Proc. R. Soc.* B, **177**, 161–76.
Hirst, J. M., Stedman, O. J. & Hurst, G. W. (1967). Long-distance spore transport: Vertical sections of Spore Clouds over the sea. *J. gen. Microbiol.* **48**, 357–77.
Hocquette, M., Géhu, J. M. & Fauquet, M. (1965). Contribution à l'étude phytosociologique de l' estuaire de l'Authie. *Bull. Soc. bot. Nord Fr.* **18**, 114–43.
Holden, A. V. (1961). Concentration of chloride in freshwaters and rain water. *Nature* **192**, 961.
Holdgate, M. W. (1955*a*). The vegetation of some British upland fens. *J. Ecol.* **43**, 389–403.
Holdgate, M. W. (1955*b*). The vegetation of some springs and wet flushes on Tarn Moor near Orton, Westmorland. *J. Ecol.* **43**, 79–89.
Holloway, J. D. (1969). A numerical investigation of the biogeography of the butterfly fauna of India, and its relation to continental drift. *Biol. J. Linn. Soc.* **1**, 373–85.
Holloway, J. D. & Jardine, N. (1968). Two approaches to zoogeography: a study based on the distributions of butterflies, birds and bats in the Indo-Australian area. *Proc. Linn. Soc. Lond.* **179**, 153–88.
Holmen, H. (1965). Subalpine tall herb vegetation, site and standing crop. In *The Plant Cover of Sweden. Acta Phytogeogr. suec.* **50**, 314 pp.
Holmen, K. (1960). The mosses of Peary Land, North Greenland. *Meddr. Grønland,* **163** (2), 96 pp.
Holmquist, C. (1962). The relic concept – is it merely a zoogeographical conception? *Oikos,* **13**, 262–92.
Hultén, E. (1950). *Atlas of the distribution of vascular plants in North-West Europe.* Stockholm.
Hultén, E. (1954). *Artemisia norvegica* Fr. and its allies. *Nytt Mag. Bot.* **3**, 63–82.
Hultén, E. (1958). The Amphi-Atlantic Plants and their phytogeographical connections. *K. svenska Vetensk Akad. Handl.* **7** (1), 340 pp.
Hultén, E. (1964). The Circumpolar Plants. 1. Vascular cryptogams, conifers, monocotyledons. *K. svenska Vetensk Akad. Handl.* **8** (5), 279 pp.

Huynh, K-L. (1970). Le pollen du genre *Anemone* et du genre *Hepatica* (Ranunculaceae) et leur taxonomie. *Pollen Spores* **12**, 329–64.

Hyde, H. A. & Williams, D. A. (1945). Pollen of lime (*Tilia* spp). *Nature* **155**, 457.

Iglesias, C. M. (1968). Estudio de la Vegetación del Partido Judicial de Caldas de Reyes. *Universidad de Madrid Facultad de Ciencias Trabajos del Departmento de Botanica y Fisiologia Vegetal* **1**, 59–114.

Imbrie, J. & Kipp, N. G. (1971). A new micropaleontological method for quantitative paleoclimatology: application to a late Pleistocene Caribbean core. In *The Late Cenozoic Glacial Ages* (ed. by K. K. Turekian). New Haven and London.

Ingram, H. A. P. (1967). Problems of hydrology and plant distribution in mires. *J. Ecol.* **55**, 711–24.

Ingram, H. A. P., Anderson, M. C., Andrews, S. M., Chinery, J. M., Evans, G. B. & Richards, C. M. (1959). Vegetational studies at Semerwater. *The Naturalist* 1959, 113–27.

Iversen, J. (1929). Studien über die pH-Verhältnisse dänischer Gewässer und ihren Einfluss auf die Hydrophyten-Vegetation. *Bot. Tidsskr.* **40**, 277–333.

Iversen, J. (1936). Secundäres pollen als fehlerquelle. *Danm. geol. Unders.*, Ser. IV, **2** (15), 1–24.

Iversen, J. (1940). Blütenbiologische Studien. I. Dimorphie und monomorphie bei *Armeria. K. danske Vidensk. Selsk., Biol. Medd.* **15** (8), 39 pp.

Iversen, J. (1942). En pollenanalytisk Tidsfaestelse of Ferskvandslagene red Nørre Lyngby. *Medd. dansk. geol. Foren.* **10**, 130–51.

Iversen, J. (1944). *Helianthemum* som fossil glacialplante i Dänmark. *Geol. Fören. Förh. Stock.* **66**, 774–6.

Iversen, J. (1945). Conditions of life for the large herbivorous mammals in the Late-glacial Period. In *The Bison in Denmark. Danm. geol. Unders.*, Ser. 11, **73**, 62 pp.

Iversen, J. (1947). Diskussionsindlaeg i: Nordisk kvartärgeologisk möte den 5–9 november 1945. *Geol. Fören. Förh. Stock.* **69**, 241–2.

Iversen, J. (1952–3). Origin of the flora of Western Greenland in the light of pollen analysis. *Oikos*, **4**, 85–103.

Iversen, J. (1953). Radiocarbon dating of the Alleröd Period. *Science*, **118**, 9–11.

Iversen, J. (1954). The Late-glacial Flora of Denmark and its relation to climate and soil. *Danm. geol. Unders.*, Ser. 11, **80**, 87–119.

Iversen, J. (1960). Problems of the early Post-glacial forest development in Denmark. *Danm. geol. Unders.*, Ser. IV, **4** (3), 32 pp.

Iversen, J. (1964). Plant indicators of climate, soil and other factors during the Quaternary. *Rep. VIth Int. Quat. Congr.* **2**, 421–6.

Iversen, J. & Troels-Smith, J. (1950). Pollenmorfologiske definitions og typer. *Danm. geol. Unders.*, Ser. IV, **3** (8), 54 pp.

Ivimey-Cook, R. B. & Proctor, M. C. F. (1966*a*). The application of association analysis to phytosociology. *J. Ecol.* **54**, 179–92.

Ivimey-Cook, R. B. & Proctor, M. C. F. (1966*b*). The Plant Communities of The Burren, Co. Clare. *Proc. R. Ir. Acad.* B, **64**, 211–301.

Jäger, E. (1968). Die pflanzengeographische Ozeanitätsgliederung der Holarktis und die Ozeanitätsbindung der Pflanzenareale. *Feddes Repert.* **79**, 157–335.

Jahns, A. (1967). Some features of mass movement on Spitsbergen slopes. *Geogr. Annlr.* A, **49**, 213–25.

Jahns, W. (1969). Torfmoos-Gesellschaften der Esterweger Dose. *Schriften Vegetationskunde*, **4**, 49–74.

James, P. W. (1965). A new check-list of British lichens. *Lichenologist* **3**, 95–153.

Janssen, C. R. (1966). Recent pollen spectra from the deciduous and coniferous-deciduous forests of north-eastern Minnesota: a study in pollen dispersal. *Ecology* **47**, 804–25.

Janssen, C. R. (1967*a*). A Post-glacial pollen diagram from a small *Typha* swamp in Northwestern Minnesota, interpreted from pollen indicators and surface samples. *Ecol. Monogr.* **37**, 145–72.

Janssen, C. R. (1967*b*). A comparison between the regional pollen rain and the sub-recent vegetation in four major vegetation types in Minnesota (U.S.A.). *Rev. Palaeobotan. Palynol.* **2**, 331–42.

Janssen, C. R. (1970). Problems in the recognition of plant communities in pollen diagrams. *Vegetatio* **20**, 187–98.

Jardine, W. G. (1968). The 'Perth' Readvance. *Scott. J. Geol.* **4**, 185–6.

Jefferies, R. L. & Willis, A. J. (1964). Studies on the calcicole–calcifuge habit. 1. Methods of analysis of soil and plant tissue and some results of investigations of four species. *J. Ecol.* **52**, 121–38.

Jefferies, T. A. (1915). Ecology of the purple heath grass. *J. Ecol.* **3**, 93–101.

Jensen, C. (1901). Bryophyta. In *Botany of the Faeröes* **1**, 120–97.

Jessen, K. (1935). Archaeological dating in the history of North Jutland's vegetation. *Acta Archaeol.* **5**, 185–214.

Jessen, K. (1949). Studies in Late Quaternary deposits and flora-history of Ireland. *Proc. R. Ir. Acad.* B, **52**, 85–290.

Johansen, J. (1968). Gródrarleivdir (Sád) av Dvørgabjørk (*Betula nana*) i Føroyum. *Annal. societ. scient. Faeroensis* **16**, 119–28.

Johnson, R. G. (1962). Interspecific associations in Pennsylvanian fossil assemblages. *J. Geol.* **72**, 32–55.

Jonassen, H. (1950). Recent pollen sedimentation and Jutland heath diagrams. *Dansk bot. Arkiv.* **13** (7), 168 pp.

Jørgensen, P. M. (1969). *Sticta dufourii* Del. and its parasymbiont *Arthonia abelonae* P. M. Jörg in Norway. *Nova Hedwigia* **18**, 331–40.

Jørgensen, S. (1963). Early Postglacial in Aamosen Vols. I and II. *Danm. geol. Unders.* Ser. 11, **87**, 105 pp.

Julin, E. & Luther, H. (1959). Om blomning och fruktsättning *Ceratophyllum demersum* i Fennoskandien. *Bot. Notiser* **112**, 321–38.

Jurko, A. (1969). Die Weidegesellschaften des Strážover Berglandes in der Nordwestslowakei und die syntaxomischen Probleme des Cynosurion-Verbandes in den Westkarpaten. *Folia Geobot. Phytotax.* **4**, 101–32.

Jurko, A. (1971). Vegetationskundliches Material zu den Weidegesellschaften aus dem Orava-Gebiet. *Biologia* **26**, 317–34.

Kenneth, A. G. & Stirling, A. McG. (1970). Notes on the Hawkweeds (*Hieracium sensu lato*) of western Scotland. *Watsonia* **8**, 97–120.

Kershaw, A. P. (1970). A pollen diagram from Lake Euramoo, North-East Queensland, Australia. *New Phytol.* **69**, 785–805.

Kershaw, K. A. & Tallis, J. H. (1958). Pattern in a high-level *Juncus squarrosus* community. *J. Ecol.* **46**, 739–48.

King, J. & Nicholson, I. A. (1964). Grasslands of the forest and subalpine zones. In *The Vegetation of Scotland* (ed. by J. H. Burnett). Edinburgh.

King, J. E. & Kapp, R. O. (1963). Modern pollen rain studies in eastern Ontario. *Can. J. Bot.* **41**, 243–52.

Kirk, W. & Godwin, H. (1963). A Late-glacial site at Loch Droma, Ross and Cromarty. *Trans. R. Soc. Edinb.* **45**, 225–49.

Kirk, W., Rice, R. J. & Synge, F. M. (1966). Deglaciation and vertical displacement of shorelines in Wester and Easter Ross. *Trans. Inst. Br. Geogr.* **39**, 65–78.

Klötzli, G. (1970). Eichen-, Edellaub- und Bruchwälder der Britischen Inseln. *Schweiz. Zeitschr. Forstwesen* **121**, 329–66.

Knaben, G. (1950). Botanical investigations in the Middle Districts of Western Norway. *Årbok. Univ. Bergen* Nr. 8, 117 pp.

Königsson, L-K. (1968). The Holocene History of The Great Alvar of Öland. *Acta Phytogeogr. suec.* **55**, 172 pp.

Köppen, W. (1923). *Die Klimate der Erde, Grundriss der Klimakunde.* Berlin.

Krog, H. (1954). Pollen analytical investigation of a C^{14}-dated Alleröd-section from Ruds-Vedby. *Danm. geol. Unders.* Ser. II, **80**, 120–39.

Krog, H. (1959). Geological Part. In *The Reindeer in Denmark. K. danske Vidensk. Selsk., Biol. Skr.* **10** (4), 117–61.

Kubitzki, K. (1961). Zur Synchronisierung der nordwesteuropäischen Pollendiagramme (mit Beiträgen zur Waldgeschichte Nordwestdeutschlands). *Flora* **150**, 43–72.

Lambert, J. M. & Dale, M. (1964). The Use of Statistics in Phytosociology. *Adv. ecol. Res.* **2**, 59–99.

Lang, G. (1952). Zur späteiszeitlichen Vegetations- und Florengeschichte Südwestdeutschlands. *Flora* **139**, 243–94.

Lang, G. (1955). Über spätquartäre Funde von *Isoëtes* und *Najas flexilis* in Schwarzwald. *Ber. Deutsch. Bot. Ges.* **68**, 24–7.

Lang, G. (1967). Über die Geschichte von Pflanzengesellschaften auf Grund Quartärbotanischer Untersuchungen. In *Pflanzensoziologie und Palynologie* (ed. by R. Tüxen). The Hague.

Lang, G. (1970). Florengeschichte und mediterran-mittel-europäische Florenbeziehungen. *Feddes Repert.* **81**, 315–35.

Lange, B. (1963). Studies in the *Sphagnum* flora of Iceland and the Faeroes. *Bot. Tidsskr.* **59**, 220–43.

Lawrence, D. R. (1968). Taphonomy and Information Losses in Fossil Communities. *Bull. geol. soc. Amer.* **79**, 1315–30.

Leach, W. (1930). A preliminary account of the vegetation of some non-calcareous British screes. *J. Ecol.* **18**, 321–32.

Leach, W. & Polunin, N. (1932). Observations on the vegetation of Finmark. *J. Ecol.* **20**, 416–30.

Lemée, M. G. (1937). *Recherches écologiques sur la végétation du Perche.* Paris.

Lichti-Federovich, S. & Ritchie, J. C. (1965). Contemporary pollen spectra in Central Canada. II. The Forest-Grassland Transition in Manitoba. *Pollen Spores* **7**, 63–87.

Lichti-Federovich, S. & Ritchie, J. C. (1968). Recent pollen assemblages from the western interior of Canada. *Rev. Palaeobotan. Palynol.* **7**, 297–344.

Lichtwardt, R. W. (1952). A new light-weight shaft for peat samplers. *Palaeobotanist* **1**, 317–18.

Lid, J. (1958). Two glacial relics of *Dryas octopetala* and *Carex rupestris* in the forests of South-eastern Norway. *Nytt Mag. Bot.* **6**, 5–9.

Lid, J. (1959), The vascular plants of Hardangervidda, a mountain plateau of southern Norway. *Nytt Mag. Bot.* **7**, 61–128.

Livingstone, D. A. (1955*a*). A lightweight piston sampler for lake deposits. *Ecology* **36**, 137–9.

Livingstone, D. A. (1955*b*). Some pollen profiles from Arctic Alaska. *Ecology* **36**, 587–600.

Livingstone, D. A. (1968). Some interstadial and postglacial pollen diagrams from Eastern Canada. *Ecol. Monogr.* **38**, 87–125.

Livingstone, D. A. & Estes, A. H. (1967). A carbon-dated pollen diagram from the Cape Breton plateau, Nova Scotia. *Can. J. Bot.* **45**, 339–59.

Lohammar, G. (1965). The vegetation of Swedish lakes. In *The Plant Cover of Sweden. Acta Phytogeogr. suec.* **50**, 314 pp.

Lohmeyer, W. *et al.* (1962). Contribution à l'unification du système phytosociologique pour l'Europe Moyenne et Nord-Occidentale. *Melhoramento* **15**, 137–51.

Löve, D. (1970). Subarctic and subalpine: where and what? *Arctic and Alpine Research*, **2**, 63–73.

Lövkvist, B. (1962). Chromosome and differentiation studies in flowering plants of Skåne, South Sweden. 1. General aspects, Type species with coastal differentiation. *Bot. Notiser* **115**, 216–87.

Lüdi, W. & Vareschi, V. (1936). Die Verbreitung und der Pollenniederschlag der Heufieberflanzen im Hochtale von Davos. *Ber. geobot. Forsch Inst. Rübel* f.d. 1935, 47–112.

Lund, J. W. G. (1961). The algae of the Malham Tarn district. *Field Studies* **1** (3), 85–119.

Lundh, A. (1951). Studies on the vegetation and hydrochemistry of Scanian lakes. III. Distribution of macrophytes and some algal groups. *Bot. Notiser (Suppl.)*, **3** (1), 138 pp.

Lundqvist, Jan (1962). Patterned ground and related frost phenomenon in Sweden. *Sver. geol. Unders.* Ser. C, Årb. **55** (7), 101 pp.

Lundqvist, Jan (1967). Submoräna sediment i Jämtlands Län. *Sver. geol. Unders.* Ser. C, Årb. **61** (3), 267 pp.

Lundqvist, Jan & Bengtsson, K. (1970). The Red Snow – a meteorological and pollen-analytical study of longtransported material from snowfalls in Sweden. *Geol. Fören. Förh. Stock.* **92**, 288–301.

Lundqvist, Jim (1968). Plant cover and environment of steep hillsides in Pite Lappmark. *Acta Phytogeogr. suec.* **53**, 153 pp.

Lye, K. A. (1966). A quantitative and qualitative investigation of oceanic bryophyte communities and their relation to the environment. *Nytt Mag. Bot.* **13**, 87–133.

Lye, K. A. (1967*a*). Studies in the growth and development of oceanic bryophyte communities. *Svensk bot. Tidskr.* **61**, 297–310.

Lye, K. A. (1967*b*). En ny inndeling av Norges plantegeografiske element. *Blyttia* **25**, 88–123.

Lye, K. A. (1969). The distribution and ecology of *Sphaerophorus melanocarpus*. *Svensk bot. Tidskr.* **63**, 300–318.

Mackereth, F. J. H. (1966). Some chemical observations on Post-glacial lake sediments. *Phil. Trans. R. Soc.* B, **250**, 165–213.

Maher, L. J. (1963). Pollen analyses of surface materials from the Southern San Juan Mountains, Colorado. *Bull. geol. soc. Amer.* **74**, 1485–504.

Maher, L. J. (1964). *Ephedra* pollen in sediments of the Great Lakes Region. *Ecology* **45**, 391–5.

Malloch, A. J. C. (1971). Vegetation of the maritime clifftops of the Lizard and Land's End Peninsulas, West Cornwall. *New Phytol.* **70**, 1155–97.

Malmer, N. (1962). Studies on mire vegetation in the Archaean area of Southwestern Götaland (Southern Sweden). 1. Vegetation and habitat conditions of the Akhult mire. *Op. bot. Soc. bot. Lund,* **7** (1), 322 pp.

Malmer, N. (1965). The Southern Mires. In *The Plant Cover of Sweden. Acta Phytogeogr. suec.* **50**, 314 pp.

Malmer, N. (1968). Über die Gliederung der Oxycocco–Sphagnetea und der Scheuchzerio–Caricetea fuscae in Südschweden. In *Pflanzensoziologische Systematik* (ed. by R. Tüxen). The Hague.

Mamakova, K. (1968). Lille Bukken and Lerøy – two pollen diagrams from Western Norway. *Årbok. Univ. Bergen*, Nr. 4, 42 pp.

Mangerud, J. (1970). Late Weichselian vegetation and ice-front oscillations in the Bergen District, Western Norway. *Norsk. geogr. Tidsskr.* **24**, 121–48.

Manley, G. (1945). Meteorological observations on Dun Fell, 2735 feet. *Quat. J. R. met. Soc.* **68**, 151–65.

Manley, G. (1952). *Climate and the British Scene.* London.

Manley, G. (1964). The evolution of the climatic environment. In *The British Isles: a systematic geography* (ed. by J. W. Watson & J. B. Sissons). Edinburgh.

Manum, S. (1962). Studies in the Tertiary flora of Spitsbergen, with notes on Tertiary floras of Ellesmere Island, Greenland, and Iceland. *Norsk Polarinst. Skrift.* **125**, 127 pp.

Martin, N. M. (1938). Some observations on the epiphytic moss flora of trees in Argyll. *J. Ecol.* **26**, 82–95.

Matthews, J. R. (1937). Geographical relationships of the British Flora. *J. Ecol.* **25**, 1–90.

Matthews, J. R. (1955). *Origin and distribution of the British Flora.* London.

McAndrews, J. H. (1966). Postglacial history of Prairie, Savanna and Forest in Northwestern Minnesota. *Mem. Torrey bot. Club* **22** (2), 72 pp.

McAndrews, J. H. (1967). Pollen analysis and vegetational history of the Itasca region, Minnesota. In *Quaternary Paleoecology* (ed. by E. J. Cushing & H. E. Wright). New Haven and London.

McCann, S. B. (1966). The main Post-glacial raised shoreline of Western Scotland from the Firth of Lorne to Loch Broom. *Trans. Inst. Br. Geogr.* **39**, 87–99.

McIntosh, R. P. (1962). Raunkiaer's 'Law of Frequency'. *Ecology* **43**, 533–5.

McIntosh, R. P. (1967). The continuum concept of vegetation. *Bot. Rev.* **33**, 130–87.

McVean, D. N. (1955). Notes on the vegetation of Iceland. *Trans. Proc. bot. soc. Edinb.* **36**, 320–38.

McVean, D. N. (1958*a*). Snow cover and vegetation in the Scottish Highlands. *Weather* **13**, 197–200.

McVean, D. N. (1958*b*). Island vegetation of some West Highland Fresh-water Lochs. *Trans. Proc. bot. soc. Edinb.* **37**, 200–208.

McVean, D. N. (1961*a*). Flora and vegetation of the islands of St Kilda and North Rona in 1958. *J. Ecol.* **49**, 39–54.

McVean, D. N. (1961*b*). Post-glacial history of juniper in Scotland. *Proc. Linn. Soc., Lond.* **172**, 53–5.

McVean, D. N. (1964). Woodland and Scrub. In *The Vegetation of Scotland* (ed. by J. H. Burnett). Edinburgh.

McVean, D. N. & Lockie, J. D. (1969). *Ecology and land use in Upland Scotland.* Edinburgh.

McVean, D. N. & Ratcliffe, D. A. (1962). *Plant Communities of the Scottish Highlands.* H.M.S.O. London.

Megard, R. O. (1964). Biostratigraphic history of Dead Man Lake, Chuska Mountains, New Mexico. *Ecology* **45**, 529–46.

Megard, R. O. (1967). Late-Quaternary cladocera of Lake Zeribar, Western Iran. *Ecology* **48**, 179–89.

Meisel, K. (1969). Zur Gliederung und Ökologie der Wiesen im nordwest deutschen Flachland. *Schriften Vegetationskunde* **4**, 23–48.

Menke, B. (1963). Beiträge zur Geschichte der *Erica* – Heiden Nordwestdeutschlands. *Flora* **153**, 521–48.

Menke, B. (1969). Vegetationskundliche und vegetationsgeschichtliche Untersuchungen an Strandwällen. *Mitt. flor.-soz. ArbGemein*, N.F. **14**, 95–120.

Meusel, H., Jäger, E. & Weinert, E. (1965). *Vergleichende Chorologie der Zentraleuropäischen Flora.* Jena.

Miller, T. G. (1965). Time in stratigraphy. *Palaeontology* **8**, 111–31.

Mitchell, G. F. (1954). Late-Glacial Flora of Ireland. *Danm. geol. Unders.* Ser. 11, No. 80, 73–86.

Mitchell, G. F. (1958). A late-glacial deposit near Ballaugh, Isle of Man. *New Phytol.* **57**, 256–63.

Moar, N. T. (1969*a*). Late-Weichselian and Flandrian pollen diagrams from South-West Scotland. *New Phytol.* **68**, 433–67.

Moar, N. T. (1969*b*). Two pollen diagrams from the mainland, Orkney Islands. *New Phytol.* **68**, 201–8.

Moe, D. (1970). The Post-glacial immigration of *Picea abies* into Fennoscandia. *Bot. Notiser* **123**, 61–6.

Molenaar, J. G. de (1968). A contribution to the phytogeography of the Angmagssalik Area, East Greenland, with special reference to chionophily. *Acta bot. neerl.* **17**, 333–9.

Mooney, H. A. & Billings, W. D. (1961). Comparative physiological ecology of Arctic and Alpine populations of *Oxyria digyna*. *Ecol. Monogr.* **31**, 1–29.

Moore, J. J. (1960). A re-survey of the vegetation of the district lying south of Dublin (1905–56). *Proc. R. Irish Acad.* B, **61**, 1–36.

Moore, J. J. (1962). The Braun-Blanquet system: A reassessment. *J. Ecol.* **50**, 761–70.

Moore, J. J. (1968). A classification of the bogs and wet heaths of Northern Europe (Oxycocco–Sphagnetea Br.-Bl. et Tx. 1943). In *Pflanzensoziologische Systematik* (ed. by R. Tüxen). The Hague.

Moore, J. J., Fitzsimmons, P., Lambe, E. & White, J. (1970). A comparison and evaluation of some phytosociological techniques. *Vegetatio* **20**, 1–20.

Moore, J. J. & O'Sullivan, A. (1970). A comparison between the results of the Braun-Blanquet method and those of 'cluster analysis'. In *Gesellschaftsmorphologie (Strukturforschung)* (ed. by R. Tüxen). The Hague.

Moore, P. D. (1970). Studies in the vegetational history of Mid-Wales. II. The late-glacial period in Cardiganshire. *New Phytol.* **69**, 363–75.

Mörnsjö, T. (1969). Studies on the vegetation and development of a peatland in Scania, South Sweden. *Op. bot. Soc. bot. Lund.* **24**, 187 pp.

Morrison, M. E. S. (1959). The ecology of a raised bog in Co. Tyrone, Northern Ireland. *Proc. R. Ir. Acad.* B, **60**, 291–308.

Morrison, M. E. S. & Stephens, N. (1965). A submerged late-Quaternary deposit at Roddans Port on the north-east coast of Ireland. *Phil. Trans. R. Soc.* B, **249**, 221–55.

Mosimann, J. E. (1965). Statistical methods for the pollen analyst: Multinomial and negative multinomial techniques. In *Handbook of Paleontological Techniques* (ed. by B. Kummel & D. M. Raup). San Francisco.

Mullenders, W. (1962). Les relations entra la végétation et les spectres polliniques en Forêt du Mont-Dieu. *Bull. Soc. r. bot. Belg.* **94**, 131–8.

Müller, H. (1953). Zur spät- und nacheiszeitlichen Vegetationsgeschichte des mitteldeutschen Trockengebiets. *Nova Acta Leop. Carol.* (N.F.), **16**, 1–67.

Müller-Stoll, W. R. (1956). Über das Verhalten der Exine nonaperturater Angiospermen-pollen bei Quellung und Keimung. *Grana Palynol.* **1** (2), 38–58.

Murray, C. W. (1970). Isle of Raasay, Inverness-shire 28th June – 5th July. *Watsonia* **8**, 190–1.

Murray, W. H. (1966). *The Hebrides.* London.

Neves, R. & Sullivan, H. J. (1964). Modification of fossil spore exines associated with the presence of pyrite crystals. *Micropaleontology* **10**, 443–52.

Newey, W. W. (1970). Pollen analysis of Late-Weichselian deposits at Corstorphine, Edinburgh. *New Phytol.* **69**, 1167–77.

Nicholson, I. A. (1970). Some effects of animal grazing and browsing on vegetation. *Trans. Proc. bot. soc. Edinb.* **41**, 85–94.

Nilsson, T. (1964). Standardpollendiagramme und C^{14}-Datierrungen aus dem Ageröds Mosse im Mittleren Schonen. *Lunds Univ. Årsskr.*, N.F. 2, **59** (7), 52 pp.

Nordhagen, R. (1922). Vegetationstudien auf der Insel Utsire in westlichen Norwegen. *Årbok. Mus. Bergen*, Nr. 1, 149 pp.

Nordhagen, R. (1927). Die Vegetation und Flora des Sylenegebietes. 1. Die Vegetation. *Skr. norsk Vidensk.-Akad. I. Mat.-Nat.*, No. 1, 612 pp.

Nordhagen, R. (1936). Versuch einer neuen Einteilung der subalpinen-alpinen Vegetation Norwegens. *Årbok. Mus. Bergen*, Nr. 7, 88 pp.

Nordhagen, R. (1940). Studien über die maritime Vegetation Norwegens. 1. Die Pflanzengesellschaften der Tangwälle. *Årbok. Mus. Bergen*, Nr. 2, 123 pp.

Nordhagen, R. (1943). Sikilsdalen og Norges Fjellbeiter. *Bergens Museum Skrifter* **22**, 607 pp.

Nordhagen, R. (1954). Some new observations concerning the geographic distribution and ecology of *Arenaria humifusa* Wg. in Norway as compared with *Arenaria norvegica* Gunn. *Bot. Tidsskr.* **51**, 248–62.

Nordhagen, R. (1955), Kobresieto-Dryadion in Northern Scandinavia. *Svensk bot. Tidskr.* **49**, 63–87.

Nyholm, E. (1954–69). *Illustrated Moss Flora of Fennoscandia* 11, Musci. Parts 1–6. Lund.

Oberdorfer, E. (1957). Süddeutsche Pflanzengesellschaften. *Pflanzensoziologie* **10**, 564 pp.

Oberdorfer, E. (1970). *Pflanzensoziologische Exkursionsflora für Süddeutschland.* Stuttgart.

Oberdorfer, E., Görs, S., Kornek, D., Lohmeyer, W., Müller, Th., Philippi, G. & Seibert, P. (1967). Systematische Übersicht der westdeutschen Phanerogamen- und Gefässkryptogamen-Gesellschaften. Ein Diskussionsentwurf. *Schriften Vegetationskunde* **2**, 7–62.

Ogden, J. G. (1967). Radiocarbon and pollen evidence for a sudden change in climate in the Great Lakes Region approximately 10000 years ago. In *Quaternary Paleoecology* (ed. by E. J. Cushing & H. E. Wright). New Haven and London.

Ogden, J. G. (1969). Correlation of contemporary and Late Pleistocene pollen records in the reconstruction of Postglacial environments in Northeastern North America. *Mitt. Int. Verein. Limnol.* **17**, 64–77.

Oldfield, F. (1959). The pollen morphology of some of the West European Ericales. *Pollen Spores* **1**, 19–48.

Oldfield, F. (1960). Studies in the Post-glacial history of British Vegetation: Lowland Lonsdale. *New Phytol.* **59**, 192–217.

Oldfield, F. (1970). Some aspects of scale and complexity in pollen-analytically based palaeoecology. *Pollen Spores* **12**, 163–71.

Olsson, I. U. (1968). Modern aspects of radiocarbon datings. *Earth Sci. Rev.* **4**, 203–18.

Ostenfeld, C. H. (1908). The Land-Vegetation of the Faeröes. In *Botany of the Faeröes* **3**, 867–1026. Copenhagen and London.

O'Sullivan, A. M. (1968*a*). Irish Molinietalia communities in relation to those of the Atlantic region of Europe. In *Pflanzensoziologische Systematik* (ed. by R. Tüxen). The Hague.

O'Sullivan, A. M. (1968*b*). A phytosociological survey of Irish grassland. In *Pflanzensoziologie und Landschaftsökologie* (ed. by R. Tüxen). The Hague.

Paton, J. A. (1965). *Census Catalogue of British Hepatics.* (4th edition). Ipswich.

Paton, J. A. & Corley, M. F. V. (1969). *Haplomitrium hookeri* (Sm.) Nees in alpine habitats in Scotland. *Trans. Br. bryol. Soc.* **5**, 827–8.

Patton, D. (1923). The vegetation of Beinn Laoigh. *Rep. botl. Soc. Exch. Club Br.* **7**, 268–319.

Peach, B. N., Horne, J., Woodward, H. B., Clough, C. T., Harker, A. & Wedd, C. B. (1910). *The geology of Glenelg, Lochalsh and southeast part of Skye.* Memoir Geological Survey. London.

Pears, N. V. (1967). Present tree-lines of the Cairngorm Mountains, Scotland. *J. Ecol.* **55**, 815–29.

Pearsall, W. H. (1941). The 'mosses' of the Stainmore district. *J. Ecol.* **29**, 161–75.

Pearsall, W. H. (1950) *Mountains and Moorlands.* London.

Pearsall, W. H. (1956). Two blanket-bogs in Sutherland. *J. Ecol.* **44**, 493–516.

Pennington, W. (1964). Pollen analysis from the deposits of six upland tarns in the Lake District. *Phil. Trans. R. Soc.* B, **248**, 205–44.

Pennington, W. (1970). Vegetation History in the North-West of England: a regional synthesis. In *Studies in the Vegetational History of the British Isles* (ed. by D. Walker & R. G. West). Cambridge.

Pennington, W. & Bonny, A. P. (1970). Absolute pollen diagram from the British Late-glacial. *Nature* **226**, 871–73.

Pennington, W. & Lishman, J. P. (1971). Iodine in lake sediments in Northern England and Scotland. *Biol. Rev.* **46**, 279–313.

Penny, L. F. (1964). A review of the Last Glaciation in Great Britain. *Proc. Yorks. geol. Soc.* **34**, 387–411.

Persson, Å. (1961). Mire and spring vegetation in an area north of Lake Torneträsk, Torne Lappmark, Sweden. *Op. bot. Soc. bot. Lund* **6** (1), 187 pp.

Persson, Å. (1964). The vegetation at the margin of the receding glacier Skaftafellsjökull, south-eastern Iceland. *Bot. Notiser* **117**, 323–54.

Phemister, J. (1960). *British Regional Geology, Scotland: The Northern Highlands.* H.M.S.O. Edinburgh.

Philippi, G. (1965). Moosgesellschaften des morschen Holzes und des Rohhumus im Schwarzwald, in der Rhön, in Weserbergland und im Harz. *Nova Hedwigia* **9**, 185–232.

Pierce, R. L. (1959). Converting coordinates for microscope-stage scales. *Micropaleontology* **5**, 377–8.

Pigott, C. D. (1956). The vegetation of Upper Teesdale in the Northern Pennines, *J. Ecol.* **44**, 545–86.

Pigott, C. D. (1958). *Polemonium caeruleum* L. *J. Ecol.* **46**, 507–25.

Pigott, C. D. (1969). The status of *Tilia cordata* and *T. platyphyllos* on the Derbyshire limestone. *J. Ecol.* **57**, 491–504.

Pigott, C. D. & Pigott, M. E. (1963). Late-glacial and Post-glacial deposits at Malham, Yorkshire. *New Phytol.* **62**, 317–34.

Pigott, C. D. & Walters, S. M. (1954). On the interpretation of the discontinuous distribution shown by certain British species of open habitats. *J. Ecol.* **42**, 95–116.

Pilcher, J. R. (1968). Some applications of scanning electron microscopy to the study of modern and fossil pollen. *Ulster Journ. Archaeology* **31**, 87–92.

Podpera, J. (1954). *Conspectus Muscorum Europaeorum.* Prague.

Pohl, F. (1937). Die pollenerzeugung der Windblüter. *Beih. bot. Centralblatt* **56**(A), 365–470.

Polunin, N. (1945). Plant life in Kongsfjord, West Spitsbergen. *J. Ecol.* **33**, 82–108.

Poore, M. E. D. (1955*a*). The use of phytosociological methods in ecological investigations. II. Practical issues involved in an attempt to apply the Braun-Blanquet System. *J. Ecol.* **43**, 245–69.

Poore, M. E. D. (1955*b*). The use of phytosociological methods in ecological investigations. I. The Braun-Blanquet System. *J. Ecol.* **43**, 226–44.

Poore, M. E. D. (1955*c*). The use of phytosociological methods in ecological investigations. III. Practical application. *J. Ecol.* **43**, 606–51.

Poore, M. E. D. (1956). The use of phytosociological methods in ecological investigations. IV. General discussion of phytosociological problems. *J. Ecol.* **44**, 28–50.

Poore, M. E. D. (1962). The method of successive approximation in descriptive ecology. *Adv. ecol. Res.* **1**, 35–68.

Poore, M. E. D. & McVean, D. N. (1957). A new approach to Scottish mountain vegetation. *J. Ecol.* **45**, 401–39.

Praglowski, J. R. (1962). Notes on the pollen morphology of Swedish trees and shrubs. *Grana Palynol.* **3** (2), 45–65.

Praglowski, J. & Erdtman, G. (1969). On the morphology of the pollen grains in *Armeria sibirica* in specimens from between longitude 30° W and 60° E. *Grana Palynol.* **9** (1–3), 72–91.

Proctor, J. (1971). The plant ecology of serpentine. II. Plant response to serpentine soils. *J. Ecol.* **59**, 397–410.

Proctor, J. & Woodell, S. R. J. (1971). The plant ecology of serpentine. I. Serpentine vegetation of England and Scotland. *J. Ecol.* **59**, 375–96.

Proctor, M. C. F. (1959). A note on *Acrocladium trifarium* (W. & M.) Richards & Wallace in Ireland. *Trans. Br. bryol. Soc.* **3**, 571–4.

Proctor, M. C. F. (1962). A sketch of the epiphytic bryophyte communities of the Dartmoor oakwoods. *Rep. Trans. Devon Ass. Advmt. Sci.* **94**, 531–54.

Proctor, M. C. F. (1964). The phytogeography of Dartmoor bryophytes. In *Dartmoor Essays* (ed. by I. G. Simmons). Torquay.

Proctor, M. C. F. (1967). The distribution of British liverworts: a statistical analysis. *J. Ecol.* **55**, 119–35.

Proctor, M. C. F. & Lambert, C. A. (1961). Pollen spectra from recent *Helianthemum* communities. *New Phytol.* **60**, 21–6.

Rampton, V. (1971). Late Quaternary Vegetational and Climatic History of the Snag-Klutlan Area, Southwestern Yukon Territory, Canada. *Bull. geol. soc. Amer.* **82**, 959—78.

Ratcliffe, D. A. (1959). The vegetation of the Carneddau, North Wales. 1. Grasslands, heaths and bogs. *J. Ecol.* **47**, 371–413.

Ratcliffe, D. A. (1960). The Mountain Flora of Lakeland. *Proc. bot. soc. Br. Isl.* **4**, 1–25.

Ratcliffe, D. A. (1964). Mires and bogs. In *The Vegetation of Scotland* (ed. by J. H. Burnett). Edinburgh.

Ratcliffe, D. A. (1968). An ecological account of Atlantic bryophytes in the British Isles. *New Phytol.* **67**, 365–439.

Ratcliffe, D. A. & Walker, D. (1958). The Silver Flowe, Galloway, Scotland. *J. Ecol.* **46**, 407–45.

Raunkiaer, C. (1934). *The life forms of plants and statistical plant geography.* Oxford.

Raven, J. E. (1952). *Koenigia islandica* L. in Scotland. *Watsonia*, **2**, 188–90.

Reitsma, Tj. (1966). Pollen morphology of some European Rosaceae. *Acta bot. neerl.* **15**, 290–307.

Reyre, Y. (1968). La sculpture de l'exine des pollens des gymnospermes et des chlamydospermes et son utilisation dans l'identification des pollens fossiles. *Pollen Spores* **10**, 197–220.

Richards, P. W. (1938). The bryophyte communities of a Killarney oakwood. *Annls. bryol.* **11**, 108–30.

Richey, J. E. (1961). *British Regional Geology, Scotland: The Tertiary Volcanic Districts.* H.M.S.O. Edinburgh.

Ritchie, J. C. & Lichti-Federovich, S. (1967). Pollen dispersal phenomena in Arctic-Subarctic Canada. *Rev. Palaeobotan. Palynol.* **3**, 255–66.

Rodriguez, F. B. (1966). La Végétation de Galicia. *An. Inst. bot. A. J. Cavanillo*, **24**, 1–306.

Rogers, D. J. (1970). A preliminary ordination study of forest vegetation in the Kirchleerau area of the Swiss Midland. *Ber. Geobot. Inst. ETH.* **40**, 28–78.

Roisin, P. (1969). *Le Domaine Phytogéographique Atlantique D'Europe.* Gembloux.

Roland, F. (1969). Étude de l'ultrastructure des apertures: III. Compléments fournis par le microscope électronique a Balayage. *Pollen Spores* **11**, 475–98.

Rossignol, M. (1961). Analyse pollinique de sédiments marins quaternaires en Israel. 1. Sédiments récents. *Pollen Spores* **5**, 301–24.

Round, F. E. (1961). The diatoms of a core from Esthwaite water. *New Phytol.* **60**, 43–59.

Rouse, G. E. & Srivastava, S. K. (1970). Detailed morphology, taxonomy, and distribution of *Pistillipollenites macgregorii. Can. J. Bot.* **48**, 287–92.

Rowley, J. R. & Dahl, A. O. (1956). Modifications in design and use of the Livingstone piston sampler. *Ecology* **37**, 849–51.

Rowley, J. R. & Erdtman, G. (1967). Sporoderm in *Populus* and *Salix. Grana Palynol.* **7** (2–3), 517–67.

Rune, O. (1965). The mountain regions of Lappland. In *The Plant Cover of Sweden. Acta Phytogeogr. suec.* **50**, 314 pp.

Rybniček, K. (1964). Die Braunmoorgesellschaften der Böhmischmährischen Höhe (Tschechoslowakei) und die Problematik ihrer Klassifikation. *Preslia* **36**, 403–15.

Rybniček, K. (1966). Glacial relics in the Bryoflora of the Highlands Českomoravská vrchovina (Bohemian-Moravian Highlands); Their Habitat and Cenotaxonomic Value. *Folia Geobot. Phytotax.* **1**, 101–19.

Rybniček, K. (1970). *Rhynchospora alba* (L.) Vahl, its distribution, communities and habitat conditions in Czechoslovakia, Part 2. *Folia Geobot. Phytotax.* **5**, 221–63.

Ryvarden, L. & Kaland, P. E. (1968). *Artemisia norvegica* Fr. funnet i Rogaland (foreløpig meddelelse). *Blyttia* **26**, 75–84.

Salmi, M. (1963). On the subfossil *Pediastrum* algae and molluscs in the Late-Quaternary sediments of Finnish Lappland. *Arch. Soc.* 'Vanamo', **18**, 105–20.

Salmi, M. (1969). Pölysateiden geologisesta merkityksestä Suomessa. *Geologi* **21**, 1–5.

Samuelsson, G. (1934). Die Verbreitung der höheren Wasserpflanzen in Nord Europa. *Acta Phytogeogr. suec.* **6**, 211 pp.

Sangster, A. G. & Dale, H. M. (1961). A preliminary Study of differential pollen grain preservation. *Can. J. Bot.* **39**, 35–43.

Sangster, A. G. & Dale, H. M. (1964). Pollen grain preservation of underrepresented species in fossil spectra. *Can. J. Bot.* **42**, 437–49.

Sarjeant, W. A. S. & Strachan, I. (1968). Freshwater acritarchs in Pleistocene peats from Staffordshire, England. *Grana Palynol.* **8** (1), 204–9.

Schoof-van Pelt, M. & Westhoff, V. (1969). Stradlingsgesellschaften seichter Gewässer in Irland (Littorelletea). *Mitt. flor.-soz. ArbGemein*, N.F. **14**, 211–23.

Schuster, R. M., Steere, W. C. & Thomson, J. W. (1959). The terrestrial cryptogams of Northern Ellesmere Island. *Nat. Mus. Canada Bull.* **164**, 132 pp.

Scott, G. A. M. (1963*a*). The ecology of shingle-beach plants. *J. Ecol.* **51**, 517–27.

Scott, G. A. M. (1963*b*). *Mertensia maritima* (L.) S. F. Gray. *J. Ecol.* **51**, 733–42.

Scott, G. H. (1963). Uniformitarianism, the Uniformity of Nature, and Paleoecology. *N.Z. J. Geol. Geophys.* **6**, 510–27.

Seddon, B. (1962). Late-glacial deposits at Llyn Dwythwch and Nant Ffrancon, Caernarvonshire. *Phil. Trans. R. Soc.* B, **244**, 459–81.

Seddon, B. (1965). Occurrence of *Isoetes echinospora* in eutrophic waters in Wales. *Ecology* **46**, 747–8.

Seddon, B. (1967). The lacustrine environment in relation to macrophytic vegetation. In *Quaternary Paleoecology* (ed. by E. J. Cushing & H. E. Wright). New Haven and London.

Segal, S. (1966). Ecological studies of peat-bog vegetation in the north-western part of the Province of Overijsel (The Netherlands). *Wentia* **15**, 109–41.

Segal, S. (1969). *Ecological notes on wall vegetation.* The Hague.

Selander, S. (1950). Floristic phytogeography of South-Western Lule Lappmark (Swedish Lappland). *Acta Phytogeogr. suec.* **27**, 200 pp.

Sheikh, K. H. (1970). The responses of *Molinia caerulea* and *Erica tetralix* to soil aeration and related factors. III. Effects of different gas concentrations on growth in solution culture; and general conclusions. *J. Ecol.* **58**, 141–54.

Shimwell, D. W. (1969). The Status of the Class Elyno-Seslerietea Br.-Bl. 1948 in the British Isles. *Mitt. flor.-soz. ArbGemein*, N.F. **14**, 309–21.

Shimwell, D. W. (1971). Festuco-Brometea Br.-Bl. and R. Tx. 1943 in the British Isles: The Phytogeography and Phytosociology of limestone grasslands. *Vegetatio* **23**, 1–28, 29–60.

Shotton, F. W. & West, R. G. (1969). Appendix B1. Stratigraphical table of the British Quaternary. In Recommendations on stratigraphical usage (Geological Society of London). *Proc. Geol. Soc. Lond.* **1656**, 139–66.

Singh, G. (1970). Late-glacial vegetational history of Lecale, Co. Down. *Proc. R. Ir. Acad.* B, **69**, 189–216.

Sissingh, G. (1969). Über die systematische Gliederung von Trittpflanzen-Gesellschaften. *Mitt. flor.-soz Arb-Gemein*, N.F. **14**, 179–92.

Sissons, J. B. (1967*a*). *The evolution of Scotland's Scenery.* Edinburgh.

Sissons, J. B. (1967*b*). Glacial stages and radiocarbon dates in Scotland. *Scott. J. Geol.* **3**, 375–81.

Sjörs, H. (1948). Myrvegetation i Bergslagen. *Acta Phytogeogr. suec.* **21**, 299 pp.

Sjörs, H. (1950*a*). On the relation between vegetation and electrolytes in North Swedish mire waters. *Oikos*, **2**, 241–58.

Sjörs, H. (1950*b*). Regional studies in North Swedish mire vegetation. *Bot. Notiser*, **103**, 173–222.

Sjörs, H. (1954). Slatteränger i Grangärde Finnmark. *Acta Phytogeogr. suec.* **34**, 135 pp.

Skogen, A. (1965). Flora og vegetasjon i Ørland herred, Sør-Trondelag. *Årbok 1965 for Det Kgl. Norske Videnskabers Selskab Muscet*, 13–124.

Skogen, A. (1966). *Pedicularis silvatica* L. ssp. *hibernica* D. A. Webb, ny for Norge. *Blyttia* **24**, 361–7.

Slesser, M. (1970). *The Island of Skye.* The Scottish Mountaineering Trust. Edinburgh.

Smith, A. G. (1958). Two lacustrine deposits in the south of the English Lake District. *New Phytol.* **57**, 363–86.

Smith, A. G. (1961). Canons Lough, Kilrea, Co. Derry: stratigraphy and pollen analysis. *Proc. R. Ir. Acad.* B, **61**, 369–83.

Smith, A. G. (1965). Problems of inertia and threshold related to post-Glacial habitat changes. *Proc. R. Soc.* B, **161**, 331–42.

Snaydon, R. W. & Bradshaw, A. D. (1961). Differential responses to calcium within the species *Festuca ovina* L. *New Phytol.* **60**, 219–31.

Snow Survey of Great Britain (1948–56) *J. Glaciol.* and *Met. Mag.*

Sonesson, M. (1968). Pollen zones at Abisko, Torne Lappmark, Sweden. *Bot. Notiser* **121**, 491–500.

Sonesson, M. (1969). Studies on mire vegetation in the Torneträsk area, North Sweden. II. Winter condidions of the Poor Mires. *Bot. Notiser* **122**, 481–511.

Sonesson, M. (1970). Studies on mire vegetation in the Torneträsk Area, Northern Sweden. III. Communities of the Poor Mires. *Op. bot. Soc. bot. Lund* **26**, 120 pp.

Sörensen, T. (1942). Untersuchungen über die Therophytengesellschaften auf den isländischen Lehmflächen ('Flags'). *K. danske Vicensk. Selsk., Biol. Skr.* **2** (2), 1–30.

Sorsa, P. (1964). Studies on the spore morphology of Fennoscandian fern species. *Annls. bot. fenn.* **1**, 179–201.

Sorsa, P. (1968). Pollen morphology of four *Sedum telephium* L. subspecies studied by means of Normarski's interference-contrast equipment. *Annls. bot. fenn.* **5**, 98–101.

Sparling, J. H. (1967). The occurrence of *Schoenus nigricans* L. in blanket bogs. *J. Ecol.* **55**, 1–13, 15–31.

Sparling, J. H. (1968). *Schoenus nigricans* L. *J. Ecol.* **56**, 883–99.

Spence, D. H. N. (1957). Studies on the vegetation of Shetland. I. The serpentine debris vegetation in Unst. *J. Ecol.* **45**, 917–45.

Spence, D. H. N. (1960). Studies on the vegetation of Shetland. III. Scrub in Shetland and in South Uist, Outer Hebrides. *J. Ecol.* **48**, 73–95.

Spence, D. H. N. (1964). The macrophytic vegetation of fresh-water lochs, swamps and associated fens. In *The Vegetation of Scotland* (ed. by J. H. Burnett). Edinburgh.

Spence, D. H. N. (1967). Factors controlling the distribution of freshwater macrophytes with particular reference to the lochs of Scotland. *J. Ecol.* **55**, 147–70.

Spence, D. H. N. (1970). Scottish Serpentine Vegetation. *Oikos*, **21**, 22–31.

Srodon, A. (1960). Pollen spectra from Spitsbergen. *Folia quatern.* **3**, 1–17.

Stamer, R. (1967). Vegetationskundliche Untersuchungen an Schlatts der Osenberge und des Ahlhorner Forstes. *Mitt. flor.-soz. ArbGemein*, N.F. **11–12**, 28–47.

Stanley, E. A. (1966). The problem of reworked pollen and spores in marine sediments. *Marine Palynology*, **4**, 397–408.

Steeves, M. W. & Barghoorn, E. S. (1959). The pollen of *Ephedra*. *J. Arnold Arbor.* **40**, 221–55.

Steindórsson, S. (1945). Studies on the vegetation of the Central Highlands of Iceland. In *The Botany of Iceland*, **3** (4), 345–547. Copenhagen.

Steindórsson, S. (1963). Um gródur i Papey. *Náttúrufraedingurinn*, **33**, 214–32.

Stix, E. (1960). Pollermorphologische Untersuchungen an Compositen. *Grana Palynol.* **2** (2), 41–114.

Stork, A. (1963). Plant immigration in front of retreating glaciers with examples from the Kebnekajse area, northern Sweden. *Geogr. Annlr.* A, **45**, 1–22.

Størmer, L. (1966). Concepts of stratigraphical classification and terminology. *Earth Sci. Rev.* **1**, 5–28.

Störmer, P. (1938). Vegetationsstudien auf der Insel Håøya im Oslofjord. *Skr. norske Vidensk.-Akad. 1. Mat.-Nat.* No. 9, 156 pp.

Störmer, P. (1969). *Mosses with a Western and Southern Distribution in Norway*. Oslo–Bergen–Tromsö.

Sugden, D. E. (1970). Landforms of deglaciation in the Cairngorm Mountains, Scotland. *Trans. Inst. Br. Geogr.* **51**, 201–19.

Suggate, R. P. & West, R. G. (1959). On the extent of the last glaciation in eastern England. *Proc. R. Soc.* B, **150**, 263–83.

Suggate, R. P. & West, R. G. (1967). The substitution of local stage names for Holocene and Post-glacial *Quaternaria*, **9**, 245–6.

Svensson, G. (1965). Vegetationsundersökningar på Store mosse. *Bot. Notiser*, **118**, 49–86.

Switsur, V. R. & West, R. G. (1972). University of Cambridge Natural Radiocarbon Measurements X. *Radiocarbon* **14**, 239–46.

Synge, F. M. & Stephens, N. (1966). Late- and Post-glacial shorelines, and ice limits in Argyll and North-East Ulster. *Trans. Inst. Br. Geogr.* **39**, 101–25.

Tallis, J. H. (1958). Studies in the biology and ecology of *Rhacomitrium lanuginosum* Brid. I. Distribution and ecology. *J. Ecol.* **46**, 271–88.

Tallis, J. H. (1969). The blanket bog vegetation of the Berwyn Mountains, North Wales. *J. Ecol.* **57**, 765–87.

Tansley, A. G. (1917). On competition between *Galium saxatile* (*G. hercynicum* Weig.) and *G. sylvestre* (*G. asperum* Schreb.) on different types of soil. *J. Ecol.* **5**, 173–9.

Tansley, A. G. (1949). *The British Islands and their Vegetation*. Cambridge.

Tauber, H. (1965). Differential pollen dispersion and the interpretation of pollen diagrams. *Danm. geol. Unders.* Ser. II, **89**, 69 pp.

Tauber, H. (1967). Investigations of the mode of pollen transfer in forested areas. *Rev. Palaeobotan. Palynol.* **3**, 277–86.

Tauber, H. (1970). The Scandinavian varve chronology and C-14 dating. In *Radiocarbon Variations and Absolute Chronology* (ed. by I. U. Olsson). Stockholm and New York.

Teichert, C. (1958). Some biostratigraphical concepts. *Bull. geol. soc. Amer.* **69**, 99–120.

Terasmae, J. (1967). Recent pollen deposition in the north-eastern district of Mackenzie (Northwest Territories, Canada). *Palaeogeogr.*, *Palaeoclimatol.*, *Palaeoecol.* **3**, 17–27.

Thomas, K. W. (1964). A new design for a peat sampler. *New Phytol.* **63**, 422–5.

Thoroddsen, Th. (1914). An account of the physical geography of Iceland, with special reference to the plant life. In *The Botany of Iceland*, **1** (2), 191–343. Copenhagen.

Thunmark, S. (1940). Orientierung über die Exkursionen des IX Internationalen Limnologenkongresse im Anebodagebiet. *Verh. int. Verein. theor. angew. Limnol.* **9**, 59–68.

Tittensor, R. M. & Steele, R. C. (1971). Plant communities of the Loch Lomond oakwoods. *J. Ecol.* **59**, 561–82.

Tralau, H. (1963). The recent and fossil distribution of some boreal and arctic montane plants in Europe. *Ark. Bot.* Ser. 2, **5**, 533–82.

Trapnell, C. G. (1933). Vegetation types in Godthaab Fjord. *J. Ecol.* **21**, 294–334.

Traverse, A. (1958). Locating plant microfossils on mixed slides. *Micropaleontology* **4**, 207–8.

Troels-Smith, J. (1955). Karakterising af løse jordarter. *Danm. geol. Unders.*, Ser. IV, **3** (10), 73 pp.

Troll, C. (1944). Strukturböden, solifluktion und frostklimate der Erde. *Geol. Rdsch.* **34**, 545–694.

Troll, K. (1925). *Ozeanische Züge im Pflanzenkleid Mitteleuropas–Freie Wege vergleichender Erdkunde*. Munich and Berlin.

Tsukada, M. (1958). Untersuchungen über das Verhältnis zwischen dem Pollengehalt der Oberflachenproben und der Vegetation des Hochlandes Shiga. *J. Osaka Cy. Univ. Inst. Polytech.* D, **9**, 217–34.

Tuomikoski, R. (1942). Untersuchungen über die Untervegetation der Bruchmoore in Ostfinnland. 1. Zur methodik der Pflanzensoziologischen Systematik. *Ann. bot. Soc.* 'Vanamo', **17** (1), 1–203.

Turner, J. (1964). Surface sample analyses from Ayrshire, Scotland. *Pollen Spores* **6**, 583–92.

Tutin, W. (1969). The usefulness of pollen analysis in interpretation of stratigraphic horizons, both Late-glacial and Post-glacial. *Mitt. Inter. Verein. Limnol.* **17**, 154–64.

Tüxen, J. (1969). Gedanken über ein System der Oxycocco-Sphagnetea Br.-Bl. & R. Tx. 1943. *Vegetatio* **19**, 181–91.

Tüxen. R. (1937). Die Pflanzengesellschaften Nordwestdeutschlands. *Mitt. flor.-soz. ArbGemein* **3**, 1–170.

Tüxen, R. (1950). Grundriss einer Systematik der nitrophilen Unkrautgesellschaften in der Eurosibirischen Region Europas. *Mitt. flor-soz. ArbGemein* N.F. **2**, 94–175.

Tüxen, R. (1955). Das system der nordwestdeutschen Pffanzengesellschaften. *Mitt. flor.-soz. ArbGemein,* N.F. **5**, 155–76.

Tüxen, R. (1970). Zur Syntaxonomie des europäischen Wirtschafts-Grünlandes (Wiesen, Weiden, Trittund Flutrasen). *Ber. Naturhist. Ges.* **114**, 77–85.

Tüxen, R. & Böttcher, H. (1969). Weide- und Wiesen-Gesellschaften (Molinio–Arrhenatheretea) in Süd-west-Island. *Berichte der Forschungs. Nedri As, Hveragerdi (Island)*, **1**, 1–31.

Tüxen, R. & Oberdorfer, E. (1958). Eurosibirische Phanerogamen–Gesellschaften Spaniens. *Veröff. geobot. Inst. Zurich.* **32**, 1–328.

Tüxen, R. & Preising, E. (1951). Erfahrungsgrundlagen für die pflanzensoziologische Kartierung des westdeutschen Grünlandes. *Angew. Pflanzen.* **4**, 28 pp.

Tyler, G. (1971). Hydrology and salinity of Baltic seashore meadows. Studies in the ecology of Baltic sea-shore meadows. III. *Oikos* **22**, 1–20.

Valentine, J. W. & Mallory, B. (1965). Recurrent groups of bonded species in mixed death assemblages. *J. Geol.* **73**, 683–701.

Valentine, J. W. & Peddicord, R. G. (1967). Evaluation of fossil assemblages by cluster analysis. *J. Paleontol.* **41**, 502–7.

Vallentyne, J. R. (1955). A modification of the Livingstone piston sampler for lake deposits. *Ecology* **36**, 139–41.

Vallentyne, J. R. (1963). Isolation of pyrite spherules from recent sediments. *Limnol. Oceanography* **8**, 16–30.

Vanden Berghen, C. (1952). Contribution à l'étude des basmarais de Belgique. *Bull. Jard. bot., Etat. Brux.* **22**, 1–64.

Vanden Berghen, C. (1958). Étude sur la végétation des dunes et des Landes de la Bretagne. *Vegetatio* **8**, 193–208.

Vanden Berghen, C. (1968). Notes sur la végétation du sudouest de la France. VI. – La végétation de la rive orientale de l'étang de Lacanau (Gironde, France). *Bull. Jard. bot., Etat. Brux.* **38**, 255–76.

Van der Hammen, Th. (1951). Late-glacial flora and peri-glacial phenomena in the Netherlands. *Leid. geol. Meded.* **17**, 71–184.

Van der Hammen, Th. & Vogel, J. C. (1966). The Susacá-interstadial and the subdivision of the Late-glacial. *Geol. en. Mijnb.* **45**, 33–5.

Van der Hammen, Th., Maarleveld, G. C., Vogel, J. C. & Zagwijn, W. H. (1967). Stratigraphy, climatic succession and radiocarbon dating of the last glacial in the Netherlands. *Geol. en Mijnb* **46**, 79–95.

van Groenewoud, H. (1965). Ordination and classification of Swiss and Canadian coniferous forests by various biometric and other methods. *Ber. Geobot. Inst. ETH.* **36**, 28–102.

Van Zeist, W. (1964). A paleobotanical study of some bogs in Western Brittany (Finistère), France. *Palaeohistoria* **10**, 157–80.

Varma, C. P. (1964). Do Dinoflagellates and Hystrichosphaerids occur in freshwater sediments? *Grana Palynol.* **5** (1), 124–8.

Vasari, Y. & Vasari, A. (1968). Late- and post-glacial macrophytic vegetation in the lochs of Northern Scotland. *Acta bot. Fenn.* **80**, 120 pp.

von Hübschmann, A. (1967). Über die Moosgesellschaften und das Vorkommen der Moose in den übrigen Pflanzengesellschaften des Moseltales. *Schriften Vegetationskunde* **2**, 63–121.

von Post, L. (1946). The prospect for pollen analysis in the study of the Earth's climatic history. *New Phytol.* **45**, 193–217.

Wagenitz, G. (1956). Pollenmorphologie der mitteleuropäischen Valerianaceen. *Flora* **143**, 473–85.

Walker, D. (1955). Studies in the post-glacial history of British vegetation. XIV. Skelsmergh Tarn and Kentmere, Westmorland. *New Phytol.* **54**, 222–54.

Walker, D. (1965). The Post-glacial period in the Langdale Fells, English Lake District. *New Phytol.* **64**, 488–510.

Walker, D. (1966). The late Quaternary history of the Cumberland lowland. *Phil. Trans. R. Soc.* B, **251**, 1–210.

Wall, D. (1967). Fossil microplankton in deep-sea cores from the Caribbean Sea. *Palaeontology* **10**, 95–123.

Wall, D. & Dale, B. (1967). The resting cysts of modern marine dinoflagellates and their palaeontological significance. *Rev. Palaeobotan. Palynol.* **2**, 349–54.

Wall, D. & Dale, B. (1968*a*). Modern dinoflagellate cysts and evolution of the Peridiniales. *Micropaleontology* **14**, 265–304.

Wall, D. & Dale, B. (1968*b*). Early Pleistocene dinoflagellates from the Royal Society Borehole at Ludham, Norfolk. *New Phytol.* **67**, 315–26.

Wall, D., Guillard, R. R. L. & Dale, B. (1967). Marine dinoflagellate cysts from resting spores. *Phycologia* **6**, 83–6.

Warburg, E. F. (1963). *Census Catalogue of British Mosses.* (3rd edition). Ipswich.

Warming, E. (1902). *Lehrbuch der ökologischen Pflanzengeographie.* Berlin.

Warren Wilson, J. (1952). Vegetation patterns associated with soil movement on Jan Mayen island. *J. Ecol.* **40**, 249–64.

Wasylikowa, K. (1964). Roslinnosc i Klimat Poznego Glacjalu W Srodkowej Polsce Na Podstawie Badan W Witowie Kolo Leczycy. *Biul. peryglac.* **13**, 261–417.

Watt, A. S. (1947). Patterns and process in the plant community. *J. Ecol.* **35**, 1–22.

Watts, W. A. (1959). Interglacial deposits at Killbeg and Newtown, Co. Waterford. *Proc. R. Ir. Acad.* B, **60**, 79–134.

Watts, W. A. (1963). Late-glacial pollen zones in Western Ireland. *Ir. Geogr.* **4**, 367–76.

Webb, D. A. (1947). The vegetation of Carrowkeel, a limestone hill in north-west Ireland. *J. Ecol.* **35**, 105–29.

Webb, D. A. (1954). Is the classification of plant communities either possible or desirable? *Bot. Tidsskr.* **51**, 362–70.

Webb, D. A. (1956). A new subspecies of *Pedicularis sylvatica* L. *Watsonia* **3**, 239–41.

Webb, D. A. & Glanville, E. V. (1962). The vegetation and flora of some islands in the Connemara lakes. *Proc. R. Ir. Acad.* B, **62**, 31–54.

Webster, J. R. (1962). The composition of wet-heath vegetation in relation to aeration of the groundwater and soil. II. Response of *Molinia caerulea* to controlled conditions of soil aeration and groundwater movement. *J. Ecol.* **50**, 639–50.

Welch, D. (1966). *Juncus squarrosus* L. *J. Ecol.* **54**, 535–48.

Welch, D. (1967). Communities containing *Juncus squarrosus* in Upper Teesdale, England. *Vegetatio* **14**, 229–40.

Welch, D. & Rawes, M. (1966). The early effects of excluding sheep from high-level grasslands in the North Pennines. *J. appl. Ecol.* **1**, 281–300.

Welten, M. (1950). Beobachtungen über den rezenten Polleniederschlag in alpiner Vegetation. *Ber. gebot. Forsch Inst. Rübel* f.d. 1949, 48–57.

Welten, M. (1957). Über das glaziale und spätglaziale Vorkommen von *Ephedra* am nordwestlichen Alpenrand. *Ber. schweiz. bot. Ges.* **67**, 33–54.

West, R. G. (1967). The Quaternary of the British Isles In *The Quaternary*, **2** (ed. by K. Rankama). London.

West, R. G. (1968). *Pleistocene geology and biology.* London.

Westhoff, V. & Den Held, A. J. (1969). *Plantengemeenschappen in Nederland.* Zutphen.

White, B. (1869). On some British Plantagines allies to *Plantago maritima. Trans. Proc. bot. soc. Edinb.* **10**, 171–3.

White, R. M. (1968). The vegetation of the Curraun Peninsula, Co. Mayo. *Ir. Nat. J.* **16**, 57–62.

Whiteside, M. C. (1965). Paleoecological studies of Potato Lake and its environs. *Ecology* **46**, 807–16.

Whittaker, R. H. (1962). Classification of natural communities. *Bot. Rev.* **28**, 1–239.

Williams, J. T. (1968). The nitrogen relations and other ecological investigations on wet fertilised meadows. *Veröff. Geobot. Inst. ETH.* **41**, 69–193.

Williams, J. T. & Varley, Y. W. (1967). Phytosociological studies of some British grasslands. 1. Upland pastures in Northern England. *Vegetatio* **15**, 169–89.

Witting, M. (1947). Katjonsbestämninger i myrvatten. *Bot. Notiser* **101**, 287–304.

Wood, K. R. (1969). The distribution of the two subspecies of *Asplenium trichomanes* L. on the Isle of Skye. Unpublished manuscript.

Wright, H. E. (1967*a*). The use of surface samples in Quaternary pollen analysis. *Rev. Palaeobotan. Palynol.* **2**, 321–30.

Wright, H. E. (1967*b*). A square-rod piston sampler for lake sediments. *J. sedim. Petrol.* **37**, 975–6.

Wright, H. E. (1968). The role of pine and spruce in the forest history of Minnesota and adjacent areas. *Ecology* **49**, 937–55.

Wright, H. E. (1971). Late Quaternary Vegetational History of North America. In *The Late Cenozoic Glacial Ages* (ed. by K. K. Turekian). New Haven and London.

Wright, H. E., Livingstone, D. A. & Cushing, E. J. (1965). Coring devices for Lake sediments. In *Handbook of Paleontological Techniques* (ed. by B. Kummel & D. M. Raup). San Francisco.

Wright, H. E., McAndrews, J. H. & Van Zeist, W. (1967). Modern pollen rain in West Iran, and its relation to plant geography and Quaternary vegetational history. *J. Ecol.* **55**, 415–43.

Wright, H. E. & Patten, H. L. (1963). The Pollen Sum. *Pollen Spores* **5**, 445–50.

Yarranton, G. A. (1967*a*). Organismal and individualistic concepts and the choice of methods of vegetation analysis. *Vegetatio* **15**, 113–16.

Yarranton, G. A. (1967*b*). A quantitative study of the bryophyte and macrolichen vegetation of the Dartmoor granite. *Lichenologist* **3**, 392–408.

Yarranton, G. A. & Beasleigh, W. J. (1968). Towards a mathematical model of limestone pavement vegetation. I. Vegetation and microtopography. *Can. J. Bot.* **46**, 1591–99.

Yarranton, G. A. & Beasleigh, W. J. (1969). Towards a mathematical model of limestone pavement vegetation. II. Microclimate, surface pH, and microtopography. *Can. J. Bot.* **47**, 959–74.

INDEX

INDEX

INDEX